DISCOVERING COMPUTERS 2018

Digital Technology, Data, and Devices

Misty E. Vermaat
Susan L. Sebok
Steven M. Freund
Jennifer T. Campbell
Mark Frydenberg

CENGAGE
Learning·

SHELLY CASHMAN SERIES·

Australia • Brazil • Mexico • Singapore • United Kingdom • United States

CENGAGE
Learning

Discovering Computers: Digital Technology, Data, and Devices
Misty E. Vermaat, Susan L. Sebok, Steven M. Freund, Jennifer T. Campbell, and Mark Frydenberg

SVP, GM Science, Technology & Math: Balraj S. Kalsi

Senior Product Director: Kathleen McMahon

Product Manager: Amanda Lyons-Li

Senior Director, Development: Julia Caballero

Senior Content Development Manager: Leigh Hefferon

Managing Developer: Emma Newsom

Associate Content Developer: Staci Eckenroth

Development Editor: Lyn Markowicz

Product Assistant: Cara Suriyamongkol

Marketing Director: Michele McTighe

Marketing Manager: Stephanie Albracht

Senior Content Project Manager: Stacey Lamodi

Art Director: Diana Graham

Text Designer: Joel Sadagursky

Cover Template Designer: Diana Graham

Cover image(s): Mario7/Shutterstock.com; Mrs. Opossum/Shutterstock.com

For product information and technology assistance, contact us at
Cengage Learning Customer & Sales Support, 1-800-354-9706

For permission to use material from this text or product, submit all requests online at **www.cengage.com/permissions**. Further permissions questions can be e-mailed to **permissionrequest@cengage.com**

Library of Congress Control Number: 2017932169

Student Edition:
ISBN: 978-1-337-28510-0

Loose-leaf Edition:
ISBN: 978-1-337-38852-8

Cengage Learning
20 Channel Center Street
Boston, MA 02210
USA

Cengage Learning is a leading provider of customized learning solutions with employees residing in nearly 40 different countries and sales in more than 125 countries around the world. Find your local representative at **www.cengage.com**.

Cengage Learning products are represented in Canada by Nelson Education, Ltd.

To learn more about Cengage Learning, visit **www.cengage.com**.

Purchase any of our products at your local college store or at our preferred online store **www.cengagebrain.com**.

Notice to the Reader

Publisher does not warrant or guarantee any of the products described herein or perform any independent analysis in connection with any of the product information contained herein. Publisher does not assume, and expressly disclaims, any obligation to obtain and include information other than that provided to it by the manufacturer. The reader is expressly warned to consider and adopt all safety precautions that might be indicated by the activities described herein and to avoid all potential hazards. By following the instructions contained herein, the reader willingly assumes all risks in connection with such instructions. The publisher makes no representations or warranties of any kind, including but not limited to, the warranties of fitness for particular purpose or merchantability, nor are any such representations implied with respect to the material set forth herein, and the publisher takes no responsibility with respect to such material. The publisher shall not be liable for any special, consequential, or exemplary damages resulting, in whole or part, from the readers' use of, or reliance upon, this material.

DISCOVERING COMPUTERS 2018
Digital Technology, Data, and Devices

Table of Contents at a Glance

DISCOVERING COMPUTERS 2018
Digital Technology, Data, and Devices

Table of Contents

Module 3

Computers and Mobile Devices: Evaluating Options for Home and Work   3-1

Module 4

Programs and Apps: Productivity, Graphics, Security, and Other Tools   4-1

Module 5

Digital Security, Ethics, and Privacy: Threats, Issues, and Defenses   5-1

Module 6

Computing Components: Processors, Memory, the Cloud, and More   6-1

Module **7**

Input and Output: Extending Capabilities of Computers and Mobile Devices   7-1

Module **8**

Digital Storage: Preserving Content Locally and on the Cloud   8-1

Module **9**

Operating Systems: Managing, Coordinating, and Monitoring Resources   9-1

Module **10**

Communicating Digital Content: Wired and Wireless Networks and Devices

10-1

Module **11**

Building Solutions: Database, System, and Application Development Tools

11-1

Module **12**

Working in the Enterprise: Systems, Certifications, and Careers   12-1

Introducing Today's Technologies:
Computers, Devices, and the Web

iStockphoto.com / Ali KeremYucel

OBJECTIVES

After completing this module, you will be able to:

1 Differentiate among laptops, tablets, desktops, and servers

2 Describe the purpose and uses of smartphones, digital cameras, portable and digital media players, e-book readers, wearable devices, and game devices

3 Describe the relationship between data and information

4 Briefly explain various input options (keyboards, pointing devices, voice and video input, and scanners), output options (printers, displays, and speakers), and storage options (hard disks, solid-state drives, USB flash drives, memory cards, optical discs, and cloud storage)

5 Differentiate the web from the Internet, and describe the relationship among the web, webpages, websites, and web servers

6 Explain the purpose of a browser, a search engine, and an online social network

7 Briefly describe digital security risks associated with viruses and other malware, privacy, your health, and the environment

8 Differentiate between an operating system and applications

9 Differentiate between wired and wireless network technologies, and identify reasons individuals and businesses use networks

10 Discuss how society uses technology in education, government, finance, retail, entertainment, health care, science, travel, publishing, and manufacturing

11 Identify technology used by home users, small/home office users, mobile users, power users, and enterprise users

Today's Technology

In the course of a day, you may … complete a homework assignment and watch a streaming video using your laptop, flip through news headlines and make dinner reservations using your tablet, search for directions and the local weather forecast while listening to music on your smartphone, edit a video on a desktop computer, and share photos online from your digital camera with family and friends. These and many other technologies are an integral part of everyday life: at school, at home, and at work (Figure 1-1).

Technology can enable you to more efficiently and effectively access and search for information; share personal ideas, photos, and videos with friends, family, and others; communicate with and meet other people; manage finances; shop for goods and services; play games or access other sources of entertainment; keep your life and activities organized; and conduct business activities. People who can accomplish these types of tasks using technology often are said to be tech savvy.

Figure 1-1   People use a variety of computers, mobile devices, and apps every day.

Because technology changes, you must keep up with the changes to remain digitally literate. *Digital literacy* involves having a current knowledge and understanding of computers, mobile devices, the web, and related technologies. This book presents the knowledge you need to be digitally literate today.

As you read this first module, keep in mind it is an overview. Most of the terms and concepts introduced in this module will be discussed in more depth later in the book.

Computers

A **computer** is an electronic device, operating under the control of instructions stored in its own memory, that can accept data (*input*), process the data according to specified rules, produce information (*output*), and store the information for future use (Figure 1-2). Computers contain many electric, electronic, and mechanical components known as *hardware*.

Electronic components in computers process data using instructions, which are the steps that tell the computer how to perform a particular task. A collection of related instructions organized for a common purpose is referred to as software or a program. Using software, you can complete a variety of activities, such as search for information, type a paper, balance a budget, create a presentation, or play a game.

Figure 1-2 A laptop is a widely used type of computer.
mama_mia / Shutterstock.com

One popular category of computer is the personal computer. A *personal computer* (PC) is a computer that can perform all of its input, processing, output, and storage activities by itself and is intended to be used by one person at a time. Most personal computers today also can communicate with other computers and devices.

Types of personal computers include laptops, tablets, and desktops, with the first two sometimes called mobile computers. A *mobile computer* is a portable personal computer, designed so that a user can carry it from place to place. A *user* is anyone who interacts with a computer or mobile device, or utilizes the information it generates.

Laptops

A **laptop**, also called a *notebook computer*, is a thin, lightweight mobile computer with a screen in its lid and a keyboard in its base (shown in Figure 1-2). Designed to fit on your lap and for easy transport, most laptops weigh up to 7 pounds (varying by manufacturer and specifications). A laptop that is less than one inch thick and weighs about three pounds or less sometimes is referred to as an ultrathin laptop. Most laptops can operate on batteries or a power supply or both.

Tablets

Usually smaller than a laptop but larger than a phone, a **tablet** is a thin, lighter-weight mobile computer that has a touch screen (read How To 1-1 for ways to interact with a touch screen). A popular style of tablet is the slate, which does not contain a physical keyboard (Figure 1-3). Like laptops, tablets run on batteries or a power supply or both; however, batteries in a tablet typically last longer than those in laptops.

Figure 1-3 A slate tablet.
Denys Prykhodov / Shutterstock.com

CONSIDER THIS

If a slate tablet has no keyboard, how do you type on it?

You can use your fingers to press keys on a keyboard that appears on the screen, called an on-screen keyboard, or you can purchase a separate physical keyboard that attaches to or wirelessly communicates with the tablet. You also may be able to speak into the tablet, and your spoken words will translate to typed text.

 HOW TO 1-1

Interact with a Touch Screen

You usually can interact with a touch screen using gestures. A *gesture* is a motion you make on a touch screen with the tip of one or more fingers or your hand. Touch screens are convenient because they do not require a separate device for input. Tablets and smartphones typically have touch screens.

The table below presents common ways to interact with a touch screen.

Touch Screen Gestures

Motion	Description	Common Uses
Tap	Quickly touch and release one finger one time	Activate a link (built-in connection) Press a button Run a program or app
Double-tap	Quickly touch and release one finger two times	Run a program or app Zoom in (show a smaller area on the screen, so that contents appear larger) at the location of the double-tap
Press and hold	Press and hold one finger to cause an action to occur, or until an action occurs	Display a shortcut menu (immediate access to allowable actions) Activate a mode enabling you to move an item with one finger to a new location
Drag, or slide	Press and hold one finger on an object and then move the finger to the new location	Move an item around the screen Scroll
Swipe	Press and hold one finger and then move the finger horizontally or vertically on the screen	Scroll Display a bar that contains commands on an edge of the screen
Stretch	Move two fingers apart	Zoom in (show a smaller area on the screen, so that contents appear larger)
Pinch	Move two fingers together	Zoom out (show a larger area on the screen, so that contents appear smaller)

 Consider This: In addition to the motions listed in the table, what other motions do you think a touch screen should support?

Desktops and All-in-Ones

A **desktop**, or desktop computer, is a personal computer designed to be in a stationary location, where all of its components fit on or under a desk or table. On many desktops, the screen is housed in a display device (or simply display) that is separate from a tower, which is a case that contains the processing circuitry (Figure 1-4a). Another type of desktop called an **all-in-one** does not contain a tower and instead uses the same case to house the display and the processing circuitry (Figure 1-4b). Some desktops and all-in-ones have displays that support touch.

⚙ **BTW**

Desktop
The term, desktop, also sometimes is used to refer to an on-screen work area on laptops, tablets, and desktops.

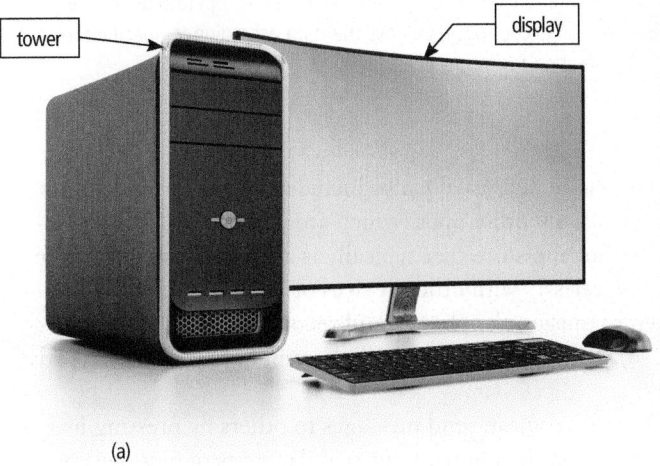

tower | display | all-in-one

(a)

(b)

Figure 1-4   Some desktops have a separate tower; all-in-ones do not.
iStockphoto.com / adventtr; Courtesy of Apple Inc.

 CONSIDER THIS

Which type of computer — laptop, tablet, or desktop — is best?
It depends on your needs. Because laptops can be as powerful as the average desktop, more people today choose laptops over desktops so that they have the added benefit of portability. Tablets are ideal for those not needing the power of a laptop or for searching for information, communicating with others, and taking notes in lectures, at meetings, conferences, and other forums where a laptop is not practical. Desktops and all-in-ones often have larger displays than laptops or tablets, which make them well suited for developing software, editing large documents, or creating images and videos.

Servers

A **server** is a computer dedicated to providing one or more services to other computers or devices on a network. A **network** is a collection of computers and devices connected together, often wirelessly. Services provided by servers include storing content and controlling access to hardware, software, and other resources on a network.

A server can support from two to several thousand connected computers and devices at the same time. Servers are available in a variety of sizes and types for both small and large business applications (Figure 1-5). Smaller applications, such as at home, sometimes use a high-end desktop as a server. Larger corporate, government, and web applications use powerful, expensive servers to support their daily operations.

⚙ **BTW**

Online
When a computer or device connects to a network, it is said to be online.

Mobile and Game Devices

A *mobile device* is a computing device small enough to hold in your hand. Because of their reduced size, the screens on mobile devices are small — often between 3 and 5 inches.

Figure 1-5   A server provides services to other computers or devices on a network.
iStockphoto.com / GuidoVrola

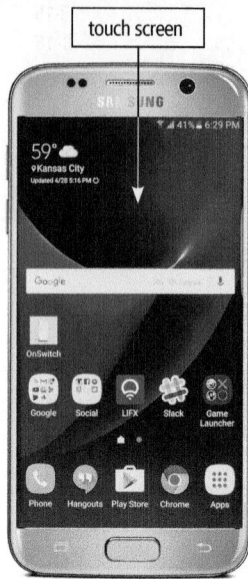

touch screen

Figure 1-6 Most smartphones have a touch screen.
iStockphoto.com / cincila

Some mobile devices are Internet capable, meaning that they can connect to the Internet wirelessly. You often can exchange information between the Internet and a mobile device or between a computer or network and a mobile device. Popular types of mobile devices are smartphones, digital cameras, portable and digital media players, e-book readers, and wearable devices.

CONSIDER THIS

Are mobile devices computers?
The mobile devices discussed in this section can be categorized as computers because they operate under the control of instructions stored in their own memory, can accept data, process the data according to specified rules, produce or display information, and store the information for future use.

Smartphones

A **smartphone** is an Internet-capable phone that usually also includes a calendar, an address book, a calculator, a notepad, games, and several other apps (which are programs on the smartphone). Other apps are available through an app store that typically is associated with the phone.

Smartphones typically communicate wirelessly with other devices or computers. With most smartphone models, you also can listen to music, take photos, and record videos. Most smartphones have a touch screen (Figure 1-6). A few models have built-in mini keyboards or keypads that contain both numbers and letters.

Instead of calling someone's phone to talk, you can send messages to others by pressing images of keys and icons on an on-screen keyboard on the phone. Four popular types of messages that you can send with smartphones include voice messages, text messages, picture messages, and video messages.

- A *voice mail message* is a short audio recording sent to or from a smartphone or other mobile device.
- A *text message* is a short note, typically fewer than 300 characters, sent to or from a smartphone or other mobile device.
- A *picture message* is a photo or other image, sometimes along with sound and text, sent to or from a smartphone or other mobile device.
- A *video message* is a short video clip, usually about 30 seconds, sent to or from a smartphone or other mobile device.

Read Ethics & Issues 1-1 to consider whether it should be legal to use a hands-free device, such as a smartphone, while driving.

ETHICS & ISSUES 1-1

Should It Be Legal to Use a Hands-Free Device while Driving?
Your new vehicle includes a sophisticated hands-free system that enables you to connect a mobile device to the vehicle's sound system. In addition to making phone calls without holding your device, you also can use this technology to read and respond to text messages or to update your Facebook status using speech-to-text, which converts your spoken words to text. Is this technology safe to use?

The debate about hands-free device safety elicits different points of view from vehicle insurance companies, consumer safety groups, and the telecommunications industry. AAA (American Automobile Association) conducted a study to measure the mental effect of using hands-free devices while driving. The conclusions indicated that drivers using hands-free devices are distracted, miss visual clues, and have slower reaction times. Others claim that drivers can be just as easily distracted if they are discussing business or emotional matters with passengers in the vehicle. The National Highway Traffic Safety Administration estimates that more than 3,000 fatalities occur each year due to "distracted driving."

Some states have outlawed any use of mobile phones while driving, while others ban users from sending text messages and/or require drivers to use hands-free devices while driving. Some vehicles contain technology that can restrict or block mobile phone usage while the vehicle is in motion.

Consider This: Do you believe you are distracted if you use hands-free devices while driving? Why or why not? Do you think auto manufacturers should continue to include hands-free device technology in vehicles? Why or why not? Would you use in-vehicle technology that limited your device usage while driving?

Digital Cameras

A **digital camera** is a device that allows you to take photos and store the photographed images digitally (Figure 1-7). A smart digital camera also can communicate wirelessly with other devices and include apps similar to those on a smartphone. Many mobile computers and devices, such as tablets and smartphones, include at least one integrated digital camera.

Digital cameras typically allow you to review, and sometimes modify, images while they are in the camera. You also can transfer images from a digital camera to a computer or device, so that you can review, modify, share, organize, or print the images. Digital cameras often can connect to or communicate wirelessly with a computer, a Smart TV (discussed later in the module), a printer, or the Internet, enabling you to access the photos on the camera without using a cable. Some also can record videos. Many digital cameras also have built-in GPS (discussed later in this module), giving them the capability to record the exact location where a photo was taken and store these details with the photo.

Figure 1-7 With a digital camera, you can view photographed images immediately through a small screen on the camera to see if the photo is worth keeping.
iStockphoto.com / seen0001

Portable and Digital Media Players

A **portable media player** is a mobile device on which you can store, organize, and play or view digital media (Figure 1-8). *Digital media* includes music, photos, and videos. Thus, portable media players enable you to listen to music, view photos, and watch videos, movies, and television shows. With most, you transfer the digital media from a computer or the web, if the device is Internet capable, to the portable media player. Some enable you to play the media while it streams, that is, while it transfers to the player.

Portable media players usually require a set of *earbuds*, which are small speakers that rest inside each ear canal. Some portable media player models have a touch screen, while others have a pad that you operate with a thumb or finger, so that you can navigate through digital media, adjust volume, and customize settings. Some portable media players also offer a calendar, address book, games, and other apps (discussed later in this module).

Portable media players are a mobile type of digital media player. A *digital media player* or *streaming media player* is a device, typically used in a home, that streams digital media from a computer or network to a television, projector, or some other entertainment device.

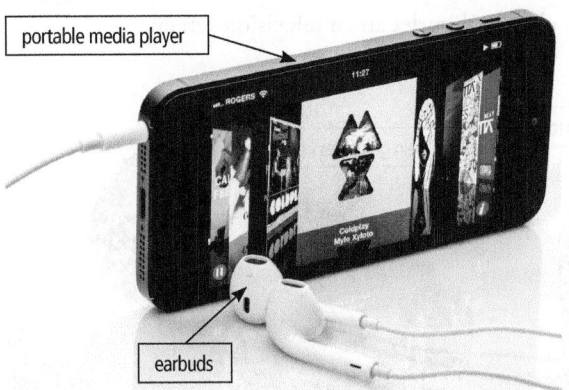

portable media player

earbuds

digital media player

Figure 1-8 Portable media players typically include a set of earbuds. Digital media players stream media to a home entertainment device.
iStockphoto.com / Onfokus; iStockphoto.com / marvinh

E-Book Readers

An **e-book reader** (short for electronic book reader), or *e-reader*, is a mobile device that is used primarily for reading e-books (Figure 1-9). An *e-book*, or digital book, is an electronic version of a printed book, readable on computers and other digital devices. In addition to books, you typically can purchase and read other forms of digital media such as newspapers and magazines.

Most e-book reader models have a touch screen, and some are Internet capable. These devices usually are smaller than tablets but larger than smartphones.

Wearable Devices

A **wearable device** or *wearable* is a small, mobile computing consumer device designed to be worn (Figure 1-10). These devices often communicate with a mobile device or computer.

Two popular wearable devices are activity trackers and smartwatches. Activity trackers monitor heart rate, measure pulse, count steps, and track sleep patterns. In addition to keeping time, a smartwatch can communicate with a smartphone to make and answer phone calls, read and send messages, access the web, play music, work with apps, such as fitness trackers and GPS, and more.

Figure 1-9   An e-book reader.
iStockphoto.com / hocus-focus

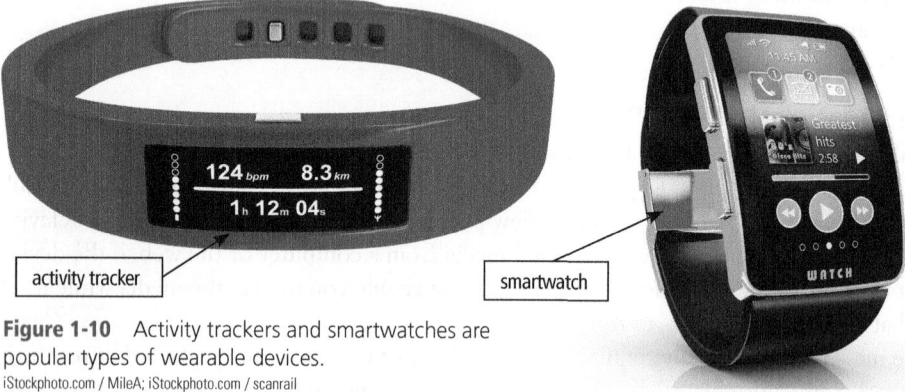

Figure 1-10   Activity trackers and smartwatches are popular types of wearable devices.
iStockphoto.com / MileA; iStockphoto.com / scanrail

Game Devices

A **game console** is a mobile computing device designed for single-player or multiplayer video games. Gamers often connect the game console to a television so that they can view their game-play on the television's screen (Figure 1-11). Many game console models are Internet capable and also allow you to listen to music and watch movies or view photos. Typically weighing between three and eleven pounds, the compact size of game consoles makes them easy to use at home, in the car, in a hotel, or any location that has an electrical outlet and a television screen.

Figure 1-11   Game consoles often connect to a television; handheld game devices contain a built-in screen.
iStockphoto.com / pagadesign;
iStockphoto.com / AnthonyRosenberg

A handheld game device is small enough to fit in one hand, making it more portable than the game console. Because of their reduced size, the screens are small — similar in size to some smartphone screens. Some handheld game device models are Internet capable and also can communicate wirelessly with other similar devices for multiplayer gaming.

 CONSIDER THIS

Are digital cameras, portable media players, e-book readers, and handheld game devices becoming obsolete as more and more smartphones and tablets include their functionality?

Many smartphones and tablets enable you to take and store photos; store, organize, and play or view your digital media; read e-books; and play games. This trend of computers and devices with technologies that overlap, called **digital device convergence**, means that consumers may need fewer devices for the functionality that they require.

Still, consumers may purchase separate stand-alone devices (i.e., a separate digital camera, portable media player, etc.) for a variety of reasons. The stand-alone device (i.e., a digital camera) may have more features and functionality than the combined device offers (i.e., a smartphone). You might want to be able to use both devices at the same time; for example, you might send text messages on the phone while reading a book on an e-book reader. Or, you might want protection if your combined device (i.e., smartphone) breaks. For example, you still can listen to music on a portable media player if your smartphone becomes nonfunctional.

Tech Feature 1-1: Gaming and Digital Home

Technology has made homes entertaining, efficient, and safe. Read Tech Feature 1-1 to learn how game devices provide entertainment and education, and home automation offers convenience and significant cost savings.

 TECH FEATURE 1-1

Gaming and Digital Home

Academic researchers developed the first video games in the 1950s as part of their studies of artificial intelligence and simulations, and their work was applied and expanded commercially to early home consoles and arcade games. The concept of home automation can be traced back to 1898 when Nikola Tesla invented the first remote control. The following sections describe how these two technologies are used today.

Gaming

Video gamers spend billions of dollars each year making the most of their downtime with game consoles and devices. An estimated 1.2 billion people worldwide are active video gamers, half of whom play at least 2 hours per day. The popularity is due, in large part, to the social aspect of gathering families and friends to play together as a group or online with one another and those around the world. The wide variety of categories offers a gaming experience for practically everyone in genres such as adventure, education, fitness, puzzles, sports, role-playing, and simulation.

- **Obtaining Games:** Gamers have several options available for obtaining games. For tablets and smartphones, they can download games from an app store to a mobile computer or device. For game consoles,

they can purchase or rent discs or other media that contain games, download or transfer them from online stores, or sign up for cloud services that stream or transfer games on demand.

- **Accessories and Input Techniques:** The more popular game consoles work with a wide variety of accessories and input techniques for directing movements and actions of on-screen players and objects. They include gamepads, voice commands, and fitness accessories, some of which are shown here. Although many games are played using a controller, several game consoles operate by allowing the player to be the controller.

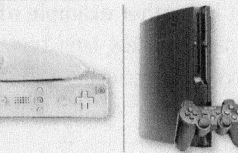

iStockphoto.com / Florea Marius Catalin; iStockphoto.com / Brandon Alms; iStockphoto.com / Lee Pettet; iStockphoto.com / Craig Veltri; Courtesy of DDR Game

Home Automation

New home builders and existing homeowners are integrating features that automate a wide variety of tasks, save time and money, and enhance the overall at-home environment.

(continued)

- **Lighting:** Controlling lighting is one of the more common uses of technology in the home. Remotes turn light fixtures on and off, and motion sensors turn on lights when a car or a visitor approaches the driveway or walkway.

- **Thermostats:** Programmable thermostats adjust to seasonal needs and can be set to control temperatures in individual rooms. Homeowners can use their smartphones to monitor heating and cooling systems, adjust temperatures, and manage energy consumption.

- **Appliances:** Smart appliances, such as dishwashers, can be programmed to run at nonpeak electrical times. Coffeemakers can turn on at set times and shut off if an overheating coffeepot has been left on accidentally. Refrigerators can track expiration dates and create shopping lists.

- **Security:** Security systems can detect break-ins at doors and heat from fires, and they can send text and

email messages to alert a homeowner when someone has entered or left the home. Surveillance cameras keep a watchful eye on the premises and interior rooms; homeowners can view the images on televisions and computers within the house or on a webpage when they are away from home.

- **Remotes:** Many people are turning to using their smartphones and tablets to control all the devices in the room. Users enjoy the convenience of customizing apps to operate their television, DVR, and security system and to perform other functions anywhere in the home.

DavidEwingPhotography / Shutterstock.com; Poulsons Photography / Shutterstock.com; Anthony Berenyi / Shutterstock.com

iStockphoto.com / Christian J. Stewart; Mmaxer / Shutterstock. com; iStockphoto.com / Nastco; © ESPN

✸ **Consider This:** How has your life become more efficient, safe, and enjoyable by using home automation and entertainment features? Why do you think gaming is so popular? Can you think of any downsides?

Data and Information

Computers process data (input) into information (output) and often store the data and resulting information for future use. *Data* is a collection of unprocessed items, which can include text, numbers, images, audio, and video. *Information* conveys meaning to users. Both business and home users can make well-informed decisions because they have instant access to information from anywhere in the world.

Many daily activities either involve the use of or depend on information from a computer. For example, as shown in Figure 1-12, computers process several data items to print information in the form of a cash register receipt.

✸ **CONSIDER THIS**

What is another example of data and its corresponding information?
Your name, address, term, course names, course sections, course grades, and course credits all represent data that is processed to generate your semester grade report. Other information on the grade report includes results of calculations, such as total semester hours, grade point average, and total credits.

Input

Users have a variety of input options for entering data into a computer, many of which involve using an input device. An **input device** is any hardware component that allows you to enter data and instructions into a computer or mobile device. The following sections discuss common input methods.

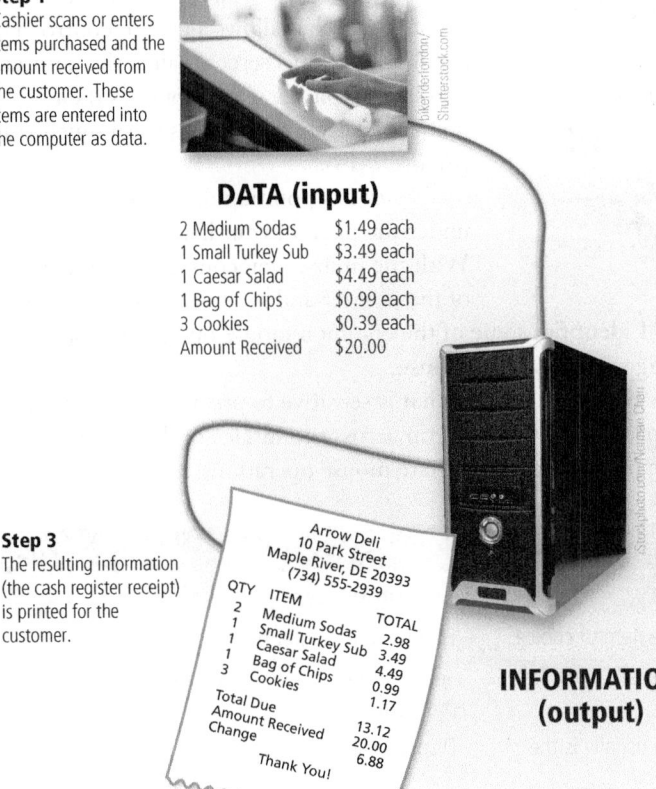

Step 1
Cashier scans or enters items purchased and the amount received from the customer. These items are entered into the computer as data.

DATA (input)

2 Medium Sodas	$1.49 each
1 Small Turkey Sub	$3.49 each
1 Caesar Salad	$4.49 each
1 Bag of Chips	$0.99 each
3 Cookies	$0.39 each
Amount Received	$20.00

Step 2
The computer receives the entered data, stores it, processes the data into information (the receipt), and stores the resulting information.

STORAGE and PROCESSES

- Stores entered data.
- Computes each item's total price by multiplying the quantity ordered by the item price (i.e., 2 * 1.49 = 2.98).
- Organizes data.
- Sums all item total prices to determine order total due from customer (13.12).
- Calculates change due to customer by subtracting the order total from amount received (20.00 - 13.12 = 6.88).
- Stores resulting information.

Step 3
The resulting information (the cash register receipt) is printed for the customer.

Arrow Deli
10 Park Street
Maple River, DE 20393
(734) 555-2939

QTY	ITEM	TOTAL
2	Medium Sodas	2.98
1	Small Turkey Sub	3.49
1	Caesar Salad	4.49
1	Bag of Chips	0.99
3	Cookies	1.17
Total Due		13.12
Amount Received		20.00
Change		6.88

Thank You!

INFORMATION (output)

Figure 1-12 A computer processes data into information. In this simplified example, the item ordered, item price, quantity ordered, and amount received all represent data (input). The computer processes the data to produce the cash register receipt (information, or output).

Keyboards A *keyboard* contains keys you press to enter data and instructions into a computer or mobile device (Figure 1-13). All desktop keyboards have a typing area that includes letters of the alphabet, numbers, punctuation marks, and other basic keys. Some users prefer a wireless keyboard because it eliminates the clutter of a cord.

Keyboards for desktops contain more keys than keyboards on mobile computers and devices. To provide the same functionality as a desktop keyboard, many of the keys on mobile computers and devices serve two or three purposes. On a laptop, for example, you often use the same keys to type numbers and to show various areas on a screen, switching a key's purpose by pressing a separate key first.

Instead of a physical keyboard, users also can enter data via an on-screen keyboard or a virtual keyboard, which is a keyboard that projects from a device to a flat surface.

desktop keyboard

laptop keyboard

Figure 1-13 Users have a variety of options for entering typed text.
skyfotostock / Shutterstock.com; Africa Studio / Shutterstock.com; Billion Photos / Shutterstock.com; David Lichtneker / Alamy Stock Photo; Courtesy of Virtual Devices

on-screen keyboard

mini keyboard

virtual keyboard

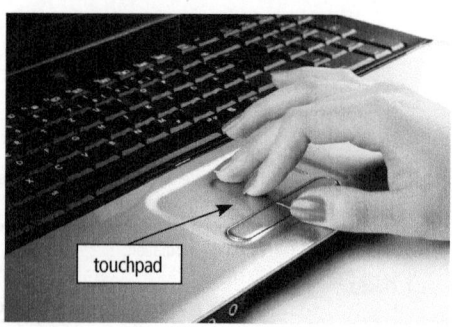

touchpad

mouse

Figure 1-14 A mouse and a touchpad.
iStockphoto.com / PhotoTalk;
iStockphoto.com / deepblue4you

Pointing Devices A pointing device is an input device that allows a user to control a small symbol on a screen, called the pointer. Desktops typically use a mouse as their pointing device, and laptops use a touchpad (Figure 1-14).

A *mouse* is a pointing device that fits under the palm of your hand comfortably. With the mouse, you control movement of the pointer and send instructions to the computer or mobile device. Table 1-1 identifies some of the common mouse operations. Like keyboards, some users prefer working with a wireless mouse.

A *touchpad* is a small, flat, rectangular pointing device that is sensitive to pressure and motion. To control the pointer with a touchpad, slide your fingertip across the surface of the pad. On most touchpads, you also can tap the pad's surface to imitate mouse operations, such as clicking.

Table 1-1	Mouse Operations	
Operation	**Description**	**Common Uses**
Point	Move the mouse until the pointer is positioned on the item of choice.	Position the pointer on the screen.
Click	Press and release the primary mouse button, which usually is the left mouse button.	Select or deselect items on the screen or run a program or feature.
Right-click	Press and release the secondary mouse button, which usually is the right mouse button.	Display a shortcut menu.
Double-click	Quickly press and release the primary mouse button twice without moving the mouse.	Run a program or program feature.
Drag	Point to an item, hold down the primary mouse button, move the item to the desired location on the screen, and then release the mouse button.	Move an object from one location to another or draw pictures.

Voice and Video Input Some mobile devices and computers enable you to speak data instructions using voice input and to capture live full-motion images using video input. With your smartphone, for example, you may be able to use your voice to send a text message, schedule an appointment, and dial a phone number. Or, you may opt for video calling instead of a voice phone call, so that you and the person you called can see each other as you chat on a computer or mobile device. As in this example, video input usually works in conjunction with voice input. For voice input, you use a microphone, and for video input you use a webcam (Figure 1-15).

microphone built into phone

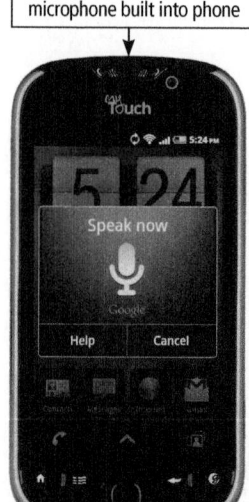

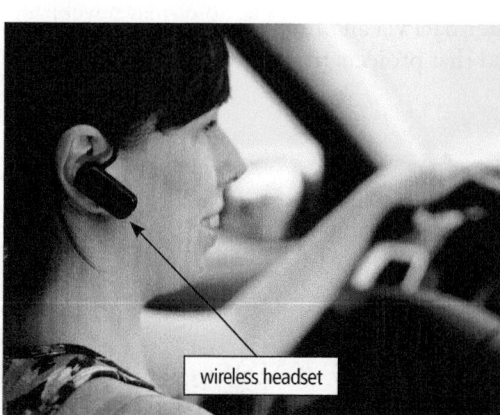

wireless headset

webcam

Figure 1-15 You can speak instructions into a microphone or wireless headset and capture live video on a webcam for a video call.
iStockphoto.com / Stephen Krow; iStockphoto.com / pierrephoto; iStockphoto.com / SuprijonoSuharjoto

A *microphone* is an input device that enables you to speak into a computer or mobile device. Many computers and most mobile devices contain built-in microphones. You also can talk into a *headset*, which contains both a microphone and a speaker. Many headsets can communicate wirelessly with the computer or mobile device. A *webcam* is a digital video (DV) camera that allows you to capture video and usually audio input for your computer or mobile device.

Scanners   A *scanner* is a light-sensing input device that converts printed text and images into a form the computer can process (Figure 1-16). A popular type of scanner works in a manner similar to a copy machine, except that instead of creating a paper copy of the document or photo, it stores the scanned document or photo electronically.

Figure 1-16   A scanner.
iStockphoto.com / EdgarasMarozas

Output

Users have a variety of output options to convey text, graphics, audio, and video — many of which involve using an output device. An **output device** is any hardware component that conveys information from a computer or mobile device to one or more people. The following sections discuss common output methods.

Printers   A **printer** is an output device that produces text and graphics on a physical medium, such as paper or other material (Figure 1-17). Printed content sometimes is referred to as a *hard copy* or *printout*. Most printers today print text and graphics in both black-and-white and color on a variety of paper types with many capable of printing lab-quality photos. A variety of printers support wireless printing, where a computer or other device communicates wirelessly with the printer.

A *3-D printer* can print solid objects, such as clothing, prosthetics, eyewear, implants, toys, parts, prototypes, and more. 3-D (three-dimensional) printers may use a variety of substances, including plastic, nylon, wood, bronze, and copper, to print the layers that create a 3-D model.

printed 3-D model

printed photo

Figure 1-17   A printer can produce a variety of printed output including photos and 3-D solid objects.
Courtesy of Epson America, Inc.; Tinxi / Shutterstock.com

Displays   A display is an output device that visually conveys text, graphics, and video information. Displays consist of a screen and the components that produce the information on the screen. The display for a desktop usually is a monitor, which is a separate, physical device. Mobile computers and devices typically integrate the display in their same physical case (Figure 1-18). Many displays have touch screens.

smartphone display

digital camera display

tablet display

laptop display

monitor display

Figure 1-18 Displays vary depending on the computer or mobile device.

iStockphoto.com / Sebastien Cote; David Lentz / Photos.com; Dmitry Rukhlenko / Photos.com; Steve Allen / Dreamstime.com; Pakhnyushcha / Shutterstock.com

Home users sometimes use a digital television or a Smart TV as a display. A *Smart TV* is an Internet-capable high-definition television (HDTV) on which you can use the Internet to watch video, listen to the radio, play games, and communicate with others — all while watching a television show.

☀ **CONSIDER THIS**

What can you do to ease eyestrain while using a computer or mobile device?
Position the display about 20 degrees below eye level. Clean the screen regularly. Blink your eyes every five seconds. Adjust the room lighting. Face into an open space beyond the screen. Use larger fonts or zoom the display. Take an eye break every 30 minutes. If you wear glasses, ask your doctor about computer glasses.

headphones

Figure 1-19 In a crowded environment where speakers are not practical, users can wear headphones to hear music, voice, and other audio.

iStockphoto.com / Photo_Alto

Speakers, Earbuds, and Headphones Speakers allow you to hear audio, that is, music, voice, and other sounds. Most personal computers and mobile devices have a small internal speaker. Many users attach higher-quality speakers to their computers and mobile devices, including game consoles.

So that only you can hear sound, you can listen through earbuds (shown earlier in this module in Figure 1-8) or headphones, which cover or are placed outside of the ear (Figure 1-19). Both earbuds and headphones usually include noise-cancelling technology to reduce the interference of sounds from the surrounding environment. To eliminate the clutter of cords, users can opt for wireless speakers or wireless headphones.

☀ **CONSIDER THIS**

How can you protect your hearing when using earbuds or headphones?
The lower the volume levels, the less potential hearing damage. Decrease the volume until people near you cannot hear the sound from your earbuds or headphones. Consider using a high-quality set of headphones with noise-cancelling technology. These headphones have improved sound quality so that you do not need to turn up the volume as loud. They also have a better design with a closer fit, which reduces the volume required for optimal listening. Noise-cancelling technology eliminates the external noise, allowing you to reduce the volume level needed. Lastly, if you intend to listen to music through earbuds or headphones for hours at a time, consider listening at only 30 percent maximum volume, because listening for extended periods of time at a high volume may be unsafe for your ears.

Memory and Storage

Memory consists of electronic components that store instructions waiting to be executed and the data needed by those instructions. Although some forms of memory are permanent, most memory keeps data and instructions temporarily, which means its contents are erased when the computer is shut off.

Storage, by contrast, holds data, instructions, and information for future use. For example, computers can store hundreds or millions of student names and addresses permanently. A computer keeps data, instructions, and information on **storage media**. Examples of local storage media includes hard disks, solid-state drives, USB (universal serial bus) flash drives, memory cards, and optical discs. The amount of storage for each type of storage media varies, but hard disks and solid-state drives generally have the largest capacities, followed by optical discs, USB flash drives, and memory cards. Some storage media are portable, meaning you can remove the medium from one computer and carry it to another computer.

A **storage device** records (writes) and/or retrieves (reads) items to and from storage media. Storage devices often also function as a source of input and output because they transfer items from storage to memory and vice versa. Drives and readers/writers, which are types of storage devices, accept a specific kind of storage media. For example, a DVD drive (storage device) accepts a DVD (storage media).

Hard Disks   A *hard disk* is a storage device that contains one or more inflexible, circular platters that use magnetic particles to store data, instructions, and information. The entire device is enclosed in an airtight, sealed case to protect it from contamination. Laptops and desktops often contain at least one hard disk that is mounted inside the computer's case (Figure 1-20).

Solid-State Drives   A *solid-state drive* (SSD) is a storage device that typically uses flash memory to store data, instructions, and information. Flash memory contains no moving parts, making it more durable and shock resistant than other types of media. For this reason, manufacturers typically offer SSDs as an option instead of hard disks in their laptops, tablets, and desktops (Figure 1-21).

hard disk is positioned in base of laptop

Figure 1-20   A hard disk mounted inside a laptop's case.
iStockphoto.com / Brian Balster

hard disk contains moving parts

SSD contains no moving parts

Figure 1-21   A solid-state drive (SSD) is about the same size as a laptop hard disk.
iStockphoto.com / ludinko

CONSIDER THIS

What is an external hard drive?
An external hard drive is a separate, portable, freestanding hard disk or SSD that usually connects to the computer with a cable (Figure 1-22). As with an internal hard disk or SSD, the entire external hard drive is enclosed in an airtight, sealed case.

external hard drive connected to laptop

Figure 1-22   A external hard drive is a separate, freestanding storage device.

iStockphoto.com / muratsarica

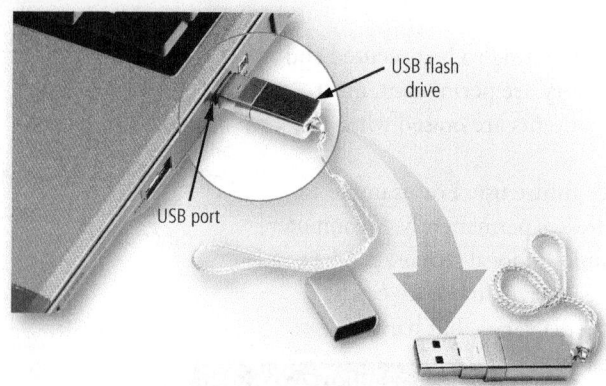

Figure 1-23 You insert a USB flash drive in a USB port on a computer.
Pakhnyushcha / Shutterstock.com

USB Flash Drives   A *USB flash drive* is a portable flash memory storage device that you plug in a USB port, which is a special, easily accessible opening on a computer or mobile device (Figure 1-23). USB flash drives are convenient for mobile users because they are small and lightweight enough to be transported on a keychain or in a pocket.

Memory Cards   A *memory card* is removable flash memory, usually no bigger than 1.5 inches in height or width, that you insert in and remove from a slot in a computer, mobile device, or card reader/writer (Figure 1-24). With a card reader/writer, you can transfer the stored items, such as digital photos, from a memory card to a computer or printer that does not have a built-in card slot.

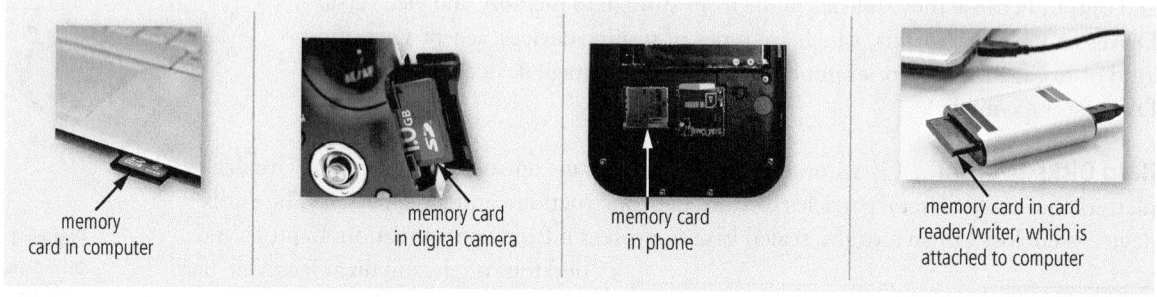

Figure 1-24 Computers and mobile devices use a variety of styles of memory cards to store documents, photos, and other items.
Verisakeet / Fotolia LLC; Sonar / Fotolia LLC; Courtesy of Mark Frydenberg: uwimages / Fotolia LLC

✳ CONSIDER THIS

What is the general use for each type of local storage media?
Hard disks and SSDs store software and all types of user files. A *file* is a named collection of stored data, instructions, or information and can contain text, images, audio, and video. Memory cards and USB flash drives store files you intend to transport from one location to another, such as a homework assignment or photos. Optical discs generally store software, photos, movies, and music.

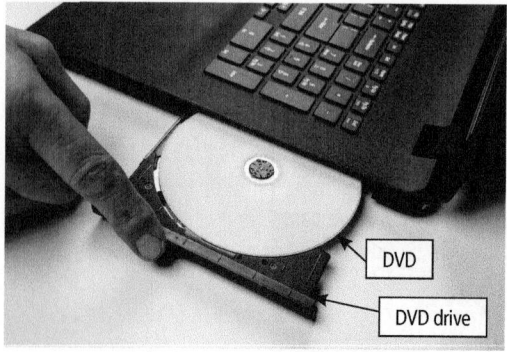

Figure 1-25 You can insert a DVD in a DVD drive on a computer. Some computers have DVD slots instead of DVD drives.
iStockphoto.com / MagMos

Optical Discs   An *optical disc* is a type of storage media that consists of a flat, round, portable metal disc made of metal, plastic, and lacquer that is written and read by a laser. CDs (compact discs) and DVDs (digital versatile discs) (Figure 1-25) are two types of optical discs.

Cloud Storage   Instead of storing data, instructions, and information locally on a hard drive or other media, some users opt for cloud storage. **Cloud storage** is an Internet service that provides remote storage to computer users. For example, Figure 1-26 shows JustCloud, which provides cloud storage solutions to home and business users.

Types of services offered by cloud storage providers vary. Some provide storage for specific types of media, such as photos, whereas others store any content and provide backup services. A **backup** is a duplicate of content on a storage medium that you can use in case the original is lost, damaged, or destroyed. Read Secure IT 1-1 for suggestions for backing up your computers and mobile devices.

Figure 1-26 JustCloud is an example of a website that provides cloud storage solutions to home and business users.
Source: JustCloud.com

✸ SECURE IT 1-1

Backing Up Computers and Mobile Devices

Power outages, hardware failure, theft, and many other factors can cause loss of data, instructions, or information on a computer or mobile device. To protect against loss, you should back up the contents of storage media regularly. Backing up can provide peace of mind and save hours of work attempting to recover important material in the event of a mishap.

A backup plan for laptop and desktop computers could include the following:

- Use a backup program, either included with your computer's operating system or one that you purchased separately, to copy the contents of your entire hard drive to a separate device.

- Regularly copy music, photos, videos, documents, and other important items to an external hard drive, a USB flash drive, or a DVD.

- Subscribe to a cloud storage provider.

- Schedule your files to be backed up regularly.

Backup plans for mobile devices are less specific. Apps for backing up your smartphone or tablet's content are available. You also can back up a mobile device to your computer's hard drive using synchronization software that runs on your computer (synchronization software is discussed later in this module). Some mobile device manufacturers, such as Apple, provide cloud storage solutions to owners of their devices. Other services allow subscribers to use another computer as a backup storage location. Overall, the best advice is to back up often using a variety of methods.

✸ **Consider This:** Do you back up files regularly? If not, why not? What would you do if you had no backup and then discovered that your computer or mobile device had failed?

cloud storage provider

Courtesy of Western Digital Corporation; iStockphoto.com / Stephen Krow

The Web

The World Wide Web (or web, for short) is a global library of information available to anyone connected to the Internet. The **Internet** is a worldwide collection of computer networks that connects millions of businesses, government agencies, educational institutions, and individuals (Figure 1-27).

Figure 1-27 The Internet is the largest computer network, connecting millions of computers and devices around the world.

Mmaxer / Shutterstock.com; Alfonso de Tomas / Shutterstock.com; SSSCCC / Shutterstock.com; iStockphoto.com / PetarChernaev; amfoto / Shutterstock. com; iStockphoto.com / Oleksiy Mark; iStockphoto.com / Oleksiy Mark; iStockphoto.com / sweetym; Oleksiy Mark / Shutterstock.com; iStockphoto.com / Stephen Krow; iStockphoto.com / Skip O'Donnell; Source: Apple Inc; iStockphoto.com / Skip O'Donnell; Source: Nutrition Blog Network; iStockphoto.com / AyaazRattansi; Oleksiy Mark / Shutterstock.com

 CONSIDER THIS ──────────────────────

How do I access the Internet?

Businesses, called Internet service providers (ISPs), offer users and organizations access to the Internet free or for a fee. By subscribing to an ISP, you can connect to the Internet through your computers and mobile devices.

Many everyday devices and objects or "things" are equipped with sensors that transmit data to and from the Internet. The term, the Internet of Things (IoT), is used to collectively refer to this communications capability. The IoT includes activity trackers, smartwatches, thermostats, alarm clocks, coffeemakers, appliances, and more.

 CONSIDER THIS ──────────────────────

Are the web and Internet the same?

No. The Internet provides more than 3.5 billion home and business users around the world access to a variety of services. The web is one of the widely used services of the Internet. Other popular services include email, instant messaging, VoIP, and FTP (all discussed later in this module).

People around the world access the web to accomplish the following types of online tasks:

- Search for information
- Conduct research
- Communicate with and meet other people
- Share information, photos, and videos with others
- Access news, weather, and sports
- Participate in online training

- Shop for goods and services
- Play games with others
- Download or listen to music
- Watch videos
- Download or read books
- Make reservations

 **BTW**

Downloading

Downloading is the process of transferring existing content stored on a server or other computer or device to your device via a network.

The **web** consists of a worldwide collection of electronic documents. Each electronic document on the web is called a **webpage**, which can contain text, graphics, audio, and video (Figure 1-28). A **website** is a collection of related webpages, which are stored on a web server. A **web server** is a computer that delivers requested webpages to your computer or mobile device.

Webpages often contain links. A *link*, short for *hyperlink*, is a built-in connection to other documents, graphics, audio files, videos, webpages, or websites. To activate an item associated with a link, you click the link. In Figure 1-28, for example, clicking the audio link connects to a live radio show so that you can hear the broadcast. A text link often changes color after you click it to remind you visually that you previously have visited the webpage or downloaded the content associated with the link.

Figure 1-28 Webpages, such as the one shown here, can display text, graphics, audio, and video on a computer or mobile device. Pointing to a link on the screen typically changes the shape of the pointer to a small hand with a pointing index finger.
Source: WTMJ

Links allow you to obtain information in a nonlinear way. That is, instead of accessing topics in a specified order, you move directly to a topic of interest. Some people use the phrase *surfing the web* to refer to the activity of using links to explore the web.

Browsing the Web

A **browser** is software that enables users with an Internet connection to access and view webpages on a computer or mobile device. Some widely used browsers include Chrome, Edge, Firefox, and Safari. Read How To 1-2 for instructions about using a browser to display a webpage on a computer or mobile device.

HOW TO 1-2

Use a Browser to Display a Webpage
The following steps describe how to use a browser to display a webpage on a computer or mobile device:

1. Run a browser. (Running programs and apps is discussed later in this module.)
2. If necessary, click the address bar to select it and any previously displayed web address it may contain. (A *web address* is a unique address that identifies a webpage.)

3. In the address bar, type the web address of the webpage you want to visit and then press the ENTER key or click the Go (or similar) button to display the webpage. For example, www.cengagebrain.com is a valid web address, which displays the CengageBrain webpage shown in the figure below. (Module 2 discusses the components of a web address.)

4. If necessary, scroll to view the entire webpage. You can scroll either by sliding your finger across a touch screen or by using a pointing device, such as a mouse, to drag the scroll bar.
5. Click links on the webpage to navigate to the link's destination.

   Consider This: What should you do if the web address you enter does not display a webpage or you receive an error message?

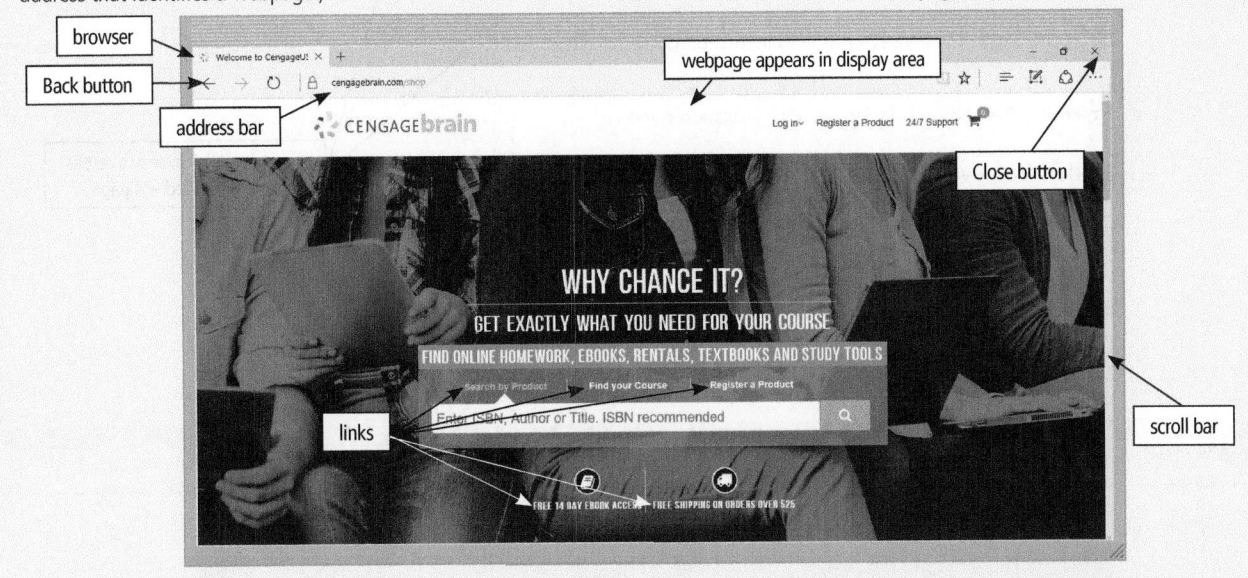

Searching the Web

A primary reason that people use the web is to search for specific information, including text, photos, music, and videos. The first step in successful searching is to identify the main idea or concept in the topic about which you are seeking information. Determine any synonyms, alternate spellings, or variant word forms for the topic. Then, use a search engine, such as Google, to help you locate the information. A **search engine** is software that finds websites, webpages, images, videos, news, maps, and other information related to a specific topic. Read How To 1-3 for instructions about how to perform a basic web search using a search engine on a computer or mobile device.

✺ HOW TO 1-3

Perform a Basic Web Search

The following steps describe how to use a search engine on a computer or mobile device to perform a basic web search:

1. Run a browser. (Running programs and apps is discussed later in this module.)

2. Display the search engine's webpage on the screen by entering its web address in the address bar. For example, you could type `google.com` to access the Google search engine, or `bing.com` to access the Bing search engine, or `yahoo.com` to access the Yahoo! search engine.

3. Click the Search box and then type the desired search text in the Search box. The more descriptive the search text, the easier it will be to locate the desired search results. As the figure shows, the search engine may provide search text suggestions as you type search text in the Search box.

4. To display search results based on your typed search text, press the ENTER key or click the Search button. To display search results based on one of the suggestions provided by the search engine, click the desired search text suggestion.

5. Scroll through the search results and then click a search result to display the corresponding webpage.

6. To return to the search results, click the Back button in the browser or on the mobile device, which typically looks like a left-pointing arrow.

✺ **Consider This:** What search text would you enter to locate the admission criteria for your school?

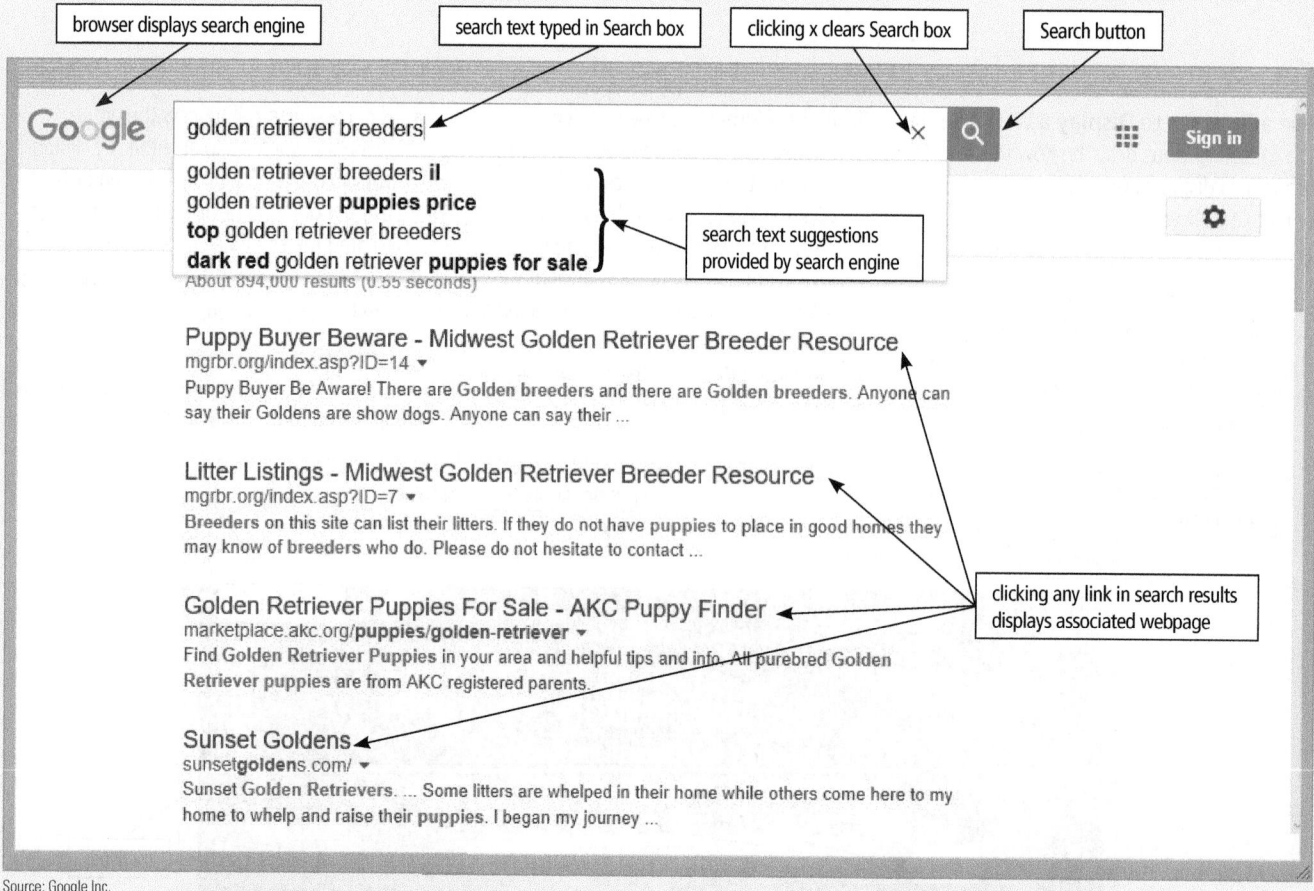

browser displays search engine

search text typed in Search box

clicking x clears Search box

Search button

search text suggestions provided by search engine

clicking any link in search results displays associated webpage

Source: Google Inc.

Online Social Networks

An **online social network**, also called a *social networking site*, is a website that encourages members in its online community to share their interests, ideas, stories, photos, music, and videos with other registered users (Figure 1-29). Popular online social networks include Facebook, Twitter, and LinkedIn.

Some online social networks have no specialized audience; others are more focused. A photo sharing site, for example, is a specific type of online social network that allows users to create an online photo album and store and share their digital photos. Similarly, a video sharing site is a type of online social network that enables users to store and share their personal videos. Read Ethics & Issues 1-2 to consider whether you should be required to obtain permission before posting photos of others.

Figure 1-29 When Facebook users share, comment on, or "like" a post, the post appears on their own personal Facebook pages.
iStockphoto.com / RossHelen

 CONSIDER THIS

How do Facebook, Twitter, and LinkedIn differ?

With Facebook, you share messages, interests, activities, events, photos, and other personal information — called posts — with family and friends. You also can 'like' pages of celebrities, companies, products, etc., so that posts from others who like the same items will appear along with your other activities on Facebook. With Twitter, you 'follow' people, companies, and organizations in which you have an interest. Twitter enables you to stay current with the daily activities of those you are following via their Tweets, which are short posts (messages) that Twitter users broadcast for all their followers.

On LinkedIn, you share professional interests, education, and employment history, and add colleagues or coworkers to your list of contacts. You can include recommendations from people who know you professionally. Many employers post jobs using LinkedIn and consider information in your profile as your online resume.

 BTW

Blogs

Posts on Twitter also form a blog, because of its journal format with the most recent entry at the top.

 ETHICS & ISSUES 1-2

Should You Be Required to Obtain Permission before Posting Photos of Others?

Your friends and followers on online social networks instantly can view photos you post. If others appear in the photo and you post it without their permission, they might feel you have violated their privacy. Tagging people in a photo may create a link to their social network profiles, exposing their identity. Depending on your privacy settings, your friends' contacts can view a photo you post and/or share the photo without your permission.

You may be able to adjust tagging rules in the privacy settings of your online social network account. For example, you can use Facebook's privacy settings to approve all photos in which others tag you. The person posting the photo still can upload the photo, but the photo's tag will not be linked to your social media account until you approve the tag. Facebook also allows you to report a photo as abusive if you feel it portrays you negatively or if the person who posted it refuses to remove it upon request. Facebook's own Statement of Rights and Responsibilities states that "You will not tag users ... without their consent."

People may not want photos of themselves posted for a variety reasons. They may have professional contacts as friends on their online social network and do not want to show themselves in a personal setting. Others may not be concerned with personal photos of themselves but do not want their children's photos shared online. Or, they simply may find the photo unflattering. A poll by Sophos stated that more than 90 percent of respondents felt they should be asked before someone posts a photo of them online. Eight percent of respondents felt that it should be illegal to do so.

Consider This: Is it ever acceptable to post photos of others without permission? Why or why not? Has someone posted or tagged you in a photo that you did not want others to see? How did you handle the situation? If asked to remove a photo or tag, would you respect the person's feelings and honor the request? What restrictions and policies should online social networks have about posting photos of others?

Internet Communications

As mentioned earlier, the web is only one of the services on the Internet. Other services on the Internet facilitate communications among users, including the following:

- Email allows you to send messages to and receive messages and files from other users via a computer network.
- With messaging services, you can have a real-time typed conversation with another connected user (real-time means that both of you are online at the same time).
- VoIP (Voice over Internet Protocol) enables users to speak to other users over the Internet (discussed further in later modules).
- With FTP (File Transfer Protocol), users can transfer items to and from other computers on the Internet (discussed further in later modules).

Digital Security and Privacy

People rely on computers to create, store, and manage their information. To safeguard this information, it is important that users protect their computers and mobile devices. Users also should be aware of health risks and environmental issues associated with using computers and mobile devices.

BTW

Malware
A recent study by Statista reports that security software blocks more than one million malware attacks every day.

Viruses and Other Malware

Malware, short for malicious software, is software that typically acts without a user's knowledge and deliberately alters the computer's or mobile device's operations. Examples of malware include viruses, worms, trojan horses, rootkits, spyware, adware, and zombies. Each of these types of malware attacks your computer or mobile device differently. Some are harmless pranks that temporarily freeze, play sounds, or display messages on your computer or mobile device. Others destroy or corrupt data, instructions, and information stored on the infected computer or mobile device. If you notice any unusual changes in the performance of your computer or mobile device, it may be infected with malware. Read Secure IT 1-2 for ways to protect computers from viruses and other malware.

SECURE IT 1-2

Protection from Viruses and Other Malware

It is impossible to ensure a virus or malware never will attack a computer, but you can take steps to protect your computer by following these practices:

- **Use virus protection software.** Install a reputable antivirus program and then scan the entire computer to be certain it is free of viruses and other malware. Update the antivirus program and the virus signatures (known specific patterns of viruses) regularly.
- **Use a firewall.** Set up a hardware firewall or install a software firewall that protects your network's resources from outside intrusions.
- **Be suspicious of all unsolicited email and text messages.** Never open an email message unless you are expecting it, *and* it is from a trusted source. When in doubt, ask the sender to confirm the message is legitimate before you open it. Be especially

cautious when deciding whether to click links in email and text messages or to open attachments.

- **Disconnect your computer from the Internet.** If you do not need Internet access, disconnect the computer from the Internet. Some security experts recommend disconnecting from the network before opening email attachments.
- **Download software with caution.** Download programs or apps only from websites you trust, especially those with music and video sharing software.
- **Close spyware windows.** If you suspect a pop-up window (a rectangular area that suddenly appears on your screen) may be spyware, close the window. Never click an Agree or OK button in a suspicious window.
- **Before using any removable media, scan it for malware.** Follow this

procedure even for shrink-wrapped software from major developers. Some commercial software has been infected and distributed to unsuspecting users. Never start a computer with removable media inserted in the computer unless you are certain the media are uninfected.

- **Keep current.** Install the latest updates for your computer software. Stay informed about new virus alerts and virus hoaxes.
- **Back up regularly.** In the event your computer becomes unusable due to a virus attack or other malware, you will be able to restore operations if you have a clean (uninfected) backup.

Consider This: What precautions do you take to prevent viruses and other malware from infecting your computer? What new steps will you take to attempt to protect your computer?

Privacy

Nearly every life event is stored in a computer somewhere ... in medical records, credit reports, tax records, etc. In many instances, where personal and confidential records were not protected properly, individuals have found their privacy violated and identities stolen. Some techniques you can use to protect yourself from identity theft include shredding financial documents before discarding them, never clicking links in unsolicited email messages, and enrolling in a credit monitoring service.

Adults, teens, and children around the world are using online social networks to share their photos, videos, journals, music, and other personal information publicly. Some of these unsuspecting, innocent computer users have fallen victim to crimes committed by dangerous strangers. Protect yourself and your dependents from these criminals by being cautious in email messages and on websites. For example, do not share information that would allow others to identify or locate you, and do not disclose identification numbers, user names, passwords, or other personal security details. A user name is a unique combination of characters, such as letters of the alphabet or numbers, that identifies one specific user. A password is a private combination of characters associated with a user name. Read Secure IT 1-3 for tips on creating strong passwords.

 SECURE IT 1-3

Creating Strong Passwords

A good password is easy for you to remember but difficult for criminals and password-breaking software to guess. Use these guidelines to create effective, strong passwords:

- **Personal information:** Avoid using any part of your first or last name, your family members' or pets' names, phone number, street address, license plate number, Social Security number, or birth date.
- **Length and Difficulty:** Use at least eight characters, including a variety of uppercase and lowercase letters, numbers, punctuation marks, and symbols. Select characters located on different parts of the keyboard, not the ones you commonly use or that are adjacent to each other. Criminals often use software that converts common words to symbols, so their program might generate

the passwords GoToSleep and Go2Sleep as possibilities to guess.

- **Modify:** Change your password frequently, at least every three months.
- **Variation:** Do not use the same password for all websites you access. Once criminals have stolen a password, they attempt to use that password for other accounts they find on your computer or mobile device, especially banking websites.
- **Passphrase:** A passphrase, which is similar to a password, consists of several words separated by spaces. Security experts recommend misspelling a few of the words and adding several numerals. For example, the phrase, "Create a strong password," could become the passphrase, "Creaet a strang pasword42."
- **Common sequences:** Avoid numbers or letters in easily recognized patterns, such

as "asdfjkl;," "12345678," "09870987," or "abcdefg." Also, do not spell words backward, use common abbreviations, or repeat strings of letters or numbers.

- **Manage:** Do not keep your passwords in your wallet, on a sheet of paper near your computer, or in a text file on your computer or mobile device. Memorize all of your passwords, or store them securely using a password management app on your computer or mobile device. Additional information about password management software is provided in Module 5.
- **Test:** Use online tools to evaluate password strength.

Consider This: How strong are your passwords? How will you modify your passwords using some of these guidelines?

Health Concerns

Prolonged or improper computer and mobile device use can lead to injuries or disorders of the hands, wrists, elbows, eyes, neck, and back. Computer and mobile device users can protect themselves from these health risks through proper workplace design, good posture while at the computer, and appropriately spaced work breaks.

With the growing use of earbuds and headphones, some users are experiencing hearing loss. Ways to protect your hearing when using these devices were presented earlier in this module.

Two behavioral health risks are technology addiction and technology overload. Technology addiction occurs when someone becomes obsessed with using technology. Individuals suffering from technology overload feel distressed when deprived of computers and mobile devices. Once recognized, both technology addiction and technology overload are treatable disorders.

Environmental Issues

Manufacturing processes for computers and mobile devices, along with *e-waste* (discarded computers and mobile devices), are depleting natural resources and polluting the environment. When computers and mobile devices are stored in basements or other locations, disposed of in landfills, or burned in incinerators, they can release toxic materials and potentially dangerous levels of lead, mercury, and flame retardants.

Green computing involves reducing the electricity consumed and environmental waste generated when using a computer. Strategies that support green computing include recycling, using energy-efficient hardware and energy-saving features, regulating manufacturing processes, extending the life of computers, and immediately donating or properly disposing of replaced computers. When you purchase a new computer, some retailers offer to dispose of your old computer properly.

✱ **CONSIDER THIS**

How can you contribute to green computing?
Some habits you can alter that will help reduce the environmental impact of computing include the following:

1. Do not leave a computer or device running overnight.
2. Turn off your monitor, printer, and other devices when you are not using them.
3. Use energy-efficient hardware.
4. Use paperless methods to communicate.
5. Recycle paper and buy recycled paper.
6. Recycle toner, computers, mobile devices, printers, and other devices.
7. Telecommute.
8. Use videoconferencing and VoIP for meetings.

Programs and Apps

Software, also called a **program**, consists of a series of related instructions, organized for a common purpose, that tells the computer what tasks to perform and how to perform them.

Two categories of software are system software and application software (or applications). System software consists of the programs that control or maintain the operations of the computer and its devices. Operating systems are a widely recognized example of system software. Other types of system software, sometimes called tools, enable you to perform maintenance-type tasks usually related to managing devices, media, and programs used by computers and mobile devices. The next sections discuss operating systems and applications.

Operating Systems

An *operating system* is a set of programs that coordinates all the activities among computer or mobile device hardware. It provides a means for users to communicate with the computer or mobile device and other software. Many of today's computers and mobile devices use a version of Microsoft's Windows, Apple's macOS, Apple's iOS, or Google's Android (Figure 1-30).

To use an application, your computer or mobile device must be running an operating system.

Figure 1-30 Shown here are the macOS and Windows operating systems for laptops and desktops and the Android and iOS operating systems for smartphones. You interact with these operating system interfaces by clicking or tapping their icons or tiles.
Courtesy of Apple Inc.; Ivan Garcia / Shutterstock.com; Courtesy of Apple Inc.; Courtesy of Microsoft

Applications

An **application** (or **app** for short) consists of programs designed to make users more productive and/or assist them with personal tasks. Browsers, discussed in an earlier section, are an example of an application that enables users with an Internet connection to access and view webpages. Table 1-2 identifies the categories of applications with samples of ones commonly used in each category.

Table 1-2   Categories of Applications

Category	Sample Applications	Sample Uses
Productivity	Word Processing	Create letters, reports, and other documents.
	Presentation	Create visual aids for presentations.
	Schedule and Contact Management	Organize appointments and contact lists.
	Personal Finance	Balance checkbook, pay bills, and track income and expenses.
Graphics and Media	Photo Editing	Modify digital photos, i.e., crop, remove red-eye, etc.
	Video and Audio Editing	Modify recorded movie clips, add music, etc.
	Media Player	View images, listen to audio/music, watch videos.
Personal Interest	Travel, Mapping, and Navigation	View maps, obtain route directions, locate points of interest.
	Reference	Look up material in dictionaries, encyclopedias, etc.
	Educational	Learn through tutors and prepare for tests.
	Entertainment	Receive entertainment news alerts, check movie times and reviews, play games.
Communications	Browser	Access and view webpages.
	Email	Send and receive messages.
	VoIP	Speak to other users over the Internet.
	FTP	Transfer items to and from other computers on the Internet.
Security	Antivirus	Protect a computer against viruses.
	Personal Firewall	Detect and protect against unauthorized intrusions.
	Spyware, Adware, and Other Malware Removers	Detect and delete spyware, adware, and other malware.
File, System, and Disk Management	File Manager	Display and organize files on storage media.
	Search	Locate files and other items on storage media.
	Image Viewer	Display, copy, and print contents of graphics files.
	Screen Saver	Shows moving image or blank screen if no keyboard or mouse activity occurs.

Applications include programs stored on a computer, as well as those on a mobile device or delivered to your device over the Internet.

- A *desktop app* is an application stored on a computer.
- A *web app* is an application stored on a web server that you access through a browser.
- A *mobile app* is an application you download from a mobile device's app store or other location on the Internet to a smartphone or other mobile device.

Some applications are available as both a web app and a mobile app. In this case, you typically can sync (or match) the data and activity between the web app and the mobile app, which is discussed later in this module.

Installing and Running Programs

Installing a program is the process of setting up the program to work with a computer or mobile device, printer, and/or other hardware. When you buy a computer or mobile device, it usually has some software, such as an operating system, preinstalled on its internal media so that you can use the computer or mobile device the first time you turn it on.

Installed operating systems often include applications such as a browser, media player, and calculator. To use additional desktop apps on a computer, you usually need to install the software. Mobile apps typically install automatically after you transfer the app's files to your mobile device from its website. You usually do not need to install web apps before you can run them.

Once installed, you run a program so that you can interact with it. When you instruct a computer or mobile device to run a program, the computer or mobile device *loads* it, which means the program's instructions are copied from storage to memory. Once in memory, the computer or mobile device can carry out, or execute, the instructions in the program so that you can use it.

You interact with a program through its user interface. The *user interface* controls how you enter data and instructions and how information is displayed on the screen. Often, you work with icons or tiles (shown previously in Figure 1-30), which are miniature images that link to programs, media, documents, or other objects.

 CONSIDER THIS

How do you know if a program will run on your computer?
When you buy a computer, you can find a list of the computer's specifications on the box, the manufacturer's website, or the order summary. Similarly, when you buy software, the box or the product's website will list specifications and minimum requirements for memory, speed, and more. Your computer's specifications should be the same as or greater than the software specifications. Ensure the software will run on your computer before making a purchase, because many retailers will not allow you to return software.

Developing Programs and Apps

A *software developer*, sometimes called a developer or programmer, is someone who develops programs and apps or writes the instructions that direct the computer or mobile device to process data into information. When writing instructions, a developer must be sure the program or app works properly so that the computer or mobile device generates the desired results. Complex programs can require thousands to millions of instructions.

Software developers use a programming language or application development tool to create programs and apps. Popular programming languages include C++, Java, JavaScript, Visual C#, and Visual Basic. Figure 1-31 shows some of the Visual Basic instructions a software developer may write to create a simple payroll program.

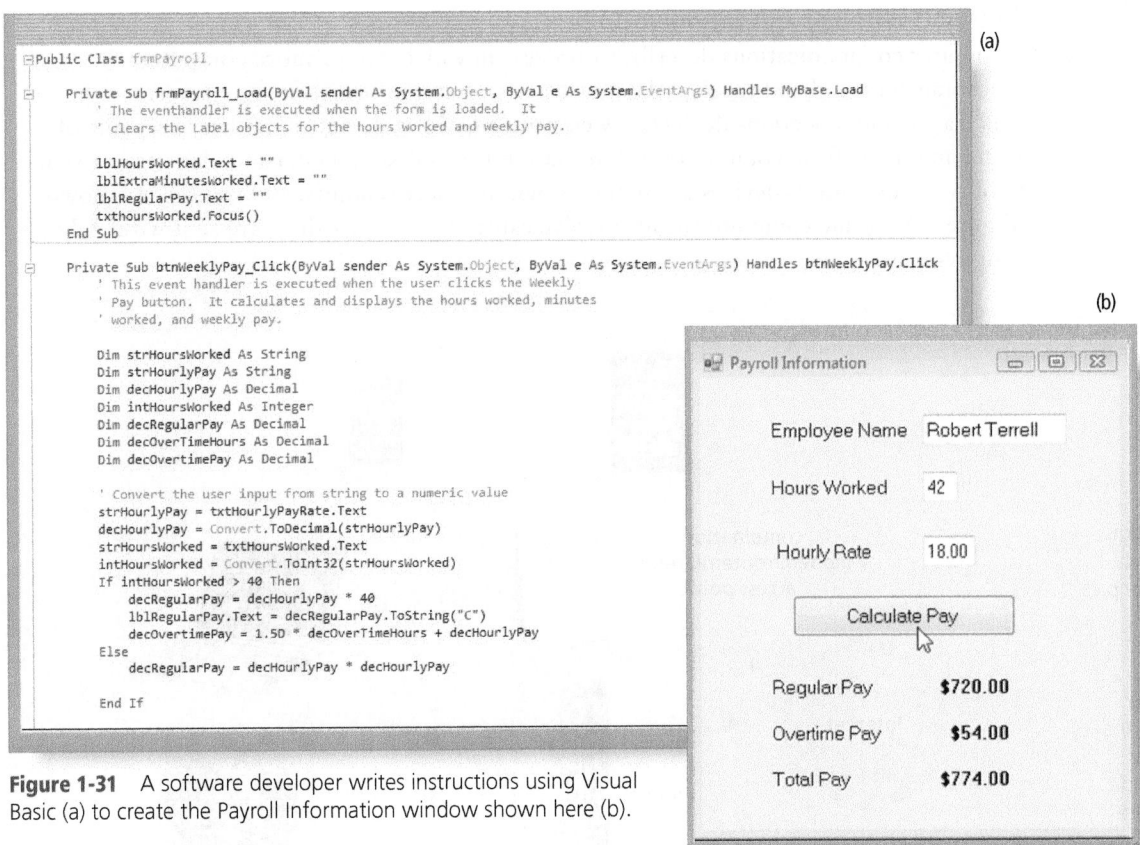

```
Public Class frmPayroll

    Private Sub frmPayroll_Load(ByVal sender As System.Object, ByVal e As System.EventArgs) Handles MyBase.Load
        ' The eventhandler is executed when the form is loaded.  It
        ' clears the Label objects for the hours worked and weekly pay.

        lblHoursWorked.Text = ""
        lblExtraMinutesWorked.Text = ""
        lblRegularPay.Text = ""
        txthoursWorked.Focus()
    End Sub

    Private Sub btnWeeklyPay_Click(ByVal sender As System.Object, ByVal e As System.EventArgs) Handles btnWeeklyPay.Click
        ' This event handler is executed when the user clicks the Weekly
        ' Pay button.  It calculates and displays the hours worked, minutes
        ' worked, and weekly pay.

        Dim strHoursWorked As String
        Dim strHourlyPay As String
        Dim decHourlyPay As Decimal
        Dim intHoursWorked As Integer
        Dim decRegularPay As Decimal
        Dim decOverTimeHours As Decimal
        Dim decOvertimePay As Decimal

        ' Convert the user input from string to a numeric value
        strHourlyPay = txtHourlyPayRate.Text
        decHourlyPay = Convert.ToDecimal(strHourlyPay)
        strHoursWorked = txtHoursWorked.Text
        intHoursWorked = Convert.ToInt32(strHoursWorked)
        If intHoursWorked > 40 Then
            decRegularPay = decHourlyPay * 40
            lblRegularPay.Text = decRegularPay.ToString("C")
            decOvertimePay = 1.50 * decOverTimeHours + decHourlyPay
        Else
            decRegularPay = decHourlyPay * decHourlyPay

        End If
```

(a)

(b)

Payroll Information

Employee Name	Robert Terrell
Hours Worked	42
Hourly Rate	18.00

Calculate Pay

Regular Pay	$720.00
Overtime Pay	$54.00
Total Pay	$774.00

Figure 1-31 A software developer writes instructions using Visual Basic (a) to create the Payroll Information window shown here (b).

Communications and Networks

Communications technologies are everywhere. Many require that you subscribe to an Internet service provider. With others, an organization such as a business or school provides communications services to employees, students, or customers.

In the course of a day, it is likely you use, or use information generated by, one or more of the communications technologies in Table 1-3.

Table 1-3   Uses of Communications Technologies

Type	Brief Description
Chat rooms	Real-time typed conversation among two or more people on a computers or mobile devices connected to a network
Email	Transmission of messages and files via a computer network
Fax	Transmission and receipt of documents over telephone lines
FTP	Permits users to transfer files to and from servers on the Internet
GPS	Navigation system that assists users with determining their location, ascertaining directions, and more
Instant messaging	Real-time typed conversation with another connected user where you also can exchange photos, videos, and other content
Internet	Worldwide collection of networks that links millions of businesses, government agencies, educational institutions, and individuals
Newsgroups	Online areas in which users have written discussions about a particular subject
RSS	Specification that enables web content to be distributed to subscribers
Videoconference	Real-time meeting between two or more geographically separated people who use a network to transmit audio and video
Voice mail	Allows users to leave a voice message for one or more people
VoIP	Conversation that takes place over the Internet using a telephone connected to a computer, mobile device, or other device
Wireless Internet access points	Enables users with computers and mobile devices to connect to the Internet wirelessly
Wireless messaging services	Send and receive wireless messages to and from smartphones, mobile phones, handheld game devices, and other mobile devices using text messaging and picture/video messaging

Wired and Wireless Communications

Computer communications describes a process in which two or more computers or devices transfer (send and receive) data, instructions, and information over transmission media via a communications device(s). A **communications device** is hardware capable of transferring items from computers and devices to transmission media and vice versa. Examples of communications devices are modems, wireless access points, and routers. As shown in Figure 1-32, some communications involve cables and wires; others are sent wirelessly through the air.

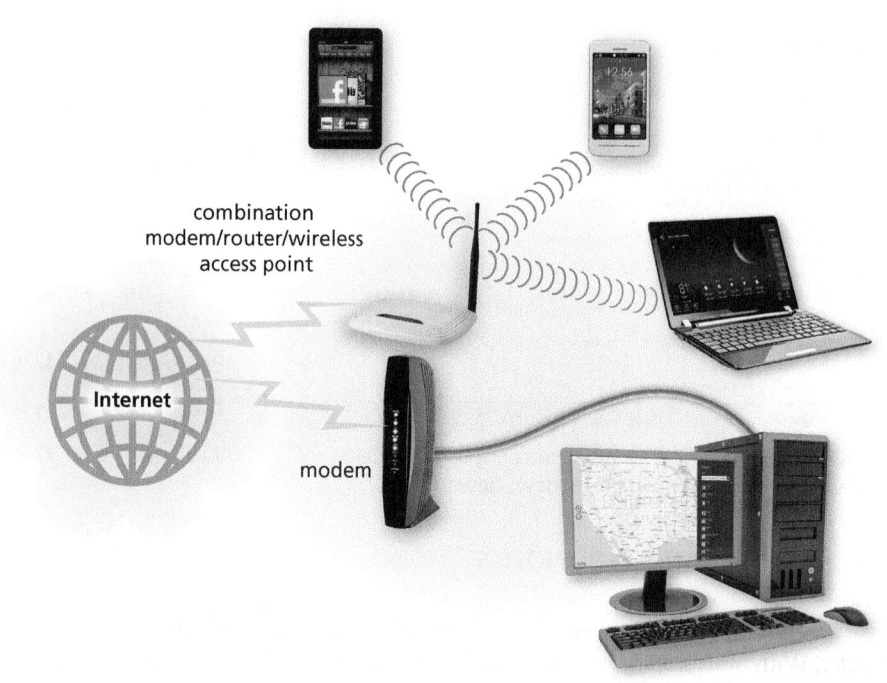

Figure 1-32   Modems, wireless access points, and routers are examples of communications devices that enable communications between computers/mobile devices and the Internet. Notice that some computers and devices communicate via wires, and others communicate wirelessly.
iStockphoto.com / Petar Chernaev; iStockphoto.com / Oleksiy Mark; Patryk Kosmider / Shutterstock.com.; Pablo Eder / Shutterstock.com; iStockphoto.com / 123render.; iStockphoto.com / aquarius83men

Wired communications often use some form of telephone wiring, coaxial cable, or fiber-optic cables to send communications signals. The wiring or cables typically are used within buildings or underground between buildings.

Because it is more convenient than installing wires and cables, many users opt for wireless communications, which sends signals through the air or space. Examples of wireless communications technologies include Wi-Fi, Bluetooth, and cellular radio, which are discussed below:

- **Wi-Fi** uses radio signals to provide high-speed Internet and network connections to computers and devices capable of communicating via Wi-Fi. Most computers and many mobile devices, such as smartphones and portable media players, can connect to a Wi-Fi network.
- **Bluetooth** uses short-range radio signals to enable Bluetooth-enabled computers and devices to communicate with each other. For example, Bluetooth headsets allow you to connect a Bluetooth-enabled phone to a headset wirelessly.
- Cellular radio uses the cellular network to enable high-speed Internet connections to devices with built-in compatible technology, such as smartphones. Cellular network providers use the categories 3G, 4G, and 5G to denote cellular transmission speeds, with 5G being the fastest.

Wi-Fi and Bluetooth are both hot spot technologies. A *hot spot* is a wireless network that provides Internet connections to mobile computers and devices. Wi-Fi hot spots provide wireless network connections to users in public locations, such as airports and airplanes, train stations, hotels, convention centers, schools, campgrounds, marinas, shopping malls, bookstores, libraries, restaurants, coffee shops, and more. Bluetooth hot spots provide location-based services, such as sending coupons or menus, to users whose Bluetooth-enabled devices enter the coverage range.

Networks

A **network** is a collection of computers and devices connected together, often wirelessly, via communications devices and transmission media. Networks allow computers to share *resources*, such as hardware, software, data, and information. Sharing resources saves time and money. In many networks, one or more computers act as a server. The server controls access to the resources on a network. The other computers on the network, called clients, request resources from the server (Figure 1-33). The major differences between the server and client computers are that the server typically has more power, more storage space, and expanded communications capabilities.

Many homes and most businesses and schools network their computers and devices. Most allow users to connect their computers wirelessly to the network. Users often are required to sign in to, or log on, a network, which means they enter a user name and password (or other credentials) to access the network and its resources.

 BTW
The Internet
The world's largest computer network is the Internet.

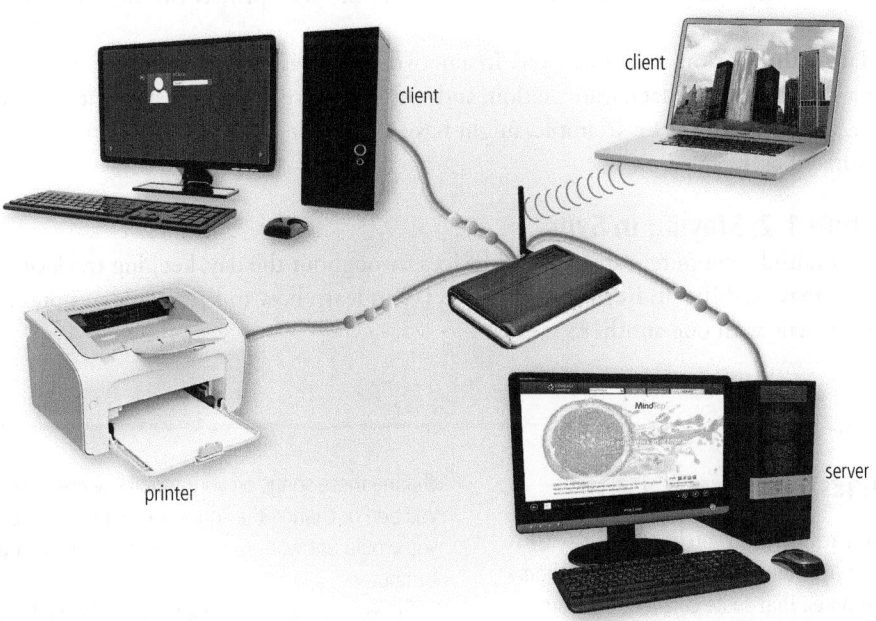

Figure 1-33 A server manages the resources on a network, and clients access the resources on the server. This network enables three separate computers to share the same printer, one wirelessly.

iStockphoto.com / sweetym; iStockphoto.com / skodonnell; Jennifer Nickert / Shutterstock.com; Serg64 / Shutterstock.com; Oleksiy Mark / Shutterstock.com

Home Networks Home networks save the home user money and provide many conveniences. Each networked computer or mobile device on a home network has the following capabilities:

- Connect to the Internet at the same time
- Share a single high-speed Internet connection
- Access photos, music, videos, and other content on computers and devices throughout the house
- Share devices such as a printer, scanner, or external hard drive
- Play multiplayer games with players on other computers and mobile devices in the house
- Connect game consoles to the Internet
- Subscribe to and use VoIP
- Interact with other devices in a smart home (such as thermostats, lighting controls, etc.)

Home networks usually are small, existing within a single structure, and use wireless technologies such as those shown previously in Figure 1-32. You do not need extensive knowledge of networks to set up a home network. You will need a communications device, such as a router, which usually includes setup instructions. Most operating systems also provide tools enabling you easily to connect all the computers and devices in your house.

Business Networks Business and school networks can be small, such as in a room or building, or widespread, connecting computers and devices across a city, country, or the globe. Some reasons that businesses network their computers and devices together include the following:

- **Facilitate communications.** Using a network, employees and customers communicate efficiently and easily via email, messaging services, blogs, online social networks, video calls, online meetings, videoconferencing, VoIP, and more.
- **Share hardware.** In a networked environment, each computer on the network can access the hardware on the network, instead of providing each user with the same piece of hardware. For example, computer and mobile device users can access the laser printer on the network, as they need it.
- **Share data, information, and software.** In a networked environment, any authorized computer user can access data, information, and software stored on other computers on the network. A large company, for example, might have a database of customer information that any authorized user can access.

Tech Feature 1-2: Staying in Sync

If you use multiple computers and mobile devices throughout the day, keeping track of common files may be difficult. Read Tech Feature 1-2 to learn how to keep your computers and devices in sync with one another.

 TECH FEATURE 1-2 ─────────────────────────────

Staying in Sync

Assume that each morning you begin the day by checking your appointment calendar on your home or office computer. That same calendar appears on your smartphone, so that you can view your schedule throughout the day. If you add, change, or delete appointments using the smartphone, however, you may need to update the calendar on your computer to reflect these edits. When you **synchronize**, or **sync**, computers and mobile devices, you match the files in two or more locations with each other, as shown in the figure below. Along with appointments, other commonly synced files from a smartphone are photos, email messages, music, apps, contacts, calendars, and ringtones.

Syncing can be a one-way or a two-way process. With a one-way sync, also called mirroring, you add, change, or delete files in a destination location, called the *target*, without altering the same files in the original location, called the *source*. For example, you may have a large collection of music stored on your home computer (the source), and you often copy some of these songs to your mobile device (the target). If you add or delete songs from your computer, you also will want to add or

change these songs on your mobile device. If, however, you add or change the songs on your mobile device, you would not want to make these changes on your computer.

In two-way sync, any change made in one location also is made in any other sync location. For example, you and your friends may be working together to create one document reflecting your combined ideas. This document could be stored on a network or on cloud storage on the Internet. Your collaboration efforts should reflect the latest edits each person has made to the file.

You can use wired or wireless methods to sync. In a wired setup, cables connect one device to another, which allows for reliable data transfer. While wireless syncing offers convenience and automation, possible issues include battery drain and low signal strength when the devices are not close to one another. Strategies for keeping your files in sync include the following:

- **Use a cable and software.** Syncing photos from a camera or a smartphone to a computer frees up memory on the mobile device and creates a backup of these files. You easily can transfer photos using a data sync cable and synchronization software. Be

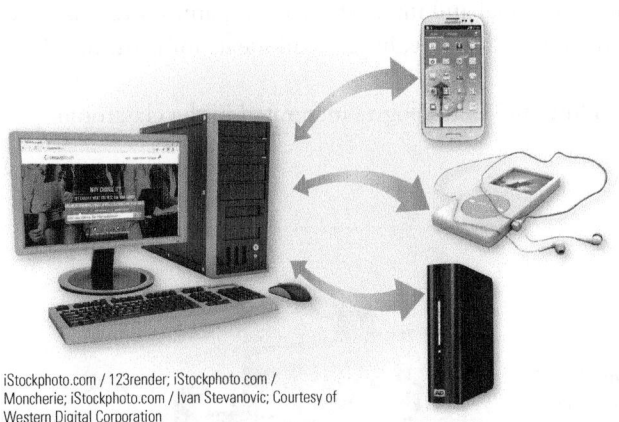

iStockphoto.com / 123render; iStockphoto.com / Moncherie; iStockphoto.com / Ivan Stevanovic; Courtesy of Western Digital Corporation

certain not to disconnect the mobile device from the computer until the sync is complete. You also can copy your photos and documents from the computer to a smartphone, an external hard drive, a USB flash drive, or some other portable storage device.

- **Use cloud storage.** Cloud storage can provide a convenient method of syncing files stored on multiple computers and accessing them from most devices with Internet access. Several cloud storage providers offer a small amount of storage space at no cost and additional storage for a nominal fee per month or per year. Each provider has specific features, but most allow users to share files with other users, preview file contents, set passwords, and control who has permission to edit the files.

- **Use web apps.** By using web apps for email, contacts, and calendars, your information is stored online, so that it is accessible anywhere you have an Internet connection and can sync with multiple devices.

 Consider This: Synchronization is an effective method of organizing and sharing common files. What files have you synced, such as photos, music, and email messages? Which sync method did you use?

Technology Uses

Technology has changed society today as much as the industrial revolution changed society in the eighteenth and nineteenth centuries. People interact directly with technology in fields such as education, government, finance, retail, entertainment, health care, science, travel, publishing, and manufacturing.

✳ CONSIDER THIS

How does technology impact crowdsourcing?
Crowdsourcing is the practice of involving a large group of people — the crowd — to collectively contribute time, services, funds, expertise, or ideas to a project, cause, or other goal. Many crowdsourcing activities today are organized and promoted via online social networks, websites, or apps. For example, you can create a fundraising campaign, share traffic updates, support entrepreneurs starting businesses, or hire a private driver.

Education/Tech Feature 1-3: Digital School

Educators and teaching institutions use technology to assist with education. Most equip labs and classrooms with laptops or desktops. Some even provide computers or mobile devices to students. Many require students to have a mobile computer or mobile device to access the school's network or Internet wirelessly, or to access digital content provided by a textbook publisher. To promote the use of technology in education, vendors often offer substantial student discounts on hardware and software.

Educators may use a course management system, sometimes called a learning management system, which is software that contains tools for class preparation, distribution, and management. For example, through the course management system, students access course materials, grades, assessments, and a variety of collaboration tools.

Many schools offer distance learning classes, where the delivery of education occurs at one place while the learning occurs at other locations. Distance learning courses provide time, distance, and place advantages for students who live far from a campus or work full time.

A few schools offer entire degrees online. National and international companies offer distance learning training because it eliminates the costs of airfare, hotels, and meals for centralized training sessions.

Read Tech Feature 1-3 to learn about additional technologies integrated in the classroom.

 TECH FEATURE 1-3

Digital School

Technology and education intersect in today's classrooms. Students can use a variety of devices, apps, and websites to collaborate and obtain content, while teachers can share information in most content areas to engage students and enhance the learning process. Digital technology offers flexibility and a revised classroom setting.

- **Mobile devices and tablets:** Schools are updating their computer labs by eliminating rows of desktops and allowing students to bring their own devices into the room and also into their classrooms, a practice often referred to as *BYOD* (bring your own device).

- **Virtual field trips:** Virtual tours of museums, ancient sites, and galleries allow audiences to see exhibits, examine paintings, and explore historical objects. After viewing 360-degree panoramas of such places as Colonial Williamsburg and Machu Picchu, students can interact with experts via online social networks and videoconferencing.

- **Games and simulations:** Game design theory can help engage students and reinforce key concepts. When students master one set of objectives in a particular topic, they can progress to more advanced levels. They can receive instant feedback and recognition for their accomplishments, collaborate with teammates, repeat play to achieve higher scores, and document their experiences. Researchers claim that students are more likely to pursue challenging subject matter when it is offered in a gaming setting.

- **Interactive whiteboards:** Teachers and students can write directly on an interactive display, shown in the figure, which is a touch-sensitive device resembling a dry-erase board. It displays images on a connected computer screen. Touch gestures are used to zoom, erase, and annotate displayed content.

Used with permission of SMART Technologies ULC (www.smarttech.com). SMART Board and the SMART logo are trademarks of SMART Technologies ULC and may be registered in the European Union, Canada, the United States and other countries.

- **Share projects:** Effective movies can bring the words in a textbook to life. Students can create scripts and then use animation software or a video camera to tell stories that apply the concepts they have learned and upload them to media sharing websites. They also can write blogs, design graphics, and conduct interviews to apply and share the concepts they have learned in the classroom.

- **3-D printers:** Low-cost 3-D printers created for the classroom and libraries are becoming popular, especially in science and engineering classes. Geology students can create topography models, biology students can examine cross sections of organs, architecture students can print prototypes of their designs, and history students can create artifacts.

Consider This: Which digital technologies have you used in your classrooms? Did they help you learn and retain information presented? If so, how?

Government

Most government offices have websites to provide citizens with up-to-date information. People in the United States access government websites to view census data, file taxes, apply for permits and licenses, pay parking tickets, buy stamps, report crimes, apply for financial aid, and renew vehicle registrations and driver's licenses.

Employees of government agencies use computers as part of their daily routine. North American 911 call centers use computers to dispatch calls for fire, police, and medical assistance. Military and other agency officials use the U.S. Department of Homeland Security's network of information about domestic security threats to help protect against terrorist attacks. Law enforcement officers have online access to the FBI's National Crime Information Center (NCIC) through in-vehicle laptops, fingerprint readers, and mobile devices (Figure 1-34). The NCIC contains more than 12 million missing persons and criminal records, including names, fingerprints, parole/probation records, mug shots, and other information.

Finance

Many people and companies use online banking or finance software to pay bills, track personal income and expenses, manage investments, and evaluate financial plans. The difference between using a financial institutions' website versus finance software on your computer is that all your account information is stored on the bank's computer instead of your computer. The advantage is you can access your financial records from anywhere in the world.

Investors often use online investing to buy and sell stocks and bonds — without using a broker. With online investing, the transaction fee for each trade usually is much less than when trading through a broker.

Figure 1-34   Law enforcement officials use computers and mobile devices to access emergency, missing person, and criminal records in computer networks in local, state, and federal agencies.
iStockphoto.com / jacomstephens

Retail

You can purchase just about any product or service on the web, including groceries, flowers, books, computers and mobile devices, music, movies, airline tickets, and concert tickets. To purchase from an online retailer, a customer visits the business's storefront, which contains product descriptions, images, and a shopping cart. The shopping cart allows the customer to collect purchases. When ready to complete the sale, the customer enters personal data and the method of payment, which should be through a secure Internet connection. Figure 1-35 illustrates the steps involved when a customer purchases from an online retailer.

Purchasing from an Online Retailer

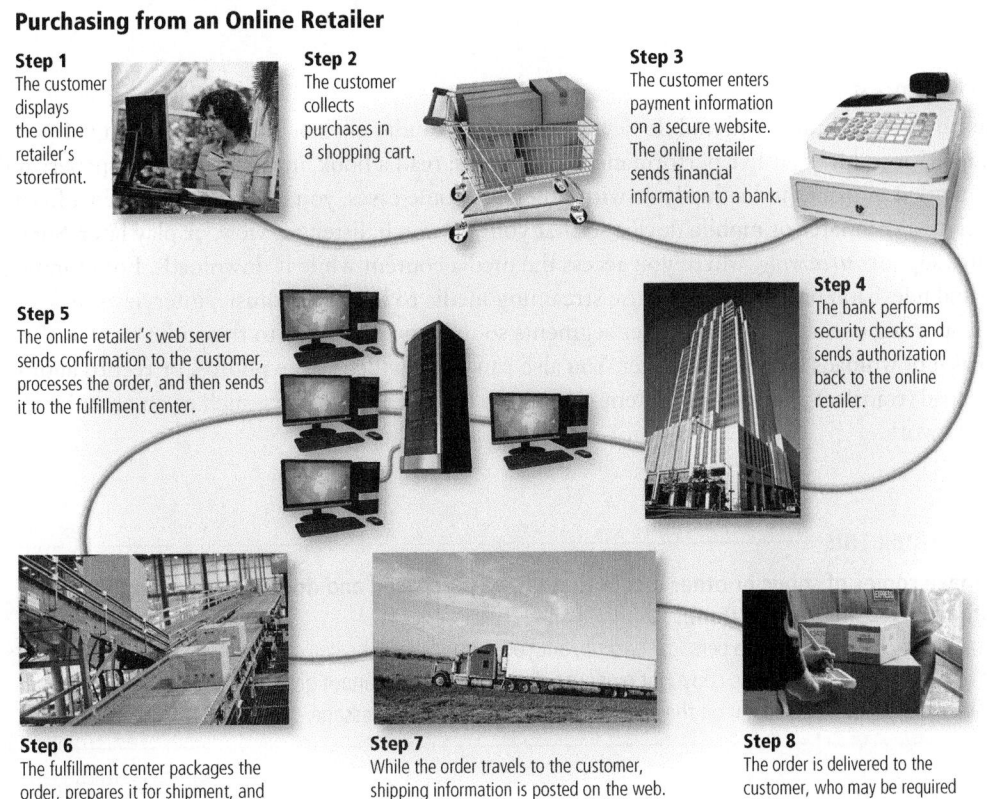

Step 1
The customer displays the online retailer's storefront.

Step 2
The customer collects purchases in a shopping cart.

Step 3
The customer enters payment information on a secure website. The online retailer sends financial information to a bank.

Step 4
The bank performs security checks and sends authorization back to the online retailer.

Step 5
The online retailer's web server sends confirmation to the customer, processes the order, and then sends it to the fulfillment center.

Step 6
The fulfillment center packages the order, prepares it for shipment, and then sends a report to the server where records are updated.

Step 7
While the order travels to the customer, shipping information is posted on the web.

Step 8
The order is delivered to the customer, who may be required to sign a handheld device or document to acknowledge receipt.

Figure 1-35   This figure shows the steps involved when a customer purchases from an online retailer.
Comstock Images / Getty Images; iStockphoto.com / Mark Evans; iStockphoto.com / AndyL; iStockphoto.com / Mlenny Photography; Oleksiy Mark / Photos.com; Oleksiy Mark / Shutterstock.com.; iStockphoto.com / MotoEd; iStockphoto.com / Oksana Perkins; iStockphoto.com / stevecoleimages

Many mobile apps make your shopping experience more convenient. Some enable you to manage rewards, use coupons, locate stores, or enable mobile payments where you can pay for goods and services directly from your phone or other mobile device. Other mobile apps will check a product's price and availability at stores in your local area or online. Read Secure IT 1-4 for tips about shopping safely online.

 **SECURE IT 1-4**

Shopping Safely Online

Browsing electronic storefronts and making online purchases can be convenient and economical, but the experience can be a disaster if you encounter unscrupulous vendors. These tips can help you enjoy a safe and productive online shopping trip.

- **Read customer reviews.** Shoppers frequently post comments about merchandise quality, pricing, and shipping. Their evaluations may help you decide whether a company is legitimate. Be aware, however, that the Federal Trade Commission has sued companies for posting false positive reviews and that some companies remove negative comments. Make it a habit to rate merchants as often as possible so that others can learn from your experiences.
- **Look for seals of approval.** Online businesses can display seals if they have met

rigorous standards. Some unscrupulous merchants, however, will place the seals on their websites even if they have not been approved. To check a seal's legitimacy, click the logo and be certain you are directed to the issuing agency's website to verify the seal is valid.

- **Create a strong password and password questions.** If the merchant requires you to create a user name and password, be certain to develop a long, complex password with at least eight characters that include letters, numbers, and special characters. (Refer to Secure IT 1-3 earlier in this module for guidance on creating a strong password.) The website also may ask for answers to security questions; if so, do not supply information that hackers could locate easily, such as your high school, place of birth, or family members' or pets' names.

- **Check website details.** Locate the vendor's privacy policy to learn how your information will be stored. Also, look for phone numbers, physical addresses, and email addresses to contact the vendor if questions arise about damaged goods or billing discrepancies.
- **Beware of requests to supply further information.** After you have placed an order, you may receive an email message asking you to confirm the transaction or to supply additional account information. A reputable business will not solicit these requests, so do not reply to the message.

 Consider This: Have you made online purchases? If so, have you followed the precautions listed here? How will you change your activities the next time you shop online?

Entertainment

You can use computers and mobile devices to listen to audio clips or live audio; watch video clips, television shows, or live performances and events; read a book, magazine, or newspaper; and play a myriad of games individually or with others. In some cases, you download the media from the web to a computer or mobile device so that you can watch, listen to, view, or play later. Some websites support *streaming*, where you access the media content while it downloads. For example, radio and television broadcasts often use streaming media to broadcast music, interviews, talk shows, sporting events, news, and other segments so that you can listen to the audio or view the video as it downloads to your computer. You also can create videos, take photos, or record audio and upload (transfer) your media content to the web to share with others, such as on an online social network.

 CONSIDER THIS

Can I make copies of songs or other media that I have purchased and downloaded from a legitimate website, such as iTunes?
You typically can make a copy as a personal backup, but you cannot share the copy with others in any format unless you have legal permission from the copyright owner to do so. That is, you cannot give someone a CD copy, nor can you share a digital file by posting it on the web or sending it as an email message.

Health Care

Nearly every area of health care today uses computers. Whether you are visiting a family doctor for a regular checkup, having lab work or an outpatient test, filling a prescription, or being rushed in for emergency surgery, the medical staff around you will be using computers for various purposes:

- Hospitals and doctors use computers and mobile devices to maintain and access patient records (Figure 1-36).
- Computers and mobile devices monitor patients' vital signs in hospital rooms and at home; patients use computers to manage health conditions, such as diabetes.
- Robots deliver medication to nurses' stations in hospitals.
- Computers and computerized devices assist doctors, nurses, and technicians with medical tests.
- Doctors use the web and medical software to assist with researching and diagnosing health conditions.
- Doctors use email, text messaging, and other communications services to correspond with patients.
- Patients use computers and mobile devices to refill prescriptions, and pharmacists use computers to file insurance claims and provide customers with vital information about their medications.
- Surgeons implant computerized devices, such as pacemakers, that allow patients to live longer.
- Surgeons use computer-controlled devices to provide them with greater precision during operations, such as for laser eye surgery and robot-assisted heart surgery.
- Medical staff use virtual reality (VR) to simulate education and training environments, such as for practicing surgeries, and patients use VR for recovery treatments, such as in rehabilitation and behavior therapy.
- Medical staff create labels for medicine, hospital ID bracelets, and more, enabling staff to verify dosage and access patient records by scanning the label.

Figure 1-36 Doctors, nurses, technicians, and other medical staff use computers and computerized devices to assist with medical tests.
iStockphoto.com / Neustockimage

Science

All branches of science, from biology to astronomy to meteorology, use computers to assist them with collecting, analyzing, and modeling data. Scientists also use the Internet to communicate with colleagues around the world. Breakthroughs in surgery, medicine, and treatments often result from scientists' use of computers. Tiny computers now imitate functions of the central nervous system, retina of the eye, and cochlea of the ear. A cochlear implant allows a deaf person to distinguish sounds. Electrodes implanted in the brain stop tremors associated with Parkinson's disease.

A *neural network* is a system that attempts to imitate the behavior of the human brain. Scientists create neural networks by connecting thousands of processors together much like the neurons in the brain are connected. The capability of a personal computer to recognize spoken words is a direct result of scientific experimentation with neural networks.

Travel

Whether traveling by car or plane, your goal is to arrive safely at your destination. As you make the journey, you may interact with a navigation system or GPS, which uses satellite signals to determine a geographic location. GPS technology also assists people with creating maps, determining the best route between two points, locating a lost person or stolen object, monitoring a person's or object's movement, determining altitude, calculating speed, and finding points of interest. Vehicles manufactured today typically include some type of onboard navigation system (Figure 1-37) or the capability of communicating with a smartphone or other mobile device's built-in navigation system.

In preparing for a trip, you may need to reserve a car, hotel, or flight. Many websites offer these services to the public where you can search for and compare flights and prices, order airline tickets, or reserve a rental car. You also can print driving directions and maps from the web.

Figure 1-37   Many vehicles include an onboard navigation system.
kaczor58 / Shutterstock.com

Publishing

Many publishers of books, magazines, newspapers, music, film, and video make their works available online. Organizations and individuals publish their thoughts and ideas using a blog, podcast, or wiki.

- A *blog* is an informal website consisting of time-stamped articles (posts) in a diary or journal format, usually listed in reverse chronological order. Posts can contain text, photos, links, and more. For example, Figure 1-38 shows the Nutrition Blog Network, in which registered dietitians post articles about nutrition. As others read articles in your blog, you can enable them to reply with their own thoughts. A blog that contains video is called a video blog.

- Podcasts are a popular way to distribute audio or video on the web. A *podcast* is recorded media that users can download or stream to a computer or portable media player. Examples of podcasts include lectures, political messages, radio shows, and commentaries. Podcasters register their podcasts so that subscribers can select content to automatically download when they are connected.

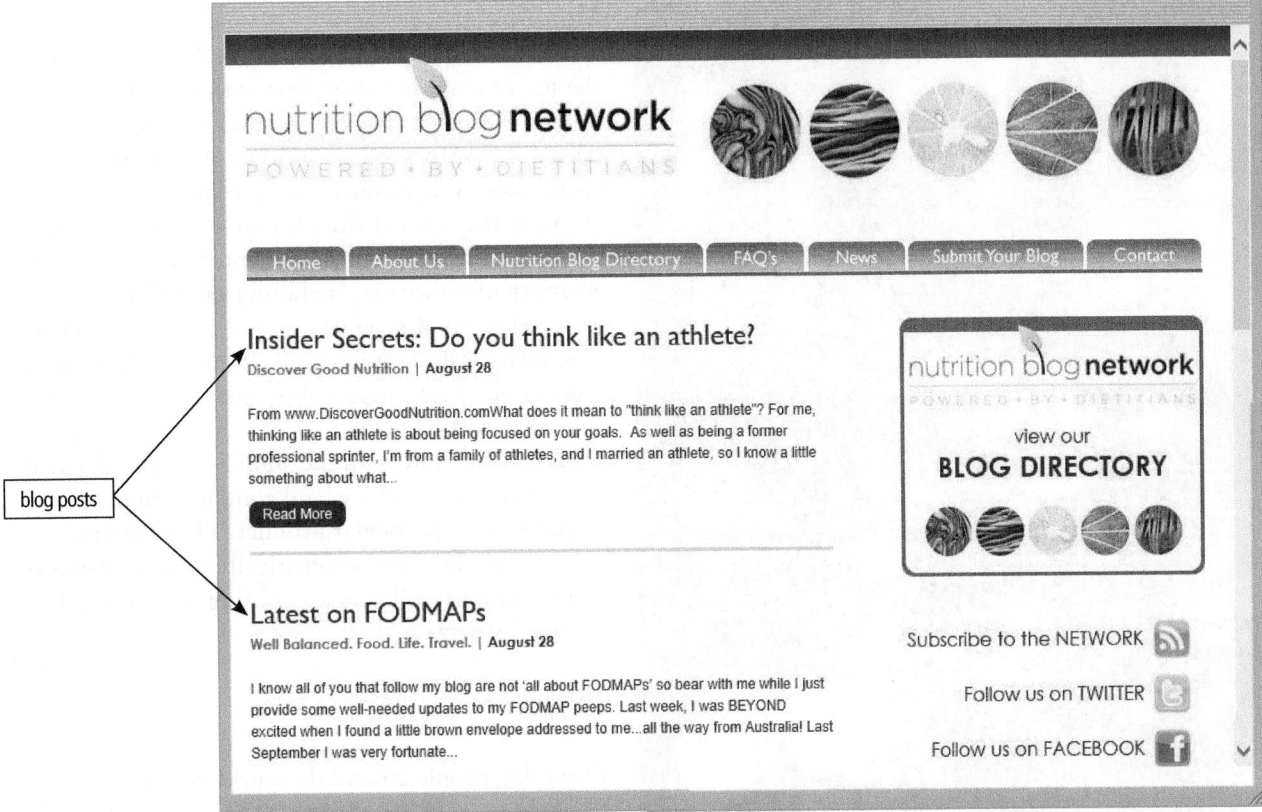

Figure 1-38 Any group or individual can create a blog, so that they can share thoughts and ideas.
Source: Nutrition Blog Network

- A *wiki* is a collaborative website that allows users to create, add to, modify, or delete the content via their browser. Many wikis are open to modification by the general public. The difference between a wiki and a blog is that users cannot modify original posts made by a blogger. Read Ethics & Issues 1-3 for an issue related to using wikis as a source for research.

✳ ETHICS & ISSUES 1-3

Should Wikis Be Allowed as Valid Sources for Academic Research?

As wikis have grown in number, size, and popularity, many educators and librarians have shunned them as valid sources of research. While some wikis are tightly controlled with a limited number of contributors and expert editors, these wikis usually focus on narrowly defined, specialized topics. Most large, multi-topic online wikis, such as Wikipedia, often involve thousands of editors, many of whom remain anonymous.

Critics of wikis cite the lack of certified academic credentials by the editors, as well as potential political or gender bias by contributors. Wikis also are subject to vandalism. Vandals' motives vary; some enter false information to discredit the wiki and others for humorous results. On occasion, rival political factions have falsified or embellished wiki entries in an attempt to give their candidate an advantage. Some wiki supporters argue that most wikis provide adequate controls to correct false or misleading content quickly and to punish those who submit it. One popular wiki now requires an experienced editor to verify changes made to certain types of articles. Other wiki protection methods include locking articles from editing, creating a list of recently edited articles, enabling readers to report vandalism, and allowing people to be notified about changes to a wiki page that they have edited or that is about them. Some proponents propose that people should use wikis as a starting point for researching a fact, but that they should verify the fact using traditional sources.

✳ **Consider This:** Should instructors allow wikis as valid sources for academic research? Why or why not? Would you submit a paper to your instructor that cites a wiki as a source? Why or why not? What policies might wikis enforce that could garner more confidence from the public? If a wiki provided verification of the credentials of the author, would you trust the wiki more? Why or why not?

Figure 1-39 Automotive factories use industrial robots to weld car bodies.
Betastock / Shutterstock.com

Manufacturing

Computer-aided manufacturing (CAM) refers to the use of computers to assist with manufacturing processes, such as fabrication and assembly. Industries use CAM to reduce product development costs, shorten a product's time to market, and stay ahead of the competition. Often, robots carry out processes in a CAM environment. CAM is used by a variety of industries, including oil drilling, power generation, food production, and automobile manufacturing. Automobile plants, for example, have an entire line of industrial robots that assemble a car (Figure 1-39).

Special computers on the shop floor record actual labor, material, machine, and computer time used to manufacture a particular product. The computers process this data and automatically update inventory, production, payroll, and accounting records on the company's network.

Technology Users

Every day, people around the world use various technologies at home, at work, and at school. Depending on the hardware, software, and communications requirements, these users generally can be classified in one of five categories. Keep in mind that a single user may fall into more than one category.

- A *home user* is any person who spends time using technology at home. Parents, children, teenagers, grandparents, singles, couples, etc., are all examples of home users.
- A *small/home office user* includes employees of companies with fewer than 50 employees, as well as the self-employed who work from home. Small offices include local law practices, accounting offices, travel agencies, and florists.
- A *mobile user* includes any person who works with computers or mobile devices while away from a main office, home, or school. Examples of mobile users are sales representatives, real estate agents, insurance agents, meter readers, package delivery people, journalists, consultants, and students.
- A *power user* is a user who requires the capabilities of a powerful computer. Examples of power users include engineers, scientists, architects, game designers, and graphic artists.
- An enterprise has hundreds or thousands of employees or customers who work in or do business with offices across a region, the country, or the world. Each employee or customer who uses computers, mobile devices, and other technology in the enterprise is an *enterprise user*.

Table 1-4 illustrates the range of hardware, programs/apps, and communications forms used in each of these categories.

Table 1-4 Categories of Users

User	Sample Hardware	Sample Desktop Apps	Sample Mobile or Web Apps	Forms of Communications
All Users 	Smartphone Digital camera Printer	Word processing Schedule and contact management Browser Security	Alarm clock Calculator News, weather, sports Reference Finance	Email Online social networks Blogs
Home User	Laptop, tablet, or desktop Portable media player and earbuds or headphones Game console E-book reader Wearable device Webcam Headset	Personal finance Photo and video editing Media player Educational Entertainment	Banking Travel Mapping Navigation Health and fitness Retail Media sharing Educational	Messaging VoIP
Small/Home Office User	Desktop(s) or laptop(s) Server Webcam Scanner	Spreadsheet Database Accounting	Travel Mapping	Messaging VoIP FTP
Mobile User	Laptop or tablet Video projector Wireless headset	Note taking Presentation Educational Entertainment	Travel Mapping Navigation Retail Educational	
Power User	Desktop Scanner	Desktop publishing Multimedia authoring Computer-aided design Photo, audio, video editing		FTP Videoconferencing
Enterprise User	Server Desktop(s) or laptop(s) Industry-specific handheld computer Webcam Scanner	Spreadsheet Database Accounting	Travel Mapping Navigation	Messaging VoIP FTP Videoconferencing

✓ Summary

Module 1 introduced you to basic computer concepts. You learned about laptops, tablets, desktops, servers, smartphones, digital cameras, portable media players, e-book readers, and game devices. The module introduced various methods for input, output, memory, and storage. It discussed the Internet, browsing and searching the web, and online social networks. Next, the module introduced digital security and safety risks and precautions, along with various types of programs, applications, communications, and networks. The many different uses of technology applications in society also were presented, along with types of users. This module is an overview. Many of the terms and concepts introduced will be discussed further in later modules.

Study Guide

The Study Guide reinforces material you should know after reading this module.

Instructions: Answer the questions below using the format that helps you remember best or that is required by your instructor. Possible formats may include one or more of these options: write the answers; create a document that contains the answers; record answers as audio or video using a webcam, smartphone, or portable media player; post answers on a blog, wiki, or website; or highlight answers in the book/e-book.

1. Define the term, digital literacy.

2. Define the terms, computer, hardware, and user.

3. Differentiate between a PC and a mobile computer. A laptop also is known as a(n) ___ computer.

4. Describe the characteristics and features of a tablet. List several touch screen gestures.

5. Explain the difference between a desktop and an all-in-one. What additional meaning does the term, desktop, sometimes have?

6. Define the term, server. What services does a server provide?

7. Explain whether or not a mobile device is a computer.

8. List characteristics of a smartphone.

9. Differentiate among voice mail, text, picture, and video messages.

10. Describe the purpose of these mobile devices: digital cameras, portable and digital media players, e-book readers, wearable devices, and game devices.

11. Describe the trend of digital device convergence and how it applies to mobile devices.

12. Describe uses of technology in home automation.

13. Differentiate between data and information. Give an example of each.

14. Define the terms, input and output. List several types of input devices and output devices.

15. Describe the purpose of a pointing device. Give an example.

16. List the hardware you can use to input and view output for voice and video.

17. Differentiate between memory and storage.

18. A computer keeps data, instructions, and information on ___ media. Give some examples.

19. Define the term, cloud storage. Describe the types of services offered by cloud storage providers.

20. Describe components of a backup plan. How do backup plans for mobile devices and personal computers differ?

21. Differentiate between the web and the Internet.

22. Describe the Internet. Define the Internet of Things. Identify reasons people use the Internet.

23. The ___ consists of a worldwide collection of electronic documents. What is each electronic document called?

24. What is a browser? Describe the purpose of a search engine.

25. Explain the purpose of an online social network.

26. Differentiate between the services and uses of Facebook, Twitter, and LinkedIn.

27. List services of the Internet that facilitate communications.

28. Define the term, malware. List ways you can protect yourself from malware.

29. What privacy risks are involved with using technology? List guidelines for creating a strong password.

30. Explain physical and behavioral health risks associated with using computers.

31. Describe strategies that support green computing.

32. Define the term, software. Software also is called a(n) ___.

33. Define the term, operating system. List popular operating systems for computers and mobile devices.

34. Differentiate between desktop, web, and mobile apps.

35. What is the role of a software developer?

36. Define the term, communications device. List examples of wireless communications technologies.

37. Define the term, hot spot.

38. Describe how homes and businesses use networks.

39. Explain what occurs when you synchronize computers and mobile devices.

40. Describe crowdsourcing with respect to technology.

41. List ways that schools use technology to enhance education.

42. Identify how the following industries use technology: government, financial, retail, entertainment, health care, science, travel, publishing, and manufacturing.

43. Describe how you might use blogs, podcasts, and wikis to publish content.

44. Differentiate among the following technology user types: home user, small/home office user, mobile user, power user, and enterprise user.

Key Terms

You should be able to define the Primary Terms and be familiar with the Secondary Terms listed below.

Primary Terms (shown in **bold-black** characters in the module)

all-in-one (1-5)
app (1-25)
application (1-25)
backup (1-16)
Bluetooth (1-28)
browser (1-19)
cloud storage (1-16)
communications
  device (1-28)
computer (1-3)
desktop (1-5)

digital camera (1-7)
digital device
  convergence (1-9)
e-book reader (1-8)
game console (1-8)
green computing (1-24)
hard drive (1-15)
input device (1-10)
Internet (1-17)
laptop (1-3)
memory (1-15)

network (1-5)
online social network (1-21)
output device (1-13)
portable media player (1-7)
printer (1-13)
program (1-24)
search engine (1-20)
server (1-5)
smartphone (1-6)
software (1-24)
storage device (1-15)

storage media (1-15)
sync (1-30)
synchronize (1-30)
tablet (1-3)
wearable device (1-8)
web (1-18)
web server (1-18)
webpage (1-18)
website (1-18)
Wi-Fi (1-28)

Secondary Terms (shown in *italic* characters in the module)

3-D printer (1-13)
blog (1-36)
click (1-12)
computer-aided manufacturing (1-38)
crowdsourcing (1-31)
data (1-10)
desktop app (1-26)
digital literacy (1-3)
digital media (1-7)
digital media player (1-7)
double-click (1-12)
double-tap (1-4)
downloading (1-18)
drag (1-4, 1-12)
earbuds (1-7)
e-book (1-8)
enterprise user (1-38)
e-reader (1-8)
e-waste (1-24)
file (1-16)
gesture (1-4)
hard copy (1-13)

hard disk (1-15)
hardware (1-3)
headset (1-13)
home user (1-38)
hot spot (1-28)
hyperlink (1-18)
information (1-10)
input (1-3)
keyboard (1-11)
link (1-18)
loads (1-26)
malware (1-22)
memory card (1-16)
microphone (1-13)
mobile app (1-26)
mobile computer (1-3)
mobile device (1-5)
mobile user (1-38)
mouse (1-12)
neural network (1-36)
notebook computer (1-3)
operating system (1-24)

optical disc (1-16)
output (1-3)
personal computer (1-3)
picture message (1-6)
pinch (1-4)
podcast (1-36)
point (1-12)
power user (1-38)
press and hold (1-4)
printout (1-13)
resources (1-29)
right-click (1-12)
scanner (1-13)
slide (1-4)
small/home office user (1-38)
Smart TV (1-14)
social networking site (1-21)
software developer (1-26)
solid-state drive (1-15)
streaming (1-34)
streaming media player (1-7)
stretch (1-4)

surfing the web (1-19)
swipe (1-4)
tap (1-4)
text message (1-6)
touchpad (1-12)
USB flash drive (1-16)
user (1-3)
user interface (1-26)
video message (1-6)
voice mail message (1-6)
wearable (1-8)
web address (1-19)
web app (1-26)
webcam (1-13)
wiki (1-37)

Courtesy of Apple Inc.

STUDENT ASSIGNMENTS

Checkpoint   The Checkpoint exercises test your knowledge of the module concepts.

True/False   Mark T for True and F for False. If False, rewrite the statement so that it is True.

_____ 1. Although some forms of memory are permanent, most memory keeps data and instructions temporarily, meaning its contents are erased when the computer is turned off.

_____ 2. An all-in-one contains a separate tower.

_____ 3. A smartphone is a small, mobile computing consumer device designed to be worn.

_____ 4. Data conveys meaning to users, and information is a collection of unprocessed items, which can include text, numbers, images, audio, and video.

_____ 5. Earbuds are a type of input device.

_____ 6. A scanner is a light-sensing output device.

_____ 7. One way to protect your computer from malware is to scan any removable media before using it.

_____ 8. A solid-state drive contains one or more inflexible, circular platters that use magnetic particles to store data, instructions, and information.

_____ 9. The terms, web and Internet, are interchangeable.

_____ 10. Electronic components in computers process data using instructions, which are the steps that tell the computer how to perform a particular task.

_____ 11. Operating systems are a widely recognized example of system software.

_____ 12. You usually do not need to install web apps before you can run them.

Matching   Match the terms with their definitions.

_____ 1. all-in-one

_____ 2. digital device convergence

_____ 3. file

_____ 4. Internet of Things

_____ 5. operating system

_____ 6. server

_____ 7. software

_____ 8. solid-state drive

_____ 9. storage device

_____ 10. touchpad

a. term that describes the trend of computers and devices with technologies that overlap

b. small, flat, rectangular pointing device that is sensitive to pressure and motion

c. series of related instructions, organized for a common purpose, that tells the computer what tasks to perform and how to perform them

d. component that records and/or retrieves items to and from storage media

e. storage device that typically uses flash memory to store data, instructions, and information

f. everyday devices and objects equipped with sensors that transmit data to and from the Internet

g. computer that is dedicated to providing one or more services to other computers or devices on a network

h. type of desktop computer that does not contain a tower and instead uses the same case to house the display and the processing circuitry

i. named collection of stored data, instructions, or information

j. set of programs that coordinates all the activities among computer or mobile device hardware

The Problem Solving exercises extend your knowledge of module concepts by seeking solutions to practical problems with technology that you may encounter at home, school, or work. The Collaboration exercise should be completed with a team.

Problem Solving

Instructions: You often can solve problems with technology in multiple ways. Determine a solution to the problems in these exercises by using one or more resources available to you (such as a computer or mobile device, articles on the web or in print, blogs, podcasts, videos, television, user guides, other individuals, electronics or computer stores, etc.). Describe your solution, along with the resource(s) used, in the format requested by your instructor (brief report, presentation, discussion, blog post, video, or other means).

Personal

1. **Shopping for Software**   You are shopping for software that will assist you with your home's interior design. The package for the program you would like to purchase states that it was designed for the most recent version of Windows, but an older version is installed on your computer. How can you determine whether the program will run on your computer?

2. **Bad Directions**   You are driving to your friend's house and are using your smartphone for directions. While approaching your destination, you realize that your smartphone app instructed you to turn the wrong way on your friend's street. How could this have happened?

3. **Bank Account Postings**   While reviewing your checking account balance online, you notice that debit card purchases have not posted to your account for the past several days. Because you use online banking to balance your account, you become concerned about your unknown account balance. What steps will you take to correct this situation?

4. **Trial Expired**   You have been using an app on your mobile device for a 30-day trial period. Now that the 30 days have expired, the app is requesting that you to pay to continue accessing your data. What are your next steps? What steps could you have taken to preserve your data before the trial period expired?

5. **Problematic Camera**   After charging your digital camera battery overnight, you insert the battery and turn on the camera only to find that it is reporting a low battery. Seconds later, the camera shuts off automatically. What might be wrong?

Professional

6. **Discarding Old Computer Equipment**   Your company has given you a new laptop to replace the outdated desktop you have been using. Because of the negative environmental impact of discarding the old computer in the trash, your supervisor asked you to suggest options for its disposal. How will you respond?

7. **Dead Battery**   While traveling for business, you realize that you forgot to bring the battery charger for your laptop. Knowing that you need to use the laptop to deliver a presentation tomorrow, what steps will you take tonight to make sure you have enough battery power?

8. **Cannot Share Photos**   You are attempting to send photos of a house for sale in an email message to your real estate partner. Each time you attempt to send the email message, you receive an automatic response stating that the files are too large. What are your next steps?

9. **Incorrect Sign-In Credentials**   Upon returning to the office from a well-deserved, two-week vacation, you turn on your computer. When you enter your user name and password, an error message appears stating that your password is incorrect. What are your next steps?

10. **Synchronization Error**   You added appointments to the calendar on your computer, but these appointments are not synchronizing with your smartphone. Your calendar has synchronized with your smartphone in the past, but it has stopped working without explanation. What are your next steps?

Collaboration

11. **Technology in Health Care**   Your primary care physician is moving from a shared office so that he can open his own practice. He mentioned that he would like to use technology in his office that not only will improve the patient experience, but also make his job easier. Form a team of three people to determine the types of technology your physician can use in his new office. One team member should research ways that technology can help improve patient check-in and billing. Another team member should research the types of technology your physician can use while he is working with patients, and the third team member should research any additional technology that can be used in the office to improve the patient experience.

✸ How To: Your Turn

The How To: Your Turn exercises present general guidelines for fundamental skills when using a computer or mobile device and then require that you determine how to apply these general guidelines to a specific program or situation.

Instructions: You often can complete tasks using technology in multiple ways. Figure out how to perform the tasks described in these exercises by using one or more resources available to you (such as a computer or mobile device, articles on the web or in print, online or program help, user guides, blogs, podcasts, videos, other individuals, trial and error, etc.). Summarize your 'how to' steps, along with the resource(s) used, in the format requested by your instructor (brief report, presentation, discussion, blog post, video, or other means).

❶ Sign Up for a Microsoft Account

A Microsoft account provides access to several Microsoft services. These services include access to resources, such as a free email account, cloud storage, a location to store information about your contacts, and an online calendar. You will need a Microsoft account to complete some of the exercises in this book. The following steps guide you through the process of signing up for a Microsoft account.

a. Run a browser and navigate to www.outlook.com.
b. Click the link and then follow the on-screen instructions to sign up for a free Microsoft account.
c. Browse the resources available to you in your Microsoft account.
d. If assigned by your instructor, compose and send a new email message from your Microsoft account to your instructor stating that you have signed up for a Microsoft account successfully.
e. Add your instructor's contact information. Next, add contact information for at least three more people.
f. Add your birthday to the calendar.
g. Edit your Microsoft account profile to add more contact and work information.

Exercises

1. If necessary, navigate to and view your new outlook.com email account. What are some ways to prevent junk email messages using the mail settings? What is junk email?
2. What is OneDrive? How much space do you have available on OneDrive to post files?
3. How can you see yourself using the various features in your newly created Microsoft account?

❷ Connect to a Wireless Network

Wireless networks are available in many homes and businesses. Connecting to a wireless network can provide you with high-speed access to the Internet and other network resources. The following steps guide you through the process of connecting to a wireless network from a computer or mobile device.

a. If necessary, turn on your computer or mobile device and make sure wireless functionality is enabled.
b. Obtain the name of the wireless network to which you want to connect. **Note:** *You should connect only to wireless networks for which you have permission.*
c. On your computer or mobile device, view the list of available wireless networks.
d. Select the wireless network to which you want to connect.
e. If necessary, enter the requested security information, such as an encryption key or a password.
f. Run a browser to test your connection to the wireless network.

Exercises

1. Why should you not connect to a wireless network unless you have permission?
2. What is the name of the wireless network to which you connected?
3. Why might you connect to a wireless network on your smartphone instead of using your mobile data plan?

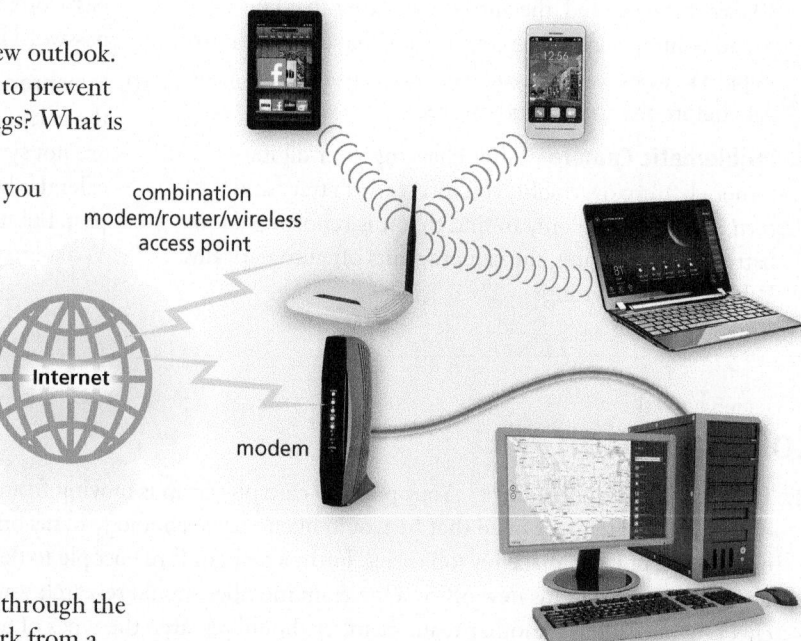

combination modem/router/wireless access point

Internet

modem

How To: Your Turn

❸ Manage Your Calendar

Individuals are choosing to use calendars on computers and mobile devices to keep track of events in their personal and professional lives more easily. In addition, students might use calendars to keep track of their class schedules. The following steps guide you through the process of managing your computer or mobile device's calendar.

a. Run the calendar app (usually by clicking its icon or tile on the home screen).

b. To add a new appointment, click the Add or New Appointment button or icon and then enter the title or subject of the appointment, its date, time, location, and other information. Click the Save button or icon on the New Appointment screen to save the information to your calendar.

c. Specify repeating information for appointments that occur at the same time over multiple occurrences, such as a class that meets every Tuesday from 10:00 a.m. to 11:00 a.m.

d. View your appointments on a daily, weekly, or monthly calendar by clicking the appropriate choice in the calendar app.

e. To edit an appointment, meeting, or event on your calendar, open the item by clicking it, make the necessary changes and then save the changes.

f. To delete an appointment, meeting, or event on your calendar, open the item by clicking it and then click the button to delete it. If necessary, confirm the deletion. If you are attempting to delete a recurring item on the calendar, the calendar app may ask whether you want to delete the one occurrence or the entire series of appointments, meetings, or events.

Exercises

1. In addition to your class schedule, what other recurring appointments might you add to your calendar?

2. Many calendar apps have a feature that can remind you of upcoming appointments in advance. How far in advance do you think you should be reminded of upcoming appointments?

3. How can you synchronize the calendar on your mobile device with the calendar on your home computer?

❹ Back Up Photos from a Phone or Tablet

Many individuals take photos using mobile devices such as phones and tablets. Many, however, neglect to realize the importance of backing up these files. A backup of the photos will be useful if you lose your mobile device, upgrade it to a newer model, or the device becomes damaged. While many mobile devices have built-in capabilities to back up photos to the cloud or to a desktop or laptop, it is important to make sure these features are configured properly. The following steps guide you through the process of backing up photos from a phone or tablet.

Backing Up to the Cloud

a. If necessary, install and sign in to an app on a phone or tablet that can back up photos to the cloud. Make sure the service you use gives you enough storage space for the photos you intend to upload.

b. Follow the instructions in the app and configure it to back up the photos at an interval of your choosing. Some options might include:
   • Back up all photos at certain intervals (such as one time per day or one time per week)
   • Back up photos as you take them
   • Back up photos stored in specific folders

c. If you are using a mobile device with a data plan, consider specifying whether you want the backup to occur only when you are connected to Wi-Fi. Backing up using your phone or tablet's data plan may result in additional charges if you inadvertently exceed your quota.

d. Verify all photos have been backed up to the cloud service.

Backing Up to a Computer

a. Use the USB cable that came with your phone or tablet to connect it to the computer to which you want to back up the photos.

b. After the computer has recognized that a phone or tablet is connected, navigate to the drive on the computer representing the phone or tablet and then navigate to the folder containing the photos. If your phone or tablet stores photos on both internal storage and a memory card, remember to back up your photos from both locations.

c. Drag the photos from the location on your phone or tablet to a folder on your computer that will store the backed up files.

d. When the files have finished backing up to the computer, close all open folder windows on the computer and then safely disconnect the phone or tablet from the computer.

Exercises

1. How often do you think you should back up your photos? Why?

2. When backing up photos, why might it be better to connect your phone or tablet to the computer using a cable instead of inserting the memory card from the phone or tablet into the computer?

3. Compare and contrast three apps or services that can back up photos from your phone or tablet to the cloud. Which one would you choose, and why?

✳ Internet Research

The Internet Research exercises broaden your understanding of module concepts by requiring that you search for information on the web.

Instructions: Use a search engine or another search tool to locate the information requested or answers to questions presented in the exercises. Describe your findings, along with the search term(s) you used and your web source(s), in the format requested by your instructor (brief report, presentation, discussion, blog post, video, or other means).

1 Making Use of the Web
Informational and Research

Informational and research websites contain factual information and include reference works such as libraries, encyclopedias, dictionaries, directories, and guides. More than three billion people worldwide use the Internet, and Google is one of the websites they visit most often. Google reports that people perform more than two trillion searches per year using its Google Search. In How To 1-2 and How To 1-3 in this module, you learned how to use a browser to display a webpage on a computer or mobile device and to perform a basic web search using a search engine.

Research This: Using a browser and search engine, find the answers to the following questions. (1) Search for the top five informational websites and top five research websites. What types of information or research does each present? What search text did you use? (2) Visit Google's website and locate the company's early philosophy: "Ten things we know to be true." What are five of these values? What is the goal of the "Made with Code" initiative? (3) Visit the Engadget website and read at least three reviews of tablets. Create a table listing the product name, price, battery life, pros, and cons. (4) Locate articles about using hands-free devices for conversations while driving. Which states have passed legislation to restrict drivers' use of hands-free devices while driving? Describe the features found in the sophisticated hands-free system of one of this year's vehicles.

2 Social Media
Online Social Networks

Online social networks are a central communications tool and the primary source of news and information for many people. Historians place the birth of online social networking with the BBS (Bulletin Board System), where users communicated with a central computer and sent messages to other BBS members and also downloaded files and games. The next phase of online social networks evolved when CompuServe, AOL (America Online), and Prodigy were among the services linking people with similar interests. Today's online social networks share many of the same basic principles by allowing members to communicate common interests, play games, and share photos, videos, and music. Some of these online social networks are for personal use, while others are for entrepreneurs, business owners, and professionals to share job-related topics.

Research This: Compare the features of the top personal online social networks, and create a table listing the number of active members in the United States and worldwide, the number of years the sites have existed, the more popular features, and the amount of content, such as photos, news stories, and links, that is shared each month. What types of advertisements are featured at each of these sites? Which sites are marketed toward younger and older users? Then, research the online social networks used for business. How does their content differ from that found on the personal online social networks? How many companies use these sites as a recruiting tool? How many native languages are supported? How are professionals using these websites to find potential clients and business partners?

3 Search Skills
Selecting Search Terms

Search text that you send to a search engine, such as Google, Bing, or Yahoo!, impacts the quality of your search results. Rather than typing a long question in the search box, you may improve your results if you select the question's most important words as your search text. For example, instead of typing the entire question "How many users currently are on Facebook?" as your search text, type the following as your search text: facebook users current. Many search engines consider common words — such as how, are,

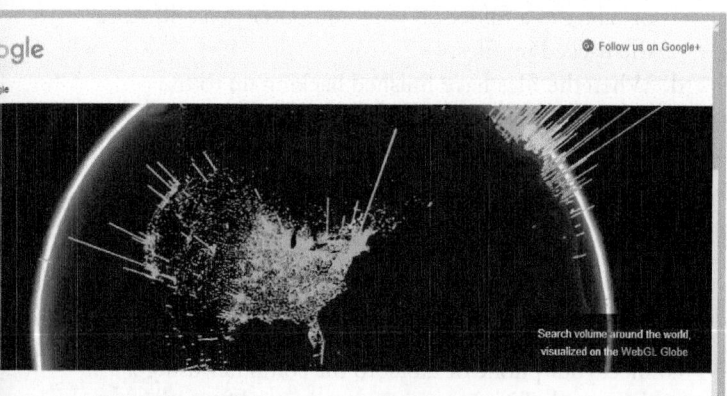

gle   ⊕ Follow us on Google+

Search volume around the world, visualized on the WebGL Globe

e's mission is to organize the world's information and make it universally accessible and useful.

Products · Company

Source: Google, Inc.

Internet Research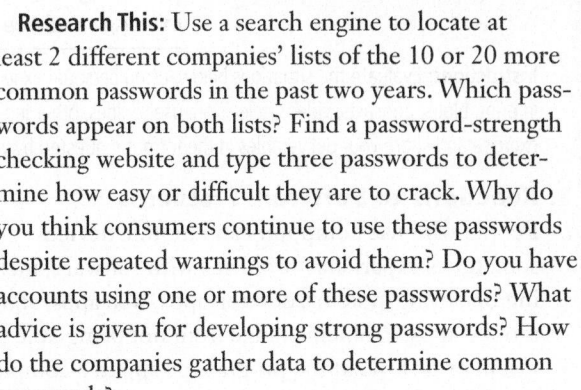

and on — as stop words, or words that a search engine ignores when performing a search.

Place the most specific or important word (facebook) first in your search text and then follow it with additional words to narrow the results. To see if rearranging the order of the words yields different results, type the following: current users facebook. Some search results from both queries likely will overlap. Many search engines assist you by automatically completing terms as you type them and will display a list of popular alternatives from which you can select. Sometimes, replacing a search term with a synonym will improve your results. For example, try using the search text, facebook users, followed by the current year instead of the using the word, current. Most search engines are not case sensitive; that is, they do not distinguish between uppercase and lowercase characters.

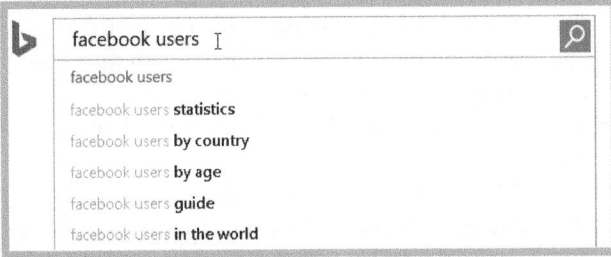

Research This: Create search text using the techniques described above, and type it into a search engine to find answers to these questions. (1) Which English words are stop words for Google? (2) What is the largest solid-state drive available? (3) How many hours per day on average do teens spend playing video games? (4) When is the next update to the Android mobile operating system expected to be released?

④ Security
Passwords

Secure IT 1-3 in this module offers advice about creating secure passwords when registering for websites. Despite suggestions and constant reminders from security experts to develop and then periodically change passwords, users continue to create weak passwords. These common passwords are broken easily and, therefore, never should be used. For many years, the most common passwords have been the word, password, and the number sequences 123456 and 12345678.

Research This: Use a search engine to locate at least 2 different companies' lists of the 10 or 20 more common passwords in the past two years. Which passwords appear on both lists? Find a password-strength checking website and type three passwords to determine how easy or difficult they are to crack. Why do you think consumers continue to use these passwords despite repeated warnings to avoid them? Do you have accounts using one or more of these passwords? What advice is given for developing strong passwords? How do the companies gather data to determine common passwords?

⑤ Cloud Services
Cloud Storage (IaaS)

Cloud storage providers offer online access to hardware for storing files, and web and mobile apps to access, back up, and manage files. Cloud storage is an example of IaaS (infrastructure as a service), a service of cloud computing that allows individuals and businesses to use a vendor's hardware to manage their computing needs.

Cloud storage providers offer both free and paid service plans based on the amount of free storage, and some allow users to earn additional storage by recommending friends to use their services or by participating in promotional campaigns. Many cloud storage providers enable users to synchronize files across multiple devices, access files via mobile or web apps, share files with team members, and maintain previous versions of files. Some provide built-in access to web-based productivity software or integrate with third-party web and mobile apps.

Research This: (1) Use a search engine to find three popular cloud storage providers. Create accounts and try each for a period specified by your instructor. In a table, summarize their features, including amount of free storage available (offered or earned), restrictions on file sizes you can upload, ease of use of web and mobile apps, operating systems or devices supported, cost of paid plans, and additional services provided for a fee. (2) Many cloud storage providers offer several gigabytes of free storage to their users. What is the largest amount of free storage you can find? Who is the provider? Can you identify any drawbacks to using this service?

✴ Critical Thinking

The Critical Thinking exercises challenge your assessment and decision-making skills by presenting real-world situations associated with module concepts. The Collaboration exercise should be completed with a team.

Instructions: Evaluate the situations below, using personal experiences and one or more resources available to you (such as articles on the web or in print, blogs, podcasts, videos, television, user guides, other individuals, electronics or computer stores, etc.). Perform the tasks requested in each exercise and share your deliverables in the format requested by your instructor (brief report, presentation, discussion, blog post, video, or other means).

1. Reactions to Software Problems

People who use computers and mobile devices sometimes experience problems with software, including operating systems, desktop apps, web apps, and mobile apps. Problems range from not being able to install or download the program or app to a computer or mobile device, to a program or an app producing unanticipated results. Depending on the situation, these problems can result in user stress. Many people believe reactions to software problems tend to be more extreme than reactions to problems with other tools.

Do This: Evaluate situations in which you have seen people react to program and app problems on their computers and mobile devices. Discuss how these users can reduce their frustration when dealing with such problems. How did you react when you were frustrated by problems with a program or an app? What did you do to solve the problem?

2. Energy Efficiency

Increases in energy prices lead many individuals to look at purchasing energy-efficient computers and devices. Energy-efficient models often look and perform similarly to equivalent computers or devices that use more energy.

Do This: Find two computers or devices of identical configuration, where the only difference is energy consumption. How much energy does the energy-efficient model save? Are energy-efficient computers and devices more or less expensive? Will the difference in cost (if any) affect your purchasing decision? How else might you be able to change your settings on your existing computer or device to save energy? Use the web to locate articles that recommend energy-efficient products and that provide tips about additional ways to save energy.

3. Case Study

Family-Owned Coffee Shop You are the new manager for a family-owned coffee shop. The previous manager tracked all of the data on paper. You realize that using technology will increase your efficiency and enable you to communicate better with the owners, employees, and customers. At the next business meeting, you will share ideas of how you will use technology.

Do This: To prepare for the meeting, you compile the following: differences between input and output, a list of the types of data you can use as input, and a list of the types of information you can produce as output. You include the types of computers, mobile devices, and other technologies you will use to enter data and produce the information. Incorporate your own experiences and user reviews of the devices.

Collaboration

4. Recommending Technology Solutions People use computers and mobile devices in a variety of fields, including travel, manufacturing, and more. Although the way people use computers and mobile devices varies, each use involves hardware, programs and apps, and some type of communications method, such as the Internet or cellular network.

Do This: Form a three-member team and choose a field in which you all are interested. Assign one member to investigate hardware, another to investigate programs and apps, and the third member to investigate communications methods used in the field. Locate user reviews and articles by industry experts. Each team member should develop a list of related items that may be used. After the investigation, create a hypothetical business or organization in the field. Recommend specific hardware, programs or apps, and communications capabilities that would be best for the network or organization. Include comparisons of specific items, as well as costs. Be sure to summarize your investigations, describe the hypothetical business or organization, and outline and support your recommendations.

iStockphoto.com / adventtr

Connecting and Communicating Online: The Internet, Websites, and Media

2

nmedia / Shutterstock.com

OBJECTIVES

After completing this module, you will be able to:

1 Discuss the evolution of the Internet

2 Briefly describe various broadband Internet connections

3 Describe the purpose of an IP address and its relationship to a domain name

4 Describe features of browsers and identify the components of a web address

5 Describe ways to compose effective search text

6 Explain benefits and risks of using online social networks

7 Describe uses of various types of websites: search engines; online social networks; informational and research; media sharing; bookmarking; news, weather, sports, and other mass media; educational; business, governmental, and organizational; blogs; wikis and collaboration; health and fitness; science; entertainment; banking and finance; travel and tourism; mapping; retail and auctions; careers and employment; e-commerce; portals; content aggregation; and website creation and management

8 Explain how the web uses graphics, animation, audio, video, and virtual reality

9 Explain how email, email lists, Internet messaging, chat rooms, online discussions, VoIP, and FTP work

10 Identify the rules of netiquette

The Internet

One of the major reasons business, home, and other users purchase computers and mobile devices is for Internet access. Recall from Module 1 that the Internet is a worldwide collection of networks that connects millions of businesses, government agencies, educational institutions, and individuals. Each of the networks on the Internet provides resources that add to the abundance of goods, services, and information accessible via the Internet.

Today, billions of home and business users around the world access a variety of services on the Internet using computers and mobile devices. The web, messaging, and video communications are some of the more widely used Internet services (Figure 2-1). Other Internet services include

access information

send or post messages

video call

Figure 2-1 People around the world use the Internet in daily activities, such as accessing information, exchanging messages, and conversing with others from their computers and mobile devices.

chat rooms, discussion forums, and file transfer. To enhance your understanding of Internet services, the module begins by discussing the history of the Internet and how the Internet works and then explains each of these services.

Evolution of the Internet

The Internet has its roots in a networking project started by the Pentagon's Advanced Research Projects Agency (ARPA), an agency of the U.S. Department of Defense. ARPA's goal was to build a network that (1) allowed scientists at different physical locations to share information and work together on military and scientific projects and (2) could function even if part of the network were disabled or destroyed by a disaster such as a nuclear attack. That network, called *ARPANET*, became functional in September 1969, linking scientific and academic researchers across the United States.

The original ARPANET consisted of four main computers, one each located at the University of California at Los Angeles, the University of California at Santa Barbara, the Stanford Research Institute, and the University of Utah. Each of these computers served as a host on the network. A *host* is any computer or device that provides services and connections to other computers or devices on a network. A web server is an example of a host. Hosts often use high-speed communications to transfer data and messages over a network. By 1984, ARPANET had more than 1,000 individual computers linked as hosts. Today, millions of hosts connect to this network, which now is known as the Internet.

The Internet consists of many local, regional, national, and international networks. Both public and private organizations own networks on the Internet. These networks, along with phone companies, cable and satellite companies, and the government, all contribute toward the internal structure of the Internet.

 CONSIDER THIS

Who owns the Internet?
No single person, company, institution, or government agency owns the Internet. Each organization on the Internet is responsible only for maintaining its own network.

The World Wide Web Consortium (*W3C*), however, oversees research and sets standards and guidelines for many areas of the Internet. The mission of the W3C is to ensure the continued growth of the web. More than 400 organizations from around the world are members of the W3C, providing advice, defining standards, and addressing other issues.

Connecting to the Internet

Users can connect their computers and mobile devices to the Internet through wired or wireless technology and then access its services free or for a fee. With wired connections, a computer or device physically attaches via a cable or wire to a communications device, such as a modem, that transmits data and other items over transmission media to the Internet. For wireless connections, many mobile computers and devices include the necessary built-in technology so that they can transmit data and other items wirelessly. Computers without this capability can use a wireless modem or other communications device that enables wireless connectivity. A *wireless modem*, for example, uses a wireless communications technology (such as cellular radio, satellite, or Wi-Fi) to connect to the Internet. Figure 2-2 shows examples of modems. The wireless modem shown in the figure is known as a *dongle*, which is a small device that connects to a computer and enables additional functions when attached.

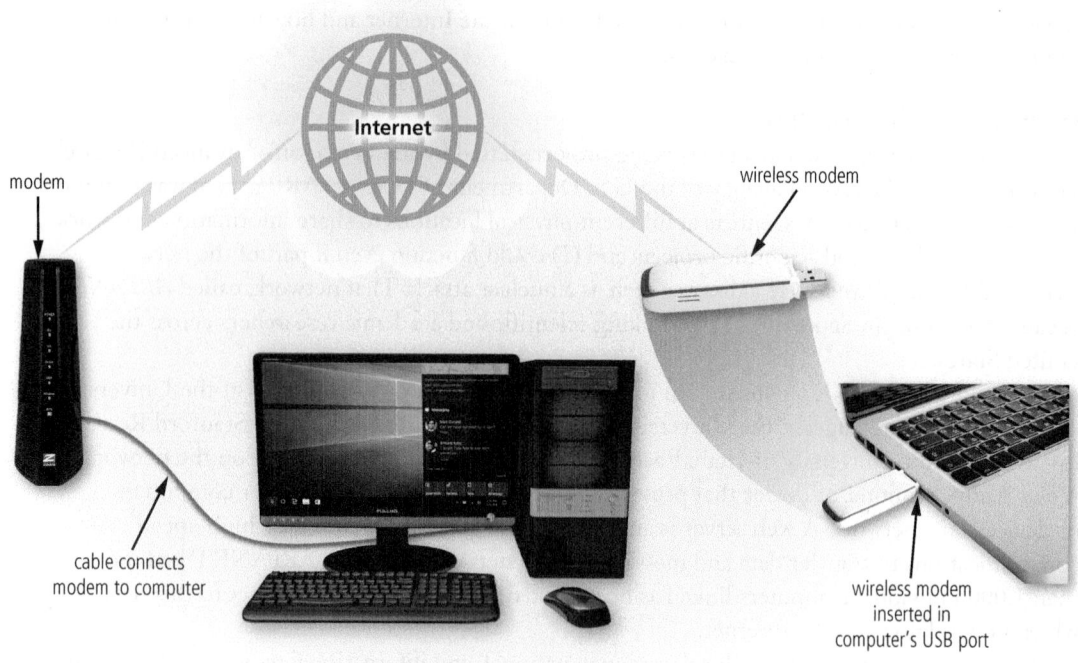

Figure 2-2   Using a modem is one way to connect computers and mobile devices to the Internet.
Courtesy of Zoom Telephonics Inc; Oleksiy Mark / Shutterstock.com; Source: Microsoft; Kristina Postnikova / Shutterstock.com; Kristina Postnikova / Shutterstock.com; DR / Fotolia LLC

Today, users often connect to the Internet via *broadband* Internet service because of its fast data transfer speeds and its always-on connection. Through broadband Internet service, users can download webpages quickly, play online games, communicate in real time with others, and more. Table 2-1 shows examples of popular wired and wireless broadband Internet service technologies for home and small business users.

	Technology	Description
Wired	*Cable Internet service*	Provides high-speed Internet access through the cable television network via a cable modem
	DSL (digital subscriber line)	Provides high-speed Internet connections through the telephone network via a DSL modem
	Fiber to the Premises (FTTP)	Uses fiber-optic cable to provide high-speed Internet access often via a modem
Wireless	**Wi-Fi** (wireless fidelity)	Uses radio signals to provide high-speed Internet connections to computers and devices with built-in Wi-Fi capability or a communications device that enables Wi-Fi connectivity
	Mobile broadband	Offers high-speed Internet connections over the cellular radio network to computers and devices with built-in compatible technology (such as 3G, 4G, or 5G) or a wireless modem or other communications device
	Fixed wireless	Provides high-speed Internet connections using a dish-shaped antenna on a building, such as a house or business, to communicate with a tower location via radio signals
	Satellite Internet service	Provides high-speed Internet connections via satellite to a satellite dish that communicates with a satellite modem

Table 2-1   Popular Broadband Internet Service Technologies

Many public locations, such as shopping malls, coffee shops, restaurants, schools, airports, hotels, and city parks have Wi-Fi hot spots. Recall that a *hot spot* is a wireless network that provides Internet connections to mobile computers and devices. Although most hot spots enable unrestricted or open access, some require that users agree to terms of service, obtain a password (for example, from the hotel's front desk), or perform some other action in order to connect to the Internet. Read Secure IT 2-1 for ways to use a public Wi-Fi hot spot safely.

✳ SECURE IT 2-1

Using Public Wi-Fi Hot Spots Safely

Connecting wirelessly to a public hot spot at your local coffee shop or at the airport can be convenient and practical. Using this free service can be risky, however, because cybercriminals may lurk in public Wi-Fi hot spots, hoping to gain access to confidential information on your computer or mobile device. Follow these guidelines for a safer browsing experience:

- **Avoid typing passwords and financial information.** Identity thieves are on the lookout for people who sign in to accounts, enter their credit card account numbers in shopping websites, or conduct online banking transactions. If you must type this personal information, be certain the website's web address begins with https, signifying a secure connection. If the website's web address changes to http, indicating an unsecure connection, sign out to end your Internet session immediately.

- **Sign out of websites.** When finished using an account, sign out of it and close the window.

- **Disable your wireless connection.** If you have finished working online but still need to use the computer, disconnect from the wireless connection.

- **Do not leave your computer or mobile device unattended.** It may seem obvious, but always stay with your computer or mobile device. Turning your back to talk with a friend or to refill your coffee gives thieves a few seconds to steal sensitive information that may be displayed on the screen.

- **Beware of over-the-shoulder snoopers.** The person sitting behind you may be watching or using a camera phone to record your keystrokes, read your email messages and online social network posts, and view your photos and videos.

✳ **Consider This:** How will you apply these precautions the next time you use a public Wi-Fi hot spot? Should businesses post signs alerting customers about Wi-Fi security issues?

DeiMosz / Shutterstock.com

Home and small business users can share and provide wireless Internet connections by creating their own Wi-Fi hot spot through a communications device in the home or business that is connected to broadband Internet service. Instead of a stationary Wi-Fi hot spot, some users opt to create mobile hot spots through mobile broadband Internet service via a separate communications device or a tethered Internet-capable device (Figure 2-3). *Tethering* transforms a smartphone or Internet-capable tablet into a portable communications device that shares its Internet access with other computers and devices wirelessly. Users may pay additional fees for mobile hot spot and tethering services.

Employees and students typically connect their computers and mobile devices to the Internet wirelessly through a business or school network, which, in turn, usually connects to a high-speed Internet service. When away from the office, home, or school, mobile users often access the Internet using Wi-Fi, mobile hot spots, or tethering services. Hotels and airports often provide wireless Internet connections as a free service to travelers. Many hotels have computers in their lobbies for customers to check email, browse the web, or print travel documents. Customers often bring their laptops or tablets to coffee shops, restaurants, libraries, hotels, and malls that offer free Wi-Fi as a service to their patrons.

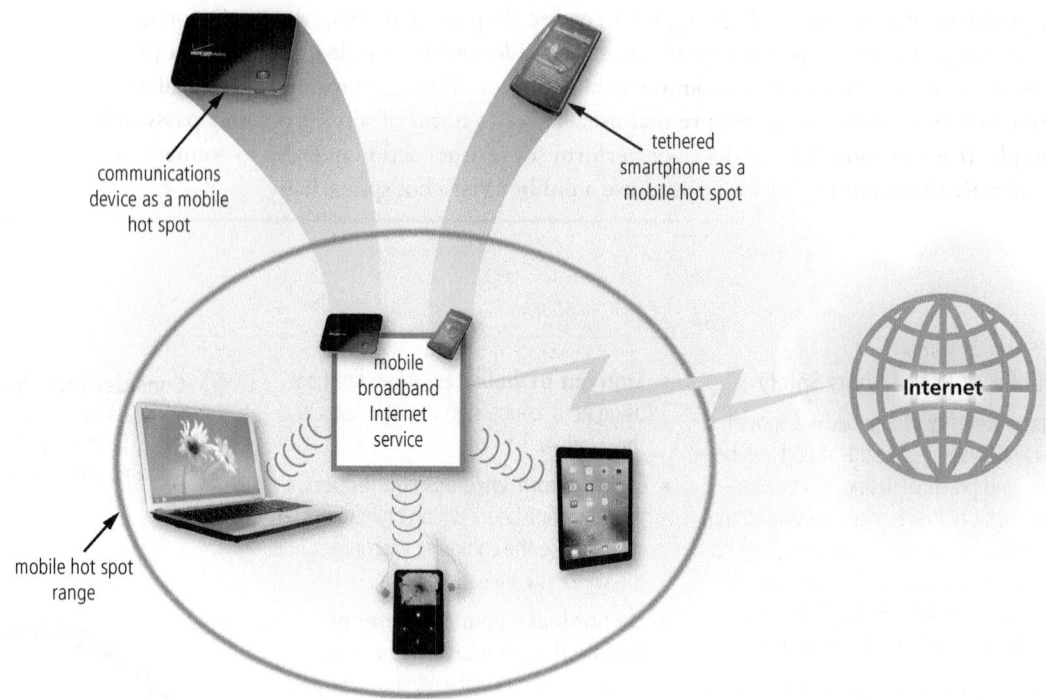

Figure 2-3   You can create a mobile hot spot using a communications device or by tethering a smartphone.

Courtesy of Verizon Wireless; figarro / Can Stock Photo; iStockphoto.com / Mlenny; amfoto / Shutterstock.com; Alex Staroseltsev / Shutterstock.com; Source: Microsoft

 CONSIDER THIS

Does everyone use broadband Internet?

No. Some home users connect computers and devices to the Internet via slower-speed dial-up access because of its lower cost or because broadband access is not available where they live. Dial-up access takes place when a modem in a computer connects to the Internet via a standard telephone line that transmits data and information using an *analog* (continuous wave pattern) signal.

Internet Service Providers

An **Internet service provider (ISP)**, sometimes called an Internet access provider, is a business that provides individuals and organizations access to the Internet free or for a fee. ISPs often charge a fixed amount for an Internet connection, offering customers a variety of plans based on desired speeds, bandwidth, and services. In addition to Internet access, ISPs may include additional services, such as email and online storage.

Bandwidth is a measure of the capability of a network to send and receive data. A high bandwidth connection transmits more data than a low bandwidth connection during the same time period. Data sizes typically are stated in terms of megabytes and gigabytes. A *megabyte* (**MB**) is equal to approximately one million characters, and a *gigabyte* (**GB**) is equal to approximately one billion characters. Table 2-2 shows approximate data usage for various Internet activities.

 BTW

Byte
A byte is the basic storage unit on a computer or mobile device and represents a single character.

Table 2-2   Data Usage Examples

Activity	Quantity	Approximate Data Usage
Send and receive email messages (with no attachments)	100 messages	3–6 MB
Post on online social networks (text only)	100 posts	25–50 MB
Upload or download photos	50 photos	50 MB
Send and receive email messages (with attachments)	100 messages	0.75–1 GB
Visit webpages	200 visits	1 GB
Talk with others using VoIP (without video)	1 hour	1.25 GB
Listen to streaming music	1 hour	1–2 GB
Play online games	1 hour	1.75 GB
Watch smaller, standard-quality streaming video	1 hour	2–5 GB
Download apps, games, music, e-books	25 downloads	3 GB
Talk with others using VoIP (with video)	1 hour	5–7.5 GB
Watch HD streaming video	1 hour	5–20 GB

 CONSIDER THIS

Does the term, data, have multiple meanings?
In the technology field, as discussed in Module 1, data can refer to unprocessed items that computers often process into information. Data also refers to the content that is stored on media or transmitted over a network. For example, when you select a data plan for your smartphone, the mobile service provider typically limits the amount of data (number of bytes) you can transfer each month depending on the plan you selected.

Wi-Fi networks often provide free Internet access, while some charge a daily or per use fee. Instead of locating a hot spot, some users prefer to subscribe to a mobile service provider, such as Verizon Wireless, so that they can access the Internet wherever they have mobile phone access. A **mobile service provider**, sometimes called a *wireless data provider*, is an ISP that offers wireless Internet access to computers and mobile devices with the necessary built-in wireless capability (such as Wi-Fi), wireless modems, or other communications devices that enable wireless connectivity. An antenna on or built into the computer or device, wireless modem, or communications device typically sends signals through the airwaves to communicate with a mobile service provider.

How Data Travels the Internet

Computers and devices connected to the Internet work together to transfer data around the world using servers and clients and various wired and wireless transmission media. On the Internet, your computer or device is a client that can access data and services on a variety of servers. Wired transmission media includes phone line, coaxial cable, and fiber-optic cable. Wireless transmission media includes radio waves and satellite signals.

The inner structure of the Internet works much like a transportation system. Just as interstate highways connect major cities and carry the bulk of the automotive traffic across the country, several main transmission media carry the heaviest amount of **traffic**, or communications activity, on the Internet. These major carriers of network traffic are known collectively as the *Internet backbone*.

In the United States, the transmission media that make up the Internet backbone exchange data at several different major cities across the country. That is, they transfer data from one network to another until reaching the final destination (Figure 2-4).

How a Home User's Request for a Webpage Might Travel the Internet Using Cable Internet Service

Step 1
You send a request to the Internet. For example, you enter the web address of a webpage you want to visit in the address bar of your browser.

Step 2
A cable modem transfers the computer's digital signals to the cable television line in your house.

Step 3
Your request (digital signals) travels through cable television lines to a central cable system, which is shared by up to 500 homes in a neighborhood.

Step 4
The central cable system sends your request over high-speed fiber-optic lines to the cable operator, who often also is the ISP.

Step 6
The server retrieves the requested webpage and sends it back through the Internet backbone to your computer.

Step 5
The ISP routes your request through the Internet backbone to the destination server (in this example, the server that contains the requested webpage).

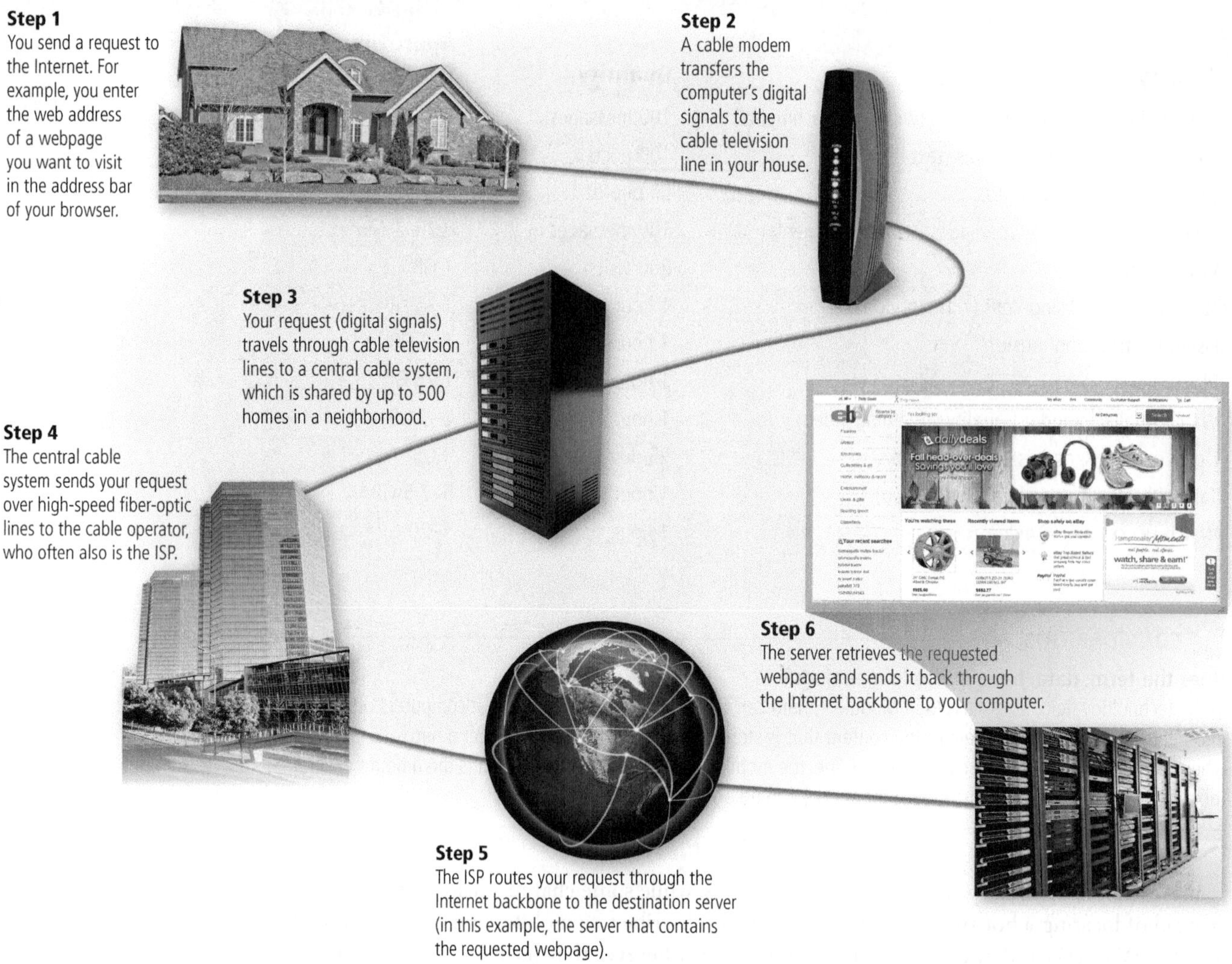

Figure 2-4   This figure shows how a home user's request for eBay's webpage might travel the Internet using cable Internet service.
romakoma / Shutterstock.com; Pablo Eder / Shutterstock.com; dotshock / Shutterstock.com; TonyV3112 / Shutterstock.com; iStockphoto.com / loops7; iStockphoto.com / luismmolina; Source: eBay

IP Addresses and Domain Names

The Internet relies on an addressing system much like the postal service to send data to a computer or device at a specific destination. An **IP address**, short for Internet Protocol address, is a sequence of numbers that uniquely identifies the location of each computer or device connected to the Internet or any other network.

The Internet uses two IP addressing schemes: IPv4 and IPv6. Due to the growth of the Internet, the original IPv4 addresses began dwindling in availability. The IPv6 scheme increased the available number of IP addresses exponentially. Because lengthy IP addresses can be difficult to remember, the Internet supports domain names. A **domain name** is a text-based name that corresponds to the IP address of a server, such as a web server that hosts a website (Figure 2-5). A domain name is part of the web address that you type in a browser's address bar to access a website.

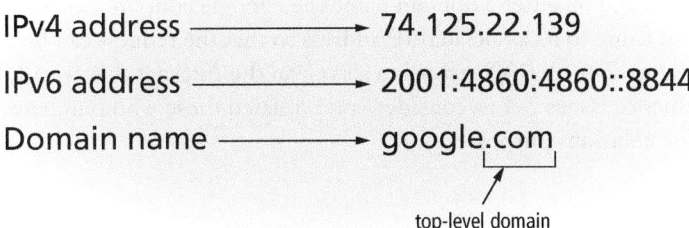

IPv4 address ⟶ 74.125.22.139

IPv6 address ⟶ 2001:4860:4860::8844

Domain name ⟶ google.com
└─ top-level domain

Figure 2-5 The IPv4 and IPv6 addresses, along with the domain name for Google's website.

The suffix of the domain name, called the *top-level domain* (*TLD*), identifies the type of organization associated with the domain. In Figure 2-5, for example, the .com is the TLD. Table 2-3 lists some of the popular TLDs. New TLDs are introduced to give individuals and businesses flexibility and creativity when purchasing domain names. For example, .biz, .museum, .name, .pro, .technology, and .travel have been introduced as TLDs within recent years.

The organization that approves and controls TLDs is the *Public Technical Identifiers (PTI)*. This nonprofit organization is an affiliate of *ICANN* (pronounced EYE-can), which stands for Internet Corporation for Assigned Names and Numbers. ICANN previously managed the domain names. For websites outside the United States, the suffix of the domain name may include a country code TLD (*ccTLD*), which is a two-letter country code, such as au for Australia. For example, www.philips.com.au is the domain name for Philips Australia. Read How To 2-1 to learn how to register a domain name.

Table 2-3	Popular TLDs
TLD	**Intended Purpose**
.biz	Businesses
.com	Commercial organizations, businesses, and companies
.edu	Educational institutions
.gov	Government agencies
.mil	Military organizations
.museum	Museums and individual museum professionals
.name	Individuals
.net	Network providers or commercial companies
.org	Nonprofit organizations
.pro	Licensed professionals
.technology	Technology information
.travel	Entities whose primary area of activity is in the travel industry

---

✳ HOW TO 2-1

Register a Domain Name

Individuals and companies register domain names so that people can find their websites easily using a browser. You register a domain name through a *registrar,* which is an organization that sells and manages domain names. When creating a website to post online, register a domain name that is easy to remember so that visitors can navigate to your website quickly. The following steps describe how to register a domain name.

1. Run a browser.
2. Use a search engine to locate a domain name registrar and then navigate to the website. You may want to evaluate several domain name registrars before deciding which one to use. Domain name registrars often offer various pricing models for registering domain names.
3. Perform a search on the domain name registrar's website for the domain name you wish to register. If the domain name is not available or costs too much, continue searching for a domain name that is available and within your price range, or explore various TLDs. For example, if the domain name you wish to register is not available or is too expensive with the .com TLD, consider using another TLD, such as .net or .org.
4. Follow the steps on the domain name registrar's website to select and complete the purchase and registration of the desired domain name.

✳ **Consider This:** What domain name based on your name would you register for your personal website? If your preferred domain name is not available, what are three alternative domain names you would consider?

The *domain name system* (*DNS*) is the method that the Internet uses to store domain names and their corresponding IP addresses. When you enter a domain name (i.e., google.com) in a browser, a DNS server translates the domain name to its associated IP address so that the request can be routed to the correct computer (Figure 2-6). A *DNS server* is a server on the Internet that usually is associated with an ISP. Read Ethics & Issues 2-1 to consider issues related those who purchase unused or lapsed domain names for nefarious purposes.

How a Browser Displays a Requested Webpage

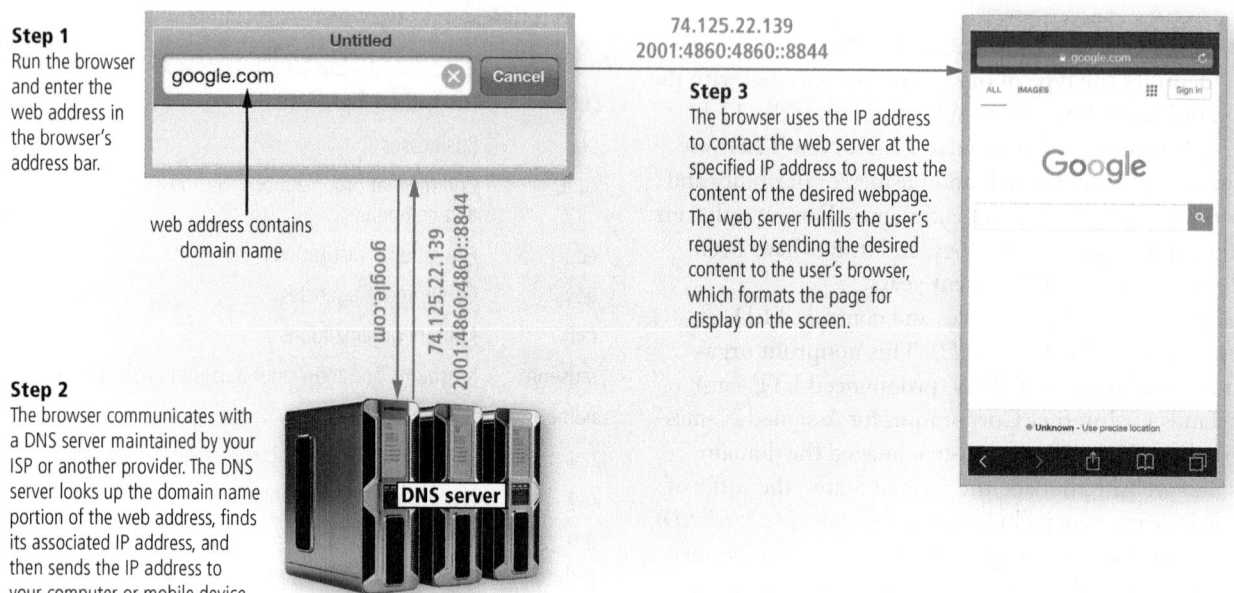

Step 1
Run the browser and enter the web address in the browser's address bar.

web address contains domain name

Step 2
The browser communicates with a DNS server maintained by your ISP or another provider. The DNS server looks up the domain name portion of the web address, finds its associated IP address, and then sends the IP address to your computer or mobile device.

74.125.22.139
2001:4860:4860::8844

Step 3
The browser uses the IP address to contact the web server at the specified IP address to request the content of the desired webpage. The web server fulfills the user's request by sending the desired content to the user's browser, which formats the page for display on the screen.

Figure 2-6   This figure shows how a user's entered domain name (google.com) uses a DNS server to display a webpage (Google, in this case).
Apple Inc.; Sashkin / Shutterstock.com; Source: Google Inc.

ETHICS & ISSUES 2-1

Should Cybersquatters Be Prosecuted?
You learn from a registrar that a domain name containing your company name is not available. When you enter the web address in a browser, a webpage appears that contains ads, false content, or a notice that the domain is available for purchase, likely from a cyber-squatter. Cybersquatters purchase unused or lapsed domain names so that they can profit from selling them; they sometimes will sell you the domain name, but some take advantage of people trying to reach a more popular website to promote their own business or needs. An example occurred when a politician registered several domain names that included his opponents' names and redirected them to his own campaign's website.

Website owners periodically must renew domain names. Cybersquatters look for out-of-date registrations and buy them so that the original website owner must buy them back. Cybersquatters often purchase domain names with common words, alternate spellings of trademarked terms, or celebrity names. With the constant increase of new TLDs, cybersquatting cases are on the rise. Experts recommend purchasing your domain name with as many TLDs as you can afford, as well as to register your own name and that of your children.

More than 15 years ago, lawmakers enacted the *Anticybersquatting Consumer Protection Act* (ACPA). The ACPA's goal is to protect trademark owners from having to pay a cybersquatter for a domain name that includes their trademark. To win a case against a cybersquatter, the owners must prove that the cybersquatters acted in bad faith, meaning they tried knowingly to profit from purchasing a domain name with a trademarked term, or a common misspelling or nickname of a trademarked term. Critics say that the ACPA prohibits free speech and free market.

Consider This: Should cybersquatting be illegal? Why or why not? Is it ethical to profit from cybersquatting? Why or why not? How should companies protect their brands when registering for domain names?

The World Wide Web

While the Internet was developed in the late 1960s, the World Wide Web emerged in the early 1990s as an easier way to access online information using a browser. Since then, it has grown phenomenally to become one of the more widely used services on the Internet.

As discussed in Module 1, the **World Wide Web (WWW)**, or web, consists of a worldwide collection of electronic documents. Each electronic document on the web is called a **webpage**, which can contain text, graphics, animation, audio, and video. Some webpages are static (fixed); others are dynamic (changing). Visitors to a *static webpage* all see the same content each time they view the webpage. With a *dynamic webpage*, by contrast, the content of the webpage is regenerated each time a user displays it. Dynamic webpages may contain customized content, such as the current date and time of day, desired stock quotes, weather for a region, or ticket availability for flights. The time required to download a webpage varies depending on the speed of the Internet connection and the amount of graphics and other media involved.

A website is a collection of related webpages and associated items, such as documents and photos, stored on a web server. A web server is a computer that delivers requested webpages to your computer or mobile device. The same web server can store multiple websites.

HTML (Hypertext Markup Language) is a set of symbols that developers use to specify the headings, paragraphs, images, links, and other content elements that a webpage contains. HTML is one of the core technologies for developing webpages, along with *CSS (cascading style sheets)* to specify the content's design and appearance and *JavaScript* to add interactivity. As these technologies matured in the early 2000s, many online social networks and collaboration tools were introduced. These websites were among the first interactive applications that allowed users to create and share content online.

Navigating the Web

Recall from Module 1 that a browser is an application that enables users with an Internet connection to access and view webpages on a computer or mobile device. Internet-capable mobile devices such as smartphones use a special type of browser, called a *mobile browser*, which is designed for their smaller screens and limited computing power. Many websites can detect if you are accessing their content on a mobile device (Figure 2-7).

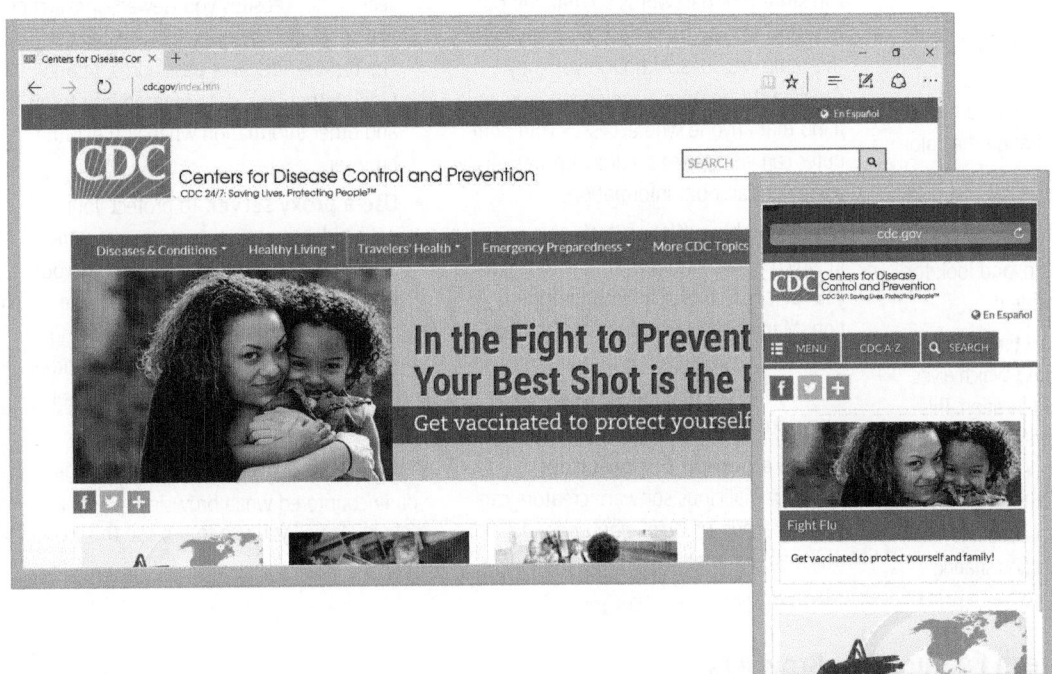

BTW

Web vs. Internet
Recall that the terms, web and Internet, should not be used interchangeably. The World Wide Web is a service of the Internet.

Figure 2-7 Many websites, such as the Centers for Disease Control and Prevention shown here, provide a mobile version that is designed specifically for display on a mobile browser.
Source: Centers for Disease Control and Prevention

When you run a browser, it may retrieve and display a starting webpage, sometimes called a home page. The initial home page that is displayed is specified in the browser. You can change your browser's home page at any time through its settings, options, or similar commands.

Another use of the term, **home page**, refers to the first page that is displayed on a website. Similar to a book cover or a table of contents, a website's home page provides information about its purpose and content. Many websites allow you to personalize the home page so that it contains areas of interest to you.

Current browsers typically support **tabbed browsing**, where the top of the browser shows a tab (similar to a file folder tab) for each webpage you display (shown in Figure 2-7). To move from one displayed webpage to another, you click the tab in the browser. Tabbed browsing allows users to have multiple home pages that automatically are displayed when the browser runs. You also can organize tabs in a group, called a tab group, and save the group as a favorite, so that at any time you can display all tabs at once. You also can click and drag a tab outside of the browser window boundaries to view the corresponding page in a new browser window, or you can drag a tab from one browser window to another.

Because some websites attempt to track your browsing habits or gather personal information, current browsers usually include a feature that allows you to disable and/or more tightly control the dissemination of your browsing habits and personal information. Read Secure IT 2-2 for safe browsing tips.

 SECURE IT 2-2

Safe Browsing Techniques

Browsing the web is similar to crossing a busy street: you need to exercise caution and look carefully for unexpected traffic. Because cyber-criminals are on the lookout to prey upon unsuspecting users, you should follow these guidelines when browsing:

- **Verify the website is safe.** Type the website address of your email, banking, online social network, and other personal accounts directly in a browser; never visit these websites merely by clicking links found in email messages. Before you sign in, double-check the web address to verify it is correct. Browsers may change the color of some of the text in the address bar to verify the website is legitimate. Also, check that the web address begins with https instead of the less secure http, and look for a closed padlock symbol beside it.

- **Turn off location sharing.** At times, you may want allow *location sharing*, which gives websites access to your current location. This feature is handy when you want to obtain current weather conditions or use a navigation app. This information could be misused by dishonest individuals, however, so it is recommended you turn off location sharing.

- **Clear your browsing history.** A copy of every website you visit is stored in the browser's *cache* (pronounced cash) folder. If you perform online banking or view your credit card transactions, the cache could contain personal information, such as passwords and account numbers. You can specify to clear cache automatically each time you exit a browser.

- **Never store passwords.** Many browsers can store your passwords so that you do not need to type them each time you visit the same websites. Although you may consider this feature a convenience, keep in mind that anyone who accesses your computer can view these secure websites easily using your account information.

- **Use a phishing filter.** *Phishing* is a scam in which a perpetrator attempts to obtain your personal and/or financial information. Many browsers include a *phishing filter*, which is a program that warns or blocks you from potentially fraudulent or suspicious websites.

- **Enable a pop-up or pop-under blocker.** Malicious software creators can develop a *pop-up ad* or *pop-under ad*, which are Internet advertisements that

suddenly appear in a new window on top of or behind a webpage displayed in a browser. A **pop-up blocker** is a filtering program that stops pop-up ads from displaying on webpages; similarly a *pop-under blocker* stops pop-under ads. Many browsers include these blockers. You also can download them from the web at no cost.

- **Use private browsing.** Prevent people using your computer or mobile device from seeing the websites you viewed or searches you conducted by using *private browsing*. The browser discards passwords, temporary Internet files, data entered into forms, and other information when you exit the browser.

- **Use a proxy server.** To protect your online identity, use a *proxy server*, which is another computer that screens all your incoming and outgoing messages. The proxy server will prevent your browsing history, passwords, user names, and other personal information from being revealed.

 Consider This: Which pop-ups have you encountered while browsing? What new techniques will you use to browse the web safely?

Tech Feature 2-1: Browsers

The decision of which browser to use is a topic of discussion among computer experts and novices alike. Read Tech Feature 2-1 to learn about features of specific browsers.

Browsers

All browsers can retrieve and display webpages, but their features and ease of use vary. Many factors can affect the decision to choose the browser that best fits your needs.

Configuring Options

Users can customize some settings to improve their browsing experience, such as those listed below.

- **Favorites**, also called *bookmarks*, are links to preferred websites. When you add a website to the list of favorites, you can visit that website simply by clicking its name in a list instead of typing its web address. Favorites can be organized into folders, alphabetized, and sorted by date or how frequently you view the websites.

- Security features, such as filters and secure connections, help protect you from fraudulent and malicious websites that might attempt to steal your identity and personal information. These features also can block websites you do not want to be displayed and can instruct the browser to save passwords.

- Privacy features help prevent thieves from accessing information about your browsing history, such as websites you have visited, data about your browsing session, and content you have seen on specific webpages.

Obtaining Browsers

A browser often is included in the operating system of a computer or mobile device. For example, many computer manufacturers include Edge when they install Windows and include Safari when they install macOS. Use a search engine to locate the browser you want to install, and visit its website to download the most recent version. Most browsers are available for download at no cost. Keep your browser up to date to prevent security holes. You can set your browser to perform updates automatically.

Making a Decision

Selecting the best browser for your needs involves some careful thought. You may decide to install several and then use each one for specific needs. Perform some research to compare browsers and then consider the following factors:

- How old is your computer or mobile device? A newer browser may not work properly on older hardware.

- How much memory is in your computer or mobile device? Some browsers work best with a lot of memory.

- Which operating system are you using? Some browsers are available for specific operating systems. For example, Edge is available only for Windows operating systems.

- What do you want the browser to do? Some browsers are best suited for performing simple searches, while others excel when running websites containing media.

Specific Browsers

- **Chrome:** Google's Chrome was first released in 2008. This free browser is available for Windows, macOS, and Linux, and it must be downloaded and installed. Chrome has independent tabbed browsing; if one tab experiences a problem, the other tabs continue to function.

- **Edge:** Edge is a Microsoft browser included in the Windows operating system. It is the default browser for Windows on most devices and is not compatible with prior versions of Windows. Features include integration with Cortana and OneDrive, along with annotation and reading tools.

- **Firefox:** Developed by the Mozilla Corporation for Windows, macOS, and Linux, Firefox is known for its extensive array of plug-ins (discussed later in the module). This free browser was first released in 2004 and must be downloaded and installed. It has enhanced privacy and security features, a spelling checker, tabbed browsing, and a password manager.

- **Opera:** This second-oldest browser is free, fast, and small. Used on both computers and mobile devices, Opera must be downloaded and installed. It began as a research project in Norway in 1994 and introduced several features found on most of today's browsers.

- **Safari:** Preinstalled on Apple computers and devices, Safari has been the default browser for macOS since 2003 and is relatively new to Windows. The browser has built-in sharing with online social networks, fast performance, parental controls, and ease of use.

Mobile Browsers

Many browsers are included by default with some mobile devices and smartphones. Their features vary greatly. Some allow users to zoom and use keyboard shortcuts with most websites, while others display only websites optimized for mobile devices. The more popular mobile browsers are Chrome, Firefox, Edge, Safari, and Opera Mini.

⚙ **Consider This:** Which browser or browsers have you used? Would you consider using another browser? Why or why not? When first invented, their only function was to browse the web. Can you recommend a more descriptive name for today's browsers?

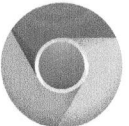

Chrome

Edge

Firefox

Opera

Safari

Google Inc.; Microsoft; Mozilla Foundation; Opera Software; Apple Inc.

Web Addresses

A webpage has a unique address, called a **web address** or *URL* (Uniform Resource Locator). For example, the web address of http://www.nps.gov identifies the U.S. Department of the Interior National Park Service home page. A browser retrieves a webpage using its web address.

If you know the web address of a webpage, you can type it in the address bar of the browser. For example, if you type the address http://www.nps.gov/history/preserve-places.htm in the address bar and then press the ENTER key or click the Search, Go, or similar button, the browser downloads and displays the associated webpage (Figure 2-8). The path, history/preserve-places.htm, in this web address identifies a webpage that is specified in a file named preserve-places.htm, which is located in a folder named history on the web server www.nps.gov that hosts the website for the nps.gov domain. When you enter this web address, after obtaining the IP address for the nps.gov domain name, the browser sends a request to the web server to retrieve the webpage named preserve-places.htm, and delivers it to your browser to be displayed.

 CONSIDER THIS

Although you entered the web address correctly, your screen does not match Figure 2-8. Why?
Organizations may update or redesign their websites, which may cause your screens to look different from those shown in this book.

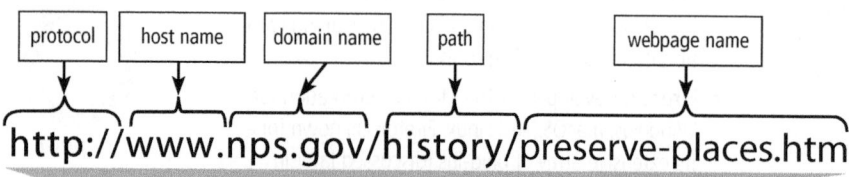

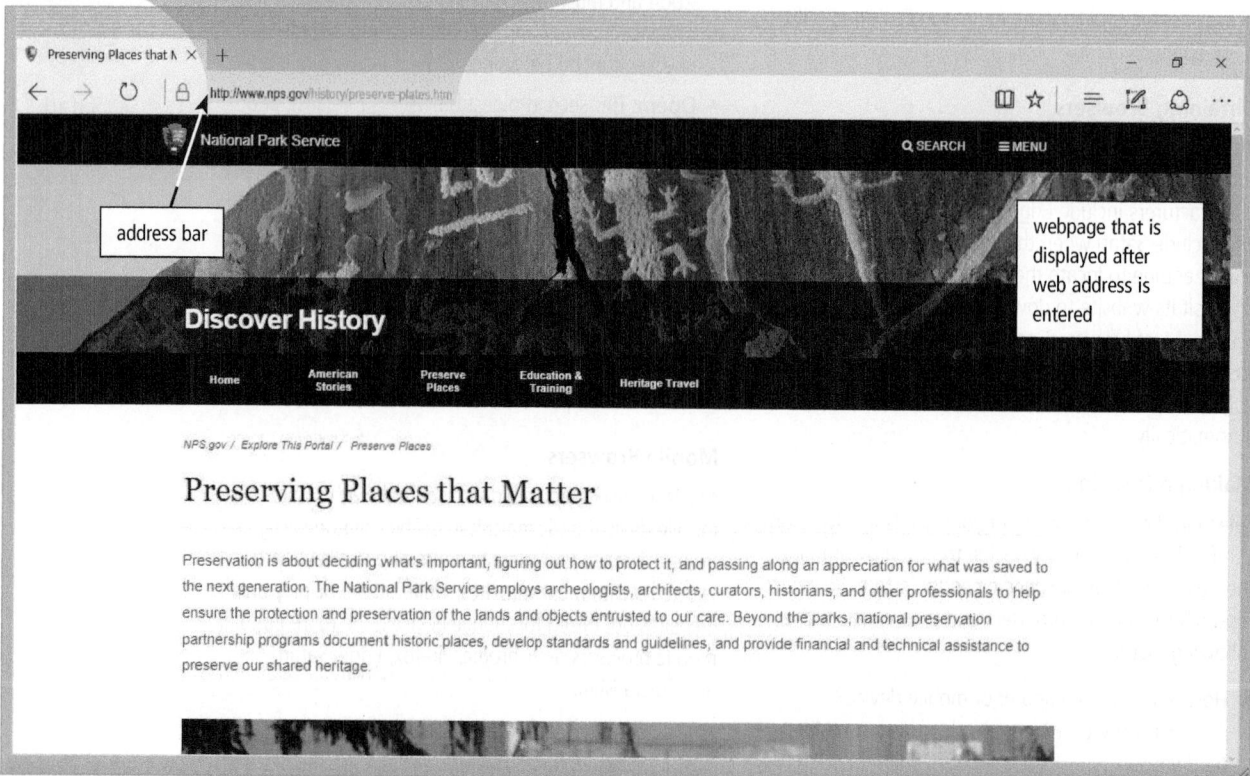

Figure 2-8   After entering http://www.nps.gov/history/preserve-places.htm in the address bar and then pressing the ENTER key or clicking the Search, Go, or similar button in a browser, the U.S. Department of the Interior National Park Service home page shown here is displayed.

Source: National Park Service U.S. Department of the Interior

A web address consists of a protocol, domain name, and sometimes the host name, path to a specific webpage, or file name of the webpage. The *http*, which stands for Hypertext Transfer Protocol, is a set of rules that defines how webpages transfer on the Internet. Many web addresses begin with http:// as the protocol. The text between the protocol and the domain name, called the host name, identifies the type of Internet server or the name of the web server. The www, for example, indicates a web server.

 CONSIDER THIS

Do you need to type the protocol and host name in a web address?
Many browsers and websites do not require that you enter the http:// or the host name www in the web address. For example, you could enter nps.gov instead of http://www.nps.gov. As you begin typing a web address or if you enter an incorrect web address, browsers often display a list of similar addresses or related websites from which you can select. If, however, the host name is not www, you will need to type the host name as part of the web address. For example, the web address of schools.nyc.gov for the New York City schools website does not contain a www and, thus, requires entry of the entire web address.

When you enter a web address in a browser, you request, or pull, information from a web server. Another way users can pull content is by subscribing to a *web feed*, which contains links to or information about updated or changed content on a website. Mass media, blogs, and online social networks often provide web feeds, saving users the time spent checking the websites for updated content. Most browsers contain the capability to read web feeds.

Web Apps and Mobile Apps

Recall from Module 1 that a web app is an application stored on a web server that you access through a browser. Users typically interact with web apps directly on a website, which is hosted on a web server. Web apps usually store users' data and information on their hosts' servers. Computer and mobile device users can keep their files on the cloud, a practice that is known as *cloud storage*.

Many web apps are available at no cost. Others offer access to basic components of their web apps free and charge for access to premium features. Many include advertisements in the free version and charge for an advertisement-free version. Some allow you to use a web app at no cost and then pay a fee when a certain action occurs. For example, you can prepare your tax return for free, but if you elect to print it or file it electronically, you pay a minimal fee.

A *mobile app* is an application you download from a mobile device's app store or other location on the Internet to a smartphone or other mobile device. More specifically, a *mobile web app* is a web app developed for use on a mobile device. Mobile apps often take advantage of features of the device, such as touch screens, digital cameras, microphones, and embedded GPS receivers, to enable you to enter and capture data.

 CONSIDER THIS

What are GPS receivers?
GPS (global positioning system) is a navigation system that consists of one or more earth-based receivers that accept and analyze signals sent by satellites in order to determine the receiver's geographic location. A **GPS receiver** is a handheld, mountable, or embedded device that contains an antenna, a radio receiver, and a processor. Most smartphones include embedded GPS receivers so that users can determine their location, obtain directions, and locate points of interest.
  GPS receivers determine their location on Earth by analyzing at least 3 separate satellite signals from 24 satellites in orbit.

Web apps and mobile apps often work together (Figure 2-9). You might access your cloud storage website from a laptop or desktop. The cloud storage website hosts web apps to upload, download, browse, organize, and view files from your computer. The website also may provide a mobile app that you install on a smartphone so that you can access the same information or perform the same tasks from a mobile device. Because the data and information for each app is stored on the cloud, all data is synchronized and accessible from anywhere you have an Internet connection, regardless of the computer or device used. The functionality of the app across computers and devices generally is the same, although the mobile app sometimes has fewer features. Some tasks may be easier to accomplish on one device or the other. For example, if a lot of typing is required, you may opt to use the web app on a laptop so that you can use a standard keyboard.

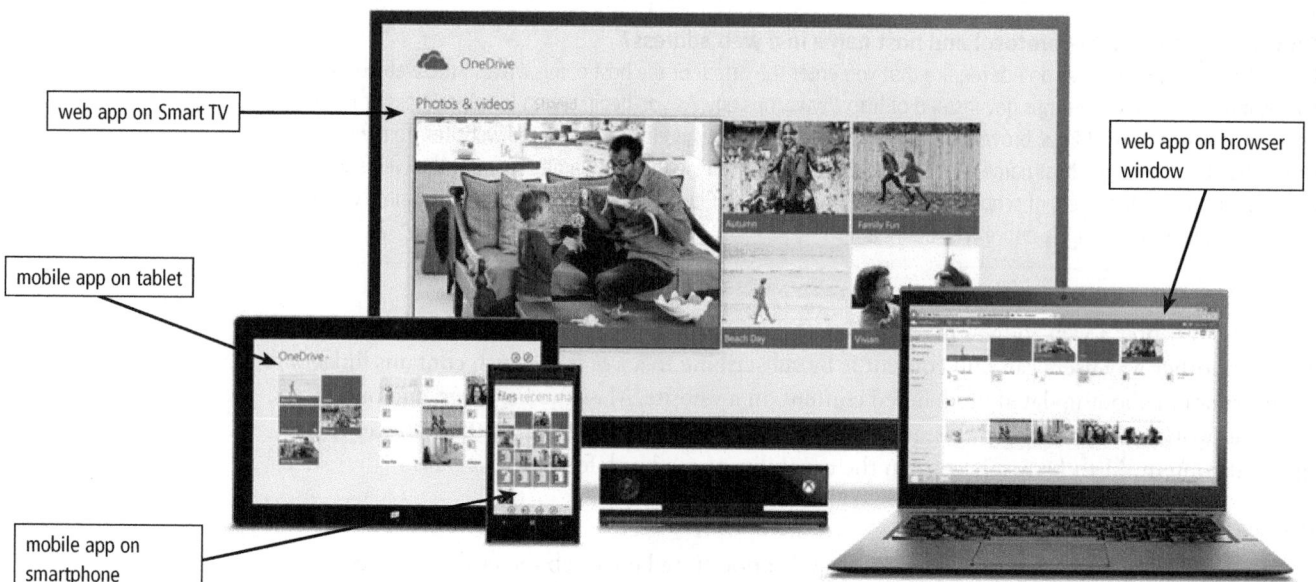

web app on Smart TV

web app on browser window

mobile app on tablet

mobile app on smartphone

Figure 2-9 Web and mobile apps often work together, enabling you to access your content from a variety of computers and devices.
Courtesy of Microsoft Corporation

Types of Websites

The web contains several types of websites: search engines; online social networks; informational and research; media sharing; bookmarking; news, weather, sports, and other mass media; educational; business, governmental, and organizational; blogs; wikis and collaboration; health and fitness; science; entertainment; banking and finance; travel and tourism; mapping; retail and auctions; careers and employment; e-commerce; portals; content aggregation; and website creation and management. Many websites fall into more than one of these types. All of these websites can be accessed from computers or mobile devices but often are formatted differently and may have different features on mobile devices. A search engine on a smartphone, for example, may include an option to dial the phone number of a company rather than display the phone number in the search results.

Search Engines

A web **search engine** is software that finds websites, webpages, images, videos, news, maps, and other information related to a specific topic. You also can use a search engine to solve mathematical equations, define words, and more.

Thousands of search engines are available. Some search engines, such as Bing, Google, and Yahoo!, are helpful in locating information on the web for which you do not know an exact web address or are not seeking a specific website. Those that work with GPS devices or services are location based, meaning they display results related to the device's current geographical position. For example, when using your smartphone, typing the words, gas stations near me, into a search engine may display all gas stations within a certain distance of your current location. Some search engines restrict search results to a specific type of information, such as items updated within the past six months or images that contain a certain color.

Search engines typically allow you to search for one or more of the following items:

- Audio: music, songs, recordings, and sounds
- Blogs: specific opinions and ideas of others
- Businesses: addresses and phone numbers
- Images: photos, diagrams, and drawings
- Maps: maps of a business or address, or driving directions to a destination
- Publications: news articles, journals, and books
- Shipments: track locations of packages in transit to specific destinations
- Transportation: Directions, routes, and arrival and departure times
- Videos: home videos, music videos, television programs, and movie clips
- Weather: local and worldwide conditions and forecasts

Search engines require that you enter a word or phrase, called *search text*, to describe the item you want to find. Search text can be broad, such as spring break destinations, or more specific, such as walt disney world. Search text generally is not case sensitive, so you can enter all the letters in lower case. If you misspell search text, search engines typically correct the misspelling or identify alternative search text. Some also provide suggested search text, links, and/or images as you type your search text.

Depending on the search text, search engines may respond with thousands to billions of search results, sometimes called *hits*. The content of the search results varies depending on the type of information you are seeking and your search text. Some search results contain links to webpages or articles; others are media, such as images or videos. Most search engines sequence the search results based on how close the words in the search text are to one another in the titles and descriptions of the results. They also may use a popularity ranking algorithm based on how frequently the webpage is referenced or linked from other websites. Thus, the first few links probably contain more relevant information.

If you enter a phrase with spaces between the words in search text, most search engines display results that include all of the important words in the phrase, which are called, *keywords*. Because keywords describe content, search engines exclude articles, conjunctions, and other similar words (e.g., to, the, and) when looking for search results. Table 2-4 lists some operators you can use

Table 2-4	Search Engine Operators		
Operator	**Description**	**Examples**	**Explanation**
Space or +	Display search results that include specific words.	art + music art music	Results have both words, art and music, in any order,
OR	Display search results that include only one word from a list.	dog OR puppy	Results have either the word, dog, or the word, puppy.
		dog OR puppy OR canine	Results have the word, dog, or the word, puppy, or the word, canine.
( )	Combine search results that include specific words with those that include only one word from a list.	Kalamazoo Michigan (pizza OR subs)	Results include both words, Kalamazoo Michigan, and either the word, pizza, or the word, subs.
–	Exclude a word from search results.	automobile-convertible	Results include the word, automobile, but do not include the word, convertible.
" "	Search for an exact phrase in a certain order.	"19th century literature"	Results include the exact phrase, 19th century literature.
*	Substitute characters in place of the asterisk.	writer*	Results include any word that begins with the text, writer (e.g., writer, writers, writer's)

in search text to refine searches. Instead of working with operators to refine search text, many search engines provide an advanced search feature or search tools that assist with limiting search results based on items such as date, TLD, language, and other characteristics.

 CONSIDER THIS ─────────────────────────────────

How can you improve search results?

You may find that many items listed in the search results have little or no bearing on the item you are seeking. You can eliminate superfluous items in search results by carefully crafting search text and using search operators to limit search results. Other techniques you can use to improve your searches include the following:

- Use specific nouns.
- Put the most important terms first in the search text.
- List all possible spellings, for example, email, e-mail. Note, however, that many search engines will correct common misspellings.
- Before using a search engine, read its Help information.
- If the search is unsuccessful with one search engine, try another.
- Practice search techniques by performing the Internet Research: Search Skills exercise in each module of this book.

Subject Directories   A *subject directory* classifies webpages in an organized set of categories, such as sports or shopping, and related subcategories. A subject directory provides categorized lists of links arranged by subject. Using a subject directory, you locate a particular topic by clicking links through different levels, moving from the general to the specific. A disadvantage with a subject directory is that users sometimes have difficulty deciding which categories to choose as they work through the menus of links presented.

Tech Feature 2-2: Online Social Networks

Recall from Module 1 that an online social network, or social networking site, is a website that encourages members in its online community to share their interests, ideas, stories, photos, music, and videos with other registered users. Some online social networks also enable users to communicate through text, voice, and video chat, and play games together online. You interact with an online social network through a website or mobile app on your computer or mobile device. Read Tech Feature 2-2 for features and uses of popular online social networks.

 CONSIDER THIS ─────────────────────────────────

What are the various kinds of social media?

Social media consists of content that users create and share online, such as photos, videos, music, links, blog posts, Tweets, wiki entries, podcasts, and status updates. Social media websites facilitate the creation or publishing of social media online and include media sharing sites (for photo, video, and audio files), bookmarking sites, blogs and microblogs, wikis, podcasts, online social networks, and online gaming sites.

Online Social Networks

People you know through personal and professional circles form your social networks. You share common interests, work or spend leisure time together, and know many of one another's friends. Online social networks allow you to manage your social networks online.

Your account on an online social network includes profile information, such as your name, location, photos, and personal and professional interests. You might create accounts on several online social networks to separate your personal and professional activities. Online social networks allow you to view the profiles of other users and designate them as your *friends* or contacts. Some sites, such as Facebook and LinkedIn, require friends to confirm a friendship, while others, such as Twitter and Google+, allow users to follow one another without confirmation.

iStockphoto.com / bombuscreative

You can expand your online social network by viewing your friends' friends and then, in turn, designating some of them as your friends. Friends of your friends and their friends form your *extended contacts*.

- Extended contacts on a personal online social network, such as Facebook, can introduce you to others at your college or from your hometown, connect you with long-distance friends or relatives, or enable you to stay in touch with those who have interests similar to yours.

- Extended contacts on a professional online social network, such as LinkedIn, can introduce you to people who work at companies where you might be seeking employment. You can share employment history and skills in your profile, enabling potential employers who look at your profile to learn about your specific skills.

Read Secure IT 2-3 for tips about securing your privacy when using online social networks.

Personal Uses

Personal uses of online social networks include sharing photos and videos, greetings, or status updates. A *status*

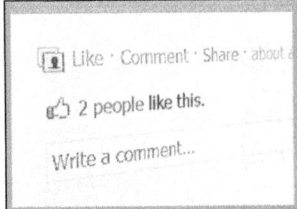

iStockphoto.com / Stratol

update informs friends about what you are doing. You can *like*, or show appreciation for, online content such as photos or videos on online

social networks such as Facebook and Google+. When you do, people who see the same content will know that you liked it, and the person who posted it is notified. All of your updates, likes, posts, and events appear in the activity stream associated with your account. Activity updates from friends may appear on a separate page associated with your account, often called a *news feed*.

On many online social networks, updates can include hashtags to identify their topics. A **hashtag** is a word(s) preceded by a # symbol that describes or categorizes a post. Users can search for posts on a topic by searching for a hashtag. Some online social networks list trending topics based on popular hashtags. Many television broadcasts, advertisements, and businesses post hashtags to encourage viewers and customers to share comments on Twitter or Facebook.

When accessing an online social network with a GPS-enabled mobile device, the location where you check in may be revealed as part of a status update. An online social network's mobile app can share your location with friends, find others nearby, and alert you to promotional deals from local businesses.

Business Uses

Businesses use online social networks to connect with their customers, provide promotional offers, and offer targeted advertising. For example, users who recommend online content about travel services may see travel-related advertising on their online social network's webpage.

Businesses also use data from online social networks to better connect with and understand customers. They can review comments from customers about their experiences using companies' products or services. Monitoring these feeds continuously gives companies immediate feedback from customers.

Nonprofit organizations use online social networks to promote activities and causes, accept donations, and allow volunteers to contact one another online.

⚙ **Consider This:** How can businesses and individuals use online social networks to bring people together in support of a common goal? What benefits and risks are involved when using online social networks?

Follow button

Natee Meepian / Shutterstock.com

 **SECURE IT 2-3**

Privacy and Security Risks with Online Social Networks

Online social networks can be excellent places to share messages, photos, and videos. They can, however, be risky places to divulge personal information. Follow these tips to help protect against thieves who are following the network traffic and attempting to invade private facets of your life.

- **Register with caution.** During the registration process, provide only necessary information. Do not disclose your birthdate, age, place of birth, or the city where you currently are living. If an email address is required, consider using a new address so that the online social network cannot access your email address book. Online social networks occasionally ask users to enter their email address and password to determine if their friends also are members of the network. In turn, the network obtains access to contacts in your address book and can send spam (unsolicited email messages) to your friends.

- **Manage your profile.** Check for privacy settings, usually found on the Settings or Options tabs, to set permissions so that you can control who can review your profile and photos, determine how people can search for you and make comments, and if desired, block certain people from viewing your page. Be aware that online social networks may change privacy settings. Periodically check your settings to ensure you have the most up-to-date settings.

- **Choose friends carefully.** You may receive a friend request that appears to be from someone you know. In reality, this message may originate from an identity thief who created a fake profile in an attempt to obtain your personal information. Confirm with the sender that the request is legitimate.

- **Limit friends.** While many online social networks encourage the practice, do not try to gather too many friends in your social network. Some experts believe that a functional online social network should not exceed 150 people. Occasionally review what your friends are posting about you.

- **Divulge only relevant information.** Write details about yourself that are relevant to the reasons you are participating in an online social network. When posting information, be aware that the message may be accessible publicly and associated with your identity permanently. Do not post anything you would not want to be made public.

- **Be leery of urgent requests for help.** Avoid responding to emergency pleas for financial assistance from alleged family members. In addition, do not reply to messages concerning lotteries you did not enter and fabulous deals that sound too good to be true.

- **Read the privacy policy.** Evaluate the website's privacy policy, which describes how it uses your personal information. For example, if you watch a video while signed in to your account, an external website or app may have access to this information and post this activity as an entry in both your activity stream and your friends' news feeds.

✳ **Consider This:** Should online social networks do a better job of telling their users what information is safe or unsafe to share? What role should parents play in overseeing their child's involvement in online social networks?

Informational and Research

An informational and research website contains factual information. Examples include libraries, encyclopedias, dictionaries, directories, guides (Figure 2-10), and other types of reference. You can find guides on numerous topics, such as health and medicine, research paper documentation styles, and grammar rules. Many of the other types of websites identified in this section also are used to research information.

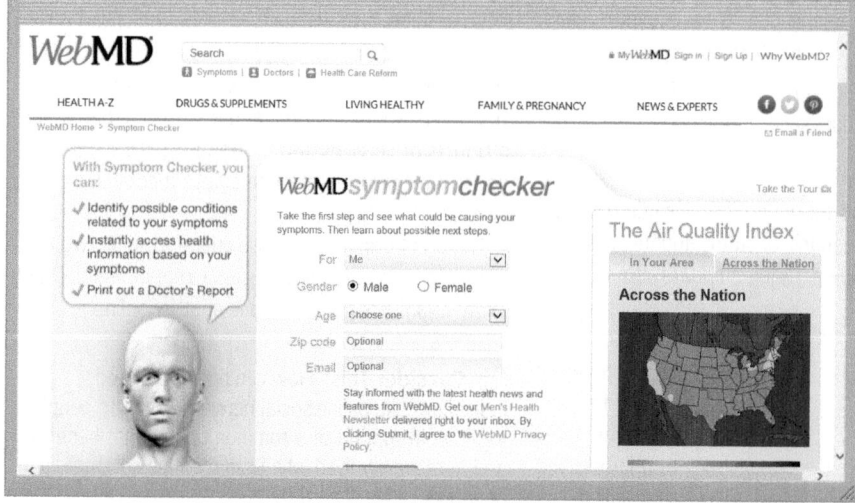

Figure 2-10 You can research health conditions from your symptoms on a medical website, such as WebMD.
Source: WebMD, LLC

The Internet, Websites, and Media

Media Sharing

A *media sharing site* is a website that enables members to manage media such as photos, videos, and music. These websites are sometimes called photo sharing sites, video sharing sites (Figure 2-11), and music sharing sites, respectively. Media sharing sites, which may be free or charge a fee, provide a quick and efficient way to upload, organize, store, and download media.

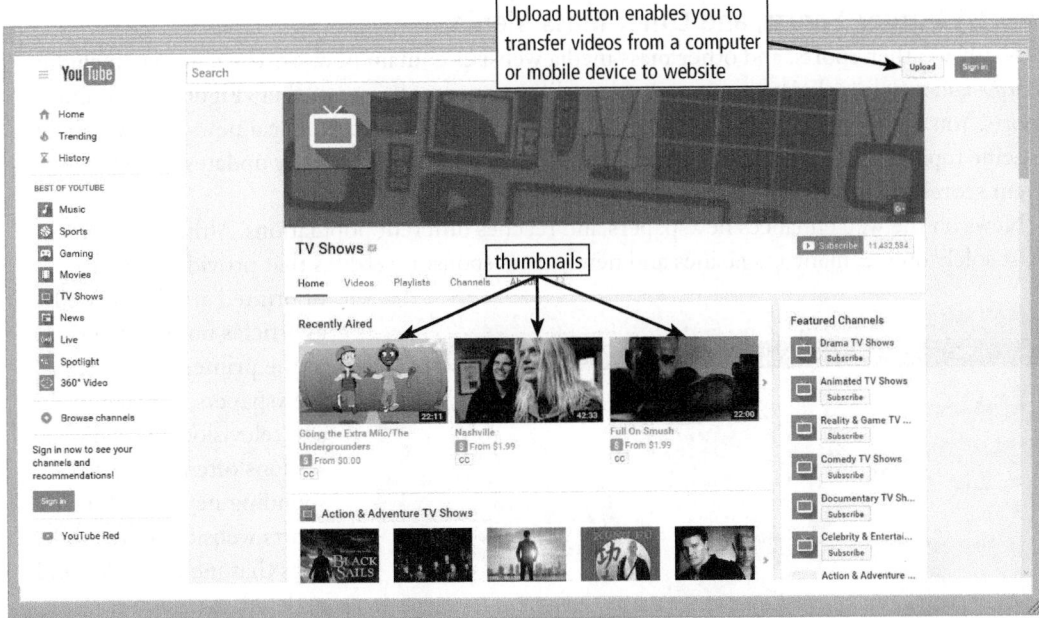

Figure 2-11 YouTube is an example of a video sharing site. You click the thumbnail to view the video.
Source: YouTube, Inc.

 CONSIDER THIS

Why would you use a media sharing site instead of an online social network?
Although the lines between media sharing sites and online social networks are becoming blurred, some users chose a traditional media sharing site if they simply want to post photos, videos, or music to share with others and do not require the full functionality of an online social network. Before you allow someone to take your photo or record video of you, however, remember that the photo or video may be posted on a media sharing site. These photos or videos may be accessible publicly and associated with your identity for a long time. Also, once posted, you may be giving up certain rights to the media. Further, do not post photos or videos that are protected by copyright.

Bookmarking

A *bookmarking site* is a website that enables members to organize, tag, and share links to media and other online content (Figure 2-12). A **tag** is a short descriptive label that you assign to webpages, photos, videos, blog posts, email messages, social media messages, and other digital content so that it is easier locate at a later time. Many websites and web apps support tagging, which enables users to organize their online content.

Figure 2-12 Pinterest is an example of a bookmarking site.
Courtesy of Pinterest

CONSIDER THIS

What is a hashtag?
On Twitter and other online social networks, a hashtag is a descriptive word or phrase (without spaces between words) that starts with the hash symbol (#). Hashtags allow users to classify posts related to a particular topic.

News, Weather, Sports, and Other Mass Media

News, weather, sports, and other mass media websites contain newsworthy material, including stories and articles relating to current events, life, money, politics, weather (Figure 2-13), and sports. You often can customize these websites so that you can receive local news or news about specific topics. Some provide a means to send you alerts, such as weather updates or sporting event scores, via text or email messages.

News on the web enhances newspapers and reaches different populations. Although some exist solely online, many magazines and newspapers sponsor websites that provide summaries of printed articles, as well as articles not included in the printed versions. Newspapers, magazines, and television and radio stations often have corresponding news, weather, or sports websites and mobile apps that include video and updated, extended coverage beyond the information available in a printed newspaper or daily television newscast. Read Ethics & Issues 2-2 to consider the issues related to using fake names on websites.

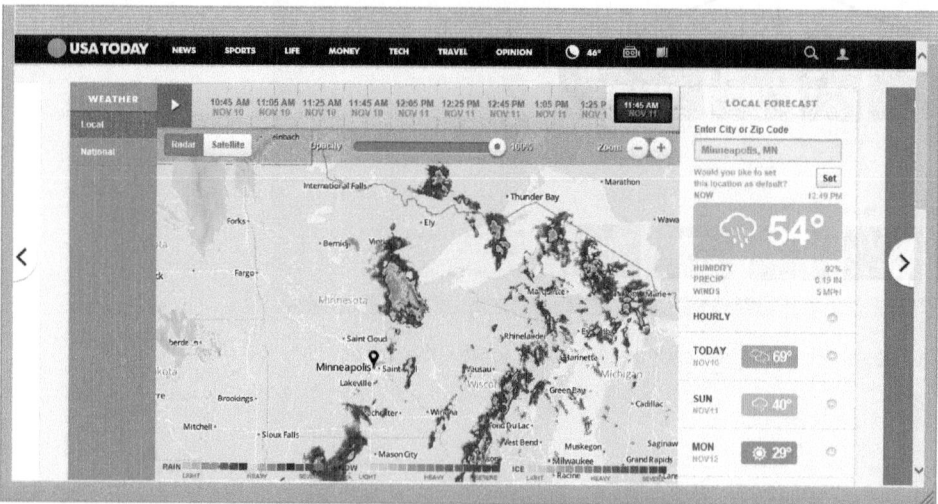

Figure 2-13   Forecasts, radar, and other weather conditions are available on the WEATHER webpage on USA TODAY's website.
Source: Gannett

 ETHICS & ISSUES 2-2

Is It Ethical to Use a Fake Name or ID on a Website?
You are signing up for an account on an online social network, an online dating website, or a news website that enables you to post comments. Should you use your real name?

Many argue that it is harmless to protect your anonymity by using a fake name but believe that it is not right to create a fake profile to mislead others or leave malicious comments on a website. The latter has become so prevalent that terms have emerged to describe this behavior. For example, *catfishing* is when someone creates a fake online social network or online dating profile and forms relationships with unsuspecting users. A *troll* is a user who posts negative, inflammatory comments on a blog post or article with the intent of inciting other users.

One website creates very thorough, but completely fake, personas, which include email addresses, Social Security numbers, phone numbers, and more. Although law enforcement has raised concerns over the potential misuses of fake profiles, it technically is legal, even though the names and personas are not real. Legitimate uses for fake name generators include testers of large databases, such as ones for hospitals.

Facebook currently requires members to use their real names. Twitter's policy is that anyone can create a fake account, but it has a verification process to identify the official account of a celebrity or public figure. Most fake Twitter accounts are harmless and often are flattering. Although some argue that creating a fake account constitutes identity theft, unless the intent is to harm or embarrass the real person, it is not unethical or illegal. When a journalist created a fake account for a politician and posted discriminatory quotes and Tweets in the politician's name, many considered it an ethics violation, because journalists are supposed to report the truth.

 Consider This: Is it ever acceptable to use a fake name online? Why or why not? Is it unethical to create fake personas for others to use? Why or why not? Should websites require you to use a real name, or have a verification process? Why or why not?

Educational

An educational website offers exciting, challenging avenues for formal and informal teaching and learning. The web contains thousands of tutorials, from learning how to build a website to learning how to cook a meal. For a more structured learning experience, companies provide online training to employees, and colleges offer online classes and degrees. Instructors often use the web to enhance classroom teaching by publishing course materials, grades, and other pertinent class information.

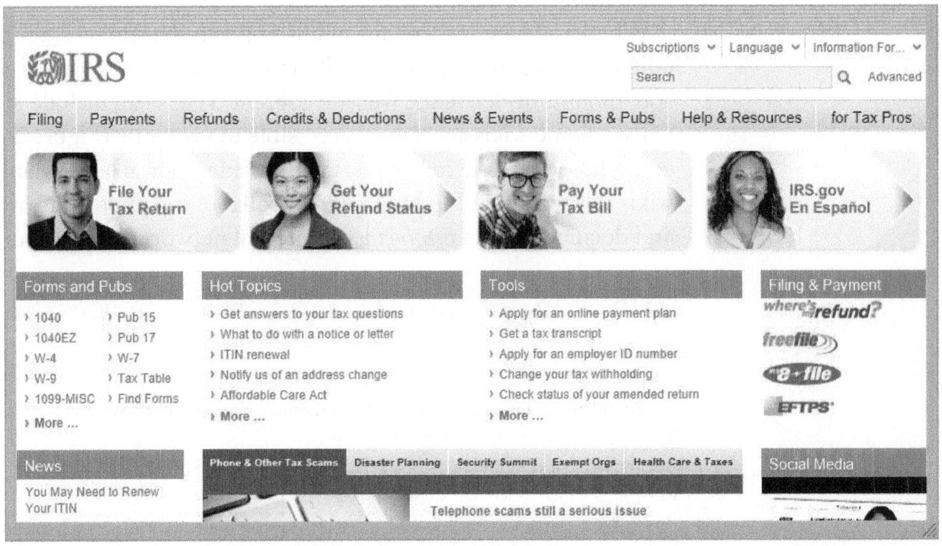

Business, Governmental, and Organizational

A business website contains content that increases brand awareness, provides company background or other information, and/or promotes or sells products or services. Nearly every enterprise has a business website. Examples include Allstate Insurance Company, Apple Inc., General Motors Corporation, Kraft Foods Inc., and Walt Disney Company.

Most United States government agencies have websites providing citizens with information, such as census data, or assistance, such as filing taxes (Figure 2-14). Many other types of organizations use the web for a variety of reasons. For example, nonprofit organizations raise funds for a cause, and advocacy groups present their views or opinions.

Figure 2-14 Government agencies, such as the IRS webpage shown here, have websites providing assistance and information to citizens.
Source: IRS

Blogs

As described in Module 1, a **blog** (short for weblog) is an informal website consisting of time-stamped articles, or posts, in a diary or journal format, usually listed in reverse chronological order. The term *blogosphere* refers to the worldwide collection of blogs. A blog that contains video sometimes is called a video blog, or vlog. A *microblog* allows users to publish short messages usually less than 10,000 characters, for others to read. The collection of a user's Tweets, or posts on Twitter, for example, forms a microblog (Figure 2-15).

Similar to an editorial section in a newspaper, blogs reflect the interests, opinions, and personalities of the author, called the **blogger**. Some blogs allow readers to add comments on blog posts, which then are published on the blog for all visitors to see. Blogs have become an important means of online communications. Businesses create blogs to communicate with employees, customers, and vendors. They may post announcements of new information on a corporate blog. Teachers create blogs to collaborate with other teachers and students. Home users create blogs to share aspects of their personal lives with family, friends, and others.

a Tweet presents current events and scientific news

Figure 2-15 When you 'follow' @NASA on Twitter, you will see Tweets such as the one shown here in your account's timeline, along with Tweets from others whom you are following.
Source: Twitter

CONSIDER THIS

How can you locate Tweets about certain topics?
When searching Twitter, you can use hashtags to find related posts. Similarly, you can tag any word(s) in your Tweets by typing it as a hashtag, such as #college.

Wikis and Collaboration

Whereas a blog is a tool for publishing and sharing messages, a wiki enables users to organize, edit, and share information. A **wiki** is a type of collaborative website that allows users to create, add, modify, or delete the website content. Wikis can include articles, documents, photos, or videos. Some wikis are public, accessible to everyone (Figure 2-16). Others are private so that content is accessible only to certain individuals or groups. Many companies, for example, set up wikis as an intranet for employees to collaborate on projects or access information, procedures, and documents. (An *intranet* is an internal network that uses Internet technologies.)

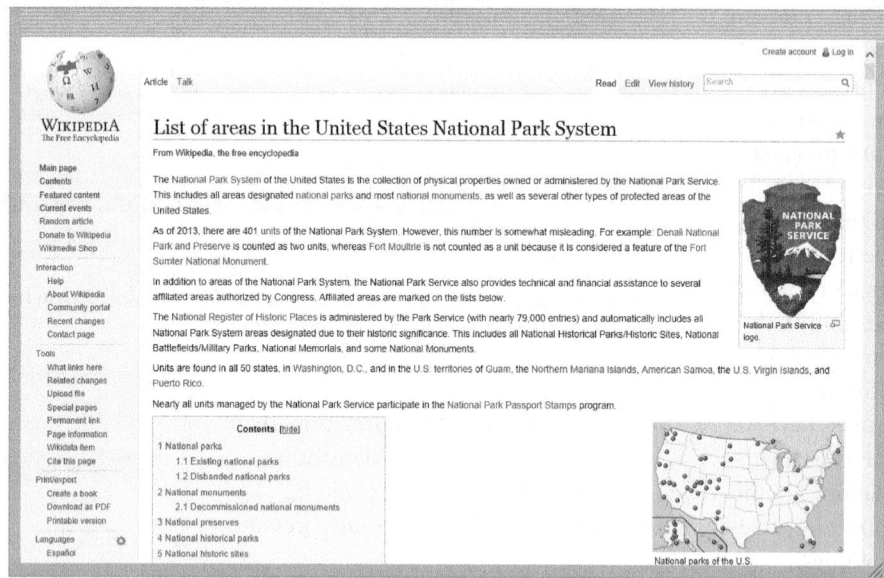

Figure 2-16   Wikipedia is a popular public wiki.
Source: Wikimedia Foundation

Contributors to a wiki typically must register before they can edit content or add comments. Wikis usually hold edits on a webpage until an editor or website manager can review them for accuracy. Unregistered users typically can review the content but cannot edit it or add comments.

Other types of collaboration websites enable users to share and edit any type of project — including documents, photos, videos, designs, prototypes, calendars, and more, often at the same time. On these websites, comments or edits are seen by other connected users. Most of these websites also enable users to communicate via text chat, and some provide a whiteboard capability for sharing drawings or sketches.

Health and Fitness

Many websites provide up-to-date medical, fitness, nutrition, or exercise information for public access. Some offer users the capability of listening to health-related seminars and discussions. Consumers, however, should verify the online medical information they read with a personal physician. Health service organizations store your personal health history, including prescriptions, lab test results, doctor visits, allergies, and immunizations. Doctors use the web to assist with researching and diagnosing health conditions.

Science

Several websites contain information about space exploration, astronomy, physics, earth sciences, microgravity, robotics, and other branches of science. Scientists use online social networks to collaborate on the web. Nonprofit science organizations use the web to seek public donations to support research.

Entertainment

An entertainment website offers music, videos, shows, performances, events, sports, games, and more in an interactive and engaging environment. Many entertainment websites support streaming media. **Streaming** is the process of transferring data in a continuous and even flow, which allows users to access and use a file while it is transmitting. You can listen to streaming audio or watch streaming video, such as a live performance or broadcast, as it downloads to your computer, mobile device, or an Internet-connected television.

Sophisticated entertainment websites often partner with other technologies. For example, you can cast your vote on a competition-themed television show via your phone or online social network account.

Banking and Finance

Online banking and online trading enable users to access their financial records from anywhere in the world, as long as they have an Internet connection. Using online banking, users can access accounts, pay bills, transfer funds, calculate mortgage payments, and manage other financial activities from their computer or mobile device (Figure 2-17). With online trading, users can invest in stocks, options, bonds, treasuries, certificates of deposit, money market accounts, annuities, mutual funds, and so on, without using a broker. Read Secure IT 2-4 for tips about protecting your bank accounts and other personal information from identity theft.

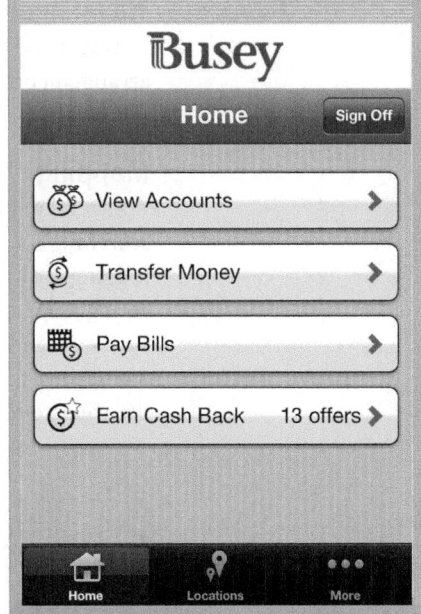

Figure 2-17 Many banks, such as Busey shown here, provide mobile versions of their online banking website so that users can manage financial accounts from their mobile devices.
Source: First Busey Corporation

 SECURE IT 2-4

Protecting Yourself from Identity Theft

The fastest growing crime in the United States is identity theft. More than nine million people fall victim each year, with the unauthorized use of an existing credit card accounting for much of the problem. The National Crime Victimization Survey reports that household identity theft losses amount to more than $13 billion each year, and that figure does not account for the aggravation and time required to repair the accounts. Practice these techniques to thwart attempts to steal your personal data:

- Do not click links in or reply to spam for any reason.
- Install a personal firewall (software that protects network resources from outside intrusions).
- Clear or disable web cookies (small text files that web servers store on a computer) in your browser. This action might prevent some cookie-based websites from functioning, but you will be able to decide which cookies to accept or reject.
- Turn off file and printer sharing on your Internet connection.

- Set up a free email account. Use this email address for merchant forms.
- Sign up for email filtering through your ISP or use an anti-spam program.
- Shred financial documents before you discard them.
- Provide only the required information on website forms.
- Avoid checking your email or performing banking activities on public computers. These computers are notorious for running tracking software such as *keyloggers*, which record keystrokes in a hidden file. If you must use a public computer for critical activities, be certain to sign out of any password-protected website and to clear the browser's cache.
- Request a free copy of your medical records each year from the Medical Information Bureau.
- Obtain your credit report once a year from each of the three major credit reporting agencies and correct any errors. Enroll in a credit monitoring service.
- Request, in writing, to be removed from mailing lists.

- Place your phone number on the National Do Not Call Registry.
- Avoid shopping club and buyer cards.
- Do not write your phone number on charge or credit receipts. Ask merchants not to write this number or any other personal information, especially your Social Security number and driver's license number, on the back of your personal checks.
- Do not preprint your phone number or Social Security number on personal checks.
- Fill in only the required information on rebate, warranty, and registration forms.
- Learn how to block your phone number from displaying on the receiver's system.

If your identity has been stolen, immediately change any passwords that may have been compromised. If you have disclosed your debit or credit card numbers, contact your financial institutions. You also should visit the Federal Trade Commission website or call the FTC help line.

✳ **Consider This:** Do you know anyone who has been a victim of identity theft? What steps will you take to protect your identity using some of these guidelines?

Travel and Tourism

Travel and tourism websites enable users to research travel options and make travel arrangements. On these websites, you typically can read travel reviews, search for and compare flights and prices, order airline tickets, book a room, or reserve a rental car.

Mapping

Several mapping website and web apps exist that enable you to display up-to-date maps by searching for an address, postal code, phone number, or point of interest (such as an airport, lodging, or historical site). The maps can be displayed in a variety of views, including terrain, aerial, maps, streets, buildings, traffic, and weather. These websites also provide directions when a user enters a starting and destination point (Figure 2-18). Many work with GPS to determine where a user is located, eliminating the need for a user to enter the starting point and enabling the website to recommend nearby points of interest.

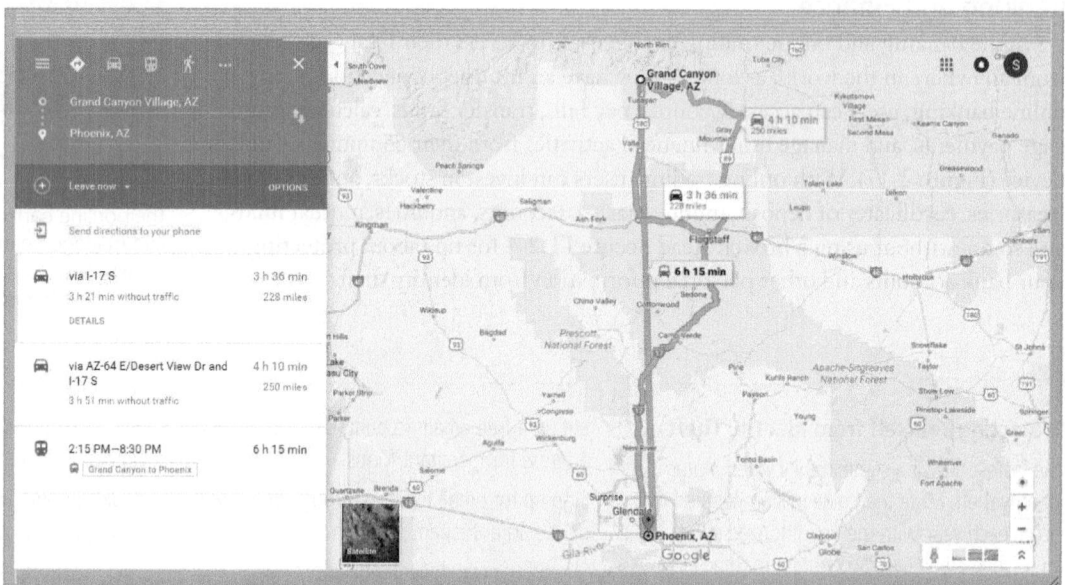

Figure 2-18 Using mapping web apps, such as Google Maps shown here, you can obtain driving directions from one destination to another.
Source: Google Inc.

Retail and Auctions

You can purchase just about any product or service on the web, a process that sometimes is called *e-retail* (short for electronic retail). To purchase online, the customer visits the business's *electronic storefront*, which contains product descriptions, images, and a shopping cart (Figure 2-19). A *shopping cart* allows the customer to collect items to purchase. When ready to complete the sale, the customer enters personal data and the method of payment, which should be through a secure Internet connection.

With an **online auction**, users bid on an item being sold by someone else. The highest bidder at the end of the bidding period purchases the item. eBay is one of the more popular online auction websites.

shopping cart

Figure 2-19   Shown here is Amazon's storefront for books, with recommendations in a variety of categories.
Source: Amazon.com, Inc.

 **CONSIDER THIS**

Is it safe to enter financial information online?

As an alternative to entering credit card, bank account, or other financial information online, some shopping and auction websites allow consumers to use an online payment service, such as PayPal. To use an online payment service, you create an account that is linked to your credit card or funds at a financial institution. When you make a purchase, you use your online payment service account, which manages the payment transaction without revealing your financial information.

Careers and Employment

You can search the web for career information and job openings. Job search websites list thousands of openings in hundreds of fields, companies, and locations. This information may include required training and education, salary data, working conditions, job descriptions, and more. In addition, many organizations advertise careers on their websites.

When a company contacts you for an interview, learn as much about the company and the industry as possible before the interview. Many have websites with detailed company profiles.

E-Commerce

E-commerce, short for electronic commerce, is a business transaction that occurs over an electronic network, such as the Internet. Anyone with access to a computer or mobile device, an Internet connection, and a means to pay for purchased goods or services can participate in e-commerce. Some people use the term *m-commerce* (mobile commerce) to identify e-commerce that takes place using mobile devices. Popular uses of e-commerce by consumers include shopping and auctions, finance, travel, entertainment, and health.

Three types of e-commerce websites are business-to-consumer, consumer-to-consumer, and business-to-business.

- *Business-to-consumer (B2C) e-commerce* consists of the sale of goods and services to the general public, such as at a shopping website.
- *Consumer-to-consumer (C2C) e-commerce* occurs when one consumer sells directly to another, such as in an online auction.
- *Business-to-business (B2B) e-commerce* occurs when businesses provide goods and services to other businesses, such as online advertising, recruiting, credit, sales, market research, technical support, and training.

Portals

A **portal** is a website that offers a variety of Internet services from a single, convenient location (Figure 2-20). A wireless portal is a portal designed for Internet-capable mobile devices. Most portals offer these free services: search engine; news, sports, and weather; web publishing; yellow pages; stock quotes; maps; shopping; and email and other communications services.

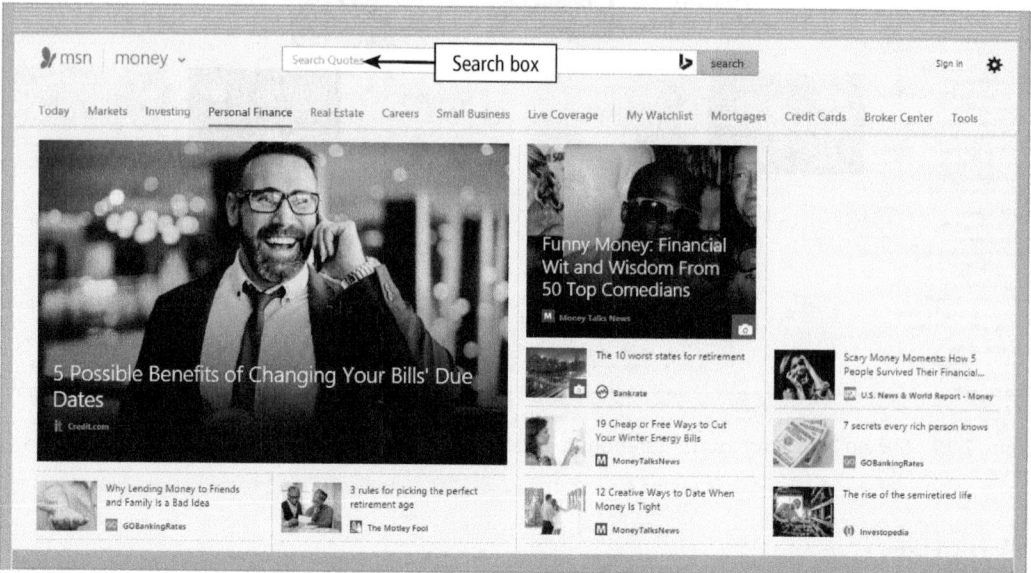

Figure 2-20 Portals, such as MSN, offer a variety of Internet services from a single location.
Source: Microsoft Corporation

Content Aggregation

A **content aggregation** website or web app, sometimes called a *curation website*, allows users to collect and compile content from a variety of websites about a particular topic or theme (Figure 2-21). Types of content that may be compiled includes news, reviews, images, videos, podcasts (discussed later in this module), and blogs. Content aggregation websites save users time because they need to visit only one website (the content aggregation website) instead of visiting multiple websites to obtain information.

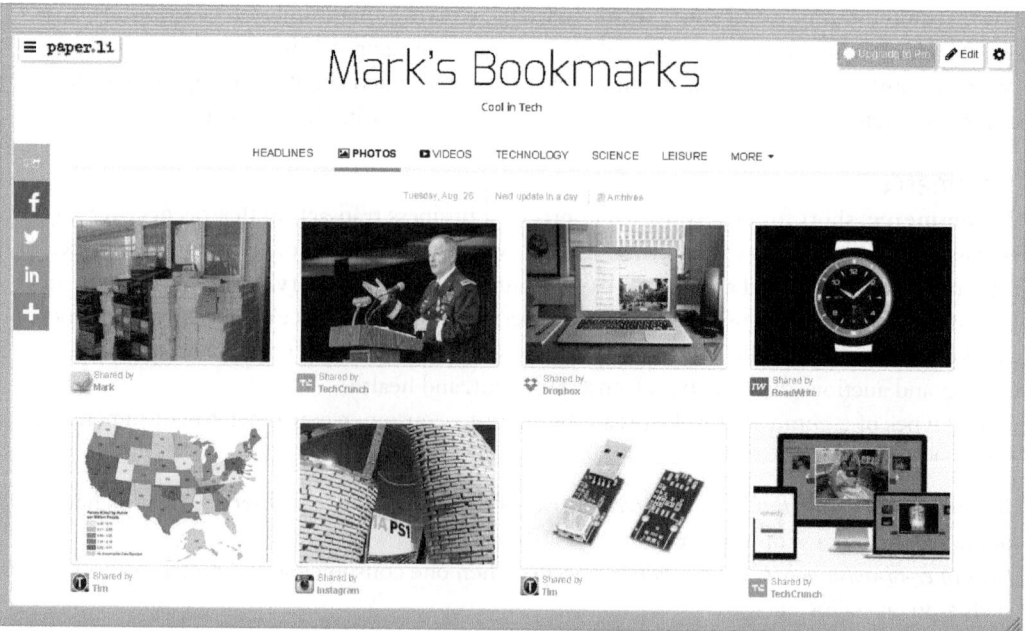

Figure 2-21 A content aggregation web app that compiles news and features from a variety of online sources.
Source: SmallRivers

Website Creation and Content Management

By creating their own websites, businesses and individuals can convey information to billions of people. The content of the webpages ranges from news stories to product information to blogs to surveys. Web creation and content management system sites provide tools that support the steps in **web publishing**, which is the creation and maintenance of websites. To create a website, you do not have to be a computer programmer. For the small business or home user, web publishing is fairly easy as long as you have the proper tools. Table 2-5 outlines the five main steps in web publishing.

Table 2-5 Steps in Web Publishing	
Step	**Description**
1. Plan the website.	Identify the purpose of the website and the characteristics of the people you want to visit the website.
	Determine ways to differentiate your website from other similar ones.
	Decide how visitors will navigate the website.
	Register the desired domain name.
2. Design the website.	Design the appearance and layout of elements on the website.
	Decide colors and formats.
	Determine content for links, text, graphics, animation, audio, video, virtual reality, and blogs.
	You may need specific hardware, such as a digital camera, webcam, video camera, scanner, and/or audio recorder.
	You also may need software that enables you to create images or edit photos, audio, and video.
3. Create the website.	To create a website, you have several options:
	a. Use the features of a word processing program that enable you to create basic webpages from documents containing text and graphics.
	b. Use a *content management system*, which is a tool that assists users with creating, editing, and hosting content on a website.
	c. Use website authoring software to create more sophisticated websites that include text, graphics, animation, audio, video, special effects, and links.
	d. More advanced users create sophisticated websites by using a special type of software, called a text editor, to enter codes that instruct the browser how to display the text, images, and links on a webpage.
	e. For advanced features, such as managing users, passwords, chat rooms, and email, you may need to purchase specialized website management software.
4. Host the website.	Options for transferring the webpages from your computer to a web server include the following:
	a. A *web hosting service* provides storage space on a web server for a reasonable monthly fee.
	b. Many ISPs offer web hosting services to their customers for free or for a monthly fee.
	c. Online content management systems usually include hosting services for free or for a fee, depending on features and amount of storage used.
5. Maintain the website.	Visit the website regularly to ensure its contents are current and all links work properly.
	Create surveys on the website to test user satisfaction and solicit feedback.
	Run analytics to track visitors to the website and measure statistics about its usage.

Some websites are dedicated to one portion of web publishing; others provide a variety of web publishing tools, including website design, content management, web hosting, website marketing, website analytics, survey development, and more. Because users view websites on a variety of computers and devices, many website developers use an approach called **responsive web design** (RWD) that adapts the layout of the website to fit the screen on which it is being displayed.

CONSIDER THIS

Can you assume that content on a website is correct and accurate?
No. Any person, company, or organization can publish a webpage on the Internet. No one oversees the content of these webpages.

Use the criteria below to evaluate a website or webpage before relying on its content.

- Affiliation: A reputable institution should support the website without bias in the information.
- Audience: The website should be written at an appropriate level.
- Authority: The website should list the author and the appropriate credentials.
- Content: The website should be well organized and the links should work.
- Currency: The information on the webpage should be current.
- Design: The pages at the website should download quickly, be visually pleasing, and be easy to navigate.
- Objectivity: The website should contain little advertising and be free of bias.

Digital Media on the Web

Most webpages include *multimedia*, which refers to any application that combines text with media. Media includes graphics, animation, audio, video, and/or virtual reality. The sections that follow discuss how the web uses these types of media.

Graphics

A **graphic** is a visual representation of nontext information, such as a drawing, chart, or photo. Many webpages use colorful graphics to convey messages (Figure 2-22). As shown in the figure, some websites use thumbnails on their pages because larger graphics can be time-consuming to display. A *thumbnail* is a small version of a larger image. You usually can click a thumbnail to display the image in full size.

Figure 2-22 Many webpages use colorful graphics to convey messages. For example, the variety of colors, images, shapes, and thumbnails on the San Diego Zoo webpage visually separate and draw attention to areas of the webpage, making the webpage more dynamic and enticing.
Source: Zoological Society of San Diego

The web often uses infographics to present concepts, products, and news. An *infographic* (short for information graphic) is a visual representation of data or information, designed to communicate quickly, simplify complex concepts, or present patterns or trends (Figure 2-23). Many forms of infographics exist: maps, signs, charts, and diagrams.

Of the graphics formats for displaying images on the web (Table 2-6), the JPEG and PNG formats are more common. *JPEG* (pronounced JAY-peg) is a compressed graphics format that attempts to reach a balance between image quality and file size. With JPG files, the more compressed the file, the smaller the image and the lower the quality. *PNG* (pronounced ping) is a patent-free compressed graphics format that restores all image details when the file is viewed. That is, the PNG format does not lose image quality during compression.

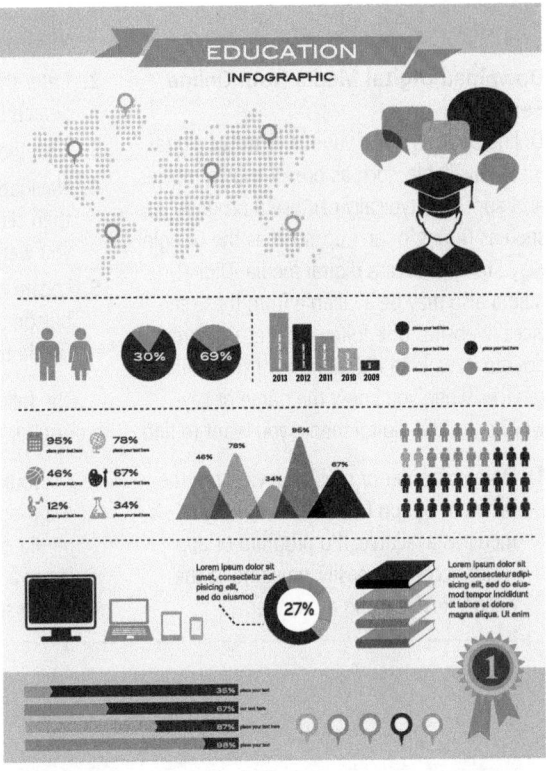

Figure 2-23   An infographic presents complex concepts at a glance.
Marish / Shutterstock.com

Table 2-6	Graphics Formats Used on the Web	
Abbreviation	**Name**	**Uses**
BMP	Bitmap	Desktop backgrounds Scanned images
GIF	Graphics Interchange Format	Images with few colors Simple diagrams Shapes
JPEG	Joint Photographic Experts Group	Digital camera photos Game screenshots Movie still shots
PNG	Portable Network Graphics	Comic-style drawings Line art Web graphics
TIFF	Tagged Image File Format	Photos used in printing industry

Animation   Many webpages use *animation*, which is the appearance of motion created by displaying a series of still images in sequence. For example, text that animates by scrolling across the screen can serve as a ticker to display stock updates, news, sports scores, weather, or other information. Web-based games often use animation.

Audio

On the web, you can listen to audio clips and live audio. *Audio* includes music, speech, or any other sound. Simple applications consist of individual audio files available for download to a computer or device. Once downloaded, you can play (listen to) the content of these files. Read How To 2-2 for instructions about downloading digital media from online services. Other applications use streaming audio so that you can listen to the audio while it downloads.

 **HOW TO 2-2**

Download Digital Media from Online Services

Online services make various forms of digital media available, such as books, music, movies, and apps. You typically can use a program, such as iTunes, or an app, such as the Google Play Store, to access digital media. Digital media also may be available from these services' websites. The following steps describe how to download digital media from online services when you know the name or key-word(s) for the digital media you want to find.

1. On a computer or mobile device, run the program or app from which the digital media is available. If a program or app is not accessible easily, navigate to the online service using a browser.

2. Enter the name or keyword(s) in the Search box.
3. Click the Search button to perform the search.
4. Navigate through the search results and then click the search result for the item you want to download.
5. Locate and then click the Download button or link to download the digital media to your computer or mobile device.

The following steps describe how to browse for and download digital media.

1. On your computer or mobile device, run the program or app from which the digital media is available. If a program or app is not accessible easily, navigate to the online service using a browser.

2. Click the category corresponding to the type of digital media you want to browse. Common categories include music, movies, books, and apps.
3. Browse the items in the category.
4. When you find an item you want to down-load, click the item to display additional information.
5. Look for and then click the Download but-ton or link to download the digital media to your computer or mobile device.

Consider This: In addition to the online services listed in this box, what are three additional resources from which you can download digital media?

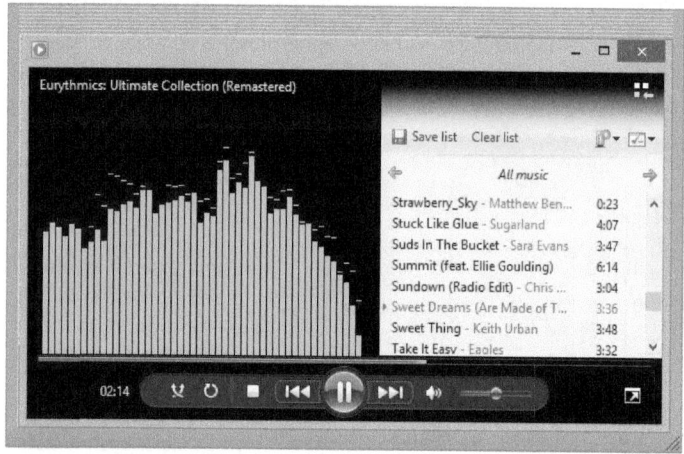

Figure 2-24   Windows Media Player is a popular media player, through which you can listen to music and watch video.
Source: Microsoft Corporation

Audio files are compressed to reduce their file sizes. For example, the *MP3* format reduces an audio file to about one-tenth its original size, while preserving much of the original quality of the sound.

To listen to an audio file on your computer, you need special software called a *media player*. Most current operating systems contain a media player; for example, the Windows operating system includes Windows Media Player (Figure 2-24). Some audio files, however, might require you to download a media player. Media players available for download include iTunes, RealPlayer, and VLC Player. You can download media players free from the web.

Video

On the web, you can view video clips or watch live video. *Video* consists of images displayed in motion. Most video also has accompanying audio. You also can upload, share, or view video clips at a video sharing site. Educators, politicians, and businesses use video blogs and video podcasts to engage students, voters, and consumers.

Simple video applications on the web consist of individual video files, such as movie or television clips, that you must download completely before you can play them on a computer or mobile device. Video files often are compressed because they are quite large in size. Videos posted to the web often are short in length, usually less than 10 minutes, because they can take a long time to download. As with streaming audio files, streaming video files allows you to view longer or live videos by playing them as they download to your computer.

Virtual Reality   **Virtual reality** (VR) is the use of computers to simulate a real or imagined environment that appears as a three-dimensional (3-D) space. VR involves the display of 3-D images that users explore and manipulate interactively. Using special VR software, a developer creates an entire 3-D environment that contains infinite space and depth, called a VR world

(Figure 2-25). A VR world on the web, for example, might show a house for sale where potential buyers walk through rooms in the VR house by sliding their finger on a touch screen or moving an input device forward, backward, or to the side. Users also can wear a special headset viewer to experience a 3-D virtual world.

In addition to games and simulations, many practical applications of VR also exist. Science educators create VR models of molecules, organisms, and other structures for students to examine. Companies use VR to showcase products or create advertisements. Architects create VR models of buildings and rooms so that clients can see how a completed construction project will look before it is built.

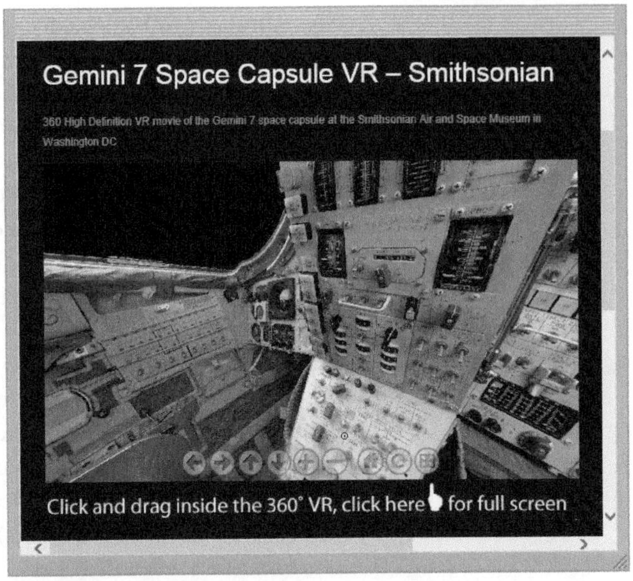

Plug-Ins

Most browsers have the capability of displaying basic multimedia elements on a webpage. Sometimes, however, a browser requires an additional program, called a plug-in, to display multimedia. A *plug-in*, or add-on, is a program that extends the capability of a browser. For example, your browser may require Adobe Reader to view and print PDF files. You typically can download plug-ins at no cost from various websites. Some plug-ins run on all types of computers and mobile devices; others have special versions for mobile devices.

Some mobile devices and browsers, however, do not support plug-ins. For this reason, web developers are using newer technologies to create websites that display correctly in both desktop and mobile browsers; these technologies generally do not require the use of plug-ins to display media.

Figure 2-25 Users can explore a VR world using a touch screen or their input device. For example, users can explore the inside of the Gemini 7 space capsule, located at the Smithsonian Air and Space Museum in Washington, D.C., from their computer or mobile device.
Source: World VR

Other Internet Services

As previously mentioned, the web is only one of the many services on the Internet. Other Internet services include the following: email, email lists, Internet messaging, chat rooms, online discussions, VoIP (Voice over IP), and FTP (File Transfer Protocol).

Email

Email (short for electronic mail) is the transmission of messages and files via a computer network. Email was one of the original services on the Internet, enabling scientists and researchers working on government-sponsored projects to communicate with colleagues at other locations.

You use an **email program** to create, send, receive, forward, store, print, and delete email messages. Email programs are available as desktop apps, web apps, and mobile apps. An email message can be simple text or can include an attachment such as a document, a graphic, an audio clip, or a video clip.

Just as you address a letter when using the postal system, you address an email message with the email address of your intended recipient. Likewise, when someone sends you a message, he or she must have your email address.

An *email address* is a combination of a user name and a domain name that identifies a user so that he or she can receive Internet email. A **user name** is a unique combination of characters, such as letters of the alphabet and/or numbers, that identifies a specific user. Your user name must be different from the other user names in the same domain. For example, a user named Rick Claremont whose server has a domain name of esite.com might want to select rclaremont as his user name. If esite.com already has an rclaremont (for Rita Claremont) user name, then Rick will have to select a different user name, such as rick.claremont or rclaremont2.

Sometimes, organizations decide the format of user names for new users so that the user names are consistent across the company. In many cases, however, users select their own user names, often selecting a nickname or any other combination of characters for their user name. Many users select a combination of their first and last names so that others can remember it easily.

In an Internet email address, an @ (pronounced at) symbol separates the user name from the domain name. Your service provider supplies the domain name. A possible email address for Rick Claremont would be rclaremont@esite.com, which would be read as follows: R Claremont at e site dot com. Most email programs allow you to create a *contacts list* or *address book*, which contains names, addresses, phone numbers, email addresses, and other details about people with whom you communicate.

Figure 2-26 illustrates how an email message may travel from a sender to a receiver. When you send an email message, an outgoing mail server determines how to route the message through the Internet and then sends the message. As you receive email messages, an incoming mail server holds the messages in your mailbox until you use your email program to retrieve them. Most email programs have a mail notification alert that informs you via a message and/or sound when you receive a new email message(s).

How an Email Message May Travel from a Sender to a Receiver

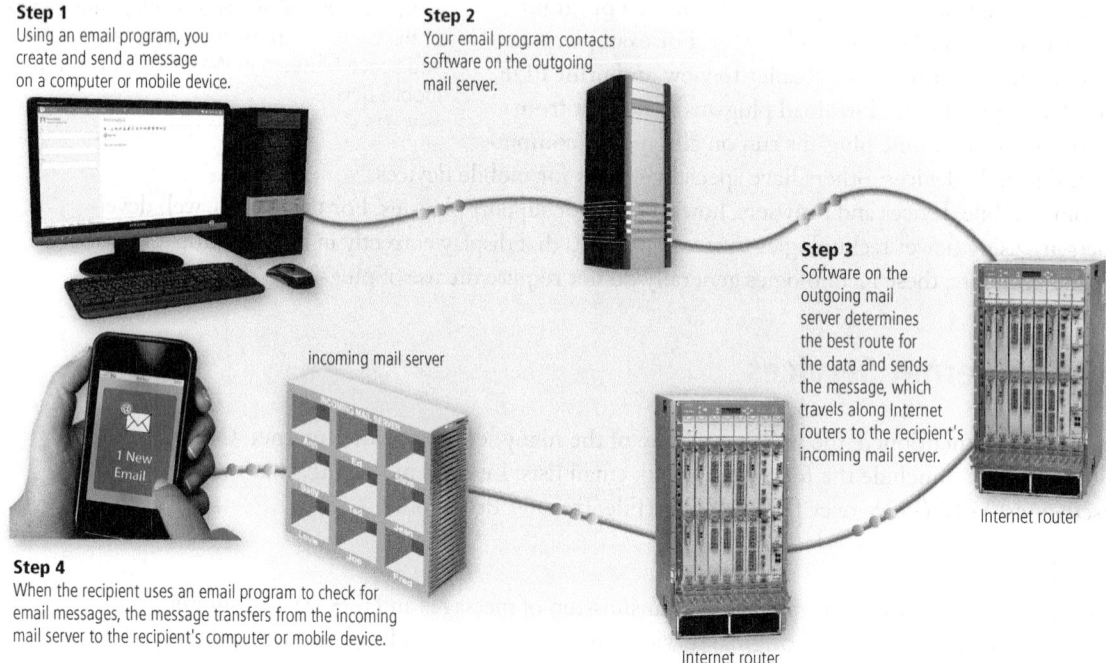

Step 1
Using an email program, you create and send a message on a computer or mobile device.

Step 2
Your email program contacts software on the outgoing mail server.

Step 3
Software on the outgoing mail server determines the best route for the data and sends the message, which travels along Internet routers to the recipient's incoming mail server.

incoming mail server

Internet router

Step 4
When the recipient uses an email program to check for email messages, the message transfers from the incoming mail server to the recipient's computer or mobile device.

Internet router

Figure 2-26   This figure shows how an email message may travel from a sender to a receiver.
Oleksiy Mark / Shutterstock.com; iStockphoto.com / luismmolina; Courtesy of Juniper Networks; iStockphoto.com / hocus-focus

---

✳ **CONSIDER THIS**

What are good practices to follow when using email?

1. Keep messages brief.
2. Respond to messages in a timely manner, but consider the consequences of writing controversial or negative words.
3. Use proper grammar, spelling, and punctuation.
4. Never respond to unsolicited messages.
5. Use meaningful subject lines.
6. Read the message before you send it.
7. Use email when you want a written record of a communication.
8. To manage the number of message you receive, unsubscribe from unwanted mailing lists, delete unneeded messages, and move important messages to an appropriate folder.

Email Lists

An **email list**, or electronic mailing list, is a group of email addresses used for mass distribution of a message. When a message is sent to an email list, each person on the list receives a copy of the message in his or her mailbox. Users may elect to receive the messages immediately or in a digest form sent at a specified interval, such as daily or after a number of messages have accumulated. You *subscribe* to an email list by adding your email address to the mailing list, which is stored on a list server. To remove your name, you *unsubscribe* from the mailing list.

The original use of email lists, such as *LISTSERV*, allowed any subscriber to send a message, which created a discussion-type forum among all subscribers via email. Some mailing lists today, such as those shown in Figure 2-27, however, are one-way communications and do not allow subscribers to send messages. Many companies and organizations subscribe to an email marketing and mailing service, such as Constant Contact. *Email marketing services* allow organizations to create campaigns, and then send them by email to everyone whose name is on a list for distribution. These services allow users to opt out from receiving future messages, forward messages to others, and track the number of people who opened the message.

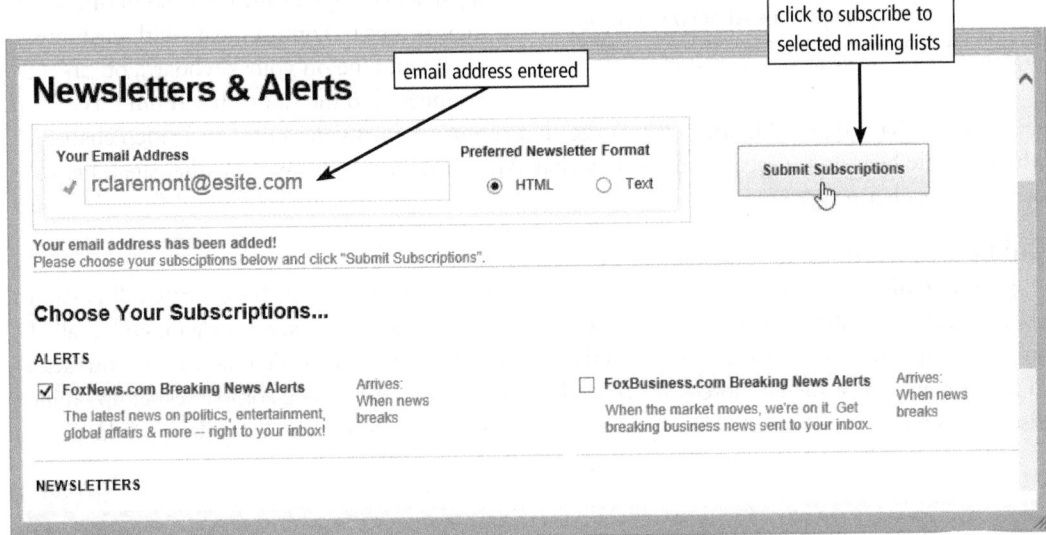

Figure 2-27   When you subscribe to a mailing list, you and all others in the list receive messages from the website. Shown here is a user who receives newsletters and alerts from FoxNews.com.

Source: FOX News Network, LLC

Internet Messaging

Internet messaging services, which often occur in real-time, are communications services that notify you when one or more of your established contacts are online and then allows you to exchange messages or files or join a private chat room with them (Figure 2-28). *Real time* means that you and the people with whom you are conversing are online at the same time. Some Internet messaging services support voice and video conversations, allow you to send photos or other documents to a recipient, listen to streaming music, and play games with another online contact.

For real-time Internet messaging to work, both parties must be online at the same time. Also, the receiver of a message must be willing to accept messages. To use an Internet messaging service, you may have to install messenger software or an app on the computer or mobile device, such as a smartphone, you plan to use.

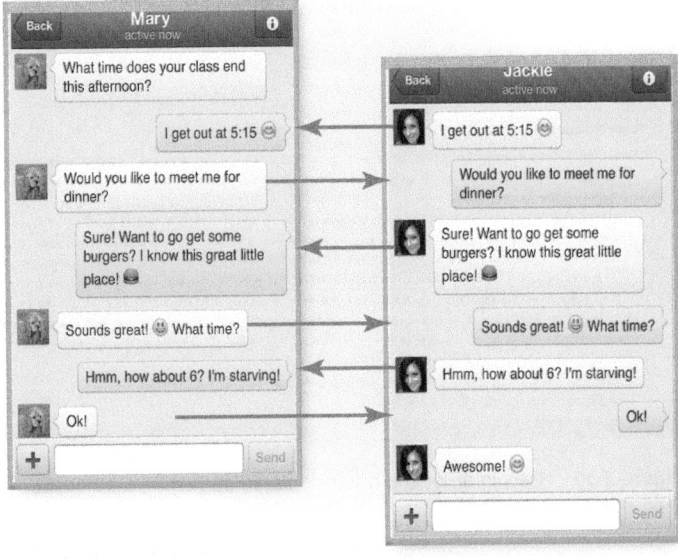

Figure 2-28   With Internet messaging services, you and the person(s) with whom you are conversing are online at the same time. The conversation appears on all parties' screens at the same time. Shown here is Facebook messenger.

iStockphoto.com / Petar Chernaev; iStockphoto.com / Oleksiy Mark

Figure 2-29   As you type, others in the same chat room see what you have typed.
ARENA Creative / Shutterstock.com; topseller / Shutterstock.com; Alex Staroseltsev / Shutterstock.com; Oleksiy Mark / Shutterstock.com; Oleksiy Mark / Shutterstock.com; Tom Wang / Shutterstock.com; vlad_star / Shutterstock.com; artjazz / Shutterstock.com

Many online social networks include a messaging feature. To ensure successful communications, all individuals on the friend list need to use the same or a compatible messenger.

Chat Rooms

A **chat** is a real-time typed conversation that takes place on a computer or mobile device with many other online users. A **chat room** is a website or application that permits users to chat with others who are online at the same time. A server echoes the user's message to everyone in the chat room. Anyone in the chat room can participate in the conversation, which usually is specific to a particular topic. Businesses sometimes use chat rooms to communicate with customers.

As you type on your keyboard, others connected to the same chat room server also see what you have typed (Figure 2-29). Some chat rooms support voice chats and video chats, in which people hear or see each other as they chat. Most browsers today include the capability to connect to a chat server.

Online Discussions

An **online discussion**, or *discussion forum*, is an online area in which users have written discussions about a particular subject (Figure 2-30). To participate in a discussion, a user posts a message, called an article, and other users read and reply to the message. A *thread*, or threaded discussion, consists of the original article and all subsequent related replies. For example, some companies set up online discussions for their customers to ask questions or share information about using their products.

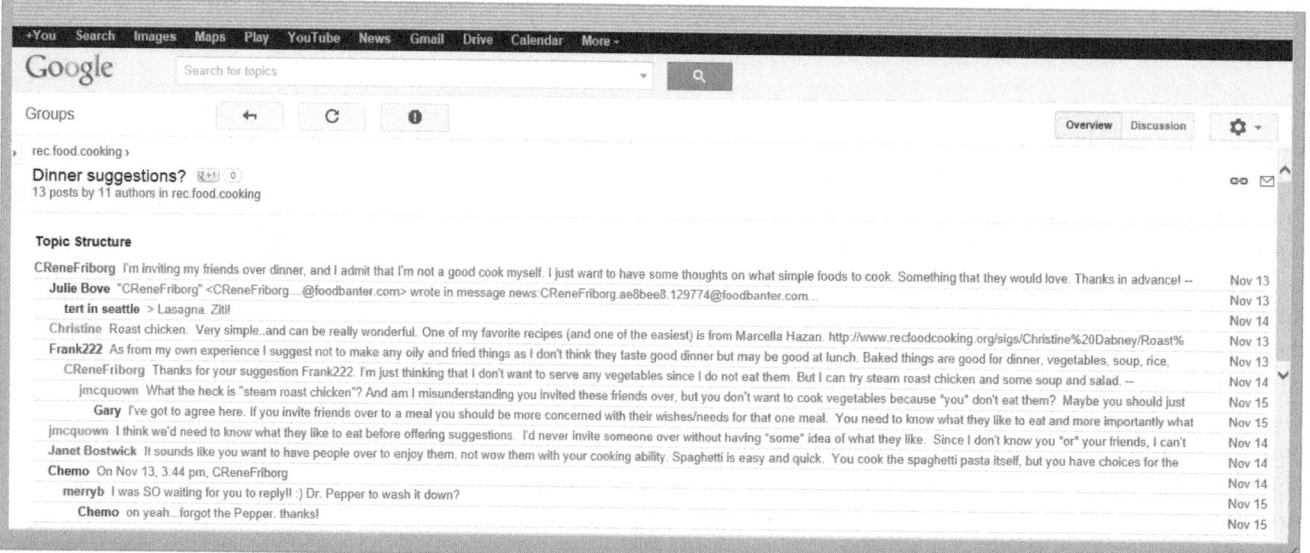

Figure 2-30   Users in an online discussion read and reply to other users' messages.
Source: Google Inc.

Some discussion forums require that you enter a user name and password to participate in the discussion. For example, an online discussion for students taking a college course may require a user name and password to access the discussion. This ensures that only students in the course participate in the discussion. Posts in an online discussion usually are stored for a certain amount of time, such as a semester, in this example.

VoIP

VoIP, short for Voice over IP (Internet Protocol), enables users to speak to other users via their Internet connection. That is, VoIP uses the Internet (instead of the public switched telephone network) to connect a calling party to one or more local or long-distance called parties.

To place an Internet phone call, you need a broadband network connection, a microphone and speaker, both of which are included with a standard computer or mobile device, and VoIP software, such as Skype. Some VoIP services require that you purchase a separate phone and VoIP router and that you subscribe to their service. Others offer certain services free and require a subscription for additional services. Read How To 2-3 for instructions about how to set up a personal VoIP service and make a call.

BTW
VoIP Microphone
You also can use a headset connected to or that communicates with your computer or mobile device.

 HOW TO 2-3 ————————————————————————

Set Up a Personal VoIP Service and Make a Call

VoIP services enable you to make free video or voice calls to others around the world. In many cases, the person you are calling also must use the same VoIP service. The following steps describe how to set up a VoIP service and make a call.

1. If you do not know the VoIP service you want to use, search for a program or app that enables you to place and receive VoIP calls.

2. If necessary, download the program or app for the VoIP service you will use.

3. Most VoIP services require you to have an account with their service before you can place or receive a call. When you run the VoIP program or app, search for the button or link to create a new account. Follow

the steps in the program or app to finish creating the account.

4. Once the account has been created, if necessary, sign in to the VoIP service with your user name and password.

5. Make sure the person you are calling also has an account with the same VoIP service. You should know at least one person using this service to successfully place a call. VoIP services typically allow you to locate and call someone by entering their user name or adding them to your list of contacts. If necessary, add the person you want to call to your list of contacts.

6. On the list of contacts, select the person you want to call and then click the appropriate button to place the call.

7. When the other person answers, you can start your voice or video call.

8. When you are ready to end the call, click the button to end the call.

9. When you are finished using the VoIP service, you should sign out of and exit the VoIP program or app.

✹ **Consider This:** Survey your friends and family to see if they use a VoIP service. If so, which service is the most popular among them?

Source: Microsoft

FTP

FTP (File Transfer Protocol) is an Internet standard that permits file uploading and downloading to and from other computers on the Internet. *Uploading* is the process of transferring files from a computer or mobile device to a server on the Internet. Recall that downloading is the process of transferring files from a server on the Internet to your computer or mobile device. Webpage developers, for example, often use FTP to upload their webpages to a web server.

Many operating systems include FTP capabilities. If yours does not, you can download FTP programs from the web, usually for a small fee.

An *FTP server* is a computer that allows users to upload and/or download files using FTP. An FTP site is a collection of files that reside on an FTP server. Many FTP sites have *anonymous FTP*, whereby anyone can transfer some, if not all, available files. Some FTP sites restrict file transfers to those who have authorized accounts (user names and passwords) on the FTP server. For example, web developers upload their website files to a web server using FTP.

Tech Feature 2-3: Digital Communications

Home users, small/home office users, mobile users, power users, and enterprise users interact with technology for many reasons, including communication, productivity, and information. Read Tech Feature 2-3 for examples of how a home user might interact with digital communications.

TECH FEATURE 2-3

Digital Communications

This scenario, which assumes you are a home user with a busy family, presents situations and questions regarding technology use during a single day.

7:30 a.m. You notice a leaky pipe under the kitchen sink. Your regular plumber recently has retired. On your smartphone, you run an app that enables you to use search criteria, GPS, and user reviews. You find a local plumber who has many positive reviews and tap the phone number on the smartphone touch screen to place the call. You leave a message explaining the problem and asking the plumber to call you back.
✹ How can you evaluate reviews for authenticity and bias? How might an app provider use your location information in ways you have not authorized?

8:45 a.m. The plumber calls you back to schedule an appointment time. You open your laptop and use the electronic calendar web app your entire family uses to keep track of appointments. You find a time that works for both of you and update the electronic calendar.
✹ What features enable multiple users, such as those in a family or small business, to use an electronic calendar? What issues may occur from using a shared calendar?

10:00 a.m. You have a freelance job blogging for a local florist. You are required to post twice weekly to the florist's blog about agreed-upon topics. You use a wiki to confirm the symbolic meaning of different types of roses so that you can include that in your next blog post. You sign in to the blog's content management system and submit your post to the blog.
✹ What responsibility do bloggers have to post accurate, verified information? Should users rely on wikis or blogs to verify content?

iStockphoto.com/pierrephoto

11:00 a.m. While you are driving to a doctor's appointment, you receive several text messages on your smartphone. You use your Bluetooth headset and your smartphone's speech-to-text feature to respond to the text messages without taking your eyes off the road.
✹ Is it legal in your state to use hands-free devices while driving? What, if any, are the consequences of noncompliance?

1:00 p.m. Back at home, you flip through today's mail. You received a bill for your monthly mortgage payment. Using your laptop, you navigate to your bank's website and schedule a recurring payment for the mortgage to ensure you never will be late on a payment.
✹ What precautions should you take when accessing financial information and authorizing payments on the web?

Dr. Cloud / Shutterstock.com

5:30 p.m. Unsure of what to make for dinner, you use your tablet to view recipes you bookmarked on a bookmarking website. You verify that you have the ingredients on hand and follow the recipe on your tablet as you prepare dinner.
✹ Who owns the content posted to social networking or bookmarking websites? What risks are involved with using these types of websites?

Khakimullin Aleksandr/Shutterstock.com

8:30 p.m. While helping your daughter with her math homework, you discover a website that includes the answers to questions asked in her textbook. You have a discussion with your daughter about ethical issues surrounding posting and using that type of content.
✹ Should students receive punishment for using answers they find on a website?

9:00 p.m. You sit down to watch your favorite vocal competition reality show, streaming live through your Smart TV. The show enables you to send a text message to vote for your favorite contestant. You debate between two popular singers, then finally send your vote via text message.
✹ How else do television, movie, and other entertainment websites use the Internet to interact with viewers or listeners?

10:30 p.m. You use the calendar app on your smartphone to confirm your schedule for tomorrow and then head to bed.
✹ How does technology enhance the daily life of a home user?

Netiquette

Netiquette, which is short for Internet etiquette, is the code of acceptable behaviors users should follow while on the Internet; that is, it is the conduct expected of individuals while online. Netiquette includes rules for all aspects of the Internet, including the web, social media, Internet messaging, chat rooms, online discussions, and FTP. Figure 2-31 outlines some of the rules of netiquette, with respect to online communications. Read Ethics & Issues 2-3 to consider issues related to an extreme misuse of online communications — cyberbullying.

Netiquette Guidelines for Online Communications
Golden Rule: Treat others as you would like them to treat you.

Be polite. Avoid offensive language.

Avoid sending or posting *flames*, which are abusive or insulting messages. Do not participate in *flame wars*, which are exchanges of flames.

Be careful when using sarcasm and humor, as it might be misinterpreted.

Do not use all capital letters, which is the equivalent of SHOUTING!

Use **emoticons** and **emojis** to express emotion. Popular emoticons include:

:) Smile   :| Indifference   :o Surprised   :(Frown   :\ Undecided   ;) Wink

Popular emojis include:

Lack of knowledge   Approval   Tears of joy   Love   Happiness   Boredom

Use abbreviations and acronyms for phrases:

| BTW | by the way | IMHO | in my humble opinion | FWIW | for what it's worth |
| FYI | for your information | TTFN | ta ta for now | TYVM | thank you very much |

Clearly identify a *spoiler*, which is a message that reveals an outcome to a game or ending to a movie or program.

Be forgiving of other's mistakes.

Read the *FAQ* (frequently asked questions), if one exists.

Figure 2-31   Some of the rules of netiquette, with respect to online communications.
Source: Microsoft

☀ ETHICS & ISSUES 2-3

Who Is Responsible for Monitoring Cyberbullying?
Sending or forwarding threatening text messages, posting embarrassing or altered pictures of someone without his or her permission, or setting up a fake online social network page where others make cruel comments and spread rumors about someone all are examples of cyberbullying. *Cyberbullying* is harassment using technology, often involving teens and preteens. Unlike verbal bullying, the perpetrators can hide behind the anonymity of the Internet and can reach a wide audience quickly. Victims cannot just walk away or ignore bullying that comes in the form of text messages, email, or online social network posts.

Cyberbullying often takes place outside of school hours on personal devices or computers not owned or monitored by a school. Yet the ramifications affect the victim at school. Schools struggle to come up with policies. Many schools are adopting policies that include consequences for any form of student-to-student bullying, even using nonschool resources, if it contributes to a hostile environment for any student or group of students. Some schools specify that students who retaliate against anyone who reports instances of bullying or cyberbullying will receive punishment.

Anti-bullying laws vary from state to state and often do not include specific language about cyberbullying. One argument against criminalizing cyberbullying is the protection of free speech. Awareness campaigns, school policies, and parent monitoring of technology use are some ways to attempt to prevent cyberbullying. These methods are not always effective. The impact on the victim can lead to poor grades, health issues, mental health concerns, and even suicide.

☀ **Consider This:** Should schools be responsible for punishing students who cyberbully other students outside of school? Why or why not? What role can parents play in reducing cyberbullying? What are the positive and negative aspects of the freedom to be anonymous on the Internet?

✔ Summary

Module 2 presented the evolution of the Internet, along with various ways to connect to the Internet, how data travels the Internet, and how the Internet works with domain names and IP addresses. It discussed the web at length, including topics such as browsing, navigating, web addresses, web apps and mobile apps, searching, and online social networks. It presented various types of websites and media on the web. It also introduced other services available on the Internet, such as email, email lists, Internet messaging, chat rooms, online discussions, VoIP, and FTP. Finally, the module listed rules of netiquette.

Study Guide

The Study Guide exercise reinforces material you should know after reading this module.

Instructions: Answer the questions below using the format that helps you remember best or that is required by your instructor. Possible formats may include one or more of these options: write the answers; create a document that contains the answers; record answers as audio or video using a webcam, smartphone, or portable media player; post answers on a blog, wiki, or website; or highlight answers in the book/e-book.

1. Explain how ARPANET contributed to the growth of the Internet.

2. Describe the role of a host on a network.

3. Identify the role of the W3C.

4. Define the terms, dongle and broadband. List popular wired and wireless broadband Internet services.

5. State the purpose of a hot spot, and list tips for using hot spots safely.

6. ISP stands for _____.

7. Briefly describe how data and information travel the Internet.

8. Describe the purpose and composition of an IP address. Differentiate between IPv4 and IPv6.

9. Define the term, domain name. List general steps to register for a domain name.

10. Identify the purpose of several generic TLDs. Identify PTI's role with TLDs.

11. Describe how and why cybersquatters register domain names.

12. State the purpose of a DNS server.

13. Differentiate between static and dynamic webpages.

14. Distinguish among the web, a webpage, a website, and a web server.

15. Describe why webpage developers use HTML, CSS, and JavaScript.

16. Explain the purpose of a browser. Describe the function of tabbed browsing.

17. List ways you can browse safely.

18. Name examples of popular browsers for personal computers and mobile devices.

19. Define the term, web address. Name a synonym.

20. Name and give examples of the components of a web address.

21. Describe the purpose of a web feed.

22. Explain the relationship between web and mobile apps.

23. Describe the purpose of GPS receivers, and why manufacturers embed them in smartphones.

24. Describe how to use a search engine. What are some ways you can refine a search?

25. Besides webpages, identify other items a search engine can find.

26. Differentiate between a search engine and a subject directory.

27. Explain how to use an online social network for personal or business use.

28. List ways to use online social networks securely.

29. Describe the purpose of these types of websites: informational and research; media sharing; bookmarking; news, weather, sports, and other mass media; educational; business, governmental, and organizational; blogs; wikis and collaboration; health and fitness; science; entertainment; banking and finance; travel and tourism; mapping; retail and auctions; careers and employment; e-commerce; portals; content aggregation; and website creation and management.

30. Is it ethical to use a fake name online? Why or why not? List techniques to protect yourself from identity theft.

31. Describe the uses of tags.

32. Define the term, e-commerce. Differentiate among B2C, C2C, and B2B e-commerce.

33. List uses and benefits of content aggregation websites and apps.

34. Identify and briefly describe the steps in web publishing.

35. The _____ web design approach adapts the layout of the website to fit the screen on which it is being displayed.

36. List the seven criteria for evaluating a website's content.

37. _____ refers to any application that combines text with media.

38. Explain how webpages use graphics, animation, audio, video, virtual reality, and plug-ins.

39. Define the terms, thumbnail and infographic.

40. Name the types of graphics formats used on the web and how they use compression.

41. List general steps to download digital media.

42. Describe the purpose of these Internet services and explain how each works: email, email lists, Internet messaging, chat rooms, online discussions, VoIP, and FTP.

43. Describe the components of an email address.

44. _____ refers to Internet communications in which both parties communicate at the same time.

45. List steps to set up a personal VoIP service and make a call.

46. Describe how a home user interacts with digital communications.

47. Define the term, netiquette.

48. Describe cyberbullying, and explain why it is difficult to catch the perpetrators.

You should be able to define the Primary Terms and be familiar with the Secondary Terms listed below.

Key Terms

Primary Terms   (shown in **bold-black** characters in the module)

blog (2-23)
blogger (2-23)
chat (2-36)
chat room (2-36)
Chrome (2-13)
content aggregation (2-28)
domain name (2-8)
e-commerce (2-27)
Edge (2-13)
email (2-33)
email list (2-35)
email program (2-33)
emojis (2-39)
emoticons (2-39)

favorites (2-13)
Firefox (2-13)
FTP (2-37)
GB (2-6)
GPS (2-15)
GPS receiver (2-15)
graphic (2-30)
hashtag (2-19)
home page (2-12)
HTML (2-11)
Internet messaging (2-35)
Internet service provider (ISP) (2-6)
IP address (2-8)

MB (2-6)
mobile service provider (2-7)
netiquette (2-38)
online auction (2-26)
online discussion (2-36)
Opera (2-13)
pop-up blocker (2-12)
portal (2-28)
responsive web design (2-29)
Safari (2-13)
search engine (2-16)
social media (2-18)

streaming (2-25)
tabbed browsing (2-12)
tag (2-21)
traffic (2-7)
user name (2-33)
virtual reality (2-32)
VoIP (2-37)
web address (2-14)
web publishing (2-29)
webpage (2-11)
wiki (2-24)
World Wide Web (WWW) (2-11)

Secondary Terms   (shown in *italic* characters in the module)

address book (2-34)
analog (2-6)
animation (2-31)
anonymous FTP (2-37)
Anticybersquatting Consumer Protection Act (2-10)
ARPANET (2-3)
audio (2-31)
bandwidth (2-6)
blogosphere (2-23)
bookmarks (2-13)
bookmarking site (2-21)
broadband (2-4)
business-to-business (B2B) e-commerce (2-27)
business-to-consumer (B2C) e-commerce (2-27)
cable Internet service (2-4)
cache (2-12)
catfishing (2-22)
ccTLD (2-9)
cloud storage (2-15)
consumer-to-consumer (C2C) e-commerce (2-27)
contacts list (2-34)
content management system (2-29)
CSS (cascading style sheets) (2-11)
curation website (2-28)
cyberbullying (2-39)
discussion forum (2-36)
DNS server (2-10)
domain name system (DNS) (2-10)
dongle (2-3)

DSL (2-4)
dynamic webpage (2-11)
electronic storefront (2-26)
e-retail (2-26)
email address (2-33)
email marketing services (2-35)
extended contacts (2-19)
FAQ (2-39)
Fiber to the Premises (FTTP) (2-4)
fixed wireless (2-4)
flames (2-39)
flame wars (2-39)
friends (2-19)
FTP server (2-37)
gigabyte (2-6)
bits (2-17)
host (2-3)
hot spot (2-5)
http (2-15)
ICANN (2-9)
infographic (2-31)
Internet backbone (2-7)
intranet (2-24)
JavaScript (2-11)
JPEG (2-31)
keyloggers (2-25)
keywords (2-17)
like (2-19)
LISTSERV (2-35)
location sharing (2-12)
m-commerce (2-27)
media player (2-32)
media sharing site (2-21)

megabyte (2-6)
microblog (2-23)
mobile app (2-15)
mobile broadband (2-4)
mobile browser (2-11)
mobile web app (2-15)
MP3 (2-32)
multimedia (2-30)
phishing (2-12)
phishing filter (2-12)
plug-in (2-33)
PNG (2-31)
pop-under ad (2-12)
pop-up ad (2-12)
private browsing (2-12)
Public Technical Identifiers (PTI) (2-9)
real time (2-35)
registrar (2-9)
satellite Internet service (2-4)
search text (2-17)

shopping cart (2-26)
spoiler (2-39)
static webpage (2-11)
status update (2-19)
subscribe (2-35)
subject directory (2-18)
tethering (2-5)
thread (2-36)
thumbnail (2-30)
top-level domain (TLD) (2-9)
troll (2-22)
unsubscribe (2-35)
uploading (2-37)
URL (2-14)
video (2-32)
W3C (2-3)
web feed (2-15)
web hosting service (2-29)
wireless data provider (2-7)
wireless modem (2-3)

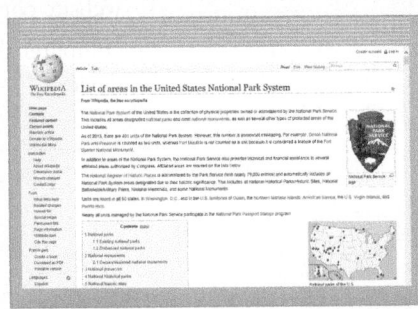

Source: Wikimedia Foundation

Checkpoint

The Checkpoint exercises test your knowledge of the module concepts.

True/False
Mark T for True and F for False. If False, rewrite the statement so that it is True.

_____ 1. No single person or government agency controls or owns the Internet.

_____ 2. The W3C is responsible for maintaining all networks and content on the Internet.

_____ 3. Users typically pay additional fees for mobile hot spot and tethering services.

_____ 4. A gigabyte (GB) is the basic storage unit on a computer or mobile device and represents a single character.

_____ 5. Developers use HTML, CSS, and JavaScript to create webpages and help users share content online.

_____ 6. Most browsers are available for download at no cost.

_____ 7. Mobile apps sometimes have fewer features than a web app.

_____ 8. A subject directory is software that finds websites, webpages, images, videos, maps, and other information related to a specific topic.

_____ 9. When you post digital content online, it is a good idea to tag it so that it is easy to locate and organize.

_____ 10. The term, blogosphere, refers to the worldwide collection of blogs.

_____ 11. Tethering is the process of transferring data in a continuous and even flow, which allows users to access and use a file while it is transmitting.

_____ 12. One way to protect yourself from identity theft online is to retain all your cookies in your browser.

Matching
Match the terms with their definitions.

_____ 1. catfishing

_____ 2. chat

_____ 3. curation website

_____ 4. cyberbullying

_____ 5. domain name

_____ 6. Internet backbone

_____ 7. tag

_____ 8. tethering

_____ 9. web serve

_____ 10. wiki

a. real-time typed conversation that takes place on a computer or mobile device with many other online users

b. term used to refer to the major carriers of network traffic

c. online practice of creating a fake profile to form relationships with unsuspecting users

d. short descriptive label that you assign to digital content so that it is easier to locate at a later time

e. harassment, often involving teens and preteens, using technology

f. website or web app that allows users to collect and compile content from a variety of websites about a particular topic or theme

g. technique that transforms a smartphone or Internet-capable tablet into a portable communications device that shares its Internet access with other computers and devices wirelessly

h. text-based name that corresponds to the IP address of a server that hosts a website

i. collaborative website that allows users to create, add, modify, or delete website content via a browser

j. computer that delivers requested webpages to your computer or mobile device

The Problem Solving exercises extend your knowledge of module concepts by seeking solutions to practical problems with technology that you may encounter at home, school, work, or with nonprofit organizations. The Collaboration exercise should be completed with a team.

Problem Solving ☀

Instructions: You often can solve problems with technology in multiple ways. Determine a solution to the problems in these exercises by using one or more resources available to you (such as a computer or mobile device, articles on the web or in print, blogs, podcasts, videos, television, user guides, other individuals, electronics or computer stores, etc.). Describe your solution, along with the resource(s) used, in the format requested by your instructor (brief report, presentation, discussion, blog post, video, or other means).

Personal

1. **Cyberbullying Message**   While reviewing the email messages in your email account, you notice one that you interpret as cyberbullying. You do not recognize the sender of the email message, but you still take it seriously. What are your next steps?

2. **Unsolicited Friend Requests**   You recently signed up for an account on Facebook. When you log in periodically, you find that people you do not know are requesting to be your friend. How should you respond?

3. **Unexpected Search Engine**   A class project requires that you conduct research on the web. After typing the web address for Google's home page and pressing the **ENTER** key, your browser redirects you to a different search engine. What could be wrong?

4. **Images Do Not Appear**   When you navigate to a webpage, you notice that no images are appearing. You successfully have viewed webpages with images in the past and are not sure why images suddenly are not appearing. What steps will you take to show the images?

Source: Twitter

5. **Social Media Password**   Your social media password has been saved on your computer for quite some time and the browser has been signing you in automatically. After deleting your browsing history and saved information from your browser, the online social network began prompting you again for your password, which you have forgotten. What are your next steps?

Professional

6. **Suspicious Website Visits**   The director of your company's information technology department sent you an email message stating that you have been spending an excessive amount of time viewing websites not related to your job. You periodically visit websites not related to work, but only on breaks, which the company allows. How does he know your web browsing habits? How will you respond to this claim?

7. **Automatic Response**   When you return from vacation, a colleague informs you that when she sent email messages to your email address, she would not always receive your automatic response stating that you were out of the office. Why might your email program not respond automatically to every email message received?

8. **Email Message Formatting**   A friend sent an email message containing a photo to your email account at work. Upon receiving the email message, the photo does not appear. You also notice that email messages never show any formatting, such as different fonts, font sizes, and font colors. What might be causing this?

9. **Mobile Hot Spot Not Found**   Your supervisor gave you a mobile hot spot to use while you are traveling to a conference in another state. When you attempt to connect to the hot spot with your computer, tablet, and phone, none of the devices is able to find any wireless networks. What might be the problem, and what are your next steps?

10. **Sporadic Email Message Delivery**   The email program on your computer has been displaying new messages only every hour, on the hour. Historically, new email messages would arrive and be displayed immediately upon being sent by the sender. Furthermore, your coworkers claim that they sometimes do not receive your email messages until hours after you send them. What might be the problem?

Collaboration

11. **Technology in Transportation**   Your project team has been assigned to present a business proposal to a group of potential investors. Because the presentation will take place in Kansas City, Missouri, you will need to transport people and ship some materials to that location. Form a team of three people and determine how to use technology to ship materials and how to make travel arrangements. One team member should research the steps required to use a website to make flight reservations, one team member should determine the steps necessary to print a package shipping label from his or her computer and track the package while it is en route, and another team member should find directions from Kansas City International Airport to a nearby hotel.

✷ How To: Your Turn

The How To: Your Turn exercises present general guidelines for fundamental skills when using a computer or mobile device and then require that you determine how to apply these general guidelines to a specific program or situation.

Instructions: You often can complete tasks using technology in multiple ways. Figure out how to perform the tasks described in these exercises by using one or more resources available to you (such as a computer or mobile device, articles on the web or in print, online or program help, user guides, blogs, podcasts, videos, other individuals, trial and error, etc.). Summarize your 'how to' steps, along with the resource(s) used, in the format requested by your instructor (brief report, presentation, discussion, blog post, video, or other means).

① View Current Virus Threats

One important way to protect your computer or mobile device from viruses is to be aware of current threats. Several websites exist that not only provide a list of current virus threats but also describe how best to protect your computer or mobile device from these threats. As new virus threats are introduced, it is important to make sure your antivirus program is updated and running properly. The following steps describe how to view a list of current virus threats.

a. Run a browser and then navigate to a search engine of your choice.
b. Perform a search for websites that display current virus threats.
c. Review the search results and visit at least two websites that display current virus threats.
d. View the list of virus threats on each of these websites.

or

a. Run a browser and then navigate to a search engine of your choice.
b. Perform a search for websites created by companies that make antivirus software. Some companies that make antivirus software include Symantec, McAfee, and Microsoft.
c. Navigate to one of these company's websites and then search for a link to a webpage displaying current virus threats.
d. Click the link to display current virus threats.

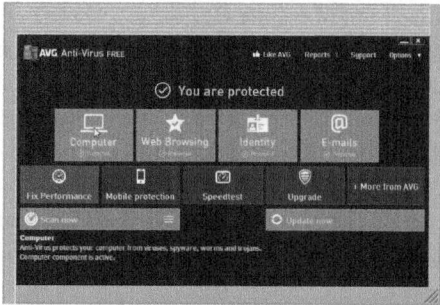

Courtesy of Checkpoint Software Technologies Ltd.

Exercises

1. Which websites did you access? Compare these websites and determine which you think provided the most helpful information. Why, in your opinion, does the website you chose provide the best information?
2. Has your computer or mobile device ever been infected with a virus? If so, what steps have you taken to remove the virus?
3. Is your computer or mobile device adequately protected from viruses? What steps do you take to keep your computer safe?

② View and Manage Data Usage

Many people have limited data plans, so it is important to know how to view the amount of data you have used on your phone or tablet when you are not connected to the Internet using a Wi-Fi connection. If you are using a phone or tablet where Wi-Fi is available, you should strongly consider using the Wi-Fi connection not only to limit data plan usage, but also to experience faster speed. If you find that your data usage is high each month, you may be able to see which apps are using the most data and adjust usage of those apps accordingly. The following steps guide you through the process of viewing and managing data usage.

a. Display the settings on your mobile device.
b. Select the option to view data usage.
c. If necessary, tap the option to display a list of apps and how much data each app uses. If necessary, select the time period for which you want to see the data usage.
d. If you notice an app using a large amount of data, tap the icon to see details for that app. If necessary, disable background data transfer for the app. Background data transfer is data the app downloads and uploads even while you are not actively using the app.
e. If you want your mobile device to notify you when you are approaching your monthly data limit, set the necessary notification option and select a value below your monthly data limit in the appropriate area.
f. If you want your mobile device to turn off data (this does not include Wi-Fi) when you reach a certain limit, set the necessary option and then select a value that is just less than your monthly data limit to ensure you never reach or exceed the limit.
g. Save all changes.

How To: Your Turn ✸

Exercises

1. Do you have a data limit on your mobile data plan? If so, what is it?
2. When you enter an area with Wi-Fi, do you configure your mobile device to connect to the Wi-Fi? Why or why not?
3. Review the mobile data usage on your mobile device. Which app uses the most data? Which app uses the least data?

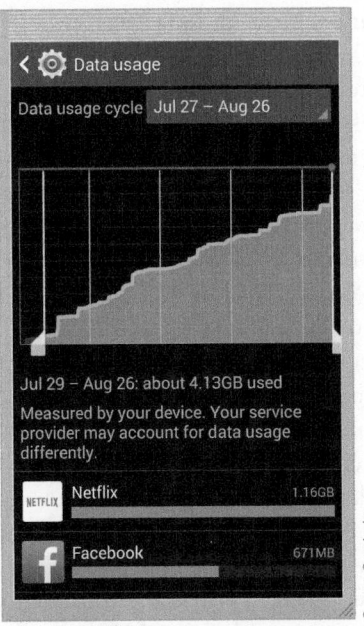

Source: Google, Inc.

❸ Search for a Job Online

If you know the company for which you would like to work, you may be able to visit that company's website and search for a webpage with current job postings. If you would like to search for openings in multiple companies, consider using a job search website. The following steps guide you through the process of searching for a job online.

a. Run a browser.
b. Use a search engine to locate a job search website and then navigate to the website.
c. Many job search websites allow you to search for jobs by criteria, such as keyword, category, or location. If you are searching for a job in a specific field, enter relevant keyword(s) (i.e., software developer) or select an appropriate category (i.e., technology). To limit your search results to a specific geographical area, specify a location (i.e., Atlanta).
d. Some websites allow you to search for jobs based on additional criteria, such as company, salary, job type, education, and experience. Specify these additional criteria by performing an advanced search.
e. After entering the job search criteria, begin the search.
f. When the search results appear, scroll through the results. To find out more about a particular job, click the job listing.
g. If desired, follow the instructions in the job listing to apply for the job.

Exercises

1. Review three job search websites. Which one did you like the best? Why?
2. Which keywords would you use on a job search website to search for a job in your desired field?
3. Before completing this exercise, had you ever searched for a job online? Do you think it is better to search for a job using a job search website, or by vising company websites directly and viewing their job postings? Justify your answer.

✳ Internet Research

The Internet Research exercises broaden your understanding of module concepts by requiring that you search for information on the web.

Instructions: Use a search engine or another search tool to locate the information requested or answers to questions presented in the exercises. Describe your findings, along with the search term(s) you used and your web source(s), in the format requested by your instructor (brief report, presentation, discussion, blog post, video, or other means).

1 Making Use of the Web
Online Social Networks and Media Sharing

Every second, an average of 6,000 Tweets are created and 5,000 Facebook statuses are updated. With these impressive numbers, it is no wonder that online social media have become ubiquitous throughout the world. Twitter, Facebook, and other online social networks, especially those discussed in Tech Feature 2-2 in this module, are popular among users of all ages. Likewise, media sharing sites, such as YouTube, which is shown in Figure 2-11 in this module, are popular means of managing and sharing photos, videos, and music.

Research This: Visit two of the websites discussed in Tech Feature 2-2 or other online social networks and

Source: Facebook

create a profile if you do not currently have one. What personal information is required to join? Does either website ask for personal information that you are uncomfortable sharing? How does the content of these two websites differ? Which features are beneficial for casual users, and which are targeted toward business or professional users? Then, visit two social media sites. What personal information is required to join? Are these websites supported by advertisements? Locate the instructions for posting media. Are these instructions straightforward? Is there a limit on the number and/or size of media files a user can post?

2 Social Media
Funding and Generating Income

Most social media companies have invested millions of dollars to develop and maintain their websites. Unlike other commercial media, such as television, radio, and newspapers, advertisements generally are not used to fund the majority of operating

costs, nor are users required to pay monthly or annual fees for basic services that they receive at no cost. One method that social media sites use to generate start-up and ongoing subsidies is through venture capitalists' funding. These investors scrutinize business plans and market trends in an effort to locate Internet start-up companies with the potential to generate substantial returns. Once the businesses are running, additional monies are needed to maintain and improve the websites. At this point, some websites display advertisements. The charge for companies to place an advertisement generally increases as the number of subscribers grows. Another method of generating income is to charge users for accessing premium content. Online dating services use this tactic successfully, for they allow people to browse online profiles free of charge but require them to pay to contact a potential dating match.

Research This: Locate venture capitalists who are seeking Internet start-up companies. Which criteria do they use to make investment decisions? Who are the successful venture capitalists, and which companies have they funded? Which types of advertisements are displayed? How does the content of these ads pertain to the demographics and interests of users?

3 Search Skills
Understand Search Results

Search results display the most relevant results first. Search results may include links to websites, news stories, images, videos, maps, and information from Wikipedia and other online databases. Results also may show links to similar searches, related people, or posts from online social networks or social media sites.

Because many search engines rely on advertising for revenue, some search results are paid advertisements. Companies and organizations may pay search providers to display links to their websites prominently in the search results when search text contains words relevant to their products and services. Paid ads often appear at the top or along the side of a search results page. A search results page may display an icon or use shading to specify that the search result is an advertisement.

Internet Research ✷

When evaluating the reliability of search results, consider the sources of the information provided. Specialized information such as medical advice or stock performance should come from recognizable sources, while you might rely on reviews from customers when selecting a restaurant or purchasing a smartphone.

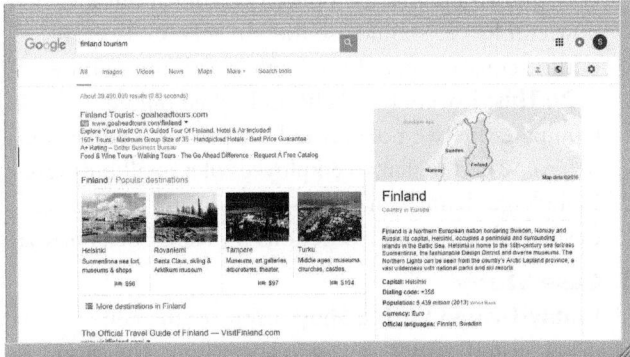

Source: Google

Research This: Type each search text phrase listed in the paragraph below into the search boxes in Bing, Google, and Yahoo! and then take a screenshot of the first webpage of search results from each. Compare them, identifying ads, news, images, videos, social media results, information from online databases, search tools, and common links that both search engines returned. Which search engine's results do you find more useful in each case? Why?

Type the following search text: (1) internet service providers, (2) google corporate headquarters, (3) flights from boston to los angeles, and (4) identity theft.

④ Security
Thermal Heat Signatures
Cybercriminals may lurk in public Wi-Fi hot spots, as you learned in Secure IT 2-1 in this module. These thieves also may be on the lookout for customers entering their PIN at keypads near cash registers or at ATMs. Body heat from fingers touching the keys remains for a short time, and a device with infrared-scanning capabilities can detect which keys are warmer than others. This device, which is readily available for purchase at cell phone accessories

stores, snaps on the back of cell phones. It captures the thermal heat signatures, with the most recently touched keys glowing red and the cooler keys glowing light green. The thief, therefore, knows which keys comprise the PIN and the sequence of numbers by looking at the intensity of colors on the infrared scan.

Research This: How much does a thermal imaging cell phone case cost? Which brand of phone is more commonly used to capture thermal imaging? What steps can consumers take to thwart thieves using infrared scanning? Which key materials are less apt to retain the thermal signatures: metal, rubber, or plastic? Researchers from which university published a paper discussing thermal camera-based attacks?

⑤ Cloud Services
Collaboration and Productivity (SaaS)
Microsoft's Office Online and Google Docs are online productivity suites for creating documents, presentations, spreadsheets, and other projects. Microsoft and Google offer these apps as part of their respective cloud storage services. Because documents are stored on the cloud, you can access them from any computer or device connected to the Internet.

These are examples of SaaS (software as a service), a service of cloud computing that allows access to software using a browser, without the need to install software on a computer or device. As providers update their software, users receive the latest version upon signing in. SaaS apps often allow users to collaborate and share their work with others. Many providers offer SaaS titles at no cost; others require users to purchase a subscription or pay for features they use.

Research This: (1) Sign up for accounts on Microsoft OneDrive and Google Drive to create and store documents with Office Online and Google Docs. With each app, create a document, share it with another user, and edit it simultaneously. What is an advantage of sharing documents over sending the files by email to collaborators? (2) How do Microsoft Office Online and Google Docs compare with Microsoft Office installed on your computer? What features are available on the cloud that are not possible on a desktop version?

✳ Critical Thinking

The Critical Thinking exercises challenge your assessment and decision-making skills by presenting real-world situations associated with module concepts. The Collaboration exercise should be completed with a team.

Instructions: Evaluate the situations below, using personal experiences and one or more resources available to you (such as articles on the web or in print, blogs, podcasts, videos, television, user guides, other individuals, electronics or computer stores, etc.). Perform the tasks requested in each exercise and share your deliverables in the format requested by your instructor (brief report, presentation, discussion, blog post, video, or other means).

1. Mobile Browser Comparison

Although most mobile devices include a mobile browser, users have the option of downloading and installing other browsers.

Source: Google Inc.

Do This: Evaluate and compare reviews of at least four mobile browsers, such as Google Chrome, Dolphin, Firefox, Mercury, Opera, or Safari. Discuss the major differences among the browsers you researched, including number and types of features, which devices are compatible, how they display webpages, security features, and the speed at which they perform. Discuss any experiences you or your classmates have had with various browsers. Include in your discussion which mobile browser you would recommend and why.

2. Acceptable Use Policy

Most businesses provide Wi-Fi and Internet access, as well as compatible computers or devices, to employees while they are at work. While the intention is for employees to use the Internet for work-related purposes, employees often find it easy to become distracted with other activities on the Internet, such as social media, checking personal email messages, playing games, or visiting websites for entertainment. These activities can degrade Internet access for others or lead to poor performance, as well as expose the company to malware or other risks. Many businesses create an acceptable use policy (AUP) that outlines how employees should use the Internet. It also may outline consequences for unauthorized Internet use.

Do This: Locate two AUPs published online. Compare the two policies and then create a policy you believe would be fair to employees of a small business. Include guidelines for Internet use during breaks, use of smartphones, and restrictions for using social media.

3. Case Study

Family-Owned Coffee Shop   You are the new manager for a family-owned coffee shop. The shop needs a website. You prepare information about the website to present at the next business meeting.

Do This: First, you plan the website by determining its purpose and audience. Use a search engine to locate two coffee shop websites, and print their home pages. Identify what you like and do not like about each. Think about the design of your website, and select the colors you would recommend. Describe the types of media you would include on the webpage and give specific examples, such as a logo, photos or a slide show, or links to videos. Make a sketch of the home page layout, including navigation, media, and text. Research content management systems. Evaluate whether you could use a preformatted template to meet your needs, and find what types of customization options are available. Determine whether you need a separate ISP for hosting the website, and calculate the costs. List ways you will maintain and update the site content.

Collaboration

4. Website Evaluation   You and three teammates want to open a new chain of fast food sandwich shops. You envision a website that includes a menu, nutritional options, and allergy information, and that has regular promotions and special offers.

Do This: With your teammates, evaluate existing fast food and sandwich websites by comparing the advantages and disadvantages of each. Assign each member the task of evaluating one chain. Team members should print the home page of the assigned website and evaluate each restaurant's website. Pay particular attention to the following areas: (1) design, (2) ease of use, (3) menu, (4) nutritional information, (5) allergy information, (6) special offers, (7) location information and directions, and (8) hours and contact information. Summarize your evaluations and rank the websites in terms of their effectiveness. Be sure to include brief explanations supporting your rankings.

Computers and Mobile Devices:
Evaluating Options for Home and Work

iStockphoto.com / scanrail

OBJECTIVES

After completing this module, you will be able to:

1 Describe the characteristics and uses of laptops, tablets, desktops, and all-in-ones

2 Describe the characteristics and types of servers

3 Differentiate among POS terminals, ATMs, and self-service kiosks

4 Describe cloud computing and identify its uses

5 Describe the characteristics and uses of smartphones, digital cameras, portable and digital media players, e-book readers, and wearable devices

6 Describe the characteristics of and ways to interact with game devices, including gamepads, joysticks and wheels, dance pads, and motion-sensing controllers

7 Identify uses of embedded computers

8 Differentiate a port from a connector, identify various ports and connectors, and differentiate among Bluetooth, Wi-Fi, and NFC wireless device connections

9 Identify safeguards against hardware theft and vandalism and hardware failure

10 Discuss ways to prevent health-related injuries and disorders caused from technology use, and describe ways to design a workplace ergonomically

Computers and Mobile Devices

As Module 1 discussed, a **computer** is an electronic device, operating under the control of instructions stored in its own memory, that can accept data (input), process the data according to specified rules, produce information (output), and store the information for future use. A **mobile device** is a computing device small enough to hold in your hand. Types of computers and mobiles devices include laptops, tablets, and desktops; servers and terminals; smartphones, digital cameras, e-book readers, portable and digital media players, and wearable devices; game devices; and embedded computers. Figure 3-1 shows a variety of computers and mobile devices.

In addition to discussing features, functions, and purchasing guidelines of computers and mobile devices, this module also presents ways to connect peripheral devices, protect computers and mobile devices from theft and failure, and minimize your health risks while using computers and mobile devices.

Figure 3-1 Computers and mobile devices are available in a variety of shapes and sizes.
iStockphoto.com / scanrail; iStockphoto.com / Chesky_W; iStockphoto.com / hocus-focus; iStockphoto.com / Courtesy of Samsung / Gregory_DUBUS; iStockphoto.com / scanrail; Courtesy of Apple, Inc.; iStockphoto.com / cincila

Mobile Computers and Desktops

A **mobile computer** is a portable personal computer, such as a laptop or tablet, designed so that a user easily can carry it from place to place, whereas a desktop is designed to be in a stationary location. A *personal computer* (PC) is a mobile computer or desktop that can perform all of its input, processing, output, and storage activities by itself and is intended to be used by one person at a time. Personal computers often are differentiated by the type of operating system they use, with Windows and Mac operating systems leading the market share. Companies such as Acer, Dell, Lenovo, HP (Hewlett-Packard), and Samsung sell personal computers that use the Windows operating system, and Apple sells personal computers that use the Mac operating system. Other operating systems for personal computers include Linux and Chrome OS.

Read Secure IT 3-1 for suggestions about how to avoid malware infections on your computers and mobile devices.

 BTW

PC
The term, PC, sometimes is used to describe a computer that runs a Windows operating system.

 SECURE IT 3-1

Avoid Malware Infections

Some websites contain tempting offers to download free games and music, install toolbars that offer convenience, enter contests, and receive coupons on your computers or mobile devices. Danger, however, may lurk in those files, for they secretly could install malware with effects ranging from a mild annoyance to a severe problem such as identity theft. Recall that malware is malicious software that acts without your knowledge and deliberately alters operations of your computer or mobile device. As a general rule, do not install or download unfamiliar software. Follow these guidelines to minimize the chance of your computer or mobile device becoming infected with malware:

- **Social media:** Malware authors often focus on social media, with the goal of stealing personal information, such as passwords, profiles, contact lists, and credit card account details. Their websites urge unsuspecting users to take surveys, click links to obtain free merchandise and games, and download antivirus programs. Ignore these deceitful tactics.
- **Email:** Spam (unsolicited email messages) can be loaded with malware, but even email messages from friends can be a culprit. If the message does not contain a

subject line or contains links or an attachment, exercise caution. One option is to save the attachment to your computer so that antivirus software can scan the file for possible malware before you open it. Your best practice is to avoid opening suspicious email messages at all costs.

- **Flash memory storage:** Colleagues and friends may hand you a USB flash drive or memory card with software, photos, and other files. Scan these media with security software before opening any files.
- **Pop-up windows:** At times, a window may open suddenly (called a pop-up window), with a warning that your computer is infected with a virus or that a security breach has occurred, and then make an urgent request to download free software to scan your computer or mobile device and correct the alleged problem. Beware. Many of these offers actually are rogue security software that will infect a computer.
- **Websites:** Websites you visit or pop-up windows may present instructions to download new software or update current programs installed on a computer or mobile device. If you are uncertain of their legitimacy, exit and research the software

by reading reviews online before you decide to install it.

- **Software:** Occasionally, some seemingly safe software attempts to install malware. Even worse, some software touted as offering malware protection actually installs more malware. Always obtain software from reputable sources and, if possible, update software directly from manufacturers' websites. Consider using the custom installation option to ensure that only the desired software is installed. Read the permissions dialog boxes that are displayed on your screen before clicking the OK or Agree buttons. If you are uncertain about the messages you are viewing, cancel the installation.
- **Smartphones:** Malware creators are targeting smartphones, particularly those using the Android operating system. While most smartphones are unprotected now, savvy users are obtaining protection from malware attacks. Read reviews before downloading antimalware apps from trusted sources.

✳ **Consider This:** What online activities might cause malware to be installed on your computer? Which specific websites provide reputable antimalware apps for mobile devices? What new techniques will you use to avoid malware?

✺ CONSIDER THIS

What is inside a personal computer?

The electronic components and circuitry of a personal computer usually are part of or are connected to a motherboard (Figure 3-2). A *motherboard*, sometimes called a system board, is the main circuit board of the personal computer. Many electronic components attach to the motherboard; others are built into it. Two main components on the motherboard are the processor and memory. Many motherboards also integrate sound, video, and networking capabilities.

A *processor,* also called a *CPU* (central processing unit), is the electronic component that interprets and carries out the basic instructions that operate a computer. Memory consists of electronic components that store instructions waiting to be executed and data needed by those instructions.

motherboard

Figure 3-2 Shown here is a partial motherboard in a laptop.
rawgroup / Fotolia LLC

Laptops, Tablets, and Other Mobile Computers

A **laptop**, also called a *notebook computer*, is a thin, lightweight mobile computer with a screen in its lid and a keyboard in its base (Figure 3-3). Designed to fit on your lap and for easy transport, most laptops weigh up to 7 pounds (varying by manufacturer and specifications) and can be as powerful as the average desktop.

Laptops have input devices, such as a keyboard, touchpad, and webcam; output devices, such as a screen and speakers; a storage device(s), such as a hard drive and maybe an optical disc drive; and usually built-in wireless communications capability. Some laptops have touch screens. Most can operate on batteries and a power supply. Read Ethics & Issues 3-1 to consider issues related to laptops and other devices with cameras.

Ultrathin laptops weigh less than traditional laptops, usually have a longer battery life, and generally run the Windows operating system. In order to minimize their thickness, many ultrathin laptops have fewer ports than traditional laptops and often require the use of special dongles to attach cables that connect to external displays or a network. (Recall that a dongle is a small device that connects to a computer and enables additional functions when attached.)

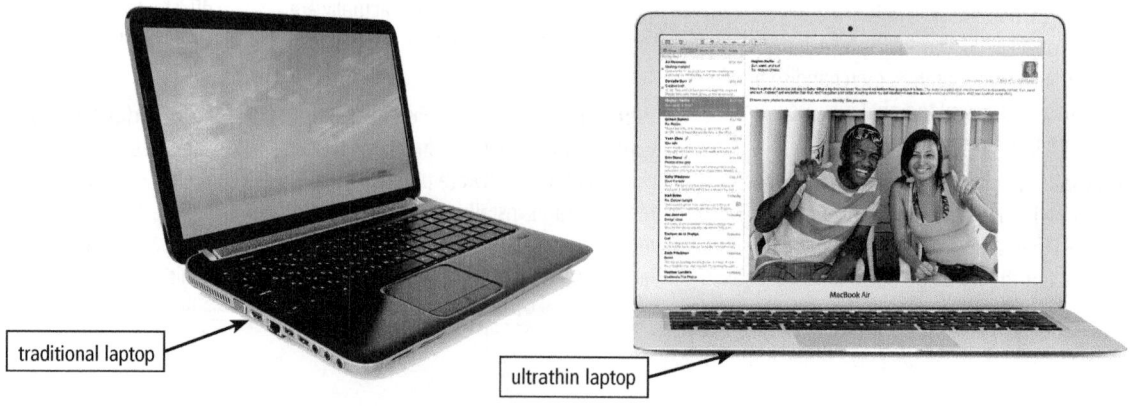

traditional laptop

ultrathin laptop

Figure 3-3 Traditional laptops weigh more than ultrathin laptops.
Julia Nikitina / Shutterstock.com; Courtesy of Apple Inc.

✱ ETHICS & ISSUES 3-1

What Punishment for Webcam Spying Is Appropriate?

Microphones, digital cameras, and webcams have many practical and harmless uses. These technologies also can leave you open to spying. For example, one school district used software, which was supposed to track the school-distributed laptops in case of theft, to take photos and screen captures of students. In another instance, a person noticed that when she gave a customer service rep access to her computer, he turned on her webcam without asking for her permission.

Cybercriminals can use spy tools that take photos, or record video or audio, without turning on a light or other notification that indicates your camera or microphone is in use. The Flame virus is one way for spy tools to infect your computer. Security experts recommend using a sticker to cover your webcam, and inserting a dummy plug in the microphone port when you are not using it. These technologies also allow people to take photos or videos in a public setting and share them without your knowledge. A director at the American Civil Liberties Union stated that when you are in a public place, people have the right to photograph you. Privacy advocates criticize *Google Street View*, however, which takes images captured using moving vehicles equipped with GPS and cameras and then creates a panoramic view of an area, including people entering and exiting buildings or relaxing on a beach.

Many states' laws do not cover these types of acts. Massachusetts, however, passed a law that made secretly taking photos or videos that focused on people's private body parts a criminal offense. Lawmakers continue to debate and expand current laws, as well as pass new ones.

✱ **Consider This:** Should webcam spying punishments be comparable to other types of spying? Why or why not? What kind of privacy should you expect when you are in a public place?

Tablets   Usually smaller than a laptop but larger than a phone, a **tablet** is a thin, lighter-weight mobile computer that has a touch screen.

Two popular form factors (shapes and sizes) of tablets are the slate and convertible (Figure 3-4). Resembling a letter-sized pad, a *slate tablet* is a type of tablet that does not contain a physical keyboard. A *convertible tablet* is a tablet that has a screen it its lid and a keyboard in its base, with the lid and base connected by a swivel-type hinge. You can use a convertible tablet like a traditional laptop, or you can rotate the display and fold it down over the keyboard so that it looks like a slate tablet. As with laptops, tablets run on batteries or a power supply or both; however, batteries in a tablet typically last longer than those in laptops.

Some tablets include a *stylus*, which looks like a small ink pen, that you can use instead of a fingertip to enter data, make selections, or draw on a touch screen. A stylus may include buttons you can press to simulate clicking a mouse. As an alternative to interacting with the touch screen, some users prefer to purchase a separate physical keyboard that attaches to or wirelessly communicates with the tablet (shown with the slate tablet in Figure 3-4).

Tablets are useful especially for taking notes in class, at meetings, at conferences, and in other forums where the standard laptop is not practical. Because slate tablets can have a more durable construction, they often are used in the medical field and other areas where exposure to germs, heat, humidity, dust, and other contaminants is greater.

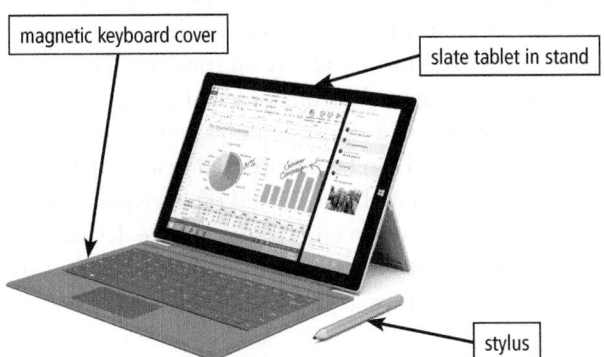

Figure 3-4   Examples of slate and convertible tablets.
Courtesy of Microsoft; iStockphoto.com / rasslava

CONSIDER THIS

What is a phablet?

Some manufacturers use the term, *phablet*, to refer to a device that combines features of a smartphone with a tablet (Figure 3-5). These devices are larger than smartphones but smaller than full-sized tablets. The screen on a phablet usually measures five to seven inches diagonally. Some include a stylus.

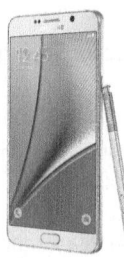

Figure 3-5 A phablet combines features of a smartphone and a tablet.
Courtesy of SAMSUNG

Figure 3-6 This handheld computer is a lightweight computer that enables warehouse employees to take inventory and check supplies.
iStockphoto.com / Ermin Gutenberger

Handheld Computers

A *handheld computer* is a computer small enough to fit in one hand. Many handheld computers communicate wirelessly with other devices or computers. Some handheld computers have miniature or specialized keyboards. Others have a touch screen and also include a stylus for input.

Many handheld computers are industry-specific and serve the needs of mobile employees, such as parcel delivery people or warehouse employees (Figure 3-6), whose jobs require them to move from place to place. Handheld computers often send data wirelessly to central office computers.

stick computer

Figure 3-7 Stick computers are approximately the same size as USB flash drives and can connect to an HDMI port on a TV or computer monitor.
Courtesy of Intel Corporation

Stick Computers

A **stick computer**, also referred to as a PC stick, is a small computer which usually is the same size as, or a little larger than, a USB flash drive (Figure 3-7). Stick computers typically plug into an HDMI port (discussed later in this module) on a computer monitor or a television and can run operating systems and apps similar to those that run on desktops and laptops. Most users rely on stick computers to browse the web, stream media, run apps, and play games. Although not as powerful as most desktops and laptops, stick computers are small and can be transported easily. Stick computers have very limited storage and often require you to save your files online or on an external storage device. Despite the limitations of these devices, they are inexpensive when compared to desktops, laptops, and tablets.

Tech Feature 3-1: Mobile Computer Buyer's Guide

If you need computing capability while traveling and during lectures or meetings, you may find a laptop or tablet to be an appropriate choice. Read Tech Feature 3-1 for tips to consider when purchasing a mobile computer.

Mobile Computer Buyer's Guide

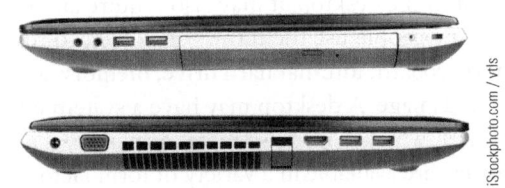
iStockphoto.com / vrts

With the abundance of mobile computer manufacturers, research each before making a purchase. The following are purchasing considerations unique to mobile computers.

1. **Determine which mobile computer form factor fits your needs**. Consider a tablet or ultrathin laptop if you require a lightweight device and the most mobility. If you require additional ports or want the computer's capabilities to be more comparable to a desktop, consider purchasing a traditional laptop.

2. **Consider a mobile computer with a sufficiently large screen**. Laptops and tablets are available with various screen sizes. For example, most traditional and ultrathin laptop screens range in size from 11 to 17 inches, while most tablet screens range in size from 7 to 12 inches.

3. **Experiment with different keyboards and pointing devices**. Mobile computers often vary in size, and for that reason have different keyboard layouts. Familiarize yourself with the keyboard layout of the computer you want to purchase, and make sure it is right for you. If you have large fingers, for example, you should not purchase a computer with a small, condensed keyboard. Laptops typically include a touchpad to control the pointer. Tablets have a touch screen and an on-screen keyboard.

4. **Consider processor, memory, and storage upgrades at the time of purchase**. As with a desktop, upgrading a mobile computer's memory and internal storage may be less expensive at the time of initial purchase. Some internal storage is custom designed for mobile computer manufacturers, meaning an upgrade might not be available in the future.

5. **The availability of built-in ports and slots is important**. Determine which ports and slots (discussed later in this module) you require on the mobile computer. If you plan to transfer photos from a digital camera using a memory card, consider a mobile computer with a built-in card slot compatible with your digital camera's memory card. If you plan to connect devices such as a printer or USB flash drive to your mobile computer, consider purchasing one with a sufficient number of USB ports. In addition, evaluate mobile computers with ports enabling you to connect an external monitor.

6. **If you plan to use your mobile computer for a long time without access to an electrical outlet, or if the battery life for the mobile computer you want to purchase is not sufficient, consider purchasing a second battery**. Some mobile computers, such as most tablets and ultrathin laptops, have built-in batteries that can be replaced only by a qualified technician. In that case, you might look into options for external battery packs or power sources.

7. **Purchase a well-padded and well-designed carrying case that is comfortable and ergonomic**. An amply padded carrying case will protect your mobile computer from the bumps it may receive while traveling. A well-designed carrying case will have room for accessories such as USB flash drives, pens, and paperwork. Although a mobile computer may be small enough to fit in a handbag, make sure that the bag has sufficient padding to protect the computer. Test the carrying case with the laptop inside to ensure it is comfortable and ergonomic.

8. **If you plan to connect your mobile computer to a video projector, make sure the mobile computer is compatible with the video projector**. You should check, for example, to be sure that your mobile computer will allow you to display an image on the screen and projection device at the same time. Also, ensure that the mobile computer has the ports required or that you have the necessary dongle and cables to connect to the video projector.

 Consider This: Based on your current computing needs, should you purchase a traditional laptop, ultrathin laptop, or tablet? What are the specifications of the mobile computer you would purchase?

Desktops and All-in-Ones

A **desktop**, or desktop computer, is a personal computer designed to be in a stationary location, where all of its components fit on or under a desk or table (Figure 3-8). Components that typically occupy space outside of a desktop include peripheral devices such as a keyboard, mouse,

BTW
Monitor Speakers
Many monitors have integrated speakers.

and webcam (input devices); speakers and printer (output devices); external hard drive (storage device); and possibly a router and/or modem (communications devices). Depending on the form factor of the desktop, it may also require an external monitor.

Some people use the term, *system unit,* to refer to the case that contains and protects the motherboard, internal hard drive, memory, and other electronic components of the computer from damage. A desktop may have a system unit tower that is a separate device from a monitor. A *tower,* which is made of metal or plastic, is a frame that houses the system unit on a desktop. Towers are available in a variety of form factors. Although they can range in height from 12 inches to 30 inches or more, the trend is toward smaller desktop tower form factors. An **all-in-one** (AIO) or *all-in-one desktop,* by contrast, does not have a tower and instead houses the display, system unit, and possibly an optical drive, in the same case.

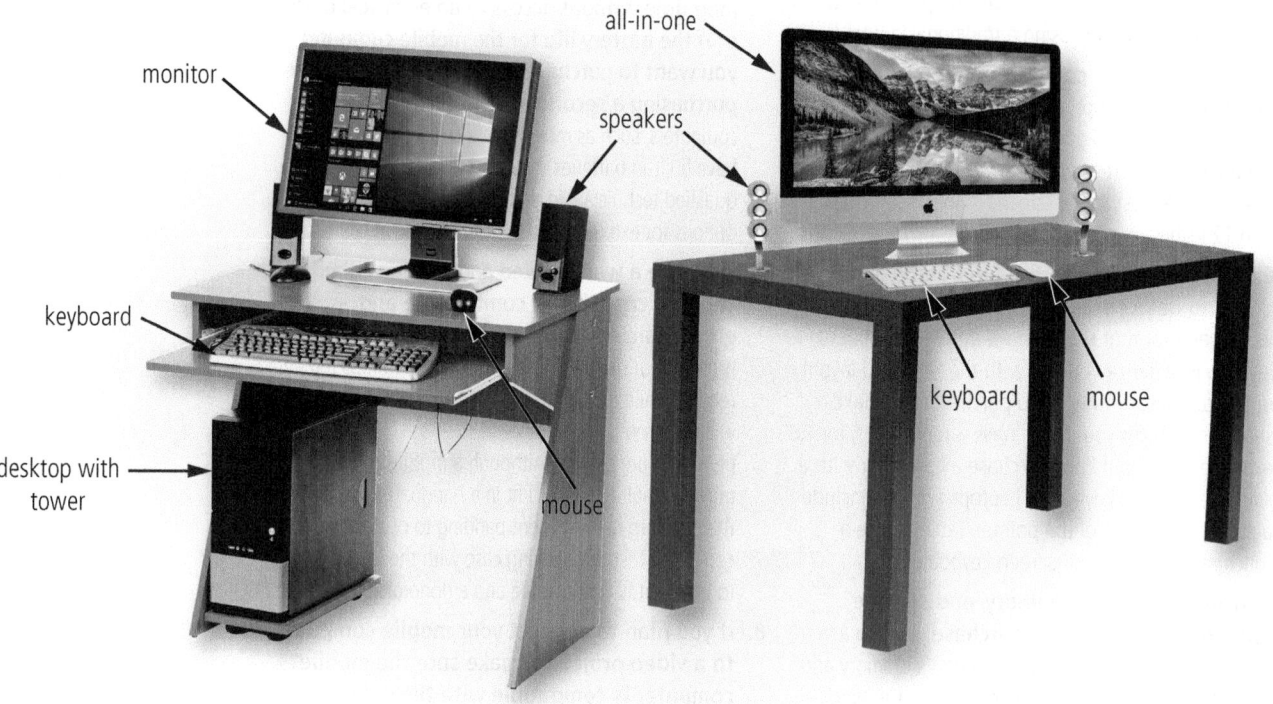

Figure 3-8   The desktop with a tower shown in this figure is a Windows computer, and the all-in-one is a Mac computer.

George Dolgikh / Shutterstock.com; Courtesy of Apple Inc. / iStockphoto.com / Evgeny Kuklev; Source: Microsoft

 CONSIDER THIS

Who uses desktops?

Home and business users who do not require the portability of a mobile computer may work with desktops for their everyday computing needs. Gaming enthusiasts often choose a *gaming desktop,* which offers high-quality audio, video, and graphics with optimal performance for sophisticated single-user and networked or Internet multiplayer games. Power users may work with a high-end desktop, sometimes called a *workstation,* that is designed to handle intense calculations and sophisticated graphics. For example, architects use powerful desktops to design buildings and homes, and graphic artists use them to create computer-animated special effects for full-length motion pictures and video games. Some users configure a desktop to function as a server on a network (servers are discussed later in this module).

Tech Feature 3-2: Desktop Buyer's Guide

Desktops are a suitable option if you work mostly in one place and have plenty of space in a work area. Read Tech Feature 3-2 for tips to consider when purchasing a desktop.

 TECH FEATURE 3-2

Desktop Buyer's Guide

Today, desktop manufacturers emphasize desktop style by offering bright colors, trendy displays, and theme-based towers so that the computer looks attractive if it is in an area of high visibility. If you have decided that a desktop is most suited to your technology needs, the next step is to determine specific software, hardware, peripheral devices, and services to purchase, as well as where to buy the computer. The following considerations will help you determine the appropriate desktop to purchase.

1. **Determine the specific software to use on the desktop**. Decide which software contains the features necessary for the tasks you want to perform. Your hardware requirements depend on the minimum requirements of the software you plan to use on the desktop.

2. **Know the system requirements of the operating system**. Determine the operating system you want to use because this also dictates hardware requirements. If, however, you purchase a new desktop, chances are it will include the latest version of your preferred operating system (Windows, macOS, or Linux).

3. **Look for bundled software**. Purchasing software at the same time you purchase a desktop may be less expensive than purchasing the software at a later date.

4. **Avoid purchasing the least powerful desktop available**. Technology changes rapidly, which means a desktop that seems powerful enough today may not serve your computing needs in the future. Purchasing a desktop with the most memory, largest hard drive capacity, and fastest processor you can afford will help delay obsolescence.

5. **Consider upgrades to the keyboard, mouse, monitor, printer, microphone, and speakers**. You use these peripheral devices to interact with the desktop, so make sure they meet your standards.

6. **Consider a touch screen monitor**. A touch screen monitor will enable you to interact with the latest operating systems and apps using touch input.

7. **Evaluate all-in-ones, which may be less expensive than purchasing a tower and monitor separately**. In addition, all-in-ones take up less space and often look more attractive than desktops with separate towers.

8. **If you are buying a new desktop, you have several purchasing options:** buy directly from a school bookstore, a local computer dealer, or a large retail store, or order from a vendor by mail, phone, or the web. Each purchasing option has its advantages. Explore each option to find the best combination of price and service.

9. **Be aware of additional costs**. Along with the desktop itself, you also may need to make extra purchases. For example, you might purchase computer furniture, an uninterruptable power supply (UPS) or surge protector (discussed later in the module), an external hard drive, a printer, a router, or a USB flash drive.

10. **If you use your computer for business or require fast resolution of major computer problems, consider purchasing an extended warranty or a service plan through a local dealer or third-party company**. Most extended warranties cover the repair and replacement of computer components beyond the standard warranty.

✹ **Consider This:** Shop around for a desktop that meets your current needs. Which desktop would you purchase? Why?

Alexey Salo / Photos.com

Table 3-1 Dedicated Servers

Type	Main Service Provided
Application server	Stores and runs apps
Backup server	Backs up and restores files, folders, and media
Database server	Stores and provides access to a database
Domain name server	Stores domain names and their corresponding IP addresses
File server (or storage server)	Stores and manages files
FTP server	Stores files for user upload or download via FTP
Game server	Provides a central location for online gaming
Home server	Provides storage, Internet connections, or other services to computers and devices in a household
List server	Stores and manages email lists
Mail server	Stores and delivers email messages
Network server	Manages network traffic
Print server	Manages printers and documents being printed
Web server	Stores and delivers requested webpages to a computer via a browser

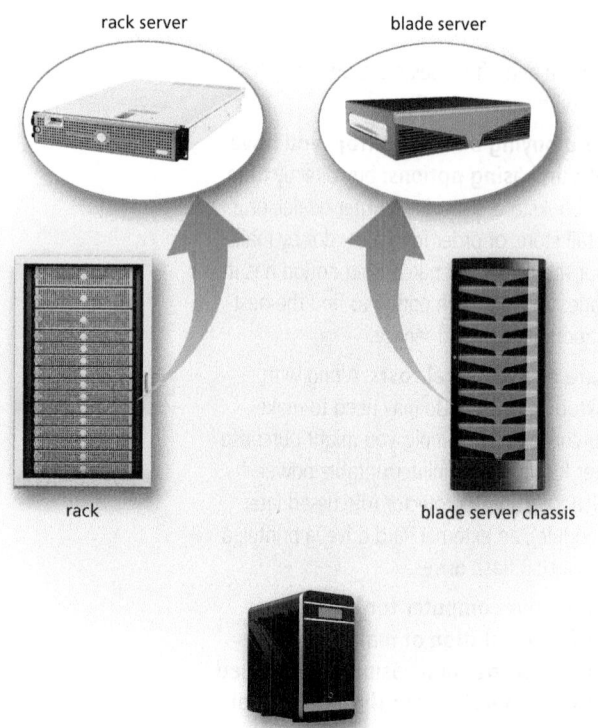

Figure 3-9 Shown here are a rack server, blade server, and tower server.
iStockphoto.com / Godfried Edelman; iStockphoto.com / luismmolina; iStockphoto.com / evirgen; iStockphoto.com / Alexander Shirokov; iStockphoto.com / luismmolina

Servers

A **server** is a computer dedicated to providing one or more services to other computers or devices on a network. Services provided by servers include storing content and controlling access to hardware, software, and other resources on a network. In many cases, a server accesses data, information, and programs on another server. In other cases, personal computers, devices, or terminals (discussed in the next section) access data, information, and programs on a server. Servers can support from two to several thousand connected computers or devices at the same time.

Some servers, called dedicated servers, perform a specific service and can be placed with other dedicated servers to perform multiple services (Table 3-1). Each type of dedicated server uses software designed specifically to manage its service. Dedicated servers typically require a faster processor, more memory, and additional storage.

Servers typically include a processor, memory, storage, and network connections. Depending on its function, a server may or may not require a monitor or an input device. Some servers are controlled from remote computers. Form factors for servers include rack server, blade server, and tower server, which are shown in Figure 3-9 and briefly described below.

- A *rack server*, sometimes called a rack-mounted server, is a server that is housed in a slot (bay) on a metal frame (rack). A rack can contain multiple servers, each in a different bay. The rack is fastened in place to a flat surface.
- A *blade server* is a server in the form of a single circuit board, or blade. The individual blades insert in a blade server chassis that can hold many blades. Like a rack server, the chassis is fastened in place to a flat surface.
- A *tower server* is a server built into an upright cabinet (tower) that stands alone. The tower can be similar in size and shape to a desktop tower or larger.

 CONSIDER THIS

Which server should you use?
Home or small business users and organizations with ample floor space often choose tower servers. (Some home users even use a desktop tower or powerful laptop to act as a home server.) Data centers and other organizations looking to conserve floor space often choose rack servers or blade servers. Organizations that require a large quantity of servers usually opt for blade servers.

Some organizations use virtualization to improve utilization of technology. *Virtualization* is the practice of sharing or pooling computing resources, such as servers and storage devices. *Server virtualization* uses software to enable a physical server to emulate the hardware and computing capabilities of one or more servers, known as virtual servers. Users can use software to configure the storage, processing power, memory, operating system, and other characteristics of virtual servers. From the end user's point of view, a virtual server behaves just like a physical server. The advantages are that a virtual server can be created and configured quickly, does not require a new physical server, and is easier to manage. Cloud computing, discussed later in this module, uses server virtualization.

Major corporations use server farms, mainframes, or other types of servers for business activities to process everyday transactions. A *server farm* is a network of several servers together in a single location. Server farms make it possible to combine the power of multiple servers. A *mainframe* is a large, expensive, powerful server that can handle hundreds or thousands of connected users simultaneously. Enterprises use server farms, mainframes, or other large servers to bill millions of customers, prepare payroll for thousands of employees, and manage millions of items in inventory.

Terminals

A *terminal* is a computer, usually with limited processing power, that enables users to send data to and/or receive information from a server, or host computer. The host computer processes the data and then, if necessary, sends information (output) back to the terminal. Terminals may include a monitor and/or touch screen, keyboard, and memory.

A *thin client* is a terminal that looks like a desktop but has limited capabilities and components. Because thin clients typically do not contain a hard drive, they run programs and access data on a network or the Internet. Public locations, such as libraries and schools, and enterprises sometimes use thin clients because they cost less, are easier to maintain, last longer, use less power, and are less susceptible to malware attacks than desktops.

Special-purpose terminals perform specific tasks and contain features uniquely designed for use in a particular industry. Three widely used special-purpose terminals are point-of-sale (POS) terminals, ATMs, and self-service kiosks.

Point-of-Sale Terminals

The location in a retail or grocery store where a consumer pays for goods or services is the point of sale (POS). Most retail stores use a *POS terminal* to record purchases, process credit or debit cards, and update inventory.

In a grocery store, the POS terminal is a combination of an electronic cash register, bar code reader, and printer (Figure 3-10). A *bar code reader* is an input device that uses laser beams to read bar codes on products. When the checkout clerk or customer scans the bar code on the grocery item, the computer uses the manufacturer name and item numbers to look up the price of the item and the complete product name. Then, the price of the item shows on the display device, the name of the item and its price print on a receipt, and the item being sold is recorded so that the inventory can be updated. Thus, the output from a POS terminal serves as input to other computers to maintain sales records, update inventory, verify credit, and perform other activities associated with the sales

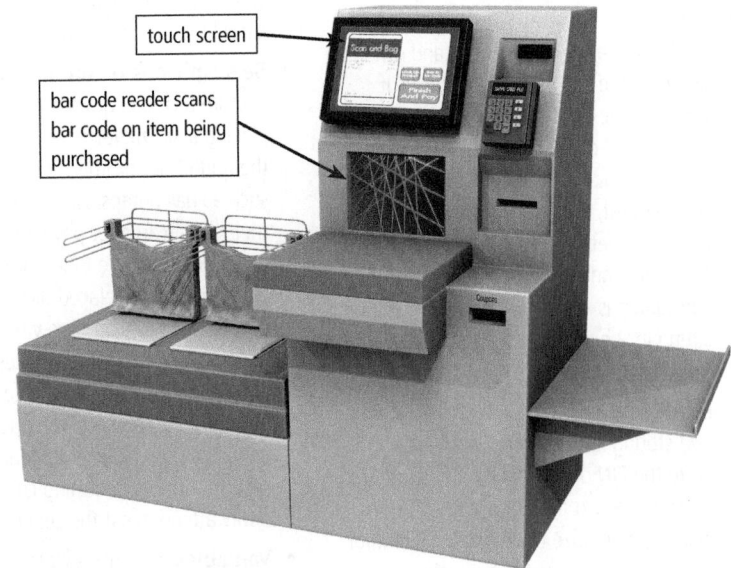

Figure 3-10 Many grocery stores offer self-service checkouts, where consumers use POS terminals to scan purchases, scan their store or saver card and coupons, and then pay for the goods.

Valentyna Chukhlyebova / Shutterstock.com; iStockphoto.com / OOone transactions that are critical to running the business. Some POS terminals are Internet capable, which allows updates to inventory at geographically separate locations.

Many POS terminals handle credit card or debit card payments. After swiping your card through the reader, the POS terminal connects to a system that authenticates the purchase. Once the transaction is approved, the terminal prints a receipt for the customer.

ATMs

An *ATM* (automated teller machine) is a self-service banking terminal that connects to a host computer through a network (Figure 3-11). Banks place ATMs in public locations, including grocery stores, convenience stores, retail outlets, shopping malls, sports and concert venues, and gas stations, so that customers can access their bank accounts conveniently.

Using an ATM, people withdraw and deposit money, transfer funds, or inquire about an account balance. Some ATMs have a touch screen; others have special buttons or keypads for entering data. To access a bank account, you insert a plastic bank card in the ATM's card reader. The ATM asks you to enter a numeric password, called a *PIN* (personal identification number), which verifies that you are the holder of the bank card. When your transaction is complete, the ATM prints a receipt for your records. Read Secure IT 3-2 for ATM safety tips.

Figure 3-11 An ATM is a self-service banking terminal that allows customers to access their bank accounts.
bankerwin / Fotolia LLC

✹ SECURE IT 3-2

ATM Safety

Visiting an ATM to withdraw or deposit money is convenient, but it also is ripe with potential for criminal activity. Avoid being a victim by exercising common sense and following these guidelines.

- **Location:** Choose an ATM in a well-lit public area away from bushes and dividers and near the entrance of a building. If using a drive-up ATM, keep the engine running and doors locked, roll windows up while waiting for the ATM to process your request, and leave adequate room to maneuver between your vehicle and the one in the lane in front of you. Observe your surroundings and be suspicious of people sitting in vehicles or loitering nearby.

- **ATM card and PIN:** Handle the ATM card like cash by keeping it in a safe location and storing it in a protective sleeve. Do not write the PIN on the back of the card or store it in a text file on your smartphone; instead, memorize the numbers. (For information about password manager apps, read Secure IT 5-3 in Module 5.) Report a lost or stolen card immediately.

- **Transaction:** Minimize time by having the ATM card ready as you approach the

machine. Do not allow people to watch your activity. Cover the keypad or screen with one hand as you enter the PIN, and use your body to block as much of the area as possible. If the ATM screen appears different, behaves unusually, or offers options with which you are unfamiliar or uncomfortable, cancel the transaction and leave the area.

- **Be suspicious of skimmers:** Thieves can capture a credit card number and PIN by placing a *skimmer* on an ATM (shown in the figure) or on other self-service stations, such as gas pumps, where users swipe their credit cards for payment. Sophisticated skimmers are Bluetooth enabled or are entire panels placed directly on top of the ATM faces and are virtually undetectable. Less-technical devices are false card readers secured to the card slot with double-sided tape and a hidden camera or an overlay on the keypad. Many ATMs have security stickers informing customers to notify attendants if the seal is broken.

- **Valuables:** Expensive clothes and jewelry can be incentives to potential assailants. Dress modestly and leave jewels at home.

- **Exiting:** Do not count cash in public; immediately put it in your pocket or

fold it in your hand. If you receive a receipt, take it with you and do not discard it in a trash can near the area. As you leave, be certain you are not being followed. If you suspect someone is tracking you, immediately walk to a populated area or business, or drive to a police or fire station.

- **Statements:** Review your balances and bank statements frequently. Be certain all deposits and withdrawals are listed, and look for unusual or unfamiliar activity.

✹ **Consider This:** Which of these tips do you follow, and how will you change your behavior the next time you visit an ATM or other self-service stations? Which ATMs in your neighborhood appear to be in safe locations?

Self-Service Kiosks

A self-service *kiosk* is a freestanding terminal that usually has a touch screen for user interaction. Table 3-2 identifies several widely used self-service kiosks. Because users interact with self-service kiosks independently, without a salesperson nearby, it is important the kiosk is simple and easy to use. In many cases, a web app or mobile app can extend or enhance the capability of the kiosk. For example, you can reserve an item via the app on a computer or mobile device and then use the kiosk to finalize the transaction.

Table 3-2	Self-Service Kiosks
Type	**Typical Services Provided**
Financial kiosk	Pay bills, add money to prepaid cards and phone plans, and perform other financial activities.
Photo kiosk	Print photos from digital images. Some allow editing of digital photos. Users may print directly at the kiosk or may send an order to a photo lab to be printed.
Ticket kiosk	Print tickets. Located in airports, amusement parks, movie theaters, rental companies, and train stations.
Vending kiosk	Dispense item after payment is received. Examples include DVD rentals and license plate renewals.
Visitor kiosk	Manage and track visitors upon check-in. Located in businesses, police stations, schools, hospitals, and other areas where access is controlled or registration is required.

A *DVD kiosk*, for example, is a self-service DVD rental machine that connects to a host computer through a network (Figure 3-12). DVD kiosks are associated with a particular vendor. To rent a movie online, for example, a customer establishes an account or connects to an existing account on the vendor's website, selects the desired movie, and then chooses a nearby DVD kiosk where the movie will be retrieved. Customers also usually can select movies directly at the DVD kiosk via a touch screen or some other input device on the kiosk. After presenting identifying information and swiping a credit card through the reader, the DVD kiosk dispenses the rented movie to the customer. The customer returns it to any of the vendor's nationwide DVD kiosks, at which time the customer's account is charged a fee based on the time elapsed.

Figure 3-12 A DVD kiosk is a self-service DVD rental terminal.
Courtesy of Redbox

Supercomputers

A *supercomputer* is the fastest, most powerful computer — and the most expensive (Figure 3-13). Supercomputers are capable of processing many trillions of instructions in a single second. With weights that exceed 100 tons, these computers can store more than 20,000 times the data and information of an average desktop.

Applications requiring complex, sophisticated mathematical calculations use supercomputers. For example, large-scale simulations and applications in medicine, aerospace, automotive design, online banking, weather forecasting, nuclear energy research, and petroleum exploration use a supercomputer.

Figure 3-13   Supercomputers can process more than one quadrillion instructions in a single second.
Los Alamos National Laboratory

Cloud Computing

BTW

The Cloud
The cloud-shaped symbol, which today universally represents cloud computing, stems from early diagrams that visually portrayed the Internet as a cloud, intangible and widespread.

Cloud computing refers to an environment that provides resources and services accessed via the Internet (Figure 3-14). Resources include email messages, schedules, music, photos, videos, games, websites, programs, web apps, servers, storage, and more. Services include accessing software, storing files online, and configuring an environment of servers for optimal performance. That is, instead of accessing these resources and services locally, you access them on the cloud. For example, you use cloud computing capabilities when you store or access documents, photos, videos, and other media online; use programs and apps online (i.e., email, productivity, games, etc.); and share ideas, opinions, and content with others online (i.e., online social networks).

Businesses use cloud computing to more efficiently manage resources, such as servers and programs, by shifting usage and consumption of these resources from a local environment to the Internet. For example, an employee working during the day in California could use computing resources located in an office in Paris that is closed for the evening. When the company uses the computing resources, it pays a fee that is based on the amount of computing time and other resources it consumes, much in the way that consumers pay utility companies for the amount of electricity used.

Cloud computing allows a company to diversify its network and server infrastructure. Some cloud computing services automatically add more network and server capacity to a company's website as demand for services of the website increases. The network and server capacity may be duplicated around the world so that, for example, an outage of a single server does not affect the company's operations.

✸ **CONSIDER THIS** ──────────────────────────────

Are all cloud services available to everyone?
Some cloud services are public and others are private. A public cloud is made available free or for a fee to the general public or a large group, usually by a cloud service provider. A private cloud is dedicated to a single organization. Some cloud services are hybrid, combining two or more cloud types.

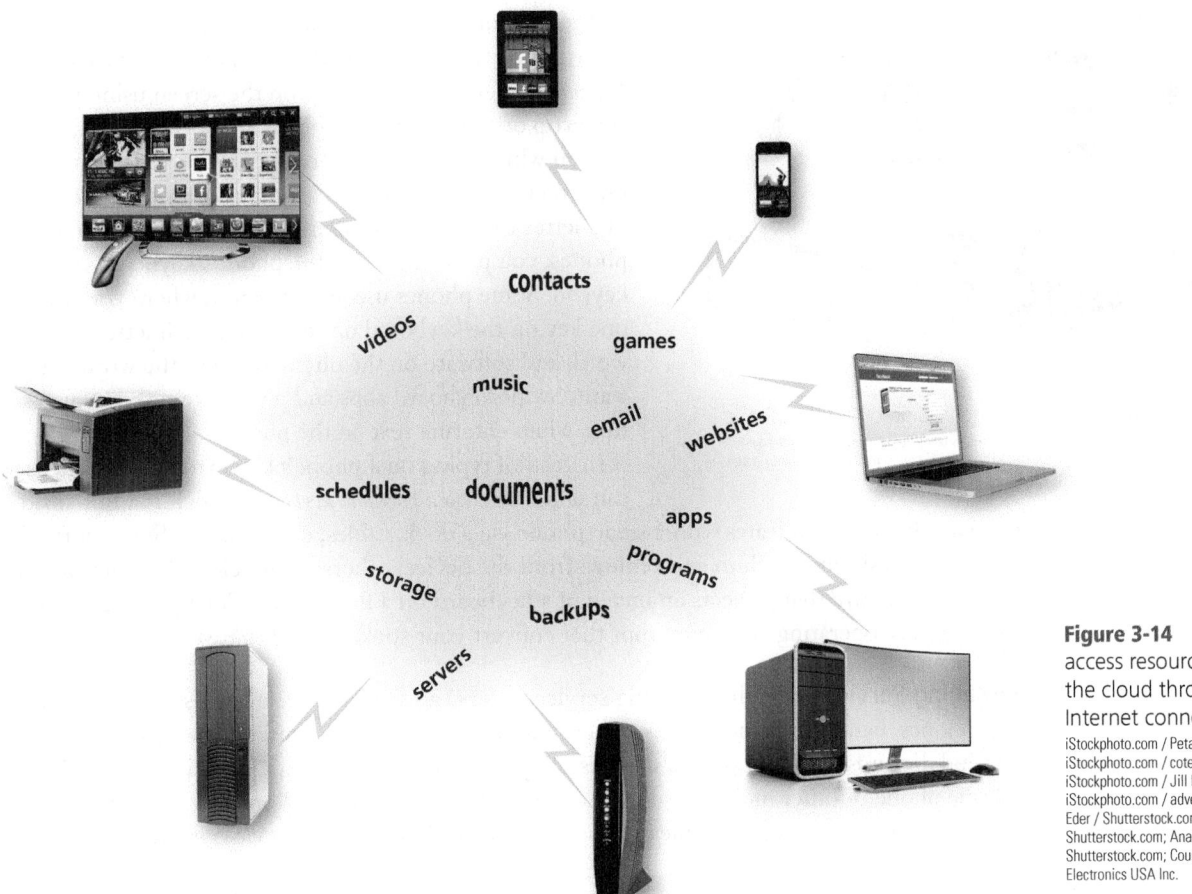

Figure 3-14 Users access resources on the cloud through their Internet connections.
iStockphoto.com / Petar Chernaev; iStockphoto.com / cotesebastien; iStockphoto.com / Jill Fromer; iStockphoto.com / adventtr; Pablo Eder / Shutterstock.com; Peter Gudella / Shutterstock.com; Anan Chincho / Shutterstock.com; Courtesy of LG Electronics USA Inc.

Mobile Devices

A mobile device is a computing device small enough to hold in your hand. Because of their reduced size, the screens on mobile devices are small — often between 3 and 5 inches. Popular types of mobile devices are smartphones, digital cameras, portable and digital media players, e-book readers, and wearable devices.

Smartphones

A **smartphone** is an Internet-capable phone that usually also includes a calendar, an address book, a calculator, a notepad, games, browser, and numerous other apps. In addition to basic phone capabilities, many smartphones include these features:

- Send and receive email messages and access the web — via Wi-Fi or a mobile data plan
- Communicate wirelessly with other devices or computers
- Function as a portable media player
- Include one or more built-in digital cameras
- Talk directly into the smartphone's microphone or into a Bluetooth headset that wirelessly communicates with the phone
- Conduct live video calls, where the parties can see each other as they speak
- Receive GPS signals to determine a user's current location
- Synchronize data and information with a computer or another mobile device
- Support voice control so that you can speak instructions to the phone and it speaks responses back to you
- Connect to external devices wirelessly, such as via Bluetooth
- Serve as a wireless access point

Many smartphones have touch screens. Instead of or in addition to an on-screen keyboard, some have a built-in mini keyboard on the front of the phone or a keyboard that slides in and out from behind the phone. Others have keypads that contain both numbers and letters. Some also include a stylus.

on-screen keyboard   swipe keyboard app   mini keyboard   keypad

slide out keyboard   portable keyboard   virtual keyboard   speech to text

Figure 3-15   A variety of options for typing on a smartphone.

iStockphoto.com / TommL; Courtesy of Nuance; FreezeFrameStudio / Photos.com; iStockphoto.com / webphotographeer; Courtesy of Jorno; Scanrail/Fotolia LLC; iStockphoto.com / Giorgio Magini; Courtesy of Virtual Devices; Courtesy of Blackberry

A variety of options are available for typing on a smartphone (Figure 3-15). Many can display an *on-screen keyboard*, where you press keys on the screen using your fingertip or a stylus. Some phones support a *swipe keyboard app*, on which users enter words by tracing a path on an on-screen keyboard with their fingertip or stylus from one letter to the next in a continuous motion. With other phones, you press letters on the phone's keyboard or keypad. Some phones use *predictive text*, where you press one key on the keyboard or keypad for each letter in a word, and software on the phone predicts the word you want. Swipe keyboard apps and predictive text save users time when entering text on the phone.

Instead of typing on a phone's keyboard or keypad, users can enter text via a *portable keyboard*, which is a full-sized keyboard that communicates with a smartphone via a dock, cables, or wirelessly. Some portable keyboards physically attach to and remove from the device; others are wireless. Another option is a *virtual keyboard* that projects an image of a keyboard on a flat surface. Finally, some phones work with the operating system or apps that convert your spoken word to text.

Messaging Services   With messaging services, users can send and receive messages to and from smartphones, handheld game devices, other mobile devices, and computers. The type of messages you send depends primarily on the services offered by the mobile service provider that works with the phone or other mobile device you select. Many users have unlimited wireless messaging plans, while others pay a fee per message sent or received. Messaging services include text and picture/video.

With text messaging service, or *SMS (short message service)*, users can send and receive short text messages, typically fewer than 300 characters, on a phone or other mobile device or computer. Text message services typically provide users with several options for sending and receiving messages, including:

- Mobile to mobile: Send a message from your mobile device to another mobile device.
- Mobile to email: Send a message from your mobile device to any email address.
- Mobile to provider: Send a message by entering a *common short code* (CSC), which is a four- or five-digit number assigned to a specific content or mobile service provider, sometimes followed by the message, for example, to a vote for a television program contestant or donate to a charity.
- Web to mobile: Send a message from a website to a mobile device or notification from a website to a mobile device with messages of breaking news and other updates, such as sports scores, stock prices, weather forecasts, incoming email messages, game notifications, and more.

✳ CONSIDER THIS

What is the difference between push and pull notifications?

A *push notification*, sometimes called a server push, is a message that initiates from the sending location (such as a server) without a request from the receiver. With a *pull notification*, by contrast, receiver requests information from the sending location.

With picture messaging service, users can send photos and audio files, as well as short text messages, to a phone or other mobile device or computer. With video messaging services, users can send short video clips, usually about 30 seconds in length, in addition to all picture messaging services. Smartphones and other mobile devices with picture/video messaging services, also called *MMS (multimedia message service)*, typically have a digital camera built into the device. Users who expect to receive numerous picture/video messages should verify the phone has sufficient memory. Picture/video message services typically provide users these options for sending and receiving messages:

- Mobile to mobile: Send the picture/video from your mobile device to another mobile device.
- Mobile to email: Send the picture/video from your mobile device to any email address.

If you send a picture message to a phone that does not have picture/video messaging capability, the phone usually displays a text message directing the user to a webpage that contains the picture/video message. Some online social networks allow you to send a picture/video message directly to your online profile.

 BTW

Analog vs. Digital
Human speech is analog because it uses continuous (wave form) signals that vary in strength and quality. Most computers and electronic devices are digital, which use only two discrete states: on and off.

 **CONSIDER THIS**

Do you need a messaging service to send a text or picture/video message?
Instead of using a messaging plan from your mobile service provider, you can use a mobile messaging app to send and receive text, picture, and other message from users. Many messaging apps also provide group chat capabilities. Most messaging apps can be downloaded to your mobile device at no cost.

Voice mail, which functions much like an answering machine, allows someone to leave a voice message for one or more people. Unlike answering machines, however, a computer in the voice mail system converts an analog voice message into digital form. Once digitized, the message is stored in a voice mailbox. A voice mailbox is a storage location on a hard drive in the voice mail system. To help users manage voice mail messages, some systems offer visual voice mail. With *visual voice mail*, users can view message details, such as the length of calls and, in some cases, read message contents instead of listening to them. Some voice mail systems can convert a voice mail message to a text message for display on a computer or mobile device, such as a smartphone, which you then can manage like any other text message.

Messaging services and voice mail systems also may be able to send messages to groups of phone numbers or email addresses. Read Secure IT 3-3 for tips about safely using smartphones and other mobile devices in public.

 SECURE IT 3-3

Safe Mobile Device Use in Public Areas

Sending a text message, updating a Facebook status, posting a Tweet, selecting a new playlist, and checking email messages are tasks you may perform using a mobile device many times each day. They all require some concentration as you focus on the device, usually while looking downward, and they distract you from events occurring around you. Using technology responsibly and safely can prevent theft and injuries.

One common method of thwarting a smartphone thief is to avoid using the phone to check the time. Potential thieves randomly ask people for the correct time. If a person stops and takes a phone out of a pocket or purse, the thief glances at the make and model and decides if it is worth snatching.

Bus stops and train stations are common places for mobile device theft. People in these locations tend to use their smartphones to check schedules, send text messages, and make phone calls. Headphones and earbuds are giveaways that you are using a mobile device and may not be focused on your surroundings. Recent studies show that more than 100 mobile phones are stolen every minute in the United States. Thieves are likely to snatch the devices while the doors are closing just before the train or bus departs from a station so that the victim is unable to pursue the thief. To decrease the chance of theft or pickpocketing, keep your mobile device(s) in a front pocket or in a zippered backpack. Keep your head up and stay aware of your surroundings. If possible, when in public, avoid using accessories that indicate the type of device to which they are connected.

Cognitive psychologists have studied the effects of inattentional blindness, which occurs when a person's attention is diverted while performing a natural activity, such as walking. The researchers have determined that diverted attention is particularly pronounced when people are talking on a mobile phone and, to a lesser extent, using a portable media player. Emergency room reports indicate that distracted walking accidents are on the rise, especially when people trip over cracks in sidewalks or run into fixed objects, such as parked cars and telephone poles.

Consider This: Do you know anyone who has had a mobile device stolen? If so, how did the theft occur? Have you ever experienced inattentional blindness or distracted walking?

Digital Cameras

A **digital camera** is a mobile device that allows users to take photos and store the photographed images digitally. A *smart digital camera* also can communicate wirelessly with other devices and can include apps similar to those on a smartphone. Mobile computers and devices, such as smartphones and tablets, often include at least one integrated digital camera.

 CONSIDER THIS

Do you need a digital camera if you have a camera built into your mobile phone?
If you use a camera only for posts on social media sites, then you may choose to use your mobile phone's built-in camera. If, however, you want increased zoom capabilities, more powerful flash, image stabilization, manual control of settings, and to reduce the drain on your phone's battery, then you may want to opt for a separate digital camera.

In addition to cameras built into phones and other devices, types of digital cameras include point-and-shoot cameras and SLR cameras (Figure 3-16). A *point-and-shoot camera is* an affordable and lightweight digital camera with lenses built into it and a screen that displays an approximation of the image to be photographed. Point-and-shoot cameras, which range in size and features, provide acceptable quality photographic images for the home or small office user. An *SLR camera* (single-lens reflex camera), by contrast, is a high-end digital camera that has interchangeable lenses and uses a mirror to display on its screen an exact replica of the image to be photographed. SLR cameras are much heavier and larger than point-and-shoot cameras. They also can be quite expensive, with a variety of available lens sizes and other attachments.

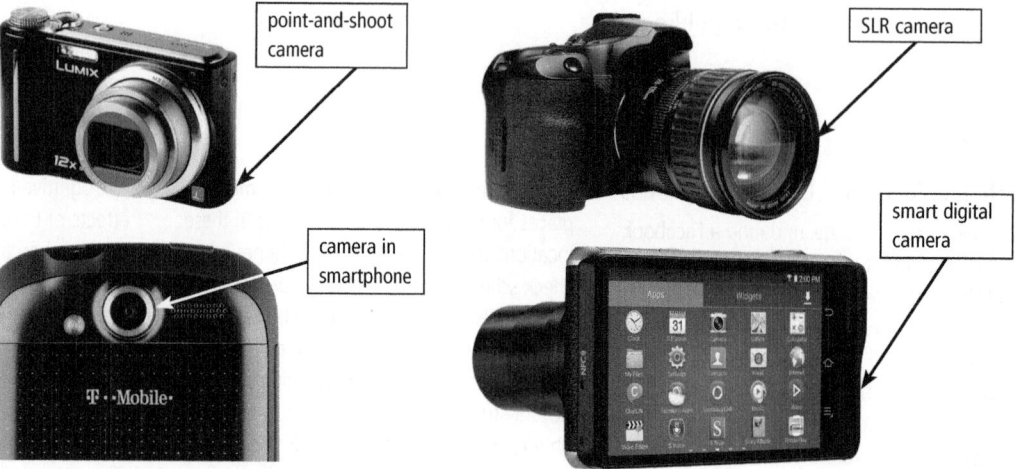

Figure 3-16 SLR digital cameras have lenses and other attachments, whereas the lenses on point-and-shoot cameras are built into the device. Many smartphones also have built-in digital cameras.
iStockphoto.com / andrew-thief;
Pawel Gaul / Photos.com;
iStockphoto.com / Stephen Krow;
Courtesy of Samsung

Most point-and-shoot cameras include zoom and autofocus capability, use a built-in flash, store images on memory cards, and enable you to view and sometimes edit images directly on the camera. Many can take video in addition to still photos. Some are equipped with GPS, giving them the capability to record the exact location where a photo was taken and then store these details with the photo. Others are waterproof. Figure 3-17 illustrates how a point-and-shoot digital camera might work.

How a Digital Camera Might Work

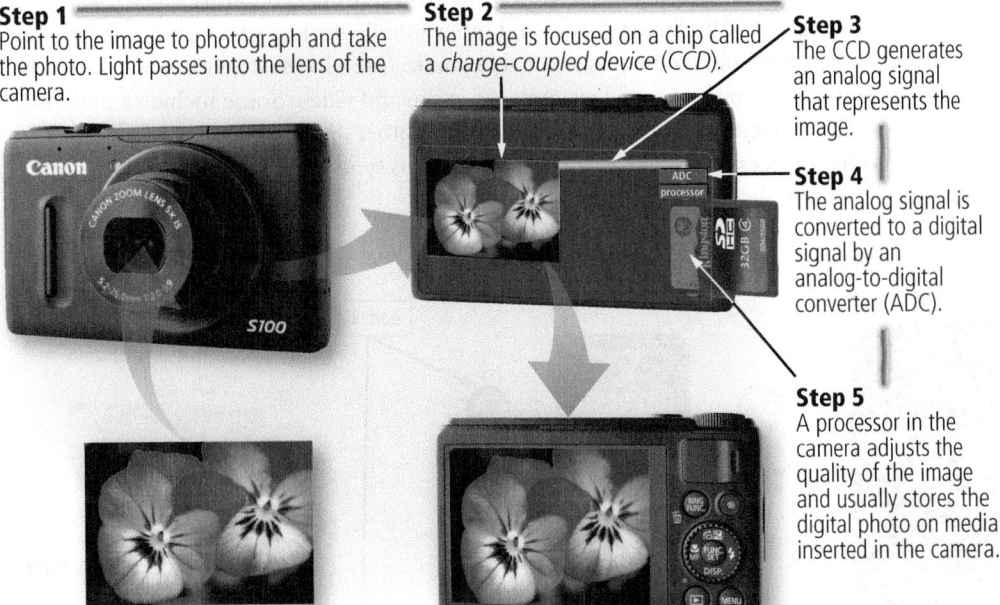

Step 1
Point to the image to photograph and take the photo. Light passes into the lens of the camera.

Step 2
The image is focused on a chip called a *charge-coupled device (CCD)*.

Step 3
The CCD generates an analog signal that represents the image.

Step 4
The analog signal is converted to a digital signal by an analog-to-digital converter (ADC).

Step 5
A processor in the camera adjusts the quality of the image and usually stores the digital photo on media inserted in the camera.

Figure 3-17 This figure shows how a point-and-shoot digital camera might work.
iStockphoto.com / David Birkbeck; iStockphoto.com / David Birkbeck; Johan Larson / Shutterstock.com; Courtesy of Kingston Technology Company, Inc

Smart digital cameras include all the features of point-and-shoot cameras and also enable you to connect wirelessly via Wi-Fi. Using the wireless capability, you instantly can save captured photos or videos on a networked computer or the cloud, share them on your online social network, upload them to a video sharing site, send them via email, and more. With a smart digital camera, you typically can download apps (just like on a smartphone) from an app store.

Digital cameras store captured images on storage media in the camera or on some type of memory card. Although most cameras enable you to review, edit, print, and share photos directly from the camera, some users prefer to transfer photos from a digital camera or the memory card to a computer's hard drive to perform these tasks.

Photo Quality   Resolution affects the quality of digital camera photos. **Resolution** is the number of horizontal and vertical pixels in a display. A *pixel* (short for picture element) is the smallest element in an electronic image (Figure 3-18). Digital camera resolution typically is stated in *megapixels* (*MP*), or millions of pixels. For example, a 16 MP resolution means 16 million pixels. The greater the number of pixels the camera uses to capture a picture, the better the quality of the picture but the larger the file size and the more expensive the camera. Most digital cameras provide a means to adjust the resolution. At a lower resolution, you can capture and store more images in the camera.

The actual photographed resolution is known as the *optical resolution*. Some manufacturers state enhanced resolution, instead of, or in addition to, optical resolution. The *enhanced resolution* usually is higher because it uses a special formula to add pixels between those generated by the optical resolution. Be aware that some manufacturers compute a digital camera's megapixels from the enhanced resolution, instead of optical resolution.

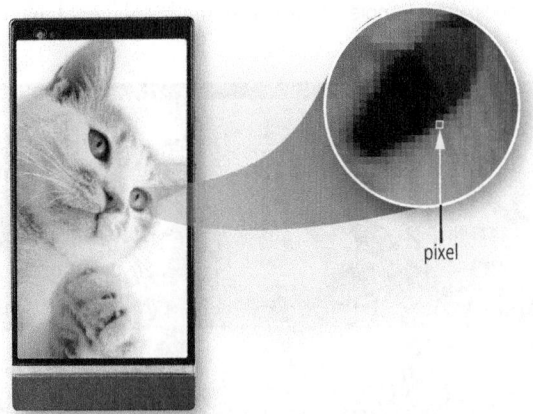

Figure 3-18 A pixel is the smallest element in an electronic image.
Lingong / Dreamstime.com

Portable and Digital Media Players

A **portable media player** is a mobile device on which you can store, organize, and play or view digital media (Figure 3-19). Smartphones and other mobile devices often can function as a portable media player. Portable media players enable you to listen to music; view photos; watch videos, movies, and television shows; and even record audio and video. Some include a digital camera and also offer a calendar, address book, games, and other apps. Others communicate wirelessly with other devices or computers and enable you to synchronize your digital media with a computer, another mobile device, or cloud storage.

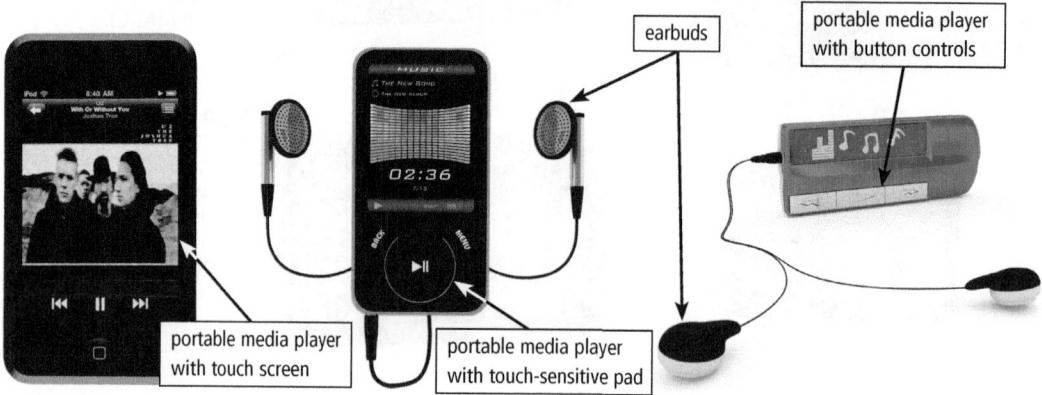

Figure 3-19 Some portable media players have touch screens; others have touch-sensitive pads or buttons that enable you to access your media library.

iStockphoto.com / Stephen Krow; iStockphoto.com / rzelich; iStockphoto.com / AleksVF

Portable media players usually require a set of *earbuds*, which are small speakers that rest inside each ear canal. Available in a variety of sizes and colors, some portable media player models have a touch screen. Others have a *touch-sensitive pad*, which is an input device that contains buttons and/or wheels you operate with a thumb or finger. Using the touch-sensitive pad, you can scroll through and play music; view pictures; watch videos or movies; navigate through song, picture, or movie lists; display a menu; adjust volume; customize settings; and perform other actions. Some portable media players have only button controls.

Portable media players are a mobile type of digital media player. A **digital media player** or *streaming media player* is a device, typically used in a home, that streams digital media from a computer or network to a television, projector, or some other entertainment device (Figure 3-20). Some can stream from the Internet, enabling users to access video on websites. Some users opt for a digital media player instead of subscribing to cable or satellite subscription services to watch television programs.

Your collection of stored digital media is called a *media library*. Portable media players and some digital media players house your media library on a storage device in the player and/or on some type of memory card. With most, you transfer the digital media from a computer or the Internet, if the device is Internet capable, to the player's media library. Read How To 2-2 in Module 2 for instructions about how to download digital media from online services.

Figure 3-20 A digital media player streams media to a home entertainment device.

Courtesy of Apple, Inc.

Tech Feature 3-3: Mobile Device Buyer's Guide

When purchasing a smartphone, digital camera, or portable or digital media player, you should consider several factors. Read Tech Feature 3-3 for tips to consider when purchasing these mobile devices.

 TECH FEATURE 3-3

Mobile Device Buyer's Guide

Mobile devices such as smartphones, digital cameras, and portable and digital media players are extremely popular. Research the manufacturers and then consider the following guidelines before purchasing a mobile device.

Smartphone Purchase Guidelines

1. Choose a mobile service provider and plan that satisfies your needs and budget. Choose a sufficient voice, text, and data plan that is appropriate.

2. Decide on the size, style, and weight of the smartphone that will work best for you.

3. Determine whether you prefer an on-screen keyboard, keypad, or mini keyboard.

4. Select a smartphone that is compatible with the program you want to use for synchronizing your email messages, contacts, calendar, and other data.

5. Choose a smartphone with sufficient battery life that meets your lifestyle.

6. Make sure your smartphone has enough memory and storage for contacts, email messages, photos, videos, and apps.

7. Consider purchasing accessories such as extra batteries, earbuds, screen protectors, and carrying cases.

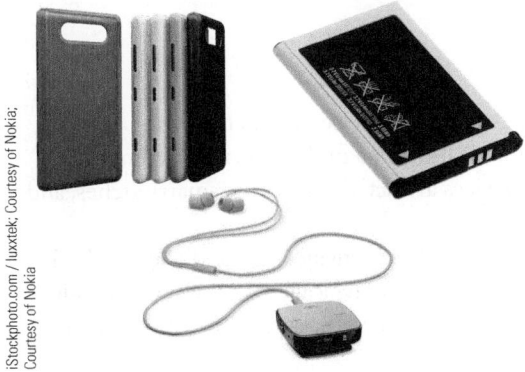

iStockphoto.com / luxxtek; Courtesy of Nokia; Courtesy of Nokia

Digital Camera Purchase Guidelines

1. Determine the type of digital camera that meets your needs, such as a point-and-shoot camera or SLR camera.

2. Choose a camera with an appropriate resolution.

3. Evaluate memory cards, because different cameras require different memory cards.

4. Consider a camera with built-in photo editing features.

5. Make sure that you can see the screen easily.

6. If the photos you plan to take will require you to zoom, choose a camera with an appropriate optical zoom.

7. Purchase accessories such as extra batteries and battery chargers, extra memory cards, lenses, and carrying cases.

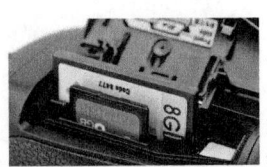

iStockphoto.com / tomprout

iStockphoto.com / Vasiliki Varvaki

Portable or Digital Media Player Purchase Guidelines

1. Choose a device with sufficient storage capacity for your media library and apps.

2. Consider how the portable or digital media player will connect to the Internet. Some devices connect using a wired and/or wireless connection. Choose a player that is compatible with the type of connection you can provide.

3. Read reviews about sound quality. If you are purchasing a portable device, consider higher-quality earbuds, headphones, or external speakers.

iStockphoto.com / Olga Popova; iStockphoto.com / Olga Popova; Terry Morris / Photos.com

4. Select a player that is compatible with other devices you already own.

5. Consider additional memory cards to increase the storage capacity of your portable or digital media player.

6. Consider the accessories. If your portable or digital media player connects to a television or other display, consider purchasing a keyboard so that you can type easily. If the device is portable, consider additional batteries or a protective case.

Consider This: Although most smartphones also can function as digital media players and digital cameras, would you have a separate digital media player and digital camera? Why?

Figure 3-21   E-book readers enable you to read e-books and other digital publications such as newspapers and magazines.

iStockphoto.com / Petar Chernaev

E-Book Readers

An **e-book reader** (short for electronic book reader), or *e-reader*, is a mobile device that is used primarily for reading e-books and other digital publications (Figure 3-21). An *e-book*, or digital book, is an electronic version of a printed book, readable on computers and other mobile devices. Digital publications include books, newspapers, and magazines. Mobile computers and devices that display text also can function as e-book readers.

E-book readers usually are smaller than tablets but larger than smartphones. Most e-book reader models can store thousands of books, have a touch screen, and are Internet capable with built-in wireless technology. You use an on-screen keyboard to navigate, search, make selections, take notes, and highlight. Some have a *text-to-speech feature*, where the device speaks the contents of the printed page. E-book readers are available with an electronic paper black-and-white screen or with a color screen. Most have settings to adjust text size and for various lighting conditions, such as bright sunlight or dim lighting. Batteries usually have a long life, providing more than 75 hours of use before needing to be recharged.

Similar to how a portable media player stores digital media, e-book readers store digital publications in a library on a storage device in the e-book reader and/or on memory cards. You typically transfer the digital publication from a computer or the Internet, if the device is Internet capable, to the e-book reader.

 BTW

Electronic Paper Screen
Some users of e-books prefer the electronic paper black-and-white screen over the models with color screens because the electronic paper resembles a paper page from a book.

 CONSIDER THIS

Do you need a separate e-book reader if you have a tablet or other device that can function as an e-book reader?
If you want the flexibility of reading on one device while using a tablet or other device for separate tasks, you will want to purchase a separate e-book reader. Also, e-book readers have a design suited for optimal readability of on-screen text and a longer battery life.

Wearable Devices

A **wearable device** or *wearable* is a small, mobile computing device designed to be worn by a consumer (Figure 3-22). These devices often communicate with a mobile device or computer using Bluetooth. Three popular types of wearable devices are activity trackers, smartwatches, and smart glasses.

An *activity tracker* is a wearable device that monitors fitness-related activities such as distance walked, heart rate, pulse, calories consumed, and sleep patterns. These devices typically sync, usually wirelessly, with a web or mobile app on your computer or mobile device to extend the capability of the wearable device.

A *smartwatch* is a wearable device that, in addition to keeping time, can communicate wirelessly with a smartphone to make and answer phone calls, read and send messages, access the web, play music, work with apps such as fitness trackers and GPS, and more. Most include a touch screen.

activity tracker communicates with
health fitness app on smartphone

smartwatch wirelessly communicates
with compatible smartphone

smart glasses respond to voice instruction to access apps

Figure 3-22 Three popular wearable devices include activity trackers, smartwatches, and smart glasses.
iStockphoto.com / Petar Chernaev; iStockphoto.com / Chesky_W; iStockphoto.com / scanrail; iStockphoto.com / Wavebreak; Source: Microsoft

Smart glasses, also called *smart eyewear* or augmented reality glasses, are wearable head-mounted eyeglass-type devices that enable the user to view information or take photos and videos that are projected to a miniature screen in the user's field of vision. For example, the device wearer could run an app while wearing smart glasses that display flight status information when he or she walks into an airport. Users control the device through voice commands or by touching controls on its frame. Some smart glasses also include mobile apps, such as fitness trackers and GPS.

Game Devices

A **game console** is a mobile computing device designed for single-player or multiplayer video games. Gamers often connect the game console to a television or a monitor so that they can view gameplay on the screen. Some models also allow you to listen to music and watch movies or view photos. Typically weighing between 3 and 11 pounds, many game console models include storage for games and other media. Optical disc drives in the game consoles provide access to games and movies on optical disc. Some use memory cards and accept USB flash drives. Game consoles that are Internet capable enable gamers to download games, stream games or movies, and play with others online. Some gamers connect keyboards or webcams so that they more easily can send text messages or conduct video chats with other gamers.

A **handheld game device** is a small mobile device that contains a screen, speakers, controls, and game console all in one unit. Some include a stylus. Some handheld game device models have touch screens and built-in digital cameras. Some are Internet capable for downloading games and apps. Most handheld game devices can communicate wirelessly with other similar devices for multiplayer gaming.

With a game console or computer video game, players direct movements and actions of on-screen objects via a controller, voice, or air gestures. Game controllers include gamepads, joysticks and wheels, dance pads, and a variety of motion-sensing controllers (Figure 3-23).

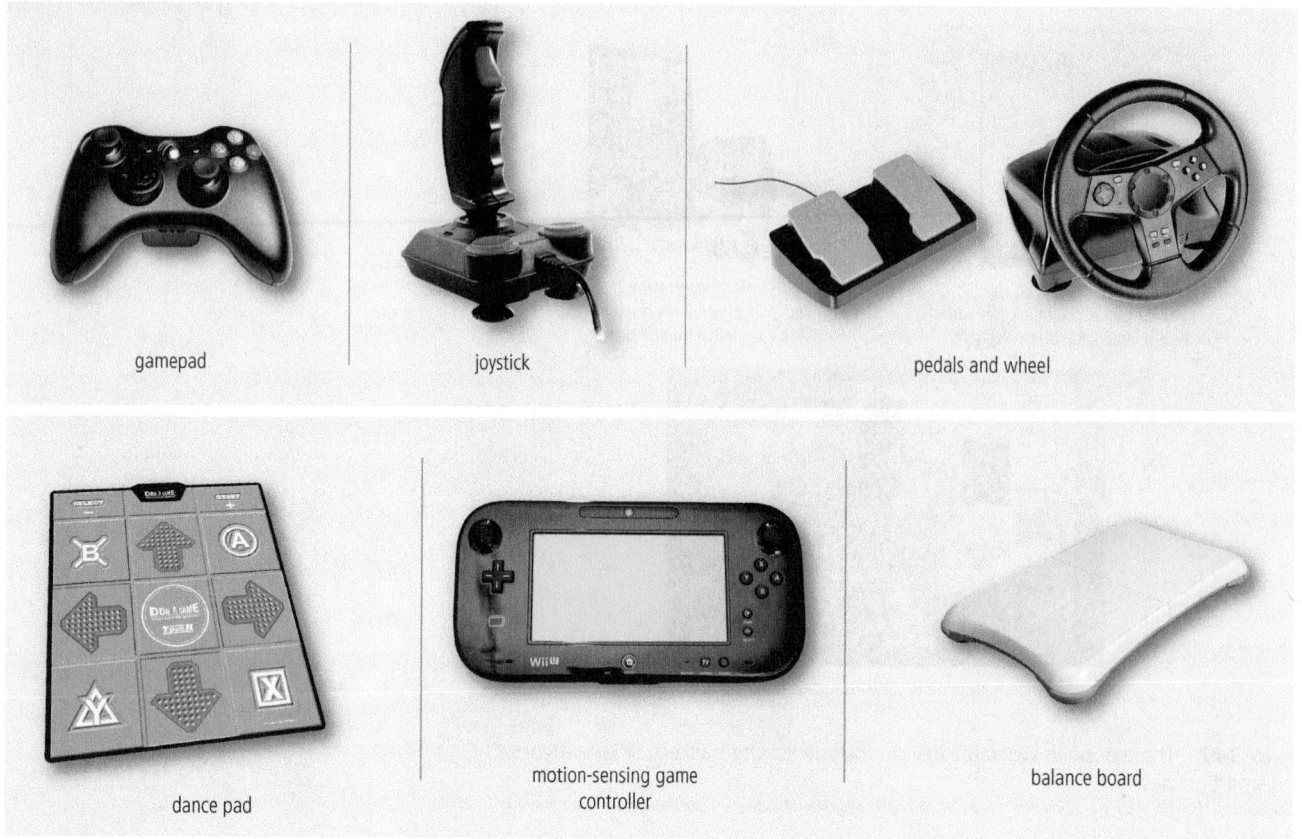

gamepad

joystick

pedals and wheel

dance pad

motion-sensing game controller

balance board

Figure 3-23 Gamers have a variety of ways to direct movements and actions of on-screen objects.
iStockphoto.com / peng wu; aquariagirl1970 / Shutterstock.com; George Dolgikh / Shutterstock.com; Courtesy of DDR Game; Tinxi / Shutterstock.com; Stuartkey / Dreamstime.com

The following list describes each of these types of game controllers. Most communicate via wired or wireless technology.

- A *gamepad*, which is held with both hands, controls the movement and actions of players or objects in video games or computer games. On the gamepad, users press buttons with their thumbs or move sticks in various directions to trigger events. Several gamepads can communicate with the game console simultaneously for multiplayer gaming.
- Users running flight and driving simulation software often use a joystick or wheel. A *joystick* is a handheld vertical lever, mounted on a base, that you move in different directions to control the actions of the simulated vehicle or player. The lever usually includes buttons, called triggers, that you press to initiate certain events. A *wheel* is a steering-wheel-type input device that users turn to simulate driving a car, truck, or other vehicle. Most wheels also include foot pedals for acceleration and braking actions.
- A *dance pad* is a flat, electronic device divided into panels that users press with their feet in response to instructions from a music video game. These games test the user's ability to step on the correct panel at the correct time, following a pattern that is synchronized with the rhythm or beat of a song.
- A *motion-sensing game controller* allows users to guide on-screen elements with air gestures, that is, by moving their body or a handheld input device through the air. Some motion-sensing game controllers are sold with a particular type of game; others are general purpose. Sports games, for example, use motion-sensing game controllers, such as baseball bats and golf clubs. With general-purpose motion-sensing game controllers, you simulate batting, golfing, and other actions with a universal handheld device or no device at all. Some motion-sensing game controllers also function as gamepads.

- Other controllers include those used for music and fitness games. Controllers that resemble musical instruments, such as guitars, drums, keyboards, and microphones work with music video games that enable game players to create sounds and music by playing the instrument. Fitness games often communicate with a *balance board*, which is shaped like a weight scale and contains sensors that measure a game player's balance and weight.

Embedded Computers

An **embedded computer** is a special-purpose computer that functions as a component in a larger product. Embedded computers are everywhere — at home, in your car, and at work. The following list identifies a variety of everyday products that contain embedded computers.

- **Consumer electronics:** Mobile phones, digital phones, digital televisions, cameras, video recorders, DVD players and recorders, answering machines
- **Home automation devices:** Thermostats, sprinkling systems, security systems, vacuum systems, appliances, lights
- **Automobiles:** Antilock brakes, engine control modules, electronic stability control, airbag control unit, cruise control, navigation systems and GPS receivers
- **Process controllers and robotics:** Remote monitoring systems, power monitors, machine controllers, medical devices
- **Computer devices and office machines:** Keyboards, printers, fax and copy machines

Because embedded computers are components in larger products, they usually are small and have limited hardware. These computers perform various functions, depending on the requirements of the product in which they reside. Embedded computers in printers, for example, monitor the amount of paper in the tray, check the ink or toner level, signal if a paper jam has occurred, and so on. Figure 3-24 shows some of the many embedded computers in vehicles. Read Ethics & Issues 3-2 to consider whether in-vehicle technology fosters a false sense of security.

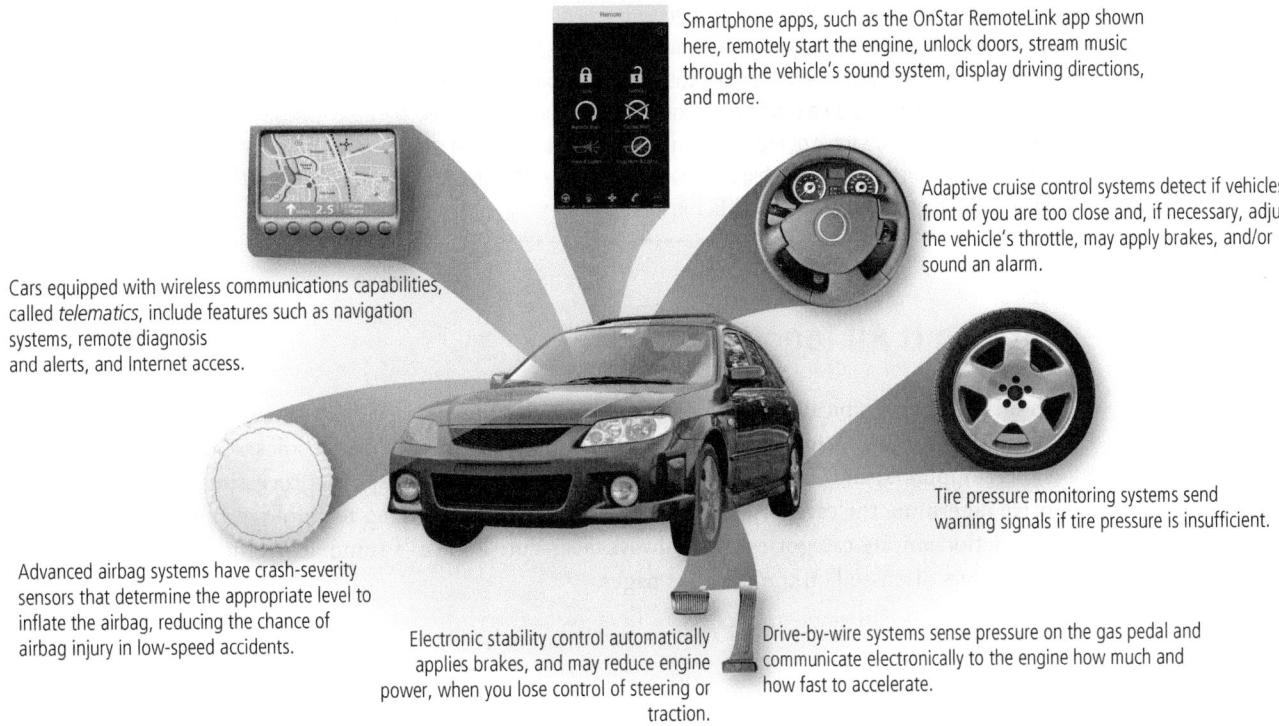

Smartphone apps, such as the OnStar RemoteLink app shown here, remotely start the engine, unlock doors, stream music through the vehicle's sound system, display driving directions, and more.

Adaptive cruise control systems detect if vehicles in front of you are too close and, if necessary, adjust the vehicle's throttle, may apply brakes, and/or sound an alarm.

Cars equipped with wireless communications capabilities, called *telematics*, include features such as navigation systems, remote diagnosis and alerts, and Internet access.

Tire pressure monitoring systems send warning signals if tire pressure is insufficient.

Advanced airbag systems have crash-severity sensors that determine the appropriate level to inflate the airbag, reducing the chance of airbag injury in low-speed accidents.

Electronic stability control automatically applies brakes, and may reduce engine power, when you lose control of steering or traction.

Drive-by-wire systems sense pressure on the gas pedal and communicate electronically to the engine how much and how fast to accelerate.

Figure 3-24   Some of the embedded computers designed to improve your safety, security, and performance in today's vehicles.

Nir Levy / Shutterstock.com; Santiago Cornejo / Shutterstock.com; iStockphoto.com / narvikk; iStockphoto.com / kenneth-cheung; iStockphoto.com / Marcin Laska; iStockphoto.com / pagadesign; Source: OnStar, LLC

ETHICS & ISSUES 3-2

Does In-Vehicle Technology Foster a False Sense of Security?

Embedded computers in vehicles can guide you when backing out of a driveway, warn you if a vehicle or object is in your blind spot, or alert you to unsafe road conditions. Apps can track gas mileage or notify you when your car needs an oil change or other services. Recently, all new cars were required to include electronic stability control, which can assist with steering the car in case of skidding, and backup cameras. Other technologies adjust vehicle speed or headlight usage, and can even activate the

brakes. All of this technology is intended to make driving safer.

Critics of in-vehicle technology claim that it can provide drivers with a false sense of security. If you rely on a sensor for assistance while backing up, parking, or changing lanes, for example, you may miss other obstructions that could cause a crash. Reliance on electronic stability control or other crash-avoidance technologies may cause you to drive faster than conditions allow or to pay less attention to the distance between your vehicle and others.

The effect on new, teen drivers is especially of concern. If teens learn to drive using

vehicles equipped with features such as video rearview mirrors, they may be unable to drive older, less-equipped vehicles safely. Many apps and devices help parents protect their teens while driving. Apps can program mobile devices to block incoming calls or text messages while the vehicle is moving. GPS can track a vehicle's location and speed. Sensors can monitor seatbelt usage and number of passengers in the vehicle.

 Consider This: Does in-vehicle technology make driving safer? Why or why not? What basic skills should all drivers have, regardless of their vehicle's technology?

CONSIDER THIS

Can embedded computers use the Internet to communicate with other computers and devices?

Many already do, on a small scale. For example, a Smart TV enables you to browse the web, stream video from online media services, listen to Internet radio, communicate with others on social media sites, play online games, and more — all while watching a television show.

A trend, called the *Internet of Things*, describes an environment where processors are embedded in every product imaginable (things), and those 'things' communicate with one another via the Internet (i.e., alarm clocks, coffeemakers, apps, vehicles, refrigerators, phones, washing machines, doorbells, streetlights, thermostats, navigation systems, etc.). For example, when your refrigerator detects the milk is low, it sends your phone a text message that you need milk and adds a 'buy milk' task to your scheduling app. On the drive home, your phone determines the closest grocery store that has the lowest milk price and sends the address of that grocery store to your vehicle's navigation system, which, in turn, gives you directions to the store. In the store, your phone directs you to the dairy aisle, where it receives an electronic coupon from the store for the milk. Because this type of environment provides an efficient means to track or monitor status, inventory, behavior, and more — without human intervention — it sometimes is referred to as machine-to-machine (M2M) communications. For additional information about the Internet of Things, read Tech Feature 6-1 in Module 6.

Putting It All Together

Industry experts typically classify computers and mobile devices in six categories: personal computers (desktop), mobile computers and mobile devices, game consoles, servers, supercomputers, and embedded computers. A computer's size, speed, processing power, and price determine the category it best fits. Due to rapidly changing technology, however, the distinction among categories is not always clear-cut. Table 3-3 summarizes the categories of computers discussed on the previous pages.

Table 3-3   Categories of Computers and Mobile Devices

Category	Physical Size	Number of Simultaneously Connected Users	General Price Range
Personal computers (desktop)	Fits on a desk	Usually one (can be more if networked)	Several hundred to several thousand dollars
Mobile computers and mobile devices	Fits on your lap or in your hand	Usually one	Less than a hundred dollars to several thousand dollars
Game consoles	Small box or handheld device	One to several	Several hundred dollars or less
Servers	Small cabinet to roomful of equipment	Two to thousands	Several hundred to several million dollars
Supercomputers	Full room of equipment	Hundreds to thousands	Half a million to several billion dollars
Embedded computers	Miniature	Usually one	Embedded in the price of the product

Ports and Connections

Computers and mobile devices connect to peripheral devices through ports or by using wireless technologies. A **port** is the point at which a peripheral device (i.e., keyboard, printer, monitor, etc.) attaches to or communicates with a computer or mobile device so that the peripheral device can send data to or receive information from the computer or mobile device. Most computers and mobile devices have ports (Figure 3-25). Some ports have a micro or mini version for mobile devices because of the smaller sizes of these devices.

⚙ **BTW**

Jack vs. Port
Instead of the term, port, the term, *jack*, sometimes is used to identify audio and video ports (i.e., audio jack or video jack).

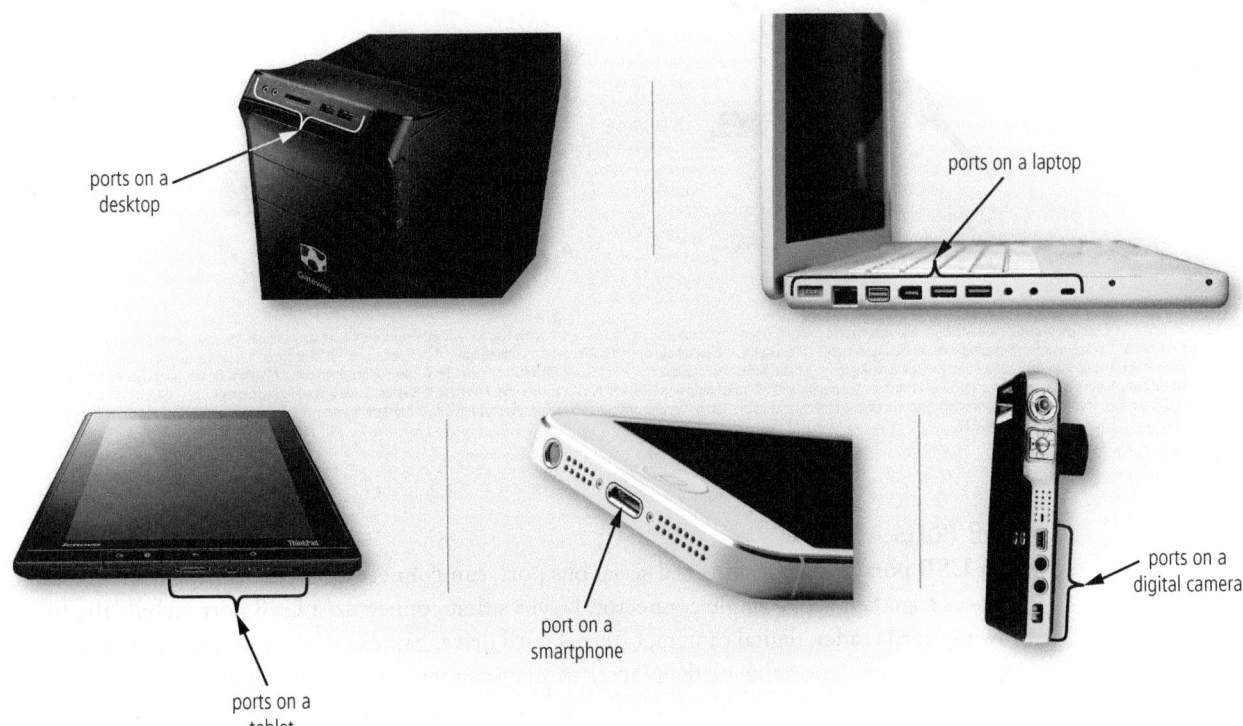

ports on a desktop

ports on a laptop

ports on a tablet

port on a smartphone

ports on a digital camera

Figure 3-25   Most computers and mobile devices have ports so that you can connect the computer or device to peripherals.
Courtesy of Gateway; Ultraone / Dreamstime.com; Courtesy of Lenovo; iStockphoto.com / Nikada; eduard ionescu / Shutterstock.com

A **connector** joins a cable to a port. A connector at one end of a cable attaches to a port on the computer or mobile device, and a connector at the other end of the cable attaches to a port on the peripheral device. Table 3-4 shows a variety of ports you may find on a computer or mobile device. USB and Thunderbolt are more general-purpose ports that allow connections to a wide variety of devices; other ports are more specific and connect a single type of device.

Table 3-4 Popular Ports and Connectors

Port Type	Connector Photo	Port Photo	Port Type	Connector Photo	Port Photo
DisplayPort (audio/video)			Mini USB		
DVI (digital video interface)			Mini HDMI (audio/video)		
HDMI (audio/video)			Network (Ethernet)		
Headphones			Speaker		
Lightning			Thunderbolt		
Microphone			USB (Type A)		
Micro USB			USB (Type B)		
Mini DisplayPort			USB (Type C)		
			VGA		

Steveheap / Dreamstime.com; iStockphoto.com / Hans Martens; iStockphoto.com / Ksenia Krylova; iStockphoto.com / Lusoimages; Jorge Salcedo / Shutterstock.com; Aarrows / Dreamstime.com; iStockphoto.com / Lusoimages; Pcheruvi / Dreamstime.com; iStockphoto.com / Potapova Vaeriya; iStockphoto.com / Jivko Kazakov; iStockphoto.com / TimArbaev; iStockphoto.com / Ashok Rodrigues; iStockphoto.com / Jon Larson; Aarrows / Dreamstime.com; iStockphoto.com / Denis Sokolov; Germán Ariel Berra / Shutterstock.com; Aarrows / Dreamstime.com; iStockphoto.com / Li Ding; iStockphoto.com / TimArbaev; iStockphoto.com / Matthew Brown; Jorge Salcedo /Shutterstock.com; Pcheruvi / Dreamstime.com; Anton Malcev / Photos.com; iStockphoto.com / alexander kirch; iStockphoto.com / Nick Smith; iStockphoto.com / Mohamed Badawi; Jorge Salcedo /Shutterstock.com / iStockphoto.com / Brandon Laufenberg; getIT / Shutterstock.com; stavklem / Shutterstock.com; iStockphoto.com / Lusoimages; lexan / Shutterstock.com; iStockphoto.com / NikiLitov; iStockphoto.com / Peter Hermus; Jarp / Fotolia LLC; Courtesy of Samsung; iStockphoto.com / ruslan117; iStockphoto.com / ruslan117

USB Ports

A **USB port**, short for universal serial bus port, can connect up to 127 different peripheral devices together with a single connector. Devices that connect to a USB port include the following: card reader, digital camera, external hard drive, game console, joystick, modem, mouse, optical disc drive, portable media player, printer, scanner, smartphone, digital camera, speakers, USB flash drive, and webcam. In addition to computers and mobile devices, you find USB ports in vehicles, airplane seats, and other public locations.

Several USB versions have been released, with newer versions (i.e., USB 3.0) transferring data and information faster than earlier ones (i.e., USB 2.0). Newer versions are *backward compatible*, which means they support older USB devices as well as newer ones. Keep in mind, though, that older USB devices do not run any faster in a newer USB port. In addition to transferring data, cables plugged into USB ports also may be able to transfer power to recharge many smartphones and tablets. Newer versions of USB can charge connected mobile devices even when the computer is not in use.

To attach multiple peripheral devices using a single USB port, you can use a USB hub. A *USB hub* is a device that plugs in a USB port on the computer or mobile device and contains multiple USB ports, into which you plug cables from USB devices. Some USB hubs are wireless. That is, a receiver plugs into a USB port on the computer and the USB hub communicates wirelessly with the receiver. Read Secure IT 3-4 for tips when using USB charging stations.

 SECURE IT 3-4

**Public USB Charging Stations —
Safe or Not?**

Although you might be tempted to recharge your smartphone or mobile device at a public charging station, think twice before plugging your USB cable into the charging kiosk's port. The station may be *juice jacking*, which occurs when a hacker steals data from or transfers malware to the device via a USB cable at a charging station. (A hacker is someone who accesses a computer or network illegally.)

This process is possible because the USB cable is used for two purposes: supplying power and syncing data. It can occur within

one minute after plugging into the charger. Anything on the device is susceptible, including photos, contacts, and music, and some malware can create a full backup of your data, leaving you prone to identity theft. Once the phone or mobile device is infected, it can continue to transmit data via Wi-Fi. Security experts claim that the only method of erasing this malware is to restore the device to its factory settings.

Charging stations are common in airports, business centers, and conference rooms. While most are safe, you can reduce the possibility of juice jacking by taking these precautions:

- Use a travel charger, also called a power bank, which can recharge a device several times before needing recharging itself.
- Keep the phone or mobile device locked so that it requires a password to sync data with another device. Turning off the device while charging may not provide sufficient protection against accessing the storage media.
- Use a power-only USB cable that does not allow data transmission.

✸ **Consider This:** Should warning signs be posted by public charging stations? Would you use a public charging kiosk if your smartphone or mobile device was running low on battery power?

Port Replicators and Docking Stations

Instead of connecting peripheral devices directly to ports on a mobile computer, some mobile users prefer the flexibility of port replicators and docking stations. A *port replicator* is an external device that provides connections to peripheral devices through ports built into the device. The mobile user accesses peripheral devices by connecting the port replicator to a USB port or a special port on the mobile computer. Port replicators sometimes disable ports on the mobile computer to prevent conflicts among the devices on the computer and port replicator.

A docking station is similar to a port replicator, but it has more functionality. A *docking station*, which is an external device that attaches to a mobile computer or device, contains a power connection and provides connections to peripheral devices (Figure 3-26). Docking stations also may include slots for memory cards, optical disc drives, and other devices. With the mobile computer or device in the docking station, users can work with a full-sized keyboard, a mouse, and other desktop peripheral devices from their laptop or tablet.

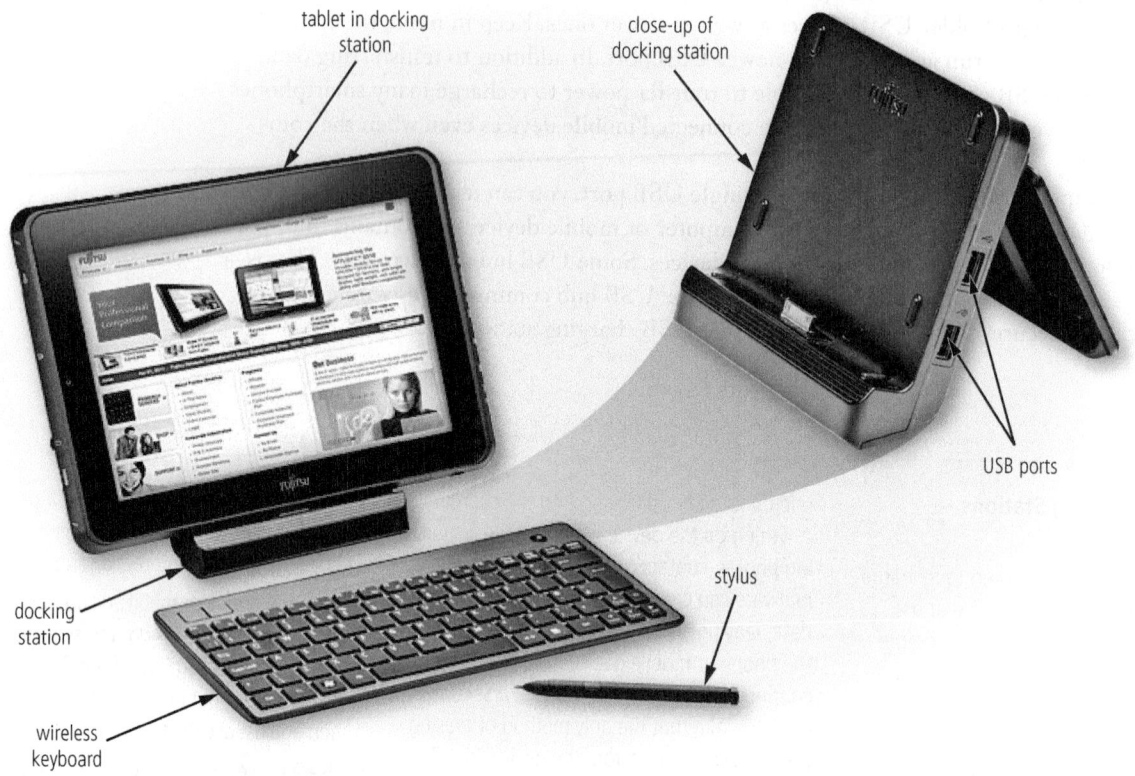

Figure 3-26   Docking stations often are used with tablets and other mobile computers, providing connections to peripheral devices.
Courtesy of Fujitsu Technology Solutions

Wireless Device Connections

Instead of connecting computers and mobile devices to peripheral devices with a cable, some peripheral devices use wireless communications technologies, such as Bluetooth, Wi-Fi, and NFC.

Bluetooth   **Bluetooth** technology uses short-range radio signals to transmit data between two Bluetooth-enabled computers or devices. In addition to computers, mobile devices and many peripheral devices, such as a mouse, keyboard, printer, or headset, and many vehicles and consumer electronics are Bluetooth enabled. Bluetooth devices have to be within about 33 feet of each other, but the range can be extended with additional equipment. If you have a computer that is not Bluetooth enabled, you can purchase a Bluetooth wireless port adapter that will convert an existing USB port into a Bluetooth port. Read How To 3-1 for instructions about setting up two Bluetooth devices to communicate with each other.

Wi-Fi   Short for wireless fidelity, **Wi-Fi** uses radio signals that conform to 802.11 standards, which were developed by the Institute of Electrical and Electronics Engineers (IEEE).

Computers and devices that have the appropriate Wi-Fi capability can communicate via radio waves with other Wi-Fi computers or devices. Most mobile computers and devices are

Wi-Fi enabled, along with routers and other communications devices. For successful Wi-Fi communications in open or outdoor areas free from interference, the Wi-Fi computers or devices should be within 300 feet of each other. In closed areas, the wireless range is about 100 feet. To obtain communications at the maximum distances, you may need to install extra hardware. Read How To 3-2 for instructions about connecting a phone to a Wi-Fi network.

 HOW TO 3-1

Pair Bluetooth Devices

Before two Bluetooth devices will communicate with each other, they might need to be paired. *Pairing* is the process of initiating contact between two Bluetooth devices and allowing them to communicate with each other. It is important to have the documentation for the Bluetooth devices you are pairing readily available. The following steps will help you pair two Bluetooth devices.

1. Make sure the devices you intend to pair are charged completely or plugged into an external power source.

2. Turn on the devices to pair, ensuring they are within your immediate reach.

3. If necessary, enable Bluetooth on the devices you are pairing.

4. Place one device in *discoverable mode*, which means it is waiting for another Bluetooth device to locate its signal. If you are connecting a smartphone to a Bluetooth headset, for example, the smartphone would need to be in discoverable mode.

5. Refer to the other device's documentation and follow the necessary steps to locate the discoverable device from the other device you are pairing.

6. After no more than about 30 seconds, the devices should initiate communications.

7. You may be required to enter a passkey (similar to a PIN) on one device for the other device with which you are pairing. For example, if you are pairing a smartphone with a Bluetooth headset, you may be required to enter the Bluetooth headset's passkey on the smartphone. In this case, you would refer to the Bluetooth headset's documentation to obtain the passkey. Common passkeys are 0000 and 1234.

8. After entering the correct passkey, the two devices should be paired successfully.

Consider This: Why is a passkey required when pairing two Bluetooth devices? Do you need to pair Bluetooth devices before each use?

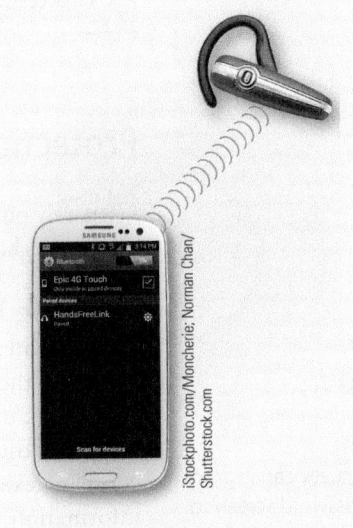

iStockphoto.com/Moncherie; Norman Chan/Shutterstock.com

 HOW TO 3-2

Connect Your Phone to a Wi-Fi Network to Save Data Charges

Many of today's data plans limit the amount of data you can transfer each month on your mobile service provider's network. Connecting a smartphone to a Wi-Fi network enables you to transfer data without using your phone's data plan and risking costly overages. The following steps describe how to connect your phone to a Wi-Fi network.

1. Make sure you are in a location where a Wi-Fi network is available. Obtain any necessary information you need to connect to the Wi-Fi network.

2. Navigate to the settings on your phone.

3. Locate and enable Wi-Fi in your phone's settings.

4. When your phone displays a list of available wireless networks, choose the network to which you want to connect.

5. If necessary, enter any additional information, such as a password, required to connect to the network.

6. Your phone should indicate when it successfully is connected to the network.

7. When you are finished using the Wi-Fi connection or are not within range of the Wi-Fi network, disable Wi-Fi on your phone to help conserve battery life.

Consider This: If you have a data plan allowing unlimited data and you are within range of a Wi-Fi network, is it better to use your mobile service provider's network or the Wi-Fi network? Why?

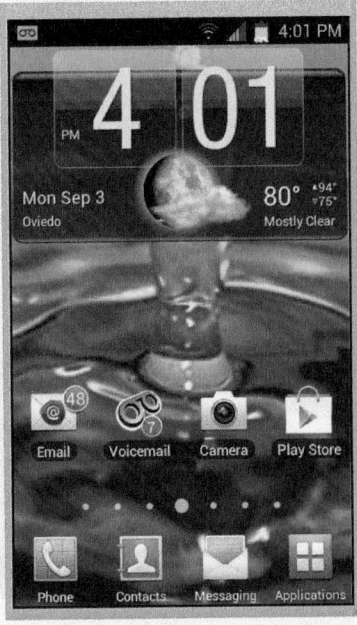

Google Inc.

NFC NFC (near field communications) uses close-range radio signals to transmit data between two NFC-enabled devices. Examples of NFC-enabled devices include smartphones, digital cameras, computers, televisions, and terminals. Other objects, such as credit cards and tickets, also use NFC technology. For successful communications, the devices either touch or are within an inch or two of each other.

 CONSIDER THIS

What are some uses of NFC devices?

- Pay for goods and services (i.e., smartphone to terminal)
- Share contacts, photos, and other files (i.e., smartphone to smartphone or digital camera to television)
- Download apps (i.e., computer to smartphone)
- Gain access or admittance (i.e., smartphone to terminal)

Protecting Hardware

Users rely on computers and mobile devices to create, store, and manage important information. Thus, you should take measures to protect computers and devices from theft, vandalism, and failure.

Hardware Theft and Vandalism

Companies, schools, and other organizations that house many computers are at risk of hardware theft and vandalism, especially those with smaller computers that easily can fit in a backpack or briefcase. Mobile users are susceptible to hardware theft because the size and weight of their computers and devices make them easy to steal. Thieves may target laptops of company executives so that they can use the stolen computer to access confidential company information illegally.

To help reduce the chances of theft, companies and schools use a variety of security measures. Physical access controls, such as locked doors and windows, usually are adequate to protect the equipment. Many businesses, schools, and some homeowners install alarm systems for additional security. School computer labs and other facilities with a large number of semifrequent users often attach additional physical security devices, such as cables that lock the equipment to a desk, cabinet, or floor. Mobile users sometimes lock their mobile computers temporarily to a stationary object, for example, a table in a hotel room. Small locking devices also exist that require a key to access a hard drive or optical disc drive.

 **BTW**

Lost Computers or Devices
You usually can instruct the password screen to display your name and phone number, so that a Good Samaritan can return a lost computer or device to you.

Users also can install a security or device-tracking app on their mobile computers and devices. Some security apps shut down the computer and sound an alarm if the computer moves beyond a specified distance. Others can be configured to photograph the thieves when they use the computer. Device-tracking apps use GPS, Wi-Fi, IP addresses, and other means to determine the location of a lost or stolen computer or device.

Users can configure computers and mobile devices to require identification before allowing access. For example, you can require entry of a user name and password to use the computer or device. Some computers and mobile devices have built-in or attached fingerprint readers (Figure 3-27), which can be used to verify a user's identity before allowing access. A *fingerprint reader*

Figure 3-27 Some mobile computers and devices include fingerprint readers, which can be used to verify a user's identity.

fingerprint reader

captures curves and indentations of a fingerprint. This type of security does not prevent theft, but it renders the computer or device useless if it is stolen.

Hardware Failure

Hardware can fail for a variety of reasons: aging hardware; random events, such as electrical power problems; and even errors in programs or apps. Not only could hardware failure require you to replace or repair a computer or mobile device, but it also can cause loss of software, data, and information.

One of the more common causes of system failure is an electrical power variation, which can cause loss of data and loss of equipment. If computers and mobile devices are connected to a network, a single power disturbance can damage multiple devices at once. Electrical disturbances that can cause damage include undervoltages and overvoltages.

- An **undervoltage** occurs when the electrical supply or voltage drops, often defined as more than five percent, below the normal volts. A *brownout* is a prolonged (more than a minute) undervoltage. A *blackout* is a complete power failure. Undervoltages can cause data loss but generally do not cause equipment damage.
- An **overvoltage**, or **power surge**, occurs when the incoming electrical supply or voltage increases, often defined as more than five percent, above the normal volts. A momentary overvoltage, called a *spike*, occurs when the increase in power lasts for less than one millisecond (thousandth of a second). Uncontrollable disturbances such as lightning bolts can cause spikes. Overvoltages can cause immediate and permanent damage to hardware.

To protect against electrical power variations, use a surge protector. A **surge protector**, also called a *surge suppressor*, uses electrical components to provide a stable current flow and minimize the chances of an overvoltage reaching the computer and other electronic equipment (Figure 3-28). Sometimes resembling a power strip, the computer and other devices plug in the surge protector, which plugs in the power source.

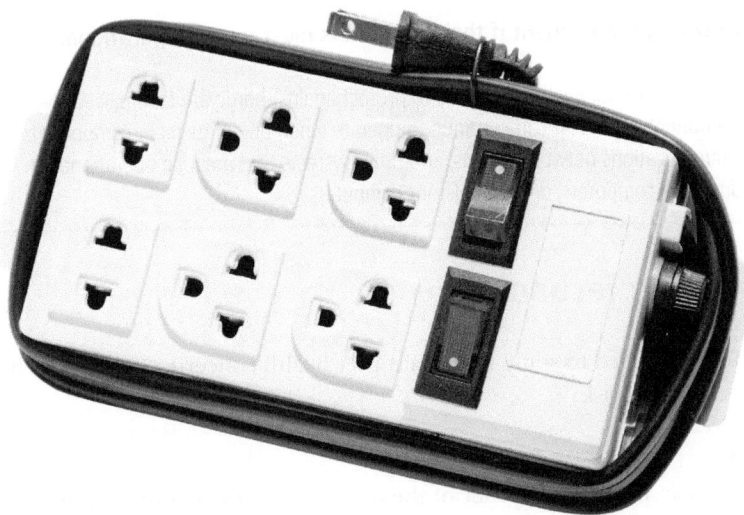

Figure 3-28 Circuits inside a surge protector safeguard against electrical power variations.
iStockphoto.com / missisya

The surge protector absorbs small overvoltages — generally without damage to the computer and equipment. To protect the computer and other equipment from large overvoltages, such as those caused by a lightning strike, some surge protectors stop working completely when an overvoltage reaches a certain level. Surge protectors also usually protect the computer from undervoltages. No surge protectors are 100 percent effective. Large power surges can bypass the protector. Repeated small overvoltages can weaken a surge protector permanently. Some experts recommend replacing a surge protector every two to three years.

For additional electrical protection, some users connect an uninterruptible power supply to the computer. An **uninterruptible power supply (UPS)** is a device that contains surge protection circuits and one or more batteries that can provide power during a temporary or permanent loss of power (Figure 3-29). A UPS connects your computer and a power source.

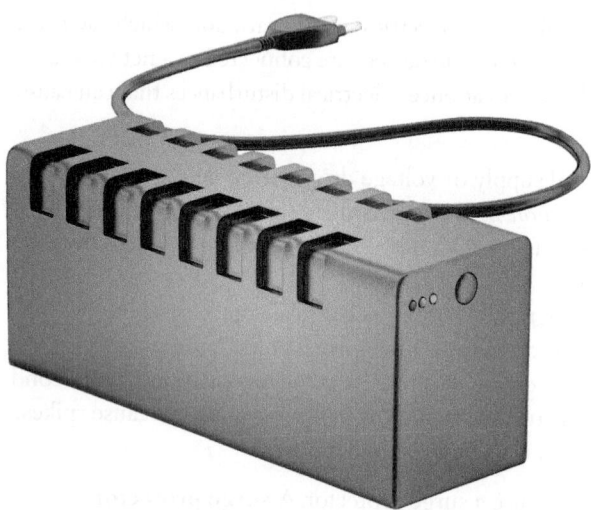

Figure 3-29   If power fails, a UPS uses batteries to provide electricity for a limited amount of time.
rendeep kumar r / Shutterstock.com

 CONSIDER THIS

What other measures can organizations implement if their computers must remain operational at all times?

Some companies use duplicate components or duplicate computers to protect against hardware failure. A *fault-tolerant computer* has duplicate components so that it can continue to operate when one of its main components fails. Airline reservation systems, communications networks, ATMs, and other systems that must be operational at all times use duplicate components, duplicate computers, or fault-tolerant computers.

Health Concerns of Using Technology

The widespread use of technology has led to some important user health concerns. You should be proactive and minimize your chance of risk.

Repetitive Strain Injuries

A *repetitive strain injury* (*RSI*) is an injury or disorder of the muscles, nerves, tendons, ligaments, and joints. Technology-related RSIs include tendonitis and carpal tunnel syndrome.

- Tendonitis is inflammation of a tendon due to repeated motion or stress on that tendon.
- Carpal tunnel syndrome (CTS) is inflammation of the nerve that connects the forearm to the palm of the hand.

Repeated or forceful bending of the wrist can cause tendonitis of the wrist or CTS. Symptoms of tendonitis of the wrist include extreme pain that extends from the forearm to the hand, along with tingling in the fingers. Symptoms of CTS include burning pain when the nerve is compressed, along with numbness and tingling in the thumb and first two fingers.

Long-term computer work can lead to tendonitis or CTS. Factors that cause these disorders include prolonged typing, prolonged mouse usage, or continual shifting between the mouse and the keyboard. If untreated, these disorders can lead to permanent physical damage.

CONSIDER THIS

What can you do to prevent technology-related tendonitis or CTS?

Follow these precautions:

- Take frequent breaks to exercise your hands and arms (Figure 3-30).
- Do not rest your wrists on the edge of a desk. Instead, place a wrist rest between the keyboard and the edge of your desk.
- Place the mouse at least six inches from the edge of the desk. In this position, your wrist is flat on the desk.
- Minimize the number of times you switch between the mouse and the keyboard.
- Keep your forearms and wrists level so that your wrists do not bend.
- Avoid using the heel of your hand as a pivot point while typing or using the mouse.
- Keep your shoulders, arms, hands, and wrists relaxed while you work.
- Maintain good posture.
- Stop working if you experience pain or fatigue.

Hand Exercises
- Spread fingers apart for several seconds while keeping wrists straight.
- Gently push back fingers and then thumb.
- Dangle arms loosely at sides and then shake arms and hands.

Figure 3-30   To reduce the chance of developing tendonitis or carpal tunnel syndrome, take frequent breaks during computer sessions to exercise your hands and arms.
iStockphoto.com / Denis Kartavenko; Scanrail1 / Shutterstock.com

Other Physical Risks

With the growing use of earbuds and headphones in computers and mobile devices, some users are experiencing hearing loss. Read How To 3-3 for guidelines for evaluating earbuds and headphones.

HOW TO 3-3

Evaluate Earbuds and Headphones

Earbuds and headphones are used to listen to music and other audio files on computers and mobile devices. Selecting the proper product not only depends on the style you prefer, but also the type of audio you will be playing. Prices for earbuds and headphones can range from only a few dollars to several hundred dollars, so it is important to know what you are purchasing. The following guidelines describe what to look for when evaluating earbuds and headphones.

- Determine which style you prefer. Earbuds rest inside your ear, while headphones rest over your ear. Experiment with both types and determine which is more comfortable for you.

- Determine the quality you desire. If you listen to music casually and typically do not notice variations in sound quality, a higher-end product might not be necessary. Alternatively, if sound quality is important, you may consider a more expensive set. Note that a higher price does not always indicate better quality; read online product reviews for information about the sound quality of various products.

- Decide whether you would like a noise cancelling feature. *Noise cancelling* helps block external noise while you are listening to the audio on your device. Noise cancelling headphones sometimes require batteries, and you are able to turn the noise

cancelling feature on and off. If you will be listening to audio in locations where you also need to hear what is going on around you, consider purchasing a product without this feature.

- Determine whether you prefer wired or wireless headphones. Wireless headphones might be more expensive, but will allow you to travel farther from your device.

Consider This: Based on your preferences and needs, which type of product (earbuds or headphones) is best for you? Locate a product online that meets your specifications. What brand is it? How much does it cost? Where is this product available?

Techniques to Ease Eyestrain

- Every 10 to 15 minutes, take an eye break.
  - Look into the distance and focus on an object for 20 to 30 seconds.
  - Roll your eyes in a complete circle.
  - Close your eyes and rest them for at least one minute.
- Blink your eyes every five seconds.
- Place your display about an arm's length away from your eyes with the top of the screen at or below eye level.
- Use large fonts.
- If you wear glasses, ask your doctor about computer glasses.
- Adjust the lighting.

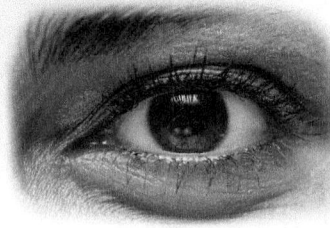

Figure 3-31 Following these tips may help reduce eyestrain while using technology.
grublee / Shutterstock.com

Computer vision syndrome (*CVS*) is a technology-related health condition that affects eyesight. You may have CVS if you have sore, tired, burning, itching, or dry eyes; blurred or double vision after prolonged staring at a display device; headache or sore neck; difficulty shifting focus between a display device and documents; difficulty focusing on the screen image; color fringes or after-images when you look away from the display device; and increased sensitivity to light. Eyestrain associated with CVS is not thought to have serious or long-term consequences. Figure 3-31 outlines some techniques you can use to ease eyestrain.

People who spend their workday using the computer sometimes complain of lower back pain, muscle fatigue, and emotional fatigue. Lower back pain sometimes is caused from poor posture. Always sit properly in the chair while you work. To alleviate back pain, muscle fatigue, and emotional fatigue, take a 15- to 30-minute break every 2 hours — stand up, walk around, stretch, and relax.

Another way to help prevent these injuries is to be sure your workplace is designed ergonomically. **Ergonomics** is an applied science devoted to incorporating comfort, efficiency, and safety into the design of items in the workplace. Ergonomic studies have shown that using the correct type and configuration of chair, keyboard, display, and work surface helps users work comfortably and efficiently and helps protect their health (Figure 3-32). You can hire an ergonomic consultant to evaluate your workplace and recommend changes.

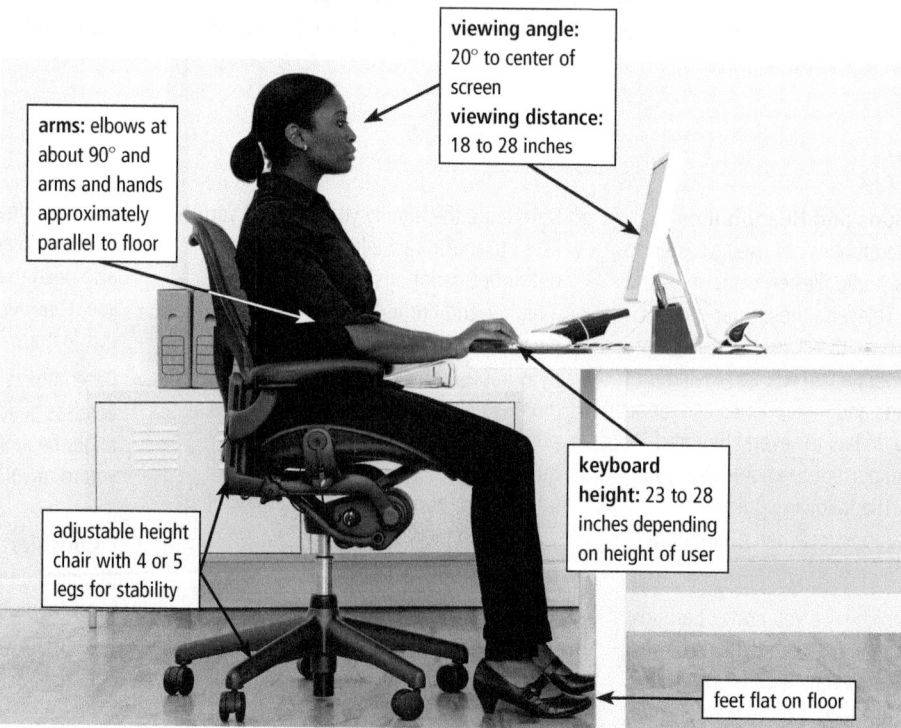

arms: elbows at about 90° and arms and hands approximately parallel to floor

viewing angle: 20° to center of screen

viewing distance: 18 to 28 inches

keyboard height: 23 to 28 inches depending on height of user

adjustable height chair with 4 or 5 legs for stability

feet flat on floor

Figure 3-32 A well designed work area should be flexible to allow adjustments to the height and build of different individuals.
Science Photo Library / Alamy Stock Photo

Behavioral Health Risks

Some technology users become obsessed with computers, mobile devices, and the Internet. **Technology addiction** occurs when technology use consumes someone's entire social life. Technology addiction is a growing health problem, but it can be treated through therapy and support groups.

People suffering from *technology overload* feel distressed when deprived of technology, even for a short length of time, or feel overwhelmed with the amount of technology they are required to manage. To cope with the feelings of distraction and to control the impact that technology can have on work and relationships, set aside technology-free time.

 CONSIDER THIS ─────────────────────────────

How can you tell if you are addicted to technology?

Symptoms of a user with technology addiction include the following:

- Craves computer time
- Overjoyed when using a computer or mobile device
- Unable to stop using technology
- Irritable when not using technology
- Neglects family and friends
- Problems at work or school

 CONSIDER THIS ─────────────────────────────

What is digital distraction?

Digital distraction is the practice of using and relying on technology so much that you do not pay enough attention to normal, everyday activities. Digital distraction might be characterized by somebody using a smartphone while having dinner with one or more other people, using a laptop for nonacademic purposes while attending a course, or individuals in the same room consumed by their smartphones or other mobile devices instead of communicating directly with those present. Digital distraction can cause negative side effects, such as lower grades in class, strained relationships, or the inability to be aware of your surroundings. Some consider digital distraction to be a health risk.

 Summary

This module presented characteristics of and purchasing guidelines for laptops, tablets, desktops, smartphones, digital cameras, and portable and digital media players. It also discussed servers, supercomputers, point-of-sale terminals, ATMs, self-service kiosks, e-book readers, wearable devices, game devices, embedded computers, and cloud computing. It presented a variety of ports and connections, ways to protect hardware, and health concerns of using technology use along with preventive measures.

STUDENT ASSIGNMENTS

Study Guide The Study Guide reinforces material you should know after reading this module.

Instructions: Answer the questions below using the format that helps you remember best or that is required by your instructor. Possible formats may include one or more of these options: write the answers; create a document that contains the answers; record answers as audio or video using a webcam, smartphone, or portable media player; post answers on a blog, wiki, or website; or highlight answers in the book/e-book.

1. List types of computers and mobile devices.

2. Describe how personal computers often are differentiated.

3. Explain how to avoid malware infections.

4. Define the term, motherboard.

5. Describe the roles of the processor and memory.

6. Differentiate among traditional and ultrathin laptops, tablets, phablets, handheld computers, and stick computers.

7. To interact with a tablet, you may use a touch screen or a(n) _____.

8. List steps to protect yourself from webcam spying.

9. List considerations when purchasing a mobile computer. Explain the importance of built-in ports and slots.

10. A(n) _____ desktop may be less expensive and take up less space.

11. Identify types of desktop users and explain how each user's computer needs may differ.

12. Identify how you can purchase the appropriate desktop computer for your needs.

13. Describe the purpose and functions of a server. Differentiate among rack, blade, and tower servers.

14. Define virtualization as it relates to servers. Define the terms, server farm and mainframe.

15. Define the terms, terminal and thin client. List the advantages of a thin client.

16. Identify situations where POS terminals, ATMs, and self-service kiosks might be used. List ATM safety guidelines.

17. A(n) _____ is used to solve complex, sophisticated mathematical calculations, such as those used in petroleum exploration.

18. List cloud computing resources. Describe how businesses use cloud computing to manage resources.

19. List types of mobile devices. Describe features of a smartphone.

20. Explain the issues surrounding the recycling of e-waste.

21. Identify methods for typing on a smartphone.

22. List options provided by text, picture/video message, and voicemail services.

23. Distinguish between push and pull notifications.

24. What are some dangers of inattentional blindness?

25. Define the term, digital distraction.

26. Describe the types of digital cameras, how they store captured images, and how to transfer photos to a computer.

27. Explain how resolution affects digital picture quality.

28. Identify the features of portable media and digital media players.

29. List considerations when purchasing different types of mobile devices.

30. List features of e-book readers and wearable devices.

31. Identify types of game controllers.

32. List products that contain embedded computers. List the disadvantages of in-vehicle technology.

33. Describe the trend, the Internet of Things.

34. Describe categories of computers and mobile devices, and identify general characteristics of size, user type, and price.

35. Explain how a computer uses ports and connectors.

36. List devices that connect to a USB port. Explain risks of using public USB charging stations.

37. Define the term, backward compatible.

38. Distinguish between a port replicator and a docking station.

39. Describe the following technologies: Bluetooth, Wi-Fi, and NFC.

40. _____ is the process of initiating contact between two Bluetooth devices.

41. List steps to connect your phone to a Wi-Fi network.

42. List methods for securing against hardware theft and vandalism.

43. Define the terms, undervoltage and overvoltage, and explain how each can damage a computer or data.

44. Describe the purposes of surge protectors and UPS devices. Explain the purpose a fault-tolerant computer.

45. Identify causes and types of repetitive strain injuries. List symptoms of CVS.

46. List guidelines for evaluating earbuds and headphones.

47. Describe the role of ergonomics in a workplace.

48. List symptoms of technology addiction. Define the term, technology overload.

You should be able to define the Primary Terms and be familiar with the Secondary Terms listed below.

Key Terms

Primary Terms (shown in **bold-black** characters in the module)

all-in-one (3-8)
Bluetooth (3-30)
cloud computing (3-14)
computer (3-2)
computer vision syndrome (3-36)
connector (3-28)
desktop (3-7)
digital camera (3-18)
digital media player (3-20)

e-book reader (3-22)
embedded computer (3-25)
ergonomics (3-36)
game console (3-23)
handheld game device (3-23)
laptop (3-4)
mobile computer (3-3)
mobile device (3-2)

NFC (3-32)
overvoltage (3-33)
port (3-27)
portable media player (3-20)
power surge (3-33)
resolution (3-19)
server (3-10)
smartphone (3-15)
stick computer (3-6)

surge protector (3-33)
tablet (3-5)
technology addiction (3-37)
undervoltage (3-33)
uninterruptible power supply (UPS) (3-34)
USB port (3-28)
wearable device (3-22)
Wi-Fi (3-30)

Secondary Terms (shown in *italic* characters in the module)

activity tracker (3-22)
AirPods (3-20)
all-in-one desktop (3-8)
application server (3-10)
ATM (3-12)
backup server (3-10)
backward compatible (3-29)
balance board (3-25)
bar code reader (3-11)
blackout (3-33)
blade server (3-10)
brownout (3-33)
charge-coupled device (CCD) (3-19)
common short code (CSC) (3-16)
convertible tablet (3-5)
CPU (3-4)
CVS (3-36)
dance pad (3-24)
database server (3-10)
digital distraction (3-37)
discoverable mode (3-31)
docking station (3-29)
domain name server (3-10)
DVD kiosk (3-13)
earbuds (3-20)
e-book (3-22)
enhanced resolution (3-19)
e-reader (3-22)
fault-tolerant computer (3-34)
file server (3-10)
fingerprint reader (3-32)
FTP server (3-10)
game server (3-10)
gamepad (3-24)
gaming desktop (3-8)

Google Street View (3-5)
handheld computer (3-6)
home server (3-10)
Internet of Things (3-26)
jack (3-27)
joystick (3-24)
juice jacking (3-29)
kiosk (3-13)
list server (3-10)
mail server (3-10)
mainframe (3-11)
media library (3-20)
megapixel (MP) (3-19)
MMS (multimedia message service) (3-16)
motherboard (3-4)
motion-sensing game controller (3-24)
network server (3-10)
noise cancelling (3-35)
notebook computer (3-4)
on-screen keyboard (3-16)
optical resolution (3-19)
pairing (3-31)
peripheral device (3-2)
personal computer (3-3)
phablet (3-6)
PIN (3-12)
pixel (3-19)
point-and-shoot camera (3-18)
port replicator (3-29)
portable keyboard (3-16)
POS terminal (3-11)
predictive text (3-16)
print server (3-10)

processor (3-4)
pull notification (3-16)
push notification (3-16)
rack server (3-10)
repetitive strain injury (RSI) (3-34)
server farm (3-11)
server virtualization (3-11)
skimmer (3-12)
slate tablet (3-5)
SLR camera (3-18)
smart digital camera (3-18)
smart eyewear (3-23)
smart glasses (3-23)
smartwatch (3-22)
SMS (short message service) (3-16)
spike (3-33)
storage server (3-10)
streaming media player (3-20)
stylus (3-5)
supercomputer (3-13)
surge suppressor (3-33)
swipe keyboard app (3-16)

system unit (3-8)
tablet (3-5)
technology overload (3-37)
telematics (3-25)
terminal (3-11)
text-to-speech feature (3-22)
thin client (3-11)
touch-sensitive pad (3-20)
tower (3-8)
tower server (3-10)
ultrabook (3-4)
USB hub (3-29)
virtual keyboard (3-16)
virtualization (3-11)
visual voice mail (3-17)
voice mail (3-17)
wearable (3-22)
web server (3-10)
wheel (3-24)
workstation (3-8)

Courtesy of Microsoft

Checkpoint

The Checkpoint exercises test your knowledge of the module concepts.

True/False

Mark T for True and F for False. If False, rewrite the statement so that it is True.

_____ 1. Malware authors often focus on social media, with the goal of stealing personal information.

_____ 2. The disadvantages of a virtual server are that it is difficult to manage and takes a long time to create and configure.

_____ 3. A mainframe is a small terminal that looks like a desktop, but has limited capabilities and components.

_____ 4. Thin clients contain powerful hard drives.

_____ 5. Applications requiring complex, sophisticated mathematical calculations use mainframes.

_____ 6. Most computers and electronic devices are analog, which use only two discrete states: on and off.

_____ 7. SLR cameras are much heavier and larger than point-and-shoot cameras.

_____ 8. Stick computers typically are less expensive than desktops and laptops.

_____ 9. Instead of the term, port, the term, connector, sometimes is used to identify audio and video ports.

_____ 10. Newer versions of USB are backward compatible, which means they support only new USB devices, not older ones.

_____ 11. A port replicator is an external device that provides connections to peripheral devices through ports built into the device.

_____ 12. NFC uses Wi-Fi signals to transmit data between two NFC-enabled devices.

Matching

Match the terms with their definitions.

_____ 1. CPU

_____ 2. fault-tolerant computer

_____ 3. kiosk

_____ 4. motherboard

_____ 5. peripheral device

_____ 6. phablet

_____ 7. push notification

_____ 8. server virtualization

_____ 9. slate tablet

_____ 10. thin client

a. term used to refer to a device that combines the features of a smartphone with a tablet

b. computer with duplicate components so that it can continue to operate when one of its main components fail

c. tablet that does not contain a physical keyboard

d. component you connect to a computer or mobile device to expand its capabilities

e. terminal that looks like a desktop but has limited capabilities and components

f. the use of software to enable a physical server to emulate the hardware and computing capabilities of one or more servers

g. electronic component that interprets and carries out the basic instructions that operate a computer

h. freestanding terminal that usually has a touchscreen for user input

i. message that initiates from a sending location without a request from the receiver

j. the main circuit board of a personal computer

The Problem Solving exercises extend your knowledge of module concepts by seeking solutions to practical problems with technology that you may encounter at home, school, or work. The Collaboration exercise should be completed with a team.

Problem Solving

Instructions: You often can solve problems with technology in multiple ways. Determine a solution to the problems in these exercises by using one or more resources available to you (such as a computer or mobile device, articles on the web or in print, blogs, podcasts, videos, television, user guides, other individuals, electronics or computer stores, etc.). Describe your solution, along with the resource(s) used, in the format requested by your instructor (brief report, presentation, discussion, blog post, video, or other means).

Personal

1. **Slow Computer Performance**   Your computer is running exceptionally slow. Not only does it take the operating system a long time to start, but programs also are not performing as well as they used to perform. How might you resolve this?

2. **Faulty ATM**   When using an ATM to deposit a check, the ATM misreads the amount of the check and credits your account the incorrect amount. What can you do to resolve this?

Source: Google

3. **Wearable Device Not Syncing**   Your wearable device synchronized with your smartphone this morning when you turned it on, but the two devices no longer are synchronized. What might be wrong, and what are your next steps?

4. **Battery Draining Quickly**   Although the battery on your smartphone is fully charged, it drains quickly. In some instances when the phone shows that the battery has 30% remaining, it shuts down immediately. What might be wrong?

5. **Potential Virus Infection**   While using your laptop, a message is displayed stating that your computer is infected with a virus and you should click a link to download a program designed to remove the virus. How will you respond?

Professional

6. **Excessive Phone Heat**   While using your smartphone, you notice that throughout the day it gets extremely hot, making it difficult to hold up to your ear. What steps can you take to correct this problem?

7. **Server Not Connecting**   While traveling on a business trip, your phone suddenly stops synchronizing your email messages, calendar information, and contacts. Upon further investigation, you notice an error message stating that your phone is unable to connect to the server. What are your next steps?

8. **Mobile Device Synchronization**   When you plug your smartphone into your computer to synchronize the data, the computer does not recognize that the smartphone is connected. What might be the problem?

9. **Cloud Service Provider**   Your company uses a cloud service provider to back up the data on each employee's computer. Your computer recently crashed, and you need to obtain the backup data to restore to your computer; however, you are unable to connect to the cloud service provider's website. What are your next steps?

10. **Connecting to a Projector**   Your boss asked you to give a presentation to your company's board of directors. When you enter the boardroom and attempt to connect your laptop to the projector, you realize that the cable to connect your laptop to the projector does not fit in any of the ports on your laptop. What are your next steps?

Collaboration

11. **Technology in Energy Management**   Your science instructor is teaching a lesson about how technology has advanced the energy management field. Form a team of three people to prepare a brief report about how technology and energy management are connected. One team member should research how computers play a role in conserving energy. Another team member should research other types of technology present in today's homes and buildings that can conserve energy, and the third team member should research other benefits (such as cost savings) resulting from proper energy management.

 How To: Your Turn

The How To: Your Turn exercises present general guidelines for fundamental skills when using a computer or mobile device and then require that you determine how to apply these general guidelines to a specific program or situation.

Instructions: You often can complete tasks using technology in multiple ways. Figure out how to perform the tasks described in these exercises by using one or more resources available to you (such as a computer or mobile device, articles on the web or in print, online or program help, user guides, blogs, podcasts, videos, other individuals, trial and error, etc.). Summarize your 'how to' steps, along with the resource(s) used, in the format requested by your instructor (brief report, presentation, discussion, blog post, video, or other means).

1 Synchronize a Device

Synchronizing a mobile device with the cloud or a computer provides a backup location for your data should your device fail, or become lost or stolen. While companies such as Google and Apple typically will allow you to download your purchased apps again free of charge, you also should synchronize your data so that it is available in the event a problem with your device arises. The following steps guide you through the process of synchronizing a device.

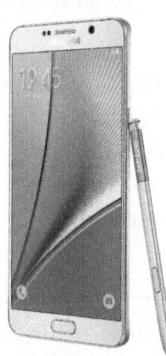

Courtesy of SAMSUNG

Synchronize with the Cloud

a. Search for an app compatible with your device that allows you to synchronize the data on your device with the cloud. Some device manufacturers, such as Apple, provide a service to synchronize your device with the cloud.
b. If necessary, download and install the app.
c. The first time you run the app, you may need to enter some personal information so that you are able to sign in and access your data in the future.
d. Configure the app to synchronize at your desired interval. If you are synchronizing a smartphone, keep in mind that synchronizing with the cloud will require a data plan. Be sure your data plan supports the amount of data that will be synchronized.
e. Once you have configured the synchronization settings successfully, select the option to manually synchronize your device at this time.

Synchronize with a Computer

a. Install and run the app designed to synchronize your device with your computer. For instance, iTunes is used to synchronize Apple devices with a computer.
b. Connect the device to the computer using the synchronization cable provided.
c. When the synchronization is complete, a message will inform you that it is safe to disconnect the device. Do not disconnect the device before the synchronization is complete, as that may damage the data on the device.

Retrieve Synchronized Data

If you lose your device or the data on your device, you can retrieve the data previously synchronized. To retrieve data synchronized previously, follow the instructions in the program or app used to synchronize your data.

Exercises

1. What type of device are you attempting to synchronize? What programs and apps are available to synchronize your device with the cloud? What programs and apps are available to synchronize your device with a computer?
2. Which program or app did you use to synchronize your device? Why did you choose that program or app instead of the others?
3. How long did it take to synchronize your device? What data on your device did the program or app synchronize?

2 Find, Download, and Read an E-Book on an E-Book Reader

Most e-book readers enable you to find and download new e-books without having to connect to a computer first. To search for and download an e-book, you need to establish an Internet connection through either Wi-Fi or a mobile data plan. The following steps guide you through the process of finding, downloading, and reading an e-book on an e-book reader.

a. Turn on your e-book reader and establish an Internet connection.
b. Navigate to the store on your e-book reader where you can search for and download e-books.
c. Locate the option to search available e-books and then enter the desired search text. You usually can search by the book's title, author, or genre.
d. Perform the search and then browse the search results for the book you want to download and install.
e. Select the option to download the book. Please note that many books cost money to download. If your payment information was entered previously, you may be charged for downloading this e-book. If you do not want to be charged, locate and download an e-book that is free.

How To: Your Turn

f. When the download is complete, return to your list of installed e-books.

g. Select the e-book you have just downloaded to read the e-book.

Exercises

1. What type of e-book reader do you have? Are you happy with the selection of e-books on your e-book reader?

2. In addition to e-book readers, what other types of devices allow you to read e-books?

3. Do e-books cost more or less than traditional print books? What are the advantages and disadvantages of using e-books?

iStockphoto.com / Petar Chernaev

③ Manage Power for Mobile Computers and Devices

Configuring power management settings on mobile computers and devices will help ensure your battery life is maximized. The following steps guide you through the process of configuring power management features on mobile computers and devices.

a. Display the Control Panel or Settings on your mobile computer or device.

b. Click the option to display power management or battery settings.

c. If necessary, select a power plan setting to view or modify.

d. Make the necessary adjustments to the settings that affect power consumption. For example, configure the display to dim or turn off after 30 seconds of inactivity. This will allow you enough time to read what is on the screen without having to touch the screen or move the mouse.

e. Save all changes.

Exercises

1. What power management settings have you configured on your mobile computer or device?

2. Compare battery life on your device before and after configuring power management settings. Have you noticed an improvement in battery life? If so, how vmuch?

3. What other power management settings are you able to configure on your mobile computer or device?

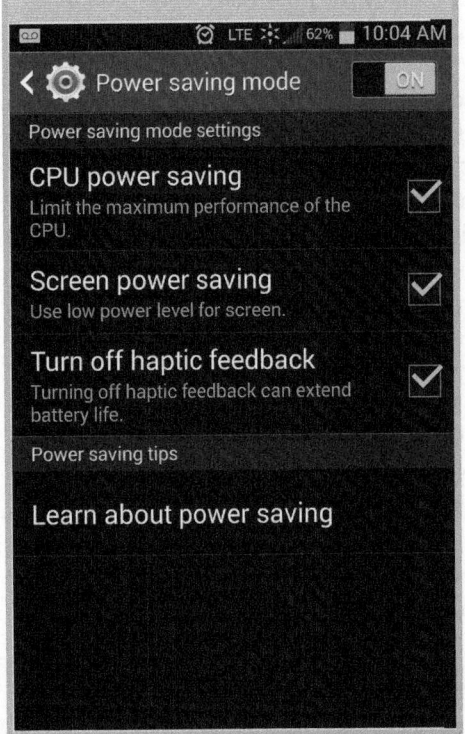

Google Inc.

✹ Internet Research

The Internet Research exercises broaden your understanding of module concepts by requiring that you search for information on the web.

Instructions: Use a search engine or another search tool to locate the information requested or answers to questions presented in the exercises. Describe your findings, along with the search term(s) you used and your web source(s), in the format requested by your instructor (brief report, presentation, discussion, blog post, video, or other means).

1 Making Use of the Web
Retail and Auctions

E-retailers are changing the ways consumers shop for goods. One market research firm reports that nearly three-fourths of shoppers complete one-half of all their transactions online. As shoppers grow increasingly loyal to e-commerce, retail websites have become more sophisticated, and brick-and-mortar stores have adapted to the online presence. Approximately 90 percent of smartphone owners use their devices to compare prices, locate promotional offers, and determine directions and store hours.

Online auctions offer another convenient method of shopping for and selling practically anything imaginable. Most auction sites organize products in categories and provide photos and descriptions. eBay is one of thousands of Internet auction websites and is the world's largest personal online trading community. In addition, craigslist is a free online equivalent of classified advertisements.

Research This: (a) Visit two retail websites and search for the latest e-book readers. Which features do these websites offer compared with the same offerings in brick-and-mortar stores? What are the advantages and disadvantages of shopping online? What policies do these websites offer for returning items? Which items have you purchased online?

(b) Visit an auction website and search for two objects pertaining to your favorite musical artist, sports team, or celebrity. For example, search for an autographed photo or ticket stubs. Describe these two items. How many people have bid on these items? Who are the sellers? What are the opening and current bids?

Source: eBay

2 Social Media
Product Ratings and Reviews

Businesses know that using social media is an efficient and effective method of building brand loyalty and promoting the exchange of ideas. The informal communication between consumers and company representatives can help maintain credibility and promote trust. According to a recent study, more than 70 percent of American Internet users visit online social networks, and 65 percent of these people discover particular brands, products, and services by reading material posted on these websites. Twitter, Facebook, and other social media often are used to befriend customers, give a positive feeling about services and goods, engage readers, and market new ideas. Subscribers share their opinions, thoughts, and experiences, either positive or negative, through product and service reviews.

Research This: Visit at least three Twitter, Facebook, or other online social network sites and review the content. How many Twitter followers or Facebook 'likes' does the website have? Identify three organizations, businesses, products, or causes that have a presence on Facebook, Twitter, or other online social networks. How many followers or fans do they have? Which posts are engaging and promote positive attitudes about the company and the products or services offered? How many user-generated reviews and product ratings are shown? How do the online social networks encourage sharing opinions? In which ways do the companies respond to and interact with followers and fans? If negative posts are written, does the company respond professionally and positively?

3 Search Skills
Search Operators

Search engines provide operators, or special symbols, that will help narrow down search results. Use quotation marks around search text to search for an exact word or phrase. For example, type the following as your search text: "wireless communications technologies" (be sure to include the quotation marks) to search for those three words in that exact order. Search results will display matching pages with the quoted search phrase highlighted or in bold.

To match one or more words in a phrase, you can use an asterisk (*), also called a wildcard operator, as part of your search text. Each asterisk represents one or more

Internet Research

words. For example, type the following as your search text: "wireless * technologies" (with the quotation marks) to find search results that match wireless communications technologies, wireless Internet technologies, wireless and related technologies, and others. If you are searching for a phrase or quotation with many words, consider using the asterisk wildcard operator in place of some of the words in the search text. This technique is useful if you have a quotation, and you want to find out who said it or where it may have appeared.

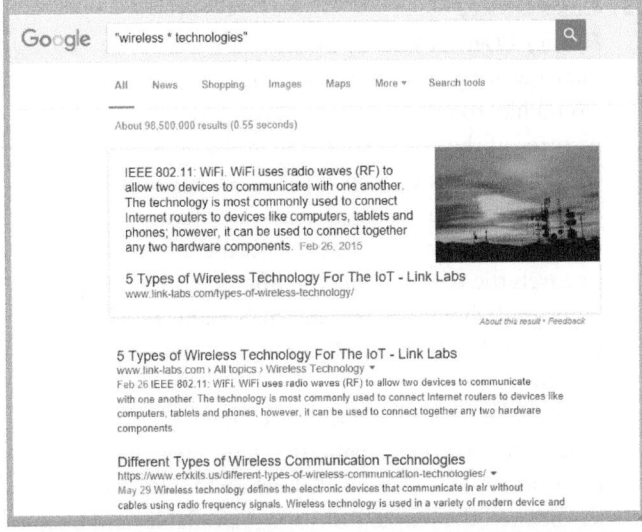

Source: Google

Research This: Create search queries using quotation marks and/or the wildcard operator to answer the following questions and use a search engine to find the answers. (1) Someone once said, "Life is not fair, get used to it." Who was it? (2) What are three websites containing digital camera reviews? (3) How do businesses use near field communications? (4) Find five different words that complete the phrase, handheld ___ devices, by typing appropriate search text into a search engine.

❹ Security
Surge Protection

Surge protectors and uninterruptible power supplies offer protection from electrical power surges, as you learned in the Protecting Hardware section of this module. While these surges are part of everyday life, they are more likely to occur during thunderstorms and peak energy consumption periods. These unavoidable occurrences can damage or ruin sensitive electronic equipment. The processor in a computer is particularly sensitive to the fluctuations in current. When shopping for a surge protector, purchase the best product you can afford. Typically, the amount of protection offered by a surge protector is proportional to its cost. That is, the more expensive the surge protector, the more protection it offers.

Research This: Visit an electronics store or view websites with a variety of surge protectors from several manufacturers. Read the packaging or specifications to determine many of the features. Compare at least three surge protectors by creating a table using these headings: manufacturer, model, price, Joule rating (a Joule is the unit of energy the device can absorb before it can be damaged; the higher the Joule rating, the better the protection), warranty, energy-absorption rating, response time, and other features. Which surge protector do you recommend? Why?

❺ Cloud Services Data
Providers and Mashups (DaaS)

The web has made it possible for many information providers to make business, housing, weather, demographic, and other data available on demand to third parties. Accessing online data on demand is an example of DaaS (data as a service), a service of cloud computing that provides current data over the Internet for download, analysis, or use in new applications.

Mashups are apps that combine data from one or more online data providers. Mapping mashups are popular because users can visualize locations associated with data originating from a variety of online sources, including real estate listings, crime statistics, current Tweets, live traffic conditions, or digital photos.

Research This: (1) Use a search engine to find two different online data markets. Write a report sharing the sources or focus of information each provides, the availability of visualization tools to preview data, and how developers can access or incorporate the data into their own apps and websites. (2) Use a search engine to find a popular mapping mashup based on data from one of the sources listed above, or another topic. Identify the provider of the data and the provider of the maps on which the data is displayed. (3) Use a search engine to find an app or website that will help you create your own map mashup showing locations of your online data: Facebook friends, Flickr or Instagram photos, or Tweets. Take a screenshot of the mashup you made.

✳ Critical Thinking

The Critical Thinking exercises challenge your assessment and decision-making skills by presenting real-world situations associated with module concepts. The Collaboration exercise should be completed with a team.

Instructions: Evaluate the situations below, using personal experiences and one or more resources available to you (such as articles on the web or in print, blogs, podcasts, videos, television, user guides, other individuals, electronics or computer stores, etc.). Perform the tasks requested in each exercise and share your deliverables in the format requested by your instructor (brief report, presentation, discussion, blog post, video, or other means).

1. Technology Purchases

You are the director of information technology at a company that specializes in designing and selling customizable sportswear for local high school and college sports teams. Most of the technology equipment is out of date and must be replaced. You need to evaluate the requirements of individual employees so that you can order replacements.

Do This: Determine the type of computer or mobile device that might be most appropriate for the following employees: a graphic designer who exclusively works in the office, a cashier who is responsible for assisting customers with purchases, and a sales representative who travels to various locations and needs wireless communications capabilities. Consider the varying requirements of each, including mobility, security, and processing capabilities. Discuss various options that might work for each user, and considerations when purchasing each type of device.

2. Game Devices

You manage a youth recreation center and have been given a grant to purchase a game console and accessories, along with fitness games, for use at the center.

Do This: Use the web to research three popular recent game consoles. Choose five characteristics to compare the game consoles, such as Internet capabilities, multiplayer game support, storage capacity, television connection, and game controllers. Research fitness games for each console and what accessories are needed to run the games. Determine the goals of each game, such as skill-building, weight loss, or entertainment. Read user reviews of each game, as well

as professional reviews by gaming industry experts. If possible, survey your friends and classmates to learn about their experiences with each game, such as heart rate while playing the games, any fitness goals reached, and their enjoyment of the game.

3. Case Study

Family-Owned Coffee Shop You are the new manager for a family-owned coffee shop. The owners would like to purchase a digital camera to upload pictures of the coffee shop, its products, and its employees to its Facebook page and its website.

Do This: You need to prepare information about digital camera options to present to the owners. First, research the cost and quality differences between point-and-shoot cameras and SLR cameras. Use the web to find a recent model of both camera types and compare the reviews, as well as the costs, for each. Make a list of additional features, such as video capabilities, editing capabilities, lens, megapixels, GPS, flash, and zoom. Determine how each camera stores the images, the amount of storage available, and how to transfer images to a computer or mobile device. Explore whether software is included with the camera that can be used to edit, store, or organize the images after they are transferred to a computer. Compare your findings with the camera capabilities of a recent model smartphone. Determine what type of camera would be best for the coffee shop's needs and the capabilities that are most important.

Courtesy of Samsung

Collaboration

4. **National Security Uses for Technology**   Technology is an integral part of military operations. Many military research projects use simulators that resemble civilian computer games. Your company has been contacted by the Department of Defense for a research project.

Do This: Form a four-member team, and then form two two-member groups. Assign each group one of the following topics to research: (1) How have mobile computers and cloud computing affected issues of national security? (2) How can the utilization of microchips worn by soldiers, or wearable computers, be integrated into civilian use? Meet with your team and discuss your findings. Determine any advantages or disadvantages, as well as any legal ramifications that may arise.

Programs and Apps: Productivity, Graphics, Security, and Other Tools

4

sdecoret / Shutterstock.com

OBJECTIVES

After completing this module, you will be able to:

1. Identify the general categories of programs and apps
2. Describe how an operating system interacts with applications and hardware
3. Differentiate among the ways you can acquire programs and apps: retail, custom, web app, mobile app, mobile web app, shareware, freeware, open source, and public-domain
4. Identify the key features of productivity applications: word processing, presentation, spreadsheet, database, note taking, text editor, calendar and contact management, project management, accounting, personal finance, legal, tax preparation, document conversion and readers, and enterprise computing
5. Identify the key features of graphics and media applications: computer-aided design, desktop publishing, paint/image editing, photo editing and photo management, video and audio editing, multimedia and website authoring, media player, and augmented and virtual reality
6. Identify the uses of personal interest applications: lifestyle, medical, entertainment, convenience, and education
7. Identify the purpose of software used in communications
8. Identify the key features of security tools: personal firewall, antivirus programs, malware removers, and Internet filters
9. Identify the key features of file, disk, and system management tools: file manager, search, image viewer, uninstaller, disk cleanup, disk defragmenter, screen saver, file compression, PC maintenance, backup and restore, and power management

Programs and Apps

Using programs and apps, you can accomplish a variety of tasks on computers and mobile devices (Figure 4-1). Recall from Module 1 that a **program**, or **software**, consists of a series of related instructions, organized for a common purpose, that tells the computer what tasks to perform and how to perform them. An **application**, or **app**, sometimes called *application software*, consists of programs designed to make users more productive and/or assist them with personal tasks.

An *operating system* is a set of programs that coordinates all the activities among computer or mobile device hardware. Other programs, often called *tools* or *utilities*, enable you to perform maintenance-type tasks usually related to managing devices, media, and programs used by computers and mobile devices. The operating system and other tools are collectively known as *system software* because they consist of the programs that control or maintain the operations of the computer and its devices.

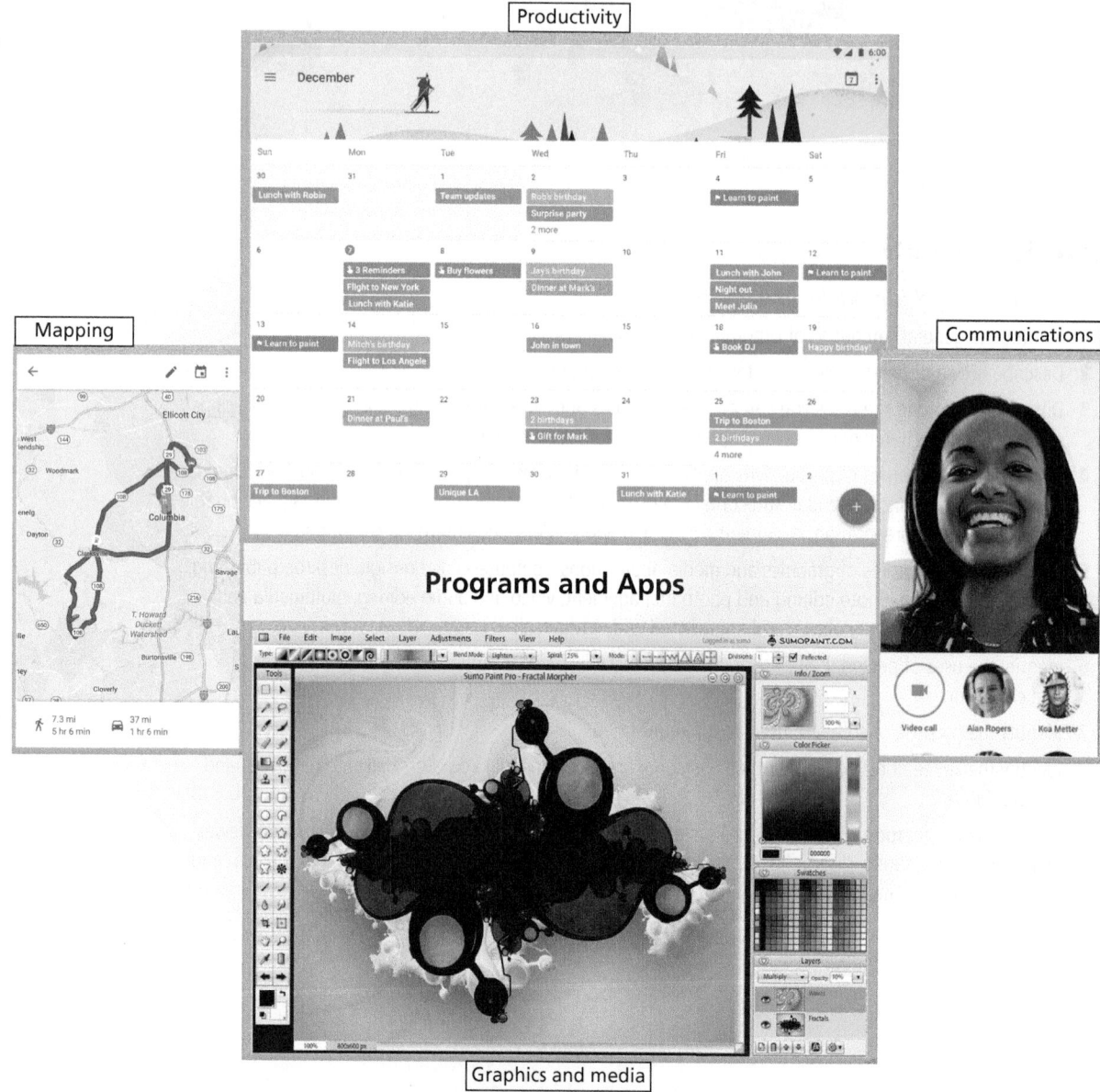

Figure 4-1   Users work with a variety of programs and apps, some of which are shown in this figure.
Source: Google, Sumopaint

Role of the Operating System

To use applications, such as a browser or word processing program, on a desktop or laptop, your computer must be running an operating system. Similarly, a mobile device must be running an operating system to run a mobile app, such as a navigation or messaging app. Desktop operating systems include macOS, Windows, Linux, and Chrome OS. Mobile operating systems include Android, iOS, and Windows (Mobile Edition). The operating system, therefore, serves as the interface between the user, the applications and other programs, and the computer's or mobile device's hardware (Figure 4-2).

An Example of How an Operating System Interacts with a User, an Application, and Hardware

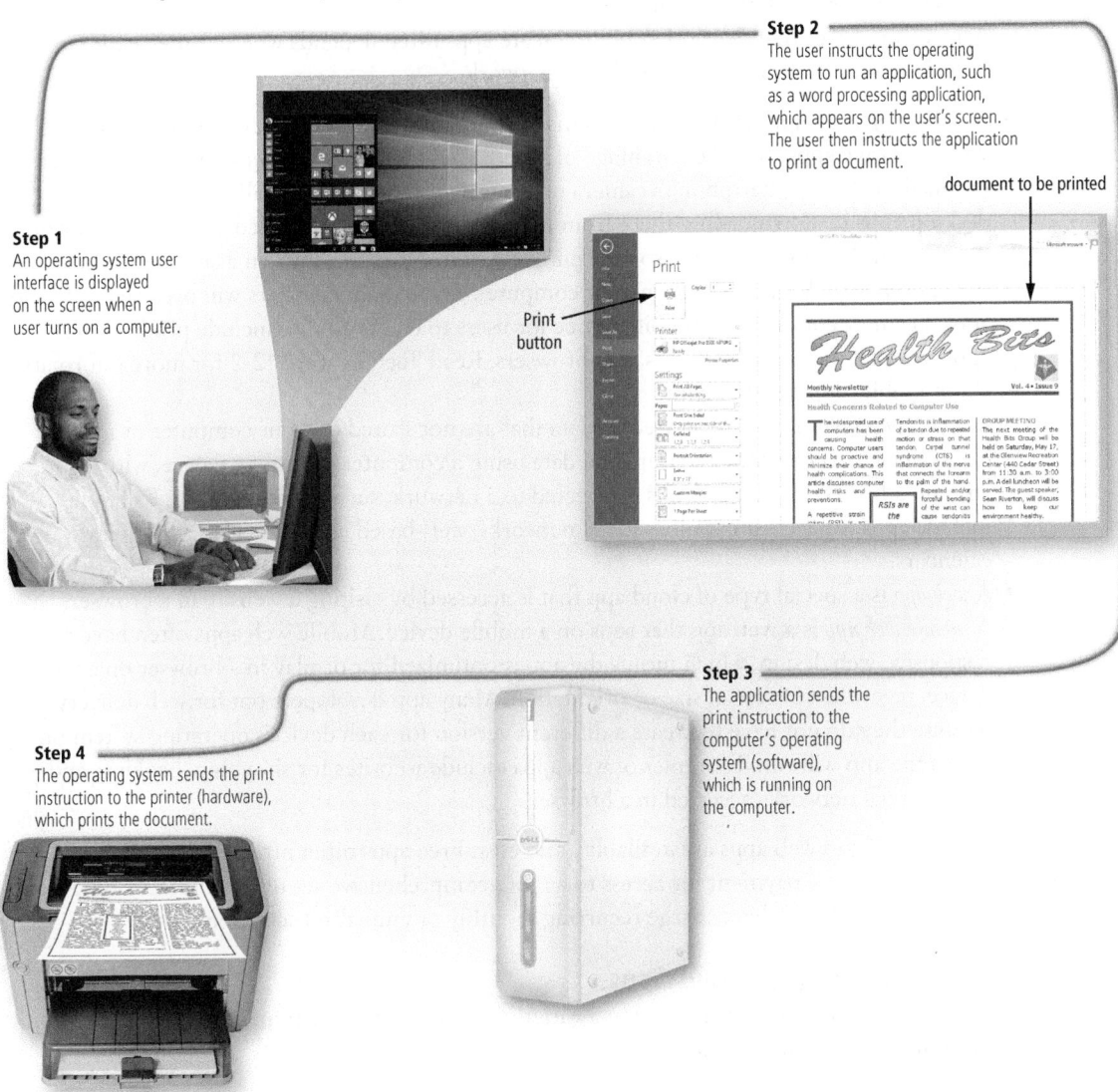

Step 2
The user instructs the operating system to run an application, such as a word processing application, which appears on the user's screen. The user then instructs the application to print a document.

document to be printed

Step 1
An operating system user interface is displayed on the screen when a user turns on a computer.

Print button

Step 3
The application sends the print instruction to the computer's operating system (software), which is running on the computer.

Step 4
The operating system sends the print instruction to the printer (hardware), which prints the document.

Figure 4-2   This figure shows how the operating system is the interface between the user, the application(s) and other programs, and the hardware.

photoguy_76 / Fotolia LLC; restyler / Shutterstock.com; StockLite / Shutterstock.com; Source: Microsoft

Each time you start a computer or mobile device, the operating system is loaded (copied) from the computer's hard drive or mobile device's storage media into memory. Once the operating system is loaded, it coordinates all the activities of the computer or mobile device. This includes running applications and transferring data among input and output devices and memory. While the computer or mobile device is running, the operating system remains in memory.

Interacting with Programs and Apps

Developers create software for specific computers or devices (desktop or mobile), and distribute software as native apps, cloud apps, or web apps, depending on requirements for how users will interact with them. A *desktop app* runs on a desktop or laptop computer. A *mobile app* runs on a mobile device.

Recall from Module 1 that you usually do not need to install desktop or mobile apps on a compatible computer or mobile device. Installing is the process of setting up the software to work with a computer or mobile device and its connected hardware. Mobile apps typically install automatically after you download them from the device's app store. You usually do not need to install web apps before you can use them, but you may need to install plug-ins, such as Java or Flash, so that they work in your browser.

The technologies that developers use to create apps often depends whether they will be installed on a user's device or accessed via a network.

- A *native app* is an app written for a specific platform and installed on a computer or mobile device. Native apps can take advantage of specific features of the devices on which they are installed, such as a smartphone's camera or contacts list. You may install native mobile or desktop apps by downloading them from an app store, sometimes called a *marketplace*, or other location on the Internet. You also may purchase native desktop apps on a storage medium, such as CD or DVD, to install on your computer. Some manufacturers will preinstall selected apps on a new computer or mobile device for users to try. Examples include productivity applications, single-player games, and browsers. Read Tech Feature 12-2 for more information about mobile app development.
- A *cloud app* makes use of software and data that are not stored on your computer or mobile device. You can access the software and data using a computer or mobile device, with or without a browser, as long as it is connected to a network, such as the Internet. Examples include apps for accessing online social networks, web-based email services, and online calendars.
- A *web app* is a special type of cloud app that is accessed by visiting a website in a browser.
- A *mobile web app* is a web app that runs on a mobile device. Mobile web apps often have a responsive web design, which means the app is optimized for display in a browser on a mobile device, regardless of screen size or orientation. Many app developers opt for web delivery because they do not have to create a different version for each device's operating system on which the app will run. Examples of web apps include websites for shopping, banking, and online social networks accessed in a browser.

Many cloud and web apps are available at no cost. Free apps often provide access to basic features and require payment for access to a more comprehensive set of capabilities. Some charge a one-time fee, while others charge recurring monthly or annual subscription fees.

Distributing Programs and Apps

Programs and apps are distributed in a variety of forms: retail, custom, shareware, freeware, open source, and public domain.

- *Retail software* is mass-produced, copyrighted software that meets the needs of a wide variety of users, not just a single user or company. Some retail software, such as an operating system, is preinstalled on new computers and mobile devices. You also can purchase retail software from local stores and on the web. With online purchases, you may be able to download purchased programs immediately instead of waiting for the software to arrive by mail.
- *Custom software* performs functions specific to a business or industry. Sometimes a company cannot locate retail software that meets its unique requirements. In this case, the company may hire software developers to create specialized custom software. Custom software usually costs more than retail software.

BTW

Trial Versions
Some retail and other programs have a *trial version*, which is an application you can use at no charge for a limited time to see if it meets your needs. Some trial versions have limited functionality.

- *Shareware* is copyrighted software that is distributed at no cost for a trial period. To use a shareware program beyond that period, you send payment to the software developer, or you might be billed automatically unless you cancel within a specified period of time. Some developers trust users to send payment if software use extends beyond the stated trial period. Others render the software useless if no payment is received after the trial period expires. In some cases, a scaled-down version of the software is distributed free, and payment entitles the user to the fully functional product.
- *Freeware* is copyrighted software provided at no cost by an individual or a company that retains all rights to the software. Thus, software developers typically cannot incorporate freeware in applications they intend to sell. The word, free, in freeware indicates the software has no charge.
- *Open source software* is software provided for use, modification, and redistribution. This software may have restrictions from the copyright holder regarding modification of the software's internal instructions and its redistribution. For example, developers may be required to provide the source code when distributing an application and may be restricted from charging a fee to those who use it. Open source software usually can be downloaded from a web server on the Internet, often at no cost. Promoters of open source software state two main advantages: a community of developers contribute enhancements to the software for all to use, and customers can personalize the software to meet their needs.
- *Public-domain software* has been donated for public use and has no copyright restrictions. Anyone can copy or distribute public-domain software to others at no cost.

 BTW
Copyright
A copyright gives authors, artists, and other creators of original work exclusive rights to duplicate, publish, and sell their materials.

 CONSIDER THIS

What is software as a service?
Software as a service (*SaaS*) describes a model for distributing software in which a software provider hosts applications on a server and makes them available to users via the Internet. The server can be configured with additional processing or storage capabilities as needs increase. SaaS providers often deliver their applications as cloud apps. Editing projects or photos, sending email messages, and managing finances are common consumer tasks with SaaS. For an exercise related to SaaS, see the Internet Research: Cloud Services exercise at the end of this module.

 BTW
Syncing Apps
When you install an app on one computer or device, it also will install automatically on any other computers and devices on the same subscription plan.

Thousands of shareware, freeware, and public-domain programs are available from websites on the Internet for users to download. Examples include communications, graphics, and game programs. Read Secure IT 4-1 for tips about safely downloading shareware, freeware, or public-domain software.

 SECURE IT 4-1

Downloading Software and Apps Safely
Websites and app stores tempt potential customers with catchy offers for software promising to speed up their computers or to obtain the latest versions of games and music. The temptation to download shareware, freeware, and public-domain software is high, especially when the cost of such useful or fun programs or apps is free or extremely reasonable. This action could be dangerous, however, because some programs or apps may contain viruses, malware, or adware just waiting to be installed on an unsuspecting user's computer or mobile device.

Before downloading any software, consider these factors when downloading shareware, freeware, or public-domain software:

- Choose apps from Google Play for Android devices or the App Store for Apple devices. These stores require apps to pass rigorous tests before they are published. Choose software from reputable shareware, freeware, and public-domain download websites that offer products for your computer or device.
- Be wary of apps that do not have many reviews or apps that were added recently, unless you can verify the developer or publisher. Search for reviews from reputable websites.

Obtain the latest versions of shareware, freeware, and public-domain software and apps. Many developers update their programs frequently in an effort to include new features and to thwart viruses. If you follow these tips, you may find some of the best software bargains in the marketplace.

⚙ **Consider This:** Look for a popular game for your computer or mobile device from an app store or through shareware, freeware, or public-domain software download websites. What information might persuade you that it is safe to install? Did you ever unknowingly install software that contained a virus or malware? How did you discover and then remedy the situation?

Installing and Updating Programs and Apps

During installation of software or before the first use, a program or app may ask you to register and/or activate the software. *Software registration* typically is optional and usually involves submitting your name and other personal information to the software manufacturer or developer. Registering the software often entitles you to product support. *Product activation* is a technique that some software manufacturers use to ensure that you do not install the software on more computers than legally licensed. Usually, the software can be run a preset number of times, has limited functionality, or does not function until you activate it via the Internet or by phone. Thus, activation is a required process for programs that request it. Some software allows multiple activations; for example, you can install it and run it on a laptop and a desktop at the same time. Registering and/or activating software also usually entitles you to free program updates for a specified time period, such as a year.

Many desktop and mobile apps use an *automatic update* feature, where the updates can be configured to download and install automatically. With web apps, by contrast, you always access the latest version when you run it in a browser.

 CONSIDER THIS

What is a license agreement?

A *license agreement*, sometimes called an end-user license agreement (*EULA*), is the right to use a program or app. The license agreement provides specific conditions for use of the software, which a user typically must accept before using the software (Figure 4-3). Unless otherwise specified by a license agreement, you do not have the right to copy, loan, borrow, rent, or in any way distribute programs or apps. Doing so is a violation of copyright law; it also is a federal crime.

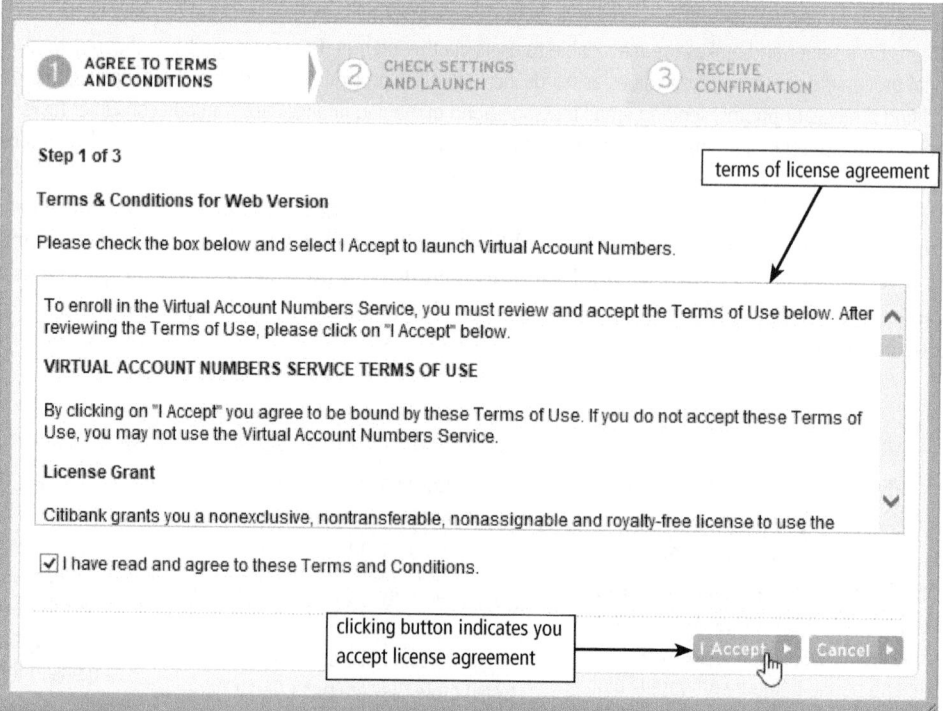

Figure 4-3   A user must accept the terms in a license agreement before using the software.
Source: Citigroup Inc.

Categories of Programs and Apps

With programs and apps, you can work on a variety of projects — such as creating letters, memos, reports, and other documents; developing presentations; preparing and filing taxes; drawing and altering images; recording and enhancing audio and video clips; obtaining directions or maps; playing games individually or with others; composing email messages; protecting computers and mobile devices from malware; organizing media; locating files; and much more. Table 4-1 categorizes popular categories of programs and apps by their general use.

Table 4-1 Programs and Apps by Category	
Category	**Types of Programs and Apps**
Productivity (Business and Personal)	• Word Processing • Accounting • Presentation • Personal Finance • Spreadsheet • Legal • Database • Tax Preparation • Note Taking • Document Management • Calendar and Contact Management • Support Services • Project Management • Enterprise Computing
Graphics and Media	• Computer-Aided Design (CAD) • Video and Audio Editing • Desktop Publishing • Multimedia and Website Authoring • Paint/Image Editing • Media Player • Photo Editing and Photo Management • Augmented and Virtual Reality • Clip Art/Image Gallery
Personal Interest	• Lifestyle • Entertainment • Mapping • Convenience • Medical • Education
Communications	• Blog • File Transfer • Browser • Internet Phone • Chat Room • Internet Messaging • Online Discussion • Mobile Messaging • Email • Videoconference
Security	• Personal Firewall • Malware Removers • Antivirus • Internet Filters
File, Disk, and System Management	• File Manager • Screen Saver • Search • File Compression • Image Viewer • PC Maintenance • Uninstaller • Backup and Restore • Disk Cleanup • Power Management • Disk Defragmenter

✳ **CONSIDER THIS**

Are the categories of programs and apps shown in Table 4-1 mutually exclusive?
Programs and apps listed in one category may be used in other categories. For example, photo editing applications, which appear in the graphics and media category, often also are used for business or personal productivity. Additionally, the programs and apps in the last three categories (communications; security; and file, disk, and system management) often are used in conjunction with or to support programs and apps in the first three categories (productivity, graphics and media, and personal interest). For example, email appears in the communications category but also is a productivity application.

Productivity Applications

Productivity applications can assist you in becoming more effective and efficient while performing daily activities at work, school, and home. Productivity applications include word processing, presentation, spreadsheet, database, note taking, calendar and contact management, project management, accounting, personal finance, legal, tax preparation, document management, and enterprise computing.

A variety of manufacturers offer productivity apps in each of these areas, ranging from desktop to mobile to web and cloud apps. Many have a desktop version and a corresponding mobile version adapted for smaller screen sizes and/or touch screens.

Developing Projects

With productivity applications, users often create, edit, format, save, and share projects. Projects include documents, presentations, spreadsheets, notes, calendars, contact lists, budgets, drawings, and more.

During the process of developing a project, you likely will switch back and forth among the following activities.

1. When you *create* a project, you enter text or numbers, insert images, add contacts, schedule appointments, and perform other tasks using a variety of input methods, such as a keyboard, a mouse, touch, or voice.
2. To *edit* a project means to make changes to its existing content. Common editing tasks include inserting, deleting, cutting, copying, and pasting.
   a. Inserting involves adding text, images, or other content.
   b. Deleting involves removing text, images, or other content.
   c. Cutting is the process of removing content and storing it in a temporary storage location, called a *clipboard*.
   d. Copying is the process of placing content on a clipboard, with the content remaining in the project. Read Ethics & Issues 4-1 for a discussion about unethical copying.
   e. Pasting is the process of transferring content from a clipboard to a specific location in a project.

BTW

Keyboard Shortcuts
In many desktop apps, you can use keyboard shortcuts for cut, copy, and paste commands, instead of selecting those items from a graphical user interface. Press CTRL+X for cut, CTRL+C for copy, and CTRL+V for paste in Windows, or press COMMAND+X for cut, COMMAND+C for copy, and COMMAND+V for paste, on computers running macOS.

⊛ ETHICS & ISSUES 4-1

What Can Schools and Employers Do to Prevent Internet Plagiarism?
The Internet has made it easier for students and employees to plagiarize; in contrast, it also provides tools that schools and employers can use to detect illegal copying. Schools often have specific rules about what constitutes plagiarism. Employees, such as journalists, are expected to follow ethical guidelines when copying or citing content.

The Internet offers many ways for students to cheat intentionally, including websites that allow you to purchase a research paper. Students may not realize that copying information without properly citing it also is plagiarism. Students who intentionally plagiarize

blame competition. Teachers have several tools to catch plagiarists, including services that compare papers to others on the Internet and produce a report highlighting content resembling previously published writing.

A journalist might be expected not only to produce multiple articles daily, but also to use social media to keep readers engaged. This pressure tempts some journalists to copy content, sometimes without giving credit or linking to the original source. The laws against plagiarism are the same whether copying content from a respected news source, a personal blog, or social media. The pressures of time and expectations of content can create high-profile cases of plagiarism that affect not

only the journalist but the news source for which he or she writes.

Some argue that the best way to prevent cheating is to educate. First, teach the values and discuss the consequences of cheating. Next, teach how to cite sources properly and summarize information. Before copying or paraphrasing another person's work, contact him or her to request permission. When in doubt, check with a librarian, editor, or instructor.

⊛ **Consider This:** How should educators and employers deal with plagiarism? Should schools use a paper-comparison service in an attempt to stop cheating? Why or why not? Does linking to the original source excuse a journalist who copies content? Why or why not?

3. When users *format* a project, they change its appearance. Formatting is important because the overall look of a project significantly can affect its capability to communicate information clearly. Examples of formatting tasks are changing the font, font size, and font style (Figure 4-4).

   a. A *font* is a name assigned to a specific design of characters. Cambria and Calibri are examples of fonts.

   b. *Font size* indicates the size of the characters in a particular font. Font size is gauged by a measurement system called points. A single point is about 1/72 of an inch in height.

   c. A *font style* adds emphasis to a font. Bold, italic, underline, and color are examples of font styles.

4. During the process of creating, editing, and formatting a project, the computer or mobile device holds it in memory. To keep the project for future use requires that you save it. When you *save* a project, the computer transfers the project from memory to a local storage medium, such as a USB flash drive or hard drive, or the cloud, so that you can retrieve it later.

5. You can distribute a project as a hard copy or electronically. A *hard copy* is information that exists on a physical medium, such as paper. To generate a hard copy, you *print* a project. Sending electronic files via email or posting them for others to view, on websites for example, saves paper and printer supplies. Many users opt for electronic distribution because it contributes to green computing.

Figure 4-4   The Cambria and Calibri fonts are shown in two font sizes and a variety of font styles.

⚙ CONSIDER THIS

How are productivity web apps different from productivity desktop apps?

Some word processing, spreadsheet, and presentation software applications are available as web apps. These online versions often have limited functionality compared to their desktop counterparts. They allow users to share projects with other users and enable many users to edit them at the same time.

Online productivity apps save your work on the cloud instantly as you type. Both the apps and the documents created with them are stored on the cloud. In contrast, desktop apps are installed on your computer. Documents created with desktop apps may be stored on your computer, on the cloud, or synchronized between both locations. Many desktop productivity programs have an AutoSave feature that automatically saves open projects to your computer's storage at specified time intervals, such as every 10 minutes. Saving your work frequently ensures that the majority of your work will not be lost in the event of a system failure or power loss.

 **CONSIDER THIS**

What is a clip art/image gallery?

Applications often include a **clip art/image gallery**, which is a collection of clip art and photos. Many clip art/image galleries also provide fonts, animations, sounds, video clips, and audio clips. You can use the images, fonts, and other items from the clip art/image gallery in all types of projects, including documents, brochures, worksheets, and slide shows.

Word Processing

Word processing software, sometimes called a word processor, is an application that allows users to create and manipulate documents containing text and sometimes graphics (Figure 4-5). People use word processing software to develop documents such as letters, memos, reports, mailing labels, and newsletters.

Word processing software has many features to create professional and visually appealing documents. For example, you can change the font, size, and color of characters; apply special effects, such as three-dimensional shadows; use built-in styles to format documents; and organize text in newspaper-style columns.

Word processing software allows users to incorporate graphics, such as digital photos and clip art, in documents. In Figure 4-5, a user inserted an image of a tractor in the document.

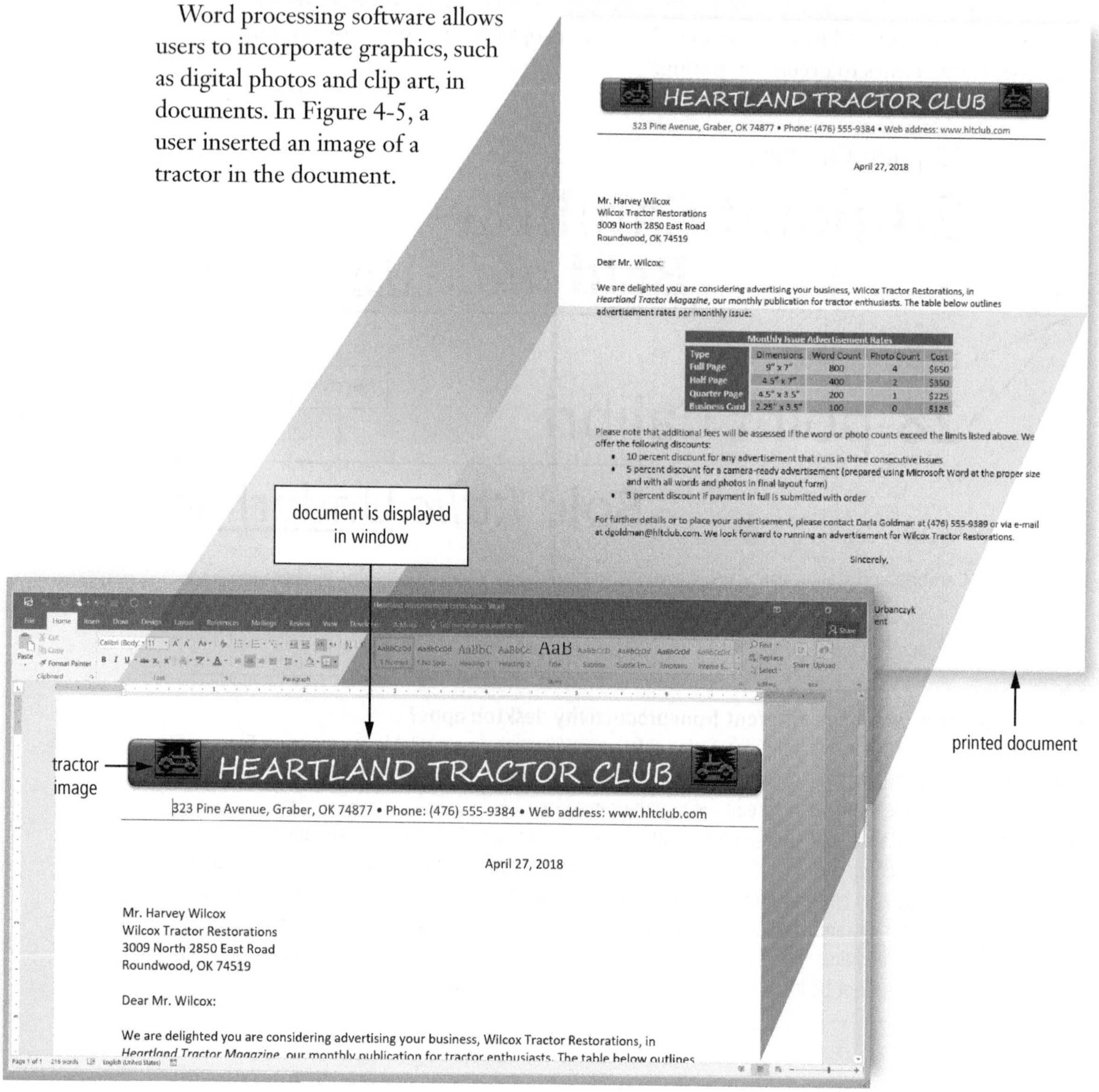

document is displayed in window

printed document

tractor image

Figure 4-5 Word processing software enables users to create professional and visually appealing documents.

Source: Microsoft

With word processing software, you easily can modify the appearance of an image after inserting it in the document.

The page setup feature of word processing software allows you to define the size of the paper on which to print and to specify the margins. A feature, called wordwrap, allows users to type words in a paragraph continually without pressing the ENTER key at the end of each line. While you edit a paragraph or change the paragraph margins, the words in the paragraph automatically wrap, or reflow, within the paragraph. As you type more lines of text than can be displayed on the screen, the top portion of the document moves upward, or scrolls, off the screen.

Word processing software typically includes tools to assist you with the writing process. For example, a spelling checker reviews the document for spelling errors. A grammar checker detects passive voice, run-on sentences, and grammatical errors. A format checker identifies extraneous spaces, capitalization errors, and more. A bibliography tool can generate and format a bibliography from information provided about references cited in a paper.

Presentation

Presentation software is an application that allows users to create visual aids for presentations to communicate ideas, messages, and other information to a group. The presentations can be viewed as slides, sometimes called a *slide show*, that are displayed on a large monitor or on a projection screen from a computer or mobile device.

Presentation software typically provides a variety of predefined presentation formats that suggest complementary colors for backgrounds, text, and graphical accents on the slides. This software also provides a variety of layouts for each slide, such as a title slide, a two-column slide, a slide with clip art, a chart, a table, or a diagram, along with tools for arranging text in various configurations (Figure 4-6).

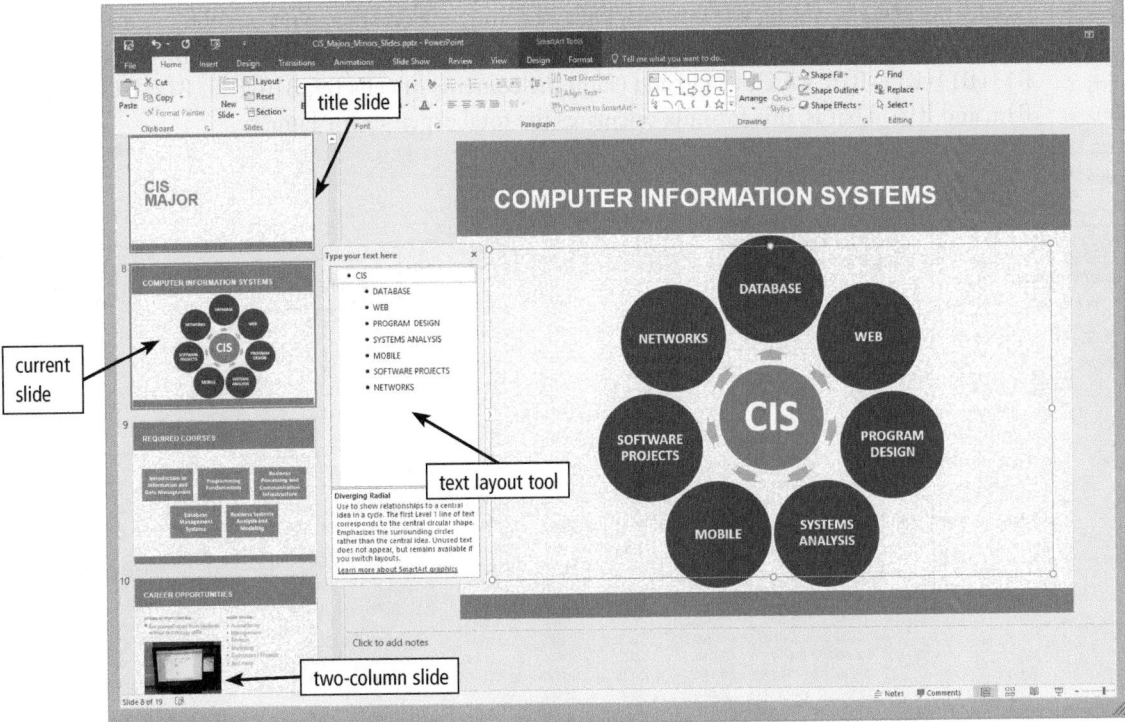

Figure 4-6 Presentation software provides tools for creating slides with content arranged in a variety of formats.
Source: Courtesy of Mark Frydenberg; Microsoft

When building a presentation, users can set the slide timing so that the presentation automatically displays the next slide after a preset delay. Presentation software allows you to apply special effects to the transition between slides. One slide, for example, might fade away as the next slide appears.

Presentation software typically includes images, photos, video clips, and audio clips to enhance presentations. Some presentation software offers a media search tool to help users locate online images or videos to include in their slides.

You can view or print a finished presentation in a variety of formats, including a hard copy outline of text from each slide and handouts that show completed slides. Presentation software also incorporates features such as checking spelling, formatting, researching, and creating webpages from existing slide shows.

Spreadsheet

Spreadsheet software is an application that allows users to organize data in columns and rows and perform calculations on the data. These columns and rows collectively are called a **worksheet**. Most spreadsheet software has basic features to help users create, edit, and format worksheets. A spreadsheet file also is known as a workbook because it can contain thousands of related individual worksheets. Data is organized vertically in columns and horizontally in rows on each worksheet (Figure 4-7).

Each worksheet usually can have thousands of columns and rows. One or more letters identify each column, and a number identifies each row. Only a small fraction of these columns and rows are visible on the screen at one time. Scrolling through the worksheet displays different parts of it on the screen.

A cell is the intersection of a column and row. The spreadsheet software identifies cells by the column and row in which they are located. For example, the intersection of column B and row 4 is referred to as cell B4. As shown in Figure 4-7, cell B4 contains the number, $1,000.29, which represents the wages for January.

Many of the worksheet cells shown in Figure 4-7 contain a number, called a value, that can be used in a calculation. Other cells, however, contain formulas that calculate values. A formula performs calculations on the data in the worksheet and displays the resulting value in a cell, usually the cell containing the formula. When creating a worksheet, you can enter your own formulas. In Figure 4-7, for example, cell B17 could contain the formula =B9+B10+B11+B12+B13+B14+B15+B16, which would add (sum) the contents of cells B9, B10, B11, B12, B13, B14, B15, and B16. That is, this formula calculates the total expenses for January.

BTW

Formulas
In many spreadsheet apps, a formula begins with an equal sign (=).

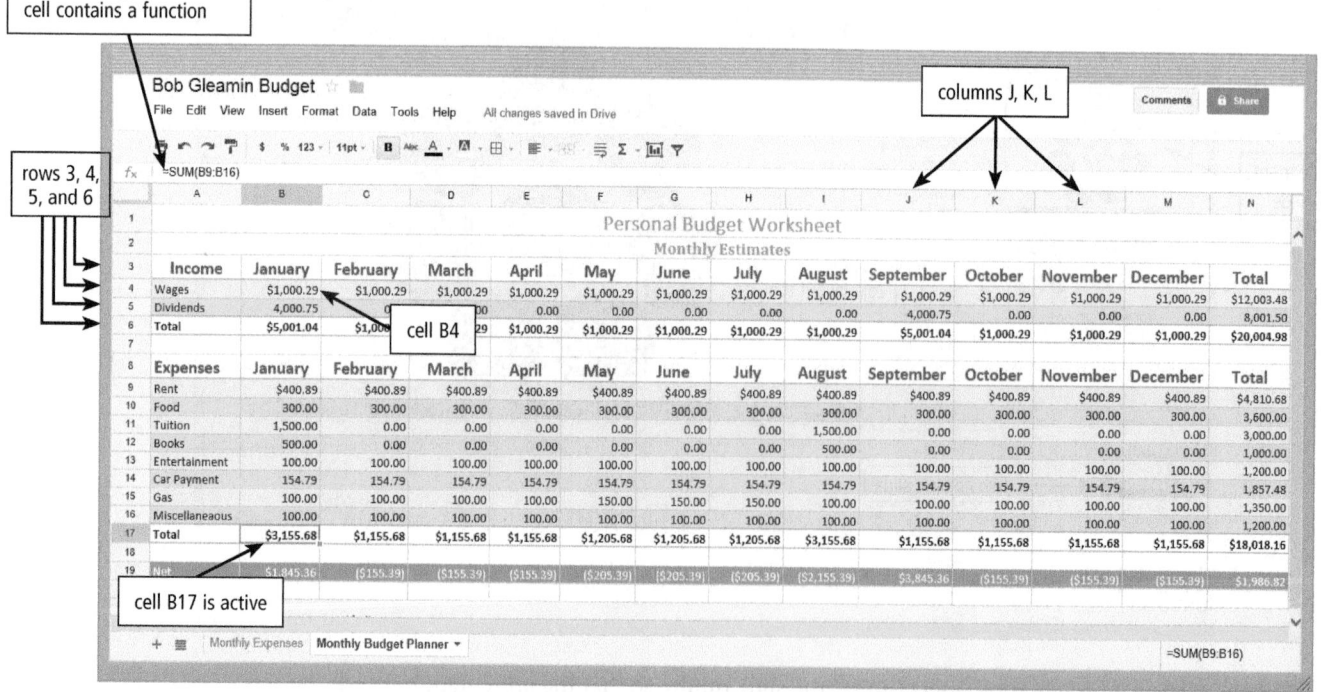

Figure 4-7   With spreadsheet software, you create worksheets that contain data arranged in columns and rows, and you can perform calculations on the data in the worksheets.

Source: Google Inc.

A *function* is a predefined formula that performs a calculation, such as adding the values in a group of cells or generating a value, such as the current time or date. For example, =SUM(B9:B16) is a formula that uses the SUM function to instruct the spreadsheet application to add all of the numbers in the range of cells B9 through B16. Spreadsheet applications contain many built-in functions to perform financial, mathematical, logical, date and time, and other calculations. Many spreadsheet applications allow users to write their own customized functions to perform special purpose calculations.

One of the more powerful features of spreadsheet software is its capability to recalculate the rest of the worksheet when data in a cell changes. Spreadsheet software's capability of recalculating data also makes it a valuable budgeting, forecasting, and decision-making tool. Another standard feature of spreadsheet software is charting, which depicts the data in graphical form, such as bar charts or pie charts. A visual representation of data through charts often makes it easier for users to see at a glance the relationship among the numbers.

Database

A **database** is a collection of data organized in a manner that allows access, retrieval, and use of that data. In a manual database, you might record data on paper and store it in a filing cabinet. With a database stored electronically, such as the one shown in Figure 4-8, the computer stores the data on a storage medium, such as a hard drive or flash drive, or the cloud.

Database software is an application that allows users to create, access, and manage a database. Using database software, you can add, change, and delete data in a database; sort and retrieve data from the database; and create forms and reports using the data in the database.

With most personal computer database programs, a database consists of a collection of tables, organized in rows and columns. Each row, called a record, contains data about a given item in the database, such as a person, product, object, or event. Each column, called a field, contains a specific category of data within a record. The Publishing database shown in Figure 4-8 consists of two tables: a Customer table and a Book Rep table. The Customer table contains 15 records (rows), each storing data about one customer. The customer data is grouped into 10 fields (columns): CU # (customer number), Customer Name, Street, City, State, Postal Code, Amount

BTW

Web Databases
Much of the information you access on the web — including photos, videos, movies, job listings, reservation details, and class registrations — is stored in databases. Read Tech Feature 11-1 for more information about web databases.

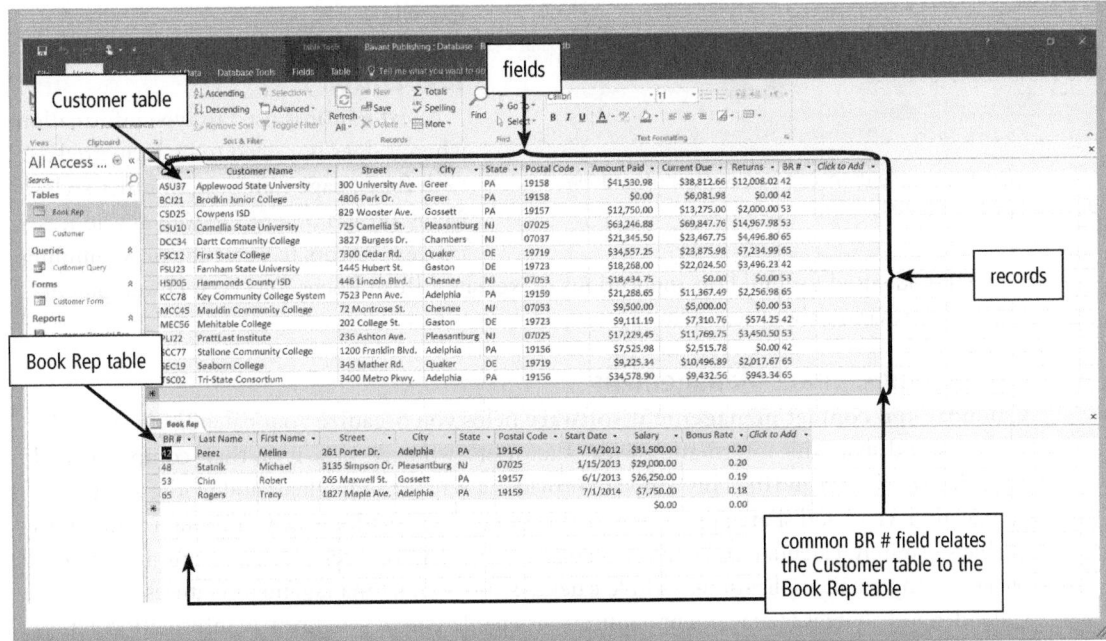

Figure 4-8   This database contains two tables: one for customers and one for book reps. The Customer table has 15 records and 10 fields; the Book Rep table has 4 records and 10 fields.
Source: Microsoft

Paid, Current Due, Returns, and BR # (book rep number). The Current Due field, for instance, contains the amount of money the customer owes the publisher. The Customer and Book Rep tables relate to each other through a common field, BR # (book rep number).

Users run queries to retrieve data. A query is a request for specific data from the database. For example, a query might request a list of customers whose balance is greater than $20,000. After obtaining the results of a query, database applications can present them on the screen, send them to a printer, or save them in a file.

 CONSIDER THIS

When should you use a database instead of a spreadsheet program?
Although databases and spreadsheets both store data, these programs have different purposes and capabilities. Spreadsheet programs are ideal for calculating results or creating charts from value in the worksheet. You should use a database program, however, if want to collect, reorganize and filter data, and/or create reports from the data.

Note Taking

Note taking software is an application that enables users to enter typed text, handwritten comments, drawings, sketches, photos, and links anywhere on a page and then save the page as part of a notebook (Figure 4-9). Users also can include audio recordings as part of their notes. Some enable users to sync their notes to the cloud so that they can access the notes on any computer or mobile device. Many note taking applications also include a calendar feature.

Users find note taking software convenient during meetings, class lectures and conferences, and in libraries and other settings where they would record written notes in a notebook.

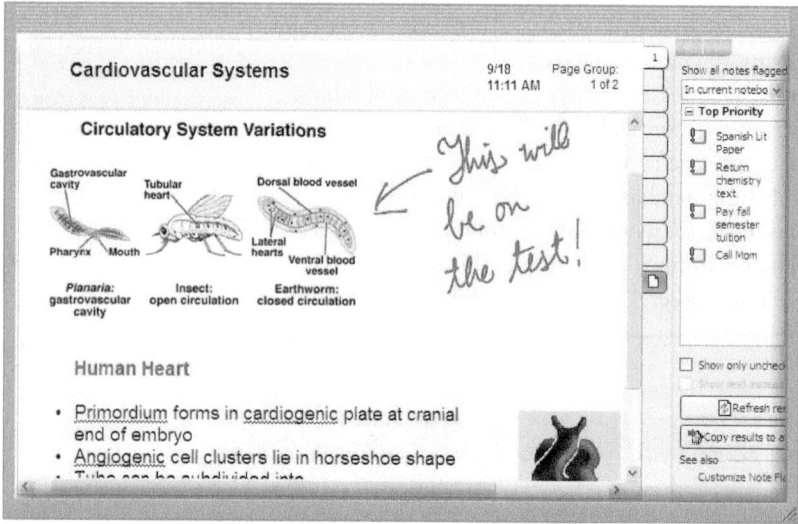

Figure 4-9   With note taking software, mobile users can handwrite notes, draw sketches, insert photos and links, and type text.
Source: Microsoft

Text Editor

A text editor is used to type information when it does not need to be formatted with fonts, page numbers, or other styles. Many programmers and web developers use text editors to enter the programming or HTML code used for building applications or websites. Read Focus On: Web Development for more information about text editors.

Calendar and Contact Management

Calendar and contact management software helps you organize your calendar, keep track of contacts, and share this information with other users, who can view it on their computers and mobile devices (Figure 4-10). This software provides a way for individuals and workgroups to organize, find, view, and share appointment and contact information easily. Although sometimes available separately, calendar and contact management software often exists as a unit in a single program. Many email applications include calendar and contact management features.

Calendar and contact management applications enable you to synchronize information across all of your computers and mobile devices so that you always have the latest version of any updated information.

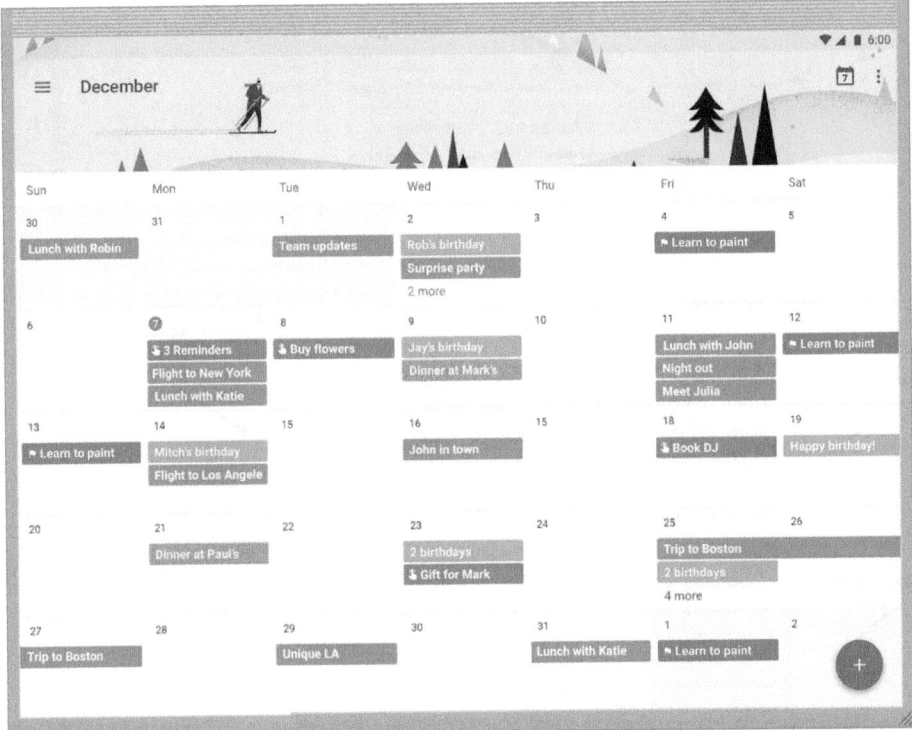

Figure 4-10   Users access their calendars on computers and mobile devices.
Google Inc.

Software Suite

A **software suite** is a collection of individual related applications available together as a unit. Productivity software suites typically include, at a minimum, word processing, presentation, spreadsheet, and email applications. While several productivity suites are designed to be installed on a local computer, some are available as web apps and enable you to share projects stored on the cloud to collaborate with other users.

CONSIDER THIS

Why would you use a software suite instead of a stand-alone application?
Software suites offer three major advantages: ease of use, integration, and lower cost.
- Software suites provide ease of use because the applications in the suite normally use a consistent interface and share features, such as clip art and spelling checker.
- Applications in a software suite often are integrated, which makes it easy to share information among them. For example, you can copy a chart on a worksheet created in a spreadsheet program and paste it into a slide created with presentation software.
- When you purchase a software suite, the suite usually costs significantly less than purchasing each application individually, or as stand-alone applications.

Project Management

Project management software is an application that allows a user to plan, schedule, track, and analyze the events, resources, and costs of a project. Project management software helps users manage project variables, such as the tasks required to complete a project and the allotted time and resources for each, allowing them to complete a project on time and within budget. A marketing manager, for example, might use project management software to schedule the processes required in a product launch (Figure 4-11).

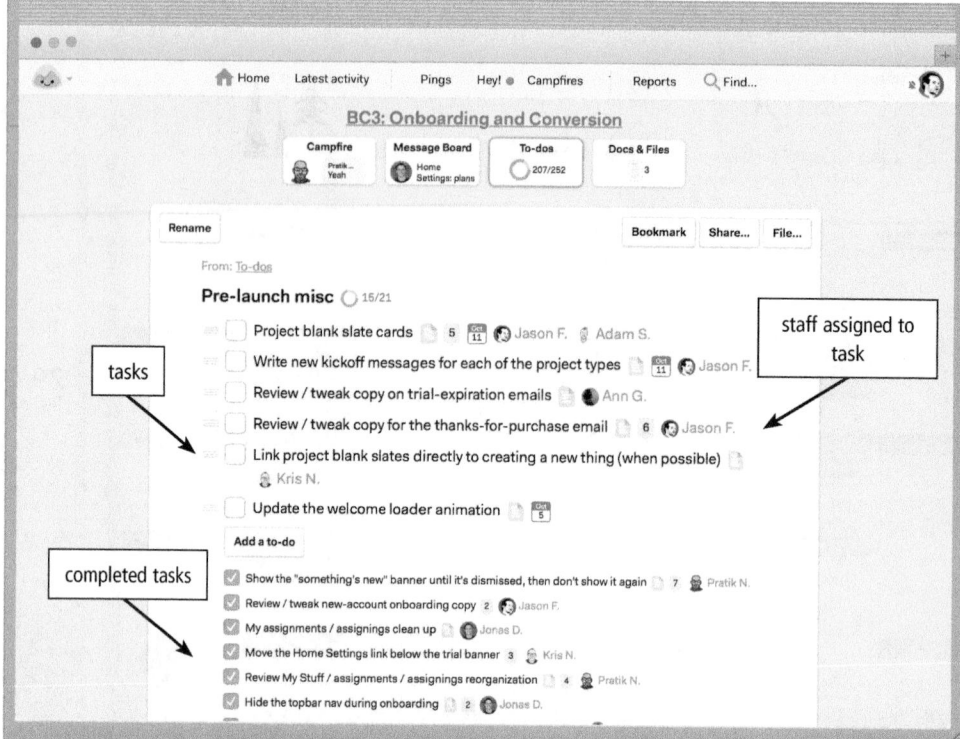

Figure 4-11 With project management software, you can plan and schedule the tasks and resources required in a project.
Courtesy of Basecamp

✳ **CONSIDER THIS**

Does the term, project, have two meanings in the technology field?
Yes. As discussed earlier in this module, a project can be a deliverable you create using application software, such as a document, presentation, spreadsheet, notes, calendar, contact list, budget, and more. A project also describe the collection of tasks and processes required to develop a solution to a problem.

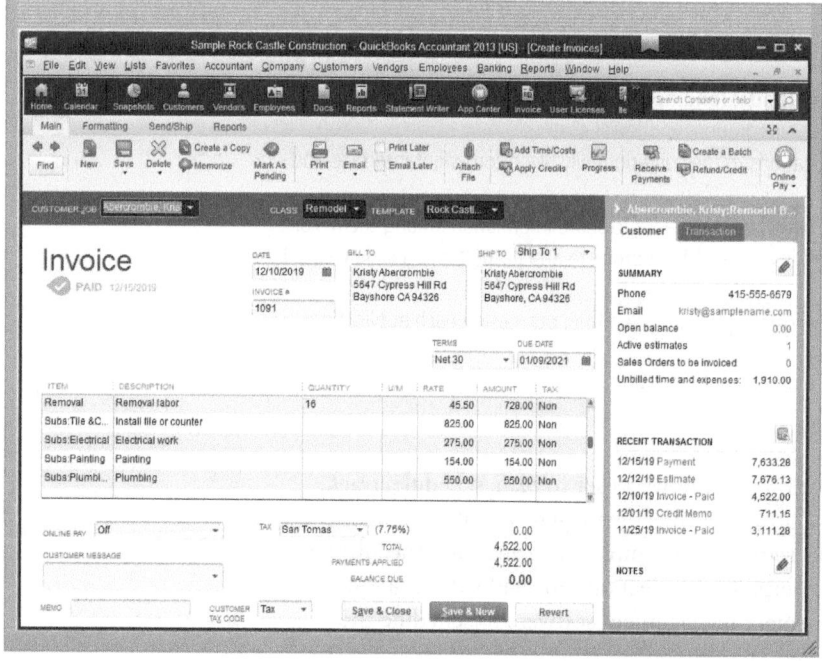

Figure 4-12 Accounting software helps businesses record and report their financial transactions.
Courtesy of Intuit

Accounting

Accounting software is an application that helps businesses of all sizes record and report their financial transactions. With accounting software, business users perform accounting activities related to the general ledger, accounts receivable, accounts payable, purchasing, invoicing (Figure 4-12), and payroll functions. Accounting software also enables business users to write and print checks, track checking account activity, and update and reconcile balances on demand.

Most accounting software supports online credit checks, bill payment, direct deposit, and payroll services. Some offer more complex features, such as job costing and estimating, time tracking, multiple company reporting, foreign currency reporting, and forecasting the amount of raw materials needed for products. The cost of accounting software for small businesses ranges from less than one hundred to several thousand dollars. Accounting software for large businesses can cost several hundred thousand dollars.

Personal Finance

Personal finance software is a simplified accounting application that helps home users and small/home office users balance their checkbooks, pay bills, track personal income and expenses, verify account balances, transfer funds, track investments, and evaluate financial plans (Figure 4-13). Personal finance software helps determine where, and for what purpose, you are spending money so that you can manage your finances.

Most personal finance software includes financial planning features, such as analyzing home and personal loans, preparing income taxes, and managing retirement savings. Other features include managing home inventory and setting up budgets. Most of these applications also offer a variety of online services, such as online banking and online investing. Read Secure IT 4-2 for safety tips when using personal finance apps on your smartphone or other mobile device.

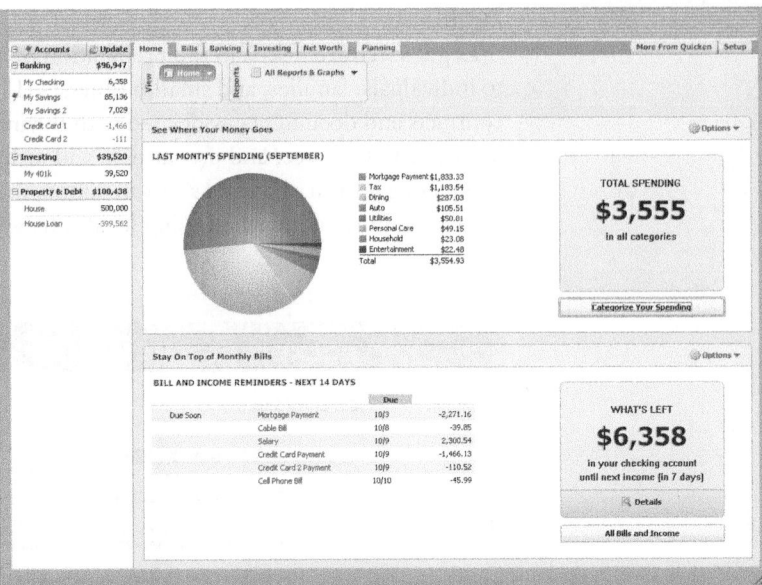

Figure 4-13   Personal finance software assists home users with tracking personal accounts.
Courtesy of Intuit

SECURE IT 4-2

Using Personal Finance Apps Safely

Personal finance apps offer convenient and easy methods to pay bills, deposit checks, examine account balances, verify payments, and transfer funds. They also are magnets for cybercriminals to snatch an unsuspecting user's personal information and send it to someone else anywhere in the world, who then can use the information for monetary transactions. Nearly one-third of malware banking apps target customers in the United States with malicious instructions that invade their smartphones and gain access to information stored on their devices. Users in Brazil, Australia, and France also are becoming extremely popular targets for banking thieves. By using caution and common sense, however, users can take steps to safeguard their funds and their identities by following these practices:

- **Evaluate the apps.** Fraudulent apps may resemble legitimate apps from financial

institutions. They often, however, are riddled with misspellings and awkward sentences. In addition, legitimate companies rarely promote downloading an app from a pop-up or pop-under advertisement. If you want an app from a bank or other financial institution, visit that company's website for instructions about downloading and installing its authentic apps.

- **Use strong passwords to access the apps.** Many of the more secure personal finance apps have dual passwords that involve typing a string of characters and also validating a picture. In addition, be certain to password protect your mobile device.

- **Guard your smartphone.** According to Consumer Reports, more than 5.2 million Americans lost or had their phones stolen in a recent year. That number decreased by more than 1 million from a previous year. The study credited the decrease in numbers

to the use of apps available to help users locate missing phones. Many phones also have a kill switch that renders the phone inoperable or remotely wipes the phone's data after too many unsuccessful login attempts. You still should take caution when storing personal information on your phone to protect your identity in the event that your mobile device is lost or stolen.

- **Verify the transactions.** Always verify your transactions by scrutinizing monthly statements. In addition, periodically check balances and alert your financial institution if any activity seems abnormal.

Consider This: Have you used finance apps? If so, which ones? When conducting transactions, do you follow some of the tips described in this box? If not, would you consider downloading an app to complete some common banking transactions? Why or why not?

Legal

Legal software assists in the preparation of legal documents and provides legal information to individuals, families, and small businesses (Figure 4-14). Legal software provides standard contracts and documents associated with buying, selling, and renting property; estate planning; marriage and divorce; and preparing a will or living trust. By answering a series of questions or completing a form, the legal software tailors the legal document to specific needs. Many lawyers offer assistance online when using legal software web apps.

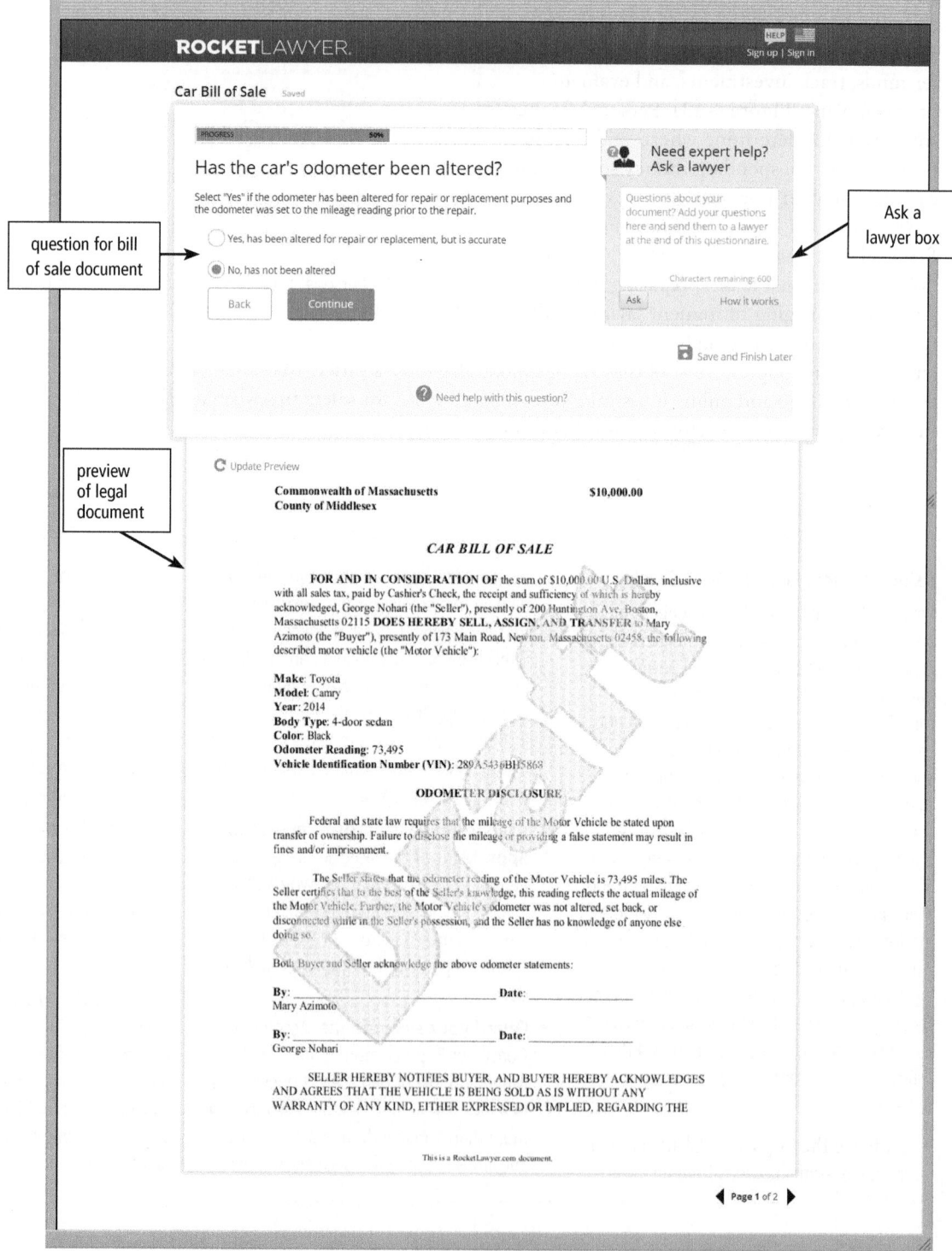

Figure 4-14   Legal software assists individuals, families, and small businesses in the preparation of legal documents.

Source: RocketLawyer

Tax Preparation

Tax preparation software is an application that can guide individuals, families, or small businesses through the process of filing federal and state taxes (Figure 4-15). These programs forecast tax liability and offer money-saving tax tips, designed to lower your tax bill. After you answer a series of questions and complete basic forms, the software creates and analyzes your tax forms to search for missed potential errors and deduction opportunities.

Once the forms are complete, you can print any necessary paperwork; then, they are ready for filing. Some tax preparation programs also allow you to file your tax forms electronically, a process called *e-filing*.

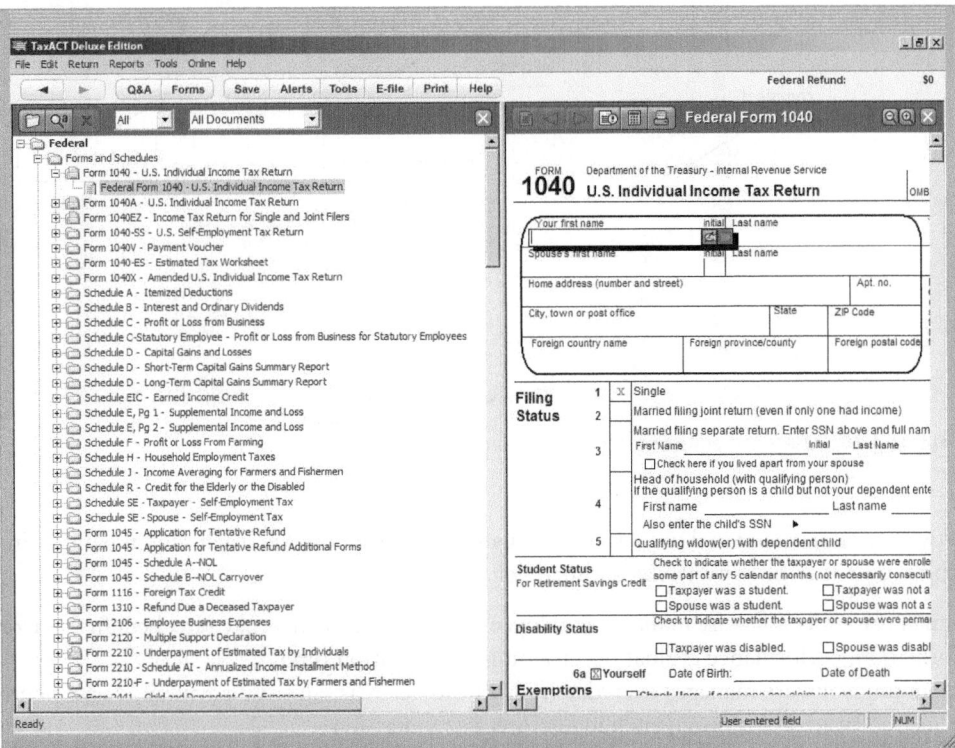

Figure 4-15 Tax preparation software guides individuals, families, or small businesses through the process of filing federal taxes.
Source: 2nd Story Software

Document Conversion and Readers

Document conversion software saves documents created in any application into a common format that has the same appearance as the original document. A popular image file format used to save converted documents is **PDF** (Portable Document Format), developed by Adobe Systems. Productivity applications, such as word processing and spreadsheet programs, often integrate the ability to save a project in PDF format. To interact with a PDF file, you need a PDF reader application, such as Adobe Reader, which can be downloaded free from Adobe's website. With a document reader, you can view, create, search, convert, annotate, edit, share, and print documents (Figure 4-16). You do not need the software that created the original document. Some readers allow you to complete forms and add your signature to documents.

Enterprise Computing

A large organization, commonly referred to as an enterprise, requires special computing solutions because of its size and geographic distribution. A typical enterprise consists of a wide variety of departments, centers, and divisions — collectively known as functional units. Nearly every enterprise has the following functional units: human resources, accounting and finance, engineering or product development, manufacturing, marketing, sales, distribution, customer service, and information technology.

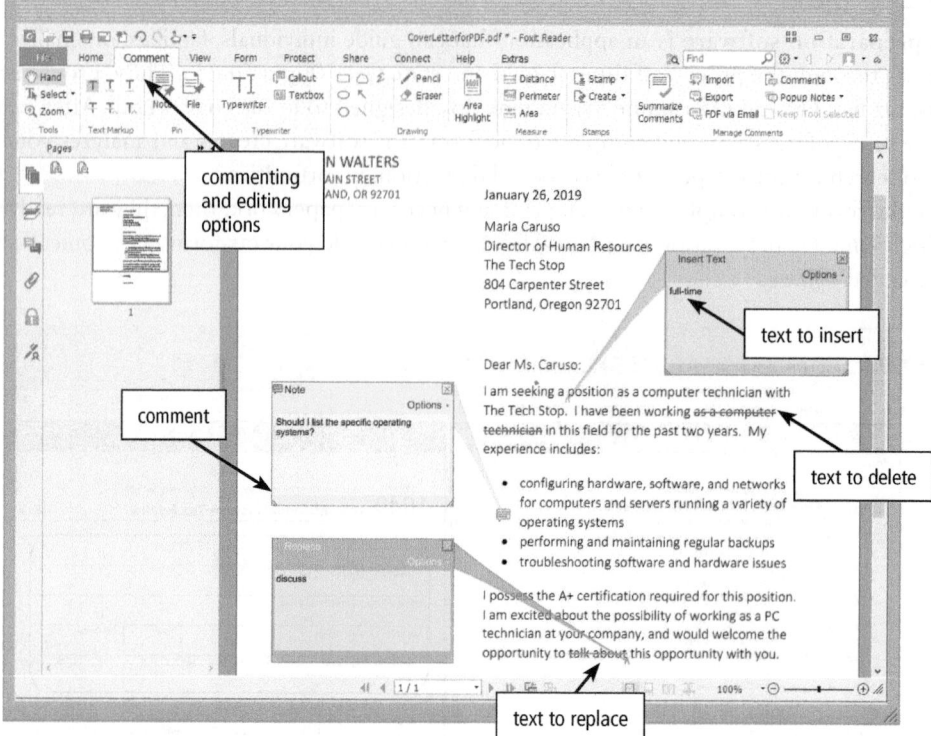

Figure 4-16   Users can edit content and add comments to a PDF document.
Source: FoxIt Reader

Software used in functional units is not mutually exclusive; however, each functional unit in an enterprise uses specific software, as outlined below.

- Human resources software manages employee information, such as pay rate, benefits, personal information, performance evaluations, training, and vacation time.
- Accounting software manages everyday transactions, such as sales and payments to suppliers. Finance software helps managers budget, forecast, and analyze.
- Engineering or product development software allows engineers to develop plans for new products and test their product designs.
- Manufacturing software assists in the assembly process, as well as in scheduling and managing the inventory of parts and products.
- Marketing software allows marketing personnel to create marketing campaigns, target demographics, and track their effectiveness.
- Sales software enables the salesforce to manage contacts, schedule meetings, log customer interactions, manage product information, and take customer orders.
- Distribution software analyzes and tracks inventory and manages product shipping status.
- Customer service software manages the day-to-day interactions with customers, such as phone calls, email messages, web interactions, and messaging sessions.
- Information technology staff use a variety of programs and apps to maintain and secure the hardware and software in an enterprise.

Tech Feature 4-1: Web and Mobile Apps for Personal and Business Productivity

A variety of applications provide a service intended to make business or personal tasks easier to accomplish. Some applications focus on a single service, while others provide several services in a single application. Read Tech Feature 4-1 to learn about some popular web and mobile apps for personal and business productivity.

Web and Mobile Apps for Personal and Business Productivity

Whether you are checking appointments, sending or reading email messages, arranging travel, banking or looking up information online, making a purchase, scanning QR (quick response) codes or bar codes, or checking in with friends on online social networks, web and mobile apps can assist your personal and business productivity.

Calendar and Email

Maintaining a calendar and checking email messages are common tasks of calendar and email web and mobile apps. Calendar apps keep track of your appointments and synchronize information entered on a mobile device with your online or desktop calendar software. Email apps integrate with your device's address book to facilitate sending messages to people whose names are stored in your device's contact list, and allow you to access and send photos stored in your device's photo gallery.

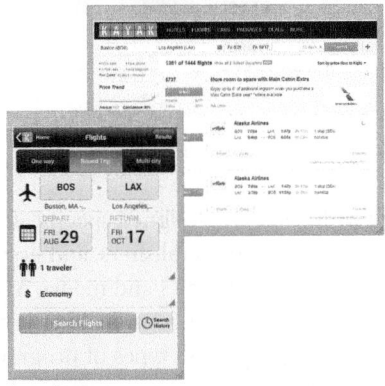

Source: Kayak

Travel

Purchasing flights, hotels, rental cars, or travel services is a common online task for personal and business travelers. Travel apps display available options and allow you to filter results. Many allow you to share travel plans with your online social networks.

Financial

You can access bank accounts or investments using a financial app. Financial mobile apps track expenses as you spend money and notify you when a bill is due. To help secure information, financial mobile apps can disable access if your device is stolen or lost. Some banking mobile apps allow you to upload a photo of a check taken with the device's camera to process the deposit.

Reference

Dictionaries, encyclopedias, books, and directories are available online as reference apps. Many have associated mobile apps that format information for mobile devices or take advantage of their features. For example, rather than typing a search term in a dictionary web app to look up its definition, a mobile app also might offer voice input. On the mobile version of an encyclopedia app, you might shake the device to display random topics or redisplay the app's home screen. Some reference mobile apps also can download information directly to your phone for offline access.

Retail

Online marketplaces and payment services support buying and selling items and transferring funds from one party to another. Marketplace apps enable customers to research products, submit or examine product reviews, and make purchases. A retail store mobile app might use a device's GPS to offer special deals closest to the customer's location. You also might use a device's camera to scan a product's bar code and then place the item in a shopping cart. Payment services allow customers to send money or pay for items using mobile devices. Read Secure IT 4-3 for safety tips when using payment apps.

Scanning

Scanning apps use a mobile device's camera to scan a QR code or bar code. A **QR code** is a square-shaped graphic that represents a web address or other information. A QR code reader app scans a QR code, and then displays its corresponding information. Some messaging apps provide codes representing contact information. By scanning the code displayed on the screen of a friend's mobile device, you can add your friend's contact information to your contacts or online social network. A bar code scanner reads a bar code and may provide product information, price, or reviews. Some supermarkets provide shopping apps for customers to scan bar codes of items they purchase. These apps create a customized shopping list, ordering items by their aisle location in the store, to provide a more efficient shopping experience.

Online Social Networks

Many users connect with family, friends, and coworkers using online social network mobile apps. Online social network web apps often integrate instant messaging and video chat communications. Mobile apps allow users to include photos and videos in updates made from their devices.

Consider This: Compare the web and mobile versions of the same app for personal and business productivity. Which features are common to both? Which features in the mobile version are not found in the web version? Which features in the web version are not found in the mobile version? Why do you think the developers made these decisions? Which features would you like to see that are missing from either version of the app?

iStockphoto.com / Franckreporter

SECURE IT 4-3

Avoiding Risks Using Payment Apps

Paying for coffee at the local coffee shop or buying tools at the hardware store has become streamlined with the advent of mobile payment apps. Each month, more than one million Starbucks customers use their smartphones instead of using cash or credit cards to pay for their orders, and many merchants are accepting this form of payment as mobile wallet apps become more secure. Users must download a mobile wallet app, such as Apple Pay or Android Pay, in order to pay with their smartphones. Using the mobile wallet app, they scan their smartphones near a reader at the POS terminal to complete the transaction, rather than handing a credit card to a clerk. Contrast this practice with the process at many restaurants, where employees often must take credit cards away from the table to complete the transaction; an unscrupulous employee would then have full access to the personal information on the cards.

Mobile payment providers state that the use of their apps is more secure than using credit cards. The apps use a payment system on phones equipped with an NFC chip, which stores data that is transmitted to a contactless terminal and verified as a legitimate sale. A smartphone user never enters an account number at the cash register because all financial information is stored on the mobile payment system. If, however, an unauthorized charge is made, the Electronic Fund Transfer Act protects users as long as the claim is made promptly, generally within two days.

If you use your smartphone to make purchases, follow this advice from the security experts:

• Use a password on your phone.

• Select an approved payment app from your device's app store that requires you to enter a password to start the transaction.

• Use a secure Internet connection when making a purchase online. When using a mobile web app, be sure that the browser shows https:// in the website's web address and a padlock symbol appears.

• Be vigilant about checking receipts and mobile transactions against monthly statements from the credit card company.

Consider This: Have you ever made a purchase using a mobile payment app? If so, how does the experience compare to paying with a credit card? Under what circumstances are you more likely to pay using your smartphone?

Google Inc.

Graphics and Media Applications

In addition to productivity applications, many people work with software designed specifically for their field of work. Power users, such as engineers, architects, desktop publishers, and graphic artists, often use sophisticated software that allows them to work with graphics and media. Many of these applications incorporate user-friendly interfaces or scaled-down versions, making it possible for the home and small business users also to create projects using these types of programs.

Graphics and media applications include computer-aided design, desktop publishing, paint/image editing, photo editing and photo management, video and audio editing, multimedia and website authoring, media players, and augmented and virtual reality applications.

Computer-Aided Design

Computer-aided design (CAD) software is a type of application that assists professionals and designers in creating engineering, architectural, and scientific designs and models (Figure 4-17). For example, engineers create design plans for vehicles and security systems. Architects design building structures and floor plans. Scientists design drawings of molecular structures.

Three-dimensional CAD programs allow designers to rotate designs of 3-D objects

Figure 4-17   Computer-aided design software is used to create three-dimensional models.
Source: Autocad

to view them from any angle. Some CAD software even can generate material lists for building designs.

Home and small business users work with less sophisticated design and modeling software. These applications usually contain thousands of predrawn plans that users can customize to meet their needs. For example, *home design/landscaping software* is an application that assists users with the design, remodeling, or improvement of a home, deck, or landscape.

Desktop Publishing

Desktop publishing software (DTP software) is an application that enables designers to create sophisticated publications that contain text, graphics, and many colors. Professional DTP software is ideal for the production of high-quality color projects, such as textbooks, corporate newsletters, marketing literature, product catalogs, and annual reports. Designers and graphic artists can print finished publications on a color printer, take them to a professional printer, or post them on the web in a format that can be viewed by those without DTP software.

Home and small business users create newsletters, brochures, flyers, advertisements, postcards, greeting cards, letterhead, business cards, banners, calendars, logos, and webpages using personal DTP software (Figure 4-18). Although many word processing programs include DTP features, home and small business users often prefer to create DTP projects using DTP software because of its enhanced features. These programs typically guide you through the development of a project by asking a series of questions. Then, you can print a finished publication on a color printer or post it on the web.

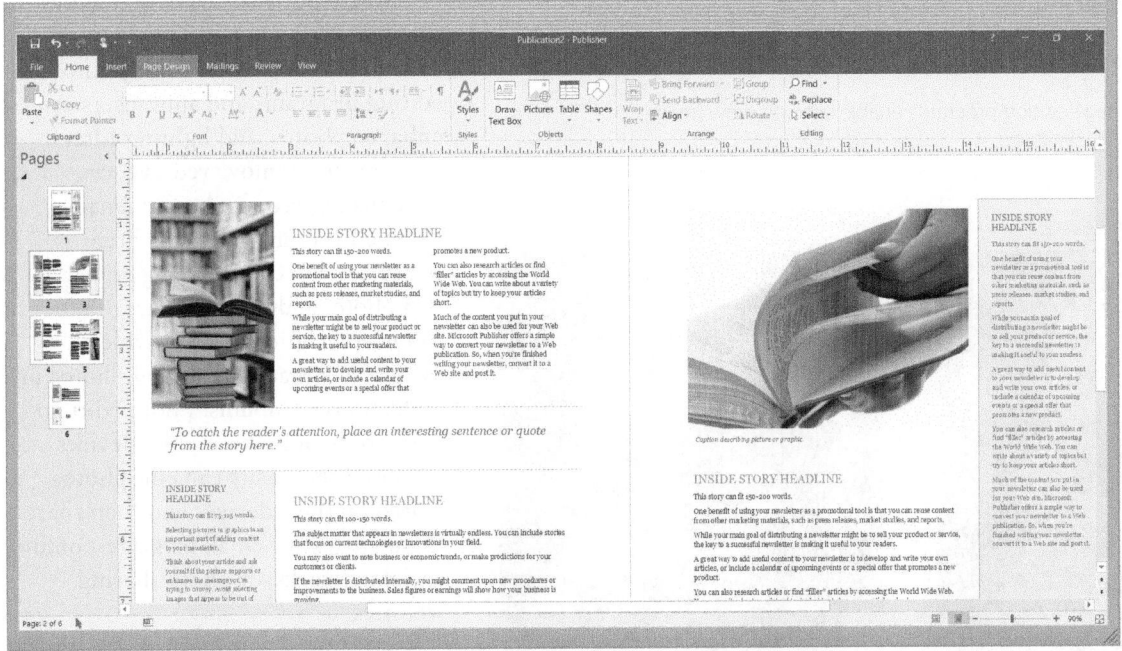

Figure 4-18   With personal DTP software, such as Microsoft Publisher shown here, home users can create newsletters.
Source: Microsoft

Many personal DTP programs also include paint/image editing software and photo editing and photo management software (discussed next), enabling users to embellish their publications with images.

Paint/Image Editing

Graphic artists, multimedia professionals, technical illustrators, and desktop publishers use paint software and image editing software to create and modify graphics, such as those used in DTP projects and webpages. **Paint software**, also called *illustration software*, is an application that

 BTW

Built-In Image Editing
Word processing, presentation, and other productivity applications usually include basic image editing capabilities.

allows users to draw pictures, shapes, and other graphics with various on-screen tools, such as a pen, brush, eyedropper, and paint bucket. **Image editing software** is an application that provides the capabilities of paint software and also includes the capability to enhance and modify existing photos and images. Modifications can include adjusting or enhancing image colors, adding special effects such as shadows and glows, creating animations, and image stitching (combining multiple images into a larger image).

Figure 4-19   Paint/image editing programs enable users to draw images.
Source: DrawPlus X5 Serif (Europe) Ltd, | www.serif.com

Paint/image editing software for the home or small business user provides an easy-to-use interface; includes various simplified tools that allow you to draw pictures, shapes, and other images (Figure 4-19); and provides the capability of modifying existing graphics and photos. These products also include many templates to assist you in adding images to projects, such as greeting cards, banners, calendars, signs, labels, business cards, and letterhead.

Photo Editing and Photo Management

Photo editing software is a type of image editing software that allows users to edit and modify the appearance of digital photos. With photo editing programs and apps, users can enhance photos, add lighting filters, crop images, remove red-eye, create collages, crop and resize images, color-correct images, straighten images, remove or rearrange objects in a photo, and more (Figure 4–20). Many applications also provide a means for organizing digital photos in collections or albums. Photo editing apps are popular on mobile devices because users easily can edit photos stored on their devices and then share them via text or email messages, online social networks, or photo sharing websites.

Read How To 4-1 for instructions about editing and sharing photos. Read Ethics & Issues 4-2 to consider issues related to altering digital photos.

With **photo management software**, you can view, organize, sort, catalog, print, and share digital photos. Some photo editing software includes photo management functionality. Many online photo sharing services enable you to organize your photos in albums by selecting photos and adding captions.

Figure 4-20   With photo editing software, users can edit digital photos, such as by adjusting the appearance of images as shown here.
Source: Google, Courtesy Mark Frydenberg

HOW TO 4-1

Edit and Share Photos

When you take a photo using a digital camera or smartphone, you sometimes may want to edit the photo to remove unwanted areas, correct imperfections, or change its size. Before editing a photo, you first should make a backup of the original photo. The table below describes common ways to edit photos using a photo editing app.

After you have edited a photo to your satisfaction, you may want to share the photo with others. Many mobile devices, as well as most photo editing desktop apps, have built-in options that allow you to share photos. To share a photo on a mobile device or from within a photo editing app, follow these steps:

1. Open the photo to share.
2. Select the sharing option in the photo editing app or on the mobile device.
3. Choose the method by which to share the photo. Common ways to share photos include sending the photo as an email attachment, posting the photo to an online social network or photo sharing website, storing the photo on the cloud, and sending the photo as a picture message to another mobile device.

✹ **Consider This:** Examine your digital camera or mobile device with a camera. Which of the photo editing features discussed here does it have? Did you notice any photo editing features in addition to those listed here?

ACTION	PURPOSE	STEPS
Crop	Removes unwanted areas of a photo	1. Select cropping tool. 2. Adjust photo border to define area(s) of the photo to keep and discard.
Remove *red-eye*	Removes the appearance of red eyes caused by the camera flash	1. Select red-eye removal tool. 2. Tap or click areas of the photo with the red-eye effect *or* drag a border around the affected areas.
Resize	Changes the physical dimensions of the photo	1. Select resizing tool. 2. Drag sizing handles to increase or decrease the photo's dimensions *or* type the desired height and width in the appropriate text boxes.
Compress	Decreases the photo's file size	1. Select option to compress photo. 2. Choose desired level of compression.
Adjust *sharpness*	Increases or decreases crispness of objects in the photo	1. Select option to adjust sharpness. 2. Drag sharpness slider to desired value *or* type the desired sharpness level into appropriate text box.
Adjust *brightness*	Adjusts lightness or darkness in the photo	1. Select option to adjust brightness. 2. Drag brightness slider to desired value *or* type the desired brightness level into appropriate text box.
Adjust *contrast*	Adjusts the difference in appearance between light and dark areas of the photo	1. Select option to adjust contrast. 2. Drag contrast slider to desired value *or* type the desired contrast level into appropriate text box.

✹ **ETHICS & ISSUES 4-2**

Is It Ethical to Alter Digital Photos?

Many commercial artists, photojournalists, and creators of magazine covers and billboards use photo editing software to alter digital photos. Artists use photo editing software to enhance digital photos by changing colors, adding or removing objects, and more. When does photo manipulation become unethical?

In several high-profile cases, news sources published intentionally altered photos that misrepresented the facts, in one case publishing photos of an aging world leader edited to remove his hearing aid. One school received criticism when it altered necklines on yearbook photos to be more modest. Real estate agents on occasion have altered photos of homes for online listings or print brochures. Also making news are celebrity or model photos that artists retouch to change their physical appearance.

The National Press Photographers Association expresses reservations about digital altering and subscribes to the following belief: "As [photo]journalists we believe the guiding principle of our profession is accuracy; therefore, we believe it is wrong to alter the content of a photo in any way … that deceives the public." Yet, some insist that the extent to which a photo "deceives the public" is in the eye of the beholder. Many differentiate between technical manipulation to improve photo quality and an intent to deceive, such as placing two people in the same photo to make it appear as if they were together at an event. . Some governments are attempting to legislate photo manipulation.

✹ **Consider This:** Is it ethical to alter digital photos? Why or why not? Does the answer depend on the reason for the alteration, the extent of the alteration, or some other factor? Should magazines stop altering pictures of people to change their appearance? Why or why not?

Video and Audio Editing

Video editing software is an application that allows users to modify a segment of a video, called a clip. For example, users can reduce the length of a video clip, reorder a series of clips, or add special effects, such as words that move across the screen. Video editing software typically includes audio editing capabilities. **Audio editing software** is an application that enables users to modify audio clips, produce studio-quality soundtracks, and add audio to video clips (Figure 4-21). Most television shows and movies and many online videos are created or enhanced using video and audio editing software. Audio and video editing apps allow users to edit audio or video files recorded with their mobile devices.

Some operating systems include video editing and audio editing applications.

Figure 4-21 With audio editing software, users modify audio clips.
Source: Adobe Systems Incorporated

Multimedia and Website Authoring

Multimedia authoring software allows users to combine text, graphics, audio, video, and animation in an interactive application. With this software, users control the placement of text and images and the duration of sounds, video, and animation. Training centers, educational institutions, and online magazine publishers use multimedia authoring software to develop interactive applications. These applications may be distributed on an optical disc, over a local area network, or online.

Website authoring software helps users create business websites for a variety of purposes, such as online stores, restaurants, small businesses, or personal interests, generally without requiring advanced HTML skills. Users can create pages by dragging and dropping content elements, such as images, videos, maps, blog posts, and other content (Figure 4-22). Some website authoring software create websites that appear properly on both desktop or laptop computers and smartphones. In addition, some of these applications are installed on a user's computer, while others are accessed through a web app running in a browser.

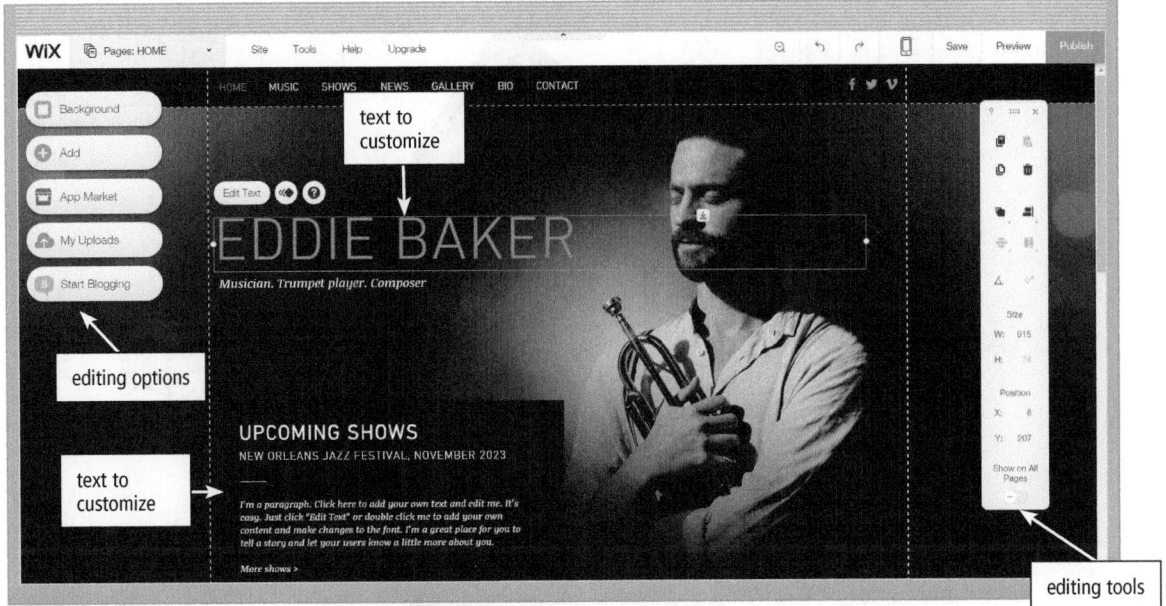

Figure 4-22   Website authoring software allows you to create engaging personal and business websites by adding your text, images, and videos to existing website templates.
Courtesy of Wix Inc.

 **CONSIDER THIS**

What are computer-based training, web-based training, and massive open online courses?
Computer-based training (CBT) is a type of education in which students learn by using and completing exercises with instructional software. *Web-based training (WBT)* is a type of CBT that uses Internet technology to deliver the training. CBT and WBT typically consist of self-directed, self-paced instruction about a topic. WBT is popular in business, industry, and schools for teaching new skills or enhancing existing skills of employees, teachers, and students.

A massive open online course (MOOC) offers access to quality education anywhere the Internet is available through a combination of video instruction and interaction with an instructor and students in an online classroom. The MOOC format can vary depending upon the subject matter and instructor's expertise, but most involve videos of lectures, assigned readings, assignments, and interactive discussions. Some instructors open their courses to anyone interested in attending, and they invite people to share the course content. Other instructors, however, keep the course closed and maintain strict control of their resources. Khan Academy is one of the more popular MOOCs, and the short video instructions on thousands of topics have been translated into 40 languages.

Media Player

A **media player** is a program that allows you to view images and animations, listen to audio, and watch video files on your computer or mobile device. Media players also may enable you to organize media files by genre, artist, or other category; create playlists; convert files to different formats; connect to and purchase media from an online media store or marketplace; stream radio stations' broadcasting over the Internet; download podcasts; burn audio CDs; and transfer media to portable media players.

Augmented and Virtual Reality

An **augmented reality app** overlays information and digital content on top of physical objects or locations. Some augmented reality mobile apps overlay media or other digital content over an image on the screen.

Figure 4-23 shows the use of augmented reality in medical education. A user scans a target image using an augmented reality app, and the app overlays 3-D graphics of the human body. By changing the angle, or zooming in and out, the user can visualize various muscles, organs, and systems of the human body.

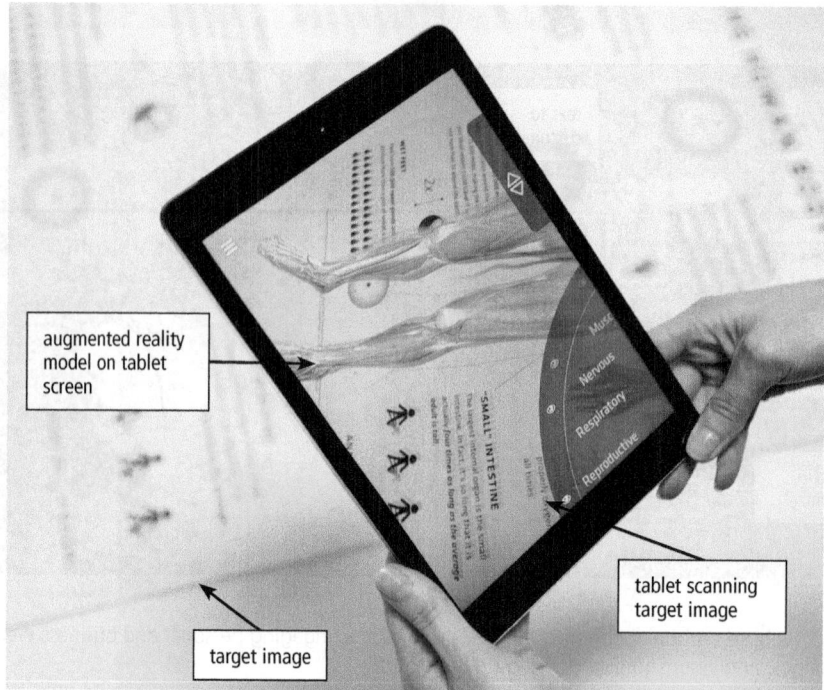

Figure 4-23 Scanning a target image with a tablet or smartphone displays an interactive model of the human body in this augmented reality app used for medical education.
Source: Daqri, Inc.

A **virtual reality app** provides an immersive user experience. Some require a specialized viewer, which may have a built-in display, or make use of a smartphone to display 360-degree images or video content. Popular applications of virtual reality include gaming, health care, fashion, business, and training. The military uses virtual reality for training soldiers for combat by simulating real-world environments. Using virtual reality simulations, soldiers learn to fly planes, respond to medical situations on a battlefield, and drive military vehicles without placing themselves in danger.

Personal Interest Applications

Countless desktop, mobile, and web apps are designed specifically for lifestyle, medical, entertainment, convenience, or education activities. Most of the programs in this category are relatively inexpensive; many are free or open source, and available for download from web sites or a device's app store. Some applications focus on a single service, while others provide several services in a single application.

- Lifestyle applications: Access the latest news or sports scores, check the weather forecast, compose music, research genealogy, find recipes, meet or chat with friends online near you, or locate nearby restaurants, gas stations, or points of interest.
- Medical applications: Research symptoms, establish a fitness or health program, track exercise activity, refill prescriptions, count calories, or monitor sleep patterns.
- Entertainment applications: Listen to music or the radio, view photos, watch videos or shows, read a book or other publication, organize and track fantasy sports teams, and play games individually or with others.

- Convenience applications: Obtain driving directions or your current location, convert speech to text instead of typing, set an alarm or timer, check the time, calculate a tip, use your phone as a flashlight, or use a personal assistant that acts on your voice commands (read How To 4-2 for instructions about using personal assistant apps).
- Education applications: Access how-to guides, learn or fine-tune a particular skill, follow a tutorial, run a simulation, assist children with reading and other elementary skills, or support academics.

 HOW TO 4-2

Use Features in Voice Command Personal Assistant and Mobile Search Apps

Many mobile operating systems include a virtual personal assistant that processes voice commands and performs certain tasks. Some mobile search apps also act on spoken commands. For example, you can issue voice commands to set an alarm, add an appointment to your calendar, send a text message, or run an app. The table below describes ways to use features in voice command personal assistant apps.

Task	Sample Voice Command(s)
Activate your device's personal assistant	"Hey, Siri." "OK, Google."
Change phone settings	"Turn on Wi-Fi." "Increase brightness."
Dial a number	"Call Madelyn's Cell." "Dial 407-555-8275."
Obtain information	"When was George Washington born?"
Obtain driving instructions	"Navigate to 123 Main Street, Orlando, Florida."
Run an app	"Run calendar."
Schedule a meeting	"Schedule a meeting with Traci at the library at 3:00 p.m. tomorrow."
Send a text message	"Text Samuel meet me at the pool."
Set a reminder	"Remind me to go grocery shopping on Tuesday."
Set a timer	"Set timer for five minutes."
Set an alarm	"Set an alarm for 6:00 a.m. tomorrow."

Consider This: Use a search engine to find a complete list of voice commands available for your phone. Try speaking some commands that you have not used before. Which ones might be the most useful for you?

Tech Feature 4-2: Web and Mobile Apps for Media and Personal Interest

A variety of applications provide a service intended to make media and personal interest tasks easier to accomplish. Some applications focus on a single service, while others provide several services in a single application. Read Tech Feature 4-2 to learn about some popular web and mobile apps for media and personal interests.

TECH FEATURE 4-2

Web and Mobile Apps for Media and Personal Interests

Whether sharing, digital photos or other media, streaming audio and video, or playing games by yourself or with others, countless web and mobile apps are available to meet your needs. You also can use web and mobile apps to look up news, sports, and weather; obtain maps and directions; help you reach your health and fitness goals; and assist you with academic objectives.

Media Sharing

With media sharing mobile apps, you use the digital camera on your mobile device to take quality photos and/or videos and then instantly can share the photos or videos on online social networks. Using the corresponding media sharing web app, you can categorize, tag, organize, and rank the media posted by you, your friends, and your contacts.

Streaming Audio and Video

Podcasts, video blogs, clips or episodes from a television show, or even entire movies are available through a variety of streaming media web and mobile apps. Some services are available only with membership, and may charge a monthly fee. Others are free, but include ads. Streaming media enables you to view and listen to content without downloading it to your computer or device. Because streaming media can consume large amounts of data, however, many users will stream media when connected to a Wi-Fi network and download media to the device's storage for listening on the go.

Gaming

Gaming web and mobile apps often offer a social component, enabling you to chat within the game environment, find friends who play the same game apps, and post your scores on social media. Word, puzzle, and board games are just some examples of apps you can play by yourself or with friends or others using the same apps.

News, Sports, and Weather

Many apps provide access to the latest news, stories, current events, sports scores, sporting events, and weather forecasts. Some of these mobile apps use GPS technology to provide current or customized information based on the location of your mobile device. You also can configure these apps to deliver text messages and other types of alerts to your device when certain events occur, such as when a football team scores a touchdown or when severe weather is near.

Source: Instagram

Mapping

Using your mobile device's GPS capability, you can use mapping mobile apps to obtain directions, maps, and recommendations for restaurants or other points of interest based on your current location. Some apps help you to track the locations of your friends based on their GPS signals (if they enable you to do so). Web apps help you decide on a route, print directions or a map, and even find amenities along your route, such as public rest stops or restaurants.

Health and Fitness

Losing weight, training for a race, or following a low-calorie diet are some uses of health and fitness apps. Using a mobile device as a pedometer or GPS receiver can help you count your steps or create a map of a route you run and then update your profile with the data it tracked. You can use corresponding web apps

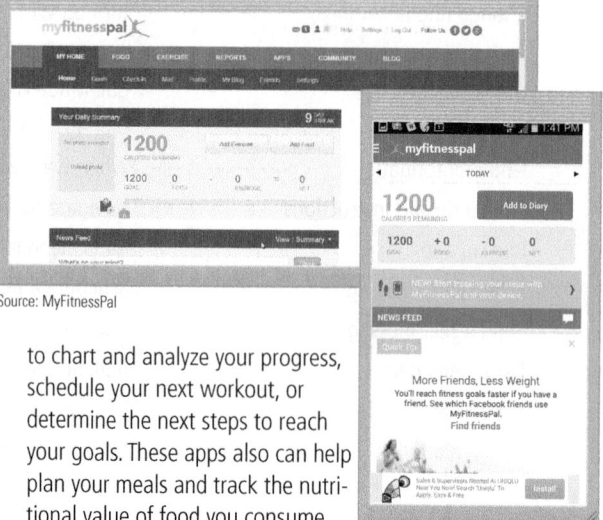

Source: MyFitnessPal

to chart and analyze your progress, schedule your next workout, or determine the next steps to reach your goals. These apps also can help plan your meals and track the nutritional value of food you consume.

Academic

Schools often subscribe to educational apps that provide students with games, quizzes, and lessons about course topics. Using these apps, teachers can keep track of students' progress and pinpoint areas where they may need extra help. You also can access complete college or high school courses and take advantage of free or fee-based digital content provided by publishers and teachers.

 Consider This: Which web and mobile apps have you used for media sharing; streaming audio and video; gaming; news, sports, and weather; mapping; health and fitness; and education? Which will you try others after reading this tech feature?

Communications Applications

Earlier modules presented a variety of communications applications, many of which are summarized in Table 4-2. Many of these are available as free web apps, as desktop apps available from download sites, or as mobile apps from the device's app store.

 BTW

Mobile Communications Apps
Most of the communications apps in Table 4-2 are available as mobile apps, as well.

Table 4-2   Communications Applications

Blog
- Time-stamped articles, or posts, in diary or journal format, usually listed in reverse chronological order
- Bloggers (author) use blogging software to create/maintain blog
  - Some blog services provide blogging software so users do not have to install it on their own servers

Browser
- Allows users to access and view webpages on the Internet
- Requires browser software
  - Integrated in most operating systems
  - Many alternative browsers are available

Chat
- Real-time, online typed conversation with one or more users
- Requires chat client software
  - Integrated in some operating systems and built into some websites
  - Included with some paid ISPs

Online Discussion
- Online forums where users have written discussions
- May require a reader program to manage and follow discussion posts
- Integrated in some operating systems, email programs, online social networks, and browsers

Email
- Messages and files sent via a network, such as the Internet
- Requires an email desktop, web or mobile app
  - Integrated in many software suites and operating systems
  - Available free at portals on the web
  - Included with a paid ISP

File Transfer
- Method of uploading files to and downloading files from servers on the Internet
- May require an FTP client program
  - Integrated in some operating systems
  - Many applications (such as web authoring software) that require frequent transfer of files to the Internet have built-in FTP capabilities

Internet Phone
- Allows users to speak to other users via an Internet connection
- Requires a microphone, a speaker, a high-speed Internet connection, and VoIP software
  - Some subscription services also require a separate phone and VoIP router
  - With a webcam, some services also support video chat or videoconferences

Internet Messaging
- Real-time exchange of messages, files, images, audio, and/or video with another online user
- Requires messaging software
- Provided by some online social networks
- Also available as a browser plug-in

Mobile (Text) Messaging
- Short text, picture, or video messages sent and received, mainly on mobile devices over a mobile carrier's network
- May require messaging plan from mobile service provider
- Requires messaging software
- Integrated in most mobile devices

Videoconference
- Meeting between geographically separated people who use a network to transmit video/audio
- Requires videoconferencing software, a microphone, a speaker, and a webcam

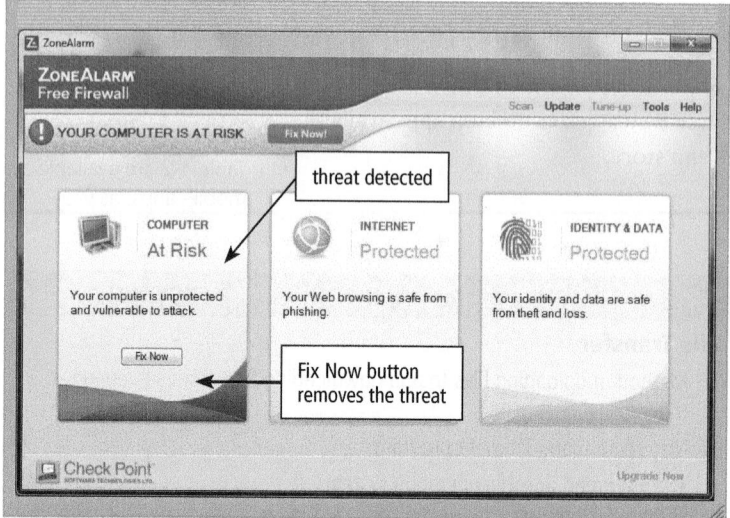

Figure 4-24 This personal firewall detected a threat to the computer and provided a means to remove the threat.
Courtesy of Checkpoint Software Technologies Ltd.

Security Tools

To protect your computers and mobile devices, you can use one or more security tools. Security tools include personal firewalls, antivirus programs, malware removers, and Internet filters. Although some of these tools are included with the operating system, you also can purchase stand-alone programs that offer improvements or added functionality.

Personal Firewall

A **personal firewall** is a security tool that detects and protects a personal computer and its data from unauthorized intrusions (Figure 4-24). Personal firewalls constantly monitor all transmissions to and from a computer or mobile device and may inform a user of attempted intrusions. When connected to the Internet, your computer or mobile device is vulnerable to attacks from hackers who try to access a computer or network illegally. These attacks may destroy your data, steal information, damage your computer, or carry out some other malicious action.

 CONSIDER THIS

What is a hardware firewall?
A *hardware firewall* is a device intended to stop network intrusions before they attempt to affect your computer or network maliciously. Many routers also can function as a hardware firewall.

 **BTW**

Security Suites
A *security suite* is a collection of individual security tools available together as a unit. These programs often are called Internet security programs.

Tech Feature 4-3: Viruses and Malware

A computer **virus** is a potentially damaging program that affects a computer or device negatively by altering the way it works. This occurs without the user's knowledge or permission. Once the virus is in a computer or device, it can spread and may damage your files, programs and apps, and operating system. Read Tech Feature 4-3 to learn more about viruses and other malware.

 TECH FEATURE 4-3

Viruses and Malware

Viruses do not generate by chance. The programmer of a virus, known as a virus author, intentionally writes a virus program. Writing a virus program usually requires significant programming skills. The virus author ensures the virus can replicate itself, conceal itself, monitor for certain events, and then deliver its payload. A *payload* is the destructive event or prank the virus delivers. Viruses can infect all types of computers and devices. Most variations of viruses have two phases involved in their execution: infection and delivery.

The first step in the infection phase is activation of the virus. The most common way viruses spread is by users running infected programs or apps. During the infection phase, viruses typically perform one or more of the following actions:

1. First, a virus replicates by attaching itself to program files. A macro virus hides in a macro, which is a standard feature of many productivity applications, such as word processing and spreadsheet apps. A boot sector virus targets the computer's start-up files. A file virus attaches itself to program files. The next time an infected program or app is run, the virus executes and infects the computer or device.

2. Viruses conceal themselves to avoid detection. A stealth virus disguises itself by hiding in fake code sections, which it inserts within working code in a file. A polymorphic virus actually changes its code as it delivers the infection.

3. Finally, viruses watch for a certain condition or event and activate when that condition or event occurs. The event might be starting the computer or device, or reaching a date on the system clock. A logic bomb activates when it detects a specific condition (say, a name deleted from the employee list). A time bomb is a logic bomb that activates on a particular date or time. If the triggering condition does not exist, the virus simply replicates.

During the delivery phase, the virus unleashes its payload, which might be a harmless prank that displays a meaningless message — or it might be destructive, corrupting or deleting data and files. The most dangerous viruses do not have an obvious payload. Instead, they quietly modify files. One way antivirus software detects computer viruses is by monitoring files for unknown changes.

In addition to viruses, other malware includes worms, trojan horse programs, and rootkits.

- A *worm* resides in active memory and replicates itself over a network to infect computers and devices, using up system resources and possibly shutting down the system.
- A *trojan horse* is a destructive program disguised as a real program, such as a screen saver. When a user runs a seemingly innocent program, a trojan horse hiding inside can capture information, such as user names and passwords, from your computer or enable someone to control your computer remotely. Unlike viruses, trojan horses do not replicate themselves.

- A *rootkit* is a program that easily can hide and allow someone to take full control of your computer from a remote location, often for nefarious purposes. For example, a rootkit can hide in a folder on your computer. The folder appears empty because the rootkit has instructed your computer not to display the contents of the folder. Rootkits can be very dangerous and often require special software to detect and remove.

Studies show that malware can infect an unprotected computer within minutes after connecting to the Internet. Due to the increasing threat of viruses attacking your computer, it is more important than ever to protect your computer from viruses and other malware. Secure IT 1-2 in Module 1 lists steps you can follow to protect your computer from a virus infection.

✳ **Consider This:** If your computer or mobile device is infected with a virus or malware, how will you know? How will you find instructions for removing a virus?

Signs of Virus and Malware Infection

- An unusual message or image is displayed on the computer screen.
- An unusual sound or music plays randomly.
- The available memory is less than what should be available.
- A program or file suddenly is missing, or an unknown program or file mysteriously appears.
- The computer's security tools, such as antivirus software or firewall, become disabled.

- The size of a file changes without explanation.
- A file becomes corrupted.
- A program will not run.
- The computer operates much slower than usual.
- Your browser displays pop-ups that you cannot close or webpages you did not request when you are online.

Antivirus Programs

To protect a computer or mobile device from virus attacks, users should install an antivirus program and keep it updated by purchasing revisions or upgrades to the software. An **antivirus program** protects a computer against viruses by identifying and removing any computer viruses found in memory, on storage media, or on incoming files (Figure 4-25). Antivirus programs scan for programs that attempt to modify a computer's start-up files, the operating system, and other programs that normally are read from but not modified. In addition, many antivirus programs automatically scan files downloaded from the web, email attachments, opened files, and all types of removable media inserted in the computer or mobile device.

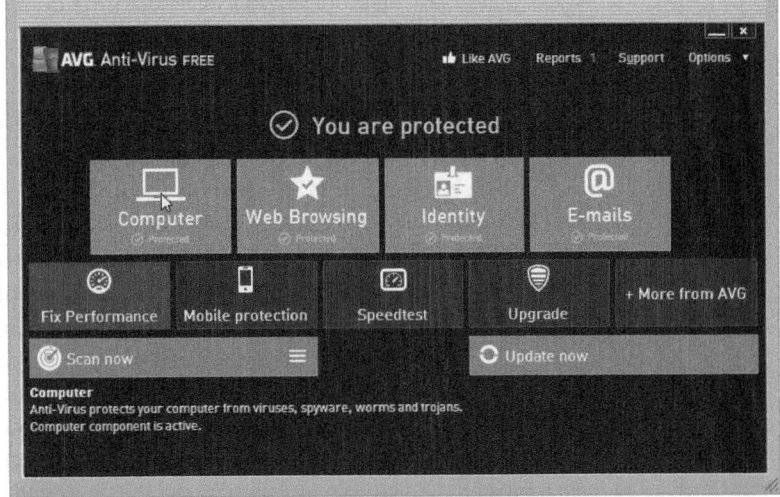

Figure 4-25   An antivirus program scans memory, media, and incoming email messages and attachments for viruses and attempts to remove any viruses it finds.
Courtesy of Checkpoint Software Technologies Ltd.

BTW

Antivirus and Malware Detection Programs
You should run only one antivirus program on your computer or mobile device; however, you can run more than one malware detection program.

If an antivirus program identifies an infected file, it attempts to remove the malware. If the antivirus program cannot remove the infection, it often quarantines the infected file. A *quarantine* is a separate area of a hard drive that holds the infected file until the infection can be removed. This step ensures other files will not become infected. Quarantined files remain on your computer or mobile device until you delete them or restore them.

Most antivirus programs also include protection against other malware, such as worms, trojan horses, and spyware. When you purchase a new computer, it may include a trial version of antivirus software. Many email servers also have antivirus programs installed to check incoming and outgoing email messages for viruses and other malware. Read Secure IT 4-4 for tips about recognizing virus hoaxes.

SECURE IT 4-4

Recognizing Virus Hoaxes

Computer hoaxes spread across the Internet in record time and often are the source of urban legends. These hoaxes take several forms and often disappear for months or years at a time, only to resurface some time later.

Most alarming to some users are the computer virus hoaxes that warn a computer is infected and needs immediate attention. Some warnings state the problem is so severe that the computer or device will explode or that the entire hard drive will be erased in a matter of

seconds. The warnings cite prominent companies, such as Microsoft and Intel Security. These messages claim to offer a solution to the problem, generally requesting a fee for a program to download. Snopes.com compiles these hoaxes and describes their sources and histories.

In reality, these fake messages are generated by unscrupulous scammers preying upon gullible people who panic and follow the directions in the message. These users divulge credit card information and then often download files riddled with viruses.

If you receive one of these virus hoaxes, never respond to the message. Instead, delete it. Most importantly, never forward it to an unsuspecting friend or coworker. If you receive the virus hoax from someone you know, send him or her a separate email message with information about the hoax.

Consider This: Have you ever received a virus hoax? If so, what action did you take?

 CONSIDER THIS

How do antivirus programs detect viruses?

Many antivirus programs identify viruses by looking for virus signatures. A *virus signature*, also called a virus definition, is a known specific pattern of virus code. Computer users should update their antivirus program's signature files regularly. This extremely important activity allows the antivirus program to protect against viruses written since the antivirus program was released and/or its last update. Most antivirus programs contain an automatic update feature or regularly prompts users to download the updated virus signatures, usually at least once a week. The vendor usually provides this service to registered users at no cost for a specified time.

Spyware, Adware, and Other Malware Removers

Spyware is a type of program placed on a computer or mobile device without the user's knowledge that secretly collects information about the user and then communicates the information it collects to some outside source while the user is online. Some vendors or employers use spyware to collect information about program usage or employees. Internet advertising firms often collect information about users' browsing habits. Spyware can enter your computer when you install a new program, through a graphic on a webpage or in an email message, or through malware.

Adware is a type of program that displays an online advertisement in a banner or pop-up or pop-under window on webpages, email messages, or other Internet services. Sometimes, Internet advertising firms hide spyware in adware. A **spyware remover** is a type of program that detects and deletes spyware and similar programs. An **adware remover** is a program that detects and deletes adware. Malware removers detect and delete spyware, adware, and other malware. Read Secure IT 4-5 for measures you can take to protect your mobile device from malware.

CONSIDER THIS

Are cookies spyware?

A *cookie* is a small text file that a web server may place on your computer or mobile device when you view a webpage. Websites may use cookies to remember information such as items placed in a shopping cart, user names, names, or addresses typed when completing an online form, and whether or not you are currently signed in to a website. Cookies typically expire after a short period, such as 30 days. Most websites include information about their use of cookies in their privacy policies. Cookies are not considered spyware because website developers do not attempt to conceal the cookies.

 SECURE IT 4-5

Malware Risks to Mobile Devices

Practically every smartphone is vulnerable to hacking attacks. Threats to smartphones and mobile devices are growing in record numbers due to the rising popularity of these products and the variety of marketplace sources for downloading apps.

One of the biggest concerns about mobile apps is that they might contain malware that enables your device to "spy" on you. When you download an app, you also may give the app permission to access some of the capabilities or content of a smartphone, such as the camera, current location, calendar, contacts, or call history. One case was reported where malware enabled a flashlight app to access

a device's camera. When the user accessed a banking app to scan a check for deposit, the flashlight app sent a photo of the check to a remote server. As a result, personal bank account information was transmitted without the user's knowledge. Other apps have been reported to contain malware that turned on a microphone without users knowing, thereby enabling others to remotely listen in on conversations.

Smartphone users can take several precautions to guard against malware threats. They include:

- Read reviews of apps and the companies that create them before downloading the apps to your mobile device.

- Use mobile malware and antivirus protection.
- Grant apps access to only the data or phone capabilities needed to run.
- Turn off or delete apps that you do not use regularly.
- Keep the operating system and apps up to date.
- Enable the screen lock feature, and use a strong password to unlock the device.
- Reset the mobile device to factory settings before selling or trading it in.

✸ **Consider This:** Which of these guidelines do you follow now when using your smartphone or mobile device? How will you modify your usage after reading these tips?

Internet Filters

Filters are programs that remove or block certain items from being displayed. Four widely used Internet filters are anti-spam programs, web filters, phishing filters, and pop-up and pop-under blockers.

Anti-Spam Programs   Spam is an unsolicited email message or posting sent to many recipients or forums at once. Spam is considered Internet junk mail. The content of spam ranges from selling a product or service, to promoting a business opportunity, to advertising offensive material. Spam also may contain links or attachments that contain malware.

An **anti-spam program** is a filtering program that attempts to remove spam before it reaches your inbox or forum. If your email program does not filter spam, many anti-spam programs are available at no cost on the web. ISPs often filter spam as a service for their subscribers.

Web Filters   **Web filtering software** is a program that restricts access to certain material on the web. Some restrict access to specific websites; others filter websites that use certain words or phrases. Many businesses use web filtering software to limit employees' web access. Some schools, libraries, and parents use this software to restrict access to websites that are not educational.

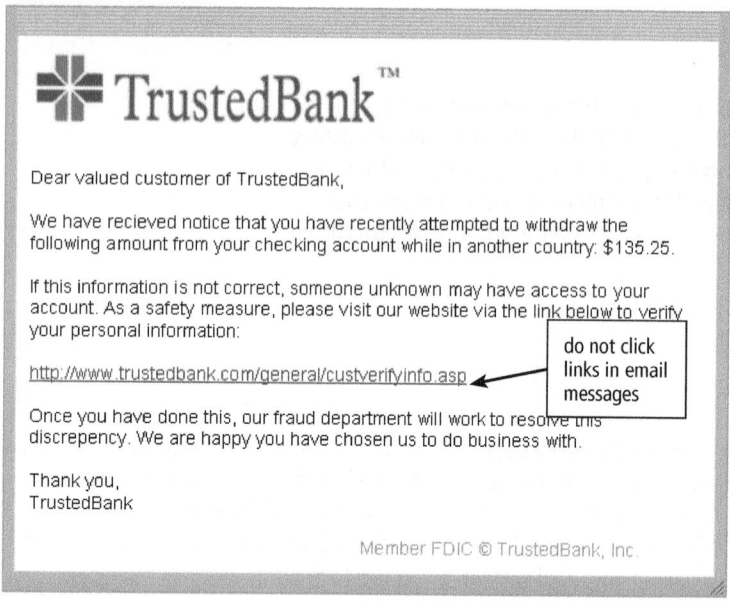

Figure 4-26 An example of a phishing email message.
Source: Andrew Levine

Phishing Filters　**Phishing** is a scam in which a perpetrator sends an official-looking email message that attempts to obtain your personal and/or financial information (Figure 4-26). Some phishing messages ask you to reply with your information; others direct you to a phony website or a pop-up or pop-under window that looks like a legitimate website, which then collects your information.

A **phishing filter** is a program that warns or blocks you from potentially fraudulent or suspicious websites. Some browsers include phishing filters.

Pop-Up and Pop-Under Blockers　A *pop-up ad* is an Internet advertisement that suddenly appears in a new window on top of a webpage. Similarly, a *pop-under ad* is an Internet advertisement that is hidden behind the browser window so that it will be viewed when users close their browser windows. A **pop-up blocker** or **pop-under blocker** is a filtering program that stops pop-up or pop-under ads from displaying on webpages. Many browsers include these blockers. You also can download pop-up and pop-under blockers from the web at no cost.

File, Disk, and System Management Tools

To perform maintenance-type tasks related to managing a computer, its devices, or its programs, you can use one or more file, disk, and system management tools. Functions provided by these tools include the following: managing files, searching, viewing images, uninstalling software, cleaning up disks, defragmenting disks, setting up screen savers, compressing files, maintaining a personal computer, and backing up files and disks. Although some of these tools are included with the operating system, you also can purchase stand-alone programs that offer improvements or added functionality.

Figure 4-27 With a file manager, you can view folders and different types of files containing documents, photos, and music. In this case, thumbnails of photos are displayed.
Source: Microsoft

File Manager

A **file manager** is a tool that performs functions related to file management. Some of the file management functions that a file manager performs are displaying a list of files on a storage medium (Figure 4-27); organizing files in folders; and copying, renaming, deleting, moving, and sorting files. A **folder** is a specific named location on a storage medium that contains related files. Most operating systems typically include a file manager.

Search

A **search tool** is a program, usually included with an operating system, that attempts to locate a file, contact, calendar event, app or any other item stored on your computer or mobile device based on criteria you specify (Figure 4-28). Search tools can look through documents, photos, music, calendars, contacts, and other items on your computer or mobile device and/or on the Internet, combining search results in a single location.

Search tools typically use an index to assist with locating items quickly. An *index* stores a variety of information about a file, including its name, date created, date modified, author name, and so on. When you enter search criteria, instead of looking through every file and folder on the storage medium, the search tool looks through the index first to find a match. Each entry in the index contains a link to the actual file on the storage media for easy retrieval.

Image Viewer

An **image viewer** is a tool that allows users to display, copy, and print the contents of a graphics file, such as a photo (Figure 4-29). With an image viewer, users can see

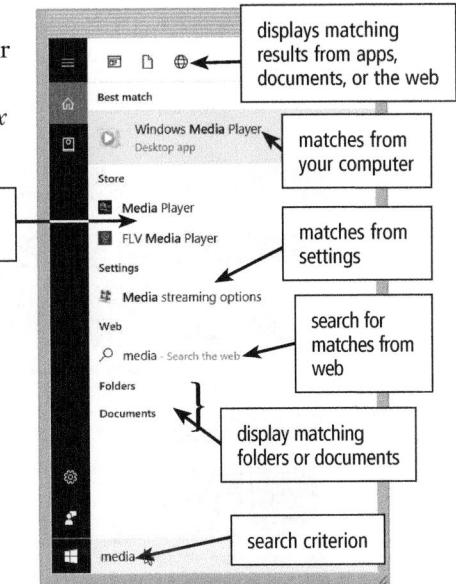

Figure 4-28   Search tools locate apps, folders, files, settings, and other items on your device or the web that match a search criteria
Source: Microsoft

Figure 4-29   An image viewer allows users to see the contents of a photo file.
Source: Microsoft

images without having to open them in a paint or image editing program. Many image viewers include some photo editing capabilities. Most operating systems include an image viewer.

Uninstaller

An **uninstaller** is a tool that removes a program, as well as any associated entries in the system files. When you install a program, the operating system records the information it uses to run the software in the system files. The uninstaller deletes files and folders from the hard drive, as well as removes program entries from the system files. Read How To 4-3 for instructions about uninstalling programs and removing apps from your computers and mobile devices.

 HOW TO 4-3

Uninstall a Program or Remove an App
Uninstalling unwanted programs and apps will save storage space on your computer or mobile device and maximize its performance. The following steps describe how to uninstall a program or remove an app.

Windows
1. Open the Control Panel.
2. Click the option to uninstall a program.
3. Click to select the program to uninstall.
4. Click the Uninstall button and then follow the prompts on the screen.

Mac
1. Open the Finder.
2. Click Applications in the left pane.
3. Locate the app you wish to uninstall.
4. Drag the app's icon to the Trash.

iOS
1. Press and hold the icon for the app you wish to delete until the app icons begin to animate.
2. Tap the X on the icon for the app you wish to uninstall from your device.

Android
1. Display the Settings menu.
2. Locate the Application manager to display a list of installed applications.
3. Tap the application to uninstall.
4. Tap the Uninstall button.
5. Tap the OK button.

Consider This: For what reason might you uninstall an app from your computer or mobile device?

CONSIDER THIS

Can you use a file manager to delete a program?
If an uninstaller exists and you remove software from a computer by deleting the files and folders associated with the program without running the uninstaller, the system file entries might not be updated. This may cause the operating system to display error messages when you start the computer.

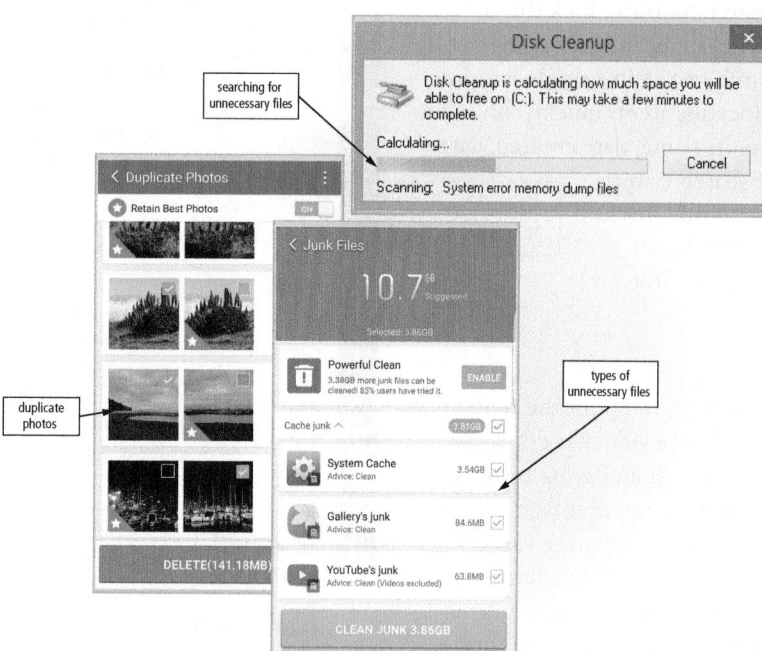

Figure 4-30 A disk cleanup tool searches for and removes unnecessary files on a computer or mobile device.
Source: CleanMaster; Microsoft

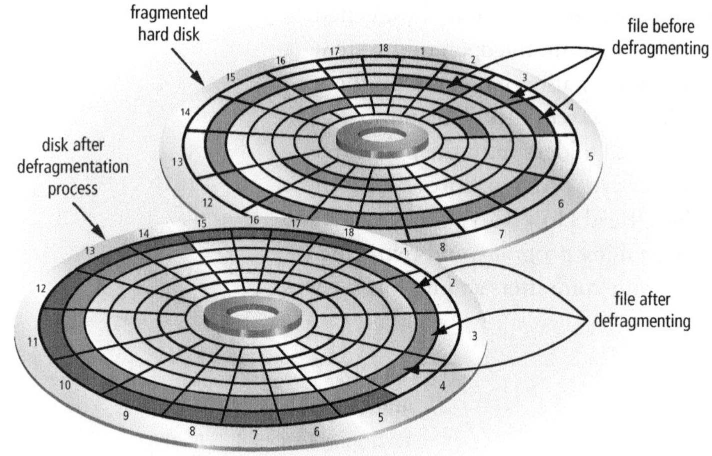

Figure 4-31 A fragmented hard disk has many files stored in noncontiguous sectors. Defragmenting reorganizes the files so that they are located in contiguous sectors, which speeds access time.

Disk Cleanup

A **disk cleanup** tool searches for and removes unnecessary files on computers and mobile devices. Unnecessary files may include downloaded program files, temporary Internet files, deleted files, and unused program files. Operating systems usually include a disk cleanup tool. Disk cleanup tools for mobile devices often locate duplicate files or photos, or large files that a user might want to delete (Figure 4-30).

Disk Defragmenter

A **disk defragmenter** is a tool that reorganizes the files and unused space on a computer's hard disk so that the operating system accesses data more quickly and programs run faster. When an operating system stores data on a hard disk, it places the data in the first available sector (a storage location on a disk in the shape of an arc). The operating system attempts to place data in sectors that are contiguous (next to each other), but this is not always possible. When the contents of a file are scattered across two or more noncontiguous sectors, the file is fragmented.

Fragmentation slows down file access and, thus, the performance of the entire computer. Defragmenting the hard disk, or reorganizing it so that the files are stored in contiguous sectors, solves this problem (Figure 4-31). Operating systems usually include a disk defragmenter.

You do not need to defragment an SSD (solid-state drive). Solid-state drives use a different process to optimize performance. When you delete a file from an SSD, most operating systems mark the locations where it was stored as "not in use" and erase the content so that those locations can be overwritten.

Screen Saver

A **screen saver** is a tool that causes a display device's screen to show a moving image or blank screen if no keyboard or mouse activity occurs for a specified time. When you press a key on the keyboard, tap the screen, or move the mouse, the screen saver disappears and the screen returns to the previous state.

File Compression

A **file compression tool** shrinks the size of a file(s). A compressed file takes up less storage space than the original file. You may need to compress a file so that it will fit on a smaller storage medium, such as a USB flash drive. When you select multiple files or folders to include in a compressed file, the file compression tool will group all of them into one compressed file. Sending a compressed file as an attachment to an email message is often preferable to attaching several files individually.

Compressed files sometimes are called **zipped files**. When you receive or download a compressed file, you must uncompress it. To **uncompress** (or unzip or expand) a file, you restore the file(s) or folder(s) it contains to their original form. Most operating systems include file compression and uncompression capabilities.

PC Maintenance

A **PC maintenance tool** is a program that identifies and fixes operating system problems, detects and repairs drive problems, and includes the capability of improving a computer's performance. Additionally, some personal computer maintenance utilities continuously monitor a computer while you use it to identify and repair problems before they occur.

Backup and Restore

A **backup tool** allows users to copy, or back up, selected files or the contents of an entire storage medium to another storage location, such as another hard drive, optical disc, USB flash drive, or the cloud. Many backup programs compress files during the backup process so they require less storage space than the original files.

Because they are compressed, you usually cannot use backup files in their backed up form. In the event you need to use a backup file, a **restore tool** reverses the process and returns backed up files to their original form. Backup tools work with a restore tool. You should back up files and storage devices regularly in the event your originals are lost, damaged, or destroyed.

 CONSIDER THIS

What is the difference between a cloud backup service and a cloud storage service?
The major difference is that cloud backup services automatically back up all user files, servers, applications, and settings to the cloud in case of hard drive failure or some other disaster. Users specify the locations of files and folders to back up and may schedule whether to back up files continuously or at scheduled times. Files usually are compressed and transferred securely to the cloud, and prior versions are retained in case they need to be recovered. Users can access copies of the saved files from their computer or mobile device.

Cloud storage services, on the other hand, do not automatically back up all files. They make some files available to access across many devices, and users are able to share them with others. Users typically specify one folder on their hard drive for a cloud storage service to save on the cloud; changes to the contents of that folder then will be saved on the cloud and replicated to other devices. Many cloud storage services retain only the most recent version of a file, overwriting any previous versions.

Consumers often take advantage of cloud storage as an easy way to back up their documents, music, videos, photos, and other personal files, while enterprise and professional users with more demanding requirements will employ cloud backup services to back up all of the files on their computers.

Power Management

A **power management tool** monitors a laptop or mobile device's battery usage, showing apps that consume the most battery power, displaying battery usage data since the device was last charged, and estimating usage time remaining. Power management apps can enable power saving mode automatically when a device's battery runs low so that the battery will last longer until charged. Typically, devices in power saving mode operate without Internet connectivity and diminish display brightness to save remaining battery power.

Summary

This module presented a variety of programs and apps available for computers and mobile devices. You learned about the role of the operating system and the various ways software is distributed and created. The module presented the features of a variety of productivity applications, graphics and media applications, and personal interest applications. It reviewed several communications applications and then presented features of a variety of security tools and file, disk, and system management tools.

Study Guide

The Study Guide reinforces material you should know after reading this module.

Instructions: Answer the questions below using the format that helps you remember best or that is required by your instructor. Possible formats may include one or more of these options: write the answers; create a document that contains the answers; record answers as audio or video using a webcam, smartphone, or portable media player; post answers on a blog, wiki, or website; or highlight answers in the book/e-book.

1. List categories of programs and apps. _____ is another word for program.

2. Define these terms: operating system, tools, and system software.

3. List examples of desktop and mobile operating systems.

4. Describe how an operating system interacts with the computer.

5. _____ software performs functions specific to a business or industry.

6. Differentiate among mobile apps, native apps, cloud apps, and web apps.

7. List any restrictions for shareware, freeware, open source, and public-domain software.

8. Explain considerations for safely downloading software and apps.

9. Describe steps to register and activate software.

10. Explain the purpose of a license agreement.

11. List types of productivity applications.

12. Describe the activities that occur during project development.

13. Differentiate among font, font size, and font style.

14. Explain the impact of the Internet on plagiarism.

15. Applications often include a(n) _____ gallery, which is a collection of clip art and photos.

16. Identify functions of the following software: word processing, presentation, spreadsheet, database, note taking, text editor, calendar and contact management, software suite, project management, accounting, personal finance, legal, tax preparation, document conversion and readers, and enterprise computing.

17. Identify tools word processing programs provide that can assist you when writing.

18. Define the following terms: worksheet and function.

19. Describe when you should use a database and when to use a spreadsheet.

20. List advantages of using a software suite.

21. Identify ways you can manage a project using project management software.

22. List safety considerations when using personal finance apps.

23. Name the types of software used by various functional units in an enterprise.

24. Identify functions of the following apps: calendar and email, travel, financial, reference, retail, scanning, and online social networks.

25. Identify risks when using payment apps.

26. Identify functions of the following software: computer-aided design, desktop publishing, paint/image editing, photo editing and photo management, video and audio editing, multimedia and website authoring, media player, and augmented and virtual reality.

27. List ways to edit digital photos. Identify issues surrounding altered digital photos.

28. _____ authoring software allows users to combine text, graphics, audio, video, and animation in an interactive application.

29. Define these terms: CBT, WBT, and MOOC.

30. List types of personal interest applications.

31. Describe ways to use voice command personal assistant apps.

32. Identify functions of the following apps: media sharing; streaming audio and video; gaming; news, sports, and weather; mapping; health and fitness; and academic.

33. Identify types of communications applications.

34. List issues surrounding an email provider scanning users' email messages.

35. Identify functions of the following tools: personal firewalls, hardware firewalls, antivirus programs, malware removers, and Internet filters.

36. Describe ways a virus infects programs or apps.

37. List types of malware. Identify signs of a virus infection.

38. Explain the risks of and how to avoid computer virus hoaxes.

39. A virus _____ is a known specific pattern of virus code. Differentiate between spyware and adware.

40. Identify ways to avoid malware when using a mobile device.

41. List and describe five types of Internet filters.

42. Identify functions of the following tools: file manager, search, image viewer, uninstaller, disk cleanup, disk defragmenter, screen saver, file compression, PC maintenance, backup and restore, and power management tools.

43. Define the terms, folder and index.

44. List steps to uninstall a program or remove an app.

45. Describe the disk defragmentation process.

46. Compressed files sometimes are called _____ files.

47. List storage media for backups.

You should be able to define the Primary Terms and be familiar with the Secondary Terms listed below.

Key Terms

Primary Terms (shown in **bold-black** characters in the module)

accounting software (4-16)
adware remover (4-34)
anti-spam program (4-35)
antivirus program (4-33)
app (4-2)
application (4-2)
augmented reality app (4-27)
audio editing software (4-26)
backup tool (4-39)
calendar and contact management software (4-14)
clip art/image gallery (4-10)
computer-aided design (4-22)
database (4-13)
database software (4-13)
desktop publishing software (4-23)

disk cleanup (4-38)
disk defragmenter (4-38)
document conversion software (4-19)
file compression tool (4-38)
file manager (4-36)
folder (4-36)
image editing software (4-24)
image viewer (4-37)
legal software (4-18)
media player (4-27)
multimedia authoring software (4-26)
note taking software (4-14)
paint software (4-23)
PC maintenance tool (4-39)
PDF (4-19)
personal finance software (4-17)

personal firewall (4-32)
phishing (4-36)
phishing filter (4-36)
photo editing software (4-24)
photo management software (4-24)
pop-under blocker (4-36)
pop-up blocker (4-36)
power management tool (4-39)
presentation software (4-11)
program (4-2)
project management software (4-15)
QR code (4-21)
restore tool (4-39)
screen saver (4-38)
search tool (4-36)
software (4-2)

software suite (4-15)
spam (4-35)
spreadsheet software (4-12)
spyware remover (4-34)
tax preparation software (4-19)
uncompress (4-38)
uninstaller (4-37)
video editing software (4-26)
virtual reality app (4-28)
virus (4-32)
web filtering software (4-35)
website authoring software (4-26)
word processing software (4-10)
worksheet (4-12)
zipped files (4-38)

Secondary Terms (shown in *italic* characters in the module)

adware (4-34)
application software (4-2)
automatic update (4-6)
brightness (4-25)
clipboard (4-8)
cloud app (4-4)
compress (4-25)
computer-based training (CBT) (4-27)
contrast (4-25)
cookie (4-35)
create (4-8)
crop (4-25)
custom software (4-4)
desktop app (4-4)
edit (4-8)
e-filing (4-19)
EULA (4-6)
font (4-9)
font size (4-9)
font style (4-9)
format (4-9)
freeware (4-5)
function (4-13)
hard copy (4-9)

hardware firewall (4-32)
home design/landscaping software (4-23)
illustration software (4-23)
index (4-37)
license agreement (4-6)
marketplace (4-4)
massive open online course (MOOC) (4-27)
mobile app (4-4)
mobile web app (4-4)
native app (4-4)
open source software (4-5)
operating system (4-2)
payload (4-32)
pop-under ad (4-36)
pop-up ad (4-36)
print (4-9)
product activation (4-6)
productivity applications (4-8)
public-domain software (4-5)
quarantine (4-34)
red-eye (4-25)
resize (4-25)
retail software (4-4)

rootkit (4-33)
save (4-9)
security suite (4-32)
shareware (4-5)
sharpness (4-25)
slide show (4-11)
software as a service (SaaS) (4-5)
software registration (4-6)
spyware (4-34)
system software (4-2)

tools (4-2)
trial version (4-4)
trojan horse (4-33)
utilities (4-2)
virus signature (4-34)
web app (4-4)
web-based training (WBT) (4-27)
worm (4-33)

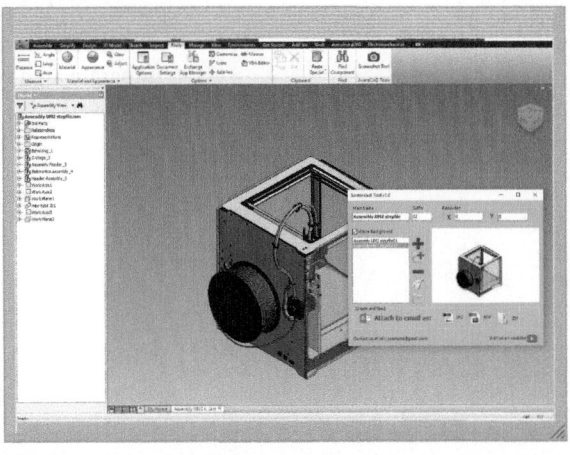

Source: Autocad

Checkpoint

The Checkpoint exercises test your knowledge of the module concepts.

True/False
Mark T for True and F for False. If False, rewrite the statement so that it is True.

_____ 1. Application software serves as the interface between the user, the apps, and the computer's or mobile device's hardware.

_____ 2. Enterprise and professional users employ cloud storage services to back up all of their files in case of disaster.

_____ 3. Open source software is mass-produced, copyrighted software that meets the needs of a wide variety of users.

_____ 4. When downloading shareware, freeware, or public-domain software, it is good practice to seek websites with ratings for and reviews of products.

_____ 5. Because they run in a browser, you always access the latest version of web apps.

_____ 6. With database software, users run functions to retrieve data.

_____ 7. Software suites offer three major advantages: lower cost, ease of use, and integration.

_____ 8. A PDF file can be viewed and printed without the software that created the original document.

_____ 9. Augmented reality apps require the use of a special viewer device to display 360-degree images or videos.

_____ 10. Many routers also can function as a hardware firewall.

_____ 11. A power management app will turn off Internet connectivity when your battery runs low.

_____ 12. Cookies typically are considered a type of spyware.

Matching
Match the terms with their definitions.

_____ 1. augmented reality

_____ 2. CBT

_____ 3. payload

_____ 4. personal firewall

_____ 5. phishing

_____ 6. QR code

_____ 7. quarantine

_____ 8. shareware

_____ 9. software as a service

_____ 10. tools

a. destructive event or prank a virus was created to deliver

b. copyrighted software that is distributed at no cost for a trial period

c. type of mobile application that overlays media or other digital content over an image on the screen

d. program that enables you to perform maintenance-type tasks usually related to managing devices, media, and programs used by computers and mobile devices

e. computing environment where an Internet server hosts and deploys applications

f. security tool that detects and protects a personal computer and its data from unauthorized intrusions

g. type of education in which students learn by using and completing exercises with instructional software

h. scam in which a perpetrator sends an official looking email message that attempts to obtain personal and/or financial information

i. square-shaped graphic that represents a web address or other information

j. separate area of a hard drive that holds an infected file until the infection can be removed

The Problem Solving exercises extend your knowledge of module concepts by seeking solutions to practical problems with technology that you may encounter at home, school, work, or with nonprofit organizations. The Collaboration exercise should be completed with a team.

Problem Solving

Instructions: You often can solve problems with technology in multiple ways. Determine a solution to the problems in these exercises by using one or more resources available to you (such as a computer or mobile device, articles on the web or in print, blogs, podcasts, videos, television, user guides, other individuals, electronics or computer stores, etc.). Describe your solution, along with the resource(s) used, in the format requested by your instructor (brief report, presentation, discussion, blog post, video, or other means).

Personal

1. **Antivirus Program Not Updating**   You are attempting to update your antivirus program with the latest virus definitions, but you receive an error message. What steps will you take to resolve this issue?

2. **Operating System Does Not Load**   Each time you turn on your computer, the operating system attempts to load for approximately 30 seconds and then the computer restarts. You have tried multiple times to turn your computer off and on, but it keeps restarting when the operating system is trying to load. What are your next steps?

3. **Unwanted Programs**   When you displayed a list of programs installed on your computer so that you

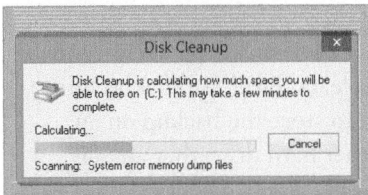

Source: Microsoft

could uninstall one, you noticed several installed programs that you do not remember installing. Why might these programs be on your computer?

4. **News Not Updating**   Each morning, you run an app on your smartphone to view the news for the current day. For the past week, however, you notice that the news displayed in the app is out of date. In fact, the app now is displaying news that is nearly one week old. Why might the app not be updating? What are your next steps?

5. **Incompatible App**   You are using your Android tablet to browse for apps in the Google Play store. You found an app you want to download, but you are unable to download it because a message states it is incompatible

with your device. Why might the app be incompatible with your device?

Professional

6. **Videoconference Freezes**   While conducting a videoconference with colleagues around the country, the audio sporadically cuts out and the video freezes. You have attempted several times to terminate and then reestablish the connection, but the same problem continues to occur. What might be the problem?

7. **License Agreement**   You are planning to work from home for several days, but you are unsure of whether you are allowed to install a program you use at work on your home computer. What steps will you take to determine whether you are allowed to install the software on your home computer?

8. **Low on Space**   The computer in your office is running low on free space. You have attempted to remove as many files as possible, but the remaining programs and files are necessary to perform your daily job functions. What steps might you take to free enough space on the computer?

9. **Unacceptable File Size**   Your boss has asked you to design a new company logo using a graphics application installed on your computer. When you save the logo and send it to your boss, she responds that the file size is too large and tells you to find a way to decrease the file size. What might you do to make the image file size smaller?

10. **Document Reader Software Cannot Open a PDF File**   Your boss sent you a PDF file for a brochure that the art department created. Your document reader software cannot open the file. What might be wrong?

Collaboration

11. **Technology in Video Production**   The admissions office at a local college is considering creating a promotional video and has asked for your help. The director of admissions would like to incorporate technology wherever possible, in hopes that it would decrease the cost of the video's production. Form a team of three people to determine what technology can be used to assist in producing the video. One team member should research the type of technology that can be used to record the video. Another team member should research software options available for video editing and the types computers or mobile devices necessary to run those applications, and the third team member should research the alternatives for publishing and distributing the video online.

✳ How To: Your Turn

The How To: Your Turn exercises present general guidelines for fundamental skills when using a computer or mobile device and then require that you determine how to apply these general guidelines to a specific program or situation.

Instructions: You often can complete tasks using technology in multiple ways. Figure out how to perform the tasks described in these exercises by using one or more resources available to you (such as a computer or mobile device, articles on the web or in print, online or program help, user guides, blogs, podcasts, videos, other individuals, trial and error, etc.). Summarize your 'how to' steps, along with the resource(s) used, in the format requested by your instructor (brief report, presentation, discussion, blog post, video, or other means).

❶ Compress/Uncompress Files and Folders

You may want to compress files if your hard drive is running out of available space. While the operating system may be able to compress some files by 50 percent or more, other files' sizes may not decrease significantly when they are compressed. Compressed files typically are stored by default in a file with a .zip file extension. The following steps describe how to compress a file or folder and then uncompress (expand or extract) the compressed file.

a. Right-click the file(s) or folders you wish to compress to display a shortcut menu.
b. Click the option to compress the file(s) or folder(s). (You may need to select a Send to or other command to display the compression options.)
c. If necessary, type the desired file name for the compressed file.
   Uncompressing (or expanding) compressed files or folders returns them to their original form. The following steps uncompress a compressed file.
a. Double-click the compressed file.
b. If necessary, click the option to uncompress (expand or extract) the file.
or
a. Right-click the compressed file to display a shortcut menu.
b. Click the option to uncompress (expand or extract) the file.

Exercises

1. In addition to the operating system's built-in functionality to compress files and folders, what other programs and apps exist that can compress files and folders?
2. In addition to trying to free space on your storage device, for what other reasons might you want to compress files and folders?
3. Try compressing various types of files on your hard drive, such as a Word document and an image. Compare the file sizes before and after compression. What did you notice with each type of file?

❷ Back Up Your Computer

Backing up your computer is an important way to protect your programs, apps, and data from loss. The frequency at which people back up their computers can vary. For instance, if you create and modify a lot of files on your computer, you may choose to back up your computer frequently. If you rarely use your computer or primarily use your computer for answering email messages and browsing the web, you might not back up your computer as often. The following steps guide you through the process of backing up a computer.

a. Decide which backup program you wish to use. Some operating systems have built-in tools you can use to back up a computer, or you can install a third-party program.
b. Run the program you will use to back up the computer.
c. If necessary, connect the storage device, such as an external hard drive, you will use to store the backup. If you plan to store the backup on an optical disc or another hard drive that already is installed, you will not need to connect an additional storage device.
d. Make sure the storage medium has enough available space for the backed up files. If you are storing the backup on optical discs, make sure you have enough optical discs for the backup.
e. Select the type of backup (full, incremental, differential, or selective) you wish to perform.
f. If you are performing a selective backup, choose the files, programs, and apps you wish to include in the backup.
g. Run the backup. The backup process may take up to several hours, depending on the number of files you are including in the backup.
h. If you are storing the backup on optical discs, the backup program may prompt you to insert new, blank optical discs throughout the backup process.
i. When the backup is complete, store the backup in a safe location. In the event you lose data or information on the computer, you will need to retrieve the backup.
j. If you are backing up on the cloud, select and open an account with a cloud backup service. Identify the files and folders to back up, and the frequency by which to copy them on the cloud.

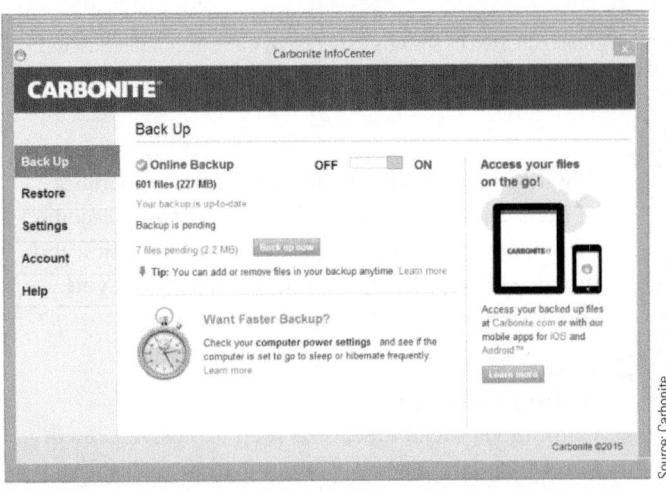

Source: Carbonite

How To: Your Turn

c. Select the option to display the calendar's sharing settings.

d. Specify with whom you want to share the calendar.

e. Determine your sharing settings for each person. For example, you may select whether a person only can view your calendar or view and edit your calendar. You also can select the level of detail you want to share with others. For example, you can share the times you are free or busy, or you can share the specific details for each appointment.

f. If necessary, repeat the two previous steps for each additional person with whom you wish to share the calendar.

g. Save the settings.

h. Verify the people with whom you shared the calendar are able to access the calendar.

Exercises

1. For what other reasons might you share your calendar?

2. In addition to the steps outlined previously, in what other ways can you share your calendar online?

3. In addition to sharing online calendars, is it possible to share calendars you create in programs such as Microsoft Outlook? If so, how?

Exercises

1. How often do you feel you should back up your computer or mobile device? Which storage medium do you feel is most appropriate? Justify your answer.

2. Research at least three programs or cloud backup services that you can use to back up your entire computer. Which products did you research? Which do you feel is the best? Why?

3. How is backing up on the cloud different from backing up files to your own storage media devices?

3 Share Your Online Calendar

If you keep track of your meetings, appointments, and other obligations using an online calendar, you might want to share your calendar with others so that they know when you are available. For instance, you might want to share your calendar with fellow employees so that they can verify your availability before scheduling meetings. Your family members may share their calendars with one another so that it is easier to plan family events when everyone is available. The following steps describe how to share your online calendar.

a. If necessary, run a browser and navigate to an online calendar.

b. Display the calendar's settings.

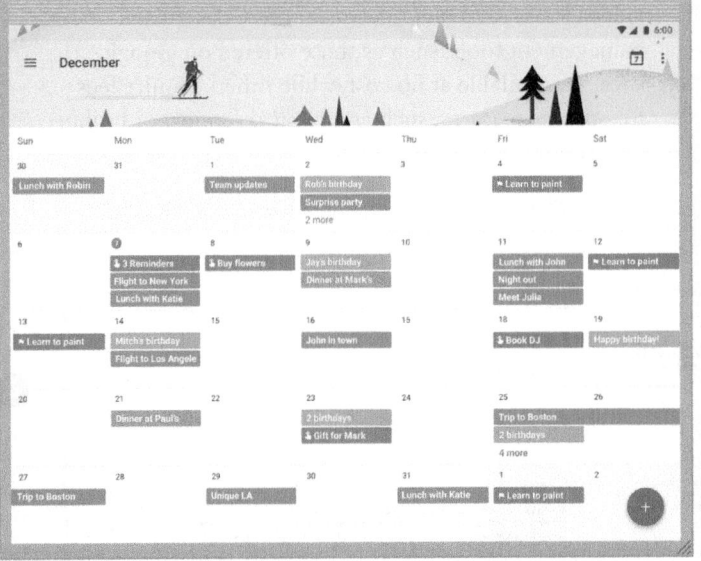

Source: Google Inc.

✺ Internet Research

The Internet Research exercises broaden your understanding of module concepts by requiring that you search for information on the web.

Instructions: Use a search engine or another search tool to locate the information requested or answers to questions presented in the exercises. Describe your findings, along with the search term(s) you used and your web source(s), in the format requested by your instructor (brief report, presentation, discussion, blog post, video, or other means).

1 Making Use of the Web
Website Creation and Management

Retailers and organizations realize the importance of having a website to promote their goods and services. An online presence helps a business connect with an audience and ultimately builds trust and respect. Innovative and dynamic websites deliver information to current and potential customers and clients. Creating these websites requires a methodology of planning, designing, creating, hosting, and maintaining. A business must identify the website's purpose, demographics of the target audience, appropriate content and functionality, page layout, and usability. Once the website is implemented, it must be monitored to determine usage. Logs list the number of visitors, the browsers they used, and usage patterns. In addition, the website should be maintained to update content and features.

Products are available to help build and manage a website. Most offer well-designed templates that can be customized to accommodate specific personal and business needs. They can include calendars, photos, videos, maps, and blogs. Some of these design and management tools, such as those offered on Google sites, are available at no cost, while others require fees for specific features, such as technical support or exclusive designs.

Source: Google Inc.

Research This: Visit Google sites and two other online content management systems for building websites. Compare these web apps by creating a table using these headings: Name, Number of Templates, Price, Maximum Storage, Customer Support, and Features.

The Features column could include the availability of items such as customizable color schemes, e-commerce, drag and drop, website logs and analytics, and mobile editing. Which website builder would you choose if you were creating a website? Why?

2 Social Media
Online Gaming

Gaming via social media has seen explosive growth in recent years, especially among adult males. Exponential gaming growth has spawned companion businesses that facilitate and manage the gaming experience. Some mobile and desktop apps provide gamers with a portal for tracking all their online gaming results in a central location that can be shared with friends and others with similar game interests. These apps integrate with the major Internet messaging services, have personalized news feeds, and incorporate a "suggestion" engine for new game discoveries. Many gaming blogs offer game tricks, work-arounds, and hidden features. Beginning gamers can engage their minds during downtime and expand their circle of online friends.

Research This: Visit at least two online social networks for gamers. How many games are shown? Which topics are featured in community discussions and live chats? Are rewards available? If so, what are they? Which online leagues and tournaments are offered? What are some of the latest news articles about specific games and the gaming industry? Have you participated in gaming online social networks? If so, which ones?

3 Search Skills
Narrowing Your Search Results

One strategy for narrowing search results is to specify what you are or are not looking for as part of your search text. Precede words with a plus sign (+) if you want to ensure that they appear in your search results, and precede a word with a minus sign (-) if you want to exclude that word from search results. For example, typing the phrase, windows +microsoft, will search for information about the operating system; typing the phrase, windows –microsoft, also will find information about windows that are made of glass.

Internet Research

Include the keyword, and, between words or phrases in search text if you want search results to include both words or phrases, or the keyword, or, if search results containing either word or phrase are acceptable. Group terms with parentheses to clarify search text. For example, type the phrase, iPhone and Google, to search for articles about smartphones and Google. Type the phrase, (phone or laptop) and Google, (including the parentheses), to search for information about phones or laptops that also mention Google.

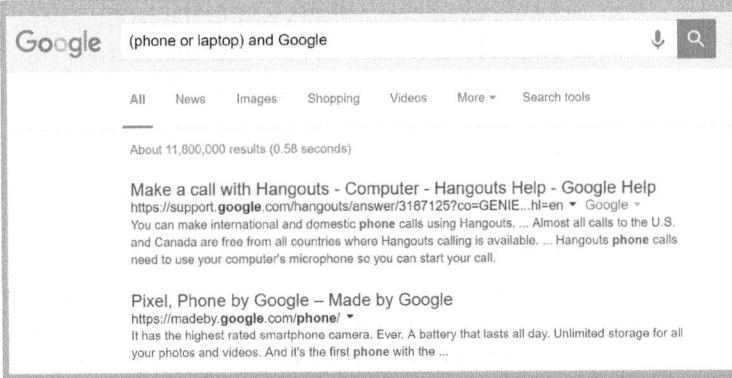

Source: Google, Inc.

Research This: Create search text using the techniques described above or in previous Search Skills exercises, and type it in a search engine to answer these questions. (1) What is an open source FTP application that has versions for both Windows and Mac? (2) Other than TurboTax, what are two examples of online tax preparation software? (3) Find reviews comparing Edge, Chrome, Safari, and Firefox browsers. (4) What are the more popular calendar management and task management apps on the Apple App Store or Google Play?

4 Security
Virus Hoaxes
Virus hoaxes are widespread and sometimes cause panic among Internet users. Secure IT 4-4 in this module gives advice on recognizing and avoiding virus hoaxes. Snopes.com provides further insight on the sources and variations of a wide variety of rumors, deceptions, and folklore.

Research This: Visit snopes.com and type the search text phrase, virus hoaxes & realities, in the Search box at the top of the page. Review the list of the more recent real (indicated by a green dot) and false (indicated by a red dot) rumors circulating on the Internet. Which are the three newest actual warnings, and which are the three latest virus hoaxes? What harm is predicted to occur if a user downloads each of these real or false viruses or views a website laden with malware? What is the origin of the website's name, Snopes?

5 Cloud Services
Photo Editing (SaaS)
Online photo editing apps provide browser-based capabilities to modify digital images and often contain many similar features as their desktop counterparts. They are an example of SaaS (software as a service), a service of cloud computing that provides access to software solutions accessed through a browser. In addition to drawing shapes, touching up colors, and adding filters to images, online photo editing apps allow users to access, store, and share their photos on the cloud. Online photo editing apps often include the capability to share photos with friends easily by sending a link, or posting the photo to online social networks.

Research This: (1) Use a search engine to research various online photo editing apps. Compare the features of two of them as you explore their capabilities. Summarize your findings in a table, regarding image formats you can import or save, sharing capabilities, special editing features, and ways to organize photos online. Which features take advantage of the fact that the app is cloud based? (2) If you have access to computers running two different operating systems, such as Windows and Mac, try running the photo editing app in a browser on both computers. What similarities and differences do you notice between the two versions?

✳ Critical Thinking

The Critical Thinking exercises challenge your assessment and decision-making skills by presenting real-world situations associated with module concepts. The Collaboration exercise should be completed with a team.

Instructions: Evaluate the situations below, using personal experiences and one or more resources available to you (such as articles on the web or in print, blogs, podcasts, videos, television, user guides, other individuals, electronics or computer stores, etc.). Perform the tasks requested in each exercise and share your deliverables in the format requested by your instructor (brief report, presentation, discussion, blog post, video, or other means).

1. File, Disk, and System Management Tools

You are the director of information technology at a company that frequently hires student interns. The interns tend to have limited experience with using file, disk, and system management tools. As part of your job, you lead workshops that teach the interns the many tasks and functions they can perform using these tools.

Do This: Choose three categories of tools, such as disk cleanup, PC maintenance, file compression, cloud storage and backup. Use the web to research popular tools or apps for each category, if they are available as part of an operating system, and the costs for each. Choose one program from each category, and read user reviews and articles by industry experts. Describe situations where you would use each type of tool. Share any experiences you have with using the tools.

2. Web and Mobile App Comparison

You recently purchased a new smartphone and want to research mobile apps that also have accompanying web apps.

Do This: Choose three categories of apps, and find an example for each that has both a free web and mobile version. Read user reviews of each app, and search for articles by industry experts. Research any known safety risks for the apps. If you determine the app is safe, have access to the appropriate device, and would like to test the mobile app, you can download it to a smartphone or other mobile device. Try accessing the web app on a computer. Using your experience or research, note the differences in functionality between the web and mobile app. Is one or the other easier to use? Why or why not?

3. Case Study

Family-Owned Coffee Shop You are the new manager for a family-owned coffee shop. The coffee shop needs productivity software in order to keep track of sales and expenses and to prepare signs to post in the store about menu items, special promotions, or events. You prepare a report to present to the owners about productivity software options to improve their business processes.

Do This: Use the web to research popular word processing, spreadsheet, presentation, and accounting software. Choose three programs from each category. List common features of each, find pricing information, and note any feedback or ratings by users. Which programs would you recommend? Why? Describe the steps involved in developing a project, using the creation of a sign for the coffee shop as an example. Identify possible uses the coffee shop may have for the spreadsheet and accounting software.

SPECIAL TODAY
COFFEE AND A MUFFIN, $2.49

Collaboration

4. Augmented and Virtual Reality in Interior Design

The manager of a home furnishings business is researching ways to use augmented or virtual reality apps to provide an enhanced customer experience at home, on their website, and in the store.

Do This: Form a three-member team and research the use of augmented or virtual reality apps. Each member of your team should choose a different type of app, such as taking panoramic photos, using virtual reality tools for interior design, and enhancing photos or maps with additional information. List ways that a home furnishings or interior design business might use each type of app as part of their business, in the store, in a mobile app, or on their website. If possible, download or access a free version of an augmented or virtual reality app from each category and spend some time using it. Read user reviews of popular apps, and search for articles by industry experts. Meet with your group to discuss your findings, and prepare a report and demonstration showing how a home furnishings business might make use of these apps.

Digital Security, Ethics, and Privacy:
Threats, Issues, and Defenses

5

iStockphoto.com / saidauita

OBJECTIVES

After completing this module, you will be able to:

1 Define the term, digital security risks, and briefly describe the types of cybercriminals

2 Describe various types of Internet and network attacks (malware, botnets, denial of service attacks, back doors, and spoofing) and explain ways to safeguard against these attacks, including firewalls

3 Discuss techniques to prevent unauthorized computer access and use, including access controls, user names, passwords, possessed objects, and biometric devices

4 Explain ways that software manufacturers protect against software piracy

5 Discuss how encryption, digital signatures, and digital certificates work

6 Identify safeguards against hardware theft, vandalism, and failure

7 Explain options available for backing up

8 Identify risks and safeguards associated with wireless communications

9 Recognize issues related to information accuracy, intellectual property rights, codes of conduct, and green computing

10 Discuss issues surrounding information privacy, including electronic profiles, cookies, phishing, spyware and adware, social engineering, privacy laws, employee monitoring, and content filtering

Digital Security Risks

Today, people rely on technology to create, store, and manage their critical information. Thus, it is important that computers and mobile devices, along with the data and programs they store, are accessible and available when needed. It also is crucial that users take measures to protect or safeguard their computers, mobile devices, data, and programs from loss, damage, and misuse. For example, organizations must ensure that sensitive data and information, such as credit records, employee and customer data, and purchase information, is secure. Home users must ensure that their credit card numbers are secure when they make online purchases.

A **digital security risk** is any event or action that could cause a loss of or damage to computer or mobile device hardware, software, data, information, or processing capability. The more common digital security risks include Internet and network attacks, unauthorized access and use, hardware theft, software theft, information theft, and system failure (Figure 5-1).

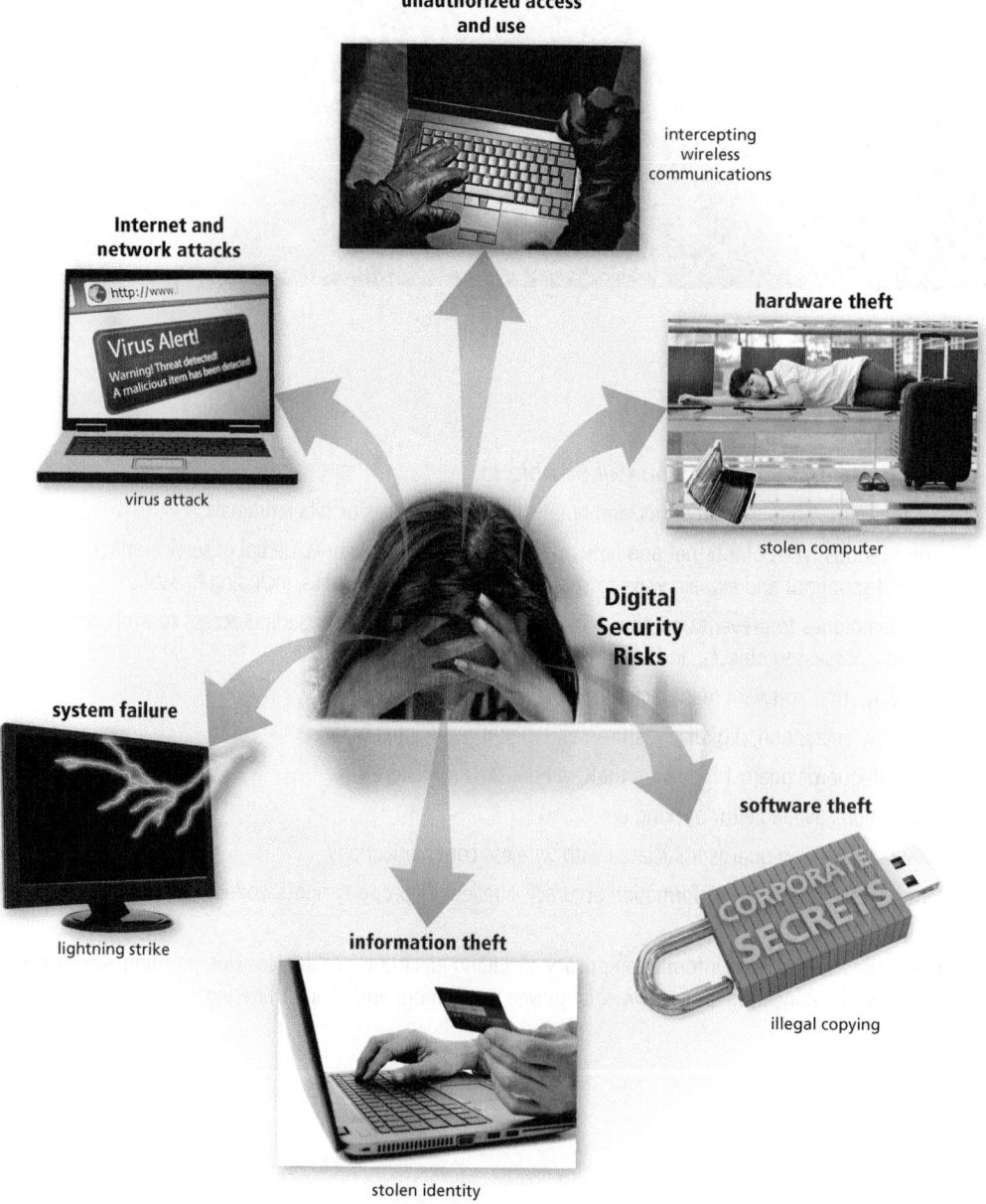

Figure 5-1   Computers and mobile devices, along with the data and programs they store, are exposed to several types of digital security risks.

jamdesign / Fotolia LLC; iStockphoto.com / BrianAJackson; iStockphoto.com / z80; iStockphoto.com / Kenishirotie; JUPITER IMAGES/ Brand X /Alamy Stock Photo

While some breaches to digital security are accidental, many are intentional. Some intruders do not disrupt a computer or device's functionality; they merely access data, information, or programs on the computer or mobile device before signing out. Other intruders indicate some evidence of their presence either by leaving a message or by deliberately altering or damaging data.

Cybercrime

An intentional breach to digital security often involves a deliberate act that is against the law. Any illegal act involving the use of a computer or related devices generally is referred to as a **computer crime**. The term **cybercrime** refers to online or Internet-based illegal acts such as distributing malicious software or committing identity theft. Software used by cybercriminals sometimes is called *crimeware*. Today, combating cybercrime is one of the FBI's top priorities.

Perpetrators of cybercrime typically fall into one of these basic categories: hacker, cracker, script kiddie, corporate spy, unethical employee, cyberextortionist, and cyberterrorist.

- The term **hacker**, although originally a complimentary word for a computer enthusiast, now has a derogatory meaning and refers to someone who accesses a computer or network illegally. Some hackers claim the intent of their security breaches is to improve security.
- A **cracker** also is someone who accesses a computer or network illegally but has the intent of destroying data, stealing information, or other malicious action. Both hackers and crackers have advanced computer and network skills.
- A **script kiddie** has the same intent as a cracker but does not have the technical skills and knowledge. Script kiddies often use prewritten hacking and cracking programs to break into computers and networks.
- Some corporate spies have excellent computer and networking skills and are hired to break into a specific computer and steal its proprietary data and information, or to help identify security risks in their own organization. Unscrupulous companies hire corporate spies, a practice known as corporate espionage, to gain a competitive advantage.
- Unethical employees may break into their employers' computers for a variety of reasons. Some simply want to exploit a security weakness. Others seek financial gains from selling confidential information. Disgruntled employees may want revenge.
- A **cyberextortionist** is someone who demands payment to stop an attack on an organization's technology infrastructure. These perpetrators threaten to expose confidential information, exploit a security flaw, or launch an attack that will compromise the organization's network — if they are not paid a sum of money.
- A **cyberterrorist** is someone who uses the Internet or network to destroy or damage computers for political reasons. The cyberterrorist might target the nation's air traffic control system, electricity-generating companies, or a telecommunications infrastructure. The term, *cyberwarfare*, describes an attack whose goal ranges from disabling a government's computer network to crippling a country. Cyberterrorism and cyberwarfare usually require a team of highly skilled individuals, millions of dollars, and several years of planning.

Some organizations hire individuals previously convicted of computer crimes to help identify security risks and implement safeguards because these individuals know how criminals attempt to breach security.

Internet and Network Attacks

Information transmitted over networks has a higher degree of security risk than information kept on an organization's premises. In an organization, network administrators usually take measures to protect a network from security risks. On the Internet, where no central administrator is present, the security risk is greater. Internet and network attacks that jeopardize security include malware, botnets, denial of service attacks, back doors, and spoofing.

Malware

Recall that **malware**, short for *malicious software*, consists of programs that act without a user's knowledge and deliberately alter the operations of computers and mobile devices. Table 5-1 summarizes common types of malware, all of which have been discussed in previous modules. Some malware contains characteristics in two or more classes. For example, a single threat could contain elements of a virus, worm, and trojan horse.

Malware can deliver its *payload*, or destructive event or prank, on a computer or mobile device in a variety of ways, such as when a user opens an infected file, runs an infected program, connects an unprotected computer or mobile device to a network, or when a certain condition or event occurs, such as the computer's clock changing to a specific date. A common way that computers and mobile devices become infected with viruses and other malware is through users opening infected email attachments (Figure 5-2). Read Secure IT 5-1 to learn about how malware can affect online gaming.

Table 5-1   Common Types of Malware

Type	Description
Adware	A program that displays an online advertisement in a banner, pop-up window, or pop-under window on webpages, email messages, or other Internet services.
Ransomware	A program that blocks or limits access to a computer, phone, or file until the user pays a specified amount of money.
Rootkit	A program that hides in a computer or mobile device and allows someone from a remote location to take full control of the computer or device.
Spyware	A program placed on a computer or mobile device without the user's knowledge that secretly collects information about the user and then communicates the information it collects to some outside source while the user is online.
Trojan horse	A program that hides within or looks like a legitimate program. Unlike a virus or worm, a trojan horse does not replicate itself to other computers or devices.
Virus	A potentially damaging program that affects, or infects, a computer or mobile device negatively by altering the way the computer or device works without the user's knowledge or permission.
Worm	A program that copies itself repeatedly, for example in memory or on a network, using up resources and possibly shutting down the computer, device, or network.

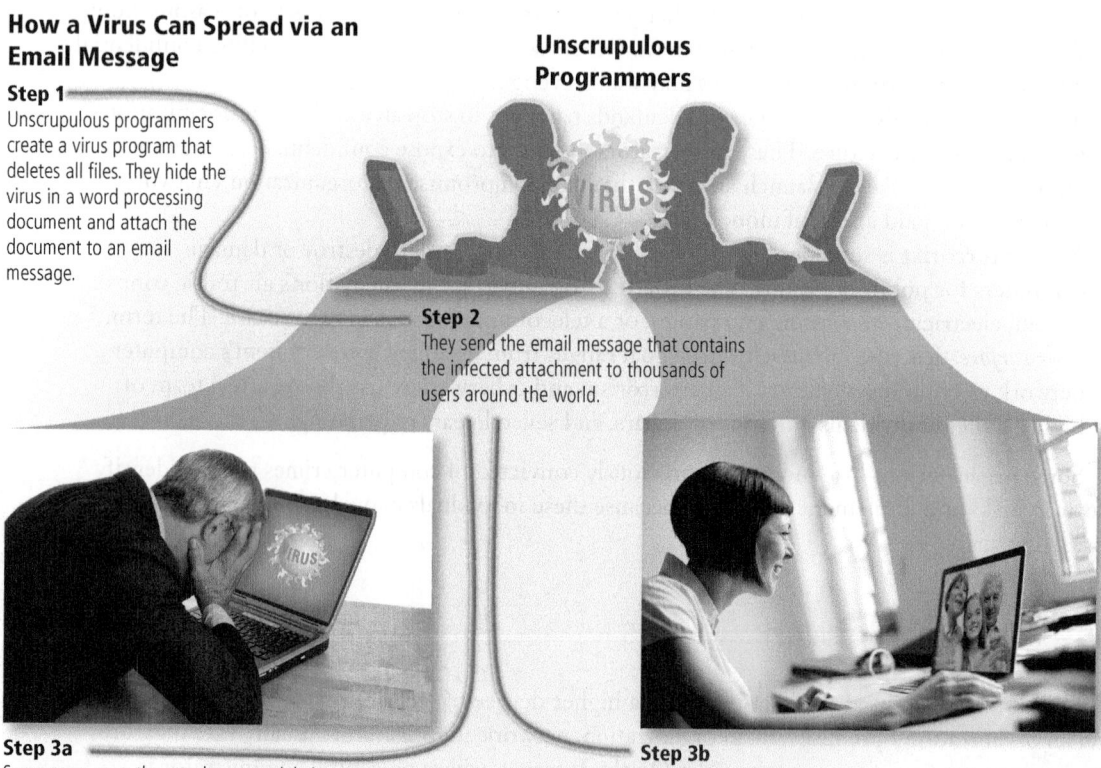

How a Virus Can Spread via an Email Message

Unscrupulous Programmers

Step 1
Unscrupulous programmers create a virus program that deletes all files. They hide the virus in a word processing document and attach the document to an email message.

Step 2
They send the email message that contains the infected attachment to thousands of users around the world.

Step 3a
Some users open the attachment and their computers become infected with the virus.

Step 3b
Other users do not recognize the name of the sender of the email message. These users do not open the email message — instead they immediately delete the email message and continue using their computers. These users' computers are not infected with the virus.

Figure 5-2 This figure shows how a virus can spread via an email message.
iStockphoto.com / Steve Cukrov; iStockphoto.com / Casarsa

CONSIDER THIS

What if you cannot remove malware?

In extreme cases, in order to remove malware from a computer or mobile device, you may need to erase, or reformat, an infected computer's hard drive, or reset a mobile device to its factory settings. For this reason, it is critical you have uninfected (clean) backups of all files. Consider creating recovery media when you purchase a new computer, and be sure to keep all installation media in the event you need to reinstall the computer's operating system and your apps. Seek advice from a technology specialist before performing a format or reformat instruction on your media.

 SECURE IT 5-1

Play It Safe to Avoid Online Gaming Risks

Gamers often understand general security issues regarding online behavior, but they may not be aware of a different set of technology and social risks they may encounter as they interact in the online world. Anyone experiencing the joys of playing games online or playing games with others through online services should realize that thieves and hackers lurking behind the scenes may take advantage of security holes and vulnerabilities that can turn a gaming session into a nightmare.

Viruses, worms, and malware can be hidden in downloaded game files, mobile apps, email message attachments, and messaging software. In addition, messages on online social networks may encourage gamers to visit fraudulent websites filled with malware. If the game requires a connection to the Internet, then any computer connected to the game's server is subject to security

cyberthreats. Thieves can take control of a remote computer that does not have a high level of security protection and use it to control other computers, or they could break into the computer and install malware to discover personal information.

Malicious users know that the gaming community uses social media intensely, so they also create accounts and attempt to mislead uninformed users into revealing personal information. The thieves may claim to have software updates and free games, when they really are luring users to bogus websites that ask users to set up profiles and accounts.

Gamers should follow these practices to increase their security:

- Before downloading any software or apps, including patches to games, or disclosing any private details, check the developer to be certain the website or the person making the request is legitimate.

- Read the permissions notices to learn what information is being requested or being collected. Avoid games requiring passwords to be saved to an online account on a smartphone.

- Exercise extreme caution if the game requires ActiveX or JavaScript to be enabled or if it must be played in administrator mode.

- Use a firewall and make exceptions to allow only trusted individuals to access your computer or mobile device when playing multiplayer online games.

- Do not share personal information with other gamers whom you meet online.

 Consider This: Have you played online games or downloaded gaming apps and followed the advice listed here? How will you change your gaming behavior now that you are aware of specific security threats?

Botnets

A **botnet**, or *zombie army*, is a group of compromised computers or mobile devices connected to a network, such as the Internet, that are used to attack other networks, usually for nefarious purposes. A compromised computer or device, known as a **zombie**, is one whose owner is unaware the computer or device is being controlled remotely by an outsider.

A *bot* is a program that performs a repetitive task on a network. Cybercriminals install malicious bots on unprotected computers and devices to create a botnet. The perpetrator then uses the botnet to send spam via email, spread viruses and other malware, or commit a distributed denial of service attack (discussed in the next section).

 CONSIDER THIS

How can you tell if your computer or mobile device is functioning as a zombie?

Your computer or mobile device may be a zombie if you notice an unusually high drive activity, a slower than normal Internet connection, or connected devices becoming increasingly unresponsive. The chances of your computer or devices becoming part of a botnet greatly increase if your devices are not protected by an effective firewall.

Denial of Service Attacks

A **denial of service attack** (**DoS attack**) is an assault whose purpose is to disrupt computer access to an Internet service, such as the web or email. Perpetrators carry out a DoS attack in a variety of ways. For example, they may use an unsuspecting computer to send an influx of confusing data messages or useless traffic to a computer network. The victim computer network slows down considerably and eventually becomes unresponsive or unavailable, blocking legitimate visitors from accessing the network.

A more devastating type of DoS attack is the *distributed DoS attack* (*DDoS attack*) in which a zombie army is used to attack computers or computer networks. DDoS attacks have been able to stop operations temporarily at numerous websites, including powerhouses such as Yahoo!, eBay, Amazon.com, and CNN.com.

The damage caused by a DoS or DDoS attack usually is extensive. During the outage, retailers lose sales from customers, news websites and search engines lose revenue from advertisers, and time-sensitive information may be delayed. Repeated attacks could tarnish reputations, causing even greater losses.

 CONSIDER THIS

Why would someone execute a Dos or DDoS attack?
Perpetrators have a variety of motives for executing a DoS or DDoS attack. Hactivists, or those who disagree with the beliefs or actions of a particular organization, claim political anger motivates their attacks. Some perpetrators use the attack as a vehicle for extortion. Others simply want the recognition, even though it is negative.

Back Doors

A **back door** is a program or set of instructions in a program that allows users to bypass security controls when accessing a program, computer, or network. Once perpetrators gain access to unsecure computers, they often install a back door or modify an existing program to include a back door, which allows them to continue to access the computer remotely without the user's knowledge. A rootkit can be a back door. Some worms leave back doors, which have been used to spread other worms or to distribute spam from the unsuspecting victim computers.

Programmers often build back doors into programs during system development. These back doors save development time because the programmer can bypass security controls while writing and testing programs. Similarly, a computer repair technician may install a back door while troubleshooting problems on a computer. If a programmer or computer repair technician fails to remove a back door, a perpetrator could use the back door to gain entry to a computer or network.

Spoofing

Spoofing is a technique intruders use to make their network or Internet transmission appear legitimate to a victim computer or network. Two common types of spoofing schemes are IP and email spoofing.

- *IP spoofing* occurs when an intruder computer fools a network into believing its IP address is associated with a trusted source. Perpetrators of IP spoofing trick their victims into interacting with the phony website. For example, the victim may provide confidential information or download files containing viruses, worms, or other malware.
- *Email spoofing* occurs when the sender's address or other components of an email header are altered so that it appears that the email message originated from a different sender. Email spoofing commonly is used in virus hoaxes, spam, and phishing scams (Figure 5-3).

Safeguards against Internet and Network Attacks

Methods that protect computers, mobile devices, and networks from attacks include the following:

- Use antivirus software.
- Be suspicious of unsolicited email attachments.
- Scan removable media for malware before using it.
- Implement firewall solutions.
- Back up regularly.

 BTW

Antivirus Programs
In addition to protecting against viruses and other malware, many antivirus programs also include protection from DoS and DDoS attacks.

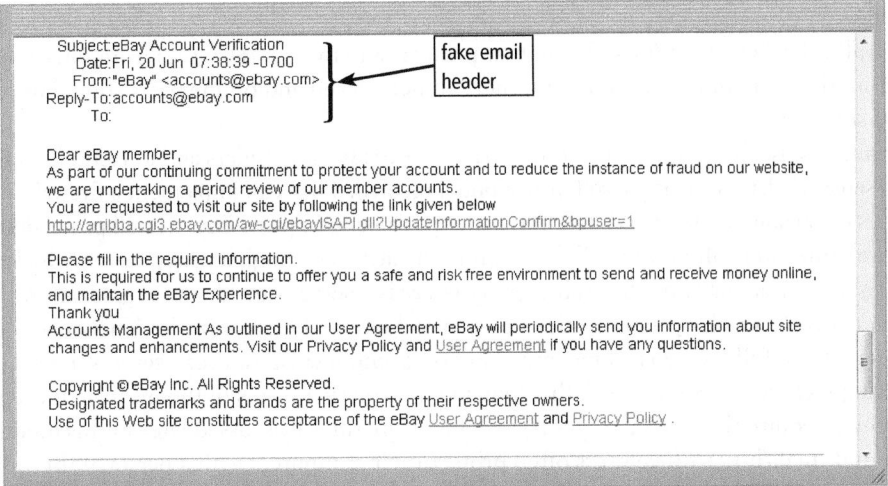

Figure 5-3 With email spoofing, the components of an email header are altered so that it appears the email message originated from a different sender.
Source: Privacy Rights Clearinghouse

Secure IT 1-2 in Module 1 provided some measures you can take to protect your computers and mobile devices from malware. Read Secure IT 5-2 for additional tips to protect home users against Internet and network attacks. The next section discusses firewalls in more depth.

 SECURE IT 5-2

Protection from Viruses and Other Malware

It is impossible to ensure a virus or malware never will attack a computer, but you can take steps to protect your computer by following these practices:

- **Use virus protection software.** Install a reputable antivirus program and then scan the entire computer to be certain it is free of viruses and other malware. Update the antivirus program and the virus signatures (known specific patterns of viruses) regularly.

- **Use a firewall.** Set up a hardware firewall or install a software firewall that protects your network's resources from outside intrusions.

- **Be suspicious of all unsolicited email and text messages.** Never open an email message unless you are expecting it, *and* it is

from a trusted source. When in doubt, ask the sender to confirm the message is legitimate before you open it. Be especially cautious when deciding whether to click links in email and text messages or to open attachments.

- **Disconnect your computer from the Internet.** If you do not need Internet access, disconnect the computer from the Internet. Some security experts recommend disconnecting from the computer network before opening email attachments.

- **Download software with caution.** Download programs or apps only from websites you trust, especially those with music and video sharing software.

- **Close spyware windows.** If you suspect a pop-up or pop-under window may be spyware, close the window. Never click an Agree or OK button in a suspicious window.

- **Before using any removable media, scan it for malware.** Follow this procedure even for shrink-wrapped software from major developers. Some commercial software has been infected and distributed to unsuspecting users. Never start a computer with removable media inserted in the computer unless you are certain the media are uninfected.

- **Keep current.** Install the latest updates for your computer software. Stay informed about new virus alerts and virus hoaxes.

- **Back up regularly.** In the event your computer becomes unusable due to a virus attack or other malware, you will be able to restore operations if you have a clean (uninfected) backup.

 Consider This: What precautions do you take to prevent viruses and other malware from infecting your computer? What new steps will you take to attempt to protect your computer?

 CONSIDER THIS

How can you determine if your computer or mobile device is vulnerable to an Internet or network attack?
You could use an **online security service**, which is a web app that evaluates your computer or mobile device to check for Internet and email vulnerabilities. The online security service then provides recommendations of how to address the vulnerabilities.

Organizations requiring assistance or information about Internet security breaches can contact or visit the website for the *Computer Emergency Response Team Coordination Center*, or *CERT/CC*, which is a federally funded Internet security research and development center.

Firewalls

A **firewall** is hardware and/or software that protects a network's resources from intrusion by users on another network, such as the Internet. All networked and online users should implement a firewall solution.

Organizations use firewalls to protect network resources from outsiders and to restrict employees' access to sensitive data, such as payroll or personnel records. They can implement a firewall solution themselves or outsource their needs to a company specializing in providing firewall protection.

Large organizations often route all their communications through a proxy server, which typically is a component of the firewall. A *proxy server* is a server outside the organization's network that controls which communications pass in and out of the organization's network. That is, a proxy server carefully screens all incoming and outgoing messages. Proxy servers use a variety of screening techniques. Some check the domain name or IP address of the message for legitimacy. Others require that the messages have digital signatures (discussed later in this module).

Home and small/home office users often protect their computers with a personal firewall. As discussed in Module 4, a **personal firewall** is a software firewall that detects and protects a personal computer and its data from unauthorized intrusions. Personal firewalls constantly monitor all transmissions to and from the computer and may inform a user of any attempted intrusions. Both Windows and Mac operating systems include firewall capabilities, including monitoring Internet traffic to and from installed applications. Read How To 5-1 for instructions about setting up a personal firewall.

Some small/home office users purchase a hardware firewall, such as a router or other device that has a built-in firewall, in addition to or instead of a personal firewall. Hardware firewalls stop malicious intrusions before they attempt to affect your computer or network. Figure 5-4 illustrates the purpose of hardware and software firewalls.

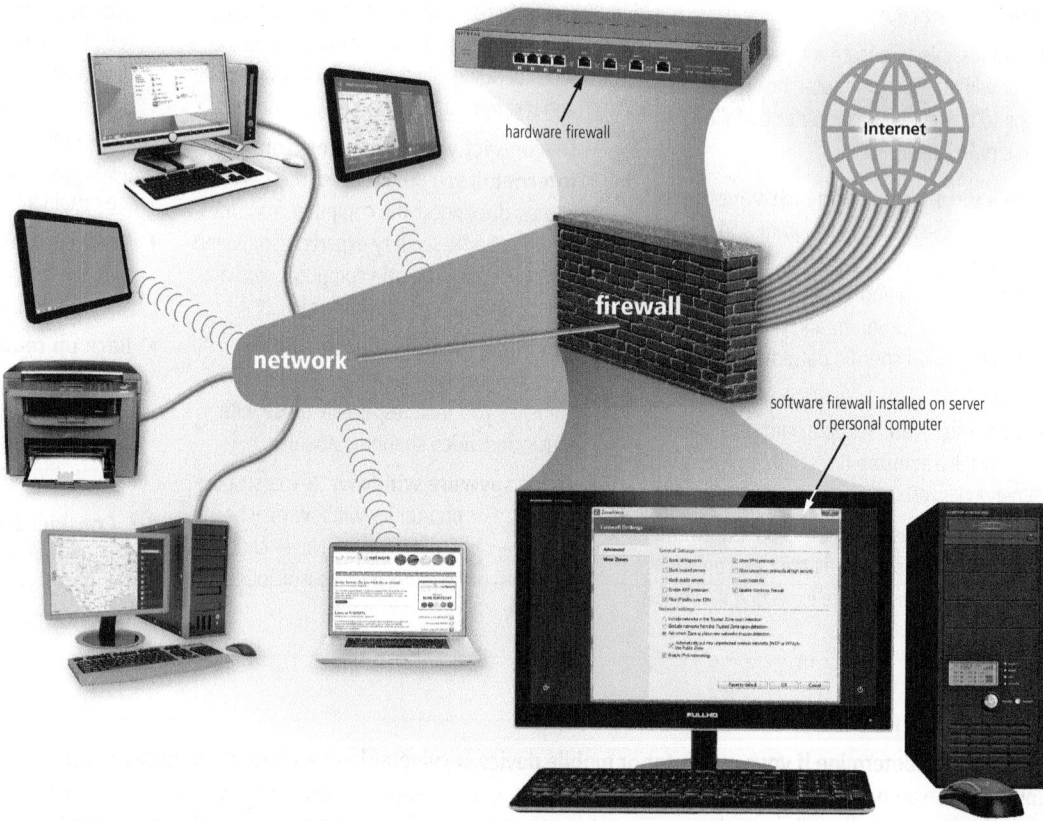

Figure 5-4 A firewall is hardware and/or software that protects a home or business's network resources from intrusion by users on another network, such as the Internet.

Courtesy of NETGEAR; Courtesy of CheckPoint Software Technologies; iStockphoto.com / skodonnell; Source: Nutrition Blog Network; iStockphoto.com / 123render; Source: Microsoft; Natalia Siverina / Shutterstock.com; iStockphoto.com / Oleksiy Mark; Source: Microsoft; iStockphoto.com / arattansi

✳ HOW TO 5-1

Set Up a Personal Firewall

A personal firewall is a program that helps protect your computer from unauthorized access by blocking certain types of communications. For example, if somebody knows the IP address of your computer and attempts to access it using a browser or other program, the personal firewall can be configured to deny the incoming connection. The following steps describe how to set up a personal firewall.

1. If your computer's operating system provides a personal firewall, locate its options in your computer's security settings. If you are using a third-party firewall that you purchased or downloaded online, you may need to disable the one that is included with the operating system because computers typically can have only one active personal firewall running at a time.

2. If you purchase a personal firewall, follow the instructions to install the program on your computer.

3. Run the personal firewall.

4. If necessary, ensure the personal firewall is enabled.

5. Review the settings for the incoming and outgoing rules. Incoming rules display programs and services that are allowed to access your computer. Outgoing rules display programs and services on your computer that are allowed to communicate with other computers and mobile devices on your network or the Internet.

6. Back up or export your current list of incoming and outgoing rules. If your computer does not function properly after you adjust the rules (in Steps 7 and 8), you will be able to restore the current rules.

7. Adjust your incoming rules to disallow devices, programs, and services you do not want accessing your computer. Be careful adjusting these settings, as adding or removing rules may hinder a legitimate program's capability to work properly.

8. Adjust your outgoing rules to allow only appropriate programs on your computer to communicate with other computers and mobile devices on your network or the Internet. Examples include a browser, email program, or other communications programs.

9. Save your settings.

10. Test programs on your computer that require Internet access. If any do not function properly, restore the list of rules you backed up or exported in Step 6.

11. Exit the personal firewall.

✳ **Consider This:** Which programs on your computer should have access to the Internet? Which programs should not?

Unauthorized Access and Use

Unauthorized access is the use of a computer or network without permission. *Unauthorized use* is the use of a computer or its data for unapproved or possibly illegal activities.

Home and business users can be a target of unauthorized access and use. Unauthorized use includes a variety of activities: an employee using an organization's computer to send personal email messages, an employee using the organization's word processing software to track his or her child's soccer league scores, or a perpetrator gaining access to a bank computer and performing an unauthorized transfer.

Safeguards against Unauthorized Access and Use

Organizations take several measures to help prevent unauthorized access and use. At a minimum, they should have a written *acceptable use policy* (*AUP*) that outlines the activities for which the computer and network may and may not be used. An organization's AUP should specify the acceptable use of technology by employees for personal reasons. Some organizations prohibit such use entirely. Others allow personal use on the employee's own time, such as a lunch hour. Whatever the policy, an organization should document and explain it to employees. The AUP also should specify the personal activities, if any, that are allowed on company time. For example, can employees check personal email messages or respond to personal text messages during work hours?

To protect your personal computer from unauthorized intrusions, you should disable file and printer sharing in your operating system (Figure 5-5). This security measure attempts to ensure that others cannot access your files or your printer. You also should be sure to use a firewall. The following sections address other techniques for protecting against unauthorized access and use. The technique(s) used should correspond to the degree of risk that is associated with the unauthorized access.

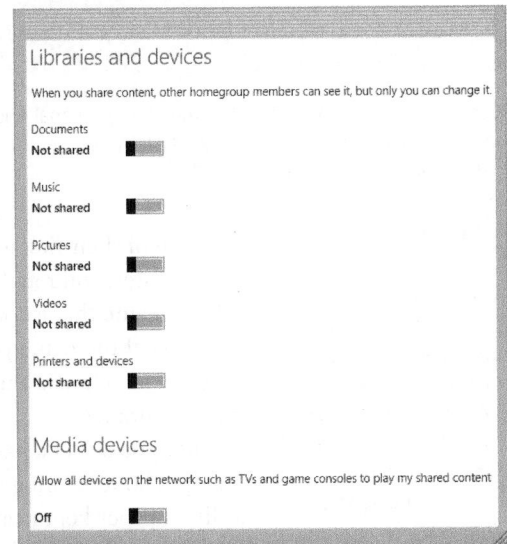

Figure 5-5   To protect files on your device's hard drive from hackers and other intruders, turn off file and printer sharing on your device.
Source: Microsoft

Access Controls

Many organizations use access controls to minimize the chance that a perpetrator intentionally may access or an employee accidentally may access confidential information on a computer, mobile device, or network. An *access control* is a security measure that defines who can access a computer, device, or network; when they can access it; and what actions they can take while accessing it. In addition, the computer, device, or network should maintain an *audit trail* that records in a file both successful and unsuccessful access attempts. An unsuccessful access attempt could result from a user mistyping his or her password, or it could result from a perpetrator trying thousands of passwords.

Organizations should investigate unsuccessful access attempts immediately to ensure they are not intentional breaches of security. They also should review successful access for irregularities, such as use of the computer after normal working hours or from remote computers. The security program can be configured to alert a security administrator whenever suspicious or irregular activities are suspected. In addition, an organization regularly should review users' access privilege levels to determine whether they still are appropriate.

User Names and Passwords

A **user name** — also called a *user ID* (identification), log on name, or sign in name — is a unique combination of characters, such as letters of the alphabet or numbers, that identifies one specific user. A **password** is a private combination of characters associated with the user name that allows access to certain computer resources.

Figure 5-6   Many websites that maintain personal and confidential data, such as Citibank's credit card system, require a user to enter a user name (user ID) and password.

Source: Citigroup Inc

Most operating systems that enable multiple users to share computers and devices or that access a home or business network require users to enter a user name and a password correctly before they can access the data, information, and programs stored on a computer, mobile device, or network. Many systems that maintain financial, personal, and other confidential information also require a user name and password as part of their sign-in procedure (Figure 5-6).

Some systems assign a user name and/or password to each user. For example, a school may use a combination of letters from a student's first and last names as a user name. For example, Brittany Stearn's user name might be stearns_brit. Some websites use your email address as the user name. Information technology (IT) departments may assign passwords so that they have a record in case the employee leaves or forgets the password.

With other systems, users select their own user names and/or passwords. Many users select a combination of their first and last names for their user names. Many online social networks, media sharing sites, and retail and other websites allow you to choose your own user name. You might select a name that is formed from parts of your real name or nickname and possibly some numbers, if the name you want is taken (such as britstearns04). If you wish to remain more anonymous, choose a user name that combines common words, or reflects your interests (such as guitarboston27).

Once you select a password, change it at regular intervals. Read Secure IT 1-3 in Module 1 for tips about creating strong passwords. Do not disclose your password to anyone or write it on a slip of paper kept near the computer, especially taped to the monitor or under the keyboard. Email and telemarketing scams often ask unsuspecting users to disclose their credit card numbers, so be wary if you did not initiate the inquiry or phone call. Read Secure IT 5-3 for tips about using a password manager.

SECURE IT 5-3

Safely Use a Password Manager

If you use the same password to access your banking, shopping, online social networks, and school accounts, you are not alone. Many people think one password is sufficient protection for all their vital online accounts, but cyberthieves are aware of this flawed thinking and take advantage of this practice. Security experts recommend using different user names and passwords for every account and changing the passwords frequently.

Keeping track of all these accounts can be an overwhelming task. A *password manager*, also called a *password organizer*, is a convenient service that stores all your account information securely. Once you select a service, you download and install the software and create one master password. The first time you view a password-protected website and enter your user name and password, the password manager saves this information. The next time you visit one of these websites or apps, the software supplies the account information automatically. Password managers use two-step verification and advanced encryption techniques (discussed later in this module) to ensure information is stored securely.

Some managers offer the option to generate random passwords, which have a unique combination of jumbled numbers and letters that are difficult for criminals to steal, for each account. Other features include the ability to auto-fill information, such as your name, address, and phone number, on forms and to provide a hint if you have forgotten your master password.

Password manager services can be free to use or may require a small annual fee. Some security experts recommend using a service that charges a fee, stating that these companies may provide more features. Before using any manager, call the company and ask about security measures, the ability to sync with multiple mobile devices, 24-hour customer service via live chat or phone, and limits on the number of passwords that can be saved.

 Consider This: Do you use a password manager? If so, do you feel secure storing all your sign in and password information in this service? If not, how do you keep track of your passwords?

 CONSIDER THIS

Why do some websites allow you to use your email address as a user name?

No two users can have the same email address; that is, your email address is unique to you. This means you can use your email address and password from one website to validate your identity on another website. Facebook, Google, and Twitter, for example, are three popular websites that provide authentication services to other applications. By using your email address (or user name) and password from one of these websites to access other websites, you do not have to create or remember separate user names and passwords for the various websites you visit.

In addition to a user name and password, some systems ask users to enter one of several pieces of personal information. Such items can include a grandparent's first name, your favorite food, your first pet's name, or the name of the elementary school you attended. These items should be facts that you easily remember but are not easy for others to discover about you when using a search engine or examining your profiles on online social networks. As with a password, if the user's response does not match information on file, the system denies access.

Passphrase   Instead of passwords, some organizations use passphrases to authenticate users. A *passphrase* is a private combination of words, often containing mixed capitalization and punctuation, associated with a user name that allows access to certain computer resources. Passphrases, which often can be up to 100 characters in length, are more secure than passwords, yet can be easy to remember because they contain words.

PIN   A **PIN** (personal identification number), sometimes called a *passcode*, is a numeric password, either assigned by a company or selected by a user. PINs provide an additional level of security. Select PINs carefully and protect them as you do any other password. For example, do not use the same four digits, sequential digits, or dates others could easily determine, such as birth dates.

⊛ BTW

Default Passwords
If a program or device has a default or preset password, such as admin, be sure to change it to prevent unauthorized access.

✳ CONSIDER THIS

Why do some websites display distorted characters you must reenter along with your password?

These websites use a CAPTCHA, which stands for Completely Automated Public Turing test to tell Computers and Humans Apart. A *CAPTCHA* is a program developed at Carnegie Mellon University that displays an image containing a series of distorted characters for a user to identify and enter in order to verify that user input is from humans and not computer programs (Figure 5-7).

A CAPTCHA is effective in blocking computer-generated attempts to access a website, because it is difficult to write programs for computers to detect distorted characters, while humans generally can recognize them. For visually impaired users or if words are too difficult to read, the CAPTCHA text can be read aloud; you also have the option of generating a new CAPTCHA.

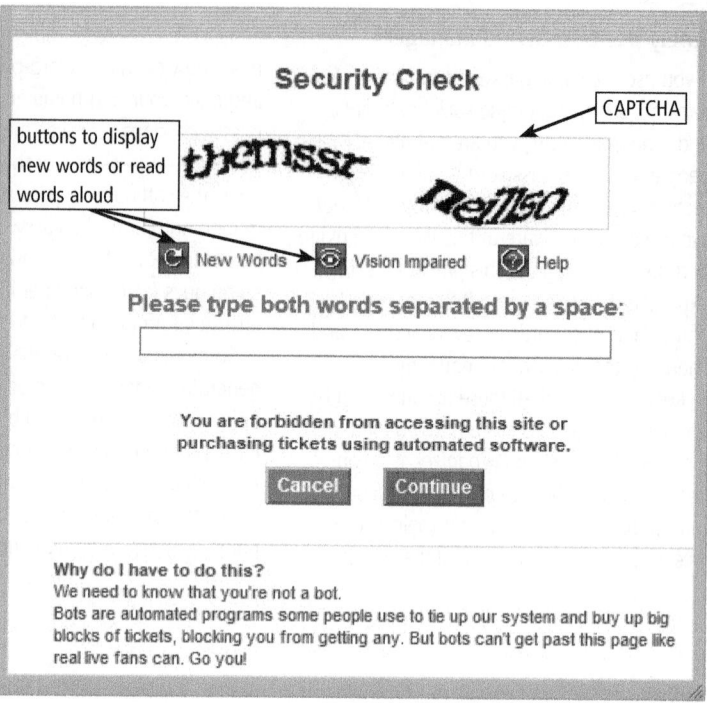

Figure 5-7   To continue with the ticket order process at the Ticketmaster website, the user must enter the characters in the CAPTCHA, which consists of the letters, themssr neillso, in this case.
Source: Carnegie Mellon University

Possessed Objects

A possessed object is any item that you must possess, or carry with you, in order to gain access to a computer or computer facility. Examples of possessed objects are badges, cards, smart cards, and keys. The card you use in an ATM (automated teller machine), for example, is a possessed object that allows access to your bank account.

Biometric Devices

A **biometric device** authenticates a person's identity by translating a personal characteristic, such as a fingerprint, into a digital code that is compared with a digital code stored in a computer or mobile device verifying a physical or behavioral characteristic. If the digital code in the computer or mobile device does not match the personal characteristic code, the computer or mobile device denies access to the individual.

Biometric devices grant access to programs, computers, or rooms using computer analysis of some biometric identifier. Examples of biometric devices and systems include fingerprint readers, face recognition systems, hand geometry systems, voice verification systems, signature verification systems, iris recognition systems, and retinal scanners.

Fingerprint Reader   A **fingerprint reader**, or fingerprint scanner, captures curves and indentations of a fingerprint (Figure 5-8). Organizations use fingerprint readers to secure doors, computers, and software. With the cost of fingerprint readers often less than $100, some home and small business users install fingerprint readers to authenticate users before they can access a personal computer. The reader also can be set up to perform different functions for different fingers; for example, one finger starts a program and another finger shuts down the computer. External fingerprint readers usually plug into a USB port.

Figure 5-8   A fingerprint reader.
Flynavyjp / Dreamstime.com

Some laptops, smartphones, and smartwatches have a built fingerprint reader. Using their fingerprint, users can unlock the computer or device, sign in to programs and websites via their fingerprint instead of entering a user name and password, and on some devices, even test their blood pressure and heart rate.

 CONSIDER THIS

What is a lock screen?
A *lock screen* is a screen that restricts access to a computer or mobile device until a user performs a certain action. Some simply require a user swipe the screen to unlock the screen. Others verify a user's identity by requiring entry of a password, PIN, or passcode; a fingerprint scan; or a gesture swipe (Figure 5-9). Gestures are motions users make on a touch screen with the tip of one or more fingers or their hand. For example, to unlock the screen on a phone, a user could connect the dots on the screen using a pattern previously defined by the user. A picture password allows the user to select an image that appears on the lock screen. The user selects a pattern of taps or gestures on the photo that the computer stores and then must repeat the pattern to unlock the screen.

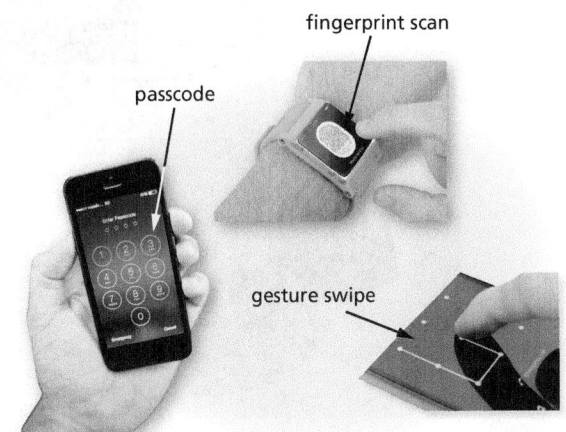

Figure 5-9 Some ways users unlock screens include entering a passcode, scanning a fingerprint, and swiping a gesture.
iStockphoto.com / franckreporter; Alexey Boldin / Shutterstock.com; iStockphoto.com / ymgerman

Face Recognition System   A *face recognition system* captures a live face image and compares it with a stored image to determine if the person is a legitimate user. Some buildings use face recognition systems to secure access to rooms. Law enforcement, surveillance systems, and airports use face recognition to protect the public. Some mobile devices use face recognition systems to unlock the device. Face recognition programs are becoming more sophisticated and can recognize people with or without glasses, makeup, or jewelry, and with new hairstyles.

Hand Geometry System   A *hand geometry system* measures the shape and size of a person's hand (Figure 5-10). Because hand geometry systems can be expensive, they often are used in larger companies to track workers' time and attendance or as security devices. Colleges use hand geometry systems to verify students' identities. Daycare centers and hospital nurseries use them to identify parents who pick up their children.

Voice Verification System   A *voice verification system* compares a person's live speech with their stored voice pattern. Larger organizations sometimes use voice verification systems as time and attendance devices. Many companies also use this technology for access to sensitive files and networks. Some financial services use voice verification systems to secure phone banking transactions.

Signature Verification System   A *signature verification system* recognizes the shape of your handwritten signature, as well as measures the pressure exerted and the motion used to write the signature. Signature verification systems use a specialized pen and tablet. Signature verification systems often are used to reduce fraud in financial institutions.

Figure 5-10 A hand geometry system verifies identity based on the shape and size of a person's hand.
Courtesy of Ingersoll Rand Security Technologies

 CONSIDER THIS

Do retailers use a signature verification system for credit card purchases?
No. With a credit card purchase, users sign their name on a signature capture pad using a stylus attached to the device. Software then transmits the signature to a central computer, where it is stored. Thus, the retailers use these systems simply to record your signature.

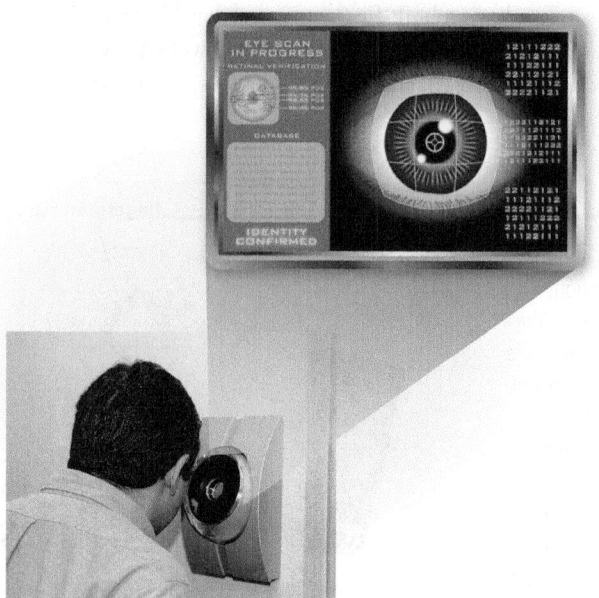

Iris Recognition System   High security areas use iris recognition systems. The camera in an iris recognition system uses iris recognition technology to read patterns in the iris of the eye (Figure 5-11). These patterns are as unique as a fingerprint. Iris recognition systems are quite expensive and are used by government security organizations, the military, and financial institutions that deal with highly sensitive data. Some organizations use retinal scanners, which work similarly but instead scan patterns of blood vessels in the back of the retina.

Figure 5-11   An iris recognition system.
iStockphoto.com / NKND200; Robert F. Balazik / Shutterstock.com

⊛ CONSIDER THIS

How popular are biometric devices?

Biometric devices are gaining popularity as a security precaution because they are a virtually foolproof method of identification and authentication. For example, some grocery stores, retail stores, and gas stations use *biometric payment*, where the customer's fingerprint is read by a fingerprint reader that is linked to a payment method, such as a checking account or credit card. Users can forget their user names and passwords. Possessed objects can be lost, copied, duplicated, or stolen. Personal characteristics, by contrast, are unique and cannot be forgotten or misplaced.

Biometric devices do have disadvantages. If you cut your finger, a fingerprint reader might reject you as a legitimate user. Hand geometry readers can transmit germs. If you are nervous, a signature might not match the one on file. If you have a sore throat, a voice recognition system might reject you. Many people are uncomfortable with the thought of using an iris scanner.

Two-Step Verification

In an attempt to further protect personal data and information from online thieves, many organizations such as financial institutions or universities that store sensitive or confidential items use a two-step verification process. With **two-step verification**, also known as *two-factor verification*, a computer or mobile device uses two separate methods, one after the next, to verify the identity of a user.

ATMs (automated teller machines) usually requires a two-step verification. Users first insert their ATM card into the ATM (Step 1) and then enter a PIN (Step 2) to access their bank account. Most debit cards and some credit cards use PINs. If someone steals these cards, the thief must enter the user's PIN to access the account.

Another use of two-step verification requires a mobile device and a computer. When users sign in to an account on a computer, they enter a user name and a password (Step 1). Next, they are prompted to enter another authentication code (Step 2), which is sent as a text or voice message or via an app on a mobile device (Figure 5-12). This second code generally is valid for a set time, sometimes only for a few minutes. If users do not sign in during this time limit, they must repeat the process and request another verification code. Microsoft and Google commonly use two-step verification when you sign in to their websites. If you sign in from a device you use frequently, you can elect to bypass this step.

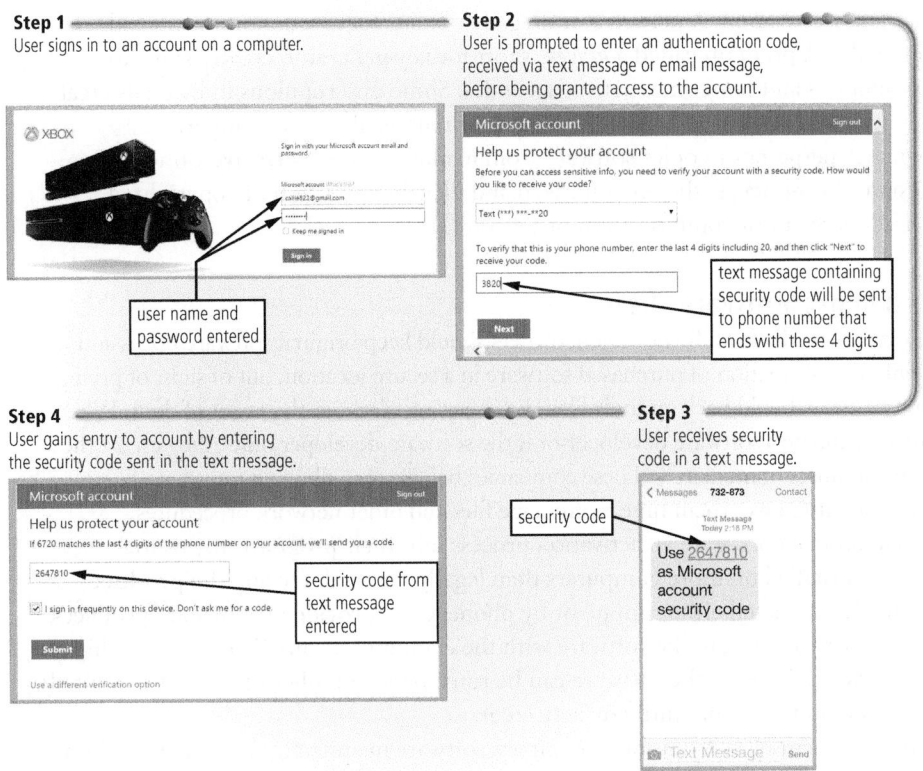

Figure 5-12   This figure shows an example of two-step authentication.
Source: Microsoft

 CONSIDER THIS

Can users circumvent the two-step verification process?
Users may be able to specify a computer or mobile device as a trusted device during a two-step verification so that future sign-in attempts on that same computer or mobile device will bypass the two-step verification. The trusted device they choose should be one they use frequently, such as their personal laptop or smartphone.

Digital Forensics

Digital forensics, also called *cyberforensics*, is the discovery, collection, and analysis of evidence found on computers and networks. Digital forensics involves the examination of media, programs, data and log files on computers, mobile devices, servers, and networks. Many areas use digital forensics, including law enforcement, criminal prosecutors, military intelligence, insurance agencies, and information security departments in the private sector.

A digital forensics examiner must have knowledge of the law, technical experience with many types of hardware and software products, superior communication skills, familiarity with corporate structures and policies, a willingness to learn and update skills, and a knack for problem solving.

Software Theft

Software theft occurs when someone steals software media, intentionally erases programs, illegally registers and/or activates a program, or illegally copies a program.

- Physically stealing software: A perpetrator physically steals the media that contains the software, or steals the hardware that contains the media that contains the software. For example, an unscrupulous library patron might steal a game CD/DVD.
- Intentionally erasing software: A perpetrator erases the media that contains the software. For example, a software developer who is terminated from a company may retaliate by removing or disabling the programs he or she has written from company computers.

 BTW

BSA
To promote understanding of software piracy, a number of major worldwide software companies formed the *Business Software Alliance* (*BSA*). The BSA operates a website and antipiracy hotlines around the world.

- Illegal registration/activation: A perpetrator illegally obtains registration numbers and/ or activation codes. A program called a *keygen*, short for key generator, creates software registration numbers and sometimes activation codes. Some unscrupulous individuals create and post keygens so that users can install software without legally purchasing it.
- Illegal copying: A perpetrator copies software from manufacturers. **Software piracy**, often referred to simply as **piracy**, is the unauthorized and illegal duplication of copyrighted software. Piracy is the most common form of software theft.

Safeguards against Software Theft

To protect software media from being stolen, owners should keep original software boxes and media or the online confirmation of purchased software in a secure location, out of sight of prying eyes. All computer users should back up their files and drives regularly, in the event of theft. When some companies terminate a software developer or if the software developer quits, they escort the employee off the premises immediately. These companies believe that allowing terminated employees to remain on the premises gives them time to sabotage files and other network procedures.

Many manufacturers incorporate an activation process into their programs to ensure the software is not installed on more computers than legally licensed. During the **product activation**, which is conducted either online or by phone, users provide the software product's identification number to associate the software with the computer or mobile device on which the software is installed. Usually, the software can be run a preset number of times, has limited functionality, or does not function until you activate it.

To further protect themselves from software piracy, software manufacturers issue users license agreements. As discussed in Module 4, a **license agreement** is the right to use software. That is, you do not own the software. The most common type of license included with software purchased by individual users is a *single-user license agreement*, also called an *end-user license agreement* (*EULA*). The license agreement provides specific conditions for use of the software, which a user must accept before using the software. These terms usually are displayed when you install the software.

Use of the software constitutes acceptance of the terms on the user's part. Figure 5-13 identifies the conditions of a typical single-user license agreement.

To support multiple users' access of software, most manufacturers sell network versions or site licenses of their software, which usually costs less than buying individual stand-alone copies of the software for each computer. A *network license* is a legal agreement that allows multiple users to access the software on the server simultaneously. The network license fee usually is based on the number of users or the number of computers attached to the network. A *site license* is a legal agreement that permits users to install the software on multiple computers — usually at a volume discount.

Typical Conditions of a Single-User License Agreement

You can...
- Install the software on only one computer or device. (Some license agreements allow users to install the software on a specified number of computers and/or mobile devices.)
- Make one copy of the software as a backup.
- Give or sell the software to another individual, but only if the software is removed from the user's computer first.

You cannot...
- Install the software on a network, such as a school computer lab.
- Give copies to friends and colleagues, while continuing to use the software.
- Export the software.
- Rent or lease the software.

Figure 5-13 A user must accept the terms of a license agreement before using the software.

✳ CONSIDER THIS

Can you install software on work computers or work-issued smartphones?
Many organizations and businesses have strict written policies governing the installation and use of software and enforce their rules by checking networked or online computers or mobile devices periodically to ensure that all software is licensed properly. If you are not completely familiar with your school's or employer's policies governing installation of software, check with the information technology department or your school's technology coordinator.

Information Theft

Information theft occurs when someone steals personal or confidential information. Both business and home users can fall victim to information theft. An unethical company executive may steal or buy stolen information to learn about a competitor. A corrupt individual may steal credit card numbers to make fraudulent purchases. Information theft often is linked to other types of cybercrime. For example, an individual first might gain unauthorized access to a computer and then steal credit card numbers stored in a firm's accounting department.

Safeguards against Information Theft

Most organizations will attempt to prevent information theft by implementing the user identification and authentication controls discussed earlier in this module. These controls are best suited for protecting information on computers located on an organization's premises. To further protect information on the Internet and networks, organizations and individuals use a variety of encryption techniques.

Encryption

Encryption is the process of converting data that is readable by humans into encoded characters to prevent unauthorized access. You treat encrypted data just like any other data. That is, you can store it or send it in an email message. To read the data, the recipient must **decrypt**, or decode it. For example, users may specify that an email application encrypt a message before sending it securely. The recipient's email application would need to decrypt the message in order for the recipient to be able to read it.

In the encryption process, the unencrypted, readable data is called *plaintext*. The encrypted (scrambled) data is called *ciphertext*. An *encryption algorithm*, or *cypher*, is a set of steps that can convert readable plaintext into unreadable ciphertext. A simple encryption algorithm might switch the order of characters or replace characters with other characters. Encryption programs typically use more than one encryption algorithm, along with an encryption key. An *encryption key* is a set of characters that the originator of the data uses to encrypt the plaintext and the recipient of the data uses to decrypt the ciphertext.

Two basic types of encryption are private key and public key. With *private key encryption*, also called *symmetric key encryption*, both the originator and the recipient use the same secret key to encrypt and decrypt the data. *Public key encryption*, also called *asymmetric key encryption*, uses two encryption keys: a public key and a private key (Figure 5-14). Public key encryption software generates both the private key and the public key. A message encrypted with a public key can be decrypted only with the

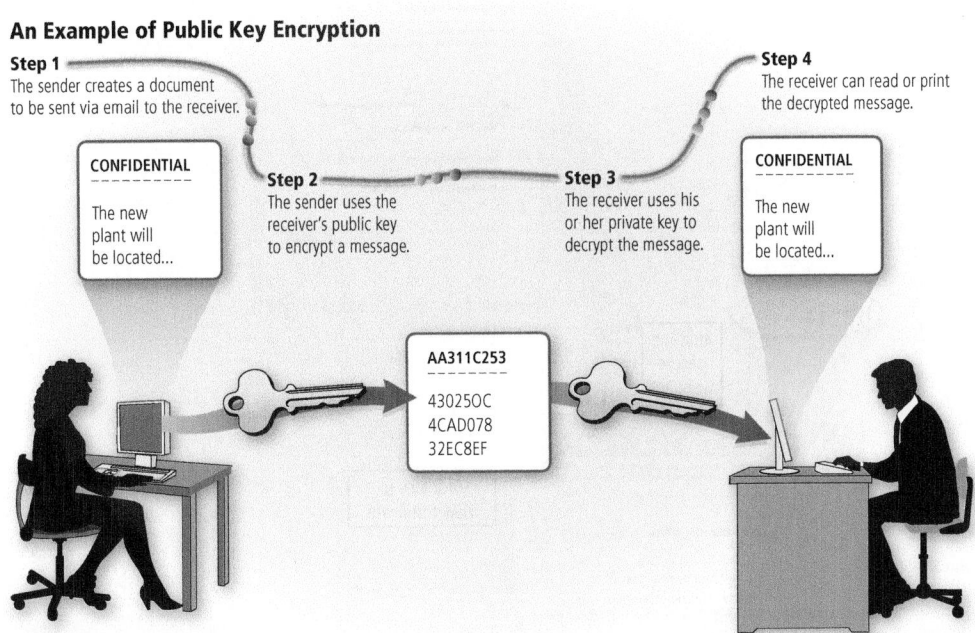

An Example of Public Key Encryption

Step 1
The sender creates a document to be sent via email to the receiver.

Step 4
The receiver can read or print the decrypted message.

CONFIDENTIAL

The new plant will be located...

Step 2
The sender uses the receiver's public key to encrypt a message.

Step 3
The receiver uses his or her private key to decrypt the message.

CONFIDENTIAL

The new plant will be located...

AA311C253

43025OC
4CAD078
32EC8EF

Figure 5-14 This figure shows an example of public key encryption.

corresponding private key, and vice versa. The public key is made known to message originators and recipients. For example, public keys may be posted on a secure webpage or a public-key server, or they may be emailed. The private key, by contrast, should be kept confidential.

Some operating systems and email programs allow you to encrypt the contents of files and messages that are stored on your computer. You also can purchase an encryption program to encrypt files. Many browsers use encryption when sending private information, such as credit card numbers, over the Internet.

Mobile users today often access their company networks through a virtual private network. When a mobile user connects to a main office using a standard Internet connection, a *virtual private network* (*VPN*) provides the mobile user with a secure connection to the company network server, as if the user has a private line. VPNs help ensure that data is safe from being intercepted by unauthorized people by encrypting data as it transmits from a laptop, smartphone, or other mobile device.

Digital Signatures and Certificates

A **digital signature** is an encrypted code that a person, website, or organization attaches to an electronic message to verify the identity of the message sender. Digital signatures often are used to ensure that an impostor is not participating in an Internet transaction. That is, digital signatures can help to prevent email forgery. A digital signature also can verify that the content of a message has not changed.

A **digital certificate** is a notice that guarantees a user or a website is legitimate. E-commerce applications commonly use digital certificates. Browsers often display a warning message if a website does not have a valid digital certificate.

A website that uses encryption techniques to secure its data is known as a **secure site** (Figure 5-15). Web addresses of secure sites often begin with https instead of http. Secure sites typically use digital certificates along with security protocols.

 CONSIDER THIS

Who issues digital certificates?
A *certificate authority* (*CA*) is an organization that issues digital certificates. Each CA is a trusted third party that takes responsibility for verifying the sender's identity before issuing a certificate. Individuals and companies can purchase digital certificates from one of more than 40 online CA providers. The cost varies depending on the desired level of data encryption, with the strongest levels recommended for financial and e-commerce transactions.

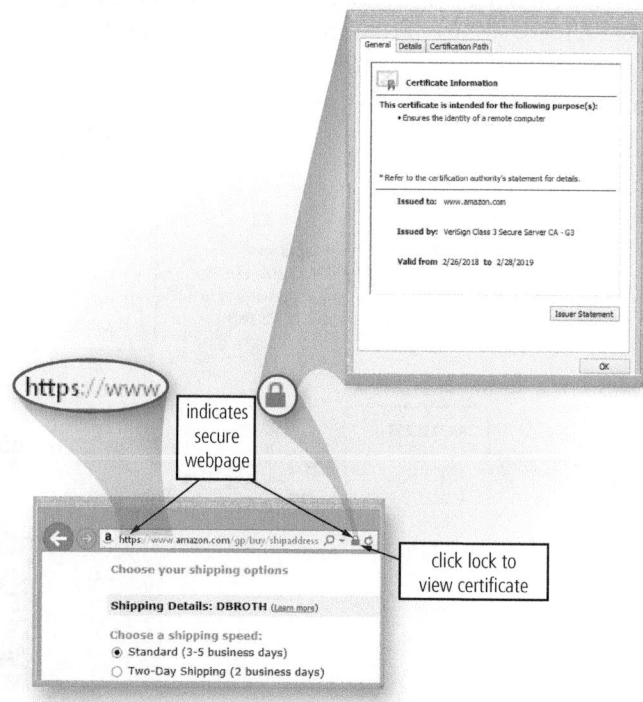

Figure 5-15 Web addresses of secure sites, such as the Amazon.com checkout, often begin with https instead of http. Browsers also often display a lock symbol in the address bar, which you usually can click to see the associated digital certificate.

Source: Amazon.com and Microsoft

Tech Feature 5-1: Cloud Data Privacy

Privacy and security concerns arise when consumers and businesses consider moving their data to an online storage service. Read Tech Feature 5-1 to learn about privacy issues surrounding cloud data storage. Read Ethics & Issues 5-1 to consider who is responsible for data left on the cloud.

 TECH FEATURE 5-1

Cloud Data Privacy

Privacy and security concerns arise when consumers and businesses consider moving their data to an online storage service. While the cloud offers a tremendous amount of storage space at a relatively low cost, the security of data and the reliability of cloud companies trigger concerns.

When people register for a cloud computing service, they sign a written contract or click an online OK or Agree button to affirm they read and understand the terms of the agreement. Any data saved on the cloud is entrusted to the third-party provider, which has a legal obligation to protect the data from security breaches. The company also must guard against data loss due to physical disasters, such as power outages, cooling failures, and fire. When data has been compromised, many states require the company to disclose the issue to the data owner promptly.

The Cloud Security Alliance (CSA) warns of hackers who register for the service with a credit card or for a free trial period and then unleash malware in an attempt to gain access to passwords. Because the registration and validation procedure for accessing the cloud is relatively anonymous, authorities can have difficulty locating the abusers.

Another concern arises when transferring data over a network to the cloud. When the data is traveling to or from a computer and the cloud service, it is subject to interception. To minimize risk, security experts emphasize that the web address of the website you are visiting must begin with https, and the data should be encrypted and authenticated.

Law enforcement's access to the data raises another security issue. Email messages stored on a private server belong to the company or individual who owns the computer, so law enforcement officials must obtain a search warrant to read a particular user's messages. In contrast, law enforcement officials can access email messages stored on the cloud by requesting the information from the company that owns the cloud service. The user might not be notified of the search until up to 90 days after the search occurred; moreover, the search may occur without limitations and may include continuous monitoring of an individual's email communications.

International laws and industry regulations protect sensitive and personal data. Germany has some of the strictest cloud data privacy laws, and, in general, the European Union's privacy regulations are more protective than those in the United States. In much of Europe, for example, consumers must agree to have their personal information collected, and they can review the data for accuracy. The education, health care, and financial services industries in the United States have strict data privacy regulations that affect cloud storage. For example, the Family Educational Rights and Privacy Act (FERPA) regulates the confidentiality of students' educational records, so colleges must obtain students' consent to share data with cloud storage providers and other third parties.

Cloud storage companies have increased their privacy and security features in recent years. Many allow consumers and businesses to protect files with passwords or require two-step authentication to access files, to delete data if a mobile device has been stolen or lost, and to delete data that has been stored past an expiration date.

✳ **Consider This:** How much of your personal data is stored on the cloud? Do you have concerns about the security of this data? Have you ever received a notice that any of your online data has been compromised? Should online social networks or email providers give more explicit notice that data is stored on the cloud? Should law enforcement officials be able to access your data without your consent? Why or why not?

iStockphoto.com / maxkabakov

ETHICS & ISSUES 5-1

Who Is Responsible for Data Left on the Cloud?

Businesses often contract with cloud storage providers for data storage. Many businesses also use cloud storage providers to store customer data. This data could include contact information, credit card numbers, and ordering history.

Ownership of cloud data becomes an issue when a cloud storage provider or the business using the cloud services closes. Other issues include what happens if the business fails to pay the cloud storage provider, or when a contract ends. Many feel that it is the responsibility of the business owner to remove and destroy company data before a contract ends. Supporters of this argument believe that cloud storage providers should not be accessing data they host. Others contend that if a business fails to remove and destroy its data before its cloud storage contract ends, cloud storage providers should return the data, or remove the data permanently.

An ongoing debate exists related to who is responsible for cloud data security. Many experts put the responsibility of securing data in the hands of the data owner. Others advocate for a shared security model, in which the cloud storage provider includes security tools, but the company provides additional security as needed.

Ownership and security of data should be included in any contract between a business and cloud storage provider. Contracts also should specify what happens in a variety of scenarios, including if either party stops its operations, or if hackers access the data.

Consider This: If a business stops its operations, who should remove its data from cloud storage? Why? If a customer does not remove its data before a contract ends, should a cloud storage provider return the data, or can it remove or sell the data? Why or why not? Who is responsible for data security? Why?

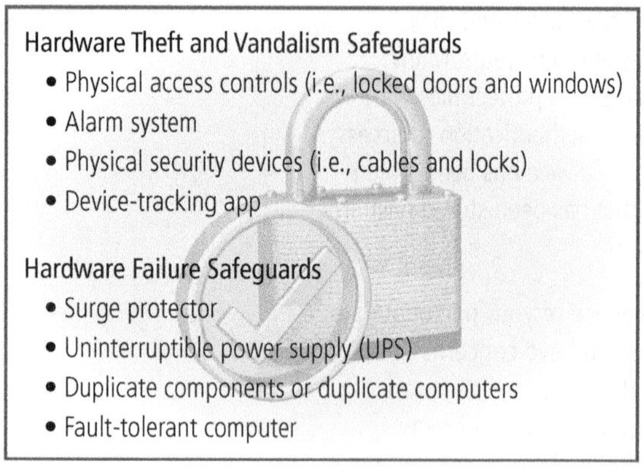

Hardware Theft and Vandalism Safeguards
- Physical access controls (i.e., locked doors and windows)
- Alarm system
- Physical security devices (i.e., cables and locks)
- Device-tracking app

Hardware Failure Safeguards
- Surge protector
- Uninterruptible power supply (UPS)
- Duplicate components or duplicate computers
- Fault-tolerant computer

Figure 5-16   Summary of safeguards against hardware theft, vandalism, and failure.
iStockphoto.com / Norebbo

Hardware Theft, Vandalism, and Failure

Users rely on computers and mobile devices to create, store, and manage important information. As discussed in Module 3, you should take measures to protect computers and devices from theft, vandalism, and failure.

Hardware theft is the act of stealing digital equipment. Hardware vandalism involves defacing or destroying digital equipment. Hardware can fail for a variety of reasons: aging hardware, natural or man-made disasters, or random events such as electrical power problems, and even errors in programs or apps. Figure 5-16 summarizes the techniques you can use to safeguard hardware from theft, vandalism, and failure.

Backing Up — The Ultimate Safeguard

To protect against data loss caused by hardware/software/information theft or system failure, users should back up computer and mobile device files regularly. As previously described, a **backup** is a duplicate of a file, program, or media that can be used if the original is lost, damaged, or destroyed; and to **back up** a file means to make a copy of it. In the case of system failure or the discovery of corrupted files, you **restore** the files by copying the backed up files to their original location on the computer or mobile device.

If you choose to back up locally, be sure to use high-quality media. A good choice for a home user might be optical discs or an external hard drive. Keep your backup media in a fireproof and heatproof safe or vault, or offsite. *Off-site* means in a location separate from where you typically store or use your computer or mobile device. Keeping backup copies off-site minimizes the chance that a single disaster, such as a fire, would destroy both the original and the backup media. An off-site location can be a safe deposit box at a bank, a briefcase, or cloud storage or cloud backup.

Cloud storage services provide storage to customers, usually along with synchronization services but often on smaller amounts of data. By contrast, cloud backup provides backup and retrieval services along with continuous data protection (discussed next) to the cloud. More customers are opting for cloud backup services because it saves them the cost of maintaining hardware (Figure 5-17).

Backup programs are available from many sources. Most operating systems include a backup program. Backup devices, such as external drives, also include backup programs. Numerous stand-alone backup tools exist. Users of a cloud backup service install software on their computers that backs up files to the cloud as they are modified.

Disc burning software writes text, graphics, audio, and video files on a recordable or rewritable disc. This software enables home users easily to back up contents of their hard drive on an optical disc (CD/DVD) and make duplicates of uncopyrighted music or movies. Disc burning software usually also includes photo editing, audio editing, and video editing capabilities.

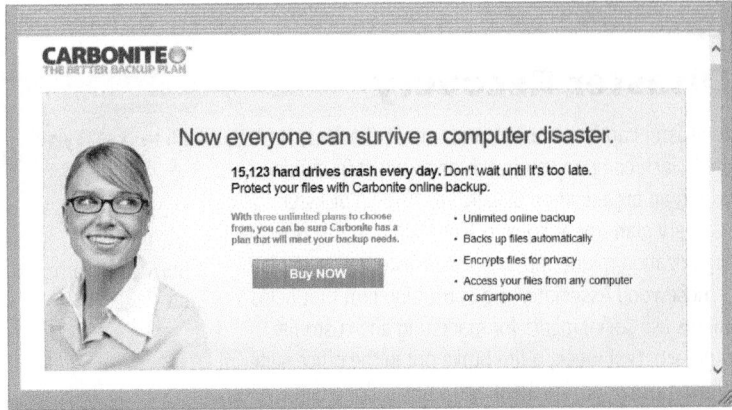

Figure 5-17 Cloud storage, such as Carbonite shown here, is a popular method for off-site backups.
Source: Carbonite, Inc.

Business and home users can perform four types of backup: full, differential, incremental, or selective. A fifth type, continuous data protection, often is used only by large enterprises to back up data to an in-house network storage device purchased and maintained by the enterprise. Cloud backup services, a sixth option, are providing continuous data protection capabilities at a lower cost. Table 5-2 summarizes the purpose, advantages, and disadvantages of each of these backup methods.

Table 5-2   Various Backup Methods

Type of Backup	Description	Advantages	Disadvantages
Full backup	Copies all of the files on media in the computer.	Fastest recovery method. All files are saved.	Longest backup time.
Differential backup	Copies only the files that have changed since the last full backup.	Fast backup method. Requires minimal storage space to back up.	Recovery is time-consuming because the last full backup plus the differential backup are needed.
Incremental backup	Copies only the files that have changed since the last full or incremental backup.	Fastest backup method. Requires minimal storage space to back up. Only most recent changes saved.	Recovery is most time-consuming because the last full backup and all incremental backups since the last full backup are needed.
Selective backup	Users choose which folders and files to include in a backup.	Fast backup method. Provides great flexibility.	Difficult to manage individual file backups. Least manageable of all the backup methods.
Continuous data protection (CDP)	All data is backed up whenever a change is made.	The only real-time backup. Very fast recovery of data.	Very expensive and requires a great amount of storage.
Cloud backup	Files are backed up to the cloud as they change.	Cloud backup provider maintains backup hardware. Files may be retrieved or restored from anywhere with an Internet connection and app on any device.	Requires an Internet connection and app, otherwise files are marked for backup when the computer goes back online.

Some users implement a three-generation backup policy to preserve three copies of important files. In a grandparent-parent-child backup scheme, full backups are made at regular (daily or weekly) intervals on removable media, most often on optical discs. The oldest saved backup is called the grandparent, the next oldest is the parent, and the current backup is the child. When a new child backup is made, the previous child backup is retained as the parent backup, the parent backup becomes the grandparent backup, and the oldest grandparent backup is discarded, and its media often is reused for a future backup.

Tech Feature 5-2: Disaster Recovery

A **disaster recovery plan** is a written plan that describes the steps an organization would take to restore its computer operations in the event of a disaster. Read Tech Feature 5-2 to learn about steps an organization takes in the event of a disaster.

 **TECH FEATURE 5-2**

Disaster Recovery

A disaster can be natural or man-made (hackers, viruses, etc.). Each company and each department or division within an organization usually has its own disaster recovery plan. The following scenario illustrates how an organization might implement a disaster recovery plan.

Rosewood Associates is a consulting firm that helps clients use social media for marketing and customer outreach. Last week, a fire broke out in the office suite above Rosewood. The heat and smoke, along with water from the sprinkler system, caused extensive damage. As a result, Rosewood must replace all computers, servers, and storage devices. Also, the company lost all of the data it had not backed up.

Rosewood currently backs up its systems daily to an internal server and weekly to a remote cloud server. Because of damage to the internal server, the company lost several days of data. Rosewood does not have a plan for replacing hardware. Thus, they will lose several additional days of productivity while purchasing, installing, and configuring new hardware.

To minimize the chance of this type of loss in the future, the company hired you as a consultant to help create a disaster recovery plan. You first discuss the types of disasters that can strike, as shown in the table. You then explain that the goal of a disaster recovery plan is to prevent, detect, and correct system threats, and to restore the most critical systems first.

A disaster recovery plan typically contains these four components: emergency plan, backup plan, recovery plan, and test plan.

Emergency Plan: An emergency plan specifies the steps Rosewood will take as soon as a disaster strikes. The emergency plan is organized by type of disaster, such as fire, flood, or earthquake, and includes:

1. Names and phone numbers of people and organizations to notify (company management, fire and police department, clients, etc.)
2. Computer equipment procedures, such as equipment or power shutoff, and file removal; employees should follow these procedures only if it is safe to do so
3. Employee evacuation procedures
4. Return procedures (who can enter the facility and what actions they are to perform)

Backup Plan: The backup plan specifies how Rosewood will use backup files and equipment to resume computer operations, and includes:

1. The location of backup data, supplies, and equipment
2. Who is responsible for gathering backup resources and transporting them to an alternate computer facility

Considerations for Disaster Recovery

Disaster Type	What to Do First	What Might Occur	What to Include in the Plan
Natural (earthquake, hurricane, tornado, etc.)	Shut off power; Evacuate, if necessary; Pay attention to advisories; Do not use phone lines if lightning occurs	Power outage; Phone lines down; Structural damage to building; Road closings, transportation interruptions; Flooding; Equipment damage	Generator; Satellite phone, list of employee phone numbers; Alternate worksite; Action to be taken if employees are not able to come to work/leave the office; Wet/dry vacuums; Make and model numbers and vendor information to get replacements
Man-made (hazardous material spill, terrorist attacks, fire, hackers, malware, etc.)	Notify authorities (fire departments, etc.) of immediate threat; Attempt to suppress fire or contain spill, if safe to do so; Evacuate, if necessary	Data loss; Dangerous conditions for employees; Criminal activity, such as data hacking and identity theft; Equipment damage	Backup data at protected site; Protective equipment and an evacuation plan; Contact law enforcement; Make and model numbers and vendor information to obtain replacements

3. The methods by which data will be restored from cloud storage
4. A schedule indicating the order and approximate time each application should be up and running

Recovery Plan: The recovery plan specifies the actions Rosewood will take to restore full computer operations. As with the emergency plan, the recovery plan differs for each type of disaster. You recommend that Rosewood set up planning committees. Each committee would be responsible for different forms of recovery, such as replacing hardware or software.

Test Plan: The test plan includes simulating various levels of disasters and recording Rosewood's ability to recover. You run a test in which the employees follow the steps in the disaster recovery plan. The test uncovers a few needed recovery actions not specified in the plan, so you modify the plan. A few days later, you run another test without giving the employees any advance notice to test the plan again.

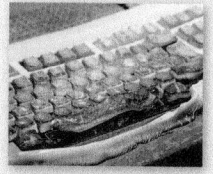

✳ **Consider This:** For what kinds of natural and man-made disasters should a company plan? What roles can cloud storage providers play in helping to recover from a disaster? How involved should employees be in developing and testing disaster recovery plans?

iStockphoto.com / Hans Laubel;
iStockphoto.com / William Sen;
Gewoldi / Photos.com

Wireless Security

Billions of home and business users have laptops, smartphones, and other mobile devices to access the Internet, send email and Internet messages, chat online, or share network connections — all wirelessly. Home users set up wireless home networks. Mobile users access wireless networks in hot spots at airports, hotels, shopping malls, bookstores, restaurants, and coffee shops. Schools have wireless networks so that students can access the school network using their mobile computers and devices as they move from building to building (Figure 5-18).

Although wireless access provides many conveniences to users, it also poses additional security risks. Some perpetrators connect to other's wireless networks to gain free Internet access; others may try to access an organization's confidential data.

To access a wireless network, the individual must be in range of the wireless network. Some intruders intercept and monitor communications as they transmit through the air. Others connect to a network through an unsecured wireless access point (WAP) or combination router/WAP. Read How To 5-2 for instructions about ways to secure a wireless network, in addition to using firewalls.

Figure 5-18 Wireless access points or routers around campus allow students to access the school network wirelessly from their classrooms, the library, dorms, and other campus locations.

Ruslan Kudrin / Shutterstock.com; Robert Kneschke / Shutterstock.com; Christopher Futcher / iStockphoto.com; Ruslan Kudrin / Shutterstock.com; Jupiterimages / Comstock; Getty Images / Thinkstock; Downunderphoto / Fotolia LLC

HOW TO 5-2

Secure Your Wireless Network
When you set up a wireless network, it is important to secure the network so that only your computers and mobile devices can connect to it. Unsecured wireless networks can be seen and accessed by neighbors and others nearby, which may make it easier for them to connect to and access the data on the computers and mobile devices on your network. The following list provides suggestions for securing your wireless network.

- Immediately upon connecting your wireless access point and/or router, change the password required to access administrative features. If the password remains at its default setting, others may possibly be able to connect to and configure your wireless network settings.

- Change the *SSID* (service set identifier), which is a network name, from the default to something that uniquely identifies your network, especially if you live in close proximity to other wireless networks.

- Do not broadcast the SSID. This will make it more difficult for others to detect your

wireless network. When you want to connect a computer or mobile device to your wireless network, it will be necessary to enter the SSID manually.

- Enable an encryption method such as WPA2 (Wi-Fi Protected Access 2), and specify a password or passphrase that is difficult for others to guess. The most secure passwords and passphrases contain more than eight characters, uppercase and lowercase letters, numbers, and special characters.

- Enable and configure the MAC (Media Access Control) address control feature. A *MAC address* is a unique hardware identifier for your computer or device. The *MAC address control* feature specifies the computers and mobile devices that can connect to your network. If a computer or device is not specified, it will not be able to connect.

- Choose a secure location for your wireless router so that unauthorized people cannot access it. Someone who has physical access to a wireless router can restore factory defaults and erase your settings.

Consider This: In addition to safeguarding the data and information on your computers from others, why else might it be a good idea to secure your wireless network?

Home   Wi-Fi   LAN   WWAN   Security   Advanced   📶 Verizon EvDO Rev Ae   Dormant
Wi-Fi

Wi-Fi Profiles

Current Profile	Secure
Selected Profile	Secure
Network Name (SSID)	smith
802.11 Mode	802.11g + 802.11b
WMM (Wi-Fi Multimedia)	Off
	With older Droids and devices that aren't working, use "Backward compatibility".
Channel	Auto
Security	WPA2
Authentication	Open Access
Network Key	68c2c067
	8 ~ 63 ASCII characters
	For greater security, use a mixture of digits, upper case, lower case, and other symbols

Update Profile   Apply   Revert

Source: Verizon Wireless

CONSIDER THIS

Can you detect if someone is accessing your wireless home network?
If you notice the speed of your wireless connection is slower than normal, it may be a sign that someone else is accessing your network. You also may notice indicator lights on your wireless router flashing rapidly when you are not connected to your wireless network. Most wireless routers have a built-in utility that allows you to view the computers and devices currently connected to your network. If you notice a computer or device that does not belong to you, consult your wireless router's documentation to determine how to remove it from the network.

Tech Feature 5-3: Mobile Security

As the number of smartphones and mobile devices in use increases, the possibility of security breaches and lost devices increases proportionally. Read Tech Feature 5-3 to learn about ways you can protect sensitive and personal data on your mobile devices.

 TECH FEATURE 5-3

Mobile Security

The consequences of losing a smartphone or mobile device are significant given the amount of storage and the variety of personal and business data stored. Symantec, one the world's leading online security companies, projects that only one-half of lost or stolen phones eventually will be returned to their owners. Chances are that the people who find the missing phones likely will have viewed much of the content on the devices in a quest to find the owners and possibly to gain access to private information.

The goal, therefore, for mobile device users is to make their data as secure as possible. Follow these steps to protect sensitive and personal data and to fight mobile cybercrime.

- **Be extra cautious locating and downloading apps.** Any device that connects to the Internet is susceptible to mobile malware. Cyberthieves target apps on widely used phones and tablets. Popular games are likely candidates to house malware, and it often is difficult to distinguish the legitimate apps from the fake apps. Obtain mobile device apps from well-known stores, and before downloading anything, read the descriptions and reviews. Look for misspellings and awkward sentence structure, which could be clues that the app is fake. If something looks awry,

do not download. Scrutinize the number and types of permissions the app is requesting. If the list seems unreasonable in length or in the personal information needed, deny permission and uninstall the app.

- **Use a PIN.** Enable the passcode feature on a mobile device as the first step in stopping prying eyes from viewing contents. This four-to-eight-digit code adds a layer of protection. Only emergency functions can be accessed without entering the correct sequence of numbers. This strong code should not be information easily guessed, such as a birthdate.

- **Turn off GPS tracking.** GPS technology can track the mobile device's location as long as it is transmitting and receiving signals to and from satellites. This feature is helpful to obtain directions from your current location, view local news and weather reports, find a lost device, summon emergency personnel, and locate missing children. Serious privacy concerns can arise, however, when the technology is used in malicious ways, such as to stalk individuals or trace their whereabouts. Unless you want to allow others to follow your locations throughout the day, disable the GPS tracking feature until needed.

- **Use mobile security software.** Protection is necessary to stop viruses and spyware and to safeguard personal and business data. Mobile security apps can allow you to lock your mobile device and SIM card remotely, erase the memory, and activate the GPS function. Other apps prevent cyberthieves from hijacking your phone and taking pictures, making recordings, placing calls to fee-imposed businesses, and sending infected messages to all individuals in your contact list. Look for security software that can back up data to a cloud

turn off location services until needed

iStockphoto.com / Henk Badenhorst; iStockphoto.com / Marcello Bortolino

account, set off a screeching alarm on the lost or stolen mobile device, offer live customer service, and provide theft, spam, virus, and malware protection.

- **Avoid clicking unsafe links.** Clicking an unknown link can lead to malicious websites. If you receive a text message from someone you do not know or an invitation to click a link, resist the urge to fulfill the request. Your financial institution never will send you a message requesting you to enter your account user name and password. Malicious links can inject malware on the mobile device to steal personal information or to create

toll fraud, which secretly contacts wireless messaging services that impose steep fees on a monthly bill.

⚙ **Consider This:** As the number of smartphones and mobile devices in use increases, the possibility of security breaches and lost devices increases proportionally. How can manufacturers and wireless carriers emphasize the importance of mobile security and convince users to take the precautions suggested in this tech feature? What mobile security safeguards have you taken to protect your smartphone or mobile device? What steps will you take after reading this tech feature?

Ethics and Society

As with any powerful technology, computers and mobile devices can be used for both good and bad intentions. The standards that determine whether an action is good or bad are known as ethics.

Technology ethics are the moral guidelines that govern the use of computers, mobile devices, information systems, and related technologies. Frequently discussed areas of computer ethics are unauthorized use of computers, mobile devices, and networks; software theft (piracy); information accuracy; intellectual property rights; codes of conduct; green computing; and information privacy. The questionnaire in Figure 5-19 raises issues in each of these areas.

Previous sections in this module discussed unauthorized use of computers, mobile devices and networks, and software theft (piracy). The following sections discuss issues related to information accuracy, intellectual property rights, codes of conduct, green computing, and information privacy.

Your Thoughts?	**Ethical**	**Unethical**
1. An organization requires employees to wear badges that track their whereabouts while at work.	☐	☐
2. A supervisor reads an employee's email message.	☐	☐
3. An employee uses his computer at work to send email messages to a friend.	☐	☐
4. An employee sends an email message to several coworkers and blind copies his supervisor.	☐	☐
5. An employee forwards an email message to a third party without permission from the sender.	☐	☐
6. An employee uses her computer at work to complete a homework assignment for school.	☐	☐
7. The vice president of your Student Government Association (SGA) downloads a photo from the web and uses it in a flyer recruiting SGA members.	☐	☐
8. A student copies text from the web and uses it in a research paper for his English Composition class.	☐	☐
9. An employee sends political campaign material to individuals on her employer's mailing list.	☐	☐
10. A company requires employees to keep personal mobile phones in a secure locker and does not permit employees to view these devices during their shifts.	☐	☐
11. An employee makes a copy of software and installs it on her home computer. No one uses her home computer while she is at work, and she uses her home computer only to finish projects from work.	☐	☐

(Continued)

Your Thoughts?

	Ethical	Unethical
12. An employee who has been laid off installs a computer virus on his employer's computer.	☐	☐
13. A person designing a webpage finds one on the web similar to his requirements, copies it, modifies it, and publishes it as his own webpage.	☐	☐
14. A student researches using only the web to write a report.	☐	☐
15. In a society in which all transactions occur online (a cashless society), the government tracks every transaction you make and automatically deducts taxes from your bank account.	☐	☐
16. Someone copies a well-known novel to the web and encourages others to read it.	☐	☐
17. A person accesses an organization's network and reports to the organization any vulnerabilities discovered.	☐	☐
18. Your friend uses a neighbor's wireless network to connect to the Internet and check email.	☐	☐
19. A company uses recycled paper to print a 50-page employee benefits manual that is distributed to 425 employees.	☐	☐
20. An employee is fired based on the content of posts on his or her online social network.	☐	☐

Figure 5-19 Indicate whether you think the situation described is ethical or unethical. Be prepared to discuss your answers.

Information Accuracy

Information accuracy is a concern today because many users access information maintained by other people or companies, such as on the Internet. Do not assume that because the information is on the web that it is correct. As discussed in Module 2, users should evaluate the value of a webpage before relying on its content. Be aware that the organization providing access to the information may not be the creator of the information. Read Secure IT 5-4 to consider the risks associated with inaccurate data.

✸ SECURE IT 5-4

Risks Associated with Inaccurate Data

Mapping and navigation software is invaluable for locating unfamiliar destinations. Problems arise, however, when satellite images are outdated or when the desired address cannot be found on a map. Inaccurate data can result in lost revenues for businesses when potential customers cannot find the storefront. It also has caused accidents when drivers followed turn-by-turn GPS directions and drove the wrong way on one-way streets, made illegal turns, or ended at ponds where a road stopped.

Business owners can report incorrect address data to some mapping services. They can, for example, state that the satellite image needs updating, their address has changed, the directions are incorrect, or the

street names are inaccurate. In some cases, the maps and addresses are updated quickly, often within a day.

Data entry errors also can lead to lost business, lawsuits, and expenses. In an extreme example, a $125 million *Mars Climate Orbiter* spacecraft was lost in space because Lockheed Martin engineers performed calculations using English units (pounds) to fire the thrusters guiding the spacecraft, but NASA engineers assumed the data was in metric units (Newtons) and sent the spacecraft 60 miles off course. In another unit conversion error, an axle broke on a Space Mountain roller coaster car at Tokyo Disneyland because it was the wrong size; the error occurred when engineers performed calculations to convert the original Space Mountain master plan from English units to metric units.

In the business world, mistakes can occur when software has not been updated or when employees are overworked, distracted, or faced with repetitive tasks. Software should have safeguards to verify valid data has been entered, such as checking that phone numbers have 10 numeric characters. Data cleaning software can eliminate duplicate database records, locate missing data, and correct discrepancies.

✸ **Consider This:** Have you ever used a mapping app or website and encountered incorrect information? Would you consider notifying mapping companies of errors in their satellite images or directions? What steps can companies take to help employees enter data accurately?

In addition to concerns about the accuracy of computer input, some individuals and organizations raise questions about the ethics of using computers to alter output, primarily graphic output, such as a retouched photo. With graphics equipment and software, users easily can digitize photos and then add, change (Figure 5-20), or remove images.

Intellectual Property Rights

Intellectual property (*IP*) refers to unique and original works, such as ideas, inventions, art, writings, processes, company and product names, and logos. *Intellectual property rights* are the rights to which creators are entitled for their work. Certain issues arise surrounding IP today because many of these works are available digitally and easily can be redistributed or altered without the creator's permission.

Figure 5-20   This digitally edited photo shows a fruit that looks like an apple on the outside and an orange on the inside.
Giuliano20 / Dreamstime.com

A *copyright* gives authors, artists, and other creators of original work exclusive rights to duplicate, publish, and sell their materials. A copyright protects any tangible form of expression. *Creative Commons* is a nonprofit organization that allows content owners to specify how their online content can be reused, if at all, on other websites. Options range from not at all to with attribution, with or without modification, and for or not for commercial purposes.

A common infringement of copyright is piracy, where people illegally copy software, movies, and music. Many areas are not clear-cut with respect to the law, because copyright law gives the public fair use to copyrighted material. The issues surround the phrase, fair use, which allows use for educational and critical purposes. This vague definition is subject to widespread interpretation and raises many questions:

- Should individuals be able to download contents of your website, modify it, and then put it on the web again as their own?
- Should a faculty member have the right to print material from the web and distribute it to all members of the class for teaching purposes only?
- Should someone be able to scan photos or pages from a book, publish them on the web, and allow others to download them?
- Should a blogger or website creator be able to include any photos they find on the web in their blogs or websites, even with attribution?
- Should someone be able to put the lyrics of a song on the web?
- Should students be able to take term papers they have written and post them on the web, making it tempting for other students to download and submit them as their own work?

These issues with copyright law led to the development of *digital rights management* (DRM), a strategy designed to prevent illegal distribution of movies, music, and other digital content.

Codes of Conduct

A **code of conduct** is a written guideline that helps determine whether a specification is ethical/unethical or allowed/not allowed. An IT code of conduct focuses on acceptable use of technology. Employers and schools often specify standards for the ethical use of technology in an IT code of conduct and then distribute these standards to employees and students (Figure 5-21). You also may find codes of conduct online that define acceptable forms of communications for websites where users post commentary or other communications, such as blogs, wikis, online discussions, and so on.

Sample IT Code of Conduct

1. Technology may not be used to harm other people.
2. Employees may not meddle in others' files.
3. Employees may use technology only for purposes in which they have been authorized.
4. Technology may not be used to steal.
5. Technology may not be used to bear false witness.
6. Employees may not copy or use software illegally.
7. Employees may not use others' technology resources without authorization.
8. Employees may not use others' intellectual property as their own.
9. Employees shall consider the social impact of programs and systems they design.
10. Employees always should use technology in a way that demonstrates consideration and respect for fellow humans.

Figure 5-21   Sample IT code of conduct employers may distribute to employees.
iStockphoto.com / Oleksiy Mark

Green Computing

People use, and often waste, resources such as electricity and paper while using technology. Recall from Module 1 that green computing involves reducing the electricity and environmental waste while using computers, mobile devices, and related technologies. Figure 5-22 summarizes measures users can take to contribute to green computing.

Personal computers, displays, printers, and other devices should comply with guidelines of the ENERGY STAR program. The United States Department of Energy (DOE) and the United States Environmental Protection Agency (EPA) developed the *ENERGY STAR program* to help reduce the amount of electricity used by computers and related devices. This program encourages manufacturers to create energy-efficient devices. For example, many devices switch to sleep or power save mode after a specified number of inactive minutes or hours. Computers and devices that meet the ENERGY STAR guidelines display an ENERGY STAR label (shown in Figure 5-22).

Green Computing Tips

1. Conserve Energy
   a. Use computers and devices that comply with the ENERGY STAR program.
   b. Do not leave a computer or device running overnight.
   c. Turn off the monitor, printer, and other devices when not in use.

2. Reduce Environmental Waste
   a. Use paperless methods to communicate.
   b. Recycle paper and buy recycled paper.
   c. Recycle toner and ink cartridges, computers, mobile devices, printers, and other devices.
   d. Telecommute.
   e. Use videoconferencing and VoIP for meetings.

Figure 5-22   A list of suggestions to make computing healthy for the environment.

US Environmental Protection Agency, ENERGY STAR program; Roman Sotola / Shutterstock.com

---

Enterprise data centers and computer facilities consume large amounts of electricity from computer hardware and associated devices and utilities, such as air conditioning, coolers, lighting, etc. Organizations can implement a variety of measures to reduce electrical waste:

- Consolidate servers by using virtualization.
- Purchase high-efficiency equipment.
- Use sleep modes and other power management features for computers and devices.
- Buy computers and devices with low power consumption processors and power supplies.
- When possible, use outside air to cool the data center or computer facility.

Some organizations continually review their *power usage effectiveness* (PUE), which is a ratio that measures how much power enters the computer facility or data center against the amount of power required to run the computers and devices.

 CONSIDER THIS ────────────────────────

Should you save out-of-date computers and devices?

Users should not store obsolete computers and devices in their basement, storage room, attic, warehouse, or any other location. Computers, monitors, and other equipment contain toxic materials and potentially dangerous elements including lead, mercury, and flame retardants. In a landfill, these materials release into the environment. Recycling and refurbishing old equipment are much safer alternatives for the environment. Manufacturers can use the millions of pounds of recycled raw materials to make products such as outdoor furniture and automotive parts. Before recycling, refurbishing, or discarding your old computer, be sure to erase, remove, or destroy its hard drive so that the information it stored remains private.

Information Privacy

Information privacy refers to the right of individuals and companies to deny or restrict the collection, use, and dissemination of information about them. Organizations often use huge databases to store records, such as employee records, medical records, financial records, and more. Much of the data is personal and confidential and should be accessible only to authorized users. Many individuals and organizations, however, question whether this data really is private. That is, some companies and individuals collect and use this information without your authorization. Websites often collect data about you, so that they can customize advertisements and send you personalized email messages. Some employers monitor your computer usage and email messages.

Figure 5-23 lists measures you can take to make your personal data more private. The following sections address techniques companies and employers use to collect your personal data.

Electronic Profiles

When you fill out a printed form, such as a magazine subscription or contest entry, or an online form to sign up for a service, create a profile on an online social network, or register a product warranty, the merchant that receives the form usually stores the information you provide in a database. Likewise, every time you click an advertisement on the web or perform a search online, your information and preferences enter a database. Some merchants may sell or share the contents of their databases with national marketing firms and Internet advertising firms. By combining this data with information from public records, such as driver's licenses and vehicle registrations, these firms can create an electronic profile of individuals. Electronic profiles may include personal details, such as your age, address, phone number, marital status, number and ages of dependents, interests, and spending habits.

Direct marketing supporters claim that using information in this way lowers overall selling costs, which lowers product prices. Critics contend that the information in an electronic profile reveals more about an individual than anyone has a right to know. They argue that companies should inform people if they plan to provide personal information to others, and people should have the right to deny such use. Many websites allow people to specify whether they want their personal information shared or preferences retained (Figure 5-24).

How to Safeguard Personal Information

1. Fill in only necessary information on rebate, warranty, and registration forms.

2. Do not preprint your phone number or Social Security number on personal checks.

3. Have an unlisted or unpublished phone number.

4. If you have Caller ID, find out how to block your number from displaying on the receiver's system.

5. Do not write your phone number on charge or credit receipts.

6. Ask merchants not to write credit card numbers, phone numbers, Social Security numbers, and driver's license numbers on the back of your personal checks.

7. Purchase goods with cash, rather than credit or checks.

8. Avoid shopping club and buyer cards.

9. View or download a copy of the information associated with your Google, Facebook, Microsoft, or other online accounts you access frequently. Disable search history, location history, and usage information sent to these websites.

10. Inform merchants that you do not want them to distribute your personal information.

11. Request, in writing, to be removed from mailing lists.

12. Obtain your credit report once a year from each of the three major credit reporting agencies (Equifax, Experian, and TransUnion) and correct any errors.

13. Request a free copy of your medical records once a year from the Medical Information Bureau.

14. Limit the amount of information you provide to websites. Fill in only required information.

15. Install a cookie manager to filter cookies.

16. Clear your browsing history when you are finished browsing.

17. Set up a free email account. Use this email address for merchant forms.

18. Turn off file and printer sharing on your Internet connection.

19. Install a personal firewall.

20. Sign up for email filtering through your ISP or use an anti-spam program.

21. Do not reply to spam for any reason.

22. Surf the web anonymously using private browsing.

Figure 5-23   Techniques to keep personal data private.
iStockphoto.com / Norebbo

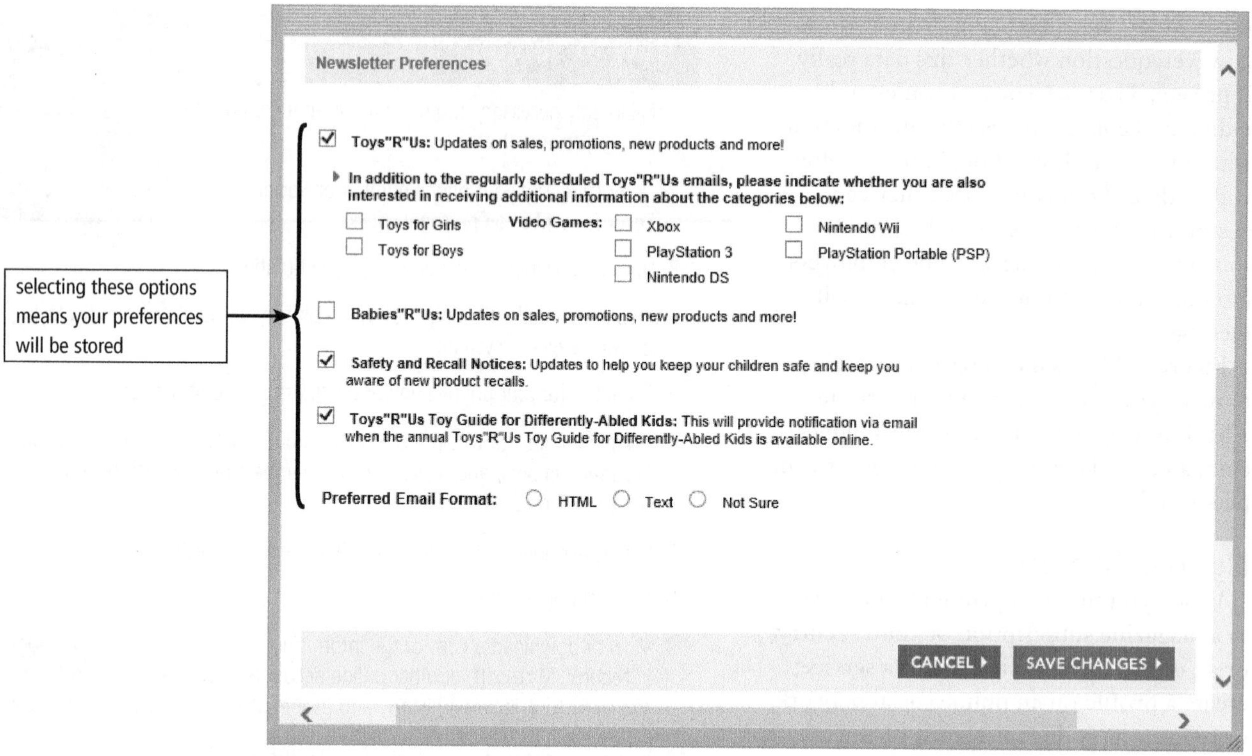

Figure 5-24   Many companies, such as Toys"R"Us shown here, allow users to specify whether they want the company to retain their preferences.
Source: Geoffrey, LLC

Cookies

A **cookie** is a small text file that a web server stores on your computer. Cookie files typically contain an identification code(s) that links to a file on a web server that contains data about you, such as your user name, postal code, or viewing preferences. Websites use cookies for a variety of purposes:

- Most websites that allow for personalization use cookies to track user preferences. These cookies may obtain their values when a user fills in an online form requesting personal information. Some websites, for example, store user names in cookies in order to display a personalized greeting that welcomes the user, by name, back to the website. Other websites allow users to customize their viewing experience with preferences, such as local news headlines, the local weather forecast, or stock quotes.
- Some websites use cookies to store user names and/or passwords, so that users do not need to enter this information every time they sign in to the website.
- Online shopping websites generally use a *session cookie* to keep track of items in a user's shopping cart. This way, users can start an order during one web session and finish it on another day in another session. Session cookies usually expire after a certain time, such as a week or a month.
- Some websites use cookies to track how often users visit a site and the webpages they visit while at the website.
- Websites may use cookies to target advertisements. These websites store a user's interests and browsing habits in the cookie.

 **CONSIDER THIS**

Do websites ever sell information stored in cookies?

Some websites sell or trade information stored in your cookies to advertisers — a practice many believe to be unethical. If you do not want personal information distributed, you should limit the amount of information you provide to a website or adjust how your browser handles cookies. You can regularly clear cookies or set your browser to accept cookies automatically, prompt if you want to accept a cookie, or disable all cookie use. Keep in mind if you disable cookie use, you may not be able to use some e-commerce websites. As an alternative, you can purchase software that selectively blocks cookies.

Many commercial websites send a cookie to your browser; your computer's hard drive then stores the cookie. The next time you visit the website, your browser retrieves the cookie from your hard drive and sends the data in the cookie to the website. Figure 5-25 illustrates how websites work with cookies. A website can read data only from its own cookie file stored on your hard drive. That is, it cannot access or view any other data on your hard drive — including another cookie file.

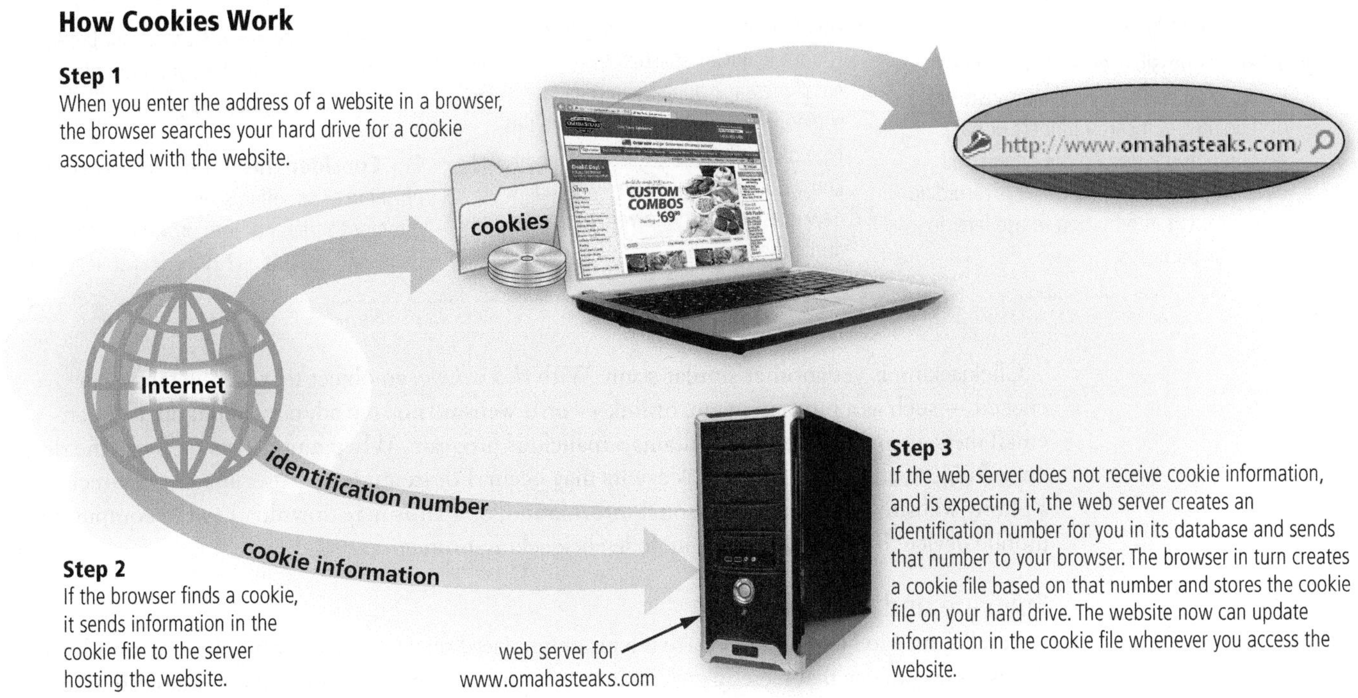

How Cookies Work

Step 1
When you enter the address of a website in a browser, the browser searches your hard drive for a cookie associated with the website.

cookies

http://www.omahasteaks.com

Internet

identification number

cookie information

Step 2
If the browser finds a cookie, it sends information in the cookie file to the server hosting the website.

web server for
www.omahasteaks.com

Step 3
If the web server does not receive cookie information, and is expecting it, the web server creates an identification number for you in its database and sends that number to your browser. The browser in turn creates a cookie file based on that number and stores the cookie file on your hard drive. The website now can update information in the cookie file whenever you access the website.

Figure 5-25 This figure shows how cookies work.
Alex Staroseltsev / Shutterstock.com; Source: Omaha Steaks International, Inc; iStockphoto.com / Norman Chan

Phishing

Recall from Module 4 that phishing is a scam in which a perpetrator sends an official looking message that attempts to obtain your personal and/or financial information. These messages look legitimate and request that you update credit card numbers, Social Security numbers, bank account numbers, passwords, or other private information. Read How To 5-3 for instructions about protecting yourself from phishing and spoofing scams.

 **HOW TO 5-3**

Protect against Phishing and Spoofing Scams

Phishing and spoofing scams can be perpetrated via email messages, websites, and even on the phone. The following guidelines will help protect you against these scams.

Phone Scams

- If you receive a phone call from someone claiming to be from a company with which you do business, record his or her name and the time of the call. Do not disclose personal or financial information to the caller. If the caller is offering a product or service and is requesting a payment, call the company back at the number you have on file, and ask to be transferred to the person who called you initially.

- Whenever possible, enter your payment information on secure websites instead of reading credit card numbers or bank account information on the phone. You never know whether the caller is recording your payment information to use later for malicious purposes.

Email Scams

- If you receive an email message from someone requesting you to verify online account or financial information, do not reply with this information.

- Never click links in email messages, even if the message appears to be from someone you know. Nor should you copy and paste the link from the email message to a browser. Instead, type the link's web address into a browser's address bar manually, and make sure you type it correctly. If you are visiting your financial institution's website, make sure the web address you enter matches the web address you have on file for them.

- Do not reply to email messages asking you for financial assistance — even if the email message appears to originate from someone you know. If you receive this type of email message from someone you know, contact the person via phone or a new email message to verify the message's authenticity.

Website Scams

- When visiting a website, such as your financial institution's website, that will require you to enter confidential information, be sure to type the web address correctly. Typing it incorrectly may take you to a phishing or spoofing website where the information you enter can be collected by an unknown party.

- Make sure websites requiring your confidential information use the https protocol.

- Websites with misspellings, poor grammar, or formatting problems may indicate a phishing website. Do not enter personal or financial information on a website that looks suspicious.

- Enable the *phishing filter* in your browser that can warn or block you from potentially fraudulent or suspicious websites.

Consider This: Have you experienced a phishing or spoofing scam? If so, how did it attempt to trick you into providing personal or financial information? How did you respond?

Clickjacking is yet another similar scam. With *clickjacking*, an object that can be tapped or clicked — such as a button, image, or link — on a website, pop-up ad, pop-under ad, or in an email message or text message contains a malicious program. When a user taps or clicks the disguised object, a variety of nefarious events may occur. For example, the user may be redirected to a phony website that requests personal information, or a virus may download to the computer or mobile device. Browsers typically include clickjacking protection.

Spyware and Adware

Recall from Module 4 that **spyware** is a program placed on a computer or mobile device without the user's knowledge that secretly collects information about the user and then communicates the information it collects to some outside source while the user is online. Some vendors or employers use spyware to collect information about program usage or employees. Internet advertising firms often collect information about users' web browsing habits. Spyware can enter your computer when you install a new program, through malware, or through a graphic on a webpage or in an email message.

Adware is a program that displays an online advertisement in a banner, a pop-up window, or pop-under window on webpages, email messages, or other Internet services. Adware on mobile phones is known as *madware*, for mobile adware. Sometimes, spyware is hidden in adware.

To remove spyware and adware, you can obtain spyware removers, adware removers, or malware removers that can detect and delete spyware and adware. Some operating systems and browsers include spyware and adware removers.

Social Engineering

As related to the use of technology, **social engineering** is defined as gaining unauthorized access to or obtaining confidential information by taking advantage of the trusting human nature of some victims and the naivety of others. Some social engineers trick their victims into revealing confidential information, such as user names and passwords, on the phone, in person, or on the Internet.

Techniques they use include pretending to be an administrator or other authoritative figure, feigning an emergency situation, or impersonating an acquaintance. Social engineers also obtain information from users who do not destroy or conceal information properly. These perpetrators sift through company dumpsters, watch or film people dialing phone numbers or using ATMs, and snoop around computers or mobile devices looking for openly displayed confidential information.

To protect yourself from social engineering scams, follow these tips:

- Verify the identity of any person or organization requesting personal or confidential information.
- When relaying personal or confidential information, ensure that only authorized people can hear your conversation.
- When personal or confidential information appears on a computer or mobile device, ensure that only authorized people can see your screen.
- Shred all sensitive or confidential documents.
- After using a public computer, clear the cache in its browser.
- Avoid using public computers to conduct banking or other sensitive transactions.

Privacy Laws

The concern about privacy has led to the enactment of federal and state laws regarding the storage and disclosure of personal data, some of which are shown in Table 5-3. Common points in some of these laws are as follows:

1. Information collected and stored about individuals should be limited to what is necessary to carry out the function of the business or government agency collecting the data.
2. Once collected, provisions should be made to protect the data so that only those employees within the organization who need access to it to perform their job duties have access to it.
3. Personal information should be released outside the organization collecting the data only when the person has agreed to its disclosure.
4. When information is collected about an individual, the individual should know that the data is being collected and have the opportunity to determine the accuracy of the data.

Read Ethics & Issues 5-2 to consider the legal issues surrounding your digital footprint.

Table 5-3 Major U.S. Government Laws Concerning Privacy

Law	Purpose
Children's Internet Protection Act	Protects minors from inappropriate content when accessing the Internet in schools and libraries
Children's Online Privacy Protection Act (COPPA)	Requires websites to protect personal information of children under 13 years of age
Computer Abuse Amendments Act	Outlaws transmission of harmful computer code, such as viruses
Digital Millennium Copyright Act (DMCA)	Makes it illegal to circumvent antipiracy schemes in commercial software; outlaws sale of devices that copy software illegally
Electronic Communications Privacy Act (ECPA)	Provides the same right of privacy protection of the postal delivery service and phone companies to various forms of electronic communications, such as voice mail, email, and mobile phones
Financial Modernization Act	Protects consumers from disclosure of their personal financial information and requires institutions to alert customers of information disclosure policies
Freedom of Information Act (FOIA)	Enables public access to most government records
HIPAA (Health Insurance Portability and Accountability Act)	Protects individuals against the wrongful disclosure of their health information
PATRIOT (Provide Appropriate Tools Required to Intercept and Obstruct Terrorism)	Gives law enforcement the right to monitor people's activities, including web and email habits
Privacy Act	Forbids federal agencies from allowing information to be used for a reason other than that for which it was collected

ETHICS & ISSUES 5-2

Do You Have the Right to Be Digitally Forgotten?
Privacy experts, such as The Institute for Responsible Online and Cell-Phone Communication (IROC2), warn that "Your digital activity is public and permanent" and is available permanently to anyone using a search engine. Does it have to be? Do you have a "right to be forgotten" as was ruled by a court in the European Union recently?

In this case, the court ordered a popular search engine to remove links to information that was "inadequate, irrelevant, or no longer relevant." The content in question included many factual articles published by a major news source. Examples included stories about a university student arrested for driving while intoxicated and a referee who lied about a

mistake. Free speech advocates criticize the law. They state that a government should not be able to deny access to accurate information. Others argue that a person should be able to request removal of information that is damaging to his or her reputation. Some are concerned that negative incidents may be necessary information for an employer to know about a job seeker, or for those considering a relationship with another person. You can never truly delete your digital footprint because everything you do online has the potential to be forwarded, captured as a screenshot, or archived in databases.

Among the debated issues is whether the rights of a private citizen should differ from those of a public figure. Many argue that different rules apply for celebrities, politicians,

and others who choose such professions. Some feel that the responsibility rests on search engines to provide methods that enable individuals to comment on, explain, or select what information is displayed when they are the subject of an Internet search. For example, Google developed the Google Inactive Account Manager, where you can specify what happens to your data after a period of inactivity.

Consider This: Does a government have a right to legislate search engine links? Why or why not? In what, if any, situations should individuals be able to request removal of digital content? Should search engines provide users with tools to control what information about them appears? Why or why not?

Content Filtering

One of the more controversial issues that surround the Internet is its widespread availability of objectionable material, such as prejudiced literature, violence, and obscene photos. Some believe that such materials should be banned. Others believe that the materials should be filtered, that is, restricted.

Content filtering is the process of restricting access to certain material. Many businesses use content filtering to limit employees' web access. These businesses argue that employees are unproductive when visiting inappropriate or objectionable websites. Some schools, libraries, and parents use content filtering to restrict access to minors. Content filtering opponents argue that banning any materials violates constitutional guarantees of free speech and personal rights. Read Ethics & Issues 5-3 to consider whether content filtering violates first amendment rights.

 ETHICS & ISSUES 5-3

Does Content Filtering in a Public Library Violate First Amendment Rights?
Among the resources libraries offer are Internet-enabled computers. The use of content filtering software on library computers controls the type of information a patron can access. Free speech advocates argue that this violates the First Amendment because it restricts library patrons from viewing certain websites and content.

The Children's Internet Protection Act (CIPA) requires that schools and libraries use content filtering software in order to receive certain federal funds. The purpose of CIPA is to restrict access to objectionable material, protect children when communicating online, prohibit children from sharing personal

information, and restrict children's identities or accounts being hacked. Proponents of CIPA claim it is necessary to protect children. CIPA does allow libraries to turn off the filters, if an adult patrons requests it. Some libraries use content filtering software on computers used only by children.

Critics of content filtering software argue that the programs do not always work as intended. They can overfilter content, blocking information or education websites based on a single word. Some websites and services that filtering software may block include online social networks, or software platforms, such as Google Drive, which students may need to access to submit assignments. Conversely, they can underfilter content, which

could result in access to webpages with inappropriate media. Others argue that it gives unequal access to students doing research who rely on library computers to do schoolwork and those who have unfiltered Internet access at home.

Libraries typically have a policy stating acceptable use of the Internet. Libraries' policies also should state whether they use content filtering software, so that the patrons are aware.

Consider This: Is it fair for a government to require that libraries use content filtering software? Why or why not? Do free speech laws cover content on the Internet? Why or why not?

Web filtering software is a program that restricts access to specified websites. Some also filter sites that use specific words (Figure 5-26). Others allow you to filter email messages, chat rooms, and programs. Many Internet security programs include a firewall, antivirus program, and filtering capabilities combined. Browsers also often include content filtering capabilities.

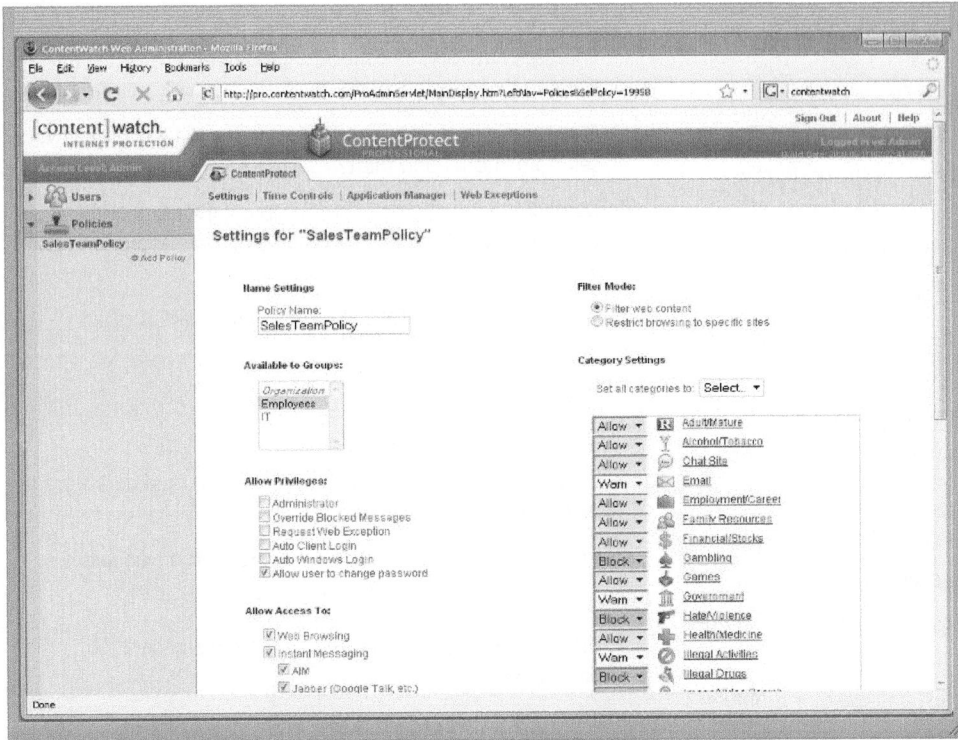

Figure 5-26   Web filtering software restricts access to specified websites.
Courtesy of ContentWatch, Inc.

Employee Monitoring

Employee monitoring involves the use of computers, mobile devices, or cameras to observe, record, and review an employee's use of a technology, including communications such as email messages, keyboard activity (used to measure productivity), and websites visited. Many programs exist that easily allow employers to monitor employees. Further, it is legal for employers to use these programs.

 **CONSIDER THIS**

Do employers have the right to read employee email messages?
Actual policies vary widely. Some organizations declare that they will review email messages regularly, and others state that email messages are private. In some states, if a company does not have a formal email policy, it can read email messages without employee notification.

🗸 Summary

This module presented a variety of digital security risks. You learned about cybercrime and cybercriminals. The module discussed risks and safeguards associated with Internet and network attacks, unauthorized access and use, software theft, information theft, and hardware theft, vandalism, and failure. It presented various backup strategies and methods of securing wireless communications. You learned about ethical issues in society and various ways to protect the privacy of personal information.

Study Guide

The Study Guide exercise reinforces material you should know after reading this module.

Instructions: Answer the questions below using the format that helps you remember best or that is required by your instructor. Possible formats may include one or more of these options: write the answers; create a document that contains the answers; record answers as audio or video using a webcam, smartphone, or portable media player; post answers on a blog, wiki, or website; or highlight answers in the book/e-book.

1. Define the terms, digital security risk, computer crime, cybercrime, and crimeware.

2. Differentiate among hackers, crackers, script kiddies, cyberextortionists, and cyberterrorists.

3. List common types of malware. A(n) ___ is the destructive event or prank malware delivers.

4. Identify risks and safety measures when gaming.

5. Define these terms: botnet, zombie, and bot.

6. Describe the damages caused by and possible motivations behind DoS and DDoS attacks.

7. A(n) ___ allows users to bypass security controls when accessing a program, computer, or network.

8. Define the term, spoofing.

9. List ways to protect against Internet and network attacks.

10. Describe the purpose of an online security service.

11. Define the terms, firewall and proxy server. List steps to set up a personal firewall.

12. Give examples of unauthorized access and use of a computer or network.

13. Identify what an AUP should specify. Why might you disable file and printer sharing?

14. Explain how an organization uses access controls and audit trails.

15. Differentiate among user names, passwords, passphrases, and pass codes.

16. List tips for using a password manager safely.

17. What is a single sign on account? PIN stands for ___.

18. Describe the purpose of a CAPTCHA.

19. Define the terms, possessed objects and biometric devices.

20. What is the purpose of a lock screen?

21. Describe how companies use the following recognition, verification, or payment systems: fingerprint, face, hand, voice, signature, and iris. List disadvantages of biometric devices.

22. Explain the two-step verification process.

23. Define the term, digital forensics. Name areas in which digital forensics are used.

24. Define the terms, software theft, keygen, and software piracy. Identify methods to prevent software theft.

25. Explain the process of product activation.

26. Describe the following license agreement types: single- or end-user, network, and site. List conditions provided in a license agreement.

27. Give examples of information theft. How can you protect yourself from information theft?

28. Describe the functions of an encryption algorithm and an encryption key. Differentiate between private and public key encryption.

29. Unencrypted data is called ___; encrypted data is called ___.

30. Describe the purpose of a VPN.

31. Define these terms: digital signature, digital certificate, and secure site.

32. List concerns and responsibilities regarding cloud data storage and privacy.

33. Describe what occurs during hardware theft or vandalism.

34. Define the terms, backup and restore.

35. List six types of backups. Describe the three-generation backup policy.

36. Identify the components of a disaster recovery plan.

37. Describe security risks associated with wireless access. Identify ways to secure your wireless network.

38. List guidelines to protect your mobile device data.

39. Describe technology ethics, information accuracy, intellectual property rights, copyrights, and codes of conduct.

40. Describe issues surrounding inaccurate data.

41. List measures users can take to contribute to green computing.

42. Explain how companies, websites, and employers might infringe on your right to information privacy.

43. Describe how the following techniques are used to collect personal data: electronic profiles, cookies, phishing, clickjacking, spyware, adware, and madware.

44. How can you protect against phishing and spoofing scams?

45. Identify methods to protect yourself from social engineering scams.

46. List examples of privacy laws. Should you be able to remove personal information from the Internet? Why or why not?

47. Describe what a company might track when monitoring employees.

48. Define and identify issues surrounding content and web filtering.

You should be able to define the Primary Terms and be familiar with the Secondary Terms listed below.

Key Terms

Primary Terms (shown in **bold-black** characters in the module)

adware (5-32)
back door (5-6)
back up (5-20)
backup (5-20)
biometric device (5-12)
botnet (5-5)
code of conduct (5-27)
computer crime (5-3)
content filtering (5-34)
cookie (5-30)
cracker (5-3)
cybercrime (5-3)
cyberextortionist (5-3)
cyberterrorist (5-3)
decrypt (5-17)

denial of service attack
   (DoS attack) (5-6)
digital certificate (5-18)
digital forensics (5-15)
digital security risk (5-2)
digital signature (5-18)
disaster recovery plan
   (5-21)
disc burning software
   (5-21)
employee monitoring
   (5-35)
encryption (5-17)
fingerprint reader (5-12)
firewall (5-8)

hacker (5-3)
information privacy (5-28)
information theft (5-17)
license agreement (5-16)
malware (5-4)
online security service
   (5-7)
password (5-10)
personal firewall (5-8)
PIN (5-11)
piracy (5-16)
product activation (5-16)
restore (5-20)
script kiddie (5-3)
secure site (5-18)

social engineering (5-32)
software piracy (5-16)
software theft (5-15)
spoofing (5-6)
spyware (5-32)
technology ethics (5-25)
two-step verification
   (5-14)
user name (5-10)
web filtering software
   (5-35)
zombie (5-5)

Secondary Terms (shown in *italic* characters in the module)

acceptable use policy (AUP) (5-9)
access control (5-10)
adware (5-4)
asymmetric key encryption (5-17)
audit trail (5-10)
biometric payment (5-14)
bot (5-5)
*Business Software Alliance
   (BSA) (5-15)*
CAPTCHA (5-12)
CERT/CC (5-7)
certificate authority (CA) (5-18)
ciphertext (5-17)
clickjacking (5-32)
cloud backup (5-21)
*Computer Emergency Response Team
   Coordination Center (5-7)*
*continuous data protection
   (CDP) (5-21)*
copyright (5-27)
Creative Commons (5-27)
crimeware (5-3)
cyberforensics (5-15)
cyberwarfare (5-3)

cypher (5-17)
differential backup (5-21)
digital rights management (5-27)
*distributed DoS attack (DDoS
   attack) (5-6)*
email spoofing (5-6)
encryption algorithm (5-17)
encryption key (5-17)
*end-user license agreement
   (EULA) (5-16)*
ENERGY STAR program (5-28)
face recognition system (5-13)
full backup (5-21)
hand geometry system (5-13)
incremental backup (5-21)
intellectual property (IP) (5-27)
intellectual property rights (5-27)
IP spoofing (5-6)
keygen (5-16)
lock screen (5-13)
MAC address (5-23)
MAC address control (5-23)
madware (5-32)
malicious software (5-4)

network license (5-16)
off-site (5-20)
passcode (5-11)
passphrase (5-11)
password manager (5-11)
password organizer (5-11)
payload (5-4)
phishing filter (5-32)
plaintext (5-17)
*power usage effectiveness
   (PUE) (5-28)*
private key encryption (5-17)
proxy server (5-8)
public key encryption (5-17)
ransomware (5-4)
rootkit (5-4)
*selective backup
   (5-21)*
session cookie (5-30)
*signature verification
   system (5-13)*
single sign on (5-10)
*single-user license
   agreement (5-16)*

site license (5-16)
spyware (5-4)
SSID (5-23)
symmetric key encryption (5-17)
trojan horse (5-4)
two-factor verification (5-14)
unauthorized access (5-9)
unauthorized use (5-9)
user ID (5-10)
*virtual private network
   (VPN) (5-18)*
virus (5-4)
voice verification system (5-13)
worm (5-4)
zombie army (5-5)

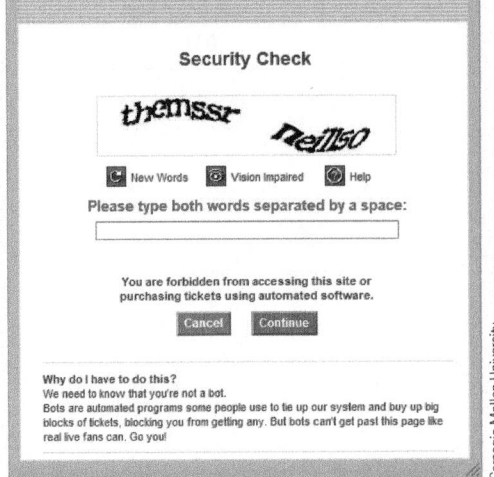

STUDENT ASSIGNMENTS

Checkpoint   The Checkpoint exercises test your knowledge of the module concepts.

True/False   Mark T for True and F for False. If False, rewrite the statement so that it is True.

_____ 1. Any illegal act involving the use of a computer or related devices generally is referred to as a crimeware.

_____ 2. A rootkit displays an online advertisement in a banner or pop-up window on webpages, email, or other Internet services.

_____ 3. Viruses, worms, and other malware can be hidden in downloaded game files and mobile apps.

_____ 4. An audit trail records in a file both successful and unsuccessful access attempts.

_____ 5. It is good practice to change your password frequently.

_____ 6. Intentionally erasing software would be considered software theft.

_____ 7. A typical license agreement allows you to rent or lease the software.

_____ 8. Unencrypted, readable data is called ciphertext.

_____ 9. Private key encryption also is called asymmetric key encryption.

_____ 10. VPNs encrypt data to help ensure that the data is safe from being intercepted by unauthorized people.

_____ 11. When data is traveling to or from a computer to a cloud service, it is subject to interception.

_____ 12. Full backups are made at regular intervals on removable media in a grandparent-parent-child backup scheme.

Matching   Match the terms with their definitions.

_____ 1. access control

_____ 2. bot

_____ 3. cookie

_____ 4. digital certificate

_____ 5. disc burning software

_____ 6. keygen

_____ 7. phishing

_____ 8. script kiddie

_____ 9. technology ethics

_____ 10. zombie

a. compromised computer or device whose owner is unaware the computer or device is being controlled remotely by an outsider

b. scam in which a perpetrator sends a message in an attempt to obtain personal or financial information

c. program that performs a repetitive task on a network

d. small text file that a web server stores on your computer

e. notice that guarantees a user or website is legitimate

f. program that writes text, graphics, audio, and video files on a recordable or rewritable disc

g. program that creates software registration numbers and sometimes activation codes

h. hacker who does not have the technical skills and knowledge of a cracker

i. security measure that defines who can access a computer, device, or network; when they can access it; and what actions they can take while accessing it

j. moral guidelines that govern the use of computers, mobile devices, information systems, and related technologies

The Problem Solving exercises extend your knowledge of module concepts by seeking solutions to practical problems with technology that you may encounter at home, school, work, or with nonprofit organizations. The Collaboration exercise should be completed with a team.

Problem Solving

Instructions: You often can solve problems with technology in multiple ways. Determine a solution to the problems in these exercises by using one or more resources available to you (such as a computer or mobile device, articles on the web or in print, blogs, podcasts, videos, television, user guides, other individuals, electronics or computer stores, etc.). Describe your solution, along with the resource(s) used, in the format requested by your instructor (brief report, presentation, discussion, blog post, video, or other means).

Personal

1. **No Browsing History**   While using the browser on your tablet, you realize that it is not keeping a history of websites you have visited. Why might this be happening, and what is the first step you will take to correct this problem?

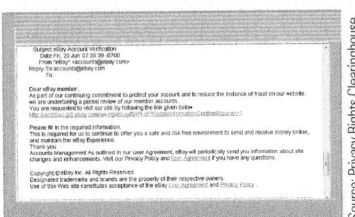

Source: Privacy Rights Clearinghouse

2. **Phishing Scam**   You just received an email message from someone requesting personal identification information. Believing the message was legitimate, you provided the requested information to the original sender. You now realize, however, that you might have fallen victim to a phishing scam. What are your next steps?

3. **Suspicious File Attachment**   You receive an email message that appears to be from someone you know. When you try to open the attachment, nothing happens. You attempt to open the attachment two more times without any success. Several minutes later, your computer is running slower and you are having trouble running apps. What might be wrong?

4. **Antivirus Software Outdated**   After starting your computer and signing in to the operating system, a message is displayed stating that your virus definitions are out of date and need to be updated. What are your next steps?

5. **Laptop's Physical Security**   You plan to start taking your laptop to school so that you can record notes in class. You want to make sure, however, that your computer is safe if you ever step away from it for a brief period of time. What steps can you take to ensure the physical security of your laptop?

Professional

6. **Corporate Firewall Interference**   You installed a new browser on your work computer because you no longer wish to use the default browser provided with the operating system. When you run the new browser, an error message appears stating that a user name and password are required to configure the firewall and allow this program to access the Internet. Why has this happened?

7. **Problems with CAPTCHA**   You are signing up for an account on a website and encounter a CAPTCHA. You attempt to type the characters you see on the screen, but an error message appears stating that you have entered the incorrect characters. You try two more times and get the same result. You are typing the characters to the best of your ability but think you still might be misreading at least one of the characters. What are your next steps?

8. **Unclear Acceptable Use Policy**   You read your company's acceptable use policy, but it is not clear about whether you are able to use the computer in your office to visit news websites on your lunch break. How can you determine whether this type of activity is allowed?

9. **Two-Step Verification Problem**   A website you are attempting to access requires two-step verification. In addition to entering your password, you also have to enter a code that it sends to you as a text message. You no longer have the same phone number, so you are unable to receive the text message. What are your next steps?

10. **Issue with Virus Protection**   You receive a notification that the antivirus program on your computer is not enabled. While attempting to enable the antivirus program, an error message is displayed stating that a problem has prevented the antivirus program from being enabled. What are your next steps?

Collaboration

11. **Technology in National and Local Security**   National and local security agencies often use technology to protect citizens. For example, computers are used to maintain a No Fly List, which contains a list of individuals not cleared to board a commercial aircraft. Form a team of three people to create a list of the various ways technology helps to keep the public safe. One team member should research how local agencies, such as police departments, use technology to ensure security. Another team member should research ways national security agencies use technology to protect the public from threats, and the last team member should research ways that private businesses use technology to enhance security. Compile these findings into a report and submit it to your instructor.

✳ How To: Your Turn

The How To: Your Turn exercises present general guidelines for fundamental skills when using a computer or mobile device and then require that you determine how to apply these general guidelines to a specific program or situation.

Instructions: You often can complete tasks using technology in multiple ways. Figure out how to perform the tasks described in these exercises by using one or more resources available to you (such as a computer or mobile device, articles on the web or in print, online or program help, user guides, blogs, podcasts, videos, other individuals, trial and error, etc.). Summarize your 'how to' steps, along with the resource(s) used, in the format requested by your instructor (brief report, presentation, discussion, blog post, video, or other means).

❶ Evaluate Your Electronic Profile

When you make purchases online, click advertisements, follow links, and complete online forms requesting information about yourself, you are adding to your electronic profile. While an electronic profile may help businesses guide you toward products and services that are of interest to you, some people view them as an invasion of privacy. The following steps guide you through the process of locating online information about yourself and taking steps to remove the information, if possible.

a. Run a browser.

b. Navigate to a search engine of your choice.

c. Perform a search for your full name.

d. In the search results, follow a link that you feel will display a webpage containing information about you. If the link's destination does not contain information about you, navigate back to the search results and follow another link.

e. Evaluate the webpage that contains information about you. If you wish to try removing the information, locate a link that allows you to contact the site owner(s) or automatically request removal of the information.

f. Request that your information be removed from the website. Some websites may not honor your request for removal. If you feel that the information must be removed, you may need to solicit legal advice.

g. If the search results display information from an account you have on an online social network, such as Facebook or LinkedIn, you may need to adjust your privacy settings so that the information is not public. If the privacy settings do not allow you to hide your information, you may need to consider deleting the account.

h. Repeat Steps d – g for the remaining search results. When you no longer see relevant search results for the search engine you used, search for other variations of your name (use your middle initial instead of your middle name, exclude your middle name, or consider using commonly used nicknames instead of your first name).

i. Use other search engines to search for different variations of your name. Some search engines uncover results that others do not.

j. If you have an account on an online social network, navigate to the website's home page and, without signing in, search for your name. If information appears that you do not want to be public, you may need to adjust your privacy settings or remove your account.

k. Follow up with requests you have made to remove your online information.

Exercises

1. What personal information have you uncovered online? Did you have any idea that the information was there?

2. What additional steps can you take to prevent people and businesses from storing information about you?

3. What steps might you be able to take if you are unsuccessful with your attempts to remove online information that identifies you?

iStockphoto.com / maxkabakov

❷ Update Virus Definitions

In addition to installing or activating an antivirus program on your computer or mobile device to keep it safe from viruses, it also is necessary to keep the virus definitions updated so that the antivirus program can search for and detect new viruses on your computer or mobile device. New virus definitions can be released as often as once per day, depending on the number of new viruses that are created. Antivirus programs either can search for and install new virus definitions automatically at specified intervals, or you can update the virus signatures manually. The following steps describe how to update the virus definitions for an antivirus program.

Update Virus Definitions Manually

a. If necessary, establish an Internet connection so that you will be able to update the virus definitions.
b. Run an antivirus program.
c. Click the button to check for updated virus definitions.
d. If new virus definitions are available for the antivirus program, click the link to download the definitions to the computer or mobile device.
e. When the update is complete, click the button to scan the computer or mobile device for viruses.

Configure Automatic Updates for Virus Definitions

a. If necessary, establish an Internet connection so that you will be able to update the virus definitions.
b. Run an antivirus program.
c. Click the option to update virus definitions automatically.
d. Click the option to display the virus definition update schedule.
e. To provide the maximum protection from viruses, configure the antivirus program to update definitions as frequently as possible.
f. After configuring the update schedule, click the button to update virus definitions manually.
g. When the update is complete, click the button to scan the computer or mobile device for viruses.

Exercises

1. What antivirus program, if any, currently is installed on your computer? Is it scheduled to update virus definitions automatically?
2. In addition to downloading and installing virus definitions from within the antivirus program, are other ways available to obtain the latest virus definitions?
3. In addition to keeping the antivirus program's virus definitions current, what other ways can you protect a computer or mobile device from viruses?

How To: Your Turn ✳

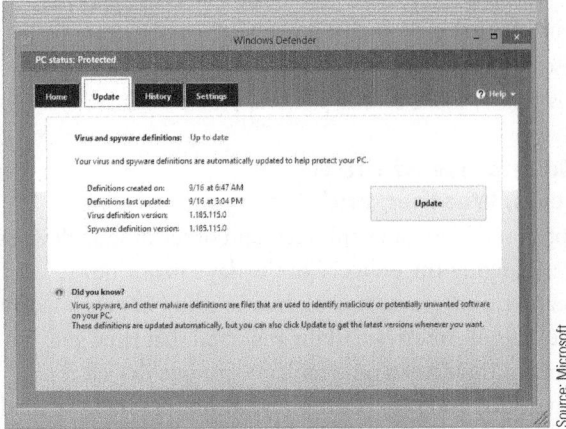

Source: Microsoft

③ Clear Your Browsing History

A browser keeps track of the webpages that you have visited previously unless you have changed your settings. Although you can clear the browsing history on your computer or mobile device, your Internet service provider still may have logs that show a history of websites you have visited. The following steps guide you through the process of clearing your browsing history.

a. Run the browser.
b. Display the browser's settings.
c. If necessary, navigate to the settings that configure the browser's security settings. These settings often are found in the Security, Safety, or Privacy category.
d. Select the option to delete the browsing history. In addition to deleting the list of websites you have visited, you also may be able to clear passwords the browser has remembered, clear cookies and temporary internet files, clear data you entered in forms, and clear a history of downloads.
e. When the browsing history has been deleted, run the browser again.
f. Follow the above steps for each additional browser you have installed on your computer or mobile device.

Exercises

1. What are some reasons why you might want to delete your browsing history?
2. Can you configure your browser to automatically delete your browsing history? If so, how?
3. What are the advantages of keeping your browsing history? If you do keep your browsing history, how long do you keep it?

✳ Internet Research

The Internet Research exercises broaden your understanding of module concepts by requiring that you search for information on the web.

Instructions: Use a search engine or another search tool to locate the information requested or answers to questions presented in the exercises. Describe your findings, along with the search term(s) you used and your web source(s), in the format requested by your instructor (brief report, presentation, discussion, blog post, video, or other means).

1 Making Use of the Web
News, Weather, and Sports

Apps on tablets, smartphones, and other mobile devices are changing the delivery of the day's major news, weather, and sports stories. In one study, approximately one-half of American adults reported that they get some of their news on a tablet or mobile device. They view video and photos from eyewitnesses and fans, read analyses from investigators and coaches, and comment on stories. Men and college-educated people are the heaviest users of mobile news websites, and they are likely to read in-depth investigations and analyses. Online social networks also are a major source of information for many people.

Research This: (a) Visit two news websites or apps and locate one national event covered in both sources. Compare the coverage of the two stories. What information is provided in addition to the text, such as video, graphics, or links to related articles? Which story offers a better analysis? Which source is easier to navigate and read? Then, using another website or app, locate and read today's top international news story. What did you learn by reading the story? Were you aware of this event prior to reading the online story? Does the coverage include videos and photos to increase your comprehension?

(b) Visit a weather website or app and obtain the five-day forecast for your hometown. Include details about information that supplements the current and forecast conditions, such as a pollen or air quality index, storm tracking, travel advisories, or season summaries.

(c) Visit a sports website or app and read the first story reported. Describe the coverage of this event. Which sources are quoted in the story? Which links are included to other stories? Describe the features provided on this website, such as the ability to chat, customize the page for your favorite teams, or share the content with media sharing sites.

2 Social Media
Unauthorized Access

Sharing photos on your social media sites of yesterday's visit to the ballpark might be at the top of today's to-do list, but these images might be just the clues cyberthieves need to access your account. Facebook, in particular, is one website that scammers and advertisers use to gather information regarding your whereabouts and your personal life. Their malicious attacks begin with a visit to your timeline or other record of your activities. Searching for keywords on your page, they send targeted messages appearing to originate from trusted friends. If you open their attachments or click their links, you have given these unscrupulous individuals access to your account. In addition, you may think you have crafted a password no one could guess. With your page open for others to view, however, the thieves scour the contents in hopes of locating starting clues, such as children's names, anniversary dates, and pet breeds, which could be hints to cracking your password.

Research This: In the Help section of an online social network you use, search for information about changing your profile's security and privacy settings. What steps can you take to mitigate the chance of becoming the victim of a hack? For example, can you adjust the connection settings to restrict who can see stories, send friend requests and messages, or search for you by name or contact information? Can you hide certain posts or block people from posting on your page? Can you report posts if they violate the website's terms? What are other potential threats to someone accessing your account?

Source: National Weather Service

3 Search Skills
Social Media Search

Search engines provide access to millions of search results by finding webpages, documents, images, or

Internet Research ✳

other information that match the search text you provide. Recommendations from people who use social media to share what they have read can be a possible alternative to using a search engine. People who take the time to Tweet pin an article or image on Twitter or Pinterest often do so because they found it useful, and hope others will as well.

To search Twitter, type the search text, search twitter, in a search engine to find the web address for the Twitter Search website, or sign in to Twitter with your credentials. In the Search Twitter text box, type the search text. For example, type the text, best mapping app, to find recommendations of links to articles or websites about mapping apps. You also can search Twitter for hashtags (a keyword preceded by a # symbol) to find Tweets about current events or popular discussion topics.

To search Pinterest, sign in to your Pinterest account and then type the search text into the search box. For example, type the search text, information security, into the search box to view related pins from Pinterest users. Pinterest users often pin links to infographics, images, and websites.

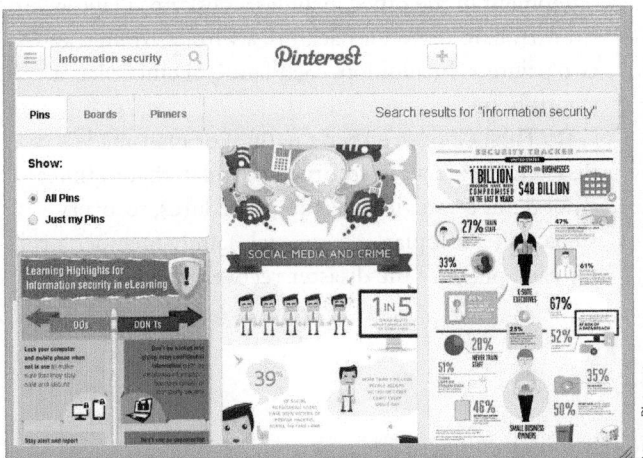

Source: Pinterest

Research This: Use Twitter and Pinterest to search for information about the following topics and then compare your results with those you would find using a search engine such as Bing, Google, or Yahoo!. (1) green computing, (2) computer virus, (3) cybercrime, and (4) malware. How are the results different? What type of information are you more likely to find on Twitter, on Pinterest, and using a search engine?

4 Security
Digital Certificates and Signatures

Digital certificates and signatures detect a sender's identity and verify a document's authenticity. In this module you learned that many e-commerce companies use them in an attempt to prevent digital eavesdroppers from intercepting confidential information. The online certificate authority (CA) vendors generate these certificates using a standard, called X.509, which is coordinated by the International Telecommunication Union and uses algorithms and encryption technology to identify the documents.

Research This: Visit websites of at least two companies that issue digital certificates. Compare products offered, prices, and certificate features. What length of time is needed to issue a certificate? What is a green address bar, and when is one issued? What business or organization validation is required? Then, visit websites of at least two companies that provide digital signatures. Compare signing and sending requirements, types of supported signatures, and available security features. Which documents are required to obtain a digital signature? When would a business need a Class 2 rather than a Class 3 digital signature?

5 Cloud Services
Cloud Security (SecaaS)

Antivirus software offers regular, automatic updates in order to protect a server, computer, or device from viruses, malware, or other attacks. Antivirus software is an example of cloud security, or security as a service (SecaaS), a service of cloud computing that delivers virus definitions and security software to users over the Internet as updates become available, with no intervention from users. Security as a service is a special case of software as a service, but is limited to security software solutions.

Individuals and enterprise users take advantage of antivirus software and security updates. Enterprise cloud users interact with cloud security solutions via a web interface to configure apps that provide protection to email servers, preventing spam before it arrives, keeping data secure, and watching for online threats and viruses. As the use of cloud-based resources continues, the market for security as a service solutions is expected to increase significantly in coming years.

Research This: (1) Use a search engine to find two different providers of security as a service solutions. Research the different solutions they provide, and report your findings. (2) How are enterprise security requirements different from those of individual users?

✳ Critical Thinking

The Critical Thinking exercises challenge your assessment and decision-making skills by presenting real-world situations associated with module concepts. The Collaboration exercise should be completed with a team.

Instructions: Evaluate the situations below, using personal experiences and one or more resources available to you (such as articles on the web or in print, blogs, podcasts, videos, television, user guides, other individuals, electronics or computer stores, etc.). Perform the tasks requested in each exercise and share your deliverables in the format requested by your instructor (brief report, presentation, discussion, blog post, video, or other means).

1. Online Gaming Safety

You and your friend frequently play a popular online role-playing game. Your friend's computer had a virus recently, which was traced back to a malware-infected website. Your friend tells you that she visited the website after following a link while playing the game. What risks are involved when playing online games?

Do This: Use the web to find articles about incidents of malware infections associated with online gaming. Research tips for increasing security when playing online games. Did you find other threats and security tips in addition to the ones mentioned in this module? Have you ever downloaded updates to a game? If so, how did you ensure the updates were safe? Locate a list of games that are known to cause malware infections. Share your findings and any online gaming security problems you have experienced with the class.

2. Ensuring Safety and Security Online

You work in the information technology department for a large enterprise. An increasing number of users are contacting the help desk complaining about slow computer performance. Help desk representatives frequently attribute the decreased performance to malware. Although the help desk has installed security software on each computer, users also must practice safe computing. Your manager asked you to prepare information that teaches employees how to guard against malware and other security threats.

Do This: Include information such as how to determine if a website is safe, how to identify email and other spoofing schemes, guidelines for downloading programs and apps, email attachment safety, and how to avoid phishing scams. Create a list of how organizations use common safeguards to protect other users on the network, such as firewalls, proxy servers, user names and passwords, access controls, and audit trails.

3. Case Study

Family-Owned Coffee Shop You are the new manager for a family-owned coffee shop. The shop's owners asked you to develop a disaster recovery plan for its office. The office consists of two back rooms: one room is the office, with all of the electronic equipment and paper files; the other is for storage of nonelectronic equipment. You, your sister, and your cousin who is graduating with a bachelor's degree in information technology (IT) work in the office. The electronic equipment in the office includes a desktop, a laptop, an external hard drive for backups, a wireless router, and two printers. In addition, each family member has a smartphone.

Do This: Choose either a natural or man-made disaster. Create a disaster recovery plan that outlines emergency strategies, backup procedures, recovery steps, and a test plan. Assign each family member a role for each phase of the disaster recovery plan.

Collaboration

4. Implementing Biometric Security

You are the chief technology officer of a large company. You have been reading an article about computer security that discussed several examples of security breaches, including thieves breaking into an office and stealing expensive equipment, and a recently terminated employee gaining access to the office after hours and corrupting data. Because of these incidents, your company would like to start using biometric devices to increase its security.

Do This: Form a three-member team and research the use of biometric devices to protect equipment and data. Each member of your team should choose a different type of biometric device, such as fingerprint readers, face recognition systems, and hand geometry systems. Find products for each device type, and research costs and user reviews. Search for articles by industry experts. Would you recommend using the biometric device for security purposes? Why or why not? Meet with your team, discuss and compile your findings, and then share with the class.

Courtesy of Ingersoll Rand Security Technologies

Technology Timeline

1937 Dr. John V. Atanasoff and Clifford Berry design and build the first electronic digital computer. Their machine, the Atanasoff-Berry-Computer, or ABC, provides the foundation for advances in electronic digital computers.

1945 John von Neumann poses in front of the electronic computer built at the Institute for Advanced Study. This computer and its von Neumann architecture served as the prototype for subsequent stored program computers worldwide.

1947 William Shockley, John Bardeen, and Walter Brattain invent the transfer resistance device, eventually called the transistor. The transistor would revolutionize computers, proving much more reliable than vacuum tubes.

1952 Dr. Grace Hopper considers the concept of reusable software in her paper, "The Education of a Computer." The paper describes how to program a computer with symbolic notation instead of detailed machine language.

AP Images/Frederick News-Post (2); J. R. Eyerman/The LIFE Picture Collection/Getty Images

Photo: Alan Richards, from the Shelby White and Leon Levy Archives Center, Institute for Advanced Study, Princeton, NJ, USA (2)

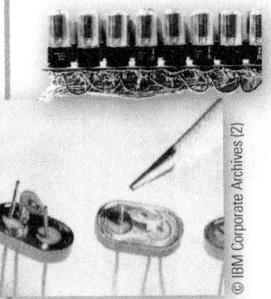

© IBM Corporate Archives (2)

Courtesy of Hagley Museum and Library

1937 1943 1945 1946 1947 1951 1952 1953

Bletchley Park Trust/SSPL/The Image Works

From the Collections of the University of Pennsylvania Archives

© IBM Corporate Archives

Pictures From History/The Image Works

Courtesy Unisys Corporation

1943 During World War II, British scientist Alan Turing designs the Colossus, an electronic computer created for the military to break German codes. The computer's existence is kept secret until the 1970s.

1946 Dr. John W. Mauchly and J. Presper Eckert, Jr. complete work on the first large-scale electronic, general-purpose digital computer. The ENIAC (Electronic Numerical Integrator And Computer) weighs 30 tons, contains 18,000 vacuum tubes, occupies a 30 × 50 foot space, and consumes 160 kilowatts of power.

1951 The first commercially available electronic digital computer, the UNIVAC I (UNIVersal Automatic Computer), is introduced by Remington Rand. Public awareness of computers increases when the UNIVAC I correctly predicts that Dwight D. Eisenhower will win the presidential election.

1953 Core memory, developed in the early 1950s, provides much larger storage capacity than vacuum tube memory.

1953 The IBM model 650 is one of the first widely used computers. The computer is so successful that IBM manufactures more than 1,000. IBM will dominate the mainframe market for the next decade.

1957 The IBM 305 RAMAC computer is the first to use magnetic disk for external storage. The computer provides storage capacity similar to magnetic tape that previously was used but offers the advantage of semi-random access capability.

1959 More than 200 programming languages have been created.

1959 IBM introduces two smaller, desk-sized computers: the IBM 1401 for business and the IBM 1620 for scientists.

1965 Dr. John Kemeny of Dartmouth leads the development of the BASIC programming language.

1968 In a letter to the editor titled, "GO TO Statements Considered Harmful," Dr. Edsger Dijkstra introduces the concept of structured programming, developing standards for constructing computer programs.

Courtesy of Dartmouth College

© IBM Corporate Archives

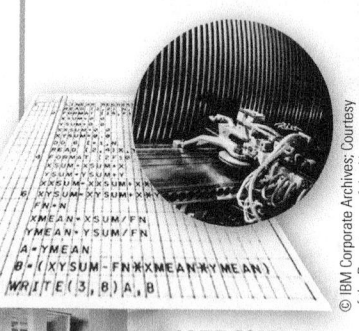

© IBM Corporate Archives; Courtesy of the Department of the Navy

1957 FORTRAN (FORmula TRANslation), an efficient, easy-to-use programming language, is introduced by John Backus.

© IBM Corporate Archives

1965 Digital Equipment Corporation (DEC) introduces the first microcomputer, the PDP-8. The machine is used extensively as an interface for time-sharing systems.

Courtesy of Hewlett-Packard Company

1968 Computer Science Corporation (CSC) becomes the first software company listed on the New York Stock Exchange.

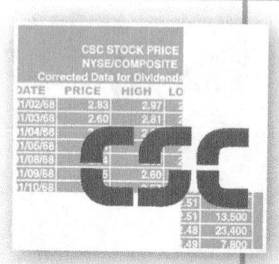

| 1957 | 1958 | 1959 | 1960 | 1964 | 1965 | 1967 | 1968 |

Courtesy of Texas Instruments (2)

1958 Jack Kilby of Texas Instruments invents the integrated circuit, which lays the foundation for high-speed computers and large-capacity memory. Computers built with transistors mark the beginning of the second generation of computer hardware.

Courtesy of Hagley Museum and Library

1960 COBOL, a high-level business application language, is developed by a committee headed by Dr. Grace Hopper.

Source: Indiana University – School of Informatics at IUPUI

Douglas Englebart
Image

Douglas Engelbart's Picture
Start Over: Profile for Engelbart

1964 The number of computers has grown to 18,000. Third-generation computers, with their controlling circuitry stored on chips, are introduced. The IBM System/360 computer is the first family of compatible machines, merging science and business lines.

1967 Douglas Engelbart applies for a patent for his wooden mouse.

© IBM Corporate Archives

1968 Alan Shugart at IBM demonstrates the first regular use of an 8-inch floppy disk.

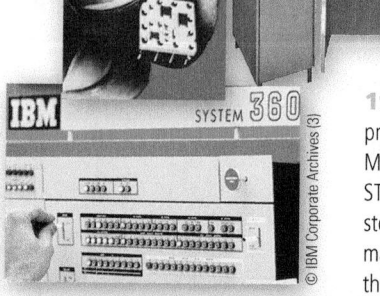

© IBM Corporate Archives (3)

1964 IBM introduces the term, word processing, for the first time with its Magnetic Tape/Selectric Typewriter (MT/ST). The MT/ST was the first reusable storage medium that allowed typed material to be edited without requiring that the document be retyped.

1969 Under pressure from the industry, IBM announces that some of its software will be priced separately from the computer hardware, allowing software firms to emerge in the industry.

© IBM Corporate Archives

1969 The ARPANET network is established, which eventually grows to become the Internet.

1975 MITS, Inc. advertises one of the first microcomputers, the Altair. The Altair is sold in kits for less than $400, and within the first three months 4,000 orders are taken.

LiPo Ching/MCT/Newscom

1975 Ethernet, the first local area network (LAN), is developed at Xerox PARC (Palo Alto Research Center) by Robert Metcalfe.

iStockphoto.com/LongHa2006

1976 Steve Jobs and Steve Wozniak build the first Apple computer. A subsequent version, the Apple II, is an immediate success. Adopted by elementary schools, high schools, and colleges, for many students, the Apple II is their first contact with the world of computers.

Bettmann/Getty Images

1980 IBM offers Microsoft Corporation cofounder, Bill Gates, the opportunity to develop the operating system for the soon-to-be announced IBM personal computer. With the development of MS-DOS, Microsoft achieves tremendous growth and success.

Corbis Premium Historical/Getty Images

1980 Alan Shugart presents the Winchester hard disk, revolutionizing storage for personal computers.

Courtesy of IBM Corporate Archives

| 1969 | 1970 | 1971 | 1975 | 1976 | 1979 | 1980 | 1981 |

© IBM Corporate Archives

1970 Fourth-generation computers, built with chips that use LSI (large-scale integration) arrive. While the chips used in 1965 contained up to 1,000 circuits, the LSI chip contains as many as 15,000.

Courtesy of Intel Corporation (2)

1971 Dr. Ted Hoff of Intel Corporation develops a microprocessor, or microprogrammable computer chip, the Intel 4004.

1979 VisiCalc, a spreadsheet program written by Bob Frankston and Dan Bricklin, is introduced.

1979 The first public online information services, CompuServe and the Source, are founded.

1981 The IBM PC is introduced, signaling IBM's entrance into the personal computer marketplace. The IBM PC quickly garners the largest share of the personal computer market and becomes the personal computer of choice in business.

Courtesy of IBM Corporate Archives

1981 The first computer virus, Elk Cloner, is spread via Apple II floppy disks, which contained the operating system. A short rhyme would appear on the screen when the user pressed the Reset button after the 50th boot of an infected disk.

iStockphoto.com/Rebekkah_ann

Lane V. Erickson/Shutterstock.com
Courtesy of Microsoft® Corporation

1986 Microsoft has public stock offering and raises approximately $61 million.

1988 Microsoft surpasses Lotus Development Corporation to become the world's top software vendor.

1991 Kodak announces the first digital SLR (single-lens reflex) camera. The Kodak DCS 100 is developed mostly for photojournalism purposes and stores the photos and batteries in a separate unit.

NMPFT/SSPL / The Image Works

3.275 Million

1982 3,275,000 personal computers are sold, almost 3,000,000 more than in 1981.

1982 Hayes introduces the 300 bps smart modem. The modem is an immediate success.

1982 Compaq, Inc. is founded to develop and market IBM-compatible PCs.

Courtesy of Hewlett-Packard Company

1991 World Wide Web Consortium releases standards that describe a framework for linking documents on different computers.

1982	**1983**	**1984**	**1986**	**1988**	**1989**	**1991**

1983 Instead of choosing a person for its annual award, TIME magazine names the computer Machine of the Year for 1982, acknowledging the impact of computers on society.

iStockphoto.com/audioundwerbung

Apple

1984 Apple introduces the Macintosh computer, which incorporates a unique, easy-to-learn, graphical user interface.

1989 Nintendo introduces the Game Boy, its first handheld game console.

SSPL / The Image Works

© IBM Corporate Archives

1983 Lotus Development Corporation is founded. Its spreadsheet software, Lotus 1-2-3, which combines spreadsheet, graphics, and database programs in one package, becomes the best-selling program for IBM personal computers.

Courtesy of Hewlett-Packard Company

1984 Hewlett-Packard announces the first LaserJet printer for personal computers.

Hank Morgan / Science Source

1989 While working at CERN, Switzerland, Tim Berners-Lee invents the World Wide Web.

1989 The Intel 486 becomes the world's first 1,000,000 transistor microprocessor. It executes 15,000,000 instructions per second — four times as fast as its predecessor, the 80386 chip.

Courtesy of Intel Corporation

1993 Microsoft releases Microsoft Office 3 Professional, the first version of Microsoft Office for the Windows operating system.

1993 Several companies introduce computers using the Pentium processor from Intel. The Pentium chip contains 3.1 million transistors and is capable of performing 112,000,000 instructions per second.

Source: amazon.com

1994 Amazon is founded and later begins business as an online bookstore. Amazon eventually expands to sell products of all types and facilitates the buying and selling of new and used goods. Today, Amazon employs more than 88,400 people.

Source: Linux

1994 Linus Torvalds creates the Linux kernel, a UNIX-like operating system that he releases free across the Internet for further enhancement by other programmers.

1995 eBay, an online auction website, is founded. Providing an online venue for people to buy and sell goods, it quickly becomes the world's largest online marketplace as it approaches 100 million active users worldwide.

AP Images/Nigel Treblin/dapd

Source: Oracle

1995 Sun Microsystems launches Java, an object-oriented programming language that allows users to write one program for a variety of computer platforms.

1995 Microsoft releases Windows 95, a major upgrade to its Windows operating system. Windows 95 consists of more than 10,000,000 lines of computer instructions developed by 300 person-years of effort.

1992 1993 1994 1995

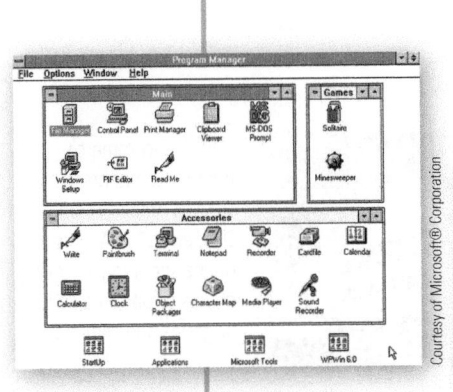
Courtesy of Microsoft® Corporation

1992 Microsoft releases Windows 3.1, the latest version of its Windows operating system. Windows 3.1 offers improvements such as TrueType fonts, multimedia capability, and object linking and embedding (OLE). In two months, 3,000,000 copies of Windows 3.1 are sold.

1993 The U.S. Air Force completes the Global Positioning System by launching its 24th Navstar satellite into orbit. Today, GPS receivers can be found in cars, laptops, and smartphones.

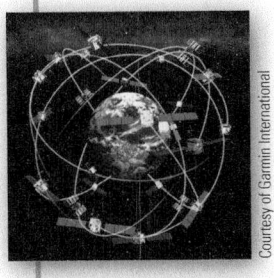
Courtesy of Garmin International

Orhan Cam/Shutterstock.com

1993 The White House launches its website, which includes an interactive citizens' handbook and White House history and tours.

1994 Jim Clark and Marc Andreessen found Netscape and launch Netscape Navigator 1.0, a browser.

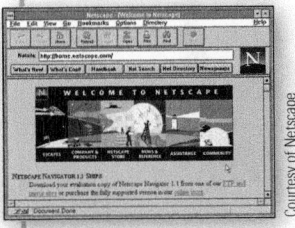
Courtesy of Netscape Communications Corporation

1994 Apple introduces the first digital camera intended for consumers. The Apple QuickTake 100 is connected to home computers using a serial cable.

Courtesy of Mark D. Martin

1994 Yahoo!, a popular search engine and portal, is founded by two Stanford Ph.D. students as a way to keep track of their personal interests on the Internet. Currently, Yahoo! has approximately 11,500 employees in 25 countries, provinces, and territories.

AP Images/Paul Sakuma

1997 Intel introduces the Pentium II processor with 7.5 million transistors. The new processor, which incorporates MMX technology, processes video, audio, and graphics data more efficiently and supports programs such as movie editing, gaming, and more.

Courtesy of Intel Corporation

1999 Intel introduces the Pentium III processor. This processor succeeds the Pentium II and can process 3-D graphics more quickly. The Pentium III processor contains between 9.5 and 44 million transistors.

Courtesy of Intel Corporation

1999 Governments and businesses frantically work to make their computers Y2K (Year 2000) compliant, spending more than $500 billion worldwide.

Y2K COMPLIANT

1997 Microsoft releases Internet Explorer 4.0 and seizes a key place in the Internet arena.

AP Images

1999 Open source software, such as the Linux operating system and the Apache web server created by unpaid volunteers, begins to gain wide acceptance among computer users.

KK Tan/Shutterstock.com

1996   1997   1998   1999

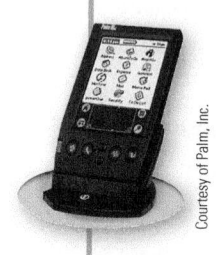

Courtesy of Palm, Inc.

1996 U.S. Robotics introduces the PalmPilot, an inexpensive user-friendly personal digital assistant (PDA).

1996 Microsoft releases Windows NT 4.0, an operating system for client-server networks.

Box shot reprinted with permission from Microsoft Corporation.

Google

Courtesy of Google, Inc.

1998 Google files for incorporation and is now the most used search engine, capturing more than 60 percent of the market over other search engines.

Brad Cherson / Alamy Stock Photo

1998 E-commerce booms. Companies such as Amazon.com, Dell, and E*TRADE spur online shopping, allowing buyers to obtain a variety of goods and services.

iStockphoto.com/juniorbeep

1998 Apple introduces the iMac, the next version of its popular Macintosh computer. The iMac wins customers with its futuristic design, see-through case, and easy setup.

Source: Napster

2000 Shawn Fanning, 19, and his company, Napster, turn the music industry upside down by developing software that allows computer users to swap music files with one another without going through a centralized file server.

Courtesy of Intel Corporation

2001 Intel unveils its Pentium 4 chip with clock speeds starting at 1.4 GHz. The Pentium 4 includes 42 million transistors.

2002 Digital video cameras, DVD burners, easy-to-use video editing software, and improvements in storage capabilities allow the average computer user to create Hollywood-like videos with introductions, conclusions, rearranged scenes, music, and voice-over.

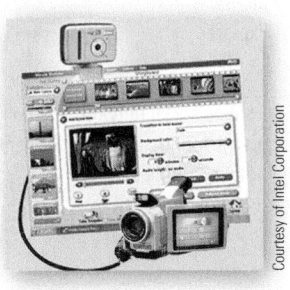

Courtesy of Intel Corporation

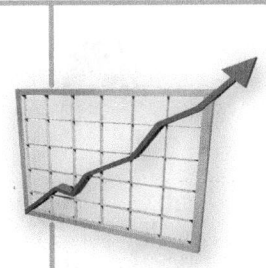

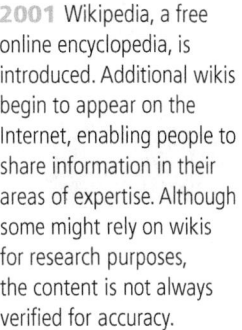

Wikimedia Foundation

2001 Wikipedia, a free online encyclopedia, is introduced. Additional wikis begin to appear on the Internet, enabling people to share information in their areas of expertise. Although some might rely on wikis for research purposes, the content is not always verified for accuracy.

2002 After several years of negligible sales, the Tablet PC is reintroduced to meet the needs of a more targeted audience.

Courtesy of ViewSonic® Corporation

2000 E-commerce achieves mainstream acceptance. Annual e-commerce sales exceed $100 billion, and Internet advertising expenditures reach more than $5 billion.

2000   2001   2002

2000 Dot-com (Internet based) companies go out of business at a record pace — nearly one per day — as financial investors withhold funding due to the companies' unprofitability.

Microsoft® .net

2002 Microsoft launches its .NET strategy, which is a new environment for developing and running software applications featuring ease of development of web-based services.

Tatiana Popova / Shutterstock.com

2002 DVD burners begin to replace CD burners (CD-RW). DVDs can store up to eight times as much data as CDs. Uses include storing home movies, music, photos, and backups.

Kenneth Murray / Science Source

2000 Telemedicine uses satellite technology and videoconferencing to broadcast consultations and to perform distant surgeries. Robots are used for complex and precise tasks.

2002 Intel ships its revamped Pentium 4 chip with the 0.13 micron processor and Hyper-Threading (HT) Technology, operating at speeds of 3.06 GHz. This new development eventually will enable processors with a billion transistors to operate at 20 GHz.

Courtesy of Intel Corporation

2004 Mozilla releases its first version of the Firefox browser. Firefox provides innovative features that enhance the browsing experience for users, including tabbed browsing and a Search box. Firefox quickly gains popularity and takes market share away from Microsoft's Internet Explorer.

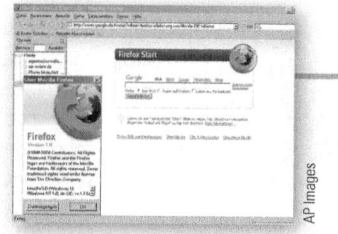

AP Images

2004 Facebook, an online social network originally available only to college students, is founded. Facebook eventually opens registration to all people and immediately grows to more than 110 million users.

Courtesy of Facebook

2004 Sony unveils the PlayStation Portable (PSP). This handheld game console is the first to use optical discs.

Issei Kato IK/CP/ Reuters

2004 Companies such as RealNetworks, Microsoft, Sony, and Walmart stake out turf in the online music store business started by Apple.

2004 Flat-panel LCD monitors overtake bulky CRT monitors as the popular choice of computer users.

2004 Linux, an open source operating system, makes major inroads into the server market as a viable alternative to Microsoft Windows Server 2003, Sun's Solaris, and UNIX.

2004 106 million, or 53 percent, of the 200 million online population in America accesses the Internet via broadband.

Source: Linux

2003

2004

Nick Koudis/Getty Images

Mannie Garcia/Reuters/Newscom

2003 In an attempt to maintain their current business model of selling songs, the Recording Industry Association of America (RIAA) files more than 250 lawsuits against individual computer users who offer copyrighted music over peer-to-peer networks.

2003 Wireless computers and devices, such as keyboards, mouse devices, home networks, and wireless Internet access points become commonplace.

wavebreakmedia/Shutterstock.com; Fuse/Getty Images; iStockphoto.com/hocus-pocus; StockLite /Shutterstock.com; iStockphoto.com/LifesizeImages

Courtesy of Palm Inc.

2004 USB flash drives become a cost-effective way to transport data and information from one computer to another.

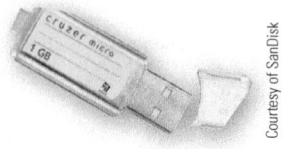

Courtesy of SanDisk Corporation

2004 Major retailers begin requiring suppliers to include radio frequency identification (RFID) tags or microchips with antennas, which can be as small as one-third of a millimeter across, in the goods they sell.

Courtesy of Intermec Technologies

2004 The smartphone overtakes the PDA as the mobile device of choice.

Courtesy of Palm Inc.

2004 Apple introduces the sleek all-in-one iMac G5. The new computer's display device contains the system unit.

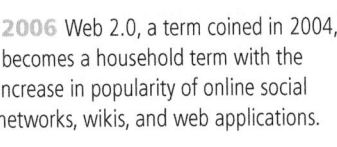

Source: YouTube

2005 YouTube, an online community for video sharing, is founded. YouTube includes content such as home videos, movie previews, and clips from television shows. In November 2006, Google acquires YouTube.

iStockphoto.com/Lpettet

2006 Sony launches its PlayStation 3. New features include a Blu-ray Disc player, high-definition capabilities, and always-on online connectivity.

2006 Apple begins selling Macintosh computers with Intel microprocessors.

2006 Web 2.0, a term coined in 2004, becomes a household term with the increase in popularity of online social networks, wikis, and web applications.

Courtesy of Intel Corporation

iStockphoto.com / robyannucci

Video iPod

Handout/Newscom/Tribune News Service/USA

2005 Apple releases the latest version of its popular pocket-sized iPod portable media player. First it played songs, then photos, then podcasts, and now, in addition, up to 150 hours of music videos and television shows on a 2.5″ color display.

2006 Nintendo releases the Nintendo DS Lite, a handheld game console with new features such as dual screens and improved graphics and sound.

Toru Hanai/Reuters

2005   2006

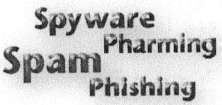

2005 Spam, spyware, phishing, and pharming take center stage, along with viruses and other malware, as major nuisances to the 801 million computer users worldwide.

2005 Blogging and podcasting become mainstream methods for distributing information via the web.

2005 Microsoft releases the Xbox 360, its latest game console. Features include the capability to play music, display photos, and communicate with computers and other Xbox gamers.

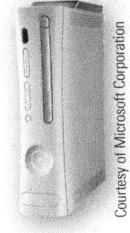

Courtesy of Microsoft Corporation

Courtesy of Intel Corporation

2006 Intel introduces its Core 2 Duo processor family. Boasting record-breaking performance while using less power, the family consists of five desktop computer processors and five mobile computer processors. The desktop processor includes 291 million transistors, yet uses 40 percent less power than the Pentium processor.

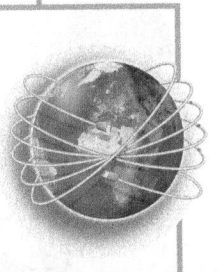

2006 IBM produces the fastest supercomputer, Blue Gene/L. It can perform approximately 28 trillion calculations in the time it takes you to blink your eye, or about one-tenth of a second.

Issei Kato (JAPAN)/Reuters

2006 Nintendo Wii is introduced and immediately becomes a leader in game consoles. The Wii is being used in revolutionary ways, such as training surgeons.

2007 Intel introduces Core 2 Quad, a four-core processor made for dual-processor servers and desktop computers. The larger number of cores allows for more energy-efficient performance and optimizes battery performance in laptops.

Courtesy of Intel Corporation

2007 VoIP (Voice over Internet Protocol) providers expand usage to include Wi-Fi phones. The phones enable high-quality service through a Wireless-G network and high-speed Internet connection.

Courtesy of Belkin International

2007 Apple releases its Mac OS X version 10.5 "Leopard" operating system, available in a desktop version and server version. The system includes a significantly revised desktop, with a semitransparent menu bar and an updated search tool that incorporates the same visual navigation interface as iTunes.

oliver feedham/ Alamy Stock Photo

2007 Apple introduces the iPhone and sells 270,000 phones in the first 2 days. iPhone uses iTouch technology that allows you to make a call simply by tapping a name or number in your address book. In addition, it stores and plays music like an iPod. Also, Apple sells its one billionth song on iTunes.

Neville Elder/Corbis Historical/ Getty Images

2008 Smartphones become smarter. Smartphones introduced this year include enhanced features such as touch screens with multi-touch technology, mobile TV, tactile feedback, improved graphics, GPS receivers, and better cameras.

AP Images/Mark Lennihan

Courtesy of Microsoft Corporation

2008 Bill Gates retires from Microsoft. He continues as chairman and advisor on key development projects.

2008 Google releases its new browser. Google Chrome uses an entirely unique interface and offers other features such as dynamic tabs, crash control, and application shortcuts.

Source: Google

chrome

2007

2008

2007 Half of the world's population uses mobile phones. More and more people are using a mobile phone in lieu of a landline in their home.

iStockphoto.com/Sean Locke

2007 Blu-ray Discs increase in popularity, overcoming and replacing HD DVD in less than one year. A Blu-ray Disc can store approximately 9 hours of high-definition (HD) video on a 50 GB disc or approximately 23 hours of standard-definition (SD) video.

Helene Rogers/Art Directors & Trips Photo/AGE Fotostock

Rfimages /Shutterstock.com

2007 Wi-Fi hot spots are popular in a variety of locations. People bring their computers to coffeehouses, fast food restaurants, or bookstores to access the Internet wirelessly, either free or for a small fee.

2008 Netflix, an online movie rental company, and TiVo, a company manufacturing digital video recorders (DVRs), make Netflix movies and television episodes available on TiVo DVRs.

Source: Netflix

2008 Computer manufacturers begin to offer solid-state drives (SSDs) instead of hard disks, mostly in laptops. Although SSDs have a lower storage capacity, are more expensive, and slightly more susceptible to failure, they are significantly faster.

Norman Chan/Dreamstime .com

iStockphoto.com

2008 WiMAX goes live! The advantage of this technology is the capability to access video, music, voice, and video calls wherever and whenever desired. Average download speeds are between 2 Mbps and 4 Mbps. By year's end, Sprint has approximately 100 million users on its network.

Source: Intel Corporation

2009 Intel releases the Core i5 and Core i7 line of processors. These processors offer increased performance for some of the more demanding tasks. Intel also enhances its Core processor family by releasing multi-core processors, designed to increase the number of instructions that can be processed at a given time.

Courtesy of Intel Corporation

2009 Computers and mobile devices promote fitness by offering games and programs to help users exercise and track their progress. These games and programs also are used to assist with physical rehabilitation.

Stuartkey/ Dreamstime.com

2009 Online social networks revolutionize communications. Schools, radio stations, and other organizations develop pages on popular online social networks, such as Facebook, creating closer connections with their stakeholders.

Google docs
Source: Google

2009 Web apps continue to increase in popularity. Web apps make it easier to perform tasks such as word processing, photo editing, and tax preparation without installing software on your computer.

2009 In June 2009, federal law requires that all full-power television stations broadcast only in digital format. Analog television owners are required to purchase a converter box to view over-the-air digital programming.

Courtesy of Coby Electronics Corporation

2011 Netbooks offer a smaller, lighter alternative to laptops. Netbooks have screens between seven and ten inches and are used mostly for browsing the web and communicating online.

Source: Verizon Wireless

2011 More than 200 types of mobile devices are using Google Android, an operating system originally designed for mobile devices.

iStockphoto.com /Brightrock

2011 A new generation of browsers is released to support HTML5, enabling webpages to contain more vivid, dynamic content.

HTML 5
HTML5 Logo by World Wide Web Consortium

2011 E-books and e-book readers explode in popularity. Many novels, textbooks, and other publications now are available digitally and can be read on an e-book reader, computer, or mobile device.

iStockphoto.com /MichaelJay

iStockphoto.com /EdStock

2011 Steve Jobs, a cofounder of Apple, passes away after a long battle with cancer. Jobs is remembered for revolutionizing the computer and music industries.

2009   2010   2011

Source: Seagate Technology LLC

2010 Hard disk capacity continues to increase at an exponential rate, with the largest hard disks storing more than 2.5 TB of data and information.

2011 Google introduces its Google+ online social network and integrates it across many of its products and services.

Source: Google

Source: AMD

2010 AMD develops a 12-core processor, which contains two 6-core processors, each on an individual chip. Power consumption is similar to that of a 6-core processor but offers reduced clock speed.

2010 Apple releases the iPad, a revolutionary mobile device with a 9.7-inch multi-touch screen. The iPad boasts up to 10 hours of battery life, connects wirelessly to the Internet, and is capable of running thousands of apps.

iStockphoto.com / hanibaram

2010 Kinect for Xbox 360 changes the way people play video games. Game players now can interact with the game with a series of sensors, as well as a camera, tracking their movements in 3-D.

Courtesy of Microsoft Corporation

Source: Lenovo

2011 Intel introduces Ultrabooks, which are powerful, lightweight alternatives to laptops. Ultrabooks normally weigh three pounds or less, have great performance and battery life, and are usually less than one inch thick.

2012 Microsoft announces the Surface, a tablet designed to compete with Apple's iPad. The Surface has a built-in stand, runs the Windows 8 operating system and its apps, and supports a cover that also can serve as a keyboard.

2012 Microsoft releases Windows 8, its newest version of the Windows operating system. Windows 8 boasts a completely redesigned interface and supports touch input.

2012 Apple releases the iPhone 5. This newest iPhone has a four-inch screen, contains a new, smaller connector, and uses Apple's A6 processor.

Source: Apple

2013 Twitter users generate more than 500 million Tweets per day.

2013 Amazon announces it will use drones to deliver packages to its customers.

Courtesy of Amazon

2013 Sony releases the PlayStation 4 (PS4) game console and Microsoft releases the Xbox One game console.

2013 Tablet sales grow at a faster rate than personal computer sales ever grew.

iStockphoto.com/franckreporter

2012

2013

2012 Google's Android surpasses Apple's iOS as the most popular operating system used on smartphones. Although the iPhone still is the bestselling smartphone, competing products are gaining market share quickly.

Source: Google

2012 Microsoft releases Office 2013. Office 365, which uses the familiar Office 2013 interface, also is released, allowing users to use their Microsoft accounts to access Office apps from computers that do not have Office installed.

Source: Windows

2012 Nintendo releases the Wii U game console.

2013 Samsung releases the Galaxy Gear, a smartwatch that synchronizes with a Samsung Galaxy smartphone using Bluetooth technology.

Ivan Garcia/Shutterstock.com

2013 Windows 8.1, a significant update to Microsoft's Windows 8 operating system, is released.

Source: Windows

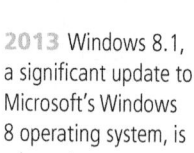
iStockphoto.com/Mlenny

2013 Apple releases the iPhone 5S, the first iPhone with TouchID. TouchID verifies a user's identity using an integrated fingerprint reader.

2013 QR codes rapidly gain in popularity, giving mobile device users an easy way to access web content.

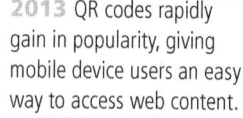

Source: qr-code-generator.com

2013 Many consumers prefer tablets for their mobile computing needs. Tablets provide ultimate portability while still allowing users to access a vast array of apps, as well as access to the Internet and their email messages.

iStockphoto.com/mozcann

Green Computing

2014 Individuals and enterprises increase their focus on green computing. Computer manufacturers not only sell more energy-efficient hardware, they also provide easy ways in which customers can recycle their old computers and devices.

2014 Solid-state storage is becoming more popular, with storage capacities increasing and prices decreasing.

Scanrail1/
Shutterstock.com

2014 Apple releases the Apple Watch, a wearable device that runs apps and can monitor various aspects of your health and fitness.

Courtesy of Apple, Inc.

2014 Decreases in storage costs and increases in Internet connection speeds persuade more users to use cloud storage for their data. Cloud storage also provides users with the convenience of accessing their files from almost anywhere.

2015 3-D printing decreases in price and increases in popularity.

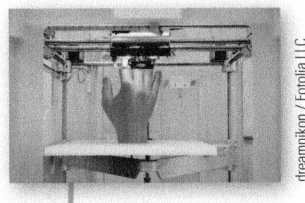

dreamnikon / Fotolia LLC

iStockphoto.com / xefstock

2015 Microsoft releases Windows 10, the latest version of its operating system. Windows 10 expands on many of the new features introduced in Windows 8, and also brings back popular features, such as the Start menu, from previous versions of Windows.

2015 Individuals and families are increasingly turning to streaming video on the Internet and abandoning their cable companies.

2014   2015

2014 Bitcoin continues to grow as a digital currency and online payment system.

Courtesy of Mark Frydenberg

2014 Apple releases the iPhone 6 and iPhone 6 Plus. Both devices have significantly larger screens than its predecessors.

Courtesy of Apple, Inc.

2014 Televisions with features such as curved screens and Ultra HD displays begin to increase in popularity.

iStockphoto.com / JazzIRT

iStockphoto.com / ferrantraite

2014 Google Glass goes on sale to the public in the United States.

2014 Amazon drops the price of its Fire Phone to $0.99, possibly indicating that apps and services are valued more than the device.

iStockphoto.com / Ilya_Starikov

2015 Emerging protocols, such as LTE-A and Wi-Fi 802.11 ac, ad, aq, and ah, increase performance on mobile and wireless networks.

2015 Approximately 91% of all Internet traffic is video, including HD and 3-D video.

2015 Microsoft releases Office 2016, which includes new productivity software and application updates.

2016 Microsoft releases the Windows 10 Anniversary Update, which is the second significant update to Windows 10 since its release in July 2015. This update includes new features, such as Sticky Notes, dark-mode themed apps, an emoji keyboard, and an updated Start menu.

iStockphoto.com / ymgerman

2016 Virtual Reality (VR) headsets are exploding in popularity, and many game consoles and smartphones are taking advantage by supporting this technology. Popular VR headsets include Google Cardboard, Oculus Rift, Samsung Gear VR, and HTC Vive.

iStockphoto.com / Christopher Ames

2016 Apple releases its newest iPhone, the iPhone 7. One of the most significant updates to this model is the removal of the traditional headphone jack. Those who wish to use headphones with this iPhone either must use an adapter, purchase wireless headphones, or purchase headphones that can connect to the iPhone's Lightning port.

iStockphoto.com / Leszek Kobusinski

2016 Several companies, such as Tesla and Google, are making advances with self-driving cars. These cars not only will be designed to improve safety as they navigate streets and highways, but also to provide flexible transportation for those who otherwise would lack transportation. Tesla announces that all Tesla vehicles produced in their factory will include the necessary hardware for self-driving capability.

iStockphoto.com / Jason Doiy

2017 Devices supporting Internet connectivity continue to appear on the market. Some researchers estimate that the number of Internet of Things (IoT) connected devices will surpass 38 billion by the end of the decade.

iStockphoto.com / mathisworks

2017 Nintendo releases the Switch, its newest game console. The Nintendo Switch can connect to a dock that is connected to a television, or it can be removed from the dock and used in portable mode. Multiple players also can gather with their devices for multiplayer games.

Barone Firenze / Shutterstock.com

2017 Intelligent personal assistants, which can help individuals find information or complete tasks, are becoming more prominent and are including more features. Popular intelligent personal assistants include Siri, Samsung S Voice, Microsoft Cortana, Amazon Alexa, and Google Assistant.

George W. Bailey / Shutterstock.com

iStockphoto.com / baranozdemir

2017 Payments apps explode in popularity and widely are used by many people to transfer money electronically. In addition, email services, such as Gmail, and online social networks, such as Facebook, provide the capability for users to send money via electronic messages.

2016

2017

iStockphoto.com / agnormark

2016 The popularity of drones quickly increases, causing concern for the Federal Aviation Administration (FAA). The FAA introduced regulations limiting who can operate drones, as well as where and when they can be operated. Some experts predict that the number of drones will increase tenfold by the end of the decade.

iStockphoto.com / Maxiphoto

2016 An increasing number of manufacturers, including Apple, Dell, HP, and Samsung, are using the USB-C connector for connectivity and power. This new connector is reversible, which allows it to connect regardless of the connector being right-side up or upside down. USB-C ports support a multitude of peripherals; they also can be used for charging a device.

iStockphoto.com / belekekin

2016 Scientists and medical professionals continue the biological and biomedical use of 3D printing to help patients in need. 3-D printing is becoming more widely used to create body parts, such as hands, arms, and legs, as well as tissue and cells. 3-D printers also can be used to print surgical tools, which cost only a fraction of their stainless steel equivalents.

2016 Google introduces two new smartphones, the Pixel and Pixel XL. These phones contain features such as Google Assistant, a fingerprint sensor on the back of the phone, high-quality front and rear cameras, unlimited cloud storage for photos and videos, and support for virtual reality.

Paul Stringer / Shutterstock.com

iStockphoto.com / 3alexd

2017 The number of worldwide Internet users exceeds 3.3 billion.

iStockphoto.com / kasto80

2017 Worldwide sales of electric vehicles inch toward five million. Electric vehicles, which are connected to a power source to charge onboard batteries, provide their owners with significant fuel savings and are much less damaging to the environment. An increasing number of municipalities and businesses are providing charging stations for electric vehicles. These stations can be used for free or for a fee.

iStockphoto.com / audioundwerbung

2017 Home automation becomes less expensive and more popular. An increasing number of individuals are installing hardware in their homes that enable them to control devices such as lights, garage doors, irrigation systems, coffeemakers, alarm systems, surveillance cameras, and air conditioners.

2017 Smartphone manufacturers continue to research the feasibility of using foldable screens on their devices. One main benefit of foldable screens is that devices with larger displays can be folded to fit in a smaller space, such as a wallet, purse, or pocket.

Computing Components:
Processors, Memory, the Cloud, and More

6

iStockphoto.com / nmlfd

OBJECTIVES

After completing this module, you will be able to:

1 Describe the various computer and mobile device cases and the contents they protect

2 Describe multi-core processors, the components of a processor, and the four steps in a machine cycle

3 Identify characteristics of various personal computer processors on the market today, and describe the ways processors are cooled

4 Describe what is meant by the Internet of Things

5 Explain the advantages and services of cloud computing

6 Define a bit, and describe how a series of bits represents data

7 Explain how program and application instructions transfer in and out of memory

8 Differentiate among the various types of memory: RAM, cache, ROM, flash memory, and CMOS

9 Describe the purpose of adapter cards and USB adapters

10 Explain the function of a bus

11 Explain the purpose of a power supply and batteries

12 Describe how to care for computers and mobile devices

Inside the Case

Whether you are a home user or a business user, you most likely will purchase a new computer or mobile device, or upgrade an existing computer at some time in the future. Thus, you should understand the purpose of each component in a computer or mobile device. As Module 1 discussed, computers and mobile devices include components that are used for input, processing, output, storage, and communications. Many of these components are inside the case that contains and protects the electronics of the computer or mobile device from damage. These cases, which are made of metal or plastic, are available in a variety of shapes and sizes (Figure 6-1).

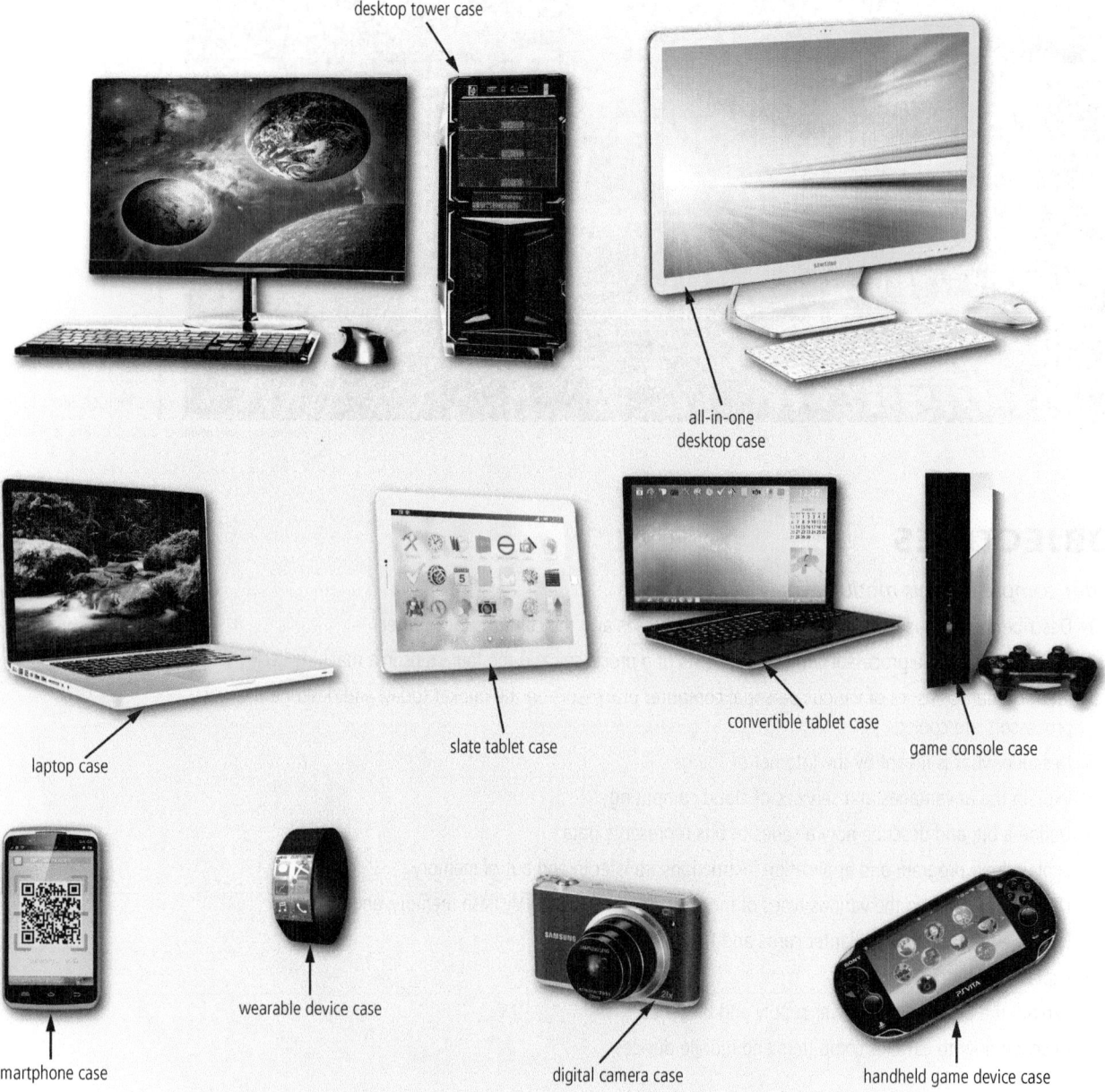

Figure 6-1   Cases for computers and mobile devices are available in a variety of shapes and sizes.

- Recall that the term, *system unit* (or *chassis*), refers to the case on a desktop that contains and protects the motherboard, hard drive, memory, and other electronic components. Some desktops have a tower system unit that is a device separate from the monitor. Others that house the display and the system unit in the same case are called an all-in-one. Peripheral devices normally occupy space outside the system unit and communicate with the system unit using wired or wireless technology.
- On most laptops, including ultrathin laptops, the keyboard and pointing device often occupy the area on top of the case, and the display attaches to the case by hinges.
- With a slate tablet, which typically does not include a physical keyboard, the case is behind the display. Keyboard options for slate tablets include an on-screen keyboard, a wireless keyboard, or a keyboard that attaches to the slate via a clip, magnets, or other mechanism. On a convertible tablet, by contrast, the case is positioned below a keyboard, providing functionality similar to a laptop. The difference is that the display attaches to the case with a swivel-type hinge, enabling the user to rotate the display and fold it down over the keyboard to look like a slate tablet.
- With game consoles, the input and output devices, such as controllers and a television, reside outside the case.
- Like a slate tablet, the case on a smartphone often is behind the display.
- The case on wearable devices, portable media players, digital cameras, and handheld game devices typically consumes the entire device and houses the display and input devices.

At some point, you might have to open the case on a desktop or access panels on a laptop to replace or install a new electronic component, or hire a professional to assist with this task. For this reason, you should be familiar with the electronic components inside the case, some of which are shown in Figure 6-2 and discussed in this module. Read Secure IT 6-1 for tips related to protecting your computers and mobile devices from theft.

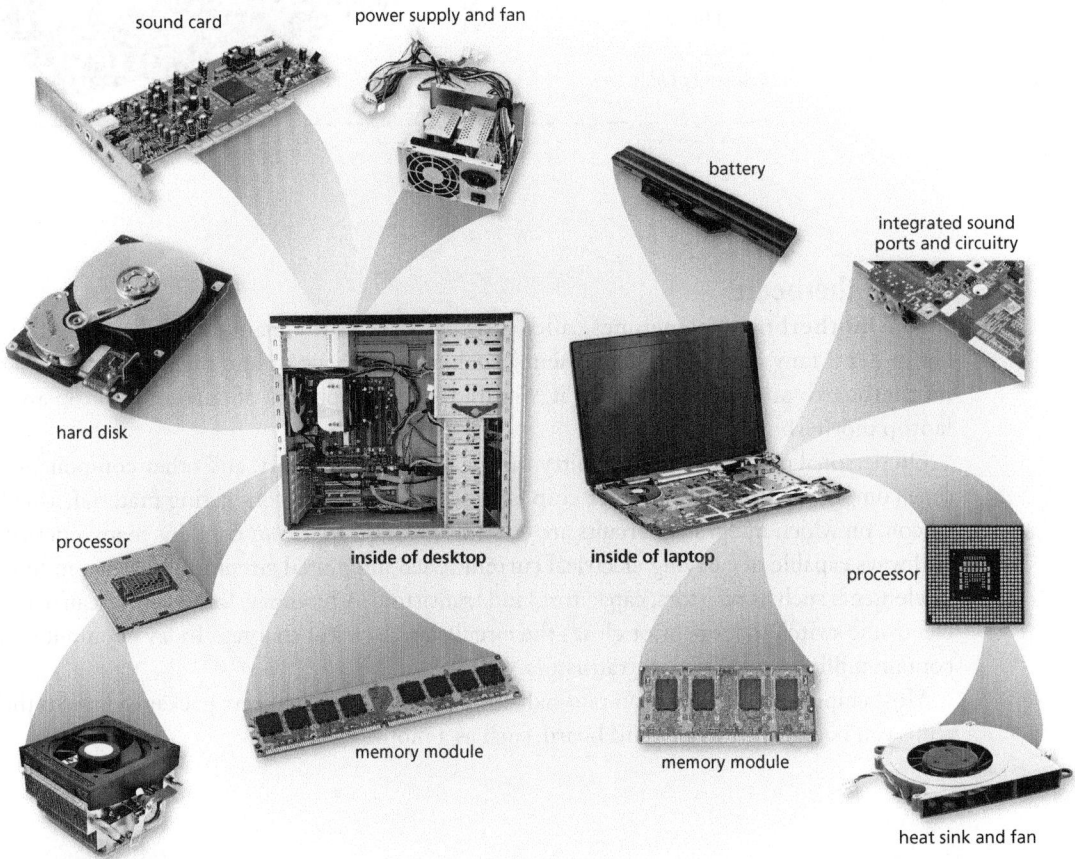

Figure 6-2   This figure shows typical components in a higher-end desktop and laptop. Many basic desktops have integrated video and sound capability, similar to the laptop image shown here.

⚙ SECURE IT 6-1

Securing Computers and Mobile Devices

Millions of smartphones, mobile devices, and computers are stolen in the United States every year, but only a small percent of these devices are recovered. Many devices can help deter potential thieves and also help trace and recover stolen goods. The following products may be useful in securing and tracking hardware.

- **Clamps, cables, and locks:** Lock kits include mounting plates, glue, cables, and padlocks to protect desktops, monitors, laptops, and peripheral devices.

- **Intrusion detection:** Thieves do not need to remove a computer from an office building or school to commit their crimes; instead, they can open the case on a desktop or server on site and then remove a hard drive or other expensive component. To prevent such tampering, hardware manufacturers have developed an alarm system to install in the case. If the computer is moved or the case is opened, an ear-piercing alarm sounds and a security company is alerted.

- **Tracking software:** Many smartphones and mobile devices have software that shows the approximate location of devices and computers. The owner can issue commands remotely to have the device play a sound, lock the screen, display a message, or erase all personal information.

- **Asset tags:** Metal security plates affixed to hardware contain unique bar codes that are registered to the owner and are stored in a security company's database. If a lost or stolen device is recovered, the finder can call the phone number on the tag, and the company will notify the owner.

- **Personal safes:** Protective cases that are approximately the size of a cereal box can store a smartphone, keys, tablet, and other valuables. The attached security cable can

be secured to a stationary object, such as a chair or table. Some personal safes have built-in electronic locks; others can be secured with a combination lock. The safe can be useful in a hotel room, at the gym, or on campus.

⚙ **Consider This:** Have you seen any of these security devices at school or at businesses? If so, where? Do you know someone whose computer or mobile device was lost or stolen? If so, was the hardware recovered? What other measures can organizations take to prevent security breaches?

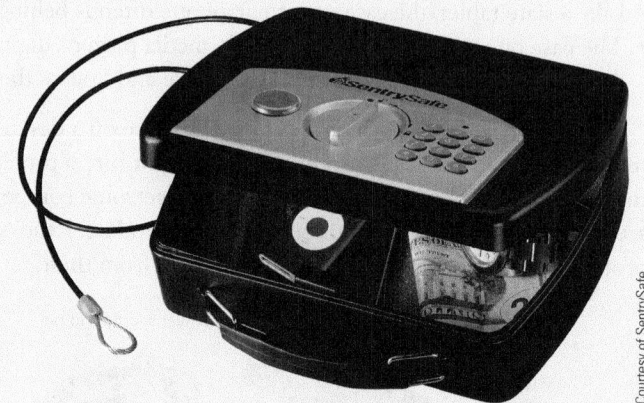

Courtesy of SentrySafe

The Motherboard

The **motherboard**, sometimes called a *system board*, is the main circuit board of the computer. Many electronic components, such as the processor and memory, attach to the motherboard; others are built into it. Figure 6-3 shows photos of current desktop and laptop motherboards.

On personal computers, the circuitry for the processor, memory, and other components reside on a computer chip(s). A computer **chip** is a small piece of semiconducting material, usually silicon, on which integrated circuits are etched. An *integrated circuit* contains many microscopic pathways capable of carrying electrical current. Each integrated circuit can contain millions of elements such as resistors, capacitors, and transistors. A *transistor*, for example, can act as an electronic switch that opens or closes the circuit for electrical charges. Today's computer chips contain millions or billions of transistors.

Most chips are no bigger than one-half-inch square. Manufacturers package chips so that the chips can be attached to a circuit board, such as a motherboard.

Figure 6-3   A desktop motherboard and a laptop motherboard.
Courtesy of GIGABYTE Technologies; iStockphoto.com / RAW group

Processors

The **processor**, also called the **central processing unit (CPU)**, interprets and carries out the basic instructions that operate a computer. The processor significantly impacts overall computing power and manages most of a computer's operations. On larger computers, such as mainframes and supercomputers, the various functions performed by the processor extend over many separate chips and often multiple circuit boards. On a personal computer, all functions of the processor usually are on a single chip. Some computer and chip manufacturers use the term, *microprocessor*, to refer to a personal computer processor chip.

Most processor chip manufacturers now offer multi-core processors. A processor core, or simply core, contains the circuitry necessary to execute instructions. The operating system views each processor core as a separate processor. A **multi-core processor** is a single chip with two or more separate processor cores. Multi-core processors are used in all sizes of computers. Read Secure IT 6-2 to learn how chips can help to identify and secure animals.

 BTW

Single-Board Computers
A single-board computer has all components on one, small circuit board. These components might include the processor and memory. Single-board computers often are much less expensive than desktops and laptops.

 CONSIDER THIS ⎯⎯⎯⎯⎯⎯⎯⎯⎯⎯⎯⎯⎯⎯⎯⎯⎯⎯⎯⎯⎯⎯

Are multi-core processors better than single-core processors?
Each processor core on a multi-core processor generally runs at a slower speed than a single-core processor, but multi-core processors typically increase overall performance. For example, although a dual-core processor does not double the processing speed of a single-core processor, it can approach those speeds. The performance increase is especially noticeable when users are running multiple programs simultaneously, such as antivirus software, word processing software, email program, browser, media player, and photo editing software. Multi-core processors also are more energy efficient than separate multiple processors, requiring lower levels of power consumption and emitting less heat inside the case.

SECURE IT 6-2

Chip Implants Secure Animals' Identity

The search for lost dogs or cats can be traumatic for their owners. The animals' safe return home may be based on data stored on a chip that veterinarians have implanted under the skin, usually at the neck or shoulder blades.

The chip — sometimes called a microchip because it is so small (about the size of a grain of rice) — has a unique number that is registered to the owner's name and address. It contains an antenna and transponder encased in a glass tube. The antenna receives low-frequency radio waves when a scanning device passes over the chip, and the transponder sends a signal with the chip's number back to the scanner.

Shelters and animal control centers routinely scan runaway pets for chips in an attempt to reunite animals with their owners. Most shelters require pets to have the implant before the animals are adopted or before a once-lost pet is returned to its owner. Some veterinarians also scan new pets for chips to ensure the animal does not belong to someone else.

Some pet owners are concerned that microchipping can cause health problems, particularly if the chip moves from its original injection site. Most humane societies and veterinarians, however, state that no long-term adverse health effects or discomfort occurs.

Microchips also are implanted or attached externally in other animals, including horses, elephants, cows, birds, fish, lizards, and snakes. Breeders, farmers, and animal associations implant the chips to deter thieves. Chips also can monitor an animal's temperature, so that a farmer can prevent the spread of disease by identifying and removing an ill animal from a herd.

Researchers, including those at the U.S. Fish and Wildlife Service, also use this technology to track migration of wild animals, reptiles, and fish. They study how these species interact with their environment, and conservation authorities can identify endangered species, such as sea turtles, that have been confiscated from smugglers.

⚙ **Consider This:** Do you have or know anyone who has a pet that has been implanted with a chip? If so, why do you think they did it? Besides possible health problems, why might some people oppose mandatory animal chipping? Do you think people someday might choose to have a chip implanted to eliminate the need to carry identification? Why or why not?

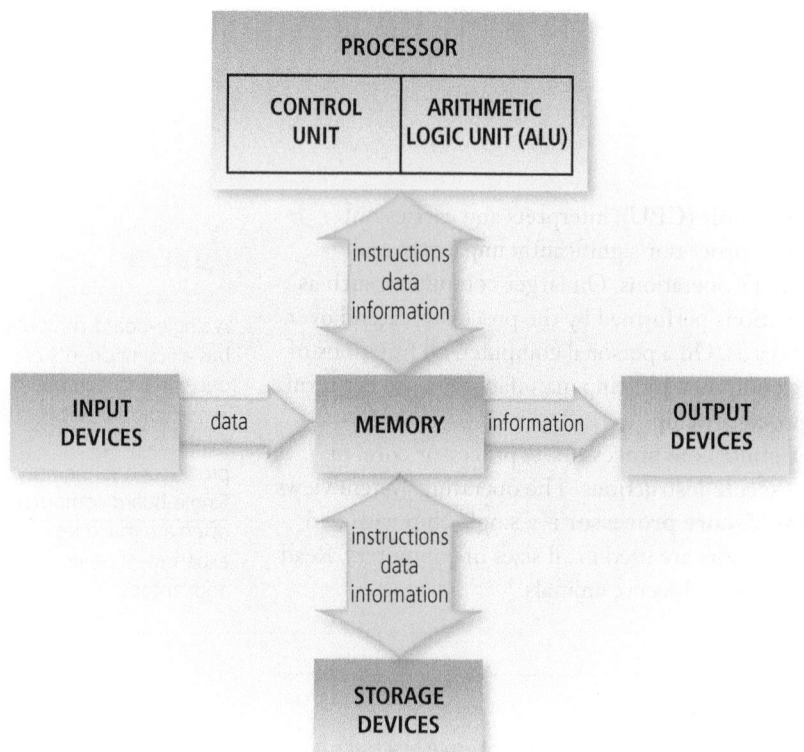

Figure 6-4   Most devices connected to the computer communicate with the processor to carry out a task.

Processors contain a control unit and an arithmetic logic unit (ALU). These two components work together to perform processing operations. Figure 6-4 illustrates how other devices connected to the computer communicate with the processor to carry out a task. When a user runs an application, for example, its instructions transfer from a storage device to memory. Data needed by programs and applications enters memory from either an input device or a storage device. The control unit interprets and executes instructions in memory, and the arithmetic logic unit performs calculations on the data in memory. Resulting information is stored in memory, from which it can be sent to an output device or a storage device for future access, as needed.

The Control Unit

The **control unit** is the component of the processor that directs and coordinates most of the operations in the computer. That is, it interprets each instruction issued by a program or an application and then initiates the appropriate action to carry out the instruction. Types of internal components that the control unit directs include the arithmetic logic unit, registers, and buses, each discussed in this module.

The Arithmetic Logic Unit

The **arithmetic logic unit** (*ALU*), another component of the processor, performs arithmetic, comparison, and other operations.

Arithmetic operations include basic calculations, such as addition, subtraction, multiplication, and division. *Comparison operations* involve comparing one data item with another to determine whether the first item is greater than, equal to, or less than the other item. Depending on the result of the comparison, different actions may occur. For example, to determine if an employee should receive overtime pay, software instructs the ALU to compare the number of hours an employee worked during the week with the regular time hours allowed (e.g., 40 hours). If the hours worked exceed 40, for example, software instructs the ALU to perform calculations that compute the overtime wage.

Machine Cycle

For every instruction, a processor repeats a set of four basic operations, which comprise a *machine cycle:* (1) fetching, (2) decoding, (3) executing, and, if necessary, (4) storing.

- *Fetching* is the process of obtaining a program or an application instruction or data item from memory.
- *Decoding* refers to the process of translating the instruction into signals the computer can execute.
- *Executing* is the process of carrying out the commands.
- *Storing*, in this context, means writing the result to memory (not to a storage medium).

Figure 6-5 illustrates the steps in a machine cycle. In some computers, the processor fetches, decodes, executes, and stores only one instruction at a time. With others, the processor fetches a second instruction before the first instruction completes its machine cycle, resulting in faster processing. Some use multiple processors simultaneously to increase processing times.

The Steps in a Machine Cycle

Using a calculator app, a student enters a calculation. The app sends the calculation to the computer's memory for processing.

Step 1
The control unit fetches the calculation's instructions and data from memory.

Step 2
The control unit decodes the calculation's instructions and sends the instructions and data to the ALU.

Step 3
The ALU performs calculations on the data.

Step 4
The results of the calculation are stored in memory.

The results in memory appear on the screen of the monitor.

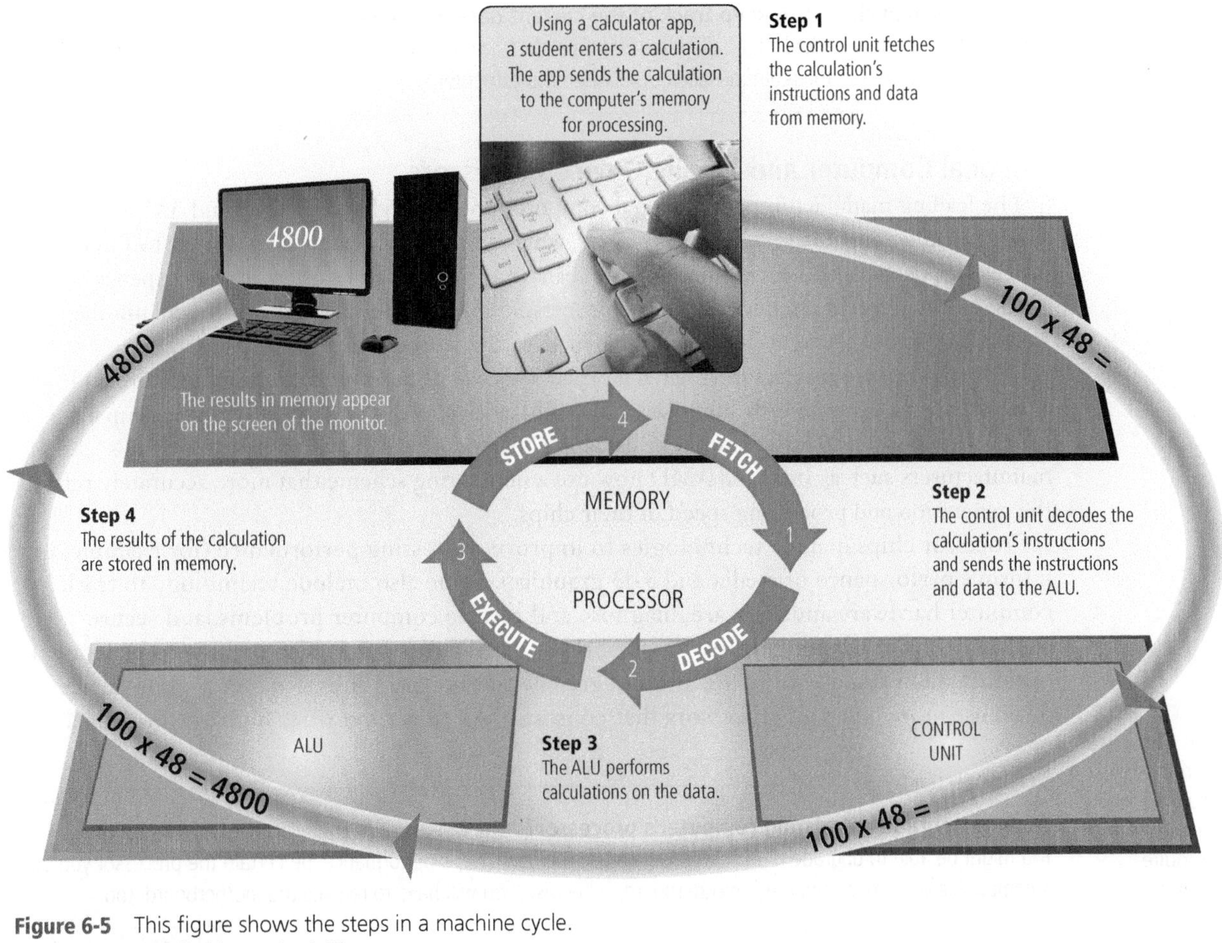

Figure 6-5   This figure shows the steps in a machine cycle.

Registers

A processor contains small, high-speed storage locations, called *registers*, that temporarily hold data and instructions. Registers are part of the processor, not part of memory or a permanent storage device. Processors have many different types of registers, each with a specific storage function. Register functions include storing the location from where an instruction was fetched, storing an instruction while the control unit decodes it, storing data while the ALU calculates it, and storing the results of a calculation.

The System Clock

The processor relies on a small quartz crystal circuit called the **system clock** to control the timing of all computer operations. Just as your heart beats at a regular rate to keep your body functioning, the system clock generates regular electronic pulses, or ticks, that set the operating pace of components of the system unit.

Each tick equates to a *clock cycle*. Processors today typically are *superscalar*, which means they can execute more than one instruction per clock cycle.

The pace of the system clock, called the **clock speed**, is measured by the number of ticks per second. Current personal computer processors have clock speeds in the gigahertz range. Giga is a prefix that stands for billion, and a *hertz* is one cycle per second. Thus, one **gigahertz (GHz)** equals one billion ticks of the system clock per second. A computer that operates at 3 GHz has 3 billion (giga) clock cycles in one second (hertz).

The faster the clock speed, the more instructions the processor can execute per second. The speed of the system clock is just one factor that influences a computer's performance. Other factors, such as the type of processor chip, amount of cache, memory access time, bus width, and bus clock speed, are discussed later in this module.

 CONSIDER THIS

Does the system clock also keep track of the current date and time?
No, a separate battery-backed chip, called the *real-time clock*, keeps track of the date and time in a computer. The battery continues to run the real-time clock even when the computer is off.

Personal Computer and Mobile Device Processors

The leading manufacturers of personal computer processor chips are Intel and AMD. AMD manufactures *Intel-compatible processors*, which have an internal design similar to Intel processors, perform the same functions, and can be as powerful, but often are less expensive. These manufacturers often identify their processor chips by a model name or model number. Read How To 6-1 for items to consider when selecting a processor for a computer.

In the past, chip manufacturers listed a processor's clock speed in marketing literature and advertisements. As previously mentioned, though, clock speed is only one factor that impacts processing speed in today's computers. To help consumers evaluate various processors, manufacturers such as Intel and AMD now use a numbering scheme that more accurately reflects the generation and processing speed of their chips.

Processor chips include technologies to improve processing performance (for example, to improve performance of media and 3-D graphics). Some also include technology to track computer hardware and software, diagnose and resolve computer problems, and secure computers from outside threats. Processors for mobile computers also include technology to optimize and extend battery life and integrate wireless capabilities. Smaller mobile devices often use more compact processors that consume less power, yet offer high performance.

 CONSIDER THIS

Can you upgrade an existing computer's processor?
You might be able to upgrade a processor to increase the computer's performance. Be certain the processor you buy is compatible with your computer's motherboard; otherwise, you will have to replace the motherboard, too.

 **BTW**

System Clock and Peripheral Devices
The speed of the system clock has no effect on peripheral devices, such as a printer or hard drive.

BTW

Mobile Device Cooling
Mobile devices often use low-voltage processors, which have such low power demands that they do not require additional cooling.

HOW TO 6-1

Select the Right Processor

When you are shopping for a new computer, it is important to select one with a processor that will meet your needs. For example, some processors are designed for home users, some are designed for power users, and others are designed for mobile users. Performing basic research before you shop for a new computer can help you select the most appropriate processor. The following steps describe how to select the right processor.

1. **Determine your needs.** Think about how you will use your computer and the programs and applications you plan to run. If you will be using your computer for basic tasks, such as web browsing or checking email, you may require a less expensive processor than a user who will be running many programs and applications simultaneously.

2. **Determine your current processor.** If you are replacing your existing computer with a new computer, determine the processor in your existing computer so that you can make sure the new processor is better and faster than the one in use currently.

3. **Research processor models.** While shopping for computers in your price range, pay attention to the types of processors they include. Visit the processor manufacturer's website and verify that the processor will meet your computing needs adequately. Reviewing the minimum system requirements on the programs and apps you wish to run may help you determine the processor you need. Choose a processor that exceeds the minimum system requirements of the programs and apps you wish to run, but remember that it is not always

necessary to purchase the most expensive computer with the fastest processor.

Consider This: What type of processor is in your current computer? If you were to upgrade your processor, which one would you choose? Why?

Courtesy of Intel

Processor Cooling

Processor chips for laptops, desktops, and servers can generate quite a bit of heat, which could cause the chip to malfunction or fail. Although the power supply on some computers contains a main fan to generate airflow, today's personal computer processors often require additional cooling. Some computer cases locate additional fans near certain components, such as a processor, to provide additional cooling. Heat sinks, liquid cooling technologies, and cooling mats often are used to help further dissipate processor heat.

A *heat sink* is a small ceramic or metal component with fins on its surface that absorbs and disperses heat produced by electrical components, such as a processor. Many heat sinks have fans to help distribute air dissipated by the heat sink. Some heat sinks are packaged as part of a processor chip. Others are installed on the top or the side of the chip (Figure 6-6).

Some computers use liquid cooling technology to reduce the temperature of a processor. *Liquid cooling technology* uses a continuous flow of fluid(s), such as water and glycol, in a process that transfers the heated fluid away from the processor to a radiator-type grill, which cools the liquid, and then returns the cooled fluid to the processor.

Laptop users sometimes use a cooling pad to help further reduce the heat generated by their computer. A *cooling pad* rests below a laptop and protects the computer from overheating and also the user's lap from excessive heat (Figure 6-7). Some cooling pads contain a small fan to transfer heat away from the laptop. These types of cooling pads often draw power from a USB port. Instead of using power, other pads absorb heat through a conductive material inside the pad.

Figure 6-6   This photo shows a heat sink being attached to the top of a processor to prevent the chip from overheating.
Claudio Bravo / Shutterstock.com

Figure 6-7   A laptop cooling pad helps reduce heat generated by a laptop.
Courtesy of Targus Group International, Inc; Courtesy of Targus Group International, Inc.

Tech Feature 6-1: The Internet of Things

The *Internet of Things (IoT)* describes a computing environment where everyday objects, or things, are connected to the Internet.

Sensors connected to these objects may gather, share, transmit, and receive data about the objects with other devices or servers online. Users can access the data or control individual objects using web or mobile apps. Read Tech Feature 6-1 to learn about types of devices used as things and technologies used to enable the IoT. Read Ethics & Issues 6-1 to consider whether the IoT discriminates, and read Secure IT 6-3 for privacy issues related to the IoT.

 TECH FEATURE 6-1

The Internet of Things

Analysts predict that the IoT will be a multitrillion-dollar business as the number of "smart" devices and things connected to the Internet continues to increase. As watches, thermostats, fitness trackers, appliances, irrigation systems, clothing, and other "things" become equipped with sensors that can transmit data to and from the Internet, keeping every "thing" connected could become one of the world's largest industries.

From Devices to Things

Computers and mobile devices are not the only things that connect to the Internet. You can buy a thermostat, such as the one from Nest Labs shown in the figure, that allows you to adjust the temperature of your home from anywhere using an app on your smartphone. The thermostat contains a temperature sensor that can send and receive data. A wireless chip attached to your medicine bottle can send text messages to remind you to take your medication and then contact your pharmacy to refill the prescription when it is due for a refill. Smart trash cans in public places have sensors that monitor the amount of trash deposited and then send a message notifying owners when the containers need to be emptied. This saves garbage collectors from checking the containers every day; instead, they can empty the containers only when receiving a message that they are full.

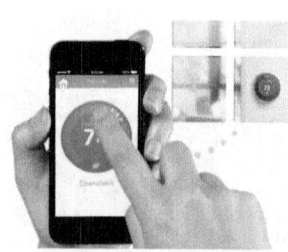
Source: Nest Labs

Wearable technology, such as smartwatches and wristbands, can track your pulse and heart rate, as well as accept calls and display notifications from a smartphone. Many public buses and subways have GPS sensors that report their locations so that travelers can track them with mobile apps. Retailers can use beacons, which are devices that send low-energy Bluetooth signals to nearby smartphones, to notify customers who use a payment app such as Paypal, of personalized offers in their stores. Washers and dryers in many college dormitory laundry rooms are connected to sensors that report the availability of an individual machine. Students can visit a website, use a mobile app, or request text message alerts to locate available machines before carrying their laundry to the laundry room.

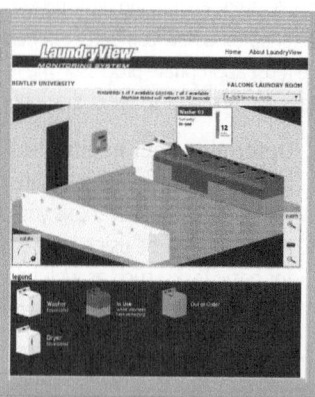
Source: Mac-Gray Corporation

Technologies Enable the IoT

The IoT brings together several recent technology developments. Communications technologies, such as Bluetooth, RFID tags, near-field communications (NFC) tags, and sensors tracking heat (temperature), light, weight, or location have become readily available. Sensors and tags can transmit messages to a server on the Internet over a wireless network at frequent intervals for analysis and storage. Developments in Big Data have made it possible to access, store, and process all of this data reported by sensors efficiently. (To learn more about Big Data, read Tech Feature 11-2 in Module 11.) Mobile service providers offer connectivity to a variety of devices at broadband speeds, so transmitting and retrieving data can take place quickly. The size and cost of wireless radios has decreased, enabling more things to have embedded sensors, tags, and transmitters.

The capability of computers, devices, and everyday objects to communicate with one another over the Internet has opened new possibilities for both consumers and the enterprise to be more productive, efficient, and informed.

 **Consider This:** Research one of the smart products described in the "From Devices to Things" section of this tech feature. Who manufactures or uses it? How does it work? What are the benefits of such a smart product? What object or thing do you wish was connected to the Internet? What data would you like it to send or capture? How might an app help you to control this object or access information about it? How would this improve your life?

ETHICS & ISSUES 6-1

Does the Internet of Things Discriminate?

Technology experts expect that the advantages brought by the expansion of the IoT will enhance the comfort, safety, and efficiency of a large population across the globe. Where does that leave people who are struggling to make ends meet? What about those who live in developing countries?

Among the IoT technologies that exist or are in development include the following examples. Students can find accurate information quickly and use cloud-based apps to store data so that it is accessible. The coordination of traffic lights based on GPS data will lead to a lessening of commute times. Wearable and implanted devices can collect and communicate health-related data. Sensors that monitor temperature, air and water quality and usage, and more will reduce home ownership costs and security risks. Agricultural devices can monitor, track, and provide assessment of livestock and crops to lower costs and improve access to food.

Individuals or countries that cannot afford these and other IoT-related technologies may feel a negative impact as others take advantage of the effects brought by these technologies. Students without access to these technologies could be at a disadvantage. Workers with shorter travel times may enjoy a better quality of life. Those who cannot afford health-related devices may be at higher risk for illnesses or medical complications. Home-owners without IoT-enabled homes may be more prone to dangers, such as fires. Countries involved in agricultural exporting may lose business as others are able to reduce costs.

As costs of these technologies decrease, it is likely that the divide between the more and less fortunate will decrease. Awareness of the impact of the inequalities also may give rise to nonprofits or organizations that focus on providing IoT technologies to a larger population.

Consider This: In what other ways will IoT affect individuals and countries who cannot afford these technologies? What responsibility exists to make IoT technologies available to all?

SECURE IT 6-3

Does the Internet of Things Encroach on Privacy?

Being digitally observed in the connected world is inescapable. Every day, smart electric meters, wearable technology, and vehicles' black boxes submit data about us as part of the IoT. Researchers predict billions of devices will be part of the IoT by the end of this decade. With all these devices in nearly every facet of our daily lives, data is being accumulated and sold to health care providers, home security businesses, utility companies, and researchers.

Savvy consumers can take some steps to attempt to limit exposure to data collection. They can enable privacy settings, for example, but that does not guarantee that data is not being gathered, transmitted, and compiled. The report of Smart TVs secretly collecting data about audiences' viewing habits sparked privacy and security concerns. Consumers need to urge companies to design products with built-in privacy protections. These devices could have default settings that prevent the sharing of data until obtaining the consumer's consent. Companies should explain what data is being collected and whether it will be used to help people live more productive lives or to create personal profiles that predict behavior. In addition, companies bear the responsibility of ensuring sensitive data being collected is kept secure and confidential.

Privacy and security concerns abound with the IoT, but most consumers and technology experts believe that the security, health, and productivity benefits of this technology outweigh the potential risks.

Consider This: Should companies inform consumers about the data being collected in homes, vehicles, schools, and workplaces? What role should governmental agencies, such as the Federal Trade Commission, play in overseeing companies' secure products and commercial data collection techniques?

Cloud Computing

Recall that cloud computing refers to an environment of servers that house and provide access to resources users access via the Internet. Home and business users choose cloud computing for a variety of reasons:

- **Accessibility:** Data and/or applications are available worldwide from any computer or device with an Internet connection.
- **Cost savings:** The expense of software and high-end hardware, such as fast processors and high-capacity memory and storage devices, shifts away from the user.
- **Space savings:** Floor space required for servers, storages devices, and other hardware shifts away from the user.
- **Scalability:** Provides the flexibility to increase or decrease computing requirements as needed.

Cloud computing consists of a front end and a back end, connected to each other through a network. The front end includes the hardware and software with which a user interacts to access the cloud. For example, a user might access a resource on the cloud through a browser on a laptop. The back end consists of the servers and storage devices that manage and store the resources accessed by users.

Tech Feature 6-2: Cloud Computing Services

Cloud computing allows companies to outsource, or contract to third-party providers, elements of their information technology infrastructure. They pay only for the computing power, storage, bandwidth, and access to applications that they actually use. As a result, companies need not make large investments in equipment or the staff to support it. Read Tech Feature 6-2 to learn about available types of cloud computing services.

 TECH FEATURE 6-2

Cloud Computing Services

Consumers and organizations rely on cloud computing services to manage IT infrastructure (infrastructure as a service), provide applications (software as a service), access online data (data as a service), and create, test, and deploy applications using web-based development tools (platform as a service).

Infrastructure as a Service

IaaS (*infrastructure as a service*) uses software to emulate hardware capabilities, enabling companies to scale, or adjust up or down, storage, processing power, or bandwidth as needed. For example, retailers may need to increase these capabilities to accommodate additional traffic to their websites during busy holiday shopping seasons. When the season ends, retailers easily can reduce these settings.

Two specific instances of IaaS are storage as a service and desktop as a service:

- **Storage as a Service:** Cloud storage providers offer file management services such as storing files online, system backup, and archiving earlier versions of files. Cloud storage is especially useful to tablet and smartphone users, because it enables them to access their files from all of their devices.

- **Desktop as a Service:** Some companies specify the applications, security settings, and computing resources available to employees on their desktop computers. These images, or configurations, provide a common desktop work environment available to employees across an entire organization. Because the desktop and its applications appear to be installed on the user's own computer, desktop as a service also is known as a *virtual desktop*.

Software as a Service

SaaS (*software as a service*) describes a computing environment where an Internet server hosts and deploys applications. Editing documents or photos, sending email messages, and managing finances are common consumer tasks of SaaS applications. A pioneering provider of SaaS applications for companies is Salesforce (shown in the figure in this tech feature), which offers customer relationship management (CRM) software. Salesforce users subscribe to modules to handle tasks such as sales and marketing campaigns and customer services.

Data as a Service

Government agencies, companies, and social media sites make data available for developers to incorporate in applications or to use when making business decisions and plans. *DaaS* (*data as a service*) allows users and applications to access a company's data. *Mashups* are applications that incorporate data from multiple providers into a new application. Displaying homes or crime statistics on a map are examples of mashups that require data from real estate, police records, and mapping providers.

Platform as a Service

Application developers need to maintain computers running specific hardware, operating systems, development tools, databases, and other software. *PaaS* (*platform as a service*) allows developers to create, test, and run their solutions on a cloud platform without having to purchase or configure the underlying hardware and software.

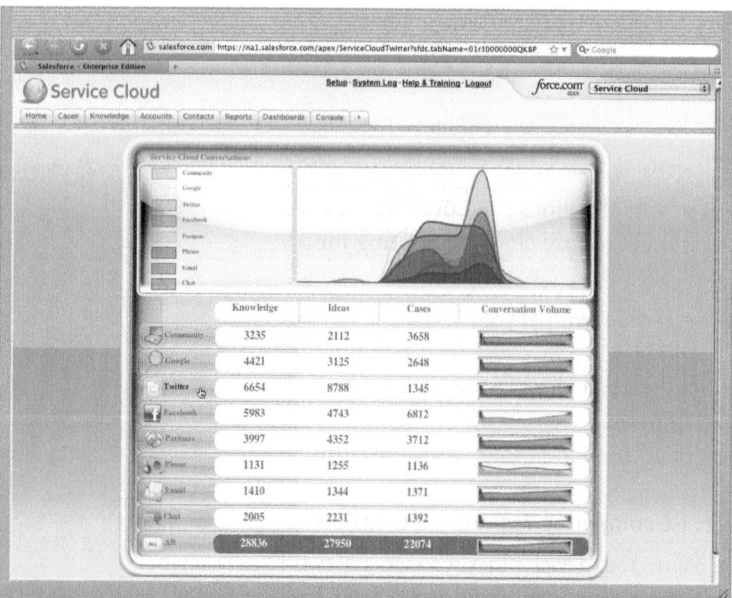

Source: Courtesy Salesforce.com

🌠 **Consider This:** Cloud computing services are based on a "pay as you go" model. How are cloud services different from desktop or mobile applications? What services are customers paying for from an SaaS provider? Under what circumstances might it be advantageous to purchase an external hard drive to store your files, rather than storing them on a third-party server on the cloud?

Data Representation

To understand how a computer processes data, you should know how a computer represents data. People communicate through speech by combining words into sentences. Human speech is **analog** because it uses continuous (wave form) signals that vary in strength and quality. Most computers are **digital**. They recognize only two discrete states: on and off. The two digits, 0 and 1, easily can represent these two states (Figure 6-8). The digit 0 represents the electronic state of off (absence of an electronic charge). The digit 1 represents the electronic state of on (presence of an electronic charge).

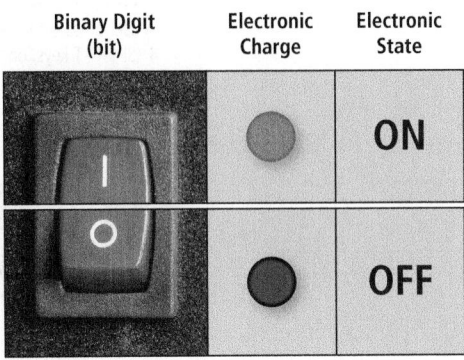

Figure 6-8 The circuitry in a computer or mobile device represents the on or the off states electronically by the presence or absence of an electronic charge.
iStockphoto.com / rjmiz

Bits and Bytes

When people count, they use the 10 digits in the decimal system (0 through 9). The computer, by contrast, uses a binary system because it recognizes only two states. The **binary system** is a number system that has just two unique digits, 0 and 1, called bits. A **bit** (short for *binary digit*) is the smallest unit of data the computer can process. By itself, a bit is not very informative.

When 8 bits are grouped together as a unit, they form a **byte**. A byte provides enough different combinations of 0s and 1s to represent 256 different characters. These characters include numbers, uppercase and lowercase letters of the alphabet, punctuation marks, and other keyboard symbols, such as an asterisk (*), ampersand (&), and dollar sign ($).

Coding Schemes

The combinations of 0s and 1s that represent uppercase and lowercase letters, numbers, and special symbols are defined by patterns called a coding scheme. Coding schemes map a set of *alphanumeric characters* (letters and numbers) and special symbols to a sequence of numeric values that a computer can process. *ASCII* (pronounced ASK-ee), which stands for American Standard Code for Information Interchange, is the most widely used coding scheme to represent a set of characters. In the ASCII coding scheme, for example, the alphabetic character E is represented as 01000101; the symbolic character * is represented as 00101010; the numeric character 6 is represented as 00110110 (Figure 6-9).

When you press a key on a keyboard, a chip in the keyboard converts the key's electronic signal into a special code, called a scan code, that is sent to the electronic circuitry

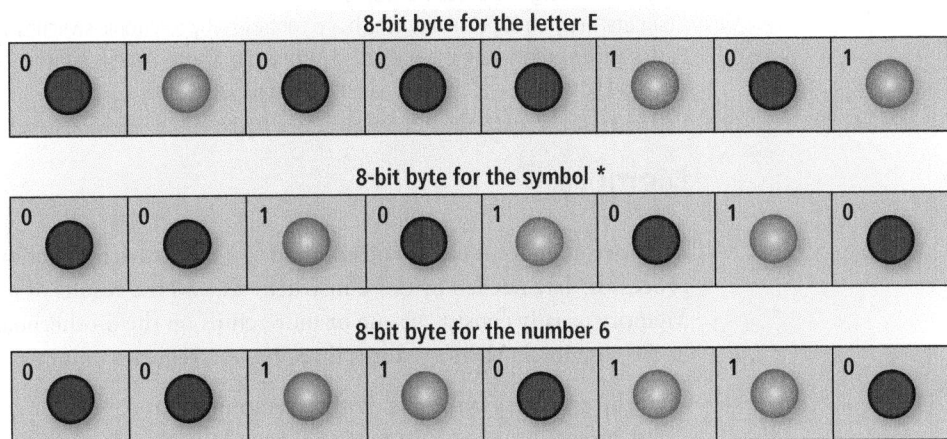

8-bit byte for the letter E

8-bit byte for the symbol *

8-bit byte for the number 6

Figure 6-9 Eight bits grouped together as a unit are called a byte. A byte represents a single character in the computer or mobile device.

in the computer. Then, the electronic circuitry in the computer converts the scan code into its ASCII binary form and stores it as a byte value in its memory for processing. When processing is finished, the computer converts the byte into a human-recognizable number, letter of the alphabet, or special character that is displayed on a screen or is printed (Figure 6-10). All of these conversions take place so quickly that you do not realize they are occurring.

How a Letter Is Converted to Binary Form and Back

Step 1

A user presses the capital letter **T** (SHIFT+T keys) on the keyboard, which in turn creates a special code, called a scan code, for the capital letter **T**.

Step 2

The scan code for the capital letter **T** is sent to the electronic circuitry in the computer.

Step 4

After processing, the binary code for the capital letter **T** is converted to an image and displayed on the output device.

Step 3

The electronic circuitry in the computer converts the scan code for the capital letter **T** to its ASCII binary code (01010100) and stores it in memory for processing.

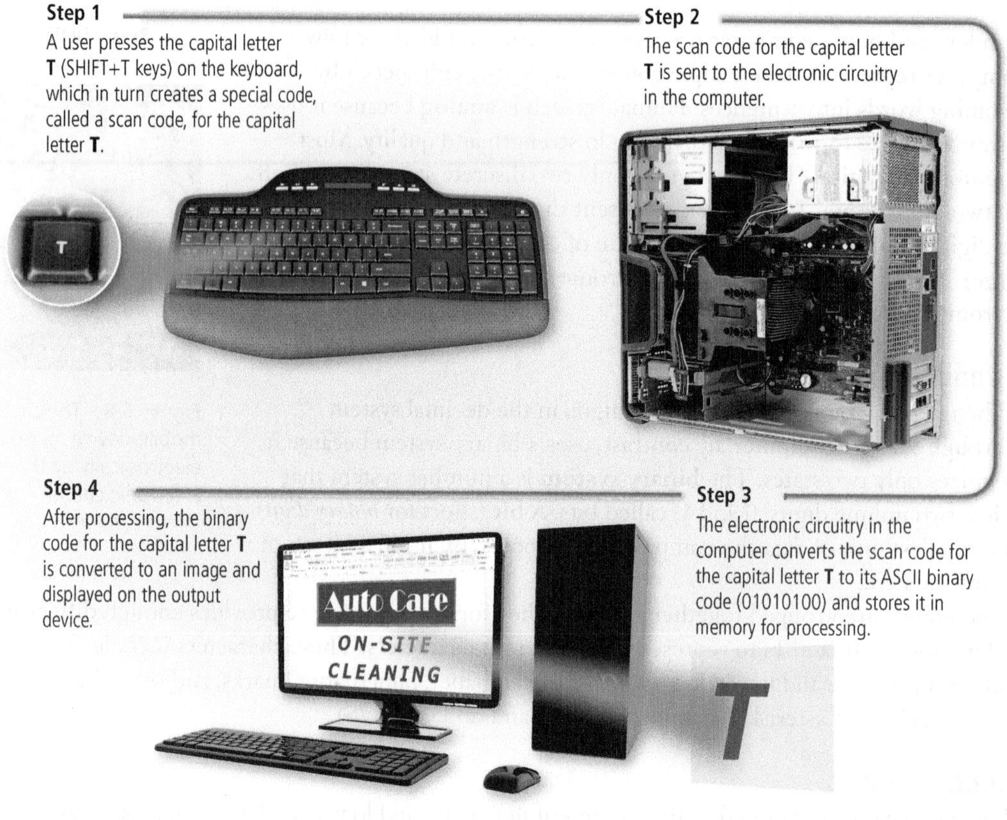

Figure 6-10   This figure shows how a letter is converted to binary form and back.
Chiyacat / Shutterstock.com; Kitch Bain / Shutterstock.com; Source: Microsoft; iStockphoto.com / sweetym

 CONSIDER THIS

Why are coding schemes necessary?
Computers rely on logic circuits, which are controlled by electronic switches whose state can be either on or off. Each switch's on/off state is represented by one bit, whose value is either 0 or 1. Coding schemes translate real-world data into a form that computers can process easily.

Memory

Memory consists of electronic components that store instructions waiting to be executed by the processor, data needed by those instructions, and the results of processing the data (information). Memory usually consists of one or more chips on the motherboard or some other circuit board in the computer. Memory stores three basic categories of items:

1. The operating system and other programs that control or maintain the computer and its devices
2. Applications that carry out a specific task, such as word processing
3. The data being processed by the applications and the resulting information

This role of memory to store both data and programs is known as the *stored program concept*.

Bytes and Addressable Memory

A byte (character) is the basic storage unit in memory. When an application's instructions and data are transferred to memory from storage devices, the instructions and data exist as bytes. Each byte resides temporarily in a location in memory that has an *address*. Simply put, an address is a unique number that identifies the location of a byte in memory. To access data or instructions in memory, the computer references the addresses that contain bytes of data. The photo in Figure 6-11 shows how seats in a stadium are similar to addresses in memory: (1) a seat, which is identified by a unique seat number, holds one person at a time, and a location in memory, which is identified by a unique address, holds a single byte, and (2) both a seat, identified by a seat number, and a byte, identified by an address, can be empty.

Manufacturers state the size of memory in terms of the number of bytes it has available for storage. Common sizes for memory are in the gigabyte range. A *gigabyte* (*GB*) equals approximately 1 billion bytes.

seat J20 is empty

seat J21 is occupied

Figure 6-11   Seats in a stadium are similar to addresses in memory: a seat holds one person at a time, and a location in memory holds a single byte; and both a seat and a byte can be empty.

iStockphoto.com / GeorgePeters

Types of Memory

Computers and mobile devices contain two types of memory: volatile and nonvolatile. When the computer's power is turned off, *volatile memory* loses its contents. *Nonvolatile memory*, by contrast, does not lose its contents when power is removed from the computer. Thus, volatile memory is temporary and nonvolatile memory is permanent. RAM is the most common type of volatile memory. Examples of nonvolatile memory include ROM, flash memory, and CMOS. The following sections discuss these types of memory.

RAM

Users typically are referring to RAM when discussing computer and mobile device memory. **RAM** (*random access memory*), also called *main memory*, consists of memory chips that can be read from and written to by the processor and other devices. When you turn on power to a computer or mobile device, certain operating system files (such as the files that determine how the desktop or home screen appears) load into RAM from a storage device such as a hard drive. These files remain in RAM as long as the computer or mobile device has continuous power. As additional applications and data are requested, they also load into RAM from storage.

The processor interprets and executes a program or application's instructions while the program or application is in RAM. During this time, the contents of RAM may change (Figure 6-12). RAM can accommodate multiple programs and applications simultaneously.

How Program Instructions Transfer in and out of RAM

Step 1
When you start the computer, certain operating system files are loaded into RAM from the hard drive. The operating system displays the user interface on the screen.

Step 2
When you run a browser, the application's instructions are loaded into RAM from the hard drive. The browser and certain operating system instructions are in RAM. The browser window appears on the screen.

Step 3
When you run a paint application, the application's instructions are loaded into RAM from the hard drive. The paint application, along with the browser and certain operating system instructions, are in RAM. The paint application window appears on the screen.

Step 4
When you exit an application, such as the browser, its instructions are removed from RAM. The browser no longer is displayed on the screen.

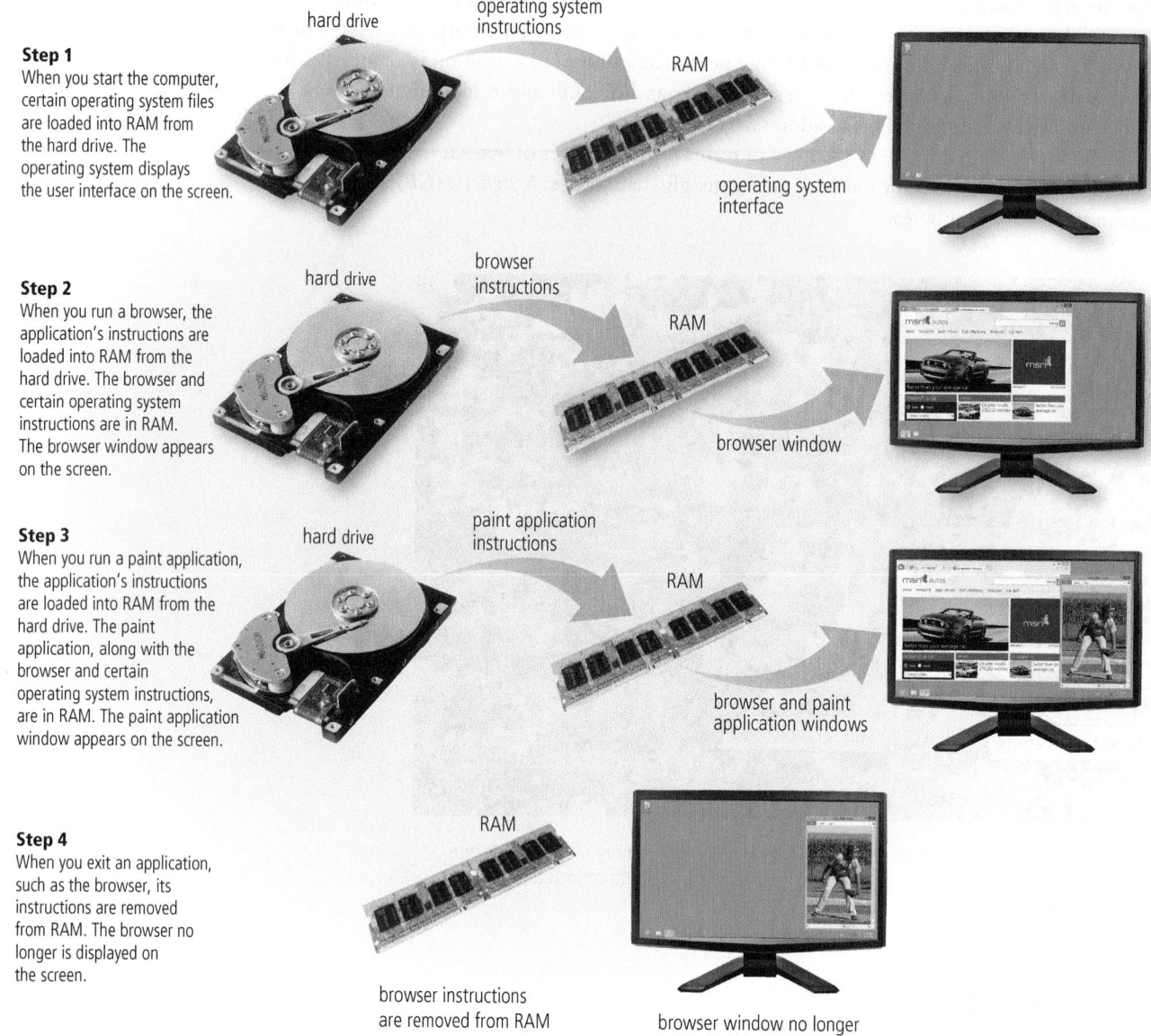

Figure 6-12   This figure shows how program and application instructions transfer in and out of RAM.
Gilmanshin / Shutterstock.com; TungCheung / Shutterstock.com; Vladyslav Starozhylov / Shutterstock.com; Source: Microsoft

Most RAM is volatile, which means it loses its contents when the power is removed from the computer. For this reason, you must save any data, instructions, and information you may need in the future. Saving is the process of copying data, instructions, and information from RAM to a storage device such as a hard drive.

Types of RAM   Two common types of RAM are dynamic RAM and static RAM:

- *Dynamic RAM* (*DRAM* pronounced DEE-ram) chips must be reenergized constantly or they lose their contents. Many variations of DRAM chips exist, most of which are faster than the basic DRAM (Table 6-1).
- *Static RAM* (*SRAM* pronounced ESS-ram) chips are faster and more reliable than any variation of DRAM chips. These chips do not have to be reenergized as often as DRAM chips; hence, the term, static. SRAM chips, however, are much more expensive than DRAM chips. Special applications, such as cache, use SRAM chips. A later section in this module discusses cache.

Read How To 6-2 for instructions about determining memory requirements.

Table 6-1   Common DRAM Variations

Name	Comments
SDRAM (Synchronous DRAM)	• Synchronized to the system clock • Much faster than DRAM
DDR SDRAM (Double Data Rate SDRAM)	• Transfers data twice, instead of once, for each clock cycle • Faster than SDRAM
DDR2	• Second generation of DDR • Faster than DDR
DDR3	• Third generation of DDR • Designed for computers with multi-core processors • Faster than DDR2
DDR4	• Fourth generation of DDR • Faster than DDR3
RDRAM (Rambus DRAM)	• Much faster than SDRAM

 BTW

DDR5
The specifications for DDR5, the fifth generation of DDR, currently are under development. DDR5 DRAM is expected to be in use by the end of the decade.

✸ HOW TO 6-2

Determine Memory Requirements
If you are shopping for a new computer or looking to upgrade your existing computer, be sure that it will have sufficient memory. When a computer has insufficient memory, its performance can slow significantly. On the other hand, it would be an unnecessary expense to purchase a computer with more memory than you will ever use. The following steps describe how to determine memory requirements.

1. If you are upgrading the memory in your existing computer, determine the following:
   a. Amount of memory currently installed
   b. Amount of memory the computer can support
   c. Type of memory module(s) currently installed
   d. Whether memory modules must be installed in pairs
   e. Number of available slots for memory modules

2. Determine the amount of memory your computer requires by checking the memory requirements for the operating system and programs and applications you plan to run. You can find the system requirements, which will specify the memory requirements, on product packaging or on a software manufacturer's website. If you are planning to upgrade your computer and the amount of memory you require exceeds the amount of memory your computer currently can support, you may need to purchase a new computer. If you are purchasing a new computer, view the computer's specifications to make sure it has sufficient memory. Some online vendors offer a web app that will check the configuration on your computer to determine the memory modules that are compatible and offer options to you for purchase.

3. Once you have determined your memory requirements, you are ready to purchase the memory modules. Memory modules are available for purchase in many computer and electronic stores, directly from computer manufacturers, and on various websites. When you are purchasing memory modules, keep the following in mind:
   a. Many types of memory modules are available. Purchase a type, size, and speed that is compatible with your computer.
   b. If your computer requires that you install memory in pairs, be sure to purchase two memory modules that are the same type, size, and speed.
   c. Do not purchase more memory modules than you have slots available. You may need to remove existing memory modules to make room for new memory modules.

✸ **Consider This:** How much memory would be appropriate for your computer based on your current computing needs?

Memory Modules   RAM chips usually reside on a memory module, which is a small circuit board. Memory slots on the motherboard hold memory modules.

Two types of memory modules are SIMMs and DIMMs (Figure 6-13). A *SIMM* (single inline memory module) has pins on opposite sides of the circuit board that connect together to form a single set of contacts. With a *DIMM* (dual inline memory module), by contrast, the pins on opposite sides of the circuit board do not connect and, thus, form two sets of contacts.

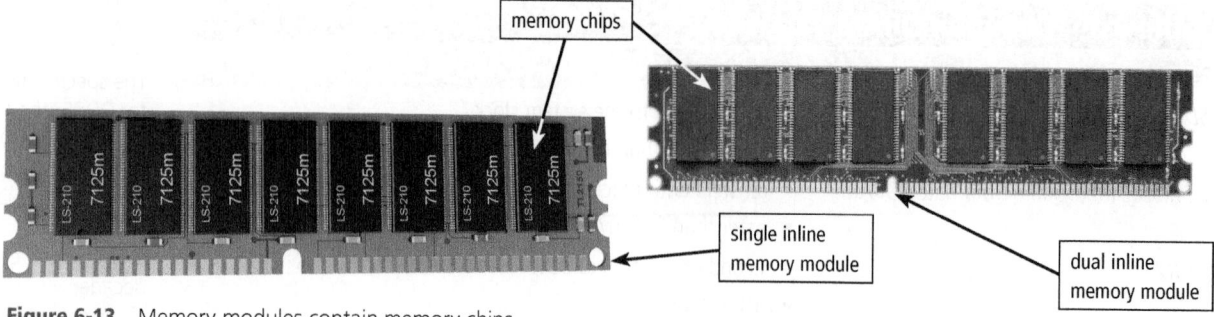

Figure 6-13 Memory modules contain memory chips.
Mykola / Shutterstock.com; TerryM / Shutterstock.com

Cache

Most of today's computers improve their processing times with **cache** (pronounced cash), which is a temporary storage area. Two common types of cache are memory cache and disk cache. This module discusses memory cache. Module 8 discusses disk cache.

Memory cache helps speed the processes of the computer because it stores frequently used instructions and data. Most personal computers today have two types of memory cache: Level 1 (L1) cache and Level 2 (L2) cache. Some also have Level 3 (L3) cache.

BTW

L2 Cache
When discussing cache, most users are referring to L2 cache.

BTW

L4 Cache
L4 cache is used with some newer processor and does not reside on the processor.

- *L1 cache* is built directly on the processor chip. L1 cache usually has a very small capacity.
- *L2 cache* is slightly slower than L1 cache but has a much larger capacity. Current processors include *advanced transfer cache* (*ATC*), a type of L2 cache built directly on the processor chip. Processors that use ATC perform at much faster rates than those that do not use it.
- *L3 cache* is a cache on the motherboard that is separate from the processor chip.

When the processor needs an instruction or data, it searches memory in this order: L1 cache, then L2 cache, then L3 cache (if it exists), then RAM — with a greater delay in processing for each level of memory it must search (Figure 6-14). If the instruction or data is not found in memory, then it must search a slower speed storage medium, such as a hard drive or optical disc.

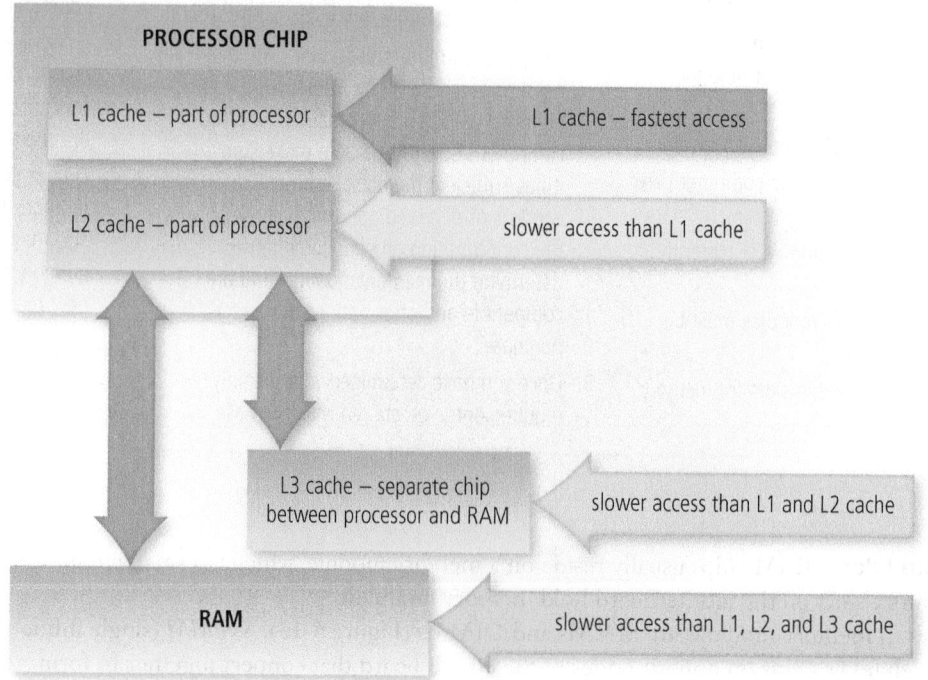

Figure 6-14 Memory cache helps speed processing times when the processor requests data, instructions, or information.

ROM

Read-only memory (ROM pronounced rahm) refers to memory chips storing permanent data and instructions. The data on most ROM chips cannot be modified — hence, the name read-only. ROM is nonvolatile, which means its contents are not lost when power is removed from the computer. In addition to computers and mobile devices, many peripheral devices contain ROM chips. For example, ROM chips in printers contain data for fonts.

Manufacturers of ROM chips often record data, instructions, or information on the chips when they manufacture the chips. These ROM chips, called **firmware**, contain permanently written data, instructions, or information, such as a computer or mobile device's start-up instructions.

Flash Memory

Flash memory is a type of nonvolatile memory that can be erased electronically and rewritten. Most computers use flash memory to hold their start-up instructions because it allows the computer to update its contents easily. For example, when the computer changes from standard time to daylight savings time, the contents of a flash memory chip (and the real-time clock chip) change to reflect the new time.

Flash memory chips also store data and programs on many mobile devices and peripheral devices, such as smartphones, portable media players, printers, digital cameras, automotive devices, and digital voice recorders. When you enter names and addresses in a smartphone, for example, a flash memory chip stores the data. Some portable media players store music on flash memory chips; others store music on tiny hard drives or memory cards. Memory cards contain flash memory on a removable device instead of a chip. Read Secure IT 6-4 for tips about deleting data on a smartphone.

 SECURE IT 6-4

Wiping Mobile Phone Memory

If you ever have lent your smartphone to someone, left it sitting on your desk at school or work, or placed it in your car's center console at valet parking, you might have provided someone access without your consent to all your personal data stored on that device. A thief can plug a small device, called a *Cellular Seizure Investigation (CSI) stick,* into the phone and then download sensitive data in seconds.

While this unscrupulous activity seems alarming, a similar action occurs every day when smartphone users recycle or sell their devices without wiping all their personal records from memory. A person buying or acquiring the phone then can access the sensitive data left in memory. Some recyclers claim that 95 percent of

the mobile phones they receive are not completely cleaned.

A kill switch allows smartphone owners to delete all data or to disable their devices remotely in the event of theft or loss. Since 2015, all smartphones sold in California must include this device, and federal and other state lawmakers have proposed requiring all manufacturers to include this switch in their products.

Deleting all data from a mobile phone's memory is a relatively simple process, but it is not a universal procedure. Each device has its own set of steps described in the owner's manual or online. In general, users must locate their device's settings area on a menu and then look for a reset command. Most electronics manufacturers post instructions for this process on their websites. Mobile

phone retailers often can offer help in clearing personal data; if you resort to this measure, be certain to watch the sales associate perform this action. If your mobile phone has a SIM or memory card, remove and destroy it if you are not going to transfer it to another phone. Employees who use their phone to access email messages on corporate servers sometimes are required to enter a passcode on the phone so that if it is lost or stolen, the data can be wiped remotely.

Consider This: Have you ever wiped the memory of your mobile phone? What action would you take if you received or bought a used mobile phone and then discovered the previous owner's personal information stored in memory? Should lawmakers require smartphone manufacturers to include a kill switch in their products? Why or why not?

CMOS

Some RAM chips, flash memory chips, and other memory chips use complementary metal-oxide semiconductor (*CMOS* pronounced *SEE-moss*) technology because it provides high speeds and consumes little power. CMOS technology uses battery power to retain information even when the power to the computer is off. Battery-backed CMOS memory chips, for example, can keep the calendar, date, and time current even when the computer is off. The flash memory chips that store a computer's start-up information often use CMOS technology.

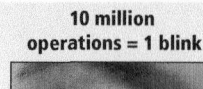
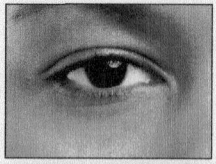
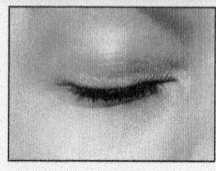

10 million operations = 1 blink

Figure 6-15 It takes about one-tenth of a second to blink your eye, in which time a computer can perform some operations 10 million times.

iStockphoto.com / drbimages;
iStockphoto.com / drbimages

Memory Access Times

Access time is the amount of time it takes the processor to read data, instructions, and information from memory. A computer's access time directly affects how fast the computer processes data. For example, accessing data in memory can be more than 200,000 times faster than accessing data on a hard disk because of the mechanical motion of the hard disk.

Today's manufacturers use a variety of terminology to state access times (Table 6-2). Some use fractions of a second, which for memory occurs in nanoseconds. A *nanosecond* (abbreviated *ns*) is one billionth of a second. A nanosecond is extremely fast (Figure 6-15). In fact, electricity travels about one foot in a nanosecond.

Table 6-2	Access Time Terminology	
Term	**Abbreviation**	**Speed**
Millisecond	ms	One-thousandth of a second
Microsecond	μs	One-millionth of a second
Nanosecond	ns	One-billionth of a second
Picosecond	ps	One-trillionth of a second

 CONSIDER THIS

What if a manufacturer states access times in megahertz instead of fractions of a second?
Some manufacturers state access times in MHz; for example, 800 MHz DDR2 SDRAM. If a manufacturer states access time in megahertz, you can convert it to nanoseconds by dividing 1 billion ns by the megahertz number. For example, 800 MHz equals approximately 1.25 ns (1,000,000,000/800,000,000). The higher the megahertz, the faster the access time; conversely, the lower the nanoseconds, the faster the access time.

While access times of memory greatly affect overall computer performance, manufacturers and retailers often list a computer's memory in terms of its size, not its access time. For example, an advertisement might describe a computer as having 16 GB of RAM.

Adapters

Although the circuitry in many of today's computers integrates all the necessary functionality, some require additional capabilities in the form of adapters. Desktops and servers use adapter cards; mobile computers use USB adapters.

Adapter Cards

An **adapter card**, sometimes called an *expansion card* or *adapter board*, is a circuit board that enhances the functions of a component of a desktop or server system unit and/or provides connections to peripheral devices. An **expansion slot** is a socket on a desktop or server motherboard that can hold an adapter card. Figure 6-16 shows some adapter cards in expansion slots on a desktop motherboard.

Two popular adapter cards are sound cards and video cards. A *sound card* enhances the sound-generating capabilities of a personal computer by allowing sound to be input through a microphone and output through external speakers or headphones. A *video card*, also called a *graphics card*, converts computer output into a video signal that travels through a cable to the monitor, which displays an image on the screen. Table 6-3 identifies the purpose of some adapter cards. Sometimes, all functionality is built in the adapter card. With others, a cable connects the adapter card to a device, such as a digital video camera, outside the computer.

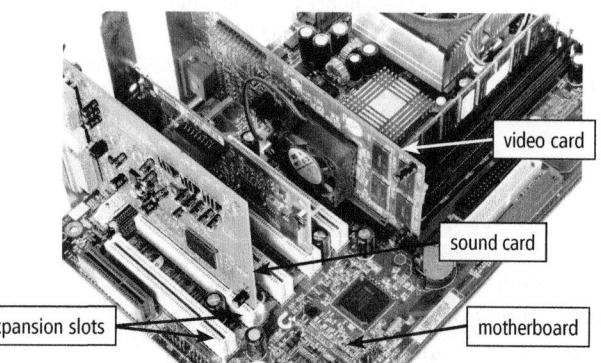

video card
sound card
expansion slots
motherboard

Figure 6-16 Cards inserted in expansion slots on a desktop motherboard.
Olga Lipatova / Shutterstock.com

Table 6-3   Adapter Cards

Type	Purpose
Bluetooth	Enables Bluetooth connectivity
MIDI	Connects to musical instruments
Modem	Connects to transmission media, such as cable television lines or phone lines
Network	Provides network connections, such as to an Ethernet port
Sound	Connects to speakers or a microphone
TV tuner	Allows viewing of digital television broadcasts on a monitor
USB	Connects to high-speed USB ports
Video	Provides enhanced graphics capabilities, such as accelerated processing or the ability to connect a second monitor
Video capture	Connects to a digital video camera

Today's computers support **Plug and Play** technology, which means the computer automatically can recognize peripheral devices as you install them. Plug and Play support means you can plug in a device and then immediately begin using it. Read Secure IT 6-5 for issues related to Plug and Play technology.

 SECURE IT 6-5

Plug and Play Security Flaws

Plug and Play technology allows your computer to recognize peripheral devices and begin using them immediately after they are installed. This support permits computers to connect and communicate with devices easily, but it also creates security flaws that allow hackers to take control of security systems, routers, Smart TVs, printers, webcams, and other devices connected to the Internet.

According to Rapid7, a security firm that uncovered these defects, between 40 and 50 million devices are susceptible to remote attacks. Rapid7 has developed a scanner tool to check vulnerabilities and identify affected hardware. Security experts recommend turning off or disabling any Plug and Play device not being used on a network that accesses the Internet.

Consider This: Would you consider checking your home network to discover Plug and Play security weaknesses or disabling devices? What steps can manufacturers take to minimize these vulnerabilities?

USB Adapters

Because of their smaller size, mobile computers typically do not have expansion slots. Instead, users can purchase a **USB adapter**, which is a dongle that plugs into a USB port, enhances functions of a mobile computer, and/or provides connections to peripheral devices (Figure 6-17). USB adapters can be used to add memory, communications, multimedia, security, and storage capabilities to mobile computers. A USB flash drive is a common USB adapter that provides computers and mobile devices with additional storage capability as long as it is plugged in. Read Ethics & Issues 6-2 to consider whether manufacturers should eliminate proprietary connectors.

Unlike adapter cards that require you to open the system unit and install the card on the motherboard, you can change a removable flash memory device without having to open the system unit or restart the computer. This feature, called *hot plugging*, allows you to insert and remove a device while the computer is running (be sure, though, to stop or eject the device before removing it).

Figure 6-17 A USB adapter inserts into a USB port on a computer or mobile device.
vetkit / Shutterstock.com; vetkit / Shutterstock.com

ETHICS & ISSUES 6-2

Should Manufacturers Eliminate Proprietary Connectors?

If you need to replace the cable that connects your mobile device to a USB port, you might have a choice of many makes, models, and prices. Some devices, however, require the use of proprietary connectors, limiting your options to those manufacturers who make connectors that match the port on your mobile device.

When Apple released the iPhone 5, for example, it required the use of a proprietary connector that was incompatible with connectors used with prior iPhone models and other Apple devices. Apple developed

the connector, called Lightning, in part to eliminate problems caused by attempts to attach the cord the wrong way. With Lightning, users can attach the cord in either direction without causing damage to the port or device. Critics argue that requiring customers to purchase proprietary connectors increases the cost of purchasing or upgrading a mobile device.

The International Electronics Commission (IEC) is working with major technology providers to make micro USB the universal connector standard used to charge mobile devices. This type of universal standard has several advantages. It will save customers

money because they will not have to purchase a new connector with their new device, even if it is a different brand. A universal standard connector also will enable users with different device models to share connectors. The environment will benefit because fewer outdated or incompatible cords will find their way into landfills. Further, the manufacturing process will generate less waste because fewer cords will be required.

Consider This: Should customers pressure manufacturers to use a universal connector standard? Why or why not? Would you consider the connector type when purchasing a new phone? Why or why not?

Buses

As explained earlier in this module, a computer processes and stores data as a series of electronic bits. These bits transfer internally within the circuitry of the computer along electrical channels. Each channel, called a **bus**, allows the various devices both inside and attached to the system unit to communicate with one another. Just as vehicles travel on a highway to move from one destination to another, bits travel on a bus (Figure 6-18).

Buses are used to transfer bits from input devices to memory, from memory to the processor, from the processor to memory, and from memory to output or storage devices. Buses consist of a data bus and an address bus. The *data bus* is used to transfer actual data, and the *address bus* is used to transfer information about where the data should reside in memory.

Bus Width

The size of a bus, called the *bus width*, determines the number of bits that the computer can transmit at one time. For example, a 32-bit bus can transmit 32 bits (4 bytes) at a time. On a 64-bit bus, bits transmit from one location to another 64 bits (8 bytes) at a time. The larger the number of bits handled by the bus, the faster the computer transfers data. Using the highway analogy again, assume that one lane on a highway can carry one bit. A 32-bit bus is like a 32-lane highway. A 64-bit bus is like a 64-lane highway.

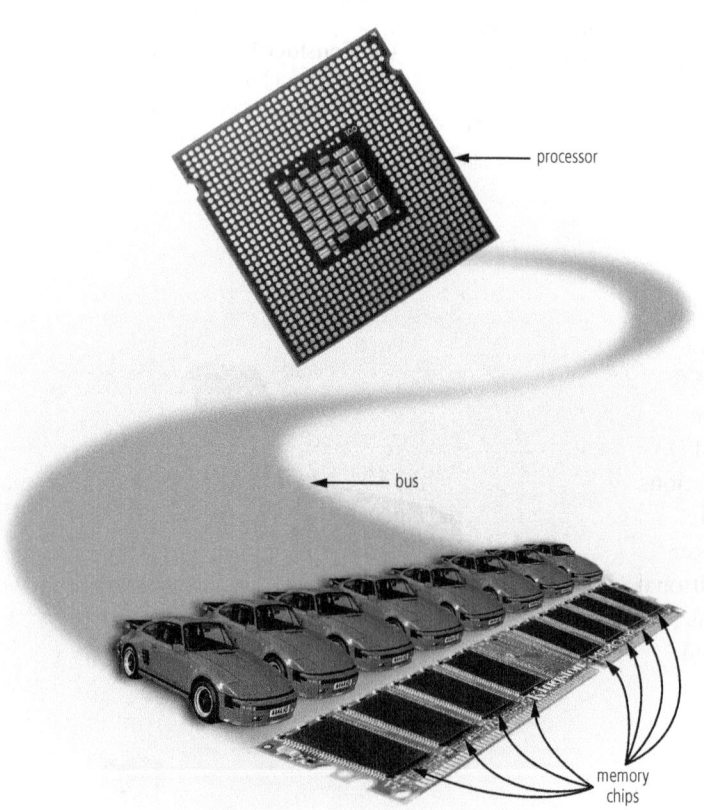

processor

bus

memory chips

Figure 6-18 Just as vehicles travel on a highway, bits travel on a bus. Buses are used to transfer bits from input devices to memory, from memory to the processor, from the processor to memory, and from memory to output or storage devices.

divgradcurl / Shutterstock.com

If a number in memory occupies 8 bytes, or 64 bits, the computer must transmit it in two separate steps when using a 32-bit bus: once for the first 32 bits and once for the second 32 bits. Using a 64-bit bus, the computer can transmit the number in a single step, transferring all 64 bits at once. The wider the bus, the fewer number of transfer steps required and the faster the transfer of data. Most personal computers today use a 64-bit bus.

In conjunction with the bus width, many computer professionals refer to a computer's word size. **Word size** is the number of bits the processor can interpret and execute at a given time. That is, a 64-bit processor can manipulate 64 bits at a time. Computers with a larger word size can process more data in the same amount of time than computers with a smaller word size. In most computers, the word size is the same as the bus width.

 CONSIDER THIS

How is bus speed measured?
Every bus also has a clock speed. Just like the processor, manufacturers state the clock speed for a bus in hertz. The higher the bus clock speed, the faster the transmission of data, which results in programs running faster.

Types of Buses

A computer has a system bus, possibly a backside bus, and an expansion bus.

- A *system bus*, also called the *front side bus* (*FSB*), is part of the motherboard and connects the processor to main memory.
- A *backside bus* (*BSB*) connects the processor to cache.
- An *expansion bus* allows the processor to communicate with peripheral devices.

When computer professionals use the term, bus, by itself, they usually are referring to the system bus.

Power Supply and Batteries

Many personal computers plug in standard wall outlets, which supply an alternating current (AC) of 115 to 120 volts. This type of power is unsuitable for use with a computer or mobile device, which requires a direct current (DC) ranging from 5 to more than 15 volts. The **power supply** or laptop AC adapter converts the wall outlet AC power into DC power (Figure 6-19). Different motherboards and computers require different wattages on the power supply. If a power supply is not providing the necessary power, the computer will not function properly.

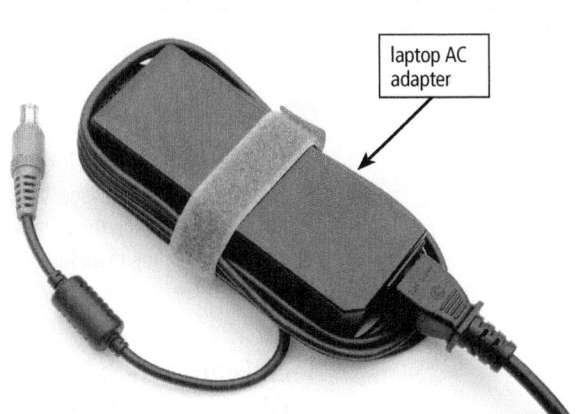

desktop power supply

laptop AC adapter

Figure 6-19   Examples of desktop power supply and laptop AC adapter.
Robert Babczynski / Shutterstock.com; iStockphoto.com / Freer Law

Built into the power supply is a fan that keeps the power supply cool. Some have variable speed fans that change speed or stop running, depending on temperature in the case. Many newer computers have additional fans near certain components in the system unit, such as the processor, hard drive, and ports. Some users install more fans to help dissipate heat generated by the components of the computer.

 CONSIDER THIS ————————————————————————————

How many fans are in a desktop case?

Most have at least three fans: one in the power supply, one in the case, and one on the processor heat sink. In addition, you also might find a fan on a video card or other adapter card. While some computers contain fans that are designed to be quiet or operate in quiet mode, others allow you to turn off noisy fans until they are needed. You also can purchase programs that slow or stop the fan until the temperature reaches a certain level.

Some external peripheral devices, such as a cable modem, speakers, or a printer, have an AC adapter, which is an external power supply. One end of the AC adapter plugs in the wall outlet and the other end attaches to the peripheral. The AC adapter converts the AC power into the DC power that the peripheral requires, and also often charges the battery in a mobile computer or device.

Mobile computers and devices can run using either a power supply or batteries. The batteries typically are rechargeable lithium-ion batteries (Figure 6-20). Many newer mobile devices and computers, such as some ultrathin laptops, do not have removable batteries.

Figure 6-20   Rechargeable batteries for mobile computers and devices.
Thejipen / Dreamstime.com; Anaken2012 / Dreamstime.com

 CONSIDER THIS ————————————————————————————

How often do batteries for mobile computers and devices need to be replaced?

Battery life depends on usage. While some may last several years, you may need to replace a battery much sooner than that. When the battery no longer can hold a charge, you should replace it with a battery made by, or recommended by, the manufacturer of the computer or device.

Tech Feature 6-3: Proper Care for Computers and Mobile Devices

Taking proper care of computers and mobile devices not only will help prolong their life, but also will keep them running optimally. Read Tech Feature 6-3 to learn about properly caring for computers and mobile devices.

TECH FEATURE 6-3

Proper Care for Computers and Mobile Devices

Caring for a computer or mobile device requires keeping hardware in good condition and maintaining programs and apps.

Hardware Maintenance

Before performing any of the following steps to care for your computer or mobile device, turn off and unplug the device from its power source. If the computer or mobile device has a removable battery, you also should remove the battery. You also should consider disconnecting all peripheral devices. All hardware maintenance should be performed in an area that is clean and free from clutter.

- Use a damp cloth to clean the screen gently. Do not use any special cleaners to clean the display, as they may damage the display. Water is sufficient to remove dust and most dirt. Read How To 6-3 for additional ways to protect screens and replace them if necessary.

- If the computer or mobile device has a keyboard, use a can of compressed air to free the keyboard from any dirt and debris that might interfere with the operation of the keys or pose a risk of getting inside the computer or mobile device. When using compressed air, hold the can upright, and not at an angle or upside down, when dispensing the air. Holding the can at an angle or upside down can cause the can to dispense a very cold liquid instead of air, which can damage components in your computer or mobile device.

- If you are transporting a laptop, be sure to store it in a case with plenty of padding. If you are using a mobile device, protect it with a case. A case will protect the device better in the event you drop it and may make it easier for you to grip the device while using it.

- If the computer or mobile device has an air vent where a fan removes heat, make sure the vent is free of dust and debris. A blocked vent can prohibit heat from escaping, which ultimately can cause the computer or mobile device to overheat. If the air vent is dirty, contact a trained professional to have it cleaned properly. Improperly cleaning an air vent can

Raw Group / Shutterstock.com

result in more debris entering the computer or mobile device.

- When you insert media such as an optical disc or USB flash drive, be sure the media is clean. Inserting dirty media can damage a computer or mobile device's internal components.

Software Maintenance

Maintaining the software on your computers and mobile devices can help them run optimally. While no specific recommendation exists for the frequency with which you should perform the following actions, you should do so if you begin to notice a decline in your computer or mobile device's performance.

- Uninstall programs and remove apps you no longer need on your computer or mobile device. These programs and apps may consume a significant amount of space on your storage medium and decrease the performance of your computer or mobile device. More information about uninstalling programs and removing apps can be found in How To 4-3 in Module 4.

- If you are using a desktop or laptop with a hard disk, defragment the computer's hard disk if you notice a decline in the computer's performance. More information about defragmenting can be found in the Disk Defragmenter section in Module 4.

- Install programs and apps only from reputable software manufacturers. In addition, make sure you are installing the program or app from the original installation media, the software manufacturer's website, or your mobile device's app store or marketplace. You also should read reviews for programs and apps before you download and/or install them to make sure the program or app will meet your needs.

Consider This: In addition to the methods mentioned in this tech feature, what other ways can you care for your computer or mobile device?

iStockphoto.com / jfmdesign

CONSIDER THIS

How does an antistatic wristband work?

When working with electronic components, such as a motherboard, you should wear an antistatic wristband. An *antistatic wristband* is a bracelet designed to protect electronics from an electrostatic discharge by preventing a buildup of static electricity on a user. The wristband has an attached clip that you connect to any bare metal surface, which acts as a ground.

 HOW TO 6-3

Protect and Replace Screens

One way to protect the screen on your mobile device is to use a screen protector. A *screen protector* is a thin plastic film that adheres to the screen of your device. While screen protectors may not protect the screen if you drop your device or an object impacts it with excessive force, it will protect the screen from minor scratches obtained through normal use. Screen protectors often can be purchased from the same place you bought your mobile device and also are available online. If you cannot find a screen protector that is the exact same size as the screen on your mobile device, you can purchase a larger one and then trim it to fit your screen.

In the event the screen on your mobile device breaks, the following steps will guide you through the process of replacing it. Even if your device continues to work with a broken screen, you still should replace it as soon as possible to avoid injury. **NOTE: Screen replacement should be attempted only by advanced users. If you are uncomfortable following these steps,** **seek help from a trained professional. In addition, the exact steps to replace a broken screen can vary with each device. If the steps for your device vary from the steps listed below, follow the instructions from your device's manufacturer.**

1. Back up the data on your mobile device before starting a screen replacement. While a successful screen replacement should not threaten the data, it is a good idea to keep a backup in case a problem arises unexpectedly.

2. Turn off the mobile device and disconnect it from all power sources. If the device uses a removable battery, remove it.

3. Protect your hands and eyes before beginning glass replacement.

4. If possible, carefully remove all pieces of broken glass. Consider using compressed air to remove any dust.

5. Remove the display assembly. Refer to your device's documentation for information about removing the display. You may need a small, nonmagnetic screwdriver and/or metal or plastic tool to remove the assembly. If the display assembly is connected to the mobile device with a cable, carefully disconnect the cable.

6. Unpack the new screen and connect it to the mobile device, connecting any necessary cables.

7. Reassemble the mobile device, reconnect the power source and/or the battery, and turn on the device.

🌼 **Consider This:** Why might you replace a cracked screen instead of replacing the entire mobile device?

iStockPhoto.com / deepblue4you

✔ Summary

This module presented the various components inside computers and mobile devices. It discussed types of processors, steps in a machine cycle, and processor cooling methods. You learned about advantages and services of cloud computing. The module discussed how memory stores data and described various types of memory. You learned about adapters, buses, power supplies and batteries, and ways to care for computers and mobile devices.

The Study Guide reinforces material you should know after reading this module.   **Study Guide**

Instructions: Answer the questions below using the format that helps you remember best or that is required by your instructor. Possible formats may include one or more of these options: write the answers; create a document that contains the answers; record answers as audio or video using a webcam, smartphone, or portable media player; post answers on a blog, wiki, or website; or highlight answers in the book/e-book.

1. Describe the hardware referred to by the terms, system unit and chassis.

2. Name the typical location of the case for a laptop, slate tablet, convertible tablet, game console, smartphone, wearable device, portable media player, digital camera, and handheld game device.

3. List products for securing and tracking hardware and how each is used.

4. Define the terms, motherboard, chip, integrated circuit, and transistor.

5. Describe the purpose of the processor and how multi- and single-core processors differ.

6. Describe the difference between a single-board computer and a traditional desktop.

7. Describe how a chip can be used to locate a lost animal.

8. Explain the role of the control unit and ALU in performing computer operations.

9. Describe what happens during each step in the machine cycle.

10. Define these terms: registers, system clock, and superscalar. Describe how clock speed is measured.

11. List two leading manufacturers of personal computer processor chips.

12. List the steps required to select the right processor.

13. List technologies that processor chips often include.

14. List options for cooling a processor, and describe how each works.

15. Define the term, Internet of Things (IoT). List IoT-enabled devices and technologies.

16. Explain how smart cities might use the Internet of Things.

17. Describe issues related to access and privacy regarding IoT.

18. Explain why a home or business user might choose cloud computing.

19. Describe services offered with cloud computing.

20. Human speech is ___ because it uses continuous (wave form) signals that vary in strength and quality. Most computers are ___, meaning that they recognize only two discrete states: on and off.

21. Define the terms, bit and byte. Describe the binary system and the ASCII coding scheme.

22. List categories of items stored in memory. Explain how manufacturers state memory size.

23. Differentiate between volatile and nonvolatile memory. List an example of each.

24. Describe how RAM works. List two types of RAM.

25. Explain how to determine memory requirements.

26. Describe the function of a memory module. List two types of memory modules.

27. Describe how a computer uses cache. Differentiate among L1, L2, and L3 cache.

28. Describe what is stored in ROM. ___ are ROM chips that contain permanently written data, instructions, or information.

29. Identify uses for flash memory.

30. List methods to wipe the memory of a mobile device when recycling or selling.

31. Describe CMOS technology and its possible uses.

32. Define the term, access time. List different methods used to state access time.

33. Describe the purpose of an adapter card and the role of an expansion slot.

34. List the various types of adapter cards.

35. Explain Plug and Play technology.

36. List security concerns regarding Plug and Play technology.

37. Describe the functions of USB adapters.

38. Explain the advantages of using a universal standard connector.

39. Define the term, hot plugging.

40. Identify the role of a bus. Differentiate between a data bus and an address bus.

41. Describe how bus width and word size affect and are used to measure computer speed.

42. List types of buses and describe the purpose of each.

43. Explain how a power supply converts AC current into DC current.

44. Explain the purpose of and roles of fans in power supplies, and how many might be in a desktop case.

45. Explain how to maintain hardware and software on your computer or mobile device.

46. A(n) ___ wristband is a bracelet designed to protect electronics from an electrostatic discharge by preventing a buildup of static electricity on a user.

47. List steps and precautions to take when replacing the screen on a mobile device.

STUDENT ASSIGNMENTS

Key Terms

You should be able to define the Primary Terms and be familiar with the Secondary Terms listed below.

Primary Terms   (shown in **bold-black** characters in the module)

access time (6-20)
adapter card (6-20)
analog (6-13)
arithmetic logic unit (6-7)
binary system (6-13)
bit (6-13)
bus (6-22)
byte (6-13)

cache (6-18)
central processing unit
   (CPU) (6-5)
chip (6-4)
clock speed (6-8)
control unit (6-6)
digital (6-13)
expansion slot (6-20)

firmware (6-19)
flash memory (6-19)
gigahertz (GHz) (6-8)
memory (6-14)
memory cache (6-18)
motherboard (6-4)
multi-core processor (6-5)
Plug and Play (6-21)

power supply (6-23)
processor (6-5)
RAM (6-15)
read-only memory
   (ROM) (6-19)
system clock (6-8)
USB adapter (6-21)
word size (6-23)

Secondary Terms   (shown in *italic* characters in the module)

adapter board (6-20)
address (6-14)
address bus (6-22)
advanced transfer cache (ATC) (6-18)
alphanumeric characters (6-13)
ALU (6-7)
antistatic wristband (6-26)
arithmetic operations (6-7)
ASCII (6-13)
backside bus (BSB) (6-23)
binary digit (6-13)
bus width (6-22)
Cellular Seizure Investigation (CSI)
   stick (6-19)
chassis (6-3)
clock cycle (6-8)
CMOS (6-19)
comparison operations (6-7)
cooling pad (6-9)

DaaS (data as a service) (6-12)
data bus (6-22)
DDR SDRAM (6-17)
DDR2 (6-17)
DDR3 (6-17)
DDR4 (6-17)
decoding (6-7)
DIMM (6-17)
dynamic RAM (DRAM) (6-16)
executing (6-7)
expansion bus (6-23)
expansion card (6-20)
fetching (6-7)
front side bus (FSB) (6-23)
gigabyte (GB) (6-15)
graphics card (6-20)
heat sink (6-9)
hertz (6-8)
hot plugging (6-21)

IaaS (infrastructure as a service)
   (6-12)
integrated circuit (6-4)
Intel-compatible processors (6-8)
Internet of Things (IoT) (6-9)
L1 cache (6-18)
L2 cache (6-18)
L3 cache (6-18)
L4 cache (6-18)
liquid cooling technology (6-9)
machine cycle (6-7)
main memory (6-15)
mashups (6-12)
microprocessor (6-5)
nanosecond (ns) (6-20)
nonvolatile memory (6-15)
PaaS (platform as a service) (6-12)
random access memory (6-15)
RDRAM (6-17)

real-time clock (6-8)
registers (6-8)
screen protector (6-26)
SDRAM (6-17)
SIMM (6-17)
software as a service (SaaS) (6-12)
sound card (6-20)
static RAM (SRAM) (6-16)
stored program concept (6-14)
storing (6-7)
superscalar (6-8)
system board (6-4)
system bus (6-23)
system unit (6-3)
transistor (6-4)
video card (6-20)
virtual desktop (6-12)
volatile memory (6-15)

Robert Babczynski / Shutterstock.com

The Checkpoint exercises test your knowledge of the module concepts. _____

Checkpoint

True/False
True/False Mark T for True and F for False. If False, rewrite the statement so that it is True.

1. The motherboard also is called a system board.
2. A single-board computer often is more expensive than a traditional desktop computer.
3. A dual-core processor doubles the processing speed of a single-core processor.
4. In general, multi-core processors are less energy efficient than separate multiple processors.
5. The system clock keeps track of the date and time in a computer.
6. In cloud computing, the back end consists of the servers and storage devices that manage and store the resources accessed by users.
7. In the binary system, the digit 1 represents the absence of an electronic charge.
8. Most RAM is nonvolatile.
9. The processor interprets and executes a program or application's instructions while the program or application is in nonvolatile memory.
10. ROM chips also are called firmware.
11. As with processors, manufacturers state the clock speed for a bus in hertz.
12. The power supply converts the wall outlet AC power into DC power.

Matching
Match the terms with their definitions.

_____ 1. ASCII
_____ 2. bus width
_____ 3. chip
_____ 4. control unit
_____ 5. firmware
_____ 6. IaaS
_____ 7. motherboard
_____ 8. registers
_____ 9. transistor
_____ 10. word size

a. small, high-speed storage locations contained in a processor
b. component of the computer that directs and coordinates most of the operations in the computer
c. widely used coding scheme to represent a set of characters
d. the main circuit board of the computer
e. integrated circuit component that acts as an electronic switch that opens or closes the circuit for electrical charges
f. ROM chips that contain permanently written data, instructions, or information
g. determines the number of bits that the computer can transmit at one time
h. the use of software to emulate hardware capabilities, enabling computers to scale, or adjust up or down, storage, processing power, or bandwidth as needed
i. small piece of semiconducting materials, usually silicon, on which integrated circuits are etched
j. number of bits the processor can interpret and execute at a given time

STUDENT ASSIGNMENTS

❋ Problem Solving

The Problem Solving exercises extend your knowledge of module concepts by seeking solutions to practical problems with technology that you may encounter at home, school, work, or with nonprofit organizations. The Collaboration exercise should be completed with a team.

Instructions: You often can solve problems with technology in multiple ways. Determine a solution to the problems in these exercises by using one or more resources available to you (such as a computer or mobile device, articles on the web or in print, blogs, podcasts, videos, television, user guides, other individuals, electronics or computer stores, etc.). Describe your solution, along with the resource(s) used, in the format requested by your instructor (brief report, presentation, discussion, blog post, video, or other means).

Personal

1. **No Matching Port** Your uncle has given you a new monitor for your computer. When you attempt to connect it, you notice that none of the ports on the back of your computer is able to accept the connector at the end of the monitor's cable. What are your next steps?

2. **Incompatible Power Adapter** While using your laptop, you notice the battery life is running low. When you plug in the AC adapter that was included with the laptop, an error message is displayed stating that the AC adapter is incompatible. You unplug the AC adapter and plug it back in, but the same message keeps appearing. Why might this be happening?

iStockphoto.com / Freer Law

3. **Nonworking Fan** Each time you turn on your computer, you hear the noise generated by the fans in the system unit. Recently, however, you turned on the computer and noticed that the noise was not as loud and that the fan in the back of the system unit was not spinning. What are your next steps?

4. **Missing Smartphone** You have just returned from the mall and seem to have forgotten your smartphone. You checked all over your house and your car, and it is nowhere to be found. What are your next steps?

5. **Low Battery Life** You have had your laptop for more than one year and notice that your battery is losing its charge more quickly than normal. What are some ways you can conserve battery life so that your smartphone does not lose its charge as quickly?

Professional

6. **Determining Memory Requirements** Your computer has been running slowly and you suspect it is because it is low on memory. You review the computer's hardware configuration and find that the computer has only 4 GB of RAM. How can you determine how much memory your computer should have to run properly?

7. **Selecting the Right Processor** Your boss has given you permission to purchase a new processor for your aging desktop computer, but many models are available. What steps will you take to make sure you purchase the processor that is best for you?

8. **Plug and Play Error** You have connected an external hard drive to your computer so that you can back up your important files, but the computer is not recognizing the external hard drive when it is connected. What might be wrong?

9. **Internet Access Unavailable** You are using a cloud storage provider to save files you want to use both at work and at home, so that you do not have to carry a USB flash drive back and forth with your files. When you arrive at work, you notice that your Internet connection is unavailable and you are unable to access the files stored on the cloud. What steps can you take to prevent this in the future?

10. **System Password** You started working at a company to replace someone who has just been terminated. When you turn on your computer, which previously was used by the terminated employee, the computer immediately asks for a system password. You do not know the password but need to access the computer so that you can start working. What are your next steps?

Collaboration

11. **Technology in Publishing** You have been hired to select employees for the IT (information technology) department in a start-up publishing company. Before you can begin hiring employees, you must familiarize yourself with the technology requirements in the publishing industry. Form a team of three people to compose a plan for creating the IT department. One team member should research the hardware requirements for people working in the publishing industry. Another team member should research the types of software used in this industry, and the third team member should compile a list of interview questions to ask each candidate.

The How To: Your Turn exercises present general guidelines for fundamental skills when using a computer or mobile device and then require that you determine how to apply these general guidelines to a specific program or situation.

How To: Your Turn

Instructions: You often can complete tasks using technology in multiple ways. Figure out how to perform the tasks described in these exercises by using one or more resources available to you (such as a computer or mobile device, articles on the web or in print, online or program help, user guides, blogs, podcasts, videos, other individuals, trial and error, etc.). Summarize your 'how to' steps, along with the resource(s) used, in the format requested by your instructor (brief report, presentation, discussion, blog post, video, or other means).

❶ Conserve Battery Life of Mobile Computers and Devices

As consumers rely on mobile computers and devices more and more every day, it is increasingly important for the battery life on these devices to support high usage demands. Unfortunately, battery life on these devices often is not sufficient for many users to make it throughout the day with moderate activity on their devices. For this reason, it is important to conserve battery life so that a mobile computer or device can remain functional until it is possible to connect it to a battery charger. The following steps guide you through the process of conserving battery life on mobile computers and devices:

a. When you first obtain a new mobile computer or device or purchase a new battery for your computer or mobile device, charge the battery completely. Most new mobile computers and devices will indicate how long to charge the battery before its first use. Refrain from using the device before the battery is fully charged.

b. Charge the battery only when it is drained completely. Many batteries on computers and mobile devices can be charged only a certain number of times before they fail completely. For this reason, you should charge batteries only when absolutely necessary.

c. When you charge your mobile computer or device, try not to unplug the battery charger until the battery is charged completely.

d. Use the battery charger supplied with the mobile computer or device. Connecting inexpensive battery chargers from other vendors may damage the battery.

e. If you want to use the mobile computer or device while it is plugged in to an external power source, remove the battery, if possible, if it is fully charged. Leaving the mobile computer or device connected to an external power source while the battery has a full charge can shorten the life of the battery.

f. If you are using a laptop or tablet, disable Wi-Fi and Bluetooth unless you are using them.

g. Adjust the display's brightness. Brighter displays consume more battery life, so keep the display as dim as you can without having to strain your eyes.

h. Download and install an app that will inform you which other apps are running and consuming battery life. If an app does not need to run, you should exit it so that the app does not consume your battery.

i. Avoid turning your mobile computer or device on and off multiple times per day. The power-saving features on mobile computers and devices often require less power than turning on your computer or mobile device from a powered-off state.

j. Turn off automatic app update capabilities on your phone or mobile device, so that your device is not constantly checking for new apps and downloading them to your device.

Exercises

1. What other ways can you think of to conserve the battery life on your mobile computer or device?
2. Approximately how long do batteries on your mobile computers and devices last before they no longer are able to hold a charge?
3. What else can shorten the battery life on a mobile computer or device?

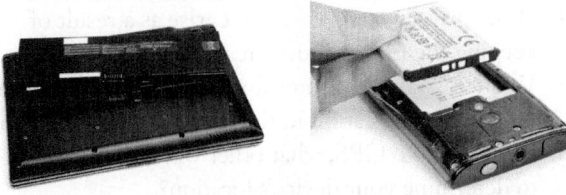

Thejipen / Dreamstime.com; Anaken2012 / Dreamstime.com

❷ Locate a Lost Mobile Computer or Device

Mobile computers and devices sometimes contain a feature that can help you locate it in the event you lose it. If the device does not contain this feature, you may be able to download and install an app that can help you track its location. The following steps guide you through the process of locating a lost mobile computer or device.

✳ How To: Your Turn

a. Before you lose or misplace a mobile computer or device, enable the feature that allows you to track its location remotely.

b. Make sure the GPS feature on your device is enabled. If GPS is not enabled, the device might be more difficult to locate.

c. If you lose your smartphone, try calling it to see if someone answers. He or she may have located your misplaced phone. If nobody answers, send it a text message inquiring about the phone's location.

d. If you lose a device, you can run an app or navigate to a website that will enable you to track the device's location. The device's location typically will be displayed on a map and include the approximate address.

e. If the device is in an unfamiliar location, use a service such as Google Maps to obtain driving directions to the location.

f. If the device is in a location other than where you originally lost it, exercise extreme caution while trying to retrieve your device. You might consider contacting a local law enforcement agency to accompany you while trying to retrieve your device.

g. If you are unable to track your device using the above suggestions, consider contacting your mobile service provider to see if they have a way to locate the device.

iStockphoto.com / Krystian Nawrocki

Exercises

1. What privacy concerns might arise as a result of keeping the GPS feature on a device enabled?

2. What are names of some apps that can help you track your device's location in the event it is lost or stolen?

3. In addition to GPS, what other ways might you be able to determine your device's location?

❸ Run Diagnostic Tools and Check for Computer Hardware Errors

If your computer is not functioning properly and you believe the problem is related to the computer's hardware, you can run diagnostic tools to check for hardware errors. If the diagnostic tool identifies a hardware error, you then can communicate information about the error to technical support personnel so that they either can correct the problem or suggest replacing the problematic hardware. The following steps guide

you through the process of running diagnostic tools and checking for hardware errors.

Obtain Diagnostic Tools

Your computer may have included diagnostic tools you can use to check for hardware errors. If it did not include diagnostic tools, follow these steps to download diagnostic tools from the computer manufacturer's website:

a. Navigate to the computer manufacturer's website.

b. Click the necessary links to display information about the computer.

c. Click the link to display a page containing drivers and/or downloads for the computer's model.

d. Browse for a diagnostic tool that you can download to your computer.

e. Some diagnostic tools can run within the operating system, and some require that you copy them to an optical disc or USB flash drive so that you can start the computer from this media and run the diagnostic tools. If necessary, copy the diagnostic tools to an optical disc or USB flash drive.

Run Diagnostic Tools

a. Run the program containing the diagnostic tools. If you copied the diagnostic tools to an optical disc or USB flash drive, restart the computer with the optical disc or USB flash drive inserted, and be sure to select the option to boot (start) from that device.

b. Select the option to scan all computer hardware for errors.

c. Begin the scan. Please note that because the program is scanning all hardware, it may take some time to complete. Some specific tests during the scan will require input from you, so watch the computer closely while the scan is in progress.

d. When the scan is complete, note any errors and, if desired, report them to the computer manufacturer's technical support team.

e. When the scan is complete, if necessary, restart the computer.

Exercises

1. What might cause you to use diagnostic tools to scan a computer for hardware errors?

2. After scanning your computer for hardware errors, were any found?

3. In addition to downloading drivers from the computer manufacturer's website, do any other websites offer tools to help you diagnose your computer hardware problems? If so, what are examples?

The Internet Research exercises broaden your understanding of module concepts by requiring that you search for information on the web.

Internet Research

Instructions: Use a search engine or another search tool to locate the information requested or answers to questions presented in the exercises. Describe your findings, along with the search term(s) you used and your web source(s), in the format requested by your instructor (brief report, presentation, discussion, blog post, video, or other means).

1 Making Use of the Web
Content Aggregation and Curation

Locating valuable information to read on particular topics or to share with your online social network may take some effort. To help find material, you may want to use content aggregation, an automated process that uses keywords to gather and filter materials someone else has written or produced on the Internet. Another option is content curation, which is a manual process of acquiring this information and then expanding the content into original and useful material to post. A good content curator can edit the content to share, add annotations and notes, give attributions to the original source, and provide additional viewpoints. As a starting point, Twitter and blog feeds, bookmarking tools such as StumbleUpon, and services that provide email notifications, such as Google Alerts, provide the opportunity to view webpages, photos, videos, and additional material about celebrities, sports, politics, businesses, and other people and subjects.

Research This: (a) Visit StumbleUpon and two other bookmarking services. If necessary, sign in to these services and compare the features. How do users select the categories to view? What information is required to create a profile? What opportunities for feedback are provided? What procedure would users follow to delete their profiles and terminate their accounts?

(b) Visit Google Alerts and two other email alerting services. If necessary, create an alert for at least two words for which you would want to receive email notifications. What options are available to customize these alerts? For example, can you specify the frequency of the alerts, the

types of websites to search, the geographical region, or the number of messages sent?

2 Social Media
Social Media Feedback

Companies review the conversations, comments, complaints, and feedback written on online social networks to obtain valuable information that ultimately enhances developing or improving products and services. In some cases, companies have asked consumers to view videos of product demonstrations, Tweet their immediate impressions, and suggest improvements. Small companies with limited marketing and advertising budgets, in particular, increasingly view social media as an inexpensive means of building relationships with and among customers. Social media users interact with others who have similar interests and exchange information about their experiences. In general, companies have found that customers are eager to provide feedback and recommend improvements.

Research This: View at least two automotive websites and describe the social media that are featured. Choose one of the websites and review the content. What topics are being discussed? In which ways is the company encouraging participation, such as by sponsoring contests or providing opportunities for consumers to upload photos and videos? Can consumers create an account to share advice, rate and review vehicles, and discuss mechanical issues?

3 Search Skills
Limiting Search Results by Website, Date, and Location

You can instruct a search engine to look for results on a specific website that match your search text. To do so, in your search text include the operator site: followed by a domain name you would like to search, with no spaces between the colon and the domain name. For example, to read articles from the Cnet website about solid state drives, type the search text, site:cnet.com "solid state drives".

Some search engines provide additional search tools to specify a date range such as the past day, week, or month, to limit your results. Limiting search results by date can help you to find current information because the search engine will return results published

Source: StumbleUpon

✳ Internet Research

during a specified period. Providing a location or ZIP code as search options will limit search results to the geographic area you specify. Location search can help you find results for a specific area, such as computer stores in Boise, Idaho.

Source: Google

Research This: Create search text using the techniques described above or in previous Search Skills exercises, and type it in a search engine to answer these questions. (1) Find information on Intel's website about core I7 processors that was posted within the past month. (2) Where in your local area can you recycle used computer equipment and electronics? (3) Find reviews of digital cameras posted within the past week. (4) Which laptops reviewed during the past six months have the longest battery life?

❹ Security
Securing Devices

More than 3 million smartphones are stolen each year, according to a *Consumer Reports* survey. In addition, 1.4 million smartphone users never have recovered a lost phone. Secure IT 6-1 in this module describes categories of products that can help secure and track hardware that has been stolen or lost.

Research This: Which apps are available for your smartphone to erase data remotely? Which location-tracking apps allow you to take a photo of the thief and then send an email message that contains the image to you automatically? If your device is lost and you file a police report, you will need the device's serial number. Locate that number now and write it on a piece of paper. Also, locate the phone's

15-digit International Mobile Equipment Identity (IMEI) number and record that number. Store the document with these two numbers in a secure location. In addition, research the efforts by the U.S. Federal Communications Commission (FCC) and the Cellular Telecommunications Industry Association (CTIA) to create a centralized database of lost and stolen mobile phones. What is the status of this database? What legislation has been proposed or passed that requires wireless carriers and phone manufacturers to develop technological solutions that can curb the growing problem of violent smartphone theft?

❺ Cloud Services
Public, Private, Hybrid, and Personal Clouds (IaaS)

When deciding how to host data and apps on the cloud, companies often choose between sharing a server on the cloud with other organizations, configuring a dedicated server on the cloud, or using both options. Companies must consider the type of data involved and the level of security required to keep it safe. Public, private, and hybrid clouds are examples of IaaS (infrastructure as a service), a service of cloud computing that uses a provider's hardware to manage, store and access files and apps over the Internet. On a public cloud, several companies store data or apps on the same physical server on the cloud. On a private cloud, a company has its own servers in the cloud to host its apps and data. On a hybrid cloud, organizations may host confidential data on a private cloud and rely on a public cloud for information that does not require such a high degree of security.

Individual users may set up a personal cloud by purchasing a networked hard drive. A networked hard drive connects directly to a router, providing access to its files over the Internet. This is a useful solution for having access to files from several devices.

Research This: (1) Use a search engine to find IaaS providers that offer public, private, and hybrid cloud solutions. Summarize the different solutions they provide. (2) Under what circumstances might an individual or enterprise set up a public, private, or hybrid cloud? (3) Research networked hard drive models from different manufacturers. Compare their costs, storage sizes, and additional features to consider when creating a personal cloud. (4) When might you create a personal cloud instead of using a cloud storage provider?

The Critical Thinking exercises challenge your assessment and decision-making skills by presenting real-world situations associated with module concepts. The Collaboration exercise should be completed with a team.

Critical Thinking

Instructions: Evaluate the situations below, using personal experiences and one or more resources available to you (such as articles on the web or in print, blogs, podcasts, videos, television, user guides, other individuals, electronics or computer stores, etc.). Perform the tasks requested in each exercise and share your deliverables in the format requested by your instructor (brief report, presentation, discussion, blog post, video, or other means).

1. Cloud Storage

The owner of the motorcycle repair shop where you work as a part-time office manager is seeking alternatives to using a network server to store and back up files. She asks you to investigate the feasibility of using cloud storage, rather than purchasing additional storage media for the company's computers, mobile devices, and network servers.

Do This: Analyze the advantages and disadvantages of using cloud storage. Include in your discussion security concerns, costs, and a comparison between two different cloud storage offerings. Which company offers the better arrangement? Why? Explore one other area of cloud computing, such as SaaS (software as a service), and determine how the service might benefit the shop. Find three providers of the cloud service and compare prices, user reviews, and features. List the risks and benefits of using the cloud for storage and other services.

2. Upgrading Memory

You are an IT consultant at a bank. An analyst at the bank is complaining that her laptop is performing slowly. You determine that the laptop's memory is insufficient for the complex calculations and reports the analyst is running.

Do This: Search the web to learn more about current memory modules available to increase memory capacity. Evaluate the differences among various options, including type, size, speed, and price. Find articles from industry experts that list methods and recommendations for upgrading a laptop's memory. Also determine how to add memory to a laptop, obtaining answers to the following questions: How can you determine the type and correct amount of memory to add? Why should you not purchase more memory than your computer can support? How do you determine the available slots for memory modules? What safety measures should you take when upgrading memory? Is it better to upgrade the memory or purchase a new laptop?

3. Case Study

Family-Owned Coffee Shop   You are the new manager for a family-owned coffee shop. You recently purchased replacement smartphones for yourself and another employee, along with an upgraded tablet that the staff can use. Because you are discarding the outdated devices, the coffee shop's owners are concerned about how to secure and protect data when selling, donating, or recycling the devices. The owners asked you to prepare information they can use in a notice to educate the shop's employees about keeping data secure when discarding a device.

Do This: Determine the possible steps needed to wipe the memory and storage media in the devices. What kind of data is important to delete? Why? What are the risks of not wiping the memory and storage media in a device before you discard it? What responsibility does the coffee shop have to protect customers' personal data? Why? Does choosing whether to sell, donate, or recycle the devices change your approach and need to wipe the devices' memory? Why or why not?

TerryM / Shutterstock.com

Collaboration

4. **Mobile Device Batteries**   You work in the IT department for a large publishing company that just purchased new tablets for all employees. The department manager asked you to prepare information about how to conserve the battery life of the tablets.

Do This: Form a three-member team. Each member of your team should choose a different type of tablet. Find information about the battery life for each device type, including recommendations for use by the manufacturer and user reviews of the device and its chargers. Research apps that track battery life. Search for articles by industry experts that give tips on conserving the battery life of a tablet. Meet with your team, and discuss and compile your findings. Which tablet would you recommend? Why? How does the charger affect the battery life? What did you learn about battery conservation? Which apps would you recommend? Why?

Input and Output: Extending Capabilities of Computers and Mobile Devices

7

Nina Masic / Alamy Stock Photo

OBJECTIVES

After completing this module, you will be able to:

1 Differentiate among various types of keyboards: standard, compact, on-screen, virtual, ergonomic, gaming, and wireless

2 Describe characteristics of various pointing devices: mouse, touchpad, and trackball

3 Describe various uses of touch screens

4 Describe various types of pen input: stylus, digital pen, and graphics tablet

5 Describe various uses of motion input, voice input, and video input

6 Differentiate among various scanners and reading devices: optical scanners, optical readers, bar code readers, RFID readers, magstripe readers, MICR readers, and data collection devices

7 Identify the types of output

8 Explain the characteristics of various displays

9 Summarize the various types of printers: ink-jet printers, photo printers, laser printers, all-in-one printers, 3-D printers, thermal printers, mobile printers, label printers, plotters and large-format printers, and impact printers

10 Identify the purpose and features of speakers, headphones and earbuds, data projectors, interactive whiteboards, and force-feedback game controllers and tactile output

11 Identify various assistive technology input and output methods

What Is Input?

Input is any data and instructions entered into the memory of a computer. Figure 7-1 shows a variety of options for entering data and instructions into a computer.

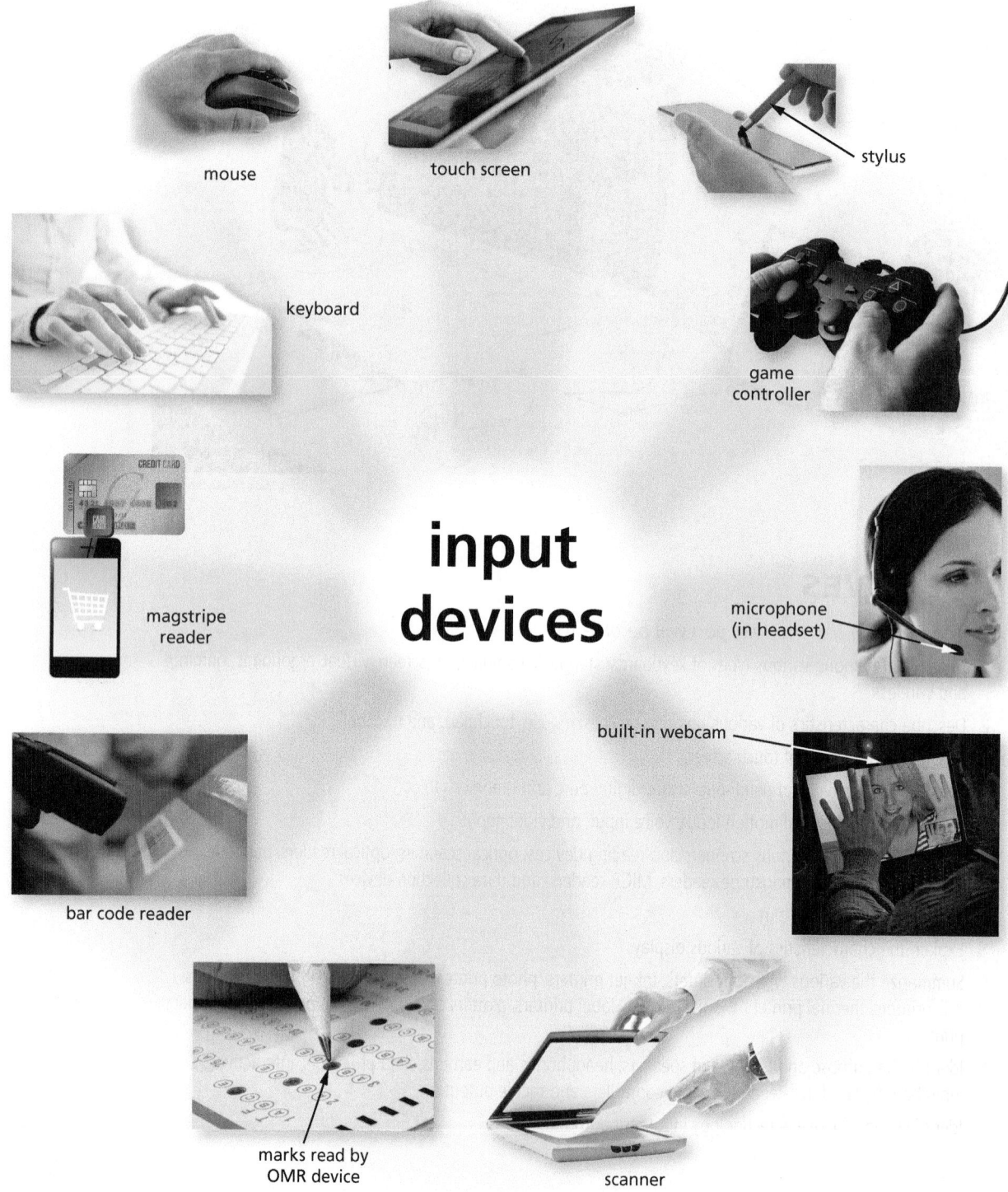

Figure 7-1   Users can enter data and instructions into computers and mobile devices in a variety of ways.

As discussed in Module 1, *data* is a collection of unprocessed items, including text, numbers, images, audio, and video. Once data is in memory, a computer or mobile device interprets and executes instructions to process the data into information. Instructions that a computer or mobile device processes can be in the form of software (programs and apps), commands, and user responses.

- *Software* is a series of related instructions, organized for a common purpose, that tells a computer or mobile device what tasks to perform and how to perform them. When software developers write programs or apps, they usually enter the instructions into the computer or mobile device by using a keyboard, mouse, or other input method. The software developer then stores the program or app in a file that a user can execute (run). When a user runs a program or app, the computer or mobile device loads the program or app from a storage medium into memory. Thus, a program or app is entered into a computer's or mobile device's memory.
- A *command* is an instruction that causes a program or app to perform a specific action. Programs and apps respond to commands that a user issues. Users issue commands in a variety of ways, which include touching an area on a screen, pressing keys on the keyboard, clicking a mouse button to control a pointer on the screen, or speaking into a microphone.
- A *user response* is an instruction a user issues by responding to a message displayed by a program or app. A response to the message instructs the program or app to perform certain actions. For example, when a program or app asks the question, 'Do you want to save the changes made to this file?', and you respond with the instruction of 'Yes', the program or app will save the file with the changes you made. If you respond with the instruction of 'No', the program or app will not save your changes before exiting.

Commonly used input methods include the keyboard, pointing devices, touch screens, pen input, motion input, voice input, video input, and scanners and reading devices. This module discusses each of these input methods.

Keyboards

Most computers and mobile devices include a keyboard or keyboarding capabilities. As discussed in previous modules, a **keyboard** is an input device that contains keys you press to enter data and instructions into a computer or mobile device. Nearly all keyboards have a typing area, function keys, toggle keys, and navigation keys (Figure 7-2). Many also include media control buttons, Internet control buttons, and other special keys. Others may include a fingerprint reader or a pointing device.

- The typing area includes letters of the alphabet, numbers, punctuation marks, and other basic keys. Read Secure IT 7-1 to learn about software that can track your keystrokes.
- *Function keys*, which are labeled with the letter F followed by a number, are special keys programmed to issue commands to a computer. The command associated with a function key may vary, depending on the program or app you are using.
- A *toggle key* is a key that switches between two states each time a user presses the key. CAPS LOCK and NUM LOCK are examples of toggle keys. Many mobile devices have keys that toggle the display of alphabetic, numeric, and symbols on touch keyboards in order to display more characters and symbols on a keyboard with fewer keys.
- Users can press the navigation keys, such as arrow keys and PAGE UP/PG UP and PAGE DOWN/PG DN on the keyboard, to move the insertion point in a program or app left, right, up, or down.
- A *keyboard shortcut* is one or more keyboard keys that you press to perform an operating system or application-related task. Some keyboard shortcuts are unique to a particular application or operating system.
- Media control buttons allow you to control a media player program, access the computer's optical disc drive, and adjust speaker volume.
- Internet control buttons allow you to run an email application, run a browser, and search the web.

 BTW

Insertion Point
The *insertion point*, also known as a *cursor* in some programs or apps, is a symbol on the screen, usually a blinking vertical bar, that indicates where the next character you type will appear.

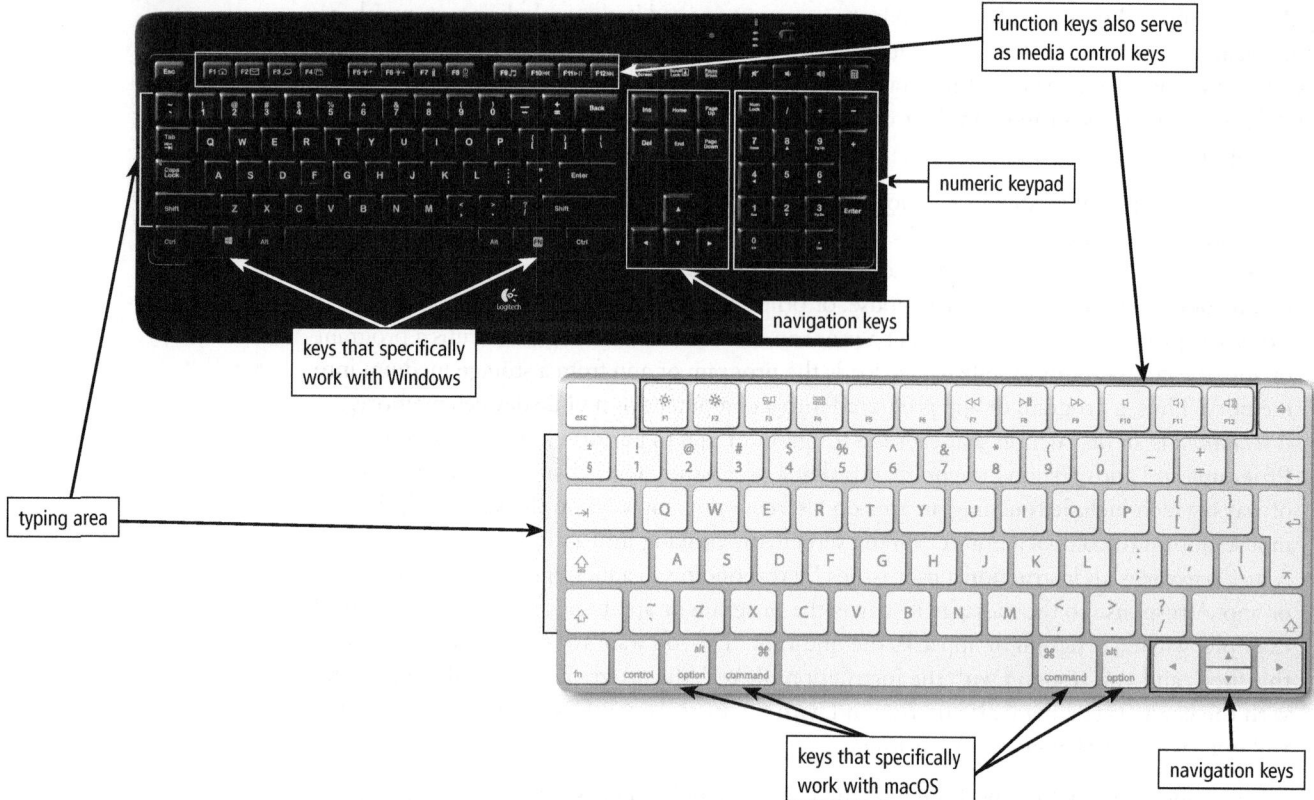

Figure 7-2   On a standard keyboard, you type using keys in the typing area and on the numeric keypad. Some of the keys on standard keyboards differ, depending on the operating system with which they are designed to work.

Courtesy of Logitech; GreenLandStudio / Shutterstock.com

✴ SECURE IT 7-1

Keyboard Monitoring

Some employers and parents want to monitor everything that has been entered into a computer to ensure that employees and children are using the computer for appropriate purposes. They may use *keyboard monitoring software*, also called *keylogging software*, to accomplish this task. This software runs undetected and stores every keystroke in a file for later retrieval.

These programs have both criminal and beneficial purposes. When used in a positive fashion, employers can measure the efficiency of data entry personnel. This software also can verify that employees are not releasing company secrets, are not viewing personal or inappropriate content on work computers, and are not engaging in activities that could subject the company to harassment, hacking, or other similar charges. Employers sometimes use the software to troubleshoot technical problems and to back up their networks. Parents, likewise, can verify their children are using the home computer safely and are not

visiting inappropriate websites. Educators and researchers can capture students' input to analyze how well they are learning a second language or improving their typing skills. This software also can monitor activity in chat rooms and other similar locations.

When used for malicious purposes, criminals use the programs on both public and private computers to capture user names, passwords, credit card numbers, and other sensitive data and then use this data to access financial accounts and private networks.

Many keylogging programs are available, and they perform a variety of functions. Some simply record keystrokes in a hidden file stored on a hard drive that can be accessed by supplying the correct password. More sophisticated programs record software used, websites visited, and periodic screenshots and then transmit this data to a remote computer.

It can be difficult to locate keylogging software on a computer, but taking these steps may help detect these programs:

- **Run detection software regularly.** Several antivirus and spyware detection programs check for known keylogging programs.

- **Review hard drive files.** Regularly look at the most recent files and note any that are updated continually. These files might be the keylogging software's logs.

- **Check running programs.** Periodically examine which software is loaded from the computer's hard drive into memory when you start the computer and which are running while you are using the computer. If you are uncertain of any program names, perform a search to learn the software's function and if it is a known keylogging program.

✴ **Consider This:** Do you know anyone who has installed keylogging software or who has found keylogging software installed on his or her computer? Is keylogging software an invasion of privacy? Should employers inform employees if the software is installed? Why or why not?

Types of Keyboards

Desktops include a standard keyboard. Standard keyboards typically have from 101 to 105 keys, which often include function keys along the top and a numeric keypad on the right (shown in the top keyboard in Figure 7-2).

As discussed in previous modules, you have a variety of keyboard options for mobile computers and devices (Figure 7-3). These devices often use a *compact keyboard*, which is smaller than a standard keyboard and usually does not include the numeric keypad or navigation keys. Typically, the keys on a compact keyboard serve two or three purposes in order to provide the same functionality as standard keyboards. Some compact keyboards are built into the computer or mobile device and/or are permanently attached with hinges, a sliding mechanism, or some other technique. Other compact keyboards are separate devices that communicate wirelessly or attach to the computer or device with a magnet, clip, or other mechanism. Some users prefer to work with on-screen or virtual keyboards instead of a physical keyboard. Others, however, prefer to use a standard keyboard with their mobile devices because these keyboards provide added functionality and tactile comfort.

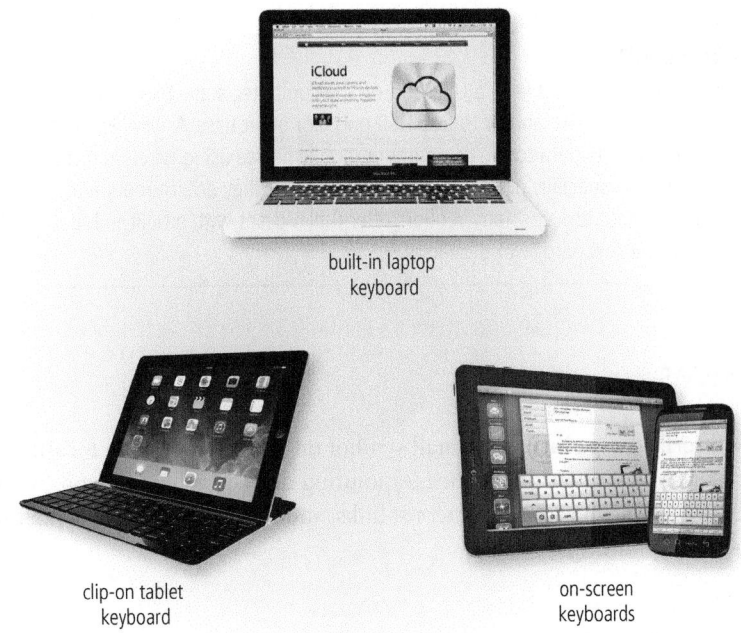

built-in laptop
keyboard

clip-on tablet
keyboard

on-screen
keyboards

Figure 7-3 Users have a variety of keyboard options for mobile computers and devices.

iStockphoto.com / EricVega; iStockphoto.com / pictafolio; Courtesy of Logitech

---

✿ CONSIDER THIS

What is the rationale for the arrangement of keys in the typing area?

The keys originally were arranged on old mechanical typewriters to separate frequently used keys, which caused typists to slow down. This arrangement, called a QWERTY keyboard because the six first letters on the top row of letter keys spell QWERTY, reduced the frequency with which the mechanical levers jammed.

An *ergonomic keyboard* has a design that reduces the chance of repetitive strain injuries (RSIs) of the wrist and hand (Figure 7-4). Recall that the goal of ergonomics is to incorporate comfort, efficiency, and safety in the design of the workplace. Even keyboards that are not ergonomically designed attempt to offer a user more comfort by including a wrist rest.

Figure 7-4   An ergonomic keyboard.
Dmitry Melnikov / Shutterstock.com

A *gaming keyboard* is a keyboard designed specifically for users who enjoy playing games on the computer. Gaming keyboards typically include programmable keys so that gamers can customize the keyboard to the game being played. The keys on gaming keyboards light up so that the keys are visible in all lighting conditions. Some have small displays that show important game statistics, such as time or targets remaining.

 CONSIDER THIS

Why use a wireless keyboard?
Although some keyboards connect via a cable to a USB port on the computer, some users choose a wireless keyboard to eliminate the clutter of a cord and/or to free USB ports for other uses. A *wireless keyboard* is a battery-powered device that transmits data to the computer or mobile device using wireless technology. For example, Bluetooth keyboards are especially popular with tablets because they do not require a USB port and are easy to pair with computers and devices. Many vendors offer tablet cases with a built-in Bluetooth keyboard so that you easily can transport a keyboard with the tablet.

Pointing Devices

In a graphical user interface, a **pointer** is a small symbol on the screen whose location and shape change as a user moves a pointing device. A pointing device can enable you to select text, graphics, and other objects, such as buttons, icons, links, and menu commands. The following pages discuss a variety of pointing devices.

Mouse

A **mouse** is a pointing device that fits under the palm of your hand comfortably. As you move a mouse, the pointer on the screen also moves. The bottom of a mouse is flat and contains a mechanism that detects movement of the mouse. Desktop users have an optical mouse or a touch mouse, both of which can be placed on nearly all types of flat surfaces (Figure 7-5).

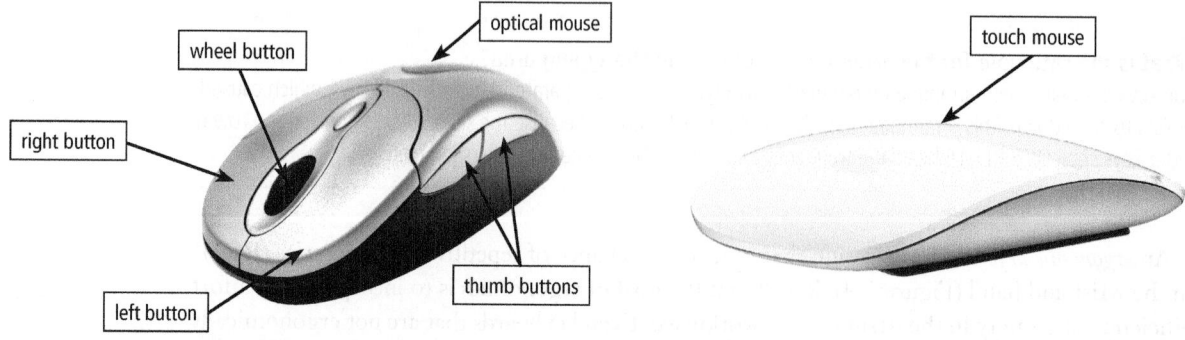

Figure 7-5   An optical mouse has buttons. A touch mouse often has no buttons.
Anton Derevschuk / Shutterstock.com; Courtesy of Apple, Inc.

An *optical mouse* uses optical sensors that emit and sense light to detect the mouse's movement. Similarly, a *laser mouse* uses laser sensors that emit and sense light to detect the mouse's movement. Some mouse devices use a combination of both technologies. The top and sides of an optical or laser mouse may have one to four buttons; some may also have a small wheel. Some are more sensitive than others for users requiring more precision, such as graphic artists, engineers, or game players.

A *touch mouse* is a touch-sensitive mouse that recognizes touch gestures, in addition to detecting movement of the mouse and traditional click and scroll operations. For example, you press a location on a touch mouse to simulate a click, sweep your thumb on the mouse to scroll pages, or slide multiple fingers across the mouse to zoom.

As with keyboards, you can purchase an ergonomic mouse to help reduce the chance of RSIs or to reduce pain and discomfort associated with RSIs.

 CONSIDER THIS

Why use a wireless mouse?
As with keyboards, some users choose a wireless mouse to eliminate the clutter of a cord. A *wireless mouse* is a battery-powered device that transmits data using wireless technology. A wireless mouse typically transmits data to a receiver that plugs in a USB port or uses Bluetooth technology to pair with the device.

Touchpad

A **touchpad** is a small, flat, rectangular pointing device that is sensitive to pressure and motion (Figure 7-6). Touchpads are found most often on laptops and convertible tablets. Desktop users who prefer the convenience of a touchpad can purchase a separate touchpad, which usually communicates wirelessly with the computer.

To move the pointer using a touchpad, slide your fingertip across the surface of the pad. Some touchpads have one or more buttons around the edge of the pad that work like mouse buttons; others have no buttons. On most touchpads, you also can tap the pad's surface to imitate mouse operations, such as clicking. Some touchpads also recognize touch gestures, such as swipe, pinch, and stretch motions.

 BTW
Trackpad
Apple uses the term, *trackpad*, to refer to the touchpad on its laptops.

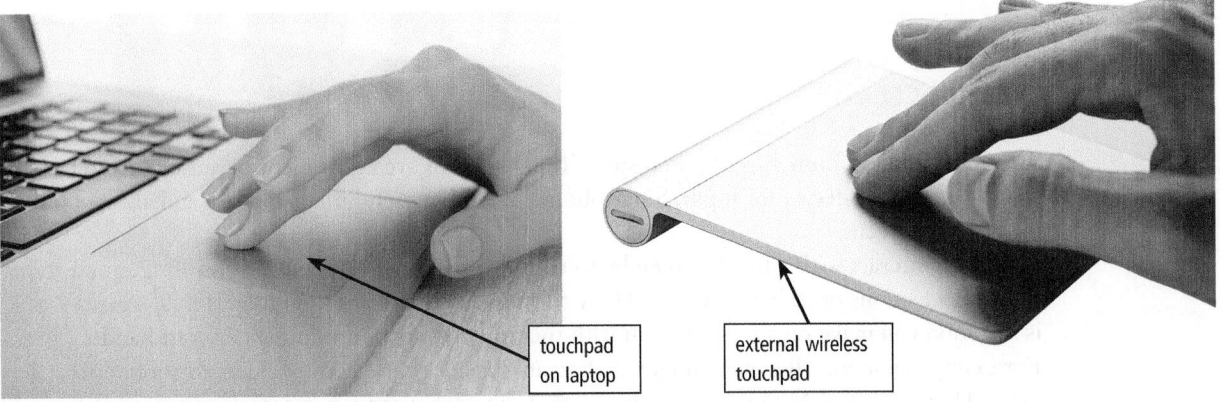

touchpad on laptop

external wireless touchpad

Figure 7-6 Laptop users often use the touchpad to control movement of the pointer. You also can purchase an external wireless touchpad for use with desktops and tablets.
Africa Studio / Shutterstock.com; iStockphoto.com / Goldmund

 CONSIDER THIS

What is a pointing stick?
Some mobile computer keyboards contain a pointing stick, which is a pressure-sensitive pointing device shaped like a pencil eraser positioned between its keys. To move the pointer using a pointing stick, you push the pointing stick with a finger.

Trackball

A **trackball** is a stationary pointing device with a ball on its top or side. The ball in most trackballs is about the size of a Ping-Pong ball. Some devices, called a trackball mouse, combine the functionality of both a trackball and a mouse (Figure 7-7).

Figure 7-7   Shown here is a trackball mouse, which is a single device that provides the functionality of both a trackball and a mouse.
iStockphoto.com / peng wu

To move the pointer using a trackball, you rotate the ball with your thumb, fingers, or the palm of your hand. In addition to the ball, a trackball usually has one or more buttons that work like mouse buttons.

 CONSIDER THIS

Why use a trackball instead of a mouse?
For users who have limited desk space, a trackball is a good alternative to a mouse because the device is stationary. Keep in mind, however, that a trackball requires frequent cleaning because it picks up oils from fingers and dust from the environment.

Touch Screens

A **touch screen** is a touch-sensitive display. Touch screens are convenient because they do not require a separate device for input. Smartphones and tablets, and many laptops and all-in-ones offer touch screens.

You can interact with a touch screen by touching areas of the screen with your finger or a stylus to make selections or to begin typing. Many touch screens also respond to gestures. A *gesture* is a motion you make on a touch screen with the tip of one or more fingers or your hand. For example, you can slide your finger to drag an object or pinch your fingers to zoom out. (Read How To 1-1 in Module 1 for a description of widely used touch screen gestures.)

Touch screens that recognize multiple points of contact at the same time are known as *multi-touch*. Because gestures often require the use of multiple fingers (points of contact), touch screens that support gestures are multi-touch.

Tech Feature 7-1: Touch Input

Many new computers and devices are using touch as a primary method of input. In fact, newer operating systems are optimizing their user interfaces for touch input. Read Tech Feature 7-1 to learn about various devices that use touch input.

TECH FEATURE 7-1

Touch Input

Devices that utilize touch input include monitors for desktops and screens on laptops and tablets, smartphones, wearable devices, portable media players, digital cameras, tablets, kiosks, and navigation systems.

Desktop Monitors and Screens on Laptops and Tablets

An increasing number of desktop monitors and screens on laptops and tablets support touch input. These touch-enabled monitors and screens allow users to interact with the operating system without a keyboard or pointing device. Instead of using a mouse to click an object on the screen, users simply can tap or double-tap the item they otherwise would have clicked. For example, users can tap or double-tap an icon to run a program or an application, slide their finger to scroll, or use their finger to drag items across the screen.

Smartphones

Smartphones are becoming more functional, lighter weight, and now typically do not include a physical keyboard. Touch input can help smartphone manufacturers achieve all these goals. The gestures you might perform on a smartphone that supports touch input include tapping to run an app, sliding or swiping to scroll, and pinching and stretching to zoom. The absence of a physical keyboard makes it more difficult to type without looking at the screen, so it is not advisable to use a smartphone when performing actions that require undivided attention, such as driving a car or walking.

Wearable Devices

Wearable devices, such as smartwatches, do not have room for a physical keyboard, so they mainly rely on touch input. The gestures you might perform on a wearable device include tapping to make a selection, and sliding or swiping to scroll through the various screens.

Portable Media Players

Portable media players widely use touch as the primary method of input so that the size of the screen on the device is maximized. That is, space on the device does not have to be dedicated to other controls, such as buttons or click wheels. Users slide and swipe to browse their music libraries on their portable media players and then tap to select the song they want to play.

While songs are playing, users can tap the screen to display controls so that they can pause or stop the song, navigate to another song, or adjust the volume.

Digital Cameras

As digital cameras start to include built-in features to browse through and edit photos without requiring a computer, touch input helps digital camera users perform these functions with greater accuracy. For example, you can perform gestures such as swiping left and right on the screen to browse your photos, tapping the screen to identify the area on which you wish to focus when taking a picture, pinching and stretching to zoom while viewing photos, tapping areas of photos to remove red-eye, and dragging borders of photos to crop them.

Kiosks

Touch input also is used on devices where a keyboard and pointing device might not endure its high volume of use. Kiosks, such as those at an airport allowing you to check in for a flight, can be used by hundreds of people per day. Because kiosks are designed to help you perform a specific function as quickly as possible, touch input is ideal for their user-friendly interfaces. Users typically interact with kiosks by tapping various areas of the screen to select options (as discussed in Module 3). If typing is required, an on-screen keyboard is displayed so that users can enter information, such as their name or a confirmation number. Kiosks requiring sensitive or a significant amount of input also might include a separate keyboard and pointing device. For example, ATMs with touch screens often have a separate keypad to enter your PIN so that others are not able to see what you are typing.

Navigation Systems

Navigation systems in cars and other vehicles use touch input because typing on a separate keyboard is not wise while operating a vehicle. Navigation system users can perform actions such as tapping to enter a destination address, dragging to display different areas of the map, or pinching and stretching to zoom. Operating a navigation system with touch input requires you to take your eyes off the road to interact with the device, so you should operate a navigation system only while your vehicle is parked or stopped. To reduce the chances of driver distraction, some built-in navigation systems reduce functionality while the vehicle is in motion.

Consider This: Do you find it is easier to use touch input instead of using a keyboard or mouse? Does your answer depend on the type of device you are using or the task you are trying to accomplish? Why?

What is the purpose of a touch-sensitive pad?
Portable media players that do not have touch screens typically have a touch-sensitive pad. A *touch-sensitive pad* is an input device that contains buttons and/or wheels you operate with a thumb or other finger. Using the touch-sensitive pad, you can scroll through and play music; view photos; watch videos or movies; navigate through song, photo, or movie lists; display a menu; adjust volume; customize settings; and perform other actions. For example, users can rotate a portable media player's touch-sensitive pad to browse through the device's playlists and press the pad's buttons to play or pause media (Figure 7-8).

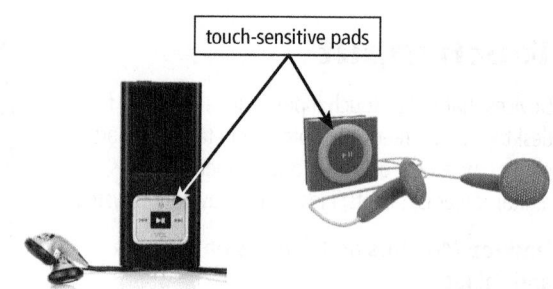

Figure 7-8 You use your thumb or finger to rotate or press buttons on a touch-sensitive pad, which commonly is found on portable media players.
iStockphoto.com / milindri; iStockphoto.com / Lusoimages

Pen Input

Some displays and mobile devices support pen input. With **pen input**, you touch a stylus or digital pen on a flat surface to write, draw, or make selections.

Stylus

A **stylus** is a small metal or plastic device that looks like a tiny ink pen but uses pressure instead of ink (Figure 7-9). Nearly all tablets and mobile devices, some laptop screens, and a few desktop monitors have touch screens that support pen input, in addition to touch input. These computers and devices may include a stylus. Some stylus designs include buttons you can press to simulate clicking a mouse.

Figure 7-9 You use a stylus to write, draw, or make selections on a touch screen that supports pen input.
iStockphoto.com / pixelfit; iStockphoto.com / pictafolio; iStockphoto.com / tirc83

To capture a handwritten signature, a user writes his or her name on a **signature capture pad** with a stylus that is attached to the device. Software then transmits the signature to a central computer, where the signature is stored. Retailers use signature capture pads to record purchasers' signatures. Signature capture pads often work with POS (point-of-sale) terminals and include a magstripe card reader, discussed later in the module.

Digital Pen

A **digital pen**, which is slightly larger than a stylus, is an input device that captures and converts a user's handwriting or drawings into a digital format, which users can upload (transfer) to a computer or mobile device. Some require the user to write or draw on special paper or a tablet; others can write or draw on any surface (Figure 7-10).

Once uploaded, *handwriting recognition software* on the computer or mobile device translates the handwritten letters and symbols created on the screen into typed text or objects that the computer or device can process. For this reason, digital pens most often are used for taking notes. Some are battery operated or USB powered; others use wireless technology, such as Bluetooth. Read Ethics & Issues 7-1 to consider whether you should take notes electronically or by hand.

Figure 7-10 Users take notes with a digital pen and then upload the notes to a computer or mobile device, where software translates the notes to typed text.
Courtesy of LiveScribe

digital pen

✸ ETHICS & ISSUES 7-1

Is It More Efficient to Take Notes by Hand or with a Digital Device?
When an instructor starts a lecture, he or she looks out at the classroom to see some students bent over a tablet, others frantically typing on a laptop, and still others using pen and paper to take notes. Which method is most effective for retaining knowledge?

A recent study concluded that students who used traditional pen and paper to take notes in class and while studying had better understanding and recall of information. The study concluded that when taking notes on a laptop, students tended to write down the speaker's exact words. Taking notes longhand required students to process the information, use their

own words, and select what information is important enough to write down. Tablet users tended to have a mix of both transcribed and selected content. Regardless of the note-taking method, students performed equally when asked to recall factual information. Laptop users, however, were less able to answer conceptual or interpretive questions than those who took notes longhand.

Another concern when using laptops and mobile devices in a classroom is distractibility. Students may receive notifications about activity on an online social network, or use Internet messaging or text messaging to communicate with others about unrelated topics. Research shows that laptop users have unrelated

programs or apps on their screen up to 40 percent of class time. Many instructors encourage students to use their computers and mobile devices for class related purposes. For example, some encourage students to Tweet answers to questions or research articles to support a fact or opinion. Others provide access to online forums in order for students to communicate with one another during or after class.

✸ **Consider This:** Should instructors inform students about the benefits of longhand note taking? Why or why not? Should students be required to take notes longhand? Why or why not? How else might you use your computer or mobile device during class time to further your own learning?

Graphics Tablet

To use pen input on a computer that does not have a touch screen, you can attach a graphics tablet to the computer. A **graphics tablet**, also called a *digitizer*, is an electronic plastic board that detects and converts movements of a stylus or digital pen into digital signals that are sent to the computer (Figure 7-11). Each location on the graphics tablet corresponds to a specific location on the screen. Architects, mapmakers, designers, and artists, for example, use graphics tablets to create images, sketches, or designs.

Motion, Voice, and Video Input

Many of today's computers, mobile devices, and game devices support motion, voice, and video input. The following sections discuss each of these input methods.

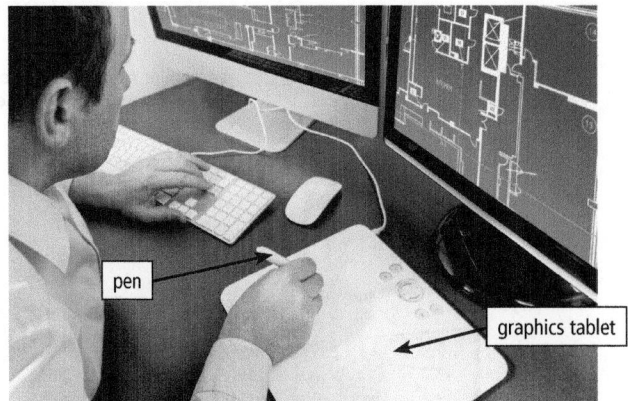

pen

graphics tablet

Figure 7-11 Architects use a graphics tablet to create blueprints.
iStockphoto.com / small_frog

Tech Feature 7-2: Motion Input

With *motion input*, sometimes called *gesture recognition*, users can guide on-screen elements using air gestures. *Air gestures* involve moving your body or a handheld input device through the air. With motion input, a device containing a camera detects your gesture and then converts it to a digital signal that is sent to a computer, mobile, or game device. For example, gamers can swing their arm or a controller to simulate rolling a bowling ball down a lane toward the pins. Read Tech Feature 7-2 to learn how a variety of fields use motion input.

⚜ **TECH FEATURE 7-2**

Motion Input

Until a few years ago, the idea of controlling a computer by waving your hands was seen only in Hollywood science fiction movies. Today, the entertainment industry (such as for gaming and animating movies), the military, athletics, and the medical field have found uses for motion input.

Motion-sensing devices communicate with a game console or a personal computer using wired or wireless technology. The console or computer translates a player's natural gestures, facial movements, and full-body motion into input. Although these devices originally were intended for gaming, developers are working on adapting them or using similar technology outside of the gaming and entertainment industries.

Entertainment

Motion-sensing game controllers enable a user to guide on-screen elements by moving a handheld input device through the air. Examples include handheld devices that enable gamers to use sweeping arm movements to simulate sports activities, such as a golf swing (shown in the figure below), balance boards that judge stability and motion when holding yoga poses, and remote control attachments, such as a steering wheel used to guide a car along a race course.

Some controllers track peripheral motion within a specific area. With these devices, users can move their finger to draw or move their whole body to dance or exercise. Some use a device that can track

controller translates motion of golf swing to move the golf ball on the screen

screen shows the position and movements of the avatar

player moves controller to simulate a golf swing

small finger gestures, enabling users to be more precise in their movements.

Facial motion capture converts people's facial movements into a digital format while they talk, smile, and more. Animators, for example, use the digital data to simulate facial movements to create realistic gaming avatars or computer-generated characters in movies. Facial movements, however, are more subtle and difficult to detect. Thus, the technology used for capturing facial motions requires more precision and a higher resolution than that required by gaming devices.

Military

Military uses of motion input include training, such as flight simulation or weapon usage. To ensure safety, trainees maneuver a helicopter or other device using motion input from a remote location. Motion input also aids in physical rehabilitation for wounded soldiers by providing a method for conducting physical therapy exercises outside of a military hospital. Another use of motion input is to assist in recovery from post-traumatic stress disorder. Sufferers of this ailment can use avatars and simulators to work through scenarios in a comfortable environment.

Athletics

Coaches and sports trainers use motion input to improve athletes' performance and to correct inefficient or injury-causing motions. Analyzing the arc of a pitcher's arm, and factoring the speed of the motion and the trajectory of the ball, can help improve a pitcher's accuracy and speed. Combining the athlete's motion input with complex algorithms can pinpoint areas in which the athlete can improve.

Medical Field

The medical field also uses motion input for training. For example, surgeons can practice new technologies in a simulated environment. Using motion input that enhances movements, surgeons also can operate less invasively. Surgeons even operate remotely, enabling experts to manipulate surgical devices and share their expertise to save lives around the world. Sports medicine specialists use motion input to assess injuries, determine treatment, and assist in physical therapy.

⚜ **Consider This:** Have you used a motion-sensing device or game controller? What were your impressions? What security issues surround military use of motion input? What issues might the medical field encounter when using motion input?

Voice and Audio Input

Voice input is the process of entering input by speaking into a microphone. The microphone may be built in the computer or device, in a headset, or an external peripheral device that sits on top of a desk or other surface. Some external microphones have a cable that attaches to a port on a computer; others communicate using wireless technology, such as Bluetooth.

Uses of voice input include Internet messaging that supports voice conversations, chat rooms that support voice chats, video calls, videoconferencing, VoIP, and voice recognition. Recall that VoIP enables users to speak to other users via their Internet connection. **Voice recognition**, also called *speech recognition*, is the computer or mobile device's capability of distinguishing spoken words. Some computers and mobile devices make use of built-in and third-party voice recognition applications, which have a natural language interface (Figure 7-12). A *voice recognition application* allows users to dictate text and enter instructions by speaking into a microphone.

Figure 7-12 With Siri, you can speak instructions and commands to the smartphone and its apps. As shown here, the user asks Siri about the weather, to which Siri replies by speaking a message and displaying the forecast.
Can Yesil/Shutterstock.com; Courtesy of Apple Inc.

On mobile devices, these applications allow users to speak simple, task-based instructions to the device, such as setting an alarm, entering a calendar appointment, or making a call. Some mobile devices have a *speech-to-text* feature, which recognizes a user's spoken words and enters them into email messages, text messages, or other applications that support typed text entry.

Audio Input Voice input is part of a larger category of input called audio input. *Audio input* is the process of entering any sound into the computer, such as speech, music, and sound effects. To enter high-quality sound into computer, the computer uses a sound card or integrated sound capability. Users enter sound into computers and mobile devices via devices such as microphones, CD/DVD/Blu-ray Disc players, or radios, each of which plugs in a port on the computer or device.

Some users also record live music and other sound effects into a computer by connecting external music devices, such as an electronic keyboard (Figure 7-13), guitar, drums, harmonica, and microphones, to a computer. Music production software allows users to record, compose, mix, and edit music and sounds. For example, music production software enables you to change the speed, add notes, or rearrange the score to produce an entirely new arrangement.

Figure 7-13 This sound engineer uses a computer to mix music.
iStockphoto.com / Chris Schmidt

 CONSIDER THIS

How do external music devices connect to a computer?
External music devices typically connect to USB and MIDI ports. When purchasing a music device, check its specifications for the type(s) of ports to which it connects.

Tech Feature 7-3: Digital Video Technology

Video input is the process of capturing full-motion images and storing them on a computer or mobile device's storage medium, such as a hard drive or optical disc. A **digital video (DV) camera** records video as digital signals, which you can transfer directly to a computer or mobile device with the appropriate connection. Read Tech Feature 7-3 to learn the steps involved in using DV technology.

✦ TECH FEATURE 7-3

Digital Video Technology

Everywhere you look, people are capturing videos using DV cameras and mobile devices with built-in digital cameras. Using **DV technology**, you can input, edit, manage, publish, and share your videos. You can enhance digital videos by adding scrolling titles and transitions, cutting out or adding scenes, and adding background music and voice-over narration. The following sections outline the steps involved in the process of using DV technology.

Step 1: Select a DV Camera

DV cameras range from inexpensive consumer versions to high-end DV camera models that support Blu-ray or HDV standards. Many mobile devices allow you to record digital video that you later can transmit to your computer or email from the device. When selecting a DV camera, consider features such as zoom, sound quality, editing capabilities, and resolution.

Step 2: Record a Video

With most DV cameras, you have a choice of recording programs that include different combinations of camera settings. These programs enable you to adjust the exposure and other functions to match the recording environment. You also have the ability to select special digital effects, such as fade, wipe, and black and white.

Step 3: Transfer and Manage Videos

You can connect most video cameras and mobile devices to a computer using a USB port. With many devices, you can transfer the videos to a media sharing or an online social network. Before doing this, however, consider the frame rate and video file format. The *frame rate* of a video refers to the number of frames per second (fps). A smaller frame rate results in a smaller file size for the video, but playback of the video will not be as smooth as one recorded with a higher frame rate. A video file format holds the video information in a manner specified by a vendor.

Step 4: Edit a Video

When editing, you first split the video into smaller pieces, or scenes, that you can manipulate easily. Most video editing software automatically splits the video into scenes at locations that you specify. After splitting, you should delete, or prune, unwanted scenes or portions of scenes. You can crop (or resize) scenes, and add logos, special effects, or titles. Special effects include warping, changing from color to black and white, morphing, or zoom motion. *Morphing* transforms one video image into another image over the course of several frames of video.

The next step is to add audio effects, including voice-over narration and background music. Using many video editing programs, you can add more tracks, or layers, of sound to a video in addition to the sound that the video camera or mobile device recorded. Adding audio tracks enables you to set a mood by providing background music or sounds. In the final step, you use video editing software to combine the scenes into a complete video by ordering scenes and adding transition effects. Transition effect options include fades, wipes, blurs, bursts, ruptures, and erosions.

Step 5: Distribute a Video

Some mobile devices allow you to upload video directly to video sharing and online social networks, as well as to send a video message. You can save digital video to media such as a DVD or Blu-ray Disc and package it for individual distribution or sale.

✸ **Consider This:** If your computer or mobile device is capable of recording video, how often and for what purposes do you generally record videos? What settings can you adjust to improve the quality of the video? Which file format does your mobile device use to save video files?

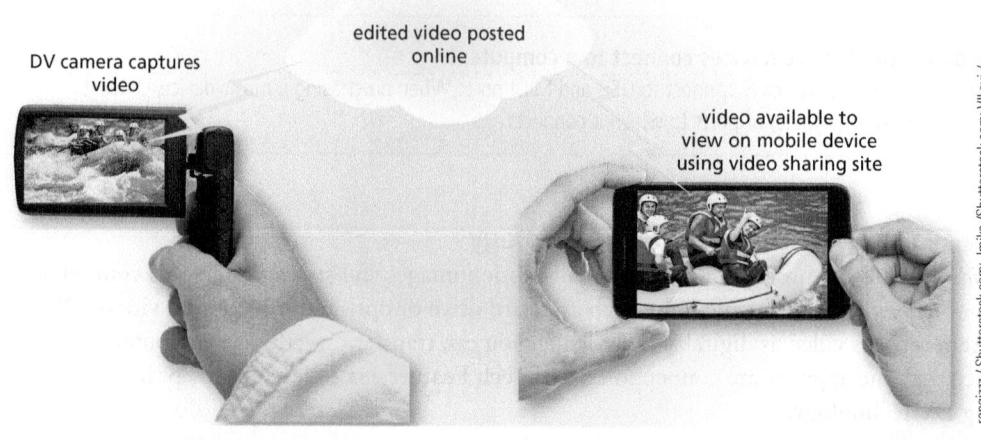

DV camera captures video

edited video posted online

video available to view on mobile device using video sharing site

Webcams and Integrated DV Cameras

A **webcam** is a type of DV camera that enables you to capture video and still images, and usually audio input, for viewing or manipulation on a computer or mobile device. Some webcams are separate peripheral devices, which usually attach to the top of a desktop monitor. Many laptops, tablets, and smartphones have built-in webcams. Smartphones and other mobile devices have built-in integrated DV cameras.

Using a webcam or integrated DV camera, you can send email messages with video attachments, broadcast live images or video over the Internet, conduct videoconferences, and make video calls. During a **video call**, all parties see one another as they communicate over the Internet. (Figure 7-1 at the beginning of this module shows a built-in webcam being used for a video call.)

Where video calls usually are for personal use, videoconferences typically are for business use. A **videoconference** is a meeting between two or more geographically separated people who use a network or the Internet to transmit audio and video data (Figure 7-14). To participate in a videoconference using a computer, you need videoconferencing software or access to a videoconferencing web app, along with a microphone, speakers, and a video camera attached to or built into a computer. As you speak, members of the meeting hear your voice on their speakers. Any image in front of the video camera, such as a person's face, appears in a window on each participant's screen.

Figure 7-14   To save on travel expenses, many large businesses use videoconferencing.
Idprod / Fotolia LLC

You can configure some webcams to display the images they capture remotely on a webpage, or via an app on a mobile device. This use of a webcam attracts website visitors by showing images that change regularly. Home or small business users might use webcams to show a work in progress, weather and traffic information, or employees at work; they also might use it as a security system. Some websites have live webcams that display still pictures and update the displayed image at a specified time or time intervals, such as every 15 seconds. A *streaming cam* has the illusion of moving images because it sends a continual stream of still images. Read Secure IT 7-2 to learn about security issues related to using webcams.

 SECURE IT 7-2

Digital Video Security

Sales of home security systems are on the rise due to their low costs and easy setup. These systems use cameras and sensors to monitor activity, and most send a message via mobile phone to alert a user of movement and entrance or exit into the dwelling and send the webcam's live feed of the scene.

This use of webcams serves a practical use in a private setting. Similarly, webcams in public areas, such as shopping malls, parking lots, and school cafeterias, help with surveillance measures and record everyday activity.

Webcam use, however, is criticized when the live feeds are used in a manner without the recorded parties' consent. Ethics and Issues 3-1 in Module 3 discusses the appropriate punishment for webcam spying, citing examples of criminals who hacked into home computers and streamed live video feeds, school administrators who took 66,000

pictures and screen captures of students using school-distributed laptops at home, and rent-to-own stores that rented laptops with spyware that captured photos of customers in their homes. DV recorders also are hidden in products resembling remote car keys, wall and desk clocks, sunglasses, smoke detectors, and electrical boxes.

If you have a webcam, follow these measures to prevent its unauthorized use:

- **Unplug the webcam.** This obvious suggestion offers the most secure solution. If the webcam is not connected to the computer, it cannot reveal what is occurring in front of the lens.

- **Cover the lens and plug the microphone.** Place a piece of black electrical tape over the lens, and insert a dummy plug in the microphone port. This solution is ideal for tablets and laptops equipped with cameras.

- **Register the hardware.** Hardware manufacturers continually update their firmware to fix issues. If you register your product, the companies can notify you of known security holes and offer updates to download.

- **Use a strong password.** When connecting a webcam to a network, you may need to configure the device for features such as sending an email or text message when motion is detected. If you are prompted to create a password, be certain it can resist hackers and malicious software. Read Secure IT 1-3 in Module 1 for tips about creating strong passwords.

✷ **Consider This:** If you have a webcam, what actions will you take to protect your privacy? Should you be warned of webcam use when you are in a public area? If so, how can these warnings be given? Would you consider buying a DV recorder for surveillance purposes?

✷ **CONSIDER THIS**

Do Drones Use Cameras?
A **drone**, also technically known as an *unmanned aerial vehicle* (*UAV*), is an aircraft that operates by an onboard computer and GPS, a remote control device, and/or an app on a computer or mobile device. While drones originally were used by the military, today they have a variety of business and personal applications including search and rescue, traffic and weather monitoring, surveillance, disaster relief, assisting farmers, delivery of goods, and aerial photography/videography (Figure 7-15).

drone camera

smartphone shows video being recorded by drone camera

Figure 7-15   This figure shows how you can watch video as it is captured by the drone camera directly on the smartphone attached to the remote control.
iStockphoto.com / Franck-Boston

Scanners and Reading Devices

Some input devices save users time by capturing data directly from a *source document*, which is the original form of the data. Examples of source documents include time cards, order forms, invoices, paychecks, advertisements, brochures, photos, inventory tags, or any other document that contains data to be processed.

Devices that can capture data directly from a source document include optical scanners, optical readers, bar code readers, RFID (radio frequency identification) readers, magstripe (magnetic stripe card) readers, and MICR (magnetic-ink character recognition) readers.

Optical Scanners

An optical scanner, usually called a **scanner**, is a light-sensing input device that reads printed text and graphics and then translates the results into a form the computer can process. A flatbed scanner works in a manner similar to a copy machine except it creates a file of the document in memory instead of a paper copy (Figure 7-16). Once you scan a picture or document, you can display the scanned object on the screen, modify its appearance, store it on a storage medium, print it, attach it to an email message, include it in another document, or post it on a website or photo community for everyone to see.

How a Flatbed Scanner Works

Step 1
Place the document to be scanned face down on the glass window. Using buttons on the scanner or the scanner program, start the scanning process.

Step 2
The scanner converts the document content to digital information, which is transmitted through the cable to the computer's memory and saved on the computer's hard drive.

Step 3
Once in the computer, users can display the image, print it, send it in an email message, include it in a document, or post it on a webpage or photo community.

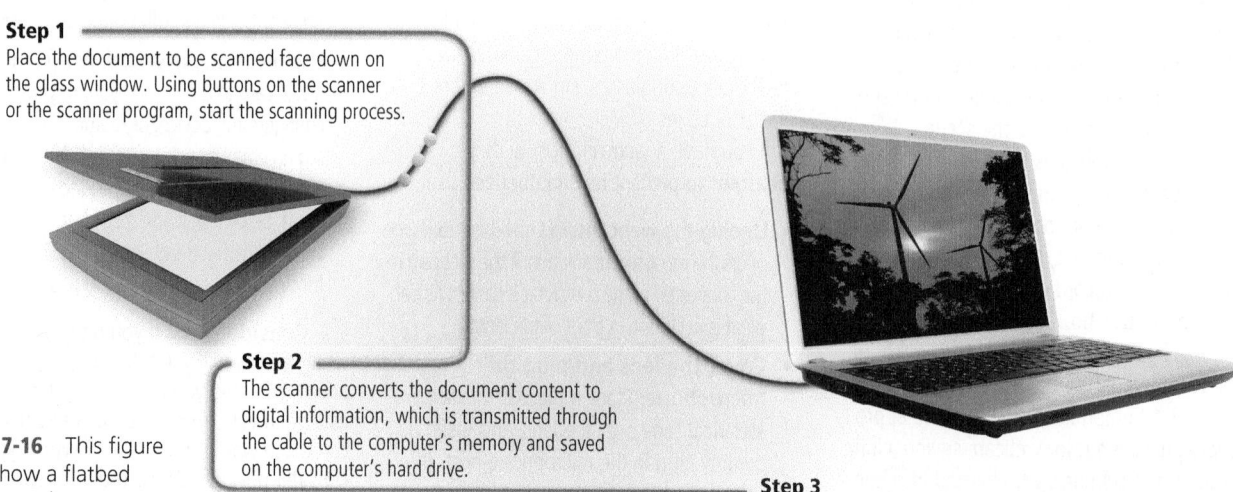

Figure 7-16   This figure shows how a flatbed scanner works.
Mile Atanasov / Shutterstock.com;
Alex Staroseltsev / Shutterstock.com

The quality of a scanner is measured by its resolution, that is, the number of bits it stores in a pixel and the number of pixels per inch. The higher each number, the better the quality, but the more expensive the scanner.

Many scanners include *OCR* (optical character recognition) *software*, which can read and convert text documents into electronic files. OCR software converts a scanned image into a text file that can be edited, for example, with a word processing application.

 **CONSIDER THIS**

How can you improve the quality of scanned documents?
Place a blank sheet of paper behind translucent papers, newspapers, and other transparent types of paper. If the original is crooked, draw a line on the back at the bottom of the image. Use that mark to align the original on the scanner. Use photo editing software to fix imperfections in images.

Optical Readers

An optical reader is a device that uses a light source to read characters, marks, and codes and then converts them into digital data that a computer can process. Two technologies used by optical readers are optical character recognition (OCR) and optical mark recognition (OMR).

- Most **OCR devices** include a small optical scanner for reading characters and sophisticated software to analyze what is read. OCR devices range from large machines that can read thousands of documents per minute to handheld wands that read one document at a time. OCR devices read printed characters in a special font.
- **OMR devices** read hand-drawn marks, such as small circles or rectangles. A person places these marks on a form, such as a test, survey, or questionnaire answer sheet (shown in Figure 7-1 at the beginning of this module).

Bar Code Readers

A **bar code reader**, also called a *bar code scanner*, is an optical reader that uses laser beams to read bar codes (Figure 7-17). A **bar code** is an identification code that often consists of either a set of vertical lines and spaces of different widths or a two-dimensional pattern of dots, squares, and other images. The bar code represents data that identifies the manufacturer and the item.

Figure 7-17 A bar code reader uses laser beams to read bar codes on products such as clothing, shown here.
iStockphoto.com / klaptoman

Manufacturers print a bar code either on a product's package or on a label that is affixed to a product, such as groceries, books, clothing, vehicles, mail, and packages. Each industry uses its own type of bar code. The United States Postal Service (USPS) uses a POSTNET bar code. Retail and grocery stores use the *UPC* (*Universal Product Code*) bar code.

A **QR code** (quick response code) is known as a 2-D bar code because it stores information in both a vertical and horizontal direction in a square-shaped graphic that represents a web address or other content, such as contacts or phone numbers (Figure 7-18). QR codes can be

Figure 7-18 This customer pays her bills by scanning an on-screen QR code.
iStockphoto.com / gpointstudio

read with a QR bar code reader or a QR code reader app on a smartphone or other mobile device. All types of material, from posters to textbooks to merchandise, include QR codes that consumers scan to obtain additional information, which may be in the form of a website or may display text for the user to read. For information about safely scanning QR codes, read Secure IT 7-3.

✹ SECURE IT 7-3

Safely Scanning QR Codes

QR codes have come a long way since their first use, which was in tracking parts used to manufacture Japanese cars. Now they are used to market, educate, and entertain. Every industry has found some benefit of using innovative and creative QR technology to benefit workers and the public. They have become a necessary method of providing additional information about exhibits, downloading apps, displaying videos, advertising items, and performing thousands of other functions.

As with most computer applications, however, users must be cautious by scrutinizing the QR codes they see, in an attempt to thwart malicious attacks. Follow these guidelines to use QR codes safely:

- **Scan trustworthy sources.** In general, QR codes in books, magazines, and newspapers are safe. Posters on the street or on leaflets handed out on street corners, however, may not be as secure. Verify the source of the codes before scanning them.
- **Verify the web address.** Most QR code reader apps show the address of the website that will be displayed. If you do not recognize the domain name or the web address looks suspicious, do not grant permission.
- **Choose a reputable QR scanner.** Visit trustworthy Android marketplaces and the iTunes Store for safe QR apps. Look for safety features that will check the authenticity of destination websites, issue

warnings for malicious QR codes, display a preview of each code, and block unsafe websites.

- **Do not supply personal information.** If the QR code directs you to a website displaying a form, do not enter personal or financial data unless you are certain that the website is safe, secure, and authentic.
- **Check for tampering.** Verify the QR code is original. Unscrupulous people may place a fraudulent sticker over the printed code.

✹ **Consider This:** Where have you seen QR codes? Have you scanned any? If so, what information have you obtained? Have you followed any of the security precautions listed above? If not, which will you now follow?

Figure 7-19 This electronic key system locks and unlocks doors using RFID technology.
iStockphoto.com / iggy1965

RFID Readers

RFID (radio frequency identification) is a technology that uses radio signals to communicate with a tag placed in or attached to an object, an animal, or a person. RFID tags, which contain a memory chip and an antenna, are available in many shapes and sizes. An **RFID reader** reads information on the tag via radio waves. RFID readers can be handheld devices or mounted in a stationary object, such as a doorway.

Uses of RFID include tagging and updating inventory (as an alternative to bar code identification); tracking times of runners in a marathon; tracking location of people, airline baggage, and misplaced or stolen goods; checking lift tickets of skiers; gauging temperature and pressure of tires on a vehicle; checking out library books; providing access to rooms or buildings (Figure 7-19); managing purchases; and tracking payment as vehicles pass through booths on tollway systems.

Magstripe Readers

A **magstripe reader**, short for *magnetic stripe card reader*, reads the magnetic stripe on the back of credit cards, entertainment cards, bank cards, identification cards, and other similar cards (Figure 7-20). The stripe contains information identifying you and the card issuer. Some information stored in the stripe may include your name, account number, the card's expiration date, and a country code.

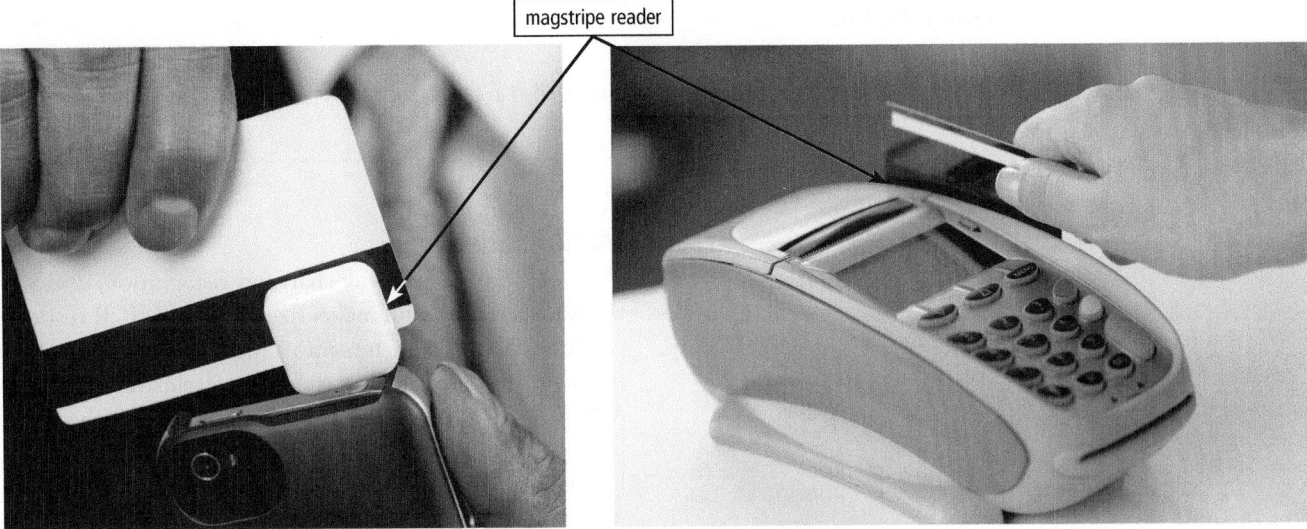

Figure 7-20   A magstripe reader reads information encoded on the stripe on the back of a credit card.
EdBockStock / Shutterstock.com; iStockphoto.com / hocus-focus

Most magstripe readers are separate devices that communicate with a POS terminal, such as those in retail stores. Home or small business users, however, may attach a small plastic magstripe reader to a smartphone or tablet so that they can accept payments using a mobile app. When a credit card is swiped through a magstripe reader, it reads the information stored on the magnetic stripe on the card. Read Secure IT 7-4 for tips about how to protect credit cards from scanning devices.

 SECURE IT 7-4

Protecting Credit Cards from Scanning Devices

One-third of the 775 million credit and debit cards issued in the United States are likely targets for high-tech thieves who can steal the account information quickly and silently. RFID technology embedded in these cards transmits signals with the coded account information to scanners, which thieves place in their coat pockets, purses, and other nonmetallic containers. Some signals have a range as far as 30 feet, so that the electronic pickpockets simply walk among crowds in search of obtaining these radio waves.

The RFID technology embedded in the credit cards is approximately the size of a postage stamp. It consists of a coil of wire connected to an electronic circuit that generates a pattern of electrical pulses with coded account information

unique to a specific card. An antenna transmits these radio waves to a scanner.

The radio waves do not penetrate metal or water easily. You, consequently, can protect these cards and documents by wrapping them in aluminum foil or placing them near water bottles. Security experts also recommend stacking several credit cards in an attempt to scramble the signals. Place the cards in your wallet with the magnetic stripe facing inside. RFID-blocking wallets also are manufactured to prevent scanners from obtaining the emitted signals.

To determine if your credit or debit card has this RFID technology, look for the words, PayPass, PayWave, Blink, or a radio wave symbol, as shown in the figure. If you do not see this information, call customer service or search the company's website. This technology also is found in passports, driver's licenses,

hotel room keys, and university and employee identification cards, so you may need to protect these documents and cards from electronic pickpockets, too.

⁂ **Consider This:** Are any of your credit or debit cards or personal documents embedded with RFID technology? If so, what precautions will you take to block the signals from scanners?

CONSIDER THIS ─────────────────────────────

Why are some magnetic stripes not readable by a magstripe reader?

If the magstripe reader rejects the card, it is possible that the magnetic stripe is scratched, dirty, or erased. Exposure to a magnet or magnetic field can erase the contents of a card's magnetic stripe.

 CONSIDER THIS ─────────────────────────────

What is a smart card?

A smart card stores data on an integrated circuit embedded in a card, such as a credit card. Module 8 discusses smart cards in more depth.

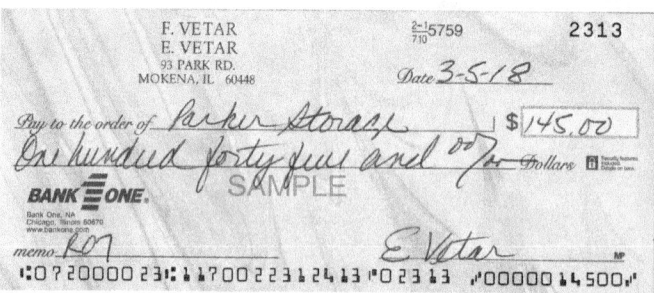

Figure 7-21 The MICR characters preprinted on the check represent the bank routing number, customer account number, and check number. The amount of the check in the lower-right corner is added after the check is cashed.

Figure 7-22 An employee in a warehouse uses this data collection device to scan items, which wirelessly transmits information about the scanned item to the store's inventory system.

endostock / Fotolia LLC

MICR Readers

An *MICR* (magnetic-ink character recognition) *device* reads text printed with magnetized ink. An MICR reader converts MICR characters into a form the computer can process. The banking industry almost exclusively uses MICR for check processing. Each check in your checkbook has precoded MICR characters beginning at the lower-left edge (Figure 7-21).

When a bank receives a check for payment, it uses an MICR inscriber to print the amount of the check in MICR characters in the lower-right corner. Each check is inserted in an MICR reader, which sends the check information — including the amount of the check — to a computer for processing.

Data Collection Devices

Instead of reading or scanning data from a source document, a *data collection device* obtains data directly at the location where the transaction or event takes place. For example, employees use bar code readers, hand-held computers, or other mobile devices to collect data wirelessly (Figure 7-22). These types of data collection devices are used in restaurants, grocery stores, factories, warehouses, the outdoors, or other locations where heat, humidity, and cleanliness are not easy to control. For example, factories and retail stores use data collection devices to take inventory and order products.

Data collection devices and many mobile computers and devices have the capability of wirelessly transmitting data over a network or the Internet. Increasingly more users today send data wirelessly to central office computers using these devices.

What Is Output?

Output is data that has been processed into a useful form. Recall that computers process data (input) into information (output). The form of output varies, depending on the hardware and software being used and the requirements of the user. Users view or watch output on a screen, print it, or hear it through speakers, headphones, or earbuds. While working with a computer or mobile device, a user encounters four basic types of output: text, graphics, audio, and video (Figure 7-23). Very often, a single form of output, such as a webpage, includes more than one of these types of output.

Text

Graphics

Audio

Video

Figure 7-23 Four types of output are text, graphics, audio, and video.

iStockphoto.com / DenTv; martinlisner / Fotolia LLC; iStockphoto.com / tomasworks; iStockphoto.com / rzelich; Courtesy of Apple, Inc.; iStockphoto.com / scanrail; JAKKRIT SAELAO / Shutterstock.com; iStockphoto.com / cotesebastien; Vladyslav Starozhylov / Shutterstock.com; Courtesy of Epson America, Inc.; sam100 / Shutterstock.com; iStockphoto.com / rzelich; iStockphoto.com /pictafolio; iStockphoto.com / pagadesign; iStockphoto.com / Oleksiy Mark; Terrie L. Zeller/ Shutterstock.com

- **Text:** Examples of output that primarily contain text are text messages, Internet messages, memos, letters, press releases, reports, classified advertisements, envelopes, and mailing labels. On the web, users read blogs, news and magazine articles, books, television show transcripts, stock quotes, speeches, and lectures.
- **Graphics:** Many forms of output include graphics to enhance visual appeal and convey information. Business letters have logos. Reports include charts. Newsletters use drawings, clip art, and photos. Users print high-quality photos taken with a digital camera. Many websites use animation.
- **Audio:** Users download their favorite songs and listen to the music. Software, such as games, encyclopedias, and simulations, often include musical accompaniments and audio clips, such as narrations and speeches. On the web, users listen to radio broadcasts, audio clips, podcasts, sporting events, news, music, and concerts. They also use VoIP.
- **Video:** As with audio, software and websites often include video clips and video blogs. Users watch news reports, movies, sporting events, weather conditions, and live performances on a computer or mobile device. They attach a video camera to a computer or mobile device to watch video or programs.

 CONSIDER THIS

Are storage devices categorized as input or output devices?
When storage devices write on storage media, they are creating output. Similarly, when storage devices read from storage media, they function as a source of input. Nevertheless, they are categorized as storage devices, not as input or output devices.

Common methods of output include displays, printers, speakers, headphones and earbuds, data projectors, interactive whiteboards, and force-feedback game controllers and tactile output. The following sections discuss each of these output devices.

Displays

A *display device*, or simply **display**, is an output device that visually conveys text, graphics, and video information. Sometimes called *soft copy*, information on a display exists electronically and appears for a temporary period. Displays consist of a screen and the components that produce the information on the screen. Most current displays are a type of *flat-panel display*, which means they have a shallow depth and a flat screen. Figure 7-24 shows displays for a variety of computers and mobile devices.

Desktops often use a monitor as their display. A **monitor** is a display that is packaged as a separate peripheral device. Some monitors have a tilt-and-swivel base, which allows you to adjust the angle of the screen to minimize neck strain and reduce glare from overhead lighting. With some, you also can rotate the screen. Adjustable monitor

monitor display
laptop display
digital camera display
navigation system display
handheld game device display
smartphone display

Figure 7-24 A variety of displays.

stands allow you to adjust the height of the monitor. Monitor controls enable you to adjust the brightness, contrast, positioning, height, and width of images. Some have touch screens, integrated speakers, and/or a built-in webcam. Today's monitors have a small footprint; that is, they do not take up much desk space. For additional space savings, some monitors are wall mountable.

Most mobile computers and devices integrate the display and other components into the case. Size of these displays varies depending on the mobile computer or device. Some mobile computers and many mobile devices have touch screens. Traditional laptops have a display that attaches with a hinge to the case. (Read How To 7-1 to learn how to connect a laptop to an external display.) Tablets are available with two types of displays: one that attaches with a hinge and one built into the top of the case. Some smartphone and digital camera displays also attach with a hinge to the device. On other smartphones and most portable media players, digital cameras, and handheld game consoles, the display is built into the case. Some vehicles integrate a display in the dashboard, enabling drivers to control audio, video, navigation, temperature, and other settings.

BTW
Measuring Displays
You measure the screen on a monitor, laptop, tablet, smartphone, or other mobile device the same way you measure a television; that is, you measure diagonally from one corner to the other.

 HOW TO 7-1

Connect a Laptop to an External Display
When you are using a laptop, you may need to connect it to an external display for a variety of reasons. If you are giving a presentation, connecting a laptop to a projector or television will allow attendees to view presentation slides or other media content. If you use your laptop at a desk, you might want to connect it to a larger display so that you can more easily see the content without straining your eyes, or you may want to work with two open programs simultaneously with one displaying on the laptop screen and the other on the external display. The following steps describe how to connect a laptop to an external display.

1. Verify that your laptop is compatible with the external display.
2. Make sure that you have a cable that can connect from a port on your laptop to a port or cable connected to the external display. If not, you may need to purchase an adapter.
3. Verify that your laptop supports a screen resolution that the external display also supports.

4. Use the cable to connect your laptop's video port to the video input port for the external display.
5. External displays often have multiple video input ports; make sure the external display is configured to display the content from the port to which your laptop is connected.
6. If necessary, configure the laptop to display content on the external display. This often can be done by pressing a key on

the keyboard or accessing the operating system's display settings.
7. If necessary, change the screen resolution on the laptop so that the contents display properly on the external display.

⚙ **Consider This:** What are some other reasons why you might want to connect your laptop to an external display?

Goygel-Sokol Dmitry / Shutterstock.com

Display Technologies

Many desktop monitors, along with the screens on mobile computers and devices, use some type of LCD technology. An **LCD** (*liquid crystal display*) sandwiches a liquid compound between two sheets of material that presents sharp, flicker-free images on a screen when illuminated. The light source, called the *backlight*, often uses either CCFL (cold cathode fluorescent lamp) or *LED* (light-emitting diode) technology.

A display that uses LED for the backlight often is called an *LED display* or an LED LCD display. LED displays consume less power, last longer, and are thinner, lighter, and brighter than a display that uses CCFL technology, but they also may be more expensive. Screens in laptops and mobile devices often use LED backlight technology.

LCD displays typically produce color using *active-matrix*, or *TFT* (thin-film transistor), technology, which uses a separate transistor to apply charges to each liquid crystal cell and, thus, displays high-quality color that is viewable from all angles. Several types of active matrix displays, or panels, are available, with some providing higher quality than others.

Instead of LCD or traditional LED, some displays use OLED technology. *OLED* (organic LED) uses organic molecules that are self-illuminating and, thus, do not require a backlight. OLED displays consume less power and produce an even brighter, easier-to-read display than LCD or LED displays, but they can have a shorter life span. OLEDs also can be fabricated on thin, flexible surfaces.

Many mobile computers and devices use either AMOLED or Retina Display technology. An *AMOLED* (active-matrix OLED) screen uses both active-matrix and OLED technologies, combining the benefits of high-quality viewing from all angles with lower power consumption. Variations of AMOLED provide different levels of viewing quality. *Retina Display*, developed by Apple, produces vibrant colors and supports viewing from all angles because the LCD technology is built into the screen instead of behind it and contains more pixels per inch of display. Recall that a *pixel* (short for picture element) is a single point in an electronic image.

Display Quality

The quality of a display depends primarily on its resolution, response time, brightness, dot pitch, and contrast ratio.

- **Resolution** is the number of horizontal and vertical pixels in a display. For example, a monitor or screen that has a 1600 × 900 resolution displays up to 1600 pixels per horizontal row and 900 pixels per vertical row, for a total of 1,440,000 pixels to create a screen image. A higher resolution uses a greater number of pixels and, thus, provides a smoother, sharper, and clearer image. As the resolution increases, however, some items on the screen appear smaller.

  Displays are optimized for a specific resolution, called the *native resolution*. Although you can change the resolution to any setting, for best results, use the monitor or screen's native resolution setting.
- *Response time* of a display refers to the time in milliseconds (ms) that it takes to turn a pixel on or off. Response times of displays typically range from 2 to 12 ms. The lower the number, the faster the response time.
- Brightness of a display is measured in nits. A *nit* is a unit of visible light intensity equal to one candela (formerly called candlepower) per square meter. The *candela* is the standard unit of luminous intensity. Displays today typically range from 250 to 700 nits. The higher the nits, the brighter the images.
- *Dot pitch*, sometimes called *pixel pitch*, is the distance in millimeters between pixels on a display. Text created with a smaller dot pitch is easier to read. Advertisements normally specify a display's dot pitch or pixel pitch. Average dot pitch on a display should be .28 mm or lower. The lower the number, the sharper the image.
- *Contrast ratio* describes the difference in light intensity between the brightest white and darkest black that can be produced on a display. Contrast ratios today range from 500:1 to 3000:1. Higher contrast ratios represent colors better.

Graphics Chips, Ports, and Flat-Panel Monitors   A cable on a monitor plugs in a port on the computer, which enables communications from a graphics chip. This chip, called the *graphics processing unit* (GPU), controls the manipulation and display of graphics on a display device. The GPU either is integrated on the motherboard or resides on a video card in a slot on the motherboard.

Today's monitors use a digital signal to produce a picture. To display the highest quality images, the monitor should plug in a DVI port, an HDMI port, or a DisplayPort.

- A *DVI (Digital Video Interface) port* enables digital signals to transmit directly to a monitor.
- An *HDMI (High-Definition Media Interface) port* combines DVI with high-definition (HD) television, audio, and video. Some ultrathin laptops have mini-HDMI ports that require the use of an adapter (or dongle) when connecting to a standard-size HDMI display.
- A *DisplayPort* is an alternative to DVI that also supports high-definition audio and video.

Over the years, several video standards have been developed to define the resolution, aspect ratio, number of colors, and other display properties. The *aspect ratio* defines a display's width relative to its height. A 2:1 aspect ratio, for example, means the display is twice as wide as it is tall. The aspect ratio for a *widescreen monitor* is 16:9 or 16:10. Some displays support multiple video standards. For a display to show images as defined by a video standard, both the display and GPU must support the same video standard.

DTVs and Smart TVs

Home users sometimes use a digital television (DTV) as a display. Gamers also use a television as their output device. They plug one end of a cable in the game console and the other end in the video port on the television.

HDTV (*high-definition television*) is the most advanced form of digital television, working with digital broadcast signals, transmitting digital sound, supporting wide screens, and providing high resolutions. A *Smart TV* is an Internet-enabled HDTV from which you can browse the web, stream video from online media services, listen to Internet radio, communicate with others on online social media, play online games, and more — all while watching a television show (Figure 7-25). Using a Smart TV, you can stream content from the TV to other Internet-enabled devices, such as a tablet or smartphone, and use cloud storage services to share content.

DTVs often use LCD, LED, or plasma technology. A *plasma display* uses gas plasma technology, which sandwiches a layer of gas between two glass plates. When voltage is applied, the gas releases ultraviolet (UV) light. This UV light causes the pixels on the screen to glow and form an image. Read Ethics & Issues 7-2 to consider the effects of radiation from monitors and other devices.

Figure 7-25   Smart TVs enable you to connect to the Internet and/or watch television shows.
Courtesy of LG Electronics USA Inc.

 ETHICS & ISSUES 7-2

Should We Be Concerned with Hardware Radiation?

When you work on a computer or talk on a mobile phone, could you be at risk from harmful radiation? Every electronic device emits some level of radiation. While the amounts for computers and mobile devices may not be harmful in low doses, some critics argue that constant exposure, such as sitting in an office all day or wearing a Bluetooth headset for several hours at a time, can cause levels of radiation that, over time, may cause cancer or other health concerns. In addition to the computer itself, peripheral devices, such as printers, along with the wireless or cordless methods to connect the devices, emit

radiation. Research is inconclusive about safe levels and long-term risks. Most agree that it is not the level from any one device, but rather the cumulative effect from long-term exposure (several hours a day over many years) to multiple devices simultaneously that causes harm.

You can protect yourself and minimize your risks. Replace older equipment, such as CRT (cathode-ray tube) monitors, with devices such as LCD monitors, which meet current emission standards. Sit back from your monitor as far as possible, and place a barrier between your computer and your lap. Move other electronic sources, such as hard drives and printers, as far away as possible. Minimize your wireless

connections, such as a wireless keyboard or a wireless mouse. Remove your Bluetooth headset when not in use, and frequently switch the headset from one ear to the other. Turn off devices when not in use. Recycle or donate older, unused devices to eliminate any radiation exposure from older devices, even when they are not in use.

Consider This: Do you consider computers and mobile devices to be harmful to your health? Why or why not? Would you change your electronic device usage, change your habits, or rearrange your computer work area to minimize your risk? Why or why not? What modifications can you make?

CONSIDER THIS

Can you view the output from your display remotely?
With a television streaming media device, you can view and control a home DVR or television from a remote computer or mobile device.

Printers

A **printer** is an output device that produces text and graphics on a physical medium, such as paper. Printed information (hard copy) exists physically and is a more permanent form of output than that presented on a display (soft copy).

A hard copy, also called a *printout*, is either in portrait or landscape orientation. A printout in *portrait orientation* is taller than it is wide, with information printed across the shorter width of the paper. A printout in *landscape orientation* is wider than it is tall, with information printed across the widest part of the paper. Letters, reports, and books typically use portrait orientation. Spreadsheets, slide shows, and graphics often use landscape orientation.

 CONSIDER THIS

Can you print documents and photos from a mobile computer and device without physically connecting to the printer with a cable?
Yes. Many printers contain memory card slots, so that you can remove the memory card from a camera, insert it in the printer, and print photos directly from the card. You also can connect a printer to a wireless network so that devices with a Wi-Fi connection can print wirelessly. With *Bluetooth printing*, a computer or other device transmits output to a printer via radio waves. The computer or other device and the printer do not have to be aligned with each other; rather, they need to be within an approximate 30-foot range. Read How To 7-2 for instructions about printing from a smartphone or tablet.

 **HOW TO 7-2**

Print from a Smartphone or Tablet
As smartphones and tablets become more widely used and packed with features, you may need to print items stored on these devices. For example, you may capture a great photo while spending time with your family and want to print the photo to place on your desk, or you may take notes on your tablet and want to print a hard copy. You have several options available to print from a smartphone or tablet. The method you use will depend primarily on the type of mobile device and printer you are using, and the printer must support printing from a mobile device. The following steps describe how to print from a smartphone or tablet:

1. Verify your mobile device or tablet is connected to the same network as the printer.
2. If necessary, download and install an app on your device or tablet to enable you to print. The printer's documentation will inform you if you need an app and, if so, where to obtain it.
3. When you are viewing the item that you want to print on your smartphone or tablet, select the option to print on your printer and then retrieve the printout.

In addition to using an app or built-in features on your mobile device or computer to print, you may be able to configure your printer so that you can attach files and send them to a specified email address. The following steps describe how to use this feature on supported printers:

1. Access your printer's settings and make sure the printer is connected to your network.
2. Configure the option to set up an email address for receiving print jobs and write down that email address.
3. On your computer or mobile device, send the file you want to print as an attachment to an email message addressed to the email address determined in Step 2.
4. When the printer receives the email message with the file attachment, it will print the file.

If your mobile device or printer does not support wireless printing, you also can print by transferring the file from your smartphone or tablet to your laptop, desktop, or printer. The following steps describe how to print from a smartphone or tablet when wireless printing is not supported:

1. Remove the memory card from your smartphone or tablet and insert it into your laptop, desktop, or printer. *Note:* If your smartphone or tablet does not have a removable memory card, you can connect the smartphone or tablet to a desktop, laptop, or printer using the USB cable included with your device.
2. On the laptop, desktop, or printer, navigate to and select the file you want to print, and then select the option to print the file.
3. When the printer stops, safely remove the memory card from the laptop, desktop, or printer and insert it in your smartphone or tablet.

 Consider This: What are some other reasons why you might want to print from a smartphone or tablet?

To meet the range of printing needs from home users to enterprise users, many different types and styles of printers exist with varying speeds, capabilities, and printing methods. Figure 7-26 presents a list of questions to help you determine the printer best suited to your needs.

Nonimpact Printers

A **nonimpact printer** forms characters and graphics on a piece of paper without actually contacting the paper. Some spray ink, while others use heat or pressure to create images.

Commonly used nonimpact printers are ink-jet printers, photo printers, laser printers, all-in-one printers, 3-D printers, thermal printers, mobile printers, label printers, plotters, and large-format printers.

Ink-Jet Printers

An **ink-jet printer** is a type of nonimpact printer that forms characters and graphics by spraying tiny drops of liquid ink onto a piece of paper. Ink-jet printers have become a popular type of color printer for use in the home.

Ink-jet printers produce text and graphics in both black-and-white and color on a variety of paper types and sizes (Figure 7-27). These printers normally use individual sheets of paper stored in one or two removable or stationary trays. Most ink-jet printers can print lab-quality photos. Ink-jet printers also print on other materials, such as envelopes, labels, index cards, greeting card paper (card stock), transparencies, and iron-on T-shirt transfers. Many ink-jet printers include software for creating greeting cards, banners, business cards, and letterhead.

The speed of an ink-jet printer is measured by the number of pages per minute (ppm) it can print. Graphics and colors print at a slower rate than text.

1. What is my budget?
2. How fast must my printer print?
3. Do I need a color printer?
4. What is the cost per page for printing?
5. Do I need multiple copies of documents?
6. Will I print graphics?
7. Do I want to print photos?
8. Do I want to print directly from a memory card?
9. What types of paper does the printer use?
10. What sizes of paper does the printer accept?
11. Do I want to print on both sides of the paper?
12. How much paper can the printer tray hold?
13. Will the printer work with my computer and software?
14. How much do supplies such as ink, toner, and paper cost?
15. Can the printer print on envelopes?
16. How many envelopes can the printer print at a time?
17. How much do I print now, and how much will I be printing in a year or two?
18. Will the printer be connected to a network?
19. Do I want wireless printing capability?

Figure 7-26 Questions to consider before purchasing a printer.

Figure 7-27 Ink-jet printers are a popular type of color printer used at home and in the office.

Courtesy of Epson America, Inc.; iStockphoto.com / JurgaR; Courtesy of Xerox Corporation; iStockphoto.com / JurgaR; Courtesy of Xerox Corporation

✳ **CONSIDER THIS**

How does resolution affect print quality?

As with many other input and output devices, one factor that determines the quality of an ink-jet printer is its resolution. Printer resolution is measured by the number of *dots per inch* (*dpi*) a printer can print. With an ink-jet printer, a dot is a drop of ink. A higher dpi means the print quality is higher because the drops of ink are smaller and more drops fit in an area.

The difference in quality becomes noticeable when the size of the printed image increases. That is, a wallet-sized image printed at 1200 dpi may look similar in quality to one printed at 2400 dpi. When you increase the size of the image, to 8 × 10 for example, the printout of the 1200 dpi resolution may look grainier than the one printed using a 2400 dpi resolution.

Ink Cartridges   The printhead mechanism in an ink-jet printer contains ink-filled cartridges. Each cartridge has fifty to several hundred small ink holes, or nozzles. The steps in Figure 7-28 illustrate how a drop of ink appears on a page. The ink propels through any combination of the nozzles to form a character or image on the paper.

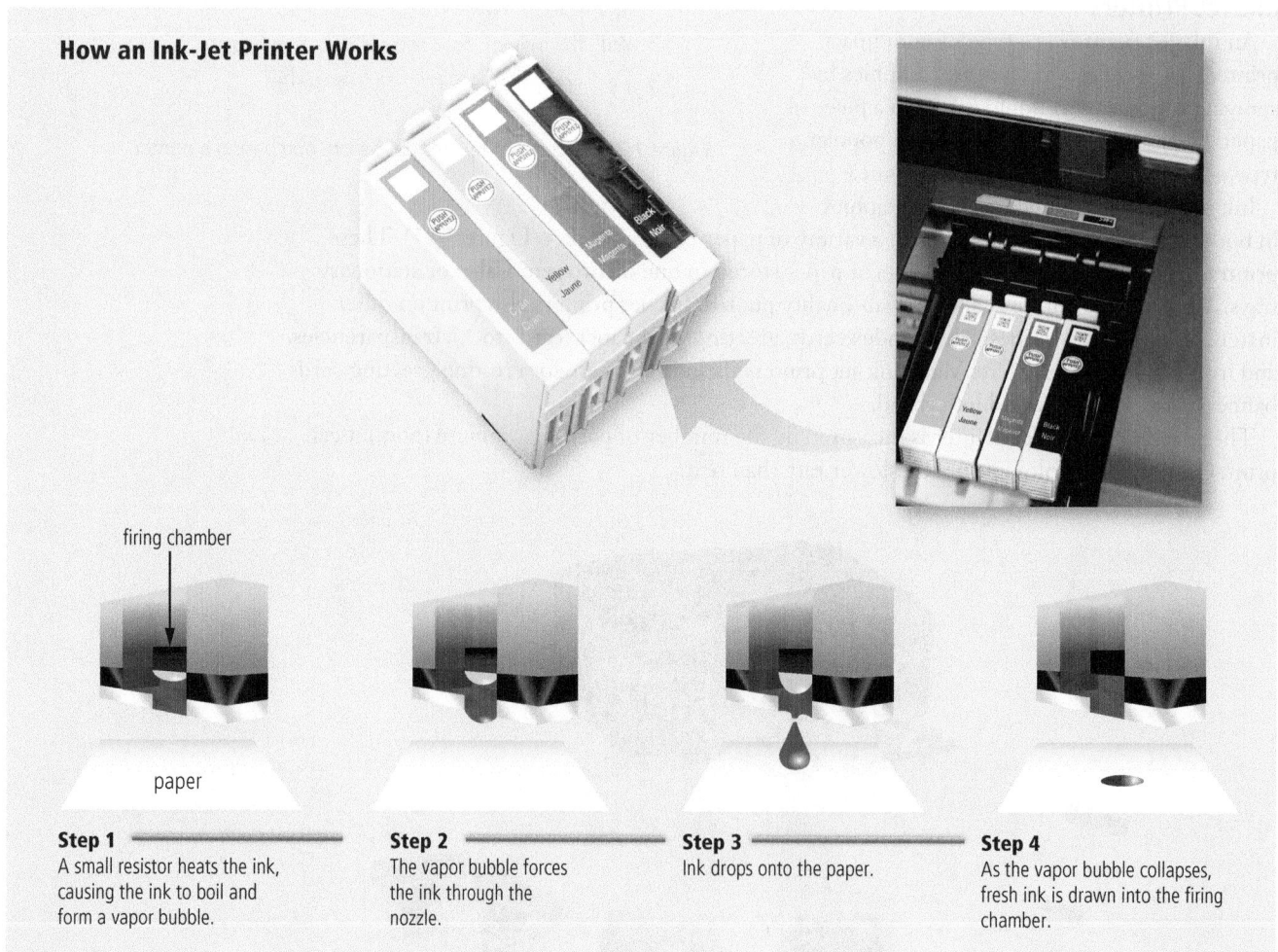

How an Ink-Jet Printer Works

firing chamber

paper

Step 1 — A small resistor heats the ink, causing the ink to boil and form a vapor bubble.

Step 2 — The vapor bubble forces the ink through the nozzle.

Step 3 — Ink drops onto the paper.

Step 4 — As the vapor bubble collapses, fresh ink is drawn into the firing chamber.

Figure 7-28   This figure shows how an ink-jet printer works.
BoyanDimitrov / Shutterstock.com; Almaamor / Dreamstime.com

When the cartridge runs out of ink, you simply replace the cartridge. Most ink-jet printers use two or more ink cartridges, one containing black ink and the other(s) containing colors. Some color cartridges contain a variety of ink colors; others contain only a single color. Consider the number of ink cartridges a printer requires, along with the cost of the cartridges, when purchasing a printer. To reduce the expense of purchasing cartridges, some users opt to purchase refilled cartridges or have empty cartridges refilled by a third-party vendor.

Photo Printers

A **photo printer** is a color printer that produces lab-quality photos (Figure 7-29). Some photo printers print just one or two sizes of photos, for example, 3 × 5 inches and 4 × 6 inches. Others print up to 8 × 10 or even larger. Some even print panoramic photos. Generally, the more sizes the printer prints, the more expensive the printer.

Figure 7-29 A photo printer.
iStockphoto.com / Ambrits

Many photo printers use ink-jet technology. With models that can print letter-sized documents, users connect the photo printer to their computer and use it for all their printing needs. For a few hundred dollars, this type of photo printer is ideal for the home or small business user.

Laser Printers

A **laser printer** is a high-speed, high-quality nonimpact printer (Figure 7-30). Laser printers are available in both black-and-white and color models. A laser printer for personal computers ordinarily uses individual 8 1/2 × 11-inch sheets of paper stored in one or more removable trays that slide in the printer case.

Laser printers print text and graphics in high-quality resolutions. While laser printers usually cost more than ink-jet printers, many models are available at affordable prices for the home user. Laser printers usually print at faster speeds than ink-jet printers.

Depending on the quality, speed, and type of laser printer, the cost ranges from a few hundred to a few thousand dollars for the home and small office user, and several hundred thousand dollars for the enterprise user.

When printing a document, laser printers process and store the entire page before they actually print it. For this reason, laser printers sometimes are called page printers. Storing a page before printing requires that the laser printer has a certain amount of memory in the device. The more memory in the printer, the faster it usually can print.

Operating in a manner similar to a copy machine, a laser printer creates images using a laser beam and powdered ink, called *toner*. The laser beam produces an image on a drum inside the printer. The light of the laser alters the electrical charge on the drum wherever it hits. When this occurs, the toner sticks to the drum and then transfers to the paper through a combination of pressure and heat (Figure 7-31). When the toner runs out, you replace the toner cartridge.

Figure 7-30 A laser printer.
Courtesy of Xerox Corporation

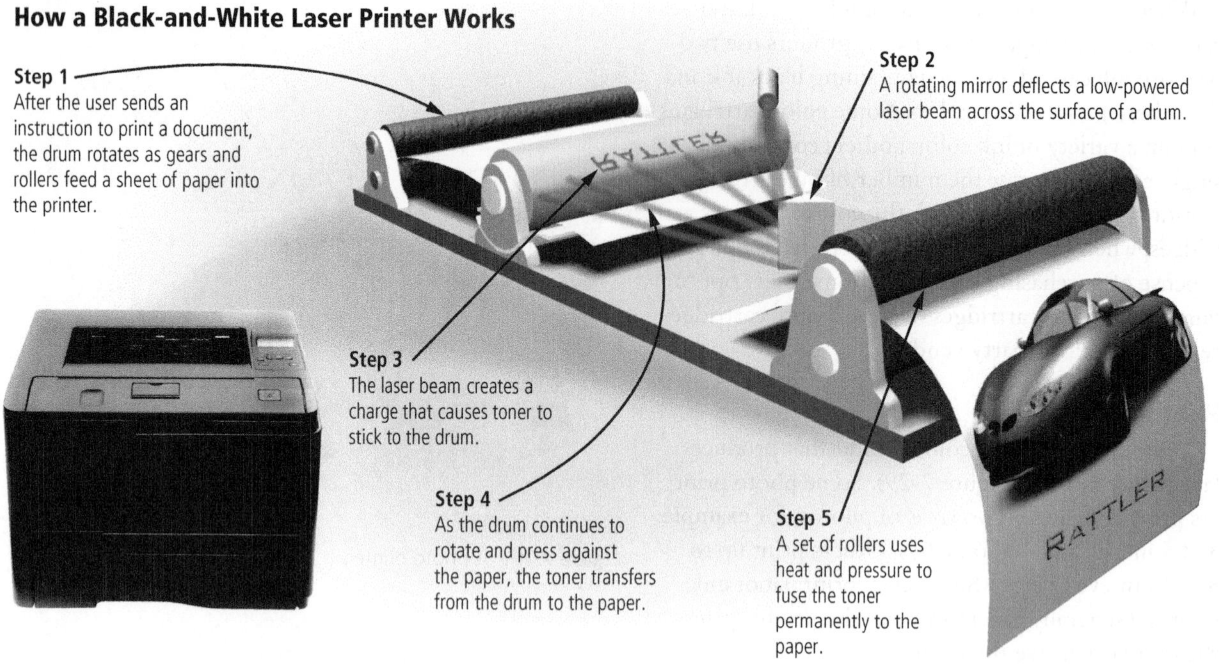

How a Black-and-White Laser Printer Works

Step 1
After the user sends an instruction to print a document, the drum rotates as gears and rollers feed a sheet of paper into the printer.

Step 2
A rotating mirror deflects a low-powered laser beam across the surface of a drum.

Step 3
The laser beam creates a charge that causes toner to stick to the drum.

Step 4
As the drum continues to rotate and press against the paper, the toner transfers from the drum to the paper.

Step 5
A set of rollers uses heat and pressure to fuse the toner permanently to the paper.

Figure 7-31   This figure shows how a black-and-white laser printer works.
PaPicasso / Shutterstock.com

Figure 7-32   An all-in-one printer.
Courtesy of Epson America, Inc.

All-in-One Printers

An **all-in-one printer**, also called a *multifunction printer* (MFP), is a single device that looks like a printer or a copy machine but provides the functionality of a printer, scanner, copy machine, and perhaps a fax machine (Figure 7-32). Some use color ink-jet printer technology, while others use laser technology.

🔅 CONSIDER THIS

Who uses all-in-one printers?
Small/home office users have all-in-one printers because these devices require less space than having a separate printer, scanner, copy machine, and fax machine. Another advantage of these devices is they are significantly less expensive than if you purchase each device separately. If the device breaks down, however, you lose all four functions, which is the primary disadvantage.

3-D Printers

A **3-D printer** uses a process called additive manufacturing to create an object by adding material to a three-dimensional object, one horizontal layer at a time. 3-D printers can print solid objects, such as clothing, prosthetics, eyewear, implants, toys, parts, prototypes, and more (Figure 7-33).

Using a digital model scanned from an existing item or created with CAD (computer-aided design) software, 3-D printers begin creating an object at the bottom and add layers of material to the object until it is complete. Depending on the type of printer, the layers are built and blended seamlessly using a variety of substances including liquid polymer, gel, resin, edible food, ceramics, plastic, nylon, wood, bronze, and copper.

In the past, 3-D printers were quite expensive and used only by large enterprises. Today, consumers work with more affordable desktop 3-D printers to create hundreds of thousands of everyday objects including custom toys, cups, household tools, kitchen utensils, storage boxes, replacement parts, game pieces, and more. For those users who do not feel comfortable creating a digital model, 3-D printer manufacturers typically provide downloadable patterns, and online community members often share patterns for free.

Figure 7-33   A 3-D printer creates a rib cage from the digital model.
iStockphoto.com / belekekin

Small and large businesses use 3-D printing in a variety of fields, including medical, automotive, aerospace, art, architecture, and manufacturing. For example, Boeing uses more than 50,000 parts created with 3-D printing for its civilian and military aircraft, Nike develops prototypes of its shoes, and surgeons implant prosthetic body parts, including ribs and other bones, into patients. Researchers claim that in the near future, 3-D printers will be able to replicate practically any object that can be scanned or designed.

Thermal Printers

A **thermal printer** generates images by pushing electrically heated pins against heat-sensitive paper. Basic thermal printers are inexpensive, but the print quality is low, the images tend to fade over time, and thermal paper can be expensive. Self-service gas pumps often print gas receipts using a built-in, lower-quality thermal printer. Many POS terminals in retail and grocery stores also print purchase receipts on thermal paper.

Some thermal printers have high print quality and can print at much faster rates than ink-jet and laser printers. A *dye-sublimation printer*, sometimes called a *digital photo printer*, uses heat to transfer colored dye to specially coated paper. Photography studios, medical labs, security identification systems, and other professional applications requiring high image quality use dye-sublimation printers that can cost thousands of dollars (Figure 7-34). Dye-sublimation printers for the home or small business user, by contrast, typically are much slower and less expensive than their professional counterparts. Some are small enough for the mobile user to carry in a briefcase.

Figure 7-34   A dye-sublimation printer.
Courtesy of Mitsubishi Electric Visual Solutions America, Inc..

Mobile Printers

A **mobile printer** is a small, lightweight, battery-powered printer that allows a mobile user to print from a laptop, smartphone, or other mobile device while traveling (Figure 7-35). Barely wider than the paper on which they print, mobile printers fit easily in a briefcase alongside a laptop.

Mobile printers mainly use ink-jet or thermal technology. Many connect to a USB port. Others have a built-in wireless port through which they communicate with the computer.

Figure 7-35   A mobile printer is small enough to fit in a backpack.
Courtesy of Brother International Corporation

Figure 7-36   A label printer.
iStockphoto.com / ZavgSG

Label Printers

A **label printer** is a small printer that prints on an adhesive-type material that can be placed on a variety of items, such as envelopes, packages, optical discs, photos, and file folders (Figure 7-36). Most label printers also print bar codes. Label printers typically use thermal technology.

Plotters and Large-Format Printers

A **plotter** is a are sophisticated printer used to produce high-quality drawings, such as blueprints, maps, and circuit diagrams. These printers are used in specialized fields such as engineering and drafting and usually are very costly. Current plotters use a row of charged wires (called styli) to draw an electrostatic pattern on specially coated paper and then fuse toner to the pattern. The printed image consists of a series of very small dots, which provides high-quality output.

Using ink-jet printer technology, but on a much larger scale, a **large-format printer** creates photo-realistic-quality color prints. Graphic artists use these high-cost, high-performance printers for signs, posters, and other professional quality displays (Figure 7-37).

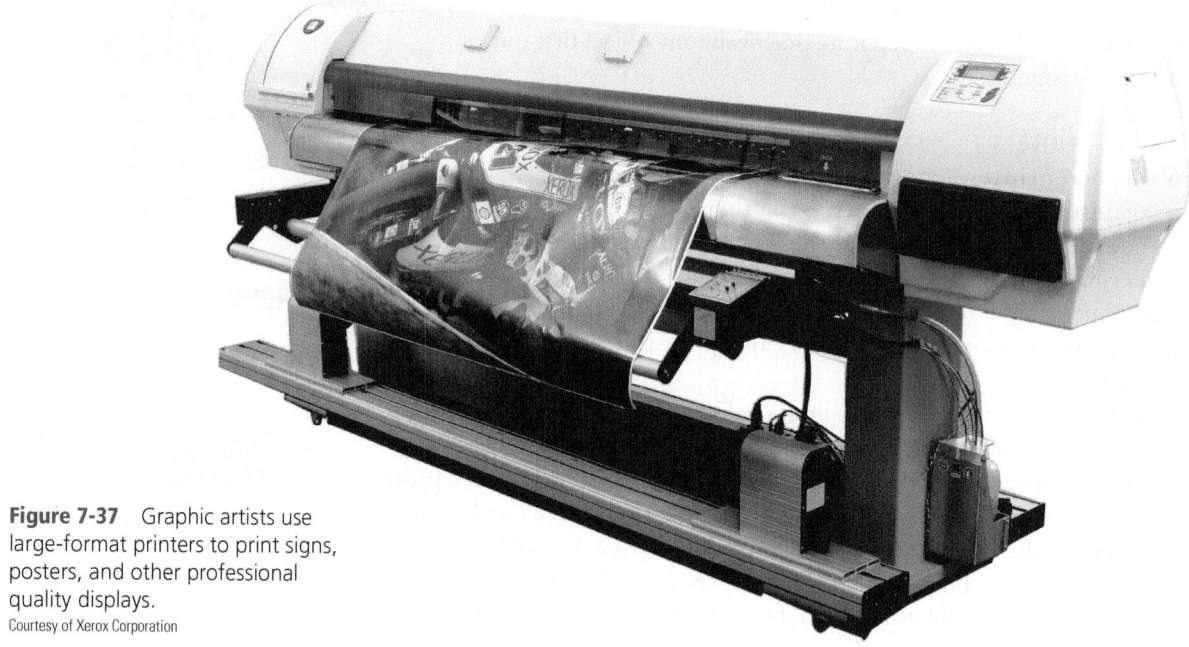

Figure 7-37   Graphic artists use large-format printers to print signs, posters, and other professional quality displays.
Courtesy of Xerox Corporation

Impact Printers

An **impact printer** forms characters and graphics on a piece of paper by striking a mechanism against an inked ribbon that physically contacts the paper. Impact printers characteristically are noisy because of this striking activity (Figure 7-38). Impact printers are ideal for printing multi part forms because they print through many layers of paper easily. Factories, warehouses, and retail counters may use impact printers because these printers withstand dusty environments, vibrations, and extreme temperatures.

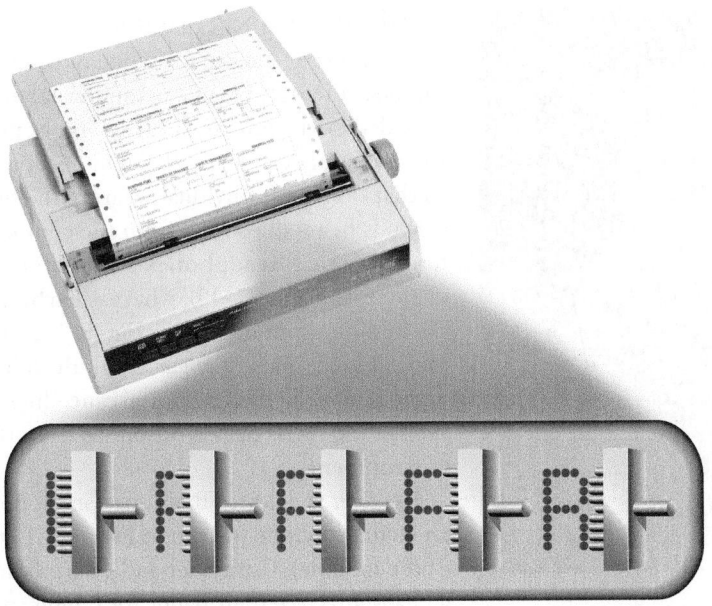

Figure 7-38   An impact printer produces printed images when tiny pins strike an inked ribbon.
Courtesy of Oki Data Americas, Inc.

Other Output Devices

In addition to displays and printers, other output devices are available for specific uses and applications. These include speakers, headphones and earbuds, data projectors, interactive whiteboards, and force-feedback game controllers and tactile output.

Speakers

Most personal computers and mobile devices have a small internal speaker that usually emits only low-quality sound. Thus, many users attach surround sound **speakers** or speaker systems to their computers, game consoles, and mobile devices to generate higher-quality sounds for playing games, interacting with media presentations, listening to music, and viewing movies (Figure 7-39).

Most surround sound computer speaker systems include one or two center speakers and two or more *satellite speakers* that are positioned so that sound emits from all directions. Speakers typically have tone and volume controls, allowing users to adjust settings. To boost the low bass sounds, surround sound speaker systems also include a *subwoofer*.

In some configurations, a cable connects the speakers or the subwoofer to a port on the computer or device. With wireless speakers, however, a transmitter connects to a port on the computer, which wirelessly communicates with the speakers.

Figure 7-39   Users often attach high-quality surround sound speaker systems to their computers, game consoles, and mobile devices.
Courtesy of Logitech

 CONSIDER THIS

What do the numbers mean in surround sound configurations?
The first number refers to the number of speakers, and the second number refers to the number of subwoofers. For example, a 2.1 speaker system contains two speakers and one subwoofer. A 5.1 speaker system has five speakers (i.e., four satellite speakers, one center speaker) and one subwoofer. A 7.2 speaker system has seven speakers (i.e., four satellite speakers, two side speakers, one center speaker) and two subwoofers.

Headphones and Earbuds

When using speakers, anyone in listening distance can hear the output. In a computer laboratory or other crowded environment, speakers might not be practical. Instead, users can listen through headphones or earbuds so that only the individual wearing the headphones or earbuds hears the sound from the computer. The difference is that **headphones** cover or are placed outside of the ear (Figure 7-40), whereas **earbuds** (shown with the audio output devices in Figure 7-23 earlier in the module) rest inside the ear canal. Both headphones and earbuds usually include noise-cancelling technology to reduce the interference of sounds from the surrounding environment.

A *headset* is a device that functions as both headphones and a microphone (shown in Figure 7-1 at the beginning of the module). Computer and smartphone users wear a headset to free their hands for typing and other activities while talking or listening to audio output. Many headsets communicate wirelessly with the computer or mobile device.

Figure 7-40 In a crowded environment where speakers are not practical, users can wear headphones to hear audio output.
Terrie L. Zeller / Shutterstock.com

As an alternative to headphones, earbuds, or headsets, you can listen to audio from mobile devices, such as a portable media player or smartphone, through speakers in a vehicle or on a stereo system at home or work. Or, you can purchase speakers specifically designed to play audio from the device.

Data Projectors

A **data projector** is a device that projects the text and images displaying on a computer or mobile device screen on a larger screen so that an audience can see the image clearly (Figure 7-41). For example, many classrooms use data projectors so that all students easily can see an instructor's presentation on the screen.

data projector

Figure 7-41 A data projector projects an image from a computer or mobile device screen on a larger screen so that an audience easily can see the image.
iStockphoto.com / poba; iStockphoto.com / Michal_edo

Some data projectors are large devices that attach to a ceiling or wall in an auditorium. Others, designed for the mobile user, are small portable devices that can be transported easily. Two types of smaller, lower-cost units are LCD projectors and DLP projectors.

- An *LCD projector*, which uses liquid crystal display technology, attaches directly to a computer or mobile device and uses its own light source to display the information shown on the computer screen. Because LCD projectors tend to produce lower-quality images, users often prefer DLP projectors for their sharper, brighter images.
- A *digital light processing (DLP) projector* uses tiny mirrors to reflect light, which produces crisp, bright, colorful images that remain in focus and can be seen clearly, even in a well-lit room. Some newer televisions use DLP instead of LCD or plasma technology.

Interactive Whiteboards

An **interactive whiteboard** is a touch-sensitive device, resembling a dry-erase board, that displays the image on a connected computer screen, usually via a projector. A presenter controls the program by clicking a remote control, touching the whiteboard, drawing on or erasing the whiteboard with a special digital pen and eraser, or writing on a special tablet. Notes written on the interactive whiteboard can be saved directly on the computer and/or printed. Interactive whiteboards are used frequently in classrooms as a teaching tool (Figure 7-42), during meetings as a collaboration tool, and to enhance delivery of presentations.

Figure 7-42   Teachers and students can write directly on an interactive whiteboard, or they can write on a slate that communicates wirelessly with the whiteboard.
Source: SMART Technologies

Force-Feedback Game Controllers and Tactile Output

Joysticks, wheels, gamepads, and motion-sensing game controllers are input devices used to control movements and actions of a player or object in computer games, simulations, and video games. These devices also function as output devices when they include *force feedback*, which is a technology that sends resistance to the device in response to actions of the user (Figure 7-43). For example, as you use the simulation software to drive from a smooth road onto a gravel alley, the steering wheel trembles or vibrates, making the driving experience as realistic as possible. These devices also are used in practical training applications, such as in the military and aviation.

Figure 7-43 Gaming devices often use force feedback, giving the user a realistic experience.
Vetkit / Dreamstime.com; shutswis / Shutterstock.com; Robseguin / Dreamstime.com

Some input devices, such as a mouse, and mobile devices, such as a smartphone, include *tactile output* that provides the user with a physical response from the device. For example, users may sense a bumping feeling on their hand while scrolling through a smartphone's contact list.

Assistive Technology Input and Output

The ever-increasing presence of computers in everyone's lives has generated an awareness of the need to address computing requirements for those who have or may develop physical limitations. The **Americans with Disabilities Act (ADA)** requires any company with 15 or more employees to make reasonable attempts to accommodate the needs of physically challenged workers.

Besides voice recognition, which is ideal for blind or visually impaired users, several other input options are available. Users with limited hand mobility who want to use a keyboard can use an on-screen keyboard or a keyboard with larger keys. Users with limited hand movement can use a head-mounted pointer to control the pointer or insertion point (Figure 7-44). To simulate the functions of a mouse button, a user works with switches that control the pointer. The switch might be a hand pad, a foot pedal, a receptor that detects facial motions, or a pneumatic instrument controlled by puffs of air.

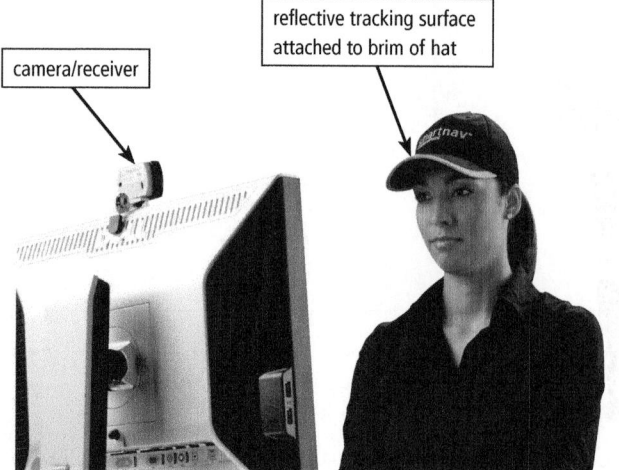

camera/receiver

reflective tracking surface attached to brim of hat

Figure 7-44 A camera/receiver mounted on the monitor tracks the position of the head-mounted pointer, which is the reflective material on the brim of the hat. As the user moves her head, the pointer on the screen also moves.
Courtesy of NaturalPoint, Inc.

For users with mobility, hearing, or vision disabilities, many different types of output options are available. Hearing-impaired users, for example, can instruct programs to display words instead of sounds. Visually impaired users can change screen settings, such as increasing the size or changing the color of the text to make the words easier to read. Instead of using a monitor, blind users can work with voice output. That is, the computer speaks out loud the information that appears on the screen. Another alternative is a Braille printer, which prints information on paper in Braille (Figure 7-45).

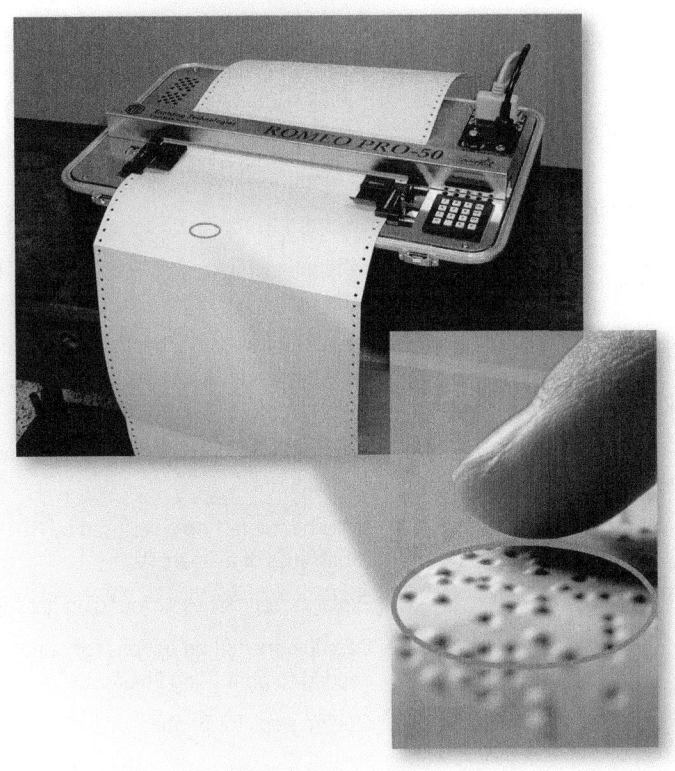

Figure 7-45   A Braille printer.
Courtesy of Enabling Technologies; Don Farrall / Getty Images

✅ Summary

This module presented a variety of options for input and output. Input options included the keyboard, mouse and other pointing devices, touch screens, pen input, motion input, voice input, video input, and scanners and reading devices. Output options included displays, printers, speakers, headphones and earbuds, data projectors, interactive whiteboards, and force-feedback game controllers and tactile output. The module also presented several assistive technology options for input and output.

Study Guide

The Study Guide reinforces material you should know after reading this module.

Instructions: Answer the questions below using the format that helps you remember best or that is required by your instructor. Possible formats may include one or more of these options: write the answers; create a document that contains the answers; record answers as audio or video using a webcam, smartphone, or portable media player; post answers on a blog, wiki, or website; or highlight answers in the book/e-book.

1. ___ is any data and instructions entered into the memory of a computer.

2. Define these terms: data, software, and command. Give an example of a user response.

3. List features that are common to most keyboards. Describe how to use a keyboard shortcut.

4. Explain the criminal and beneficial purposes of keyboard monitoring software.

5. Differentiate among compact, ergonomic, gaming, and wireless keyboards.

6. Define the term, pointer. Name objects a pointing device can select.

7. List different mouse types.

8. Describe the following input devices: touchpad, pointing stick, and trackball.

9. Explain how to interact with a touch screen.

10. Describe how desktop monitors, laptop and mobile device screens, smartphones, wearable devices, portable media players, digital cameras, kiosks, and navigation systems use touch input.

11. List methods and devices for using pen input. Define the term, digitizer.

12. Explain how hand-writing notes during class could impact your knowledge retention.

13. Define the term, motion input. Describe how the entertainment industry, the military, athletics, and the medical field use motion input.

14. Name hardware and devices used for voice and audio input.

15. Outline steps involved in using DV technology.

16. Explain what occurs during a videoconference and the technology needed.

17. Define the term, drone. Identify some uses of drones.

18. Outline steps to secure your privacy when using a device with a webcam.

19. Describe types of scanners and reading devices.

20. A(n) ___ code stores information that can correspond to a web address or other content.

21. List guidelines for safely scanning QR codes.

22. List uses of RFID technology, and list uses for magstripe readers.

23. List guidelines to protect your credit card from scanning devices.

24. Describe how a bank uses MICR technology.

25. Give examples of data collection devices and describe how they are used.

26. Define the term, output. List types and methods of output.

27. Define the terms, display and monitor. Describe different types of monitors.

28. List steps to connect a laptop to an external display.

29. Differentiate among LCD, CCFL, LED, TFT, OLED, and AMOLED technologies.

30. Describe how display quality is determined. Define these terms: resolution, response time, nit, candela, dot pitch, and contrast ratio.

31. Explain the purpose of the GPU. List and describe port types for monitors.

32. Describe the technologies used by HDTV. Explain the capabilities of a Smart TV.

33. Explain safety issues surrounding hardware radiation.

34. Describe orientation options for printouts. Explain what is needed to print using Bluetooth.

35. Outline steps for printing from a smartphone or tablet.

36. Explain how an ink-jet printer works, and describe the mechanics of the ink cartridge.

37. Explain how resolution affects printer quality.

38. Compare the price and quality of laser printers to ink-jet printers.

39. Describe the following printer types: photo, all-in-one, 3-D, thermal, mobile, label, plotter, and impact.

40. Explain how computers and mobile devices use speakers, such as satellite speakers, to emit sound.

41. Differentiate among headphones, earbuds, and headsets.

42. Define the term, data projector. Differentiate between LCD and DLP projector technology.

43. Describe uses of interactive whiteboards and force-feedback game controllers. Define the term, tactile output.

44. List types of assistive technologies for input and output.

You should be able to define the Primary Terms and be familiar with the Secondary Terms listed below.

Key Terms

Primary Terms (shown in **bold-black** characters in the module)

3-D printer (7-30)
all-in-one printer (7-30)
Americans with Disabilities Act (ADA) (7-36)
bar code (7-17)
bar code reader (7-17)
data projector (7-34)
digital pen (7-10)
digital video (DV) camera (7-13)
display (7-22)
drone (7-16)
DV technology (7-14)
earbuds (7-34)

graphics tablet (7-11)
HDTV (7-25)
headphones (7-34)
impact printer (7-32)
ink-jet printer (7-27)
input (7-2)
interactive whiteboard (7-35)
keyboard (7-3)
label printer (7-32)
large-format printer (7-32)
laser printer (7-29)
LCD (7-23)
magstripe reader (7-19)

mobile printer (7-31)
monitor (7-22)
mouse (7-6)
nonimpact printer (7-27)
OCR devices (7-17)
OMR devices (7-17)
output (7-20)
pen input (7-10)
photo printer (7-29)
plotter (7-32)
pointer (7-6)
printer (7-26)
QR code (7-17)
resolution (7-24)

RFID (7-18)
RFID reader (7-18)
scanner (7-16)
signature capture pad (7-10)
speakers (7-33)
stylus (7-10)
thermal printer (7-31)
touch screen (7-8)
touchpad (7-7)
trackball (7-8)
video call (7-15)
videoconference (7-15)
voice recognition (7-13)
webcam (7-15)

Secondary Terms (shown in *italic* characters in the module)

active-matrix (7-24)
air gestures (7-11)
AMOLED (7-24)
aspect ratio (7-25)
audio input (7-13)
backlight (7-23)
bar code scanner (7-17)
Bluetooth printing (7-26)
candela (7-24)
command (7-3)
compact keyboard (7-5)
contrast ratio (7-24)
cursor (7-3)
data (7-3)
data collection device (7-20)
digital light processing (DLP) projector (7-35)
digital photo printer (7-31)
digitizer (7-11)
display device (7-22)
DisplayPort (7-24)
dot pitch (7-24)
dots per inch (dpi) (7-28)
DVI (Digital Video Interface) port (7-24)
dye-sublimation printer (7-31)
ergonomic keyboard (7-5)
flat-panel display (7-22)
force feedback (7-36)
frame rate (7-14)

function keys (7-3)
gaming keyboard (7-6)
gesture (7-8)
gesture recognition (7-11)
graphics processing unit (7-24)
handwriting recognition software (7-11)
HDMI (High-Definition Media Interface) port (7-24)
headset (7-34)
high-definition television (7-25)
insertion point (7-3)
keyboard monitoring software (7-4)
keyboard shortcut (7-3)
keylogging software (7-4)
landscape orientation (7-26)
laser mouse (7-7)
LCD projector (7-35)
LED (7-23)
LED display (7-23)
liquid crystal display (7-23)
magnetic stripe card reader (7-19)
MICR device (7-20)
morphing (7-14)
motion input (7-11)
multifunction printer (7-30)
multi-touch (7-8)
native resolution (7-24)
nit (7-24)
OCR software (7-17)

OLED (7-24)
optical mouse (7-7)
pixel (7-24)
pixel pitch (7-24)
plasma display (7-25)
portrait orientation (7-26)
printout (7-26)
response time (7-24)
Retina Display (7-24)
satellite speakers (7-33)
Smart TV (7-25)
soft copy (7-22)
software (7-3)
source document (7-16)
speech recognition (7-13)
speech-to-text (7-13)
streaming cam (7-15)

subwoofer (7-33)
tactile output (7-36)
TFT (7-24)
toggle key (7-3)
toner (7-29)
touch mouse (7-7)
touch-sensitive pad (7-10)
trackpad (7-7)
unmanned aerial vehicle (UAV) (7-16)
UPC (Universal Product Code) (7-17)
user response (7-3)
video input (7-13)
voice input (7-13)
voice recognition application (7-13)
widescreen monitor (7-25)
wireless keyboard (7-6)
wireless mouse (7-7)

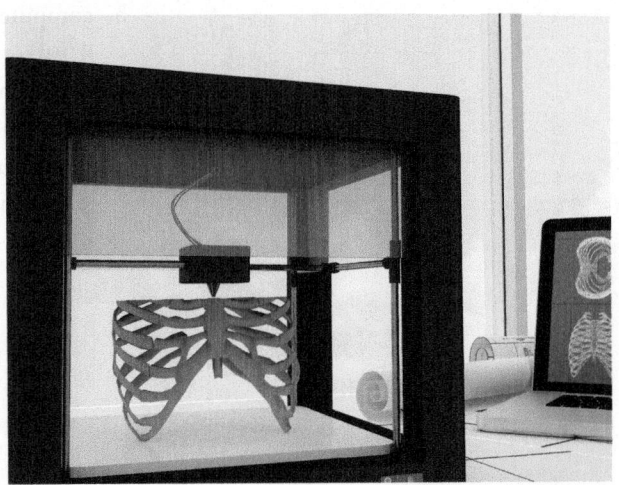

iStockphoto.com / belekekin

STUDENT ASSIGNMENTS

Checkpoint   The Checkpoint exercises test your knowledge of the module concepts.

True/False   Mark T for True and F for False. If False, rewrite the statement so that it is True.

_____ 1. CAPS LOCK and NUM LOCK are two examples of toggle keys.

_____ 2. Keylogging software runs undetected and stores every keystroke in a file for later retrieval.

_____ 3. Wearable devices mainly rely upon touch input.

_____ 4. A smaller frame rate results in a smaller file size for a video, as well as a smoother playback.

_____ 5. Optical character recognition (OCR) and optical mark recognition (OMR) are two technologies used by QR code readers.

_____ 6. A magstripe reader reads the preprinted characters on the bottom of a check.

_____ 7. LCD stands for liquid crystal display.

_____ 8. In terms of response time, the lower the number, the faster the response time.

_____ 9. Contrast ratio defines a display's width relative to its height.

_____ 10. A 3-D printer creates an object by using ink cartridges.

_____ 11. Printer resolution is measured by the number of pixels per inch a printer can print.

_____ 12. A dye-sublimation printer uses heat to transfer colored dye to specially coated paper.

Matching   Match the terms with their definitions.

_____ 1. command

_____ 2. drone

_____ 3. headset

_____ 4. interactive whiteboard

_____ 5. keyboard shortcut

_____ 6. multi-touch

_____ 7. scanner

_____ 8. stylus

_____ 9. touchpad

_____ 10. voice recognition

a. small metal or plastic device that looks like a tiny ink pen but uses pressure instead of ink

b. small, flat, rectangular pointing device that is sensitive to pressure and motion

c. touch screen capability of recognizing more than one point of contact at the same time

d. device that functions as both headphones and a microphone

e. touch-sensitive device that displays the image on a connected computer screen, usually via projector

f. aircraft that operates by an onboard computer and GPS, a remote control device, and/or an app on a computer or mobile device

g. instruction that causes a program or app to perform a specific action

h. computer or mobile device's capability of distinguishing spoken words

i. light-sensing input device that reads printed text and graphics and then translates the result into a form the computer can process

j. one or more keyboard keys that you press to perform an operating system or application-related task

The Problem Solving exercises extend your knowledge of module concepts by seeking solutions to practical problems with technology that you may encounter at home, school, or work. The Collaboration exercise should be completed with a team.

Problem Solving

Instructions: You often can solve problems with technology in multiple ways. Determine a solution to the problems in these exercises by using one or more resources available to you (such as a computer or mobile device, articles on the web or in print, blogs, podcasts, videos, television, user guides, other individuals, electronics or computer stores, etc.). Describe your solution, along with the resource(s) used, in the format requested by your instructor (brief report, presentation, discussion, blog post, video, or other means).

Personal

1. **Assistive Technologies**   You have just purchased a new computer and, because of a visual impairment, you are having trouble reading the information on the screen. What are your next steps?

2. **Smart TV Issues**   You are watching a movie on your Smart TV using a streaming media service. Every few minutes, a message is displayed on the TV stating that the movie is buffering. Why might this be happening, and what can you do to resolve this issue?

© Courtesy of LG Electronics USA Inc.

3. **Touch Gestures Not Working**   You are using the stretch touch gesture to zoom on your mobile device. Each time you perform the gesture, however, instead of zooming, one of your fingers appears to be dragging an item around the screen. What might be the problem?

4. **Dim Screen**   While using your laptop, the screen suddenly becomes dim. You set the brightness to its highest setting before it dimmed and wonder why it suddenly changed. After resetting the brightness to its highest setting, you continue working. What might have caused the screen to dim?

5. **Malfunctioning Earbud**   While listening to music on your portable media player, one side of the earbuds suddenly stops working. What might have caused this?

Professional

6. **Printer Problem**   You are attempting to print on a wireless printer from your laptop, but each time you click the Print button, you receive an error message that the printer is not connected. What are your next steps?

7. **Projector Resolution Issue**   You are preparing for a meeting in your company's conference room and have connected your laptop to the projector. When the projector displays the information from your laptop screen, the resolution drops significantly and not everything fits on the screen. What steps can you take to correct this problem?

8. **Fingerprints Not Recognized**   To increase security, your company now requires employees to sign in to their computer accounts using a fingerprint reader instead of entering a user name and password. This past weekend, you cut the finger you use to sign in, and your computer now does not recognize your fingerprint. As a result, you are unable to access your computer. What are your next steps?

9. **Access Denied**   Your company uses security badges with embedded RFID tags to authenticate the rooms to which employees have access. This badge also grants employees access to the company's parking lot. When arriving at work one morning, you wave your badge in front of the RFID reader, but the gate that allows access to the parking lot does not open. In addition, a red light blinks on the RFID reader. What are your next steps?

10. **Monitors Reversed**   You have two monitors on your desk at work: the monitor on the left is your primary monitor and displays the taskbar and the applications you currently are using, and you typically use the monitor on the right to display an email program. When you arrive at work and sign in to your Windows account, you realize that the monitor on the right is now the primary monitor. What might have happened?

Collaboration

11. **Technology in Finance**   Technology enables individuals and businesses to conduct transactions in the finance industry with great convenience and speed; however, many individuals do not realize the extent to which technology impacts the industry. Form a team of three people to learn more about the important role that technology plays in today's finance industry. One team member should research the different ways that technology impacts and improves personal financial transactions, such as home banking. Another team member should research how large businesses use technology to manage their finances, and the other team member should research the different ways technology has helped improve the stock market. Write a brief report summarizing your findings.

✸ How To: Your Turn

The How To: Your Turn exercises present general guidelines for fundamental skills when using a computer or mobile device and then require that you determine how to apply these general guidelines to a specific program or situation.

Instructions: You often can complete tasks using technology in multiple ways. Figure out how to perform the tasks described in these exercises by using one or more resources available to you (such as a computer or mobile device, articles on the web or in print, online or program help, user guides, blogs, podcasts, videos, other individuals, trial and error, etc.). Summarize your 'how to' steps, along with the resource(s) used, in the format requested by your instructor (brief report, presentation, discussion, blog post, video, or other means).

① Record and Edit a Video

After recording a video, you may want to edit it before sharing it with others. For example, you might want to remove portions of the video, add special effects, or play an audio track instead of the audio recorded with the video. The following steps guide you through the process of recording and editing a video.

Record a Video

a. Verify your camera's battery is charged and that the device has sufficient space available to store the video you are about to record.

b. If you plan to record the video from one location, consider placing the camera on a stable surface.

c. If you intend to record outside where it is windy, shield the camera from the wind.

d. Start the recording.

e. If you plan to move the camera during recording, do so with slow, smooth movements.

f. Stop the recording.

Edit a Video

a. If you are using video editing software on your computer, transfer the video to the computer. If you are using video editing capabilities on your mobile device, run the video editing app.

b. Make a copy of the video so that you can revert to the original if you make a mistake.

c. Run a video editing program on your computer and open the video.

d. To trim a video — that is, remove portions from the beginning and/or end of the video — click the command to trim the video. Select the new starting and ending position for the video.

e. To add a special effect to the video, select the location in the video where you want to add the special effect, and then click the command corresponding to the special effect you want to add.

f. To add music that will play while the video is playing, click the command to add a separate audio track to the video. Next, navigate to and select the music file you want to add. Finally, select the starting and ending locations in the video for the music.

g. Preview the video, save your changes, and exit the program.

Exercises

1. Why might you want to trim a video?
2. What type of device do you use to record videos? Why?
3. Compare and contrast at least three programs or apps that can be used to edit videos. Which one do you prefer? Why?

② Save as or Print to a PDF File

In an effort to conserve paper, many applications, such as Microsoft Office, have a built-in feature enabling users to print soft copies in various formats, such as PDF. When you save as or print to a PDF file (both saving as or printing to PDF produce the same results), anyone with an app capable of reading PDF files will be able the view the file without necessarily having to open it in the same program from which it was created. Several free apps you can use to view PDF files are available. The following steps guide you through the process of printing to a PDF file.

a. Verify the app from which you want to print has a built-in feature to save files in or print files to PDF format. If this feature is not available, search for and install an app that enables you to save files to or print files in PDF format.

b. Open the file you want to save in or print to PDF format.

c. If you want to save the file as a PDF format, display the app's Save As dialog box and check if PDF is one of the available file types.

d. If you want to print the file to a PDF, display the screen to print the file and select the appropriate printer to print the file to PDF.

e. Click the button to save or print the file.

f. Specify a file name and save location for the PDF file.

Exercises

1. What are some applications you can use to view PDF files?
2. In addition to saving paper, what are some other reasons why you might save or print to a PDF?

How To: Your Turn

3 Take Screenshots

Many computer and mobile device operating systems allow you to take screenshots, which are snapshots of the screen that are saved as an image. In addition, third-party programs and apps also allow you to take screenshots. The following steps guide you through the process of taking a screenshot on your computer or mobile device.

a. If you wish to use a third-party app to take a screenshot, search for, download, and install the desired app. Next, run the app and review the required steps to take the screenshot.

b. Display the desired programs, apps, or windows on the screen of which you want to take a screenshot.

c. Issue the command to take the screenshot. On computers, you may need to press a specific key combination (such as CTRL+PRINT SCREEN). On mobile devices, you may need to press specific buttons at the same time (such as the Home button and the Power button) or perform a specific hand gesture (such as swiping your hand across the screen).

d. Locate the screenshot. If you used a third-party app, it may be displayed immediately upon taking the screenshot. If you used an operating system such as Windows or macOS, you may need to run another app (such as Microsoft Word) and paste the image into the document. If you took the screenshot on a mobile device, you may be able to locate the screenshot in the image gallery.

Exercises

1. What are at least three reasons why you may need to take a screenshot?

2. Why might you want to use a third-party program or app to take a screenshot instead of using the computer or device's built-in function?

3. If you take a screenshot of an entire screen but require information on only a section of the screen, what steps can you take to manipulate the screenshot so that it shows only the section of the screen you desire?

4 Share a Photo or Video from Your Mobile Device with an Online Social Network

If you take a photo or record a video on your mobile device and want to share it with your friends, you might consider uploading it to an online social network. This exercise describes two common ways to share a photo or video from your mobile device to an online social network.

Share Button

You may be able to share photos or videos with an online social network easily by using the Share button. To use the Share button, you must have the online social network account to which you want to share properly configured on your mobile device. The following steps guide you through the process of sharing a photo or video from your mobile device with an online social network using the Share button.

a. Locate and display the photo or video on your mobile device that you want to share with the online social network.

b. Tap the Share button.

c. Tap the desired online social network with which you want to share the photo or video.

d. If desired, type a caption or message to share with the photo or video.

e. Tap the necessary button to share the photo or video.

Uploading Photos or Videos Manually

If you are unable to share your photo or video using the Share button, you can sign in to the online social network and upload it manually. The following steps guide you through the process of sharing a photo or video on an online social network by uploading it manually to your online social network account.

a. If necessary, take a photo or record a video you want to share.

b. Using an app installed on your mobile device or the online social network's website, sign in to your account on the online social network on which you want to share the photo or video.

c. Tap the appropriate button to post or share a photo or video.

d. Navigate to and select the photo or video you want to share.

e. If desired, type a caption or message to share with the photo or video.

f. Tap the necessary button to share the photo or video.

Exercises

1. What types of photos or videos do you share with online social networks?

2. Research the potential privacy risks associated with uploading photos or videos of yourself or your family. Are you comfortable sharing photos or videos on online social networks? Why or why not?

3. Why might individuals want to share photos and videos on online social networks instead of using other methods such as sending them as attachments to email messages?

✳ Internet Research

The Internet Research exercises broaden your understanding of module concepts by requiring that you search for information on the web.

Instructions: Use a search engine or another search tool to locate the information requested or answers to questions presented in the exercises. Describe your findings, along with the search term(s) you used and your web source(s), in the format requested by your instructor (brief report, presentation, discussion, blog post, video, or other means).

① Making Use of the Web
Health and Fitness

More than 75 percent of Internet users search online for health information, and their most commonly researched topics are specific diseases or conditions, treatments and procedures, and doctors or other health professionals. One-half of these online diagnosticians say that the information they found for themselves or someone else led them to seek medical attention.

Fitness websites and apps can provide guidance and motivation for all fitness levels and lifestyles. Expert advice is offered for designing customized workout routines, maintaining a nutritious diet, and buying equipment. Other features include downloadable MP3 workouts, videos demonstrating correct exercise techniques, and the ability to locate a virtual supportive workout buddy. Users often can set goals and then track their performance and overall progress with logs and detailed graphs.

Research This: (a) Visit WebMD and two other health websites and describe the features of each. Which of the three is the most user-friendly? Why? Search for the difference between the flu and a cold. Describe the symptoms of each and the recommended foods to eat when you are suffering from either ailment.

(b) Visit WebMD and two fitness websites. What similar features do these websites have, such as fitness tools, effective exercises, and food planners? Which website is the easiest to navigate? Why? Which articles, planners, and tools would you use to start or continue your fitness routines?

② Social Media
Online Social Networks

Aspiring musicians have turned to online social networks to break into the music business and to promote their material. Musical artists are urged to develop accounts on YouTube, Facebook, OurStage, MP3.com, Twitter, Myspace, Last.fm, PureVolume, and other online social networks to interact and stay connected with their fans. They can post information about concerts and album releases and sell concert tickets. They also can add music that fans can listen to, download at no charge, or purchase. Some online social networks sponsor contests for bands to showcase their talents and vie for fans' votes to play live at a local venue. Others are crowd-funding websites where bands can ask fans to pledge a specific amount of money to support the artists' creative efforts.

Research This: View at least two websites that allow listeners to recommend music and share playlists. What similarities and differences do these websites have? Locate one of your favorite artists on an online social network and describe the content displayed. For example, are concerts and new releases being promoted? Then, search for and view at least two musician websites. What types of music are available? Which new artists and songs did you hear?

③ Search Skills
News Search

Performing a news search using a search engine will limit search results to news stories that appeared

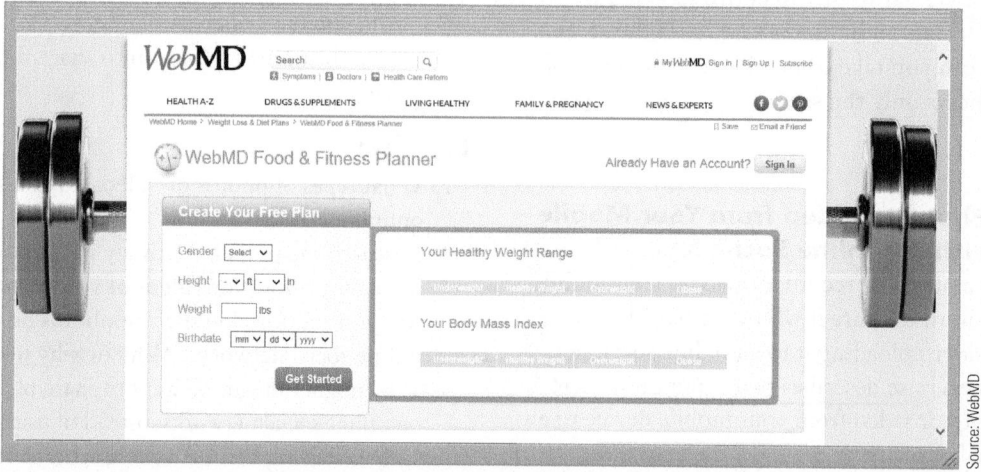

Source: WebMD

Internet Research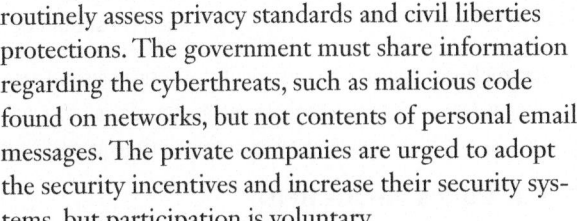

recently or in the past in newspapers and magazines, news websites, and other electronic media news sources. To search for news articles about assistive technology devices, for example, type the search text, assistive technology devices, in the search engine's search box and then click the News link on the search page. You may narrow the results by specifying a date range or location. Click the search button to see the results.

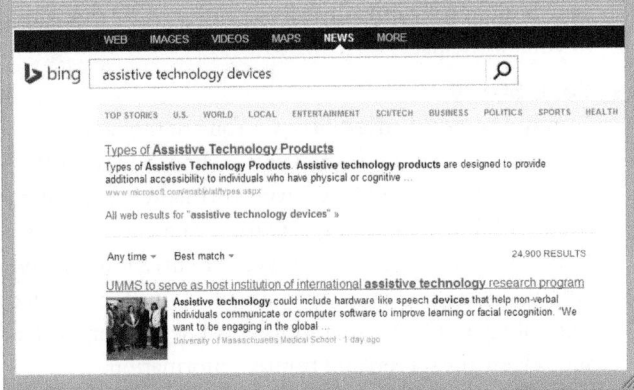

Source: Microsoft

Research This: Create search text using the techniques described above or in previous Search Skills exercises, and type it into a search engine to answer these questions. Present a summary of your findings. (1) Find news articles about the enterprise uses of 3-D printing. (2) Find news articles suggesting capabilities to be included in the next iPhone. (3) Find a news story published within the past week describing how any company uses QR codes. (4) Select a technology company and then find news stories about its financial earnings during the past three months.

4 Security
Passwords
The Office of Cyber and Infrastructure Analysis (OCIA), a division of the U.S. Department of Homeland Security, strives to thwart and respond to physical or cyberthreats and hazards. Part of the office's role is to implement two policies: (1) Presidential Policy Directive 21 - Critical Infrastructure Security and Resilience and (2) Executive Order 13636 - Improving Critical Infrastructure Cybersecurity. These two policies are designed to strengthen and secure the country's critical physical assets and services, such as air traffic control, natural gas supplies, water treatment, power plants, and finance, which are likely targets of cyberattacks. Federal agencies must comply with and routinely assess privacy standards and civil liberties protections. The government must share information regarding the cyberthreats, such as malicious code found on networks, but not contents of personal email messages. The private companies are urged to adopt the security incentives and increase their security systems, but participation is voluntary.

Research This: Locate Presidential Policy Directive 21 - Critical Infrastructure Security and Resilience and Executive Order 13636 - Improving Critical Infrastructure Cybersecurity and read their contents. Then, research news articles describing lawmakers' and businesses' support and criticism of these orders. What components are proposed to increase the nation's cybersecurity? What positions do the Internet Security Alliance and The Internet Association take on this matter? What efforts has Congress made to pass legislation addressing computer security?

5 Cloud Services
Virtualization (IaaS)
An online business's website receives higher traffic during peak holiday shopping times. Purchasing and configuring additional servers to meet this demand for the short term can be an expensive task for companies managing complex computing environments. To minimize cost and maximize performance, companies often use virtualization software rather than purchasing and installing additional memory, storage, or processing power. Virtualization software allows one physical machine to emulate the capabilities of one or more servers. Virtualization is an example of infrastructure as a service (IaaS), a service of cloud computing that allows users to configure a computing environment's hardware, devices, storage, and operating systems using software. Amazon Web Services (AWS) and Microsoft Azure are two cloud providers of virtualization services.

Research This: (1) Use a search engine to find current articles, websites, or reviews of the virtualization offerings of Amazon Web Services and Microsoft Azure. (2) Find a case study about a company using Amazon's or Microsoft's virtualization services, summarize the problem the company was trying to solve, and describe how virtualization played a part in solving it. (3) Refer to the Module 6 Internet Research activity on private, public, and hybrid clouds. Why is running a private cloud in a virtualized environment a popular cloud computing solution?

✳ Critical Thinking

The Critical Thinking exercises challenge your assessment and decision-making skills by presenting real-world situations associated with module concepts. The Collaboration exercise should be completed with a team.

Instructions: Evaluate the situations below, using personal experiences and one or more resources available to you (such as articles on the web or in print, blogs, podcasts, videos, television, user guides, other individuals, electronics or computer stores, etc.). Perform the tasks requested in each exercise and share your deliverables in the format requested by your instructor (brief report, presentation, discussion, blog post, video, or other means).

1. Bar Codes versus RFID

You work as an efficiency analyst at one of the largest retail companies in the world, with multiple stores in every state, as well as in many other countries. For the past 25 years, the company has used bar code readers at checkout counters that scan the bar code on products to determine from a database the price to charge customers and to keep a record of inventory. The company is considering replacing the bar codes and bar code readers with RFID.

Do This: Analyze and discuss the impact such a change would have on the company, its suppliers, and its customers. Include in your discussion any security risks. Find two examples of RFID readers and compare prices, user reviews, and features. Are handheld options for RFID readers available for store clerks to use on the store floor or for customer checkout? Compile your findings. List advantages and disadvantages of implementing RFID. Include information about reliability and costs.

2. Carpal Tunnel Syndrome

While attending college for the past two years, you have worked part-time as a data entry clerk. Recently, you began to feel a pain in your right wrist. Your doctor diagnosed the problem as carpal tunnel syndrome, which is the most well-known of a series of musculoskeletal disorders that fall under the umbrella of repetitive strain injuries (RSIs). Your doctor made several recommendations to relieve the pain. You want to learn more about this debilitating injury.

Do This: Use the web to investigate carpal tunnel syndrome. Research the carpal tunnel syndrome warning signs and risk factors. Find suggestions about proper workstation ergonomics to avoid carpal tunnel syndrome. Evaluate the differences among various treatment options. Does insurance typically cover treatment? Include in your discussion the average length of time of recovery. How should you change your workspace to help heal and prevent further damage? Should the company's insurance pay for changes to your workspace? Why or why not?

3. Case Study

Family-Owned Coffee Shop   You are the new manager for a family-owned coffee shop. You recently hired a part-time employee, who is visually impaired, to assist with record-keeping activities. The coffee shop's owners have asked you to assess their current input and output devices and make recommendations for assistive technologies. The new employee will need to enter data and review on-screen and printed information.

Do This: Use the web to find information about assistive input devices, such as voice recognition and larger keyboards. Research output devices, such as large-screen monitors and Braille printers. In addition to devices, research assistive software that you can install on existing computers, devices, and POS terminals shared by others. Find reviews from users of these assistive devices. Research costs for implementation, and find information about any grants your company can apply for as a nonprofit to ease the costs. Compile your findings.

Don Farrall / Getty Images

Collaboration

4. Printer Comparison   You work for a local real estate agency as an IT consultant. The agency needs a new, networked printer it can use to print high-quality, custom color brochures for the homes it is showing. Each brochure is printed double-sided on glossy paper, and the agency prints an average of 200 brochures per week.

Do This: Form a three-member team. Refer to Figure 7-26 in this module, which lists several questions to consider when choosing a printer, and divide the questions among your team. Each team member should answer each question according to what the employer needs. Then, each team member should use the web to research at least two printers that meet the requirements. Meet with your team, and discuss and compile your findings. Share information about the printers you researched, describe their features, and evaluate their advantages and disadvantages. Identify any additional questions you might have for the employer, such as needs for wireless printing and printing from mobile devices. Which printer you would recommend? Why?

Digital Storage: Preserving Content Locally and on the Cloud

8

iStockphoto.com / Rawpixel

OBJECTIVES

After completing this module, you will be able to:

1 Differentiate between storage and memory
2 Describe the characteristics of internal hard disks
3 Describe the benefits of solid-state drives
4 Identify uses of external hard drives and RAID
5 Differentiate among various types of memory cards and USB flash drives
6 Discuss the benefits and uses of cloud storage
7 Describe characteristics of and differentiate among types of optical discs
8 Explain types of enterprise storage: RAID, NAS, SAN, and tape
9 Identify uses of magnetic stripe cards, smart cards, RFID tags, and NFC tags

Storage

A storage medium, also called *secondary storage*, is the physical material on which a computer keeps data, information, programs, and applications. Examples of storage media include hard disks, solid-state drives (both of which can be internal or external), memory cards, USB flash drives, optical discs, network attached storage devices, magnetic stripe cards, smart cards, RFID tags, and NFC tags. Another storage option is cloud storage, which keeps information on servers on the Internet. Because the user accesses files on cloud storage through a browser using an app from the storage provider, the actual media on which the files are stored are transparent to the user. Figure 8-1 shows a variety of storage options.

In addition to programs and apps, users store a variety of data and information on storage media in their computers and mobile devices or on cloud storage. For example, many users store digital photos, appointments, schedules, contacts, email messages, and tax records. A home user also might store budgets, bank statements, a household inventory, stock purchase records, homework assignments, recipes, music, and videos. In addition or instead, a business user stores

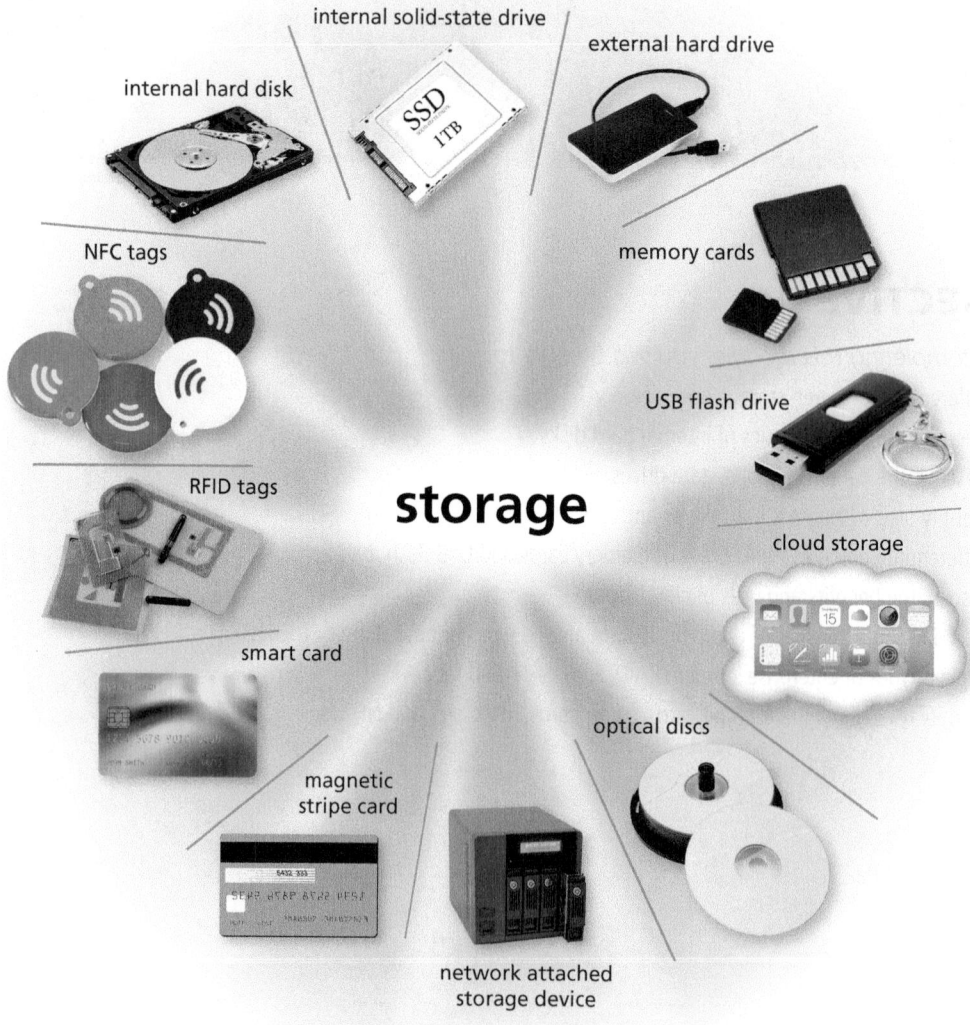

Figure 8-1   A variety of storage options.

reports, financial records, travel records, customer orders and invoices, vendor payments, payroll records, inventory records, presentations, quotations, and contracts. Business and power users store diagrams, drawings, blueprints, designs, marketing literature, corporate newsletters, and product catalogs.

A **storage device** is the hardware that records and/or retrieves items to and from storage media. **Writing** is the process of transferring data, instructions, and information from memory to a storage medium. **Reading** is the process of transferring these items from a storage medium into memory. When storage devices write on storage media, they are creating output. Similarly, when storage devices read from storage media, they function as a source of input. Nevertheless, they are categorized as storage devices, not as input or output devices.

 CONSIDER THIS

Does the amount of storage on a computer or mobile device affect the speed at which it operates?
Although the amount of storage does not directly affect the speed of a processor in a computer or mobile device, storage capacity (discussed next) could indirectly affect the overall performance. For example, a computer or mobile device with extra available storage may perform faster because the unused space can be used to hold temporary files while you browse the web and for virtual memory, discussed later in this module. Storage access times are discussed in more depth later in this module.

Storage Capacity

Capacity is the number of bytes (characters) a storage medium can hold. Recall from Module 6 that a gigabyte (GB) equals approximately 1 billion bytes. A terabyte (TB) is equal to approximately 1 trillion bytes. Table 8-1 identifies the terms manufacturers may use to define the capacity of storage media. For example, a storage medium with a capacity of 750 GB can hold approximately 750 billion bytes.

Storage requirements among users vary greatly. Home users, small/home office users, and mobile users typically have much smaller storage requirements than enterprise users. For example, home users may need 1 to 2 TB (terabytes, or trillions of bytes) of storage for all of their digital content, while enterprises may require 20 to 40 PB (petabytes, or quadrillions of bytes) of storage.

Table 8-1	Terms Used to Define Storage	
Storage Term	**Approximate Number of Bytes**	**Exact Number of Bytes**
Kilobyte (KB)	1 thousand	2^{10} or 1,024
Megabyte (MB)	1 million	2^{20} or 1,048,576
Gigabyte (GB)	1 billion	2^{30} or 1,073,741,824
Terabyte (TB)	1 trillion	2^{40} or 1,099,511,627,776
Petabyte (PB)	1 quadrillion	2^{50} or 1,125,899,906,842,624
Exabyte (EB)	1 quintillion	2^{60} or 1,152,921,504,606,846,976
Zettabyte (ZB)	1 sextillion	2^{70} or 1,180,591,620,717,411,303,424
Yottabyte (YB)	1 septillion	2^{80} or 1,208,925,819,614,629,174,706,176

 CONSIDER THIS

What can a gigabyte store?
The total number of items that can be stored in a gigabyte will vary, depending on file size, quality of media, and a variety of other factors. As a general guide, though, a gigabyte can hold approximately 500,000 pages of text, 600 medium-resolution photos, 250 songs (2 to 3 minutes each), 4 hours of low-resolution video, or 15 minutes of high-definition video.

Storage versus Memory

Items on a storage medium remain intact even when you turn off a computer or mobile device. Thus, a storage medium is nonvolatile. Most memory (i.e., RAM), by contrast, holds data and instructions temporarily and, thus, is volatile. Figure 8-2 illustrates this concept of volatility.

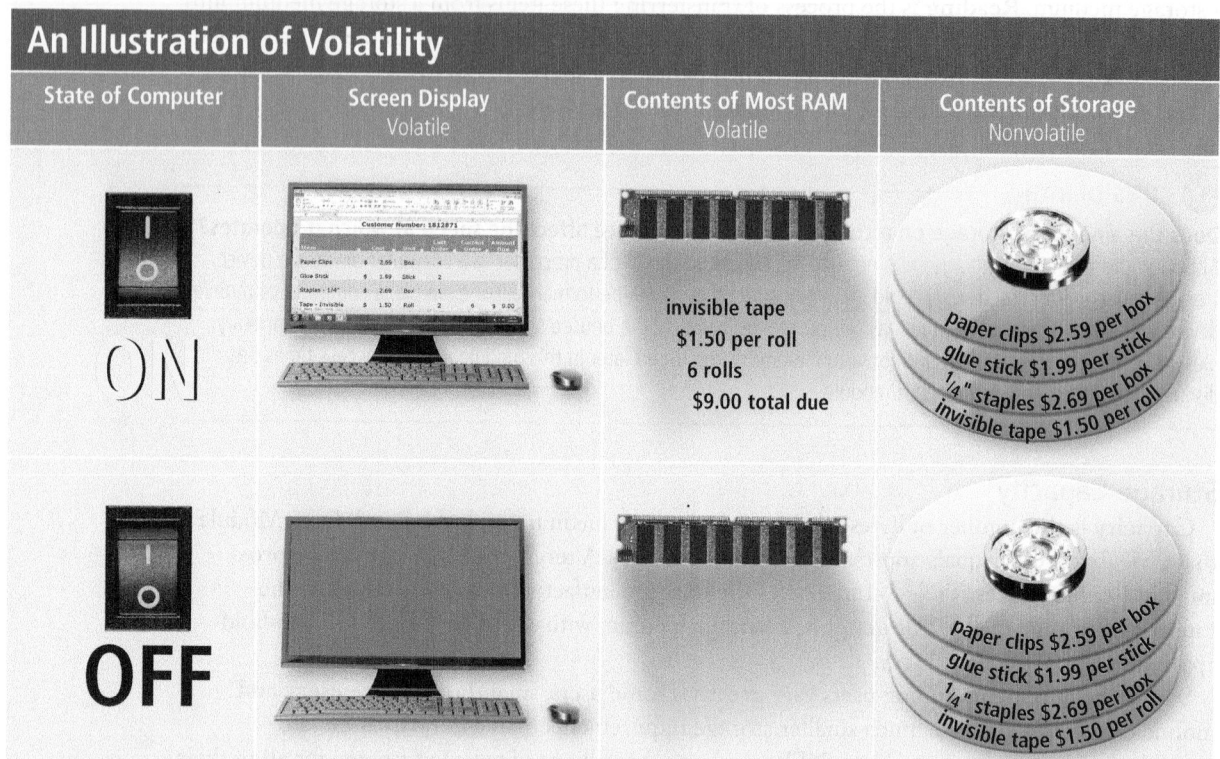

Figure 8-2   A screen display is considered volatile because its contents disappear when power is removed. Likewise, most RAM is volatile. That is, its contents are erased when power is removed from a computer or mobile device. Storage, by contrast, is nonvolatile. Its contents remain when power is off.

ImageState Royalty Free / Alamy Stock Photo; Anson0618 / Shutterstock.com; Unkas Photo / Shutterstock.com; ImageState Royalty Free / Alamy Stock Photo; Anson0618 / Shutterstock.com; Unkas Photo / Shutterstock.com; Source: Microsoft

 CONSIDER THIS

How do storage and memory interact?

When you turn on a computer or mobile device, it locates the operating system on its storage medium and loads the operating system into its memory (specifically, RAM). When you issue a command to run an application, such as a browser, the operating system locates the application on a storage medium and loads it into memory (RAM). When you are finished using the application, the operating system removes it from RAM, but the application remains on the storage medium.

A storage medium is similar to a filing cabinet that holds file folders, and memory is similar to the top of your desk. When you want to work with a file, you remove it from the filing cabinet (storage medium) and place it on your desk (memory). When you are finished with the file, you remove it from your desk (memory) and return it to the filing cabinet (storage medium).

Storage Access Times

The speed of storage devices and memory is defined by access time. **Access time** measures (1) the amount of time it takes a storage device to locate an item on a storage medium or (2) the time required to deliver an item from memory to the processor. The access time of storage devices is slow compared with the access time of memory. Memory (chips) accesses items in billionths of a second (nanoseconds). Storage devices, by contrast, access items in thousandths of a second (milliseconds) or millionths of a second (microseconds).

Instead of, or in addition to, access time, some manufacturers state a storage device's transfer rate because it affects access time. *Transfer rate* is the speed with which data, instructions, and information transfer to and from a device. Transfer rates for storage are stated in *KBps* (kilobytes per second), *MBps* (megabytes per second), and *GBps* (gigabytes per second).

Numerous types of storage media and storage devices exist to meet a variety of users' needs. Figure 8-3 shows how different types of storage media and memory compare in terms of transfer rates and uses. This module discusses these and other storage media.

Tech Feature 8-1: Media Sharing

Users often want to share photos, videos, and music they have stored on computers and mobile devices with others using social media. Read Tech Feature 8-1 to learn about sharing media.

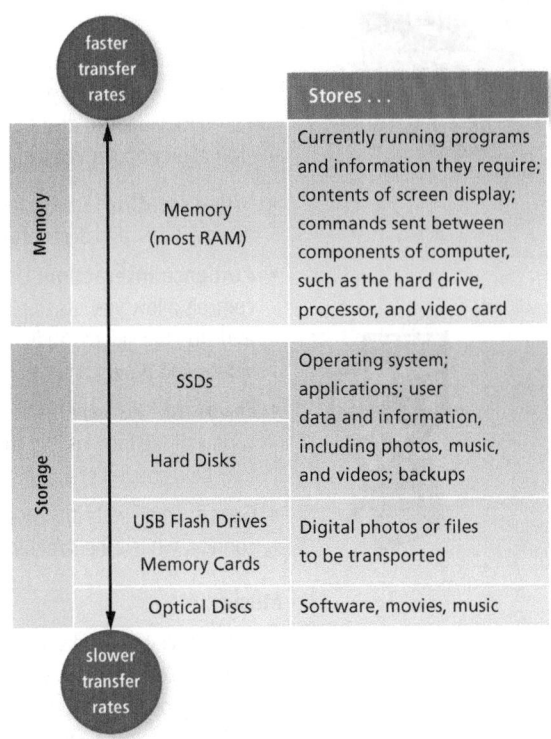

Figure 8-3   A comparison of different types of storage media and memory in terms of relative speed and uses. Memory is faster than storage but is expensive and not practical for all storage requirements. Storage is less expensive but is slower than memory.

 TECH FEATURE 8-1

Media Sharing

Online services offer a host of tools for sharing photos, video, and music with friends and family. When researching locations to share media files, ask yourself the following questions:

- **Where do my original files need to reside?** Can I upload from my computer, mobile device, or camera? Can I send via text message or email?

- **What is the cost?** Is the service free, or must I pay a monthly or annual fee? What happens to my files if I miss a payment or cancel my account?

- **How do I access and share the files safely?** Is the service password protected? Can I use Facebook, Twitter, blogs, and email to share the files?

- **What privacy rights are available?** Can I determine who can access the files and see my profile? Can I use a *geotag*, which is geographical data that can pinpoint where a photo was taken?

- **Can I annotate my media?** Does the service allow me to add notes, tags, and locations?

- **Are online reviews of the services available?** What experiences have other people had using the websites? Are they generally pleased or displeased with the service's reliability and ease of use?

- **What help and website support are available?** Does the service have an extensive Help section? Are FAQs, tutorials, and user forums posted?

Photos

Some photo sharing sites have millions of images to view and possibly download. When deciding which websites to use, consider the following factors:

- **Services:** Many services allow users to print the images. They also offer photo-customizing products.

- **Tools:** Owners can create webpages and keep photos organized by using albums, titles, and tags. They also can join forums to share experiences.

- **Features:** It is efficient if you can upload many files simultaneously in one batch. Many websites allow visitors to write comments on uploaded photos.

- **Storage space:** Some services offer unlimited storage, while others may limit members to a maximum number of stored photos or limit the total storage space.

(Continued)

iStockphoto.com / adventtr

Video

With video recording available on most smartphones and cameras, virtually anyone who owns these devices can produce videos to distribute. The following features are found on popular video sharing sites:

- **Video creation:** Editing tools allow special effects, editing, titles, and descriptions.
- **Audience interaction:** On-screen and keyboard controls allow viewers to play, pause, fast-forward, and stop the videos. Audience members can rate the videos and browse specific categories.
- **Features:** Most services accept files saved in a variety of file formats, but the maximum file size may be restricted or limited.
- **Genre:** Some websites accept a wide variety of content, while others require original work.

Maximus256 / Shutterstock.com

Music

Online social networks and personal radio stations are popular sources of music. Some of these services are for listening only, while others sell songs to download. The following features are found on music sharing sites:

- **Playlists:** Musicians and listeners can organize the songs and albums into specific categories, such as by artist or genre. In a playlist, each song can be played sequentially or shuffled to play in random order.

Dmitrydesign / Shutterstock.com

- **Compatibility:** Some file types will not play on specific mobile devices, so check permissible formats before attempting to upload or download songs.
- **Features:** Services show the album cover, list artist information, and provide song previews.
- **Titles:** Musicians use music hosting websites as a convenient method of distributing their works.

Protecting Your Rights to Files You Share

When you post your files on many media sharing sites, you can give permission to people who want to use or republish your photos, documents, or other digital content for a variety of purposes. As discussed in Module 5, Creative Commons is a rights management system that provides standard licensing options that owners of creative works may specify when granting permission for others to use their digital content. When posting and downloading media files, ensure you are not infringing on copyright protection. Creative Commons simplifies the process of asking for permission to reuse online content.

✳ **Consider This:** Have you used photo, video, or music sharing sites? If so, which ones? How did you decide the services to use? If not, would you like to try uploading or viewing one of these websites?

Hard Drives

The term, **hard drive**, refers collectively to hard disks and SSDs. Hard drives can be internal or external. That is, they can reside inside a computer or mobile device, or they can be an external device that connects to a computer or some mobile devices. The following sections discuss the characteristics of internal and external hard disks and SSDs.

Hard Disk

A **hard disk**, also called a **hard disk drive (HDD)**, is a storage device that contains one or more inflexible, circular platters that use magnetic particles to store data, instructions, and information. Depending on how the magnetic particles are aligned, they represent either a 0 bit or a 1 bit. Recall from Module 7 that a bit (binary digit) is the smallest unit of data a computer can process. Thus, the alignment of the magnetic particles represents the data.

Desktops and laptops often contain at least one hard disk. The entire hard disk is enclosed in an airtight, sealed case to protect it from contamination (Figure 8-4). Read Ethics & Issues 8-1 to consider whether governments should be able to confiscate computers and mobile devices to search the content of hard drives and other media.

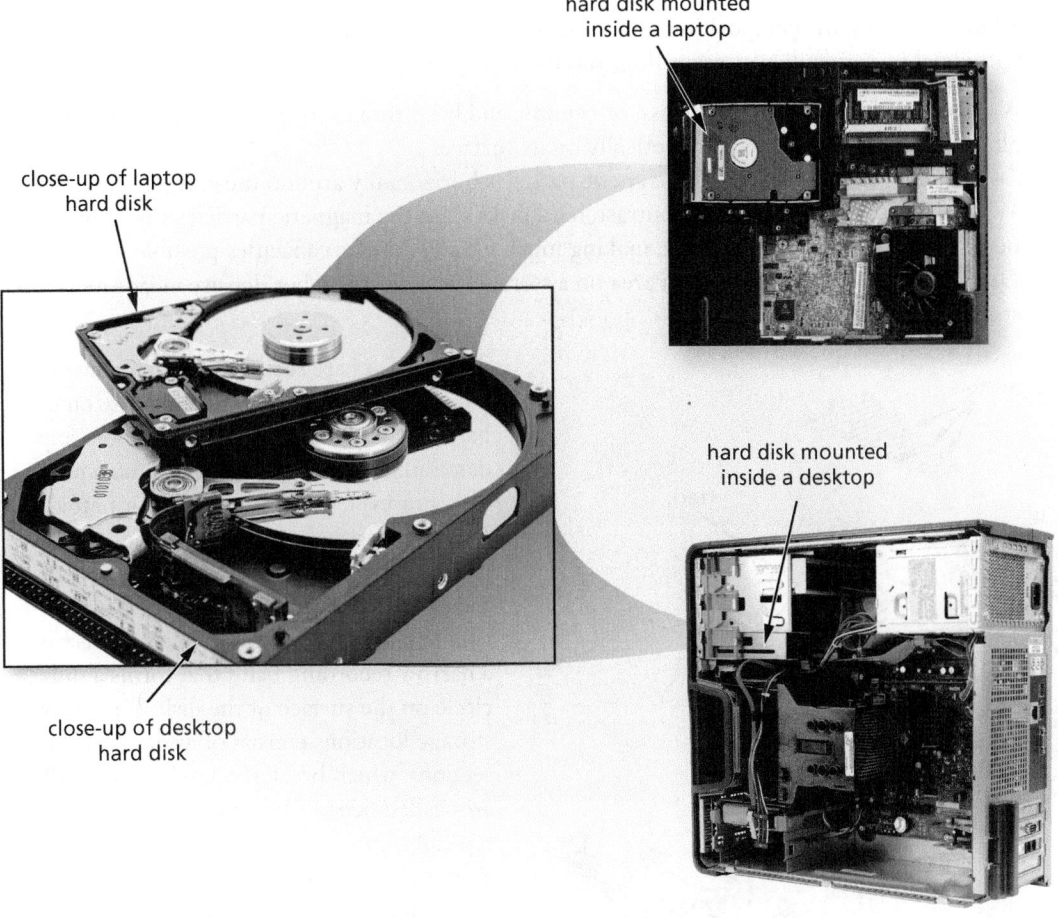

Figure 8-4   The hard disk in a personal computer is enclosed inside an airtight, sealed case. In these photos of the desktop and laptop hard disks, the top plate is removed for illustration purposes. The laptop hard disk is much smaller than the desktop hard disk.
Kitch Bain / Shutterstock.com; ludodesign / Fotolia LLC; Gertan / Shutterstock.com

---

⚛ ETHICS & ISSUES 8-1

Is Government Search and Seizure of Computers Ethical?
In the interest of national security, the Department of Homeland Security may search and seize any computer or mobile device belonging to anyone arriving in the United States. Authorities can conduct the sometimes random searches without a warrant or even a reason. Additionally, the government has taken computers from schools and libraries in a similar manner. Authorities who confiscate computers and mobile devices for an off-site inspection may hold them for any amount of time.

The Fourth Amendment protects against unreasonable search and seizure. Yet sometimes, authorities do not return the devices and provide little or no reason for the seizure. At airports and other points of entry to the country, the government considers computers and mobile devices to be containers, just as a piece of luggage is a container. Authorities, therefore, can search and seize computers and mobile devices without reasonable suspicion, just as they can with luggage.

Opponents claim that users may be unaware of some of the contents of a hard drive, such as with a shared or repurposed computer or device. Users also may not realize that the media on the computer or mobile device contains Internet search history, access to cloud storage, online social network activity, deleted email messages and documents, and drafts of email messages or documents that they never sent or saved. Opponents also claim that the government should be able to inspect the hardware but not the contents of memory or a hard drive.

Librarians and school administrators have stated that the government is invading the privacy of patrons and students. Privacy experts warn that, even without physically inspecting a computer or device, the government may still be able to access digital content you save, search for, or post.

⚛ **Consider This:** Is government search and seizure of computers without a warrant ethical? Why or why not? Do you believe a government employee should have the power to inspect the data on your mobile computer or device? Why or why not? If memories or thoughts someday are decipherable by a computer at a security checkpoint, should it be legal for the government to scan them? Why or why not?

The storage capacity of hard disks varies and is determined by the number of platters the hard disk contains, the composition of the magnetic coating on the platters, whether it uses longitudinal or perpendicular recording, and its density.

- A *platter* is made of aluminum, glass, or ceramic and has a thin coating of alloy material that allows items to be recorded magnetically on its surface.
- *Longitudinal recording* aligns the magnetic particles horizontally around the surface of the disk. With *perpendicular recording*, by contrast, hard disks align the magnetic particles vertically, or perpendicular to the disk's surface, making much greater storage capacities possible.
- *Density* is the number of bits in an area on a storage medium. A higher density means more storage capacity.

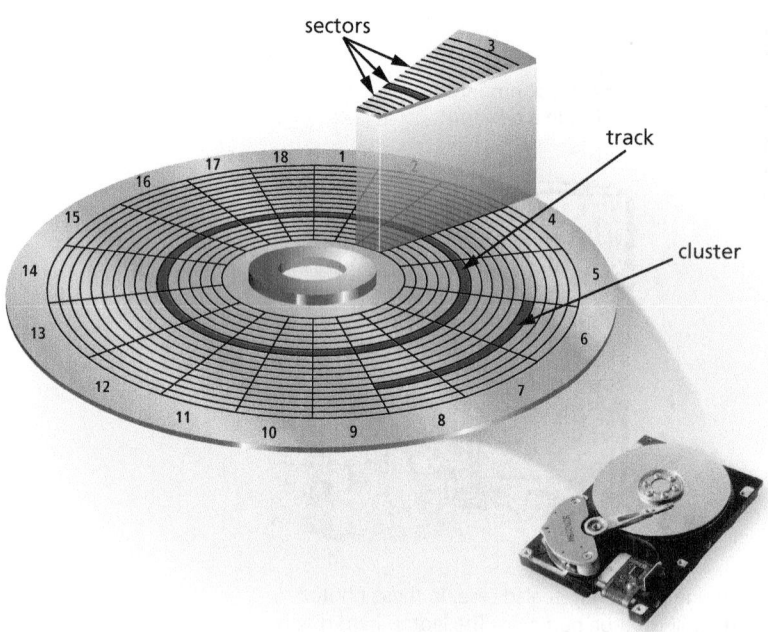

Figure 8-5   Tracks form circles on the surface of a hard disk. The disk's storage locations are divided into wedge-shaped sections, which break the tracks into small arcs called sectors. Several sectors form a cluster.

Gilmanshin / Shutterstock.com

Hard disks are read/write storage media. That is, you can read from and write on a hard disk any number of times. Before any data can be read from or written on a hard disk, however, the disk must be formatted. *Formatting* is the process of dividing the disk into tracks and sectors (Figure 8-5) so that the operating system can store and locate data and information on the disk. A *track* is a narrow recording band that forms a full circle on the surface of the disk. The disk's storage locations consist of wedge-shaped sections, which break the tracks into small arcs called *sectors*. On a hard disk, a sector typically stores up to 512 bytes of data. Sometimes, a sector has a flaw and cannot store data. When you format a disk, the operating system marks these bad sectors as unusable.

On desktops, the platters most often have a form factor (size) of approximately 3.5 inches in diameter. On laptops, mobile devices, and some servers, the form factor is 2.5 inches or less. A typical hard disk has multiple platters stacked on top of one another. Each platter has two read/write heads, one for each side. A **read/write head** is the mechanism that reads items and writes items in the drive as it barely touches the disk's recording surface. A head actuator on the hard disk attaches to arms that move the read/write heads to the proper location on the platter (Figure 8-6).

While the computer is running, the platters in the hard disk rotate at a high rate of speed. This spinning, which usually is 5,400 to 15,000 *revolutions per minute (rpm)*, allows nearly instant access to all tracks and sectors on the platters. The platters may continue to spin until power is removed from the computer, or more commonly today, the platters stop spinning or slow down after a specified time to save power. The spinning motion creates a cushion of air between the platter and its read/write head. This cushion ensures that the read/write head floats above the platter instead of making direct contact with the platter surface. The distance between the read/write head and the platter is about two-millionths of one inch.

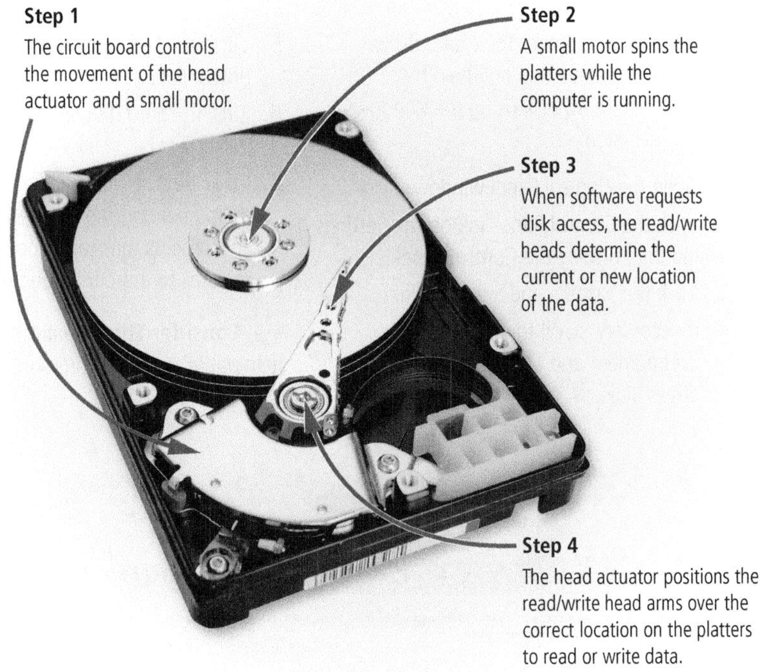

How a Hard Disk Works

Step 1
The circuit board controls the movement of the head actuator and a small motor.

Step 2
A small motor spins the platters while the computer is running.

Step 3
When software requests disk access, the read/write heads determine the current or new location of the data.

Step 4
The head actuator positions the read/write head arms over the correct location on the platters to read or write data.

Figure 8-6   This figure shows how a hard disk works.
Alias Studiot Oy / Shutterstock.com

✳ **CONSIDER THIS**

What happens if dust touches the surface of a platter on a hard disk?

Because of the close clearance between the read/write head and the platter on a hard disk, dust, dirt, hair, smoke, or any other contaminant could cause a disk to crash (Figure 8-7). A *head crash* occurs when a read/write head touches the surface of a platter, usually resulting in a loss of data or sometimes loss of the entire disk.

Although current internal hard disks are built to withstand shocks and are sealed tightly to keep out contaminants, head crashes occasionally still do occur. Thus, it is crucial that you back up a hard disk regularly.

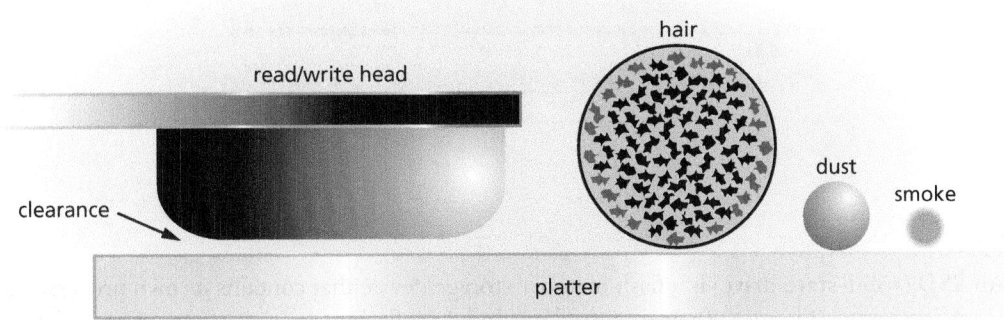

Figure 8-7   The clearance between a hard disk read/write head and the platter is about two-millionths of an inch. Any contaminant could render the disk unusable.

✳ **BTW**
Recovering Data
If you deleted a file from a hard drive and need to recover it, look in the Recycle Bin (Windows) or Trash (Macs). Several free recovery programs are available to download. As a last resort, expert commercial data recovery software is available at retail stores or through the storage manufacturer's website.

Most manufacturers guarantee their hard disks to last approximately three to five years. Many last much longer with proper care. To prevent the loss of items stored on a hard disk, you regularly should perform preventive maintenance such as defragmenting or scanning the disk for errors. Read How To 8-1 for instructions about defragmenting a hard disk.

 **HOW TO 8-1**

Defragment a Hard Disk

As discussed in Module 4, defragmenting a hard disk can improve your computer's performance by storing all related files for a particular program together. This can reduce the amount of time it takes the hard disk to locate and access the files necessary for programs to run. Windows has a built-in tool to defragment a computer's hard disk. Because the macOS defragments files automatically and writes smaller files closer together, Mac users generally do

not have to defragment their hard disks. The following steps describe how to defragment a hard disk using the Windows operating system.

1. Open the Control Panel window.
2. Click the Control Panel link on the Settings menu to display the Control Panel.
3. Click the 'System and Security' link.
4. If necessary, scroll to display the 'Defragment and optimize your drives' link.

5. Click the 'Defragment and optimize your drives' link.
6. Click the hard disk you wish to defragment.
7. Click the Optimize button to begin defragmenting the selected hard disk. This process may take from several minutes to more than one hour.

✷ **Consider This:** What other tools can help optimize the performance of your computer?

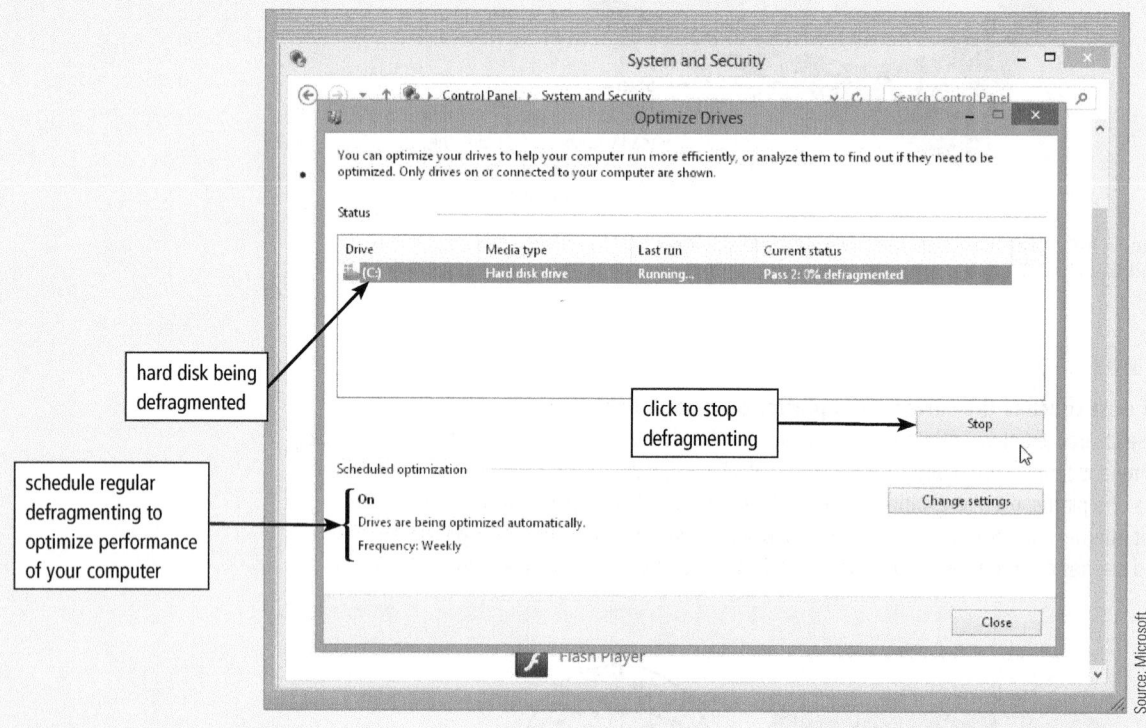

Source: Microsoft

SSDs

An **SSD (solid-state drive)** is a flash memory storage device that contains its own processor to manage its storage (Figure 8-8). As discussed in Module 6, flash memory is a type of nonvolatile memory that can be erased electronically and rewritten. Flash memory chips are a type of *solid-state media*, which means they consist entirely of electronic components, such as integrated circuits, and contain no moving parts. The lack of moving parts makes flash memory storage more durable and shock resistant than other types of media, such as magnetic hard disks or optical discs.

SSDs may be in the form of flash memory chips installed directly on a motherboard or an adapter card. They also may be housed in a separate casing that attaches to the motherboard, as shown in Figure 8-8, and are available in a variety of form factors, including 3.5 inches, 2.5 inches, and 1.8 inches. SSDs are used in all types of computers, including servers, desktops, laptops, tablets, and a variety of mobile devices, such as portable media players and DV cameras. Some computers have both a hard disk and an SSD.

SSDs have several advantages over traditional (magnetic) hard disks, including the following:

- Faster access times (can be more than 100 times faster)
- Faster transfer rates
- Quieter operation
- More durable
- Lighter weight
- Less power consumption (leads to longer battery life)
- Less heat generation
- Longer life (more than 10 times longer)
- Defragmentation is not required

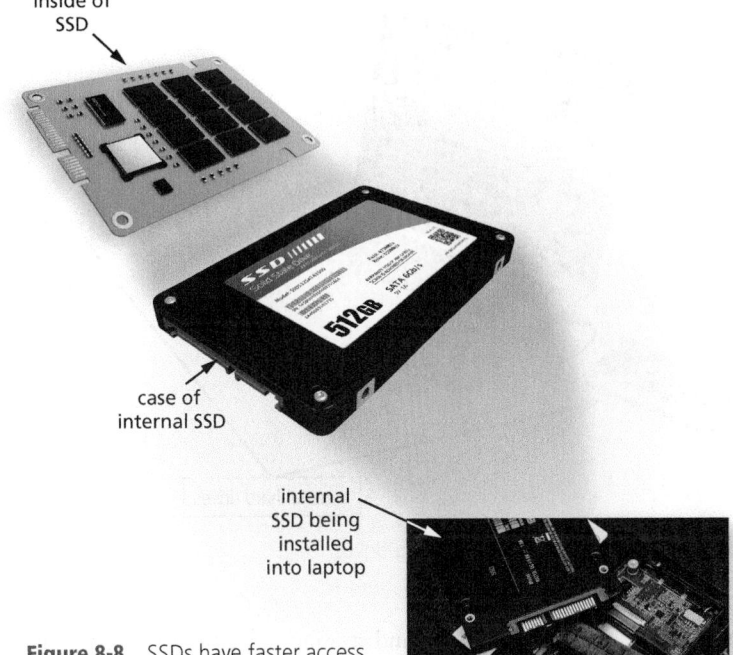

inside of SSD

case of internal SSD

internal SSD being installed into laptop

Figure 8-8 SSDs have faster access times than traditional hard disks, but they also are more expensive.
iStockphoto.com / scanrail; jules / Fotolia LLC; JIPEN / Shutterstock.com

 CONSIDER THIS

Why do SSDs have faster access times than hard disks?
Access time on a hard disk depends on the location of the data. That is, the data on the platter near the read/write head is accessed faster. The data on an SSD, by contrast, can be accessed almost instantly wherever it is located because the drive contains no moving parts.

 BTW

SSD Access Times
You do not need to defragment an SSD because the location of the stored data has no impact on its access times.

The disadvantages of SSDs are that they typically have lower storage capacities than hard disks, data recovery in the event of failure can be more difficult than for traditional hard disks, and their cost is higher per gigabyte. In order to keep the price of a laptop affordable, laptops with SSDs usually have a lower storage capacity than laptops with a traditional hard disk.

 CONSIDER THIS

Which should you use, a hard disk or SSD?
You may want to opt for a hard disk if you are looking for a looking for the lowest-cost option, use the computer or mobile device only for basic tasks at one location, or if you require a large amount of storage space on a hard drive, such as for high-end media. If you transport the computer or mobile device frequently, want faster access to stored items, need a quieter drive (such as for audio recording), you may want to choose an SSD. Another option is a dual-drive computer, that is, one that includes both a hard disk and SSD, so that you can take advantage of the benefits of both drives.

External Hard Drives

An **external hard drive** is a separate freestanding storage device that connects with a cable to a USB port or other port on a computer or mobile device (Figure 8-9). Both hard disks and SSDs are available as external hard drives.

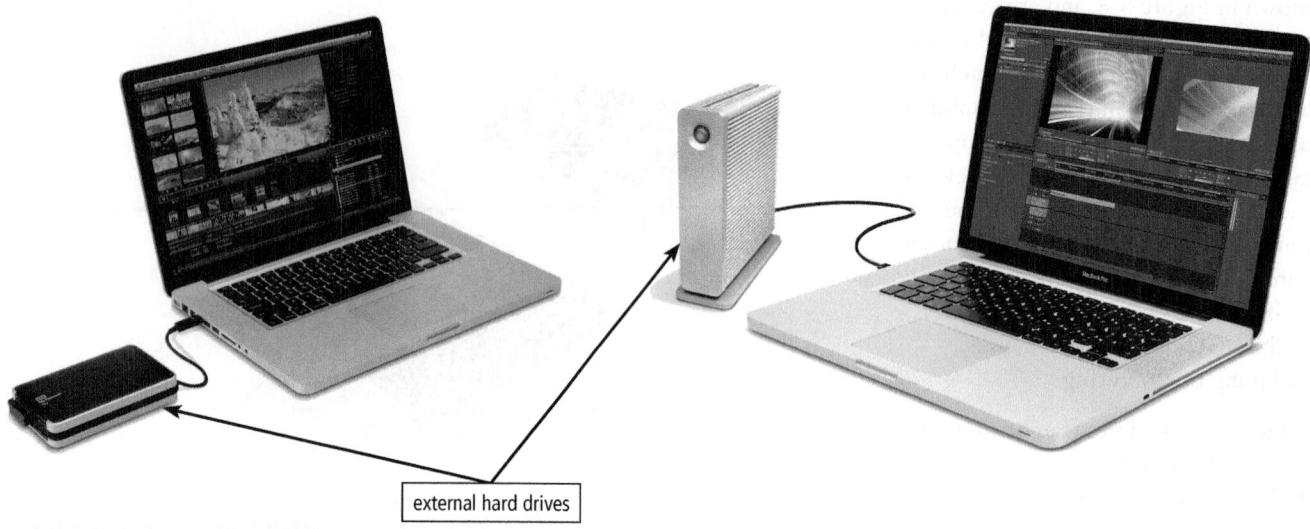

external hard drives

Figure 8-9   Examples of external hard drives.
Courtesy of Western Digital; Courtesy of LaCie

Sizes and storage capacities of external hard drives vary, with some having greater capacities than internal hard drives. Smaller external hard drives are portable and enable mobile users to transport photos and other files from one computer to another easily. As with an internal hard drive, an entire external hard drive is enclosed in an airtight, sealed case. External hard drives units can include multiple hard drives that you can use for different purposes, if desired.

 CONSIDER THIS

Why would you use an external hard drive instead of a second internal hard drive?
Although the transfer rate of external hard drives usually is slower than that of internal hard drives, external hard drives do offer many advantages over internal hard drives:

- Transport a large number of files.
- Back up important files or an entire internal hard drive (most external hard drive models include backup software).
- Easily store large audio and video files.
- Secure your data; for example, at the end of a work session, you can relocate or lock up an external hard drive, leaving no data in a computer. Read Secure IT 8-1 for instructions about encrypting files or drives to protect data.
- Add storage space to a mobile computer, such as a laptop or tablet.
- Add storage space to a desktop without having to open the case or connect to a network.

 SECURE IT 8-1

Encrypting Data and Files on Storage Devices

Hard drives and other storage devices are necessary tools for keeping, backing up, and transporting data and files. If they fall into the wrong hands, however, the data may be unprotected and subject to unrestricted access. Encryption encodes the data so that only authorized people can access the data.

Some operating systems provide a feature allowing users to encrypt individual files, folders, or the entire contents of a hard drive or external storage device. In addition, third-party programs are designed to encrypt data.

While each program may use a different method of encrypting files, they all use the process of cryptography. Mathematical functions, called algorithms, scramble the data. A password generally is needed to decrypt, or reassemble, this data. If this password is lost, the program or operating system's documentation may identify a procedure that allows users to access the encrypted files. In some cases, however, the software will not decrypt the files without the password, so people might reconsider encryption if they anticipate great risk when losing access to these files.

Encrypted files offer security, but users might notice that the operating system may require more time to open and access encrypted files. While no encryption program is infallible, security experts recommend using this process to protect individual files, folders, or entire storage media with personal or sensitive information.

Consider This: What types of files would you encrypt on media in or attached to your computer or mobile device? Would you consider not using encryption in the chance that you might lose the password?

RAID

Some personal computer manufacturers provide a hard drive configuration that connects multiple smaller hard disks or SSDs into a single unit that acts like a single large hard drive. A group of two or more integrated hard drives is called a **RAID** (redundant array of independent disks). RAID is an ideal storage solution in situations where uninterrupted access to the data is critical (Figure 8-10). Because enterprises often use RAID, the characteristics of these devices are discussed in more depth in the enterprise storage section of this module.

Figure 8-10 An example of RAID for the home or small business user.
Courtesy of LaCie

 CONSIDER THIS

How do drives connect to a computer?

A *controller*, formerly called a disk controller, consists of a special-purpose chip and electronic circuits that control the transfer of data, instructions, and information from a drive to and from the system bus and other components in the computer. The controller may be part of a drive, may be on the motherboard, or may be a separate adapter card inside the computer.

In personal computer advertisements, vendors usually state the type of interface supported by the controller. In addition to USB, which can function as an interface for an external hard drive, four other types of interfaces for use in personal computers are EIDE, SCSI, SAS, and SATA.

- *EIDE* (Enhanced Integrated Drive Electronics) is an interface that uses parallel signals to transfer data, instructions, and information. EIDE interfaces provide connections for hard disks, SSDs, RAID, optical disc drives, and tape drives.
- Like EIDE, *SCSI* (Small Computer System Interface) also uses parallel signals, but can support up to 8 or 15 peripheral devices. Supported devices include hard disks, SSDs, RAID, optical disc drives, tape drives, printers, scanners, network cards, and more.
- *SAS* (serial-attached SCSI) is a type of SCSI that uses serial signals to transfer data, instructions, and information. Advantages of SAS over parallel SCSI include thinner, longer cables; reduced interference; lower cost; support for many more connected devices at once; and faster speeds. SAS interfaces support connections to hard disks, SSDs, RAID, optical disc drives, printers, scanners, digital cameras, and other devices.
- *SATA* (Serial Advanced Technology Attachment) uses serial signals to transfer data, instructions, and information. The primary advantage of SATA interfaces is that their cables are thinner, longer, more flexible, and less susceptible to interference than cables that use parallel signals. SATA interfaces support connections to hard disks, SSDs, RAID, and optical disc drives. External drives can use the *eSATA* (external SATA) interface, which is much faster than USB.

 BTW
Serial versus Parallel
With serial transfers, data is sent one bit at a time. Parallel transfers, by contrast, send several bits at once.

Portable Flash Memory Storage

In addition to SSDs discussed in the previous section, two other widely used types of flash memory storage include memory cards and USB flash drives. Users opt for memory cards and USB flash drives because they are portable.

Memory Cards

Memory cards enable mobile users easily to transport digital photos, music, videos, or other files to and from mobile devices and computers or other devices. As mentioned in Module 1, a **memory card** is a removable flash memory storage device, usually no bigger than 1.5 inches in height or width, that you insert in and remove from a slot in a computer, mobile device, or card reader/writer (Figure 8-11).

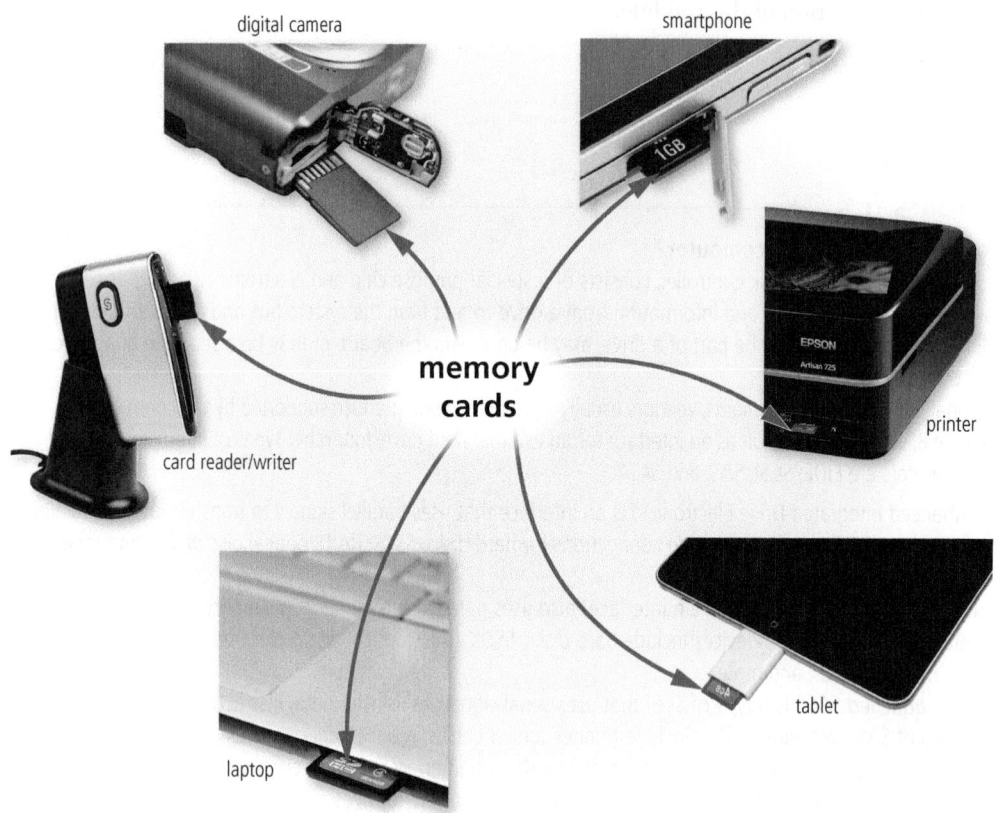

Figure 8-11   Many types of computers and devices have slots for memory cards.

iStockphoto.com / TZfoto; Courtesy of Epson America Inc; Verisakeet / Fotolia LLC; Noblige / Dreamstime.com; iStockphoto.com / brianbalster; iStockphoto.com / hanibaram

Common types of memory cards include **SDHC (Secure Digital High Capacity), SDXC (Secure Digital Expanded Capacity), miniSD, microSDHC, microSDXC, CF (CompactFlash), xD Picture Card, Memory Stick PRO Duo,** and **M2 (Memory Stick Micro)**. Capacities of memory cards vary. A slot on a computer or device often accepts multiple types of cards. For example, an SD slot will accept an SDHC and SDXC card. To read a mini or micro card in a computer, you insert it in an adapter that fits in a standard-sized slot on the computer or device (shown in Figure 8-1 at the beginning of this module).

If your computer or printer does not have a built-in card slot, you can purchase a *card reader/ writer*, which is a device that reads from and writes on memory cards. Card reader/writers usually connect to the USB port on a computer. The type of card determines the type of card reader/ writer needed. Some accept multiple types of cards; others accept one type. Figure 8-12 shows how one type of memory card works with a card reader/writer.

How SD Cards Work

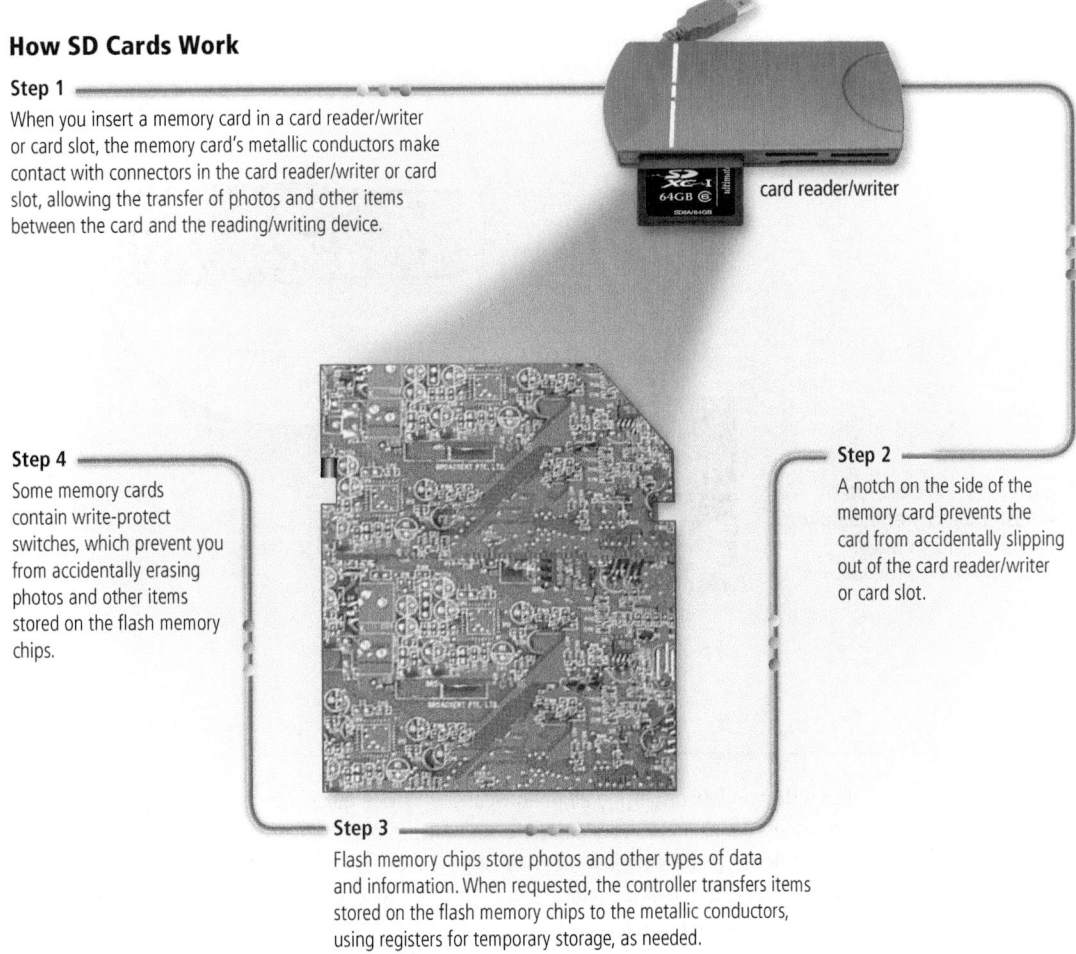

Step 1
When you insert a memory card in a card reader/writer or card slot, the memory card's metallic conductors make contact with connectors in the card reader/writer or card slot, allowing the transfer of photos and other items between the card and the reading/writing device.

card reader/writer

Step 4
Some memory cards contain write-protect switches, which prevent you from accidentally erasing photos and other items stored on the flash memory chips.

Step 2
A notch on the side of the memory card prevents the card from accidentally slipping out of the card reader/writer or card slot.

Step 3
Flash memory chips store photos and other types of data and information. When requested, the controller transfers items stored on the flash memory chips to the metallic conductors, using registers for temporary storage, as needed.

Figure 8-12   This figure shows how an SD card works.
iStockphoto.com / HugoGmez; Courtesy of Kingston Technology Company Inc.

✹ CONSIDER THIS

What is the life span of a memory card?
Depending on the card, manufacturers claim their media can last from 10 to 100 years with proper care, including the following:
• Do not bend the card.
• Avoid dropping the card.
• Keep cards away from direct sunlight.
• Do not expose cards to extreme temperatures.
• Do not remove the card while data is transferring to or from it.

USB Flash Drives

As mentioned in Module 1, a **USB flash drive**, sometimes called a *thumb drive*, is a flash memory storage device that plugs in a USB port on a computer or mobile device (Figure 8-13). USB flash drives are convenient for mobile users because they are small and lightweight enough to be transported on a keychain or in a pocket. With a USB flash drive, users easily transfer documents, photos, music, and videos from one computer to another. Storage capacities of USB flash drives vary. Read Secure IT 8-2 for pointers about safely removing a USB flash drive and other media.

Figure 8-13 A close-up of the flash memory and circuitry inside a USB flash drive.
cheyennezj / Shutterstock.com; iStockphoto.com / werny

SECURE IT 8-2

Safely Remove Media

If you are using portable flash memory storage with your computer or mobile device, you should not remove the device or media while it is in use. Likewise, you should not remove a smartphone, digital camera, or portable media player that actively is connected to your computer. Although you might not be accessing files, the operating system still might be accessing the device, and disconnecting it may damage the files.

Operating systems typically provide an option to remove or eject the device or media safely and then will notify you when the device or media no longer is in use and can be removed. To remove or eject removable storage media, follow these steps:

1. Close any files or exit any programs that are open or running on the media.

2. Open the window displaying all the drives and media connected to your computer or mobile device and then select the drive or media you want to remove safely.

3. Click the command to safely remove or eject the removable storage media. (If you are unable to locate this command, you may need to press and hold or right-click the icon representing the device or media to display a shortcut menu and then click the command to remove or eject the device or media safely.)

4. When the notification appears stating that the device or media is safe to remove or eject, disconnect or remove it from your computer. If a notification does not appear, you can disconnect or remove the device or media once it no longer appears in your operating system as connected to your computer.

These guidelines generally apply to all types of portable flash memory storage, including USB flash drives, memory cards, and solid-state drives. When handling these storage devices, do not subject them to extreme temperatures, moisture, dust, or static electricity. Store them in cases, and try to avoid dropping them.

Consider This: Do you follow the guidelines described here before disconnecting portable flash memory storage, smartphones, digital cameras, and portable media players from your computer? If not, have you encountered damaged files on your storage devices? Should storage companies provide instructions on their packaging materials about how to remove media safely?

Cloud Storage

Some users choose cloud storage in addition to storing data locally on a hard disk, SSD, or other media. As discussed in previous modules, **cloud storage** is an Internet service that provides storage to computer or mobile device users.

Cloud storage is available for home and business users, with various levels of storage services available. Cloud storage fee arrangements vary, depending on the user's storage requirements.

CONSIDER THIS

What are some advantages of cloud storage?

Users subscribe to cloud storage for a variety of reasons:

- To access files on the Internet from any computer or device that has Internet access
- To store large audio, video, and graphics files on the Internet instantaneously, instead of spending time downloading to a local hard drive or other media
- To allow others to access their files on the Internet so that others can listen to an audio file, watch a video clip, or view a photo — instead of sending the file to them via an email message
- To view time-critical data and images immediately while away from the main office or location; for example, doctors can view X-ray images from another hospital, home, or office, or while on vacation
- To store off-site backups of data
- To provide data center functions, relieving enterprises of this task

 CONSIDER THIS

What is a personal cloud?

Some hard drive manufacturers sell networked hard drives that make your data available on a cloud that exists within your home or office. That is, the networked hard drive connects directly to your router, creating a *personal cloud* that allows you to access its files over the Internet. With a personal cloud, you maintain the storage device on which the files are located versus a cloud storage provider where your files are stored on servers on the Internet that a cloud storage provider configures, maintains, and backs up.

Tech Feature 8-2: Services Offered by Cloud Storage Providers

Cloud storage provides access to your files across many devices. Read Tech Feature 8-2 to learn about services provided by cloud storage providers.

 BTW

Online Backups
Online backups are popular among both business users and consumers because they can schedule backups to take place automatically and do not need to purchase storage media. Users generally pay for backup services based on the amount of bandwidth or storage they use.

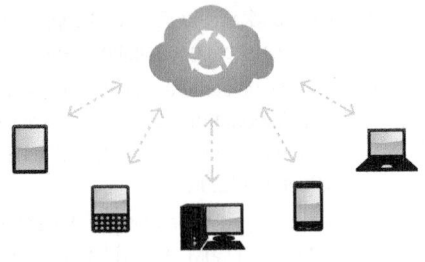 **TECH FEATURE 8-2**

Services Offered by Cloud Storage Providers

Microsoft OneDrive, Google Drive, Apple's iCloud, Amazon Cloud Drive, Dropbox, and Box are among the many options that consumers consider for cloud storage. These and other cloud storage providers enable you to synchronize files, write documents, back up files on your computer or mobile device, share project work, stream music, post photos, and play games online. Many offer a limited amount of free storage and make additional storage available for a fee.

iStockphoto.com / Aaltazar

Synchronize Files

Many cloud storage providers place a folder on your computer with contents you can synchronize across multiple devices. Other providers allow you to upload files for storage online, and download them via a web app or mobile app.

Cloud storage providers often retain previous versions of your files, in case you need to revert to an earlier one.

Write Documents

Google Drive and OneDrive provide integrated web apps to edit documents in a browser and store them on the cloud. Some third-party tools, such as Evernote, an online note taking application, synchronize your notes with popular cloud storage providers.

Back Up Files

Storing files on the cloud is an easy way to back them up in case the hard drive on your computer fails or your mobile device is lost, stolen, or damaged. Some cloud backup services, such as Carbonite, automatically copy a computer or mobile device's new or changed files to the cloud, freeing users of performing backups themselves. Backup providers generally do not synchronize files across a user's multiple devices, but only provide capabilities to store and retrieve files on the cloud.

Stream Music

You can play music and videos stored offline (i.e., on your computer or mobile devices) in places without Internet access. Many people also store their media files on the cloud, so as not to use up the limited internal storage available on mobile devices. Some services, such

(Continued)

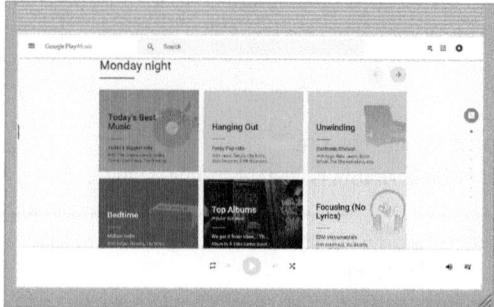

Source: Google, Inc.

as Google Play, support streaming music stored on the cloud to Android, iOS, and other devices.

Post Photos

Photo sharing sites and online social networks provide apps that support uploading photos taken with a smartphone or tablet to the cloud.

Play Games

Internet-connected game consoles enable you to save games in progress. Because game information is stored on the cloud, you can continue playing where you left off, regardless of whether you are using your own or another's game console.

Evaluating Providers

With so many providers offering free and paid cloud storage services, it is important to compare features to take advantage of the capabilities that each offers. Criteria to consider include the amount of free storage offered, the cost to purchase more if needed, and the maximum file size that each service allows you to upload. Keep the files you use most on the service on which you have the most storage space; use services that support streaming to store and play media files. Photos, songs, and videos take longer to upload than smaller text or webpage files, so it is important to select a provider whose servers have sufficient bandwidth to support large file transfers.

It also is important to read a cloud storage provider's privacy policy and terms of agreement to which you must consent before using its services. Some cloud storage providers may not guarantee the protection of the files you upload, so you still should keep a backup of the files you stored on the cloud. Read How To 8-2 to learn about selecting a cloud storage provider and deciding what to upload.

✳ **Consider This:** What are advantages of storing your files on the cloud? When does it make sense to use physical storage media, such as a USB flash drive, to store your files? Storing files on the cloud encourages collaboration and sharing. How can you share files stored on the cloud with your team members? Are you concerned about the security of your files when stored on the cloud? What information, if any, would you not store on the cloud?

✳ HOW TO 8-2

Select a Cloud Storage Provider and Decide What to Upload to the Cloud
Many people are choosing to back up data to the cloud in addition to, or instead of, backing up to storage media such as external hard drives and optical discs. Cloud storage providers enable you to synchronize data on your computers and mobile devices effortlessly to one or more servers in remote locations. Various cloud storage providers exist, and it is important to select one that adequately meets your needs. In addition to selecting a cloud storage provider, you also should decide what to upload to the cloud.

Selecting a Cloud Storage Provider
Consider the following guidelines when selecting a cloud storage provider:

- Verify the company is reputable and has been in business for an extended period of time.
- Choose a provider that encrypts your files.
- Make sure the company has not fallen victim to major security breaches.

- Determine whether the provider's service is compatible with your computer(s) and mobile device(s).
- Compare the price of various storage plans and choose a provider that offers competitive pricing.
- Verify the cloud storage provider will support the types of files you want to back up. For example, some cloud storage providers might allow you only to back up photos, so they would not be a good choice to back up your personal files, such as documents and spreadsheets.
- If desired, choose a cloud storage provider that allows you to share selected files with others.
- Consider whether the provider offers a mobile app that you can use to access your files using a mobile device.

Deciding What to Upload to the Cloud
Consider the following guidelines when determining what to upload to the cloud. Before ultimately deciding what to upload, make sure the cloud storage provider you choose will adequately protect your files.

- Consider uploading files that you cannot afford to lose, such as financial documents or scanned copies of insurance paperwork.
- Upload files that might have sentimental value, such as photos and video. In the unlikely event of a disaster that ruins your computer, mobile device, and backups you possess, the cloud storage provider will retain these files.
- Do not back up programs and apps if you have access to the installation media or files.
- If your cloud storage provider offers only a limited amount of storage space, back up only the files you are sure you will need again in the future.
- Routinely review the files you have stored on the cloud storage provider and remove files you no longer need.

✳ **Consider This:** Which of your files would you back up to the cloud? Why? After reviewing at least three cloud storage providers, which one would you choose? Why?

Optical Discs

An **optical disc** is a type of storage medium that consists of a flat, round, portable disc made of metal, plastic, and lacquer that is written and read by a laser. Optical discs used in computers typically are 4.75 inches in diameter and less than 1/20 of an inch thick. Game consoles and mobile devices, however, may use a *mini disc* that has a diameter of 3 inches or less; mini discs also work in standard-sized optical disc drives. Three widely used types of optical discs are CDs (compact discs), DVDs (digital versatile discs or sometimes digital video discs), and Blu-ray Discs.

On some computers, you push a button to slide out a tray, insert the disc, and then push the same button to close the tray; others are slot loaded, which means you insert the disc in a narrow opening on the drive (Figure 8-14). When you insert the disc, the operating system automatically may run a program, play music, or start a video on the disc. Desktops and traditional laptops usually have an optical disc drive. Ultrathin laptops, tablets, and mobile devices typically do not have an optical disc drive.

Many different formats of optical discs are available today. Some are read only, meaning users cannot write (save) on the media. Others are read/write, which allows users to save on the disc just as they save on a hard drive. With most discs, you can read and/or write on one side only. Manufacturers usually place a silk-screened label on the top layer of these single-sided discs. You insert a single-sided disc in the drive with the label side up.

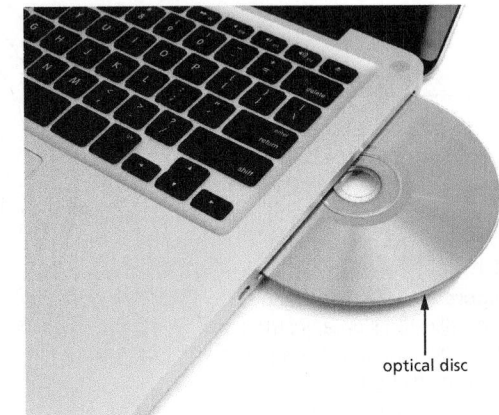

Figure 8-14   An optical disc in a disc drive.
ESB Professional / Shutterstock.com

Characteristics of Optical Discs

Optical discs store items by using microscopic pits (indentations) and lands (flat areas) that are in the middle layer of the disc (Figure 8-15). A high-powered laser light creates the pits. A lower-powered laser light reads items from the disc by reflecting light through the bottom of the disc. The reflected light is converted into a series of bits the computer can process. A land causes light to reflect, which is read as binary digit 1. Pits absorb the light; this absence of light is read as binary digit 0.

How a Laser Reads Data on an Optical Disc

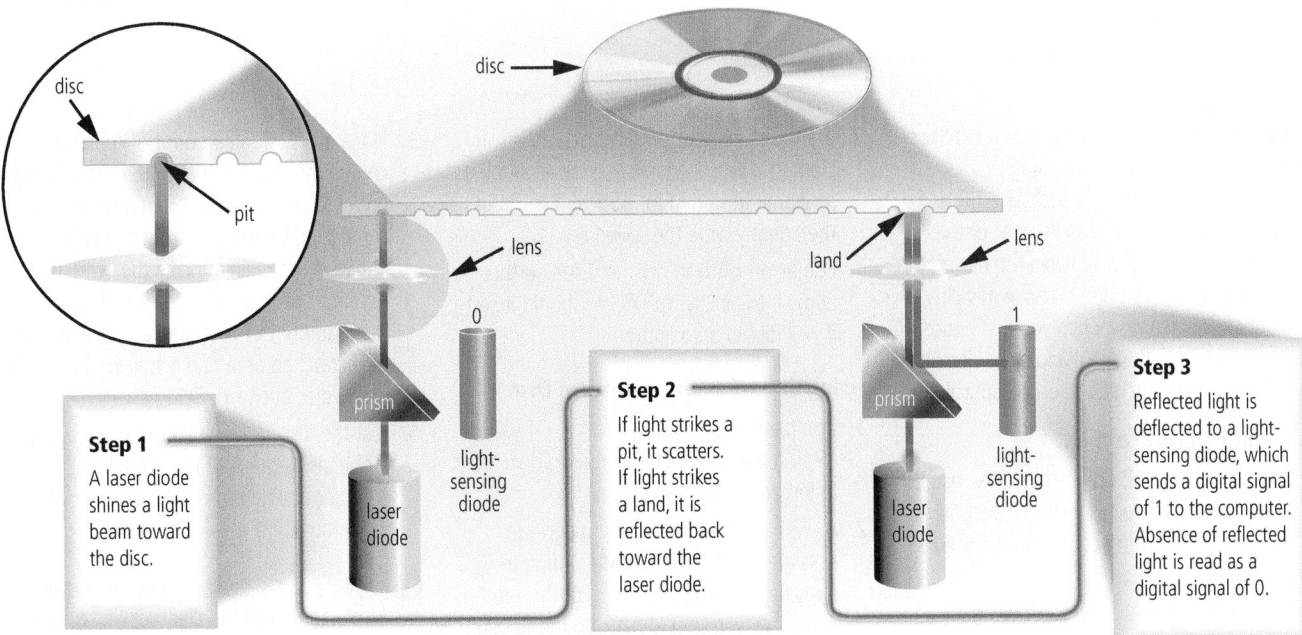

Figure 8-15   This figure shows how a laser reads data on an optical disc.

Optical discs commonly store items in a single track that spirals from the center of the disc to the edge of the disc. As with a hard disk, this single track is divided into evenly sized sectors on which items are stored (Figure 8-16).

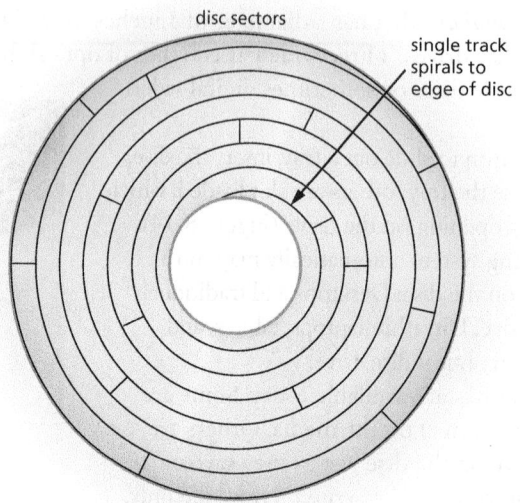

disc sectors

single track spirals to edge of disc

Figure 8-16 An optical disc typically stores data, instructions, and information in a single track that spirals from the center of the disc to the edge of the disc.

**BTW**

Transfer Rates
The original transfer rate of an optical disc was 150 KBps (kilobytes per second). Manufacturers measure all optical disc drives relative to this original speed, using an X to denote a transfer rate of 150 KBps. For example, a 48X drive has a transfer rate of 7,200 KBps (48 × 150), or 7.2 MBps.

 CONSIDER THIS

What is the life span of an optical disc?
Manufacturers claim that a properly cared for, high-quality optical disc will last 5 years but could last up to 100 years. Tips for proper care of optical discs include the following:

- Never bend a disc; it may break.
- Do not expose discs to extreme temperatures or humidity. The ideal temperature range for disc storage is 50 to 70 degrees Fahrenheit.
- Stacking discs, touching the underside of discs, or exposing them to any type of contaminant may scratch a disc. Read How To 8-3 for instructions about cleaning and fixing scratches on a disc.
- Place an optical disc in its protective case, called a *jewel case*, when you are finished using it, and store it in an upright (vertical) position.

HOW TO 8-3

Clean an Optical Disc and Fix Scratches
If you are having trouble accessing programs and files on an optical disc, such as a CD or DVD, you may need to clean the disc or fix scratches on its surface. To avoid the risk of not being able to access a disc because it is dirty, you should clean a disc when you first notice dirt on its surface. The following steps describe how to clean or fix scratches on an optical disc:

Cleaning an Optical Disc
1. While holding the disc by its edges, use compressed air to blow excess dust off of its surface. Hold the can of compressed air upright while using it.
2. Use a soft, nonabrasive cloth to gently wipe debris off of the disc's surface. Wipe the disc from the center out to its edges.

3. If any dirt remains on the disc, dip a soft cloth or cotton ball in isopropyl alcohol (or a cleaner designed for optical discs) and then gently wipe the soiled areas.
4. Use a soft cloth to dry the disc's surface or allow it to air dry. You never should insert a wet disc in a computer.

Fixing Scratches on an Optical Disc
1. Complete the previous Steps 1 – 4 to clean the disc. If it still contains scratches, follow the remaining steps.
2. As with any maintenance you perform, risks are associated with attempting to fix scratches on an optical disc. For this reason, if possible, you should back up the data on the disc before attempting to fix a scratch.

3. Place a very small amount of rubbing compound (available at a hardware store) on a soft, nonabrasive cloth and rub the compound on the disc from its center outward at the location of the scratch. If rubbing compound is not available, place a small amount of toothpaste (not a gel) on the scratched area and rub from the inside of the disc outward.
4. Test the disc. If you still are experiencing problems because of the scratch(es), consider having a professional remove the scratch.

Consider This: What other household products can be used to clean or fix scratches on an optical disc?

CDs

CDs are available in three basic formats: read-only, recordable, and rewritable.

- A **CD-ROM** (CD-read-only memory) is a type of optical disc that users can read but not write on (record) or erase — hence, the name read-only. Manufacturers write the contents of standard CD-ROMs and distribute them to consumers. A standard CD-ROM is called a *single-session disc* because manufacturers write all items on the disc at one time. Software manufacturers sometimes distribute their programs using CD-ROMs. The term, *photo CD*, sometimes is used to refer to CDs that contain only photos.

- A **CD-R** (CD-recordable) is an optical disc on which users can write once, but not erase, their own items, such as text, graphics, and audio. Because a CD-R can be written on only one time, the format of these discs sometimes is called *WORM* (write once, read many). Some CD-Rs are *multisession*, which means you can write on part of the disc at one time and another part at a later time — if the disc has free space.

- A **CD-RW** (CD-rewritable) is an erasable multisession disc users can write on multiple times. CD-RW overcomes the major disadvantage of CD-R because it allows users to write and rewrite data, instructions, and information on the CD-RW disc multiple times — instead of just once. Reliability of the disc tends to drop, however, with each successive rewrite.

A popular use of CD-RW and CD-R discs is to create audio CDs. For example, you can record your own music and save it on a CD, purchase and download songs from the web, or rearrange tracks on a purchased music CD.

 **BTW**

Burning and Ripping
The process of writing on an optical disc is called *burning*. The process of copying audio and/or video data from a purchased disc and saving it on your own media is called *ripping*.

 CONSIDER THIS

Can all CD drives read all CD formats?
A CD-ROM drive or a CD player may be able to read only CD-ROMs and sometimes CD-Rs. Because audio CDs and CD-ROMs use the same laser technology, you may be able to use a CD-ROM drive to listen to an audio CD while using the computer.

Most CD-R drives can read audio CDs, CD-ROMs, CD-Rs, and sometimes CD-RWs. Most CD-RW drives can read audio CDs, CD-ROMs, CD-Rs, and CD-RWs. To write on a CD-R disc, you must have a CD-R drive. Similarly, to write on a CD-RW disc, you must have a CD-RW drive.

DVDs

DVD quality for storing videos far surpasses that of CDs because items are stored in a slightly different manner, which enables DVDs to have greater storage capacities and higher resolutions than CDs. The first storage technique involves making the disc denser by packing the pits closer together. The second involves using two layers of pits. This technique doubles the capacity of the disc because the lower layer of pits is semitransparent, which allows the laser to read through it to the upper layer. Finally, some DVDs are double-sided. A more expensive DVD format is **Blu-ray**, which has a higher capacity and better quality than standard DVDs, especially for high-definition audio and video.

As with CDs, DVDs are available in three basic formats: read-only, recordable, and rewritable.

- A **DVD-ROM** (DVD-read-only memory) is a high-capacity optical disc that users can read but not write on or erase. Manufacturers write the contents of DVD-ROMs and distribute them to consumers. DVD-ROMs store movies, music, music videos, huge databases, and applications you install on a computer.

- **DVD-R** and **DVD+R** are competing DVD-recordable WORM formats, on which users can write once but not erase their own items, including video, audio, photos, graphics, and text.

- **DVD-RW**, **DVD+RW**, and **DVD+RAM** are competing DVD-rewritable formats that users can write on multiple times.

 **BTW**

DVD/CD-RW
Some drives, called DVD/CD-RW drives, are combination drives that read and write on DVD and CD media. Current computers that include optical drives often use these combination drives.

CONSIDER THIS

Can all DVD drives read all DVD formats?
No. In addition to DVD-ROMs, most DVD-ROM drives also can read audio CDs, CD-ROMs, CD-Rs, and CD-RWs. Recordable and rewritable DVD drives usually can read a variety of DVD and CD media. Blu-ray Disc (BD) drives and players are backward compatible with DVD and CD formats. Before investing in equipment, check to be sure it is compatible with the media on which you intend to record.

Enterprise Storage

Enterprise hardware allows large organizations to manage and store data and information using devices intended for heavy use, maximum efficiency, and maximum availability. The availability of hardware to users is a measure of how often it is online. Highly available hardware is accessible 24 hours a day, 365 days a year. To meet these needs, enterprise hardware often includes levels of *redundancy*, which means that if one component fails or malfunctions, another can assume its tasks.

Some organizations manage an enterprise storage system in-house. Others elect to offload all (or at least the backup) storage management to an outside organization or a cloud storage provider, a practice known as *outsourcing*. Enterprises use a combination of storage techniques to meet their large-scale needs, including cloud storage and some of the other previously discussed methods, along with RAID, network attached storage, storage area networks, and tape. Read Ethics & Issues 8-2 to consider issues with employees bringing their own devices into an enterprise.

ETHICS & ISSUES 8-2

Are Businesses Vulnerable when Employees Use Their Own Devices to Access Company Data?
BYOD (bring your own device) strategies enable employees to access company data from a personal smartphone, tablet, or laptop. Companies might adopt or allow a BYOD policy to save money on the cost of buying and maintaining devices. Employers might increase productivity by allowing employees to work in the environment in which they are most comfortable.

BYOD raises many privacy and security concerns. IT managers, security experts, and human resource directors work together to create and enforce a BYOD policy. BYOD guidelines should balance securing company data and preventing unauthorized network access with ensuring personal autonomy and privacy over employees' personal data. IT managers express concern over the potential need to service many different types of devices, if the company policy requires it to troubleshoot or secure employee devices. A company's security team must protect company data. In some cases, employees must install a tool to remotely wipe data, including personal data, if the device is lost, damaged, or stolen. Human resource directors help devise guidelines regarding cost-sharing and how to protect employees' private data and activities. Some industries may not be able to allow BYOD, as it may violate data privacy laws.

Many companies ban certain apps, such as gaming or file sharing, because of concerns over malware risks. In many cases, employees must agree to back up data. Employees should protect the device with a password or biometric security feature. Some companies employ a *geofence*, which is a virtual perimeter or boundary, to disable certain apps or cameras in secure areas, such as labs or meeting rooms.

Consider This: If you use your own device for work, would you be willing to give some control over the device to your company? Why or why not? Should companies be able to punish employees who violate BYOD policies? Why or why not?

Enterprise storage often uses *Fibre Channel* (FC) technology as the interface that connects the devices to the network because FC technology has much faster transmission rates than SCSI and other previously discussed interfaces.

RAID

For applications that depend on reliable data access, users must have the data available when they attempt to access it. Some manufacturers provide a type of hard drive system that connects several smaller drives into a single unit that acts like a single large hard drive. As mentioned earlier in this module, a group of two or more integrated hard drives is called a RAID (Figure 8-17). Although RAID can be more expensive than traditional hard drives, it is more reliable. Computers and enterprise storage devices often use RAID.

RAID may duplicate data, instructions, and information to improve data reliability. RAID implements duplication in different ways, depending on the storage design, or level, being used. The simplest RAID storage design is *level 1*, called *mirroring*, which writes data on two drives at the same time to duplicate the data (Figure 8-18a). A level 1 configuration enhances storage reliability because, if a drive should fail, a duplicate of the requested item is available elsewhere within the array of drives.

Other RAID levels use a technique called *striping*, which splits data, instructions, and information across multiple drives in the array (Figure 8-18b). Striping improves drive access times, but does not offer data duplication. For this reason, some RAID levels combine both mirroring and striping.

Figure 8-17   Shown here is a rack-mounted RAID chassis, including many integrated hard disks.
stavklem / Shutterstock.com

⊛ BTW
RAID Levels
Various RAID levels exist, each offering different levels of reliability and performance. Common RAID levels in use today are 0, 1, 5, and 10.

(a)

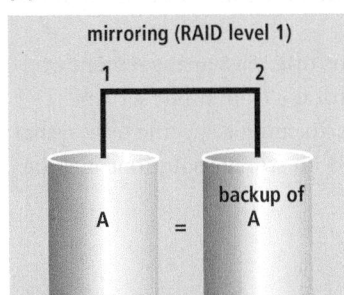

(b)

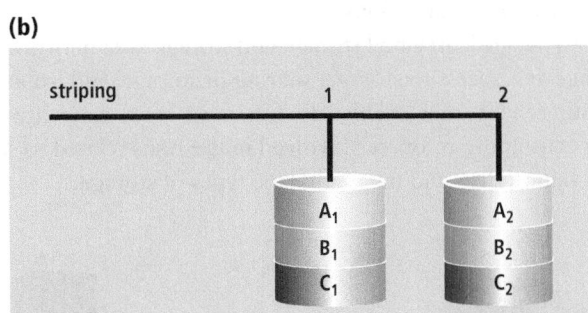

Figure 8-18   In RAID level 1, called mirroring, a backup disk exists for each drive. Other RAID levels use striping; that is, portions of each drive are placed on multiple drives.

NAS and SAN

Network attached storage (NAS) is a server that is placed on a network with the sole purpose of providing storage to users, computers, and devices attached to the network (Figure 8-19). A network attached storage server, often called a *storage appliance*, has its own IP address, usually does not have a keyboard or display, and contains at least one hard drive, often configured in a RAID. Administrators can add storage to an existing network quickly by connecting a network attached storage server to a network.

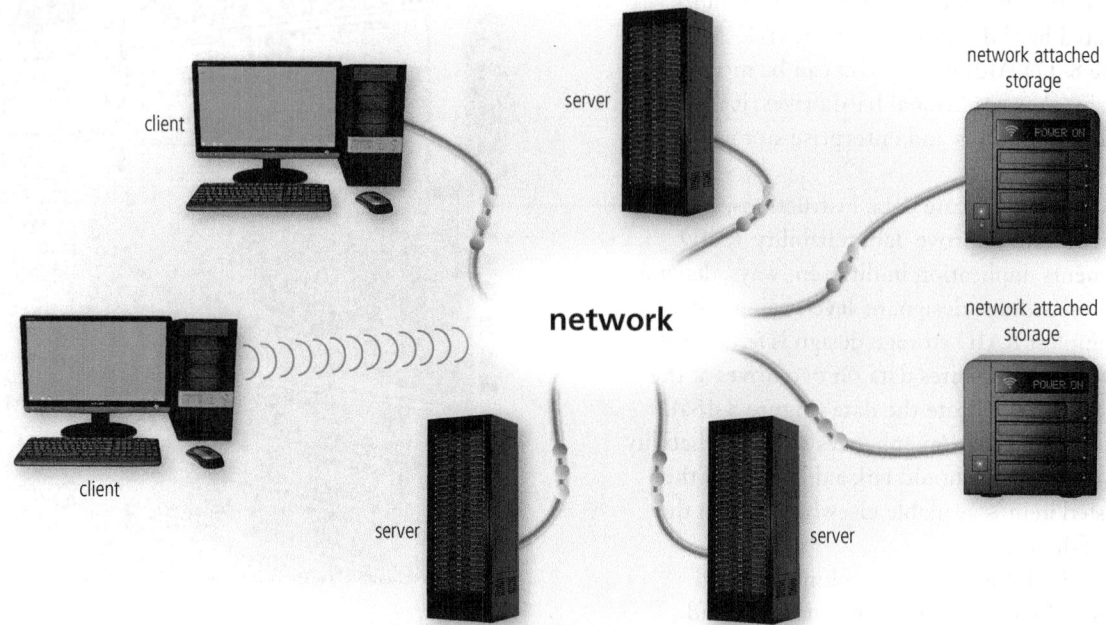

Figure 8-19 An example of how network attached storage connects on a network.
iStockphoto.com / luismmolina; lucadp / Shutterstock.com; Scanrail1 / Shutterstock.com; Source: Microsoft

A **storage area network (SAN)** is a high-speed network with the sole purpose of providing storage to other attached servers (Figure 8-20). In fact, a storage area network includes only storage devices. High-speed fiber-optic cable usually connects other networks and servers to the storage area network, so that the networks and servers have fast access to large storage capacities. A storage area network can connect to networks and other servers that are miles away using high-speed network connections.

Both network attached storage and storage area network solutions offer easy management of storage, fast access to storage, sharing of storage, and isolation of storage from other servers. Isolating the storage enables the other servers to concentrate on performing a specific task, rather than consuming resources involved in the tasks related to storage. Both storage solutions include disk, optical disc, and magnetic tape types of storage.

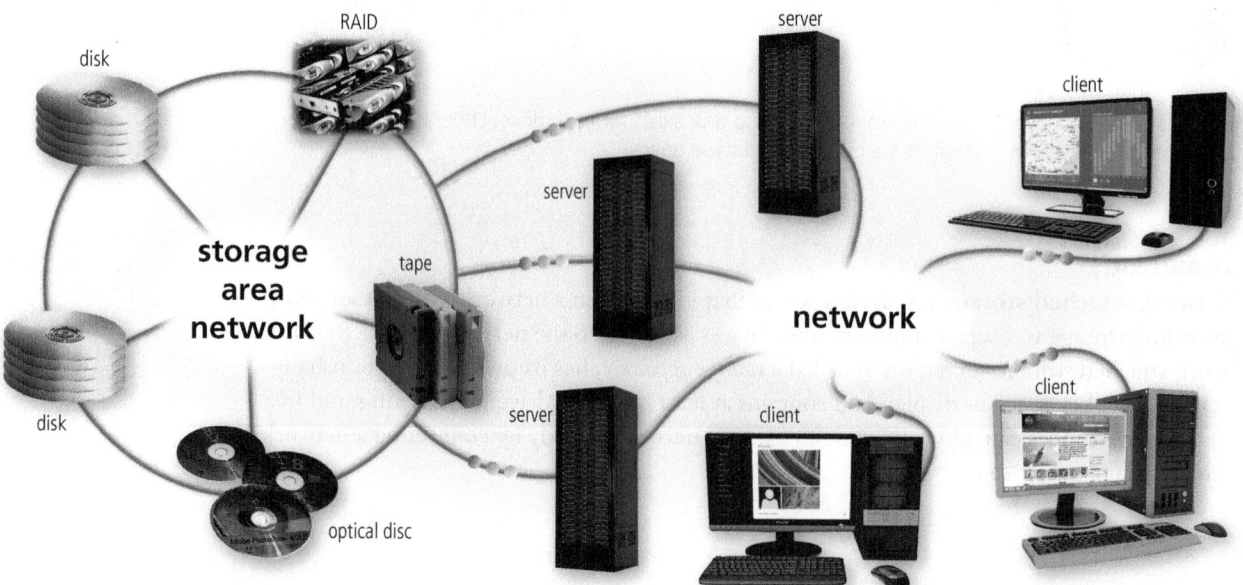

Figure 8-20 A storage area network provides centralized storage for servers and networks.
stavklem / Shutterstock.com; iStockphoto.com / luismmolina; bigmagic / Shutterstock.com; Scanrail1 / Shutterstock.com; iStockphoto.com / sweetym; iStockphoto.com / 123render; Source: Microsoft

CONSIDER THIS

Which do enterprises typically use, network attached storage or storage area networks?
Enterprises sometimes choose to implement both network attached storage and storage area network solutions. A network attached storage server is better suited for adding storage to an existing network, such as a department's file server. A company typically implements a storage area network solution as central storage for an entire enterprise.

Magnetic Tape

One of the first storage media used with enterprise computers was tape. **Tape** is a magnetically coated ribbon of plastic that is capable of storing large amounts of data and information at a low cost. Before the use of digital music players became widespread, cassette tapes were a popular medium to store music. Tape no longer is used as a primary method of storage. Instead, businesses use tape most often for long-term storage and backup.

Comparable to a cassette recorder, a *tape drive* reads from and writes on a magnetic tape. Although older computers used reel-to-reel tape drives, today's tape drives use tape cartridges. A *tape cartridge* is a small, rectangular, plastic housing for tape. Enterprises typically use a *tape library*, where individual tape cartridges are mounted in a separate cabinet. Often, a tape robot automatically retrieves tape cartridges (Figure 8-21), which are identified by location or bar code.

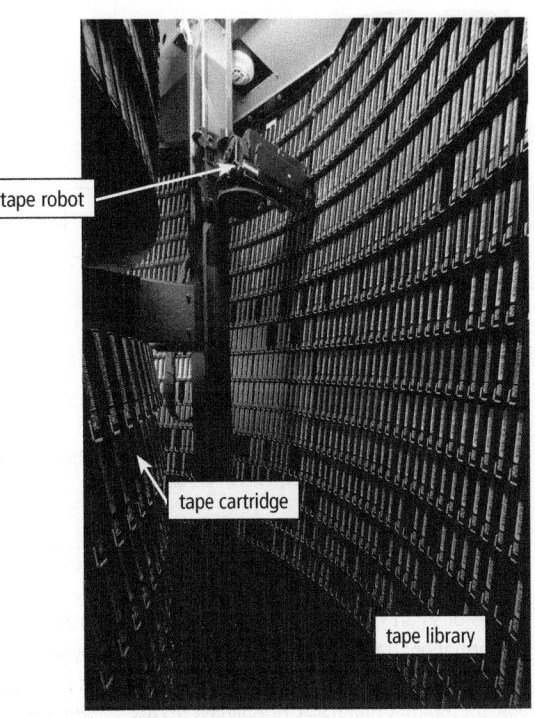

Figure 8-21 A tape robot retrieves tape cartridges.
Courtesy of Oak Ridge National Laboratory

 CONSIDER THIS

Is tape as fast as other storage techniques?
No. Tape storage requires *sequential access*, which refers to reading or writing data consecutively. In much the same way you would find a specific song on a cassette tape or videotape, you must forward or rewind to a specific position to access a specific piece of data. On a tape, for example, to access items ordered A, B, C, and D, you must pass through items A, B, and C sequentially before you can access item D.

Hard drives, flash memory storage, and optical discs all use direct access. *Direct access,* also called *random access,* means that the device can locate a particular data item or file immediately, without having to move consecutively through items stored in front of the desired data item or file. When writing or reading specific data, direct access is much faster than sequential access.

Other Types of Storage

In addition to the previously discussed types of storage, other options are available for specific uses and applications. These include magnetic stripe cards, smart cards, RFID tags, and NFC chips and tags.

Magnetic Stripe Cards

A **magnetic stripe card** is a credit card, entertainment card, bank card, or other similar card with a stripe that contains information identifying you and the card (Figure 8-22). The card issuer, such as a financial organization, encodes information in the stripe. The information in the stripe often includes your name, account number, and the card's expiration date. When you swipe the card through a magstripe reader, discussed in the previous module, it reads information stored on the stripe.

Figure 8-22 The magnetic stripe on the back of credit cards and other ID cards contain information that identifies you and the card.
iStockphoto.com / rwarnick

Smart Cards

A **smart card**, which is an alternative to a magnetic stripe card, stores data on an integrated circuit embedded in the card (Figure 8-23). Two types of smart cards, also called *chip cards*, are contact and contactless. When you insert a contact smart card in a specialized card reader, the information on the smart card is read and, if necessary, updated. Contactless smart cards communicate with a reader using a radio frequency, which means the user simply places the card near the reader.

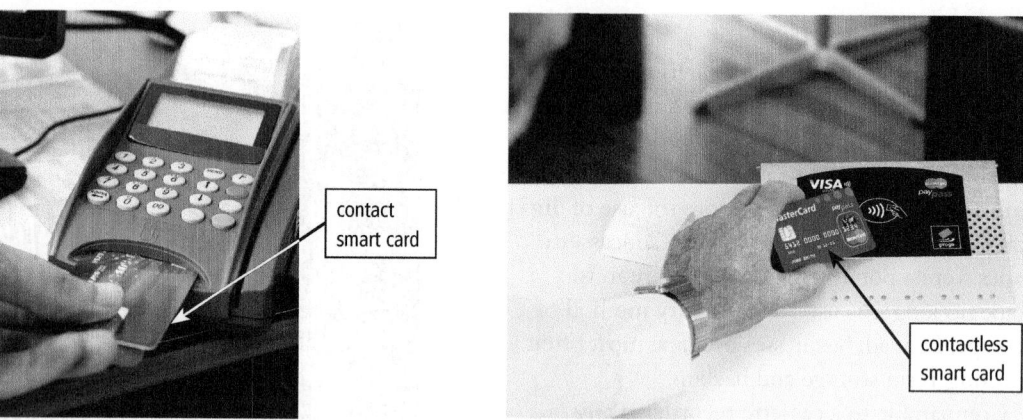

contact smart card

contactless smart card

Figure 8-23 Examples of contact and contactless smart cards and their readers.
iStockphoto.com / oytun karadayi; iStockphoto.com / audioundwerbung

 **CONSIDER THIS**

What are some uses of smart cards?
Uses of smart cards include storing medical records, vaccination data, and other health care and identification information; tracking information, such as employee attendance or customer purchases; storing a prepaid amount of money, such as for student purchases on campus or fares for public transportation; and authenticating users, such as for Internet purchases or building access. In addition, a smart card can double as an ID card or credit card. Read Secure IT 8-3 for tips about protecting your credit cards.

 **SECURE IT 8-3**

Using Credit Cards Safely

Consumers in the United States own more than 775 million credit and debit cards, and the average cardholder has multiple cards available to use. With this widespread use, the potential for theft is high.

The newest smart cards have embedded RFID tags that allow vendors to obtain the account number without physically touching the card. While this technology is convenient for both the merchant and consumer, it also enables thieves with remote scanners to capture the card's information without the owner's knowledge.

Thieves also use a handheld device to swipe the card and then obtain and store account details. This action, called *skimming*, is prevalent at gas stations, restaurants, and lounges, where unscrupulous employees sell the information to criminals who then spend your money or steal your identity.

Follow these tips to help keep your credit card account safe:

Do

- Use a card with added security features, such as a photo.

- Draw a line through blank areas on restaurant charge slips. If you have left a cash tip on the table, write the words, On Table, in the slip's tip amount section.

- Cover the keypad when entering a PIN.

- Save charge receipts and check them against monthly statements or online postings.

- Keep a record in a safe place of all your credit card numbers, expiration dates, and toll-free numbers to call if you need to report a lost or stolen card.

- Purchase an RFID-proof wallet to shield smart cards from remote readers.

- Shred new credit account mail solicitations.

- Look for skimmers, which can capture a credit card number. (Read Secure IT 3-2 in Module 3 for information about skimmers at ATMs and other self-service stations.)

Do Not

- Reveal your account number during a phone call unless you have initiated the call.

- Write your PIN on the card or on the protective envelope.

- Sign a blank charge slip.

- Carry extra cards, especially when traveling to unfamiliar locations.

- Let your card out of sight. While you may not be able to follow this advice at a restaurant when you hand the card to a server, you can be observant of employees' behaviors.

 **Consider This:** Do you know anyone who has been a victim of credit card theft? What steps will you take to use credit cards more safely after reading this information?

RFID Tags

Recall that RFID is a technology that uses radio signals to communicate with a tag placed in or attached to an object, an animal, or a person. The **RFID tag** consists of an antenna and a memory chip that contains the information to be transmitted via radio waves (Figure 8-24). An RFID reader reads the radio signals and transfers the information to a computer or computing device.

RFID tags are either passive or active. An active RFID tag contains a battery that runs the chip's circuitry and broadcasts a signal to the RFID reader. A passive RFID tag does not contain a battery and, thus,

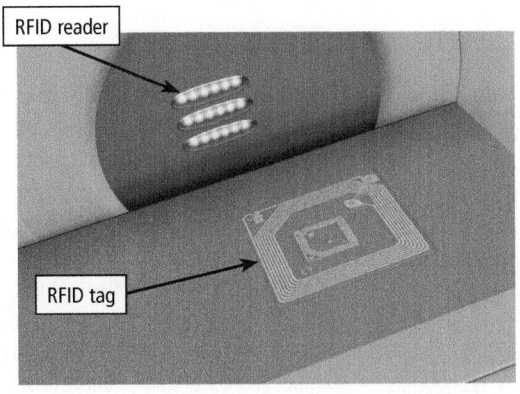

Figure 8-24 An RFID reader reads radio signals from an RFID tag that is affixed to this box.
iStockphoto.com / luismmolina

cannot send a signal until the reader activates the tag's antenna by sending out electromagnetic waves. Because passive RFID tags contain no battery, these can be small enough to be embedded in skin.

 CONSIDER THIS

How do RFID tags differ from contactless smart cards?
The physical size of the chip and storage capacities in an RFID tag typically are much smaller than the chips in contactless smart cards. The chips in RFID tags usually are read only, whereas the chips in contactless smart cards can function as a processor. Also, RFID tags often are not as secure as contactless smart cards. Thus, credit cards that contain RFID tags, called RFID-enabled credit cards, may not be as secure as those that use contactless technology.

NFC Chips and Tags

Recall that NFC is a technology (based on RFID) that uses close-range radio signals to transmit data between two NFC-enabled devices or an NFC-enabled device and an NFC tag. NFC-enabled devices include smartphones, digital cameras, computers, televisions, and terminals. An NFC-enabled device, such as a smartphone, contains an NFC chip (Figure 8-25). Other objects, such as credit cards and tickets, can contain an NFC chip. An *NFC tag*, similar to RFID tag, contains a chip and an antenna that contains information to be transmitted (shown in Figure 8-1 at the beginning of the module). Most NFC tags are self-adhesive, so that they can be attached to any location.

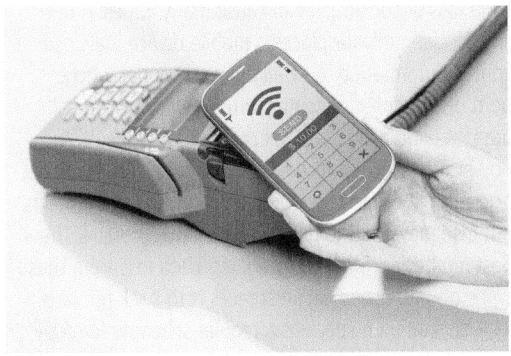

Figure 8-25 This NFC-enabled phone communicates with the NFC reader to send a mobile payment.
iStockphoto.com / scyther5

When a user places the NFC-enabled device close to another NFC-enabled device or an NFC tag, radio waves enable communications between the chips in the NFC-enabled devices or the chip in the NFC-enabled device and the NFC tag. Uses of NFC communications includes using a mobile device to pay for goods or services, displaying a webpage, making a phone call, sending a text message, or exchange contact information. Read Secure IT 8-4 for how to secure NFC transactions.

 **SECURE IT 8-4**

Keeping NFC Transactions Safe

NFC-enabled phones offer convenience when making contactless payments at the point of sale. A user simply waves his or her smartphone above a reader attached to a register, and money is deducted from a credit card or account that is registered when the NFC application is installed. The security of this technology, however, raises major issues.

Eavesdropping is one concern. The phones and the merchant's receivers need to be less than 8 inches apart to communicate with each other and complete the wireless data transfer, but even this short distance leads to vulnerabilities that allow cyberthieves to steal financial and other personal data. Attackers can stand near the sales counter to intercept the smartphone's signals or use antennas to

extend the signal's range. Another issue is data corruption and modification, when the high-tech criminals change or delete communications between the devices. Customers also are uneasy when the technology allows merchants to load coupons, advertisements, and other adware on the phone during the NFC transaction without the shopper's permission.

Hardware manufacturers and software engineers are working to improve security between the smartphones and the readers that receive the signals, but consumers need to exercise common sense and be proactive in protecting their sensitive information. They should follow these procedures in an attempt to avoid security breaches:

• Use a strong passcode on the phone and a PIN for the NFC transaction.

• Lock the phone when it has not been used for several minutes.

• Install antivirus software.

• Install an app that takes a photograph of a person trying to access a phone without permission and then sends a message to another mobile device when the phone has been stolen, or uses the phone's GPS to track its locations.

• Turn off Bluetooth discoverable status when not using this feature.

 Consider This: Have you used NFC transactions? If so, did you take any precautions to keep your data safe? If not, would you consider using NFC technology to pay for goods and services? Why or why not?

Tech Feature 8-3: Backup Plans

To protect against data loss, users should back up the contents of their storage devices regularly. Read Tech Feature 8-3 to learn about backup plans.

TECH FEATURE 8-3

Backup Plans

Data loss or corruption can cause many issues. A user who accidentally misplaces a mobile device may lose contact information. A small business owner whose hard drive is infected with a virus may lose financial data, making billing and tax preparation difficult. A power user whose office floods and ruins a desktop not only may lose work completed on complex projects but also may need to replace expensive software. The best method for protecting against data loss from these types of unforeseen circumstances is to back up data.

A backup plan specifies a regular schedule for copying and storing important data, information, apps, and programs. Organizations should state their backup plans clearly, document them in writing, and follow them consistently. Home and small business users can use a calendar app or other reminder to keep a backup schedule for their computers or mobile devices, or use a program or app that performs automatic backups. Backup plans should weigh the time and expense of performing a backup against the value of the data, information, apps, and programs. For example, a small business may perform one type of backup daily, while a home user may find that monthly backups are sufficient. Read Ethics &

Issues 8-3 to consider storage requirements for public companies.

As briefly discussed in Module 5, business and home users can use four methods for backup: full, differential, incremental, or selective. Typically, only large enterprises uses a fifth type, continuous data protection. Cloud backup services, a sixth option, provide continuous data protection capabilities at a lower cost. Users can choose to backup to external media, or, as increasingly more are choosing to do, to the cloud.

• A *full backup*, sometimes called an *archival backup*, provides the best protection against data loss because it copies all program and data files. Generally, users should perform a full backup at regular intervals, such as at the end of each week and at the end of the month.

• Between full backups, you can perform differential or incremental backups. A *differential backup* copies only the files that have changed since the last full backup. An *incremental backup* copies only the files that have changed since the last full or last incremental backup.

• A *selective backup*, sometimes called a *partial backup*, allows the user to choose specific files to back up, regardless of whether or not the files have changed since the last incremental backup.

Backup software enables you to schedule backups, select the appropriate backup type, and choose the storage media for the backup. Traditional storage media includes CDs or DVDs, external hard drives, or removable SSDs, including USB flash drives or memory cards. Whichever storage media you choose, it should be stored separately from the device you are backing up to ensure it is available in case of theft or disaster. When choosing storage media, consider price and reliability. A USB flash drive may be inexpensive, but it also could be corrupted or lost easily. Cloud storage may be more expensive, but your data will be in a remote location and accessible from anywhere at any time.

Many smartphones and other mobile devices include services that sync data to a computer or to a cloud service. To sync data to a computer, the mobile device either requires cables to connect via a USB port or uses wireless methods, such as Wi-Fi or Bluetooth. Many mobile apps sync data to web apps automatically, which means you may not need to schedule a procedure to back up items on a mobile device, such as contacts, calendars, email messages, notes, and apps. For

additional protection, however, some users still back up certain mobile data for easy retrieval if the device is lost or corrupted.

December					
MONDAY	TUESDAY	WEDNESDAY	THURSDAY	FRIDAY	SAT/SUN
28 DAILY INCREMENTAL BACKUP	**29** DAILY INCREMENTAL BACKUP	**30** END OF MONTH FULL BACKUP	**1** DAILY INCREMENTAL BACKUP	**2** WEEKLY FULL BACKUP	**3/4**
5 DAILY INCREMENTAL BACKUP	**6** DAILY INCREMENTAL BACKUP	**7** DAILY INCREMENTAL BACKUP	**8** DAILY INCREMENTAL BACKUP	**9** WEEKLY FULL BACKUP	**10/11**
12 DAILY INCREMENTAL BACKUP	**13** DAILY INCREMENTAL BACKUP	**14** DAILY INCREMENTAL BACKUP	**15** DAILY INCREMENTAL BACKUP	**16** WEEKLY FULL BACKUP	**17/18**
19 DAILY INCREMENTAL BACKUP	**20** DAILY INCREMENTAL BACKUP	**21** DAILY INCREMENTAL BACKUP	**22** DAILY INCREMENTAL BACKUP	**23** WEEKLY FULL BACKUP	**24/25**
26 DAILY INCREMENTAL BACKUP	**27** DAILY INCREMENTAL BACKUP	**28** DAILY INCREMENTAL BACKUP	**29** DAILY INCREMENTAL BACKUP	**30** END OF MONTH FULL BACKUP	**31/1**

✳ **Consider This:** Do you have a backup plan for your mobile device and/or computer? Why or why not? How often do you think you need to back up your devices? Why? What storage media is best suited for your backup needs? Why?

✳ **ETHICS & ISSUES 8-3**

How Much Data Should Companies Be Required to Keep?
More than a decade ago, after a string of corporate scandals, lawmakers enacted the *Sarbanes-Oxley (SOX) Act*. SOX provides a myriad of financial reporting requirements and guidelines for publicly traded companies. A main focus of SOX is the retention of business records. Because of SOX, companies have been confronted with massive new data storage requirements. For example, a company must retain all of its email messages just as it would other business records. Deleting stored email messages can result in a destruction of evidence infraction. Employees face penalties of up to 20 years in prison for altering or destroying records or documents.

IT departments must not only understand this complex law, but they also must ensure accuracy of financial data, determine policies for record retention, and provide storage capacity to hold all of the data.

Supporters of SOX state that it is essential to avoid corporate scandals caused by lack of accuracy in financial reporting. They also say that consumer confidence has increased because the financial statements are more transparent. Further, the financial costs for complying with SOX have decreased since companies have implemented plans. Opponents claim that the law is overreaching and costs too much for the added benefits. In addition, opponents blame the law for a decline in the number of IPOs (initial public

offerings), as well as the transfer of several large companies to foreign countries. Recently, the U.S. government passed the Jumpstart Our Business Startup (JOBS) Act. Supported by technology companies, startup businesses, and venture capitalists, the JOBS Act aims to support smaller and emerging companies. By redefining the size of companies, as well as tiers of responsibilities related to SOX, supporters of the JOBS Act hope to help new businesses grow.

✳ **Consider This:** Is the Sarbanes-Oxley Act an unfair burden on companies? Why or why not? Should the government distinguish between large and smaller companies? Why or why not? Are such laws necessary in order to protect the public? Why or why not?

✅ Summary

This module presented a variety of storage options. You learned about storage capacity and storage access times. The module discussed characteristics of hard disks, SSDs, external hard drives, and RAID. It discussed portable flash memory storage, including memory cards and USB flash drives. It presented advantages and various uses of cloud storage. Next, the module discussed characteristics of optical discs. Enterprise storage options were presented. You also learned about magnetic stripe cards, smart cards, RFID tags, and NFC chips and tags.

Study Guide

The Study Guide exercise reinforces material you should know after reading this module.

Instructions: Answer the questions below using the format that helps you remember best or that is required by your instructor. Possible formats may include one or more of these options: write the answers; create a document that contains the answers; record answers as audio or video using a webcam, smartphone, or portable media player; post answers on a blog, wiki, or website; or highlight answers in the book/e-book.

1. Define the term, secondary storage. List types of storage media.

2. Differentiate between writing and reading data to storage media.

3. ___ refers to the number of bytes a storage medium can hold. Identify terms manufacturers use to determine this.

4. Differentiate between storage and memory and describe how they interact.

5. Explain what access time measures and how transfer rates are stated.

6. Identify questions to ask before deciding how to share media files.

7. Define the term, hard drive.

8. Explain the ethical issues surrounding government search and seizure of computers.

9. List characteristics and functions of a hard disk.

10. ___ is the process of dividing the disk into tracks and sectors.

11. Define the term, read/write head.

12. List steps to defragment a hard disk.

13. Define the term, SSD. List devices that use SSDs.

14. List advantages and disadvantages of SSDs versus magnetic hard disks.

15. Define the term, external hard drive. Explain why you would use an external hard drive instead of a second internal hard drive.

16. Explain how to encrypt files.

17. RAID is an acronym for ___.

18. Explain the role of a controller for transferring data from a drive to the computer components.

19. In addition to USB, list four other types of interfaces for use in personal computers.

20. Describe memory cards and their uses. List types of memory cards.

21. Explain who might use a USB flash drive, and for what purpose.

22. Explain how to eject removable storage media safely.

23. Define the term, cloud storage. List advantages of cloud storage.

24. List uses of a personal cloud.

25. Name uses of cloud storage. Explain criteria for evaluating cloud storage providers.

26. Define the term, optical disc. List types of optical discs.

27. List characteristics of optical discs.

28. List steps for cleaning and fixing scratches on optical discs.

29. Differentiate among CD-ROM, CD-R, and CD-RW discs.

30. The process of writing on an optical disc is called ___. The process of copying audio and/or video data from a purchased disc and saving it on your own media is called ___.

31. Describe the storage techniques that make DVD storage higher capacity than CD storage.

32. Define the terms, redundancy and outsourcing, as they relate to enterprise computing.

33. Explain issues surrounding BYOD policies in the workplace.

34. List and describe the levels of RAID used in enterprises.

35. Differentiate between a network attached storage (NAS) and a storage area network (SAN).

36. Explain how enterprise computers use tape for storage.

37. Differentiate between sequential and direct access.

38. Define the terms, magnetic stripe card and smart card. Describe the uses of each.

39. List tips for using credit cards safely. ___ occurs when thieves use a handheld device to swipe the card and then obtain and store account details.

40. Differentiate between active and passive RFID tags.

41. Describe NFC technology and its uses.

42. List guidelines for conducting NFC transactions safely.

43. Describe types of backup used by business and home users. Explain considerations when creating a backup plan.

44. Explain the ethical issues surrounding the Sarbanes-Oxley Act.

STUDENT ASSIGNMENTS

You should be able to define the Primary Terms and be familiar with the Secondary Terms listed below.

Key Terms

Primary Terms (shown in **bold-black** characters in the module)

access time (8-5)
Blu-ray (8-21)
capacity (8-3)
CD-R (8-21)
CD-ROM (8-21)
CD-RW (8-21)
CF (CompactFlash) (8-14)
cloud storage (8-16)
DVD-R (8-21)
DVD-ROM (8-21)
DVD-RW (8-21)
DVD+R (8-21)

DVD+RAM (8-21)
DVD+RW (8-21)
external hard drive (8-11)
hard disk (8-6)
hard disk drive (HDD) (8-6)
hard drive (8-6)
M2 (Memory Stick Micro) (8-14)
magnetic stripe card (8-25)
memory card (8-14)
Memory Stick PRO Duo (8-14)

microSDHC (8-14)
microSDXC (8-14)
miniSD (8-14)
network attached storage (NAS) (8-23)
optical disc (8-19)
RAID (8-13)
read/write head (8-8)
reading (8-3)
RFID tag (8-27)
SDHC (Secure Digital High Capacity) (8-14)

SDXC (Secure Digital Expanded Capacity) (8-14)
smart card (8-26)
SSD (solid-state drive) (8-10)
storage area network (SAN) (8-24)
storage device (8-3)
tape (8-25)
USB flash drive (8-15)
writing (8-3)
xD Picture Card (8-14)

Secondary Terms (shown in *italic* characters in the module)

archival backup (8-28)
burning (8-21)
card reader/writer (8-14)
chip cards (8-26)
controller (8-13)
density (8-8)
differential backup (8-28)
direct access (8-25)
EIDE (8-13)
eSATA (8-13)
exabyte (EB) (8-3)
Fibre Channel (FC) (8-22)
formatting (8-8)
full backup (8-28)
GBps (8-5)
geofence (8-22)
geotag (8-5)

gigabyte (GB) (8-3)
head crash (8-9)
incremental backup (8-28)
jewel case (8-20)
KBps (8-5)
kilobyte (KB) (8-3)
level 1 (8-23)
longitudinal recording (8-8)
MBps (8-5)
megabyte (MB) (8-3)
mini disc (8-19)
mirroring (8-23)
multisession (8-21)
NFC tag (8-27)
outsourcing (8-22)
partial backup (8-28)
perpendicular recording (8-8)

personal cloud (8-17)
petabyte (PB) (8-3)
photo CD (8-21)
platter (8-8)
random access (8-25)
redundancy (8-22)
revolutions per minute (rpm) (8-8)
ripping (8-21)
Sarbanes-Oxley Act (SOX) (8-29)
SAS (serial-attached SCSI) (8-13)
SATA (8-13)
SCSI (8-13)
secondary storage (8-2)
sectors (8-8)
selective backup (8-28)
sequential access (8-25)
single-session disc (8-21)

skimming (8-26)
solid-state media (8-10)
storage appliance (8-23)
striping (8-23)
tape cartridge (8-25)
tape drive (8-25)
tape library (8-25)
terabyte (TB) (8-3)
thumb drive (8-15)
track (8-8)
transfer rate (8-5)
WORM (8-21)
yottabyte (YB) (8-3)
zettabyte (ZB) (8-3)

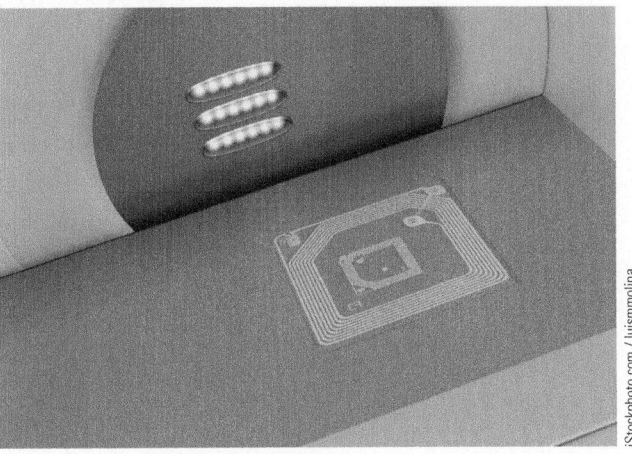

Checkpoint

The Checkpoint exercises test your knowledge of the module concepts.

True/False   Mark T for True and F for False. If False, rewrite the statement so that it is True.

_____ 1. Storage devices can be categorized as input or output devices.

_____ 2. A storage medium is volatile; that is, items stored on it remain intact even when you turn off a computer or mobile device.

_____ 3. Compared with the access time of memory, the access time of storage devices is slow.

_____ 4. On storage media, a higher density means less storage capacity.

_____ 5. Because of current standards, head crashes no longer occur.

_____ 6. The access time of a hard disk can be more than 100 times faster than an SSD.

_____ 7. While encrypted files offer greater security than unencrypted files, an operating system may require more time to open and access encrypted files.

_____ 8. While each program may use a different method of encrypting files, they all use the process of cryptography.

_____ 9. A group of two or more integrated hard drives is called a RAID.

_____ 10. When you are finished using a USB flash drive, simply remove it from the USB port.

_____ 11. Mini discs require a separate mini disc drive; that is, they do not work in standard-sized optical disc drives.

_____ 12. An active RFID tag contains a battery than runs the chip's circuitry and broadcasts a signal to the RFID reader; because they are so small, they can be embedded in skin.

Matching   Match the terms with their definitions.

_____ 1. capacity

_____ 2. controller

_____ 3. longitudinal recording

_____ 4. network attached storage

_____ 5. reading

_____ 6. ripping

_____ 7. sequential access

_____ 8. solid-state media

_____ 9. thumb drive

_____ 10. writing

a. storage method in which the magnetic particles are aligned horizontally around a disk's surface

b. server whose sole purpose is providing storage to users, computers, and devices attached to the network

c. the number of bytes a storage medium can hold

d. special-purpose chip and electronic circuits that control the transfer of data, instructions, and information from a drive to and from the system bus and other components in the computer

e. flash memory chip type that consists entirely of electronic components, such as integrated circuits, and contains no moving parts

f. flash memory storage device that plugs in a USB port on a computer or mobile device

g. process of transferring data, instructions, and information from memory to a storage medium

h. process of copying audio and/or video data from a purchased disc and saving it on your own media

i. storage technique that reads or writes data consecutively

j. process of transferring data, instructions, and information from a storage medium into memory

The Problem Solving exercises extend your knowledge of module concepts by seeking solutions to practical problems with technology that you may encounter at home, school, or work. The Collaboration exercise should be completed with a team.

Problem Solving

Instructions: You often can solve problems with technology in multiple ways. Determine a solution to the problems in these exercises by using one or more resources available to you (such as a computer or mobile device, articles on the web or in print, blogs, podcasts, videos, television, user guides, other individuals, electronics or computer stores, etc.). Describe your solution, along with the resource(s) used, in the format requested by your instructor (brief report, presentation, discussion, blog post, video, or other means).

Personal

1. **Unrecognized Storage Device**   You have connected an external storage device to your new MacBook Pro, but the operating system is not recognizing the device's contents. Instead, it asks whether you want to format the device. Why might this be happening?

2. **Second Hard Drive Connection**   While installing a second hard drive in your computer, you realize that your computer does not include a cable to connect the hard drive to the motherboard. How can you determine what type of cable to purchase?

3. **Incompatible Memory Card**   While attempting to copy files from your digital camera to your laptop, you realize that the memory card from your camera does not fit in the memory card slot on your laptop. What other steps can you take to copy the photos from the camera to the laptop?

4. **Missing Files**   You stored some files on a USB flash drive, but when you attempted to access them you noticed that they no longer were there. What might have happened, and what next steps will you take to attempt to recover these files?

 5. **Media Not Supported**   You purchased a program that came on a DVD, but your laptop does not have an optical disc drive. What next steps can you take to install this program?

ESB Professional / Shutterstock.com

Professional

6. **Inaccessible Files**   Your company requires you to store your files on a remote server so that you can access the files from any location within the company. When you sign in to another computer using your account, you cannot see your files. What might be causing this?

7. **Encrypted Storage Device**   You have purchased an external storage device so that you can back up files on your office computer. The IT department in your company informs you that you must make sure the data on the device is encrypted. What are your next steps?

8. **Alternative to Tape Storage**   Your company still uses tape storage to back up important files, but your manager has asked you to begin researching alternatives to the aging technology. What steps will you take to research current storage technologies that are suitable to store company backups?

9. **Faulty RFID Card**   You use an RFID card to obtain access to your office. When you attempt to scan your card, the RFID reader acts like it does not recognize your card is nearby. What are your next steps?

10. **Files Not Synchronizing**   You have saved files on the cloud from your home computer, but the files are not appearing on the computer in your office. What might have happened, and what steps can you take to retrieve the files?

Collaboration

11. **Technology in the Automotive Industry**   Technology is used in the automotive industry to increase speed and efficiency. Your instructor would like everyone to realize the importance of technology in this industry and the different ways it is used. Form a team of three people. One team member should investigate how technology is used to build automobiles. Another team member should investigate how technology is used to help ensure the safety of individuals working in the automobile manufacturing process, and the last team member should research how technology is used to market and sell cars. Write a brief report summarizing your findings.

✴ How To: Your Turn

The How To: Your Turn exercises present general guidelines for fundamental skills when using a computer or mobile device and then require that you determine how to apply these general guidelines to a specific program or situation.

Instructions: You often can complete tasks using technology in multiple ways. Figure out how to perform the tasks described in these exercises by using one or more resources available to you (such as a computer or mobile device, articles on the web or in print, online or program help, user guides, blogs, podcasts, videos, other individuals, trial and error, etc.). Summarize your 'how to' steps, along with the resource(s) used, in the format requested by your instructor (brief report, presentation, discussion, blog post, video, or other means).

① Determine Your Device's Storage Capacity

It may be necessary to determine your device's storage capacity before you decide to install a new operating system, program, or app, or if you want to transfer a large number of files to your computer or mobile device. For example, a new program you want to install may state that it requires a certain amount of storage capacity, so you should verify the storage capacity available on your device before deciding to purchase and install the program. One way to determine a device's total storage capacity is to review the documentation or specifications that were included with your computer or mobile device. The following steps guide you through the process of determining your device's storage capacity using other methods.

Computers

a. Open the window that shows the available storage devices on the computer.

b. Press and hold or right-click the drive for which you want to display the total storage capacity and then select the option to display the drive properties.

c. Navigate to the location showing the total storage capacity and available storage space.

or

a. Some operating systems allow you to hover your pointer over the icon representing the drive for which you want to determine the storage capacity, and the storage information will appear.

Mobile Devices

a. Display the device settings.

b. Navigate to the storage settings.

c. If necessary, navigate to the screen showing the total storage capacity and available storage space.

Exercises

1. What are other reasons why you might need to determine the total storage capacity or available storage space on your computer or mobile device?

2. Does the total storage capacity displayed on your computer or mobile device match the exact amount advertised when you purchased your computer or mobile device? If not, what might cause the discrepancy?

3. How much storage space is available on your computer or mobile device? What steps can you take if the storage on your device is almost completely used?

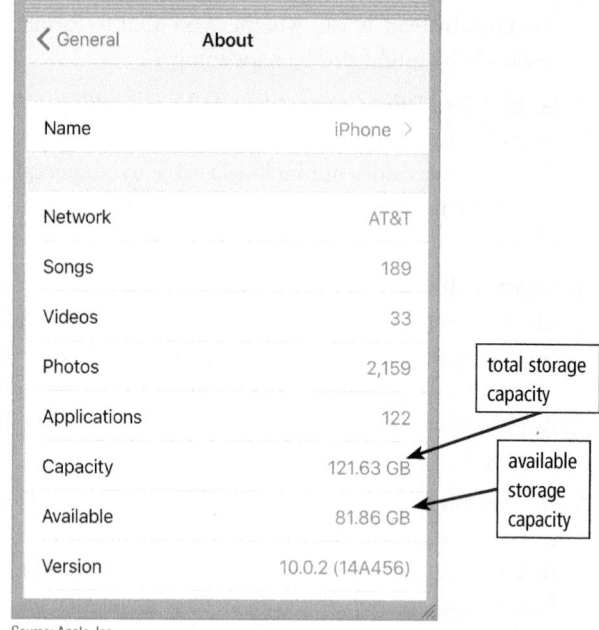

Source: Apple, Inc.

② Copy Individual Files to Another Storage Device, and Copy Files to Cloud Storage

If you save a file on your computer or mobile device and later will need to access it on another device, you likely will have to copy the file to another storage device or to the cloud so that you can access the file on the other device. The following steps guide you through the process of copying files to another storage device or to the cloud.

Copying Files to Another Storage Device

a. Navigate to the location containing the file you want to copy. If the file is on an external storage device or memory card, connect the storage device to your computer or insert the memory card into your computer's card reader. Next, navigate to the location containing the file you want to copy.

b. Navigate to the location to which you want to copy the file. If the location to which you want to copy the file is on an external storage device or on a memory card, connect the external storage device

How To: Your Turn

to your computer or insert the memory card into your computer's card reader. Next, navigate to the location to which you want to copy the file.

c. Drag the file you want to copy to the destination location. After you drag the file, make sure the file exists both in the source and destination location.

Copying Files to the Cloud

a. If necessary, sign up for an account with an online service that can store your files. Some online services store only photos and videos, while other services store all types of files, such as documents and other media files.

b. Sign in to the online service and navigate to the page where you can upload files.

c. Click the button or link to upload a file.

d. Navigate to and then click the file you want to upload.

e. Click the button or link to upload the file.

Exercises

1. What types of files might you want to copy to the cloud? Why would you copy files to the cloud instead of copying them to an external storage device?

2. What are at least three online services that allow you to store files? Are they free, or do they charge a fee? How much space do they provide? How do you obtain more storage space?

3. What steps would you take to copy a file from the cloud to your computer or mobile device?

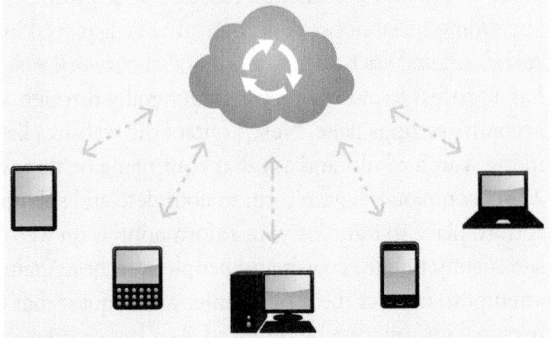

iStockphoto.com / Aaltazar

❸ Manage Space on a Storage Device

As you use your computer or mobile device, chances are that you are storing more files and installing additional programs and apps. At some point, you might require additional space or need to improve performance on your storage device. While purchasing an additional storage device might seem like the best option, ways may be available to help you manage the space on your existing storage device so that an additional purchase is not necessary. The following steps

guide you through the process of managing space on a storage device.

a. Review the files on your storage device and identify unused files you might be able to delete. Be careful not to remove files that the operating system, programs, or apps require to run properly.

b. View the list of programs and apps you have installed on your computer or mobile device. If you no longer need a program or app, uninstall it.

c. If you have files you may need in the future but not immediately, consider compressing them or copying them to an external storage device or to cloud storage. Verify the files have copied properly and then remove the files from your primary storage device.

d. If possible, defragment the storage device. If the storage device has not been defragmented recently, this process might improve performance significantly.

e. Search for and use any other tools that might be available in your operating system to maximize available space or improve performance. Note that some programs that claim to increase free space by compressing the files on your hard drive may slow your computer's performance.

f. If the above options do not increase performance enough or create sufficient free space, you might need to purchase an additional storage device.

Exercises

1. What files on your storage device might you consider deleting to save space? Why?

2. Does your computer or mobile device contain any programs or apps that you no longer need? How can you uninstall programs and apps from your computer or mobile device?

3. How does defragmentation help increase performance on your computer?

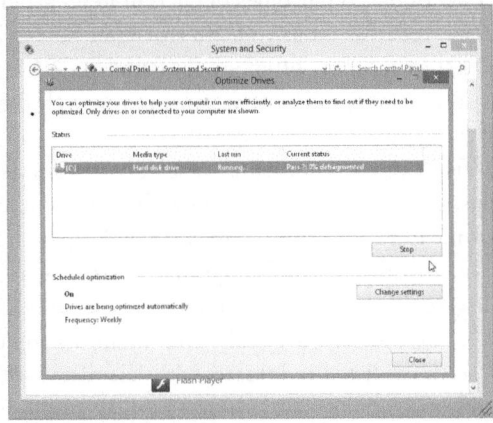

Source: Microsoft

✳ Internet Research

The Internet Research exercises broaden your understanding of module concepts by requiring that you search for information on the web.

Instructions: Use a search engine or another search tool to locate the information requested or answers to questions presented in the exercises. Describe your findings, along with the search term(s) you used and your web source(s), in the format requested by your instructor (brief report, presentation, discussion, blog post, video, or other means).

1 Making Use of the Web
Educational and Science

General reference websites, which include online encyclopedias, almanacs, and reference collections, are excellent sources of comprehensive, accurate, and organized facts on specific topics. For example, history and literary buffs can appreciate the websites that translate text, contain thousands of free books to download, and provide literary analyses. Among the more comprehensive websites are those sponsored by the American Library Association and the Library of Congress.

Answers to perplexing science questions and math problems are available on several educational websites that include practice tests, conversion tables, and current news articles. Environmental websites seek to educate and often persuade citizens to become aware of issues. The information helps consumers to make environmentally responsible purchasing decisions and urges people to become involved in solving global environmental problems. Scientists' research efforts extend beyond investigating this planet to exploring the great frontier of space. Their science websites contain information about current studies, conferences, and breakthroughs in such areas as biology, earth and ocean sciences, physics, and chemistry.

Research This: (a) Visit a general reference website and locate any free resources that you can download to your computer or mobile device. What materials are available to download? Which general topics are available? For which classes would you find the contents useful? Are you able to browse and search the collections? What types of current news articles are displayed? Are links to news stories or research articles shown? How often are they updated? Are previous stories archived so that you can research these events?

(b) Visit two environmental or science websites or apps, such as NASA, and browse their contents or download related apps. Which general topics are available for students? What types of current news articles are displayed? Are additional resources, such as videos and photos, available? Are online social network accounts listed to interact with scientists and researchers?

Source: NASA

2 Social Media
Locating Personal Information

Digital footprints tracking your Internet activity are relatively easy to find. Maintaining online anonymity is difficult to achieve once you have established online social network accounts with your actual name. While deleting an online social network account is a fairly easy process, deleting all remnants of information relating to the account can be a more difficult task. Just because you no longer can sign in to the account does not mean your posts, photos, and personal information do not exist somewhere on a website.

If you desire to remove an Internet presence for security or personal reasons, begin by searching for your name or account user names. Remove your profiles from any online social network account that is displayed in the search results. Each of the online social network websites has a process to close an account, generally through the account's settings page. Next, contact the websites listed in the search results and ask that your name be removed. Many companies have a form to complete and submit. A third place to hunt for your information is on websites listing public records and people searches. Again, attempt to contact these companies and request that your personal information be removed. As a last resort, some services will perform these tasks for a fee.

Research This: Use a search engine to locate instances of your name or user names. Did the search results list these names? If so, which online social networks or companies have records of your name? Then, search for your name on at least two websites that have public records or people databases. Did you see your name on these websites? If so, do you want the details, such as a phone number or address, available for anyone to see? If not, attempt to remove this data and write a report of the steps you took and your success in deleting the personal information.

Internet Research

❸ Search Skills
Image Search

An image search locates photos and images related to your search text or similar to other images. Click the Images link on a search engine's home page and then type the search text describing images you would like to find. For example, type the search text, solid state drive, to find photos of solid state drives. Search engines allow you to narrow your results by specifying additional conditions on the images found. These may include size (icon, wallpaper, or dimensions in pixels), color, time taken (past day, week, or month), type (photo, clip art, face, animation, or drawing), shape (wide, tall, square), usage rights (whether a photo may be reused, and under what conditions), and safe search. Safe search filters content inappropriate for minors.

Some search engines allow you to upload or specify the web address for an image, so that the search engine can locate images with similar features. Searching for similar images can be effective if the image is of a well-known person, place, or object.

Image search results usually display an arrangement of thumbnail images; click each thumbnail to see it in full size, download it, or obtain its web address from the browser's address bar.

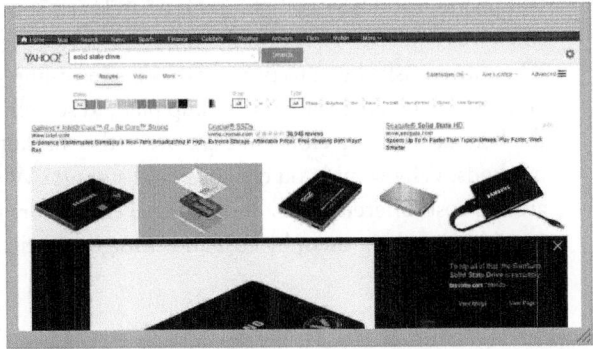

Source: Yahoo!

Research This: Create search text using the techniques described above or in previous Search Skills exercises and then type it in a search engine to find these images: (1) an RFID tag, exactly 400 × 400; (2) an external DVD drive, with a transparent background; (3) an internal hard drive, labeled for noncommercial reuse; (4) a person holding an SD card; and (5) images similar to a photo of a laptop computer (take a photo of a laptop and upload it). How successful was your image search?

Create a document containing each image, its web address, and the name or web address of the website on which it appears.

❹ Security
Degaussing Storage Media

Permanently destroying files on storage media is recommended when donating or selling a computer. Federal laws have imposed strict requirements and penalties for data security, particularly regarding health and insurance records and credit transactions. While procedures exist to restore deleted files or erased media, often companies and individuals truly desire that the data never can be recovered. Sensitive medical and financial information, in particular, should be erased so that savvy criminals and digital forensics examiners cannot recover deleted files. The U.S. Department of Defense and the National Security Agency set standards for sanitizing magnetic media and specify that degaussing, or demagnetizing, is the preferred method in lieu of permanently destroying the storage medium.

Research This: What types of degaussers are available? How do they wipe a drive's contents? How are Gauss and Oersted ratings applied? What length of time is required to degauss a drive? Some companies offer degaussing services. What procedures do they use to ensure secure practices?

❺ Cloud Services
Cloud Backups (IaaS)

Backing up files to the cloud provides a systematic way for organizations and individuals to create off-site copies of their files. Backing up files to the cloud is an example of infrastructure as a service (IaaS), a service of cloud computing which allows users to access and store files online.

Cloud backup providers offer continuous backup of new and changed files, transmitting them over a secure Internet connection. Like many cloud services, they offer a "pay as you go" pricing model, where customers subscribe to a service for a period, and pay for the features or storage they use. Many cloud backup providers offer web and mobile apps to access and restore files.

Cloud backup services differ from cloud storage services. Cloud backup services offer the software and infrastructure to back up and restore files only. They generally do not support synchronizing files across devices or sharing files with many users, which are common features of cloud storage services.

Research This: (1) Use a search engine to find two different cloud backup providers. Compare their pricing plans, storage offered, file types backed up, security features, and other services offered. (2) Why are cloud backup services attractive options for small to medium-sized businesses? (3) When is it practical to use cloud backup services, and when is it practical to use cloud storage?

✳ Critical Thinking

The Critical Thinking exercises challenge your assessment and decision-making skills by presenting real-world situations associated with module concepts. The Collaboration exercise should be completed with a team.

Instructions: Evaluate the situations below, using personal experiences and one or more resources available to you (such as articles on the web or in print, blogs, podcasts, videos, television, user guides, other individuals, electronics or computer stores, etc.). Perform the tasks requested in each exercise and share your deliverables in the format requested by your instructor (brief report, presentation, discussion, blog post, video, or other means).

1. Increasing Storage Capacity

You are the office manager at a local boutique. The store needs to increase its storage capacity, and so decides to buy an external hard drive. Your boss asks you to research access times and storage capacities of various external hard drives.

Do This: Use the web to learn more about available hard drive options. What other factors should you evaluate when determining the appropriate hard drive to purchase? Analyze the advantages and disadvantages of using external hard drives for storage. Include in your discussion backup plans, costs, and alternate options. Recommend two hard drives to your boss. Include user reviews and any information by industry experts in your comparison between the two different hard drives. Which is the best option? Why? Compile your findings.

2. NFC

Your new smartphone includes NFC capabilities. You are curious about its uses but are concerned about potential risks. Before you enable NFC and install apps that can use this technology, you want to do some research.

Do This: Use the web to find and then list current and developing uses of NFC. If possible, find reviews or blog posts about these technologies. Describe any safety issues you found in your research. List ways you can protect yourself when using NFC technology.

Locate apps that can use NFC. For what purposes can you use this new technology? What disadvantages and risks exist? How can you avoid any negative experiences and protect your data? Do any current laws govern or restrict the use of NFC for data collection? What are they? Can you provide additional potential uses for NFC at home, school, or work?

3. Case Study

Family-Owned Coffee Shop   You are the new manager for a family-owned coffee shop. The owners have asked you to create a backup plan for the shop's computers and devices. The employees in the coffee shop have access to multiple shared laptops, a desktop, and a tablet. Several employees use their own smartphones and tablets for work, according to the coffee shop's BYOD policy.

Do This: Use the web to find industry experts' recommendations for backing up data. Write a sample backup plan and schedule for the owners, and include types of backups you will use. Describe each backup type you propose and why you recommend it. Is any special software required to back up the different devices? The owners asked you to present reasons for using cloud storage as part of your backup plan. Research the benefits of using cloud storage over other backup methods. Why would you choose cloud storage? What are the cost differences? Compare three cloud storage providers, ranking them by cost and storage capacity.

Collaboration

4. Computers in Telemarketing

Your team is performing IT research for a magazine-subscription telemarketing company. The company's 150 telemarketers must make a minimum of 100 calls a day. If telemarketers do not meet the minimum number, they must finish the calls from home. The company must decide on the type of storage device to provide the telemarketers so that they can take the necessary data home. Management has narrowed the choice to three storage options: rewritable optical discs, cloud storage, or USB flash drives.

Do This: Form a three-member team and assign an option to each member. Each team member should evaluate the advantages and disadvantages. Include features such as capacity, access time, durability of media, ease of transporting between home and office, and cost. Meet with your team, and discuss and compile your findings. Which method would you recommend? Why? What are the advantages of each? Share your findings with the class.

science photo / Fotolia LLC

Operating Systems: Managing, Coordinating, and Monitoring Resources

9

iStockphoto.com / Vertigo3d

OBJECTIVES

After completing this module, you will be able to:

1 Explain the purpose of an operating system

2 Describe the start-up process and shutdown options on computers and mobile devices

3 Explain how an operating system provides a user interface, manages programs, manages memory, and coordinates tasks

4 Describe how an operating system enables users to configure devices, establish an Internet connection, and monitor performance

5 Identify file management and other tools included with an operating system, along with ways to update operating system software

6 Explain how an operating system enables users to control a network or administer security

7 Summarize the features of several desktop operating systems: Windows, macOS, UNIX, Linux, and Chrome OS

8 Briefly describe various server operating systems: Windows Server, macOS Server, UNIX, and Linux

9 Summarize the features and uses of several mobile operating systems: Google Android, Apple iOS, and Windows (Mobile Edition)

Operating Systems

When you purchase a computer or mobile device, it usually has an operating system and other tools installed. As previously discussed, the operating system and related tools collectively are known as system software because they consist of the programs that control or maintain the operations of the computer and its devices. An **operating system (OS)** is a set of programs that coordinate all the activities among computer or mobile device hardware. Other tools, which were discussed in Module 4, enable you to perform maintenance-type tasks usually related to managing devices, media, and programs used by computers and mobile devices.

Most operating systems perform similar functions that include starting and shutting down a computer or mobile device, providing a user interface, managing programs, managing memory, coordinating tasks, configuring devices, monitoring performance, establishing an Internet connection, providing file management and other device or media-related tasks, and updating operating system software. Some operating systems also allow users to control a network and administer security (Figure 9-1).

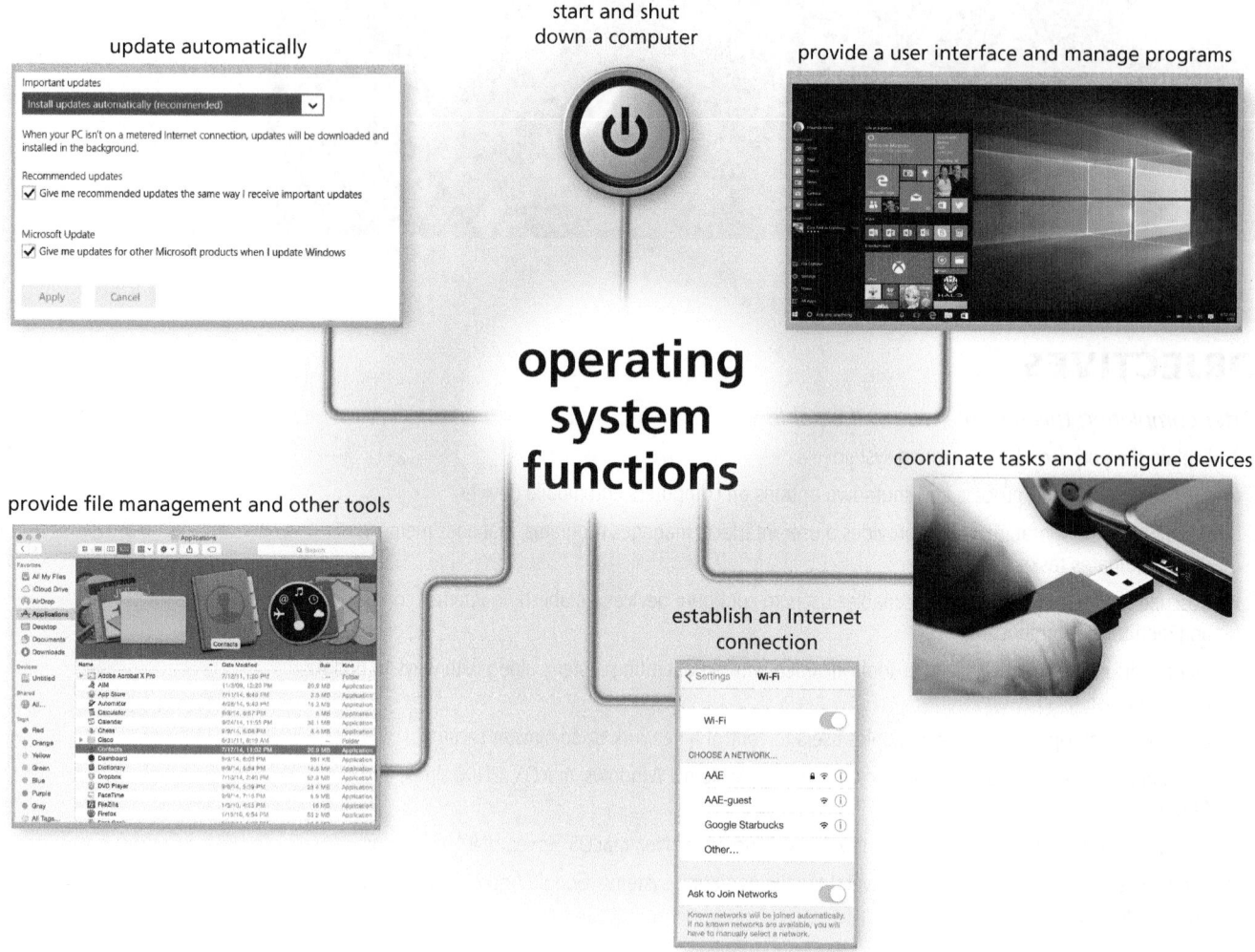

start and shut down a computer

update automatically

provide a user interface and manage programs

operating system functions

provide file management and other tools

coordinate tasks and configure devices

establish an Internet connection

Figure 9-1   Most operating systems perform similar functions, some of which are illustrated above.
Nomad_Soul / Shutterstock.com; Source: Apple Inc; Source: Microsoft

Although an operating system often can run from a USB flash drive, media in an optical drive, or an external drive, in most cases, an operating system resides inside a computer or mobile device. For example, it is installed on a hard drive in a laptop or desktop. On mobile devices, the operating system may reside on firmware in the device. *Firmware* consists of ROM chips or flash memory chips that store permanent instructions.

Operating systems often are written to run on specific types of computers, based on their computing needs and capabilities. That is, servers do not run the same operating system as tablets or laptops because these computers perform different computing tasks. For example, a tablet or laptop operating system might have a feature to turn the device off after a few minutes of inactivity in order to conserve battery power. A server, by contrast, always is plugged in and generally remains on all of the time, which means its operating system would not need this power-saving feature. The same types of computers, such as laptops, may run different operating systems. It also is possible to run more than one operating system on the same computer.

When purchasing a program or an application, you must ensure that it works with the operating system installed on your computer or mobile device. The operating system that a computer uses sometimes is called the *platform* because applications are said to run "on top of" it, or because the platform supports the applications. With purchased applications, their specifications will identify the required platform(s), or the operating system(s), on which they will run. A *cross-platform application* is an application that runs the same way on multiple operating systems.

Operating System Functions

Every computer and mobile device has an operating system. Regardless of the type of the computer or device, however, their operating systems provide many similar functions. The following sections discuss functions common to most operating systems. These functions include starting and shutting down computers and mobile devices, providing a user interface, managing programs, managing memory, coordinating tasks, configuring devices, monitoring performance, establishing an Internet connection, updating operating system software, providing file and disk management tools, controlling a network, and administering security.

Starting Computers and Mobile Devices

If a computer or mobile device is off, you press a power button to turn it on (Figure 9-2). If it is on, you may need to restart (also called reboot) the computer or mobile device for a variety of reasons. For example, you might install a new program or app, update existing software, or experience network or Internet connectivity problems. Alternatively, you might notice that the performance of the computer or device is sluggish, or it may stop responding altogether. The method you use to restart a computer or device differs, depending on the situation and also the hardware. You may be able to use operating system instructions or press keys on the keyboard to restart the computer or device. Or, you might be required to respond to on-screen prompts. Sometimes, the computer or device restarts automatically.

When you start or restart a computer or mobile device, a series of messages may appear on the screen. The actual information displayed varies depending on the make and type of the computer or mobile device and the equipment installed. The start-up process, however, is similar for large and small computers and mobile devices, as described in the following steps.

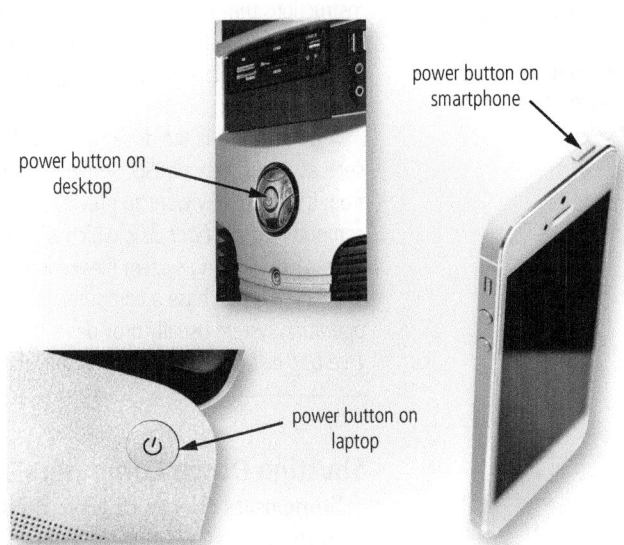

Figure 9-2 Examples of power buttons on computers and mobile devices.
Olinchuk / Shutterstock.com; iStockphoto.com / kizilkayaphotos; iStockphoto.com / Nikada

Step 1: When you turn on the computer or mobile device, the power supply or battery sends an electrical current to circuitry in the computer or mobile device.

Step 2: The charge of electricity causes the processor chip to reset itself and finds the firmware that contains start-up instructions.

Step 3: The start-up process executes a series of tests to check the various components. These tests vary depending on the type of computer or devices and can include checking the buses, system clock, adapter cards, RAM chips, mouse, keyboard, and drives. It also includes making sure that any peripheral devices are connected properly and operating correctly. If any problems are identified, the computer or device may beep, display error messages, or cease operating — depending on the severity of the problem.

Step 4: If the tests are successful, the kernel of the operating system and other frequently used instructions load from the computer or mobile device's internal storage media to its memory (RAM). The *kernel* is the core of an operating system that manages memory and devices, maintains the internal clock, runs programs, and assigns the resources, such as devices, programs, apps, data, and information. The kernel is *memory resident*, which means it remains in memory while the computer or mobile device is running. Other parts of the operating system are *nonresident*; that is, nonresident instructions remain on a storage medium until they are needed, at which time they transfer into memory (RAM).

Step 5: The operating system in memory takes control of the computer or mobile device and loads system configuration information. The operating system may verify that the person attempting to use the computer or mobile device is a legitimate user. Finally, the user interface appears on the screen, and any start-up applications, such as antivirus software, run.

 CONSIDER THIS

What is meant by the phrase, booting a computer?
The process of starting or restarting a computer or mobile device is called *booting*. Some people use the term *cold boot* to refer to the process of starting a computer or mobile device from a state when it is powered off completely. Similarly, *warm boot* refers to the process of restarting a computer or mobile device while it remains powered on.

A warm boot generally is faster than a cold boot because it skips some of the operating system start-up instructions that are included as part of a cold boot. If you suspect a hardware problem, it is recommended that you use a cold boot to start a computer or device because this process detects and checks connected hardware devices. If a program or app stops working, a warm boot often is sufficient to restart the device because this process clears memory.

A **boot drive** is the drive from which your personal computer starts, which typically is an internal hard drive, such as a hard disk or SSD. Sometimes, an internal hard drive becomes damaged and the computer cannot boot from it, or you may want to preview another operating system without installing it. In these cases, you can start the computer from a *boot disk*, which is removable media, such as a CD/DVD or USB flash drive, that contains only the necessary operating system files required to start the computer.

When you purchase a computer, it may include recovery media in the form of a CD/DVD. If it does not, the operating system usually provides a means to create one. When the word, live, is used with a type of media, such as *Live USB* or *Live CD/DVD*, this usually means the media can be used to start the computer.

 **BTW**

Recovery Media
In situations when a boot disk is required to restart a computer or device that will not start from its boot drive, the boot disk often is referred to as *recovery media*.

Shutting Down Computers and Mobile Devices

Some users choose to leave their computers or mobile devices running continually and rarely turn them off. Computers and devices that are left on always are available, and users often run back up or other similar programs while the computer or device is not being used. These users also do not need to wait for the boot process, which can be time consuming on older computers. Other users choose to shut down their computers and mobile devices regularly. These users might be concerned with security, want to reduce energy costs, or prefer to clear memory often. To turn off a computer or mobile device, you may be required to use operating system commands, press keyboard key(s), push a power button, or a combination of these methods. Read Secure IT 8-2 in Module 8 for tips on safely removing media before shutting down a computer or mobile device.

Power options include shutting down (powering off) the computer or mobile device, placing it in sleep mode, or placing it in hibernate mode. Both sleep mode and hibernate mode are designed to save time when you resume work on the computer or device. *Sleep mode* saves any open documents and running programs or apps to RAM, turns off all unneeded functions, and then places the computer in a low-power state. If, for some reason, power is removed from a computer or device that is in sleep mode, any unsaved work could be lost. *Hibernate mode*, by contrast, saves any open documents and running programs or apps to an internal hard drive before removing power from the computer or device.

The function of the power button on a computer or mobile device varies, and users typically are able to configure its default behavior. For example, you typically can place a computer or mobile device in sleep mode by quickly pressing its power button or closing its lid or cover (for example, on a laptop or a tablet). Pressing and holding down the power button may remove all power from the computer or mobile device.

⚙ **BTW**
Power Options
Some operating systems do not include sleep mode or hibernate mode functions.

Providing a User Interface

You interact with an operating system through its user interface. That is, a **user interface (UI)** controls how you enter data and instructions and how information is displayed on the screen. Two types of operating system user interfaces are graphical and command line. Operating system user interfaces often use a combination of these techniques to define how a user interacts with a computer or mobile device.

Graphical User Interface   Most users today work with a graphical user interface. With a *graphical user interface (GUI)*, you interact with menus and visual images by touching, pointing, tapping, or clicking buttons and other objects to issue commands (Figure 9-3). Many current GUI operating systems incorporate features similar to those of a browser, such as links and navigation buttons (i.e., Back button and Forward button) when navigating the computer or mobile device's storage media to locate files.

Figure 9-3   Examples of operating system graphical user interfaces on some computers and mobile devices.

Source: Apple Inc.; Carlos Osorio / Getty Images; iStockphoto.com / cincila

A graphical user interface designed for touch input sometimes is called a *touch user interface*. Some operating systems for desktops and laptops and many operating systems for mobile devices have a touch user interface.

 CONSIDER THIS ———————————————————————————————

What is a natural user interface?
With a **natural user interface** (**NUI**), users interact with the software through ordinary, intuitive behavior. NUIs are implemented in a variety of ways: touch screens (touch input), gesture recognition (motion input), speech recognition and personal assistant apps (voice input), and virtual reality (simulations).

Command-Line Interface   To configure devices, manage system resources, automate system management tasks, and troubleshoot network connections, network administrators and other technical users work with a command-line interface. In a *command-line interface*, a user types commands represented by short keywords or abbreviations (such as dir to view a directory, or list of files) or presses special keys on the keyboard (such as function keys or key combinations) to enter data and instructions (Figure 9-4).

Some people consider command-line interfaces difficult to use because they require exact spelling, form, and punctuation. Minor errors, such as a missing period, generate an error message. Command-line interfaces, however, give a user more control to manage detailed settings. When working with a command-line interface, the set of commands used to control actions is called the *command language*.

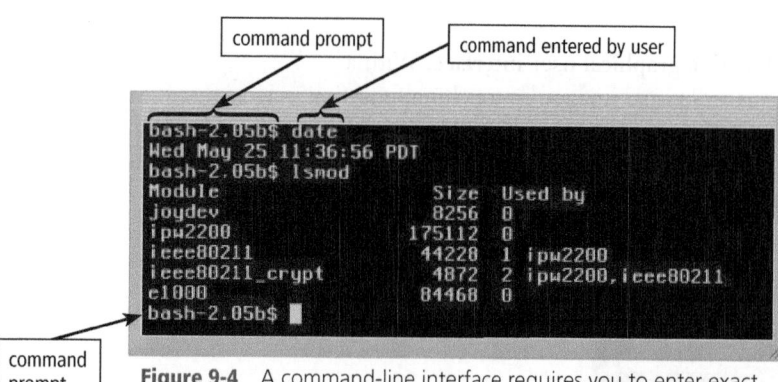

command prompt

command entered by user

command prompt

Figure 9-4   A command-line interface requires you to enter exact spelling, form, and punctuation.

Managing Programs

How an operating system handles programs directly affects your productivity. An operating system can be single-tasking or multitasking:

- A single-tasking operating system allows only one program or app to run at a time. For example, if you are using a browser and want to check email messages, you must exit the browser before you can run the email program. Operating systems on embedded computers and some mobile devices use a single tasking operating system.
- Most operating systems today are multitasking. A *multitasking* operating system allows two or more programs or apps to reside in memory at the same time. Using the example just cited, if you are working with a multitasking operating system, you do not have to exit the browser to run the email program. Both programs can run concurrently.

When a computer is running multiple programs concurrently, one program is in the foreground and the others are in the background (Figure 9-5). The one in the *foreground* is the active program, that is, the one you currently are using. The other programs running but not in use are in the *background*. The foreground program typically is displayed on the screen, and the background programs are hidden partially or completely behind the foreground program. A multitasking operating system's user interface easily allows you to switch between foreground and background programs.

Figure 9-5 The foreground application, Microsoft Word, is displayed on the screen. The other applications (Calendar, Google Maps in Edge, and File Explorer) are in the background.
donatas1205 / Shutterstock.com; Source: Google Inc.; Source: Microsoft

In addition to managing applications, an operating system manages other processes. These processes include programs or routines that provide support to other programs or hardware. Some are memory resident. Others run as they are required. Figure 9-6 shows a list of some processes running on a Windows computer; notice the list contains the applications running in Figure 9-5, as well as other programs and processes.

Some operating systems support a single user; others support thousands of users running multiple programs. A *multiuser* operating system enables two or more users to run programs simultaneously. Networks, servers, and supercomputers allow hundreds to thousands of users to connect at the same time and, thus, use multiuser operating systems.

Through the operating system, you also can install programs and apps, as well as remove them. Read How To 9-1 for instructions on removing a program or app.

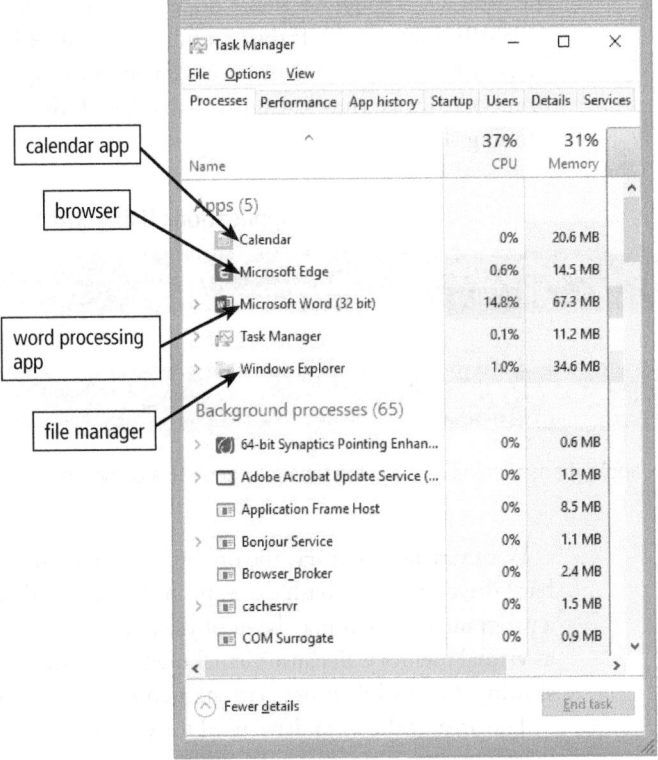

Figure 9-6 An operating system manages multiple programs and processes while you use a computer or mobile device.
Source: Microsoft

 **HOW TO 9-1**

Remove a Program or App

If you are running low on space on your computer or mobile device, you may want to remove programs and apps you no longer use. The following steps describe how to remove a program or app from your computer or mobile device:

1. Sign in to a user account that has administrative privileges; that is, the user account should have the capability to perform functions such as removing programs or apps.

2. Make sure the program or app you want to remove is not running.

3. Display the list of programs or apps installed on your computer or mobile device.

4. Select the program or app you wish to remove.

5. Click the button to remove the program or app.

6. If necessary, when the installation is complete, restart your computer or device.

7. Verify the program or app you removed no longer is on your computer or mobile device.

✳ **Consider This:** What are some other reasons why you might want to remove a program or app from your computer or mobile device?

Managing Memory

The purpose of memory management is to optimize the use of a computer or device's internal memory, i.e., RAM. As Module 6 discussed, RAM (random access memory) consists of one or more chips on the motherboard that hold items such as data and instructions while the processor interprets and executes them. The operating system allocates, or assigns, data and instructions to an area of memory while they are being processed. Then, it carefully monitors the contents of memory. Finally, the operating system releases these items from being monitored in memory when the processor no longer requires them.

If several programs or apps are running simultaneously, your computer or mobile device may use up its available RAM. For example, assume an operating system requires 2 GB of RAM to run, an antivirus program — 256 MB, a browser — 512 MB, a productivity software suite — 1 GB, and a photo editing program — 512 MB. With all these programs running simultaneously, the total RAM required would be 4.352 GB (2048 MB + 256 MB + 512 MB + 1024 MB + 512 MB) (Figure 9-7). If the computer has only 4 GB of RAM, the operating system may have to use virtual memory in order to run all of the applications at the same time. When a computer or mobile device runs low on available RAM, this often results in the computer or mobile device running sluggishly.

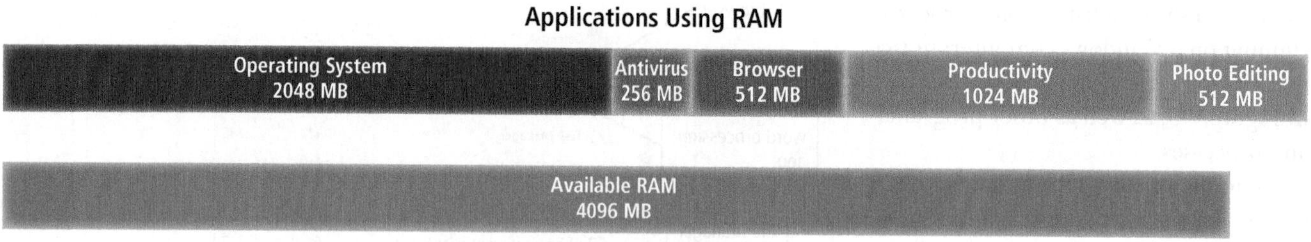

Applications Using RAM

Operating System 2048 MB	Antivirus 256 MB	Browser 512 MB	Productivity 1024 MB	Photo Editing 512 MB

Available RAM 4096 MB

Figure 9-7   Many applications running at the same time may deplete a computer's or device's available RAM.

With **virtual memory**, the operating system allocates a portion of a storage medium, such as a hard drive or a USB flash drive, to function as additional RAM (Figure 9-8). As you interact with a program, part of it may be in physical RAM, while the rest of the program is on the hard drive as virtual memory. Because virtual memory is slower than RAM, users may notice the computer slowing down while it uses virtual memory.

The area of the hard drive used for virtual memory is called a *swap file* because it swaps (exchanges) data, information, and instructions between memory and storage. A *page* is the amount of data and program instructions that can be swapped at a given time. The technique of swapping items between memory and storage, called *paging*, is a time-consuming process for the computer. When an operating system spends much of its time paging, instead of executing application software, it is said to be *thrashing*.

How a Computer Might Use Virtual Memory

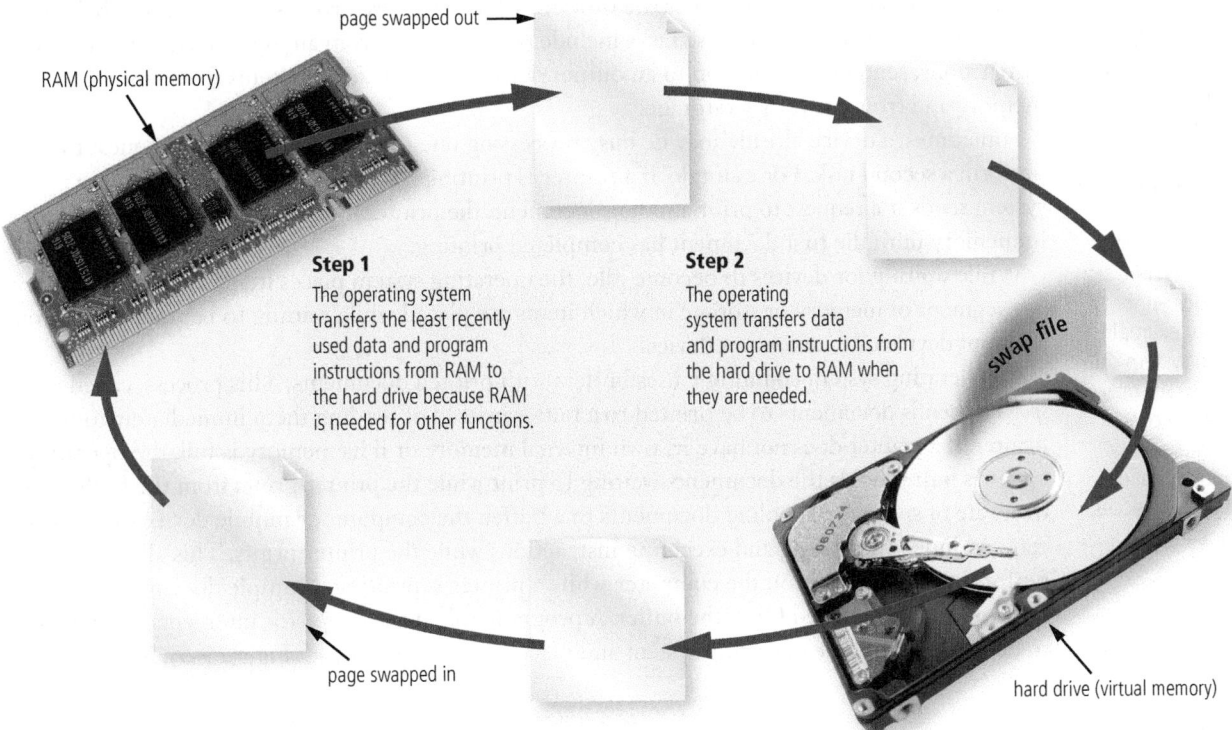

page swapped out →

RAM (physical memory)

Step 1
The operating system transfers the least recently used data and program instructions from RAM to the hard drive because RAM is needed for other functions.

Step 2
The operating system transfers data and program instructions from the hard drive to RAM when they are needed.

swap file

page swapped in

hard drive (virtual memory)

Figure 9-8 This figure shows how a computer might use virtual memory.
TungCheung / Shutterstock.com; kastianz / Shutterstock.com

✹ CONSIDER THIS

What happens if an application stops responding or the computer appears to run sluggishly?

If an application, such as a browser, has stopped responding, the operating system may be thrashing. When this occurs, try to exit the program. If that does not work, try a warm boot and then a cold boot. To help prevent future occurrences of thrashing, you might consider the following:

1. Remove unnecessary files and uninstall seldom used programs and apps. (Read How To 9-1 earlier in this module for instructions about removing programs and apps.)

2. If your computer has a hard disk (instead of an SSD), try defragmenting the hard disk. (Read How To 8-1 in Module 8 for instructions about defragmenting a hard disk.)

3. Purchase and install additional RAM.

✹ CONSIDER THIS

What if my smartphone runs out of memory?

If your smartphone or other mobile device displays a message that it is running low on memory, try the following:

1. Exit unnecessary applications that are running.

2. Restart the smartphone or mobile device.

3. Uninstall seldom used applications. (Read How To 9-1 earlier in this module for instructions about removing programs and apps.)

4. Download and install an app that identifies and removes unused files, duplicate or blurry photos, and downloaded app files you no longer need on the phone.

5. Remove unnecessary files, including photos and videos (you may want to copy them to cloud storage, a computer, or a memory card first).

6. If your smartphone supports the use of a memory card, specify that applications, photos, videos, or downloaded files should be saved on a memory card instead of the smartphone's internal memory.

BTW

Higher-Priority Tasks
A multiuser operating system does not always process tasks on a first-come, first-served basis. If a user or task has been assigned a higher priority than others by the network administrator, the operating system performs higher-priority tasks first. For example, an operating system on a corporate server may process tasks to check for incoming email more frequently than it processes tasks to access archived documents.

Coordinating Tasks

The operating system determines the order in which tasks are processed. A task, or job, is an operation the processor manages. Tasks include receiving data from an input device, processing instructions, sending information to an output device, and transferring items from storage to memory and from memory to storage.

Sometimes, a device already may be busy processing one task when it receives a request to perform a second task. For example, if a printer is printing a document when the operating system sends it a request to print another document, the printer must store the second document in memory until the first document has completed printing.

While waiting for devices to become idle, the operating system places items in buffers. A *buffer* is a segment of memory or storage in which items are placed while waiting to be transferred from an input device or to an output device.

An operating system commonly uses buffers with printed documents. This process, called *spooling*, sends documents to be printed to a buffer instead of sending them immediately to the printer. If a printer does not have its own internal memory or if its memory is full, the operating system's buffer holds the documents waiting to print while the printer prints from the buffer at its own rate of speed. By spooling documents to a buffer, the computer or mobile device's processor can continue interpreting and executing instructions while the printer prints. This allows users to perform other activities on the computer while a printer is printing. Multiple documents line up in a **queue** (pronounced Q) in the buffer. A program, called a *print spooler*, intercepts documents to be printed from the operating system and places them in the queue (Figure 9-9).

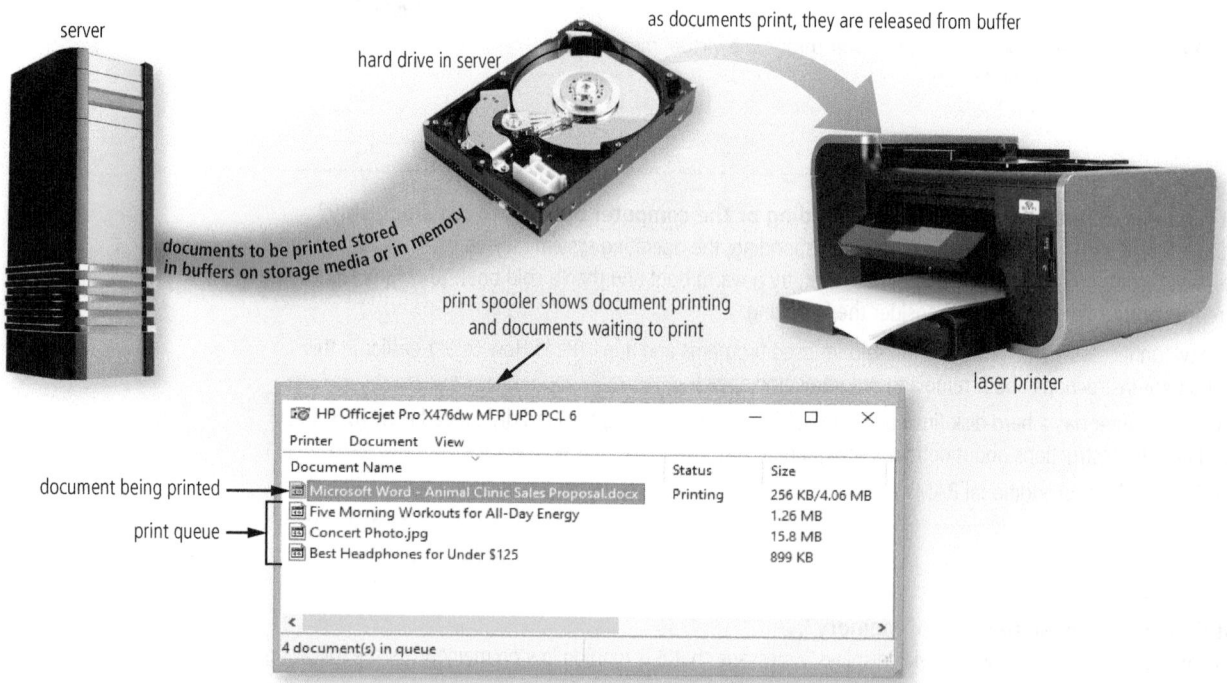

Figure 9-9   Spooling increases both processor and printer efficiency by placing documents to be printed in a buffer or on storage media before they are printed. This figure shows three documents in the queue with one document printing.

iStockphoto.com / luismmolina; iStockphoto.com / lleerogers; Kitch Bain / Shutterstock.com; Source: Microsoft

Configuring Devices

A **driver**, short for *device driver*, is a small program that tells the operating system how to communicate with a specific device. Each device connected to a computer, such as a mouse, keyboard, monitor, printer, card reader/writer, digital camera, webcam, portable media player, or smartphone, has its own specialized set of commands and, thus, requires its own specific driver. When you start a computer or connect a device via a USB port, the operating system loads the device's driver. Drivers must be installed for each connected device in order for the device to function properly. Read How To 9-2 for instructions about finding the latest drivers for devices.

✸ HOW TO 9-2

Find the Latest Drivers for Devices
Device manufacturers sometimes release updated driver versions either to correct problems with previous drivers, enhance a device's functionality, or increase compatibility with new operating system versions. The following steps describe how to find the latest drivers for devices:

1. Search for and navigate to the device manufacturer's website.

2. Click the link on the website to display the webpage containing technical support information.

3. Select or enter the device's model number to display support information for the device.

4. Browse the device's support information and then click the link or button to download the most current driver. Manufacturers often create different versions of drivers for different operating systems, so make sure you download the driver that is compatible with the operating system you currently are using.

5. When the download is complete, follow the instructions that accompanied the driver to install it.

✸ **Consider This:** What might you do if you are unable to locate your device's driver on the manufacturer's website?

If you attach a new device, such as a portable media player or smartphone, to a computer, its driver must be installed before you can use the device. Today, most devices and operating systems support Plug and Play. As discussed in Module 6, *Plug and Play* means the operating system automatically configures new devices as you install or connect them. Specifically, it assists you in the device's installation by loading the necessary drivers automatically from the device and checking for conflicts with other devices. With Plug and Play, a user plugs in a device and then immediately can begin using the device without having to configure it manually.

Monitoring Performance

Operating systems typically include a performance monitor. A **performance monitor** is a program that assesses and reports information about various computer resources and devices (Figure 9-10). For example, users can monitor the processor, drives, network, and memory usage.

The information in performance reports helps users and administrators identify a problem with resources so that they can try to resolve any issues. If a computer is running extremely slow, for example, the performance monitor may determine that the computer's memory is being used to its maximum. Thus, you might consider installing additional memory in the computer.

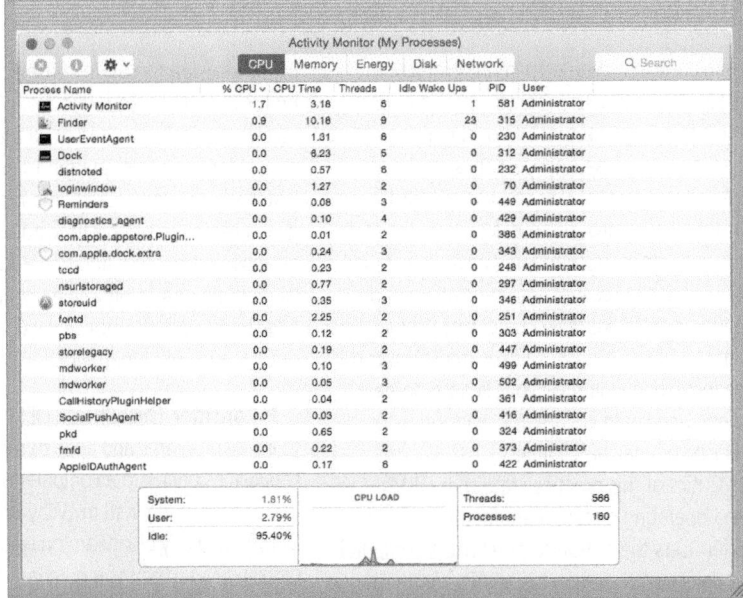

Figure 9-10   The Activity Monitor in this figure is tracking CPU (processor) usage.
Source: Apple Inc.

Establishing an Internet Connection

Operating systems typically provide a means to establish Internet connections. You can establish wired connections, such as cable and DSL, or wireless connections, such as Wi-Fi, mobile broadband, and satellite. Some connections are configured automatically as soon as you connect to the Internet. With others, you may need to set up a connection manually (Figure 9-11).

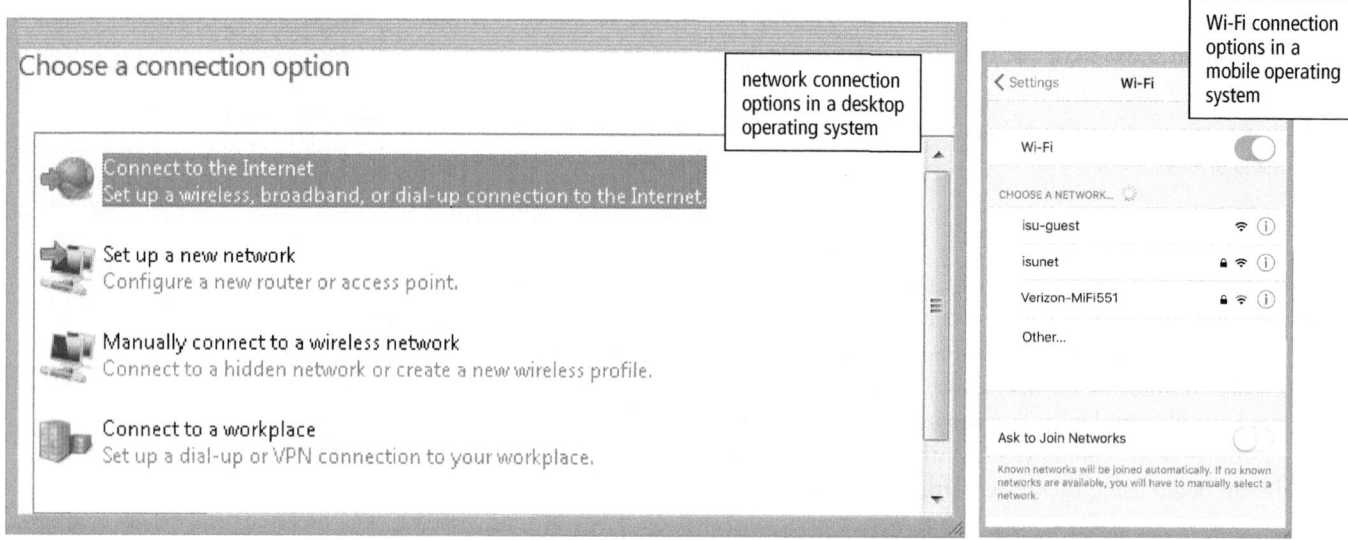

Figure 9-11   Shown here are Internet connection options for desktop and mobile operating systems.
Source: Microsoft; Source: Apple Inc.

Some operating systems also include a browser and an email program, enabling you to begin using the web and communicating with others as soon as you set up an Internet connection. Operating systems also sometimes include firewalls and other tools to protect computers and mobile devices from unauthorized intrusions and unwanted software. Read Ethics & Issues 9-1 to consider whether operating systems should include antivirus and other programs.

⚙ ETHICS & ISSUES 9-1

Should Manufacturers Include Extra Programs in Operating Systems for Computers and Mobile Devices?
OEMs (original equipment manufacturers) often include and profit from including extra programs installed with a computer or device's operating system. These additional programs and apps, often called *bloatware*, mostly are harmless. Users object to their inclusion, however, because these programs and apps take up space, may slow start-up time, and can decrease the computer or device's overall efficiency.

Bloatware can come in many forms: antivirus programs, games, productivity apps, and more. Some programs or apps cause nuisances for the user, such as those that display alarming messages about a computer's virus

protection and then offer more protection for additional costs. Programs that run when the operating system starts or run in the background cause unnecessary slowdowns. Websites exist that you can use to check your installed programs or apps against a list of those other users commonly have uninstalled, as well as the reasons for uninstalling. Independent software developers post fixes to remove bloatware. These fixes may or may not be legal, depending on your license agreement, and could violate any warranties for which you may be eligible.

Critics of this practice state that OEMs and operating system manufacturers should offer users the option to purchase a computer or device with a clean installation (without bloatware) of the operating system. A clean

install may lead to an increased cost to make up for the lost revenue the manufacturer receives by including the extra programs or apps. Many say that charging more for a clean installation is unethical. Some recommend giving users the option to install the programs or apps that provide additional functionality as plug-ins or add-ons. Open source software advocates state that these versions offer more options to avoid bloatware.

⚙ **Consider This:** Should OEMs be able to install programs and apps to run alongside capabilities built into a computer or mobile device's operating system? Why or why not? Did you find any bloatware on your computer or mobile device when you purchased it? Were you able to delete unwanted programs and apps?

Updating Operating System Software

Many programs, including operating systems, include an **automatic update** feature that regularly provides new features or corrections to the program. That is, the operating system automatically checks to see if new updates are available, and if so, downloads them from the Internet and installs them on your computer. With an operating system, these updates can include fixing program errors, improving program functionality, expanding program features, enhancing security, and modifying device drivers (Figure 9-12).

Many software makers provide free downloadable updates, sometimes called a *service pack*, to users who have registered and/ or activated their software. With operating systems, the automatic update feature can be configured to alert users when an update is available or to download and install the update automatically. Some operating systems, such as Microsoft Windows, enable automatic updates by default so that your computer or device always has the most recent features. Users can disable or defer automatic updates, if necessary, because these updates can require additional resources or potentially interfere with critical work. Users without an Internet connection usually can order the updates on an optical disc for a minimal shipping fee. Read Secure IT 9-1 for issues related to automatic updates.

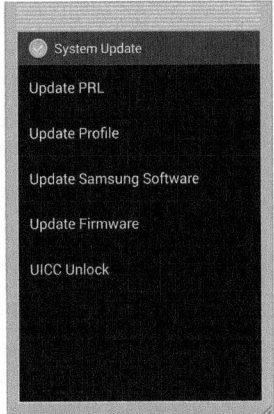

Figure 9-12 An operating system usually includes a means to download and install important updates.
Source: Google Inc.

 BTW

Bugs
An error in a program sometimes is called a *bug*.

 SECURE IT 9-1

Automatic Updates — Safe or Not?

Software updates often improve security and reliability, and they also may add significant features that optimize the computer's performance. In most cases, you have the choice either to allow the software to update automatically or to assess and then decide whether to install each update individually. Software manufacturers often recommend you download and install all available updates when they become available.

The automatic update option occasionally has caused problems. In one case, people preparing their income tax returns were unable to print forms when a leading software company issued an automatic update one week before the filing deadline. In another situation, an automatic update was installed on all computers — even those with this feature disabled. The company claimed that the update was harmless and was for the benefit of its customers. Only later did some users realize that this secret update caused serious problems. One problem, ironically, was that updates no longer could be installed on the affected computers. Customers were furious about the issues, especially because the company made the changes without informing the computer owners. One consequence of the ensuing outrage was that many people turned off the automatic update feature, fearing that future updates might cause even more damage.

Consider This: Is the automatic update feature enabled or disabled on your computer? Why? Should software companies be able to send automatic updates to your computer without your knowledge? Why or why not?

Providing File, Disk, and System Management Tools

Operating systems often provide users with a variety of tools related to managing a computer, its devices, or its programs. These file, disk, and system management tools were discussed in Module 4 and are summarized in Table 9-1. Read Secure IT 9-2 to learn more about an operating system's built-in security tools.

Table 9-1 File, Disk, and System Management Tools

Tool	Function
File Manager	Performs functions related to displaying files; organizing files in folders; and copying, renaming, deleting, moving, and sorting files
Search	Attempts to locate files on your computer or mobile device based on specified criteria
Image Viewer	Displays, copies, and prints the contents of graphics files
Uninstaller	Removes a program or app, as well as any associated entries in the system files
Disk Cleanup	Searches for and removes unnecessary files
Disk Defragmenter	Reorganizes the files and unused space on a computer's hard disk so that the operating system accesses data more quickly and programs and apps run faster
Screen Saver	Causes a display's screen to show a moving image or blank screen if no keyboard or mouse activity occurs for a specified time
File Compression	Shrinks the size of a file(s)
PC Maintenance	Identifies and fixes operating system problems, detects and repairs drive problems, and includes the capability of improving a computer's performance
Backup and Restore	Copies selected files or the contents of an entire storage medium to another storage location
Power Management	Monitors a laptop or mobile device's battery usage

---

❈ SECURE IT 9-2

Using and Evaluating an Operating System's Built-In Security Tools

Security software must run constantly to protect against new viruses and malware and spyware attacks. Operating systems can include the following security tools:

- **Firewall:** Security experts recommend using a firewall and configuring it to turn on or off automatically.

- **Automatic updating:** Security updates are issued at least once daily, and other updates are generated on an as-needed basis. Many people enjoy the convenience offered by allowing these fixes to install automatically instead of continually checking for new files to download. Users can view the update history to see when specific updates were installed. If an update caused a problem to occur, a user can uninstall these new files.

- **Antivirus software:** Many operating systems include antivirus programs that are updated regularly. Some users mistakenly think they should install and run another antivirus program simultaneously for more protection. They should not run more than one antivirus program on a computer because multiple programs might conflict with one another and slow overall performance.

- **Spyware and malware detection software:** Sophisticated malware and spyware threats are emerging at an unparalleled rate, so comprehensive spyware and malware detection software is mandatory to fend off attacks on the computer or device.

The operating system generally is scheduled to scan and update when the computer is idle, such as in the middle of the night. Overall, the security tools should run constantly and quietly in the background to ensure a safe computing experience.

❈ **Consider This:** Does your operating system have a firewall and protection against spyware and malware? Do updates occur automatically or manually? Which operating systems are more susceptible to malware attacks? Why?

Controlling a Network

Some operating systems are designed to work with a server on a network. These multiuser operating systems allow multiple users to share a printer, Internet access, files, and programs.

Some operating systems have network features built into them. In other cases, the operating system for the network is a set of programs that are separate from the operating system on the client computers or mobile devices that access the network. When not connected to the network, the client computers use their own operating system. When connected to the network, the operating system on the network may assume some of the operating system functions on the client computers or mobile devices.

The *network administrator*, the person overseeing network operations, uses the server operating system to add and remove users, computers, and other devices to and from the network. The network administrator also uses the operating system on the network to configure the network, install software, and administer network security.

Administering Security

Network administrators, as well as owners of computers, typically have an *administrator account* that enables them to access all files and programs, install programs, and specify settings that affect all users on a computer, mobile device, or network. Settings include creating user accounts and establishing permissions. These *permissions* define who can access certain resources and when they can access those resources.

For each user, the network administrator or computer owner establishes a user account. A user account enables a user to **sign in** to, or access resources on, a network or computer (Figure 9-13). Each user account typically consists of a user name and password. Recall that a **user name**, or user ID, is a unique combination of characters, such as letters of the alphabet and/or numbers, that identifies a specific user.

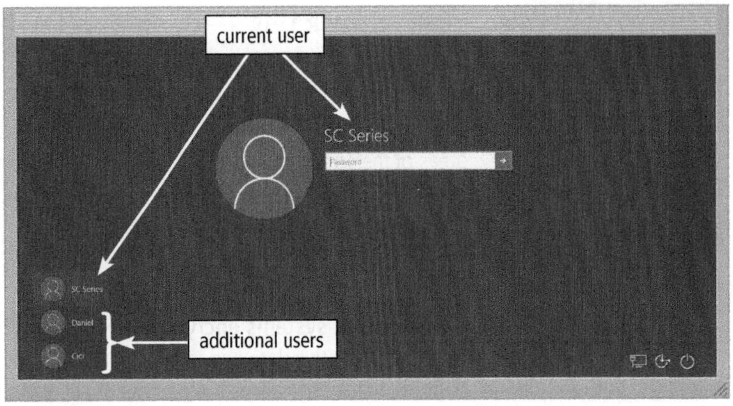

Figure 9-13   Most multiuser operating systems allow each user to sign in, which is the process of entering a user name and a password into the computer. Single-user operating systems often use a password to lock an entire device or computer.
Source: Microsoft

A **password** is a private combination of characters associated with the user name that allows access to certain computer, mobile device, or network resources. Some operating systems allow the network administrator to assign passwords to files and commands, restricting access to only authorized users. Mobile device owners often assign a password to the entire device, restricting all access until the correct password is entered. Read Secure IT 1-3 in Module 1 for tips on creating strong passwords.

To prevent unauthorized users from accessing computer resources, keep your password confidential. After entering a user name and/or password, the operating system compares the user's entry with the authorized user name(s) and password(s). If the entry matches the user name and/or password stored in a file, the operating system grants the user access. If the entry does not match, the operating system denies access to the user.

The operating system on a network records successful and unsuccessful sign-in attempts in a file. This allows the network administrator to review who is using or attempting to use the computer. The administrators also use these files to monitor computer usage. Read Ethics & Issues 9-2 to consider who is responsible for operating system security flaws.

✹ BTW

Passwords
While users type a password, most computers and mobile devices hide the actual password characters by displaying some other characters, such as asterisks (*) or dots.

✹ ETHICS & ISSUES 9-2

Should Operating System Manufacturers Be Liable for Breaches Due to Security Flaws?
If you purchase a household device with a warranty, you can hold the manufacturer responsible for replacing and fixing it. Some argue that the same product liability laws that protect consumers in other industries should apply to software. Users' devices and data are vulnerable when security flaws exist in operating systems for computers and mobile devices. A flaw in an operating system can affect the performance of the computer or mobile device and subject data to corruption or unauthorized use. A user

may not even be aware when a computer or mobile device is corrupted.

Hackers look for ways to break into a computer or mobile device using flaws in the operating system. An operating system is complex software that includes millions of lines of code. Developers write code as securely as possible, but with the volume of code, mistakes are bound to occur. Users sometimes are unaware of their own role in infecting their own computer or mobile device. Perhaps a hacker took advantage of a user with an unsecured Wi-Fi connection, or the user did not install or enable the latest updates to the operating system.

Some argue that making software manufacturers responsible for flaws will inhibit innovation. If a company spends more time looking for potential security flaws, it has less time to spend enhancing the software. In addition, some of the same features that enhance an operating system, such as web integration, increase the software's vulnerability.

✹ **Consider This:** Has your computer or mobile device become infected with malware due to a flaw in the operating system? How did you know? What responsibility does a software manufacturer have for preventing and fixing operating system flaws? Should users expect their software to be perfect? Why or why not?

CONSIDER THIS —————————————————————————————————————

What are some alternatives to passwords?

Many computers and mobile devices offer alternatives to setting and entering a password in order to gain access. Alternatives to passwords include specifying passcodes containing only numeric characters, swiping or touching areas of the screen in a specified order or pattern, or fingerprint or facial recognition.

 CONSIDER THIS —————————————————————————————————————

Do operating systems encrypt data and files?

To protect sensitive data and information further as it travels over a network, the operating system may encrypt it. Recall that *encryption* is the process of encoding data and information into an unreadable form. Administrators can specify that data be encrypted as it travels over a network to prevent unauthorized users from reading the data. When an authorized user attempts to read the data, it is automatically decrypted, or converted back into a readable form.

Types of Operating Systems

Many of the first operating systems were device dependent and proprietary. A *device-dependent* program is one that runs only on a specific type or make of computer or mobile device. *Proprietary software* is privately owned and limited to a specific vendor or computer or device model. Some operating systems still are device dependent. The trend today, however, is toward *device-independent* operating systems that run on computers and mobile devices provided by a variety of manufacturers. The advantage of device-independent operating systems is you can retain existing applications and data files even if you change computer or mobile device models or vendors.

When you purchase a new computer or mobile device, it typically has an operating system preinstalled. As new versions of the operating system are released, users often upgrade their existing computers and mobile devices to incorporate features of the new versions. Some upgrades are free; some offer an upgrade price that is less than the cost of purchasing the entire operating system.

New versions of an operating system usually are *backward compatible*, which means they recognize and work with applications written for an earlier version of the operating system (or platform). Newly developed applications may or may not be backward compatible; that is, they may or may not run on older operating systems. Further, an application may or may not be *upward compatible*, meaning it may or may not run on newer versions of an operating system.

The three basic categories of operating systems on computers and mobile devices are desktop, server, and mobile. Table 9-2 lists examples in each of these categories, which are discussed on the following pages.

Table 9-2	Examples of Operating Systems by Category
Category	**Name**
Desktop	Windows
	macOS
	UNIX
	Linux
	Chrome OS
Server	Windows Server
	macOS Server
	UNIX
	Linux
Mobile	Google Android
	Apple iOS
	Windows (Mobile Edition)

Desktop Operating Systems

A **desktop operating system**, sometimes called a *stand-alone operating system*, is a complete operating system that works on desktops, laptops, and some tablets. Desktop operating systems sometimes are called *client operating systems* because they also work in conjunction with a server operating system. Client operating systems can operate with or without a network.

Examples of the more widely used desktop operating systems are Windows, macOS, UNIX, Linux, and Chrome OS.

Windows/Tech Feature 9-1

In the mid-1980s, Microsoft developed its first version of Windows, which provided a graphical user interface. Since then, Microsoft continually has updated its Windows operating system, incorporating innovative features and functions with each subsequent version. In addition to basic capabilities, the latest versions of Windows offer these features:

- Uses tiles to access apps
- Includes the desktop interface
- Support for input via touch, mouse, and keyboard
- Email app, calendar app, and browser (*Edge*) included
- Photos, files, and settings can sync with *OneDrive*, Microsoft's cloud server
- Enhanced security through an antivirus program, firewall, and automatic updates
- Windows Store offers additional applications for purchase

Read Tech Feature 9-1 to learn more about the interface of the Windows operating system.

 BTW

Networking
Some desktop operating systems include networking capabilities, allowing the home and small business user to set up a small network.

 TECH FEATURE 9-1

Windows User Interface

The following screens show the components of the Windows interface. The Windows operating system simplifies the process of working with documents and apps by organizing the manner in which you interact with the computer.

The Windows interface includes a Start button, Start menu, tiles, and icons, as shown in the figure below. You click the Start button to display the Start menu, which allows you access to apps, tiles, folders, and files on the computer or mobile device and to run programs, search for documents and websites, customize the computer or mobile device, and obtain help. You click tiles to run apps, and double-click icons to run apps.

When you run an app in Windows, it may appear in an on-screen work area app, called the desktop, shown in the second figure in this tech feature. Many Office and Windows programs, such as Paint, contain common elements.

 BTW

PC
The term, PC, sometimes is used to describe a computer that runs a Windows operating system.

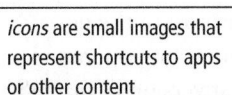
icons are small images that represent shortcuts to apps or other content

Start menu

tiles are graphical objects that represent dynamic links to apps, usually Windows Store apps

Source: Microsoft

Start button

'Search the web and Windows' box

(Continued)

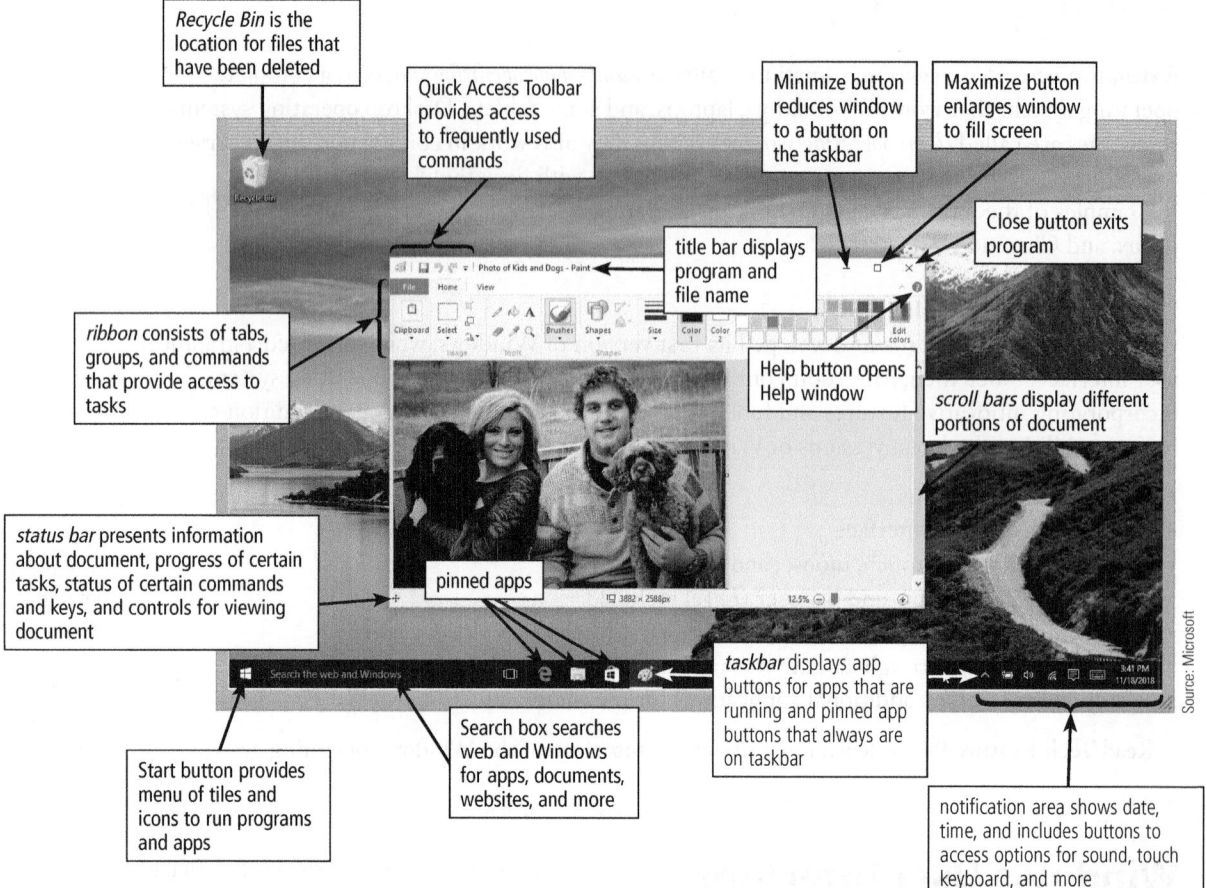

Recycle Bin is the location for files that have been deleted

Quick Access Toolbar provides access to frequently used commands

Minimize button reduces window to a button on the taskbar

Maximize button enlarges window to fill screen

Close button exits program

title bar displays program and file name

ribbon consists of tabs, groups, and commands that provide access to tasks

Help button opens Help window

scroll bars display different portions of document

status bar presents information about document, progress of certain tasks, status of certain commands and keys, and controls for viewing document

pinned apps

taskbar displays app buttons for apps that are running and pinned app buttons that always are on taskbar

Start button provides menu of tiles and icons to run programs and apps

Search box searches web and Windows for apps, documents, websites, and more

notification area shows date, time, and includes buttons to access options for sound, touch keyboard, and more

Source: Microsoft

✳ **Consider This:** Have you used Windows? If so, which version? What was your experience? What features of the Windows interface make it easy to run apps and open documents? Why? How does the ribbon help make learning a new program easier?

macOS/Tech Feature 9-2

Since it was released in 1984 with Macintosh (Mac) computers, Apple's *Macintosh operating system* has earned a reputation for its ease of use and has been the model for most of the new GUIs developed for non-Mac systems. The latest version, **macOS**, is a multitasking operating system available for computers manufactured by Apple. Features of the latest version of macOS include the following:

- Mail, calendars, contacts, and other items sync with *iCloud*, Apple's cloud server
- Communicate and play games with users of mobile devices running Apple's mobile operating system (iOS)
- Built-in Facebook and Twitter support allows you to post a status, comments, or files from any app
- Browser (*Safari*)
- Open multiple desktops at once
- Dictated words convert to text
- Support for Braille displays
- Mac App Store provides access to additional apps and software updates

Read Tech Feature 9-2 to learn more about the interface of macOS.

TECH FEATURE 9-2

macOS User Interface

The following screens show the components of the macOS user interface. macOS is installed on Apple computers, such as iMacs, MacBook Pros, MacBook Airs, Mac Pros, and Mac minis. The user interface contains components such as the Dock, icons, and windows.

The macOS user interface begins with the desktop. Many macOS programs and apps contain common elements, as shown in the desktop figure below.

You can use the Launchpad to view, organize, and run apps, as shown in the second figure below.

Consider This: How is the user interface in macOS similar to the Windows user interface? How is it different?

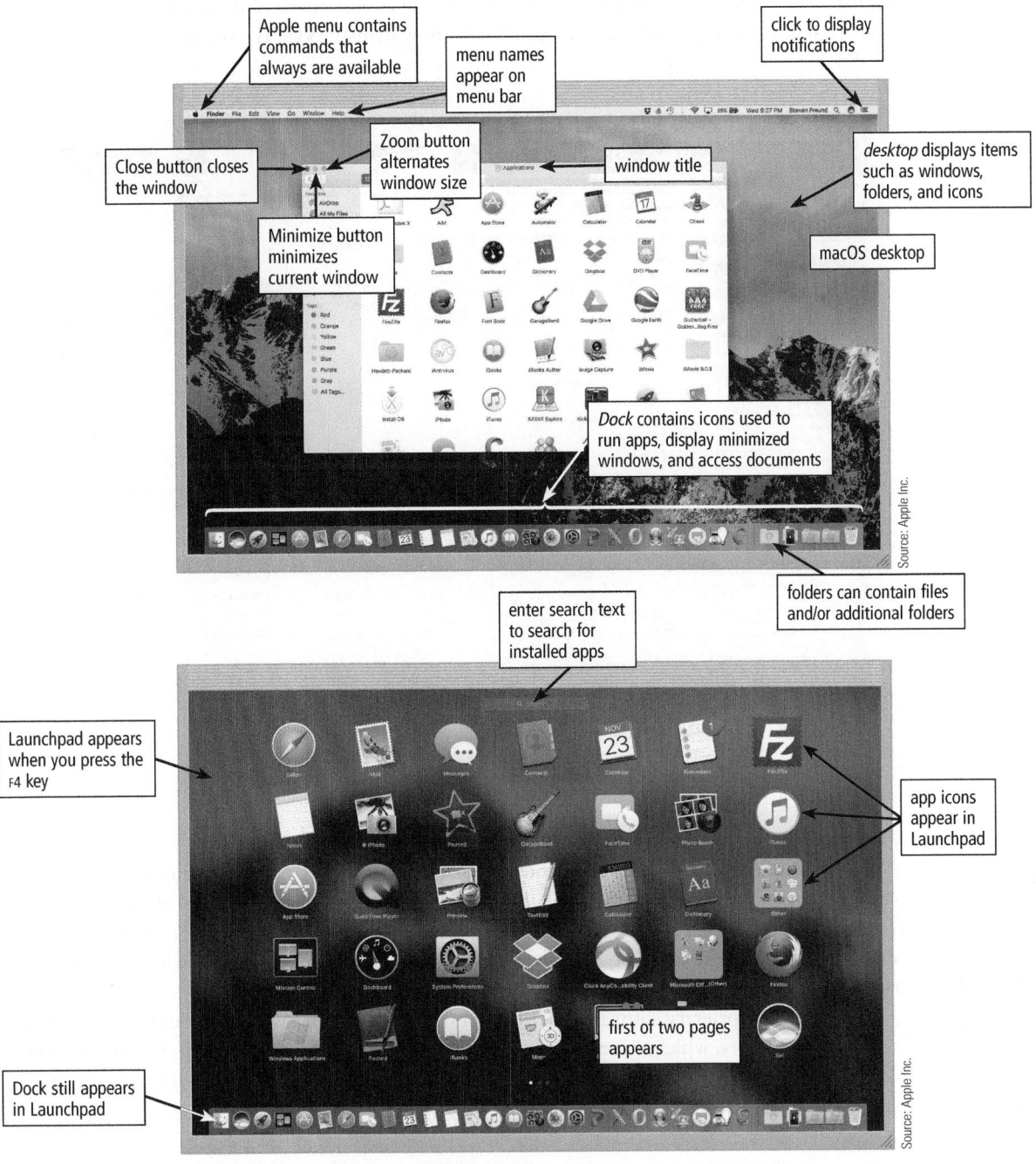

Apple menu contains commands that always are available

menu names appear on menu bar

click to display notifications

Close button closes the window

Zoom button alternates window size

window title

desktop displays items such as windows, folders, and icons

macOS desktop

Minimize button minimizes current window

Dock contains icons used to run apps, display minimized windows, and access documents

folders can contain files and/or additional folders

enter search text to search for installed apps

Launchpad appears when you press the F4 key

app icons appear in Launchpad

first of two pages appears

Dock still appears in Launchpad

Source: Apple Inc.

UNIX

UNIX (pronounced YOU-nix) is a multitasking operating system developed in the early 1970s by scientists at Bell Laboratories. Bell Labs (a subsidiary of AT&T) was prohibited from actively promoting UNIX in the commercial marketplace because of federal regulations. Bell Labs instead licensed UNIX for a low fee to numerous colleges and universities, where UNIX obtained a wide following. UNIX was implemented on many different types of computers. In the 1980s, the source code for UNIX was licensed to many hardware and software companies to customize for their devices and applications. As a result, several versions of this operating system exist, each with slightly different features or capabilities.

Today, a version of UNIX is available for most computers of all sizes. Although some versions of UNIX have a command-line interface, most versions of UNIX offer a graphical user interface (Figure 9-14). Power users often work with UNIX because of its flexibility and capabilities. An industry standards organization, *The Open Group*, now owns UNIX as a trademark.

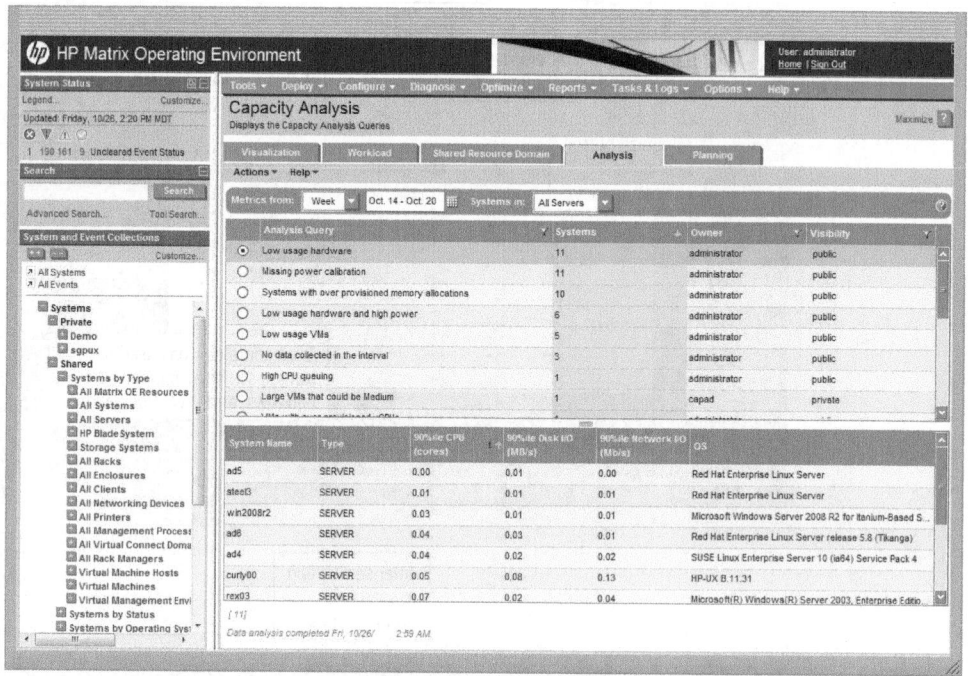

Figure 9-14 One version of the UNIX operating system.
Courtesy of Hewlett-Packard Company (Cupertino)

Linux

Linux (pronounced LINN-uks), introduced in 1991, is a popular, multitasking UNIX-based operating system that runs on a variety of personal computers, servers, devices, and single-board computers. (Recall from Module 6 that a single-board computer has all components on one, small circuit board.) In addition to the basic operating system, Linux also includes many free tools and programming languages.

Linux is not proprietary software like the operating systems discussed thus far. Instead, Linux is *open source software*, which means its code is provided for use, modification, and redistribution. Many programmers have donated time to modify and redistribute Linux to make it the most popular UNIX-based operating system.

CONSIDER THIS

Why use open source software?
Open source software has no restrictions from the copyright holder regarding modification of the software's internal instructions and may or may not have restrictions regarding redistribution of the software. Promoters of open source software state two main advantages: users who modify the software share their improvements with others, and customers can personalize the software to meet their needs. Read Secure IT 9-3 to consider security issues associated with open and closed source programs.

SECURE IT 9-3

Open Source or Closed Source — Which Is More Secure?
Supporters of open source software maintain that this type of software enables developers to create high-quality programs. Source code, along with any changes, remains public, so communities of open source software developers can examine, correct, and enhance programs. They also can make changes immediately when security issues arise.

Many proponents of open source software use Linux, which is known for its speed and stability. Of the 500 fastest supercomputers, more than 90 percent use variants of Linux. Many of these computers perform high-performance tasks, including detecting and

preventing fraud. Companies and nonprofit organizations can distribute and sell their versions of Linux, which enables those without the expertise to modify open source software and to benefit from the creative efforts of the Linux community.

Developers of closed source operating systems, on the other hand, refuse to share some or all of the code. They believe that companies and developers should be able to control, and profit from, the operating systems they create. Their philosophy may hinder third-party software developers who create programs and apps for the operating system.

Fear of viruses and other security concerns can lead some to question about whether

open source software is worthwhile. While dishonest and anonymous developers can use open source software to create programs that may be or may include malware, cryptography experts emphasize that Linux systems have fewer reported security exposures than Windows-based systems. In general, Linux systems do not run antivirus software, but they do use detection programs that check for signs of attacks and probes.

Consider This: Are the security concerns about open source software legitimate? Why or why not? Why is antivirus software not needed on Linux-based systems? Does the open source model lead to higher-quality software? Why or why not?

Linux is available in a variety of forms, known as distributions. Some distributions of Linux are command line. Others are GUI (Figure 9-15). Some companies market software that runs on their own distribution of Linux. Many application programs, tools, and plug-ins have Linux distributions.

Users obtain versions of Linux in a variety of ways. Some download it free from a provider's website and create media to install it on a computer, or they create a Live CD/DVD or Live USB from which to preview it. Others purchase optical discs from vendors who may bundle their own software with the operating system or download it from their websites. Some retailers will preinstall Linux on a new computer on request.

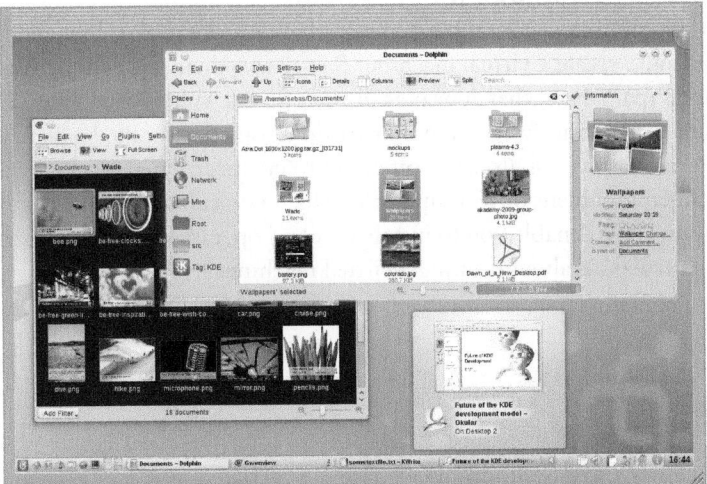

Figure 9-15 A GUI distribution of Linux.
Courtesy of KDE

Chrome OS

Chrome OS, introduced by Google, is a Linux-based operating system designed to work primarily with web apps (Figure 9-16). Apps are available through the Chrome Web Store, and data is stored on Google Drive. The only apps typically installed on the computer are the Chrome browser, a media player, and a file manager. A specialized laptop that runs Chrome OS is called a *Chromebook*, and a specialized desktop that runs Chrome OS is called a *Chromebox*. Chromebooks and Chromeboxes typically use SSDs for internal storage. Users also can run Chrome OS as a virtual machine (which is discussed in the next section).

Because computers running Chrome OS work mostly with web apps, they do not require as much internal storage capacity as other desktop operating systems discussed in this section. Their start-up and shutdown time also is considerably less than other desktop operating systems because Chrome OS uses a streamlined start-up procedure.

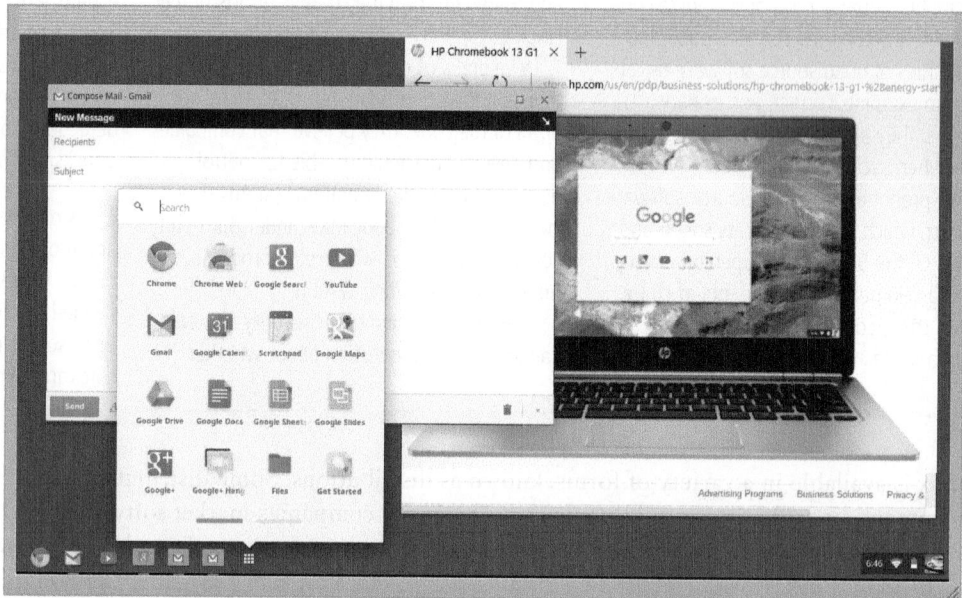

Figure 9-16   Chrome OS is a Linux-based operating system by Google.
Source: HP Development Company, L.P.

Running Multiple Desktop Operating Systems

If you want to run multiple operating systems on the same computer, you could partition the hard drive or you could create a virtual machine. *Partitioning* divides a hard drive in separate logical storage areas (partitions) that appear as distinct drives. When you partition a drive, you can install a separate operating system in each partition, sometimes called a dual boot. Because partitioning requires advanced skills, users often opt to create a virtual machine instead. A *virtual machine* (*VM*) is an environment on a computer in which you can install and run an operating system and programs. VMs enable you to install a second operating system on a computer. Read How To 9-3 for instructions about creating a virtual machine.

HOW TO 9-3

Set Up and Use a Virtual Machine
A virtual machine enables a computer to run another operating system in addition to the one installed. Various reasons exist for using a virtual machine. For example, if you are running the latest version of Windows on a computer but require an app that runs only in a previous version of Windows, you might set up a virtual machine running the previous version of Windows so that you can run the desired app. The computer still will have the latest version of Windows installed, but you easily will be able to switch to the previous version when necessary.

To set up a virtual machine, you will need the required software, as well as installation media for the operating system you want to install in the virtual machine. The following steps describe how to set up a virtual machine:

1. Obtain and install an app that creates and runs virtual machines.
2. Run the app and select the option to create a new virtual machine.
3. Specify the settings for the new virtual machine.
4. If necessary, insert the installation media for the operating system you want to run in the virtual machine.
5. Run the virtual machine. Follow the steps to install the operating system in the virtual machine.
6. When the operating system has finished installing, remove the installation media.
7. While the virtual machine is running, if desired, install any apps you want to run.
8. When you are finished using the virtual machine, shut down the operating system in the same manner you would shut down your computer.
9. Exit the virtual machine software.

After you set up the virtual machine, you can use the virtual machine any time by performing the following steps:

1. Run the virtual machine software.
2. Select the virtual machine you want to run.
3. Click the button to run the virtual machine.
4. When you are finished using the virtual machine, shut down the operating system similar to how you would shut down your computer.
5. Exit the virtual machine software.

Consider This: What are some other reasons that might require you to set up and use a virtual machine on a computer?

Server Operating Systems

A **server operating system** is a multiuser operating system that organizes and coordinates how multiple users access and share resources on a network. Client computers on a network rely on server(s) for access to resources.

Many of the desktop operating systems discussed in the previous section function as clients and work in conjunction with a server operating system. Although desktop operating systems may include networking capability, server operating systems are designed specifically to support all sizes of networks, including medium- to large-sized businesses and web servers. Server operating systems can handle high numbers of transactions, support large-scale messaging and communications, and have enhanced security and backup capabilities.

Many also support virtualization. Recall that *virtualization* is the practice of sharing or pooling computing resources, such as servers or storage devices. Through virtualization, for example, server operating systems can separate a physical server into several virtual servers. Each virtual server then can perform independent, separate functions.

Examples of server operating systems include the following:

- **Windows Server:** Developed by Microsoft, Windows Server enables organizations to manage applications and websites on-site and/or on the cloud.
- **macOS Server:** Developed by Apple, macOS Server enables organizations to collaborate, share files, host websites and mail servers, and more on Mac computers and iOS devices.
- **UNIX:** Capable of handling a high volume of transactions in a multiuser environment and working with multiple processors, UNIX often is used on web servers.
- **Linux:** Because it provides a secure, stable multiuser environment, Linux often is used on web servers and on supercomputers.

Mobile Operating Systems

The operating system on mobile devices and many consumer electronics is called a **mobile operating system** and resides on firmware. (Read Secure IT 9-4 for security issues associated with employees bringing their own mobile devices and consumer electronics to work.) Mobile

BTW

Multipurpose OS
Operating systems, such as UNIX and Linux, that function as both desktop and server operating systems sometimes are called *multipurpose operating systems*.

operating systems typically include or support the following: calendar and contact management, text messaging, email, touch screens, accelerometer (so that you can rotate the display), digital cameras, media players, speech recognition, GPS navigation, a variety of third-party apps, a browser, and wireless connectivity, such as cellular, Wi-Fi, and Bluetooth.

 SECURE IT 9-4

BYOD Security Issues

Effective BYOD (bring your own device) policies can lead to many benefits for businesses, but they also give rise to many issues that affect information security and data protection. When employees bring their smartphones, tablets, and laptops into the workplaces, the companies surrender much control over this hardware compared to devices they own.

One of the biggest problems is that employees can carry their devices everywhere outside of work. If these devices are lost or stolen, the company's sensitive information can land in the hands of criminals. Many of these allegedly lost devices are sold on online auctions and other services websites, even if

the original owners have wiped their devices remotely.

Companies need to educate employees on *mobile device management* (*MDM*). One point they need employees to know is that phishing scams abound in email messages, text messages, Facebook posts, and Tweets. Other security measures to emphasize are the need to use strong passwords, to not reveal these passwords to other employees, and to avoid apps that collect information about the user, especially those that monitor the employee's location and shopping habits.

BYOD policies should be developed that address technical, legal, and human resources issues. The language in these policies should cover these topics:

- Ensuring that work data will not be merged with the employee's personal data
- Requiring that nonemployees, such as family members who use the device, will not access work data
- Following procedures when an employee resigns or is terminated
- Alerting management immediately when the device is lost or stolen

Consider This: Do you or people you know work at a business that allow employees to bring their own devices to work? If so, do these businesses have a BYOD policy? If so, how were the policy's terms communicated? For example, were they explained verbally and available in written form?

 BTW

Android Releases
Google names its Android releases alphabetically after sweet treats, such as Gingerbread, Honeycomb, Ice Cream Sandwich, Jelly Bean, Key Lime Pie, KitKat, Lollipop, Marshmallow, and Nougat.

Popular mobile operating systems include Android, iOS, and Windows (Mobile Edition). The following sections discuss each of these operating systems.

 CONSIDER THIS

Do other mobile operating systems exist?
Yes. Several other mobile operating systems exist, although they are not as widely used as Android, iOS, and Windows (Mobile Edition). For example, *Firefox OS* is a Linux-based open source operating system that runs on smartphones and tablets developed by Mozilla. *Fire OS* is a Linux-based operating system for Amazon Kindle tablets and Amazon Fire Phones. Several phones also run a version of Linux.

Android

Android is an open source, Linux-based mobile operating system designed by Google for smartphones and tablets (Figure 9-17). A variety of manufacturers produce devices that run the Android operating system, adding their own interface elements and bundled software. As a result, an Android smartphone manufactured by Samsung may have different user interface features from one manufactured by Google.

Features unique to recent versions of the Android operating system include the following:

- *Google Assistant*, a voice recognition app, is a personal assistant for Google devices.
- Android Pay is a mobile payment app.
- *Google Play* app store provides access to apps, songs, books, and movies.
- *Google Drive* provides access to email, contacts, calendar, photos, files, and more.
- Google Photos is a photo management app.
- Face recognition or fingerprint scanner can unlock the device.
- Share contacts and other information by touching two devices together (using NFC technology).
- Speech output assists users with vision impairments.
- Voice recognition capability enables users to speak instructions.
- Built-in heart rate monitor works with phone apps.

Figure 9-17 An Android phone and tablet.
Valentin Valkov / Shutterstock.com; Courtesy of Sony Corporation

iOS

iOS (originally called iPhone OS), developed by Apple, is a proprietary mobile operating system specifically made for Apple's mobile devices (Figure 9-18). Supported devices include the iPhone, iPod Touch, and iPad. Features unique to recent versions of the iOS operating system include the following:

- *Siri*, a voice recognition app, is a personal assistant for iOS devices.
- Apple Pay is a mobile payment app.
- iCloud enables you to sync mail, calendars, contacts, and other items.
- *iTunes Store* provides access to music, books, podcasts, ringtones, and movies.
- Integrates with iPod to play music, video, and other media.
- Improves connectivity with other devices running a Mac operating system.
- Mac App Store provides access to additional apps and software updates.

Figure 9-18 An iOS phone and tablet.
Courtesy of Apple Inc.

Windows (Mobile Edition)

Windows (**Mobile Edition**), developed by Microsoft, is a proprietary mobile operating system that runs on some smartphones (Figure 9-19). Features unique to recent versions of the Windows (Mobile Edition) operating system include the following:

- *Cortana*, a voice recognition app, is a personal assistant for Windows devices.
- Sync photos, files, and settings with OneDrive.
- Use your phone as a remote control for your television.
- Access a global catalog of music, videos, or podcasts, or listen to iTunes music.
- Geofencing enables your phone to send or receive notification when you enter or exit a geographic location. (Read Ethics & Issues 8-2 in Module 8 for other uses of geofencing.)
- *Microsoft Store* provides access to additional apps and software updates.
- *Wallet* app provides a centralized location for coupons, credit cards, loyalty cards, and memberships in a single, easily accessible location.

Figure 9-19 Phone running Windows (Mobile Edition).
Valentin Valkov / Shutterstock.com

Tech Feature 9-3: Mobile versus Desktop Operating Systems

While mobile and desktop operating systems share many similarities, they also have differences designed for their operating environment. Read Tech Feature 9-3 for a comparison of mobile and desktop operating systems.

TECH FEATURE 9-3

Mobile versus Desktop Operating Systems

An operating system has the same role, whether for a desktop or mobile device. It manages operations and provides a user interface. Because of this shared role, many similarities exist between the functions of desktop and mobile operating systems. From a user's perspective, operating systems enable you to work with apps and to monitor and maintain the functions of the computer or device. Typical functions included in mobile operating systems include the following:

- Main areas, such as a desktop or home screen, enable you to access and organize apps
- Methods to return to the main area quickly
- The ability to organize the app icons or tiles in the main areas easily by moving them to pages or folders or by adding them to menus
- System tools, such as to manage battery power and Internet connections
- Options for security settings

Whether you are purchasing a computer or mobile device, the choice of an operating system plays an important role.

Historically, the two types of operating systems have had different uses and capabilities. The differences are due in part to the disparity in screen size, keyboards, and processing power. Because of convergence, as well as the increased reliance on mobile devices for communications and productivity, the use and function of mobile and desktop operating systems are becoming more similar. The prevalence of web apps and cloud storage services enables users to access the same programs and files they work with on their desktop from a mobile device. Some developers now create operating systems that share code and have common features, regardless of whether they are installed on a computer or mobile device. Features, such as tiles and icons (typically used in mobile devices), make the transition between using a mobile device and computer easier. For example, mobile device operating systems include capabilities that allow users to take advantage of the touch screen displays. As more computer desktop monitors today are touch enabled, computer users can take advantage of this feature.

Many differences exist in the way a user interacts with a mobile operating system.

- A desktop operating system may use menus, windows, and bars to run apps and to access features within apps. On a desktop, you can run multiple programs simultaneously and seamlessly due to the large screen and the use of pointing devices. This feature makes desktops more relevant than mobile operating systems to productivity and multitasking.
- A mobile operating system may have one program running at a time with others running in the background, or it may provide a means for multiple apps to run simultaneously on the screen. Quick movements and gestures are often all that you need to perform tasks on a mobile device. Mobile operating systems use technologies such as cellular, Bluetooth, Wi-Fi, GPS, and NFC to communicate with other devices and to connect to the Internet. Mobile devices also typically include cameras, video cameras, voice recorders, and sometimes speech recognition.

Consider This: What similarities have you noticed between mobile and desktop operating systems? What differences have you noticed between mobile and desktop operating systems? What features work better with a mobile versus a desktop operating system? Why? Is the convergence trend beneficial or should each device type take advantage of its strengths? Why?

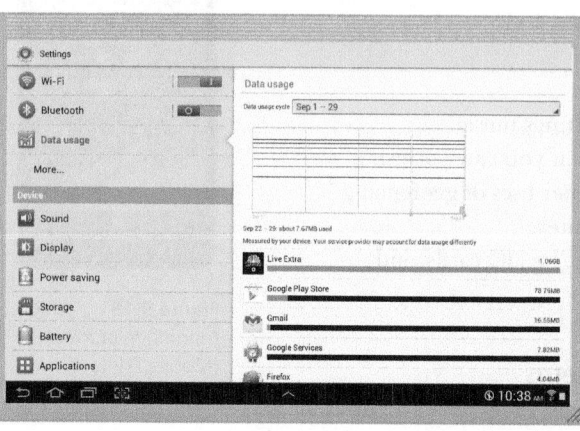

Source: Samsung

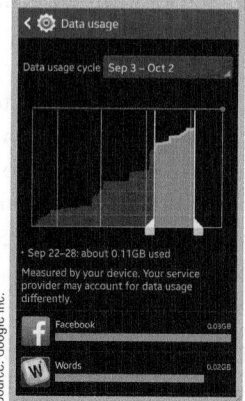

Source: Google Inc.

 **CONSIDER THIS** ————————————————

Do embedded computers use mobile operating systems?
Typically, an embedded computer uses an embedded operating system, sometimes called a *real-time operating system* (*RTOS*). Examples of products that use embedded operating systems include digital cameras, ATMs, digital photo frames, HDTV receivers, fuel pumps, ticket machines, process controllers, robotics, and automobile components. Embedded operating systems often perform a single task, usually without requiring input from a user. Several embedded operating systems are available, each intended for various uses.

 **Summary**

This module discussed the functions common to most operating systems: starting and shutting down computers and mobile devices, providing a user interface, managing programs, managing memory, coordinating tasks, configuring devices, monitoring performance, establishing an Internet connection, updating operating system software, providing file, system, and disk management tools, controlling a network, and administering security. It also presented a variety of desktop operating systems, server operating systems, and mobile operating systems.

Study Guide

The Study Guide reinforces material you should know after reading this module.

Instructions: Answer the questions below using the format that helps you remember best or that is required by your instructor. Possible formats may include one or more of these options: write the answers; create a document that contains the answers; record answers as audio or video using a webcam, smartphone, or portable media player; post answers on a blog, wiki, or website; or highlight answers in the book/e-book.

1. Define the term, operating system. List the functions of an operating system.

2. Define the term, firmware. Name another term for an operating system.

3. List methods to start a computer or device.

4. Identify the five steps in the start-up process.

5. The _____ is the core of an operating system. Differentiate between resident and nonresident, with respect to memory.

6. Explain the role of a boot drive.

7. List reasons why users might shut down computers or mobile devices regularly. Differentiate between sleep mode and hibernate mode.

8. Define the term, user interface. Distinguish between GUI, natural-user, and command-line interfaces.

9. Define the terms, foreground and background, in a multitasking operating system.

10. List steps for removing a program or app.

11. Describe how a computer manages memory. Define the term, virtual memory.

12. The technique of swapping items between memory and storage is called _____.

13. Explain what occurs during thrashing, and list steps to prevent it.

14. List actions you should take if a mobile device displays a message that it is running low on memory.

15. Explain how a computer coordinates tasks. Define these terms: buffer, spooling, and queue.

16. Describe the role of a driver. Explain how to find the latest drivers for a device.

17. Describe the role of a performance monitor.

18. Explain how an operating system establishes an Internet connection.

19. Explain the issues surrounding an operating system's inclusion of additional software.

20. Identify changes that may be made to an operating system during an automatic update. List security concerns regarding automatic updates.

21. List file and disk management tools, and describe the function of each.

22. List and describe security tools used by operating systems.

23. Describe the role of a network administrator.

24. Explain the capabilities of administrator and user accounts on a network.

25. Explain the use of permissions on a network.

26. Explain issues surrounding responsibility for operating system security flaws.

27. List alternatives to using passwords.

28. Explain how an operating system uses encryption.

29. Differentiate between device-dependent and device-independent programs.

30. Define these terms: proprietary software, backward compatible, and upward compatible.

31. List two other names for a desktop operating system.

32. Identify features of Windows. Define the term, desktop, with respect to Windows and macOS.

33. The term, _____, sometimes is used to describe a computer that runs a Windows operating system.

34. Identify features of macOS. You can use the _____ to view, organize, and run apps.

35. Describe uses and features of the UNIX operating system.

36. Define the term, open source software. _____ is an example of an open source operating system.

37. Define Raspberry Pi. List two operating systems built for Raspberry Pi.

38. Explain the issues surrounding open source versus closed source operating systems.

39. Identify features of Chrome OS.

40. Identify reasons to use a virtual machine. List steps for setting up a virtual machine.

41. Describe a server operating system. List examples of server operating systems.

42. Identify common features of mobile operating systems.

43. Explain security concerns regarding BYOD policies.

44. Differentiate among the features of the Android, iOS, and Windows (Mobile Edition) mobile operating systems.

45. List differences and similarities between how a user interacts with mobile versus desktop operating systems.

46. Describe how embedded computers use operating systems.

You should be able to define the Primary Terms and be familiar with the Secondary Terms listed below.

Key Terms

Primary Terms (shown in **bold-black** characters in the module)

Android (9-24)
automatic update (9-13)
boot drive (9-4)
Chrome OS (9-22)
desktop operating system (9-17)
driver (9-10)
iOS (9-25)

Linux (9-20)
macOS (9-18)
mobile operating system (9-23)
natural user interface (NUI) (9-6)
operating system (OS) (9-2)

password (9-15)
performance monitor (9-11)
queue (9-10)
server operating system (9-23)
sign in (9-15)
UNIX (9-20)

user interface (UI) (9-5)
user name (9-15)
virtual memory (9-8)
Windows (Mobile Edition) (9-25)

Secondary Terms (shown in *italic* characters in the module)

administrator account (9-15)
background (9-6)
backup and restore (9-14)
backward compatible (9-16)
bloatware (9-12)
boot disk (9-4)
booting (9-4)
buffer (9-10)
bug (9-13)
Chromebook (9-22)
Chromebox (9-22)
client operating systems (9-17)
cold boot (9-4)
command language (9-6)
command-line interface (9-6)
Cortana (9-25)
cross-platform application (9-3)
desktop (9-19)
device driver (9-10)
device-dependent (9-16)
device-independent (9-16)
disk cleanup (9-14)
disk defragmenter (9-14)
Dock (9-19)
Edge (9-17)
encryption (9-16)
file compression (9-14)
file manager (9-14)
Fire OS (9-24)
Firefox OS (9-24)
firmware (9-2)
foreground (9-6)
Google Assistant (9-25)

Google Drive (9-25)
Google Play (9-25)
graphical user interface (GUI) (9-5)
hibernate mode (9-5)
iCloud (9-18)
icons (9-17)
image viewer (9-14)
iTunes Store (9-25)
kernel (9-4)
Live CD/DVD (9-4)
Live USB (9-4)
Macintosh operating system (9-18)
memory resident (9-4)
Microsoft Store (9-25)
mobile device management (MDM) (9-24)
multipurpose operating systems (9-23)
multitasking (9-6)
multiuser (9-7)
network administrator (9-14)
nonresident (9-4)
OneDrive (9-17)
open source software (9-20)
page (9-8)
paging (9-8)
partitioning (9-22)
PC maintenance (9-14)
permissions (9-15)
platform (9-3)

Plug and Play (9-11)
power management (9-14)
print spooler (9-10)
proprietary software (9-16)
Raspberry Pi (9-20)
Raspbian (9-20)
real-time operating system (RTOS) (9-27)
recovery media (9-4)
Recycle Bin (9-18)
ribbon (9-18)
Safari (9-18)
screen saver (9-14)
scroll bars (9-18)
search (9-14)
service pack (9-13)
Siri (9-25)

sleep mode (9-5)
spooling (9-10)
stand-alone operating system (9-17)
status bar (9-18)
swap file (9-8)
taskbar (9-18)
The Open Group (9-20)
thrashing (9-8)
tiles (9-17)
touch user interface (9-6)
uninstaller (9-14)
upward compatible (9-16)
virtual machine (VM) (9-22)
virtualization (9-23)
Wallet (9-25)
warm boot (9-4)
Windows IoT (9-20)

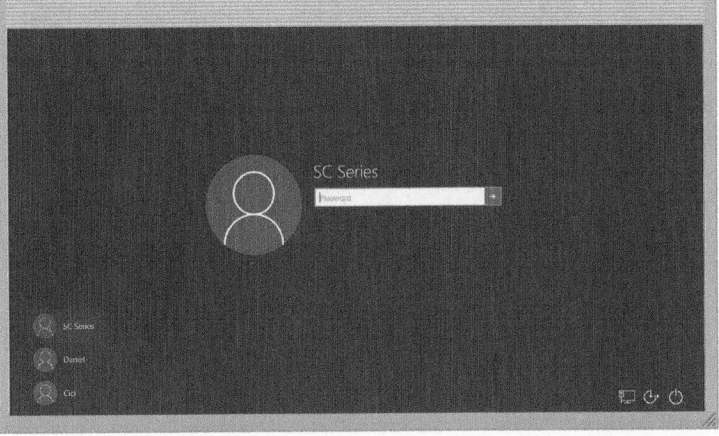

Source: Microsoft

Checkpoint   The Checkpoint exercises test your knowledge of the module concepts.

True/False   Mark T for True and F for False. If False, rewrite the statement so that it is True.

_____ 1. An operating system must reside inside a computer or mobile device; that is, it cannot run from a USB flash drive or other external drives.

_____ 2. The kernel is nonresident, which means it remains in memory while the computer or mobile device is running.

_____ 3. A user interface controls how you enter data and instructions and how information is displayed on the screen.

_____ 4. Most users today work with a command-line interface.

_____ 5. Most operating systems today are multitasking.

_____ 6. The area of the hard drive used for virtual memory is called a swap file.

_____ 7. Each device connected to a computer requires its own specific driver.

_____ 8. Hackers often look for ways to break into a computer or device using flaws in the operating system.

_____ 9. Many of the first operating systems were device dependent and proprietary.

_____ 10. An upward compatible application means it can recognize and work with applications written for an earlier version of the operating system.

_____ 11. Linux is proprietary software.

_____ 12. Operating systems that function as both desktop and server operating systems sometimes are called multipurpose operating systems.

Matching   Match the terms with their definitions.

_____ 1. bloatware

_____ 2. buffer

_____ 3. command language

_____ 4. device-independent

_____ 5. driver

_____ 6. firmware

_____ 7. open source software

_____ 8. proprietary software

_____ 9. Raspbian

_____ 10. thrashing

a. operating system problem that occurs when it spends much of its time paging, instead of executing application software

b. small program that tells the operating system how to communicate with a specific device

c. A version of Linux built for Raspberry Pi

d. software that is privately owned and limited to a specific vendor or computer or device model

e. ROM chips or flash memory chips that store permanent instructions

f. operating system that runs on computers and mobile devices provided by a variety of manufacturers

g. software whose code is provided for use, modification, and redistribution

h. additional programs and apps included with operating systems, usually for profit

i. segment of memory or storage in which items are placed while waiting to be transferred from an input device or to an output device

j. set of commands used to control actions performed in a command-line interface

The Problem Solving exercises extend your knowledge of module concepts by seeking solutions to practical problems with technology that you may encounter at home, school, or work. The Collaboration exercise should be completed with a team.

Problem Solving

Instructions: You often can solve problems with technology in multiple ways. Determine a solution to the problems in these exercises by using one or more resources available to you (such as a computer or mobile device, articles on the web or in print, blogs, podcasts, videos, television, user guides, other individuals, electronics or computer stores, etc.). Describe your solution, along with the resource(s) used, in the format requested by your instructor (brief report, presentation, discussion, blog post, video, or other means).

Personal

1. **Difficulty Signing In to Operating System**   You are attempting to sign in to your operating system, but you receive an error message stating that you have entered an invalid password. What are your next steps?

2. **Missing Customization Settings**   When you sign in to your operating system, your customized desktop background does not appear. Instead, the operating system displays the default desktop background. What might have happened?

3. **Incompatible Program**   You have upgraded to the latest version of an operating system on your computer. After the upgrade, you realize that programs that used to run without issue now do not run. What are your next steps?

4. **Insufficient Access**   You are attempting to install a program on your computer and a dialog box appears informing you that you have insufficient privileges to install the program. What might be wrong?

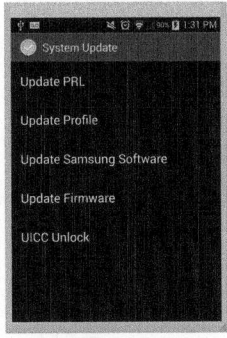

Source: Google Inc.

5. **Software Update Issues**   You have heard that new software updates are available for your operating system, but when the operating system checks for updates, it shows that no updates are available. Why might this be the case?

Professional

6. **Virtual Machine Error**   You use virtual machines on your office computer so that you can run and test software in multiple operating system versions. When you attempt to run one of the virtual machines, you receive an error message that the virtual machine already is running. You are certain that the virtual machine is not running. What steps can you take to correct the problem?

7. **Missing Files and Settings**   When you sign in to various computers at work with the credentials assigned by your IT department, you typically see all your files. When you recently signed in to the computer in your office, however, you were unable to view your files. What are your next steps?

8. **Faulty Update**   Your computer is set to install updates for the operating system, programs, and apps automatically. You have learned through your company's IT department that a recent operating system update causes a problem to occur with a program you use regularly. What are your next steps?

9. **Mobile Device Operating System Upgrade**   A notification appears on your mobile phone stating that an operating system upgrade has been downloaded and is ready to install. Your company has provided the mobile phone to you for work-related business, and you are hesitant to install the upgrade. What are your next steps?

10. **Slow System Performance**   Your office computer has been running slow lately, and you are attempting to determine the cause. What steps can you take to determine what might be slowing your computer's performance?

Collaboration

11. **Technology in Meteorology**   Your environmental sciences instructor is teaching a lesson about how technology has advanced the meteorology field. Form a team of three people to prepare a brief report about how technology and meteorology are connected. One team member should research how meteorologists predicted weather patterns before computer use became mainstream. Another team member should create a timeline illustrating when and how technology was introduced to the meteorology field, and the third team member should research the technology required for a typical news station to forecast and present the weather.

✳ How To: Your Turn

The How To: Your Turn exercises present general guidelines for fundamental skills when using a computer or mobile device and then require that you determine how to apply these general guidelines to a specific program or situation.

Instructions: You often can complete tasks using technology in multiple ways. Figure out how to perform the tasks described in these exercises by using one or more resources available to you (such as a computer or mobile device, articles on the web or in print, online or program help, user guides, blogs, podcasts, videos, other individuals, trial and error, etc.). Summarize your 'how to' steps, along with the resource(s) used, in the format requested by your instructor (brief report, presentation, discussion, blog post, video, or other means).

1 Determine Your Operating System Version

Companies such as Microsoft, Apple, and Google release new versions of operating systems periodically. Software and drivers sometimes are designed for specific operating system versions, which means you may need to determine your operating system version so that you can obtain the proper software. The following steps describe how to determine your operating system version.

a. If necessary, turn on your computer or mobile device and, if necessary, sign in to the operating system. Some operating systems will display the version when they run. If the operating system version is not displayed, continue following these steps.

b. If you are using a Mac computer, click the command on the Apple menu to display information about the computer to determine the operating system version. If you are running an operating system other than macOS, continue following these steps.

c. Display the control panel or settings for your computer or mobile device.

d. Navigate to and then click the command to display system information about the computer or device, and then locate the operating system version.

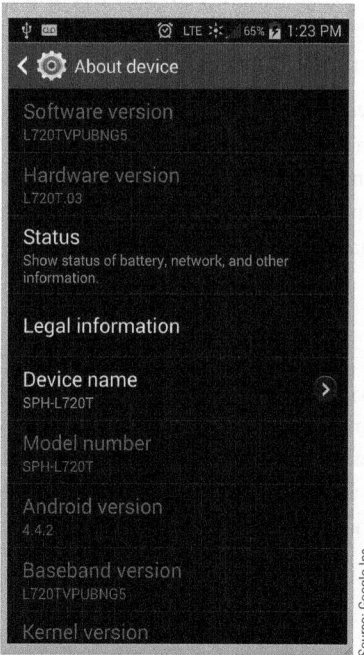

Source: Google Inc.

Exercises

1. What operating system are you running?
2. What are some other reasons why you might need to know the operating system version on your computer or mobile device?
3. What might happen if you attempt to install a program or app that is not designed for your operating system version?

2 Search for Files on a Computer

Advances in technology enable users to store a large number of files, such as documents, photos, videos, and music, on their computers. Users store contacts, appointments, email messages, and other information on mobile devices to retrieve at a later time. With all the information you can store on computers and mobile devices, it sometimes can be difficult to locate an item you need to access. Today's operating systems contain a search tool that provides an easy way to locate files stored on a computer or mobile device. To search for an item on a computer or mobile device, you should know information about the item for which you are searching. The following steps guide you through the process of searching a computer or mobile device.

a. If necessary, run the search tool on your computer or mobile device. If you are using a mobile device, such as a smartphone or tablet, you may be able to access the search tool by pressing a search button on the phone or tablet.

b. If you remember all or part of the name of the file for which you are searching, enter all or part of the file name in the search box.

c. Click the search button to display the search results. Depending upon the number of files and folders on your computer or mobile device, it may take several minutes for search results to appear.

d. If no search results are displayed, consider searching again and entering less information in the search box.

e. When you locate the file for which you are searching, you can open it either by clicking or double-clicking the file. The method you should use to open the file will depend on the operating system you are using.

How To: Your Turn ✹

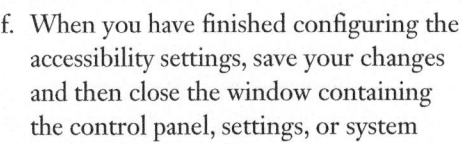

Source: Google Inc.; Source: HP Development Company, L.P.

Exercises

1. Have you used the search tool on your computer? If so, what files were you attempting to locate? If not, do you think the search tool will be helpful to you?
2. Have you used the search tool on a mobile device? What were you attempting to locate?
3. In addition to searching for files, what other items might the search tool locate?

③ Configure Accessibility Settings

Many modern operating systems allow users to configure accessibility settings to make it easier for some individuals to interact with them. Accessibility features can perform functions such as enhancing the contrast between colors on the display device, narrating text that is displayed on the screen, and allowing the user to control the pointer using keys on the keyboard. The following steps guide you through the process of configuring accessibility settings.

a. If necessary, sign in to the operating system.
b. Display your operating system's control panel, settings, or system preferences.
c. Click the command to display accessibility settings.
d. Select the accessibility setting you want to configure, and specify your desired settings.
e. Repeat the previous step for all remaining accessibility settings you want to configure.

f. When you have finished configuring the accessibility settings, save your changes and then close the window containing the control panel, settings, or system preferences.
g. If you no longer require the accessibility settings, display your operating system's control panel, settings, or system preferences, display the setting you want to disable, and then disable the setting.

Exercises

1. Accessibility settings are not only for people with impairments; these settings can make it easier for anyone to use a computer. Can you think of any accessibility settings that you might consider using to make it easier to interact with the computer?
2. Which third-party programs can provide additional features for accessibility?
3. Do you feel that the accessibility features in your computer or mobile device's operating system are sufficient? Why or why not?

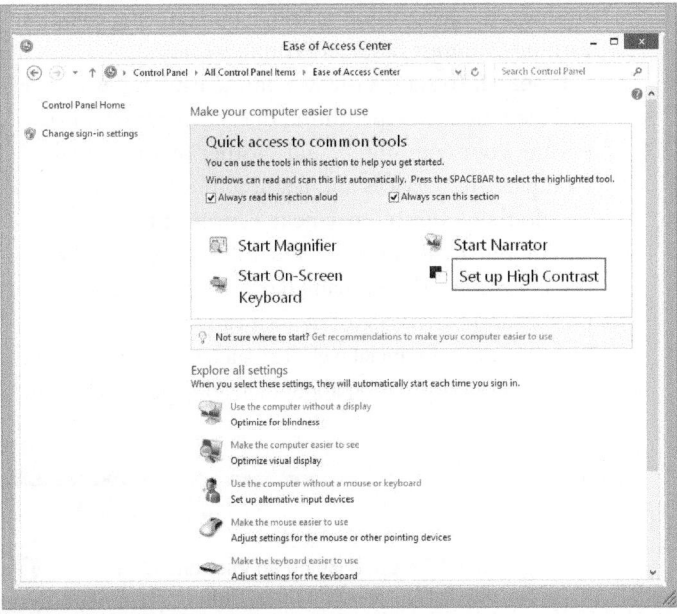

Source: Microsoft

✳ Internet Research

The Internet Research exercises broaden your understanding of module concepts by requiring that you search for information on the web.

Instructions: Use a search engine or another search tool to locate the information requested or answers to questions presented in the exercises. Describe your findings, along with the search term(s) you used and your web source(s), in the format requested by your instructor (brief report, presentation, discussion, blog post, video, or other means).

1 Making Use of the Web
Banking and Finance

Managing money and making wise investments and are among the most important skills consumers need to master. Abundant advice is available on a variety of banking and financial websites. More than 90 percent of Americans who manage household finances have enrolled in online banking programs, and more than 40 percent have used a banking app on their smartphones or mobile devices. Whether their financial institutions are a retail bank, a virtual bank, or a credit union, they enjoy the convenience of monitoring account balances, depositing checks, transferring funds, receiving text message alerts, and paying bills.

Personal finance websites provide information on portfolio management, tax preparation, real estate investing, mortgage rates, retirement planning, credit card and student loan advice, and a host of other lifestyle and educational topics. Also available are calculators to help make saving, spending, and real estate decisions. Business finance websites include market data, company earnings, interest rates, and corporate news.

Research This: (a) Visit two online banking websites: one for a financial institution that has a physical presence in your community and another that is virtual. Compare the services and featured products. For example, do they offer bill payment, retirement accounts, and mobile banking apps? What fees are charged for these services? Which bank has the highest money market and certificate of deposit rates?

(b) Visit two financial websites, such as Yahoo! Finance, that feature information about managing personal credit and debt. Read two stories discussing student loans, credit card debt, overspending, or retirement planning. According to these articles, what mistakes do people make managing their money? Who are the economic professionals writing or being quoted in the articles? What advice is given that can help you handle your expenses?

2 Social Media
Blogs

Operating systems constantly evolve as developers add new features, fix security issues, and modify functions. Computer and mobile device users need to stay abreast of these changes, especially when the updates affect performance and safety. Many blogs feature content about operating systems. Their posts cover industry news, photos, product reviews, previews of forthcoming software and hardware, and management changes. Most of these blogs are unofficial, meaning that the writers are not necessarily employees of the companies that develop the operating systems. The bloggers generally have extensive experience in the technology field and desire to share their expertise with others.

Research This: Search online for a blog that tracks features or updates to a mobile, desktop, or other operating system that you use or about which you would like more information. Report the web address of the blog, along with a summary of the most recent blog post.

3 Search Skills
Video, Audio, and Voice Search

A video search allows you to locate video files posted or shared online. Click the Videos link on a search engine's home page and then type the search text. For example, type the search text, linux tutorial, in the search box to find videos for learning about Linux. You can narrow your results by specifying additional conditions. These may include length (in minutes), time taken (such as past day, week, or month), quality, popularity (based on number of views), and source (YouTube or other websites).

To search for audio files, type the search text, audio search, in a

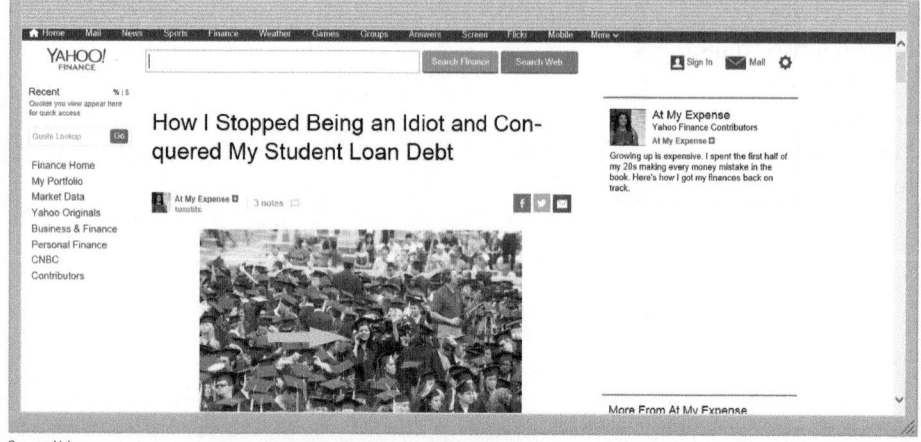

Source: Yahoo

Internet Research ☀

search engine's search box and look for a search engine that specializes in finding audio clips, streaming audio, and other audio files. Alternatively, visit a website for sharing audio and music files, and search that site directly. For example, type the search text, ios podcast, in an audio sharing site's search box to find podcasts about Apple's mobile operating system.

Some search apps allow you to speak your search text. For example, using Google, click the microphone button in the search box or say the phrase, "okay google" to activate voice search and then speak your question. The app will convert your speech to text and provide the search results.

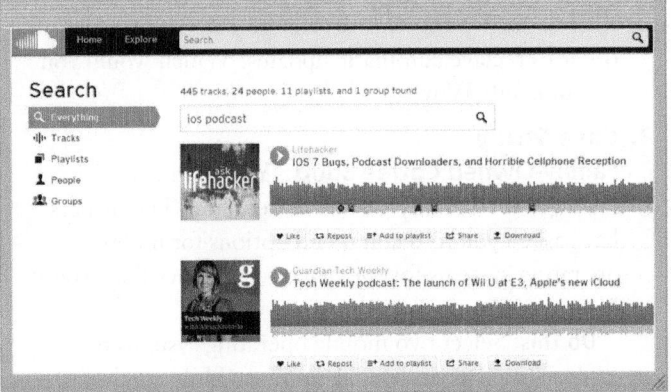

Source: SoundCloud

Research This: Using a search app that accepts voice input, either speak the search text or find an audio sharing site in which to type search text to find podcasts, audio files, or videos about these topics: (1) a video about how to manage security settings on your computer posted within the past month; (2) a video tutorial about how to use the Mac Finder, shorter than four minutes in length; (3) a video that was not posted on YouTube, describing how to partition a hard drive; and (4) audio files of Windows operating system start-up sounds.

Create a document containing the web address of each audio or video clip and the name or web address of the website on which it appears. Watch or listen to comments on how accurately they reflect your search text.

④ Security
Virus, Spyware, and Malware Protection

An operating system should include antivirus and spyware and malware detection software to fend off intrusions. The use of this security software is discussed in Secure IT 9-2 in this module. Major companies that provide this software often include information on their websites about recently discovered virus threats and hoaxes. They also track scheduled virus payload strikes and map global and regional virus attacks.

Research This: Visit at least two virus protection websites to obtain virus information. When were the latest active threats discovered and updated? What are their names and risk levels? When is the next virus payload strike scheduled? What type of malware is spreading via mobile device use? Which virus removal tools and resources are available?

⑤ Cloud Services
Cloud Development Platforms (PaaS)

Developers have many choices for the programming languages, operating systems, databases, and tools they use to create apps hosted on the cloud. Microsoft Azure, Amazon Web Services, and Google App Engine are providers of platform as a service (PaaS), a service of cloud computing that delivers tools for developing, testing, and deploying apps on the cloud.

A PaaS provider manages the computing resources required to run apps on the cloud so that developers can concentrate on writing the code, logic, interfaces, and operations of the software.

Research This: (1) Read a customer case study about Microsoft Azure, Amazon Web Services, or Google App Engine. In what industry is the customer involved? What was the challenge for which the customer was seeking a PaaS solution? How did this solution meet their needs? (2) Research one of these PaaS providers. Which operating systems and development tools does it support? How does it support scalability when additional computing resources are required? What pricing model is in place?

✸ Critical Thinking

The Critical Thinking exercises challenge your assessment and decision-making skills by presenting real-world situations associated with module concepts. The Collaboration exercise should be completed with a team.

Instructions: Evaluate the situations below, using personal experiences and one or more resources available to you (such as articles on the web or in print, blogs, podcasts, videos, television, user guides, other individuals, electronics or computer stores, etc.). Perform the tasks requested in each exercise and share your deliverables in the format requested by your instructor (brief report, presentation, discussion, blog post, video, or other means).

1. Using Operating System Tools

You are the office manager at a social media consulting business. The office recently upgraded and replaced several computers. You now are running the latest version of Windows on all of your computers. Your boss asks you to explore the various tools that are included with the operating system and to evaluate any additional needs you might have.

Do This: Use the web to learn more about the following Windows operating system tools: firewalls, automatic updates, and software that scans for viruses, spyware, and other malware. Read reviews by industry experts and users. Analyze the advantages and disadvantages of using built-in operating system tools. Do any built-in operating system tools present security concerns? If so, what would you recommend? Explore alternatives for each of the tools, and determine whether you should disable the Windows tool and if any risks exist. Compile your findings.

Source: Microsoft

2. Complete Security Solutions

Your neighbor started a new construction business. He would like to hire you to set up his new computers. His business will use the Internet to communicate with clients via email, store backups of data, and access cloud-based accounting software. The office will include two networked computers, which will share a printer and an Internet connection. In addition, he will use a tablet so that he can access the cloud-based accounting software using Wi-Fi. Because of security concerns with using the Internet, he first would like you to install a program(s) designed to protect his computers from various security threats.

Do This: Use the web to find answers to the following questions. What types of security threats exist on the Internet that could impact his business? What types of security measures should he use? Evaluate two programs that provide a comprehensive security solution. What are the programs' functions? What are their costs? Do the services charge subscription fees in order to receive automatic updates? Which would you recommend? Why?

3. Case Study

Family-Owned Coffee Shop　You are the new manager for a family-owned coffee shop. The owners have asked you to recommend options for mobile operating systems for the new smartphones they would like to purchase.

Do This: Select two mobile operating systems to explore (such as Android, Windows (Mobile Edition), and iOS). Use the web to find industry experts' recommendations and user reviews for each operating system. Include the different device types for which each is available. Examine differences in security, features, speed, and reliability. What security concerns exist? What security features enable you to protect the smartphone and its data? Which mobile operating system offers the best features? Which is considered faster and/or more reliable? Your office computers run macOS. Do compatibility issues exist with any of the mobile operating systems? If so, what are the issues? Can you find solutions that would enable you to sync data? Compile your findings.

Collaboration

4. Desktop Operating Systems

You are an analyst for a large manufacturer of laundry soaps. The company currently uses an early version of the Windows operating system on its 5,000 desktops. This year, the company plans to upgrade the operating system and, if necessary, its desktops. The company asks your team to compare the latest versions of the Windows, Mac, and Linux operating systems.

Do This: Form a three-member team and assign each member an operating system. Each member should use the web to develop a feature/benefit analysis and answer the following questions. What is the initial cost of the operating system per computer? What are the memory and storage requirements? Will the operating system require the company to purchase new computers? Which is best at protecting against viruses, spam, and spyware? Which support touch input? As a team, compile your findings and share your recommendation with the class.

Communicating Digital Content: 10
Wired and Wireless Networks and Devices

iStockphoto.com / cofotoisme

OBJECTIVES

After completing this module, you will be able to:

1 Discuss the purpose of components required for successful communications (sending device, communications device, transmission media, and receiving device) and identify various sending and receiving devices

2 Differentiate among LANs, MANs, WANs, and PANs

3 Differentiate between client/server and peer-to-peer networks

4 Explain the purpose of communications software

5 Describe various network communications standards and protocols: Ethernet, token ring, TCP/IP, Wi-Fi, LTE, Bluetooth, UWB, IrDA, RFID, and NFC

6 Describe various types of communications lines: cable, DSL, ISDN, FTTP, T-carrier, and ATM

7 Describe commonly used communications devices: broadband modems, wireless modems, wireless access points, routers, network cards, and hubs and switches

8 Discuss ways to set up and configure a home network

9 Differentiate among physical transmission media: twisted-pair cable, coaxial cable, and fiber-optic cable

10 Differentiate among wireless transmission media: infrared, broadcast radio, cellular radio, microwaves, and communications satellite

Communications

The process in which two or more computers or devices transfer data, instructions, and information is known as digital communications. Today, even the smallest computers and devices can communicate directly with one another, with hundreds of computers on a corporate network, or with millions of other computers around the globe — often via the Internet.

Figure 10-1 shows a sample communications system. Some communications involve cables and wires; others are sent wirelessly through the air. For successful communications, you need the following:

• A **sending device** that initiates an instruction to transmit data, instructions, or information
• A communications device that connects the sending device to transmission media

Communications System

Figure 10-1 A simplified example of a communications system. Some devices that serve as sending and receiving devices are (a) servers, (b) desktops, (c) laptops, (d) tablets, (e) smartphones and headsets, (f) portable media players, (g) handheld game devices, and (h) GPS receivers in vehicles. Transmission media consist of phone and power lines, cable television and other underground lines, microwave stations, and satellites.

- **Transmission media**, or a *communications channel*, on which the data, instructions, or information travel
- A communications device that connects the transmission media to a receiving device
- A **receiving device** that accepts the transmission of data, instructions, or information

As shown in Figure 10-1, all types of computers and mobile devices serve as sending and receiving devices in a communications system. This includes servers, desktops, laptops, tablets, smartphones, portable media players, handheld game devices, and GPS receivers. Communications devices, such as modems, wireless access points, and routers, connect transmission media to a sending or receiving device. Transmission media can be wired or wireless.

This module presents types of networks, along with various types of communications lines and devices, and transmission media.

Networks

As discussed in Module 1, a **network** is a collection of computers and devices connected together via communications devices and transmission media. A network can be internal to an organization or span the world by connecting to the Internet. Many home and business users create a network to facilitate communications, share hardware, share data and information, share software, and transfer funds (Figure 10-2):

- **Facilitate communications.** Using a network, people communicate efficiently and easily via email, Internet messaging, chat rooms, blogs, wikis, online social networks, video calls, online meetings, videoconferences, VoIP, text messaging, and more. Some of these communications occur within an internal network. Other times, they occur globally over the Internet.

Reasons to Use a Network

facilitate communications

transfer funds

share hardware

share data and information

share software

Figure 10-2   Networks facilitate communications; enable sharing of hardware, data and information, and software; and provide a means for transferring funds.

- **Share hardware.** Each computer or device on a network can be provided access to hardware on the network. For example, each computer and mobile device user can access a printer on the network, as they need it. Thus, home and business users create networks to save money on hardware expenses.
- **Share data and information.** Any authorized user can access data and information stored on a network. A large company, for example, might have a database of customer information. Any authorized employee can access the database using a computer or mobile device connected to the network.

  Most businesses use a standard, such as *EDI* (*electronic data interchange*), that defines how business documents travel across transmission media. For example, businesses use EDI to send bids and proposals, place and track orders, and send invoices.
- **Share software.** Users connected to a network can access software on the network. To support multiple users' software access, vendors often sell versions of their software designed to run on a network or as a web app on the Internet. These network and Internet subscription versions usually cost less than buying individual copies of the software for each computer. The license fees for these programs typically are based on the number of users or the number of computers or mobile devices attached to the network.
- **Transfer funds.** *Electronic funds transfer* (*EFT*) allows users connected to a network to exchange money from one account to another via transmission media. Both businesses and consumers use EFT. Examples include wire transfers, use of credit cards and debit cards, direct deposit of funds into bank accounts, online banking, and online bill payment.

Instead of using the Internet or investing in and administering an internal network, some companies hire a value-added network provider for network functions. A *value-added network* (*VAN*) provider is a third-party business that provides networking services such as EDI services, secure data and information transfer, storage, or email. Some VANs, such as PayPal, charge an annual or monthly fee; others charge by the service used.

 BTW

Sharing Network Software

When you use a network to share software, you sometimes have to install the software on your computer, and a server on the network manages the licenses.

CONSIDER THIS

What is an intranet?
Recognizing the efficiency and power of the Internet, many organizations apply Internet and web technologies to their internal networks. An *intranet* (intra means within) is an internal network that uses Internet technologies. Intranets generally make company information accessible to employees and facilitate collaboration within an organization. Files on an intranet generally are not accessible from the Internet.

One or more servers on an intranet host an organization's internal webpages, applications, email messages, files, and more. Users locate information, access resources, and update content on an intranet using methods similar to those used on the Internet. A company hosts its intranet on servers different from those used to host its public webpages, apps, and files.

Sometimes a company uses an *extranet* (extra means outside or beyond), which allows customers or suppliers to access part of its intranet. Package shipping companies, for example, allow customers to access their intranet via an extranet to print air bills, schedule pickups, and track shipped packages as the packages travel to their destinations.

LANs, MANs, WANs, and PANs

Networks usually are classified as a local area network, metropolitan area network, wide area network, or personal area network. The main difference among these classifications is their area of coverage.

LAN   A **local area network** (**LAN**) is a network that connects computers and devices in a limited geographical area, such as a home, school, office building (Figure 10-3), or closely positioned group of buildings. Each computer or device on the network, called a *node*, often shares resources, such as printers, large hard drives, and programs. Often, the nodes are connected via cables.

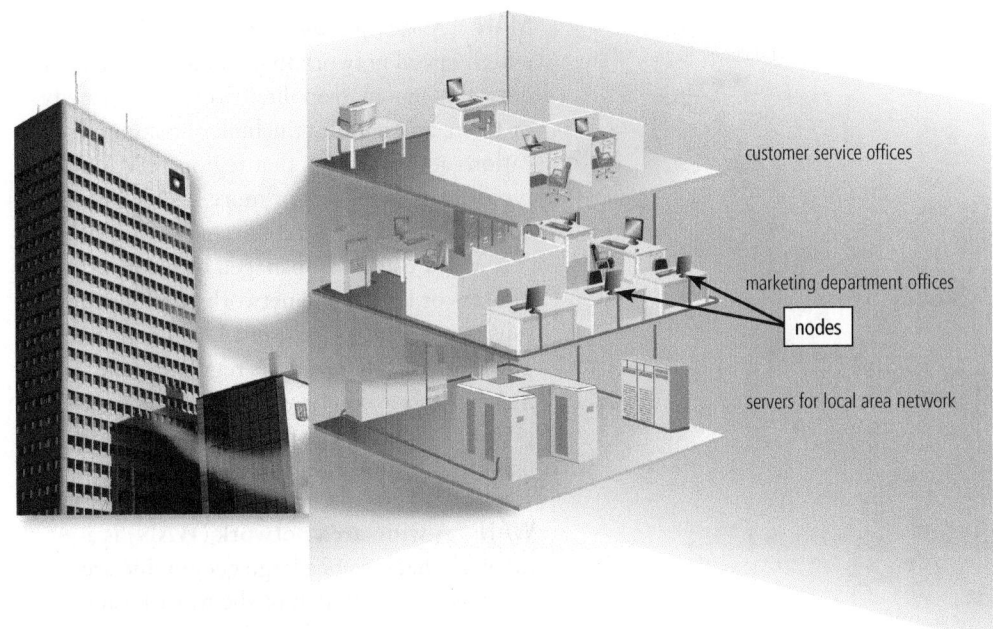

Figure 10-3 Computers and devices on different floors access the same LAN in an office building. Computers and devices on the network often are identified as nodes.
Xtuv Photography / Shutterstock.com

A **wireless LAN (WLAN)** is a LAN that uses no physical wires. Computers and devices that access a wireless LAN must have built-in wireless capability or the appropriate wireless network card, USB adapter, or other wireless device. A WLAN may communicate with a wired LAN for access to its resources, such as software, hardware, and the Internet (Figure 10-4).

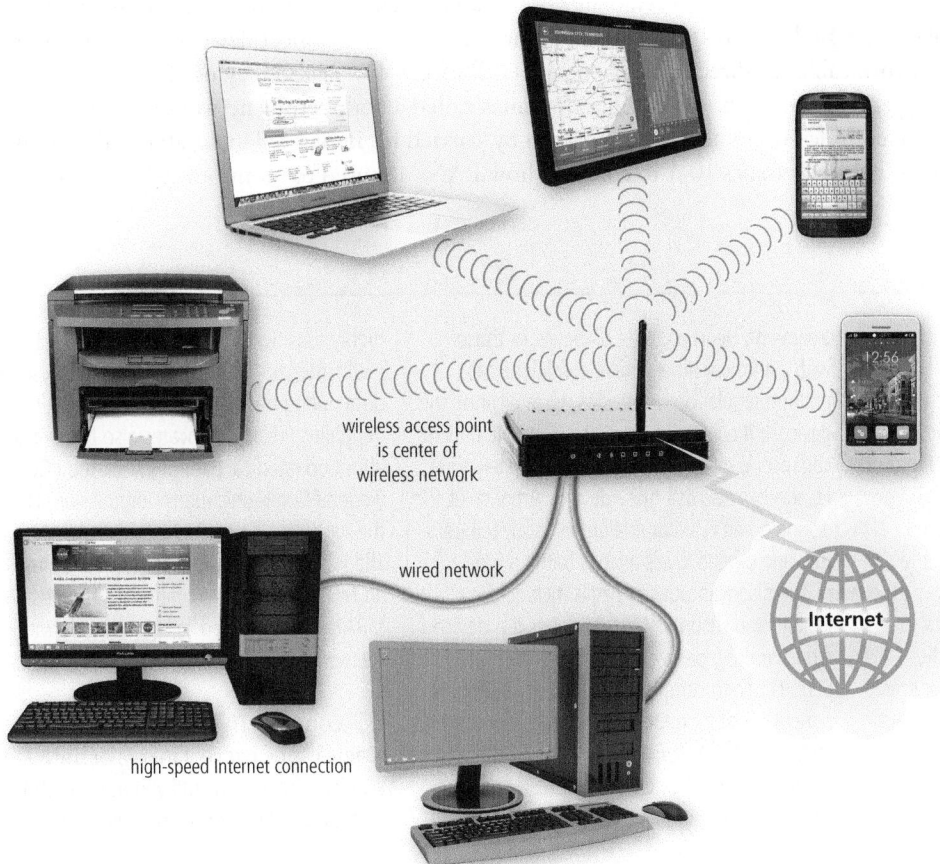

Figure 10-4 Computers and mobile devices on a WLAN may communicate via a wireless access point with a wired LAN to access its hardware, software, Internet connection, and other resources.
iStockphoto.com / SKrow; Scanrail1 / Shutterstock.com; iStockphoto.com / 123render; iStockphoto.com / pictafolio; iStockphoto.com / Moncherie; Natalia Siverina / Shutterstock.com; Ruslan Kudrin / Shutterstock.com

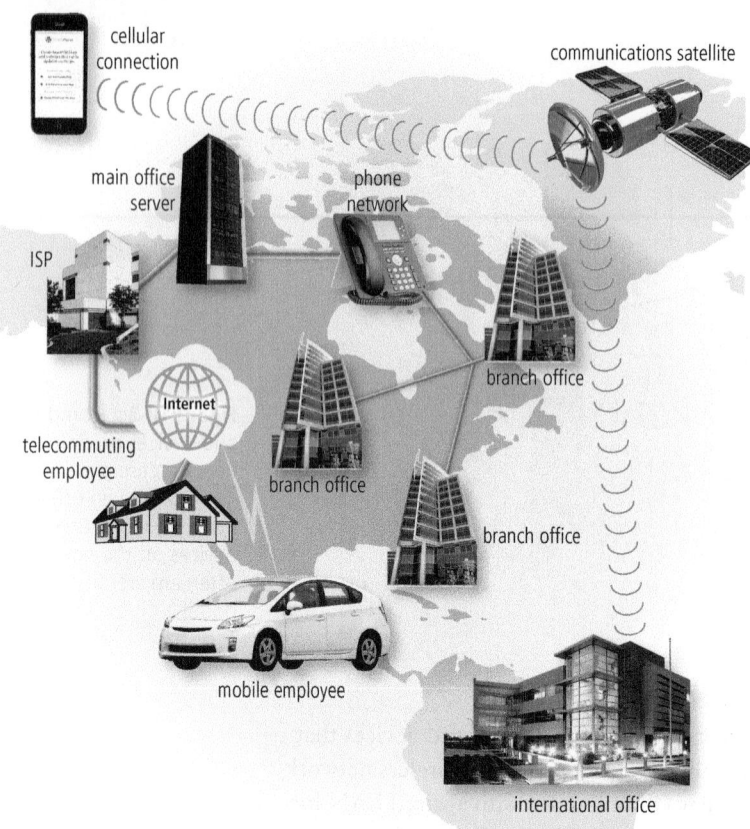

Figure 10-5 A simplified example of a WAN.

Maksim Toome / Shutterstock.com; Paul Matthew Photography / Shutterstock.com; imging / Shutterstock.com; Vtls / Shutterstock.com; iStockphoto.com / scanrail; iStockphoto.com / cotesebastien; Mmaxer / Shutterstock.com

MAN   A *metropolitan area network* (*MAN*) is a high-speed network that connects local area networks in a metropolitan area, such as a city or town, and handles the bulk of communications activity across that region. A MAN typically includes one or more LANs, but covers a smaller geographic area than a WAN.

A MAN usually is managed by a consortium of users or by a single network provider that sells the service to the users. Local and state governments, for example, regulate some MANs. Phone companies, cable television providers, and other organizations provide users with connections to the MAN.

WAN   A **wide area network** (**WAN**) is a network that covers a large geographic area (such as a city, country, or the world) using a variety of wired and wireless transmission media (Figure 10-5). A WAN can be one large network or can consist of multiple LANs connected together. The Internet is the world's largest WAN.

PAN   A **personal area network** (**PAN**) is a network that connects computers and devices in an individual's workspace using wired and wireless technology. Devices include smartphones, digital cameras, printers, and more. A PAN may connect devices through a router using network cables or directly using special USB cables. PANs also may use Bluetooth or Wi-Fi technology. A *body area network* (*BAN*), sometimes called a body sensor network (BSN), is a type of PAN that wirelessly connects sensors worn by, carried by, implanted in, or attached to a human body. Read Ethics & Issues 10-1 to consider how BANs are used to monitor medical data.

ETHICS & ISSUES 10-1

Would You Use a BAN to Monitor Medical Data?

By wearing, carrying, implanting, or attaching small devices to a person's body, medical professionals can track vital signs and monitor heart rhythms, breathing rates, and much more via a BAN, which uses low-powered sensors to collect data. The BAN sends the collected data wirelessly to an Internet-connected device, which relays the data to a medical data server. In some cases, the data transmits directly to emergency services. Some devices also automatically can dispense medications based on the data collected.

Because of these devices, a patient may not have to visit a medical facility to receive

treatment. Heart patients, diabetics, or those with asthma or other similar conditions can perform regular daily activities while wearing the device. If it collects any unusual data, the patient can receive medical resources immediately. First responders also use these devices. A fire chief, for example, can monitor firefighters' body temperature and oxygen levels as they battle a fire.

The disadvantages of BANs include data validity and security. What happens if a device stops working or its data becomes corrupt? Serious health complications could result if the patient is not monitoring conditions via another technique. For example, devices that administer medication could cause an overdose or underdose if not working properly. Medical data is

highly sensitive. An unscrupulous individual could intercept vital signs and other personal data during transfer, violating a patient's confidentiality. Privacy advocates also have concerns about nonmedical uses of BANs. The FCC (Federal Communications Commission) controls the registration of MBANs (medical BANs). The FCC regulates the radio frequency in which an MBAN can transmit data. Some types of MBANs are restricted to be used only within a licensed medical facility.

Consider This: Should insurance companies be required to pay for BANs? Why or why not? Would you use a BAN for a medical condition? Why or why not?

Network Architectures

The configuration of computers, devices, and media on a network is sometimes called the *network architecture*. Two examples of network architectures are client/server or peer-to-peer.

Client/Server   On a **client/server network**, one or more computers act as a server, and the other computers on the network request services from the server (Figure 10-6). A **server** controls access to the hardware, software, and other resources on the network and provides a centralized storage area for programs, data, and information. The **clients** are other computers and mobile devices on the network that rely on the server for its resources. For example, a server might store an organization's email messages. Clients on the network, which include any users' connected computers or mobile devices, access email messages on the server. Both wired and wireless networks can be configured as a client/server network.

Although it can connect a smaller number of computers, a client/server network architecture typically provides an efficient means to connect 10 or more computers. Most client/server networks require a person to serve as a network administrator because of the large size of the network.

As discussed in Module 3, some servers are dedicated servers that perform a specific task. For example, a network server manages network traffic (activity), and a web server delivers requested webpages to computers or mobile devices.

Peer-to-Peer   A *peer-to-peer (P2P) network* is a simple, inexpensive network architecture that typically connects fewer than 10 computers. Each computer or mobile device, called a *peer*, has equal responsibilities and capabilities, sharing hardware (such as a printer), data, or information with other computers and mobile devices on the peer-to-peer network (Figure 10-7). Peer-to-peer networks allow users to share resources and files located on their computers and to access shared resources found on other computers on the network. Peer-to-peer networks do not have a common file server. Instead, all computers can use any of the resources available on other computers on the network. For example, you might set up a P2P network between an Android tablet and a Windows laptop so that they can share files using Bluetooth or so that you can print from the tablet to a printer accessible to all devices on the network. Both wired and wireless networks can be configured as a peer-to-peer network.

P2P networks are ideal for very small businesses and home users. Some operating systems include a P2P networking tool that allows users to set up a peer-to-peer network. Many businesses also see an advantage to using P2P. That is, companies and employees can exchange files using P2P, freeing the company from maintaining a network server for this purpose. Business-to-business e-commerce websites find that P2P easily allows buyers and sellers to share company information such as product databases.

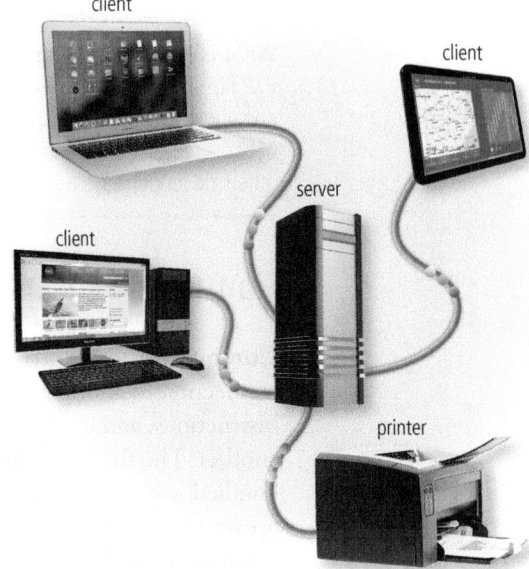

Figure 10-6   As illustrated by the communications in this simplified diagram, on a client/server network, one or more computers act as a server, and the client computers and mobile devices access the server(s). Connections can be wired or wireless and may occur through a communications device.
iStockphoto.com / scanrail; iStockphoto.com / SKrow; Scanrail1 / Shutterstock.com; Anan Chincho / Shutterstock.com; iStockphoto.com / luismmolina

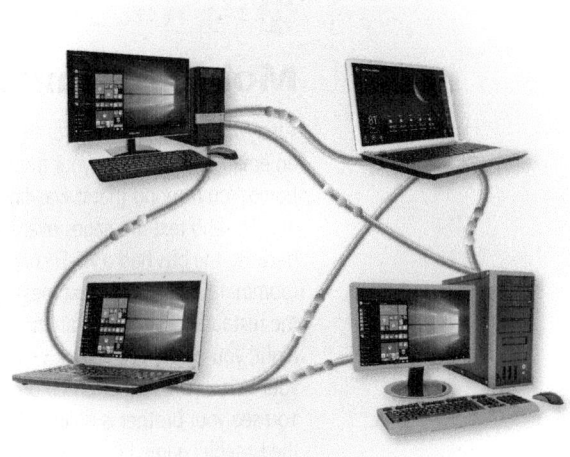

Figure 10-7   As illustrated by the communications in this simplified diagram, each computer or mobile device on a P2P network shares its hardware and software with other computers and mobile devices on the network. Connections can be wired or wireless and may occur through a communications device.
Alex Staroseltsev / Shutterstock.com; iStockphoto.com / 123render; Sergey Peterman / Shutterstock.com; Scanrail1 / Shutterstock.com; Source: Microsoft

CONSIDER THIS ────────────────────────────────────

What is P2P file sharing?

P2P file sharing, sometimes called a *file sharing network*, describes a network configuration on which users access one another's hard drives and exchange files directly via a file sharing program. As more users connect to the network, each user has access to shared files on other users' hard drives. When users sign out of the network, others no longer have access to their hard drives.

Communications Software

Communications software consists of programs and apps that (1) help users establish a connection to another computer, mobile device, or network; (2) manage the transmission of data, instructions, and information; and (3) provide an interface for users to communicate with one another. The first two often are provided by or included as tools with an operating system or bundled with a communications device. The third is provided by applications such as email, FTP, browser, discussion boards, chat rooms, Internet messaging, videoconferencing, and VoIP.

Sometimes, communications devices are preprogrammed to accomplish communications tasks. Some routers, for example, contain firmware for various protocols. Other communications devices require separate communications software to ensure proper transmission of data. Communications software works with the network standards and protocols (presented in a later section) to ensure data moves through the network or the Internet correctly.

Tech Feature 10-1: Mobile Communications

Users often communicate with one another via mobile computers and devices. Read Tech Feature 10-1 to learn about communications options for mobile devices and associated data plans.

 TECH FEATURE 10-1 ────────────────────────────────

Mobile Communications

After visiting your parents for the weekend, you receive an email message from your mom asking about your trip home. You respond that it was fine and that you were able to send text messages over the Internet to your sister because the bus had a Wi-Fi connection. Meanwhile, your roommate sends you a text message with directions to the restaurant where you are meeting for dinner. That night, you chat on Facebook with a classmate about your homework and catch up on your friends' updates. You see your brother is online and is live streaming from the baseball game he is attending. From email and text messages to voice and video calls, computers and mobile devices offer many ways to communicate.

Email is best for sharing longer, detailed messages. For shorter or time-sensitive messages, consider using the following forms of immediate communications.

Text/Picture/Video Messaging

Text, picture, and video messages often take the place of phone conversations among many people, who find exchanging these messages to be less intrusive and more efficient than voice conversations. SMS (short message service) text messages are messages of 300 or fewer characters sent from one user to another

through a mobile service provider's cell phone tower. With MMS (multimedia message service), users also can send and receive photos, videos, and audio files. Occasional users might subscribe to a text-messaging plan, where providers charge a small fee for each message sent or received. In contrast, avid users, who send frequent text, picture, or video messages, might subscribe to an unlimited plan. To avoid paying fees to mobile service providers for sending text messages, some people opt for free messaging apps and services available via third-party providers. These services send messages over the Internet rather than a provider's network. Some of these services are free when both parties subscribe. Free messaging apps often include advertising content alongside the messages.

Internet Messaging

With Internet messaging services, you can send text or media messages in real time to other online users. To access an Internet messaging service, you need the service's desktop, web, or mobile app, and an Internet connection on your computer or mobile device. Users with accounts on multiple Internet messaging services often use an Internet messaging aggregator app to manage contact lists and chat on different Internet messaging networks simultaneously.

Some providers allow you to merge your text/picture/ video (SMS and MMS) and Internet messages so that you can see messages of both types from the same contact in a single conversation.

Voice and Video Calling

VoIP services, such as Skype and FaceTime, also provide voice and video calling services over the Internet. These often are much less expensive than making phone calls over a mobile service provider's network. It also is possible to make calls from a VoIP program to a mobile or landline phone. Voice and video calling require large amounts of bandwidth. As a result, some carriers prohibit the use of calling services over their networks, requiring users to connect via Wi-Fi to make these calls. Read Ethics & Issues 10-2 to consider video calling and other issues associated with communications technologies and medical care.

© radub85 / Fotolia LLC

Data Plans

Your mobile device's data plan enables you to access the Internet through your mobile service provider's network when Wi-Fi is not available. Without a data plan, you must use Wi-Fi or a wired connection to access the Internet on your computer or mobile device. Some mobile service providers offer an unlimited data plan for your device, while many offer limited data plans. If you exceed your data limit in a given month, additional fees apply. By monitoring your data usage to see how much you use on average over a few months, you can decide on the best plan for you. Some carriers offer a shared data plan that provides an allotted amount of data to be shared across several smartphones, tablets, laptops, gaming devices, and mobile hot spots. Using Wi-Fi when available to access the Internet will save on data usage charges if you have a limited data plan.

✳ **Consider This:** Think about how you use different forms of mobile communications to share information or communicate with your family, friends, or coworkers as part of your daily routine. For what purposes do you generally send email messages or text messages? After exchanging text messages, when might you make a phone call or use VoIP service to talk in real time? Under what circumstances is each form of communication most efficient?

✳ **ETHICS & ISSUES 10-2**

Do the Benefits of Telemedicine Outweigh the Risks?

After your doctor asks you several questions, she gives you a diagnosis and sends a prescription to your local pharmacy electronically. Instead of walking out of the exam room, you turn off your tablet's webcam, receiving medical care without leaving your home. *Telemedicine* is the use of communications and information technology to provide and assist with medical care. Patients use telemedicine to communicate with a doctor, nurse, or pharmacist from their home or workplace. Healthcare professionals benefit from collaborating and consulting with specialized physicians in other locations.

Proponents of telemedicine state that its use can provide healthcare access to patients in remote areas, or those who are unable to leave their home safely. The Mayo Clinic is testing in-office kiosks which enable employees to videoconference with a medical professional to diagnose minor health conditions without the employee having to leave work. Another benefit of telemedicine is in cases where spread of infectious disease is a concern.

Some healthcare experts state that the cost of the equipment and time spent training healthcare professionals outweighs the benefits. The inability of healthcare professionals to perform hands-on tasks, such as take a temperature or examine the patient's ears or throat, can lead to misdiagnosis or an incomplete exam. If a patient requires immediate care, such as for an allergic reaction, a medical professional is not on hand to give treatment, causing delays. Insurance companies may require physicians to have medical licenses in the state where the patient resides in order to cover the expenses. Privacy advocates warn that hackers can access shared data or spy on videoconferences between doctors and patients.

✳ **Consider This:** Have you ever used telemedicine to communicate with your healthcare provider? Why or why not? Would you use a kiosk at your workplace to communicate with a healthcare provider? Why or why not? Is it practical to rely on telemedicine to provide care to people in remote areas? Why or why not?

Network Communications Standards and Protocols

Today's networks connect terminals, devices, and computers from many different manufacturers across many types of networks. For the different devices on various types of networks to be able to communicate, the network must use similar techniques of moving data through the network from one application to another.

To alleviate the problems of incompatibility and ensure that hardware and software components can be integrated into any network, various organizations such as ANSI (American National Standards Institute) and IEEE (Institute of Electrical and Electronics Engineers) propose, develop, and approve network standards. A *network standard* defines guidelines that specify the way computers access the medium to which they are connected, the type(s) of medium used, the speeds used on different types of networks, and the type(s) of physical cable and/or the wireless technology used. Hardware and software manufacturers design their products to meet the guidelines specified in a particular standard, so that their devices can communicate with the network. A standard that outlines characteristics of how two devices communicate on a network is called a *protocol*. Specifically, a protocol may define data format, coding schemes, error handling, and the sequence in which data transfers over a network.

Table 10-1 identifies some of the more widely used network communications standards and protocols for both wired and wireless networks. The following sections discuss each of these standards and protocols.

Table 10-1	Network Communications Standards and Protocols	
Name	**Type**	**Sample Usage**
Ethernet	Standard	LAN
Token ring	Standard	LAN
TCP/IP	Protocol	Internet
Wi-Fi	Standard	Hot spots
LTE	Standard	Mobile phones
Bluetooth	Protocol	Wireless headset
UWB	Standard	Inventory tracking
IrDA	Standard	Remote control
RFID	Protocol	Tollbooth
NFC	Protocol	Mobile phone payment

✷ CONSIDER THIS

Do network standards and protocols work together?
Network standards and protocols often work together to move data through a network. Some of these standards define how a network is arranged physically, while others specify how messages travel along a network. Thus, as data moves through a network from one program to another, it may use one or more of these standards.

✷ BTW

Data Transfer Rates
Mbps (megabits per second) is one million bits per second, and *Gbps* (gigabits per second) is one billion bits per second.

Ethernet

Ethernet is a network standard that specifies no central computer or device on the network (nodes) should control when data can be transmitted. That is, each node attempts to transmit data when it determines the network is available to receive communications. If two computers or devices on an Ethernet network attempt to send data at the same time, a collision will occur. When this happens, the computers or devices resend their messages until data transfer is successful.

The Ethernet standard defines guidelines for the physical configuration of a network (e.g., cabling, network devices, and nodes). Ethernet currently is the most popular network standard for LANs because it is relatively inexpensive and easy to install and maintain. Depending on the transmission media used, Ethernet networks have data transfer rates that range from 10 Mbps for home/small office users to 100 Gbps for enterprise users.

Token Ring

The **token ring** standard specifies that computers and devices on the network share or pass a special signal, called a token, in a unidirectional manner and in a preset order. A *token* is a special series of bits that functions like a ticket. The device with the token can transmit data over the network. Only one token exists per network. This ensures that only one computer transmits data at a time. Although token ring is not as widely used today, many networks use the concept of a token.

The token ring standard defines guidelines for the physical configuration of a network (e.g., cabling, network cards, and devices). Some token ring networks connect up to 72 devices. Others use a special type of wiring that allows up to 260 connections. The data transfer rate on a token ring network ranges from 4 Mbps to 16 Mbps.

TCP/IP

Short for Transmission Control Protocol/Internet Protocol, **TCP/IP** is a network protocol that defines how messages (data) are routed from one end of a network to the other. TCP/IP describes rules for dividing messages into small pieces, called *packets*; providing addresses for each packet; checking for and detecting errors; sequencing packets; and regulating the flow of messages along the network.

TCP/IP has been adopted as the network standard for Internet communications. Thus, all hosts on the Internet follow the rules defined in this standard. As shown in Figure 10-8, Internet communications also use other standards, such as the Ethernet standard, as data is routed to its destination.

When a computer sends data over the Internet, the data is divided into packets. Each packet contains the data, as well as the recipient (destination), the origin (sender), and the sequence information used to reassemble the data at the destination. Each packet travels along the fastest individual available path to the recipient's computer or mobile device via routers. This technique of breaking a message into individual packets, sending the packets along the best route available, and then reassembling the data is called *packet switching*. Read Secure IT 10-1 for another use of packets.

How Communications Standards Might Work Together

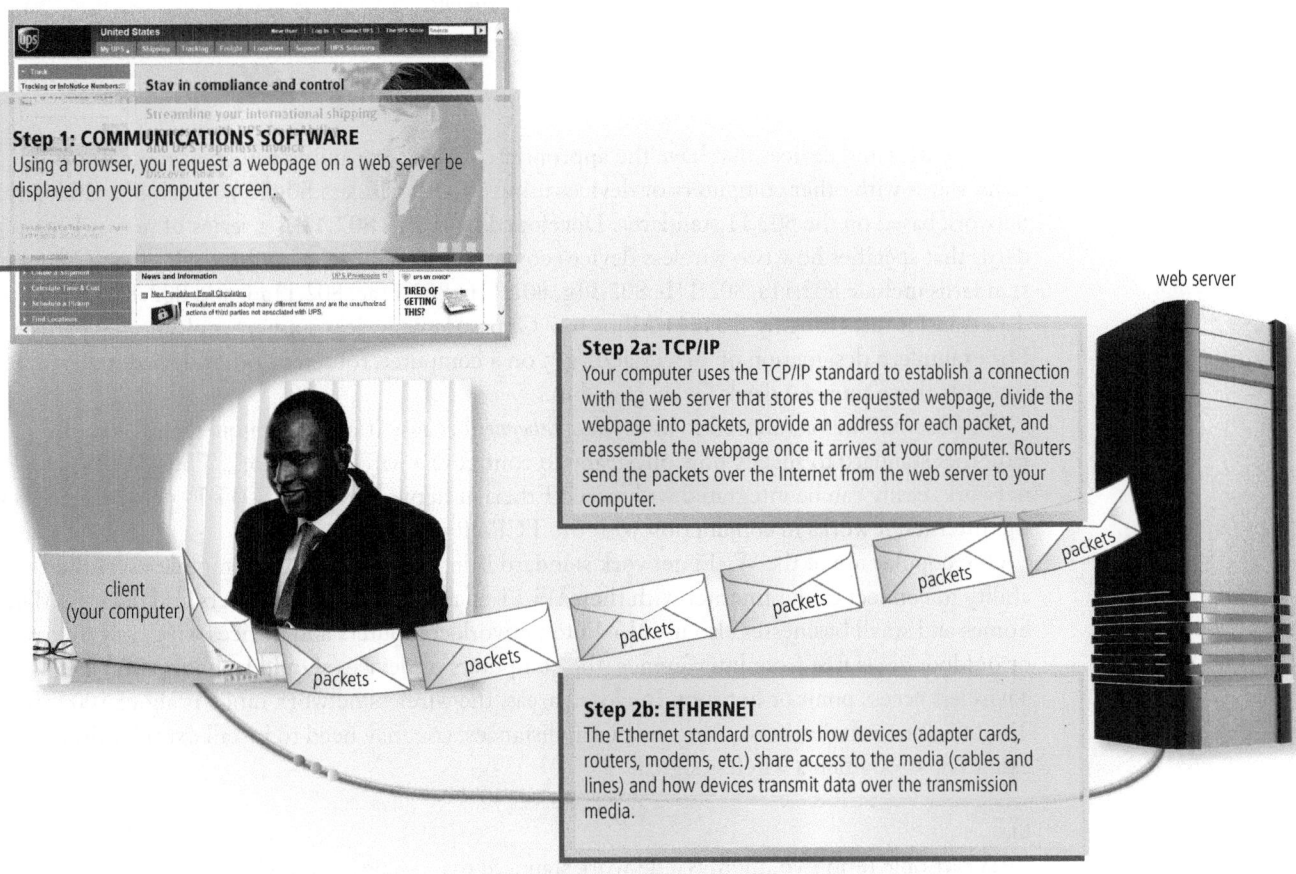

Step 1: COMMUNICATIONS SOFTWARE
Using a browser, you request a webpage on a web server be displayed on your computer screen.

web server

Step 2a: TCP/IP
Your computer uses the TCP/IP standard to establish a connection with the web server that stores the requested webpage, divide the webpage into packets, provide an address for each packet, and reassemble the webpage once it arrives at your computer. Routers send the packets over the Internet from the web server to your computer.

client (your computer)

Step 2b: ETHERNET
The Ethernet standard controls how devices (adapter cards, routers, modems, etc.) share access to the media (cables and lines) and how devices transmit data over the transmission media.

Figure 10-8   This figure illustrates how Internet communications use TCP/IP and Ethernet to ensure that data travels correctly to its destination.
lenetstan / Shutterstock.com; iStockphoto.com / luismmolina

SECURE IT 10-1

Monitoring Network Traffic

Network monitoring software constantly assesses the status of a network and sends an email or text message, usually to the network administrator, when it detects a problem. These messages may state that an outage has occurred, the server's available memory space is near capacity, a new user account has been added, or some other critical event has developed.

Monitoring software can measure the amount of network traffic, graph network usage, determine when a specific program uses the network, and show the bandwidth used by each computer or mobile device. On networks that use the TCP/IP protocol, for example, *packet sniffer software* monitors and logs packet traffic for later analysis. Packet sniffing can detect problems, such as why traffic is flowing slowly.

The software also can play a security role, including identifying unusual or excessive network activity. For example, it can flag a remote computer always connected to the network or someone making repeated attempts to sign in to an account. Hackers use packet sniffer software to hijack a computer, which means they capture a user's packets and then reconstruct the contents of webpages that were visited, obtain user names and passwords, and trace photos and videos viewed.

Consider This: How would you determine if your employer or school has network monitoring software? Would you change your computer activities, including browsing certain websites, if you knew the software could track your computer or mobile device usage?

 CONSIDER THIS

Can IP addresses be used to determine a computer or device's location?

In many cases, you can determine a computer or a device's location from its IP address. For example, if an IP address begins with 132.170, a small amount of research will uncover that the University of Central Florida assigns IP addresses beginning with these numbers; however, additional research would be necessary to determine where the computer or mobile device is located on the network. Certain websites allow visitors to find a location by entering an IP address. Some web apps infer your approximate location from your IP address when GPS is not available in order to provide you with local information or nearby search results.

Wi-Fi

Computers and devices that have the appropriate wireless capability can communicate via radio waves with other computers or devices using **Wi-Fi** (wireless fidelity), which identifies any network based on the 802.11 standards. Developed by IEEE, **802.11** is a series of network standards that specifies how two wireless devices communicate over the air with each other. Common standards include 802.11a, 802.11b, 802.11g, 802.11n, 802.11ac, 802.11ad, and 802.11af, with data transfer rates ranging from 11 Mbps to 7 Gbps. Many devices support multiple standards. For example, a designation of 802.11 ac/b/g/n on a computer, router, or other device indicates it supports those four standards (ac, b, g, and n).

Wi-Fi sometimes is referred to as *wireless Ethernet* because it uses techniques similar to the Ethernet standard to specify how physically to configure a wireless network. Thus, Wi-Fi networks easily can be integrated with wired Ethernet networks. When a Wi-Fi network accesses the Internet, it works in conjunction with the TCP/IP network standard.

One popular use of the Wi-Fi network standard is in hot spots that offer mobile users the ability to connect to the Internet with their Wi-Fi-enabled wireless computers and devices. Many homes and small businesses also use Wi-Fi to network computers and devices wirelessly. In open or outdoor areas free from interference, the computers or devices should be within 300 feet of a wireless access point or hot spot. In closed areas, the wireless network range is about 100 feet. To obtain communications at the maximum distances, you may need to install extra hardware to extend or strengthen a wireless signal.

LTE

LTE (Long Term Evolution) is a network standard that defines how high-speed cellular transmissions use broadcast radio to transmit data for mobile communications. Developed by the Third Generation Partnership Project (3GPP), LTE has the potential of 100 Mbps *downstream rate* (receiving data) and 30 Mbps *upstream rate* (sending data). Newer specifications are being developed that potentially can support a 1 Gbps downstream rate and a 500 Mbps upstream rate. Based on the TCP/IP network standard, LTE supports data, messaging, voice, and video transmissions. Many mobile service providers, such as AT&T and Verizon Wireless, offer LTE service.

Two competing standards for LTE are WiMax (Worldwide Interoperability for Microwave Access) and UMB (Ultra Mobile Broadband).

Bluetooth/Tech Feature 10-2

Bluetooth is a network protocol that defines how two Bluetooth devices use short-range radio waves to transmit data. The data transfers between devices at a rate of up to 3 Mbps. To communicate with each other, Bluetooth devices often must be within about 33 feet but can be extended to about 325 feet with additional equipment.

A Bluetooth device contains a small chip that allows it to communicate with other Bluetooth devices. For computers and devices that are not Bluetooth-enabled, you can purchase a Bluetooth wireless port adapter that will convert an existing USB port into a Bluetooth port. Most current operating systems have built-in Bluetooth support. When connecting two devices using Bluetooth, the originating device sends a code to the connecting device. The codes must match to establish the connection. Devices that share a Bluetooth connection are said to be paired. Read Tech Feature 10-2 to learn about Bluetooth uses, advantages, and disadvantages.

 TECH FEATURE 10-2

Bluetooth Technology

Most mobile devices and computers manufactured today are equipped with Bluetooth capability. One of the earliest and most popular uses of Bluetooth is to connect hands-free headsets to a mobile phone. Bluetooth has many additional uses, and device manufacturers are increasingly including Bluetooth technology.

Uses

You can use Bluetooth-enabled or Bluetooth-enhanced devices in many ways, including the following:

- Connect devices, such as mobile phones, portable media players, or GPS devices, with vehicle stereos, which use the vehicle's speakers to project sound (shown in the figure).

- Use GPS receivers to send directions to a mobile phone or GPS-enabled device.

- Transfer photos wirelessly from a digital camera to a laptop or server.

- Play music on a smartphone through the speakers on a computer or other Bluetooth-enabled device.

- Send signals between video game accessories, video game devices, and a television.

- Establish a PAN (personal area network).

- Allow communications between a computer and devices, such as a keyboard, printer, Smart TV, or mobile phone. Connecting these devices enables you to print documents, share calendar appointments, and more.

- Replace wired communications devices, such as bar code readers, with wireless devices to enhance portability.

- Transmit data from a medical device, such as a blood glucose monitor, to a mobile phone or other device.

- Change the channel, pause a program, or schedule a recording using a Bluetooth-compatible or Bluetooth-enabled television and remote control.

- Track objects that include tags or nodes used to send wireless signals read by a real-time location system.

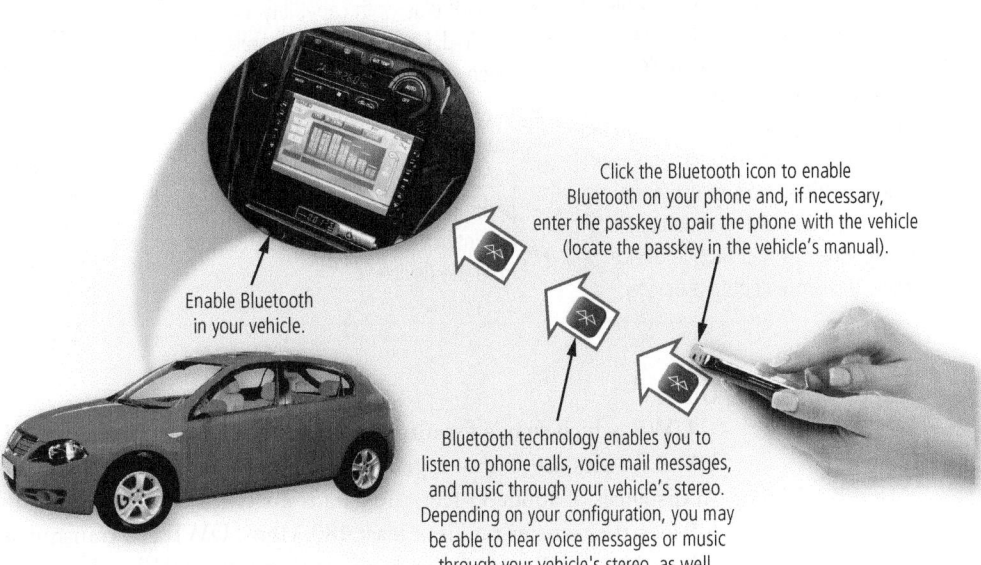

Enable Bluetooth in your vehicle.

Click the Bluetooth icon to enable Bluetooth on your phone and, if necessary, enter the passkey to pair the phone with the vehicle (locate the passkey in the vehicle's manual).

Bluetooth technology enables you to listen to phone calls, voice mail messages, and music through your vehicle's stereo. Depending on your configuration, you may be able to hear voice messages or music through your vehicle's stereo, as well.

© Fotolia LLC; Adisa / Shutterstock.com; Vartanov Anatoly / Shutterstock.com; Pakhnyushchy / Shutterstock.com

(Continued)

Advantages and Disadvantages

Advantages of using Bluetooth technology include the following:

- If a device has Bluetooth capability, using Bluetooth technology is free.

- Although Bluetooth devices need to be near each other, they do not have to be in the same room, within the same line of sight, or facing each other.

- Bluetooth devices typically require low processing power and use little energy, so using Bluetooth technology will not drain a device's battery.

- Establishing a wireless Bluetooth connection is easy. With most Bluetooth-enabled devices, you simply click a Bluetooth shortcut or icon to enable Bluetooth. Once enabled, the devices usually immediately recognize a connection. (Before initial use, you may need to pair two Bluetooth devices so that they can communicate with each other. Read How To 3-1 in Module 3 for instructions about pairing Bluetooth devices.)

- Bluetooth connections have low security risks. If you want to secure a Bluetooth channel, you would define an identification number for the connection and create a PIN that you can distribute as needed. If the secured computer or device detects an unknown Bluetooth connection, you can choose to accept or reject it. Read Secure IT 10-2 to learn about security risks associated with using Bluetooth technology.

- Bluetooth technology is standardized globally, meaning it can be used to connect devices that are not the same make or model.

- Bluetooth connections have little risk of interference with other wireless networks because the strength of the wireless signals is weak and because of frequency hopping, which changes frequency channels periodically.

One disadvantage of Bluetooth technology is its low bandwidth. Because of its slow data transfer speeds, Bluetooth technology is not an ideal solution for replacing a LAN. Because Bluetooth-enabled mobile payment services are new, security risks may exist. Most agree that the advantages of Bluetooth technology far outweigh the disadvantages.

✳ **Consider This:** Have you used Bluetooth technology to connect two devices? What devices did you connect, and what was your experience? In your opinion, what is the best reason to use Bluetooth? Why? What devices do you think will include Bluetooth technology in the future?

 SECURE IT 10-2

Preventing Bluebugging

One reason why Bluetooth technology is so popular is because connections generally have low security risks, as described in Tech Feature 10-2. Despite this advantage, security experts have seen an increase in *Bluebugging*, which occurs when cyberthieves exploit Bluetooth devices that have been paired. Smartphones and other mobile devices are discoverable to other Bluetooth devices only for a short period when they first are turned on, but during this time the hackers can intercept the signals or use hardware that has the same identifying characteristics as the smartphone or other mobile device. Once hackers have intercepted a device,

they take control and read or download personal data, place calls, monitor conversations, review text and email messages, and modify contacts.

Security experts recommend following these practices to prevent Bluebugging:

- Turn off Bluetooth capability if it is not required. Use a Bluetooth earpiece only when you need to be hands free.

- Use your device in a remote area. Bluebuggers often work in crowded and public places, such as shopping centers, parks, and public transportation, and they can intercept signals up to 30 feet away from the device.

- Prevent hackers from intercepting your device by pairing it for the first time in a secure location, such as your home.

- If Bluetooth is required, be certain the device's visibility setting is hidden and all paired devices are set to unauthorized so that the user must authorize each connection request.

- Upgrade your phone. Older devices are more vulnerable to these intrusions.

✳ **Consider This:** Have you paired your phone with any Bluetooth devices? If so, did you pair them in a private location? Which of these guidelines will you follow to attempt to prevent Bluebugging?

UWB

UWB, which stands for **ultra-wideband**, is a network standard that specifies how two UWB devices use short-range radio waves to communicate at high speeds with each other. At distances of about 33 feet, the data transfer rate is 110 Mbps. At closer distances, such as about 6.5 feet, the transfer rate is at least 480 Mbps. UWB can transmit signals through doors and other obstacles. Because of its high transfer rates, UWB is best suited for transmission of large files, such as video, graphics, and audio. Examples of UWB uses include locating and tracking inventory, equipment, or personnel (especially in remote or dangerous areas).

IrDA

Some devices, such as television remote controls, use the **IrDA** (Infrared Data Association) standard to transmit data wirelessly to each other via infrared (IR) light waves. The devices transfer data at rates from 115 Kbps (thousand bits per second) to 4 Mbps between their IrDA ports. Infrared requires *line-of-sight transmission*; that is, the sending device and the receiving device must be in line with each other so that nothing obstructs the path of the infrared light wave. Because Bluetooth and UWB do not require line-of-sight transmission, these technologies are more widespread than IrDA.

RFID

RFID (*radio frequency identification*) is a protocol that defines how a network uses radio signals to communicate with a tag placed in or attached to an object, an animal, or a person. The tag, called a transponder, consists of an antenna and a memory chip that contains the information to be transmitted via radio waves. Through an antenna, an RFID reader, also called a transceiver, reads the radio signals and transfers the information to a computer or computing device. Read Secure IT 6-2 in Module 6 for uses of animal implants.

Depending on the type of RFID reader, the distance between the tag and the reader ranges from 5 inches to 300 feet or more. Readers can be handheld or embedded in an object, such as a doorway or a tollbooth (Figure 10-9).

How Electronic RFID Toll Collection Works

Step 1
Motorist purchases an RFID transponder or RFID tag and attaches it to the vehicle's windshield.

Step 2
As the vehicle approaches the tollbooth, the RFID reader in the tollbooth sends a radio wave that activates the windshield-mounted RFID tag. The activated tag sends vehicle information to the RFID reader.

Step 3
The RFID reader sends the vehicle information to the lane controller. The lane controller, which is part of a local area network, transmits the vehicle information to a central computer that subtracts the toll from the motorist's account. If the vehicle does not have an RFID tag, a high-speed camera takes a picture of the license plate and the computer prints a violation notice, which is mailed to the motorist.

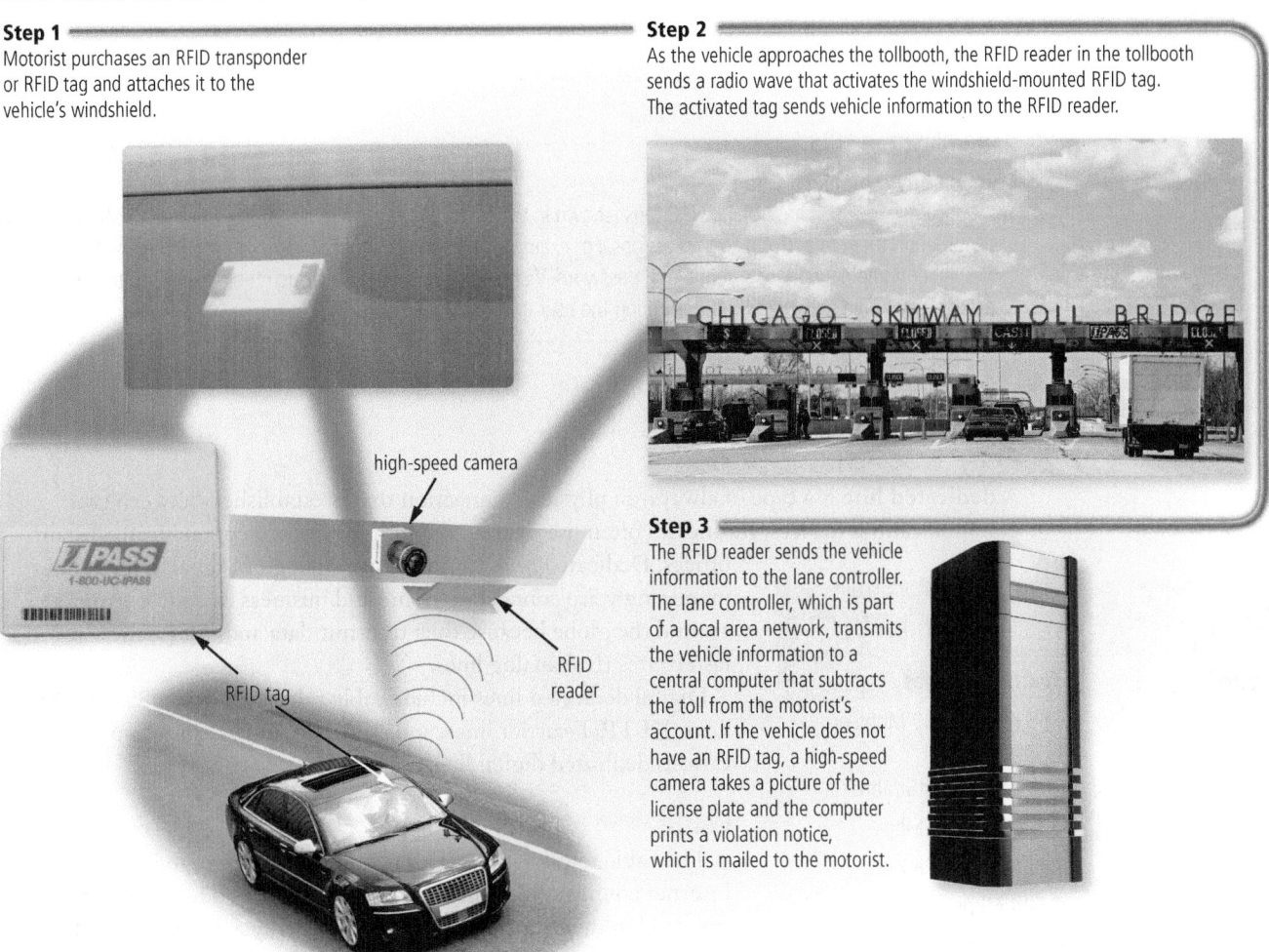

high-speed camera

RFID tag

RFID reader

Figure 10-9   This figure shows how electronic RFID toll collection works.

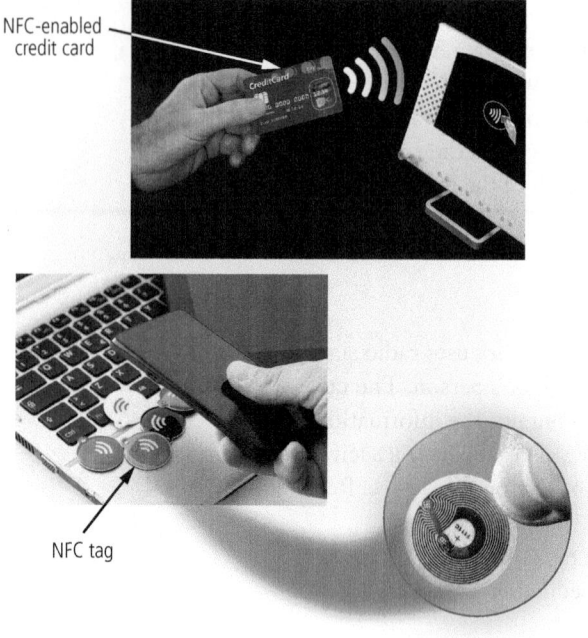

NFC-enabled credit card

NFC tag

Figure 10-10 Some objects, such as credit cards, are NFC enabled. You also can program NFC tags yourself.

Alexander Kirch / Shutterstock.com; iStockphoto.com / cheyennezj; iStockphoto.com / pierrephoto

NFC

NFC (*near field communications*) is a protocol, based on RFID, that defines how a network uses close-range radio signals to communicate between two devices or objects equipped with NFC technology (Figure 10-10). Examples of NFC-enabled devices include smartphones, digital cameras, televisions, and terminals. Credit cards, tickets, and NFC tags are examples of objects that also use NFC technology. An NFC tag is a chip that can store small amounts of data. NFC tags are in a variety of objects, such as posters, ski lift tickets, business cards, stickers, and wristbands.

For successful communications, the devices or objects touch or are placed within an inch or two of each other. For example, you can touch two NFC-enabled phones together to transfer contacts, touch an NFC-enabled phone to an NFC tag to display a map, or hold an NFC-enabled phone near a parking meter to pay for parking. Contactless payment, such as the parking meter example, is a popular use of NFC technology. Other uses of NFC technology include sharing contacts or photos, downloading apps, and gaining access or admittance.

 CONSIDER THIS ————————————————

Can you buy a blank NFC tag?
Yes. Consumers can purchase blank NFC tags (shown in the bottom photo in Figure 10-10) at a reasonable cost and easily program them to perform certain actions. For example, you can use a mobile app to program an NFC tag to contain your home network user name and password. Visitors to your home can touch their phones to the NFC tag to access your home network without entering the user name and password.

Communications Lines

A **dedicated line** is a type of always-on physical connection that is established between two communications devices. Businesses often use dedicated lines to connect geographically distant offices. Dedicated lines can be either analog or digital. Digital lines increasingly are connecting home and business users to networks around the globe because they transmit data and information at faster rates than analog lines.

Digital dedicated lines include cable television lines, DSL, ISDN lines, FTTP, T-carrier lines, and ATM. Table 10-2 shows speeds of various dedicated digital lines.

Cable

The cable television (CATV) network provides high-speed Internet connections, called *cable Internet service*. The CATV signal enters a building through a single line, usually a coaxial cable. This cable connects to a modem (discussed in the next section), which typically attaches to your computer via an Ethernet cable. Home and small business users often subscribe to cable Internet service.

Table 10-2	Speeds of Various Dedicated Digital Lines
Type of Line	**Transfer Rates**
Cable	256 Kbps to 100 Mbps or higher
DSL	256 Kbps to 8.45 Mbps
FTTP	5 Mbps to 300 Mbps
Fractional T1	128 Kbps to 768 Kbps
T1	1.544 Mbps
T3	44.736 Mbps
ATM	155 Mbps to 622 Mbps, can reach 10 Gbps

DSL

DSL (*Digital Subscriber Line*) transmits on existing standard copper phone wiring. Some DSL installations include a dial tone, providing users with both voice and data communications. These DSL installations often require that filters be installed to reduce noise interference when voice communications share the same line. DSL is a popular digital line alternative for the small business or home user.

ADSL is a popular type of DSL. As shown in Figure 10-11, *ADSL (asymmetric digital subscriber line)* is a type of DSL that supports faster downstream rates than upstream rates. ADSL is ideal for Internet access because most users download more information from the Internet than they upload.

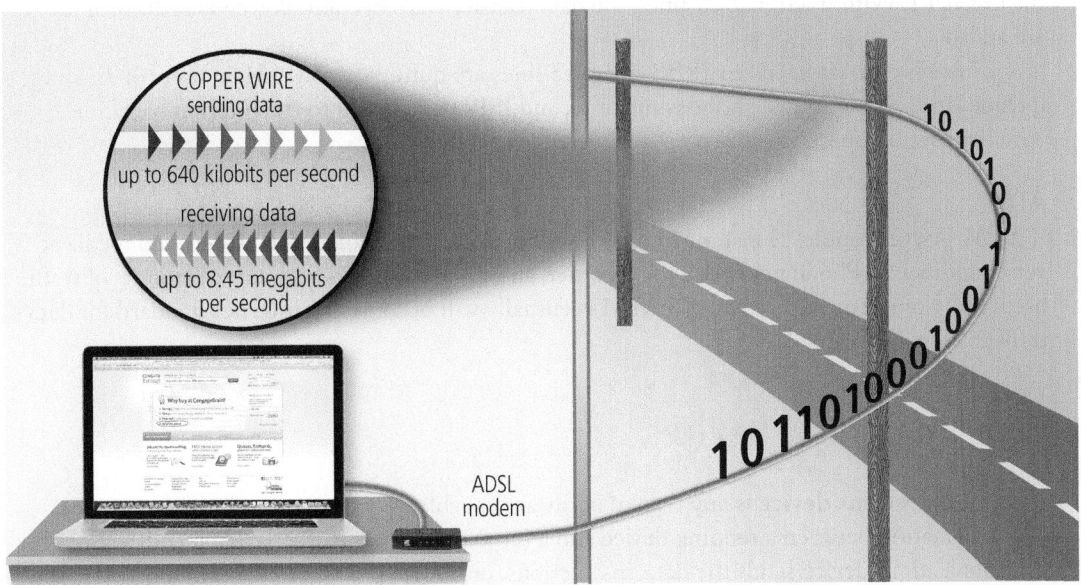

Figure 10-11   ADSL connections transmit data downstream (receiving) at a much faster rate than upstream (sending).
artjazz / Shutterstock.com

 **CONSIDER THIS**

Which is a better choice, DSL or cable Internet service?
Each has its own advantages. DSL uses a line that is not shared with other users in the neighborhood. With cable Internet service, by contrast, users might share the node with up to hundreds of other cable Internet users. Simultaneous access by many users can cause the cable Internet service to slow down. Cable Internet service, however, has widespread availability and usually has faster transmission rates.

FTTP

FTTP, which stands for **Fiber to the Premises**, uses fiber-optic cable to provide extremely high-speed Internet access to a user's physical permanent location.

- *FTTH (Fiber to the Home)* provides home users with Internet access via fiber-optic cable.
- *FTTB (Fiber to the Building)* refers to small businesses that use fiber-optic cables to access the Internet.

With FTTP service, an optical terminal at your location receives the signals and transfers them to a router connected to a computer. As the cost of installing fiber decreases, more homes and businesses are expected to choose FTTP.

T-Carrier

A **T-carrier line** is any of several types of long-distance digital phone lines that carry multiple signals over a single communications line. Whereas a standard phone line carries only one signal, digital T-carrier lines use multiplexing so that multiple signals share the line. T-carrier lines provide very fast data transfer rates. Only medium to large companies usually can afford the investment in T-carrier lines because these lines are so expensive.

The most popular T-carrier line is the *T1 line*. Businesses often use T1 lines to connect to the Internet. Home and small business users purchase *fractional T1*, in which they share a connection to the T1 line with other users. Fractional T1 is slower than a dedicated T1 line, but it also is less expensive. Users who do not have other high-speed Internet access in their areas can opt for fractional T1. With fractional T1 lines, the data transfer rates become slower as additional users are added.

A *T3 line* is equal in speed to 28 T1 lines. T3 lines are quite expensive. Main users of T3 lines include large corporations, phone companies, and ISPs connecting to the Internet backbone. The Internet backbone itself also uses T3 lines.

ATM

ATM (Asynchronous Transfer Mode) is a service that carries voice, data, video, and media at very high speeds. Phone networks, the Internet, and other networks with large amounts of traffic use ATM. Some experts predict that ATM eventually will become the Internet standard for data transmission, replacing T3 lines.

Communications Devices

A **communications device** is any type of hardware capable of transmitting data, instructions, and information between a sending device and a receiving device. At the sending end, a communications device sends the data, instructions, or information from the sending device to transmission media. At the receiving end, a communications device receives the signals from the transmission media.

The following pages describe a variety of communications devices: modems, wireless access points, routers, network cards, and hubs and switches.

Digital Modems: Cable, DSL, and ISDN

A *broadband modem*, also called a *digital modem*, is a communications device that sends and receives data and information to and from a digital line. Three types of broadband modems are cable modems, DSL modems, and ISDN modems. These modems typically include built-in Wi-Fi connectivity.

A **cable modem** is a broadband modem that sends and receives digital data over the CATV network. To access the Internet using the CATV service, as shown in Figure 10-12, the CATV provider installs a splitter inside your house. From the splitter, one part of the cable runs to your televisions and the other part connects to the cable modem. Many CATV providers include a cable modem as part of the installation; some offer a rental plan, and others require that you purchase one separately. A cable modem usually is an external device, in which one end of a cable connects to a CATV wall outlet and the other end plugs in a port on a computer.

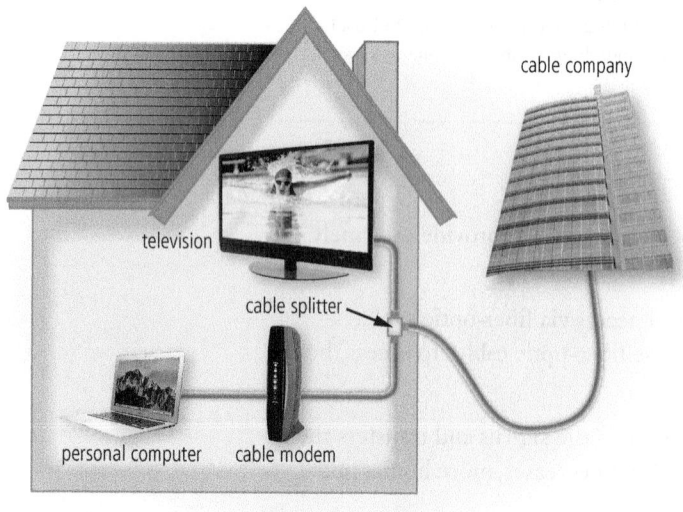

Figure 10-12 A typical cable modem installation.
tiridifilm / iStockphoto.com; image100 / Alamy Stock Photo; iStockphoto.com / SKrow; Pablo Eder / Shutterstock.com

A **DSL modem** is a broadband modem that sends digital data and information from a computer to a DSL line and receives digital data and information from a DSL line. Similarly, an *ISDN* (Integrated Services Digital Network) *modem* is a broadband modem that sends digital data and information from a computer to an ISDN line and receives digital data and information from an ISDN line. DSL and ISDN modems usually are external devices, in which one end connects to the phone line and the other end connects to a port on the computer.

BTW
Cable and DSL
Cable and DSL are more widely used than ISDN.

 CONSIDER THIS

What are dial-up modems?

A *dial-up modem* is a communications device that converts digital signals to analog signals and analog signals to digital signals, so that data can travel along an analog phone line. For example, a dial-up modem connected to a sending computer converts the computer's digital signals into analog signals. The analog signals then can travel over a standard phone line. A dial-up modem connected to a receiving computer converts the analog signals from a standard phone line into digital signals that the computer can process.

A dial-up connection must be reestablished each time the modem is used. With transfer rates of only up to 56 Kbps, dial-up connections also are much slower than broadband connections. For these reasons, dial-up connections are used only in remote areas or where high-speed or wireless options are not available.

Wireless Modems

Some mobile users have a *wireless modem* that uses a mobile service provider's network to connect to the Internet wirelessly from a computer or mobile device (Figure 10-13). Wireless modems, which have an external or built-in antenna, are available as USB adapters and other devices.

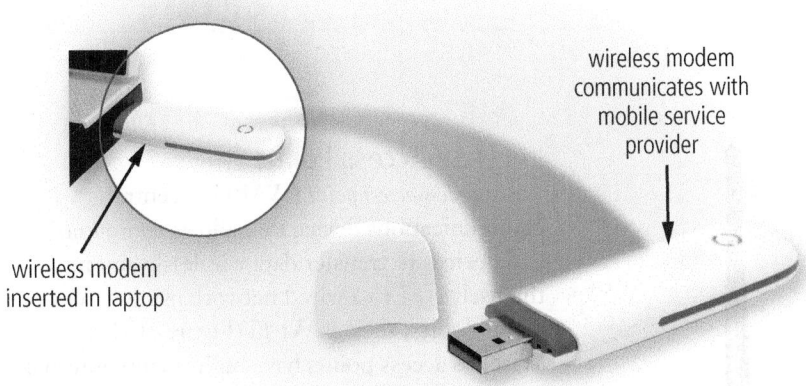

Figure 10-13 Wireless modems allow users to access the Internet wirelessly using a mobile service provider's network. Some manufacturers refer to the type of wireless modem shown in this figure as a USB modem.
iStockphoto.com / nolimitpictures

Some smartphones also can function as a wireless modem, called a *mobile hot spot*, when tethered to a personal computer or mobile device. Read How To 10-1 for instructions about using your phone as a mobile hot spot.

HOW TO 10-1

Use Your Phone as a Mobile Hot Spot

If you are in a location without a wireless Internet connection, you may be able to access the Internet from your desktop or mobile computer if you enable your smartphone as a mobile hot spot. When you enable a phone as a mobile hot spot, the phone acts as a wireless access point. You then can connect (tether) your desktop or mobile computer to the phone and utilize the data plan on your phone to access the Internet. If you have a limited data plan with your mobile service provider, you should be careful not to use your phone as a hot spot too often. While the speed from a mobile hot spot might not be as fast as your home or office network, it should be more than sufficient for performing tasks such as browsing the web or sending and receiving email messages that contain mostly text. The next steps describe how to use your phone as a mobile hot spot:

1. Contact your mobile service provider and determine whether your plan allows for your phone to be used as a mobile hot spot. Using your phone as a mobile hot spot may carry an additional monthly charge.
2. Determine whether your phone has built-in functionality to be used as a mobile hot spot. If not and if supported by your service plan, you may be able to download a separate app that allows your phone to function as a mobile hot spot.
3. Access your phone's settings and enable the mobile hot spot. Your phone should display the SSID and password to access the hot spot. Read How To 5-2 in Module 5 for additional information about SSIDs.
4. Connect to the mobile hot spot on a computer or mobile device using the SSID and password displayed in the previous step.
5. When you are finished using the hot spot, disconnect from the wireless network on your computer and disable the hot spot feature on your phone.

Consider This: How can you determine how much data you are using on your smartphone's data plan?

Peter Bernik / Shutterstock.com

Figure 10-14 Wireless access point.
iStockphoto.com / wsfurlan

Wireless Access Points

A *wireless access point* (WAP) is a central communications device that allows computers and devices to transfer data wirelessly among themselves or to a wired network using wireless technologies, such as Wi-Fi (Figure 10-14). Wireless access points have high-quality internal or external antennas for optimal signals. For the best signal, some manufacturers suggest positioning the wireless access point at the highest possible location and using a device to strengthen your wireless signal. Read How To 10-2 for tips to strengthen your wireless signal. A wireless access point either connects to a router via an Ethernet or other cable or is part of a router.

✿ HOW TO 10-2

Strengthen Your Wireless Signal

If you reside in a large apartment or house and use a wireless network, you may find that you either experience poor network performance or you are unable to access the network in certain locations. These problems may be related to a weak wireless signal in your home. Various options are available to strengthen a wireless signal to increase network performance and ensure you have a wireless connection throughout your home. The following points describe how to strengthen a wireless signal:

- If your wireless router or wireless access point has an antenna(s), make sure the antenna(s) is extended completely.

- If you are able to remove the antenna(s) from your wireless router or wireless access point, consider replacing it with a wireless signal booster. Check your device's and the

wireless signal booster's documentation to determine whether it will work with your device.

- If possible, position the wireless router or wireless access point in a central location of your home and away from appliances or other electronic devices that may degrade the signal.

- Purchase a range extender for your wireless router or wireless access point. Some range extenders are compatible only with specific wireless routers or wireless access points, and others are universal. Make sure the range extender you purchase is compatible with your device. Once installed, follow the range extender's instructions to enable it on your network.

- If you still experience problems with the strength of your wireless signal after following the suggestions above, consider

replacing your wireless router or wireless access point with a newer model.

✿ **Consider This:** What problems may arise if your wireless network's range extends beyond the confines of your home? How can you determine the range of your wireless network?

Copyright 2013 NETGEAR

Routers

A *router* is a communications device that connects multiple computers or other routers together and transmits data to its correct destination on a network. A router can be used on a network of any size. On the largest scale, routers along the Internet backbone forward data packets to their destination using the fastest available path. For smaller business and home networks, a router allows multiple computers and mobile devices to share a single broadband Internet connection, such as through a cable modem or DSL modem (Figure 10-15).

If the network has a separate router, it connects to the router via a cable. Similarly, if the network has a separate wireless access point, it connects to the router via a cable. Many users, however, opt for routers that provide additional functionality:

- A *wireless router* is a device that performs the functions of a router and also a wireless access point.
- A *broadband router* is a device that performs the functions of a router and also a broadband modem.

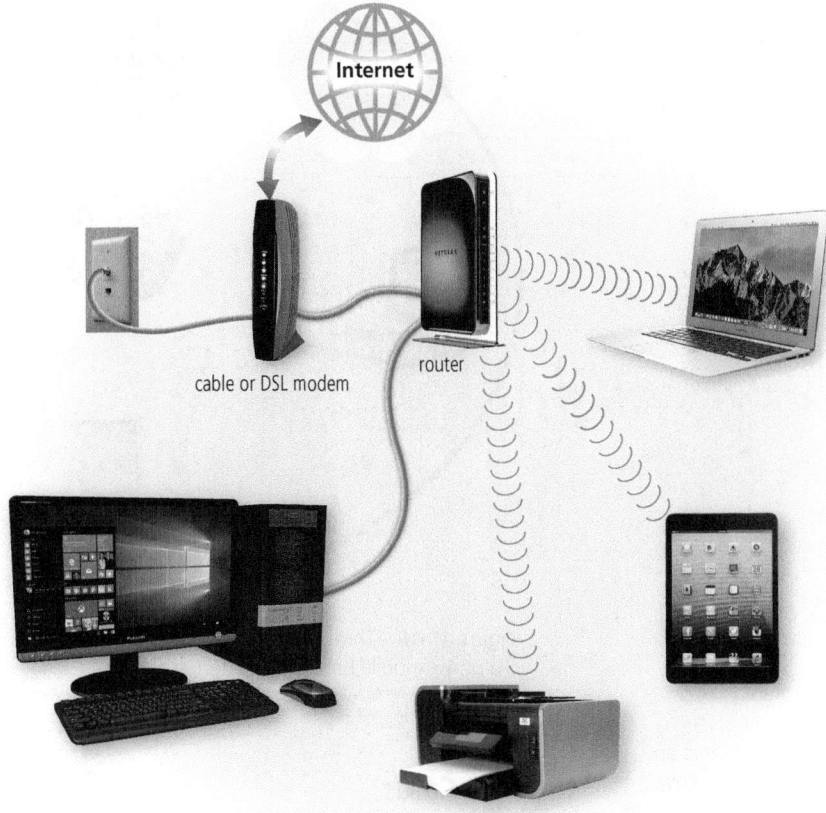

Figure 10-15   Through a router, home and small business networks can share access to a broadband Internet connection, such as through a cable or DSL modem.

Copyright 2013 NETGEAR; iStockphoto.com / SKrow; iStockphoto.com / Dane Wirtzfeld / Elerium; Kitch Bain / Shutterstock.com; Scanrail1 / Shutterstock.com; Pablo Eder / Shutterstock.com; 1125089601 / Shutterstock.com

BTW

Hardware Firewall
To prevent unauthorized users from accessing files and computers, many routers are protected by a built-in firewall, called a *hardware firewall*. Some also have built-in antivirus protection.

- A *broadband wireless router* is a device that performs the functions of a router, a wireless access point, and a cable or DSL modem.
- A *mobile broadband wireless router* is a device that performs the functions of a router, a wireless access point, and a wireless modem (Figure 10-16). Consumers use mobile broadband wireless routers to create a mobile hot spot.

These combination devices eliminate the need for a separate wireless access point and/or modem on a network. These routers also enable you easily to configure and secure the device against unauthorized access.

 CONSIDER THIS

How many connections can a router support?
Although a router may be able to connect more than 200 wired and/or wireless computers and mobile devices, the performance of the router may decline as you add connections. Some mobile service providers limit the number of connections to their mobile broadband wireless routers.

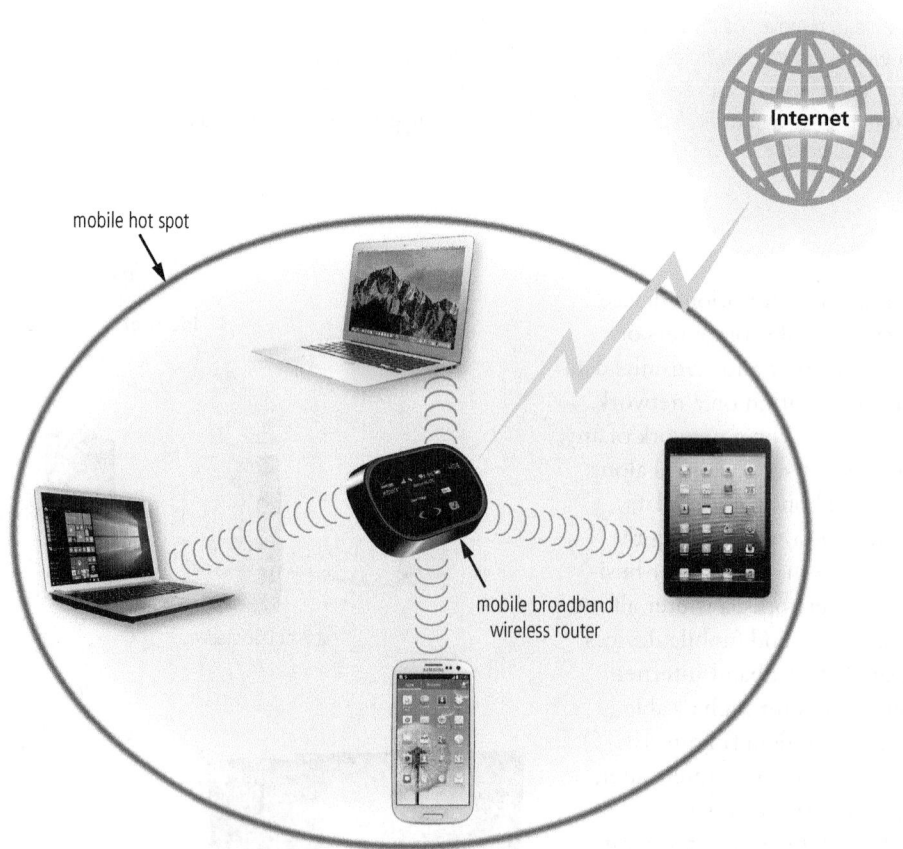

Figure 10-16 Through a mobile broadband wireless router, users can create a mobile hot spot via 3G or 4G mobile broadband Internet service.
Courtesy of Verizon Wireless; iStockphoto.com / SKrow; iStockphoto.com / Dane Wirtzfeld / Elerium; iStockphoto.com / Moncherie; Alex Staroseltsev / Shutterstock.com

BTW

Motherboards
Many computers and mobile devices have motherboards that integrate networking capability, eliminating the need for a separate network card.

Network Cards

A *network card*, sometimes called a *network interface card* (*NIC* pronounced nick), is a communications device that enables a computer or device that does not have built-in networking capability to access a network. The network card coordinates the transmission and receipt of data, instructions, and information to and from the computer or device containing the network card.

Network cards are available in a variety of styles. A network card for a desktop is an adapter card that has a port to which a cable connects (Figure 10-17). A network card for mobile computers and devices is in the form of a USB adapter or other device. A network card follows the guidelines of a particular network communications standard, such as Ethernet or token ring.

Figure 10-17   Network card for a desktop computer.
Courtesy of D-Link Corporation

Hubs and Switches

Today, thousands of computer networks exist, ranging from small networks operated by home users to global networks operated by widespread telecommunications firms. Interconnecting these many types of networks requires various types of communications devices. A *hub* or *switch* is a device that provides a central point for cables in a network (Figure 10-18). Larger networks typically use a switch, while smaller networks use a hub. Some hubs and/or switches include routers. That is, the hub or switch receives data from many directions and then forwards it to one or more destinations.

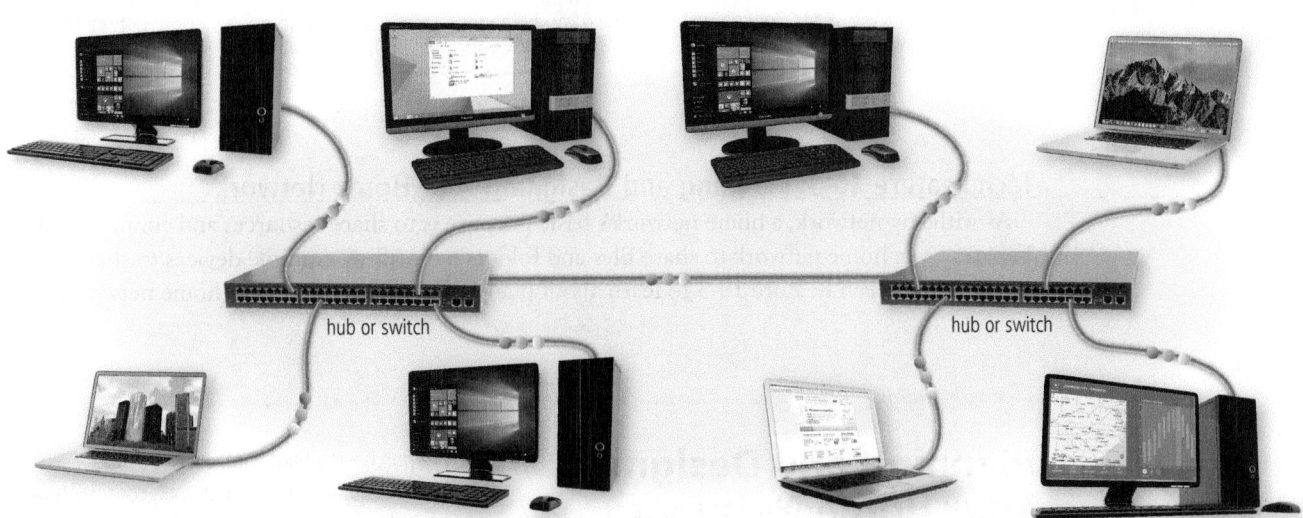

hub or switch   hub or switch

Figure 10-18   A hub or switch is a central point that connects several devices in a network together, as well as connects to other networks, as shown in this simplified diagram.
Courtesy of D-Link Corporation; iStockphoto.com / sweetym; Scanrail1 / Shutterstock.com; Scanrail1 / Shutterstock.com; iStockphoto.com / skodonnell; Natalia Siverina / Shutterstock.com; iStockphoto.com / skodonnell; iStockphoto.com / sweetym; Alex Staroseltsev / Shutterstock.com; iStockphoto.com / sweetym

Home Networks

Many home users connect multiple computers and devices together in a **home network**. Vendors typically offer home networking packages that include all the necessary hardware and software to network your home using wired or wireless techniques. You no longer need extensive knowledge of networks to set up a home network. For example, desktop operating systems often enable you to connect all computers in your house to a home network easily. Read Secure IT 10-3 to learn how to detect if an intruder is accessing your network.

 SECURE IT 10-3

Detecting an Intruder Accessing Your Wireless Home Network

One of the largest Internet security threats is *IP hijacking*, which occurs when cyberthieves tap into home routers or cable modems or other Internet access point to intercept a paid Internet service. Some cyberthieves use the connection to commit illegal acts; others just steal the Internet connection. The incidences of IP hijacking are growing, and catching thieves is a difficult task for law enforcement officials.

Unscrupulous people hijack Internet service in one of two ways. Either the network has no security, or the thieves determine the network name and password and then reprogram their modem's settings to duplicate the network's settings. The Electronic Communications Privacy Act (ECPA) and a lack of funding prevent fraud examiners from investigating and prosecuting many IP hijackers.

Experts recommend using the following steps to determine if someone is accessing a wireless network without permission:

- **Sign in to the administrative interface.** The modem's user's guide will provide instructions to view wireless clients actively using a wireless access point.

- **Count the number of connected devices.** Each device connected wirelessly to the network should be displayed in a table that shows, at a minimum, the device's name, MAC address, and IP address. (Read How To 5-2 in Module 5 for additional information about MAC address controls.) Wireless devices that might be connected to the network include smartphones, game consoles, DVD players, and other hardware. If the number of devices seems extraordinarily high, use a MAC lookup website, which can help you

to determine the manufacturer of wireless devices in the list.

- **Secure the network.** The router's manufacturer's website should provide instructions about upgrading the security strength. Change the default network name and password, and be certain to use the latest wireless encryption technology. Enable the router's firewall and, if possible, use "stealth mode" to make the network less visible to outsiders. Disable the feature that allows users to administer the router wirelessly, so that changes can be made only when using a physical connection with an Ethernet cable.

Consider This: If you use a wireless router, have you taken any of these steps to prevent IP hijacking? Which steps will you now take? Do you know anyone who has had a cyberthief access his or her network?

Tech Feature 10-3: Planning and Designing Your Home Network

As with any network, a home network's basic purpose is to share resources and connect devices. You can use a home network to share files and folders or to allow multiple devices to share a printer. Read Tech Feature 10-3 to learn about planning and designing your home network.

 TECH FEATURE 10-3

Planning and Designing Your Home Network

A home network enables you to use a common Internet connection among many computers and mobile devices. Other uses include connecting entertainment devices, such as digital video recorders (DVRs) and televisions, to the Internet and establishing a connection between devices in order to play multiplayer games.

Before purchasing hardware, or contracting a network expert to set up your network, consider how your network will be used, and by whom. Ask yourself the following questions:

- What devices will connect to the network? The number of devices, as well as the operating system or platform on which the devices operate will determine the speed and strength needed to run your wireless network.

- How large of a range do you need, and where will most of the use take place? If you have a small apartment, your needs will differ from those with a large home.

- How many users typically will be using the network, how will they use it, and for what purposes? The number of users affects the capabilities of the network and determines whether you need to define permissions for certain users or devices.

- How secure do you need your network? Hiding the network name, requiring passwords, or having a user with network administration capabilities can help ensure your network is safe from unauthorized use.

A home network can be as simple as using a cable to connect two devices. More complex home networks include wireless technologies that connect several devices to one another and to the Internet. Hardware needed for a wireless, Internet-connected home network includes the following:

- A modem, such as a cable or DSL modem, that connects to an ISP and establishes the Internet connection for the network

- A router, which establishes the connection between the Internet and all computers and devices on the home network and also enables the devices to communicate with one another

- A wireless access point, often included as part of the router, in order to connect wireless devices

- Computers and devices, such as desktops, laptops, tablets, smartphones, televisions, cable set-top boxes, or a VoIP phone, that you connect to the home network

Once you configure your wireless network, you can create user names and user groups. Names and groups establish network users, who can share files (such as documents, music, and photos), as well as devices (such as printers), with others connected to the network.

Maintaining the network involves monitoring the security settings and network activity, establishing connections to new devices as needed, and enhancing the wireless signal if necessary. Wireless home network speeds and ranges vary. The strength of the wireless signal affects the range of the network. Read How To 10-2 earlier in this module for instructions about strengthening a wireless signal.

⚙ **Consider This:** Do you have a home network? What devices are connected to it? Is your network password protected? Why or why not? Is the signal weaker in certain areas in your home? If so, where? What can you do to increase the effectiveness and security of your network?

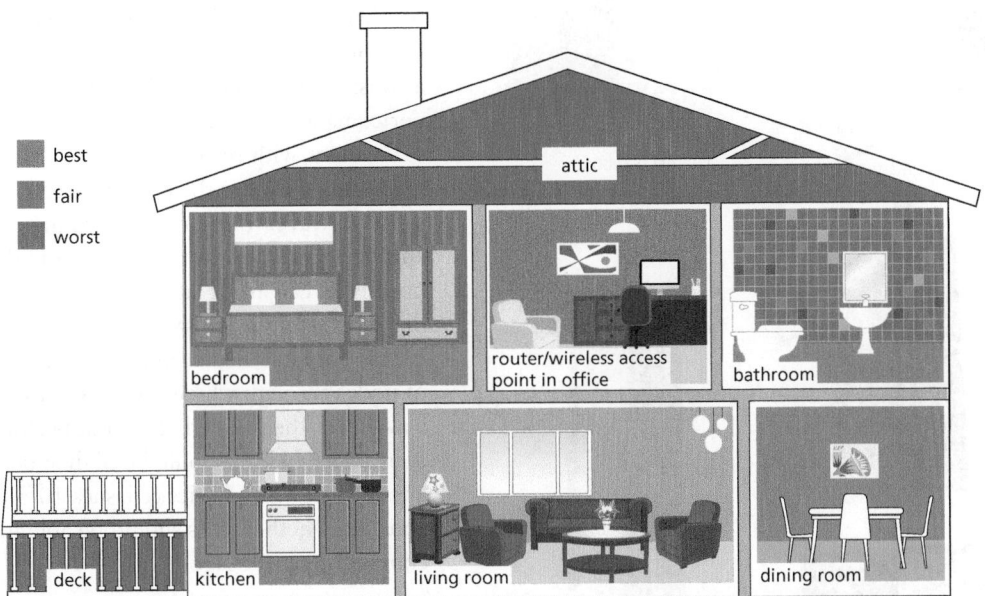

An Example of Sending a Request over the Internet Using a Variety of Transmission Media

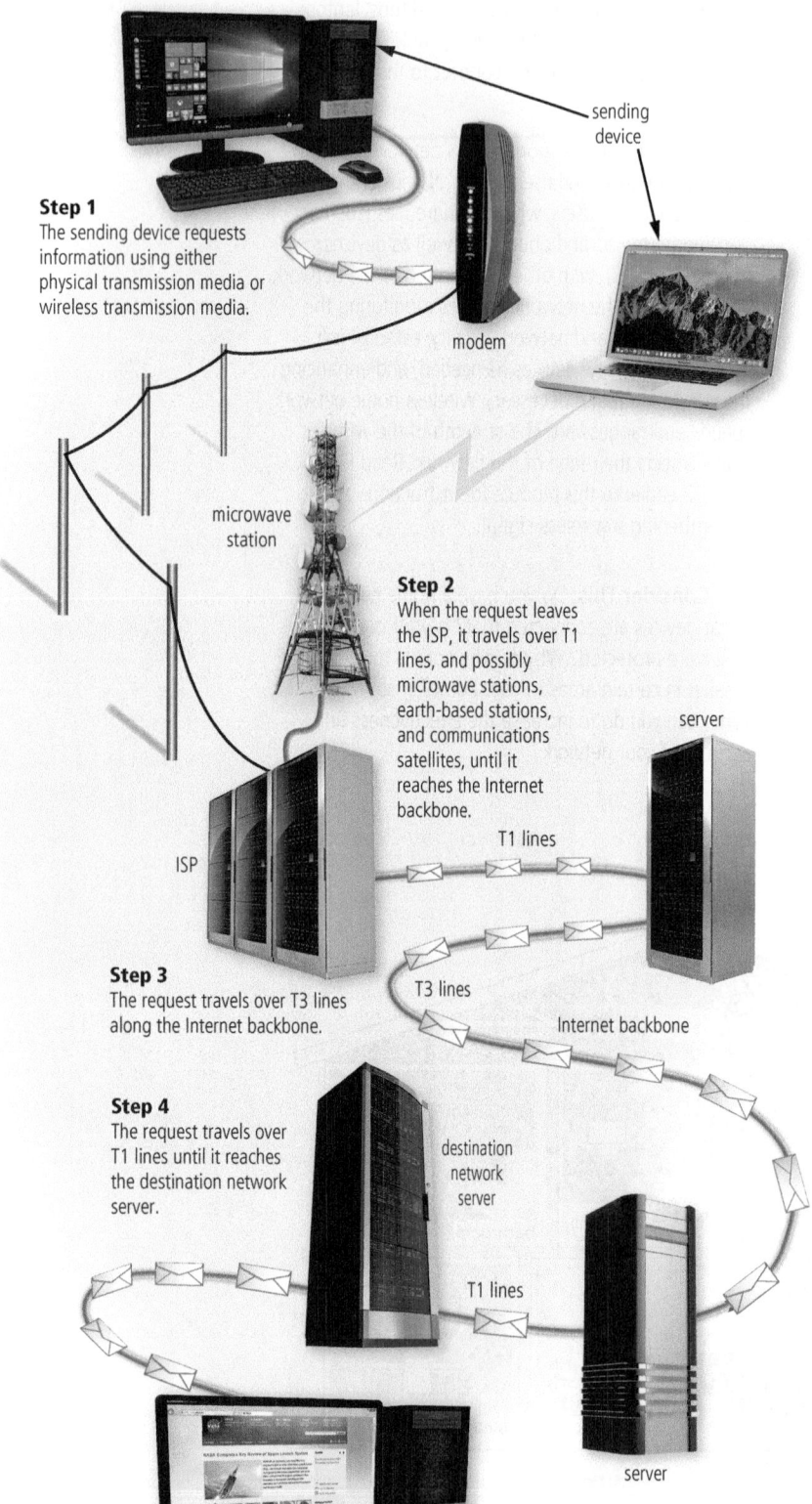

Step 1
The sending device requests information using either physical transmission media or wireless transmission media.

sending device

modem

microwave station

Step 2
When the request leaves the ISP, it travels over T1 lines, and possibly microwave stations, earth-based stations, and communications satellites, until it reaches the Internet backbone.

server

T1 lines

ISP

Step 3
The request travels over T3 lines along the Internet backbone.

T3 lines

Internet backbone

Step 4
The request travels over T1 lines until it reaches the destination network server.

destination network server

T1 lines

server

Figure 10-19 This figure shows a simplified example of sending a request over the Internet using a variety of transmission media.

Scanrail1 / Shutterstock.com; Pablo Eder / Shutterstock.com; iStockphoto.com / skodonnell; iStockphoto.com / Andrey Prokhorov; iStockphoto.com / Andrey Prokhorov; iStockphoto.com / scanrail; iStockphoto.com / luismmolina; Scanrail1 / Shutterstock.com; Alfonso de Tomas / Shutterstock.com

Transmission Media

Transmission media consist of materials or substances capable of carrying one or more communications signals. When you send data from a computer or mobile device, the signal that carries the data may travel over various transmission media. This is especially true when the transmission spans a long distance. Figure 10-19 illustrates the variety of transmission media, including both physical and wireless, used to complete a data request over the Internet. Although many media and devices are involved, the entire communications process could take less than one second.

Broadband media transmit multiple signals simultaneously. The amount of data, instructions, and information that can travel over transmission media sometimes is called the **bandwidth**. The higher the bandwidth, the more data transmitted. For transmission of text only, a lower bandwidth is acceptable. For transmission of music, graphics, photos, virtual reality images, or 3-D games, however, you need a higher bandwidth. When the bandwidth is too low for the application, you will notice a considerable slowdown in system performance.

Latency, with respect to communications, is the time it takes a signal to travel from one location to another on a network. Several factors that negatively can affect latency include the distance between the two points, the type of transmission media, and the number of nodes through which the data must travel over the network. For best performance, bandwidth should be high and latency low. Read Ethics & Issues 10-3 to consider whether ISPs should be able to control Internet usage.

Should ISPs Be Allowed to Control Your Internet Usage?

People often compare the early days of the Internet and web to a wild frontier. ISPs simply offered customers an Internet connection and exerted no control over how the customer used the connection. This is similar to a phone company, which does not control who a customer calls, the length of a call, or the reason for the call. Online gaming, VoIP, video and audio streaming, and the use of web apps and cloud services led to an increased reliance on the Internet. Because of these increases, ISPs are attempting to regulate and limit their customers' usage.

Capping is a practice ISPs use that provides a certain amount of data usage at the optimal speed. Once a customer has used his or her allotted amount, the customer's Internet access is restricted, is slowed, or incurs additional costs. *Throttling* occurs when a network reduces upload and download speeds of certain high-data users at peak times in order not to tie up network resources for a small pool of users.

Controversy surrounds capping and throttling practices. Providers argue that caps are necessary to regulate traffic and ensure equal access to the Internet for all of its users. Critics argue that ISPs use limits to unfairly increase customer fees. Legislators are attempting to resolve the issues surrounding *net neutrality*, which is the concept of an open Internet, accessible to all users, without interference from ISPs or other third-parties. Proposals include standardizing how data transfer rates are measured and involving the Federal Communications Commission (FCC). The FCC would evaluate the regulations to ensure that ISPs intend merely to regulate traffic, rather than make a profit. It would examine whether caps or throttling are appropriate for low-usage times, such as in the middle of the night, and other related issues.

⊛ **Consider This:** Should ISPs control your Internet usage? Why or why not? Are data caps at peak usage times reasonable? Why or why not? Should the government enforce net neutrality? Why or why not?

Physical Transmission Media

Physical transmission media use wire, cable, and other tangible materials to send communications signals. These wires and cables typically are used underground or within or between buildings. Ethernet and token ring LANs use physical transmission media.

Table 10-3 lists the transfer rates of LANs using various physical transmission media. The following sections discuss each of these types.

Twisted-Pair Cable

One of the more widely used transmission media for network cabling and landline phone systems is twisted-pair cable. **Twisted-pair cable** consists of one or more twisted-pair wires bundled together (Figure 10-20). Each *twisted-pair wire* consists of two separate insulated copper wires that are twisted together. The wires are twisted together to reduce **noise**, which is an electrical disturbance that can degrade communications.

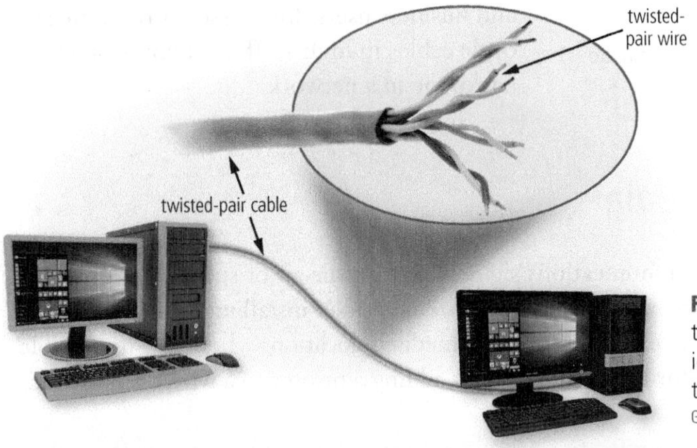

Table 10-3	Transfer Rates for Physical Transmission Media Used in LANs
Type of Cable and LAN	**Maximum Transfer Rate**
Twisted-Pair Cable	
• 10Base-T (Ethernet)	10 Mbps
• 100Base-T (Fast Ethernet)	100 Mbps
• 1000Base-T (Gigabit Ethernet)	1 Gbps
• Token ring	4 Mbps to 16 Mbps
Coaxial Cable	
• 10Base2 (ThinWire Ethernet)	10 Mbps
• 10Base5 (ThickWire Ethernet)	10 Mbps
Fiber-Optic Cable	
• 10Base-F (Ethernet)	10 Mbps
• 100Base-FX (Fast Ethernet)	100 Mbps
• FDDI (Fiber Distributed Data Interface) token ring	100 Mbps
• Gigabit Ethernet	1 Gbps
• 10-Gigabit Ethernet	10 Gbps
• 40-Gigabit Ethernet	40 Gbps
• 100-Gigabit Ethernet	100 Gbps

twisted-pair wire

twisted-pair cable

Figure 10-20 A twisted-pair cable consists of one or more twisted-pair wires. Each twisted-pair wire usually is color coded for identification. Landline phone networks and LANs often use twisted-pair cable.

Galushko Sergey / Shutterstock.com; iStockphoto.com / 123render; Scanrail1 / Shutterstock.com

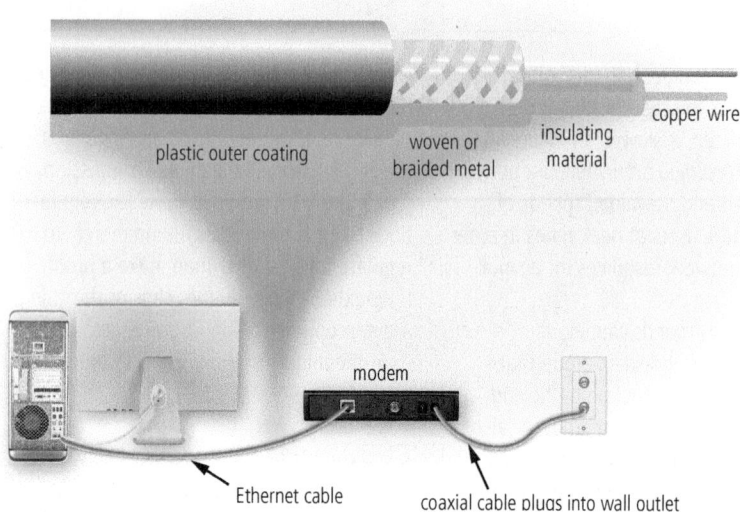

Figure 10-21 On coaxial cables, data travels through a copper wire. This simplified illustration shows a computer connected to a modem, which also is connected to the CATV network through a coaxial cable.
iStockphoto.com / THEPALMER; iStockphoto.com / Evgeny Karandaev; Courtesy of Zoom Telephonics, Inc.

Coaxial Cable

Coaxial cable, often referred to as *coax* (pronounced KO-ax), consists of a single copper wire surrounded by at least three layers: (1) an insulating material, (2) a woven or braided metal, and (3) a plastic outer coating (Figure 10-21).

CATV network wiring often uses coaxial cable because it can be cabled over longer distances than twisted-pair cable. Most of today's computer networks, however, do not use coaxial cable because other transmission media, such as fiber-optic cable, transmit signals at faster rates.

Fiber-Optic Cable

The core of a **fiber-optic cable** consists of dozens or hundreds of thin strands of glass or plastic that use light to transmit signals. Each strand, called an *optical fiber*, is as thin as a human hair. Inside the fiber-optic cable, an insulating glass cladding and a protective coating surround each optical fiber (Figure 10-22).

Fiber-optic cables have the following advantages over cables that use wire, such as twisted-pair and coaxial cables:

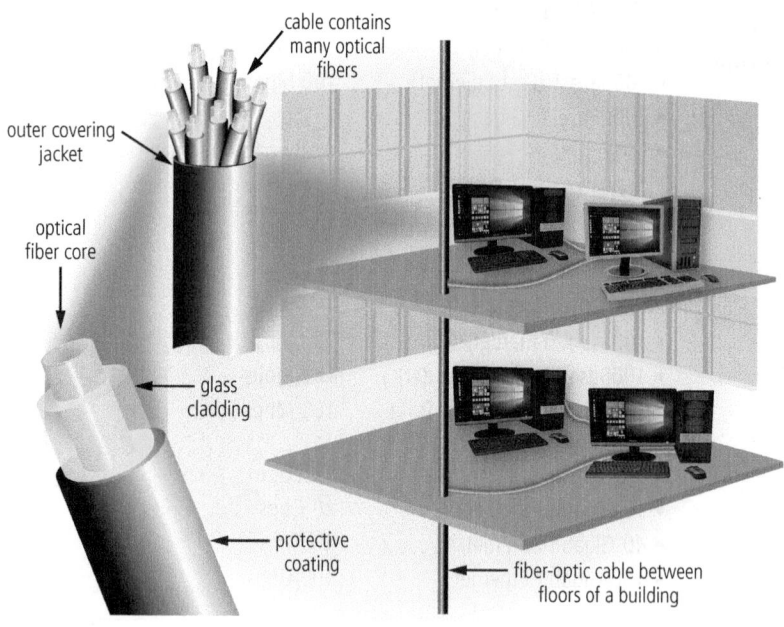

Figure 10-22 A fiber-optic cable consists of hair-thin strands of glass or plastic that carry data as pulses of light, as shown in this simplified example.
Scanrail1 / Shutterstock.com; iStockphoto.com / 123render; Scanrail1 / Shutterstock.com; Scanrail1 / Shutterstock.com

- Capability of carrying significantly more signals than wire cables
- Faster data transmission
- Less susceptible to noise (interference) from other devices, such as a copy machine
- Better security for signals during transmission because they are less susceptible to noise
- Smaller size (much thinner and lighter weight)

Disadvantages of fiber-optic cable are it costs more than twisted-pair or coaxial cable and can be difficult to install and modify. Despite these limitations, many phone companies replaced original analog phone lines with fiber-optic cables, enabling them to offer fiber-optic Internet access to home and business users. Businesses also use fiber-optic cables in high-traffic networks or as the backbone in a network.

Wireless Transmission Media

Wireless transmission media send communications signals through the air or space. Many users opt for wireless transmission media because it is more convenient than installing cables. In addition to convenience, businesses use wireless transmission media in locations where it is impossible to install cables. Read How To 10-3 for instructions about adding a printer to a wireless network.

✸ HOW TO 10-3

Add a Wireless Printer to a Home/Small Office Network

Adding a wireless printer to a home or small office network has several advantages. For example, multiple computers and mobile devices on the network can use the printer. You also can place the printer anywhere in the home or office, as long as it is within range of the wireless signal. For example, a wireless router can be on the first floor of your house, and a wireless printer can be on the second floor. The following steps describe how to add a wireless printer to a home/small office network:

1. Determine the location to install the wireless printer. This location must have an electrical outlet for the printer and also be within range of the wireless network. You can check the strength of wireless signals in your home or office by walking around

with a mobile computer or device while connected to the network and monitoring the signal strength.
2. Be sure to place the printer on a stable surface.
3. Access the printer's settings and navigate to the network settings.
4. Connect to the wireless network in your home or small office. If necessary, specify the encryption key for your network.
5. Enter any remaining required information.
6. Install the printer software on the computer(s) from which you want to print to the wireless printer. During the installation process, you will select the wireless printer that you have connected and configured. If the printer does not appear, return to Step 4 and try connecting the printer to the wireless network again.

If the problem persists, consider contacting the printer's manufacturer.
7. Verify the computers are able to print successfully to the wireless printer.

✸ **Consider This:** What are some ways to prevent some computers or mobile devices on your network from printing on your wireless printer?

iStockphoto.com / btrenkel

Types of wireless transmission media used in communications include infrared, broadcast radio, cellular radio, microwaves, and communications satellites. Table 10-4 lists transfer rates of various wireless transmission media, which are discussed in the following sections.

Infrared

As discussed earlier in the module, infrared (IR) is a wireless transmission medium that sends signals using infrared light waves. Mobile computers and devices, such as a mouse, printer, and smartphone, may have an IrDA port that enables the transfer of data from one device to another using infrared light waves.

Broadcast Radio

Broadcast radio is a wireless transmission medium that distributes radio signals through the air over long distances, such as between cities, regions, and countries, and short distances, such as within an office or home.

For radio transmissions, you need a transmitter to send the broadcast radio signal and a receiver to accept it. To receive the broadcast radio signal, the receiver has an antenna that is located in the range of the signal. Some networks use a transceiver, which both sends and receives signals from wireless devices. Broadcast radio is slower and more susceptible to noise than physical transmission media, but it provides flexibility and portability.

Bluetooth, UWB, and Wi-Fi communications technologies discussed earlier in this module use broadcast radio signals. Bluetooth and UWB are alternatives to infrared communications, with the latter designed for high-bandwidth transmissions. Hot spots use Wi-Fi.

Table 10-4	**Wireless Transmission Media Transfer Rates**	
Medium		**Maximum Transfer Transmission Rate**
Infrared		115 Kbps to 4 Mbps
Broadcast radio	• Bluetooth	1 Mbps to 24 Mbps
	• 802.11b	11 Mbps
	• 802.11a	54 Mbps
	• 802.11g	54 Mbps
	• 802.11n	300 Mbps
	• 802.11ac	500 Mbps to 1 Gbps
	• 802.11ad	up to 7 Gbps
	• UWB	110 Mbps to 480 Mbps
Cellular radio	• 2G	9.6 Kbps to 144 Kbps
	• 3G	144 Kbps to 3.84 Mbps
	• 4G	Up to 100 Mbps
Microwave radio		Up to 10 Gbps
Communications satellite		Up to 2.56 Tbps

 BTW

Data Transfer Rates
Tbps (terabits per second) is one trillion bits per second.

Cellular Radio

Cellular radio is a form of broadcast radio that is in wide use for mobile communications, specifically wireless modems and mobile phones (Figure 10-23). A mobile phone uses high-frequency radio waves to transmit voice and digital data messages. Because only a limited number of radio frequencies exist, mobile service providers reuse frequencies so that they can accommodate the large number of users. Some users install an amplifier or booster to improve the signal strength. Read Secure IT 10-4 to consider issues related to fake cell towers.

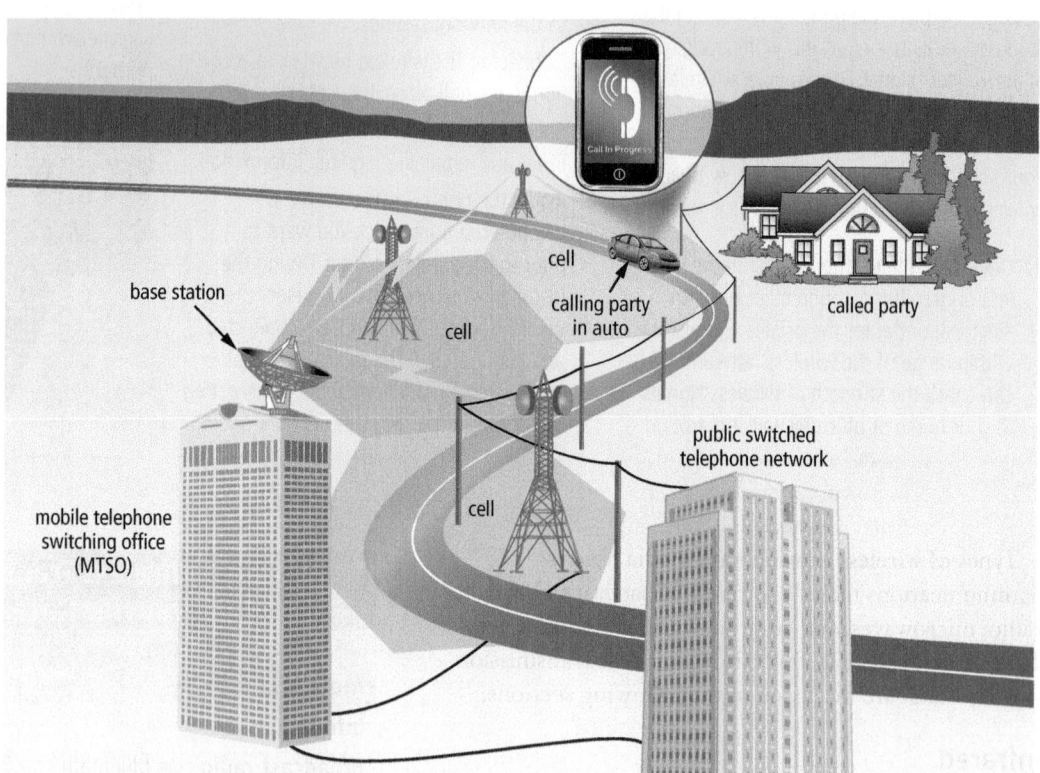

Figure 10-23   As a person with a mobile phone drives from one cell to another, the radio signals transfer from the base station (microwave station) in one cell to a base station in another cell.
Stuart Miles / Dreamstime.com

SECURE IT 10-4

Fake Cell Towers Are Tracking Devices

At least 17 cell towers located throughout the United States are intercepting mobile phone calls, according to technical security company ESD America. The company has identified these towers but does not know who owns them. It does know, however, that they do not belong to a mobile service provider or to the National Security Agency (NSA).

Every mobile device has a unique *International Mobile Subscriber Identity* (*IMSI*) that allows it to communicate with a cell tower. The interceptor technology on fake towers grasps, or catches, this IMSI signal; hence, it is known as an IMSI catcher.

According to some reports, cyberthieves can purchase IMSI catchers for $1,800 or can build the devices themselves. The interceptors, also called stingrays, slow the protocol, so consumers may notice that the display on their smartphone shows that the 4G connection has dropped to 2G and that the performance has degraded. Higher-quality interceptors, however, will not change the phone's display when the phone has been attacked.

The Federal Communications Commission (FCC) is investigating these fake towers to determine who or what entity is intercepting the calls. It has established a task force to

protect cellular networks and to address the threat of illicit IMSI catcher technology. It also is working with several industry organizations to develop new, secure cybersecurity standards. In addition, the FCC urges consumers to update their mobile devices' operating systems and apps because the latest software often addresses security vulnerabilities.

Consider This: Have you read any articles or publications disclosing the illicit and unauthorized use of IMSI catchers? Who or what organization do you think is using these interceptors?

Several categories of cellular radio transmissions exist, defining the development of cellular networks. Although the definitions of these categories may vary by mobile service providers, below are some general guidelines:

- *1G* (first generation of cellular transmissions)
    - Analog data transfer at speeds up to 14.4 Kbps
- *2G* (second generation of cellular transmissions)
    - Digital data transfer at speeds from 9.6 Kbps to 144 Kbps
    - Improved voice transmissions, added data communications, and added SMS (short message service) or text messaging services
    - Standards include *GSM* (Global System for Mobile Communications) and *GPRS* (General Packet Radio Service)
- *3G* (third generation of cellular transmissions)
    - Digital data transfer at speeds from 144 Kbps to 3.84 Mbps
    - Improved data transmissions, added MMS (multimedia message services)
    - Standards include *UMTS* (Universal Mobile Telecommunications System), CDMA (Code Division Multiple Access), EDGE (Enhanced Data GSM Environment), and EVDO (Evolution Data Optimized)
- *4G* (fourth generation of cellular transmissions)
    - Digital data transfer at speeds up to 100 Mbps
    - Improved video transmissions
    - Standards include Long Term Evolution (LTE), Ultra Mobile Broadband (*UMB*), and IEEE 802.16 (WiMAX)
- *5G* (fifth generation of cellular transmissions)
    - Future generation of cellular transmissions
    - Expected to improve bandwidth
    - Expected to provide artificial intelligence capabilities on wearable devices

Microwaves

Microwaves are radio waves that provide a high-speed signal transmission. Microwave transmission, often called *fixed wireless*, involves sending signals from one microwave station to another (Figure 10-24). A *microwave station* is an earth-based reflective dish that contains the antenna, transceivers, and other equipment necessary for microwave communications. As with infrared, microwaves use line-of-sight transmission. To avoid possible obstructions, such as buildings or mountains, microwave stations often sit on the tops of buildings, towers, or mountains.

Microwave transmission typically is used in environments where installing physical transmission media is difficult or impossible and where line-of-sight transmission is available. For example, microwave transmission is used in wide-open areas, such as deserts or lakes, between buildings in a close geographic area, or to communicate with a satellite. Current users of microwave transmission include universities, hospitals, city governments, CATV providers, and phone companies. Homes and small businesses that do not have other high-speed Internet connections available in their area also opt for lower-cost fixed wireless plans.

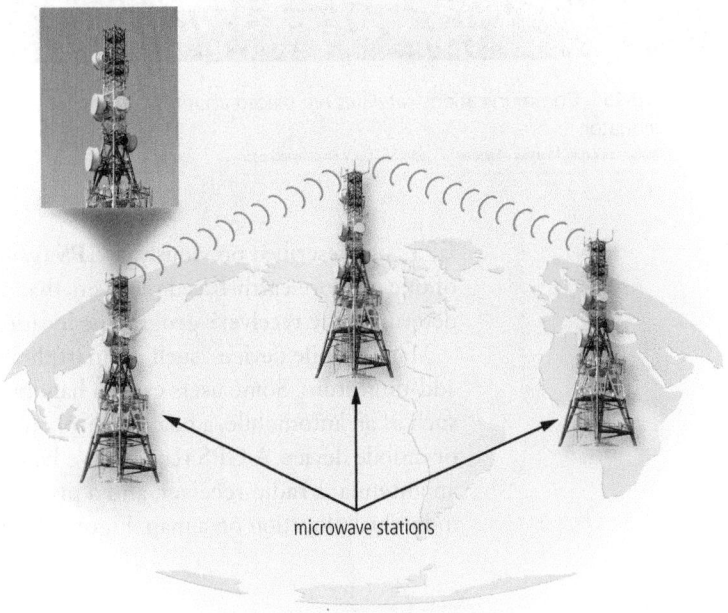

microwave stations

Figure 10-24   A microwave station is a ground-based reflective dish that contains the antenna, transceivers, and other equipment necessary for microwave communications.
Alfonso de Tomas / Shutterstock.com

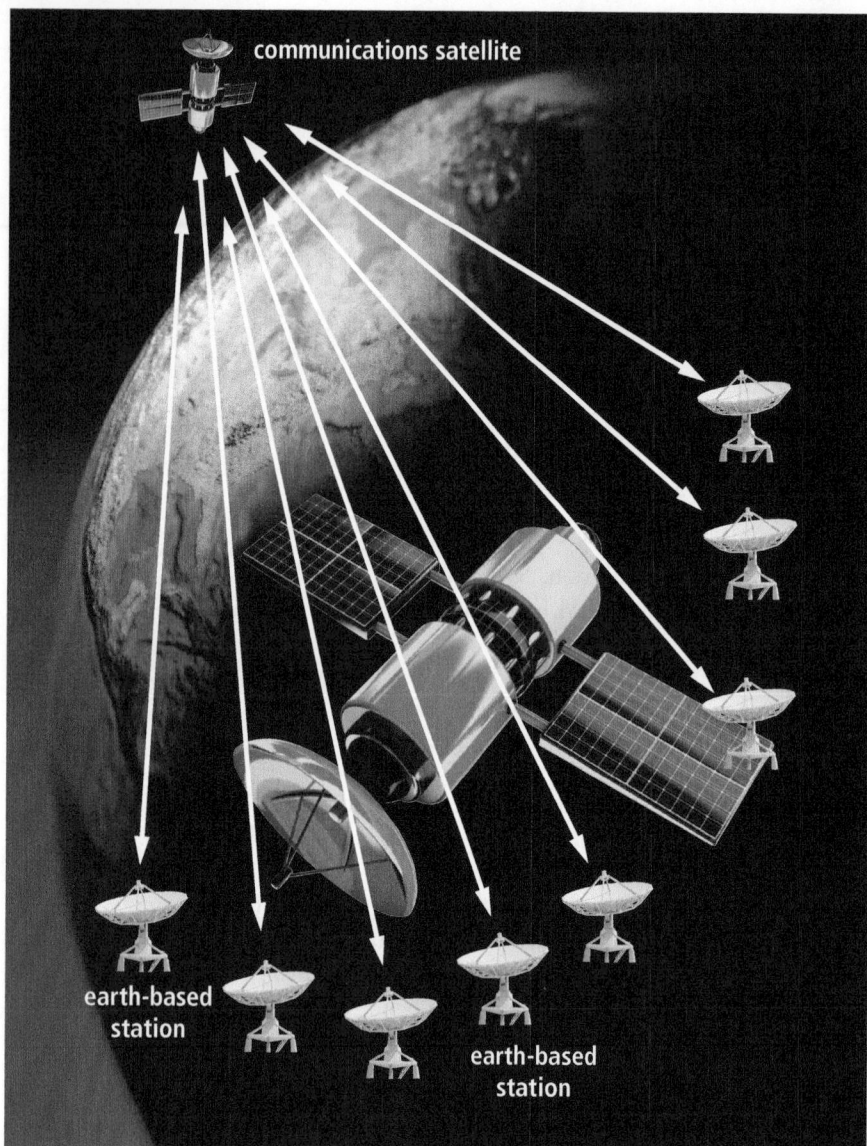

communications satellite

earth-based station

earth-based station

Figure 10-25 Communications satellites are placed about 22,300 miles above the Earth's equator.

Mmaxer / Shutterstock.com; Mmaxer / Shutterstock.com; SSSCCC / Shutterstock.com

Communications Satellite

A **communications satellite** is a space station that receives microwave signals from an earth-based station, amplifies (strengthens) the signals, and broadcasts the signals back over a wide area to any number of earth-based stations (Figure 10-25). These earth-based stations often are microwave stations. Other devices, such as smartphones and GPS receivers, also can function as earth-based stations. Transmission from an earth-based station to a satellite is an *uplink*. Transmission from a satellite to an earth-based station is a *downlink*.

Applications such as air navigation, television and radio broadcasts, weather forecasting, videoconferencing, paging, GPS, and Internet connections use communications satellites. With the proper satellite dish and a satellite modem, consumers can access the Internet using satellite technology. With satellite Internet connections, however, uplink transmissions usually are slower than downlink transmissions. This difference in speeds usually is acceptable to most Internet satellite users because they download much more data than they upload. Although a satellite Internet connection is more expensive than cable Internet or DSL connections, sometimes it is the only high-speed Internet option in remote areas.

GPS As described previously, a **GPS** (*global positioning system*) is a navigation system that consists of one or more earth-based receivers that accept and analyze signals sent by satellites in order to determine the receiver's geographic location.

Many mobile devices, such as smartphones, have GPS capability built into the device or as an add-on feature. Some users carry a handheld GPS receiver; others mount a receiver to an object such as an automobile, a boat, an airplane, farm and construction equipment, or a computer or mobile device. A GPS receiver is a handheld, mountable, or embedded device that contains an antenna, a radio receiver, and a processor. Many include a screen display that shows an individual's location on a map. Figure 10-26 shows how a GPS works.

Figure 10-26 This simplified figure shows how a GPS works.

 CONSIDER THIS

What are uses of GPS?

The first and most used application of GPS technology is to assist people with determining where they are located. The data obtained from a GPS, however, can be applied to a variety of other uses: creating a map, ascertaining the best route between two points, locating a lost person or stolen object, monitoring the movement of a person or object, determining altitude, and calculating speed.

Many vehicles use GPSs to provide drivers with directions or other information, such as alternate traffic routes, automatically call for help if the airbag is deployed, dispatch roadside assistance, unlock the driver's side door if keys are locked in the car, and track the vehicle if it is stolen. Newer GPS receivers and mobile apps that support GPS technology also provide information about nearby points of interest, such as gas stations, restaurants, and hotels. Hikers and remote campers may carry GPS receivers in case they need emergency help or directions.

Some GPS receivers work in conjunction with a cellular radio network. Parents, for example, can locate the whereabouts of a child who carries a mobile phone with GPS capability or other GPS-enabled device.

Summary

This module presented a variety of networks and communications technologies. It discussed various types of network architectures and standards and protocols. It explained communications software. Several types of communications lines and communications devices were presented. The module discussed how to create a home network. It also presented a variety of physical transmission media and wireless transmission media.

Study Guide

The Study Guide reinforces material you should know after reading this module.

Instructions: Answer the questions below using the format that helps you remember best or that is required by your instructor. Possible formats may include one or more of these options: write the answers; create a document that contains the answers; record answers as audio or video using a webcam, smartphone, or portable media player; post answers on a blog, wiki, or website; or highlight answers in the book/e-book.

1. List the device types and media you need for successful communications.

2. A(n) _____ is a collection of computers and devices connected together via communications devices and transmission media.

3. List reasons home and business users create a network. Identify how networks facilitate communications.

4. A(n) _____ is a third-party business that provides networking services, such as EDI.

5. Define the terms, intranet and extranet.

6. Differentiate among LANs, WLANs, MANs, WANs, and PANs.

7. Explain issues surrounding the use of BANs.

8. Name and describe two types of network architectures.

9. Define the terms, client and server.

10. Explain how P2P networks function, and describe the uses of P2P file sharing.

11. List functions of communications software. List and describe forms of immediate mobile communications.

12. Explain issues surrounding the use of telemedicine.

13. Define the terms, network standard and protocol. Explain whether they work together.

14. Define the term, Ethernet.

15. Explain what happens when two devices on an Ethernet attempt to send data at the same time.

16. Describe how a network transmits data using a token.

17. TCP/IP is the network standard for _____ communications. Describe how packet switching works.

18. Explain how network monitoring software and packet sniffers identify network security risks.

19. Explain whether you can use an IP address to determine a computer or device's location.

20. Describe how Wi-Fi enables users to connect to the Internet.

21. _____ is a network standard that defines how high-speed cellular transmissions use broadcast radio to transmit data for mobile communications.

22. List uses for Bluetooth devices. Name advantages and disadvantages of using Bluetooth.

23. Describe how to prevent Bluebugging.

24. Differentiate among UWB, IrDA, RFID, and NFC technologies.

25. Identify the role of a dedicated line. List types of digital dedicated lines.

26. Explain the advantages of cable Internet services and DSL.

27. List and differentiate among different T-carrier lines.

28. Define the term, communications device.

29. List and describe three widely used types of broadband modems.

30. Define the term, dial-up modem.

31. Define the terms, wireless modem and mobile hot spot.

32. List the steps to use your phone as a mobile hot spot.

33. Define the term, wireless access point. Explain how to strengthen your wireless signal.

34. Identify the role of a router. List types of routers that offer additional functionality.

35. To prevent unauthorized users from accessing files and computers, many routers are protected by a built-in _____ firewall.

36. Describe the function of a network card.

37. Identify the roles of hubs and switches on a network.

38. Explain how to determine if someone is accessing a wireless network without permission.

39. List questions to ask when planning a home network.

40. Identify hardware needed to set up a home network.

41. Define the terms, broadband, bandwidth, and latency.

42. Explain issues surrounding ISPs setting limits on Internet usage.

43. Name types of physical transmission media. Define the term, noise.

44. Identify advantages and disadvantages of fiber-optic cables.

45. List steps to add a wireless printer to a home/small office network.

46. Name types of wireless transmission media.

47. Explain how cyberthieves use fake cell towers to intercept communications.

48. Differentiate among 1G, 2G, 3G, 4G, and 5G cellular transmissions.

49. List uses of GPS.

You should be able to define the Primary Terms and be familiar with the Secondary Terms listed below.

Key Terms

Primary Terms (shown in **bold-black** characters in the module)

802.11 (10-12)
ATM (10-18)
bandwidth (10-26)
Bluetooth (10-13)
broadband (10-26)
broadcast radio (10-29)
cable modem (10-18)
cellular radio (10-30)
client/server network (10-7)
clients (10-7)
coaxial cable (10-28)
communications device (10-18)

communications satellite (10-32)
communications software (10-8)
dedicated line (10-16)
DSL (10-17)
DSL modem (10-19)
Ethernet (10-10)
fiber-optic cable (10-28)
FTTP (Fiber to the Premises) (10-17)
GPS (10-32)
home network (10-24)
IrDA (10-15)

latency (10-26)
local area network (LAN) (10-4)
LTE (10-12)
microwaves (10-31)
network (10-3)
NFC (10-16)
noise (10-27)
personal area network (PAN) (10-6)
receiving device (10-3)
RFID (10-15)
sending device (10-2)
server (10-7)

T-carrier line (10-18)
TCP/IP (10-11)
token ring (10-10)
transmission media (10-3)
twisted-pair cable (10-27)
UWB (ultra-wideband) (10-14)
wide area network (WAN) (10-6)
Wi-Fi (10-12)
wireless LAN (WLAN) (10-5)

Secondary Terms (shown in *italic* characters in the module)

1G (10-31)
2G (10-31)
3G (10-31)
4G (10-31)
5G (10-31)
ADSL (asymmetric digital subscriber line) (10-17)
Bluebugging (10-14)
body area network (BAN) (10-6)
broadband modem (10-18)
broadband router (10-21)
broadband wireless router (10-22)
cable Internet service (10-16)
capping (10-27)
coax (10-28)
communications channel (10-3)
dial-up modem (10-19)
digital modem (10-18)
Digital Subscriber Line (10-17)
downlink (10-32)
downstream rate (10-12)
EDI (electronic data interchange) (10-4)
electronic funds transfer (EFT) (10-4)
extranet (10-4)

file sharing network (10-8)
fixed wireless (10-31)
fractional T1 (10-18)
FTTB (Fiber to the Building) (10-17)
FTTH (Fiber to the Home) (10-17)
Gbps (10-10)
global positioning system (10-32)
GPRS (10-31)
GSM (10-31)
hardware firewall (10-22)
hub (10-23)
International Mobile Subscriber Identity (IMSI) (10-30)
intranet (10-4)
IP hijacking (10-24)
ISDN modem (10-19)
line-of-sight transmission (10-15)
Mbps (10-10)
metropolitan area network (MAN) (10-6)
microwave station (10-31)
mobile broadband wireless router (10-22)
mobile hot spot (10-19)
near field communications (10-16)

net neutrality (10-27)
network architecture (10-7)
network card (10-22)
network interface card (NIC) (10-22)
network monitoring software (10-12)
network standard (10-10)
node (10-4)
optical fiber (10-28)
packet sniffer software (10-12)
packet switching (10-11)
packets (10-11)
peer (10-7)
peer-to-peer (P2P) network (10-7)
protocol (10-10)
radio frequency identification (10-15)
router (10-21)

switch (10-23)
T1 line (10-18)
T3 line (10-18)
Tbps (10-29)
telemedicine (10-9)
throttling (10-27)
token (10-10)
twisted-pair wire (10-27)
UMB (10-31)
UMTS (10-31)
uplink (10-32)
upstream rate (10-13)
value-added network (VAN) (10-4)
wireless access point (10-20)
wireless Ethernet (10-12)
wireless modem (10-19)
wireless router (10-21)

Checkpoint   The Checkpoint exercises test your knowledge of the module concepts.

True/False   Mark T for True and F for False. If False, rewrite the statement so that it is True.

_____ 1. All types of computers and mobile devices serve as sending and receiving devices in a communications system.

_____ 2. Files on an intranet also are accessible from the Internet.

_____ 3. Disadvantages of BANs include data validity and security.

_____ 4. A peer-to-peer (P2P) network typically connects fewer than 10 computers.

_____ 5. Voice and video calling require large amounts of bandwidth.

_____ 6. UWB requires line-of-sight transmission, so its technology is not as widespread as IrDA.

_____ 7. For successful communications with NFC devices, the devices or objects must touch or be placed within an inch or two of each other.

_____ 8. DSL transmits on existing standard copper phone wiring.

_____ 9. Large corporations, phone networks, the Internet, and other networks with large amounts of traffic use DSL.

_____ 10. A broadband modem is a communications device that converts digital signals to analog signals and analog signals to digital signals, so that data can travel along an analog phone line.

_____ 11. Although some routers may be able to connect more than 200 wired and/or wireless computers and mobile devices, the performance of the router may decline as you add connections.

_____ 12. With satellite Internet connections, uplink transmissions usually are slower than downlink transmissions.

Matching   Match the terms with their definitions.

_____ 1. bandwidth

_____ 2. client

_____ 3. Ethernet

_____ 4. latency

_____ 5. LTE

_____ 6. packet sniffer software

_____ 7. protocol

_____ 8. network standard

_____ 9. TCP/IP

_____ 10. value-added network (VAN)

a. standard that outlines characteristics of how two devices communicate on a network

b. guidelines that specify the way computers access the medium to which they are connected, the type(s) of medium used, the speeds used on different types of networks, and the type(s) of physical cable and/or the wireless technology used

c. third-party business that provides networking services, such as EDI services, secure data and information transfer, storage, or email

d. program that monitors and logs packet traffic for later analysis

e. network protocol that defines how messages are routed from one end of a network to the other, ensuring the data arrives correctly

f. the amount of data, instructions, and information that can travel over transmission media

g. network standard that specifies no computer or device on the network should control when data can be transmitted

h. computers or mobile devices on the network that rely on the server for its resources

i. the time it takes a signal to travel from one location to another on a network

j. network standard that defines how high-speed cellular transmissions use broadcast radio to transmit data for mobile communications

The Problem Solving exercises extend your knowledge of module concepts by seeking solutions to practical problems with technology that you may encounter at home, school, or work. The Collaboration exercise should be completed with a team.

Problem Solving

Instructions: You often can solve problems with technology in multiple ways. Determine a solution to the problems in these exercises by using one or more resources available to you (such as a computer or mobile device, articles on the web or in print, blogs, podcasts, videos, television, user guides, other individuals, electronics or computer stores, etc.). Describe your solution, along with the resource(s) used, in the format requested by your instructor (brief report, presentation, discussion, blog post, video, or other means).

Personal

1. **Problems Exchanging Files**   You are attempting to use Bluetooth to send files from your phone to your computer. When you try sending the files from your phone, it does not display your computer as a device to which it can send the file. What might be the problem?

2. **Cannot Connect to Hot Spot**   You are sitting in a fast food restaurant that offers free Wi-Fi. When you search for available hot spots using your computer, the restaurant's hot spot does not appear in the computer's list of wireless networks. What are your next steps?

3. **Paired Bluetooth Devices**   You and your brother each have your Bluetooth-enabled smartphones paired with your car so that you can talk through the car's microphone and listen through its speakers. When you and your brother are both in the car at the same time, his phone rings but it is not connected to the car's audio. Why might this be the case?

4. **Slow Internet Connection**   Your Internet speed has suffered a sharp decline in performance recently. You have not added any computers or mobile devices to your house that might be accessing the network, and you are puzzled by the sudden performance problems. What might be the problem?

5. **Wireless Network Coverage**   You installed a new wireless network in your house. You notice that you sometimes have trouble connecting to the network 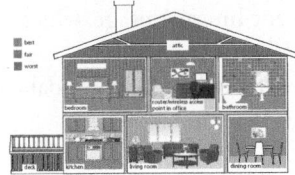 from certain locations in the house, but other times you can connect from the same location without issue. What might be causing the problem?

Professional

6. **Cannot Access Network**   You brought your personal laptop to your place of employment so that you can take care of some personal obligations while you are on lunch break. You successfully connect to your company's wireless network but are unable to access the Internet. What might be the problem?

7. **Cannot Sign In**   Your corporate network requires you to sign in with a user name and password as soon as your computer or mobile device connects. After entering your user name and password, the computer still does not connect to the network. What might be the problem?

8. **Too Many Networks**   While attempting to connect to the wireless network at your job, you notice that five different wireless networks are available. How can you determine the network to which you should connect?

9. **No Network Connection**   You have unpacked, installed, and turned on a new computer at your desk. When the operating system starts and you run the browser to display a webpage, you receive an error message stating that you are not connected to the Internet. You check the network card on the back of the computer and although the cable is plugged in, the lights next to the port are not flashing. What are your next steps?

10. **Connecting Corporate Email**   You are visiting your company's remote office for the day and realize that you do not have the necessary information to connect to their wireless network. Your boss has asked you to check your email throughout the day, so it is important that you connect to the Internet. What are your next steps?

Collaboration

11. **Technology in Agriculture**   Your employer owns hundreds of acres of orange groves and realizes labor and utility costs can be decreased by installing automated systems to manage the property. As a digitally literate employee of the organization, your supervisor asks you to research automated systems that can help decrease expenses. Form a team of three people to research automated agricultural solutions. One team member should research automated irrigation systems that water the trees only as needed. Another team member should research solutions that can keep the trees healthy and free from pests, and the third team member should create a list of reasons why these automated systems can decrease costs, bolster efficiency, and increase profit. Compile your findings and submit them to your instructor.

✳ How To: Your Turn

The How To: Your Turn exercises present general guidelines for fundamental skills when using a computer or mobile device and then require that you determine how to apply these general guidelines to a specific program or situation.

Instructions: You often can complete tasks using technology in multiple ways. Figure out how to perform the tasks described in these exercises by using one or more resources available to you (such as a computer or mobile device, articles on the web or in print, online or program help, user guides, blogs, podcasts, videos, other individuals, trial and error, etc.). Summarize your 'how to' steps, along with the resource(s) used, in the format requested by your instructor (brief report, presentation, discussion, blog post, video, or other means).

① Evaluate Internet Access Plans

If you are planning to connect to the Internet from your computer or mobile device, you will need to subscribe to an Internet access plan. Cable companies, phone companies, and mobile service providers all offer Internet access plans, so it is important to evaluate the plans in your area to determine which one is best for you. The following steps guide you through the process of evaluating Internet access plans.

a. Create a budget. Internet access plans are available for a monthly fee, so determine how much money you are able to spend for Internet access on a monthly basis.

b. Locate and list the Internet access plans available in your area. To determine Internet access plans that are available, check the local cable or phone company's website and search for available plans. You may have to enter your ZIP code to determine whether certain plans are available in your area. Alternatively, visit a local electronics store and inquire about wireless Internet access plans available in your area.

c. Compare Internet access speeds. Each Internet access plan may offer a different speed, so determine which speed is sufficient for you. If you mainly browse webpages and send or receive email messages, you may not need a plan that offers the fastest transfer rates. If you plan to download files, play online games, and watch movies on the Internet, you should consider a plan with faster transfer rates. You also should consider a plan with faster transfer rates if you will have multiple devices accessing the Internet simultaneously in your household. If an ISP offers multiple plans with a variety of transfer rates, it often will let you switch back and forth between plans without penalty so that you can find the one with the transfer rate that is best for you.

d. Check for package deals. If you already have service with an existing CATV or phone provider, they may be able to add Internet access to your current services at a reduced rate. Bundling multiple services can make each service (such as Internet access) less expensive, but you should be careful not to sign up for services you do not need.

e. Think about how much data you intend to transfer each month. Some Internet access plans limit the amount of data you can upload or download each month. While it can be difficult to determine how much data you will upload or download, you first should purchase a plan that might allow you to transfer more than you think you will need. Monitor your data usage each month and consider downgrading to a plan that provides the amount of data transfer that better represents your use.

f. Determine where you require Internet access. Some ISPs will allow you to use their hot spots for free in locations such as shopping malls, coffeehouses, and airports. Consider the additional locations from where you can access the Internet for free, and determine whether it makes the Internet access plan more desirable.

g. Consider whether a wireless Internet access plan is appropriate. While these plans can cost more and transfer rates often are not as fast, they do provide the flexibility of allowing you to connect to the Internet from almost anywhere. If you often travel and regularly need to access the Internet while away from home, a wireless Internet access plan might be right for you.

Exercises

1. What Internet access plans are available in your area?
2. Prepare a table comparing the Internet access plans in your area. Based on your current Internet usage, which plan appears to be the best? Why?
3. How can you determine approximately how much data you will transfer each month?

② Locate Hot Spots

If you are using a mobile computer or device and need to access the Internet, you will need to locate a hot spot. Hot spots are available in a variety of locations, such as coffeehouses, shopping malls, public libraries, airports, and educational institutions. Once you locate a hot spot, be sure to use it safely. Read Secure IT 2-1 in Module 2 for more information about using public Wi-Fi hot spots safely. If you plan to connect to a wireless hot spot, make sure you are authorized to connect.

For example, you should not connect to people's or businesses' hot spots without their knowledge or consent. If you are unsure of whether you are authorized to connect to a hot spot, contact someone representing the residence or business providing the hot spot. The following are guidelines that can assist you in locating a hot spot:

- Enable (turn on) your mobile computer or device's Wi-Fi and see whether it automatically detects any wireless networks. If one or more wireless networks are detected, connect to the one with the SSID that accurately describes your location. For example, if you are at a coffeehouse, the SSID of the wireless network might be the coffeehouse's name. If you unsure of the wireless network to which you should connect, contact an employee at the location and inquire. If the wireless network is protected with a password, the employee may be able to provide the password.
- You can check the location's website or app in advance to determine whether it has free Wi-Fi. For example, if you are flying out of your local airport, the airport's website might indicate whether Wi-Fi is available.
- Businesses offering free Wi-Fi sometimes have a decal on a front door or window indicating the location has Wi-Fi. If necessary, contact an employee to determine how to connect to the wireless network.
- Search for and navigate to a website that lists Wi-Fi hot spots in a particular area. These websites sometimes do not provide the most up-to-date information, so do not rely completely on the information you locate.

DeiMosz / Shutterstock.com

Exercises

1. What public hot spots are available near where you live?
2. Have you connected to a public hot spot before? If so, when?
3. What security risks may be associated with connecting to a public hot spot?

③ **Test Your Internet Speed**

Internet connection speeds will vary depending on the type of Internet connection you currently are using. If you believe your Internet speed is not what was promised by your Internet access provider, you can

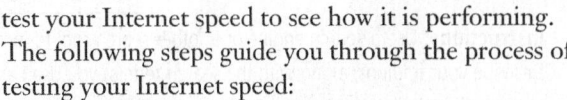

How To: Your Turn ✳

test your Internet speed to see how it is performing. The following steps guide you through the process of testing your Internet speed:

a. Turn off any computers or mobile devices that might be accessing the Internet, except for the computer on which you want to test your broadband speed.
b. If your broadband Internet service is provided through your phone company, do not talk on the phone during the test. If your CATV company provides your broadband Internet service, turn off all devices accessing the cable television. If you have cable boxes or converters, disconnect them from their power source so that they cannot communicate using the Internet connection while you are testing your broadband speed.
c. Run the browser.
d. Search for and navigate to a website that can test your Internet speed.
e. Click the button to start the test. The test may take up to one minute to complete before displaying results.
f. Internet speeds sometimes can vary with the time of day or day of the week. Repeat the previous steps to test your Internet speed at various times throughout the day, as well as on weekdays and weekends.
g. If you have any concerns regarding your Internet speed, contact your Internet access provider.

Exercises

1. What is the speed of the Internet connection on the computer or mobile device you currently are using?
2. Test your Internet speed while other computers and mobile devices also are using the Internet connection. How do the results vary from when your other devices are turned off?
3. Do you see differences in the Internet speed when you test it during the day versus at night? If so, what might explain these differences in speed?

speedtest.net

✸ Internet Research

The Internet Research exercises broaden your understanding of module concepts by requiring that you search for information on the web.

Instructions: Use a search engine or another search tool to locate the information requested or answers to questions presented in the exercises. Describe your findings, along with the search term(s) you used and your web source(s), in the format requested by your instructor (brief report, presentation, discussion, blog post, video, or other means).

1 Making Use of the Web
Blogs, Wikis, and Collaboration

Writers can publish their views and share their interests using blogs, as you learned in Module 2. The blogosphere began as an easy way for individuals to express their opinions on the web. Today, this communications vehicle has become a powerful tool for individuals, groups, and corporations to promote their ideas and to advertise their products. Individuals easily may set up a blog free or for a fee, and they do not need to have knowledge of web design or programming.

Wikis are collaborative websites. As discussed in Module 2, users can develop, modify, and delete content on these public or private websites. This information can include articles, documents, photos, and videos. Other collaboration websites, such as Google Docs, allow users to share documents and to work together in real time. All files are stored online, so participants can access these documents everywhere at any time.

Research This: (a) Visit two blogging services, such as Tumblr, WordPress, or Blogger. What steps are required to start a blog? Do these services have monthly or annual fees? Do storage limitations exist? What options are available to customize the design? Can products or services be sold or advertised? If you were to set up a blog, which topics would you cover? Could you assign your own domain name to your blog?

(b) Visit two reference wikis. Which subjects are featured? Which organizations host the websites? How are the wikis funded? Are they public or private? Who may edit the content? What procedure is used to add, modify, or delete information?

(c) Visit two collaboration websites. What features are available for sharing content, such as managing projects, scheduling, blogging, discussing forum topics,

Source: Tumblr, Inc.

publishing information, delivering announcements, or uploading photos and videos? Are chat windows and whiteboards offered? What is the charge for using these services? Do they offer a mobile app? Do members receive notifications when content is updated?

2 Social Media
Online Dating Websites

Using social media can be an excellent opportunity to unite with people who share similar interests. In some cases, local groups form for members to improve themselves and their communities. Dog owners, runners, photographers, entrepreneurs, parents, and travelers are among the thousands of groups with members who met online. In addition, more than 41 million people in the United States have subscribed to at least one of the 2,500 online dating services. Online dating can offer a safe opportunity to meet a variety of people if some practical advice is followed. Reputable dating services keep information confidential and have many members. Some have niche dating demographics, such as age, professions, religion, cultural interests, or geographical regions, and members can search for matches with desired criteria.

Research This: Search at least two online dating websites for information about these services. How many members do they have? What is the cost to join? What are the monthly membership fees? What claims do their privacy statements make about not disclosing personal information? What policies are in place to report members who have acted inappropriately?

3 Search Skills
Map Search

Search engines provide capabilities to search for maps, directions, and local attractions. Type search text in a search engine and then click the Maps link on a search engine's home page to see a map of locations for your search text. For example, type the search text, verizon wireless chicago, in the search box to find locations of Verizon Wireless stores in Chicago. Type the search text, cisco boston, to view the location of the Boston Cisco office on a map. To obtain directions, type the address to or from which to obtain directions, and specify walking, driving, or by public transportation. On mobile devices with GPS capability, you can specify to use your current location as a starting or

Internet Research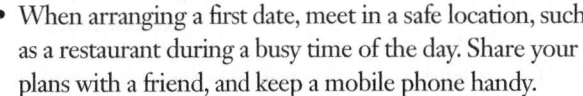

ending location. You also can search near a location. For example, type the search text, pizza near 125 high street boston, to display the names of pizza restaurants near that location. Some mapping search tools allow you to zoom, pan, and navigate a map in aerial view or street view, showing the location when looking from above or on the street.

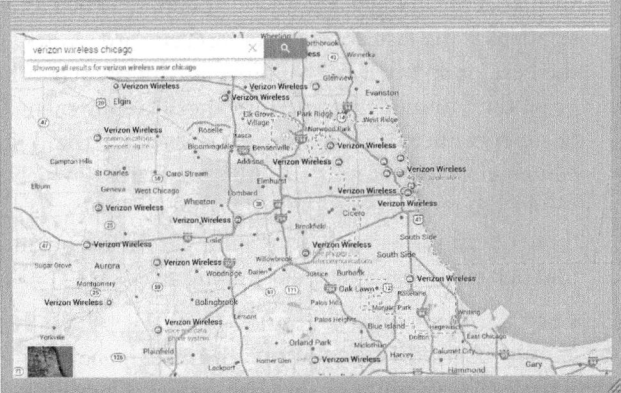

Source: Google, Inc.

Research This: Create search text using the techniques described above or in previous Search Skills exercises, and type it in a search engine to create maps that provide this information: (1) aerial and street view of your home, (2) directions to a local store that sells wireless networking equipment, (3) locations of your mobile service provider's retail stores in your current city, and (4) distance between Microsoft's headquarters in Redmond, Washington and Apple's headquarters in Cupertino, California. Take screenshots to capture and document your results.

4 Security
Online Dating Fraud

The Social Media exercise in this section discusses online dating websites. According to some of these dating services, 20 percent of people currently in committed relationships met online. While using these dating websites may result in a positive experience, the Better Business Bureau and other consumer-oriented organizations receive thousands of complaints each year about these services. Online dating fraud is rising, so security experts caution online dating members to follow safe practices, including the following:
- Compose a profile carefully, and be certain it reflects the image you want to portray. Do not post your full name, phone number, or home or work location.
- Use the service's messaging system before sending email or text messages or having a phone conversation.

- When arranging a first date, meet in a safe location, such as a restaurant during a busy time of the day. Share your plans with a friend, and keep a mobile phone handy.
- Trust your instincts. If you feel uncomfortable or threatened, leave the location and call a friend.

Research This: Visit at least two websites providing advice for online dating members. What guidance is provided in addition to the four safe practices listed above? What behaviors may signal potentially dangerous situations? Where can members verify other members' reputations? How can members report fraud and inappropriate behavior?

5 Cloud Services
Streaming Media from the Cloud (SaaS)

Streaming media allows users to play music or videos from the cloud without having to wait for the entire file to download. Streaming media is an example of software as a service (SaaS), a service of cloud computing that allows access to software apps using a browser, without the need to install software on a computer or device. Streaming media has become popular because of the decreasing cost of cloud storage; the increasing download speeds for business, home, and mobile users; and the growing number of devices available to play downloaded content.

When streaming, a provider sends the media to the user's device over the Internet in a compressed format. The user runs a media player app to uncompress the data as it arrives and then play the resulting audio data as sound; or, the user can display the resulting video data on mobile devices, computers, Smart TVs, and other devices that have an appropriate player.

Content providers, such as Netflix, Hulu, and Amazon, allow users to subscribe to their services for a monthly fee and watch videos on demand, or instantly, by streaming them to Internet-connected devices.

Individuals and businesses use streaming services to broadcast video of their events live, on the Internet in high definition. Many will use this service to broadcast presentations, product demonstrations, performances, and other events online.

Research This: (1) What file formats are used to compress audio and video files for streaming? (2) Compare the offerings of Netflix, Hulu, and Amazon for providing video on demand. Do you use any of these services? Which would you choose? Why? (3) Find a television or radio broadcast that is streamed live on the Internet and simultaneously broadcast "on air." Watch or listen to part of the live stream and then do the same for the broadcast on television or radio. How do the experiences and quality compare? What other events often are streamed live online?

✸ Critical Thinking

The Critical Thinking exercises challenge your assessment and decision-making skills by presenting real-world situations associated with module concepts. The Collaboration exercise should be completed with a team.

Instructions: Evaluate the situations below, using personal experiences and one or more resources available to you (such as articles on the web or in print, blogs, podcasts, videos, television, user guides, other individuals, electronics or computer stores, etc.). Perform the tasks requested in each exercise and share your deliverables in the format requested by your instructor (brief report, presentation, discussion, blog post, video, or other means).

1. Transmission Media

You work as an intern in the IT department for a local newspaper. The newspaper's management team recently approved a budget for redesigning the interior of its century-old building as part of an urban rehabilitation project. Because the employees at the newspaper more often use mobile devices and laptops than desktops, the newspaper plans to set up a wireless LAN.

Do This: Prepare information that summarizes the issues surrounding wireless network setup. Include the following information: What hardware is required for a wireless network? Could the thick walls in the building present a problem? If so, how can the issue be resolved? Does a wireless network present any health hazards? What security concerns exist for a wireless network? What advantages does a wireless network have over a wired network for the newspaper's needs?

iStockphoto.com / wsfurlan

2. Wireless Networking Standards

Several networking standards exist for wireless networks, including 802.11a, 802.11b, 802.11g, 802.11n, 802.11ac, 802.11ad, and 802.11af. You want to install a wireless network in your house and want to ensure that you choose the standard that best meets your needs.

Do This: Use the web to research the various wireless networking standards and answer the following questions: Which was the first developed standard?

Are any of the standards more susceptible to interference from other wireless devices in your home, such as alarm systems and mobile phones? Which standard is the fastest? Is the fastest standard always the best, or do other factors on your wireless network or on the Internet affect performance? Is equipment to support one standard more expensive than the equipment that supports the other standards? Which would you recommend? Why? Address the answers to those questions, as well as any other information you find pertinent. Compile your findings.

3. Case Study

Family-Owned Coffee Shop You are the new manager for a family-owned coffee shop. The shop's office equipment consists of a few laptops and tablets, a printer, and several smartphones. The owners have asked you to investigate how the shop might use Bluetooth technology.

Do This: Review the uses of Bluetooth technology listed in Tech Feature 10-2 in this module. Which uses might apply to the shop? Can you think of other ways the shop might use Bluetooth technology? What are the advantages of using Bluetooth technology? Use the web to find industry experts' recommendations for Bluetooth use in a small business. What other wireless technologies might the shop use? Examine issues related to bandwidth, speed, and reliability. What security concerns exist? What measures should the shop take to prevent Bluebugging? Would you recommend the shop use Bluetooth? Why or why not? Should the shop replace its LAN with Bluetooth? Why or why not? Compile your findings.

Collaboration

4. Network Security You are a network administrator for a small security firm. The company's main office includes 20 workers, most of whom use laptops. This year, the company plans to upgrade the network. The company asks your team to create a list of common network security issues, to make recommendations for hardware and software, and to create guidelines to secure the network.

Do This: Form a three-member team. As a team, list different networking security risks discussed in this module. Each member should choose a different risk to research. Members should determine the following: Describe the risk. Find an example of an industry article or blog post describing an experience with the risk. What damage was done? What steps did the network administrator take to recover from the damage, and/or prevent future attacks? What hardware or software can be used to safeguard against the risk? What guidelines for network users should be in place to help avoid the risk? As a team, compile your findings and share your recommendation with the class.

Building Solutions: Database, System, and Application Development Tools

11

OBJECTIVES

After completing this module, you will be able to:

1 Differentiate among a character, field, record, and data file and describe validation techniques

2 Differentiate between file processing systems and the database approach

3 Describe uses of web databases, types of databases, and Big Data

4 Discuss functions common to most database management systems: data dictionary, file retrieval and maintenance, data security, and backup and recovery

5 Define system development, list the system development phases, and identify the guidelines for system development

6 Discuss the importance of project management, feasibility assessment, documentation, and data and information gathering techniques

7 Discuss the purpose of and tasks conducted in each system development phase

8 Differentiate between low-level languages and procedural languages

9 Identify the benefits of object-oriented programming languages and application development tools

10 Describe various ways to develop webpages and web applications

Databases, Data, and Information

As presented in Module 4, a **database** is a collection of data organized in a manner that allows access, retrieval, and use of that data. As discussed in previous modules, data is a collection of unprocessed items, which can include text, numbers, images, audio, and video. Information is processed data; that is, it is organized, meaningful, and useful.

Computers process data in a database to generate information for users. A database at a school, for example, contains data about its students and classes (Figure 11-1).

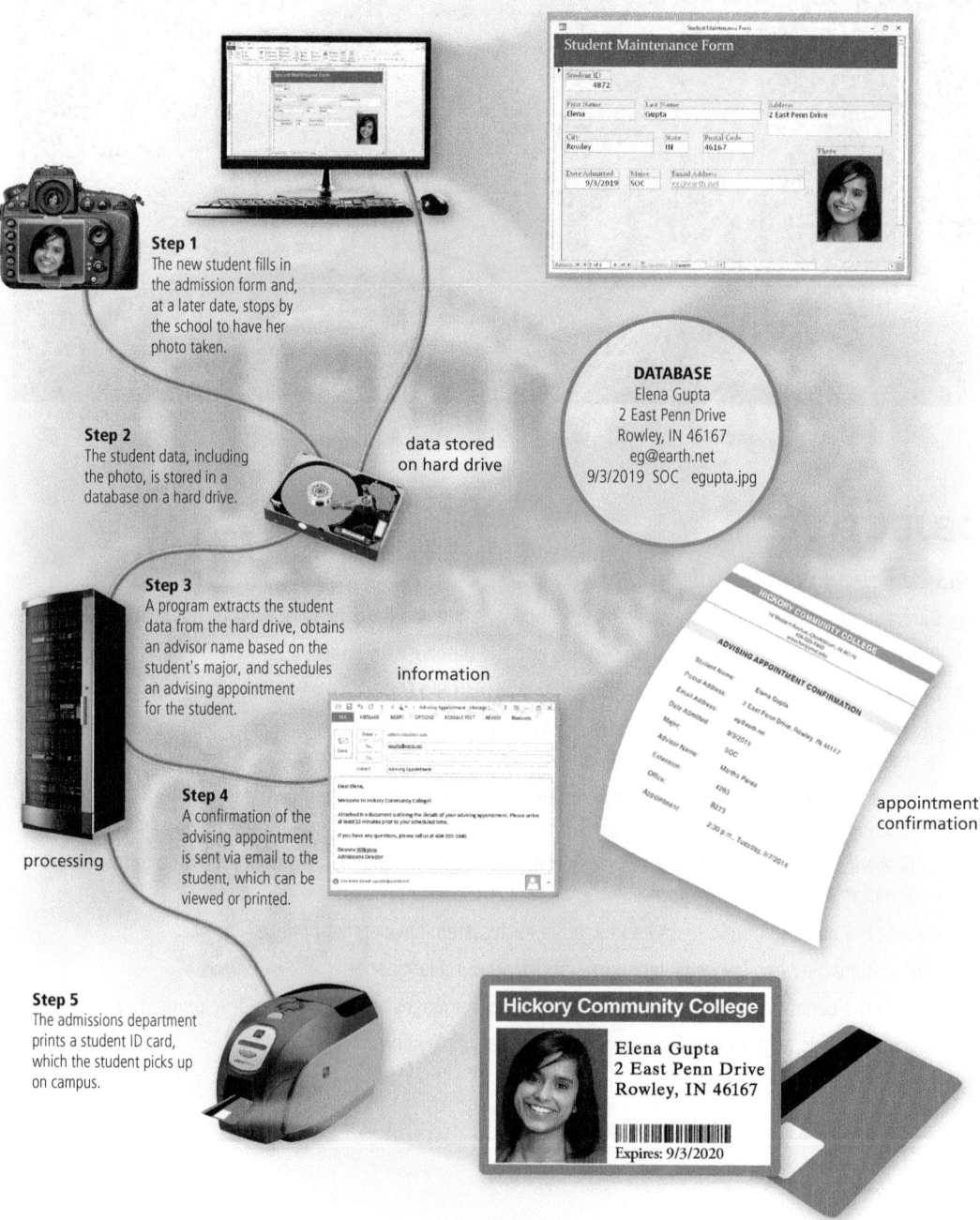

How a School's Admissions Department Might Process New Student Data into Information

Step 1
The new student fills in the admission form and, at a later date, stops by the school to have her photo taken.

Step 2
The student data, including the photo, is stored in a database on a hard drive.

data stored on hard drive

DATABASE
Elena Gupta
2 East Penn Drive
Rowley, IN 46167
eg@earth.net
9/3/2019 SOC   egupta.jpg

Step 3
A program extracts the student data from the hard drive, obtains an advisor name based on the student's major, and schedules an advising appointment for the student.

information

Step 4
A confirmation of the advising appointment is sent via email to the student, which can be viewed or printed.

processing

appointment confirmation

Step 5
The admissions department prints a student ID card, which the student picks up on campus.

Hickory Community College
Elena Gupta
2 East Penn Drive
Rowley, IN 46167
Expires: 9/3/2020

student ID encoded on magnetic stripe

Figure 11-1   This figure shows how a school's admissions department might process new student data into information.

When students are accepted to a school, they typically complete an online admission form that is displayed as a form in a browser. Students type their personal information into an online form and, at a later date, stop by the school to have their photo taken. Upon submitting the form, the page uploads the student's personal information in a database on a server at the school. When the school takes the student's photo, it also is stored in the school's database. The school's admission system assigns an ID number to the student and stores it in the database. The system then sends the student an email message with advising information. When the student's photo is taken on campus, relevant information is sent to an ID card printer, where the student's photo, name, and address is printed on the front of the card and the ID number is encoded on a magnetic stripe on the back of the card. Figure 11-1 illustrates this process.

With **database software**, often called a **database management system (DBMS)**, users create a computerized database; add, modify, and delete data in the database; sort and retrieve data from the database; and create forms and reports from the data in the database.

The Hierarchy of Data

Data is organized in levels. Information technology (IT) professionals classify data in a hierarchy. Each higher level of data consists of one or more items from the lower level. Depending on the application and the user, different terms describe the various levels of the hierarchy.

As shown in Figure 11-2, a database contains a group of related data files. A data file contains records, a record contains fields, and a field is composed of one or more characters. This sample School database contains four data files: Student, Instructor, Schedule of Classes, and Student Schedule.

- The Student file contains records about enrolled students.
- The Instructor file contains records about current instructors.
- The Schedule of Classes file contains records about class offerings in a particular semester.
- The Student Schedule file contains records about the classes in which a student is enrolled for a given semester.

 BTW

Tables
In some database programs, a data file is referred to as a table (i.e., Student table, Instructor table, etc.).

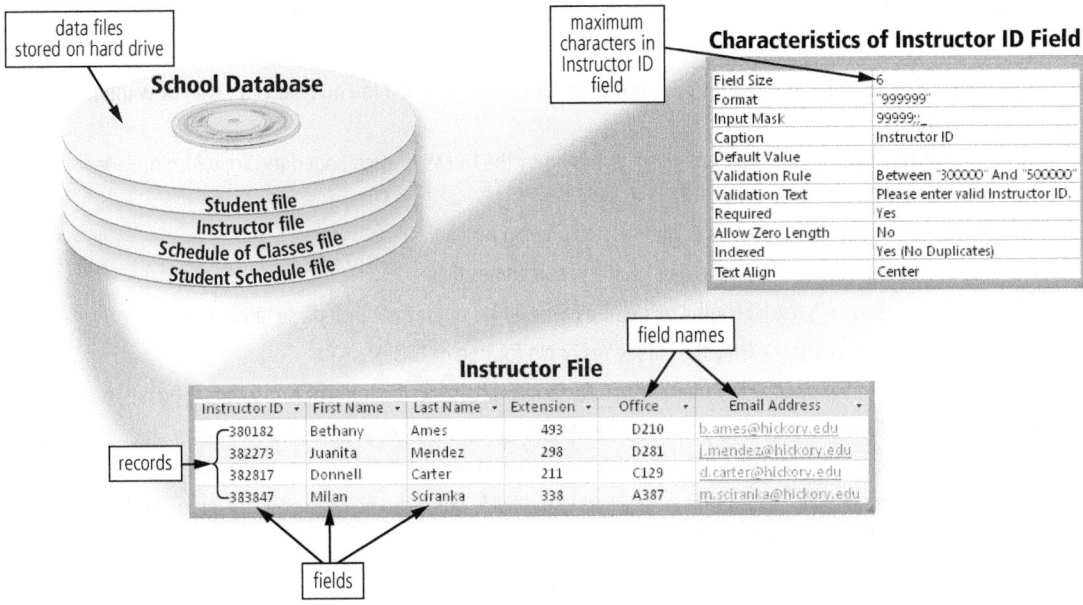

Figure 11-2 A sample school database with four data files: Student, Instructor, Schedule of Classes, and Student Schedule. The sample Instructor file contains four records. Each record contains six fields. The Instructor ID field can contain a maximum of six characters (bytes).
Source: Microsoft

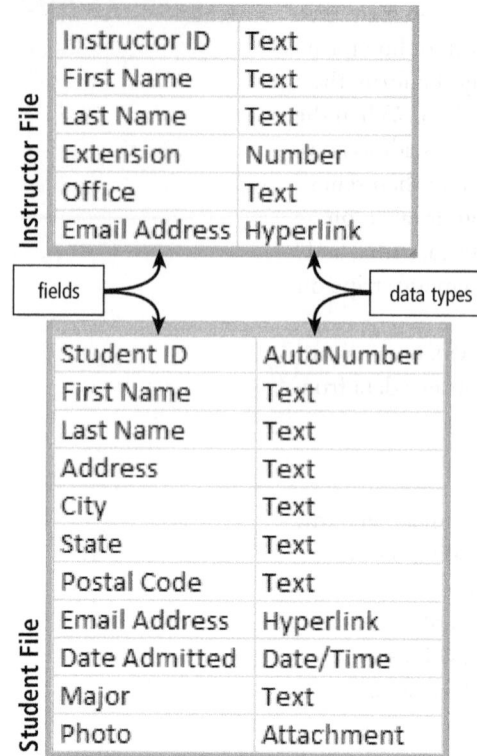

Figure 11-3 Data types of fields in the Instructor and Student files.

Characters As discussed in Module 6, a bit is the smallest unit of data the computer can process. Eight bits grouped together in a unit constitute a byte. In the ASCII coding scheme, each byte represents a single **character**, which can be a number (4), letter (R), blank space (SPACEBAR), punctuation mark (?), or other symbol (&).

Fields A **field** is a combination of one or more related characters or bytes and is the smallest unit of data a user accesses. A **field name** uniquely identifies each field. When searching for data in a database, you often specify the field name. For example, field names for the data in the Instructor file are Instructor ID, First Name, Last Name, Extension, Office, and Email Address.

A database uses a variety of characteristics, such as field size and data type, to define each field. The field size defines the maximum number of characters a field can contain. For example, the Instructor ID field contains 6 characters and thus has a field size of 6 (shown in Figure 11-2).

The **data type** specifies the kind of data a field can contain and how the field is used. Figure 11-3 identifies the data types for fields in the Instructor and Student files.

CONSIDER THIS ─────────────

What are common data types?
Common data types include the following:

- Text: Letters, numeric characters, or special characters
- Number (also called numeric values): Positive or negative numbers, and the number zero, with or without decimal points
- AutoNumber: Unique number automatically assigned by the DBMS to each added record, which provides a value that identifies the record (such as a student ID)
- Currency: Dollar and cent amounts or numbers containing decimal values
- Date (also called date/time): Month, day, year, and sometimes time
- Memo (also called long text): Lengthy text entries, which may or may not include separate paragraphs
- Yes/No (also called *Boolean*): Only the values Yes or No (or True or False)
- Hyperlink: Email address or web address that links to a webpage on the Internet or document on a network
- Object (also called *BLOB*, for binary large object): Photo, audio, video, or a document created in other programs or apps, such as word processing or spreadsheet, stored as a sequence of bytes in the database
- Attachment: Document or image that is attached to the field, which can be opened in the program that created the document or image (functions similarly to email attachments)

Records A **record** is a group of related fields. For example, a student record includes a set of fields about one student. A **primary key** is a field that uniquely identifies each record in a file. The data in a primary key is unique to a specific record. For example, the Student ID field uniquely identifies each student because no two students can have the same student ID. In some files, the primary key consists of multiple fields, called a *composite key*. For example, the primary key for the Schedule of Classes file could consist of the fields Semester Code, Class Code, and Class Section, which together would uniquely identify each class listed in a schedule.

Data Files A **data file**, often simply called a file, is a collection of related records stored on a storage medium, such as a hard drive, or on cloud storage. A Student file at a school might consist of thousands of individual student records. Each student record in the file contains the same fields. Each field, however, contains different data. Figure 11-4 shows a small sample Student file that contains four student records, each with eleven fields. A database includes a group of related data files.

Sample Student File

Student ID	First Name	Last Name	Address	City	State	Postal Code	Email Address	Date Admitted	Major	Photo
2295	Milton	Brewer	54 Lucy Court	Charlestown	IN	46176		6/10/2019	EE	mbrewer.jpg
3876	Louella	Drake	33 Timmons Place	Bonner	IN	45208	lou@world.com	8/9/2019	BIO	ldrake.jpg
3928	Adelbert	Ruiz	99 Tenth Street	Sheldon	IN	46033		10/8/2019	CT	aruiz.jpg
2872	Benjamin	Tu	2204 Elm Court	Rowley	IN	46167	tu@indi.net	9/14/2019	GEN	btu.jpg

 records   key field   fields

Figure 11-4 This sample data file, stored on a hard drive, contains four records, each with eleven fields.

✳ CONSIDER THIS
Why do some fields that store only numbers have a text data type?
Fields that contain numeric characters whose values will not be used in calculations, such as postal codes or phone numbers, usually are assigned a text data type.

File Maintenance

File maintenance refers to the procedures that keep data current. File maintenance includes adding records to, modifying records in, and deleting records from a file. Users add new records to a file when they obtain additional data that should be stored, such as data about a new student admitted to a school. Generally, users modify a record in a file for two reasons: (1) to correct inaccurate data or (2) to update old data with new data, such as replacing a student's address when she moves to a new address. When a record no longer is needed, a user deletes it from a file. For example, if a student was accepted for admission but later notifies the school that he chose to attend another college, the school might delete the student's records from its database. Read Ethics & Issues 11-1 to consider how organizations use data they collect.

ETHICS & ISSUES 11-1

What Use of Collected Data Is Fair?
A department store came under scrutiny recently for using customers' shopping habits and purchases to determine whether a customer was pregnant. The store used the data to send ads for baby products before some customers even announced that they were expecting. If you willingly purchase products at a store, can the business analyze your purchases to create a profile to use for marketing purposes? Can it sell that data to a third party?

Function creep occurs when a company uses the technology intended for one purpose for an entirely different purpose. One example of function creep is when companies use or sell customer data collected through sales transactions using customer loyalty cards or other customer tracking methods. While some

companies use data for their own purposes, such as to plan inventory or identify sales trends, others sell to data brokers or businesses that perform marketing surveys or generate credit reports. Privacy advocates are concerned about any use of personal data for purposes other than what the customer intended.

Online social networks and search engines often use activities, such as posts, pages viewed, and search terms, to suggest sponsored ads. Online vendors state that the data enables them to provide custom product suggestions and streamline ordering processes. Some customers acknowledge that a company has the right to use data to enhance the customers' experience or to make business decisions.

Many consumers would like more control over their data. The FTC Fair Information Practices (FIP) attempt to address data privacy concerns. FIP states that companies must inform customers of their data use and must allow customers to provide or deny consent. Criticisms include that the FIP guidelines are not legally binding and that other countries include more restrictions, as well as laws for regulating data collection and usage.

 Consider This: Have you experienced examples of a company using your personal data? For what purpose? Do you read a company's data privacy policy before using its website or service? Why or why not? How should the government enforce data privacy laws?

DBMSs use a variety of techniques to manage deleted or obsolete records. Sometimes, the DBMS removes the record from the file immediately, which means the deleted record cannot be restored. Other times, the record is flagged, or marked, so that the DBMS will not process it again. In this case, the DBMS places an asterisk (*) or some other character at the beginning of the record to indicate that it was deleted. DBMSs that maintain inactive data for an extended period commonly flag records. For example, a school might flag courses no longer offered or former employees no longer employed. When a DBMS flags a deleted record, the record remains physically on the drive. The record, however, is deleted logically because the DBMS will not process it. DBMSs will ignore flagged records unless an instruction is issued to process them.

 CONSIDER THIS

Can you permanently delete flagged records?
From time to time, users should run a program that removes flagged records and reorganizes current records. For example, the school may remove from the drive the names of applicants who chose to attend other schools instead. Deleting unneeded records reduces the size of files, thereby freeing up storage space.

Validating Data

Validation is the process of comparing data with a set of rules or values to determine if the data meets certain criteria. Many programs perform a validity check that analyzes data, either as you enter the data or after you enter it, to help ensure that it is valid. For instance, when an admissions department specialist adds or modifies data in a student record, the DBMS tests the entered data to verify it meets certain criteria.

If the data fails a validity check, the computer either should not allow the invalid data to be stored, or it should display an error message that instructs the user to enter the data again. Validity checks, sometimes called validation rules, reduce data entry errors and thus enhance the data's integrity.

Alphabetic/Numeric Check   An *alphabetic check* ensures that users enter only alphabetic data into a field. A *numeric check* ensures that users enter only numeric data into a field. For example, data in a First Name field should contain only characters from the alphabet. Data in a Current Enrollment field should contain integers.

Range Check   A *range check* determines whether a number is within a specified range. Assume the lowest per credit hour fee at the school is $75.00 and the highest is $370.75. A range check for the Credit Hour Fee field ensures it is a value between $75.00 and $370.75.

Consistency Check   A *consistency check* tests the data in two or more associated fields to ensure that the relationship is logical and their data is in the correct format. For example, the value in a Date Admitted field cannot occur earlier in time than a value in a Birth Date field.

Completeness Check   A *completeness check* verifies that a required field contains data. For example, some fields cannot be left blank; others require a minimum number of characters. One completeness check can ensure that data exists in a Last Name field. Another can ensure that a day, month, and year are included in a Birth Date field.

Check Digit   A *check digit* is a number(s) or character(s) that is appended to or inserted in a primary key value. A check digit often confirms the accuracy of a primary key value. Bank account, credit card, and other identification numbers often include one or more check digits.

Other Checks   DBMSs that include the hyperlink and attachment data types can perform validity checks on data entered in those fields. Hyperlink entries (web addresses and email addresses) can be tested to ensure that the address follows the correct format. Similarly, an attachment entry can be validated by confirming that the file exists.

Table 11-1 illustrates some of the validity checks just discussed and shows valid data that passes the check and invalid data that fails the check.

Table 11-1 Sample Valid and Invalid Data			
Validity Check	**Field(s) Being Checked**	**Valid Data**	**Invalid Data**
Alphabetic Check	First Name	Karen	Ka24n
Numeric Check	Current Enrollment	24	s8q
Range Check	Per Credit Hour Fee	$220.25	$2,120.00
Consistency Check	Date Admitted, Birth Date	9/19/2019 8/27/2000	9/19/2019 8/27/2020
Completeness Check	Last Name	Gupta	
Other Check	Email Address	eg@earth.net	egearth.net

File Processing Systems and Databases

Almost all applications use the file processing approach, the database approach, or a combination of both approaches to store and manage data. The next sections discuss these two approaches.

File Processing Systems

In the past, many organizations exclusively used file processing systems to store and manage data. In a typical **file processing system**, each department or area within an organization has its own set of files. The records in one file may not relate to the records in any other file. Many of these systems have two major weaknesses: redundant data and isolated data.

- **Redundant data:** Because each department or area in an organization has its own files in a file processing system, the same fields are stored in multiple files. If a file processing system is used at a school, for example, the Student file and the Student Schedule file both might store the same students' names and addresses.

  Duplicating data in this manner can increase the chance of errors. If a student changes his or her address, for example, the school must update the address in each file in which it appears. If the Address field is not changed in all the files where it is stored or is changed incorrectly in one location, then discrepancies among the files exist. This duplication also wastes resources, such as storage space and time. When new students are added or student data is modified, file maintenance tasks consume additional time because employees must update multiple files that contain the same data.

- **Isolated data:** It often is difficult to access data that is stored in separate files in different departments. Assume, for example, that the student email addresses exist in the Student files and class room numbers (locations) are in the Schedule of Classes file. To send an email message informing students about a room change, data is needed from both the Student file and the Schedule of Classes file. Sharing data from multiple, separate files to generate such a list in a file processing system often is a complicated procedure and usually requires an experienced programmer.

The Database Approach

When an organization uses a database approach, many programs and users share the data in the database. A school's database most likely, at a minimum, contains data about students, instructors, schedule of classes, and student schedules. As shown in Figure 11-5, various areas within the school share and interact with the data in this database. The database does secure its data, however, so that only authorized users can access certain data items. Read Ethics & Issues 11-2 to consider whether criminal databases are useful for law enforcement.

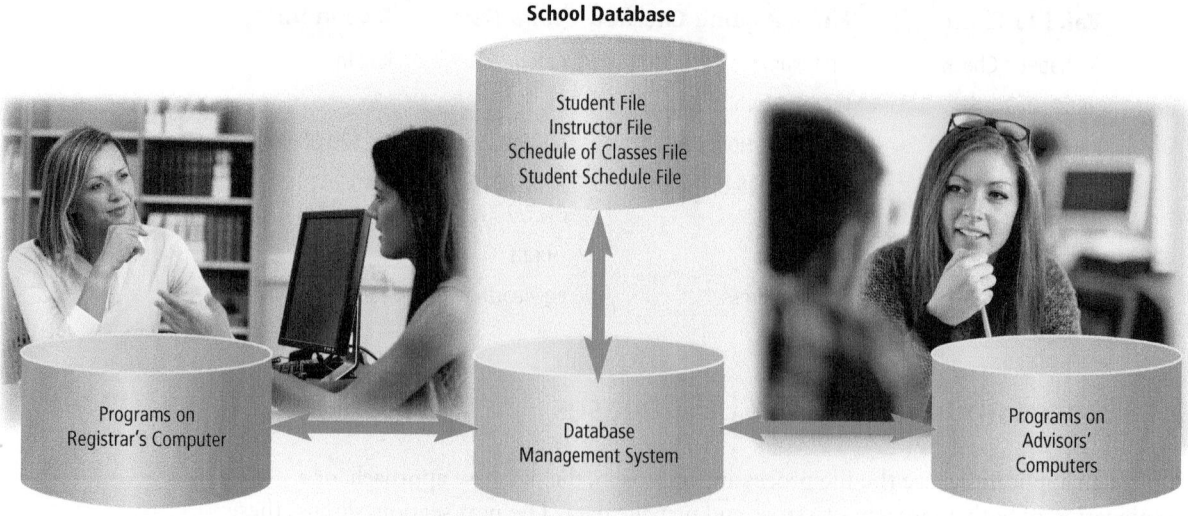

School Database

Student File
Instructor File
Schedule of Classes File
Student Schedule File

Programs on Registrar's Computer

Database Management System

Programs on Advisors' Computers

Figure 11-5 In a school's database, the computer used by the registrar and the computers used by advisors access data in the same database through the DBMS.

Does the Use of Criminal Databases Help or Hinder Investigations?
On television, detectives use databases to quickly compile a list of suspects for a crime. In these depictions, the list is complete, accurate, and leads to a speedy conviction. In reality, criminal databases are a helpful tool in solving crimes, but they are not without limitations. As with any database, the value depends on the quality of its information. If a criminal database contains data that is incomplete, inaccurate, or outdated, is it useful for law enforcement?

Many criminal databases exist at the county, state, and federal levels. Some information is mandatory, but other contributions to databases are voluntary or require only periodic updates. States' departments of correction record and share arrest records and jail time, but county or local jail records may not be included. Some courts and law enforcement use these databases for background checks to narrow a list of suspects or when determining sentencing. Others allow the use during an investigation, but findings are not admissible in court.

Megan's Law refers to a group of U.S. laws that require law enforcement agencies to share information in a national database about criminals who commit unlawful acts on children. States decide which information to make public and how to distribute the information. Often, states release criminals' names, photos, addresses, and information about the crime on a searchable, public website. Some states share information with one another regarding almost all criminals, and a few allow citizens to search for convicted criminals by name. Privacy experts feel that publishing this information makes it impossible for an offender who has served time to lead a normal life. Proponents state that the public's right to know outweighs the rights of privacy of those convicted.

✳ **Consider This:** Are criminal databases useful in law enforcement? Why or why not? Should information from criminal databases be admissible in court? Why or why not? What information should states provide to the public regarding people convicted of crimes? Why?

While a user is working with the database, the DBMS resides in the computer's memory. Instead of working directly with the DBMS, some users interact with a front end. A *front end* is a program that generally has a more user-friendly interface than the DBMS. For example, a registration department specialist interacts with the Class Registration program by filling out a form. This front-end program interacts with the DBMS, which, in turn, interacts with the database. Many programs today use forms on a webpage as their front end. An application that supports a front-end program by interacting directly with the database sometimes is called the *back end*. In this case, the DBMS is the back end.

Advantages of a Database Approach

The database approach addresses many of the weaknesses associated with file processing systems. Advantages of the database approach include the following:

- **Reduced data redundancy:** Most data items are stored in only one file, which greatly reduces duplicate data. For example, a school's database would record a student's name and address only once. When student data is entered or changed, one employee makes the change once. Figure 11-6 demonstrates the differences between how a file processing application and a database application might store data.

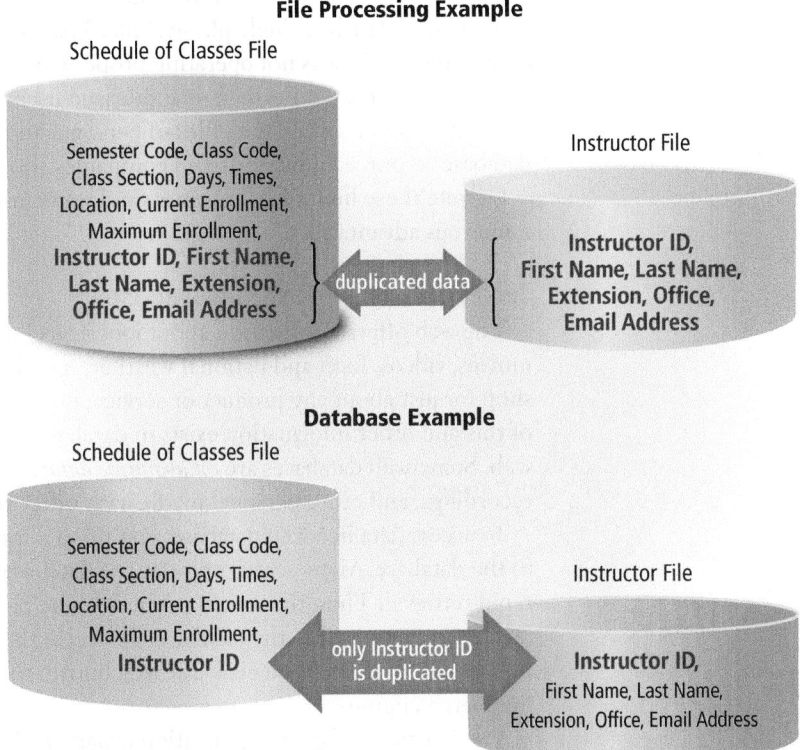

Figure 11-6   With file processing, both files contain all six instructor data fields. With a database, only the Instructor file contains the First Name, Last Name, Extension, Office, and Email Address fields. Other files, such as the Schedule of Classes file, contain only the Instructor ID — which links to the Instructor file when instructor data is needed.

- **Improved data integrity:** When users modify data in the database, they make changes to one file instead of multiple files. Thus, the database approach increases the data's integrity by reducing the possibility of introducing inconsistencies.
- **Shared data:** The data in a database environment belongs to and is shared, usually over a network, by the entire organization. This data is independent of, or separate from, the programs that access the data. Organizations that use databases typically have security settings to define who can access, add, modify, and delete the data in a database.
- **Easier access:** The database approach allows nontechnical users to access and maintain data, provided they have the necessary privileges. Many computer users also can develop smaller databases themselves, without professional assistance.
- **Reduced development time:** It often is easier and faster to develop programs that use the database approach. Many DBMSs include several tools to assist in developing programs, which further reduces the development time.

 CONSIDER THIS

Can a database eliminate redundant data completely?
No. A database reduces redundant data; it does not eliminate it. Key fields link data together in a database. For example, a Student ID field will exist in any database file that requires access to student data. Thus, a student ID is duplicated (exists in more than one file) in the database.

Disadvantages of a Database Approach A database can be more complex than a file processing system. People with special training usually develop larger databases and their associated applications. Databases also require more memory and processing power than file processing systems.

Data in a database can be more vulnerable than data in file processing systems because it can store a lot of data in a single physical file. Many users and programs share and depend on this data. If the database is not operating properly or is damaged or destroyed, users may not be able to perform their jobs. Further, unauthorized users potentially could gain access to a single database file that contains several data files of personal and confidential data. To protect their database resource, individuals and companies should establish and follow security procedures.

Despite these limitations, business and home users often work with databases because of their numerous advantages.

Tech Feature 11-1: Web Databases

The web offers information about jobs, travel destinations, television programming, photos, movies, videos, local and national weather, sporting events, and legislative information. You can shop for just about any product or service, buy or sell stocks, and make airline reservations. Much of this and other information exists in databases that are stored on or are accessible through the web. Some web databases are *collaborative databases*, where users store and share photos, videos, recordings, and other personal media with other registered users.

To access data in a web database, you fill in a form on a webpage. The webpage is the front end to the database. Many search engines use databases to store and index content from websites for rapid retrieval. Thus, the search engine's home page, containing a form in which to type search text, is the front end to the database. To access the search engine's database, you enter search text in a search form and then click a search button that instructs the form to send the search text to the search engine.

A web database for an organization usually resides on a database server. A *database server* is a computer that stores and provides access to a database. For smaller databases, many desktop database programs provide a variety of web publishing tools that enable users without computer programming experience to create a home or small office database. Read Tech Feature 11-1 to learn about types of web databases.

 **TECH FEATURE 11-1**

Web Databases

A database service, or a website that acts as a portal for a database, enables government agencies, schools, and companies to share information with a wide audience. Some web databases are accessible to the public. Examples of public databases include shopping and travel databases. Other databases contain information accessible only to authorized users. Examples of protected databases include certain government databases or entertainment and research databases that are subscription based.

Government

Government web database services can provide access to information about the government, as well as information created and used by government agencies. Some information that government agencies publish in databases is available to the public. Through these database services, for example, users can locate information about current laws. Other database services, such as those for criminal databases, allow access only to those individuals with necessary clearance. Government database services also enable officials around the world to share data.

Entertainment

You can search an entertainment web database service to find out who guest-starred on your favorite television program or locate video or audio clips. Using a subscription-based entertainment web database service allows you to access media content, such as music. These database services often enable you to create and share playlists. Entertainment professionals use subscription-based web databases to view and post casting notices or update artist profiles.

Travel

Booking online travel through a travel web database service enables you to view multiple vendors and options. You can limit a search to desired locations and dates. These database services help you find deals on air travel, car rentals, hotel rooms, and vacation packages. Travel web database services can save your personal data and travel history. These services will send notifications about upcoming travel deals and communicate changes or updates to your travel plans.

Shopping

Shopping web database services enable you to locate the right size and color, sort by price or featured products, and more. Vendors can use a web database service to show photos of items they sell and to track inventory. Some shopping database services search for bargains, presenting a variety of purchasing options so that you can find the lowest price. These database services also use your search and order history to suggest products in their databases that you may be interested in buying.

Research

You can interact with web databases to research product information when shopping for a new appliance or car. Information accessible through these web database services includes costs, safety concerns, and industry and user reviews. Some research web database services provide financial information for potential investors, including company histories and stock analysis. Research web database services are available to help you find a college or university and then provide information about admission requirements, financial information, and application advice.

Education

Teachers can search education web database services to locate and share curricula, worksheets, and lesson plans. Schools use web database services to store and distribute student contact information and grades. Students interact with web database services when signing up for their courses online. Using these services during enrollment helps a school determine when a class has reached its maximum size.

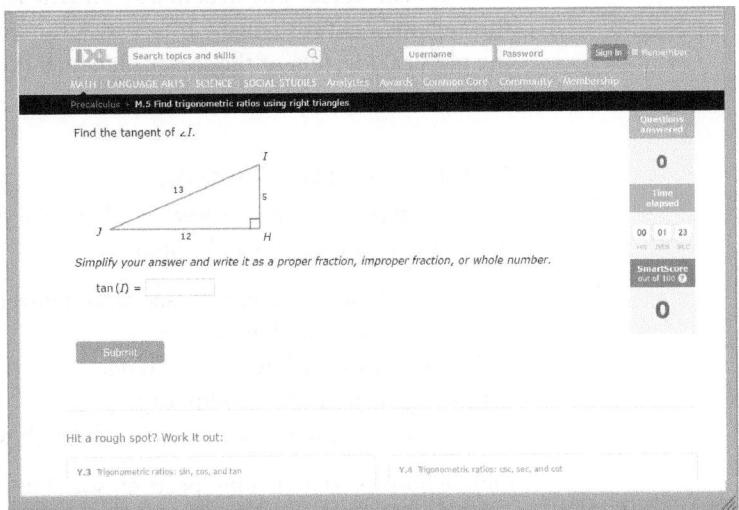

© 2016 IXL Learning.

Consider This: Which web database services have you used? How do web databases help you in your daily life? Would you use a web database for research? Why or why not?

Types of Databases

Every database and DBMS is based on a specific data model. A data model consists of rules and standards that define how the database organizes data. A **data model** defines how users view the organization of the data. It does not define how the operating system actually arranges the data on the storage media. A database typically is based on one data model. Three popular data models in use today are relational, object-oriented, and multidimensional.

Relational Database

A *relational database* is a database that stores data in tables that consist of rows and columns. In addition to storing data, a relational database also stores data relationships. A relationship is a link within the data. Applications best suited for relational databases are those whose data can be organized into a two-dimensional table, that is, tables with rows and columns. Many organizations use relational databases for payroll, accounts receivable, accounts payable, general ledger, inventory, order entry, invoicing, and other business-related functions.

Object-Oriented Database

An *object-oriented database* (*OODB*) stores data in objects. An *object* is an item that contains data, as well as the actions that read or process the data. Examples of applications appropriate for an object-oriented database include media databases that store images, audio clips, and/or video clips; groupware databases that store documents, such as schedules, calendars, manuals, memos, and reports; and CAD (computer-aided design) databases that store data about engineering, architectural, and scientific designs.

Multidimensional and Other Database Types

A *multidimensional database* stores data in dimensions. Whereas a relational database is a two-dimensional table, a multidimensional database can store more than two dimensions of data. These multiple dimensions allow users to access and analyze any view of the database data. One application that uses multidimensional databases is a data warehouse. A *data warehouse* is a huge database that stores and manages the data required to analyze historical and current transactions. The database in a data warehouse often is distributed. The data in a *distributed database* exists in many separate locations throughout a network or the Internet. Although the data is accessible through a single server, the physical location of the server on which it is stored is transparent and often unknown, to the user.

Tech Feature 11-2: Big Data

Recent technology trends have resulted in activities that generate large quantities of data. These trends include the following:

- Growth of online commerce, social, and government applications
- Increased use of mobile devices
- Emergence of the Internet of Things
- Development of cloud computing
- Availability of Internet connectivity through wired and wireless networks

Online business transactions, posts on social networks, government agencies, media and text messages from tablets and smartphones, and automated sensors produce data that is stored in databases located on servers distributed across the Internet. **Big Data** refers to large-scale data sets that require advanced technologies beyond the capabilities of typical database software to gather, store, process, retrieve, or analyze. Read Tech Feature 11-2 to learn more about characteristics and sources of Big Data, and technologies that facilitate working with large-scale distributed databases.

⊛ TECH FEATURE 11-2

Big Data

Through their daily activities, consumers, businesses, and machines produce large quantities of data to be stored on the Internet. Making sense of Big Data can provide valuable information to organizations trying to improve their business processes and make intelligent business decisions.

Characteristics of Big Data

Analysts often refer to the three V's when describing characteristics of Big Data: volume, velocity, and variety. Large-scale data sets grow in volume (how much data is generated), velocity (the rate at which data is generated), and variety (the different formats in which data can appear).

Volume refers to the amount of data that individuals and organizations generate. As data formats expand from text to images, files, audio, and video, it is common to need storage for multiple terabytes (1,000 gigabytes) of data. In the future, some organizations may require storage for petabytes (1,000 terabytes) and exabytes (1,000 petabytes) of data.

Velocity refers to the rate at which data is processed. In one day, for example, Google performs more than 7 billion searches, Facebook records more than 4.5 billion "likes," Twitter receives more than 500 million Tweets, and temperature and barometric sensors located across the world gather and transmit more than 200 million observations. In one minute, YouTube processes 300 hours of uploaded video. In one second, Amazon processes almost 400 transactions from customers during the company's sale day for its Prime customers.

Variety refers to the different formats to represent or store data for use by humans and computer applications. Some data, such as census records, stock values, and corporate sales, is structured, meaning it can be organized neatly in tables. Unstructured data generally is more complex and may include items such as Tweets, media files, Wikipedia articles, and fingerprints.

Some analysts have expanded the three V's to include veracity (how accurate the data is), value (how organizations use their data), and viability (whether organizations can make predictions based on this data).

Sources and Uses of Big Data

One way businesses generate Big Data is by capturing customer behaviors. For example, in addition to storing information about a customer's purchase, some shopping websites also gather data about how much time customers spend on a webpage, how many items they view before making a purchase, and which pages on the company's website that customers visited, in order to create a more customized experience. Amazon and other retailers compile data from customer purchases in a process called collaborative filtering to recommend related products. For example, Amazon recommends that customers who purchase a digital camera might also want to purchase a storage card or a camera case.

© 1996–2016, Amazon.com, Inc. or its affiliates.

Government agencies generate large amounts of data in real time from satellite images, social media posts, and media. By analyzing this data, they can monitor transportation systems, dispatch first responders in emergencies, and provide consumers with information to make informed choices about health care, schools, and community services.

Temperature and barometric sensors, wearable devices, and buses and trains equipped with GPS capability all transmit data over the Internet to be used in a variety of web and mobile applications.

Data Visualization

Data visualization is the process of presenting data graphically as charts, maps, or other pictorial formats in order to understand the resulting information easily. As the size of databases grows, data visualizations make it possible to interpret complex data sets, find relationships among data items, and discover patterns that can provide useful information. The "Racial Dot Map" shown in the figure is a visualization

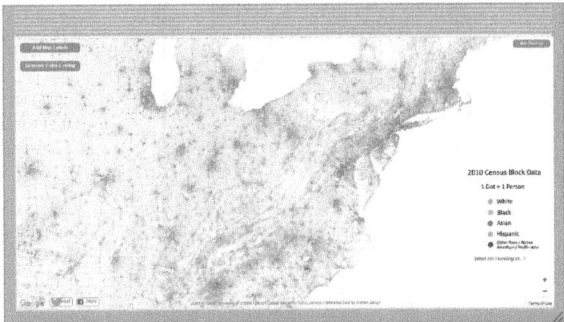
Weldon Cooper Center for Public Service, Rector and Visitors of the University of Virginia (Dustin A. Cable, creator).

that displays one dot per person in the United States. Each dot is colored by ethnicity. The figure shows the map zoomed in on the Boston area.

⊛ **Consider This:** What websites or apps do you use that generate or take advantage of Big Data? How have cloud computing, online social networks, and the Internet of Things contributed to and enabled the growth of Big Data? What visualizations have you seen that help make sense of complex data sets?

Database Management Systems

As previously discussed, a database management system (DBMS), or database program, is software that allows you to create, access, and manage a database. Managing a company's databases requires a great deal of coordination. The *database administrator (DBA)* is the person in the organization who is responsible for managing and coordinating all database activities, including development, maintenance, and permissions.

DBMSs are available for many sizes and types of computers. Whether designed for a small or large computer, most DBMSs perform common functions. The following pages discuss these functions.

BTW

Metadata
Because the data dictionary contains details about data, some call it *metadata* (meta means more comprehensive).

Data Dictionary

A **data dictionary**, sometimes called a *repository*, contains data about each file in the database and each field in those files. For each file, it stores details such as the file name, a description, the file's relationship to other files, and the number of records in the file. For each field, it stores details such as the field name, description, field type, field size, default value, validation rules, and the field's relationship to other fields. Figure 11-7 shows how a data dictionary might list data for a Student file.

A DBMS uses the data dictionary to perform validation checks to maintain the integrity of the data. When users enter data, the data dictionary verifies that the entered data matches the field's data type. For example, the data dictionary allows only dates to be entered in a Date Admitted field. The data dictionary also can limit the type of data that can be entered, often allowing a user to select from a list. For example, the data dictionary ensures that the State field contains a valid two-letter state code, such as IN, by presenting a list of valid state codes to the user.

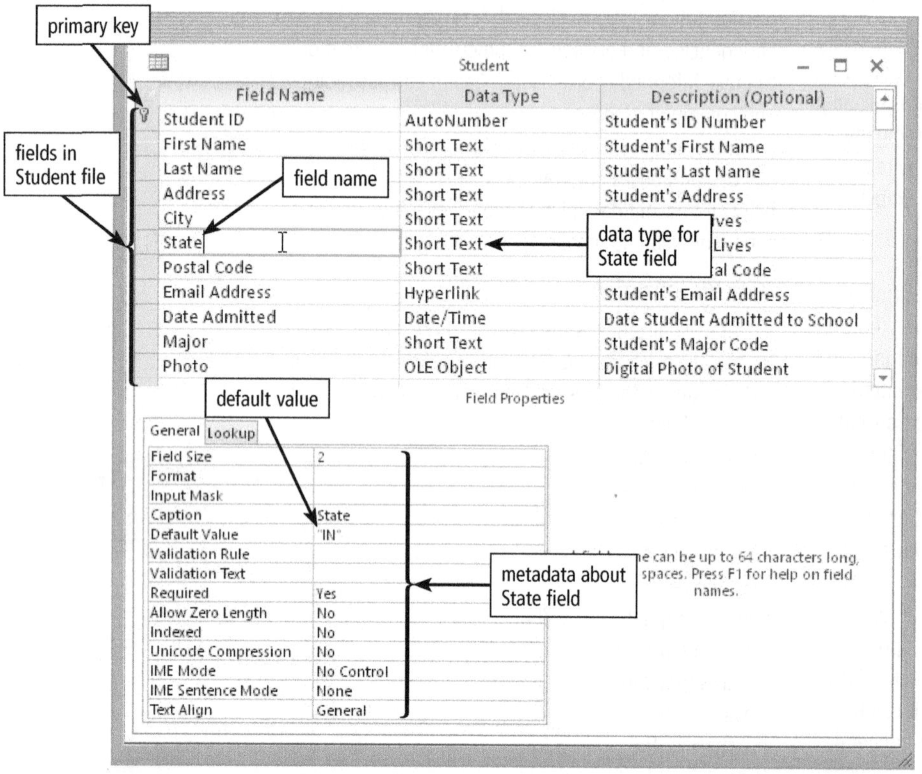

Figure 11-7   A sample data dictionary entry shows the fields in the Student file and the properties of the State field.
Source: Microsoft

File Retrieval and Maintenance

A DBMS provides several tools that allow users and programs to retrieve and maintain data in the database. To retrieve or select data in a database, you query it. A **query** is a request for specific data from the database. Users can instruct the DBMS to return or store the results of a query. The capability of querying a database is one of the more powerful database features.

A DBMS offers several methods to retrieve and maintain its data. The four more commonly used are query languages, query by example, forms, and report writers. Another method is by importing data.

Query Language   A **query language** consists of simple, English-like statements that allow users to specify the data they want to display, print, store, update, or delete. Each query language has its own formats and vocabulary.

Structured Query Language (SQL pronounced S-Q-L or sequel) is a popular query language that allows users to manage, update, and retrieve data. SQL has special keywords and rules that users include in SQL statements. Figure 11-8a shows an SQL statement that creates the results shown in Figure 11-8b.

Figure 11-8a   (SQL statement)

```
SELECT CLASS_TITLE, CLASS_SECTION,
  MAXIMUM_ENROLLMENT - CURRENT_ENROLLMENT AS SEATS_REMAINING
FROM SCHEDULE_OF_CLASSES, CLASS_CATALOG
WHERE SCHEDULE_OF_CLASSES.CLASS_CODE = CLASS_CATALOG.CLASS_CODE
ORDER BY CLASS_TITLE
```

Figure 11-8b   (SQL statement results)

Class Title	Class Section	Seats Remaining
Algebra 1	51	14
Art Appreciation	52	19
English Composition 1	02	5
Introduction to Sociology	01	14

Figure 11-8   A sample SQL statement and its results. Notice that the query results show meaningful column headings instead of the actual SQL field names.
Source: Microsoft

Query by Example   Most DBMSs include *query by example (QBE)*, a feature that has a graphical user interface to assist users with retrieving data. Figure 11-9 shows a sample QBE screen for a query that searches for and lists students majoring in sociology; that is, their Major field value is equal to SOC.

Figure 11-9a   (all records in Student table)

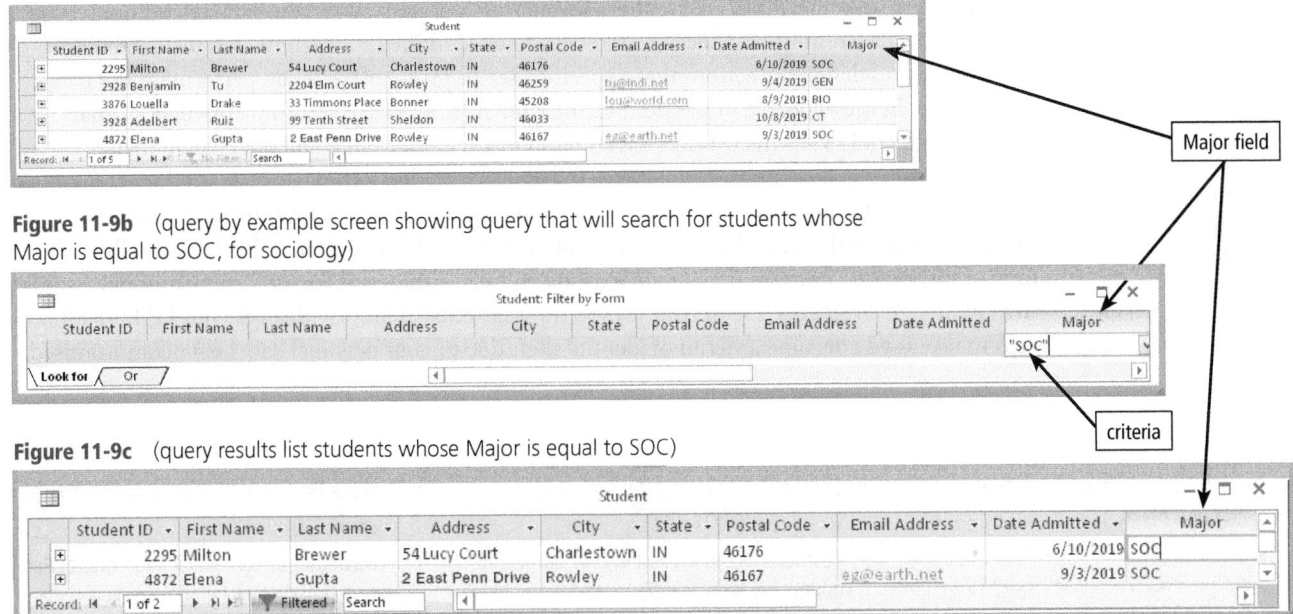

Figure 11-9b   (query by example screen showing query that will search for students whose Major is equal to SOC, for sociology)

Figure 11-9c   (query results list students whose Major is equal to SOC)

Figure 11-9   Shown here is a Microsoft Access QBE, which searches for students whose major is sociology.
Source: Microsoft

Form   A **form**, sometimes called a *data entry form*, is a window on the screen that provides areas for entering or modifying data in a database. You use forms (such as the Student Maintenance Form in Figure 11-1 at the beginning of this module) to retrieve and maintain the data in a database. To reduce data entry errors, well-designed forms should validate data as it is entered.

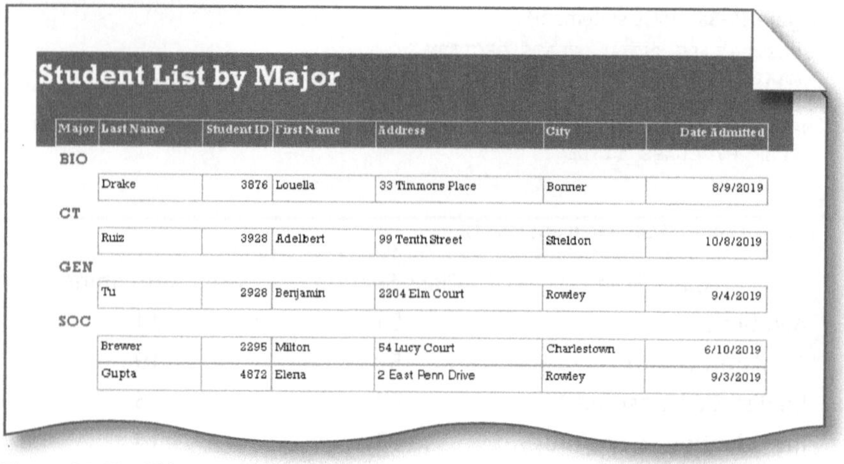

Student List by Major

Major	Last Name	Student ID	First Name	Address	City	Date Admitted
BIO						
	Drake	3876	Louella	33 Timmons Place	Bonner	8/9/2019
CT						
	Ruiz	3928	Adelbert	99 Tenth Street	Sheldon	10/8/2019
GEN						
	Tu	2928	Benjamin	2204 Elm Court	Rowley	9/4/2019
SOC						
	Brewer	2295	Milton	54 Lucy Court	Charlestown	6/10/2019
	Gupta	4872	Elena	2 East Penn Drive	Rowley	9/3/2019

Figure 11-10 This report, created in Microsoft Access, displays student information by major.
Source: Microsoft

Report Writer A **report writer,** also called a *report generator*, allows users to design a report on the screen, retrieve data into the report design, and then display or print the report (Figure 11-10). Unlike a form, you use a report writer only to retrieve data. Report writers usually allow you to format page numbers and dates; titles and column headings; subtotals and totals; and fonts, font sizes, color, and shading; and to include images. Some report writers allow you to create a report as a webpage.

Data Security

Most organizations and people realize that data is one of their more valuable assets. To ensure that data is accessible on demand, an organization must manage and protect its data just as it would any other resource. Thus, it is vital that the data is kept secure. For example, data in a database often is encrypted to prevent unauthorized users from reading its contents, and its access is restricted to only those who need to process the data.

A DBMS provides means to ensure that only authorized users can access data. In addition, most DBMSs allow different levels of access privileges to be identified for each field in the database. Access privileges define the actions that a specific user or group of users can perform on the data. For example, in the Schedule of Classes file, the student would have read-only privileges. That is, the student could view the list of classes offered in a semester but could not change them. A department head, by contrast, would have full-update privileges to classes offered during a particular semester, meaning he or she can view and modify the data. Finally, some users have no access privileges to the data; that is, they cannot view or modify any data in the database. Read How To 11-1 for ways to secure and maintain a database. Read Ethics and Issues 11-3 to consider issues surrounding governments' use of databases to track citizens' identities. Read Secure IT 11-1 for steps to take if you become a victim of identity theft due to your personal data being compromised.

BTW

Principle of Least Privilege

Many organizations adopt a *principle of least privilege policy*, where users' access privileges are limited to the lowest level necessary to perform required tasks to prevent accidental or intentional misuse of the data.

HOW TO 11-1

Secure and Maintain a Database

As you add and delete tables and records from your database, you should secure and maintain the database so that it can continue operating securely and efficiently. If you neglect to secure and maintain a database, chances increase that the data can become compromised or inaccessible. The following guidelines describe how to secure and maintain a database.

Secure the Database

- Each person accessing the database should have a profile that includes a user name, a strong password that must be changed frequently, and limits on database system-level access.
- Only administrators should have access to create and delete tables.
- Consider allowing typical users only to view or modify records.
- Restrict users to accessing only database tables and records that are necessary to perform their job function(s).
- Limit the number of unsuccessful sign-in attempts in a specified period, and record when users access the database.

Maintain the Database

- If the database contains a table that you do not need (and you do not foresee a future need for the data in that table), remove the table from the database.
- Evaluate the fields in all remaining tables and make sure they are assigned the proper data type. Make any necessary adjustments.
- Remove fields you no longer need from the tables in your database.
- If the database contains a large number of records, consider deleting records you no longer need.
- Navigate to and then click the command to compact and repair the database (if available).
- If you want to protect the data in the database, consider selecting the option to encrypt the database.

Consider This: What problems may arise from individuals or companies failing to properly secure and maintain their databases?

ETHICS & ISSUES 11-3

Should Governments Use Databases to Track and Identify Citizens?

Government agencies collect citizens' information through many methods, using data from the Social Security Administration, fingerprints captured for military or law enforcement use, and other legal methods. Governments across the world justify this type of information gathering as protection against terrorism, identity fraud, and criminal activity. What is more important — a government's obligation to protect its citizens, or an individual's right to privacy?

With global terrorism a threat and individual identity theft on the rise, many governments argue that using collected information to create national

identification (ID) cards is essential to providing national security. Privacy advocates express concerns about the effect ID cards have on civil liberties. The United States, Australia, and the United Kingdom are among countries that have resisted making national ID cards mandatory.

National ID cards can be used to verify a citizen's rights to employment, purchasing property, voting, and receiving benefits. If a citizen does not provide an ID card, he or she can then be denied those basic rights. Opponents argue not only that individual's civil rights are at risk, but that the risks of security breaches if a card is lost or stolen, or if the database itself is hacked, can lead to more problems. National ID card

processes are expensive, and the regulations around distributing and securing the cards raise further questions. The collection of biometric data, including fingerprints, DNA, iris scans, and facial or voice recognition are seen by some as security methods against fraud, and by others as invasions of privacy.

Consider This: Would you submit your DNA or other biometric data to an employer or government official? Why or why not? Are you in favor of national ID cards? Why or why not? If you were proposing legislation for ID cards, what restrictions might you impose, and what reasons would you give for their necessity?

SECURE IT 11-1

Recovering from Identity Theft

Every two seconds, someone becomes a new identity fraud victim, according to Javelin Strategy & Research. Data breaches in businesses, banks, medical centers, and schools have affected nearly 39 percent of Americans. This crime is the complaint most often reported to the Federal Trade Commission (FTC).

On average, victims of identity theft spend 25 hours settling the resulting issues. Experts recommend that people who have experienced identity theft should follow this advice as part of their resolution efforts:

• **Request a fraud alert.** Contact the fraud department at the three national credit reporting companies: Experian, Equifax, and TransUnion. (Refer to the How To: Your Turn student assignment in this module for details about contacting these agencies.) One agency should report the theft to the other two companies, but you might want to contact all three to be certain the fraud has been noted. Request that a fraud alert be placed on your accounts to help prevent credit accounts from being opened in your name. This free service requires lenders

to contact the account owners if a new request for credit is submitted. This fraud alert must be renewed every 90 days.

• **Order credit reports.** Once you file a fraud alert, you are entitled to receive a free credit report. Wait at least 30 days from the theft to obtain the report, however, because creditors may report activity on a monthly basis, and your most current report may not include current information. Request that only the last four digits of your Social Security number are shown on the report.

• **Obtain an FTC affidavit and file it with law enforcement agencies.** The FTC's Identity Theft Victim's Complaint and Affidavit is accepted as proof of your identity. Download the form from the FTC's website and then file it with the police. The form also can be used to dispute claims with creditors.

• **Report Internet crime to the Internet Crime Complaint Center.** Report stolen finances or identities and other cybercrime to the Internet Crime Complaint Center. This organization is a partnership between the Federal Bureau of Investigation and the National White Collar Crime Center.

• **Keep records of your actions.** Create a journal that records the names of people you called, phone numbers, dates, and correspondence sent.

• **Review financial accounts.** Look for unusual activity, and check to see if any accounts were opened recently. Continue reviewing the accounts even if you do not see any questionable transactions.

• **Enroll in a credit monitoring service.** Each of the three national credit reporting agencies and many credit card companies provide this service. The companies send messages to subscribers when unusual activity is detected on a credit card account to alert consumers to possible identity theft. This service can be useful for people who have large balances in savings and checking accounts, travel frequently, or fail to check their bank statements and credit reports regularly.

Consider This: Do you know someone who has been a victim of identity theft? If so, which type of fraud occurred? What activity did this person take to report this crime and to restore personal records and accounts?

Backup and Recovery

Occasionally, a database is damaged or destroyed because of hardware failure, a problem with the software, human error, or a catastrophe, such as fire or flood. A DBMS provides a variety of techniques to restore the database to a usable form in case it is damaged or destroyed.

• A backup, or copy, of the entire database should be made on a regular basis. Some DBMSs have their own built-in backup tools. Others require users to purchase a separate backup program, or use one included with the operating system.

- More complex DBMSs maintain a **log**, which is a listing of activities that modify the contents of the database. If a registration department specialist modifies a student's address, for example, the change appears in the log.

- A DBMS **recovery utility** uses logs and/or backups, and either a rollforward or a rollback technique, to restore a database when it becomes damaged or destroyed. In a *rollforward*, also called *forward recovery*, the DBMS uses the log to reenter changes made to the database since the last save or backup. In a *rollback*, also called *backward recovery*, the DBMS uses the log to undo any changes made to the database during a certain period. The rollback restores the database to its condition prior to the failure. Depending on the type of failure, the DBMS determines which type of recovery technique to use.

- **Continuous backup** is a backup plan in which changes are backed up as they are made. This backup technique can cost more than other backup strategies but is growing in popularity for businesses whose data must be available at all times, because it provides recovery of damaged data in a matter of seconds. Organizations such as hospitals, communications companies, and financial institutions often use continuous backup.

Tech Feature 11-3: Forensic Databases

The collection and analysis of biometric and other data used in criminal investigations is called *digital forensics*. By accessing data — such as fingerprints, facial and voice recognition, and handwriting analysis — stored in a structured database, investigators can significantly reduce time spent wading through hard copy files.

Databases also can increase accuracy and widen the scope of an investigation by pooling data from other counties and states into national databases. In addition to biometric data, forensic databases can include crime statistics, criminal profiles, connections among known criminals, and more. Read Tech Feature 11-3 to learn more about how scientists use forensic databases to solve crimes.

 TECH FEATURE 11-3

Forensic Databases

Mega Pixel/Shutterstock.com

The first time a fingerprint at a crime scene was used to link a suspect to a crime occurred in 1879 in Tokyo, Japan. A hospital had been burglarized, and the police had a suspicion of who had committed the crime. The swirls on a fingerprint left on a wall, however, did not match the alleged criminal's fingertip, and he was released.

The process of matching fingerprints now is performed through the FBI's Next Generation Identification (NGI) System. This system provides more accurate biometric recognition and quicker response times than the Integrated Automated Fingerprint Identification System (IAFIS) it is predicted to replace. Detectives will scan fingerprints they find at crime scenes, and the NGI computer will search the database of more than one million fingerprints from criminal and civil subjects and attempts to find similarities in the loops, arches, and whorls. The NGI's Rap Back function gives criminal justice entities, such as law enforcement agencies and parole offices, updated status notifications of crimes committed by people holding positions of trust, such as caregivers and teachers. In addition, the Interstate Photo System (IPS) facial recognition service permits police to search photo images of people associated with criminal identities.

At times, forensic scientists cannot locate fingerprints, but they do find palmprints, which burglars can leave on windows, doorknobs, window ledges, paper, and weapons. The Royal Canadian Mounted Police (RCMP) are adding palmprints to its fingerprint database. RCMP

forensic experts locate palmprints in 30 percent of the crime scenes they investigate. They are hopeful the expanded database, along with their use of sensitive Vacuum Metal Deposition (VMD) technology, will help them to recover prints from evidence in cold cases. The VMD instrument creates a vacuum, allowing metal to vaporize and adhere to fingerprint or palmprint residue on fabrics, firearms, plastic, and other nonporous and partially porous objects.

Cultura Creative (RF) / Alamy Stock Photo

✻ **Consider This:** In what other scenarios might forensic databases be useful? What additional fields could be added to forensic databases to assist criminal justice entities in their crime investigations?

System Development

An *information system* is a collection of hardware, software, data, people, and procedures that work together to produce information. As a user of technology in a business, you someday may participate in the modification of an existing information system or the development of a new one. Thus, it is important that you understand system development.

System development is a set of activities used to build an information system. System development activities often are grouped into larger categories called *phases*. This collection of phases sometimes is called the **system development life cycle** (**SDLC**). Many traditional SDLCs contain five phases (Figure 11-11):

1. Planning
2. Analysis
3. Design
4. Implementation
5. Support and Security

Each system development phase consists of a series of activities, and the phases form a loop. In theory, the five system development phases often appear sequentially, as shown in Figure 11-11. In reality, activities within adjacent phases often interact with one another, making system development a dynamic, iterative process.

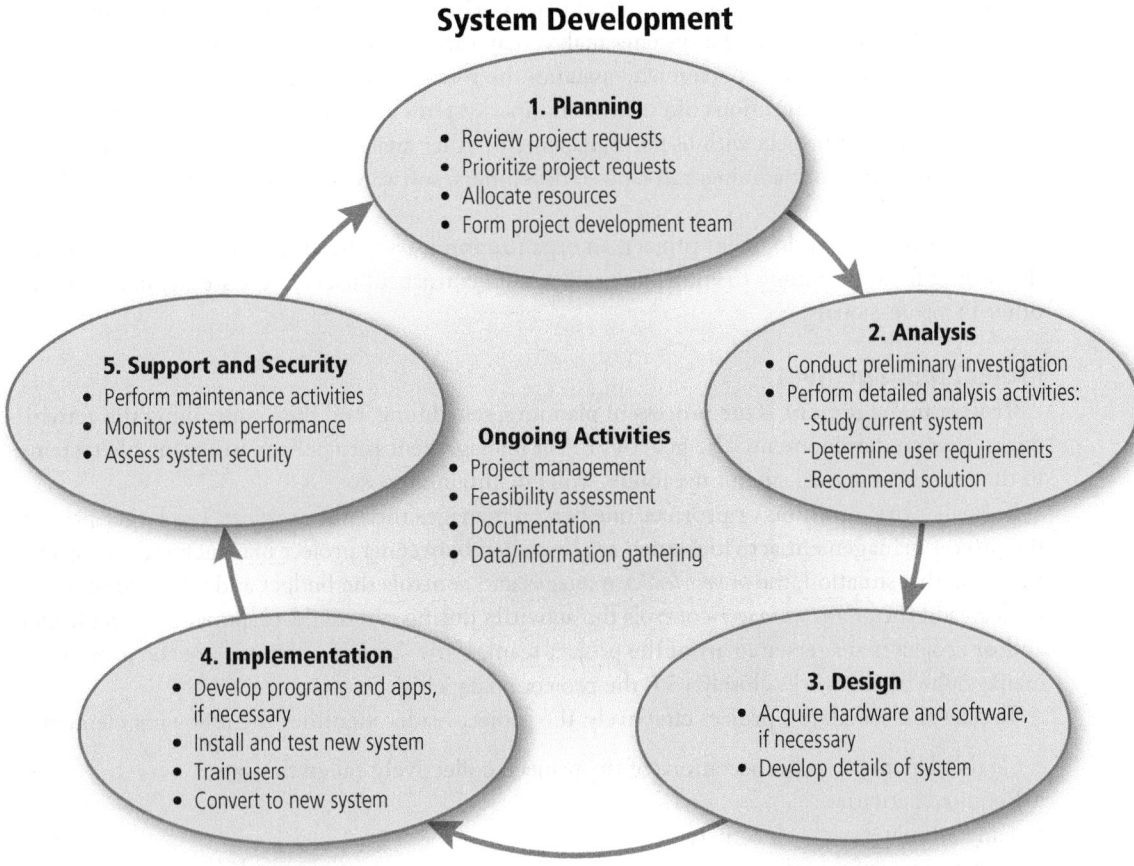

System Development

1. Planning
- Review project requests
- Prioritize project requests
- Allocate resources
- Form project development team

2. Analysis
- Conduct preliminary investigation
- Perform detailed analysis activities:
  - Study current system
  - Determine user requirements
  - Recommend solution

3. Design
- Acquire hardware and software, if necessary
- Develop details of system

4. Implementation
- Develop programs and apps, if necessary
- Install and test new system
- Train users
- Convert to new system

5. Support and Security
- Perform maintenance activities
- Monitor system performance
- Assess system security

Ongoing Activities
- Project management
- Feasibility assessment
- Documentation
- Data/information gathering

Figure 11-11 System development often consists of five phases that form a loop. Several ongoing activities also take place throughout system development.

System Development Guidelines

System development should follow three general guidelines: group activities into phases, involve users, and define standards.

1. **Group activities into phases.** Many SDLCs contain the same phases shown in Figure 11-11. Others have more or fewer phases. Regardless, all system development cycles have similar activities and tasks.
2. **Involve users.** Users include anyone for whom the system is being built. Customers, employees, students, data entry specialists, accountants, sales managers, and owners all are examples of users. Users are more apt to accept a new system if they contribute to its design.
3. **Define standards.** *Standards* are sets of rules and procedures an organization expects employees to accept and follow. Standards help people working on the same project produce consistent results.

Who Participates in System Development?

System development should involve representatives from each department in which the proposed system will be used. This includes both nontechnical users and IT professionals. Although the roles and responsibilities of members of the system development team may change from organization to organization, this module presents general descriptions of tasks for various team members.

During system development, the systems analyst meets and works with a variety of people. A **systems analyst** is responsible for designing and developing an information system. The systems analyst is the users' primary contact person. Depending on the size of the organization, the tasks performed by the systems analyst may vary. Smaller organizations may have one systems analyst or even one person who assumes the roles of both systems analyst and software developer. Larger organizations often have multiple systems analysts who discuss various aspects of the development project with users, management, other analysts, database analysts, database administrators, network administrators, web developers, software developers, vendors, and the steering committee.

For each system development project, an organization usually forms a *project team* to work on the project from beginning to end. The project team consists of users, the systems analyst, and other IT professionals.

BTW

Steering Committee
A *steering committee* is a decision-making body in an organization.

Project Management

Project management is the process of planning, scheduling, and then controlling the activities during system development. The goal of project management is to deliver an acceptable system to the user in an agreed-upon time frame, while maintaining costs.

In smaller organizations or projects, one person manages the entire project. For larger projects, the project management activities often are separated between a project manager and a project leader. In this situation, the *project leader* manages and controls the budget and schedule of the project, and the *project manager* controls the activities during system development. Project leaders and/or project managers are part of the project team. If the systems analyst is not the project manager, he or she works closely with the project manager.

To plan and schedule a project effectively, the project leader identifies the following elements:

- Goals, objectives, and expectations of the project, collectively called the *scope*
- Required activities
- Time estimates for each activity
- Cost estimates for each activity
- Order of activities
- Activities that can take place at the same time

After these items are identified, the project leader usually records them in a project plan. Project leaders can use **project management software** to assist them in planning, scheduling, and controlling development projects. One aspect of managing projects is to ensure that everyone submits deliverables on time and according to plan. A *deliverable* is any tangible item, such as a chart, diagram, report, or program file.

Gantt and PERT Charts   Popular tools used to plan and schedule the time relationships among project activities are Gantt and PERT charts (Figure 11-12).

- A *Gantt chart*, developed by Henry L. Gantt, is a bar chart that uses horizontal bars to show project phases or activities. The left side, or vertical axis, displays the list of required activities. A horizontal axis across the top or bottom of the chart represents time.
- Developed by the U.S. Department of Defense, a *PERT chart*, short for Program Evaluation and Review Technique chart, analyzes the time required to complete a task and identifies the minimum time required for an entire project.

PERT charts, sometimes called network diagrams, can be more complicated to create than Gantt charts, but are better suited than Gantt charts for planning and scheduling large, complex projects.

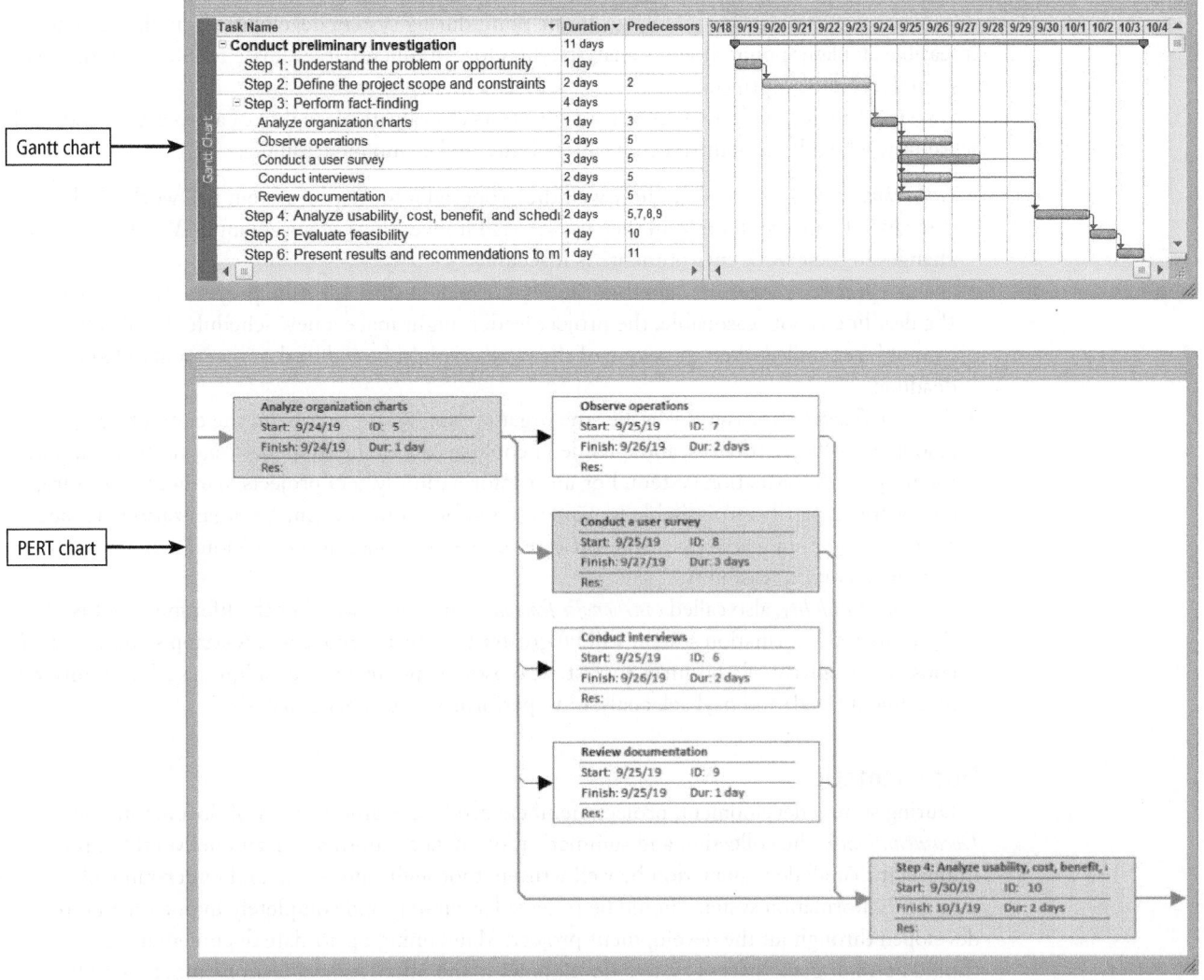

Figure 11-12   Project managers use software to create Gantt charts, PERT charts, and other charts and diagrams.

✳ **CONSIDER THIS** ──

How do project leaders adjust when a project changes?

After the project features and deadlines have been set, the project leader monitors and controls the project. Some activities take less time than originally planned. Others take longer. The project leader may realize that an activity is taking excessive time or that scope creep has begun. *Scope creep*, also called *feature creep*, occurs when one activity has led to another that was not planned originally; thus, the scope of the project now has grown.

Project leaders should use *change management*, which is the process of recognizing when a change in the project has occurred, taking actions to react to the change, and planning for opportunities because of the change. For example, the project leader may recognize the team will not be able to meet the original deadline of the project due to scope creep. Thus, the project leader may extend the deadline or may reduce the scope of the system development. If the latter occurs, the users will receive a less comprehensive system at the original deadline. In either case, the project leader revises the first project plan and presents the new plan to users for approval. It is crucial that everyone is aware of and agrees on any changes made to the project plan.

Feasibility Assessment

Feasibility is a measure of how suitable the development of a system will be to the organization. A project that is feasible at one point during system development might become infeasible at a later point. Systems analysts, therefore, frequently reevaluate feasibility during the system development project.

A systems analyst typically uses at least four tests to evaluate feasibility of a project: operational feasibility, schedule feasibility, technical feasibility, and economic feasibility.

- *Operational feasibility* measures how well the proposed information system will work. Will the users like the new system? Will they use it? Will it meet their requirements? Will it cause any changes in their work environment? Is it secure?
- *Schedule feasibility* measures whether the established deadlines for the project are reasonable. If a deadline is not reasonable, the project leader might make a new schedule. If a deadline cannot be extended, then the scope of the project might be reduced to meet a mandatory deadline.
- *Technical feasibility* measures whether the organization has or can obtain the computing resources, software services, and qualified people needed to develop, deliver, and then support the proposed information system. For most information system projects, hardware, software, and people typically are available to support an information system. An organization's choice for using computing resources and software services in-house or on the cloud may impact a system's technical feasibility.
- *Economic feasibility*, also called *cost/benefit feasibility*, measures whether the lifetime benefits of the proposed information system will be greater than its lifetime costs. A systems analyst often consults the advice of a business analyst, who uses many financial techniques, such as return on investment (ROI) and payback analysis, to perform a cost/benefit analysis.

Documentation

During system development, project members produce a large amount of documentation. *Documentation* is the collection and summarization of data, information, and deliverables. It is important that all documentation be well written, thorough, consistent, and understandable. The final information system should be reflected accurately and completely in documentation developed throughout the development project. Maintaining up-to-date documentation should be an ongoing part of system development. Too often, project team members put off documentation until the end of the project because it is time consuming, but these practices typically result in lower-quality documentation. Read How To 11-2 to learn how you can manage a project using project management software.

 **HOW TO 11-2**

Oversee a Project Using Project Management Software

Several project management programs and apps are available, some for free and others fee based. These programs and apps are designed for projects of specific sizes, so be sure to research the various programs and apps on the market and choose one that best suits your needs. To manage a project using project management software, follow these steps:

1. Make sure you understand the project in its entirety, as well as the steps you must take to bring the project to completion.

2. Determine the date by which the project must be completed.

3. Verify you have the appropriate resources (people and materials) to complete the project. If you do not have the necessary resources, obtain them, if possible.

4. Determine the order of the steps that must be taken to bring the project to completion. Identify steps that must be taken before other steps, as well as steps that can be completed at the same time as other steps.

5. Verify the feasibility of the plan.

6. During the project, it will be necessary to update the progress and possibly adjust dates. Changes to the project and its dates should be communicated to the entire project team.

 Consider This: Do you think project management software can help individuals complete a project more quickly? Why or why not?

 CONSIDER THIS

How do team members collaborate?

Conferencing software includes tools that enable users to share documents via online meetings and communicate with other connected users. When a meeting takes place on the web, it is called a *web conference*. In an online meeting, the facilitator may share a document for all participants to see at the same time. This allows the participants to edit a document and see the changes being made. Many conferencing software apps allow the facilitator to share his or her computer's desktop screen to demonstrate software apps or show webpages in real time to meeting participants. During the online meeting, participants have the ability to open a chat window and type messages to one another. Conferencing software also usually includes audio and video capabilities.

Data and Information Gathering Techniques

During system development, members of the project team gather data and information. They need accurate and timely data and information for many reasons. They must keep a project on schedule, evaluate feasibility, and be sure the system meets requirements. Systems analysts and other IT professionals use several techniques to gather data and information. They review documentation, observe, survey, interview, conduct joint-application design sessions, and research.

- **Review documentation:** By reviewing documentation such as organization charts, memos, and meeting minutes, systems analysts learn about the history of a project. Documentation also provides information about the organization, such as its operations, weaknesses, and strengths.
- **Observe:** Observing people helps systems analysts understand exactly how they perform a task. Likewise, observing a machine allows you to see how it works.
- **Survey:** To obtain data and information from a large number of people, systems analysts distribute surveys.
- **Interview:** The interview is the most important data and information gathering technique for the systems analyst. It allows the systems analyst to clarify responses and probe during face-to-face feedback.
- **JAD sessions:** Instead of a single one-on-one interview, analysts often use joint-application design sessions to gather data and information. A *joint-application design (JAD) session*, or *focus group*, consists of a series of lengthy, structured group meetings in which users and IT professionals work together to design or develop an application (Figure 11-13).
- **Research:** Newspapers, technology magazines and journals, reference books, trade shows, the web, vendors, and consultants are excellent sources of information. These sources can provide the systems analyst with information, such as the latest hardware and software products and explanations of new processes and procedures. In addition, systems analysts often collect website statistics, such as the number of visitors and most-visited webpages, etc., and then evaluate these statistics as part of their research.

Figure 11-13 During a JAD session, the systems analyst is the moderator, or leader of the discussion. Another member, called the *scribe*, records facts and action items assigned during the session.
Nyul / Dreamstime.com

 CONSIDER THIS

What circumstances initiate system development?

A user may request a new or modified information system for a variety of reasons. The most obvious reason is to correct a problem, such as an incorrect calculation or a security breach. Another reason is to improve the information system. Organizations may want to improve hardware, software, or other technology to enhance an information system.

Sometimes, situations outside the control of an organization require a modification to an information system. Corporate management or some other governing body may mandate a change. Mergers, reorganizations, and competition also can lead to change.

A user may request a new or modified information system verbally in a phone conversation or written as an email message. In larger organizations, users write a formal request for a new or modified information system, which is called a *project request* or *request for system services*. The project request becomes the first item of documentation for the project. It also triggers the first phase of system development: planning.

Planning Phase

The planning phase for a project begins when the steering committee receives a project request. This committee usually consists of five to nine people and typically includes a mix of vice presidents, managers, nonmanagement users, and IT personnel.

During the **planning phase**, four major activities are performed: (1) review and approve the project requests, (2) prioritize the project requests, (3) allocate resources, such as money, people, and equipment to approved projects, and (4) form a project development team for each approved project.

 CONSIDER THIS

How are projects prioritized?

The projects that receive the highest priority are those mandated by management or some other governing body. These requests are given immediate attention. The steering committee evaluates the remaining project requests based on their value to the organization. The steering committee approves some projects and rejects others. Of the approved projects, it is likely that only a few will begin system development immediately. Others will have to wait for additional funds or resources to become available.

Analysis Phase

The **analysis phase** consists of two major activities: (1) conduct a preliminary investigation and (2) perform detailed analysis.

The Preliminary Investigation   The main purpose of the **preliminary investigation**, sometimes called the *feasibility study*, is to determine the exact nature of the problem or improvement and decide whether it is worth pursuing. Should the organization continue to assign resources to this project? To answer this question, the systems analyst conducts a general study of the project.

The first task in the preliminary investigation is to interview the user who submitted the project request. Depending on the nature of the request, project team members may interview other users, too. In addition to interviewing, members of the project team may use other data gathering techniques, such as reviewing existing documentation. Often, the preliminary investigation is completed in just a few days.

Upon completion of the preliminary investigation, the systems analyst writes the feasibility report. This report presents the team's findings to the steering committee.

 CONSIDER THIS

Does the feasibility report always recommend that the project be continued?
In some cases, the project team may recommend to cancel the project. If the steering committee agrees, the project ends at this point. If the project team recommends continuing and the steering committee approves this recommendation, then detailed analysis begins.

Detailed Analysis   *Detailed analysis* involves three major activities: (1) study how the current system works, (2) determine the users' wants, needs, and requirements, and (3) recommend a solution. Detailed analysis sometimes is called *logical design* because the systems analysts develop the proposed solution without regard to any specific hardware or software. That is, they make no attempt to identify the procedures that should be automated and those that should be manual.

While studying the current system and identifying user requirements, the systems analyst collects a great deal of data and information. A major task for the systems analyst is to document these findings in a way that can be understood by everyone. Systems analysts use diagrams to describe the processes that transform inputs into outputs and diagrams that graphically show the flow of data in the system. Both users and IT professionals refer to this documentation.

The System Proposal   After the systems analyst has studied the current system and determined all user requirements, the next step is to communicate possible solutions for the project in a system proposal. The purpose of the system proposal is to assess the feasibility of each alternative solution and then recommend the most feasible solution for the project, which often involves modifying or expanding the current system. The systems analyst presents the system proposal to the steering committee. If the steering committee approves a solution, the project enters the design phase.

When the steering committee discusses the system proposal and decides which alternative to pursue, it considers whether to modify the existing system, buy retail software from an outside source, use web apps, build its own custom software, and/or outsource some or all of its IT needs to an outside firm. The final decision often is a mix of these options. Read Secure IT 11-2 for issues related to outsourcing.

SECURE IT 11-2

Security Issues Arising from Outsourcing

Businesses outsource noncore functions because third-party vendors may be more efficient and more cost effective than the businesses trying to perform the functions on their own. Noncore functions often include general business tasks, such as maintaining and supporting an organization's information systems and processing customer payments on websites.

Sometimes, however, when a business outsources, the external vendors are not as careful with security and customer information as the business itself might be. The business that outsources this task has spent time and effort to cultivate and then forge a relationship with

its customers, and it is in the company's best interest to treat its customers well. The outside vendor, however, has no such bond with the customers.

Security breaches might occur when work is contracted to third parties. For example, personal and confidential information about customers and employees, payroll, credit card numbers, and health records can be transferred to external hard drives or other storage media and taken outside the building. Companies should develop a computer security plan that requires safeguards on the part of the outside vendors. These procedures might include running background checks

on personnel, closely monitoring the level of database access and email messages, replacing Social Security numbers with another unique identifier, and conducting security audits. The plan also should include penalties if a security breach occurs.

⚙ **Consider This:** Does outsourcing lead to a lower level of security and privacy for customers? Why or why not? What can an organization do to ensure that vendors practice the same level of care with customer information as the organization practices? Should customers hold organizations or their vendors responsible for leaks of private customer information? Why?

Design Phase

The **design phase** consists of two major activities: (1) if necessary, acquire hardware and software and (2) develop all of the details of the new or modified information system. The systems analyst often performs these two activities at the same time instead of sequentially.

When the steering committee approves a solution, the systems analyst begins the activity of obtaining additional hardware or software or evaluating cloud providers that offer the computing services to meet the organization's needs. The systems analyst may skip this activity if the approved solution does not require new hardware or software. If this activity is required, it consists of four major tasks: (1) identify technical specifications, (2) solicit vendor proposals, (3) test and evaluate vendor proposals, and (4) make a decision.

Identify Technical Specifications   The first step in acquiring necessary hardware and software is to identify all the hardware and software requirements of the new or modified system. To do this, systems analysts use a variety of research techniques. They talk with other systems analysts, visit vendors' stores, and search the web. Many trade journals, newspapers, and magazines provide some or all of their printed content online.

After the systems analyst defines the technical requirements, the next step is to summarize these requirements for potential vendors. The systems analyst can use three basic types of documents for this purpose: an RFQ, an RFP, or an RFI.

- A *request for quotation* (*RFQ*) identifies the required product(s). With an RFQ, the vendor quotes a price for the listed product(s).
- With a *request for proposal* (*RFP*), the vendor selects the product(s) that meets specified requirements and then quotes the price(s).
- A *request for information* (*RFI*) is a less formal method that uses a standard form to request information about a product or service.

Solicit Vendor Proposals   Systems analysts send the RFQ, RFP, or RFI to potential hardware and software vendors. Another source for hardware and software products is a value-added reseller. A *value-added reseller* (*VAR*) is an organization that purchases products from manufacturers and then resells these products to the public — offering additional services with the product (Figure 11-14).

Instead of using vendors, some organizations hire an IT consultant or a group of IT consultants. An *IT consultant* is a professional who is hired based on technical expertise, including service and advice.

Test and Evaluate Vendor Proposals After sending RFQs, RFPs, or RFIs to potential vendors, the systems analyst will receive completed quotations and proposals. Evaluating the proposals and then selecting the best one often is a difficult task.

Systems analysts use many techniques to test the various software products from vendors. They obtain a list of user references from the software vendors. They also talk to current users of the software to solicit their opinions. Some vendors will provide a

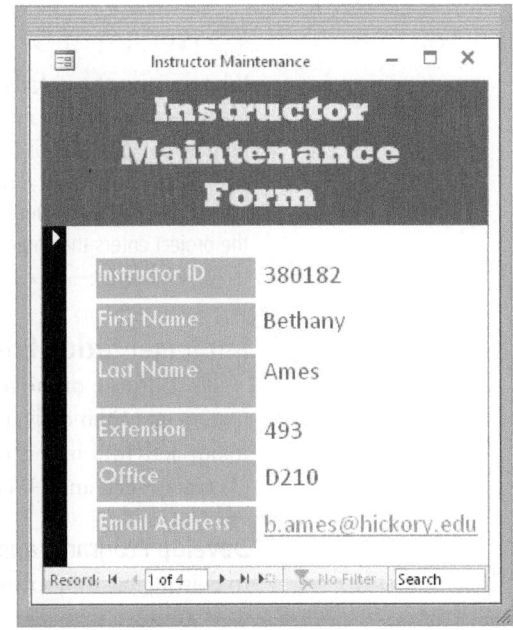

Figure 11-14 Many VARs provide complete systems, often called turnkey solutions.
Source: Magal Security Systems Ltd.

demonstration of the product(s) specified. Others supply demonstration copies or trial versions, allowing the organizations to test the software themselves.

Sometimes it is important to know whether the software can process a certain volume of transactions efficiently. In this case, the systems analyst conducts a benchmark test. A *benchmark test* measures the performance of hardware or software. For example, a benchmark test could measure the time it takes a payroll program to print 50 paychecks. Comparing the time it takes various accounting programs to print the same 50 paychecks is one way of measuring each program's performance.

Make a Decision Having rated the proposals, the systems analyst presents a recommendation to the steering committee. The recommendation could be to award a contract to a vendor or to not make any purchases at this time.

Detailed Design The next step is to develop detailed design specifications for the components in the proposed solution. The activities to be performed include developing designs for the databases, inputs, outputs, and programs.

- During database design, the systems analyst works closely with the database administrators to identify those data elements that currently exist within the organization and those that are new. The systems analyst also addresses user access privileges.
- During detailed design of inputs and outputs, the systems analyst carefully designs every menu, screen, and report specified in the requirements. The outputs often are designed first because they help define the requirements for the inputs.

The systems analyst may develop a mock-up and/or a layout chart for each input and output. A *mock-up* is a sample of the input or output that contains actual data (Figure 11-15). The systems analyst shows mock-ups to users for their approval. After users approve the mock-up, the systems analyst develops a layout chart for the software

Figure 11-15 Users provide their approval on inputs and outputs. This input screen is a mock-up (containing actual sample data) for users to review.
Source: Microsoft

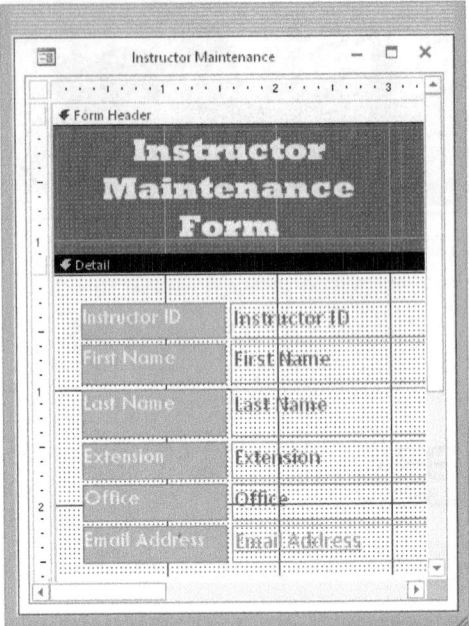

Figure 11-16 Shown here is a technical view in Access of the mock-up in Figure 11-15.
Source: Microsoft

developer. A layout chart is more technical and contains programming-like notations. Many database programs provide tools for technical design (Figure 11-16).

Other issues that must be addressed during input and output design include the types of media to use (paper, video, or audio); formats (graphical or narrative); and data entry validation techniques, which include making sure the entered data is correct (for example, a state code has to be one of the fifty valid two-letter state abbreviations).

- During program design, the systems analyst prepares the *program specification package*, which identifies required programs and the relationship among each program, as well as the input, output, and database specifications.

 CONSIDER THIS

How can systems analysts build relationships with users?
Systems analysts have much more credibility with users if the analysts understand user concerns and have empathy for how the workers are feeling. If users are involved, they are more likely to accept and use the new system — called *user buy-in*. One reason systems fail is because some systems analysts create or modify systems with little or no user participation.

Prototyping Many systems analysts today use prototypes during detailed design. A **prototype**, sometimes called a *proof of concept*, is a working model of the proposed system's essential functionality. The systems analyst actually builds a functional form of the solution during design. The main advantage of a prototype is users can work with the system before it is completed to make sure it meets their needs. As soon as users approve a prototype, systems analysts can implement a solution more quickly than without a prototype.

CONSIDER THIS

Who reviews the detailed design?
Many people should review the detailed design specifications before they are given to the programming team. The purpose of their review is to ensure the design represents a finished product that will work for the user and the development is feasible. Reviewers should include users, systems analysts, managers, IT staff, and members of the system development team. If the steering committee decides the project still is feasible, which usually is the case, the project enters the implementation phase.

Implementation Phase

The purpose of the **implementation phase** is to construct, or build, the new or modified system and then deliver it to the users. Members of the system development team perform four major activities in this phase: (1) develop programs and apps, (2) install and test the new system, (3) train users, and (4) convert to the new system.

Develop Programs and Apps If the organization purchases retail software or no modifications to existing custom software are required, the development team may skip this activity. For custom software that is new or requires modification, however, programs and apps are developed or modified either by an outside firm or in-house.

Software developers write or modify programs and apps from the program specification package created during the analysis phase. Just as system development follows an organized set of activities, so does program development. These program development activities are known as the *program development life cycle*.

What is a sandbox?

A *sandbox* is an environment that allows software developers to test their programs with fictitious data without adversely affecting other programs, information systems, or data. Sandboxes are used for testing purposes both by developers and users. Users often work with a sandbox to familiarize themselves with a new program or information system before they use it.

Install and Test the New System   If the organization acquires new hardware or software, someone must install and test it. The systems analysts should test individual programs. They also should be sure that all the programs work together in the system.

Systems analysts and users develop test data so that they can perform various tests.

- A *unit test* verifies that each individual program or object works by itself.
- A *systems test* verifies that all programs in an application work together properly.
- An *integration test* verifies that an application works with other applications.
- An *acceptance test* is performed by end users and checks the new system to ensure that it works with actual data.

Train Users   **Training** involves showing users exactly how they will use the new hardware and software in the system. Some training takes place as one-on-one sessions or classroom-style lectures (Figure 11-17). Other organizations use web-based training, which is a self-directed, self-paced online instruction method. Whichever technique is used, it should include hands-on sessions with realistic sample data. Users should practice on the actual system during training. Users also should be provided access to printed or online user manuals for reference. It is the systems analyst's responsibility to create user manuals.

Figure 11-17   Organizations must ensure that users are trained properly on the new system. One training method uses hands-on classes to learn the new system.
Goodluz / Shutterstock.com

Convert to the New System   The final implementation activity is to change from the old system to the new system. This change can take place using one or more of the following conversion strategies: direct, parallel, phased, or pilot.

- With *direct conversion*, the user stops using the old system and begins using the new system on a certain date. The advantage of this strategy is that it requires no transition costs and is a quick implementation technique. The disadvantage is that it is extremely risky and can disrupt operations seriously if the new system does not work correctly the first time.

- *Parallel conversion* consists of running the old system alongside the new system for a specified time. Results from both systems are compared. The advantage of this strategy is that you can fix any problems in the new system before you terminate the old system. The disadvantage is that it is costly to operate two systems at the same time.

- In a *phased conversion*, each location converts at a separate time. For example, an accounting system might convert its accounts receivable, accounts payable, general ledger, and payroll sites in separate phases. Each site can use a direct or parallel conversion. Larger systems with multiple sites may use a phased conversion.

- With a *pilot conversion*, only one location in the organization uses the new system — so that it can be tested. After the pilot site approves the new system, other sites convert using one of the other conversion strategies.

Support and Security Phase

The purpose of the **support and security phase** is to provide ongoing assistance for an information system and its users after the system is implemented. The support and security phase consists of three major activities: (1) perform maintenance activities, (2) monitor system performance, and (3) assess system security.

Information system maintenance activities include fixing errors in, as well as improving, a system's operations. To determine initial maintenance needs, the systems analyst should meet with users. The purpose of this meeting, often called the *post-implementation system review*, is to discover whether the information system is performing according to the users' expectations. In some cases, users would like the system to do more. Maybe they have enhancements or additional requirements that involve modifying or expanding an existing information system.

During this phase, the systems analyst monitors performance of the new or modified information system. The purpose of performance monitoring is to determine whether the system is inefficient or unstable at any point. If it is, the systems analyst must investigate solutions to make the information system more efficient and reliable — back to the planning phase.

Most organizations must deal with complex technology security issues. All elements of an information system — hardware, software, data, people, and procedures — must be secure from threats both inside and outside the enterprise. Read Secure IT 11-3 for information about an organization's technology security plan.

SECURE IT 11-3

Technology Security Plan Components

If an organization experiences a major information system disaster, a computer security plan will guide the recovery process. The document should identify all the security risks that may cause an information system asset loss and include all possible safeguards to detect, prevent, and recover from losses. It should identify all of the organization's information assets, which include hardware, software, documentation, procedures, people, data, facilities, and supplies. Key components should include securing equipment, especially laptops and mobile devices, creating a strong

disaster recovery strategy, developing a security breach detection and response plan, and providing for ongoing training.

One of the responsibilities of a chief security officer (CSO) is to protect the organization's information assets. The goal of the computer security plan is to match an appropriate level of safeguards against the identified risks. The CSO must realize that some degree of risk is unavoidable and that the more secure a system is, the more difficult it is for everyone to use. The security plan should be evaluated annually, or more frequently if information assets have changed

dramatically. Microsoft has developed a Security Development Lifecycle to guide the development, implementation, and review process. Its seven security practices phases — training, requirements, design, implementation, verification, release, and response — help increase security while reducing costs.

Consider This: What method should be used to communicate the plan to all employees and provide adequate training to ensure continued compliance? How can a CSO be assured that employees will comply with the computer security plan?

Application Development Languages and Tools

The previous sections discussed the system development phases. One activity during the implementation phase is to develop programs and apps. Although you may never write a program or app, information you request may require a software developer to create or modify a program or app. Thus, you should understand how software developers, sometimes called programmers, create programs and apps to meet information requirements.

To create a program, software developers sometimes write a program's instructions using a programming language. A **programming language** is a set of words, abbreviations, and symbols that enables a software developer to communicate instructions to a computer or mobile device. Other times, software developers use a program development tool to create a program or app. Software that provides a user-friendly environment for building programs and apps often is called an *application development tool*. An application development tool provides a means for creating, designing, editing, testing, and distributing programs and apps. Software developers use a variety of programming languages and application development tools to create programs and apps.

Several hundred programming languages exist today. Each language has its own rules, or *syntax*, for writing the instructions. Languages often are designed for specific purposes, such as scientific applications, business solutions, or webpage development. When solving a problem or building a solution, software developers often use more than one language; that is, they integrate the languages.

Procedural Languages

With a **procedural language**, a software developer writes instructions using English-like words that tell the computer what to accomplish and how to do it. For example, ADD stands for addition, or PRINT means to print. Many procedural languages also use arithmetic operators, such as * (asterisk) for multiplication and 1 (plus sign) for addition. Hundreds of procedural languages exist. Only a few, however, are used widely enough for the industry to recognize them as standards.

One example of a widely used procedural language is C. The **C** programming language, developed in the early 1970s by Dennis Ritchie at Bell Laboratories, originally was designed for writing system software. Today, many programs are written in C (Figure 11-18). C runs on almost any type of computer with any operating system, but it is used most often with the UNIX and Linux operating systems.

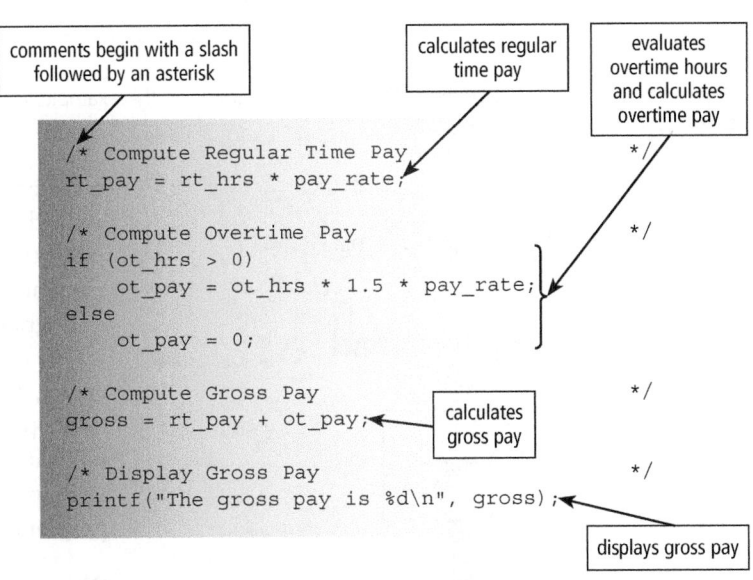

Figure 11-18 An excerpt from a C payroll program. The code shows the computations for regular time pay, overtime pay, and gross pay; the decision to evaluate the overtime hours; and the output of the gross pay.

Compilers and Interpreters Before a computer or mobile device can run (execute) a program or app created with a procedural language, system developers must convert the program into *machine language*, which is the only language the computer directly recognizes. That is, the computer cannot execute the procedural language source program. A *source program* contains the language instructions, or *code*, to be converted to machine language. For procedural languages, software developers typically use either a compiler or an interpreter to perform the conversion.

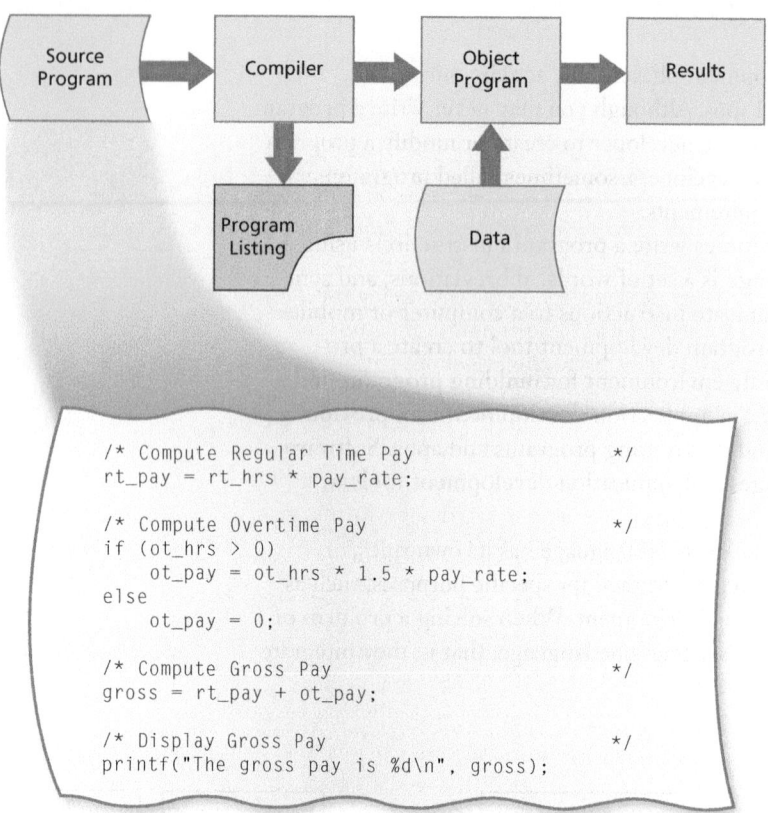

```
/* Compute Regular Time Pay          */
rt_pay = rt_hrs * pay_rate;

/* Compute Overtime Pay              */
if (ot_hrs > 0)
    ot_pay = ot_hrs * 1.5 * pay_rate;
else
    ot_pay = 0;

/* Compute Gross Pay                 */
gross = rt_pay + ot_pay;

/* Display Gross Pay                 */
printf("The gross pay is %d\n", gross);
```

Figure 11-19 A compiler converts the source program (C, in this example) into a machine language object program.

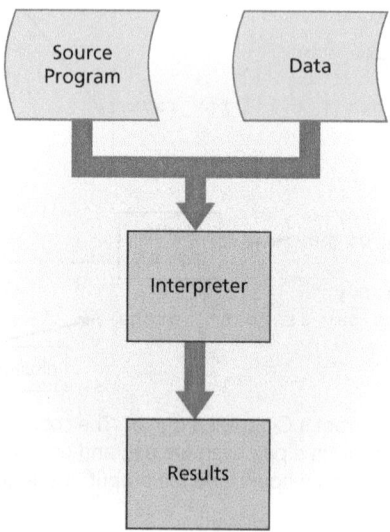

Figure 11-20 With an interpreter, one instruction of the source program at a time is converted into machine language and then immediately executed by the computer or mobile device.

- A *compiler* is a separate program that converts the entire source program into machine language before executing it. The machine language version that results from compiling the procedural language is called the *object program* or *object code*. The compiler stores the object program on storage media for execution later.

  While it is compiling the source program into the object program, the compiler checks the source program for errors. The compiler then produces a program listing that contains the source code and a list of any errors. This listing helps the software developer make necessary changes to the source code and correct errors in the program. Figure 11-19 shows the process of compiling a source program.

- An *interpreter*, by contrast, translates and executes one instruction at a time. An interpreter reads an instruction, converts it to one or more machine language instructions, and then executes those machine language instructions. It does this all before moving to the next instruction in the program. Each time the source program runs, the interpreter translates and executes it, instruction by instruction. An interpreter does not produce an object program. Figure 11-20 shows the process of interpreting a program.

  One advantage of an interpreter is that when it finds errors, it displays feedback immediately. The software developer can correct any errors before the interpreter translates the next instruction. The disadvantage is that interpreted programs do not run as fast as compiled programs.

Object-Oriented Programming Languages and Application Development Tools

System developers use an **object-oriented programming (OOP) language** or object-oriented application development tool to implement objects in a program. Recall that an object is an item that can contain both data and the procedures that read or manipulate that data. An object represents a real person, place, event, or transaction.

A major benefit of OOP is the ability to reuse and modify existing objects. For example, once a system developer creates an Employee object, it is available for use by any other existing or future program. Thus, system developers repeatedly reuse existing objects. For example, a payroll program and health benefits program both would use an Employee object. That is, the payroll program would use it to process employee paychecks, and the health benefits program would use it to process health insurance payments.

Programs developed using the object-oriented programming languages and application development tools have several advantages. The objects can be reused in many systems, are designed for repeated use, and become stable over time. In addition, developers create applications faster because they design programs using existing objects. Programming languages, such as Java and C++, and the latest versions of Visual Basic are complete OOP languages. Most object-oriented application development tools, such as Visual Studio, are referred to as an *integrated development environment* (*IDE*) because they include tools for building graphical interfaces, an editor for entering program code, a compiler and/or interpreter, and a debugger (to remove errors). Some work with a single programming language, and others support multiple languages. Read How To 11-3 for instructions about selecting the object-oriented programming language and application development tools best suited to your needs.

 HOW TO 11-3

Determine Which Object-Oriented Programming Language or Application Development Tool to Use

Software developers can choose from a variety of object-oriented programming languages and application development tools to write a program or app for a computer or mobile device. The following guidelines describe how to determine which language or tool to use:

- Determine the types of devices on which your program or app will run. For example, if you are writing an app for a mobile device, limited languages and tools may be available for you to use. If you are writing a

program or app that will run on a computer, more options will be available. Perform research and determine which types of programming languages can be used for various devices and operating systems.

- Determine the capabilities of the programming languages you are considering using. Some programming languages have greater capabilities than others.

- Consider the speed at which programs and apps run that are written in a particular programming language. For example, a program or app might run faster if it is written in one language as opposed to another.

- Consider whether you want to write a program using a text editor or an IDE. If you want to use an IDE, your choices of programming languages may be limited.

- Solicit recommendations from other developers. Explain the type of program or app you plan to write, and consider suggestions they might offer.

 Consider This: If you are forced to write a program or app using a programming language with which you are not very familiar, what resources can you utilize to obtain assistance?

 CONSIDER THIS

What is rapid application development?

RAD (*rapid application development*) is a method of developing software in which the software developer writes and implements a program in segments instead of waiting until the entire program is completed. An important concept in RAD is the use of prebuilt components. For example, software developers do not have to write code for buttons and text boxes on Windows forms because they already exist in the programming language or application development tools provided with the language. Object-oriented programming languages and application development tools work well in a RAD environment.

 CONSIDER THIS

What is agile development?

Agile development guidelines for program development emphasize adaptation of goals and continuous improvement of the software or app. Its focus is on creating a working version of software that addresses user needs, collaboration with users and stakeholders, and response to changes in technology and market needs.

Java **Java** is an object-oriented programming language developed by Sun Microsystems. Figure 11-21 shows a portion of a Java program and the window that the program displays. When software developers compile a Java program, the resulting object program is machine independent. Software developers use various Java Platform implementations, which provide application development tools for creating programs for all sizes of computers and mobile devices.

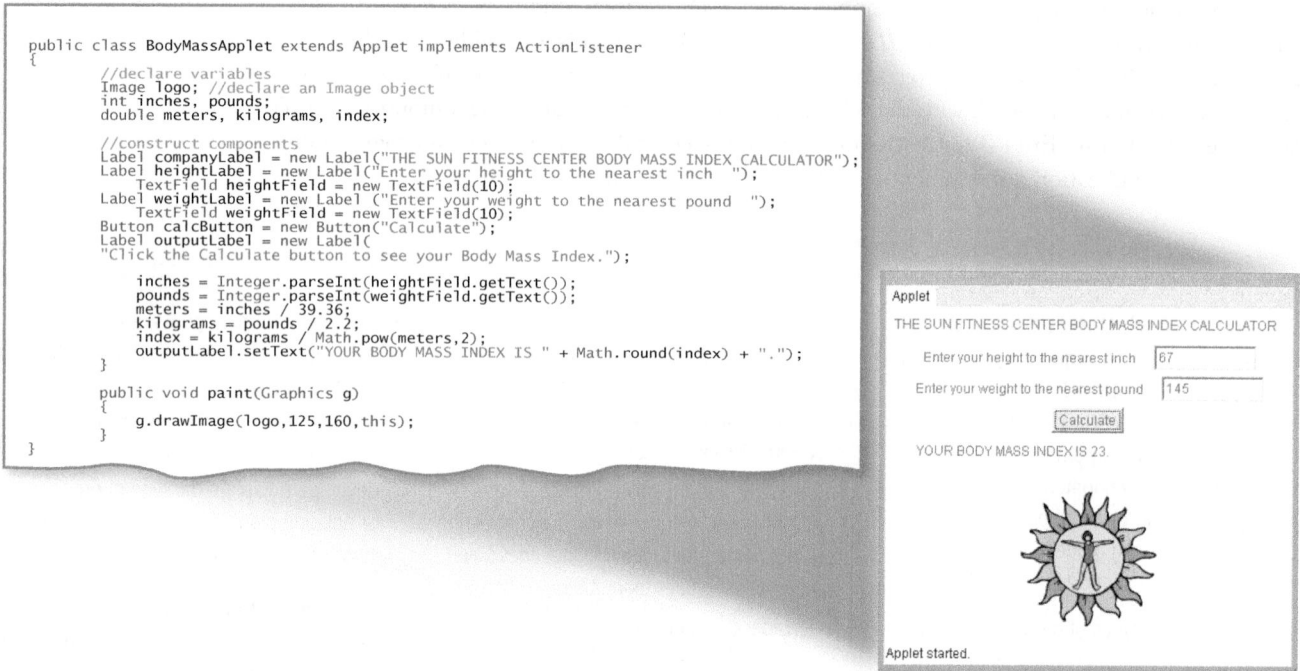

Figure 11-21 A portion of a Java program and the window the program displays.

C++ Developed in the 1980s by Bjarne Sroustrup at Bell Laboratories, **C++** (pronounced SEE-plus-plus) is an object-oriented programming language that is an extension of the C programming language. C++ includes all the elements of the C language, plus it has additional features for working with objects. Software developers commonly use C++ to develop database and web applications.

Visual Studio Developed by Microsoft, **Visual Studio** contains a suite of object-oriented application development tools that assists software developers in building programs and apps for Windows or any operating system that supports the Microsoft .NET Framework. Visual Studio also includes a set of tools for developing programs and apps that work with Microsoft's Office suite. OOPs included in the Visual Studio suite are Visual Basic, Visual C++, and Visual C#.

 CONSIDER THIS

What is .NET?

The Microsoft .NET Framework, or .NET (pronounced dot net), is a set of technologies that allows almost any type of program to run on the Internet or an internal business network, as well as stand-alone computers and mobile devices. Similarly, ASP.NET is a web application framework that provides the tools necessary for the creation of dynamic websites.

✳ BTW

Visual Basic
Visual Basic is based on the BASIC programming language, which was developed in the early 1960s. Because this language is easy to learn and use, beginning programmers often use it.

Other Languages and Application Development Tools

The following sections discuss a variety of other programming languages and application development tools.

4GLs   A **4GL** (*fourth-generation language*) is a nonprocedural language that enables users and software developers to access data in a database. With a *nonprocedural language*, the software developer writes English-like instructions or interacts with a graphical environment to retrieve data from files or a database. Many object-oriented application development tools use 4GLs. One popular 4GL is SQL. As discussed earlier in this module, SQL is a query language that allows users to manage, update, and retrieve data in a relational DBMS.

Classic Programming Languages   In addition to the programming languages discussed on the previous pages, software developers sometimes use the languages to maintain legacy systems. These languages, which include BASIC, COBOL, FORTRAN, and RPG, were more widely used in the past than they are today.

Application Generators   An application generator is a program that creates source code or machine code from a specification of the required functionality. When using an application generator, a software developer or user works with menu-driven tools and graphical user interfaces to define the desired specifications. Application generators most often are bundled with or are included as part of a DBMS. An application generator typically consists of a report writer and forms (discussed earlier in this module), and a menu generator. A menu generator enables you to create a menu for the application options.

Macros   A **macro** is a series of statements that instructs a program or app how to complete a task. Macros allow users to automate routine, repetitive, or difficult tasks in application software, such as word processing, spreadsheet (Figure 11-22), or database programs. That is, users can create simple programs within the application by writing macros. You usually create a macro in one of two ways: (1) record the macro or (2) write the macro.

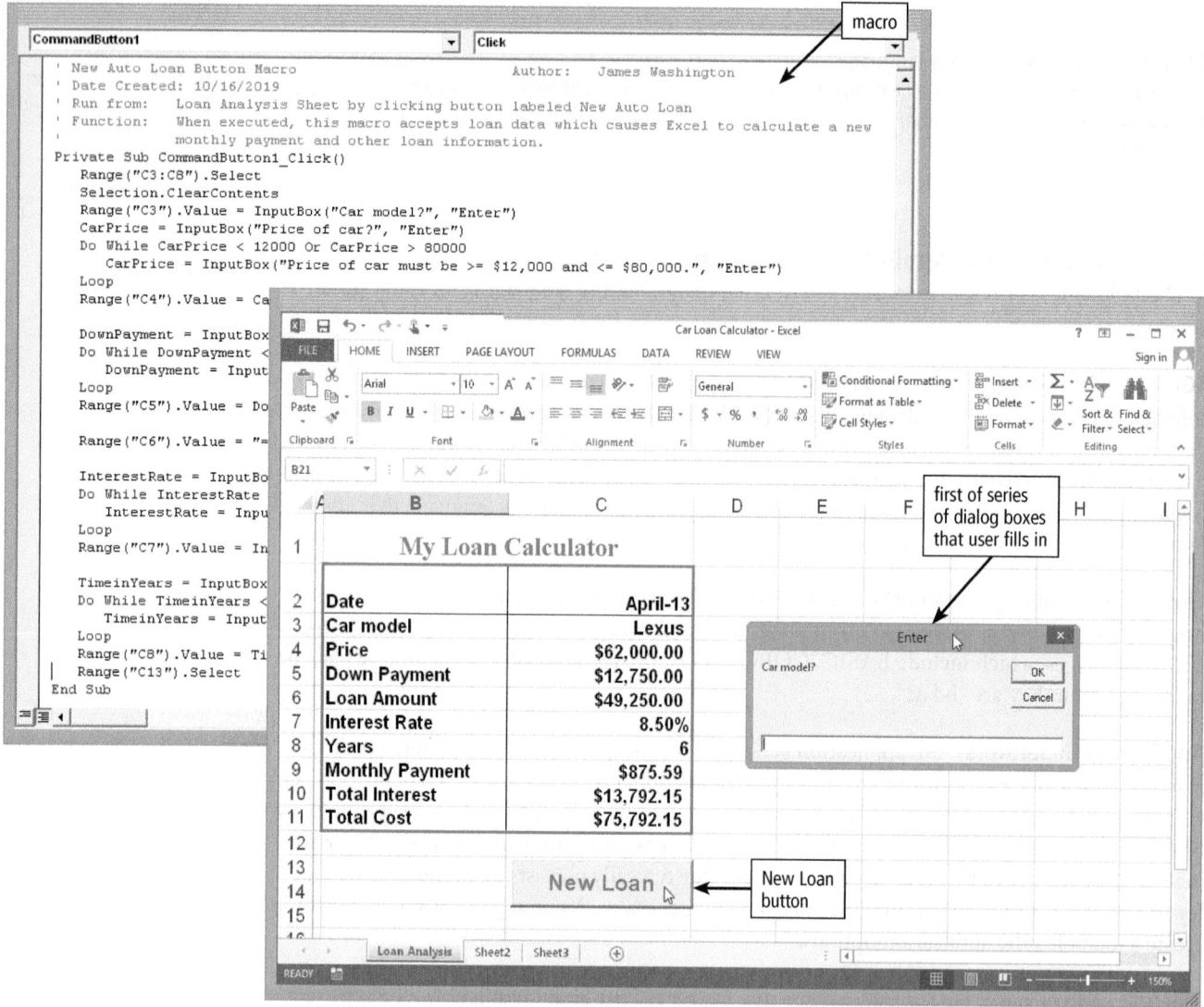

Figure 11-22   The top screen shows a macro used to automate an auto loan. After this macro is written, the user taps or clicks the New Loan button to run the macro. The bottom screen shows the macro guiding the user through part of the data entry process.
Source: Microsoft

SECURE IT 11-4

Protection from Macro Viruses

More than 20 years ago, the first macro viruses wreaked havoc with personal computers. Now, the same macro coding techniques are being used to create malware infecting smartphones. For example, the Selfmite worm sends text messages with malicious links to the owner's contacts.

As the name implies, a macro virus hides in a program's macro language. Malware authors find that one of the easiest methods of spreading viruses and worms is by distributing apps and files containing macro viruses. This type of virus is easy to write, and the damage that results from infecting

smartphones and computers can exceed millions of dollars.

Because many computers and smartphones have acquired damaging macro viruses, antivirus and productivity software companies have strengthened their efforts to prevent this malware from infecting their products. One method, for example, disables the macros, which prohibits users from running once-automated tasks on their computers. The users, however, are frustrated when they now must perform routines manually. Other prevention measures include setting the software's macro security level to high, not installing apps from unknown sources, not opening unexpected file attachments, and holding down the shift key

when opening a file that may be infected by a macro virus so that any automatic macros are prevented from running.

Many smartphone and computer users claim the software companies should make it impossible for malware authors to take advantage of security problems in the software. The software companies, however, place the blame on users who install apps and open files from unknown sources.

Consider This: Should users or software companies be held accountable for macro security threats? Why? How can smartphone and computer users best be educated about opening text messages and documents from unknown sources?

Web Development

The designers of webpages, known as *web developers*, use a variety of techniques to create and publish webpages. The following sections discuss these techniques.

HTML HTML (*Hypertext Markup Language*) is a special formatting language that software developers use to format documents for display on the web. You view a webpage written with HTML in a browser, such as Edge, Safari, Firefox, Opera, or Chrome. Figure 11-23a shows part of the HTML code used to create the webpage shown in Figure 11-23b.

Figure 11-23a   (portion of HTML code)

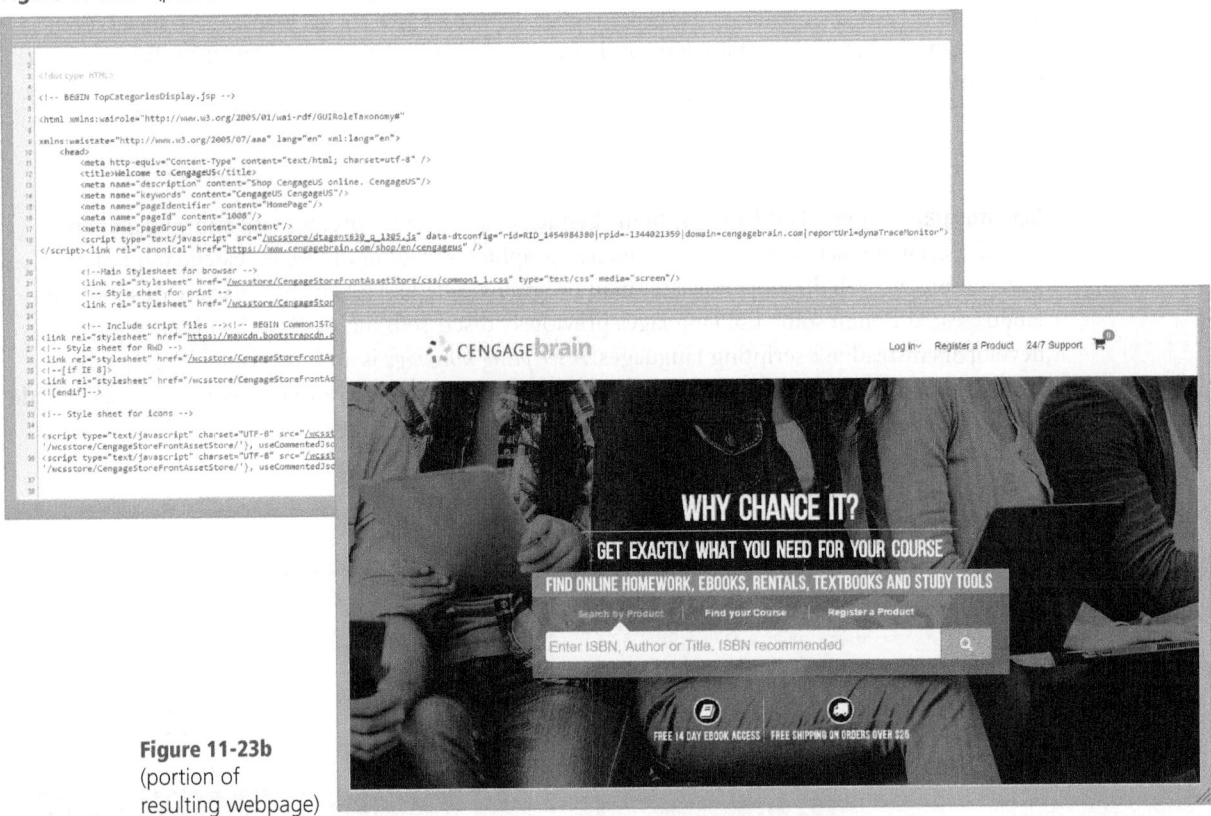

Figure 11-23b
(portion of
resulting webpage)

Figure 11-23   The portion of the HTML code in Figure 11-23a generates a portion of the Cengage Learning CengageBrain webpage shown in Figure 11-23b.

✺ CONSIDER THIS ─────────────────

Is HTML a programming language?
HTML is not actually a programming language. It is, however, a language that has specific rules for defining the placement and format of text, graphics, video, and audio on a webpage. HTML uses tags or elements, which are words, abbreviations, and symbols that specify links to other documents and indicate how a webpage is displayed when viewed on the web.

XML XML (*Extensible Markup Language*) is an increasingly popular format for sharing data that allows web developers to create tags that describe the structure of information. XML separates the webpage content from its format, allowing the browser to display the contents of a webpage in a form appropriate for the display device. For example, RSS feeds (web feeds) are represented as XML. A webpage can read the feed's content as described by XML and then apply styles and consistent formatting to each element (title, link, description) to display it within a browser.

Wireless devices use a subset of XML called WML. *WML* (*wireless markup language*) allows web developers to design pages specifically for microbrowsers. Many smartphones and other mobile devices use WML as their markup language.

 **CONSIDER THIS**

What are some applications of XML?

Two applications of XML are the RSS 2.0 and ATOM specifications. *RSS 2.0,* which stands for Really Simple Syndication, and *ATOM* are specifications that content aggregators use to distribute content to subscribers. The online publisher creates an RSS or ATOM document, called a web feed, that is made available to websites for publication. News websites, blogs, and podcasts often use web feeds to publish headlines and stories. Most browsers can read web feeds, meaning they can display titles, links, descriptions, and other information about pages identified in the feed.

Scripting and Other Web Development Languages   To add interactivity on webpages and to add special media effects, such as animated graphics, scrolling messages, calendars, and advertisements, web developers write small programs called scripts using a variety of scripting languages. Although some use languages previously discussed, such as Java and C++, many developers instead use scripting languages. A *scripting language* is an interpreted language that typically is easy to learn and use. Popular scripting and other web development languages include JavaScript (Figure 11-24), Perl, PHP, Python, and Ruby.

Figure 11-24a   (JavaScript code)

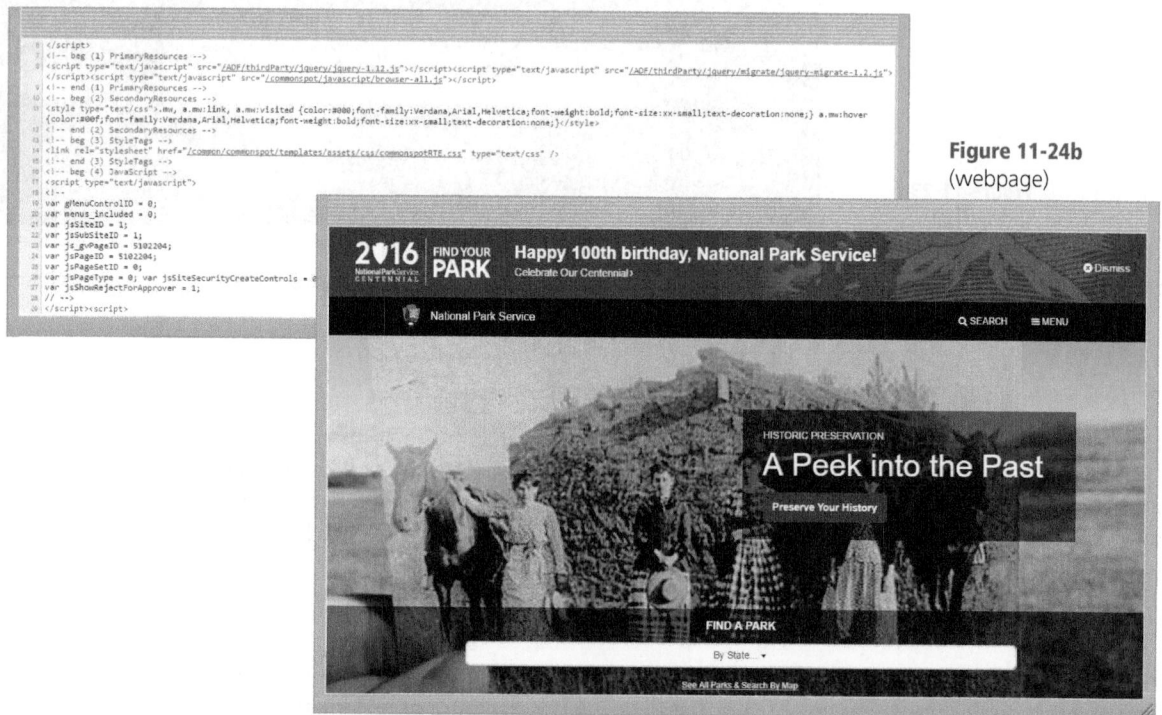

Figure 11-24b
(webpage)

Figure 11-24   Shown here is a portion of the JavaScript code and its associated National Park Service webpage.
Source: National Park Service U.S. Department of the Interior

Tech Feature 11-4: Web Application Development

Three technologies form the foundation for many web applications: HTML5 specifies the structure of content displayed on a webpage; CSS (cascading style sheets) describes the design and appearance of information on a webpage; and *JavaScript* is a scripting language that allows users to interact with a webpage's content. Many web applications also access applications running on a server, connect to a database, or access third-party content from online sources. Together, these technologies enable developers to create browser-independent web applications that run on a variety of devices.

As discussed in an earlier module, the W3C (World Wide Web Consortium) is an international organization that sets the standards for the technologies and operation of the web. In addition, it defines the standards for HTML5 and CSS. Read Tech Feature 11-4 to learn about technologies that enable developers to create browser-independent web applications.

 TECH FEATURE 11-4

Web Application Development

To develop a web application, web developers use HTML5, CSS, and JavaScript.

HTML5

HTML5 is the current HTML standard for creating websites and applications. HTML uses a set of codes called tags to instruct a browser how to structure a webpage's content. HTML tags specify the structure of content on a webpage, such as headings, paragraphs, links, or images. HTML5 includes tags for playing audio and video files without relying on the use of third-party plug-ins or modules, such as Adobe Flash, to perform these tasks. Some mobile devices and computers, such as Apple's iPhone and iPad, do not support displaying media content that requires Flash. Instead, they rely on HTML5-compliant browsers, which are capable of interpreting HTML5 tags, to handle these tasks.

Source: HTML5 Logo by World Wide WebConsortium

Additional HTML5 features include recognizing gestures, such as swipe or drag-and-drop, on mobile devices; dynamically creating graphics, such as progress bars, charts, and animations; *geolocation* (determining a user's location based on a device's GPS or connection to a cell tower); and offline storage. For example, Google Drive uses HTML5's drag-and-drop feature so that you can organize documents and uses its offline storage feature to allow you to work with your documents when you do not have an Internet connection. Twitter makes use of HTML5's geolocation feature when users search for Tweets that originate near a specific location.

These HTML5 features enable web developers to build applications that address the needs of how people use the web today and provide richer user experiences. Each browser implements the HTML5 specification differently and may not support all of its features.

CSS

While HTML describes the structure of a webpage's content as a collection of elements (such as headings, paragraphs, images, and links), CSS allows web designers to separate the code that specifies a webpage's content from the code that specifies the webpage's appearance. For example, a webpage may contain two paragraphs of text that are presented using a variety of fonts and sizes, styles, colors, borders, thicknesses, columns, or backgrounds. CSS provides web designers with precise control over a webpage's layout and allows the designers to apply different layouts to the same information for printing or for viewing in browsers on smartphones, tablets, or computers with varying screen sizes. The current version of CSS is known as CSS3 (cascading style sheets, version 3).

JavaScript

JavaScript is a programming language that adds interactivity to webpages. It often is used to check for appropriate values on web forms, display alert messages, display menus on webpages, control the appearance of a browser window, read and write cookies, display alert boxes, and detect the browser version in order to display a webpage especially designed for that browser. JavaScript code is loaded with a webpage and runs in the browser.

Developing Websites and Applications with HTML5, CSS, and JavaScript

Web developers often use tools, such as the one shown in the figure, to create their code and visualize

(continued)

what it will look like in a browser. In this example, HTML5 specifies a heading, a paragraph, and a link; CSS specifies the page background color and fonts, while JavaScript instructs the page to display an alert box when it loads.

✳ Consider This: What are two advantages and two disadvantages of writing mobile apps using HTML5, CSS, and JavaScript? Before HTML5's geolocation features, how might a web app have determined a user's approximate location? Some web-based email services, such as Gmail, use HTML5, CSS, and JavaScript. Name a feature of Gmail that might demonstrate a characteristic of each of these technologies.

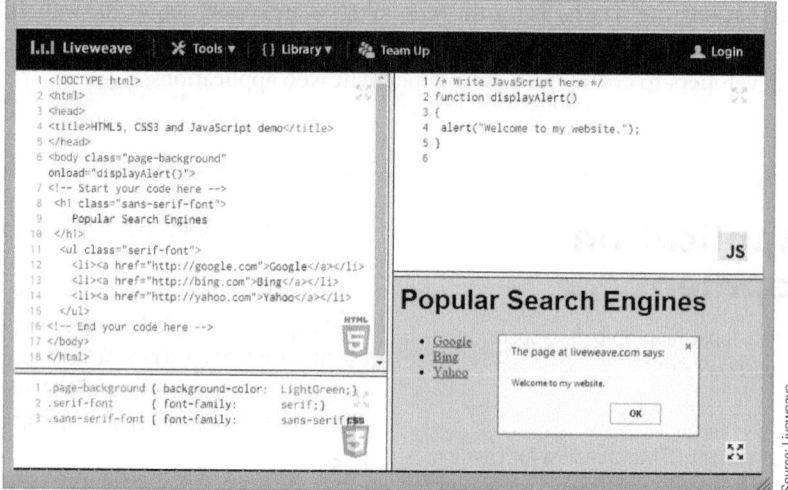

Source: Liveweave

🛡 Summary

This module discussed the hierarchy of data, ways to validate data, the advantages of the database versus the file processing approach, and characteristics of database management systems. It also discussed the system development phases and the guidelines for system development, along with activities that occur during system development, including project management, feasibility assessment, documentation, and data and information gathering. This module also reviewed various programming languages and application development tools used to create and modify computer programs. Finally, it described a variety of web development tools.

The Study Guide reinforces material you should know after reading this module.

STUDENT ASSIGNMENTS

Instructions: Answer the questions below using the format that helps you remember best or that is required by your instructor. Possible formats may include one or more of these options: write the answers; create a document that contains the answers; record answers as audio or video using a webcam, smartphone, or portable media player; post answers on a blog, wiki, or website; or highlight answers in the book/e-book.

1. Define the terms, database and database software. Identify the role of a file, record, and field in database hierarchy.

2. Define these terms: field, field name, and data type. List common data types.

3. Identify what is stored in a record. Explain the importance of a primary key.

4. Define the term, data file. Identify what is involved in file maintenance.

5. Explain the issues surrounding fair use of collected customer data.

6. Explain how a DBMS might manage deleted or obsolete records.

7. Define the term, validation. List types of validity checks and explain what occurs in each.

8. Explain the disadvantages of typical file processing systems. Describe the database approach to storing data.

9. Explain the issues surrounding use of criminal databases.

10. Differentiate between a front-end and back-end program. Explain the advantages and disadvantages of the database approach.

11. Explain how you access data in a web database. Describe the role of a database server.

12. Identify uses of web databases for government, entertainment, travel, shopping, research, and education.

13. A(n) _____ defines how users view the organization of the data. List popular examples.

14. List possible uses of an object-oriented database.

15. Explain the characteristics, sources, and uses of Big Data. Describe what occurs during data visualization.

16. Describe the role of the database administrator.

17. Define the term, data dictionary. Explain how a data dictionary helps ensure data integrity.

18. A(n) _____ is a request for specific information from a database.

19. Define the terms, query language, SQL, and QBE.

20. Define the terms, form and report writer.

21. Explain how access privileges contribute to data security. List steps to secure and maintain a database.

22. List methods to recover from identity theft. Explain issues surrounding use of national ID cards.

23. List methods to restore or backup a database. Differentiate between rollforward and rollback recovery.

24. Identify the five phases in the SDLC. Name three guidelines for system development.

25. Identify who participates in system development. Describe the responsibilities of a systems analyst.

26. Define the term, project management. List elements the project leader must identify.

27. A(n) _____ is any tangible item, such as a chart, diagram, report, or program file. List the steps involved in using project management software.

28. Describe how Gantt and PERT charts are used.

29. Define the terms, scope creep and change management.

30. Identify tests used to evaluate feasibility of a project. Explain the importance of documentation.

31. Describe ways that team members collaborate.

32. Identify data and information gathering techniques. A(n) _____ session also is called a focus group.

33. Describe circumstances that can initiate system development.

34. List the four activities of the planning phase. Explain how projects are prioritized.

35. Describe the activities of the analysis phase. List the three activities of the detailed analysis phase.

36. Explain security issues surrounding outsourcing.

37. List the two activities of the design phase. Describe how a systems analyst obtains hardware or software.

38. Differentiate among an RFQ, RFP, and RFI. Describe the roles of VARs and IT consultants when soliciting vendor proposals.

39. Explain what occurs when vendor proposals are tested and evaluated. A(n) _____ test measures the performance of hardware or software.

40. Explain the activities and users involved in the detailed design phase. Define the term, prototype.

41. List the four activities of the implementation phase.

42. List the three activities of the support and security phase. Describe components of a technology security plan.

43. Define the following terms: programming language, application development tool, and syntax.

44. Define the terms, procedural language, machine language, compiler, and interpreter. List benefits of OOP languages.

45. Describe the following: 4GLs, classic programming languages, application generators, and macros. Explain how to protect yourself from macro viruses.

46. Explain how web developers use HTML5, XML, WML, CSS, and JavaScript.

47. Describe uses of forensic databases.

Key Terms

You should be able to define the Primary Terms and be familiar with the Secondary Terms listed below.

Primary Terms (shown in **bold-black** characters in the module)

4GL (11-35)
analysis phase (11-25)
Big Data (11-12)
C (11-31)
C++ (11-34)
character (11-4)
continuous backup (11-18)
data dictionary (11-14)
data file (11-5)
data model (11-12)
data type (11-4)
database (11-2)
database management
    system (DBMS) (11-3)
database software (11-3)
design phase (11-26)

feasibility (11-20)
field (11-4)
field name (11-4)
file maintenance (11-5)
file processing system
    (11-8)
form (11-15)
HTML (11-37)
Implementation phase
    (11-28)
Java (11-34)
log (11-18)
macro (11-35)
object-oriented
    programming (OOP)
    language (11-32)

planning phase (11-24)
preliminary investigation
    (11-25)
primary key (11-5)
procedural language
    (11-31)
programming language
    (11-31)
project management
    (11-20)
project management
    software (11-20)
prototype (11-28)
query (11-14)
query language (11-15)
record (11-5)

recovery utility (11-18)
report writer (11-16)
Structured Query
    Language (SQL) (11-15)
support and security phase
    (11-30)
system development
    (11-19)
system development life
    cycle (SDLC) (11-19)
systems analyst (11-20)
training (11-29)
validation (11-6)
Visual Studio (11-34)
XML (11-37)

Secondary Terms (shown in *italic* characters in the module)

.NET (11-34)
acceptance test (11-29)
agile development (11-33)
alphabetic check (11-7)
application development tool (11-31)
ASP.NET (11-34)
ATOM (11-38)
back end (11-9)
backward recovery (11-18)
benchmark test (11-27)
BLOB (11-4)
Boolean (11-4)
change management (11-22)
code (11-31)
collaborative databases (11-10)
compiler (11-32)
completeness check (11-7)
composite key (11-5)
conferencing software (11-23)
consistency check (11-7)
cost/benefit feasibility (11-22)
data entry form (11-15)
data warehouse (11-12)
database administrator (DBA)
    (11-14)
database server (11-10)
deliverable (11-21)
detailed analysis (11-25)
digital forensics (11-18)
direct conversion (11-29)
distributed database (11-12)
documentation (11-22)
economic feasibility (11-22)

e-form (11-15)
Extensible Markup Language
    (11-37)
feasibility study (11-25)
feature creep (11-22)
focus group (11-23)
forward recovery (11-18)
fourth-generation language (11-35)
front end (11-9)
function creep (11-6)
Gantt chart (11-21)
geolocation (11-39)
Hypertext Markup
    Language (11-37)
information system (11-19)
integrated development
    environment (IDE) (11-33)
integration test (11-29)
interpreter (11-32)
IT consultant (11-27)
JavaScript (11-39)
joint-application design (JAD)
    session (11-23)
logical design (11-25)
machine language (11-31)
metadata (11-14)
mock-up (11-27)
multidimensional database (11-12)
nonprocedural language (11-35)
numeric check (11-7)
object (11-12)
object code (11-32)
object program (11-32)

object-oriented database
    (OODB) (11-12)
operational feasibility (11-22)
parallel conversion (11-30)
PERT chart (11-21)
phased conversion (11-30)
phases (11-19)
pilot conversion (11-30)
post-implementation system
    review (11-30)
principle of least privilege policy
    (11-16)
program development life cycle
    (11-28)
program specification package
    (11-28)
project leader (11-20)
project manager (11-20)
project request (11-24)
project team (11-20)
proof of concept (11-28)
query by example (QBE) (11-15)
RAD (rapid application
    development) (11-33)
range check (11-7)
relational database (11-12)
report generator (11-16)
repository (11-14)
request for information
    (RFI) (11-26)
request for proposal
    (RFP) (11-26)

request for quotation (RFQ) (11-26)
request for system services (11-24)
rollback (11-18)
rollforward (11-18)
RSS 2.0 (11-38)
sandbox (11-29)
schedule feasibility (11-22)
scope (11-20)
scope creep (11-22)
scribe (11-24)
scripting language (11-38)
source program (11-31)
standards (11-20)
steering committee (11-20)
syntax (11-31)
systems test (11-29)
user buy-in (11-28)
technical feasibility (11-22)
unit test (11-29)
value-added reseller (VAR) (11-26)
visual programming environment
    (VPE) (11-35)
visual programming language
    (11-35)
web conference (11-23)
web developers (11-37)
WML (wireless markup
    language) (11-38)

The Checkpoint exercises test your knowledge of the module concepts.

Checkpoint

True/False   Mark T for True and F for False. If False, rewrite the statement so that it is True.

_____ 1. In a data hierarchy, each higher level of data contains one or more items from the lower level.

_____ 2. A check digit often confirms the accuracy of a primary key value.

_____ 3. In a typical database system, each department or area within an organization has its own set of files.

_____ 4. In a file processing system, duplicated data can increase the chance of errors.

_____ 5. Many programs today use forms on a webpage as their front end.

_____ 6. File processing systems require more memory, storage, and processing power than a database.

_____ 7. To retrieve or select data in a database, you query it.

_____ 8. Unlike a form, you use a report writer only to retrieve data.

_____ 9. One way to secure a database is to allow only administrators to have access to create and delete tables.

_____ 10. In a rollforward, the DBMS uses the log to undo any changes made to the database during a certain period.

_____ 11. Gantt charts are better suited than PERT charts for planning and scheduling large, complex projects.

_____ 12. The planning phase begins when the steering committee receives a project request.

Matching   Match the terms with their definitions.

_____ 1. check digit

_____ 2. data type

_____ 3. feature creep

_____ 4. file maintenance

_____ 5. object

_____ 6. object program

_____ 7. primary key

_____ 8. source program

_____ 9. standards

_____ 10. validation

a. procedures that keep data current

b. item that contains data, as well as the actions that read or process the data

c. field that uniquely identifies each record in a file

d. process of comparing data with a set of rules or values to determine if the data meets certain criteria

e. language instructions, or code, to be converted to machine language

f. machine language version of a program that results from compiling the procedural language

g. number(s) or character(s) that is appended to or inserted in a primary key value

h. specifies the kind of data a field can contain and how the field is used

i. problem that occurs when one activity has led to another that was not planned originally, causing the project to grow in scope

j. sets of rules and procedures an organization expects employees to accept and follow

✳ Problem Solving

The Problem Solving exercises extend your knowledge of module concepts by seeking solutions to practical problems with technology that you may encounter at home, school, or work. The Collaboration exercise should be completed with a team.

Instructions: You often can solve problems with technology in multiple ways. Determine a solution to the problems in these exercises by using one or more resources available to you (such as a computer or mobile device, articles on the web or in print, blogs, podcasts, videos, television, user guides, other individuals, electronics or computer stores, etc.). Describe your solution, along with the resource(s) used, in the format requested by your instructor (brief report, presentation, discussion, blog post, video, or other means).

Personal

1. **No Search Results**   While searching a web database for a hotel room for an upcoming trip, a message is displayed stating that no search results match your criteria. What can you do to correct this problem?

2. **Incorrect Price**   You are shopping for groceries and, after loading all items in your cart, it is time to check out. The cashier scans your items, but you realize that the register is not reflecting an advertised discount on one of the items. Why might this be happening?

3. **Webpage Not Readable**   You are attempting to view a webpage on your smartphone, but the text is very small and you are having difficulty reading anything. It is extremely time consuming for you to zoom in and constantly scroll around the webpage to view the contents. What might be causing this?

4. **Inaccurate Credit Report**   You have obtained a free copy of your credit report and notice that multiple companies are accessing your credit report without your knowledge or permission. Your financial records are very important, and it is troubling that other companies are accessing this information. Why might this be occurring?

5. **Webpage Script**   You are viewing a webpage and have just submitted an online form. The browser does not appear to do anything for about one minute, and an error message finally appears stating that a script on the page is taking longer than expected to run. What might be wrong?

Professional

6. **Data Entry Issues**   You are in charge of adding student information to your school's database using a front end. When you attempt to enter the street address for one of the students, the entire street name does not fit in the text box. What are your next steps?

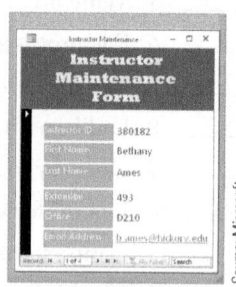

Source: Microsoft

7. **Incorrect Postal Codes**   Your company's database stores information about its customers, including their names, addresses, phone numbers, email addresses, and order history. While reviewing the database to ensure data integrity, you notice that some of the postal codes, which should be five digits, are only four digits. What might be wrong?

8. **Database Connection Error**   While interacting with a web app, an error is displayed informing you that the web app is not able to connect to the database. What might be causing this?

9. **Database Recovery**   Your boss has informed you that the main customer database for your company has become corrupt. Fortunately, you can attempt to use the recovery utility to salvage the data in the database. When you attempt to recover the database, you receive an error message that the recovery has failed. What are your next steps?

10. **Content Management System Updates**   You are attempting to update your company's website using a content management system. When you make the requested changes in the content management system, they are not reflected on the company website. What might be the problem?

Collaboration

11. **Technology in Sports**   You serve as an assistant coach for your former high school's baseball team. The head coach, whose computer is more than five years old, informs you that he would like to create an application that will allow him to keep track of his players' statistics. For instance, he would like to track each player's number of strikeouts, walks, hits, and home runs. Form a team of three people to determine the requirements for implementing his request. One team member will research the types of apps that can track this data, another team member will determine the specifications for a computer or mobile device capable of running the software and storing the data, and the other team member will determine the best way to collect the data during the game.

The How To: Your Turn exercises present general guidelines for fundamental skills when using a computer or mobile device and then require that you determine how to apply these general guidelines to a specific program or situation.

How To: Your Turn

Instructions: You often can complete tasks using technology in multiple ways. Figure out how to perform the tasks described in these exercises by using one or more resources available to you (such as a computer or mobile device, articles on the web or in print, online or program help, user guides, blogs, podcasts, videos, other individuals, trial and error, etc.). Summarize your 'how to' steps, along with the resource(s) used, in the format requested by your instructor (brief report, presentation, discussion, blog post, video, or other means).

1 Obtain and Verify the Accuracy of a Credit Report

It is important to obtain your credit report at least one time per year to verify its accuracy, as imperfections on a credit report can lead to problems such as financing being declined or higher interest rates on loans. The following steps guide you through the process of obtaining and verifying the accuracy of a credit report.

a. Run a browser and then navigate to annualcreditreport.com.

b. When you arrive at the website, verify that the browser is using the https protocol, indicating a secure connection.

c. Click the button to request the report.

d. Provide the necessary personal information.

e. Select the agency or agencies from which you want a copy of your credit report.

f. Click the button to continue to the credit reporting agency's website.

g. If necessary, enter the additional requested information to validate your request.

h. Follow the instructions on the website to finish obtaining a copy of your credit report.

i. Save and/or print a copy of the credit report. After you have obtained a copy of your credit report, verify it for accuracy. The following points describe what to look for when reviewing the report:

- Verify the list of accounts is accurate.
- Verify your payment history.
- Verify current balances are accurate.
- Review your personal information, and report any inconsistencies to the credit reporting agency.
- Review your rights under the Fair Credit Reporting Act.

Exercises

1. In addition to the reasons mentioned in this exercise, why else might you want to obtain a copy of your credit report?

2. What is a credit score? How can you obtain your credit score? What are the highest and lowest possible credit scores?

3. If you find erroneous information on your credit report, how can you make the necessary corrections?

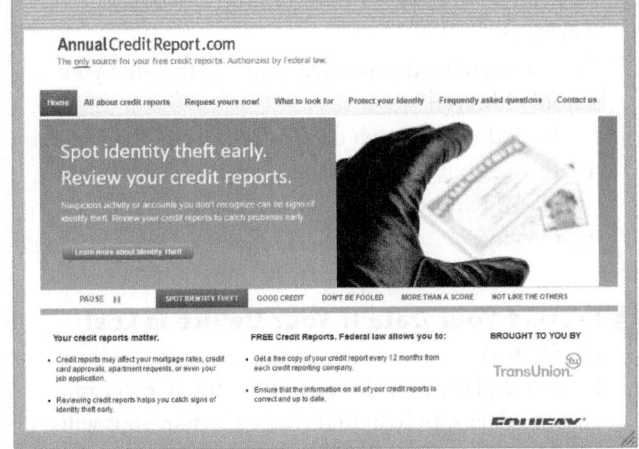

Copyright © 2016 Central Source, LLC

2 Use a Research Database

Students often use one or more research databases to locate information about a particular topic. Research databases often can be accessed in a public or school library, through a library's website, or through the research database's website. The following steps guide you through the process of using a research database:

a. Locate and then navigate to the research database that contains the information you are seeking. Consult a librarian if you need assistance in determining the exact database you should use.

b. Determine the location from which you can access the research database. For instance, you may need to access some research databases from a library computer. Other databases are accessible from anywhere if you can verify your identity as a library patron or a student. Some databases are available to the public at no charge or with no other restrictions.

c. Navigate to the research database you plan to use.

d. If the research database contains an option to perform an advanced search, click the option to perform the advanced search.

e. Specify the search criteria. Note that not all research databases will request the same search criteria. The following list contains some common criteria:

1. Keywords
2. Author
3. Publication date

✸ How To: Your Turn

4. Publication type
5. Education level
f. Run the search.
g. Browse the search results and then click the search result that interests you.

Exercises

1. Why might you want or need to use a research database?
2. What research databases are available through your school's library?
3. Evaluate three research databases that you may need to use throughout your academic career. Which one do you like the most? Why? Which one do you like the least? Why?

③ Protect Your Data If Your Device Is Lost or Stolen

If you misplace your device or it is stolen, you can use another device to help find yours. Certain apps will help you locate your device, cause your phone to ring, display an alert message, take a photo using the front or back camera, or remotely lock the device so that your data will be safe. Some apps require purchasing the full version to access advanced features, such as remotely locking or wiping your device. The following steps guide you through the process of protecting your data if your device is lost or stolen.

a. Determine whether your device has a built-in feature or app you can use to locate it in the event it is lost or stolen. If not, locate, install, and run an app that can perform this service. The app you locate and install should meet the following criteria:
1. The app should be reputable and have good reviews.
2. Reviews should contain no indication that the app is malicious.
3. The app should be able to locate, lock, and erase data from your device if it is lost or stolen.
4. You should be able to access or control your phone from a variety of devices (such as smartphones, tablets, and laptops) and operating systems (such as iOS, Android, macOS, and Windows).
5. The app should be secure so that others cannot inadvertently or maliciously control your device.
b. From the app's home screen, configure the necessary settings so that you will be able to locate and control your device if it is lost or stolen. Consider configuring the following settings:

1. Determine which ringer or sound you want to use if you are attempting to locate a lost device.
2. Specify how to instruct the device to take an appropriate action. For example, you may be able to instruct a device to play a sound (such as a siren) by sending a text message to it with certain wording, or by tapping or clicking a button on a specific website.
3. Enable the GPS feature on the device so that you will be able to see its location.
c. Make sure the data on your device is backed up regularly to a computer or to the cloud. Some devices have a feature (or apps available) to automatically back up your data in the event it is erased from your device.
d. Test the features of the app to make sure it works as intended.
e. In the event the device is lost or stolen, perform the following steps as soon as possible for the best chance at retrieving the device and its data:
1. Issue a command to the device to lock it.
2. If you are attempting to locate a phone, call it to see if someone answers. If so, try to retrieve the phone.
3. If possible, send a text message to the device with your contact information to see if someone contacts you.
4. Activate the ringer or sound on the device so that you can hear it if it is nearby.
5. If possible, access a web app or an app on another device to track the device's location using GPS.
6. If possible, take a photo with the device's front and back cameras to see if you can determine where it is located.
7. If you are unsuccessful and you think the data on the device is at risk, issue a command to the device to erase all data. Consider contacting law enforcement if you think the device was stolen.

Exercises

1. Have you ever lost or misplaced a device? If so, did you locate it? How?
2. Evaluate at least three apps that can locate and remove data from a lost or stolen device. Which ones did you evaluate? Which is your favorite? Why?
3. Some devices offer a feature that allows you to encrypt the data. Would you encrypt the data on your device? Why or why not? What are the benefits of doing so? What drawbacks exist, if any?

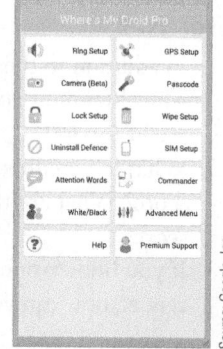

Source: Google, Inc.

The Internet Research exercises broaden your understanding of module concepts by requiring that you search for information on the web.

Internet Research

Instructions: Use a search engine or another search tool to locate the information requested or answers to questions presented in the exercises. Describe your findings, along with the search term(s) you used and your web source(s), in the format requested by your instructor (brief report, presentation, discussion, blog post, video, or other means).

1 Making Use of the Web
Entertainment

Americans, on average, spend nearly six percent of their income on entertainment, which includes tickets for concerts and movies, electronic equipment, hobbies, and services. They have scaled back their away-from-home activities in favor of in-home entertainment as they have invested in home theaters, high-speed Internet, and game consoles.

Many websites satisfy our cravings for amusement. For example, the Rock and Roll Hall of Fame and Museum has videos, stories, and a comprehensive "The Story of Rock" to enjoy. The Internet Movie Database (IMDb) has facts about more than 2.7 million movies, television shows, and entertainment programs. It also has video highlights, quotes, quizzes, and movie showtimes. Other entertainment websites have a variety of content aimed at amusing visitors and relieving boredom.

Research This: (a) Locate the Rock and Roll Hall of Fame and Museum website and view the information about the latest inductees. What is the total number of inductees? Which artists have been inducted more than once? Describe two upcoming events. Which classes are being offered in the Rock and Roll Night School?

(b) Locate the Internet Movie Database website. Take the IMDb Internet Icon Quiz. What score did you earn? What are three movies opening this week? What is the top news story of the day?

(c) Visit an entertainment website. What content is featured, such as humorous and sports video clips, photos, animations, and audio clips? What categories are available? Are advertisements included in the content? Which content is available at no cost, and which requires a fee to access?

2 Social Media
Targeted Ads

Companies collect data as people browse websites. Just seconds after individuals visit a specific webpage, advertisements are displayed matching their shopping patterns and favorite products. This tracking is prevalent in online social networks, too, as marketers match users' profiles and other posted information, such as status updates, with specific businesses. Facebook, for example, allows retailers to upload their databases containing email addresses, phone numbers, and other personal facts. This data then is compared with the Facebook users' data. When a match is found, specific advertisements are displayed. Social media may charge the advertisers each time a user clicks an ad, called CPC (cost per click) or PPC (pay per click), which could range from a few cents to several dollars. Another option is to charge for a specific number of times an ad is displayed, called CPI (cost per impression).

Research This: Locate at least two articles discussing targeting ads on online social networks. How do the businesses place their ads based on the users' online identities and profiles? What steps are taken to ensure the users' privacy? Should users expect companies to collect data about some of their online behaviors in return for using the websites at no charge?

3 Search Skills
Verifying Your Search Results

Even though a link to a website or other online resource may appear first in your list of search results, the information it presents may not be accurate. Several strategies exist to help you determine the credibility of search results. Verify the information you read by finding supporting information on other websites or by comparing search results from different search engines. Often authors will provide links to sources within or at the end of an article. Search for information about the author to help determine his or her credibility, authenticity, or objectivity. Some articles may present opinions, not facts.

If you do not recognize or have doubts about the domain name of a website you are reading, type the search text, whois, in a search engine to locate the WhoIs database. Then type the domain name of the website in question (such as cengagebrain.com) in

Source: The Rock and Roll Hall of Fame and Museum, Inc.

✺ Internet Research

the WhoIs search box to find its owner. You then can search for more information about the website's owner. If you are looking for time-sensitive information, check the date when the links or pages were updated. If a webpage is filled with ads or pop-ups, it may be a scam.

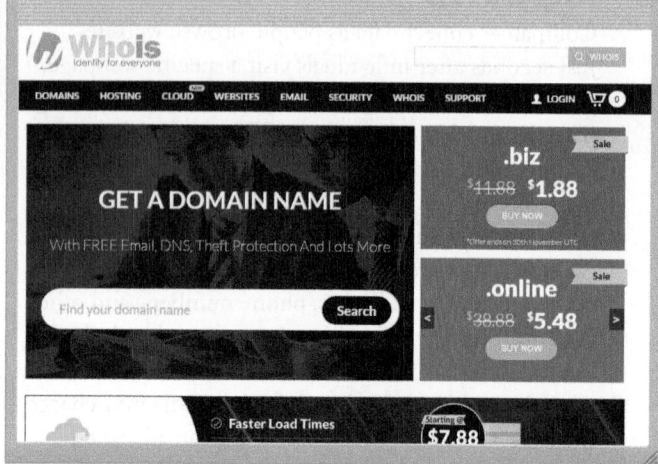

Source: WhoIs

Research This: Use a search engine to answer these questions and report your findings. (1) Find an article on Wikipedia about relational databases. What references reinforce the statements in the article? (2) Find a popular blog about CRM systems and use WhoIs to determine the blog's owner. (3) Search for a news article about web databases and then find two additional articles by the same author on a similar topic. (4) Search for information about the five most popular content management systems in use today. Do different websites give you different results? How was popularity determined?

④ Security
Selling Data

When you use supermarket loyalty cards, enter contests, complete warranty registrations, apply for credit cards, and subscribe to newsletters, businesses automatically store personal data about you, your transactions, and your preferences in their marketing databases. They often use this data to analyze sales, develop advertising campaigns, and solicit more business from you. Unbeknownst to many consumers, some companies also sell or rent this data to other businesses

for the purpose of developing interest-based or online behavioral advertising. Consumers can refuse to receive targeted email messages and marketing materials, but they often must search the websites or paper forms for check boxes to indicate these opt-out preferences. Some consumer advocates view this practice as an invasion of privacy and urge businesses to default to not adding consumers' information to databases unless the consumer opts in to receive additional materials.

Research This: Visit at least two websites that include opt-in or opt-out provisions and read the disclosure notices. What steps can you take to remove yourself from databases? Which organizations help protect consumers and offer information on maintaining online privacy? Then, search for at least two marketing companies that provide online direct advertising campaigns. How do these companies use databases to match consumers' buying preferences with targeted offers?

⑤ Cloud Services
Online Databases (DaaS)

Accessing information from online databases is an example of data as a service (DaaS), a service of cloud computing that provides data on demand for use in applications or visualizations. Federal, state, and local governments provide data online to promote transparency and enable users to perform research online. Independent data markets are websites that aggregate and offer data from leading providers, along with web-based tools for exploring, analyzing, and visualizing online data. Data providers make the data available to developers through an API (application programming interface), who incorporate the data in new products, such as web or mobile apps. Users often can explore the data through a web interface.

Research This: (1) Use a search engine to find and visit the open data site for your city, state, or country's government. Select a topic for which data is available, and use the online tools provided to explore a data set and create a visualization in the form of a map or graph. (2) Use a search engine to find and visit an independent data market website, and browse the data sets listed. Select one of the data sets and read about the data it contains. How might an app make use of this data? What pricing models are available for developers who wish to incorporate this data into their apps?

The Critical Thinking exercises challenge your assessment and decision-making skills by presenting real-world situations associated with module concepts. The Collaboration exercise should be completed with a team.

Critical Thinking

Instructions: Evaluate the situations below, using personal experiences and one or more resources available to you (such as articles on the web or in print, blogs, podcasts, videos, television, user guides, other individuals, electronics or computer stores, etc.). Perform the tasks requested in each exercise and share your deliverables in the format requested by your instructor (brief report, presentation, discussion, blog post, video, or other means).

1. Online Movie Reviews

Information about movie titles and television shows is available from the web database IMDb (Internet Movie Database). Visitors can search IMDb using by title, cast member, year produced, characters, genre, awards, or other criteria. Each movie or show's listing offers a brief description and rating and includes links to such items as summary, trivia, reviews, quotes, and even streaming video options.

Do This: Visit imdb.com and search for both recently released and classic movies. Explain the steps you used to query the movie database. Assess how complete the information provided was. Who would benefit most from using the movie database? Why? Answer the following questions about your experiences. Did the information provided differ when viewing recently released titles versus classic movies? What did you learn from your queries? Can you identify a few fields that are included in the records for each movie? What interactive features can you identify? Can you find any HTML5 features that have been incorporated?

2. Spreadsheets versus Databases

Some individuals and small organizations prefer using spreadsheets instead of databases. People who use spreadsheets might argue that similar to databases, spreadsheets have columns and rows, and you can keep track of different sets of data in individual worksheets. This is similar to how you would use tables in a database to store different data sets. In addition, some find it easier to install, use, and maintain spreadsheet software than database software. After reading this module, you are convinced that databases have additional advantages, such as the capability of storing more data and more quickly searching for data, as well as generating reports.

Do This: Prepare information aimed toward individuals who prefer spreadsheets to databases. Include reasons why it is not advisable to store large amounts of data in spreadsheets, as well as the reporting and querying capabilities of databases. Explain benefits for using a database for collaborating and sharing information among departments in a business.

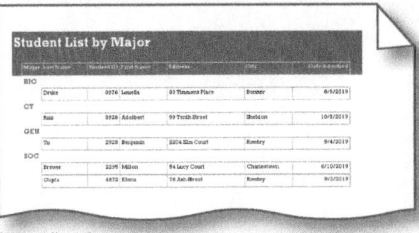

Source: Microsoft

3. Case Study

Family-Owned Coffee Shop   You are the new manager for a family-owned coffee shop. The coffee shop uses a database to store information about its inventory, prices, employees, customers, and special offers. The coffee shop's website uses information stored in the database to display products, pricing, and sales. The owners have asked you to investigate how the coffee shop should secure its database.

Do This: Using information learned in the module as well as performing additional research, prepare information about securing a database. What risks exist for databases? Who should determine the security measures to take? What should you include in the database security policy? Include recommendations for backing up data, validation, maintenance, and assigning different access levels to employees and managers. Is the coffee shop bound to uphold pricing mistakes that appear on its website? Why or why not? Compile your findings.

Collaboration

4. **System Development Life Cycle**   A major retail company has hired your team to create and implement the steps in the system development life cycle (SDLC) to create custom inventory software.

Do This: Assign SDLC steps to different teammates and compile a plan for each step. Share your findings. Does the plan contain gaps? Do any steps or tasks overlap? What guidelines should you follow during system development? What roles are needed? How might you use project management software? As a team, answer the following questions to share with the retail company: Would you use a compiler or an interpreter? Why? Would you use an object-oriented programming language? Why or why not? What types of information gathering techniques would be most effective? Why? Would you recommend outsourcing parts of the process? Why or why not? What is necessary to create a prototype of the project? Search for popular programming languages. Find industry experts' reviews of each language. Can you find an example of a program that uses each language? Which language might be best suited to this project? Why? As a team, compile your findings and share your recommendation with the class.

Working in the Enterprise:
Systems, Certifications, and Careers

12

ImageFlow / Shutterstock.com

OBJECTIVES

After completing this module, you will be able to:

1　Identify the qualities of valuable information

2　Describe various information systems used in an enterprise

3　Identify the components of and steps in information literacy

4　Describe career opportunities available in these segments of the computer industry: general business and government organizations and their IT departments; technology equipment field; software and apps field; technology service and repair field; technology sales; technology education, training, and support field; and IT consulting

5　Identify job titles and responsibilities for various technology jobs

6　Identify mobile app development strategies

7　Identify ways to prepare for certification

8　Describe the general areas of IT certification

9　Identify ways to begin a job search

10　Explain how to create a professional online presence

The Technology Industry

Nearly every job requires you to interact with technology to complete projects, exchange information with coworkers, and meet customers' needs. The technology field provides many opportunities for people of all skill levels and interests, and a demand for computer professionals continues to grow. Figure 12-1 identifies some technology-related careers available to today's college graduates. You can use both social media and job search websites to learn about technology careers and to promote yourself to potential employers. By creating a professional online presence, hiring managers can learn more about you beyond what you can convey in a traditional one-page paper resume.

Figure 12-1 The technology industry offers many rewarding careers.

iStockphoto.com / jayfish

As new technologies emerge, organizations look for potential employees who possess skills and a desire to learn and who are comfortable using all types of technology. This module discusses the various types of information systems you may encounter in an organization, as well as technology professionals with whom you might interact. It also explores current technology careers and how you can prepare for them.

Information Systems in the Enterprise

Businesses, and their employees, use many types of systems. A system is a set of components that interact to achieve a common goal. A billing system, for example, allows a company to send invoices and receive payments from customers. Through a payroll system, employees receive paychecks — often deposited directly into their bank accounts. A manufacturing system produces the goods that customers order. Very often, these systems also are information systems. Recall from Module 11 that an **information system** is a set of hardware, software, data, people, and procedures that work together to produce information. Information systems support daily, short-term, and long-range information requirements of users in a company.

To assist with sound decision making, information must have value. For it to be valuable, information should be accurate, verifiable, timely, organized, accessible, useful, and cost effective.

- Accurate information is error free. Inaccurate information can lead to incorrect decisions. For example, consumers assume their credit reports are accurate. If your credit report incorrectly shows past-due payments, a bank may not lend you money for a vehicle or a house.
- Verifiable information can be proven as correct or incorrect. For example, security personnel at an airport usually request some type of photo identification to verify that you are the person named on the ticket.
- Timely information is useful only within a specific time period. A decision to build additional schools in a particular district should be based on the most recent census report — not on one that is 10 years old. Most information loses value with time. Some information, however, such as information about trends, gains value as time passes and more information is obtained. For example, your transcript gains value as you take more classes.
- Organized information is arranged to suit the needs and requirements of the decision maker. Two different people may need the same information presented in a different manner. For example, an inventory manager may want an inventory report to list out-of-stock items first. The purchasing agent, instead, wants the report alphabetized by vendor.
- Accessible information is available when the decision maker needs it. Having to wait for information may delay an important decision. For example, a sales manager cannot decide which sales representative deserves the award for highest annual sales if the December sales have not been entered in the database yet.
- Useful information has meaning to the person who receives it. Most information is important only to certain people or groups of people. Always consider the audience when collecting and reporting information. Avoid distributing useless information. For example, an announcement of an alumni association meeting is not useful to students who have not graduated yet.
- Cost-effective information should provide more value than it costs to produce. An organization occasionally should review the information it produces to determine if it still is cost effective to produce. Some organizations create information only on demand, that is, as people request it, instead of on a regular basis. Many make information available online so that users can access it as they need it.

Functional Units

A large organization, commonly referred to as an enterprise, requires special computing solutions because of its size and geographic distribution. A typical enterprise consists of a wide variety of departments, centers, and divisions — collectively known as functional units. Examples of functional units include human resources, manufacturing, and customer service.

Some information systems are used exclusively by only one type of functional unit within the enterprise. Table 12-1 lists some of the more common information systems that are used by functional units in a typical enterprise. Other information systems that support activities of several functional units include enterprise resource planning, document management systems, and content management systems.

Table 12-1	Information Systems Used Exclusively by Functional Units in an Enterprise
Functional Unit	**Information System**
Human Resources (HR)	• *A human resources information system* (*HRIS*) manages one or more administrative human resources functions, such as maintaining and managing employee benefits, schedules, and payroll.
Engineering or Product Development	• *Computer-aided engineering* (*CAE*) aids in the development and testing of product designs, and often includes CAD (computer-aided design).
Manufacturing	• *Computer-aided manufacturing* (*CAM*) controls production equipment, such as drills, lathes, and milling machines. • *Material Requirements Planning* (*MRP*) monitors and controls inventory, material purchases, and other processes related to manufacturing operations. • *Manufacturing Resource Planning II* (*MRP II*) is an extension of MRP that also includes product packaging and shipping, machine scheduling, financial planning, demand forecasting, tracking labor productivity, and monitoring product quality.
Marketing	• Market research systems analyze data gathered from demographics and surveys. Social media marketing systems analyze data from email campaigns, online social networks, and content viewed and time spent on webpages.
Sales	• *Salesforce automation* (*SFA*) helps salespeople manage customer contacts, schedule customer meetings, log customer interactions, manage product information, and place customer orders.
Customer Service	• *Customer relationship management* (*CRM*) manages information about customers, past purchases, interests, and the day-to-day interactions, such as phone calls, email messages, web communications, and Internet messaging sessions.

Enterprise Resource Planning

Enterprise Resource Planning (**ERP**) integrates MRP II with the information flow across an organization to manage and coordinate the ongoing activities of the enterprise, including product planning, manufacturing and distribution, accounting and finance, sales, human resources, and customer support.

Advantages of ERP include complete integration of information systems across departments, better project management, and improved customer service. Complete integration means information is shared rapidly, and management receives a more complete and timely view of the organization through the information. Project management software often is standardized across an enterprise so that different parts of the enterprise easily can integrate and collaborate on their planning and logistics. Figure 12-2 illustrates how ERP encompasses all major activities of an enterprise.

planning and logistics

billing and collections

purchasing materials (MRP)

marketing

HR

customer support

distribution

payments

sales

accounting/finance

product inventory

parts inventory

production

Figure 12-2 ERP encompasses all of the major activities throughout an enterprise.

Hurst Photo / Shutterstock.com; Monkey Business Images / Shutterstock.com; iStockphoto.com / PKM1; BartlomiejMagierowski / Shutterstock.com; Inti St Clair / Getty Images; iStockphoto.com / choicegraphx; John Penezic / Shutterstock.com; lucadp / Shutterstock.com; Andresr / Shutterstock.com; baki / Shutterstock.com; StockLite / Shutterstock.com; wavebreakmedia / Shutterstock.com; Tumar / Shutterstock.com; ESB Professional / Shutterstock.com

Document Management Systems

Some organizations use document management systems to make collaboration possible among employees. A **document management system (DMS)** allows for storage and management of a company's documents, such as word processing documents, presentations, and spreadsheets. A central library stores all documents within a company or department. The system supports access control, security, version tracking of documents, and search capabilities; it also gives users the ability to check out documents to review or edit them and then check them back in when finished. This information can be used for searches within the document repository. Web-based application document management systems allow individuals and any organization to enjoy the benefits of document management systems as applications running in a browser. Users are granted access to certain parts of the repository, depending on their needs.

Content Management Systems

A **content management system (CMS)** enables and manages the publishing, modification, organization, and access of various forms of documents and other files, including media

BTW

DMS and CMS
A CMS (content
management system)
typically includes a DMS
(document management
system).

and webpages, on a network or the web. CMSs include information about the files and data (metadata). For example, the metadata for a company's employee manual may include the author's name, revision number, a brief summary, and last revision date. A CMS also provides security controls for the content, such as who is allowed to add, view, and modify content and on which content the user is allowed to perform those operations.

Users add content to a CMS through a graphical user interface or webpage. Based on the user's actions, the CMS processes content, categorizes the content, indexes the content so that it later can be searched, and stores the content. Users then access the content stored in the system through a website, company portal, or other application. Read Focus on Web Development for more information about content management systems.

CONSIDER THIS

What are uses of a CMS?

Publishing entities, such as news services, use CMSs to keep websites and web feeds up to date. As news or information is published, it is categorized and updated on the appropriate sections of the website. For example, a sportswriter may submit a story to the CMS and add metadata that indicates the story is a headline story. The CMS categorizes the story so that it is displayed as the first item with a large headline on the sports section of the website and included in the sports section's web feed. The CMS indexes the information in the story so that users who search the website based on keywords in the story will find a link to the story. Bloggers use CMSs to post to their blogs without having to format each entry manually in HTML. Blog posts can be categorized so that readers can search by category for posts on the same topic. Blogs also are searchable. Readers can use the CMS to comment on blog posts, and the blog owner may need to approve the comments before they are published.

BTW

TPS
Transaction processing
systems were among
the first computerized
systems that processed
business data. Many
people initially used the
term, data processing, to
refer to the functions of
these systems.

Other Enterprise-Wide Information Systems

Some enterprise-wide information systems focus on the collection, organization, and sharing of information so that users can make decisions based on an up-to-date and accurate view of the information. The following sections discuss these information systems.

Transaction Processing Systems   A *transaction processing system* (TPS) is an information system that captures and processes data from day-to-day business activities. Examples of transactions are deposits, payments, orders, and reservations. When you use a credit card to purchase an item, you are interacting with a transaction processing system.

Information systems use batch or online transaction processing systems (Figure 12-3). With *batch processing*, the computer collects data over time and processes all transactions later, as a group. With *online transaction processing* (*OLTP*), the computer processes each transaction as it is entered. For example, when you book a flight on the web, the airline probably uses OLTP to schedule the flight, book the flight, and send you a confirmation message.

Most transaction processing systems today use OLTP because users need information immediately. For some routine processing tasks, such as printing monthly invoices or weekly paychecks, they use batch processing.

Management Information Systems   A **management information system** (**MIS**) is an information system that generates accurate, timely, and organized information, so that managers and other users can make decisions, solve problems, supervise activities, and track progress. Management information systems often are integrated with transaction processing systems and focus on creating information that managers and other users need to perform their jobs.

A management information system creates three basic types of reports: detailed, summary, and exception (Figure 12-4). A *detailed report* usually lists just transactions. For example, a Detailed Flight Report lists the number of passengers booked for a given flight. A *summary report* consolidates data usually with totals, tables, or graphs, so that managers can review it quickly and easily. An *exception report* identifies data outside of a normal condition. These out-of-the-ordinary conditions, called the *exception criteria*, define the normal activity or status range. For example, a Premier Club Booking Exception Report notifies the airline's marketing department that some flights have not met minimum goals for booking Premier Club members.

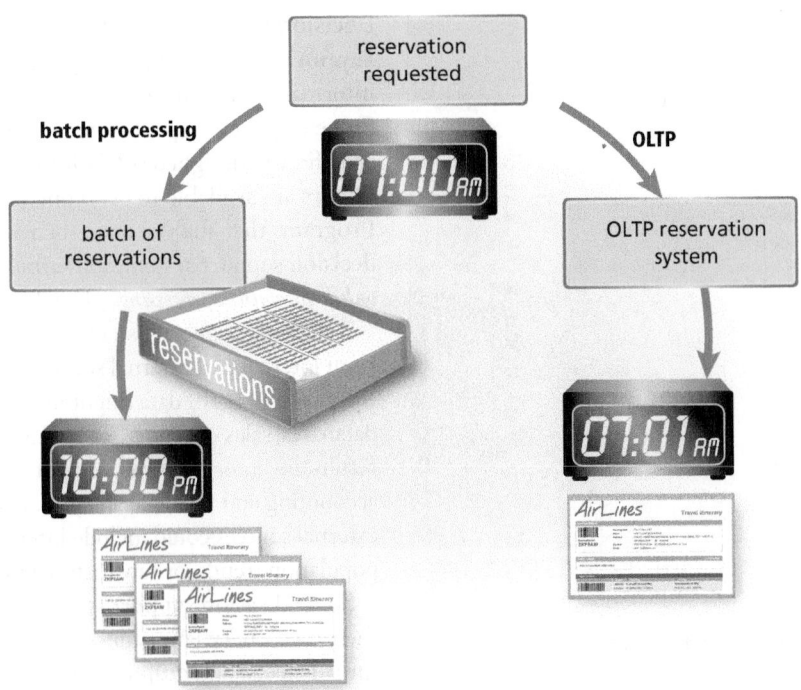

Figure 12-3 With batch processing, all reservations would be processed together at the end of the day. With OLTP, by contrast, reservations are processed immediately.

Detailed Flight Report for Flight #328				
Passenger Name	**Gender**	**Birthdate**	**Seat**	**Premier Club**
Adams, Latisha	F	4/25/92	3C	Y
Brewer, Milton	M	10/14/45	22F	N
Cam, Lin	F	12/16/91	2A	Y
Canaan, Lana	F	4/12/90	21A	N
Cole, Kristina	F	5/10/79	16C	N
Drake, Louella	F	3/4/81	4A	Y
Galens, Lynette	F	11/2/75	2C	N
Gilbert, Laura	F	2/20/78	4F	N
Henreich, Max	M	3/10/85	17C	Y
Hidalgo, Ronald	M	10/15/44	3F	Y
Marsh, Constance	F	11/5/82	2C	N
McGill, Teresa	F	2/27/73	16F	Y
Moretti, Leo	M	9/22/90	17A	Y
Nitz, Dawn	F	7/12/65	3F	N
Ruiz, Albert	M	2/13/93	10D	Y
Stein, Michelle	F	8/16/50	3A	N
Tu, Benjamin	M	1/16/77	22C	N
Van Wijk, Fred	M	6/9/89	10A	Y
Warner, Betty	F	7/1/58	16A	N

Summary Flight Report for March 30			
Flight #	**Origin/ Destination**	**Passengers**	**Premier Club Members**
1048	ORD – RSW	108	33
543	ORD – BMI	24	12
715	ORD – LAX	160	62
701	ORD – JFK	26	10

Exception Flight Report for March 30				
Flight #	**Class**	**Origin/ Destination**	**Premier Club Members**	**Premier Club Member Goal**
1048	A	ORD – RSW	1	4
701	C	ORD – JFK	3	5

Figure 12-4 Three basic types of reports generated in an MIS are detailed, summary, and exception.

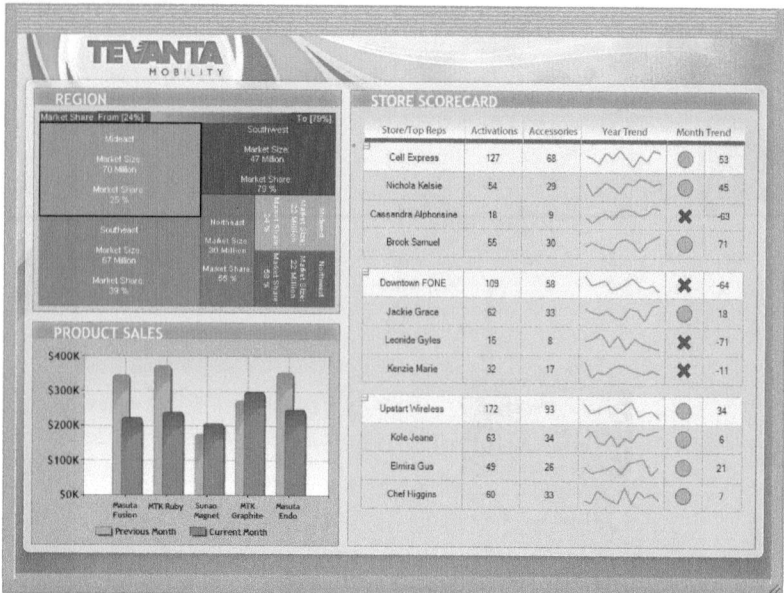

Figure 12-5   This decision support system helps managers analyze sales by product and by sales rep.
Courtesy of Dundas Data Visualation, Inc.

Decision Support Systems   A **decision support system** (DSS) helps users analyze information and make decisions (Figure 12-5). Some decision support systems are company specific and designed solely for managers. Others are available to everyone on the web. Programs that analyze data, such as those in a decision support system, sometimes are called *online analytical processing (OLAP)* programs.

A decision support system uses data from internal and external sources. Internal sources of data might include databases, sales orders, MRP and MRP II results, inventory records, or financial data from accounting and financial analyses. Data from external sources could include interest rates, population trends, or raw material pricing.

Some decision support systems include their own query languages, statistical analyses, spreadsheets, and graphics that help users retrieve data and analyze the results. Some also allow managers to create a model of the factors affecting a decision.

Expert Systems   An **expert system** is an information system that captures and stores the knowledge of human experts and then imitates human reasoning and decision making (Figure 12-6). Expert systems consist of two main components: a knowledge base and inference rules. A *knowledge base* is the combined subject knowledge and experiences of the human experts. The *inference rules* are a set of logical judgments that are applied to the knowledge base each time a user describes a situation to the expert system.

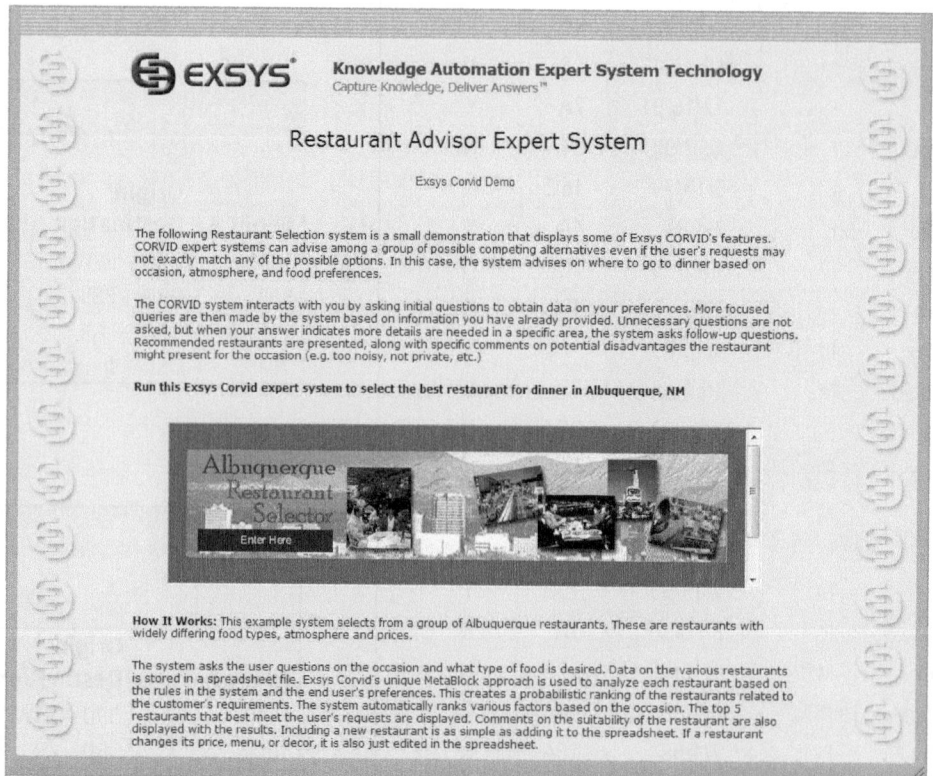

Figure 12-6   This company's restaurant advisor expert system recommends a restaurant based on a user's answers to specific questions.
Courtesy of Exsys

Expert systems help all levels of users make decisions. Enterprises employ expert systems in a variety of roles, such as answering customer questions, training new employees, and analyzing data. Expert systems also successfully have resolved such diverse problems as diagnosing illnesses, searching for oil, and making soup.

 CONSIDER THIS ―――――――――――――――――――――――――――

How do expert systems relate to artificial intelligence?
Expert systems are a component of artificial intelligence. **Artificial intelligence (AI)** is the application of human intelligence to computers. Artificial intelligence technology senses a person's actions and, based on logical assumptions and prior experience, takes the appropriate action to complete the task. Artificial intelligence has a variety of capabilities, including speech recognition, logical reasoning, and creative responses.

Tech Feature 12-1: Information Literacy

To adequately manage information, you should know how to use the five components of information literacy and also know the steps in effective research and composition. Read Tech Feature 12-1 to learn about information literacy.

 TECH FEATURE 12-1 ――――――――――――――――――――――――

Information Literacy

Managing the vast amount of information inundating us daily can be an overwhelming task, not only for those involved in technology careers but also for any digital citizen. This twenty-first century skill set, called *information literacy*, prepares students, employees, and citizens to manage information so that they can be knowledgeable decision makers.

Defining Information Literacy

When personal computers first became popular, the American Library Association was the first organization to recognize the importance of information literate citizens. As the web and the Internet became a mainstay in education, business, and home environments, experts realized that the traditional basic literacy skills of reading, writing, and arithmetic were insufficient for living a productive life. According to the Association of College & Research Libraries, also needed are lifelong skills "to locate, evaluate, and use effectively the needed information."

Information Literacy Components

An individual's quality of existence depends upon obtaining quality information. Information literate people know how to locate meaningful sources that can be used to solve problems, make decisions, and set goals. The following five categories are recognized as integral literacy components:

- **Digital literacy:** Using computers, mobile devices, the Internet, and related technologies effectively is a necessity in business and society. Also important is an understanding of the general concerns of having computers in the world, including their integration in employment and education and their effects on national and personal security.

- **Library instruction:** Undergraduates rarely seek the help of librarians when performing academic research. This lack of help may be due, in part, to the fact that the students misunderstand the role of the reference librarian. Information literate individuals use the librarians' expertise in locating relevant sources. They also understand the necessity of using citations, how information is cataloged and organized, search strategies, and the process of locating and evaluating resources.

- **Media literacy:** Skills needed to understand how mass communication and popular culture affect learning and entertainment include the ability to evaluate and analyze how music, film, video, television, and other nonprint media are used effectively to persuade and inform.

- **Numerical literacy:** The ability to use basic math skills and interpret data is essential to solving problems and communicating information. Also important are understanding how data is gathered and presented in graphs, charts, and other visuals and how to interpret and verify information presented in media.

(Continued)

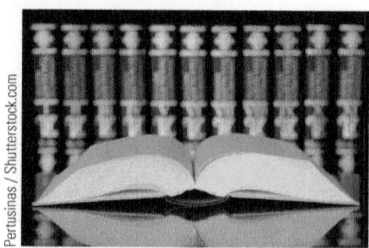

- **Traditional literacy:** Individuals who can read and understand a variety of documents are likely to complete their educations, obtain employment, and participate in community groups. They also need to think critically about the material they have read and to express their thoughts by writing and speaking coherently.

Steps in Effective Research and Composition

Locating appropriate material, organizing these sources, and producing the final document require effort and careful thought. The following paragraphs discuss steps you should take when crafting research, thinking critically, and drafting strategies:

- **Establish an appropriate topic.** Identify the purpose and audience. Determine an effective method of communicating the information, such as a written paper, oral presentation, or blog. Explore and narrow the topic so that it is manageable within time and logistical constraints. Determine the audience's familiarity with the topic and the need to find reference materials.

- **Identify sources.** Determine where to locate electronic and print resources, including websites, media, databases, and printed materials. Differentiate between primary and secondary sources, popular and scholarly articles, and current and historical materials.

- **Evaluate materials.** Analyze the sources to determine reliability, accuracy, timeliness, and bias. Compare the materials to determine if the authors agree or disagree with topics.

- **Create the final work.** Organize and integrate the source material using direct quotations, paraphrases, and summaries. Document the work to credit sources and avoid plagiarism. Integrate photos, charts, and graphs when necessary to clarify the message. Use the writing process to create, review, revise, and proofread.

✳ **Consider This:** Test your skills at effective research by examining a website for a vehicle you would consider purchasing. Describe the photos, colors, placement of objects, and description. Who is the intended audience? Is any information missing from the website? What message is the company attempting to send? Do you think the message achieves its purpose?

Technology Careers

⚙ **BTW**

New Technologies
As new technologies and trends emerge, you should stay informed about them to ensure your relevance in the technology market.

With billions of dollars in annual revenue, the technology industry is a major source of career opportunities worldwide. This industry has created thousands of high-tech career opportunities, even in organizations whose primary business is not technology-related. As technology changes, so do the available careers and requirements. New careers are available in social media and mobile technologies that did not exist a few years ago. For this reason, you should stay up to date with technology developments.

Figure 12-7 Some organizations allow employees to telecommute.
ESB Professional / Shutterstock.com

General Business and Government Organizations and Their IT Departments

Business and government organizations of all sizes use a variety of computers, mobile devices, and other technology. Most use networks to ensure seamless communications among employees, vendors, and customers. They also use webpages, email, mobile apps, online social networks, and more to communicate with the public.

Larger organizations use computers and other technology to answer and route phone calls, process orders, update inventory, and manage accounts receivable, accounts payable, billing, and payroll activities. Many use mobile devices, web conferencing, and VPNs (virtual private networks) to stay connected with employees who work in other locations or who telecommute (Figure 12-7). Read How To 12-1 for tips related to setting up a home office for telecommuting. Read Ethics & Issues 12-1 to consider whether telecommuting is good or bad for business.

✻ HOW TO 12-1

Set Up Your Home Office for Telecommuting

Telecommuting mutually benefits employers and employees. Employers do not have to pay for the physical infrastructure (including office space and parking) for the employee, and telecommuters often work more hours than those who physically commute to an office. Employees benefit from not having to commute and from having a comfortable work environment. The following guidelines describe how to set up your home office for telecommuting:

- Choose a location in your home that is free from noise and distractions. If your home is occupied by others during the hours you plan to telecommute, your office should be located away from potentially noisy areas. For example, an office next to a room where someone else is watching television may not be an ideal choice.

- Make sure your office has a comfortable desk and chair. Although it may be tempting to sit on your couch with your laptop while you work, having a professional workspace will increase productivity.

- Consider how you will store important documents: as paper copies in a file cabinet or digital documents in the cloud.

- If required, verify your office has a sufficient Internet connection. Be sure your wireless network is encrypted. Consider setting up one network for business and another for personal use or by clients.

- Make sure the office has a phone to place and receive calls and videoconferences. If you will be relying on a mobile phone, verify your phone can receive a strong signal and has a conveniently located charger and power outlet.

- Use a headset with your phone to minimize background noise.

- Obtain supplies that typically are found in an office setting, such as writing utensils, paper, tape, a stapler, paper clips, and sticky notes.

- If your employer does not provide a computer for your use, make sure your computer is sufficiently equipped to complete your job tasks. Make sure you also have accessories, such as USB flash drives and other external storage media, if necessary.

- Consider obtaining an all-in-one printer that can print, scan, and copy, as well as extra ink cartridges.

✻ **Consider This:** What other equipment, supplies, and furniture would you prefer to have in an office from where you telecommute?

✻ ETHICS & ISSUES 12-1

Is Telecommuting Good or Bad for Business?

Studies show that nearly 80 percent of workers dream of leaving the confines of an office to work from the comfort of home, at least part of the time. Although employees may view working from home as an ideal situation, some bosses do not agree. An Internet CEO, for example, made news when she reviewed data such as employees' sign-ins to the company's VPN (virtual private network) and discovered that many employees were not working during company hours. As a result, the CEO made the decision to end telecommuting at her company.

Supporters cite reduced pollution and commuting time. Other benefits include

increased productivity due to lack of office gossip and politics. Many feel that they could not be as dedicated to their jobs without telecommuting because of the flexible hours and closeness to home. Others feel that trusted employees should have the privilege if they earn it. Companies benefit by saving on resources, such as office space.

Opponents claim that some lack the self-discipline to work remotely. Employees may be distracted more easily without direct management supervision. Some workers have difficulty setting appropriate boundaries regarding childcare or other family obligations. Additionally, productivity actually may decrease if employees stagger work hours to fit their schedule, limiting times when employees can schedule meetings.

Many experienced workers agree that telecommuting cannot replace valuable face-to-face time with coworkers, vendors, and customers. Some workers fear telecommuting because they feel that the lack of a personal relationship with managers puts them at the top of the list for downsizing.

✻ **Consider This:** Is telecommuting good or bad for business? Why? Are some businesses or positions better suited for telecommuting? If so, which ones? Do some people lack the self-discipline to be productive while telecommuting? If so, how should managers determine whether to allow this practice and who may participate?

Most medium and large businesses and government organizations have an IT (information technology) department. IT staff are responsible for ensuring that all the computer operations, mobile devices, and networks run smoothly. They also determine when and if the organization requires new hardware, mobile devices, or software. Usually, these jobs are divided into the following areas:

- Management — directs the planning, research, development, evaluation, and integration of technology.
- Research and software development — analyzes, designs, develops, and implements new information technology and maintains and improves existing systems.
- Technical support services — evaluates and integrates new technologies, administers the organization's data resources, and supports the centralized computer operating system and servers.
- Operations — operates the centralized computer equipment and administers the network, including both data and voice communications.
- Training/Support — teaches employees how to use components of the information system or answers specific user questions.
- Information security services — develops and enforces policies that are designed to safeguard an organization's data and information from unauthorized users.
- Marketing/Strategy — directs and implements Internet and social media marketing, and manages customer relationships.

Technology Equipment

The *technology equipment field* consists of manufacturers and distributors of computers, mobile devices, and other hardware, such as magnetic and optical drives, monitors, printers, and communications and networking devices. In addition to the companies that make end-user equipment, thousands of companies manufacture components used inside a computer or mobile device, such as chips, motherboards, cables and connectors, and power supplies.

Available careers in this field include positions with companies that design, manufacture, and produce computers and input, output, communications, mobile, and networking devices. Careers include designing and fabricating chips, testing internal components (Figure 12-8), assembling computers and devices, and packing finished products.

Software and Apps

The *software and apps field* consists of companies that develop, manufacture, and support a wide range of software and apps for computers, the web, and mobile devices. Some companies specialize in a particular type, such as productivity software or tools, or focus on a device type. Other companies — especially larger firms, such as Microsoft — produce and sell many types of software that work with both computers and mobile devices and may use Internet services to sync data among devices or provide collaborative features.

Some employees develop desktop, cloud, web, and mobile apps, such as productivity software, games, simulations, and more; others develop operating systems and related tools. Read Secure IT 12-1 to consider how unlicensed software affects software publishers.

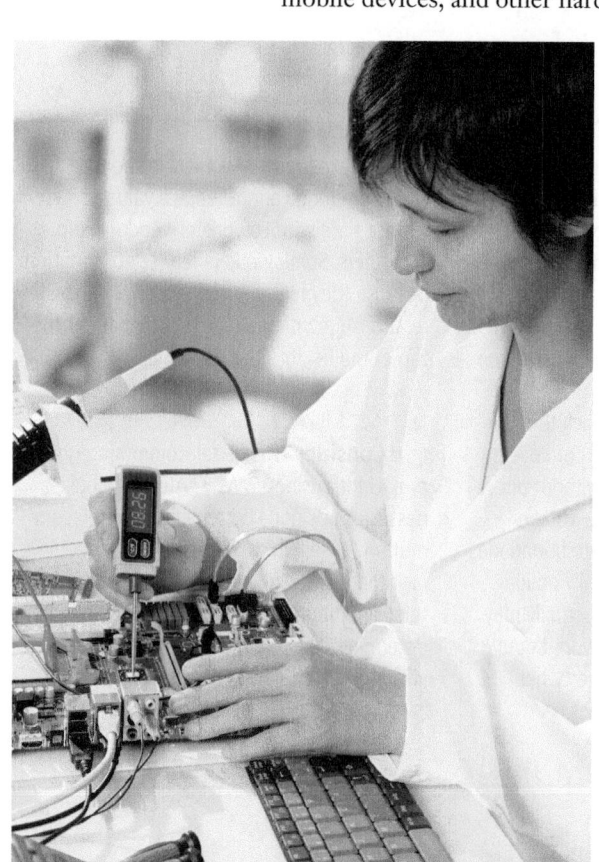

Figure 12-8 This lab technician tests internal computer components.

iStockphoto.com / anyaivanova

Using Unlicensed Software Is a Crime

Software publishers own the copyright to their products. These companies are on the lookout for copies of their software that have been duplicated, distributed, or used without their permission. The pirated software denies these publishers revenue they would have earned from sales, which they could have used to produce new products and improve current products. A recent Business Software Alliance (BSA) Global Software Survey revealed that 39 percent of all software has been installed without proper licensing, including one in five pieces in the United States. This software is valued at more than $52 billion.

Software may be considered unlicensed in a number of circumstances: it could have been downloaded illegally from file-sharing websites, it could have an expired license, or it could be installed on multiple computers when the license specifies use on only one computer. Using unlicensed software violates copyright laws and is subject to serious criminal and civil penalties up to $150,000 for each illegal copy. It is important, therefore, to understand when software can be copied legally. In most circumstances, the software owner can make one copy of the software for backup purposes. Many people make multiple copies, however, either to share or to sell. Often the sharing is done online. In one survey, more than 50 percent of students and 25 percent of instructors admitted that they have copied or would copy software illegally.

People and companies copy software illegally for a variety of reasons, insisting that software prices are too high, that software often is copied for educational or other altruistic purposes, that copied software makes people more productive, that no restrictions should be placed on the use of software after it is purchased, and that software copying is a widespread practice. They also may not be aware that their actions are illegal, but ignorance is not an excuse for illegal actions.

Along with the risk of facing litigation, people and businesses using unlicensed software risk data theft and unauthorized access to their information because they are not receiving program updates and patches that could prevent hacking attempts. If people discover unlicensed software being used on a computer at work or at school, the best practice is to report this situation to managers or IT authorities. The Business Software Alliance encourages people to call its hotline and promises to keep the information confidential.

✷ **Consider This:** What penalties should be imposed for using unlicensed software? Why? Can you counter the reasons people give for copying software illegally? How? Would you copy software illegally, even if your boss told you to copy it? Why or why not? Should software vendors be allowed to probe your computer secretly for illegally installed software? Why or why not?

Technology Service and Repair

The *technology service and repair field* provides preventive maintenance, component installation, and repair services to customers (Figure 12-9). Some technology service technicians possess general knowledge that enables them to work with a variety of devices from different manufacturers. Other technicians receive training and certifications directly from manufacturers to specialize in devices from that manufacturer. This work is best suited for those individuals who like to troubleshoot and solve problems and who have a strong background in electronics.

Many technology equipment manufacturers include diagnostic software with their computers and devices that assists technicians in identifying problems. Today's technology also allows technicians to diagnose and repair software problems from a remote location; that is, the technician accesses the user's hard drive or smartphone from a different location.

Technology Sales

Technology salespeople must possess a general understanding of technology and a specific knowledge of the product they are selling. Strong people skills are important, including a keen listening ability and superior verbal communications. Technology salespeople generally determine buyers' needs and direct buyers toward devices, computers, and apps that meet their needs.

Figure 12-9   This repair technician is replacing a laptop hard drive.
iStockphoto.com / theJIPEN

Figure 12-10   A salesperson in an electronics store shows a digital camera to customers.
dotshock / Shutterstock.com

Some salespeople work directly for technology equipment manufacturers, mobile device manufacturers, or software manufacturers. Others work for resellers, including retailers that sell personal computer products. The technology salesperson in a retail store often is a suitable entry-level job for students working toward a certificate or degree in computer-related fields (Figure 12-10). Before consulting the opinion of a salesperson, be sure to independently research the product so that you can better determine whether answers to your questions are unbiased.

Technology Education, Training, and Support

Schools, colleges, universities, and private companies all need qualified educators to provide technology-related education and training. The high demand in this field has led to a shortage of qualified instructors at the college level as instructors increasingly move to careers in private industry, which offers the promise of higher pay.

Corporate trainers teach employees how to use software and apps, design and develop systems, write programs, integrate and sync data from apps used on multiple devices, and perform other technology-related activities (Figure 12-11). Many large companies use their own training departments. Corporations usually require less educational background for trainers than educational institutions require for instructors.

Figure 12-11   A corporate trainer shows employees how to use new software.
Jenner / Fotolia LLC

In a more informal setting, a help desk specialist answers hardware, software, and networking questions in person, over the phone, or electronically via email or a chat room. Educational requirements for help desk specialists are less stringent than they are for other careers in the technology field. The help desk specialist position is an ideal entryway into the IT field.

IT Consulting

Technology professionals sometimes become IT consultants after gaining experience in one or more technology-related areas, such as software development, systems analysis and design, network configuration, developing mobile devices, using social media, or web development. An **IT consultant**, typically hired based on expertise, provides technology services to his or her clients. Large enterprises often hire teams of consultants to offer advice about technology-related concerns. IT consultants must possess strong technical skills in their specialized area and must be able to communicate effectively to clients. Read Ethics & Issues 12-2 to consider the effects of outsourcing IT jobs.

✸ ETHICS & ISSUES 12-2

Is Outsourcing Jobs Wrong?

Companies have a long history of outsourcing, or relying on outside companies to perform certain tasks. Outsourcing enables companies to find workers with specialized experience and to control costs. When a company sends jobs overseas, outsourcing becomes offshoring. A skilled computer professional in the United States typically commands a higher salary than an IT worker in other countries. To remain competitive, many companies have chosen to send computer jobs abroad.

Proponents say that the United States has a long history of outsourcing all types of work when the economics of the situation demands it. Companies feel that they have a right to choose to send business tasks abroad if it saves costs.

Foreign economies benefit when companies hire and pay workers a fair wage and provide benefits. American consumers benefit from the reduced cost of goods.

Opponents say that offshoring results in unemployment and harms the economy. Others are concerned that sensitive work, such as health record maintenance or weapons manufacturing, could place U.S. citizens at risk. Some experts state that the work done abroad should be easy to manage and quantifiable in order to ensure it meets company standards. Some companies have received negative press due to inefficiencies in call centers and customer support located abroad.

Government officials and lawmakers struggle with policies regarding offshoring, especially with regard to taxing workers.

Politicians debate whether or not companies who keep business in the United States should receive tax breaks. Many argue that the United States should require companies who hire foreign workers to pay a fair salary and provide benefits comparable to those for American workers.

✸ **Consider This:** Should the government limit a company's ability to outsource computer jobs to other countries? Why or why not? Should companies receive criticism for outsourcing jobs? Why or why not? What are some possible alternatives to outsourcing that would help to keep a company competitive? What steps can people take in their careers to avoid becoming a victim of outsourcing? Would you pay more money for goods manufactured in the United States? Why or why not?

Putting It All Together — Job Titles and Descriptions

The following sections briefly describe some of the more popular technology-related job titles for several categories of IT careers.

System Development   Careers in system development require you to analyze or create software, apps, databases, websites and web-based development platforms, and networks. Some careers are listed in Table 12-2.

Table 12-2 System Development Jobs	
Job Title	**Job Description**
Cloud Architect	Identifies business requirements, strategies, and solutions for cloud storage and services that meet a company's goals or needs
Cognitive Engineer	Develops artificial-intelligence-based machines and programs based on data analysis to mimic human thought processes
Database Designer	Specifies the structure, interface, and requirements of a large-scale database; determines security and permissions for users
Program and App Developer	Specifies, designs, implements, tests, and documents programs and apps in a variety of fields, including robotics, operating systems, animation, and applications
Systems Analyst	Works closely with users to analyze their requirements, designs and develops new information systems, and incorporates new technologies
Systems Programmer	Installs and maintains operating system software and provides technical support to the programming staff
Web Designer	Designs the layout, navigation, and overall appearance of a website with a focus on user experience; specifies a website's appearance using HTML5, JavaScript, CSS, media, and other web design technologies
Web Developer	Analyzes, develops, and supports the functionality of a website, including applications that often interact with databases or other online resources

Technology Operations   Careers in technology operations require you to have knowledge about how hardware, software, and networks function. Some careers are listed in Table 12-3.

Table 12-3 Technology Operations Jobs	
Job Title	**Job Description**
Computer Technician	Installs, maintains, and repairs hardware and servers; installs, upgrades, and configures software; troubleshoots hardware problems
Help Desk Specialist/ Help Desk Technician	Answers technology-related questions in person, on the phone, or via email or an online chat room
Network Administrator/ Engineer	Installs, configures, and maintains LANs, WANs, wireless networks, intranets, Internet systems, and network software; identifies and resolves connectivity issues
Technical Project Manager	Guides design, development, and maintenance tasks; serves as interface between programmers/developers and management

Web Marketing and Social Media   Careers in web marketing and social media require you to be knowledgeable about web-based development platforms, social media apps, and marketing strategies. Some careers are listed in Table 12-4.

Table 12-4 Web Marketing and Social Media Jobs	
Job Title	**Job Description**
Customer Relationship Management (CRM) Specialist	Integrates apps and data related to customer inquiries, purchases, support requests, and behaviors in order to provide a complete application that manages a company's relationships with its customers
Internet/Social Media Marketing Specialist	Directs and implements an organization's use of Internet and social media marketing, including Facebook pages, Twitter feeds, blogs, and online advertisements
Search Engine Optimization (SEO) Expert	Writes and develops web content and website layouts so that they will appear at the beginning of search results when users search for content
User Experience (UX) Designer	Plans and designs software and apps that consider a user's reaction to a program and its interface, including its efficiency, its effectiveness, and its ease of use

Data Storage, Retrieval, and Analysis   Careers in data storage and analysis require you to be knowledgeable about collecting, analyzing, and reporting data from databases or the web. Some careers are listed in Table 12-5.

Table 12-5 Data Storage, Retrieval, and Analysis Jobs	
Job Title	**Job Description**
Data Scientist	Uses analytics and other Big Data techniques to interpret a company's data from a variety of sources to better understand its performance, make recommendations for improvement, and predict future outcomes
Database Administrator	Creates and maintains the data dictionary; monitors database performance
Database Analyst	Uses data modeling techniques and tools to analyze and specify data usage
Digital Forensics Examiner	Collects and analyzes evidence found on computers, networks, mobile devices, and databases
Web Analytics Expert	Collects and measures Internet data, such as website traffic patterns and advertising, and develops reports that recommend strategies to maximize an organization's web presence

Information and Systems Security   Careers in information and systems security require you to be knowledgeable about potential threats to a device or network, including viruses and hacking. Security specialists need to know the tools and techniques to protect against threats. Some careers are listed in Table 12-6.

Table 12-6   Information and Systems Security Jobs

Job Title	Job Description
Computer Security Incident Responder	Creates logs, documentation, and recovery plans based on cybersecurity threats and incidents
Computer Security Specialist/ Mobile Security Specialist	Responsible for the security of data and information stored on computers and mobile devices within an organization
Digital Forensics Analyst	Inspects electronic data to recover documents and files from data storage devices that may have been damaged or deleted, in order to use them as evidence in a crime investigation
Network Security Administrator	Configures routers and firewalls; specifies web protocols and enterprise technologies
Security Analyst	Implements security procedures and methods, looks for flaws in security of a company's devices and networks, works with and trains employees at all levels, and assigns permissions and network settings
Security System Project Manager	Develops and maintains programs and tools designed to provide security to a network

App Development and Mobile Technologies   Careers in app development and mobile technologies require you to have knowledge about trends in the desktop and mobile app market, as well as the ability to develop secure apps for a variety of computers and mobile devices. Some careers are listed in Table 12-7.

Table 12-7   App Development and Mobile Technologies Jobs

Job Title	Job Description
Desktop or Mobile Application Programmer/ Developer	Converts the system design into the appropriate application development language, such as Visual Basic, Java, C#, and Objective C, and toolkits for various platforms
Games Designer/Programmer	Designs games and translates designs into a program or app using an appropriate application development language
Mobile Strategist	Integrates and expands the company's initiatives for mobile users
Mobile Technology Expert	Develops and directs an organization's mobile strategy, including marketing and app development
Virtual Reality Engineer	Designs applications that incorporate technologies (such as VR and 3-D) with tools (such as Google Cardboard) to create storytelling tools and apps

Tech Feature 12-2: Mobile App Development

When creating mobile apps, selecting a strategy to develop an app is as important as describing its capabilities. Read Tech Feature 12-2 to learn about three approaches to developing mobile apps.

 TECH FEATURE 12-2

Mobile App Development

Developers and technology managers should evaluate several possible approaches for creating mobile apps, and make a decision based on both technical and business considerations. Should they invest the time and money it takes to develop high-performing native apps for many different mobile operating systems? Would they be better off creating mobile web apps, written using standard web technologies, to run in a mobile browser? Or should they use a hybrid, or mixed, approach that can simplify the development process and lower development costs at the expense of a possible inconsistent user experience across platforms?

Native Apps

A *native app* is written for mobile devices running a particular mobile phone operating system, such as Google's Android, Apple's iOS, or Microsoft's Windows Phone. They offer fast performance and can store data for offline use. Native apps can access all of a device's content, including its contacts, calendar, and photos, and can interact with its hardware, including the microphone, camera, or accelerometer to measure movement and motion.

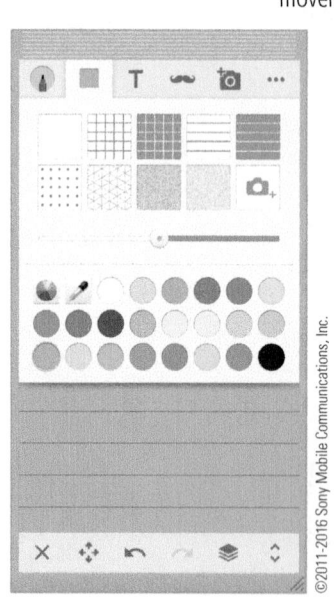

Apps developed for a specific mobile platform or device generally will not work on another without significant modification. Creating native apps requires programming languages, presentation technologies, and development tools particular to each platform.

After testing to be sure it works properly, developers deploy, or submit, a native app to an app store for approval and distribution. When deploying native apps to Google Play, Apple's App Store, or the Windows Store, developers must ensure that their apps follow rules and conditions that their publishers issue. For example, apps must run properly, may not contain offensive content, and should notify the user when requesting the current location or access to information stored on the device. Developers may pay a one-time or annual fee to publish apps in an app store. The store retains a percentage of the sales price of any apps sold as a commission.

©2011-2016 Sony Mobile Communications, Inc.

Mobile Web Apps

Mobile web apps are actually websites that provide a user experience similar to native apps. Developers write them using standard web technologies including HTML5, CSS, and JavaScript. Mobile web apps are not deployed to an app store; rather, they are deployed to a web server and users access them in a mobile browser. Users, therefore, always have access to the most recent version of an app. Creating a shortcut to the app's website and saving it as an icon or tile on a device's home screen provides easy access to the mobile web app. Many mobile web apps have a responsive web design, so that they will be displayed properly on devices with screens of different sizes.

Some companies choose to develop mobile web apps so that they can write one app that works on all devices that is not subject to the rules of an app store. Mobile web apps can access a limited set of device features, such as basic gestures, working offline, tap-to-call, and GPS, but do not have access to native features, such as the camera, microphone, accelerometer, and device notifications.

Hybrid Apps

A *hybrid app* combines features of native and mobile web apps. Like native apps, hybrid apps are developed for specific platforms and deployed to an app store. They can access many of a device's hardware features, such as its camera. Like mobile web apps, they are built with HTML5, CSS, and JavaScript. Developers use development tools to package this code with a browser and prepare it as a native app to deploy to popular app stores. In this way, hybrid apps are cross-platform, meaning the same code can run on many mobile platforms. This approach often saves development time and costs, but may not provide a consistent user experience or fast performance on all devices.

Consider This: If an app is available as both a mobile web app and in an app store for you to download, which would you be more likely to use? Why? Suppose you have a great idea for an app, and you raise enough money to hire an experienced developer to build it for you. Would you ask the developer to code it as a web, hybrid, or native app? Why? Does your choice depend on the capabilities and requirements of the app?

Technology Certifications

A certification demonstrates your knowledge in a specific area to employers or potential employers. Organizations often require technology certification to ensure quality standards and to confirm their workforce remains up to date with respect to technology.

Most certification programs do not require academic coursework. Test results alone determine certification. Few professionals, however, have the experience and skill set to take a certification exam without preparation.

To assist in preparing for a certification exam, several training options are available: self-study, online training, instructor-led training, and web resources. Authorized testing centers provide most certification exams for a fee. The exam sponsor's website typically lists testing centers near you. On the website, you can schedule and pay for your exam (Figure 12-12). At a testing center, you may use a computer to take the examination, or you may mark your answers on a form that will be read by a scanner for grading. You likely will know before you leave the testing center whether you passed the examination. Some tests are in a multiple-choice format. Others are skill based. If you do not pass an exam, you may have to pay the fee again to retake it.

Obtaining a certification requires time and money. Certifications demonstrate your commitment to your chosen area. When deciding whether to obtain a certification, consider your long-term career goals, as well as your current experience. Read evaluations of the certification to determine its value in the industry you have chosen. Examine employment projections and available job opportunities to determine if it is worth obtaining the certification.

Technology certifications are available in many areas, some of which are discussed next.

Figure 12-12 Certification exam sponsors, such as (ISC)² shown here, provide ways for you to prepare for exams, register and pay for exams, and more.
Source: (ISC)²

Application Software Certifications

Although numerous types of application software exist, several programs have achieved national recognition for use as business and graphics tools. Most sponsors of application software certifications have a partner training program and encourage computer-training centers to be authorized training representatives. A popular application software certification includes *Microsoft Office Specialist*, which tests a user's skills of Microsoft Office programs.

As with most other certifications, vendor-authorized testing facilities take registrations and administer the certification test. People with the following jobs may be interested in application software certification:

- Corporate trainers
- Help desk specialists
- Office managers/workers
- Technology sales representatives
- Technology teachers

Data Analysis and Database Certifications

Data analysis certifications focus on the discovery, collection, and analysis of evidence on computers and networks. These certifications often contain the word, forensics, in their title. Database certifications cover the tasks required to support a database management system. If you are interested in working with data analysis or database certifications, you also may benefit from certifications in hardware, networking, programming, and security.

BTW

Exam Day
Before taking a certification exam, read the instructions provided by the testing center to ensure you bring all necessary supplies, equipment, or technology. Print a copy of the directions in case your GPS device or app fails. Arrive early and silence or turn off your mobile devices. Know approximately how long the exam will take so that you can use your time wisely.

People with the following jobs may be interested in data analysis and database certification:

- Data scientist
- Database administrators
- Database analysts
- Digital forensics examiners

Hardware Certifications

Hardware certifications vary in scope from a narrow focus with an emphasis on the repair of a specific device to an integrated hardware solution that addresses a company's current and future computing needs. Obtaining an advanced certification in hardware implies that you have achieved a standard of competence in assessing a company's hardware needs, and you can implement solutions to help the company achieve its computing goals. A popular hardware certification includes *A+*, which tests knowledge of computer setup, configuration, maintenance, troubleshooting, basic networking skills, and system software.

People interested in hardware certifications also may benefit from networking and operating system software certifications, which are closely tied to advanced hardware knowledge. People with the following jobs may be interested in hardware certification:

- Cable installation technicians
- Computer repair technicians
- Corporate trainers
- Help desk specialists
- IT consultants
- System engineers and administrators

Networking Certifications

Network expertise is acquired through years of experience and training because so many variables exist for a total network solution. Obtaining an advanced certification in networking implies that you have achieved a standard of competence, enabling you to address the complex issues that arise when planning, installing, managing, and troubleshooting a network. Cisco, Novell, Sun, and others offer certifications that test knowledge of installing, configuring, operating, and administering networks.

People in the following careers may be interested in network certification:

- Hardware service technicians
- IT consultants
- Network managers
- Network engineers
- System administrators

Operating System Certifications

Several options for various knowledge levels are available to those seeking operating system certifications. These certifications focus on particular skills of the user, the operator, the system administrator, and the software engineer. IBM, Microsoft, Novell, RedHat, Sun, and others offer certifications that test knowledge of their operating systems.

If you are interested in an occupation as an operating system administrator or software engineer, you also may benefit from certifications in networking, hardware, and the Internet. These additional certifications are closely linked to the operating system and serve to broaden expertise in that area. (Read Secure IT 12-2 to learn about risks associated with users who make unauthorized modifications to operating systems.) People with the following jobs may be interested in a certification in operating systems:

- Hardware technicians
- Help desk specialists
- Network administrators

- IT consultants
- System administrators

⚙ SECURE IT 12-2

Risks of Jailbreaking and Rooting

Copyrights protect creators of original works, and digital rights management (DRM) strategies were developed to prevent people from pirating the owners' digital content. (Refer to Module 5 for details about copyrights and piracy.) Hardware manufacturers include DRM software on their products to control the apps and other programs that can be installed. When users want to run unapproved apps and customize their smartphones or mobile devices, they can make unauthorized modifications to the operating system and bypass the DRM restrictions.

This process, called *jailbreaking*, generally refers to hacking into Apple's iPhones and iPads, whereas a similar term, *rooting*, refers to products running Android and other operating systems.

When software developers create apps for Apple's iOS, Apple scrutinizes the software to ensure it adheres to strict guidelines. This review process helps maintain integrity and security. When the phone or mobile device is jailbroken, however, this reliability no longer exists. Apple states that jailbreaking causes these issues: security vulnerabilities, instability, shortened battery life, unreliable voice and

data, disruptions of services, and the inability to apply future software updates. The unauthorized modification violates the end-user license agreement (EULA), so the device may no longer be covered by the manufacturer's warranty.

❀ **Consider This:** Do you know anyone with a jailbroken smartphone or mobile device? Should Apple ease the limitations that are placed on changing iOS default settings or installing apps and other software from websites other than the App Store?

Programmer/Developer Certifications

Various certifications are available in the programmer/developer area. These certifications usually are supported with training programs that prepare applicants for the certification test. A popular specific programmer/developer certification includes *Google Apps Certified Specialist*, which tests a user's skills of administering, selling, and deploying Google Apps. A more broad development certification includes *Project Management Professional* (PMP), which tests knowledge of tasks required during system development.

If you are interested in developing applications, you also may benefit from certifications in networking and web design. These certifications are closely tied to programming and may broaden employment opportunities. People with the following jobs may be interested in a programmer/developer certification:

- Game developers
- IT consultants
- Mobile application developers
- Project leaders/managers
- Systems analyst
- Web developers

Security Certifications

Security certifications measure a candidate's ability to identify and control security risks associated with any event or action that could cause a loss of or damage to computer hardware, software, data, information, or processing capability. (Read Secure IT 12-3 to consider the effects of inadequately protected customer data.) While some security certifications focus solely on network and Internet security, others include measures to secure operating systems, application programs, and information systems, as well as the physical facility and its people. A popular specific security certification includes *Certified Information Systems Security Professional (CISSP)*, which tests in-depth knowledge of access control methods, information systems development, cryptography, operations security, physical security, and network and Internet security. Some security certifications relate specifically to the area of digital forensics.

People in the following careers may be interested in security certification:

- Information security officers and managers
- Law enforcement officials
- Military intelligence officers
- Network administrators
- Wireless network administrators
- Network security specialists
- Security administrators

Tech Feature 12-3: Drones

Drones, once a tool for hobbyists, have many practical business uses. As drone technology and usage increases, so do security concerns. Reach Tech Feature 12-3 to learn about drone usage.

 TECH FEATURE 12-3

Drones

If you stare into the sky for any length of time, you might see a drone heading your way. What began as projects for military use now are common gadgets for hobbyists. These light, relatively inexpensive, and versatile aircraft increasingly are catching the interest of businesses, the media, scientists, and law enforcement.

Also known as an unmanned aerial vehicle (UAV) or unmanned aerial system (UAS), a drone is an aircraft that operates by an onboard computer and GPS, a remote control device, and/or an app on a computer or mobile device. Most are equipped with an autopilot, a high-resolution camera, and real-time video. The drone 'pilot,' or operator, manages the controls from the ground and can watch the drone by viewing a display attached to the base station.

Dmitry Kalinovsky / Shutterstock.com

FAA Regulations

Current FAA regulations state that drones can fly no higher than 400 feet, must stay within the operator's line of sight, and cannot venture over airports or populated areas. Newer FAA regulations require registration of both the drone and the operator; they also restrict flights crossing state lines.

Commercial and Media Use

Amazon captured the media's attention when it announced plans to deliver packages using drones. The FAA opposed this proposition, stating that drones had to be flown within sight of the operator and cannot drop cargo. Other commercial and media ventures, however, use drones for a variety of purposes. Insurance companies use drones to survey storm damage to buildings and property. Sports photographers capture aerial footage, especially for events such as hang gliding, snowboarding, and downhill skiing.

Scientific Use

Their inexpensive cost makes drones ideal for cash-strapped or small-sized scientific or conservation-related use where the risk might be great, such as taking pictures in the eye of a hurricane. Farmers create aerial maps to manage crop watering and fertilizing. Conservationists track endangered species, secure protected nesting areas, and map natural resources. Scientists attach specialized diagnostic tools to measure solar reflectivity of the Amazon rain forest, use thermal imaging cameras to measure endangered plant temperatures, and measure hurricane pressures and temperatures.

Kletr / Shutterstock.com

Military, Law Enforcement, and Other Uses

Military uses of drones include surveillance of areas into which it would be unsafe to send personnel, to supply deliveries to combat areas, and even to detonate weapons. Law and safety officials also use drones effectively. Medical personnel use drones to deliver supplies to remote regions and to retrieve medical samples. Firefighters locate forest fires with drones. Law enforcement can photograph a complex crime scene from above without contaminating evidence.

☀ **Consider This:** Have you ever used a drone? If so, for what purpose? To what extent should the FAA regulate drone usage? Why? What security concerns are associated with drone usage?

✿ **SECURE IT 12-3**

Protecting Customer Data

Many for-profit and nonprofit companies and organizations have been affected by malware intrusions into their point-of-sale systems. Hackers have broken into retail servers and accessed data for millions of credit and debit card accounts. In one situation, they broke into a large entertainment company's server, disrupting service to its customers and publishing personal data for millions of customers, including passwords and possibly credit card information. The breached company allegedly waited one week to inform customers about the attack. The hackers who exposed this company's data were part of a well-known activist group that routinely targets large corporations and government agencies to expose data vulnerabilities and to protest policies. The group claimed that the company had not encrypted the exposed data properly. The group's members are unknown, so officials

are unable to hold them responsible for their actions.

Customers, however, sued the company for the breach. One lawsuit stated that the company's lack of encryption and adequate firewalls makes it responsible for the hackers' actions. Officials agreed, with one stating, "If you are responsible for so many payment card details and log-in details, then keeping that personal data secure has to be your priority." Customers held the company responsible for the delay in notification. The attack ultimately cost the company an estimated $170 million. Since the breach, the company changed its user agreement policies. The new policy states that by agreeing to use its products, users give up the right to sue for security breaches.

Thousands of other corporate security breaches have ranged from email phishing schemes to stolen equipment.

Cybersecurity risks affect all businesses because criminals know how to manipulate technology to compromise the networks and install malware. The U.S. Department of Homeland Security, U.S. Secret Service, and the National Cybersecurity and Communications Integration Center work to locate organized criminal groups, warn organizations about potential unauthorized access, and detect intrusions. They provide information about performing risk assessments, installing backup systems, and establishing security policies.

✳ **Consider This:** Should hackers be punished for exposing customer data? Why or why not? What expectations of security should customers have when they enter personal data on a website or form? Should companies be able to prevent customers from suing them? Why or why not?

Job Searching and Career Planning

Many job opportunities may exist in your industry, so it is important to narrow down the available jobs to ones for which you are qualified and in which you are interested. Tools at your disposal include the career service department at your school (Figure 12-13), career planning websites, and online social networks. Read How To 12-2 to learn how to start your job search online.

Whether you are seeking a new job or currently are employed, you may find a career planning website useful. Career planning websites often allow you to post your resume online or enter your resume information in a form at the website for potential employers to review. Many also offer mobile apps. Examples of popular career planning websites include CareerBuilder, Dice, and Monster. Use a search engine to locate these career planning websites and their mobile apps.

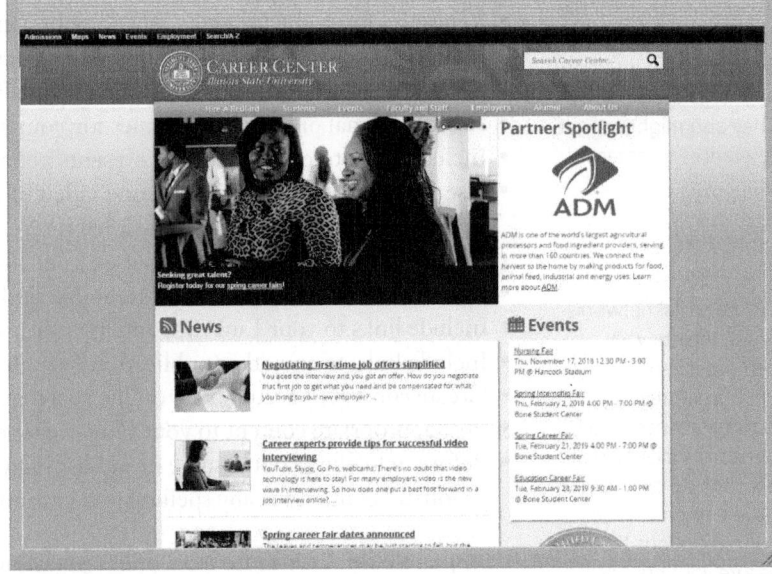

Figure 12-13   A college or university career services website, such as the Illinois State University one shown here, provides helpful career planning information.
Source: Illinois State University

HOW TO 12-2

Start Your Job Search Online
Starting your job search online will help you locate available jobs and determine whether you are qualified to apply. Performing your research online will save time applying and interviewing for jobs for which you are not qualified. The following steps describe how to start your job search online.

1. Begin your job search by reviewing the information on online social networks, job search websites, and organizations' websites. On these websites, you can learn about career opportunities and prepare for an interview.

2. Follow an organization's activity on Facebook, Twitter, LinkedIn, and other social media channels.

3. Research a company's online activity to become familiar with some of the products, services, and opportunities that they provide.

4. Visit career services websites hosted by your college or university. These websites often contain information about career fairs, resume planning workshops, and campus recruitment activities.

5. Consider visiting a career planning website. These websites offer information about available jobs and local salaries.

You also can use them to research corporate work environments, technology news, and opportunities for professional networking.

6. Upload your resume to career planning websites and job search websites. Create the resume in a word processing program and then save it in the PDF format so that it has a consistent appearance when viewed on a variety of computers or mobile devices.

✹ **Consider This:** Have you ever searched for a job online? Why or why not? If so, were you successful in finding a job for which you were qualified?

Creating a Professional Online Presence

An understanding of the web, digital media, and online social networks, such as LinkedIn, is beneficial in creating your online presence.

Recommended Online Strategies A professional online presence that positively conveys your accomplishments, skills, interests, and personality offers potential employers a more complete picture of you beyond what can be conveyed in a resume.

- Register a form of your name as a domain name and host a blog or website at that web address. If your name is not available or you do not have access to a web server, include your name as part of the web address for your website on a free service, such as Blogger or WordPress.
- Avoid informal or humorous names for your account profiles, blog title, or domain name.
- Include a photo of yourself that presents your best self.
- Use a webcam to create a 30-second video in which you introduce yourself. In the video, summarize your skills and professional interests. Post the video on YouTube or another video sharing site and include a link to it on your blog or website.
- Upload a PDF file of your resume, and include a link to it on your blog or website.
- Include links to your LinkedIn and Twitter profiles on your blog or website.
- Include links to any other publications, articles, videos, or digital content you have created.
- Create consistent accounts on online social networks.
- Post appropriate content to your blog, website, or online social networks regularly.
- Before uploading your resume or publishing your blog or website, ask at least two people to proofread content for any spelling and grammar mistakes. Keep the language professional.

Using LinkedIn LinkedIn is an online social network where professionals, such as Reid Hoffman, founder of LinkedIn (Figure 12-14), can create profiles and connect with coworkers and industry colleagues. LinkedIn uses the term, contacts, to describe the individuals in your professional network and also stores your relationship with each contact in your network.

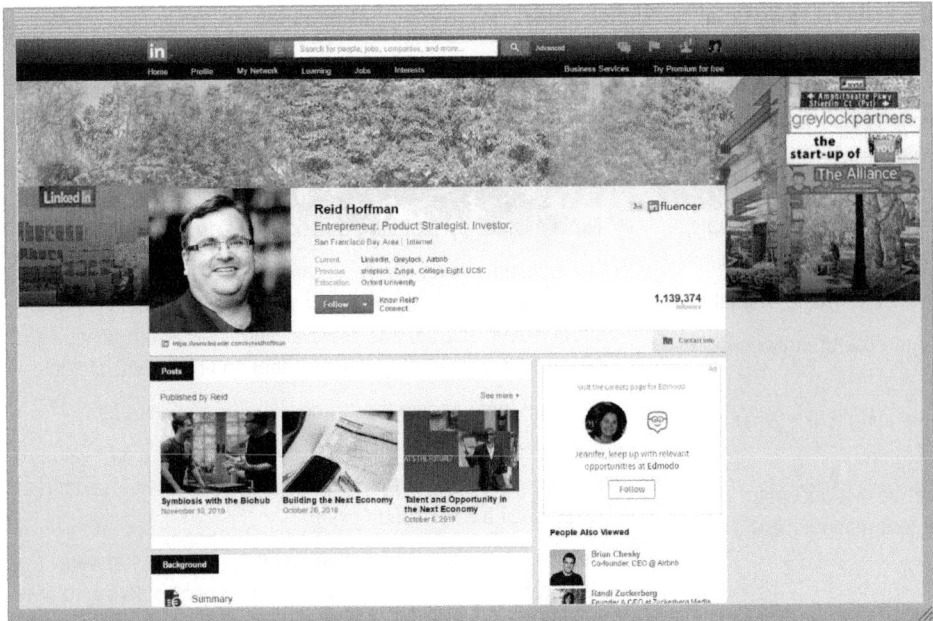

Figure 12-14   LinkedIn profile for Reid Hoffman, founder of LinkedIn.
Source: LinkedIn

Use LinkedIn to:

- Connect with or stay in touch with current and former coworkers and classmates.
- Follow companies on LinkedIn to stay informed of job openings.
- Recommend colleagues and coworkers to recognize their skills and areas of expertise.
- Use LinkedIn's employment database to learn about career opportunities. View the job listing to find the name of the person who posted the job and to determine the connections between you and those members you might want to contact in order to learn about a company or open jobs.
- Join groups of people with similar interests or experiences. For example, your school's alumni group, people who work at the same company, people looking to share experiences they had when starting their own businesses, and people who use specific apps might be willing to share their expertise.
- Consider expanding your network by connecting with your contacts' connections. If you invite an extended contact to connect, be sure to include a note that introduces yourself and indicates your professional reason for connecting.

Summary

This module discussed information systems used in an enterprise. It also presented various technology career fields and specific technology jobs. It then discussed technology certifications. Finally, it described how to begin a job search and create a professional online presence.

Study Guide
The Study Guide reinforces material you should know after reading this module.

Instructions: Answer the questions below using the format that helps you remember best or that is required by your instructor. Possible formats may include one or more of these options: write the answers; create a document that contains the answers; record answers as audio or video using a webcam, smartphone, or portable media player; post answers on a blog, wiki, or website; or highlight answers in the book/e-book.

1. A(n) _____ system is a set of hardware, software, data, people, and procedures that work together to produce information.

2. List and describe seven criteria that make information valuable.

3. Describe how functional units in an enterprise use information systems.

4. Define the term, enterprise resource planning (ERP). What are the advantages of ERP?

5. Explain the uses of and relationship between a document management system (DMS) and a content management system (CMS).

6. List uses of a CMS.

7. List transactions that may occur when using a transaction processing system (TPS). Differentiate between batch and online transaction processing.

8. Define the term, management information system (MIS). Differentiate among the three types of reports an MIS generates.

9. Describe how a decision support system (DSS) is used. OLAP stands for _____.

10. List types of internal and external sources used in a DSS.

11. A(n) _____ system is an information system that captures and stores the knowledge of human experts and then imitates human reasoning and decision making.

12. Define the terms, knowledge base, inference rules, and artificial intelligence (AI).

13. Explain FAA regulations regarding drones. Describe commercial and media, scientific, and military, law enforcement, and other drone usage.

14. List guidelines for setting up your home office for telecommuting. Explain issues surrounding telecommuting.

15. List and describe the areas typically found in an IT department.

16. Describe the technology equipment field, and list possible jobs in this area.

17. Explain different types of companies in the software and apps field.

18. Explain security issues that arise when using unlicensed software.

19. Describe the technology service and repair field. Explain how technicians use diagnostic software.

20. List criteria needed to be a technology salesperson. Describe various careers in this field.

21. Describe the role of a corporate trainer.

22. Explain the responsibilities and educational requirements of a help desk specialist.

23. Define the roles an IT consultant might fulfill.

24. Explain issues surrounding outsourcing and offshoring of jobs.

25. List requirements and available careers for the following areas: system development; technology operations; web marketing and social media; data storage, retrieval, and analysis; information and systems security; and app development and mobile technologies.

26. Describe three approaches to developing mobile apps.

27. Explain how and why an employee or employer might value or require technology certifications. What options are available to prepare for a certification exam?

28. Describe the benefits of obtaining an application software certification. List jobs that may require, or jobholders who may benefit from, obtaining this certification.

29. Explain the focus of a data analysis certification. List jobs that may require, or jobholders who may benefit from, obtaining this certification.

30. Explain why an employee might obtain an advanced hardware certification. _____ is a popular hardware certification.

31. List jobs that may require, or jobholders who may benefit from, obtaining a hardware certification.

32. Explain the expertise necessary to achieve a networking certification. List jobs that may require, or jobholders who may benefit from, obtaining this certification.

33. List options that are available for operating system certification. Name companies that offer operating system certifications.

34. List jobs that require, or jobholders who may benefit from, obtaining an operating system certification.

35. Explain security issues surrounding jailbreaking and rooting.

36. List examples of programmer/developer certifications. List jobs that may require, or jobholders who may benefit from, obtaining this certification.

37. Explain what is measured by obtaining a security certification. Name one popular specific security certification.

38. List jobs that may require, or jobholders who may benefit from, obtaining a security certification.

39. List steps to start your job search online.

40. Explain how a job seeker might use a career planning website. List examples of popular career planning websites.

41. Describe how security breaches of customer data might occur. Explain the responsibility of a company to protect its customer data.

42. List strategies to create a professional online presence. Explain how professionals use LinkedIn.

43. Explain how social media can help your job search.

44. List steps to create a professional presence on LinkedIn.

You should be able to define the Primary Terms and be familiar with the Secondary Terms listed below.

Key Terms

Primary Terms (shown in **bold-black** characters in the module)

artificial intelligence (AI) (12-9)

cloud architect (12-15)

cognitive engineer (12-15)

computer security incident responder (12-17)

computer security specialist/mobile security specialist (12-17)

computer technician (12-16)

content management system (CMS) (12-5)

customer relationship management (CRM) specialist (12-16)

data scientist (12-16)

database administrator (12-16)

database analyst (12-16)

database designer (12-15)

decision support system (12-8)

desktop or mobile application programmer/developer (12-17)

digital forensics analyst (12-17)

digital forensics examiner (12-16)

document management system (DMS) (12-5)

Enterprise Resource Planning (ERP) (12-4)

expert system (12-8)

games designer/programmer (12-17)

help desk specialist/help desk technician (12-16)

information system (12-3)

Internet/social media marketing specialist (12-16)

IT consultant (12-14)

management information system (MIS) (12-6)

mobile strategist (12-17)

mobile technology expert (12-17)

network administrator/engineer (12-16)

network security administrator (12-17)

program and app developer (12-15)

search engine optimization (SEO) expert (12-16)

security analyst (12-17)

security system project manager (12-17)

systems analyst (12-15)

systems programmer (12-15)

technical project manager (12-16)

user experience (UX) designer (12-16)

virtual reality engineer (12-17)

web analytics expert (12-16)

web designer (12-15)

web developer (12-15)

Secondary Terms (shown in *italic* characters in the module)

A+ (12-20)

batch processing (12-6)

Certified Information Systems Security Professional (CISSP) (12-21)

computer-aided engineering (CAE) (12-4)

computer-aided manufacturing (CAM) (12-4)

customer relationship management (CRM) (12-4)

detailed report (12-6)

exception criteria (12-6)

exception report (12-6)

Google Apps Certified Specialist (12-21)

human resources information system (HRIS) (12-4)

hybrid app (12-18)

inference rules (12-8)

information literacy (12-9)

jailbreaking (12-21)

knowledge base (12-8)

Manufacturing Resource Planning II (MRP II) (12-4)

Material Requirements Planning (MRP) (12-4)

Microsoft Office Specialist (12-19)

native app (12-18)

online analytical processing (OLAP) (12-8)

online transaction processing (OLTP) (12-6)

Project Management Professional (12-21)

rooting (12-21)

salesforce automation (SFA) (12-4)

software and apps field (12-12)

summary report (12-6)

technology equipment field (12-12)

technology service and repair field (12-13)

transaction processing system (TPS) (12-6)

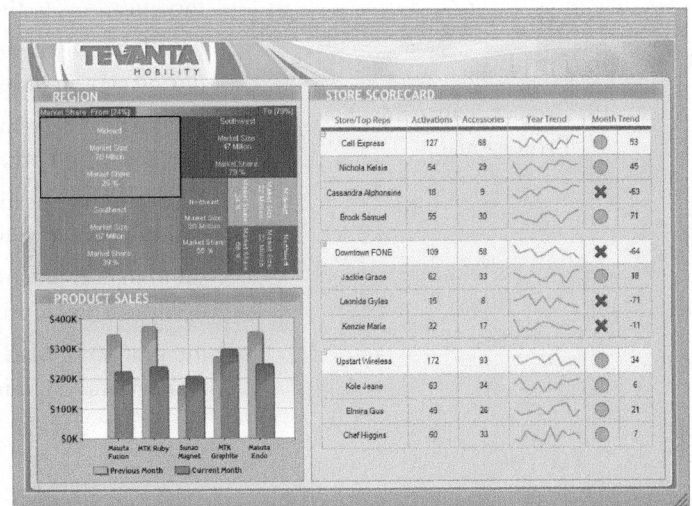

Courtesy of Dundas Data Visualation, Inc.

Checkpoint

The Checkpoint exercises test your knowledge of the module concepts.

True/False

Mark T for True and F for False. If False, rewrite the statement so that it is True.

_____ 1. Accessible information has meaning to the person who receives it.

_____ 2. A typical enterprise consists of a wide variety of departments, centers, and divisions — collectively known as functional units.

_____ 3. CMSs are popular in large part because of their ease of use; CMS operators need minimal technical skills.

_____ 4. The high cost makes drones prohibitive for cash-strapped or small scientific or conservation use.

_____ 5. In most circumstances, the licensed software owner can make multiple copies of software, for back up or to share with other users.

_____ 6. Educational requirements for help desk specialists are far more stringent than they are for other careers in the technology field.

_____ 7. Outsourcing enables companies to find workers with specialized experience and to control costs.

_____ 8. Apps developed for a specific mobile platform or device generally work on any other device without any modification.

_____ 9. Like native apps, hybrid apps are developed for specific platforms and deployed to an app store.

_____ 10. Most professionals have the experience and skill set to take a certification exam without preparation.

_____ 11. Data analysis certifications focus on the discovery, collection, and analysis of evidence on computers and networks.

_____ 12. Employers often use social media to determine if a candidate's personality would fit into the corporate culture.

Matching

Match the terms with their definitions.

_____ 1. A+

_____ 2. artificial intelligence

_____ 3. CRM

_____ 4. ERP

_____ 5. hybrid app

_____ 6. inference rules

_____ 7. jailbreaking

_____ 8. MRP

_____ 9. OLTP

_____ 10. Project Management Professional

a. processing system in which the computer processes each transaction as it is entered

b. application of human intelligence to computers

c. information system that manages information about customers, past purchases, interests, and the day-to-day interactions

d. program that combines features of native and mobile web apps

e. process of hacking into iPhones and iPads in order to make unauthorized modifications to the operating system and bypass DRM restrictions

f. broad development certification that tests knowledge of tasks required during system development

g. information systems that monitors and controls inventory, material purchases, and other processes related to manufacturing operations

h. hardware certification that tests knowledge of computer setup, configuration, maintenance, troubleshooting, basic networking skills, and system software

i. set of logical judgments that are applied to the knowledge base each time a user describes a situation to the expert system

j. integration of MRP II with the information flow across an organization to manage and coordinate the ongoing activities of the enterprise

The Problem Solving exercises extend your knowledge of module concepts by seeking solutions to practical problems with technology that you may encounter at home, school, or work. The Collaboration exercise should be completed with a team.

Problem Solving

Instructions: You often can solve problems with technology in multiple ways. Determine a solution to the problems in these exercises by using one or more resources available to you (such as a computer or mobile device, articles on the web or in print, blogs, podcasts, videos, television, user guides, other individuals, electronics or computer stores, etc.). Describe your solution, along with the resource(s) used, in the format requested by your instructor (brief report, presentation, discussion, blog post, video, or other means).

Personal

1. **Keywords for Job Search** After taking your third computer class, you realize that you would like to train people how to use computers and software. You look for a job online and are asked to enter some keywords for your job search. What keywords will you enter to find a job that allows you to train others how to use computers and software?

2. **Online Job Search** Having decided to work in the computer equipment field, you begin your job search online. In addition to looking on job search websites for available positions, where else might you find job postings?

3. **Documenting Education and Experience** You are preparing your resume to submit to a computer service and repair company. You have studied computer service and repair in various classes and want to convince your prospective employer that you are the best candidate for the job. What might convince the employer to offer you a job?

4. **Contemplating a Job Offer** After graduating from college with a degree in computer science, you send your resume to several companies. Almost immediately, you receive a job offer as a technical support representative in a midsized organization. Will you accept this job offer or wait for additional offers? Why?

5. **Appropriate Certification** Because you hope to pursue a career as a system administrator, you would like to 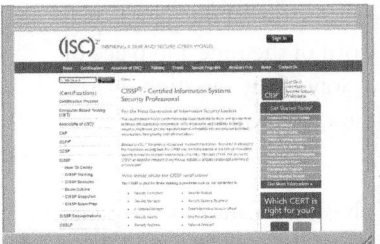 obtain a certification. Many certifications are available, but you want to choose the one(s) that will best prepare you for your future career. Which certification(s) will you consider?

Professional

6. **Staying Current with Technology** Having accepted a job as a computer salesperson, you now realize the importance of staying up to date with the latest technologies and products. What are three ways that you can stay current in the technology field while working full time?

7. **Outsourcing IT Positions** As the chief information officer for a large organization, you consider outsourcing various positions within your department to save money. What are some types of positions that can be outsourced easily? What positions might be difficult to outsource? Why?

8. **Conducting an Interview** You are preparing to conduct several interviews for candidates applying for a job as a senior systems administrator. What types of questions will you ask during the interview to determine whether they have the experience required to fulfill the job responsibilities?

9. **Tough Decision** Two top candidates who applied for a job within your organization have interviewed well, and you are having difficulty selecting which candidate should be offered the job. One candidate has several certifications and only two years of job-related experience, while the other candidate has six years of experience, but no certifications. What decision will you make, and why?

10. **Training Decision** Your boss has allocated money to allow everyone in the IT department to attend training related to their job responsibilities. While researching the training available for your job as a system administrator, you learn that you either can take a semester-long course at a local university or attend an accelerated one-week, forty-hour training course. At the end of each training session, you will be ready to become certified. Which type of training will you choose? Why?

Collaboration

11. **Technology in Architecture and Design** As a student in a drafting class, your instructor has challenged you to design your dream home by using programs and apps wherever possible. Form a team of three people that will determine how to accomplish this objective. One team member should compare and contrast two programs or apps that can be used to create a two-dimensional floor plan, another team member should compare and contrast two computer-aided design programs or apps that can create a more detailed design of the house, and the third team member should compare and contrast two programs or apps that can assist with other aspects of the design process, such as landscaping and interior design.

✱ How To: Your Turn

The How To: Your Turn exercises present general guidelines for fundamental skills when using a computer or mobile device and then require that you determine how to apply these general guidelines to a specific program or situation.

Instructions: You often can complete tasks using technology in multiple ways. Figure out how to perform the tasks described in these exercises by using one or more resources available to you (such as a computer or mobile device, articles on the web or in print, online or program help, user guides, blogs, podcasts, videos, other individuals, trial and error, etc.). Summarize your 'how to' steps, along with the resource(s) used, in the format requested by your instructor (brief report, presentation, discussion, blog post, video, or other means).

❶ Conduct an Effective Interview

Gathering information is an important task, whether you are trying to assess whether a job candidate would be a good fit for an open position, or if you need to gather feedback about a new system you are developing. An important means of gathering information is the personal interview. Interviews must be thorough and comprehensive. Prior to conducting an interview, you must determine that an interview is the best means for obtaining the information you seek. You have learned a variety of ways to obtain information, and you should use each of them appropriately. Because an interview may interrupt a person's schedule and takes time, you must be sure the information gained in the interview justifies this interruption. Once you have determined you should conduct an interview to gather information, plan to ask questions that will generate useful answers. The following steps guide you through the process of conducting an interview that ultimately will generate useful answers.

a. Your questions should directly address the goals of the interview. Do not expect the person being interviewed to provide a tutorial. Your questions must generate answers that supply you with the information you need to make a decision.

b. Your questions should be thought-provoking. In general, do not ask questions requiring a yes or no answer. Your questions should not lead the interviewee to an answer — rather, the questions should be open-ended and allow the person to develop the answer. As an interviewer, never argue with the person being interviewed, do not suggest answers or give opinions, ask straightforward questions rather than compound questions, never assign blame for any circumstance that might come up in the interview, and never interrupt while the person is talking. Finally, you, as the interviewer, should not talk much. Remember, you are conducting the interview to gain information, and it is the person you are interviewing who has that information. Let him or her talk.

c. Pay attention carefully, with your ears and your eyes. What you hear normally is most important, but body language and other movements often convey information as well. Concentrate on the interviewee — expect that you will make much more eye contact with the person than he or she will with you. Allow silences to linger — the normal impulse in a conversation is to fill the silence quickly; in an interview, however, if you are quiet, the person being interviewed might think of additional information.

d. As you listen, concentrate on the interviewee. When points are being made, do not take notes because that will distract from what the person is saying; stay focused. Once the information has been conveyed, jot down a note so that you will remember.

e. Throughout the interview, offer reinforcing comments, such as, "The way I understand what you just said is …" Make sure when you leave the interview that no misunderstandings exist between you and the person you interviewed.

f. Before you conclude the interview, be sure all your goals have been met. You may not have another opportunity to interview the person, so ensure you have asked sufficient questions to gain the information you need to make a decision.

g. After the interview, it is recommended you send a follow-up email message or letter to the person you interviewed to review the information you learned. This message or letter should invite the interviewee to correct any errors you made in summing up your findings. In addition, for all the people you interview, keep a record of the time and place of the interview. In this way, if any questions arise regarding the interview, you will have a record.

Interviewing Online

If you are not in the same physical location as the people you want to interview, it may be better to conduct the interview online. If you plan to conduct the interview online, consider the following advice:

- Plug in the computer or device so that you do not have to rely on battery power. If you must rely on battery power, be sure that the battery is fully charged.

How To: Your Turn ✳

- Use a wired Internet connection, rather than connecting to a wireless network, to minimize the risk of losing Internet connectivity during the interview.
- Select a location for the video call that has a neutral background and is free from distractions.
- Know how to initiate or receive a video call.
- Exit your email, chat, and other unnecessary applications during the interview so that you are not distracted or interrupted by alerts and notification messages.
- Test the videoconferencing software in advance to ensure the configuration works.
- Adjust the microphone, webcam, and speakers before the actual interview to ensure optimum call quality.
- Practice switching between the videoconferencing app's chat window and your desktop or a browser window, in case you want to share a link, send a file, or type a message during the interview.
- Keep your eyes focused on the webcam so that you will appear attentive.

Exercises

1. Think about the last time you were involved in an interview (either as an interviewer or an interviewee). What types of questions were you asked? Do you feel the questions solicited useful answers?
2. If you were to interview a candidate for a technology-related position, what types of questions would you ask?
3. What advantages do open-ended questions have? When might a question requiring a brief answer be appropriate?

❷ Create an Online Survey

If you want to collect information from a group of people, one way is to use an online survey. Online surveys can be sent to many individuals across the globe, allowing you to collect responses in a timely manner. Multiple web apps exist that allow you to create and distribute online surveys either for free or for a fee. Each web app has slightly different features, so evaluate various options before deciding which one to use. The following steps guide you through the process of creating an online survey.

a. Navigate to the website you want to use to create the online survey.
b. If necessary, create an account on the website hosting the web app.
c. Select the option to create a new survey.
d. Enter a descriptive title for the survey.
e. Add the appropriate instructions to the survey.
f. Add the questions to your survey. This includes:
   - Choosing the correct question type
   - Entering a descriptive question
   - If necessary, specifying the answer choices
   - Selecting whether the question is required
   - Specifying whether certain answers should prompt additional questions to appear
g. Save the survey.
h. Test the survey to make sure it functions as intended.
i. Distribute the survey to intended recipients.
j. When the due date for the survey passes, collect the survey results.

Exercises

1. What are at least three reasons you might need to distribute an online survey in your desired field?
2. Compare and contrast at least three online tools that can create and distribute surveys. Which one was your favorite? Why? Which one was your least favorite? Why? What are the differences between their free and fee-based accounts?

✳ Internet Research

The Internet Research exercises broaden your understanding of module concepts by requiring that you search for information on the web.

Instructions: Use a search engine or another search tool to locate the information requested or answers to questions presented in the exercises. Describe your findings, along with the search term(s) you used and your web source(s), in the format requested by your instructor (brief report, presentation, discussion, blog post, video, or other means).

❶ Making Use of the Web
Careers and Employment

It is a good idea to acquire information before graduation about the industry in which you would like to work. While your teachers provide valuable training and knowledge to prepare you for a career, they rarely teach you how to begin a job search. You can broaden your horizon by searching online for career information and job openings.

Career websites provide details about training and education requirements, employment outlook, industry trends, and salary data. They also offer advice on writing a cover letter and resume, applying for jobs online, networking, and preparing for an interview. When you are offered a job, turn to these websites to obtain industry salary comparisons and negotiation techniques.

Job seekers can search employment websites, such as CareerBuilder, Dice, and Monster, for specific position openings worldwide. The jobs can be sorted by category, industry, location, date posted, job title, and keywords. Some websites list job fairs and separate the listings by categories, such as entry level, part time, summer, and temporary.

Source: CareerBuilder

Research This: (a) Visit at least two career websites and review the resources. What type of career advice is given? Are aptitude tests available? What tools are provided to manage a job search, such as tips for writing a cover letter and resume, job search mistakes to avoid, search strategies, and online social network tips?

(b) Use at least two employment websites to search for three job openings in your field. Which positions are available? What are their salaries, locations, required education and experience, and job descriptions? Can job seekers post a resume? Are company profiles and salary comparison available? Do these websites have mobile apps?

❷ Social Media
Corporate Policies

Companies have created policies that employees must follow when participating in social media and online social networks. Intel, for example, considers participation in social media to be an opportunity, not a right, and requires its employees to disclose their identity, protect the company's confidential and classified information, and use common sense when writing and airing opinions. Apple employees are urged to use good judgment when using online social networks and are barred from discussing the company on their own websites and from commenting on or posting messages regarding the company and its products on any related websites.

Research This: Locate at least two corporate policies for social media participation and summarize the requirements. Do you agree with the companies' guidelines? Are the policies too lenient or too strict? What actions are taken if an employee fails to abide by the policies? In what ways may policies differ among various fields, such as in health care and education?

❸ Search Skills
Using the Web for Research

A search engine may provide targeted results from news websites, blogs, corporate websites, and other sources. In addition, research websites, digital libraries, and specialized search engines can provide valuable information when using the web for research.

Your college or university library's website may list links to online journals, magazines, films, and books that will be helpful resources. It may make available links to online research databases, such as Gartner, Factiva, LexisNexis, and ProQuest, that offer IT professionals' press releases, analysis, and case studies about companies, technologies, and industries. These sources often present valuable background information, and they offer IT professionals relevant business information to guide their decision-making.

Academic search engines, such as Google Scholar, and digital libraries, such as JSTOR (Journal Storage), provide access to academic journals and conference publications that can be useful when doing academic research. Navigating to these websites from campus may give you additional access to online research databases to which your library has a paid subscription.

Source: Gartner

Research This: Complete these tasks and report your findings. (1) Use your school library's website to find articles in online newspapers about information literacy. (2) Use a research database available from your school library's website to find an article about the fastest-growing IT careers. (3) Use a research database available from your school library's website to find an article about a company or technology discussed in this module. (4) Use Google Scholar or JSTOR to find a recent scholarly publication about rapid application development.

④ Security
Java Flaws

Microsoft, Apple, Facebook, and Twitter are among the technology companies that have experienced a series of attacks exploiting security flaws in the Java plug-in for browsers. These security intrusions appear to have originated from hackers in China, Russia, or Eastern Europe who were attempting to obtain the companies' intellectual property, sensitive data, and users' personal information. The cyberthieves bypassed Java's built-in protections and installed malware on the compromised

computers. Kaspersky Security estimates that more than one-half of the security threats can originate from Java flaws. Oracle, the company that develops Java, issues patches to address known security vulnerabilities, but the Department of Homeland Security and other experts recommend not using Java until it is needed in browsers because new attacks may occur in the popular programming language.

Research This: Locate at least two articles discussing Java security flaws. How do Oracle and other companies inform users about the need to obtain updates to fix security holes? How many devices worldwide have Java installed? How can users discover if Java is installed on their computer or mobile device and, if it is, learn how to uninstall it?

⑤ Cloud Services
Enterprise Software Apps

Many companies make use of enterprise software apps to manage customer relationship management (CRM) and Enterprise Resource Planning (ERP). The rise of cloud computing in the enterprise has resulted in these and other enterprise software apps being hosted and managed on the cloud, rather than being purchased and installed in house. Software as a service (SaaS), a service of cloud computing, provides the delivery of software applications that are stored and deployed from servers on the Internet.

Enterprise software applications are popular SaaS offerings because IT departments do not need to install the software or manage the servers on which they run; instead, they can concentrate on configuring and specifying the services that these apps provide. Their "pay as you go" model, where customers are charged only for the capabilities they use, make SaaS apps attractive from a financial perspective. Users always interact with the most up-to-date version, and because the apps are accessed in a browser, it is easy to maintain the app across large organizations.

Research This: (1) Read about Salesforce, a pioneer in cloud-based CRM applications. What services does Salesforce provide? Find a case study about Salesforce, and describe how Salesforce's cloud solutions met one of its customer's needs. (2) Read about enterprise SaaS offerings to manage business operations and customer relations. Select or compare cloud services from companies such as SAP, Microsoft, and Oracle, and prepare a summary of their offerings. What are advantages and disadvantages to companies running these apps on the cloud?

✳ Critical Thinking

The Critical Thinking exercises challenge your assessment and decision-making skills by presenting real-world situations associated with module concepts. The Collaboration exercise should be completed with a team.

Instructions: Evaluate the situations below, using personal experiences and one or more resources available to you (such as articles on the web or in print, blogs, podcasts, videos, television, user guides, other individuals, electronics or computer stores, etc.). Perform the tasks requested in each exercise and share your deliverables in the format requested by your instructor (brief report, presentation, discussion, blog post, video, or other means).

1. Offshoring and Outsourcing

The consulting company where you work as a systems analyst has refused to use offshoring, claiming management prefers to employ homeland citizens. The company's competitors have been using offshoring for some time. Your company's management team wants to discuss outsourcing the company's accounting system to an overseas firm.

Do This: Research laws, guidelines, and opinions regarding outsourcing. Address the following questions: Do you think systems should be developed entirely overseas? Why or why not? What are the major advantages and disadvantages of developing systems offshore? What security issues exist when using offshore developments? Does the United States have an obligation to help with employment overseas or in developing nations? Why or why not? What factors should a company consider when determining whether to use offshore developers?

2. Mobile App Development

Your company creates digital quizzes and study guides for nursing students. Currently you deliver these quizzes and other materials through a subscription-based website. Customers have been asking for an app that is optimized for smartphones and tablets. You have been asked to gather necessary information to start the project.

Do This: Determine which type of mobile app might be best suited to this type of product and explain why. Research other quiz and study guide apps. Read user reviews to determine what features customers might find valuable. List common features of the most highly-rated apps. What skills, hardware, and software are necessary to develop this type of app? What resources might your company have to purchase or use to develop the app? Research mobile app development jobs on an employment website to find examples of requirements for this type of job. What certifications might you look for when hiring a mobile app developer?

3. Case Study

Family-Owned Coffee Shop You are the new manager for a family-owned coffee shop. Your accountant and purchasing coordinator have expressed interest in telecommuting a few days per week. You need to present a telecommuting proposal for the next meeting of the board of directors.

Do This: Research benefits and disadvantages of allowing telecommuting. List requirements for employees to be able to work from home, including types of Internet access and hardware. Discuss security issues with allowing employees to telecommute. How can you address security concerns? List guidelines employees should follow when working from home. Should you implement a method for evaluating employee efficiency or productivity when telecommuting? Why or why not? How would you assess individual employee performance? What jobs are better suited to telecommuting? Why? Would you recommend that the coffee shop allow telecommuting? Why or why not?

Collaboration

4. Job Search

You work in the human resources department of a network security company. You currently have several openings for positions, including a network administrator, a security expert, and a help desk technician.

Do This: Form a three-member team and have each team member choose a different position. As a team, discuss any common requirements or background necessary for all of the positions based on the type of company. Each team member should list the educational background, available certifications, and other requirements for the position. Find listings for available jobs in your area. What responsibilities are listed for the position? What salary information can you locate? Create a list of information potential employees should have as part of their online profile. As a team, meet to discuss and compile your findings.

iStockPhoto.com / the_IIPEN

Developing Websites: Creating, Formatting, and Publishing Content Online

OBJECTIVES

After completing this Focus On, you will be able to:

1 Discuss tools for developing a website, such as text editors, code editors, and content management systems, and when to use each

2 Explain the uses of HTML5, CSS, and JavaScript technologies when developing websites

3 Discuss concepts related to web development, including static and dynamic content, relative and absolute references, HTML tags and attributes, and embedded and inline styles

4 Explain how to view a webpage's source code after displaying the page in a browser

5 Explain the unique role of the index.html page in a website

6 Use HTML tags to add a title, headings, paragraphs, images, links, ordered and unordered lists, and videos to a webpage

7 Use CSS to specify fonts, colors, and styles for text and background images or colors for webpages

8 Use JavaScript to display the current date and time on a webpage

9 Upload a website to a web server using an FTP program

Tools for Developing a Website

As discussed in Module 2, a website is a collection of related webpages and associated items that usually are hosted on the same web server. A web developer often creates a simple website by designing its layout, specifying the content for each web page, and typing the HTML codes, called tags, for each web page using a text editor. When developing complex websites with hundreds or thousands of pages, web developers rely on content management systems to specify the design and content of each web page. By using a content management system, advanced users and web developers can specify the appearance, structure, and behavior of a website by writing HTML and other code when developing a website. Content management system tools enable developers with knowledge of basic HTML tags to add text or media to webpages.

Text Editors

A text editor is similar to a word processing program, but it lacks most text formatting features, such as fonts, colors, margins, and paragraphs, and it saves files in a text format. A browser interprets the text file and displays the content using the formatting codes specified in the file.

Operating systems typically include a text editor. For example, Windows users may use Notepad, and macOS users may use TextEdit as their text editors. Most text editors save files in a text format automatically. Others may require additional steps to save documents in a text format.

A code editor is a type of text editor that has additional features to help web developers write the code used to develop websites and applications accurately and efficiently. For example, some code editors can display HTML code in different colors (tags might be displayed in one color, while document content is displayed in another color). In addition, code editors might improve readability of your code by applying appropriate indenting and line spacing or automatically completing HTML tags or styles as you type them. Many web developers opt to download a free or fee-based code editor with these features.

Many of the figures in this Focus On show HTML code as it appears in Brackets, a modern, open source editor built for web developers. Brackets is available for computers running both Windows and macOS. Use a search engine with the search text, download brackets editor, to locate a website from which you can download and install Brackets. Figure FO-1 shows several text and code editors.

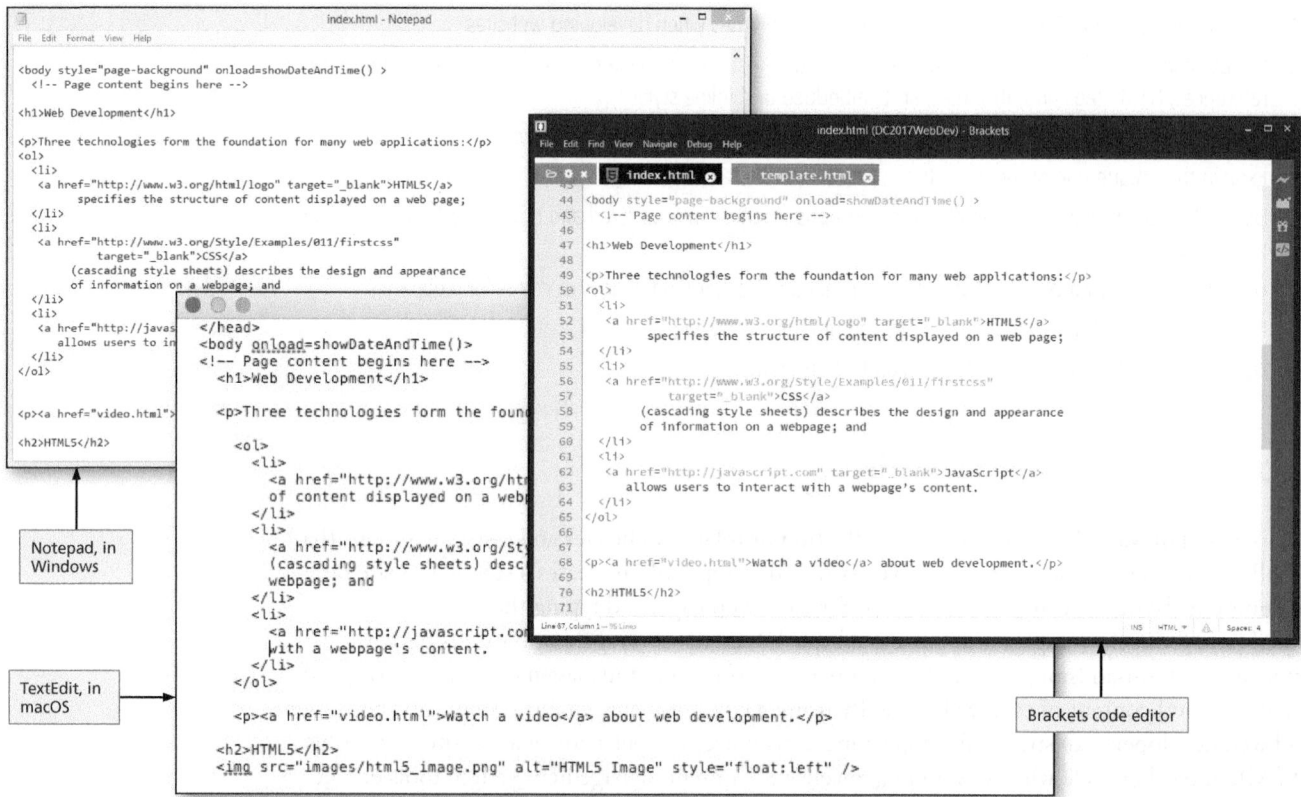

Figure FO-1   Text editors: Notepad, TextEdit, and Brackets.
Sources: Microsoft; Apple Inc.; Brackets.io

 CONSIDER THIS

If you are using a Mac, do you have to do anything special to use TextEdit to create webpages?
Yes. Depending on the version of TextEdit you are using, you may need to set preferences in TextEdit to save your webpage files in a text format. Ask your instructor, or consider using a search engine to locate websites that provide the instructions necessary for your computer. Consider using search text that includes words such as textedit, edit, and html.

✳ CONSIDER THIS

Where can you find out more about text editors and code editors that run on your computer?
Use a search engine to locate websites that provide this information. Consider using the words, text editor web design, followed by the name of your operating system, such as Windows or macOS, as your search text. If you are looking for only free text editors, consider adding the word, free, to your search text. If you need assistance selecting, downloading, and installing an editor, contact your instructor.

Content Management Systems

Developers of complex websites with hundreds or thousands of frequently updated pages, such as those of a university or online business, often make use of a content management system (CMS) to enter, modify, or delete content. A CMS is a web publishing tool that manages the publishing, modification, organization, and access of various forms of documents and other files, including media and webpages, on a network or the web. Many content management systems are open source and offer regular updates, enhancements, plug-ins, and themes for download, often at no cost. Other CMS or web publishing tools are hosted by their providers. They often provide basic capabilities at no cost and require a fee to access advanced features.

A CMS allows web developers to specify the parts of a page that are common to a website (such as a banner graphic, navigation menu, or footer information that appear on every page) so that they need to be specified only once. Many CMSs allow web developers to customize their websites by including specialized tools that can be integrated into a website to offer advanced capabilities, such as implementing shopping carts, displaying photo galleries, providing contact forms, and recording website usage.

When using a CMS, a web developer creates the theme, or design of a website, and one or more website content administrators enters its content. The CMS uses a database to store both the design and content of the website. The CMS will query the database, assemble the different parts of the page as HTML code, and then send the HTML to the user's browser for display. Many CMSs provide a variety of themes from which to choose when creating a website. Often, a web developer can customize a theme by specifying colors, banner graphics, placement of navigation menus, and other characteristics. By applying different themes, developers easily can alter the appearance of a website without modifying its content. For example, one theme may be optimized for displaying on a large screen, while another theme might display only images and text, so that the website can be displayed quickly on mobile devices. Figure FO-2 shows options for selecting a theme or configuring the appearance of a website created with the WordPress CMS.

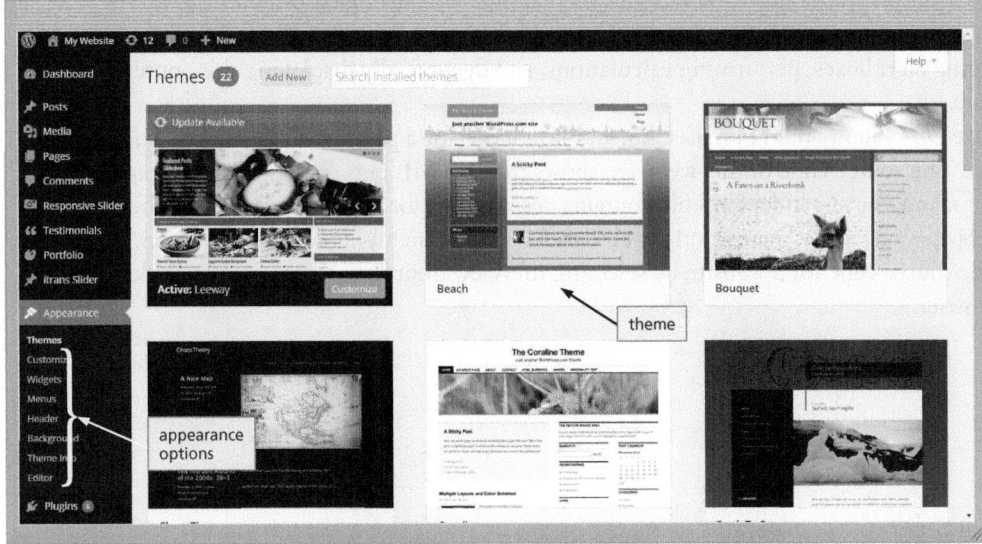

Figure FO-2   Selecting a theme for a website built with WordPress.
Source: WordPress

Table FO-1 summarizes several popular content management systems for creating websites.

Table FO-1 Popular Content Management Systems

Name	Description	Hosting	Cost
Drupal	Powerful, open source CMS often used for large-scale websites because of its capability of being customized and its efficient use of computer resources	Installed on a user's or an organization's web server	Software is free; users pay for some specialized themes or modules that provide advanced features
Google Sites	Easy-to-use web application provided by Google often used for personal or small-to-medium websites; integrates with Google apps and services	Hosted by Google	Free to build, host, and maintain sites for users with Google accounts; additional cost for customizing a domain name
Joomla!	Open source CMS often used for developing e-commerce websites, corporate websites, and online social networks	Users may install Joomla! on their own computers and host on their own servers, or use a limited version hosted by Joomla!	Software is free; users pay for some specialized themes or extensions that provide advanced features
Wix	Web-based tool for developing websites for individuals and small businesses; features App Market with tools for building online stores, photo galleries, forms, and capturing website analytics	Hosted by Wix	Free version offers basic features; advanced capabilities available for a fee

Source: WordPress

Website Technologies

Hypertext Markup Language (HTML) uses a set of codes called tags to format documents for display in a browser. The current version of HTML is HTML5. HTML tags describe the structure of the content on a webpage, including headings, paragraphs, images, and links. These tags generally occur in pairs in an HTML document, one before a content item and another after it.

A complementary technology called cascading style sheets (CSS) contains specifications for the fonts, colors, layout, and placement of these HTML elements on a webpage. The current version of CSS is CSS3.

JavaScript is a programming language for creating programs that a browser can run to generate content for a website. Uses for JavaScript include obtaining the current date and time, formatting alert boxes, performing calculations, and dynamically displaying this content on a webpage.

Figure FO-3 shows the HTML, CSS, and JavaScript for a page on the National Zoo's website. The source code of this webpage shows that HTML tags specify the paragraphs, links, list items, and images, and a CSS file contains descriptions for how to style each of the tags on the webpage. JavaScript manages the website's navigation menus and user interaction. You can view the source code for a website by selecting the View Source or 'View Source Code' option in a browser.

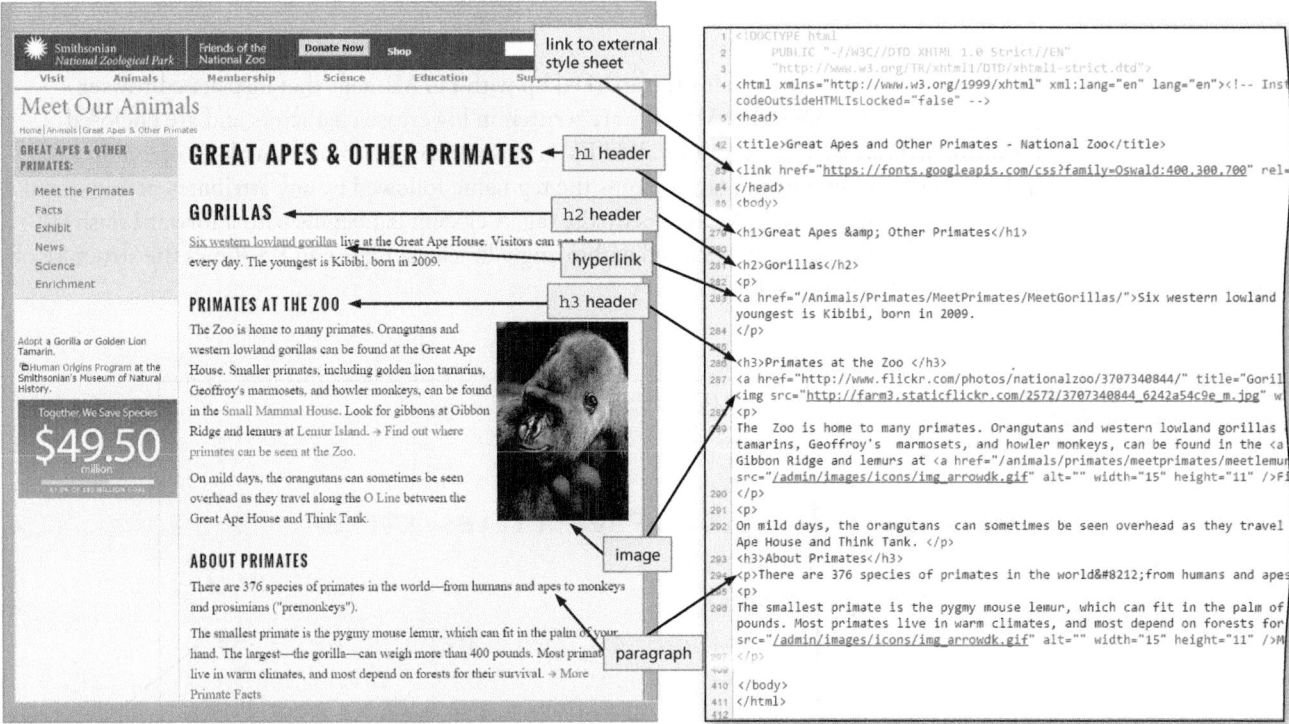

Figure FO-3 A page from the National Zoo website and its source code.
Source: National Zoo

Because screens on computers and mobile devices are of different sizes, many web developers will create webpages that have a responsive design. Responsive webpages automatically adjust the size of their content to display appropriately relative to the size of the screen of the device on which it is displayed. Figure FO-4 shows a webpage displayed in a browser on a full-size screen and the same webpage when viewed in a browser on a mobile device.

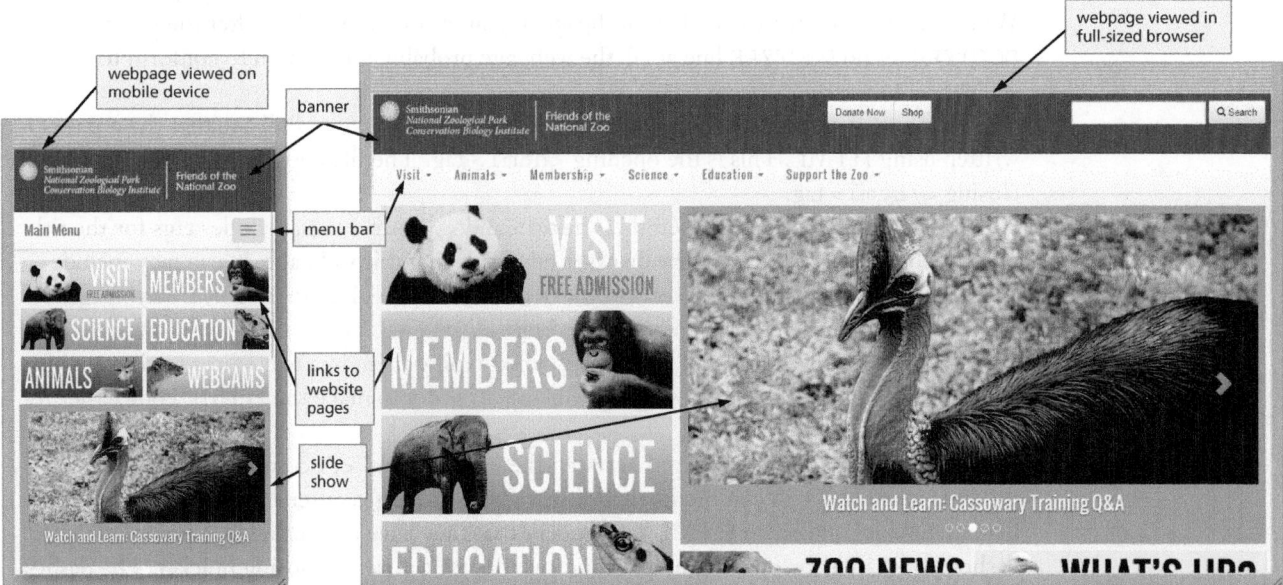

Figure FO-4 A website with responsive design, in a mobile and full-sized browser.
Source: National Zoo

Structure of a Webpage

A webpage's source code contains text marked up with HTML tags that instruct a browser how to display its content. HTML tags are written in lowercase characters and are enclosed within angle brackets (< >). Almost all HTML tags are written in pairs, with an opening tag and a closing tag. An opening tag contains the tag name followed by any attributes or additional information needed to completely specify the tag. A closing tag begins with a forward slash (/) followed by the tag name, all enclosed within angle brackets. Figure FO-5 shows the structure of a webpage coded in HTML.

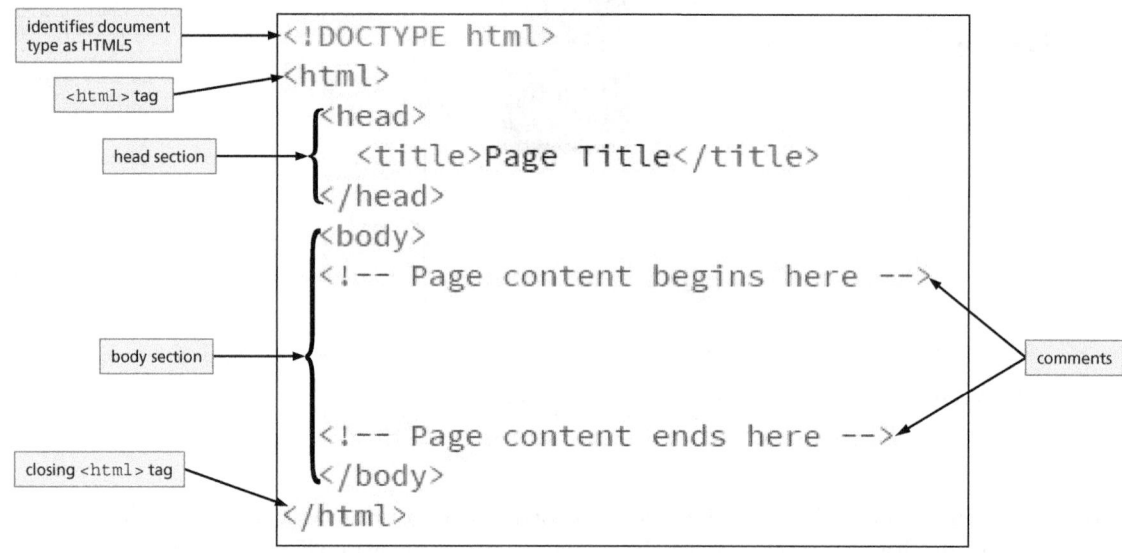

Figure FO-5   Structure of a webpage.

- As shown in Figure FO-5, the first line of code in an HTML5 webpage contains the line, `<!DOCTYPE html>`. These words identify that the document type of this page is HTML5. When viewing the source code for a webpage, if you see different values after the word `DOCTYPE`, or no `DOCTYPE` line at all, the webpage probably was written to conform to standards of an earlier version of HTML.
- The next line of code in a webpage file is always an `<html>` tag to indicate that the content is written using HTML. This is the opening `<html>` tag. The file ends with the corresponding closing `</html>` tag.
- The head section, located between the `<head>` and `</head>` tags, includes tags for the title of the webpage that appears in the browser tab displaying this webpage; it also may include styles and JavaScript. The body section, located between the `<body>` and `</body>` tags, contains the content of the webpage marked up with HTML tags.
- Sometimes a web developer will indent tags when typing them in a text editor so that opening tags and their corresponding closing tags line up, in order to make the HTML code easier for a human to read.
- The content of a webpage is placed between the `<body>` and `</body>` tags. In Figure FO-5, this area is marked with comments to indicate where the page content begins and ends. Comments look similar to HTML tags, except that they have an exclamation point and two dashes (!--) after the opening bracket and two dashes before the closing bracket. The dashes are not required, but they help improve readability. Web developers often include comments to make it easier to read and interpret the HTML code.

A browser ignores the spacing of the HTML code and any comments included in the file and renders, or displays, a webpage's content based on the meaning of the tags used to mark it up.

The World Wide Web Consortium (W3C) oversees the specification of HTML standards, and as HTML evolves, the W3C identifies some tags as deprecated, or obsolete. For example, in earlier versions of HTML, the <font> tag was used to specify the font of text on a webpage. With the development of CSS, the W3C has deprecated the <font> tag. While the <font> tag still may display text in a particular font correctly in some browsers, the preferred way to display text in a specific font is using CSS.

The W3C provides a free, online HTML5 validator application to ensure that a webpage's HTML tags follow the specifications, or rules, for HTML5. The HTML5 validator will identify any misaligned tags, deprecated tags, required attributes, or information that may be missing, as shown in Figure FO-6.

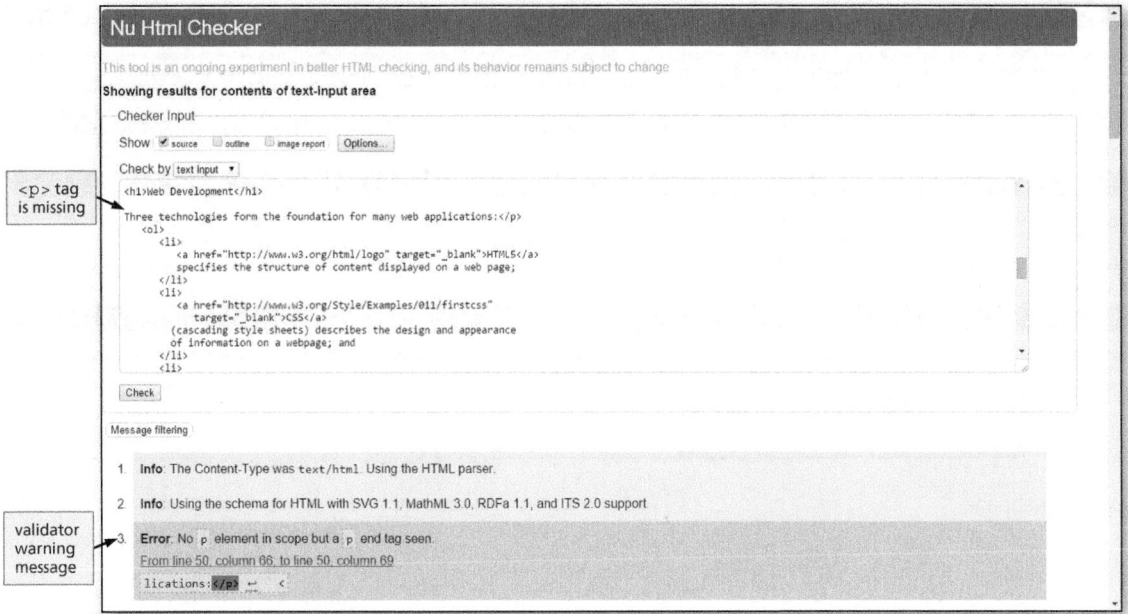

Figure FO-6 Code analyzed in an HTML5 validator.
Source: World Wide Web Consortium

✳ CONSIDER THIS

How can you find and use an HTML5 validator?
Use a search engine with the search text, W3C HTML validator, to locate the W3C Markup Validator Service. Navigate to the W3C Markup Validation Service website, and specify the web address of a webpage, upload an HTML file, or paste in the HTML code to be validated. Review the output to determine any code that needs to be corrected for the page to pass inspection. Using a validator will ensure that the code complies with HTML5 standards and that the page is displayed correctly in all HTML5-compliant browsers.

✳ CONSIDER THIS

Where can you find a list of deprecated tags in HTML5?
Use a search engine with the search text, html5 deprecated tags attributes, to locate this information.

Developing a Website

This section will guide you through the steps of developing a simple website. You will need to select, download, and install a text editor, or use Notepad for Windows or TextEdit for macOS. The website you will create in this Focus On will include two webpages, containing various headings, paragraphs of text, links, styles, images, an embedded video, and the current time and date (Figure FO-7).

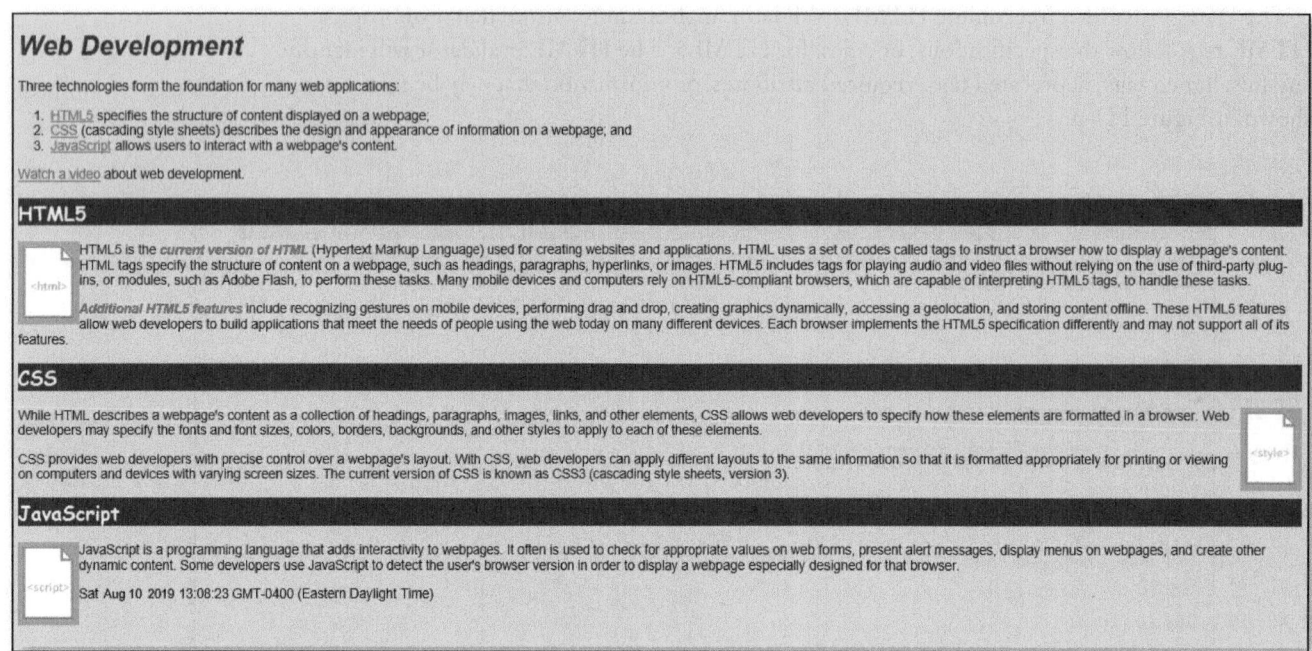

Figure FO-7a   index.html webpage.

Figure FO-7b   video.html webpage.

CONSIDER THIS ———————————————————————————

Are all webpages coded in HTML?
Yes. Many simple websites make use of static webpages, whose content changes only when a web developer updates the HTML code for each page. More complex websites often have dynamic webpages. Dynamic webpages obtain their content by running programs on a web server or on a client device, written in JavaScript running in a browser. These programs often perform calculations or interact with a database to access requested information and then generate the HTML code to display that content in a browser.

To Create the index.html File

To perform the steps in this Focus On, you will need to download the Focus On starter files from the Student Resource Center for this book. If you need assistance accessing these files, contact your instructor. Download and uncompress these files. Create a folder named website on your computer that will contain all of the files and images used in your website. Move the template.html file, startertext.txt files, and the images folder to the website folder.

The template.html file includes the webpage structure. You will open this file in a text editor and save it with the file name, index.html. The index.html file usually is the webpage displayed by default when you enter a web address that does not include the name of a specific webpage. *Why? The .html file extension indicates to the browser that the file stores the content for a webpage, so that it can open the file and display its contents. The webpage structure helps the browser identify the file as a webpage so that it can display it properly.* The following steps open the template.html file in a text editor and save it with the file name, index.html.

- Run the text editor of your choice.
- Navigate to and open the template.html file.
- If necessary, enable the word wrap feature so that you can view all the webpage text without scrolling horizontally (Figure FO-8).

Q&A Can I just navigate to the template.html file and double-click it so that it opens in a text editor?

```
1   <!DOCTYPE html>
2   <html>
3     <head>
4       <title>Page Title</title>
5     </head>
6   <body>
7   <!-- Page content begins here -->
8
9
10
11  <!-- Page content ends here -->
12  </body>
13  </html>
```
webpage structure

Figure FO-8

By default, most operating systems are configured to open files with an .html extension in a browser. If you double-click the .html file icon in a file explorer application, it is likely that the template.html file will open in your default browser instead of a text editor.

- Save the file using the file name, index.html. Do not exit the text editor. If you are running Notepad on a Windows computer, change the file type in the Save As dialog box in Notepad to All Files so that Notepad saves the file with the proper .html extension.

To Copy the Starter Text from a Source File and Paste It in the index.html File

The startertext.txt file includes all the text the webpage will display. *Why? For the purposes of this exercise, copying and pasting text from an existing file will save you from having to type all the webpage text manually.* The following steps copy the starter text from the startertext.txt file and paste it in the body section of the index.html file so that it appears in the browser's display area.

1

- Open the startertext.txt file (Figure FO-9).

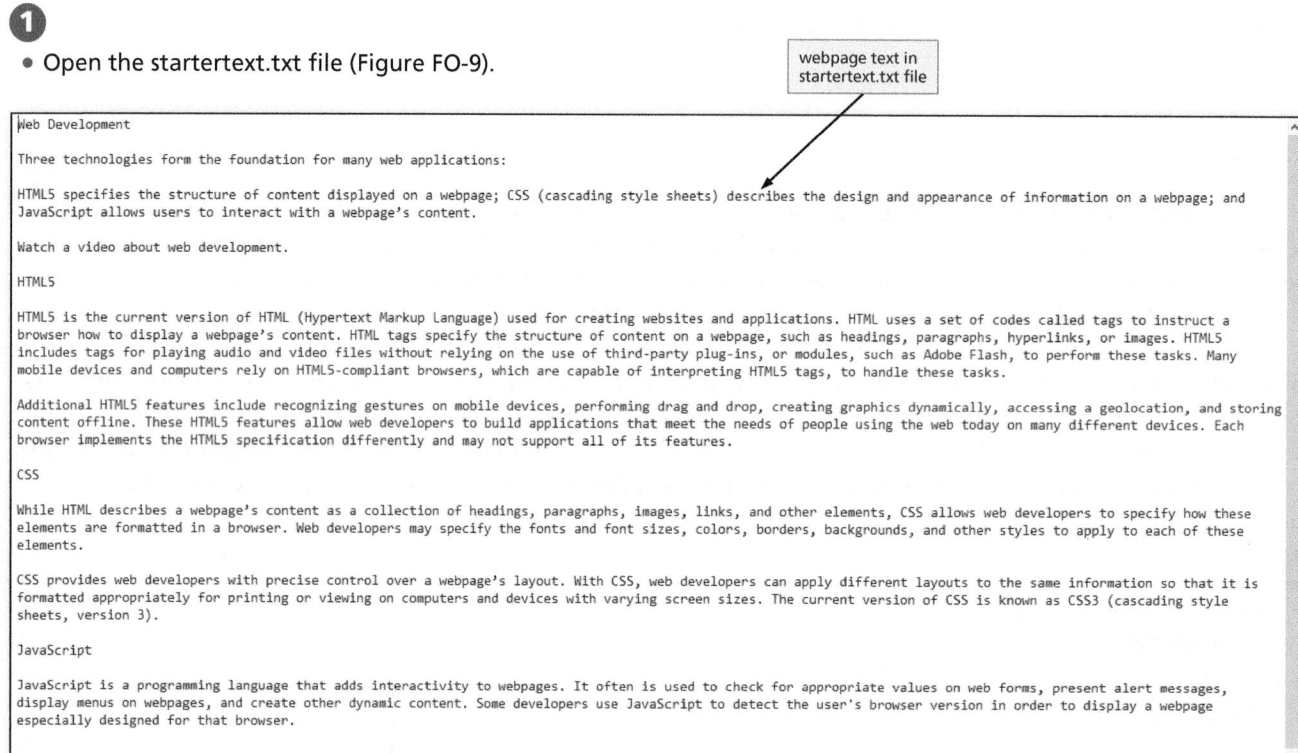

webpage text in startertext.txt file

Figure FO-9

2

- Select all the text in the startertext.txt file.
- Copy the text.
- Close the startertext.txt file.
- Display the text editor window containing the index.html file.
- Position the insertion point on blank line after the line that contains the code, `<!--Page content begins here -->` (Figure FO-10). Recall that this line is a comment; its only purpose is to make it easier for a web developer to read or understand the HTML code.

```
 1   <!DOCTYPE html>
 2 ▼ <html>
 3 ▼   <head>
 4       <title>Page Title</title>
 5     </head>
 6 ▼   <body>
 7     <!-- Page content begins here -->
 8
 9
10
11     <!-- Page content ends here -->
12     </body>
13   </html>
```

blank line where text will be inserted

Figure FO-10

3

- Paste the text you copied in Step 2 (Figure FO-11).
- Save the changes to the index.html file.

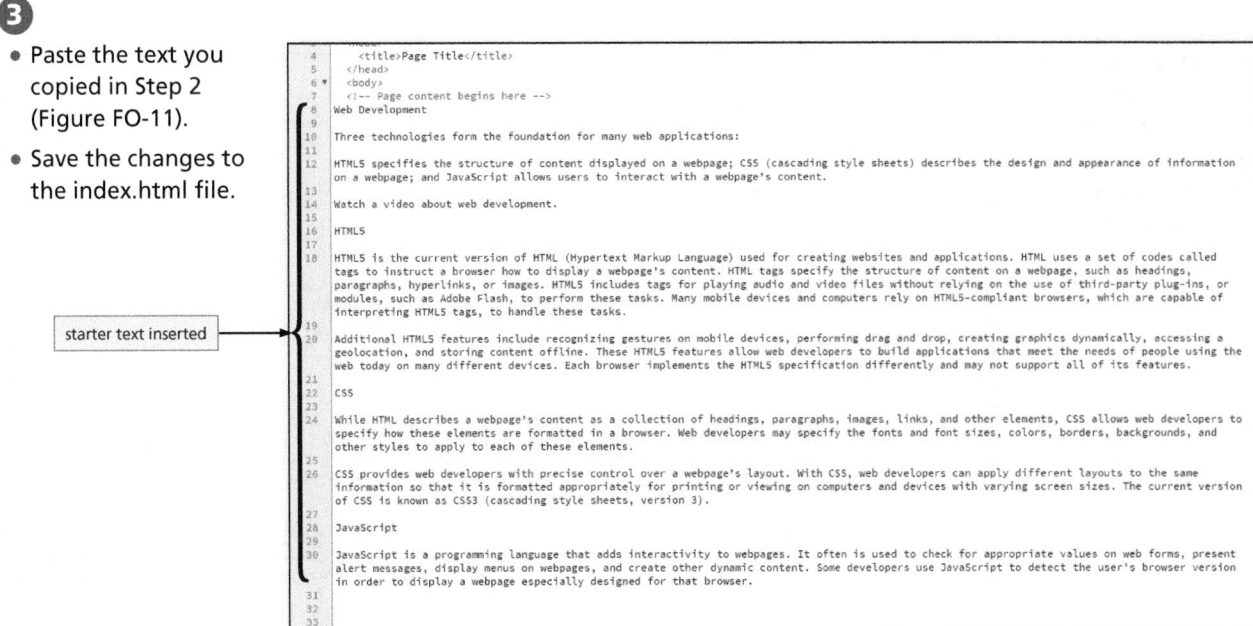

starter text inserted

Figure FO-11

To Specify the Webpage Title

As mentioned previously, the webpage title helps identify the webpage. For example, if you have multiple webpages open in the browser, each webpage's title will appear in its respective browser tab. If you save a webpage as a bookmark or favorite, by default, the browser will identify the webpage by its title. You always should assign a meaningful title to each webpage you create. *Why?* *A descriptive webpage title can help you identify a webpage without having to view its contents and also will help search engines locate the page.* The following steps add a meaningful title to the index.html webpage.

- Select the text, Page Title, that appears between the `<title>` and `</title>` tags (Figure FO-12).

existing webpage title selected between `<title>` and `</title>` tags

```
1    <!DOCTYPE html>
2 ▼  <html>
3 ▼    <head>
4        <title>Page Title</title>
5      </head>
6 ▼    <body>
7        <!-- Page content begins here -->
8  Web Development
9
10  Three technologies form the foundation for many web applications:
11
12  HTML5 specifies the structure of content displayed on a webpage; CSS (cascading style sheets) descri
    on a webpage; and JavaScript allows users to interact with a webpage's content.
13
14  Watch a video about web development.
15
16  HTML5
17
18  HTML5 is the current version of HTML (Hypertext Markup Language) used for creating websites and appl
    tags to instruct a browser how to display a webpage's content. HTML tags specify the structure of co
    paragraphs, hyperlinks, or images. HTML5 includes tags for playing audio and video files without rely
    modules, such as Adobe Flash, to perform these tasks. Many mobile devices and computers rely on HTML5
    interpreting HTML5 tags, to handle these tasks.
19
20  Additional HTML5 features include recognizing gestures on mobile devices, performing drag and drop, c
    geolocation, and storing content offline. These HTML5 features allow web developers to build applicat
    web today on many different devices. Each browser implements the HTML5 specification differently and
21
22  CSS
23
24  While HTML describes a webpage's content as a collection of headings, paragraphs, images, links, and
    specify how these elements are formatted in a browser. Web developers may specify the fonts and font
```

Figure FO-12

②

- Type **Mark's Web Development Page** as the title, replacing the name, Mark, with your first name (Figure FO-13).

```
1    <!DOCTYPE html>
2  ▼ <html>
3  ▼   <head>
4        <title>Mark's Web Development Page</title>
5      </head>
6  ▼   <body>
7        <!-- Page content begins here -->
8    Web Development
9
10   Three technologies form the foundation for many web applications:
11
12   HTML5 specifies the structure of content displayed on a webpage; CSS (cascading style sheets) descri
     on a webpage; and JavaScript allows users to interact with a webpage's content.
13
14   Watch a video about web development.
15
16   HTML5
17
18   HTML5 is the current version of HTML (Hypertext Markup Language) used for creating websites and appl
     tags to instruct a browser how to display a webpage's content. HTML tags specify the structure of co
     paragraphs, hyperlinks, or images. HTML5 includes tags for playing audio and video files without rel
     modules, such as Adobe Flash, to perform these tasks. Many mobile devices and computers rely on HTML5
     interpreting HTML5 tags, to handle these tasks.
19
20   Additional HTML5 features include recognizing gestures on mobile devices, performing drag and drop, o
     geolocation, and storing content offline. These HTML5 features allow web developers to build applica
     web today on many different devices. Each browser implements the HTML5 specification differently and
21
22   CSS
23
24   While HTML describes a webpage's content as a collection of headings, paragraphs, images, links, and
     specify how these elements are formatted in a browser. Web developers may specify the fonts and fon
```

updated webpage title

Figure FO-13

Headings

Headings indicate the different sections of a webpage. HTML supports six levels of headings, which are identified by the following tags: `<h1>`, `<h2>`, `<h3>`, `<h4>`, `<h5>`, and `<h6>`. The `<h1>` tag displays text in the largest font size for headings, and the `<h6>` tag displays text in the smallest font size for headings (Figure FO-14).

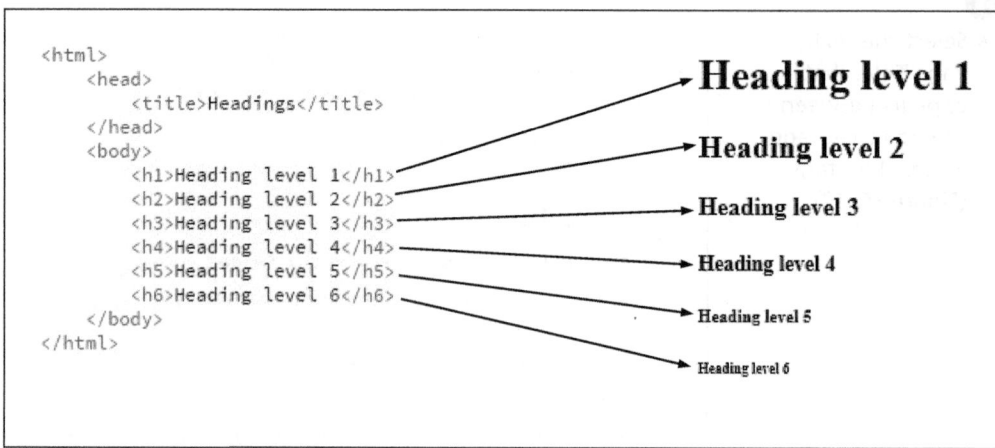

Figure FO-14

To Specify the Headings in the index.html File

The index.html file in this example will contain four headings: a heading at the top that identifies the webpage, as well as three additional headings that identify each of the three sections. ***Why?*** *Using webpage headings helps visitors identify the content they would like to read.* The following steps identify the headings in the index.html file.

1

- Position the insertion point at the beginning of the line that reads, Web Development.
- Type **<h1>** to identify where the heading begins.
- Position the insertion point at the end of the line of text that reads, Web Development.
- Type **</h1>** to identify where the heading ends. Although the browser disregards spacing, you may type blank spaces to indent this tag so it lines up with its opening <h1> tag (Figure FO-15).

```
1   <!DOCTYPE html>
2 ▼ <html>
3 ▼   <head>
4       <title>Mark's Web Development Page</title>
5     </head>
6 ▼   <body>
7     <!-- Page content begins here -->
8       <h1>Web Development</h1>
9
10  Three technologies form the foundation for many web applications:
11
12  HTML5 sp  opening    structure of content displayed on a webpage; CSS (cascading style sheets) descri
    on a web  and closing  vaScript allows users to interact with a webpage's content.
13            <h1> tags
14  Watch a video about web development.
15
16  HTML5
17
18  HTML5 is the current version of HTML (Hypertext Markup Language) used for creating websites and appl
    tags to instruct a browser how to display a webpage's content. HTML tags specify the structure of con
    paragraphs, hyperlinks, or images. HTML5 includes tags for playing audio and video files without rely
    modules, such as Adobe Flash, to perform these tasks. Many mobile devices and computers rely on HTML5
    interpreting HTML5 tags, to handle these tasks.
19
20  Additional HTML5 features include recognizing gestures on mobile devices, performing drag and drop, c
    geolocation, and storing content offline. These HTML5 features allow web developers to build applicat
    web today on many different devices. Each browser implements the HTML5 specification differently and
21
22  CSS
23
24  While HTML describes a webpage's content as a collection of headings, paragraphs, images, links, and
    these elements are formatted in a browser. developers may specify the fonts and f
```

Figure FO-15

2

- Position the insertion point at the beginning the line that reads, HTML5.
- Type **<h2>** to identify where the heading begins.
- Position the insertion point at the end of the line of text that reads, HTML5.
- Type **</h2>** to identify where the heading ends. To increase readability, you may type spaces to indent this tag so it lines up with its opening <h2> tag (Figure FO-16).

```
2 ▼ <html>
3 ▼   <head>
4       <title>Mark's Web Development Page</title>
5     </head>
6 ▼   <body>
7     <!-- Page content begins here -->
8       <h1>Web Development</h1>
9
10  Three technologies form the foundation for many web applications:
11
12  HTML5 specifies the structure of content displayed on a webpage; CSS (cascading style sheets) descri
    on a webpage; and JavaScript allows users to interact with a webpage's content.
13
14  Watch a video about web development.
15
16      <h2>HTML5</h2>
17
18  HTML5 is the current version of HTML (Hypertext Markup Language) used for creating websites and appl
    tags  opening    a browser how to display a webpage's content. HTML tags specify the structure of co
    para  and closing  links, or images. HTML5 includes tags for playing audio and video files without rel
    modu  <h2> tags   Adobe Flash, to perform these tasks. Many mobile devices and computers rely on HTML5
    interpreting HTML5 tags, to handle these tasks.
19
20  Additional HTML5 features include recognizing gestures on mobile devices, performing drag and drop, c
    geolocation, and storing content offline. These HTML5 features allow web developers to build applicat
    web today on many different devices. Each browser implements the HTML5 specification differently and
21
22  CSS
23
24  While HTML describes a webpage's content as a collection of headings, paragraphs, images, links, and
    specify how these elements are formatted in a browser. Web developers may specify the fonts and font
    other styles to apply to each of these elements.
```

Figure FO-16

- Repeat the steps in Step 2 to identify the lines that read, CSS and JavaScript, as <h2> headings, and indent each line by four spaces (Figure FO-17).

- Save the changes to the index.html file.

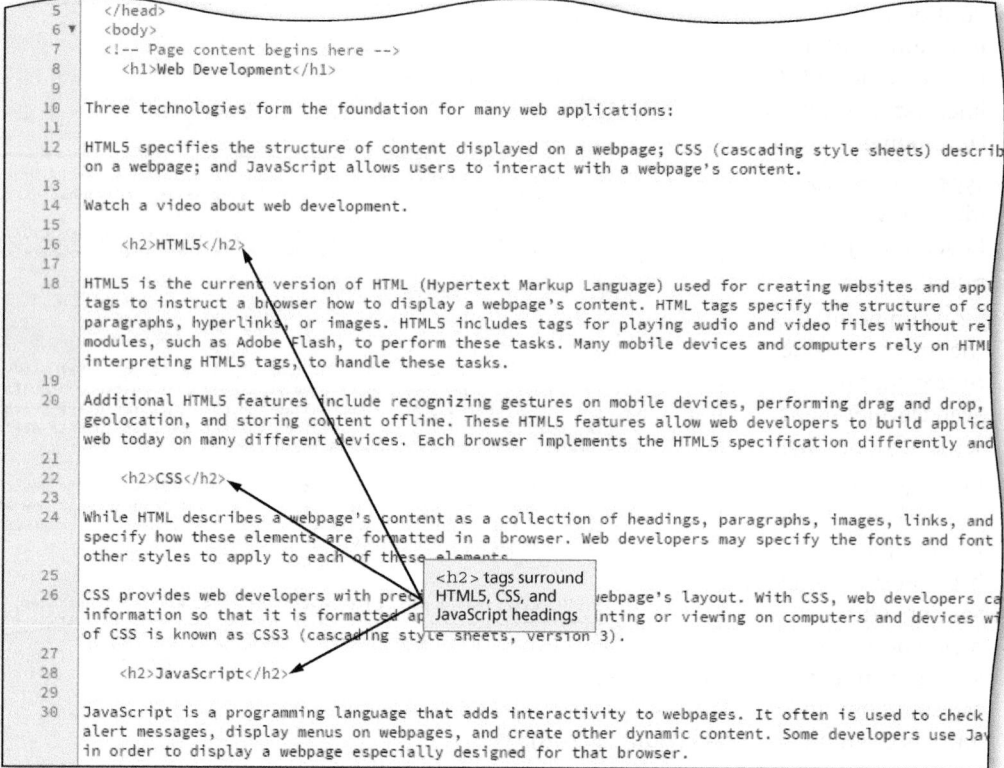

```
 5    </head>
 6 ▼  <body>
 7    <!-- Page content begins here -->
 8      <h1>Web Development</h1>
 9
10    Three technologies form the foundation for many web applications:
11
12    HTML5 specifies the structure of content displayed on a webpage; CSS (cascading style sheets) describ
      on a webpage; and JavaScript allows users to interact with a webpage's content.
13
14    Watch a video about web development.
15
16      <h2>HTML5</h2>
17
18    HTML5 is the current version of HTML (Hypertext Markup Language) used for creating websites and app
      tags to instruct a browser how to display a webpage's content. HTML tags specify the structure of co
      paragraphs, hyperlinks, or images. HTML5 includes tags for playing audio and video files without re
      modules, such as Adobe Flash, to perform these tasks. Many mobile devices and computers rely on HTM
      interpreting HTML5 tags, to handle these tasks.
19
20    Additional HTML5 features include recognizing gestures on mobile devices, performing drag and drop,
      geolocation, and storing content offline. These HTML5 features allow web developers to build applica
      web today on many different devices. Each browser implements the HTML5 specification differently and
21
22      <h2>CSS</h2>
23
24    While HTML describes a webpage's content as a collection of headings, paragraphs, images, links, and
      specify how these elements are formatted in a browser. Web developers may specify the fonts and font
      other styles to apply to each of these elements.
25
26    CSS provides web developers with pre    ┌──────────────────┐ webpage's layout. With CSS, web developers ca
      information so that it is formatted ap  │ <h2> tags surround │ nting or viewing on computers and devices w
      of CSS is known as CSS3 (cascading sty │ HTML5, CSS, and    │ version 3).
                                             │ JavaScript headings │
27                                           └──────────────────┘
28      <h2>JavaScript</h2>
29
30    JavaScript is a programming language that adds interactivity to webpages. It often is used to check
      alert messages, display menus on webpages, and create other dynamic content. Some developers use Jav
      in order to display a webpage especially designed for that browser.
```

Figure FO-17

To View the index.html Webpage in a Browser

As shown in Figure FO-18, the website folder contains one HTML file for each page and a folder called images with all of the website's images. The following steps view the index.html file in a browser. *Why? When creating a webpage, you often should view your progress in a browser to make sure the webpage appears as you intend. If you find something wrong, you should correct it before writing additional HTML code for your webpage.*

- Minimize the text editor window showing the HTML code for the index.html file.
- If necessary, navigate to the location of the index.html file (Figure FO-18).

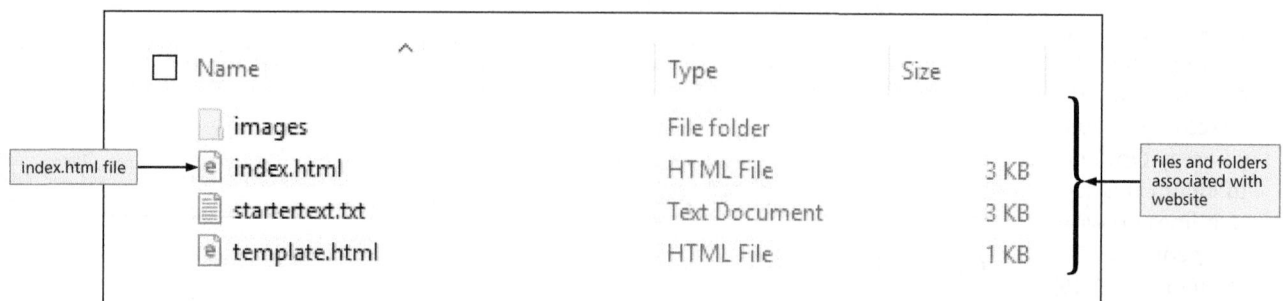

Name	Type	Size
☐ images	File folder	
index.html file → ⓔ index.html	HTML File	3 KB
📄 startertext.txt	Text Document	3 KB
ⓔ template.html	HTML File	1 KB

files and folders associated with website

Figure FO-18

2

- Double-click the index.html file to open it in a browser (Figure FO-19).

What happens if the file does not open in a browser?
You may need to run a browser first and then use the Open command in the browser to navigate to and open the index.html file.

If my computer's display device is large enough, can I arrange the windows to display both the text editor and browser side by side?
Yes.

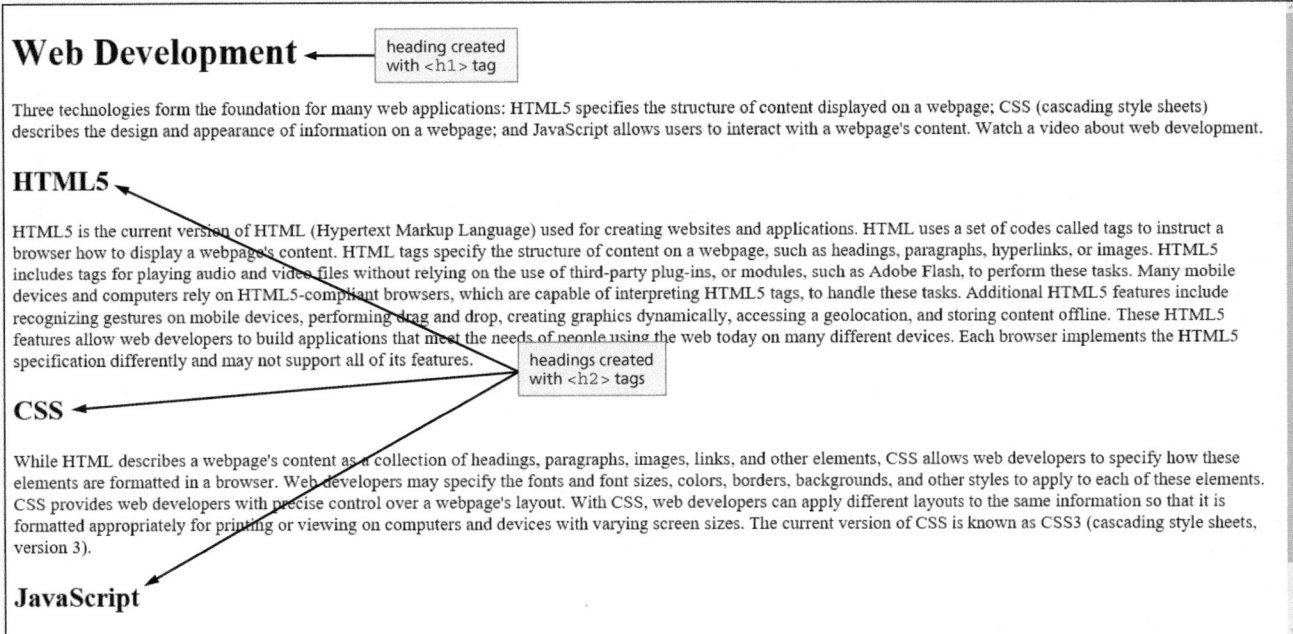

Web Development ← heading created with \<h1> tag

Three technologies form the foundation for many web applications: HTML5 specifies the structure of content displayed on a webpage; CSS (cascading style sheets) describes the design and appearance of information on a webpage; and JavaScript allows users to interact with a webpage's content. Watch a video about web development.

HTML5

HTML5 is the current version of HTML (Hypertext Markup Language) used for creating websites and applications. HTML uses a set of codes called tags to instruct a browser how to display a webpage's content. HTML tags specify the structure of content on a webpage, such as headings, paragraphs, hyperlinks, or images. HTML5 includes tags for playing audio and video files without relying on the use of third-party plug-ins, or modules, such as Adobe Flash, to perform these tasks. Many mobile devices and computers rely on HTML5-compliant browsers, which are capable of interpreting HTML5 tags, to handle these tasks. Additional HTML5 features include recognizing gestures on mobile devices, performing drag and drop, creating graphics dynamically, accessing a geolocation, and storing content offline. These HTML5 features allow web developers to build applications that meet the needs of people using the web today on many different devices. Each browser implements the HTML5 specification differently and may not support all of its features.

headings created with \<h2> tags

CSS ←

While HTML describes a webpage's content as a collection of headings, paragraphs, images, links, and other elements, CSS allows web developers to specify how these elements are formatted in a browser. Web developers may specify the fonts and font sizes, colors, borders, backgrounds, and other styles to apply to each of these elements. CSS provides web developers with precise control over a webpage's layout. With CSS, web developers can apply different layouts to the same information so that it is formatted appropriately for printing or viewing on computers and devices with varying screen sizes. The current version of CSS is known as CSS3 (cascading style sheets, version 3).

JavaScript

Figure FO-19

3

- When you are finished viewing the webpage in the browser, minimize the browser window and redisplay the text editor containing the index.html file.

Paragraphs

The \<p> and \</p> tags are used to identify the beginning and ending of paragraphs. If you have several paragraphs of text on your webpage, these tags will inform the browser to insert additional line spacing above and below the paragraph so that the text is easier to read when displayed in the browser. The browser ignores line breaks and line spacing in the HTML file, so it is important to properly define the paragraphs using the \<p> and \</p> tags. For example, even if the HTML file appears to have five distinct paragraphs, each separated by a blank line, the browser will ignore the blank lines and display everything as one, long paragraph. To display the text correctly in a browser, place \<p> and \</p> tags around each paragraph. Each \<p> tag must have a corresponding \</p> tag so that the code is HTML5-compliant.

The index.html file in this example has eight paragraphs: three below the webpage title, two below the HTML5 heading, two below the CSS heading, and one below the JavaScript heading.

To Identify the Paragraphs in the index.html File

The following steps use the <p> and </p> tags to identify each of the eight paragraphs in the index.html file. *Why?* *Using the <p> and </p> tags to format each paragraph will enhance the webpage structure and make the text more readable for the webpage visitors.*

- Position point at the beginning of the paragraph that begins with, Three technologies form the foundation....

- Type **<p>** to indicate where the paragraph begins.

- Position the insertion point at the end of the first paragraph.

- Type **</p>** to indicate the end of the paragraph. Although spacing does not matter to the browser, you may type spaces to indent this tag so that it lines up with its opening **<p>** tag (Figure FO-20).

```
 1   <!DOCTYPE html>
 2 ▼ <html>
 3 ▼   <head>
 4       <title>Mark's Web Development Page</title>
 5     </head>
 6 ▼   <body>
 7     <!-- Page content begins here -->
 8       <h1>Web Development</h1>
 9
10       <p>Three technologies form the foundation for many web applications:</p>
11
12     HTML5 specifies the structure of content displayed on a webpage; CSS (cascading style sheets) descr
       on a webpage; and JavaScript allows users to interact with a webpage's content.
13
14     Watch a video about web development.
15
16       <h2>HTML5</h2>
17
18     HTML5 is the current version of HTML (Hypertext Markup Language) used for creating websites and app
       tags to instruct a browser how to display a webpage's content. HTML tags specify the structure of co
       paragraphs, hyperlinks, or image       opening and closing       tags for playing audio and video files without re
       modules, such as Adobe Flash, to        <p> tags                 ks. Many mobile devices and computers rely on HTML
       interpreting HTML5 tags, to hand
19
20     Additional HTML5 features include recognizing gestures on mobile devices, performing drag and drop,
       geolocation, and storing content offline. These HTML5 features allow web developers to build applica
       web today on many different devices. Each browser implements the HTML5 specification differently and
21
22       <h2>CSS</h2>
23
24     While HTML describes a webpage's content as a collection of headings, paragraphs, images, links, an
       specify how these elements are formatted in a browser. Web developers may specify the fonts and for
       other styles to apply to each of these elements.
```

Figure FO-20

2

- For the remaining paragraphs in the index.html file, type **<p>** at the beginning of each paragraph and type **</p>** at the end of each paragraph. To increase readability, you may type spaces to indent this tag so that it lines up with its opening <p> tag, as shown in Figure FO-21.

- Save the changes to the index.html file.

- Refresh or reload the webpage in the browser window to verify the changes are displayed properly.

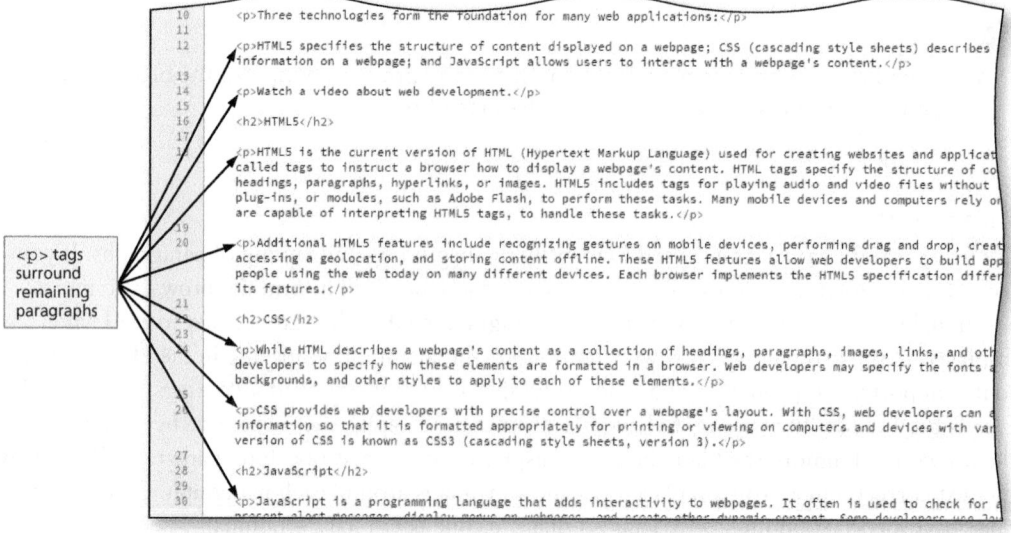

```
10       <p>Three technologies form the foundation for many web applications:</p>
11
12       <p>HTML5 specifies the structure of content displayed on a webpage; CSS (cascading style sheets) describes
         information on a webpage; and JavaScript allows users to interact with a webpage's content.</p>
13
14       <p>Watch a video about web development.</p>
15
16       <h2>HTML5</h2>
17
18       <p>HTML5 is the current version of HTML (Hypertext Markup Language) used for creating websites and applicat
         called tags to instruct a browser how to display a webpage's content. HTML tags specify the structure of co
         headings, paragraphs, hyperlinks, or images. HTML5 includes tags for playing audio and video files without
         plug-ins, or modules, such as Adobe Flash, to perform these tasks. Many mobile devices and computers rely on
         are capable of interpreting HTML5 tags, to handle these tasks.</p>
19
20       <p>Additional HTML5 features include recognizing gestures on mobile devices, performing drag and drop, creat
         accessing a geolocation, and storing content offline. These HTML5 features allow web developers to build app
         people using the web today on many different devices. Each browser implements the HTML5 specification differ
         its features.</p>
21
22       <h2>CSS</h2>
23
24       <p>While HTML describes a webpage's content as a collection of headings, paragraphs, images, links, and oth
         developers to specify how these elements are formatted in a browser. Web developers may specify the fonts a
         backgrounds, and other styles to apply to each of these elements.</p>
25
26       <p>CSS provides web developers with precise control over a webpage's layout. With CSS, web developers can a
         information so that it is formatted appropriately for printing or viewing on computers and devices with var
         version of CSS is known as CSS3 (cascading style sheets, version 3).</p>
27
28       <h2>JavaScript</h2>
29
30       <p>JavaScript is a programming language that adds interactivity to webpages. It often is used to check for
```

<p> tags surround remaining paragraphs

Figure FO-21

Q&A | I keep attempting to refresh, but my page does not change. What can I do?
Some browsers keep the content of previously loaded pages in local storage so that they will load faster when a user returns to them. Try pressing the CTRL key on the keyboard while reloading the page in order to clear any pages previously stored by the browser.

Images

Most webpages contain one or more images that add visual appeal. Images can be either photos or graphics. Some websites include a banner, or graphic that identifies the website, at the top of each page so that they are easily recognizable. While images can make a website more attractive, or help to deliver its message, remember that not all viewers may be able to see these images. For example, someone who is visually impaired or someone who has configured his or her browser so that it does not display images may be unable to view the images. For this reason, it is not advisable to use images as the only method of conveying information to website visitors.

Images are stored in files located on a web server, and references to the images appear in the HTML code using the `<img>` tag. Choose images stored in the JPEG, GIF, or PNG format (identified with a .jpg, .gif, or .png file extension), as they are the formats supported by most browsers. Webpages containing many images with large file sizes may have long load times on devices with slower Internet connections.

The Web Development webpage you are creating in this example will contain three images: one under the HTML5 heading, one under the CSS heading, and one under the JavaScript heading. When adding the HTML code for these images, you will specify attributes for each `<img>` tag to provide additional information needed for the browser to display the image. Attributes are coded within an HTML tag. Many HTML tags have attributes associated with them. See Table FO-2 at the end of this Focus On for a summary of common tags and their attributes.

Common attributes for the `<img>` tag describe the location of an image file, alternate text for the image, and a style that indicates how to position the image. For example, the `src` attribute of the `<img>` tag specifies the source location of the image; the `alt` attribute specifies alternate text, or alt text, associated with an image; and the `style` attribute provides information regarding the placement or display of an image.

This example stores its images in a folder named images that is located in the website folder, as specified in the `src` attribute.

HTML tags may have zero or more attributes. The format of an attribute is its name, followed by an equal sign, followed by the attribute's value, surrounded in quotation marks.

The `src` attribute's value refers to an image file located in the images folder.

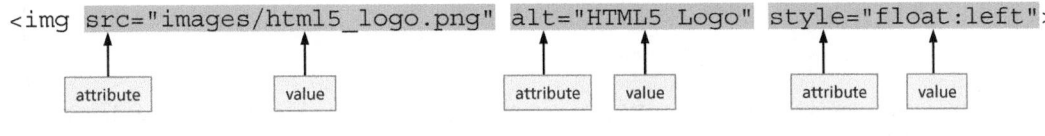

```
<img src="images/html5_logo.png" alt="HTML5 Logo" style="float:left">
```
attribute | value | attribute | value | attribute | value

 BTW

Images

Be cautious when you include images from another website. If the owner of the other website modifies the location or removes the image entirely, the image will not appear on your website. You should have permission to use all of the images and photos displayed on your website. Many search engines allow you to search for images and photos that may be used without obtaining the owner's permission.

 BTW

Photo Size

If you are trying to display photos from a digital camera or smartphone camera on your website, you should use image editing software to shrink the photos to an appropriate size, such as 300 × 400 pixels or 600 × 800 pixels. The size, or resolution, of a photo taken with an 8 megapixel camera can be approximately 2447 × 3264 pixels, which is larger than the resolution of the screens on many devices or monitors.

 **CONSIDER THIS**

Is it required to include the `alt` attribute?
The `alt` attribute is a required part of the `<img>` tag in HTML5. Many browsers display the alternate text in place of an image when they are not set to load images automatically or the file containing the image is not found. Alternate text also helps visually impaired users, who use screen reading software to navigate a website, identify the purpose of an image. Most screen reading apps will read aloud the alternate text for each image.

CONSIDER THIS ────────────────────────────────────

How does the `float:left` style display?
The `float:left` style displays the image at the upper-left corner of a block of text and displays the text around the image.

 CONSIDER THIS ────────────────────────────────────

Where is the closing tag to correspond with `<img>`?
Some tags do not have a corresponding closing tag. When no additional information is required between an opening tag and its closing tag, HTML5 omits the closing tag. In this case, the image is specified entirely by its attributes, so HTML5 does not specify a tag to close the `<img>` tag. HTML5 tags that do not require a closing tag are sometimes called one-sided tags. Other one-sided tags include `<br>` (line break) and `<hr>` (horizontal rule).

To Insert Images in the index.html File

As shown in Figure FO-18, this example stores images used in this website in a folder named images, located in the same folder as the index.html file. It is a good practice to store images used in a website in a folder separate from the HTML pages of a website so that they can be located easily. The following steps insert three images, which are located in the images folder, in the index.html file. ***Why? You will insert these images to add visual appeal to the webpage.***

1

- Locate the `<h2>HTML5</h2>` heading in the file. Position the insertion point before the first `<p>` tag that follows this heading and then press the ENTER key to insert a new line.
- Type `<img src="images/html5_image.png" alt="HTML5 Image" style="float:left">` to insert a reference to the html5_image.png file located in the images folder, set the alternate text to HTML5 Image, and position the image so that it is aligned to the left of the text below the HTML5 heading (Figure FO-22).

```
7    <!-- Page content begins here -->
8    <h1>Web Development</h1>
9
10   <p>Three technologies form the foundation for many web applications:</p>
11
12   <p>HTML5 specifies the structure of content displayed on a webpage; CSS (cascading style
     information on a webpage; and JavaScript allows users to interact with a webpage's conten
13
14   <p>Watch a video about web development.</p>
15
16   <h2>HTML5</h2>
17   <img src="images/html5_image.png" alt="HTML5 Image" style="float:left">
18
19   <p>HTML5 is the current version of HTML (Hypertext Markup Language) used for creating web
     called tags to instruct a browser how to display a webpage's content. HTML tags specify t
     headings, paragraphs, hyperlinks, or images. HTML5 includes tags for playing audio and vi
     plug-ins, or modules, such as Adobe Flash, to perform these tasks. Many mobile devices ar
     are capable of interpreting HTML5 tags, to handle these tasks.</p>
20
21   <p>Additional HTML5 features include recognizing gestures on mobile devices, performing d
     accessing a geolocation, and storing content offline. These HTML5 features allow web deve
     people using the web today on many different devices. Each browser implements the HTML5 s
```

`<img>` tag inserted

Figure FO-22

- Locate the `<h2>CSS</h2>` heading in the file. Position the insertion point before the first `<p>` tag that follows this heading and then press the ENTER key to insert a new line.

- Type `<img src="images/css_image.png" alt="CSS Image" style="float:right">` to insert a reference to the css_image.png file in the images folder, set the alternate text to CSS Image, and style the image so that it is aligned to the right of the text under the CSS heading.

- Locate the `<h2>JavaScript</h2>` heading in the file. Position the insertion point before the first `<p>` tag that follows this heading and then press the ENTER key to insert a new line.

- Type `<img src="images/js_image.png" alt="JavaScript Image" style="float:left">` to insert a reference to the js_image.png file in the images folder, set the alternate text to JavaScript Image, and align the image to the left of the text under the JavaScript heading (Figure FO-23).

- Save the changes to the index.html file.

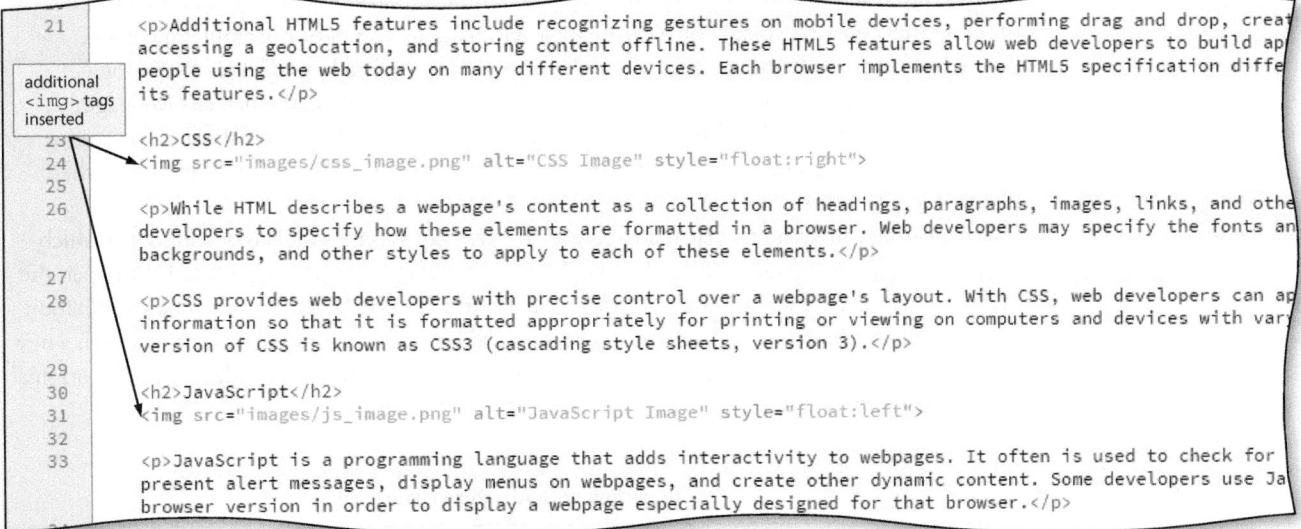

```
21    <p>Additional HTML5 features include recognizing gestures on mobile devices, performing drag and drop, crea
      accessing a geolocation, and storing content offline. These HTML5 features allow web developers to build ap
      people using the web today on many different devices. Each browser implements the HTML5 specification diffe
      its features.</p>

23    <h2>CSS</h2>
24    <img src="images/css_image.png" alt="CSS Image" style="float:right">
25
26    <p>While HTML describes a webpage's content as a collection of headings, paragraphs, images, links, and othe
      developers to specify how these elements are formatted in a browser. Web developers may specify the fonts an
      backgrounds, and other styles to apply to each of these elements.</p>

27
28    <p>CSS provides web developers with precise control over a webpage's layout. With CSS, web developers can ap
      information so that it is formatted appropriately for printing or viewing on computers and devices with var
      version of CSS is known as CSS3 (cascading style sheets, version 3).</p>

29
30    <h2>JavaScript</h2>
31    <img src="images/js_image.png" alt="JavaScript Image" style="float:left">
32
33    <p>JavaScript is a programming language that adds interactivity to webpages. It often is used to check for
      present alert messages, display menus on webpages, and create other dynamic content. Some developers use Ja
      browser version in order to display a webpage especially designed for that browser.</p>
```

additional
`<img>` tags
inserted

Figure FO- 23

- Refresh or reload the webpage in the browser window to verify the changes are displayed properly. If necessary, scroll to display the three images (Figure FO-24).

Q&A

Why are the images not being displayed?

If images are not displayed, most likely the browser cannot find them. Check that you correctly typed the code referencing the images and that the images exist in the location you specified (in this case, the images folder). Be sure that you saved the index.html file after making the changes in the previous set of steps before reloading the webpage.

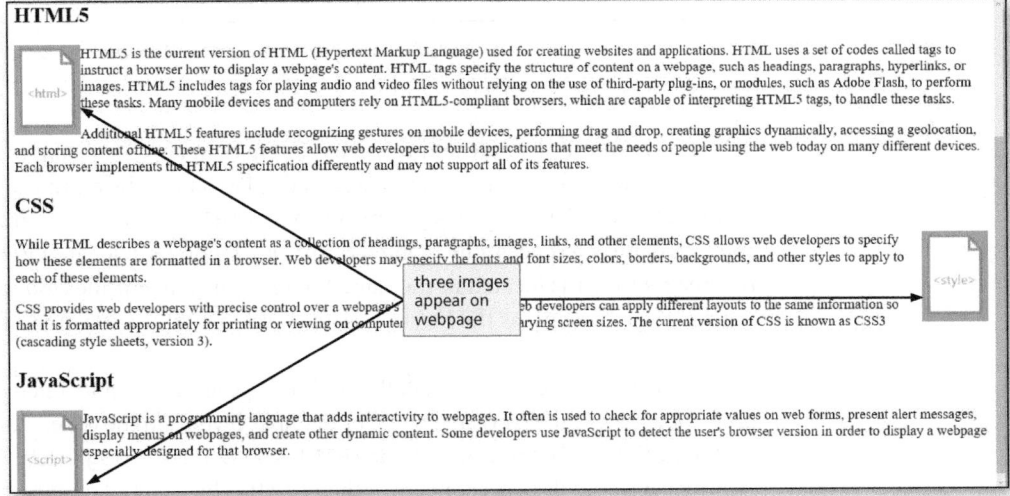

Figure FO- 24

Links

A link, or hyperlink, can be text or an image in a webpage that a user clicks to navigate to another webpage, download a file, or perform another action, such as running an email app and addressing an email message. If you want webpage visitors to be able to access other webpages in the website easily, you should include links to those pages. In addition to providing links to other pages in the website, you also can provide links to other websites. Webpages always are stored as separate files, and hypertext references to the files appear in the HTML code using the `<a>` (anchor) tag. Its `href` (hypertext reference) attribute often refers to the location of the file or webpage that you want to view or download.

The `href` attribute's value references link's the location of another webpage or file using either a relative reference or an absolute reference. Relative references identify the location of webpages and files on the current website. Absolute references are used to identify the location of webpages or files stored on other websites.

An absolute reference includes the full path, including the protocol and domain name containing the webpage, image, or file you are attempting to access (for example, the code, `<a href="http://www.google.com">Google</a>`, is a hyperlink to the Google website). If the http:// protocol is missing from an absolute reference, the desired webpage, image, or file may not load. (This also is known as a broken link.) While an absolute reference must include http://, some browsers may not display the http:// prefix in the address bar when navigating to a webpage.

When creating a link, the `target` attribute of the `<a>` tag specifies the tab or window in which the resulting webpage, image, or file will open. Use the attribute `target="_blank"` to open the linked document in a new window or tab. If you exclude the `target` attribute, the link's destination will open in the same browser tab or window. It is a good idea to open links to other websites in a new browser tab or window so that the visitor easily can return to the webpage by redisplaying the original tab or window.

Hyperlink with Absolute Reference

```
<a href="http://www.w3.org" target="_blank">HTML5</a>
```

Hyperlink with Relative Reference

```
<a href="video.html"> Watch a video</a>
```

You also can use absolute and relative references in an `<img>` tag to specify the location from where a browser should access an image to display on a website. In the HTML code, `<img src="images/html5_image.png" alt="HTML Image">`, from the previous step, the `src` attribute references a file named html5_image.png file located in the images folder, and the images folder is located in the same folder as the current file (index.html, in this case). This is a relative reference, as the location is given relative to the location of the file requesting the resource.

To display an image stored on another website, specify an absolute reference, including the http:// protocol, as part of the `src` attribute. For example, if you add the code, `<img src="https://www.w3.org/html/logo/downloads/HTML5_Logo_512.png" alt="HTML5 Logo">`, to a webpage, it would display an image of the HTML5 logo stored on the web server hosting the website at w3c.org. The image will be accessed from the web server specified in the absolute reference.

The index.html page in this example will contain four links: three links to websites about HTML5, CSS, and JavaScript, for which you will use absolute references, and one link to another webpage you will create as part of this website, for which you will use a relative reference.

To Insert a Link with an Absolute Reference

The following steps add links with absolute references to three different locations. **Why?** *Links with absolute references are required in this case because the webpages to which you are linking are not on the same website or web server as the index.html file.*

- In the second paragraph beginning, HTML5 specifies the structure, position the insertion point immediately before the H in HTML5.
- Type `<a href="http://www.w3.org/html/logo" target="_blank">` to specify the link destination and that the resulting webpage should open in a new, blank window.
- Position the insertion point after HTML5 and then type `</a>` to indicate the end of the link (Figure FO-25).

```
 8       <h1>Web Development</h1>
 9
10       <p>Three technologies form the foundation for many web applications:</p>
11
12          <p><a href="http://www.w3.org/html/logo" target="_blank">HTML5</a> specifies the structure of content displayed
            (cascading style sheets) describes the design and appearance of information on a webpage; and JavaScript allows u
            webpage's content.</p>
13
14       <p>Watch a video about web development.</p>
15
16       <h2>HTML5</h2>
17       <img src="images/html5_image.png"            le="float:left">
18
19       <p>HTML5 is the current version of HTML (Hypertext Markup Language) used for creating websites and applications. HT
            called tags to instruct a browser how to display a webpage's content. HTML tags specify the structure of content or
            headings, paragraphs, hyperlinks, or images. HTML5 includes tags for playing audio and video files without relying
            plug-ins, or modules, such as Adobe Flash, to perform these tasks. Many mobile devices and computers rely on HTML5-
            are capable of interpreting HTML5 tags, to handle these tasks.</p>
20
```

opening and closing <a> tags surround link text

Figure FO-25

- In the same paragraph, position the insertion point immediately before CSS and type `<a href="http://www.w3.org/Style/Examples/011/firstcss" target="_blank">` to specify the link destination and that the resulting webpage should open in a new, blank window.
- Position the insertion point after CSS and then type `</a>` to indicate the end of the link.
- Save the changes to the index.html file.
- Refresh or reload the webpage in the browser window to verify the changes are displayed properly.
- In the same paragraph, position the insertion point immediately before JavaScript and then type `<a href="http://javascript.com" target="_blank">` to specify the link destination and that the resulting webpage should open in a new, blank window.
- Position the insertion point after JavaScript and then type `</a>` to indicate the end of the link (Figure FO-26).
- Save the changes to the index.html file.
- Refresh or reload the webpage in the browser window to verify the changes are displayed properly.

```
 8       <h1>Web Development</h1>
 9
10       <p>Three technologies form the foundation for many web applications:</p>
11
12          <p><a href="http://www.w3.org/html/logo" target="_blank">HTML5</a> specifies the structure of content displayed on a webpage; <a
            href="http://www.w3.org/Style/Examples/011/firstcss" target="_blank">CSS</a> (cascading style sheets) describes the design and appearance
            of information on a webpage; and <a href="http://javascript.com" target="_blank">JavaScript</a> allows users to interact with a webpage's
            content.</p>
13
14       <p>Watch a video about web development.</p>
15
16       <h2>HTML5</h2>
17       <img src="images/html5_image.png" alt="HTML5 Image" style="float:left">
18
19       <p>HTML5 is the current version of HTML (Hypertext Markup Language) used for creating websites and applications. HTML uses a set of codes
            called tags to instruct a browser how to display a webpage's content. HTML tags specify the structure of content on a webpage, such as
            headings, paragraphs, hyperlinks, or images. HTML5 includes tags for                    files without relying on the use of third-party
            plug-ins, or modules, such as Adobe Flash, to perform these tasks. M                    omputers rely on HTML5-compliant browsers, which
            are capable of interpreting HTML5 tags, to handle these tasks.</p>
```

two additional <a> tags inserted

Figure FO-26

To Create the video.html File

The following steps open the startertext.txt file and save it with the file name, video.html. The Video page will contain an embedded online video.

1 Open the template.html file in a text editor.

2 Save the file with the file name, video.html.

3 Between the `<title>` and `</title>` tags, select the existing text and then type **Video Page** to replace the text.

4 Save the changes to the video.html file. Do not close the file.

To Insert a Link with a Relative Reference

The link with a relative reference to the Video webpage on the Web Development website will navigate to the video.html webpage you created in the previous set of steps. *Why? Because the webpage to which you are linking is located in the same folder as the file from which you are linking, it will be easier to create a link with a relative reference so that you do not have to indicate the entire path of the file.* The following step inserts a link with a relative reference that points to the video.html file.

1

- Display the index.html file.
- Position the insertion point immediately before the W in the paragraph beginning, Watch a video.
- Type `<a href="video.html">` to indicate the beginning of the link that will point to video.html, which is in the same folder as index.html.
- Position the insertion point after the word, video, in the same sentence and then type `</a>` to indicate the end of the link (Figure FO-27).
- Save the changes to the index.html file.
- Refresh or reload the webpage in the browser window to verify the changes are displayed properly.

Q&A How can I add an image so that a user can click it, instead of text, to navigate to another webpage?
Create the link, but include the HTML for the image tag between the `<a>` and `</a>` tags. For example:
`<a href="video.html"><img src="images/video.png" alt="video icon"></a>`
will display a video icon for the user to click to navigate to the video.html page. Be sure the video icon (video.png) is located in the website's images folder.

Figure FO-27

Unordered and Ordered Lists

Two types of lists that HTML supports are unordered and ordered, as specified by the `<ul>` and `<ol>` tags, respectively. Unordered lists display a collection of items in a list format, with each list item preceded by a bullet. Ordered lists precede each list item with a number (Figure FO-28). Both `<ul>` and `<ol>` tags require using the `<li>` tag to specify list items. List items may contain other HTML tags, such as images, hyperlinks, or formatted text.

Unordered List	

```<ul>```
  ```<li>HTML5</li>```
  ```<li>CSS</li>```
  ```<li>JavaScript</li>```
```</ul>```
	• HTML5
	• CSS
	• JavaScript

Ordered List	

```<ol>```
  ```<li>HTML5</li>```
  ```<li>CSS</li>```
  ```<li>JavaScript</li>```
```</ol>```
	1. HTML5
	2. CSS
	3. JavaScript

Figure FO-28

To Format Items in an Ordered List

The following steps format the text in the first paragraph in the Web Development webpage as an ordered list. The list will contain three list items, each identified by a number. *Why? An ordered list will display the information in this paragraph with greater visual appeal than a long, multi-line paragraph.*

- The items in this ordered list will include the three links for HTML5, CSS, and JavaScript. To change the first paragraph into an ordered list, change the first `<p>` to **`<ol>`** and the corresponding `</p>` to **`</ol>`**.
- Position the insertion point before the `<a>` tag for the HTML5 link, press the ENTER key, press the SPACEBAR two times to create an indent, and then type **`<li>`** to indicate the beginning of a list item, and then press the ENTER key.
- Position the insertion point immediately after the semicolon in the HTML5 sentence, press the ENTER key, press the SPACEBAR until the insertion point lines up with the opening `<li>` tag, and then type **`</li>`** to indicate the end of the first list item. Adjust the line spacing and indentation as necessary to match Figure FO-29.
- Press the ENTER key so that the next list item will begin on a new line in the file (Figure FO-29).

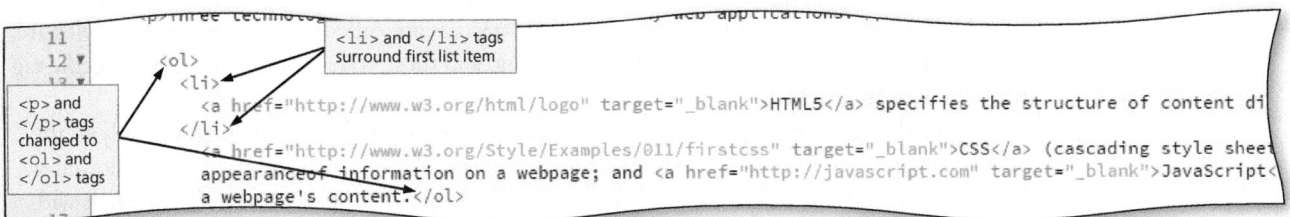

Figure FO-29

2
- Insert the remaining list items, typing the `<li>` and `</li>` tags for the CSS and JavaScript sentences.
- Adjust the line spacing and indentation so that the HTML for the ordered list looks like Figure FO-30.
- Save the changes to the index.html file.
- Refresh or reload the webpage in the browser window to verify the changes are displayed properly.

Q&A Is the spacing and indentation important?

As stated previously, browsers ignore extra blank spaces and line spaces when rendering HTML content. The spacing and indentation you are creating in the index.html file only improves the file's readability for anyone reviewing the HTML. Some text editors automatically will align or indent these tags for you.

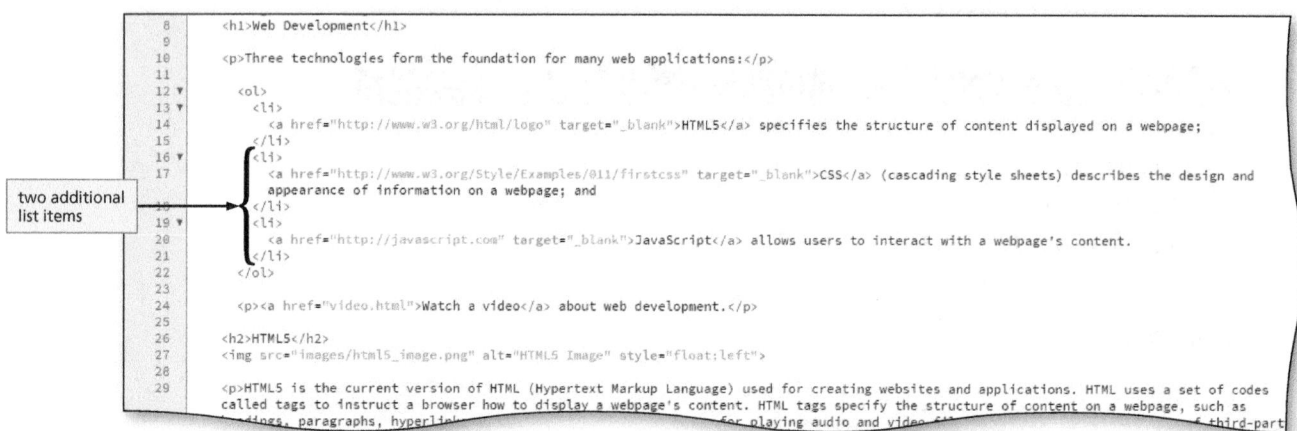

Figure FO-30

Applying Styles with CSS

While a main advantage of HTML is its capability to define webpage structure, it is not as easy to apply style elements such as fonts, font sizes, font styles, and colors. Although it is possible to customize these elements of webpages using HTML, CSS makes it easier to specify the appearance of similar elements in the same webpage or same website. For example, in a previous section you used the `<h1>` and `<h2>` tags to create four headings on the Web Development webpage. You can use CSS to specify the font, background color, and font color for all headings identified by the `<h2>` tag in the index.html webpage.

When you inserted the images previously in this Focus On, you used the `style` attribute of the `<img>` tag to indicate that you wanted the images to appear either to the left of the text or to the right of the text. (Recall that the HTML5 and JavaScript images appear to the left of the text in their respective sections, and the CSS image appears to the right of the text in the CSS section.) The styles you indicated in the `<img>` tags are called inline styles. Inline styles are identified by the `style` attribute in an HTML tag, and these styles apply only to the specific tag in which they are defined.

Embedded styles, which are defined in the head section of an HTML document, apply to the entire webpage. The format for a style's value is the style name, followed by a colon, followed by the style's value. If more than one style is specified, separate each style name and value pair with a semicolon. In this section, you will define styles to be used in the index.html file. Figure FO-31 shows the styles you will define.

style names for HTML tags use the tag names

custom style names are preceded by a period (.)

```
<style>
  h1 {
      font-family:sans-serif;
      color:navy;
      font-style:italic;
  }
  h2 {
      font-family:cursive;
      background-color: navy;
      color:papayawhip;
  }
  p {
      font-family:sans-serif;
      color:rgb(56,0,0);
  }
  ol {
      font-family:sans-serif;
      color:rgb(56,0,0);
  }
  body {
      background-color:#bbccff;
  }
  .fancy {
      font-weight:bold;
      color:red;
      font-style:italic;
  }
</style>
```

Figure FO-31

 CONSIDER THIS

Where can you find more information about CSS styles and their values?
You can use a search engine to locate websites that provide complete documentation about CSS, such as w3schools.com. Consider including words such as w3schools, css, and reference in your search text.

 CONSIDER THIS

How can you specify colors to use for backgrounds or text in an HTML file?
Most browsers recognize common color names, such as red, orange, green, and blue, along with other predefined color names, such as navy, lime green, and papaya whip. To find a list of all available color names for use on the web, use the phrase, web color names, as search text in a search engine.

You can use the `rgb()` function to specify colors by providing their red, green, and blue components as decimal values between 0 and 255, or you can use hexadecimal (base 16) values between 00 and FF. A value of 0 means the absence of a color; 255, or FF in hexadecimal, means complete fullness of a color. For example, black is specified by `rgb(0,0,0)` or the hexadecimal value #000000, red is `rgb(255,0,0)` or the hexadecimal value #FF0000, a shade of gray is indicated by the value `rgb(200,200,200)` or the hexadecimal value #C8C8C8, and white is represented by the value `rgb(255,255,255)` or the hexadecimal value #FFFFFF.

 CONSIDER THIS

Is it possible to use the same styles on all of the webpages of a website?
Yes. When creating websites with several webpages, web developers often place CSS declarations in a separate text file, called an external style sheet, so that each webpage of the website can access the same style information. External styles typically are used on large websites where web developers want a consistent style on each webpage. You can find more information about external style sheets by using a search engine with the search text, create external style sheet CSS.

To Add CSS to the index.html File

You have added all text and images to the index.html webpage and are ready to begin formatting the page using CSS. *Why? Formatting a webpage with CSS makes it more attractive and is likely to capture website visitors' attention for a longer period of time.* The following step adds embedded styles to the index.html webpage.

- Position the insertion point at the end of the `</title>` tag and then press the ENTER key.
- Type the text in Figure FO-31. Make sure you pay attention to the spacing and indentation to maximize readability (Figure FO-32).
- Save the changes to the webpage.
- Refresh or reload the webpage in the browser window to verify the changes are displayed properly.

Figure FO-32

To Add a Custom Style to the index.html File

In the previous set of steps, you specified a custom style, called `fancy`, which combines several styles to apply at the same time. Custom style names are preceded by a period (.). The period helps distinguish custom styles from styles for HTML tags, and informs the browser that the custom style will be applied to selected content on the page. When you specify a custom style name, you also must specify where in the webpage you want to apply this style. *Why? Using a custom style allows you to specify exactly where you want to use the style in the webpage. The style is not applied automatically to specific tags, as was the case with the <h1>,<h2>,<p>,<ol>, and <body> tags in the previous set of steps.* The following steps use the `<span>` tag with the `class` attribute to specify two different phrases on the page where the `fancy` custom style is to be applied.

- Position the insertion point immediately before the word, current, in the first paragraph below the HTML5 heading.
- Type `<span class="fancy">` to indicate where you want to begin applying the `fancy` custom style.
- Position the insertion point immediately after the word, HTML, in the same sentence.
- Type `</span>` to indicate where you want to stop applying the `fancy` custom style (Figure FO-33).

Figure FO-33

2

- Position the insertion point immediately before the word, Additional, in the second paragraph below the HTML5 heading.
- Type **<span class="fancy">** to indicate where you want to begin applying the fancy custom style.
- Position the insertion point immediately after the word, features, in the same sentence.
- Type **</span>** to indicate where you want to stop applying the fancy style (Figure FO-34).
- Save the changes to the index.html file.
- Refresh or reload the webpage in the browser window to verify the changes are displayed properly.

```
56   <h2>HTML5</h2>
57   <img src="images/html5_image.png" alt="HTML5 Image" style="float:left">
58
59   <p>HTML5 is the <span class="fancy">current version of HTML</span> (Hypertext Markup Language) used for creating websites and app
     HTML uses a set of codes called tags to instruct a browser how to display a webpage's content. HTML tags specify the structure o
     on a webpage, such as headings, paragraphs, hyperlinks, or images. HTML5 includes tags for playing audio and video files without
     the use of third-party plug-ins, or modules, such as Adobe Flash, to perform these tasks. Many mobile devices and computers rely
     compliant browsers, which are capable of interpreting HTML5 tags, to handle these tasks.</p>
60
61   <p><span class="fancy">Additional HTML5 features</span> include recognizing gestures on mobile devices, performing drag and drop
     graphics dynamically, accessing a geolocation, and storing content offline. These HTML5 features allow web developers to build a
     that meet the needs of people using the web today on many different devices. Each browser implements the HTML5 specification dif
     may not support all of its features.</p>
62
63   <h2>CSS</h2>
64   <img src="ima                                    " style="float:right">
65
66   <p>While HTML describes a webpage's content as a collection of headings, paragraphs, images, links, and other elements, CSS allo
     developers to specify how these elements are formatted in a browser. Web developers may specify the fonts and font sizes, colors
     backgrounds, and other styles to apply to each of these elements.</p>
67
68   <p>CSS provides web developers                    a webpage's layout. With CSS, web d                        different layouts
```

> <span> and </span> tags surround additional text to be formatted with specified fancy custom style

Figure FO-34

JavaScript

JavaScript is code that can be added to HTML documents to enhance the webpage by adding interactivity or dynamic content. JavaScript can perform simple actions, such as retrieving and displaying the current date and time, to more complex actions, such as performing calculations. In many cases, the JavaScript code appears between opening and closing <script> tags in the head section of an HTML document. In the body section, you simply reference the JavaScript code where you want the resulting content to display.

To Use JavaScript to Add the Current Date and Time

Adding the current date and time to the index.html file requires you to add code in two sections of the webpage. The following steps type the code to retrieve the current date in the head section of the index.html file (Figure FO-35a), and the code to display the retrieved date and time will be located in the body section (Figure FO-35b). **Why?** *Displaying the current date and time on a webpage suggests to visitors that the version of the webpage they are viewing is current.*

```
<script>
function showDateAndTime() {
document.getElementById("current_date").innerHTML= Date();
}
</script>
```

Figure FO-35a

```
<p id="current_date"></p>
```

Figure FO-35b

- Position the insertion point after the `</style>` tag in the head section and then press the ENTER key two times.
- Type the code shown in Figure FO-35a to enter the JavaScript code that retrieves the current date and time. Be sure to apply the same spacing, indentation, and use of uppercase and lowercase letters as shown in the figure.
- Position the insertion point immediately after the y in the `<body>` tag. Press the SPACEBAR one time and then type `onload=showDateAndTime()` to specify that you want to run the JavaScript code when the webpage loads (Figure FO-36).

```
24         color:rgb(56,0,0);
25 ▼     }
26       body {
27         background-color:#bbccff;
28 ▼     }
29       .fancy {
30         font-weight:bold;
31         color:red;
32         font-style:italic;
33       }
34     </style>
35
36 ▼   <script>
37       function showDateAndTime() {
38         document.getElementById("current_date").innerHTML = Date();
39       }
40     </script>
41
42 ▼   </head>
43     <body onload=showDateAndTime()>
44       <!-- Page content begins here -->
45       <h1>Web Development</h1>
46
47       <p>Three technologies form the foundation for many web applications:</p>
48 ▼     <ol>
49         <li>
50           <a href="http://www.w3.org/html/logo" target="_blank">HTML5</a> specifies the structure of content displayed on a webpage;
51         </li>
52 ▼       <li>
          <a href="http://www.w3...                    k">CSS</a> (cascading st...
```

JavaScript code added to head section

`<body>` tag modified to load JavaScript code when webpage loads

Figure FO-36

- Position the insertion point immediately after the last `</p>` tag in the index.html file and then press the ENTER key two times.
- Type the code shown in Figure FO-35b to specify where to display the current date (Figure FO-37).
- Save the changes to the index.html file.
- Refresh or reload the webpage in the browser window to verify the changes are displayed properly.
- Refresh or reload the page again to verify that the JavaScript updates the date and time that is displayed.

```
       <p><span class="fancy">Additional HTML5 features ... recognizing gestures on mobile devices, performing ... creating
       graphics dynamically, accessing a geolocation, and storing content offline. These HTML5 features allow web developers to build applications
       that meet the needs of people using the web today on many different devices. Each browser implements the HTML5 specification differently and
       may not support all of its features.</p>
68
69     <h2>CSS</h2>
70     <img src="images/css_image.png" alt="CSS Image" style="float:right">
71
72     <p>While HTML describes a webpage's content as a collection of headings, paragraphs, images, links, and other elements, CSS allows web
       developers to specify how these elements are formatted in a browser. Web developers may specify the fonts and font sizes, colors, borders,
       backgrounds, and other styles to apply to each of these elements.</p>
73
74     <p>CSS provides web developers with precise control over a webpage's layout. With CSS, web developers can apply different layouts to the same
       information so that it is formatted appropriately for printing or viewing on computers and devices with varying screen sizes. The current
       version of CSS is known as CSS3 (cascading style sheets, version 3).</p>
75
76     <h2>JavaScript</h2>
77     <img src="images/js_image.png" alt="JavaScript Image" style="float:left">
78
79     <p>JavaScript is a programming language that adds interactivity to webpages. It often is used to check for appropriate values on web forms,
       present alert messages, display menus on webpages, and create other dynamic content. Some developers use JavaScript to detect the user's
       browser version in order to display a webpage especially designed for that browser.</p>

       <p id="current_date"></p>

       <!-- Page content ends here -->
     </body>
85 </html>
```

`<p>` tag contains id element to display current date and time

Figure FO-37

Adding a YouTube Video to a Webpage

YouTube, a popular website with more than one billion users, contains videos about almost any topic imaginable. In addition to watching a YouTube video in a browser or using the YouTube app on a mobile device, you also can embed YouTube videos directly on a webpage. When you locate a video on that you want to include on a webpage, YouTube provides HTML code you can use to add the video to the webpage (Figure FO-38). This section adds a video about Web Development to the video.html file.

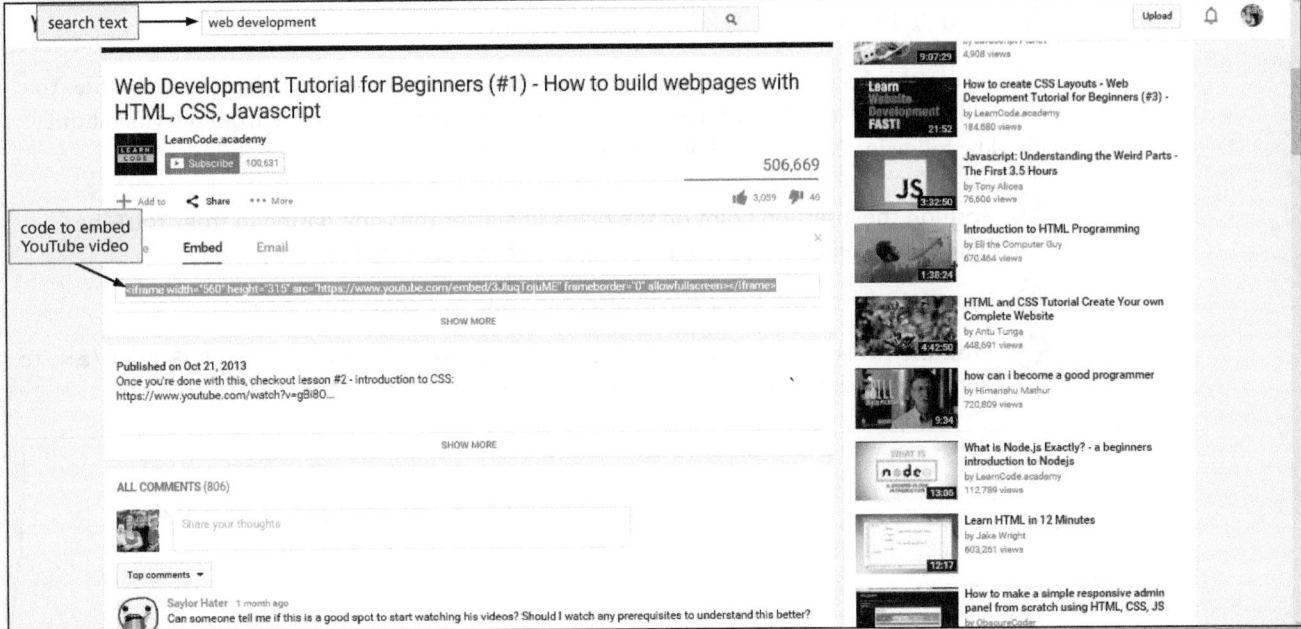

Figure FO-38
Source: YouTube

To Embed a YouTube Video in the video.html Webpage

The following steps locate a video on YouTube and embed the video in the video.html webpage. *Why? Embedding a video can add appeal to a webpage by presenting content in a format other than text and images.*

- Open a new browser tab and navigate to youtube.com.
- Use the search box on the youtube.com webpage to locate a video about web development.
- Locate the embed code. *Hint:* Click the Share link and then click the Embed link.
- Select the embed code in its entirety and then copy it to the clipboard.

2

- Display the text editor containing the code for the video.html webpage.
- Position the insertion point on a blank line immediately following the line that reads,
  `<!--Page content begins here -->`.
- Paste the contents of the clipboard (Figure FO-39).

code to embed YouTube video copied from YouTube website

```
      html>

    >Web Development</title>
5   </head>
6   <body>
7     <!-- Page content begins here -->
8       <iframe width="560" height="315" src="https://www.youtube.com/embed/3JluqTojuME" frameborder="0" allowfullscreen></iframe>
9
10
11    <!-- Page content ends here -->
12  </body>
13  </html>
```

Figure FO-39

CONSIDER THIS

What other online content can you embed on a website?

In addition to embedding videos on a website, you also may include media content, such as online calendars and documents, social media posts, images or slideshows from photo sharing websites, and maps positioned at preset locations. To include this content on a website, look for a link labeled Share or Embed or an icon displaying HTML brackets (< >) on the website containing the content. Click this link or icon, copy the embed code displayed in the browser, and paste it at the desired location in the HTML file.

To Add a Link Back to the index.html Webpage

Earlier in this Focus On, you created a link from the index.html file to the video.html file. You now will provide a link that will navigate users back to the index.html file from the video.html file. The following steps add a link to the index.html file.

1 Position the insertion point on the blank line after the code pasted in from YouTube, immediately above the `</html>` tag, and then press the ENTER key.

2 Type `<br>` to add a line break after the code to display the video.

3 Press the ENTER key two times and then type `<a href="index.html">Home</a>` to add a link back to the website's home page referenced in index.html (Figure FO-40).

```
1    <!DOCTYPE html>
2  ▼ <html>
3  ▼   <head>
4        <title>Web Development</title>
5      </head>
6  ▼   <body>
7        <!-- Page content begins here -->
8        <iframe width="560" height="315" src="https://www.youtube.com/embed/33luqTojuME" frameborder="0" allowfullscreen></iframe>
9
10       <br>
11
12       <a href="index.html">Home</a>
13
14       <!-- Page content ends here -->
15      </body>
16    </html>
```

`<br>` tag added to create line break

hyperlink to index.html webpage

Figure FO-40

To Add a Background Style to the video.html Webpage

When choosing a background image for a webpage, be sure to choose one that does not detract from the webpage content. Background images create a pattern behind a webpage's content. By default, most browsers repeat the background image both horizontally and vertically in the content area to form a tiled pattern. The following step adds an embedded style that will display a background image on the video.html webpage (Figure FO-41). **Why?** *A background image is another way to add visual appeal to a webpage. A webpage with a plain white or colored background might be less attractive than a webpage with a texture or pattern in the background.*

relative path to background image

```
<style>
  body {
    background-image:url("images/stripe_background.png");
  }
</style>
```

Figure FO-41

Focus On: Web Development

- Position the insertion point immediately after the `</title>` tag and then press the ENTER key.
- Type the code in Figure FO-41. Be sure to apply the same line spacing and indenting as shown in the figure (Figure FO-42).
- Save the changes to the video.html file.

```
1   <!DOCTYPE html>
2 ▼ <html>
3 ▼   <head>
4       <title>Web Development</title>
5     <style>
6 ▼     body  {
7         background-image:url("images/stripe_background.png");
8       }
9     </style>
10    </head>
    <body>
    <!-- Page content begins here -->
      <iframe width="560" height="315" src="https://www.youtube.com/embed/3JluqTojuME" frameborder="0" allowfullscreen></i
16    <br>
17
18    <a href="index.html">Home</a>
19
20    <!-- Page content ends here -->
```

CSS code to specify page background image

Figure FO-42

 CONSIDER THIS

Where can you find images to use as textures as the background of a webpage?
You can find background images by using a search engine to locate websites that provide these. Consider including words such as webpage, background, and textures in your search text.

To Exit the Text Editor and Preview the Webpages

When you have finished creating the webpages, the next step is to preview them in a browser before publishing them online. *Why? It is important to thoroughly preview the webpages you create to make sure all links work, all images are displayed, and the overall webpage is displayed as you intend.* The following steps exit the text editor and then load the webpages in the browser for you to preview.

- Close the video.html file in the text editor. If necessary, save the changes to the file.
- Close the index.html file in the text editor. If necessary, save the changes to the file.

- Redisplay the index.html file in the browser window. Click the Reload or Refresh button to make sure you are viewing the most current version of the webpage (Figure FO-43).

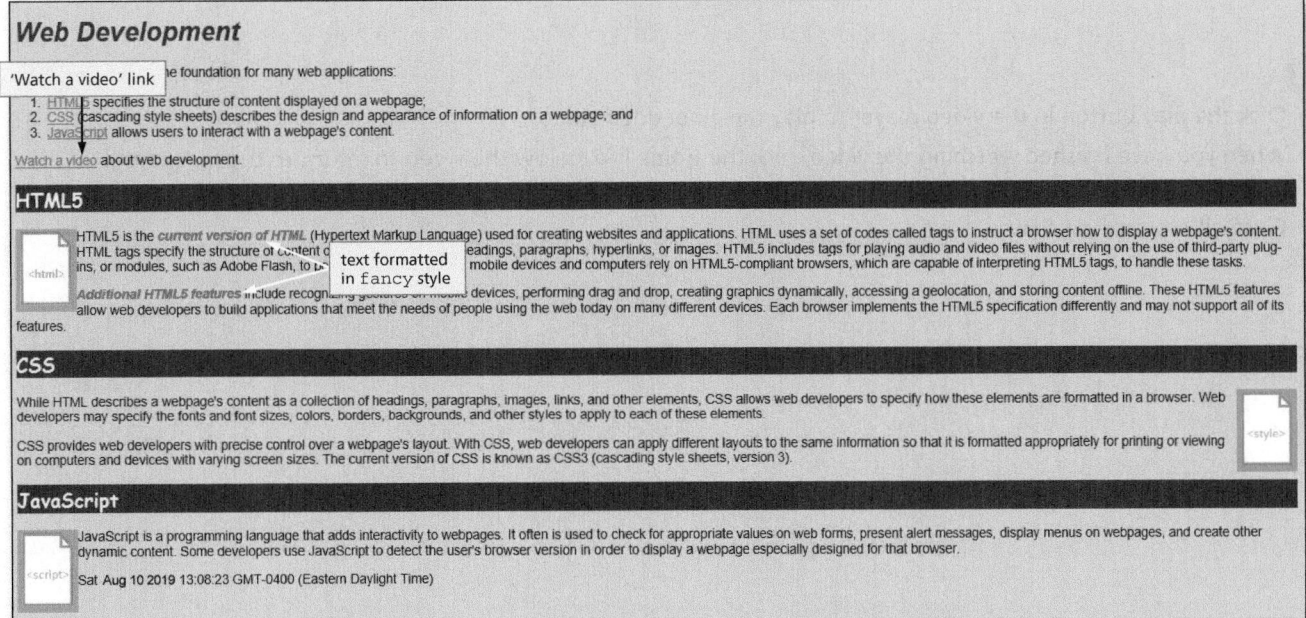

Figure FO-43

- Verify the webpage you are viewing looks the same as Figure FO-43. The headings and paragraphs should be formatted, the page should have a light blue background color, two phrases should be formatted with the custom fancy style, and the three images should have loaded.
- Click the HTML5 link to make sure it navigates to the proper destination. Then, return to the browser tab or window displaying the index.html webpage.
- Click the CSS link to make sure it navigates to the proper destination. Then, return to the browser tab or window displaying the index.html webpage.
- Click the JavaScript link to make sure it navigates to the proper destination. Then, return to the browser tab or window displaying the index.html webpage.
- Click the 'Watch a video' link to display the video.html webpage (Figure FO-44).

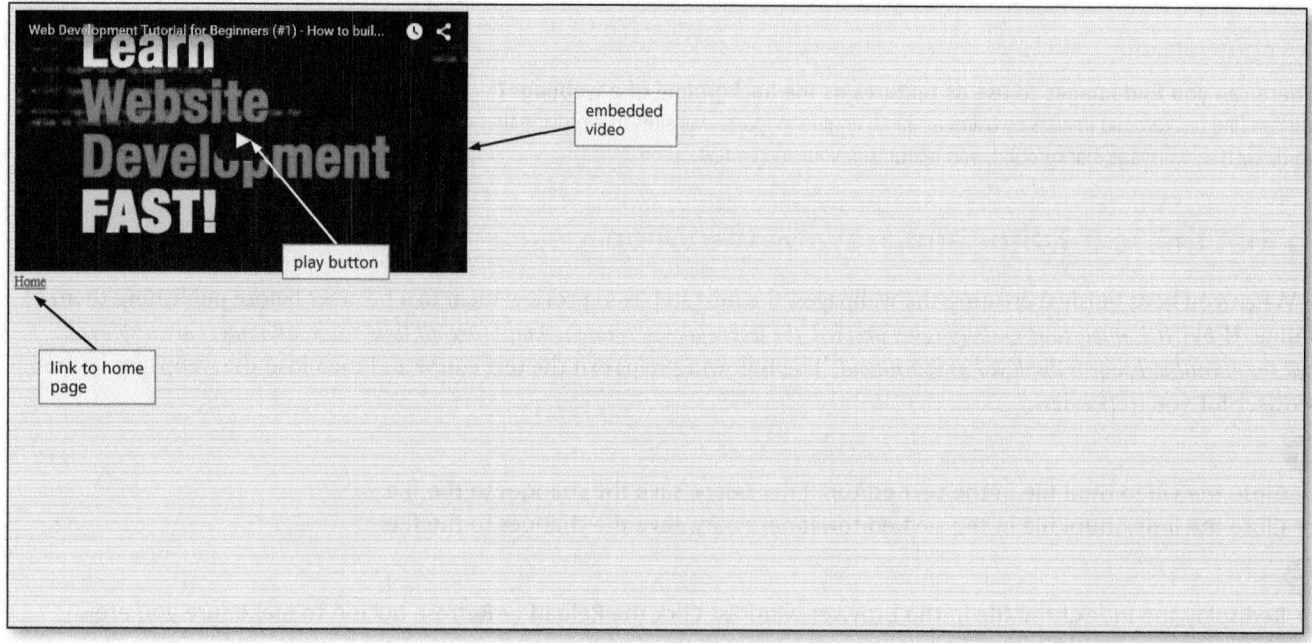

Figure FO-44

- Click the play button in the video player to play the embedded video.
- When you have finished watching the video, click the Home link below the video to return to the index.html webpage.
- Close all browser windows.

To Publish a Website Online

When you have finished testing the pages in your website, you are ready to publish them so that anyone can access them on a device connected to the Internet. *Why? Websites published on a web server are accessible online for all to see.*

To transfer the files from your local computer to a remote web server, you will need to connect to the remote web server using the File Transfer Protocol (FTP). FTP specifies rules for transferring files from one computer to another on the Internet. While it is possible to enter FTP text commands in a command window to specify how to transfer files to and from a server, most users opt to download a free FTP application, such as FileZilla or CuteFTP, which has a graphical user interface, to simplify the process.

You also will need an account on a web server in order to publish a website. If your school provides you with space to host a website, ask your instructor for the settings to connect to your account on the school's web server. In general, you will need to know the host or web server name, your user name, and your password to publish the files; you will need the web address of your website's home page to view it online. You should publish only those files related to your website assignment on your school's web server.

The following steps connect to a remote web server using an FTP application.

- Type the host name (the name of the web server) and the user name and password for the account, or set up a profile containing this information using an FTP application.
- Click the connect button to connect to the server (Figure FO-45).

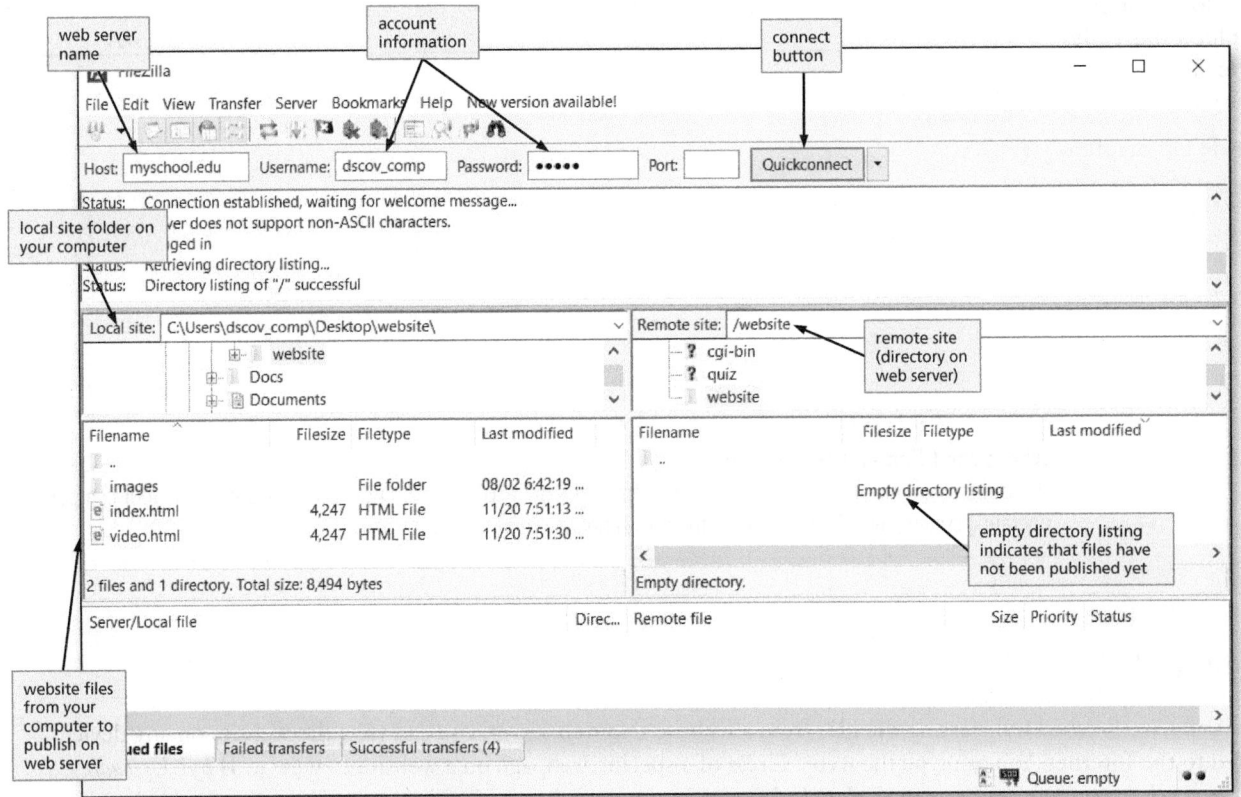

Figure FO-45
Source: Filezilla

- In the local site section of the FTP application, navigate to the website folder containing the HTML, images, and other files for the website.

- In the remote site section of the FTP application, you should see the contents of your account on the web server. No files should appear if you have not yet uploaded any.

- Select the index.html and video. html files and the images folder from the local websites section.

- Drag the selected items to the remote website section, or select the upload option to upload these files to the web server (Figure FO-46).

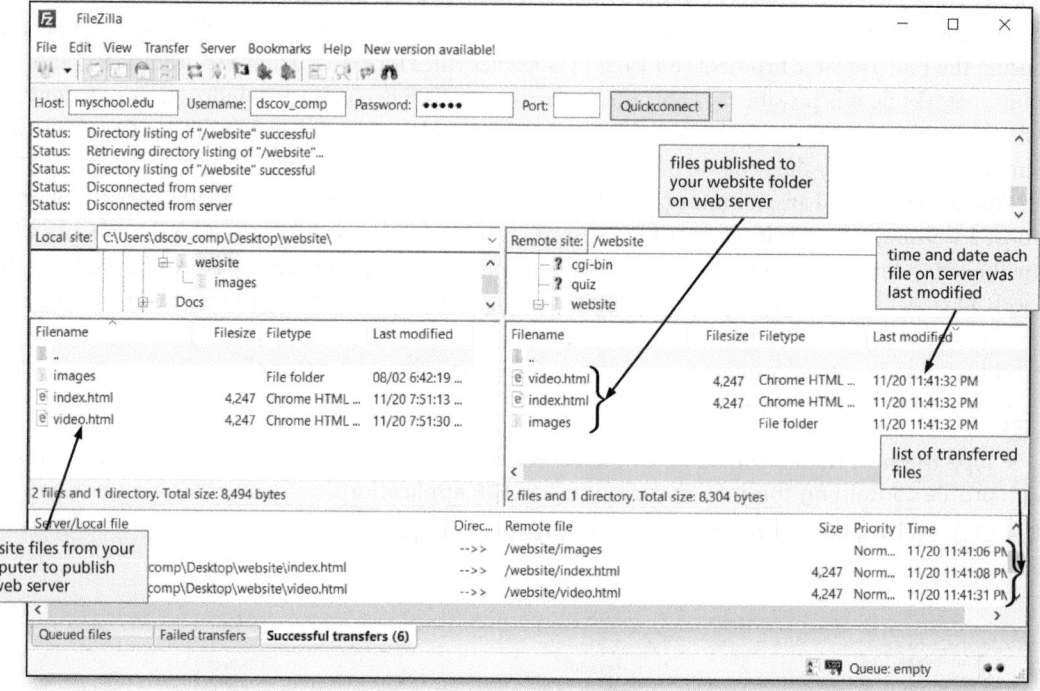

Figure FO-46
Source: Filezilla

Q&A   How do I know if my files transferred correctly?

Check the time and date and the size of the files on the server. The sizes should match the sizes of the files in your website folder. A file's time and date shows the time and date that the web server received the file.

✷ **CONSIDER THIS** ─────────

Where can I find an FTP program?

Use a search engine with the search text, free ftp program. If you wish to find a program specific to your computer's operating system, include the name of the operating system in the search text.

To View a Website Online

When you have finished transferring the files from a website to a web server, you can view the website on any device connected to the Internet. You can type the web address of a specific webpage on a website to view it. *Why? Uploading webpages to a web server allows anyone connected to the Internet to view them by entering their web address. You should view the website online to make sure it is displayed as you intend.* The following step displays the published website in a browser.

- Run a browser or open a new browser tab.
- In the address bar, type the absolute address of the website hosted on a web server. (This web address begins with http:// and includes the name of the server hosting the web site.) The website will appear (Figure FO-47).

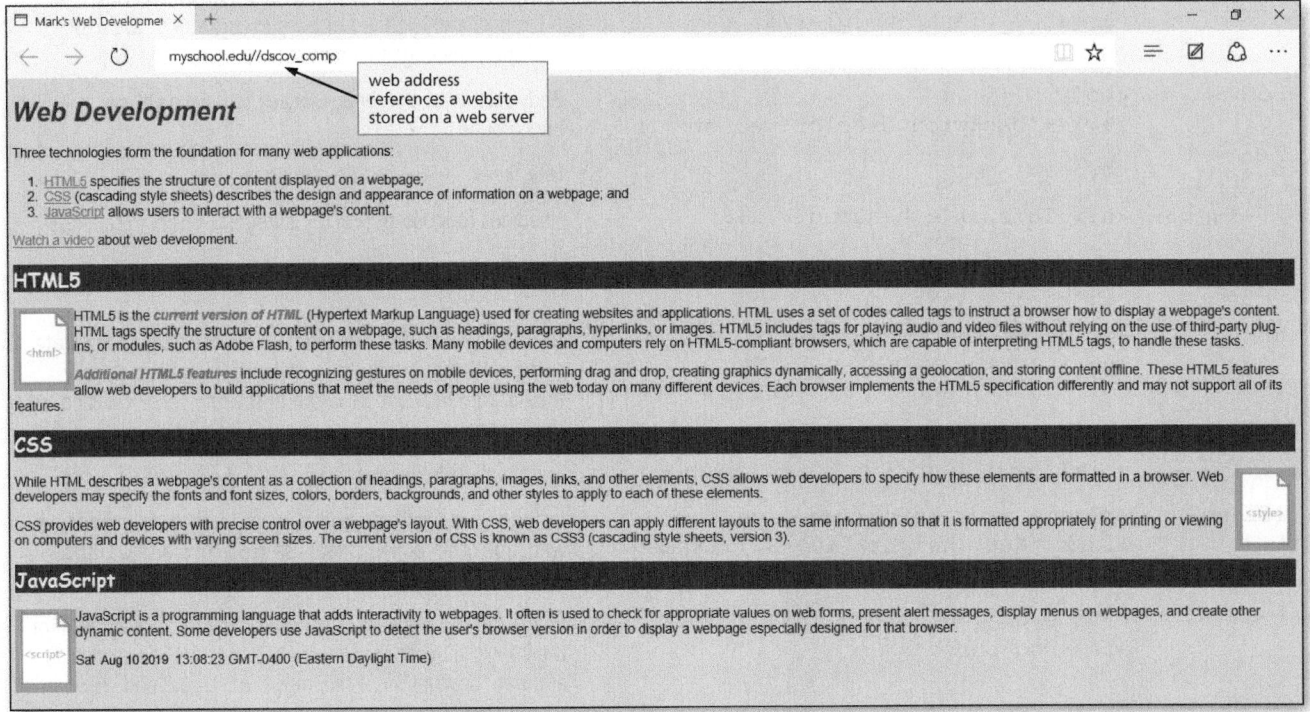

Figure FO-47

Q&A

Do I need to type index.html in the web address to view my website's home page in a browser?
No. You often can omit index.html when entering a web address in a browser. Because index.html often is the name of the first, or home, page that many websites display, a web server will look for a page with that name by default if no page name is specified in the request to locate a webpage.

What if I need or want to make changes to a website once it is published online?
Type the changes you want to make in the text editor, verify them locally in a browser, and then upload the changed files to the web server using an FTP program. Refresh or revisit the webpages in a browser to verify the changes were uploaded correctly.

Summary of Tags and Styles

This section summarizes tags and styles presented in this Focus On, as well as additional tags and styles often used when authoring webpages.

HTML5 Tags

Table FO-2 lists several HTML5 tags and notes about their usage. When a tag takes an attribute, the format is each attribute name followed by an equal sign (=), followed by its value in quotation marks, as in `<a href="http://www.google.com" target="_blank">Google</a>`. Use a search engine with the search text, basic HTML tags, to locate complete documentation online. You can add a style attribute to many of these tags.

Table FO-2   Selected HTML5 Tags

Tag	Example	Description
`<!-->`	`<!--This is a comment. -->`	Comment from web developer, ignored when page is rendered
`<a>`	`<a href="http://www.google.com" target="_blank">Google</a>`	Anchor tag, specifies a link; specify `href` (hypertext reference) and use the attribute `target="_blank"` to display the page in a new tab
`<body>`	`<body style="background-color:yellow">`	Body section of a webpage, styled to have a yellow background
` `	` `	Line break; ` ` has no closing tag
`<h1>` through `<h6>`	`<h1> This is a heading.</h1>`	Headings for content; `<h1>` is largest, `<h6>` is smallest
`<head>`	`<head> ... </head>`	Head section
`<hr>`	`<hr style="background-color: rgb(192,192,192)">`	Displays a horizontal rule (line) across the page to separate sections of content; optional style attributes may specify the background color or width of the line; `<hr>` has no closing tag
`<html>`	`<html> ... </html>`	Starts an HTML document
`<iframe>`	`<iframe src="http://cengage.com" width="600" height="400"></iframe>`	Includes content from another website, such as embedding webpage or an online video; use `height` and `width` attributes to specify the size, in pixels, of the iframe
`<img>`	`<img src="images/dog.jpg" alt="Dog photo">`	Image tag, `src` attribute specifies the source or location of the image, `alt` attribute (required in HTML5) provides an alternate description of the image, `height` and `width` specify the display size of the image in pixels; `<img>` has no closing tag

`<li>`	`<ol>`
	`  <li> Item 1</li>`
	`  <li> Item 2 </li>`
	`</ol>`
		List item, used within `<ol>` or `<ul>` tags

`<ol>`	`<ol>`
	`  <li> Item 1</li>`
	`  <li> Item 2 </li>`
	`</ol>`
		Ordered (numbered) list

`<p>`	`<p>This is a paragraph.</p>`	Paragraph
`<script>`	`<script> ... </script>`	Identifies JavaScript code; located in head section
`<span>`	`<span class="fancy">This text is formatted fancy.</span>`	Identifies content to apply a custom style

`<style>`	`<style>`
	`  h1 {`
	`    font-family:serif;`
	`    color: blue;`
	`  }`
	`</style>`
		Identifies embedded styles for tags; located in head section

`<title>`	`<title>My Website</title>`	Title of a webpage that appears in the browser tab; located in head section of document

`<ul>`	`<ul>`
	`  <li> Item 1</li>`
	`  <li> Item 2 </li>`
	`</ul>`
		Unordered (bulleted) list

Styles

Styles may appear in the style section or as part of a style attribute in almost all HTML tags, or in an external style sheet. The format for a style declaration is the style name, followed by a colon, followed by the value for the style. Table FO-3 lists examples of styles. If more than one style is used, separate each style with a semicolon. Use a search engine with the search text, css styles reference, to locate complete documentation online.

Table FO-3 Selected Styles

Style	Example	Description
`background-color`	`background-color:yellow`	Specifies the background color of elements, such as `<p>`, `<h1>`, and `<body>`
`background-image`	`background-image: url("images/stripes.jpg")`	Sets the background image of `<body>`, `<p>`, `<h1>`, and other elements to the file whose path is given in the `url()` function
`border`	`border:3px red`	Specifies a four-sided border that is 3 pixels thick
`color`	`color:blue`	Colors can be a web color name, a hexadecimal value, such as #0000FF, or an rgb value, such as `rgb(0,0,255)` that specifies the red, green, and blue components of the color
`float`	`float:left`	Specifies whether to place an element to the left or right relative to text; often used to position an image to the left or right of text.
`font-family`	`font-family:serif`	Specifies the font for a paragraph, heading, or other text element; use specific font names, such as `times`, `arial`, and `courier`, or family names, such as `serif`, `sans-serif`, `cursive`, or `monospace`
`font-size`	`font-size:10px`	Specifies font size in pixels
`font-style`	`font-style:italic`	Specifies font style; use `normal`, `italic`, or `oblique` as the value for this style
`font-weight`	`font-weight:bold`	Specifies the font weight for a paragraph, heading, or other text element; use `bold` for thick characters, or numeric values 100 through 900, in increments of 100; 400 is the same as `normal`, 700 is the same as `bold`
`text-align`	`text-align:left`	Sets alignment for `<h1>`, `<h2>`, or `<h3>` tags; values can be `left`, `center`, or `right`

Exercises

Short Answer

Consider these HTML code fragments below and then answer the questions for each.

1. `<a href="http://nationalzoo.si.edu/" target="_blank">Zoo</a>`

   In which browser window will the page appear? Is this an absolute or a relative reference? What text will appear as the link you should click?

2. `<img src="images/cat.jpg" alt="Cat">`

   Where is the cat.jpg file located within your website's development folder? What is the purpose of the attribute, `alt="Cat"`?

3. `<body style="background-color:rgb(255,0,255)">`

   What does this style specify for the body tag? What color is specified?

4. `<style> h1 { color:blue; font-family:serif } </style>`

   To which `<h1>` tags in an HTML document will this style declaration apply? What is the name of a font that a browser might use to display text in a serif font? Would you most likely find this style declaration in the head or body section of an HTML document?

5. ```
<ul>
   <li>Cake</li>
   <li>Ice Cream</li>
   <ol>
     <li>Chocolate</li>
     <li>Vanilla</li>
   </ol>
   <li>Cookies</li>
</ul>
```

   Consider the HTML5 code for a dessert menu on a restaurant's website. How does it appear in a browser?
```

How To: Your Turn

Develop a website for your online resume, for a club or organization of which you are a member, or for a small business. The website should include these features:

- At least two pages, each with different background images or colors
- An image at the top of each page that serves as a banner
- Links between the home page and other pages on the website
- Styled text (bold, italics, different fonts or colors)
- Content in an ordered or unordered list
- Embedded media content (such as a video, map, or Tweet)
- Links to your accounts on online social networks
- Links to other websites (open in a new window or tab)
- An image that, when clicked, acts as a link
- JavaScript code that displays the current date and time on a webpage

Internet Research

Many small businesses host and install a content management system in order to develop their websites. Search the web for an online content management system, such as WordPress or Google Sites. Sign up for an account so that you can create a basic website and experiment with its features. Which features of a content management system did you find most useful? How does the process of developing a website with a content management system compare with creating a website by writing HTML code? When would it be helpful to know even basic HTML code when creating a website using a content management system?

Technology Acronyms

Acronym	Description	Page
1G	first generation	10-31
2G	second generation	10-31
3-D	three-dimensional	1-13
3G	third generation	10-31
3GPP	Third Generation Partnership Project	10-12
4G	fourth generation	10-31
4GL	fourth-generation language	11-35
5G	fifth generation	10-31
AC	alternating current	6-23
ACPA	Anticybersquatting Consumer Protection Act	2-10
ADA	Americans with Disabilities Act	7-36
ADC	analog-to-digital	3-19
ADSL	asymmetric digital subscriber line	10-17
AI	artificial intelligence	12-9
AIO	all-in-one	3-8
ALU	arithmetic logic unit	6-6
AMOLED	active-matrix OLED	7-24
ANSI	American National Standards Institute	10-10
API	application programming interface	11-48
ARPA	Advanced Research Projects Agency	2-3
ASCII	American Standard Code for Information Interchange	6-13
ATC	advanced transfer cache	6-18
ATM	automated teller machine	3-12
ATM	Asynchronous Transfer Mode	10-18
AUP	acceptable use policy	5-9
B2B	business-to-business	2-27
B2C	business-to-consumer	2-27
BAN	body area network	10-6
BD	Blu-ray Disc	8-22
BLOB	binary large object	11-4
BMP	bitmap	2-31
BSA	Business Software Alliance	12-13
BSB	backside bus	6-23
BSN	body sensor network	10-6
BTW	by the way	2-39
BYOD	bring your own device	8-23

Acronym	Description	Page
C2C	consumer-to-consumer	2-27
CA	certificate authority	5-18
CAD	computer-aided design	7-30
CAE	computer-aided engineering	12-4
CAM	computer-aided manufacturing	12-4
CAPTCHA	Completely Automated Public Turing test to tell Computers and Humans Apart	5-12
CATV	cable television	10-16
CBT	computer-based training	4-27
CCFL	cold cathode fluorescent lamp	7-23
ccTLD	country code top-level domain	2-9
CD	compact disc	8-19
CDMA	Code Division Multiple Access	10-31
CDP	continuous data protection	5-21
CD-R	CD-recordable	8-21
CD-ROM	CD-read-only memory	8-21
CD-RW	CD-rewritable	8-21
CERT/CC	Computer Emergency Response Team Coordination Center	5-7
CF	CompactFlash	8-14
CIPA	Children's Internet Protection Act	5-34
CISSP	Certified Information Systems Security Professional	12-21
CMOS	complementary metal-oxide semiconductor	6-19
CMS	content management system	12-5
COPPA	Children's Online Privacy Protection Act	5-33
CPC	cost per click	11-47
CPI	cost per impression	11-47
CPU	central processing unit	6-5
CRM	customer relationship management	6-12
CRT	cathode-ray tube	7-25
CSA	Cloud Security Alliance	5-19
CSC	common short code	3-16
CSI	Cellular Seizure Investigation	6-19
CSO	chief security officer	11-31

Acronym	Description	Page
CSS	cascading style sheets	11-39
CSS3	cascading style sheets, version 3	11-39
CTIA	Cellular Telecommunications Industry Association	6-34
CTS	carpal tunnel syndrome	3-34
CVS	computer vision syndrome	3-36
DaaS	data as a service	6-12
DBA	database administrator	11-14
DBMS	database management system	11-3
DC	direct current	6-23
DDoS	distributed DoS	5-6
DDR SDRAM	Double Data Rate SDRAM	6-17
DIMM	dual inline memory module	6-17
DLP	digital light processing	7-35
DMCA	Digital Millennium Copyright Act	5-33
DMS	document management system	12-5
DNS	domain name system	2-10
DoS	denial of service	5-6
dpi	dots per inch	7-28
DRAM	dynamic RAM	6-16
DRM	digital rights management	12-21
DSL	Digital Subscriber Line	10-17
DSS	decision support system	12-8
DTP	desktop publishing	4-23
DTV	digital television	7-25
DV	digital video	7-13
DVD	digital versatile disc or digital video disc	8-19
DVD+R	DVD-recordable	8-21
DVD+RAM	DVD-random access memory	8-21
DVD+RW	DVD-rewritable	8-21
DVD-R	DVD-recordable	8-21
DVD-ROM	DVD-read-only memory	8-21
DVD-RW	DVD-rewritable	8-21
DVI	Digital Video Interface	7-24
DVR	digital video recorder	10-24
EB	exabyte	8-3
ECPA	Electronic Communications Privacy Act	5-33
EDGE	Enhanced Data GSM Environment	10-31
EDI	electronic data interchange	10-4
EFT	electronic funds transfer	10-4
EIDE	Enhanced Integrated Drive Electronics	8-13

Acronym	Description	Page
ERP	Enterprise Resource Planning	12-4
eSATA	external SATA	8-13
EULA	end-user license agreement	12-21
EVDO	Evolution Data Optimized	10-31
FAQ	frequently asked questions	2-39
FC	Fibre Channel	8-23
FDDI	Fiber Distributed Data Interface	10-27
FERPA	Family Educational Rights and Privacy Act	5-19
FIP	Fair Information Practices	11-6
FOIA	Freedom of Information Act	5-33
fps	frames per second	7-14
FSB	front side bus	6-23
FTP	File Transfer Protocol	1-22
FTTB	Fiber to the Building	10-17
FTTH	Fiber to the Home	10-17
FTTP	Fiber to the Premises	10-17
FWIW	for what it's worth	2-39
FYI	for your information	2-39
GB	gigabyte	6-15
GBps	gigabytes per second	8-5
Gbps	gigabits per second	10-10
GHz	gigahertz	6-8
GIF	Graphics Interchange Format	2-31
GPRS	General Packet Radio Service	10-31
GPS	global positioning system	10-33
GPU	graphics processing unit	7-24
GSM	Global System for Mobile Communications	10-31
GUI	graphical user interface	9-5
HD	high-definition	7-24
HDD	hard disk drive	8-6
HDMI	High-Definition Media Interface	7-24
HDTV	high-definition television	7-25
HRIS	human resources information system	12-4
HTML	Hypertext Markup Language	11-37
http	Hypertext Transfer Protocol	2-15
IaaS	infrastructure as a service	6-12
IAFIS	Integrated Automated Fingerprint Identification System	11-18
ICANN	Internet Corporation for Assigned Names and Numbers	2-9
IDE	integrated development environment	11-33

Acronym	Description	Page
IEC	International Electronics Commission	6-22
IEEE	Institute of Electrical and Electronics Engineers	10-10
IMEI	International Mobile Equipment Identity	6-34
IMHO	in my humble opinion	2-39
IMSI	International Mobile Subscriber Identity	10-30
IoT	Internet of Things	6-9
IP	Internet Protocol	10-11
IP	intellectual property	5-27
IR	infrared	10-15
IrDA	Infrared Data Association	10-15
IROC2	Institute for Responsible Online and Cell-Phone Communication	5-34
ISDN	Integrated Services Digital Network	10-19
ISP	Internet service provider	1-18
IT	information technology	6-30
JAD	joint-application design	11-23
JPEG	Joint Photographic Experts Group	2-31
KB	kilobyte	8-3
KBps	kilobytes per second	8-5
Kbps	kilobits per second	10-15
L1	Level 1	6-18
L2	Level 2	6-18
L3	Level 3	6-18
LAN	local area network	10-4
LCD	liquid crystal display	7-24
LED	light-emitting diode	7-24
LTE	Long Term Evolution	10-31
M2	Memory Stick Micro	8-14
M2M	machine-to-machine	3-26
MAC	Media Access Control	5-23
MAN	metropolitan area network	10-6
MB	megabyte	8-3
MBAN	medical body area network	10-6
MBps	megabytes per second	8-5
Mbps	megabits per second	10-10
MDM	mobile device management	9-24
MFP	multifunction printer	7-30
MICR	magnetic-ink character recognition	7-16
MIS	management information system	12-6
MMS	multimedia message service	10-31
MOOC	massive open online course	4-27

Acronym	Description	Page
MP	megapixels	3-19
MRP	Material Requirements Planning	12-4
MRP II	Manufacturing Resource Planning II	12-4
ms	millisecond	6-20
MTSO	mobile telephone switching office	10-30
NAS	network attached storage	8-23
NFC	near field communications	6-10
NGI	Next Generation Identification	11-18
NIC	network interface card	10-22
ns	nanosecond	6-20
NSA	National Security Agency	10-30
NUI	natural user interface	9-6
OCIA	Office of Cyber and Infrastructure Analysis	7-45
OCR	optical character recognition	7-17
OEM	original equipment manufacturer	9-12
OLAP	online analytical processing	12-8
OLED	organic LED	7-24
OLTP	online transaction processing	12-6
OMR	optical mark recognition	7-17
OODB	object-oriented database	11-12
OOP	object-oriented programming	11-32
OS	operating system	9-2
P2P	peer-to-peer	10-7
PaaS	platform as a service	6-12
PAN	personal area network	10-13
PATRIOT	Provide Appropriate Tools Required to Intercept and Obstruct Terrorism	5-33
PB	petabyte	8-3
PC	personal computer	1-3
PDF	Portable Document Format	4-19
PERT	Program Evaluation and Review Technique	11-21
PIN	personal identification number	3-12
PMP	Project Management Professional	12-21
PNG	Portable Network Graphics	2-31
POS	point of sale	7-10
PPC	pay per click	11-47
ppm	pages per minute	7-27
ps	picosecond	6-20
PTI	Public Technical Identifiers	2-9
PUE	power usage effectiveness	5-28
QBE	query by example	11-15
QR	quick response	7-17

Acronym	Description	Page
RAD	rapid application development	11-33
RAID	redundant array of independent disks	8-13
RAM	random access memory	6-15
RDRAM	Rambus DRAM	6-17
RFI	request for information	11-26
RFID	radio frequency identification	10-15
RFP	request for proposal	11-26
RFQ	request for quotation	11-26
ROI	return on investment	11-22
ROM	read-only memory	6-19
rpm	revolutions per minute	8-8
RSI	repetitive strain injury	3-34
RSS	Really Simple Syndication	11-38
RTOS	real-time operating system	9-26
RWD	responsive web design	2-29
SaaS	software as a service	6-12
SAN	storage area network	8-24
SAS	serial-attached SCSI	8-13
SATA	Serial Advanced Technology Attachment	8-13
SCSI	Small Computer System Interface	8-13
SDHC	Secure Digital High Capacity	8-14
SDLC	system development life cycle	11-49
SDRAM	Synchronous DRAM	6-17
SDXC	Secure Digital Expanded Capacity	8-14
SecaaS	security as a service	5-43
SEO	search engine optimization	12-16
SFA	salesforce automation	12-4
SIMM	single inline memory module	6-17
SLR	single-lens reflex	3-18
SMS	short message service	10-8
SOX	Sarbanes-Oxley	8-29
SQL	Structured Query Language	11-15
SRAM	static RAM	6-16
SSD	solid-state drive	8-10
SSID	service set identifier	5-23
TB	terabyte	8-3
Tbps	terabits per second	10-29
TCP/IP	Transmission Control Protocol/Internet Protocol	10-11
TFT	thin-film transistor	7-24
TIFF	Tagged Image File Format	2-31

Acronym	Description	Page
TLD	top-level domain	2-9
TPS	transaction processing system	12-6
TTFN	ta-ta for now	2-39
TYVM	thank you very much	2-39
UAV	unmanned aerial vehicle	12-22
UI	user interface	9-5
UMB	Ultra Mobile Broadband	10-13
UMTS	Universal Mobile Telecommunications System	10-31
UPC	Universal Product Code	7-17
UPS	uninterruptible power supply	3-34
URL	Uniform Resource Locator	2-14
USB	universal serial bus	1-15
UV	ultraviolet	7-25
UWB	ultra-wideband	10-14
UX	user experience	12-16
VAN	value-added network	10-4
VAR	value-added reseller	11-26
VM	virtual machine	9-22
VoIP	Voice over Internet Protocol	1-22
VPE	visual programming environment	11-35
VPN	virtual private network	12-10
VR	virtual reality	1-35
W3C	World Wide Web Consortium	11-39
WAN	wide area network	10-6
WAP	wireless access point	10-20
WBT	web-based training	4-27
Wi-Fi	wireless fidelity	10-12
WiMax	Worldwide Interoperability for Microwave Access	10-13
WLAN	wireless local area network	10-5
WML	wireless markup language	11-38
WORM	write once, read many	8-21
WPA2	Wi-Fi Protected Access 2	5-23
WWW	World Wide Web	2-11
XML	Extensible Markup Language	11-37
YB	yottabyte	8-3
ZB	zettabyte	8-3
μs	microsecond	6-20

Troubleshooting Computer and Mobile Device Problems

While using a computer or mobile device, at some point you probably will experience a technology problem that requires troubleshooting. Technology problems that remain unresolved may impact your ability to use your device. This appendix identifies some common problems you might experience with computers and mobile devices; it also includes some suggestions for correcting these problems. If the recommended solutions in the table below do not solve your problem, or you are uncomfortable performing any of the recommended actions, contact a repair professional (independent computer repair company, technical support department at your job or academic institution, or computer or mobile device manufacturer) for additional options.

This appendix also might assist you with completing some of the Problem Solving exercises found at the end of each module in this textbook. Table 1 contains possible solutions for problems that might occur on your computer or mobile device.

Note: The following steps are suggestions; they are not comprehensive solutions. When working with a computer or mobile device, follow all necessary safety precautions before implementing any of these recommended solutions. Contact a professional if you require additional information.

Table 1   Problems and Recommended Solutions

Problem	Desktop	Laptop	Tablet	Phone	Recommended Solution(s)
Computer or device does not turn on.	✓	✓	✓		The computer might be in sleep or hibernate mode; to wake up the computer, try pressing a key on the keyboard, pressing the power button, or tapping the touch screen if applicable.
	✓				Make sure power cables are plugged securely into the wall and the back of the computer.
		✓	✓	✓	Make sure the battery is charged if the computer or device is not connected to an external power source. If the battery is charged, connect the external AC adapter and attempt to turn on the computer or device. If the computer or device still does not turn on, the problem may be with the computer or device.
	✓	✓	✓	✓	If none of the above options resolves the issue, the power supply or AC adapter might be experiencing problems; contact a professional for assistance.
Battery does not hold a charge.		✓	✓	✓	Verify the AC adapter used to charge the battery is working properly. If the mobile computer or device can run from the AC adapter without a battery installed, the AC adapter most likely is working properly. If the AC adapter works, it may be time to replace the battery.
Computer issues a series of beeps when turned on.	✓	✓			Refer to your computer's documentation to determine what the beeps indicate, as the computer hardware may be experiencing a problem.

Problem	Desktop	Laptop	Tablet	Phone	Recommended Solution(s)
Computer or device turns on, but operating system does not run.	✓	✓	✓	✓	Disconnect all nonessential peripheral devices, remove all storage media, and then restart the computer or device.
					Restart the computer or device; if the problem persists, the operating system might need to be restored. If restoring the operating system does not work, the hard drive might be failing.
Monitor does not display anything.	✓				Verify the monitor is turned on.
					Verify the video cable is connected securely to the computer and monitor.
					Make sure the power cables are plugged securely into the wall and the back of the monitor.
					Make sure the monitor is set to the correct input source.
					Restart the computer.
					If you have access to a spare monitor, see if that monitor will work. If so, your original monitor might be faulty. If not, the problem may be with your computer's hardware or software configuration.
Screen does not display anything.		✓	✓	✓	Restart the device.
					Make sure the device is plugged in or the battery is sufficiently charged.
Keyboard or mouse does not work.	✓	✓	✓		Verify the keyboard and mouse are connected properly to the computer or device.
					If the keyboard and mouse are wireless, make sure they are turned on and contain new batteries.
					If the keyboard and mouse are wireless, attempt to pair them again with the computer or wireless receiver. Read How To 3-1 for more information.
					If you have access to a spare keyboard or mouse, see if it will work. If so, your original keyboard or mouse might be faulty. If not, the problem may be with your computer's hardware or software configuration.
		✓			Make sure the touchpad is not disabled.
Wet keyboard no longer works.	✓	✓			Turn the keyboard upside down to drain the liquid, dab wet areas with a cotton swab, and allow the keyboard to dry.
Speakers do not work.	✓	✓	✓	✓	Verify that headphones or earbuds are not connected.
					Make sure the volume is not muted and is turned up on the computer or mobile device.
	✓	✓			Verify the speakers are turned on.
					Make sure the speakers are connected properly to the computer.
					If necessary, verify the speakers are plugged in to an external power source.
Hard drive makes noise.	✓	✓			If the computer is not positioned on a flat surface, move it to a flat surface.
					If the problem persists, contact a professional.

Problem	Desktop	Laptop	Tablet	Phone	Recommended Solution(s)
Fan contains built-up dust/ does not work.	✓	✓			If possible, open the system unit and use a can of compressed air to blow the dust from the fan and away from the system unit.
	✓				Remove obvious obstructions that might be preventing the fan from functioning.
					Verify the fan is connected properly to the motherboard.
					If the fan still does not work, it may need to be replaced.
Computer or device is too hot.	✓	✓			Verify the fan or vents are not obstructed. If the fan or vents are obstructed, use a can of compressed air to blow the dust from the fan or vent and away from the computer or device or remove other obstructions.
		✓			Purchase a cooling pad that rests below the laptop and protects it from overheating.
			✓	✓	Exit apps running in the background.
					Search for and follow instructions how to clear the tablet or phone's cache memory.
					Run an app to monitor the tablet's or phone's battery performance, and exit apps that require a lot of battery power.
					Decrease the brightness of the display.
Cannot read from optical disc.	✓	✓			Clean the optical disc and try reading from it again.
					Try reading from another optical disc. If the second optical disc works, the original disc is faulty.
					If the second disc does not work, the problem may be with the optical disc drive.
External drive (USB flash drive, optical disc drive, or external hard drive) is not recognized.	✓	✓	✓		Remove the drive and insert it into a different USB port, if available.
					Remove the drive, restart the computer, and insert the drive again.
					Try connecting the drive to a different computer. If you still cannot read from the drive, it may be faulty.
Program or app does not run.	✓	✓	✓	✓	Restart the computer or device and try running the program or app again.
					If feasible, uninstall the program or app, reinstall it, and then try running it again. If the problem persists, the problem may be with the operating system's configuration.
Computer or device displays symptoms of a virus or other malware.	✓	✓	✓	✓	Make sure your antivirus software is up to date and then disconnect the computer or device from the network and run antivirus software to attempt to remove the malware. Continue running scans until no threats are detected and then reconnect the computer to the network.
					If you do not have antivirus software installed, obtain and install a reputable antivirus program or app and then scan your computer in an attempt to remove the malware. You should have only one antivirus program or app installed on your computer or mobile device at one time.
					If you are unable to remove the malware, take your computer to a professional who may be able to remove the malicious program or app.

Problem	Desktop	Laptop	Tablet	Phone	Recommended Solution(s)
Computer or device is experiencing slow performance.	✓	✓	✓		Defragment the hard disk.
	✓	✓			Uninstall programs and apps that you do not need.
					Verify your computer or device meets the minimum system requirements for the operating system and software you are running.
					If possible, purchase and install additional memory (RAM).
Screen is damaged physically.	✓	✓	✓	✓	Contact a professional to replace the screen; if the computer or device is covered under a warranty, the repair may be free.
					Replacing a broken screen on a computer or device might be more costly than replacing the computer or device; consider your options before replacing the screen.
Touch screen does not respond.	✓	✓	✓	✓	Clean the touch screen.
					Restart the computer or device.
Computer or device is wet.		✓	✓	✓	Turn off the computer or device, remove the battery, and dry off visible water with a cloth. Fill a plastic bag or box with rice, submerge the computer or device and battery into the rice so that it is surrounded completely, and then do not turn on the computer or device for at least 24 hours.
					If the computer or device does not work after it is dry, contact a professional for your options.
Computer or device does not connect to a wireless network.	✓	✓	✓	✓	Verify you are within range of a wireless access point.
					Make sure the information to connect to the wireless network is configured properly on the computer or device.
					Make sure the wireless capability on the computer or device is turned on.
Computer or device cannot synchronize with Bluetooth accessories.	✓	✓	✓	✓	Verify the Bluetooth device is turned on.
					Verify the Bluetooth functionality on your computer or device is enabled.
					Verify the computer or device has been paired properly with the accessory. Read How To 3-1 for more information.
					Make sure the Bluetooth device is charged.
Device continuously has poor mobile phone reception.			✓	✓	Restart the device.
					If you have a protective case, remove the case to see if reception improves.
					If you are using the device inside a building, try moving closer to a window or open doorway.
					Contact your wireless carrier for additional suggestions.

Index